GLENN'S

OLDSMOBILE

TUNE-UP AND REPAIR GUIDE

A
GLENN
TUNE-UP
AND
REPAIR
GUIDE

GLENN'S
OLDSMOBILE
TUNE-UP AND REPAIR GUIDE

by Harold T. Glenn

HENRY REGNERY COMPANY·CHICAGO

Library of Congress Cataloging in Publication Data
Glenn, Harold T.
  Glenn's Oldsmobile tune-up & repair guide.
  1. Oldsmobile automobile. I. Title. II. Title:
Oldsmobile tune-up & repair guide.
TL215.04G47   629.28'7'22   74-6925
ISBN: 0-8092-8320-4

Printed in the United States of America
Library of Congress Catalog Card Number 74-6925
International Standard Book Number 0-8092-8320-4

foreword

This is a comprehensive tune-up and repair guide for all Oldsmobile automobiles. It is a reference book for professional mechanics and also a completely usable manual for car owners who want to make their own repairs, those who are interested in keeping their autos running smoothly and economically, and performance-minded drivers who want to obtain as much power as possible from their engines.

The four "roadmaps" in the first chapter ("Troubleshooting") are especially important in helping to pinpoint the trouble before beginning repairs. This feature also helps to save time while repairs are in process, because it shows the mechanic what to look for as the unit is being disassembled. Many simple procedures are demonstrated that require no elaborate equipment for testing and that can be made by any interested car owner. The book includes servicing the engine, running gear, driveline, brakes, and fuel and electrical systems. Comprehensive specification tables and service information for all Oldsmobile vehicles made from 1955 to 1974 are provided.

Among the many special features of this guide is the use of step-by-step illustrated instructions. Another is the use of "exploded illustrations" of major mechanical and electrical units. There are many photographs of worn parts so that the reader will recognize such wear when he sees it. These pictures take the place of years of experience.

The author wishes to express his appreciation to the Oldsmobile Division of General Motors Corporation for its gracious assistance in furnishing material for this guide, and specifically to the following: Fritz W. Bennetts, Carlton Brechler, Steven J. Harris, and Carroll B. Sugar of the Public Relations department. Appreciation must also be expressed to the following firms, which generously loaned the author illustrations: AC Spark Plug Division; Ammco Tools, Inc.; Champion Spark Plug Company; Federal-Mogul Service; McQuay-Norris Manufacturing Company; Offenhauser Sales Corporation; Perfect Circle Division, Dana Corporation; Sun Electric Corporation; Toledo Steel Products Company.

Special thanks are due to my wife, Anna Glenn, for her gracious and devoted assistance in helping to proofread the manuscript and galley proofs and to Mark Tsunawaki for his contribution to the artwork of this book.

HAROLD T. GLENN

Books by HAROLD T. GLENN

Youth at the Wheel
Safe Living
Automechanics
Glenn's Auto Troubleshooting Guide
Exploring Power Mechanics
Automobile Engine Rebuilding and Maintenance
Automobile Power Accessories
Glenn's Auto Repair Manual
Automotive Smog Control Manual
Glenn's Emission-Control Systems
Glenn's Tune-Up and Repair Manual for American and Imported Car Emission-Control Systems
Glenn's Foreign Car Repair Manual
Glenn's Triumph Repair and Tune-Up Guide
Glenn's Alfa Romeo Repair and Tune-Up Guide
Glenn's Austin, Austin-Healey Repair and Tune-Up Guide
Glenn's Sunbeam-Hillman Repair and Tune-Up Guide
Glenn's MG, Morris and Magnette Repair and Tune-Up Guide
Glenn's Volkswagen Repair and Tune-Up Guide
Glenn's Volkswagen Repair and Tune-Up Guide (Spanish Edition)
Glenn's Mercedes-Benz Repair and Tune-Up Guide
Glenn's Foreign Carburetors and Electrical Systems Guide
Glenn's Renault Repair and Tune-Up Guide
Glenn's Jaguar Repair and Tune-Up Guide
Glenn's Volvo Repair and Tune-Up Guide
Glenn's Peugeot Repair and Tune-Up Guide
Glenn's Fiat Repair and Tune-Up Guide
Glenn's Toyota Tune-Up and Repair Guide
Glenn's Mazda Tune-Up and Repair Guide
Glenn's Chrysler Outboard Motor Repair and Tune-Up Guide for 1 & 2 Cylinder Engines
Glenn's Chrysler Outboard Motor Repair and Tune-Up Guide for 3 & 4 Cylinder Engines
Glenn's Evinrude Outboard Motor Repair and Tune-Up Guide for 1 & 2 Cylinder Engines
Glenn's Evinrude Outboard Motor Repair and Tune-Up Guide for 3 & 4 Cylinder Engines
Glenn's Johnson Outboard Motor Repair and Tune-Up Guide for 1 & 2 Cylinder Engines
Glenn's Johnson Outboard Motor Repair and Tune-Up Guide for 3 & 4 Cylinder Engines
Glenn's McCulloch Outboard Motor Repair and Tune-Up Guide
Glenn's Mercury Outboard Motor Repair and Tune-Up Guide
Glenn's Sears Outboard Motor Repair and Tune-Up Guide
Honda One-Cylinder Repair and Tune-Up Guide
Glenn's Honda Two-Cylinder Repair and Tune-Up Guide
Suzuki One-Cylinder Tune-Up and Repair Guide
Yamaha Enduro Tune-Up and Repair Guide
Triumph Two-Cylinder Motorcycle Tune-Up and Repair Guide
Glenn's Chevrolet Tune-Up and Repair Guide
Glenn Chevrolet Camaro Tune-Up and Repair Guide
Glenn's Ford/Lincoln/Mercury Tune-Up and Repair Guide
Glenn's Chrysler/Plymouth/Dodge Tune-Up and Repair Guide
Glenn's Pontiac Tune-Up and Repair Guide
Glenn's Pontiac Firebird Tune-Up and Repair Guide
Glenn's Oldsmobile Tune-Up and Repair Guide
Glenn's Buick Tune-Up and Repair Guide
Glenn's Complete Bicycle Manual

contents

1 troubleshooting

Troubleshooting must be a well thought-out procedure. To be successful with it, you must start by accurately determining the problem; then you must use a logical approach to arrive at the proper solution. Obviously, if the instructions are to be of maximum benefit as a guide, they must be fully understood and followed exactly.

ROADMAPS

When an engine does not start, the trouble must be localized to one of four general areas: cranking, ignition, fuel, and compression. Each of these areas must be systematically inspected until the trouble is located in one of them, and then detailed tests of that system must be made to isolate the part causing the starting problem.

To assist you, four roadmaps have been developed so that the testing program can be visualized in its entirety and the logical approach determined. ROADMAP ONE concerns EMERGENCY TROUBLESHOOTING, and it represents some quick and simple tests that can be made on the cranking, ignition, fuel, and compression systems to determine which one requires further investigation. ROADMAP TWO deals with a detailed inspection of the various units which make up the cranking system. ROADMAP THREE details the various tests that are used for isolating ignition system troubles, while ROADMAP FOUR covers the tests that are used to pinpoint fuel system troubles.

EMERGENCY TROUBLESHOOTING— ROADMAP ONE

In using this EMERGENCY TROUBLESHOOTING ROADMAP, proceed sequentially through each of the tests until a defect is uncovered. Then skip to the detailed testing procedure and roadmap for that system. For example, if, when using the EMERGENCY TROUBLESHOOTING ROADMAP, the first two systems, cranking and ignition, test OK, but the third test shows that there is trouble in the fuel system, then skip ROADMAPS TWO and THREE and proceed to the detailed tests under ROADMAP FOUR—FUEL SYSTEM TESTS.

①**CRANKING SYSTEM TEST:** Turn the ignition switch to the START position, and the cranking motor should crank the engine at a normal rate of speed. If it does, it is an indication that the battery, cables, starting relay, and cranking motor are in good condition. To proceed with the testing program, go on to Test ② on the EMERGENCY TROUBLESHOOTING ROADMAP.

If the cranking motor cranks the engine slowly or doesn't crank it at all, the trouble is in the cranking system, and you should proceed to ROADMAP TWO—CRANKING SYSTEM TESTS for the detailed testing procedure that will help you uncover the starting trouble.

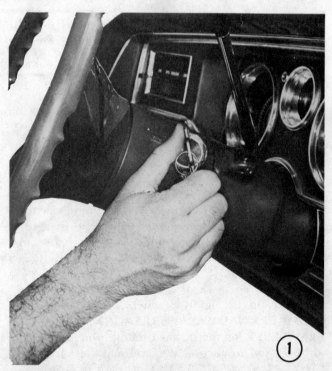

①

ROADMAP ONE — EMERGENCY TROUBLESHOOTING

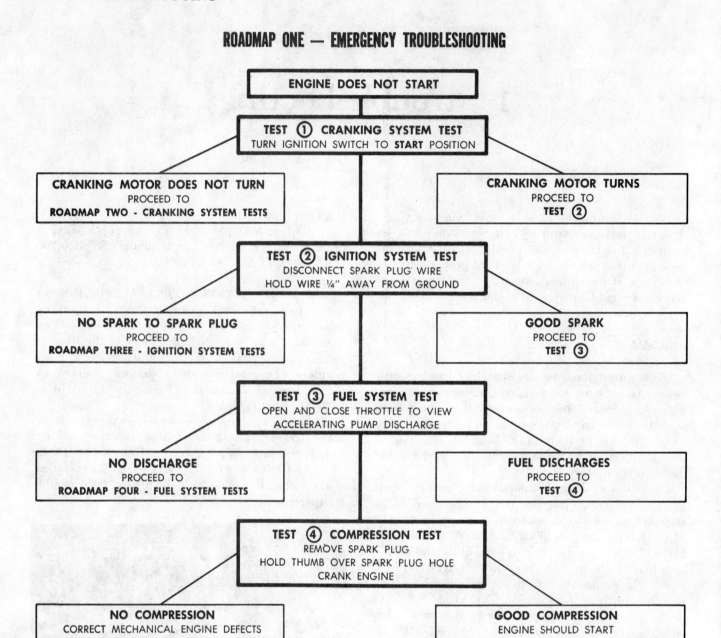

ENGINE DOES NOT START

TEST ① CRANKING SYSTEM TEST
TURN IGNITION SWITCH TO **START** POSITION

CRANKING MOTOR DOES NOT TURN
PROCEED TO
ROADMAP TWO - CRANKING SYSTEM TESTS

CRANKING MOTOR TURNS
PROCEED TO
TEST ②

TEST ② IGNITION SYSTEM TEST
DISCONNECT SPARK PLUG WIRE
HOLD WIRE ¼" AWAY FROM GROUND

NO SPARK TO SPARK PLUG
PROCEED TO
ROADMAP THREE - IGNITION SYSTEM TESTS

GOOD SPARK
PROCEED TO
TEST ③

TEST ③ FUEL SYSTEM TEST
OPEN AND CLOSE THROTTLE TO VIEW
ACCELERATING PUMP DISCHARGE

NO DISCHARGE
PROCEED TO
ROADMAP FOUR - FUEL SYSTEM TESTS

FUEL DISCHARGES
PROCEED TO
TEST ④

TEST ④ COMPRESSION TEST
REMOVE SPARK PLUG
HOLD THUMB OVER SPARK PLUG HOLE
CRANK ENGINE

NO COMPRESSION
CORRECT MECHANICAL ENGINE DEFECTS

GOOD COMPRESSION
ENGINE SHOULD START

②**IGNITION SYSTEM TEST:** Disconnect a spark plug wire and hold it about 1/4″ from a spark plug or ground. Crank the engine with the ignition switch turned ON, and a good spark should jump from the wire to the spark plug or ground. If it does, go on to Test ③ on the EMERGENCY TROUBLESHOOTING ROADMAP.

If there is no spark or the spark is very weak, the trouble is in the ignition system, and you should proceed to ROADMAP THREE—IGNITION SYSTEM TESTS for the detailed testing procedure that will help you to uncover the ignition system trouble.

③**FUEL SYSTEM TEST:** This test is to determine whether or not there is fuel in the carburetor. Remove the air cleaner, and then look down into the throat of the carburetor. Open and close the throttle several times to see if fuel is squirted out of the pump jets as shown in the accompanying illustration. *NOTE: The top of the carburetor has been removed in this illustration for photographic purposes.*

If fuel is discharged, it is an indication that there is fuel in the carburetor bowl and that the fuel system must be functioning properly; therefore, go on to Test ④ on the EMERGENCY TROUBLE-SHOOTING ROADMAP.

If no fuel is discharged from the pump jets, then

HIGH-TENSION LEAD

②

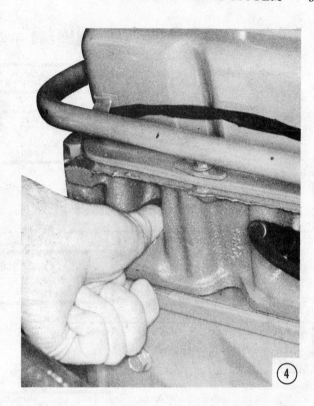

④

the trouble is in the fuel system, and you should proceed to the detailed tests on ROADMAP FOUR—FUEL SYSTEM TESTS to isolate the trouble.

④**COMPRESSION TEST:** Remove a spark plug and hold your thumb over the spark plug hole. Have someone crank the engine. You should be able to feel pressure pulses as the piston comes up on

ACCELERATOR PUMP

ACCELERATOR DISCHARGE NOZZLES

③

each of the firing strokes. It is not necessary in this rough test to determine the exact pressure, as you only have to know whether or not there is compression. Strong pressure pulses indicate that the mechanical parts of the engine are sound.

CRANKING SYSTEM TESTS—ROADMAP TWO

This roadmap provides a sequential series of tests that can be made to isolate trouble in a cranking system that does not function properly. Obviously, an engine cannot be started properly if it cannot be turned fast enough to draw in a full charge of fuel, compress it properly, and have enough voltage reserve left for igniting the mixture. The cranking system includes the cranking motor and drive, battery, starting relay, ignition switch, and the necessary wiring and cables to complete the various circuits. Vehicles with an automatic transmission have, in addition, a neutral-safety switch which prevents operation of the cranking motor in all transmission selector positions except NEUTRAL or PARK.

Every cranking motor problem falls into one of three situations: the cranking motor does not turn at all, it spins rapidly but does not crank the engine, or it cranks the engine very slowly.

ROADMAP TWO — CRANKING SYSTEM TESTS

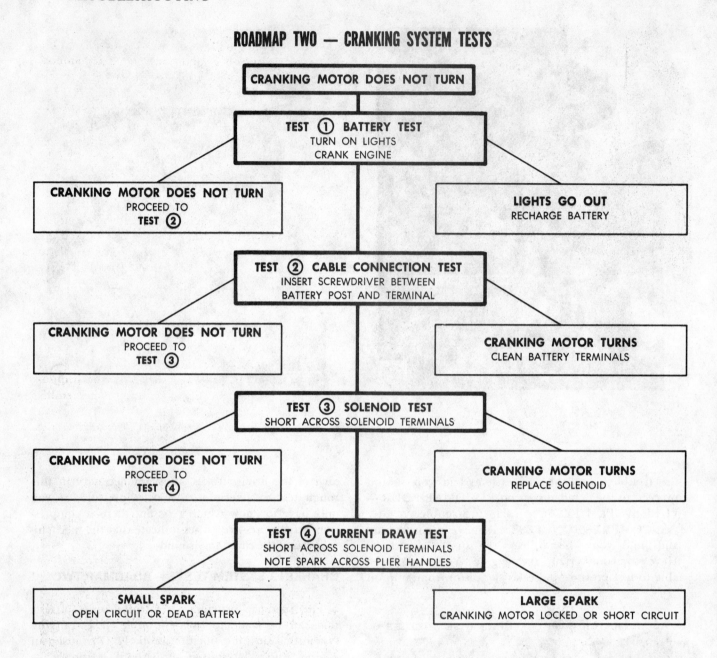

CRANKING MOTOR DOES NOT TURN

TEST ① BATTERY TEST
TURN ON LIGHTS
CRANK ENGINE

CRANKING MOTOR DOES NOT TURN
PROCEED TO
TEST ②

LIGHTS GO OUT
RECHARGE BATTERY

TEST ② CABLE CONNECTION TEST
INSERT SCREWDRIVER BETWEEN
BATTERY POST AND TERMINAL

CRANKING MOTOR DOES NOT TURN
PROCEED TO
TEST ③

CRANKING MOTOR TURNS
CLEAN BATTERY TERMINALS

TEST ③ SOLENOID TEST
SHORT ACROSS SOLENOID TERMINALS

CRANKING MOTOR DOES NOT TURN
PROCEED TO
TEST ④

CRANKING MOTOR TURNS
REPLACE SOLENOID

TEST ④ CURRENT DRAW TEST
SHORT ACROSS SOLENOID TERMINALS
NOTE SPARK ACROSS PLIER HANDLES

SMALL SPARK
OPEN CIRCUIT OR DEAD BATTERY

LARGE SPARK
CRANKING MOTOR LOCKED OR SHORT CIRCUIT

BATTERY TEST

①Turn on the headlights, and then crank the engine by turning the ignition switch to the START position. On a car with a normal electrical system, the lights will dim somewhat and the cranking motor will crank the engine at a normal rate of speed. On a vehicle with a defect, there are several possible results, depending upon the amount of charge left in the battery or the condition of the cables. If the lights go out completely or dim considerably, the battery is dead and must be recharged. If the starting relay clicks like a machine gun, the battery charge is too low to keep the starting relay engaged when the cranking motor load is connected into the circuit. If the cranking motor spins without cranking the engine, the drive is broken, and the cranking motor should be removed for repairs. If the headlights do not dim and the cranking motor does not operate, then there is an open circuit. Go on to Test ②.

CABLE CONNECTION TEST

②If the cranking motor is inoperative and the headlights do not dim, you should troubleshoot for a poor connection at the battery, starting relay, cranking motor, or neutral-safety switch. The first test is to insert a screwdriver blade tip between a battery post and cable while trying to crank the engine. If the cranking motor now turns, the battery cable connection is corroded and must be disassembled, cleaned, and reassembled. Make this screwdriver test between each of the two battery terminals. *NOTE: This is a very common cause of trouble because of the corrosive nature of battery electrolyte.* If the cranking motor still does not turn with the screwdriver blade tip between the battery post and cable, try moving the transmission selector lever from NEUTRAL to PARK to see if the neutral-safety switch is out of adjustment or has a poor connection. Sometimes jiggling the selector lever will restore a connection temporarily so that the engine can be started. If the cranking motor still does not turn, go on to Test ③.

SOLENOID TEST

③ The solenoid (sometimes called a starting relay) should be checked next by holding a pair of pliers so that the handles short across the two large cable terminals. **CAUTION: Make sure that the uninsulated pliers handles do not touch any other metallic part of the car, or sparks will fly.** You can use a heavy jumper cable or screwdriver in place of the

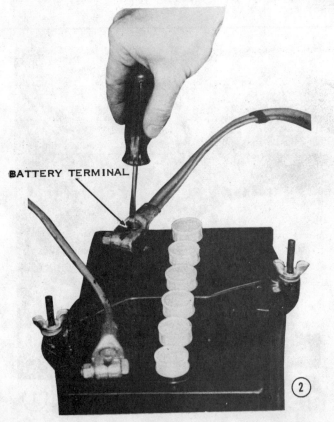

BATTERY TERMINAL

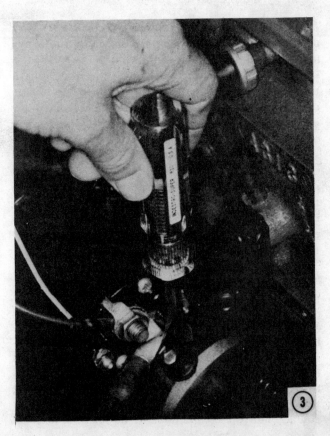

(4)

pliers to short across the terminals. **CAUTION: Don't use thin wire, as it will get very hot under the heavy load and will burn your hands.**

If the cranking motor now turns, the trouble is in the relay, which should be checked to see if the circuit from the ignition switch to the starting relay is complete. Check out this circuit by holding a piece of wire from the heavy terminal (battery) on the starting relay to the small terminal, which is the energizing circuit wire from the ignition switch. If the relay now operates, the trouble is in the circuit to the ignition switch. **CAUTION: The ignition switch must be turned to the START position in order to energize this circuit.** If the cranking motor still does not turn, go on to Test (4).

CURRENT DRAW TEST

(4) Hold the screwdriver or pair of plier handles across the two large terminals on the starting relay, as before. This time, note the size of the spark that appears as the pliers handles touch the terminals. If there is no spark or a small one, then there is a very small current draw in the cranking motor, indicating that the cranking motor brushes are making poor contact with the commutator. If the spark is large, it

indicates an excessive current draw. This can be caused by a short in the wiring inside of the cranking motor, the cranking motor drive teeth being jammed against the teeth of the flywheel, or by the existence of a hydrostatic lock. Water in the combustion chamber, being noncompressible, can prevent the engine from turning.

IGNITION SYSTEM TESTS—ROADMAP THREE

This roadmap provides a series of tests that can be used to isolate trouble in the ignition system. You must make the tests and repairs in the sequence given below to arrive at a solution to the problem. A large majority of starting troubles are caused by defects in the ignition system, and fully 90% of these troubles are the result of defective contact points.

IGNITION CIRCUIT TEST

(1) Disconnect the high-tension coil wire at the center of the distributor cap and hold it about 1/4″ from a good ground. *NOTE: If the rubber boot cannot be pushed back enough, insert a paper clip.* Turn the ignition switch to the START position and crank the engine. If there is no spark here, proceed to Test (2). If there is a good spark, and the trouble has been isolated to the ignition system, proceed to Test (5).

HIGH-TENSION COIL

(1)

ROADMAP THREE — IGNITION SYSTEM TESTS

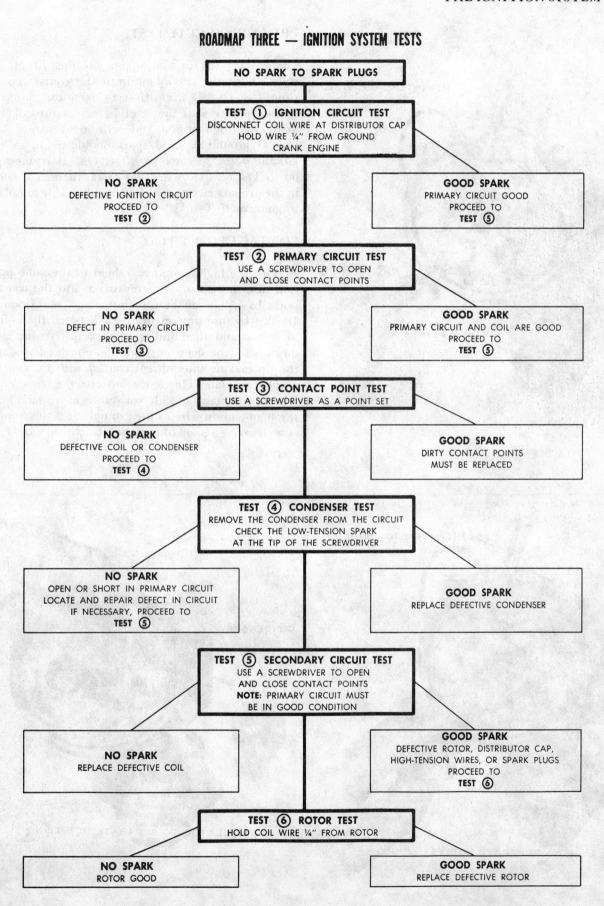

NO SPARK TO SPARK PLUGS

TEST ① IGNITION CIRCUIT TEST
DISCONNECT COIL WIRE AT DISTRIBUTOR CAP
HOLD WIRE ¼" FROM GROUND
CRANK ENGINE

NO SPARK
DEFECTIVE IGNITION CIRCUIT
PROCEED TO
TEST ②

GOOD SPARK
PRIMARY CIRCUIT GOOD
PROCEED TO
TEST ⑤

TEST ② PRIMARY CIRCUIT TEST
USE A SCREWDRIVER TO OPEN
AND CLOSE CONTACT POINTS

NO SPARK
DEFECT IN PRIMARY CIRCUIT
PROCEED TO
TEST ③

GOOD SPARK
PRIMARY CIRCUIT AND COIL ARE GOOD
PROCEED TO
TEST ⑤

TEST ③ CONTACT POINT TEST
USE A SCREWDRIVER AS A POINT SET

NO SPARK
DEFECTIVE COIL OR CONDENSER
PROCEED TO
TEST ④

GOOD SPARK
DIRTY CONTACT POINTS
MUST BE REPLACED

TEST ④ CONDENSER TEST
REMOVE THE CONDENSER FROM THE CIRCUIT
CHECK THE LOW-TENSION SPARK
AT THE TIP OF THE SCREWDRIVER

NO SPARK
OPEN OR SHORT IN PRIMARY CIRCUIT
LOCATE AND REPAIR DEFECT IN CIRCUIT
IF NECESSARY, PROCEED TO
TEST ⑤

GOOD SPARK
REPLACE DEFECTIVE CONDENSER

TEST ⑤ SECONDARY CIRCUIT TEST
USE A SCREWDRIVER TO OPEN
AND CLOSE CONTACT POINTS
NOTE: PRIMARY CIRCUIT MUST
BE IN GOOD CONDITION

NO SPARK
REPLACE DEFECTIVE COIL

GOOD SPARK
DEFECTIVE ROTOR, DISTRIBUTOR CAP,
HIGH-TENSION WIRES, OR SPARK PLUGS
PROCEED TO
TEST ⑥

TEST ⑥ ROTOR TEST
HOLD COIL WIRE ¼" FROM ROTOR

NO SPARK
ROTOR GOOD

GOOD SPARK
REPLACE DEFECTIVE ROTOR

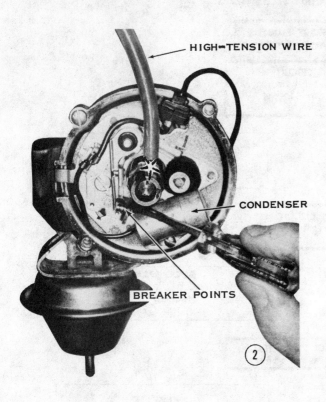

HIGH-TENSION WIRE

CONDENSER

BREAKER POINTS

②

PRIMARY CIRCUIT TEST

② Remove the distributor cap, and then lift off the rotor. Turn the crankshaft until the contact points close. Use a small screwdriver to open and close the contact points with the ignition switch turned ON. With the high-tension coil wire held about 1/4" from a ground, a good spark should jump to the ground *if the primary circuit is OK*. If it does, go on to Test ⑤. If there is no spark, there is a defect in the primary circuit, which you will be able to isolate by going on to Test ③.

CONTACT POINT TEST

③ With the high-tension wire held in the same position, use the tip of the screwdriver and the contact point base plate of the distributor as a set of points. Do this by inserting an insulator between the points as shown and then sliding the screwdriver up and down, with the shaft touching the movable point and the tip making intermittent contact with the contact point base plate. This test substitutes the screwdriver for the contact points. If you now get a spark from the high-tension wire to the ground, then the trouble is a defective set of contact points, which should be

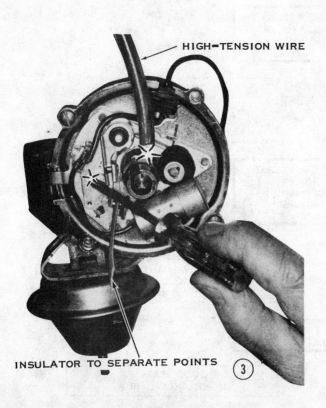

HIGH-TENSION WIRE

INSULATOR TO SEPARATE POINTS   ③

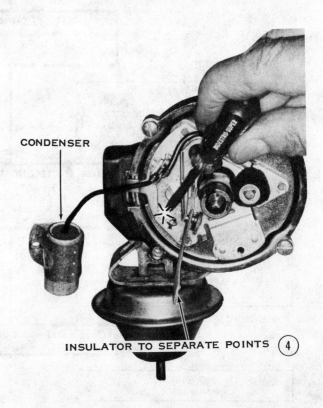

CONDENSER

INSULATOR TO SEPARATE POINTS   ④

replaced. *NOTE: If the contact points are oxidized enough, the illustrated insulator is not required, as the oxidized surfaces form their own insulator.* If there is no spark from the high-tension wire to the ground, then the trouble can be a defective coil or condenser. To check out the condenser, go on to Test ④.

CONDENSER TEST

④ Condensers give very little trouble in general service, but there is always the possibility that a condenser might short out and ground the primary circuit. There is also the possibility that one of the primary wires or connections inside of the distributor might short to ground. The most accurate way to test a condenser is with a tester manufactured for that purpose. For emergency troubleshooting, however, it is possible to check the condenser and the primary circuit insulation for a short by removing the condenser from the system, and then making a few tests with a screwdriver. **CAUTION: Make sure that the metallic case of the condenser does not touch any part of the distributor.** With an insulator between the contact points, slide the blade of a screwdriver up and down, with the shaft making contact with the movable contact point and the tip of the screwdriver making intermittent contact with the contact point base plate. This time check the low-tension spark between the screwdriver tip and the contact point base plate. You should have a spark here indicating that the primary circuit is complete through the neutral-safety switch, primary of the ignition coil, ballast resistor, and primary wiring inside of the distributor. Reconnect the condenser and, if you *now* get no low-tension spark, the condenser is shorting the circuit to ground, and it should be replaced.

If you have no low-tension spark at the screwdriver tip without the condenser in the circuit, it indicates that there is no current flowing to this point, or that there is a short circuit to ground. In this case, it is necessary to check back along the primary circuit wiring to find the defective unit which is open circuited or shorted to ground. Check by using a jumper wire and shorting each unit in turn to ground, just as you did at the movable contact point. The defective unit is the one in which you get a low-tension spark at one of its terminals and no spark at the other. As mentioned before, this can be at the ignition switch, the primary of the ignition coil, the ballast resistor, or at the primary wires in the distributor.

If the condenser and the primary circuit are OK, but the engine still does not start, the trouble can be in the secondary circuit. Proceed to Test ⑤.

SECONDARY CIRCUIT TEST

⑤ *The secondary circuit cannot be tested by emergency troubleshooting techniques unless the primary circuit has tested OK so far or has been repaired as the defects have been uncovered.* If the primary circuit tests OK, use the same test procedures as in Test ②. Hold the high-tension wire about 1/4" from a good ground while using a screwdriver to open and close the contact points. A spark at the high-tension wire indicates that the ignition coil is good but, if the engine still does not start, the trouble must be somewhere else in the secondary circuit: in the rotor, distributor cap, high-tension wires, or spark plugs. To test the rotor, go on to Test ⑥.

If no spark occurs from the high-tension wire to ground, the ignition coil is defective and should be replaced.

ROTOR TEST

⑥ Replace the rotor on the distributor shaft. Hold the high-tension coil wire about 1/4" from the rotor spring, and then crank the engine with the ignition

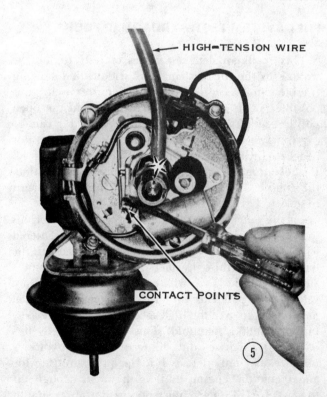

← HIGH-TENSION WIRE

CONTACT POINTS

⑤

switch turned ON. If a spark jumps to the rotor, it is shorted to ground and should be replaced. If no spark jumps to the rotor, its insulation is good and the trouble, if it still exists, must be found by inspecting the distributor cap for cracks, the high-tension wires for poor insulation, and the spark plugs for defects.

FUEL SYSTEM TESTS—ROADMAP FOUR

This roadmap details a series of tests to localize trouble in the fuel system. It is seldom that starting trouble can be caused by the carburetor itself. It is possible for an automatic choke to stick in the open position and cause starting trouble, but this can be overcome to some extent by pumping the accelerator pedal to discharge some fuel into the intake manifold. If the automatic choke sticks in the shut position, the engine will flood, and this will make it difficult to start.

On the other hand, the fuel system can be a serious source of trouble when hard starting is encountered with a hot engine. When a hot engine is shut off, the temperature within the fuel bowl may rise to 150°-200°F., and the fuel will boil. All carburetors are vented to bypass this pressure, but some of the fuel may percolate over the high-speed nozzle and overflow into the intake manifold. This raw fuel needs lots of air to vaporize and dilute it for an explosive mixture. The only remedy is to open the throttle wide and crank the engine until it draws in enough air to start. **CAUTION: Under no circumstances should**

you pump the accelerator pedal, or you will be adding fuel through the accelerating jets to compound the trouble.

Too much fuel can also enter the intake manifold, causing hot starting trouble if the needle valve and seat assembly is leaking. After an engine is shut off, the residual pressure in the fuel line forces excess fuel past the leaking needle valve, which raises the level in the fuel bowl and causes the excess to overflow into the intake manifold. Excessive amounts of fuel can also enter an engine due to a "heavy" float, which reduces its buoyancy. The result is an excessively high fuel level in the float bowl, which causes a continuous overflow.

Generally, fuel system troubles are caused by a plugged filter, a defective fuel pump, or a leak in the suction line from the fuel pump to the fuel tank. Oddly enough, the great majority of starting troubles in which the defect has been traced to the fuel system can be found to result from an empty fuel tank.

FUEL PUMP TEST

①Connect a jumper wire from the primary (distributor) side of the ignition coil to ground to keep the engine from starting. It is also possible to pull the high-tension wire out of the distributor cap and ground it. **CAUTION: Because gasoline will be flowing in the engine compartment during this test, it is very important to guard against fire by securely grounding the high-tension wire so that it cannot spark.** Disconnect the fuel line to the carburetor, position a container so that the discharged fuel can

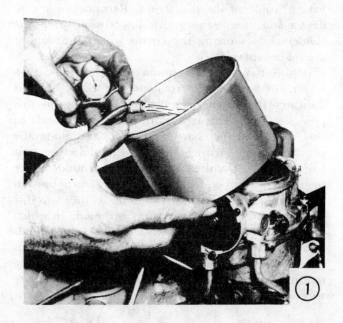

ROADMAP FOUR — FUEL SYSTEM TESTS

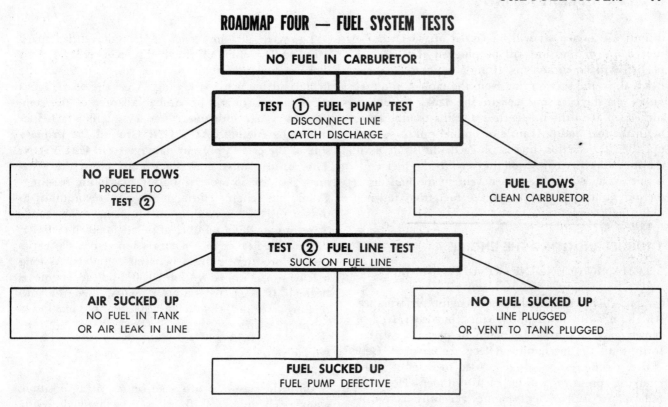

NO FUEL IN CARBURETOR

TEST ① FUEL PUMP TEST
DISCONNECT LINE
CATCH DISCHARGE

NO FUEL FLOWS
PROCEED TO
TEST ②

FUEL FLOWS
CLEAN CARBURETOR

TEST ② FUEL LINE TEST
SUCK ON FUEL LINE

AIR SUCKED UP
NO FUEL IN TANK
OR AIR LEAK IN LINE

NO FUEL SUCKED UP
LINE PLUGGED
OR VENT TO TANK PLUGGED

FUEL SUCKED UP
FUEL PUMP DEFECTIVE

be caught, and then crank the engine. A good-size stream of fuel should pulse out of the line if the fuel pump is functioning properly. Catch at least 10-15 pulses to check the possibility that the size of the stream might decrease, which would indicate a restricted line. In case the fuel line is plugged, it is possible for the fuel stream to stop entirely. If adequate fuel flows to the carburetor, and the engine still does not start, there is the possibility that a strainer in the carburetor inlet is plugged, or that the fuel inlet needle valve and seat are gummed together, which would not allow fuel to pass. Or it can be automatic choke trouble, as discussed before.

If no fuel flows, a defective fuel pump may be the cause or the line from the fuel tank to the fuel pump may be plugged or leaking air. In this case, no fuel will flow. Check out these possibilities by proceeding to Test ②.

FUEL LINE TEST

② The fuel line can be tested by sucking on it. Because of the inaccessibility of the line, it is necessary to disconnect it at the fuel pump and attach a rubber tube to it. Suck on the tube, and one of three con-

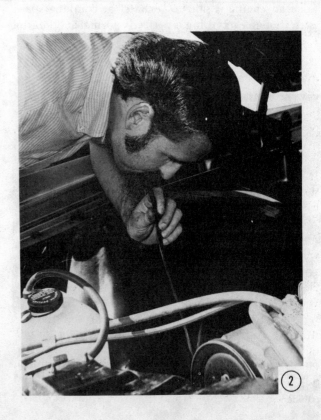

ditions will occur: air will be sucked up, fuel will be sucked up, or the line will be plugged and little or no fuel will be sucked up. If air is sucked up, there is a leak in the suction line from the tank to the fuel pump or there is no fuel in the tank. If fuel is sucked up, then the line is clear and the trouble must be in the fuel pump. If little or no fuel can be sucked up, then the suction line is plugged, the strainer in the fuel tank is clogged, or the vent to the fuel tank is not open. Without an open vent to the fuel tank, suction builds up and keeps the fuel from flowing to the fuel pump.

TROUBLESHOOTING THE ENGINE

MECHANICAL ENGINE CONDITIONS

Good compression is the key to engine performance. An engine with worn piston rings, burned valves, or blown gaskets cannot be made to perform satisfactorily until the mechanical defects are repaired. Generally, a compression gauge is used to determine the cranking pressure within each cylinder. However, today's big displacement engines generally have considerable valve overlap, and the resulting compression reading may be much lower than the manufacturer's specifications of around 150-170 psi. It is entirely possible to obtain a reading as low as 120 psi on a modern engine which is in good mechanical condition. Such an engine is said to "exhale" at cranking speed, even though everything is perfectly normal at operating speeds.

To make a compression test, remove the spark plugs and lay them out in the order of removal. This is extremely important so that you can "read" the firing end of each spark plug. After the spark plugs are removed, insert the rubber adapter of the compression gauge into one cylinder and have a helper crank the engine. **CAUTION: Ground the primary side of the coil to prevent damage to it. CAUTION: The throttle valve and choke must be in the wide-open position in order to obtain maximum readings.** Crank the engine through several revolutions to obtain the highest reading on the compression gauge or record an equal number of pulses for each cylinder.

The significance in a compression test is the variation in pressure readings between cylinders. As long as this variation is within 20-30 psi, the engine is normal. If a greater variation exists, then the low-reading cylinder should be checked by making a cylinder leak test.

LEAK TEST

With the piston at top dead center, firing position, compressed air at 60-70 psi can be applied to the cylinder through an adapter screwed into the spark plug port. On commercially built units, a gauge indicates percent of leakage. Over 20% leakage, in

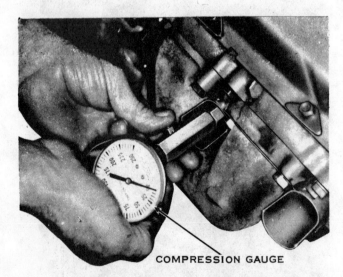

COMPRESSION GAUGE

For an engine to idle smoothly, it must have compression that does not vary over 15 psi for any cylinder. The actual reading is not as important as the amount of variance between cylinders.

HOSE

ADAPTOR

To make a leak test, introduce compressed air in a cylinder in which the piston is at TDC, firing position. Listening to the source of the leaking air will indicate the nature of the defect. In this case, a hiss through the carburetor means a leaking intake valve.

most cases, is considered excessive. It is not difficult to make your own leakage tester. All that is required is an old spark plug shell to which a tire valve has been brazed. In use, the adapter is screwed into the spark plug hole, and then compressed air to 60-70 psi is introduced.

Listening at the point from which the compressed air is escaping indicates the nature of the defect. Insert a short length of heater hose into the various areas being tested and listen at the other end. The

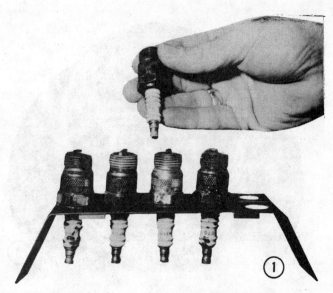

hose helps to amplify the leakage noise. Air hissing from the tail pipe indicates a leaking exhaust valve. Air heard in the carburetor air horn indicates a leaking intake valve. If you hear air hissing at the oil filler pipe, the rings are worn. If bubbles appear in the radiator, the engine has a blown head gasket or a cracked block or head.

SPARK PLUGS

① By way of confirmation, carefully examine the spark plugs you removed from the engine. Line them up in the order of removal so that you can "read" the firing end of the spark plugs and thereby ascertain what has been going on in each cylinder of the engine.

② This is the way a normal spark plug should look after use. The deposits should be dry and powdery. The hard deposits inside the shell indicate that the engine is starting to use some oil, but the condition is not serious. The most important evidence, however, is the light gray color of the porcelain, which is an

A special gauge can be used to indicate the per cent of leakage of the compressed air. This is the indication that could be expected with a normal cylinder.

indication that this spark plug has been running at the correct temperature. This means that the spark plug is one with the correct heat range and that the air-fuel mixture is correct. The combustion temperature is high enough to raise the temperature of the spark plug porcelain so that it burns off the small amount of oil that is normally present in the combustion chamber during the firing period.

③ This black, sooty condition on both the shell and porcelain is caused by an excessively rich air-fuel mixture, both at low and high speeds. The rich mixture lowers the combustion temperature so that the spark plug does not run hot enough to burn off the deposits.

④ If the deposits are formed only on the shell, it is an indication that the low-speed air-fuel mixture is too rich. With a normal mixture at high speeds, the combustion chamber temperature is high enough to burn off the deposits on the insulator.

⑤ This dark insulator, with very few deposits, indicates that the spark plug is running too cool.

This condition can be caused by low compression or by using a spark plug of an incorrect heat range. If the condition is isolated to one cylinder, low compression can be suspected. If all of the spark plugs look like this, they are probably of a heat range that is too cold.

⑥ Heavy carbon-like deposits are an indication of excessive oil consumption. This can result from worn piston rings, worn valve guides, or from a valve seal that is either worn or incorrectly installed.

⑦ This wet, fouled spark plug is not firing. Any combustion would have dried off the deposits until the spark plug looked like the one in the preceding

picture. This fouled condition of the spark plug can be caused by the wet oily deposits on the insulator shorting the high-tension spark to ground inside the shell. Or the condition can be caused by ignition trouble, in which case no high-tension pulse is delivered to the plug to fire it.

⑧ Overheating and pre-ignition are indicated by a dead white or gray insulator, which is generally blistered. The electrode gap wear rate will be considerably more than normal and, in the case of pre-ignition, will actually cause the electrodes to melt as the ones in this spark plug did. Overadvanced ignition timing, detonation from using a fuel of too-

low octane rating, an excessively lean air-fuel mixture, or cooling system troubles can cause overheating.

⑨ Excessive electrode wear results in a wide gap and, more important, the carbonized electrode surfaces form a high-resistance gap path for the spark to jump across. This condition will cause the engine to mis-fire under acceleration. If all of the spark plugs are in this condition, it can cause an increase in fuel consumption and a restricted top speed, especially so if the rest of the ignition system is not operating at maximum efficiency. The remedy, of course, is to replace the spark plugs. However, it is possible to use this spark plug if the electrodes are filed to remove the resistance surfaces and then regapped to the correct specifications.

⑩ If you find two adjacent spark plugs fouled, check for a blown cylinder head gasket or for incorrect connections of the high-tension wires to these plugs.

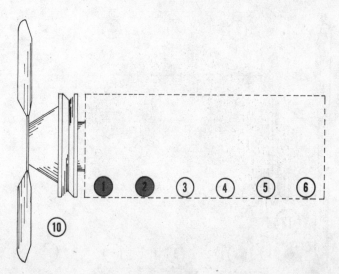

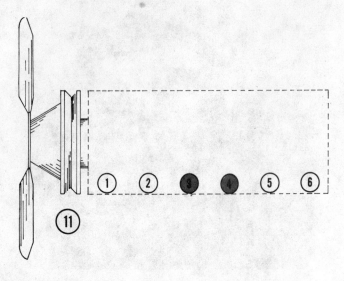

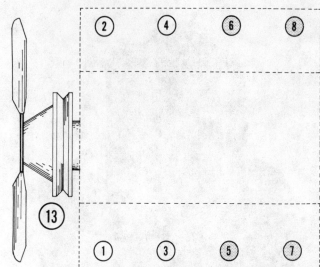

⑪ If the two center spark plugs are fouled, the cause may be raw fuel boiling out of the carburetor into the intake manifold after the engine is shut down. Such a condition can be caused by percolation, a leaking intake needle valve and seat, a heavy float, or a high fuel level.

⑫ If four spark plugs are fouled in this unusual pattern, one barrel of the carburetor is running too rich. This pattern follows the usual fuel flow in a V-8 engine.

⑬ If the four rear spark plugs are overheated, there is a possible cooling system problem. It may be necessary to reverse-flush the engine to restore circulation to the rear of the cylinder heads.

⑭ If one spark plug is overheated, check the firing order. When the burned plug is the second of two adjacent, consecutive-firing spark plugs, the overheating may be the result of crossfire. If, as in this illustration, you found that the spark plug of No. 7

cylinder was overheated, and the firing order is 1-8-4-3-6-5-7-2, the crossfire might result from the fact that cylinders Nos. 5 and 7 are adjacent to each other physically and also in the firing order. Separating the high-tension leads going to these two plugs may eliminate the problem.

VACUUM GAUGE

A vacuum gauge is a relatively inexpensive piece of test equipment that can be very handy in isolating trouble in an internal-combustion engine. As with a compression gauge, a numerical reading cannot be counted on. Instead, relative readings and typical actions of the needle provide clues to some types of troubles.

Normal idle vacuum in the intake manifold ranges from 15 to 22″ Hg. On later-model engines, lower and less steady intake manifold vacuum readings are

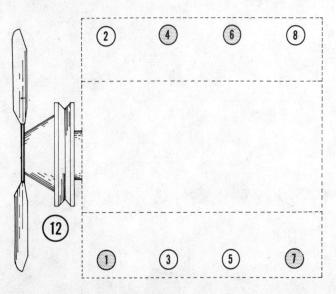

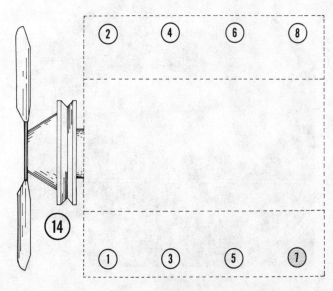

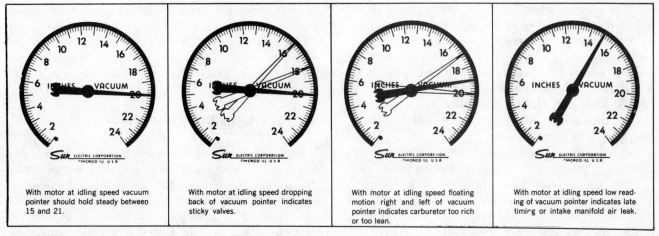

With motor at idling speed vacuum pointer should hold steady between 15 and 21.

With motor at idling speed dropping back of vacuum pointer indicates sticky valves.

With motor at idling speed floating motion right and left of vacuum pointer indicates carburetor too rich or too lean.

With motor at idling speed low reading of vacuum pointer indicates late timing or intake manifold air leak.

A vacuum gauge is a handy diagnostic tool for isolating troubles in an internal-combustion engine. The interpretations are shown under each of the gauge readings.

becoming increasingly common because of the greater use of high-lift cams and the increase in the amounts of valve overlap. Also, altitude affects a vacuum gauge reading. In mountainous areas, a vacuum gauge will read about one inch lower for each 1,000′ of elevation above sea level. It is also possible for a change in barometric pressure to affect a vacuum gauge reading, which possibility emphasizes the fact that it is much more important to watch the needle action than its actual reading. With experience, you will come to recognize easily such conditions as sticking valves, a tight valve lash adjustment, or a restriction in the exhaust system.

DYNAMOMETER TESTING

It is possible to use a vacuum gauge and a set of shorting wires as a relatively inexpensive dynamom-

eter for isolating mechanical troubles to one or more cylinders. In this test, all of the spark plugs except one are successively shorted out so that the engine is made to run on one cylinder at a time. If a vacuum gauge is connected to the intake manifold, a reading can be obtained to compare the efficiency of each cylinder. A low-reading cylinder can be the result of inefficiency in one of the three basic systems: ignition, fuel, or compression.

The ground clip of the shorting wires must be attached to a *good* ground. Start the engine and have a helper advance the throttle as you successively short out all of the cylinders, except one. It will be necessary to open the throttle wide in order to keep the engine running on one cylinder at a time. Note the

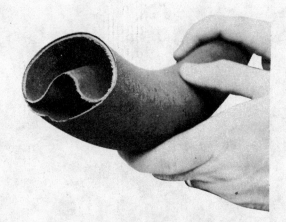

This is part of an exhaust pipe that collapsed. This kind of defect can be checked with a vacuum gauge by accelerating the engine and allowing it to return to idle. A restricted exhaust will cause a momentary stop in the return of the needle when the throttle is closed quickly.

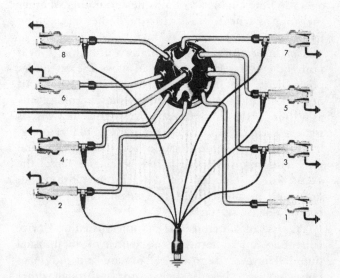

A set of shorting wires is a relatively inexpensive diagnostic tool, and very effective in isolating trouble. You will not get a shock, provided that the ground clip of the shorting wires is attached to a good ground first.

vacuum gauge reading, and then move the shorting clip from one of the spark plugs to the spark plug of the cylinder you just tested. Note the vacuum gauge reading, and then test each of the other cylinders in turn by running the engine on that one spark plug. A weak cylinder or a cylinder that is not firing is easily determined, but the most important part of this test is the ability to compare the relative power (vacuum) of each firing stroke.

Tuning on a dynamometer, when the ignition timing is adjusted with the engine running under load, is sometimes referred to as "power tuning." In practice, the engine is run at about 3,000 rpm and the distributor turned until a peak horsepower reading is obtained on a test meter. This same adjustment can be performed with the shorting wires and a vacuum gauge. With the engine running on one cylinder, adjust the position of the distributor until the vacuum gauge needle advances to its highest value.

ENGINE NOISES

Noises are generally referred to as knocks, slaps, clicks, and squeaks; they are caused by loose bearings, pistons, gears, and other moving parts of the engine. In general, the most common types of noises are either synchronized to engine speed or to one-half engine speed. Those that are timed to engine speed are sounds that have to do with the crankshaft, rods, pistons, and pins. The sounds that are emitted at one-half crankshaft speed concern valve-train noises. Whether or not the sound occurs at engine speed or one-half engine speed can usually be determined by operating the engine at a slow idle and noting whether the noise is synchronized with the flashes of a timing light.

A main bearing knock is usually a dull thud that is noticeable under load. Trying to move the car under power with the brakes applied will bring out this noise. Pull the spark plug wires from the plugs, one at a time. If the noise disappears when a plug wire is removed, then it is probably coming from that cylinder. This category would include rod bearings, piston pins, and piston slap. If a rod bearing is loose, the noise will be loudest on deceleration. Piston pin noise and piston slap are, in general, louder when a cold engine is first started.

The use of a stethoscope or other listening device will often aid in locating the source of an unusual sound. However, a great deal of care and judgment must be used, because noise travels through other metallic parts as well, parts not involved in the problem.

Carbon build-up in the combustion chamber can cause interference with a piston. Fuel pumps can knock, belts can be noisy, distributors can emit clicking noises, and generators can contribute to unusual sounds. Flywheels, clutches, transmissions, water pumps, and loose manifolds can also cause noise problems.

EXCESSIVE OIL CONSUMPTION

High oil consumption complaints are often the result of oil leaks rather than actual consumption by the engine. Therefore, before assuming that an engine is burning oil, examine the exterior for evidence of oil leaks. In analyzing the problem, consideration must be given to the fact that oil can enter the combustion chambers in only four ways: past the piston rings, through the valve guides, through the intake manifold and, if the engine is equipped with a vacuum booster pump, through a defect in the pump. Evidence of excessive oil consumption usually is in the form of carbon deposits in the exhaust outlet pipe and oil-fouled spark plugs. The following items are generally responsible for oil consumption prob-

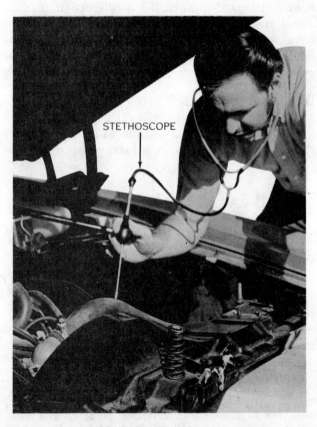

STETHOSCOPE

Engine noises can be pinpointed with a stethoscope or with a long screwdriver held to the ear.

lems: (1) a clogged positive crankcase ventilation system, (2) piston rings not sealing, (3) excessive valve stem-to-guide clearance, (4) ineffective valve stem seals, or (5) a cracked intake manifold (the type that serves as a valve chamber cover).

A quick check to determine if the PCV (Positive Crankcase Ventilation) system is working can be made by removing the oil filler cap and placing the palm of your hand over the oil filler tube opening for 30 seconds with the engine idling. If there is suction when removing your hand, the system is working. If there is pressure against your hand, the system is inoperative.

OVERHEATING

WITHOUT THE LOSS OF COOLANT

Overheating can be caused by the front of the radiator being obstructed by leaves, bugs, and/or dirt. Restricted hoses in the cooling system can affect the flow of coolant, and this is also true if the pump drive belt is loose. Any restriction in the exhaust system, too, will cause overheating. This can be a bent exhaust pipe or an exhaust control valve that is stuck in the closed position.

Circulation can also be impaired by a loose or broken pump hub or impeller, or the thermostat can be defective. The thermostat can be checked by removing it from the engine and testing it in a pail of heated water.

When the thermostat is removed for checking, inspect the casting for a foundry flash inside the manifold. This can be done by a visual inspection or by probing through the thermostat opening with a piece of welding rod or heavy wire. If there is a flash,

it will restrict the flow of coolant through the manifold, causing the coolant to boil after the engine is stopped. This condition can also cause the engine to overheat after long driving periods.

If the car is equipped with a fluid-coupling type of fan drive, check the operation of the unit as follows: (1) Run the engine at approximately 1,000 rpm until normal operating temperature is reached. This process can be speeded up by blocking off the front of the radiator with cardboard. (2) Stop the engine and, using a cloth to protect your hand, immediately check the effort required to turn the fan. If considerable effort is required, the coupling is operating satisfactorily. If very little effort is required to turn the fan, it is an indication that the coupling is not operating properly and that it should be serviced or replaced.

Retarded ignition timing and a lean air-fuel mixture will also cause overheating.

WITH LOSS OF COOLANT

When it becomes necessary to add coolant to the system at regular intervals, the cause of the trouble should be investigated. Visually inspect the radiator, pump, engine, and hoses for leaks. Check the pressure rating and operation of the radiator filler cap.

If the loss of coolant is due to an internal leak caused by a crack in the combustion chamber, the coolant will be rusty and the engine will overheat. If this is the case, evidence of the crack can be determined by looking for bubbles in the coolant as the engine is accelerated. Do this by draining the coolant to the top of the block and then removing the top hose. Add coolant until the level is even with the top of the thermostat housing. Start the engine and accelerate

The pressure rating of the radiator filler cap can be checked with a pump and gauge arrangement, as shown.

A crack in the head or block can be checked by introducing compressed air into each cylinder with the piston at TDC firing position and checking for bubbles in the coolant at the thermostat housing, as discussed in the text.

it quickly. Check the coolant surface for evidence of bubbles.

If you suspect a crack in the combustion chamber, you can introduce air pressure into each cylinder while checking the coolant at the thermostat housing for bubbles. To do this, install an air hose adapter (an old spark plug shell to which a tire valve has been brazed) in No. 1 spark plug hole. Start the test by rotating the crankshaft until No. 1 cylinder is at TDC, firing position. Check the distributor points, which should just be starting to open. Introduce air at full line pressure. Check each cylinder in turn by rotating the crankshaft until the breaker points start to open for the next cylinder in the firing order. Transfer the air hose adapter to that cylinder, and then repeat the test.

EMISSION-CONTROL SYSTEMS

There are three kinds of emissions that must be controlled on a modern engine: crankcase, exhaust, and evaporative. The troubleshooting of these systems will be covered in Chapter 3, along with the theory of operation.

FUEL AND IGNITION SYSTEM PROBLEMS

ROUGH ENGINE IDLE

A rough idle can be caused by any of numerous conditions and maladjustments of the engine. This problem is best approached by first doing a complete engine tune-up to take care of such possible ignition conditions as points and/or spark plugs burned, fouled, or improperly gapped or the ignition timing set too far advanced or retarded.

Other engine conditions which can cause a rough idle are intake manifold air leaks, uneven compression, sticking valves, and troubles in the fuel system which can affect the idle mixture. These troubles include a high fuel level, heavy float, a leaking needle valve and seat, a leaking power valve diaphragm, a restricted air filter element, automatic choke malfunctions, and poor idle mixture and/or speed adjustments.

With the advent of exhaust, evaporative, and crankcase emission control systems, the modern engine induction system has been designed with a calibrated amount of air leaking into the intake manifold. This is necessary to vent the crankcase of unburned vapors. Also, some of the late-model engines are passing intake manifold vacuum through calibrated bleeds to operate diaphragms for controlling valves in the power brakes, hand brake releasing mechanisms, heater and air conditioning door systems, and vacuum motors for regulating the temperature of the incoming air in the thermostatically controlled air cleaner. If an excessively large amount of air is bleeding into the intake manifold through a leak in one of the air hoses, by an improper vacuum connection or by an incorrectly installed part with an improper air bleed, the result will be a rough engine idle. The only way to isolate troubles of this type is to pinch off one at a time the hoses leading to the intake manifold and to note the effect on a vacuum gauge and tachometer. In the case of a vent, such as the one to the PCV valve in the manifold, pinching it off should cause a drop in engine speed of about 60 rpm. If there is no drop, then the PCV valve is plugged, and the calibrated air bleed is shut. If the drop is excessive, the PCV valve has an incorrectly calibrated air bleed.

Check for a vacuum leak in each of the other vacuum systems by pinching off each hose in turn and noting the effect of so doing on the vacuum gauge and the tachometer.

INCONSISTENT ENGINE IDLE SPEED

The most common cause of an inconsistent idle speed is sticking or binding in the throttle linkage and/or the automatic transmission throttle control and kickdown linkages. It is also possible for the

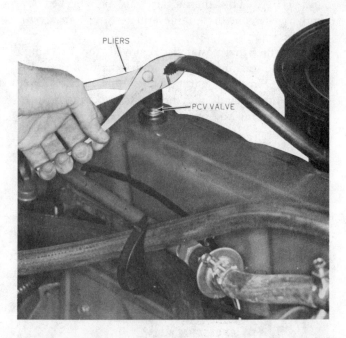

To check out the PCV system, clamp the hose shut, and the engine speed should drop about 60 rpm. **CAUTION: If the hose is old, it is better to pull it off the valve and cover the end with your finger. Clamping off an old hose will often loosen particles from the brittle inside walls, which may then plug the valve.**

carburetor throttle shaft to be either sticking or loose on the throttle lever, or to have a loose throttle plate which can shift in the body and cause this trouble.

If the carburetor is equipped with a dashpot, check the operation of the plunger for sticking or binding. Clean the end of the plunger and the plunger seat on the throttle lever. A dirty and gummy plunger and seat can cause a sticking condition.

EXCESSIVE FUEL CONSUMPTION

This condition can be the result of poor driving habits, a faulty condition of the vehicle, or inefficient engine operation. Quite often, it is a combination of all three. If the fuel consumption has been normal for some time, and then suddenly increases, defects other than the driver are indicated.

Preliminary checking should include an inspection for correct tire inflation, dragging brakes, or a fuel leak. Check for a fuel leak both with the engine running and not running. Fuel leaks show up more readily between the fuel pump and carburetor when the fuel pump is operating. On the other hand, a leak between the fuel pump and tank will not be evident when the fuel pump is operating. This is due to the vacuum that is created on the suction side of the system, which will keep the fuel from leaking.

Ignition performance can have a decided effect on gasoline mileage. Some of the factors which can adversely affect mileage are fouled or burned spark plugs, ignition system defects, and late ignition timing.

If the other factors check out or have been corrected and the fuel consumption is still excessive, then the carburetor must be overhauled. Check the power valve and the needle valve and seat for leaking. Care must be taken when making the adjustments which affect fuel consumption, such as those to the float level, automatic choke, vacuum-kick, and power valve. When checking the operation of the automatic choke, make sure that the heat tube is open and that the vacuum system works properly. Be sure to clean the filter element of the air cleaner.

ACCELERATION STUMBLE

A stumble on acceleration is generally caused by insufficient delivery of fuel during a stroke of the carburetor accelerator pump. This deficiency could be the result of too short a pump stroke or leaking accelerator pump check valves. The remedy is to remove the carburetor, clean it thoroughly (paying particular attention to the parts of the acceleration system), and then reassemble it. Be sure to make the bench adjustments, paying special attention to those which are concerned with the parts of the accelerating circuit.

It is quite possible that other systems can cause a stumble on acceleration. If the manifold heat control valve is stuck in the open position, it can cause a stumble when the engine is warming up. Trouble in the ignition system secondary circuit will also cause a stumble, but this condition may better be referred to as a miss on acceleration.

CONDITION	CAUSED BY
BURNED	Any discoloration other than a frosted slate grey shall be considered as burned points.
EXCESSIVE METAL TRANSFER OR PITTING	Incorrect alignment. Incorrect voltage regulator setting. Radio condenser installed to the distributor side of the coil. Ignition condenser of improper capacity. Extended operation of the engine at speeds other than normal.

Defective breaker points are a common cause of ignition trouble, and this, in turn, has a decided effect on the gasoline mileage obtained. This illustration shows defective breaker points and the conditions which caused them.

Engine Surge

A surging engine is one which runs as if the load on the car were being intermittently increased and decreased. This is best detected while maintaining a constant car speed. Surging can take place at any car speed. However, surging generally is detected in the mid-speed range and may not be in evidence at other speeds.

In general, surging is caused by a lean fuel condition, resulting from dirt or a restriction in the fuel system. A defective fuel pump or any condition that does not permit a normal flow of fuel mixture into the intake manifold can cause surging. Another cause, though quite remote, is a distributor vacuum-advance system that may be hunting or constantly changing the spark timing.

Poor High-Speed Performance

This problem can be caused by either the fuel system or the ignition system. A fuel system that does not supply adequate fuel for high-speed operation usually causes the engine to cut out entirely as car speed is increased. As the car slows down, a speed will be reached where operation will again be normal.

An ignition problem is usually evidenced by the engine misfiring during acceleration, but it is possible for a malfunctioning ignition system, without sufficient reserve, to pass out at higher engine speeds. Generally, the feeling is one of rough engine operation rather than of a complete cutting out.

Other conditions which should be checked for poor high-speed performance are preignition and over-advanced ignition timing. Fuel system troubles include the following: a restricted air cleaner, restricted exhaust system, defective fuel pump, clogged fuel filter in the line, and partially clogged vent in the gas tank.

Poor Low-Speed Performance

If the engine performance is sluggish at low speeds only and high-speed operation is normal, the fuel supply system must be operating satisfactorily. The spark plugs, distributor contact points, compression, and exhaust system must also be normal.

If the trouble occurs only at low speeds, it can be in the low-speed or range circuits of the carburetor, in an incorrect low-speed calibration of the distributor, or in a failure to set the ignition timing to specifications. Also, check the vacuum advance diaphragm of the distributor for a leak. If the engine is equipped with a Holley carburetor, check the distributor vacuum passages in the carburetor. An automatic transmission with a defective one-way clutch will also cause a loss of performance at low speeds.

CLOSED (HEAT ON)   OPEN (HEAT OFF)

A stumble on acceleration can be caused by a manifold heat control valve stuck in the open position. There is not enough heat supplied to the intake manifold to vaporize the fuel properly.

Improperly adjusted ignition timing has a decided effect on the performance of the engine, emissions, and gasoline mileage. Use a timing light to adjust the ignition timing to specificatins.

ENGINE STALLING

When an engine starts normally, but fails to keep running, the trouble is probably in the fuel system. If the temperature is below freezing, water in the fuel line or carburetor may have frozen, thereby restricting the flow of fuel. Stalling when cold can be caused by the fast-idle speed being too low, the choke plate sticking, an incorrect setting of the choke cover, or the choke plate pull-down adjustment being incorrect.

If a hot engine stalls and cannot be restarted, the trouble may be caused by vapor lock. Such an engine cannot usually be restarted until the vaporized fuel has condensed back into a liquid. If the hot engine stalling condition is general, the trouble can be caused by the idle speed being too low, the idle mixture being incorrectly adjusted, or the choke plate sticking partially closed.

Under certain weather conditions, an engine will run normally, both when it is cold and when it is hot, but will stall at idle or near-idle speeds during the engine warm-up period. This condition can be caused by carburetor icing, and it is most likely to occur when winter-grade gasoline (more volatile than summer grade) is used and when the atmospheric temperature ranges from 30° to 60°F. at relative humidities above 65%.

When carburetor icing occurs, moisture is drawn from the air passing through the carburetor. It condenses and forms ice on the throttle plates and the surrounding throttle body. When the throttle is almost completely closed for idling, this ice tends to bridge the gap between the throttle plate and body, thereby cutting off the air supply and causing the engine to stall. Opening the throttle for restarting breaks the ice bridge but does not eliminate the possibility of further stalling until the engine and carburetor have warmed up.

In some instances, an engine will run normally in all phases of its operation but will stall just as the car is brought to a stop. This condition usually is confined to cars equipped with an automatic transmission. Cars so equipped have an anti-stall dashpot attached to the carburetor to control the closing rate of the throttle plates. A dashpot that is out of adjustment or one that is defective generally causes this type of engine stalling. However, if the stalling is accompanied by engine roughness, a contributing cause could be a high carburetor fuel level due to a leaking needle valve and seat or to a heavy float, or a combination of dashpot adjustment and fuel level.

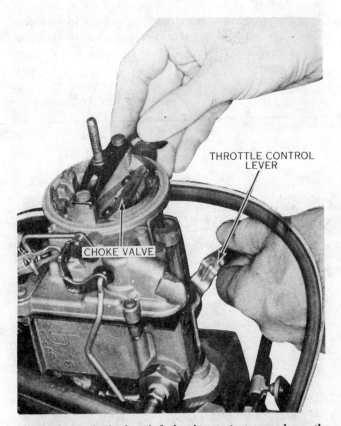

THROTTLE CONTROL LEVER

CHOKE VALVE

One way to check the air-fuel mixture is to speed up the engine and restrict the flow of air through the carburetor. This can be done by closing the choke valve partially or restricting the opening with the palm of your hand. If the mixture is too lean, restricting the air will cause the engine to speed up. If the mixture is too rich, restricting the air will cause the engine to slow down.

ENGINE STARTS HARD

When an engine is hard to start when cold but starts easily when hot, the trouble usually is caused by defects in the ignition system or by a lean supply of fuel through the carburetor. A choke coil that is set too lean, sticking choke plate, and binding choke linkage are the most common causes of this particular lean condition. If this cold-starting problem exists only when the temperature is below freezing, the most likely cause is water in the carburetor which freezes and restricts the flow of fuel.

Hard starting of a hot engine generally is caused by an oversupply of fuel through the carburetor, which results in engine flooding. The more common causes of flooding are a choke coil that is set too rich, sticking choke plate, and binding choke linkage. Flooding also can be caused by a dirty, worn, or leaking float valve needle and seat or by a sticking float. Another cause of flooding is percolation, whereby the fuel in the carburetor bowl boils over into the intake manifold. This condition, when it exists, is most likely to occur

Engine misfire is generally caused by ignition system defects. Worn-out spark plugs with corroded electrodes and an excessively wide gap can cause the engine to misfire on acceleration.

shortly after a hot engine is shut off. High fuel pump pressure occasionally contributes toward flooding.

When an engine can be started, but keeps running only when the ignition key is held in the START position, the trouble is in the ballast resistor or its circuit. If the engine does not run when the ignition key is turned to the ON position, the trouble can be caused by the idle mixture being incorrectly adjusted, the choke plate sticking, a restriction in the fuel line, or a weak fuel pump.

Engine Misfire

In most instances, this condition is caused by spark plug troubles; the plugs may be fouled, have broken insulators, be improperly gapped, or offer high resistance at the electrodes, or the wrong type may have been installed. The condition can also be caused by other defects in the ignition system secondary circuit —in the ignition coil, rotor, distributor cap, or high-tension wiring. If the condition can be traced to the primary circuit, then the trouble can be burned contact points, incorrect point dwell, incorrect point spring tension, a defective condenser, or a corroded low-tension wiring connection.

ELECTRICAL SYSTEM

BATTERY AND CHARGING SYSTEM

The charging system consists of an alternator, a regulator, a battery, a charge indicator gauge and the necessary wiring to connect the components.

Battery problems are not always due to charging system defects. Excessive use of lights and accessories while the engine is either off or running at low speed, voltage losses, corroded battery cables and connectors, low water level in the battery, or prolonged disuse of the battery which would permit a self-discharged condition are all possible reasons which should be considered when a battery is run down or low on charge.

Charging system troubles such as low alternator output or no alternator output (indicated by the indicator gauge showing discharge while the engine is running) require testing of both the alternator and the alternator regulator. Alternator regulator problems usually do not make themselves known except by their direct effect on the alternator output and, of course, eventually by creating a battery problem. Proper adjustment of the regulating units contained in the regulator assembly is very important.

Test the alternator output at the battery, with an ammeter in series between the battery cable and battery post. It is necessary to add approximately 5 amperes to the output reading obtained to cover the current draw of the gauge system, ignition system, and field circuit. If the car is equipped with a transistor ignition system, 6 amperes should be added to the output reading in order to determine the total output of the alternator.

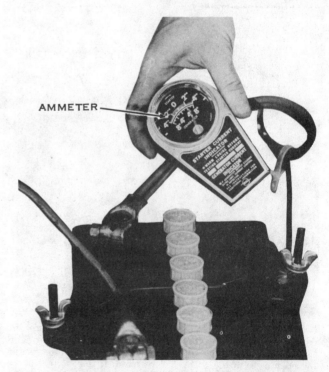

AMMETER

An induction-type ammeter can be used to measure the charging system output by holding the meter over the main wire to the battery with the engine running at a fast-idle speed.

If the output is satisfactory at the alternator, inspect and test the charging circuit wiring for excessive resistance. Inspect all wiring and connections between the alternator and the battery (insulated side) and between the battery and the alternator (ground side). Isolate the area of excessive resistance by checking the voltage drop over each of the circuit sections.

An output of 2 to 5 amperes less than specifications usually indicates an open diode. An output of approximately 10 amperes less than specifications usually indicates a shorted diode.

Noisy Alternator

When investigating the complaint of alternator noise, first try to localize and pinpoint the noise area to make sure that the alternator is at fault rather than the drive belt or water pump or another part of the engine. Start the engine and listen for the area and the type of noise. Use a stethoscope or similar sound-detection instrument to localize the noise. An alternator bearing, pump bearing, or belt noise is usually a squealing sound.

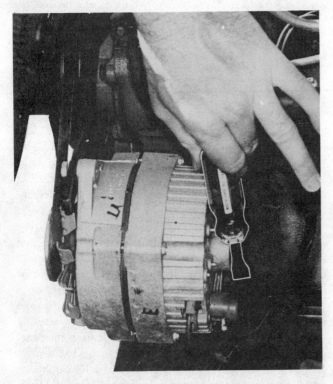

A simple check to see if the regulator contacts are in good condition is to hold a screwdriver against the end of the alternator with the ignition key in the running position but with the engine stopped. If the regulator contact points are good, the field will be energized and the screwdriver will be attracted by the resulting magnetic field. CAUTION: Don't make contact at the positive diode heat sink which is at battery voltage, or sparks will fly.

An alternator with a shorted diode will normally whine (magnetic noise) and will be most noticeable at idle speeds. Perform an alternator output test; if the output is approximately 10 amperes less than specifications, a shorted diode is indicated. To eliminate the belt as the cause of noise, apply a light amount of belt dressing. If the alternator belt is at fault, adjust the belt to specifications or replace it, if necessary. If the belt is satisfactory and the noise is believed to be in the alternator or pump, remove the alternator belt. Start the engine and listen for the noise as a double check to be sure the noise is not caused by another component. If the noise is traced to the alternator, remove it and inspect the bearings for wear, scoring, or an out-of-round condition.

TURN SIGNALS

The turn signal system includes a fuse, a flasher unit, a switch and wiring assembly, front and rear signal lights, instrument panel indicator lights, an ignition switch (accessory terminal is used as the power source), and the necessary wiring to connect the components.

As a visual aid in troubleshooting turn signal problems, connect an ammeter in series with the battery. Any indication of an excessive current draw can then be readily observed. **CAUTION: The ignition switch must be either in the ACC or ON position for the turn signal lights to operate.**

One Signal Light Fails to Operate

This type of trouble is most often the result of a burned-out bulb. If one bulb is burned out, the remaining bulb(s) will remain on but will not flash. Also, the respective right or left instrument panel indicator light will remain on. Switch failure, shorted or open wiring, loose connectors, or corroded bulb socket assemblies are other causes of inoperative signal lights.

All Signal Lights Fail to Operate

This trouble is most often the result of a blown fuse or a defective flasher unit. However, a turn signal switch failure or shorted or open wiring could also be contributing causes. As the fuse or turn signal power supply is fed from the accessory terminal of the ignition switch, check that other accessories such as the radio are operative. If other accessories are not operative, it is possible that the ignition switch may be defective.

A 12-volt test light may be substituted for a voltmeter. A voltage or test light indication should be obtained only at the connectors which lead to the lights in question. If there is voltage or a test light indication at connectors other than those for which the turn signal switch is positioned, then the turn signal switch or wiring assembly has a short circuit. If there is no voltage at the connections, then an open circuit through the switch is indicated. In either case, the switch and wiring assembly must be removed for repair or replacement.

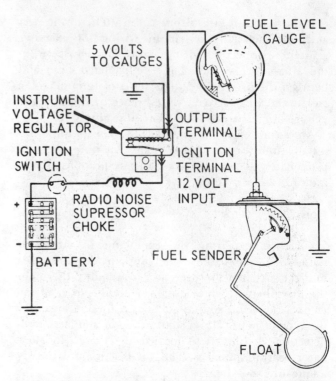

A constant voltage regulator is designed to furnish 5 volts for energizing the gauges. The battery voltage cannot be used for the gauge system because it varies with the state of charge and the charging rate of the alternator.

CONSTANT VOLTAGE SYSTEM

The constant voltage system consists of the fuel level indicator gauge, fuel tank sending unit, temperature indicator gauge, temperature sending unit, and the oil pressure indicator gauge and sending unit except on cars equipped with an oil pressure indicator light.

If all gauge indicators read maximum, the condition is caused by sticking points or an open heater winding in the CV regulator. If all gauge indicators remain on the low end of the scale, an open CV regulator or an open circuit on the input side of the regulator is the probable cause. If one or two gauge indicators register incorrectly, a defective indicator or sending unit is the most probable cause. Substitute a new fuel tank sending unit to check out a suspected gauge. Disconnect the wire from the suspected sending unit and connect it to the test unit. **CAUTION: Be sure that the test unit is grounded properly to the metal of the car.**

If the gauge indicator operation is erratic, loose wiring connectors or a defective sending unit is the most probable cause. If all gauge indicators read higher than conditions warrant, the probable cause is a

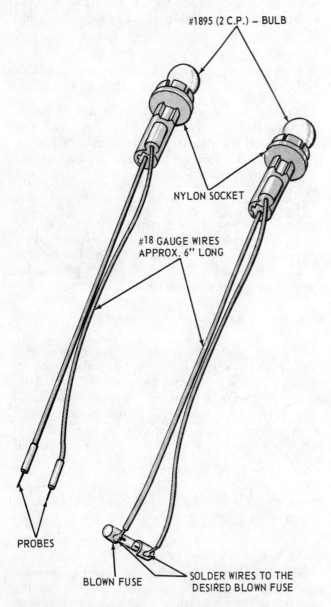

A testing probe can be made with an old socket and a bulb. This device can be used to check terminals for current without blowing out the fuse. If a similar probe is soldered to a blown fuse (right), the fuse can be inserted into the fuse receptacle of a circuit for testing so that fuses are not blown out at each test.

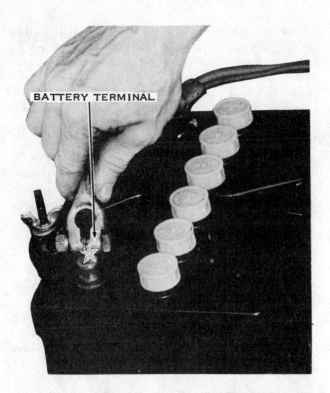

BATTERY TERMINAL

If a current drain discharges the battery, it can be checked by sparking the battery cable against the terminal post. If a spark occurs with all switches OFF, then there is a current drain in the electrical wiring of the vehicle. CAUTION: Make sure that the doors are closed when making this test, or the courtesy lights will be switched on but not lit, and you will get a misleading indication.

poor ground at the CV regulator. Clean and tighten the CV regulator ground connections, and then retest the system. If the gauge indicators still read higher than operating conditions indicate, replace the CV regulator.

TROUBLESHOOTING THE DRIVELINE

Clutch Chatters

Rapid gripping or slipping of the clutch assembly while the unit is being engaged will cause a clutch to chatter. Some of the conditions resulting in clutch chatter are release bearing binding, worn linkage, clutch pedal and assist spring being out of adjustment, loose engine mounts, and a warped or sticking clutch disc.

Clutch Drags

Clutch drag (spinning) causes clashing of the transmission gears and is most noticeable in shifting from neutral position to low or reverse gear. The condition is caused by a clutch disc that is not completely released when the pedal is fully depressed. Thus, the disc continues to rotate, being dragged around by the rotation of the flywheel. In most instances, the dragging condition is caused by excessive clutch pedal free travel.

Clutch Noisy

If the clutch pedal operation is noisy with the engine stopped, the trouble is caused by linkage requiring lubrication, linkage worn or improperly adjusted, release bearing burred and dragging on the transmission bearing retainer, or the pressure plate lugs rubbing against the cover.

If the noise occurs only when the engine is running, the condition can be caused by a misaligned engine and flywheel housing or by looseness or a worn condition of the pilot bearing. *NOTE: A faulty clutch pilot bearing is characterized by a high-pitched noise when the clutch pedal is depressed with the engine idling.*

If the noise occurs only when the clutch pedal is partially depressed, the trouble is a defective release bearing. The pedal action brings the release bearing into contact with the clutch release fingers when the pedal is partially depressed, causing the bearing to spin.

Clutch Slips

Clutch disc slippage will be encountered if the friction surface of the clutch plate fails to hold the disc against the friction face of the flywheel. If severe clutch slippage exists, a greater than normal engine speed will be noticed in high gear when the accelerator is depressed to full throttle. If the slippage is slight but continuous, it may go unnoticed until excessive temperature caused by friction results in failure of the disc and/or friction surfaces.

In most cases, slippage is caused by insufficient clutch pedal free-travel. Normal clutch disc facing wear causes a gradual reduction in free-travel and when a point of no free-travel is reached, clutch slippage will begin.

STANDARD-GEARED TRANSMISSION

The problems related to a geared transmission are the transmission jumping out of gear, excessive amount of noise, hard shifting efforts, clashing of gears when the transmission is shifted, and lubricant leakage.

Transmission Jumps Out of Gear

The gears will not slip out of low or reverse gear on cars that are equipped with a properly installed and adjusted exterior interlock linkage. This linkage has been designed to make certain the transmission low and reverse shift lever is locked in place after the clutch pedal has been fully released. If the linkage is not set properly or the linkage parts are bent or damaged, there may be a binding or interference condition that will not allow proper meshing of the transmission gears.

The transmission gears may fail to stay in mesh if the internal interlock balls are damaged, the interlock spring is weak or broken, or the notches on the cam and shaft assemblies are worn, cracked, or broken.

Transmission Noisy

To determine the cause of the noise problem, drive the car and check the operation of the transmission in each gear ratio. If the noise is present only during one specific gear ratio, it is probably caused by defective gears pertaining to that respective gear ratio. If the transmission is noisy in each gear ratio, the noise could be caused by improper lubrication, damaged bearings, flywheel housing misalignment, loose transmission mounting bolts, or damaged mainshaft or cluster gears.

Check the synchronizers for damaged parts or improper operation. Make sure that the synchronizer parts are properly assembled. The insert springs should properly secure the inserts into the insert area of the hub. The sleeve and blocking rings should be free from nicks and burrs. The splines of the hub and shaft have to be free of burrs and nicks that could restrict the hub from moving on the shaft. The cam and shaft assembly of the gear shift housing should be checked for restricted travel.

Check all the transmission and flywheel housing bolts for the proper torque. Start with the flywheel housing. **CAUTION: Make sure that the flywheel**

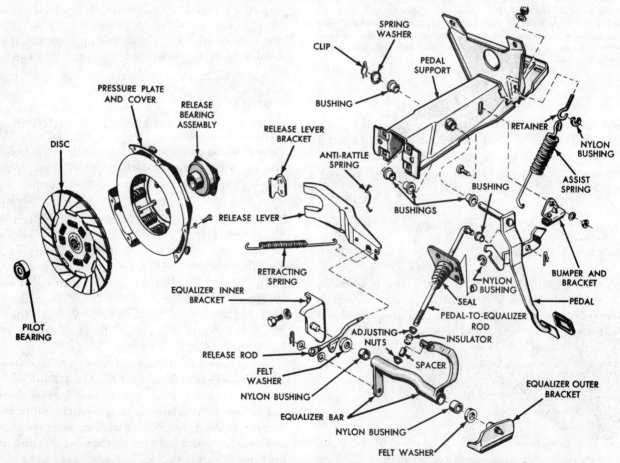

Exploded view of the clutch operating mechanism. The pedal free play should be a minimum of 1″

housing is properly positioned against the engine.
Check the torque on the engine rear mounting bolts and crossmember-to-body bolts. Loose mounting bolts allow misalignment of the transmission in relationship to the torque transfer from the engine to the transmission main drive gear. Misalignment between the flywheel housing and the engine will cause the same type of problem as loose mounting bolts.

Check the lubricant for proper level. If necessary, drain some of the old lubricant and make sure that it isn't contaminated with metal chips or dirt. The wrong type of lubricant can be a factor in causing noise.

HARD SHIFTING

Excessive shifting efforts are usually caused by an improperly adjusted clutch or transmission manual linkage. If the transmission has the exterior interlock type linkage, make sure that the cam or wedge parts are not binding and that the interlock is adjusted properly. The last items to be checked should be the internal shift linkage and synchronizers. If the problem exists only during cold weather, a pint of automatic transmission fluid may be added to the lubricant. Also, make sure that the transmission contains the specified lubricant.

If the linkage is not adjusted properly or the

ENGINE OIL
LEVEL GAUGE

TRANSMISSION
OIL LEVEL GAUGE

Details of the transmission and engine oil level gauges.

linkage is bent, there will be a binding or interference condition when shifting from one gear to another. To check this out, disconnect the linkage at the end of the steering column and move the selector lever to check for any binding condition. Next, disconnect the linkage rods at the transmission shift levers, and then try the levers for freedom of movement.

If there are no linkage problems, then the transmission will have to be disassembled in order to check the synchronizers for proper operation. Check the splines on the sleeve and hub for nicks or burrs. Make sure that the synchronizer ring is not damaged and that the inserts are properly assembled and retained in the hub by the insert springs.

AUTOMATIC TRANSMISSION

The routine for diagnosing troubles in an automatic transmission requires you to follow certain procedures. Before any repairs or adjustments are made, certain checks must be made, and then the vehicle must be taken for a road test. For example, the transmission fluid level and the manual throttle linkage adjustment must be checked before any road test is undertaken.

The sequence in which the diagnosis is performed is most important. It must follow the recommended procedures of the Diagnosis Guide, which lists the steps in the order in which they must be taken. The Guide covers the likeliest causes of troubles first, especially those which do not require opening the transmission.

AUTOMATIC TRANSMISSION DIAGNOSIS
GUIDE

1. Transmission fluid. Check the transmission fluid level. ☐ Full ☐ Overfull ☐ Low

The very first test to make of any automatic transmission complaint is that of the level and condition of the fluid. Too little fluid starves the hydraulic system and causes delay in clutch application, causing slippage. There's also danger of the pump taking in air and causing the fluid to foam, resulting in mushy application of clutches and bands and excessive wear. Too much fluid can be just as bad as too little. The gear train churns it up with the same results as the pump sucking air.

Certain fluid conditions are important to watch for, such as varnish on the dipstick, black fluid with the odor of a burned electrical coil, and friction material in the fluid. Varnish on the dipstick indicates the control valves, clutches, and gears are coated with varnish. Burned, black fluid means overheating and a clutch or band burned out.

Before checking the fluid be sure that it is warmed up. Move the selector lever through all the ranges to fill the clutches and servos. Then, with the engine idling and the selector lever in the PARK position, check the fluid level. It should be 1/4" below the FULL mark on the dipstick, but never higher than the FULL mark. If there's too much fluid, take some out. If it's low, add some.

2. Engine idle. Too high an engine idle can cause rough initial shifts because of too much control pressure in applying the clutches. Be sure the engine idle is set to specifications.   ☐ Performed

3. Linkage. Check the kickdown and manual linkage by driving the vehicle at a road speed of approximately 40 mph and then depressing the accelerator to the floorboard. The transmission should shift back to second gear.   ☐ O.K.   ☐ Other

4. Stall test. Perform a stall test to check engine performance and for any sign of transmission slippage.

After each stall test, move the selector lever to NEUTRAL with the engine running at 1,000 rpm for 15 seconds to cool the transmission. **CAUTION: Release the throttle immediately if slippage is indicated.** *NOTE: Stall-test only with the transmission at operating temperature.* **CAUTION: Don't hold the throttle open over five seconds during each test.**
☐ Performed

5. Road test. Drive the car in each range and through all shifts, including forced downshifts, observing any irregularities of performance.
☐ Road test completed

6. Shift test. The operating conditions shown on the Shift Test Chart should be checked in the order listed; by doing so, you may be able to correct a malfunction with a minor adjustment, thereby making unnecessary a major repair.

7. Pressure tests. CAUTION: The transmission must be at operating temperature. When the linkage is adjusted properly, all of the transmission shifts should occur within or close to the specified speeds. If the shifts do not occur within limits or if the transmission slips during shifts, it is necessary to attach testers to check the pressures.

Attach a tachometer gauge to the engine and pressure gauges to the control pressure outlets at the transmission, as shown. Firmly apply the parking brake, and then start the engine. Make the tests as indicated according to the type of transmission.

DUAL-COUPLING FOUR-SPEED HYDRA-MATIC AUTOMATIC TRANSMISSION—THROUGH 1960

STALL TEST

Before any tests are made, the transmission fluid must be brought up to the correct level. Then a "stall" test should be made to determine engine and transmission performance. This test must be used with moderation because considerable strain is exerted on the drive line, differential gears, and axles.

To perform the stall test, warm the engine to operating temperature, connect an electric tachometer, set the hand brake lever tightly, and apply the foot brake firmly. Place the shift control lever in the DR position and depress the accelerator pedal to the floorboard. The engine will speed up until the friction created between the torus members equals the power output of the engine. Engine efficiency can be judged by the stall speed, which should be between 1800 and 1900 rpm. If the engine speed is less than 1800 rpm, the engine is in need of a tune-up. If the engine speeds up above 2000 rpm, then the neutral clutch, the front sprag, or the rear sprag is slipping. **CAUTION: Never hold the throttle open more than 1 minute, or damage will result.** If the engine speeds up to 2000 rpm, close the throttle immediately to avoid damage to the transmission.

OIL PRESSURE TEST

Connect an oil pressure gauge to the take-off hole at the bottom of the rear pump. Start the engine and operate it for several minutes to warm the transmission oil to normal operating temperature. (Approx. 175°.) Then check the pressure in all ranges, which should be 50 psi minimum in P, N, both DR ranges, and LO, with a maximum variation of 10 psi between ranges. The pressure may be higher in R.

Drive the car on the road and check the operating pressure in DR-right position at approximately 25 mph, which should be 90-100 psi. Now, move the selector back to the DR-left position so that the transmission will shift into fourth speed. The pressure should drop to 60-70 psi. Check the pressure in R by stopping the car and setting the hand brake firmly. Place the selector lever in R, apply the foot brake, and open the accelerator half way. The pressure should increase to 145-190 psi.

ROAD TESTING

Additional troubles, such as noise, slippage, and

improper upshifts and downshifts can be checked by driving the car over a test route which includes a hilly section to test for full-throttle upshift, slippage, and forced downshifts, a level section for testing upshift points, and a quiet section for testing for noise.

The upshifts should occur at the following speeds:

Shift	Left-Drive Range		Right-Drive Range		Lo Range	
	Minimum Throttle	Full Throttle	Minimum Throttle	Full Throttle	Minimum Throttle	Full Throttle
1-2	4-9	11-15	4-9	11-15	4-9	11-15
2-3	11-15	35-40	11-15	35-40	—	42-52
3-4	17-20	65-75	—	65-75	—	65-75

The downshifts should occur at the following speeds:

Shift	Left-Drive Range		Right-Drive Range		Lo Range	
	Closed Throttle	Full Throttle	Closed Throttle	Full Throttle	Closed Throttle	Full Throttle
4-3	15-11	70-28	70-60	70-28	70-60	70-28
3-2	10-6	25-14	10-6	25-14	45-39	45-39
2-1	8-3	12-3	8-3	12-3	8-3	12-3

HYDRA-MATIC TROUBLESHOOTING CHART

Troubles & Causes

1. **Slips in 1st and 3rd**
   - 1a. Front sprag clutch slipping
   - 1b. Front sprag clutch broken
2. **Slips in or misses 2nd and 4th**
   - 2a. Front unit torus cover seals leaking
   - 2b. Front unit torus cover exhaust valves sticking or missing
   - 2c. Front unit torus cover feed restriction or leak
   - 2d. Front unit torus cover signal restriction or leak
   - 2e. Low oil pressure
   - 2f. Coupling valve sticking
   - 2g. Sticking valves or dirt in valve body
   - 2h. Coupling snap ring improperly installed, or missing
   - 2i. Limit valve defective
   - 2j. Coupling passage restricted or leaking
   - 2k. Front unit torus vanes damaged
3. **Slips in all DR ranges**
   - 3a. Manual linkage incorrectly adjusted

The main line oil pressure test chart is to be used in conjunction with the diagnosis section to aid determining the malfunctioning unit(s). To check oil pressure, remove the pipe plug from the bottom of the reverse clutch housing and connect a 300 lb. oil pressure gauge. In performing the oil pressure test it is extremely important that THE TRANSMISSION IS AT NORMAL OPERATING TEMPERATURE (APPROXIMATELY 175°).

Shop Test

ENGINE SPEED	SELECTOR LEVER POSITION	P.S.I.
460 r.p.m. in Dr Range (Parking Brake Applied)	P., N., DR., S. or Lo	50-100 p.s.i. (with not more than 10 p.s.i. difference between ranges)
2,000 r.p.m. (Rear Wheels Off Ground and Brakes Released)*	R	175-200 p.s.i.

* DO NOT STALL TEST as damage to the reverse unit may result.

Road Test

SHIFT	SELECTOR LEVER POSITION	P.S.I. **
1st, 2nd, and 3rd	DR	90-100
4th	DR	60-70

** A drop in pressure of approximately 10 p.s.i. as each shift is made is normal, but the gauge reading should stabilize after each shift is made.

Main line oil pressure test specifications for the dual-range, four-speed Hydra-Matic automatic transmission.

3b. Neutral clutch slipping or burned
3c. Neutral clutch apply restricted or leaking
3d. Incorrect number of neutral clutch plates
3e. Low oil pressure
3f. Control valve defective
3g. Torus members defective
3h. Intake pipe "O" ring damaged or missing
3i. Pressure regulator valve stuck in pump
3j. Pump slide stuck

4. Slips in 1st and 2nd, DR range
4a. Rear sprag clutch slipping or improperly assembled
4b. Rear sprag clutch broken
4c. Neutral clutch burned, restricted, or the piston is sticking

5. Slips in 3rd and 4th
5a. Rear unit clutch slipping or burned
5b. Rear unit clutch apply restricted or leaking
5c. Incorrect number of clutch plates (rear)
5d. Accumulator defective
5e. Center support, leak at 2-3 passage
5f. Low oil pressure
5g. Accumulator valve stuck—3rd only

6. Slips in 3rd or in DR-right on coast
6a. Overrun clutch slipping or burned
6b. Overrun clutch apply restricted or leaking
6c. Sticking valves or dirt in valve body
6d. Overrun clutch passage restricted or leaking

7. Slips in 1st and 2nd in LO range on coast
7a. Low servo apply restricted or leaking
7b. Low band not anchored to case or broken
7c. Low servo piston and rod binding in case of servo and accumulator body
7d. Band facing worn or loose
7e. Anchor dowel pin loose or missing in case

8. No drive in DR range
8a. Manual linkage incorrectly adjusted
8b. Manual valve not engaged with drive pin
8c. Low oil pressure
8d. Pressure regulator stuck
8e. Front pump intake pipe improperly installed
8f. Front sprag broken
8g. Front and/or rear sprag incorrectly installed
8h. Rear sprag broken
8i. Front sprag inner race broken
8j. Rear sprag outer race broken
8k. Neutral clutch plates burned
8l. Neutral clutch piston stuck
8m. Control valve defective
8n. Front pump defective

9. No upshifts or erratic operation
9a. Governor valves stuck

9b. Broken governor rings
9c. Sticking valves or dirt in valve body
9d. G-2 bushing turned
9e. Front unit internal gear bushing seized to shaft

10. Misses 2nd
10a. Governor boost valve stuck closed
10b. Transition valve stuck away from plate
10c. Sticking valves or dirt in valve body
10d. Governor sticking

11. Misses 3rd or 2-4-3
11a. Transition valve sticking
11b. Sticking valves or dirt in valve body
11c. TV adjustment—too long
11d. Rear clutch
11e. Transition valve spring weak or broken

12. Locks up in 2nd and 4th
12a. Front sprag clutch broken
12b. Overrun clutch applied or sticking

13. Locks up in 3rd and 4th
13a. Rear sprag clutch broken
13b. LO band not releasing

14. Rough 2-3 shift
14a. Accumulator valve stuck
14b. Accumulator piston stuck
14c. Accumulator gasket broken or leaking
14d. Restricted or leaking oil passages
14e. Broken accumulator spring
14f. Broken or leaking piston oil seal rings
14g. Control valve defective
14h. TV adjusted incorrectly
14i. Rear clutch pack slipping
14j. Case passages leaking or restricted

15. Upshifts high
15a. Throttle linkage adjusted too short
15b. Governor valves sticking
15c. Broken governor rings
15d. Sticking valves or dirt in valve body
15e. Leaking or restricted main line feed to governor

16. Upshifts low
16a. Throttle linkage adjusted too long
16b. Governor valves sticking
16c. Broken governor rings
16d. Sticking valves or dirt in valve body
16e. Leaking TV oil

17. No reverse, slips or locks up
17a. Manual linkage incorrectly adjusted
17b. Manual valve not engaged with drive pin
17c. Reverse piston apply restricted or leaking
17d. Low oil pressure
17e. Overrun clutch apply leaking
17f. Pressure regulator defective

17g. Neutral clutch not released

17h. Flash restricting neutral clutch exhaust port on manual body

18. Selector lever will not go into reverse

18a. Governor valves sticking

18b. Broken governor rings

18c. Reverse blocker piston stuck

18d. Manual linkage interference

19. Reverse drive in neutral

19a. Reverse stationary cone sticking

20. Delayed 1-2 shift

20a. Coupling valve sticking

20b. Governor boost valve sticking

20c. G-1 valve sticking

20d. Wrong spring on coupling valve

21. Drives in LO range only

21a. Rear sprag broken

21b. Neutral clutch not applying properly

22. No forced downshifts, 4-3 or 3-2

22a. Control valve defective

22b. Linkage improperly adjusted

23. 2-3 runaway or 2-1-3

23a. 2-3 passage in center bearing support leaking

23b. Plug out of accumulator

23c. Rear clutch burned

23d. Valve body defective

24. Will not go into P

24a. Parking links broken

24b. Interference—parking mechanical

24c. Linkage improperly adjusted

24d. Parking pawl improperly adjusted

25. Starts in 2nd speed

25a. Valves sticking

25b. Governor sticking

25c. Governor boost valve stuck

26. Drives forward in reverse and neutral

26a. Neutral clutch piston stuck in applied position

27. Lunges forward before backing up when placing selector in reverse

27a. G-2 plunger stuck in the outward position

27b. Restricted neutral clutch release oil passage

ROTO HYDRA-MATIC AUTOMATIC TRANSMISSION—1961-64

OIL PRESSURE SPECIFICATIONS

Drive Right	Minimum	Maximum
25 mph	98	111

OIL PRESSURE TROUBLESHOOTING CHART

Troubles & Causes

1. Low oil pressure

1a. Oil level too low

1b. Wrong boost plug or stuck

1c. Pressure regulator valve malfunction

1d. Strainer and "O" ring defects

1e. Manual valve misaligned with quadrant

1f. Foaming or cavitation of improper fluid

1g. Internal leak

1h. Stuck valve in control valve assembly

1i. Front pump slide stuck in the low output side

2. High oil pressure

2a. Pressure regulator valve stuck

2b. Wrong boost plug or stuck

2c. Manual valve misaligned with quadrant

2d. Stuck valve in control valve assembly

2e. Front pump slide stuck in the high output side

TRANSMISSION TROUBLESHOOTING CHART

Troubles & Causes

1. No drive in drive range

1a. Neutral clutch slipping

1b. Coupling defective

1c. Sprag assembly slipping

1d. Low oil level

1e. Low oil pressure

1f. Restricted passage in valve body

1g. Internal leak

1h. Manual linkage out of adjustment

1i. Control valve assembly defective

1j. Reverse cone sticking

2. Drive in neutral

2a. Neutral clutch

2b. Manual linkage

3. No reverse

3a. Manual linkage

3b. Low pressure

3c. Reverse cone clutch

3d. Restricted passage

3e. Neutral clutch

4. Drive in "right drive" or low range only

4a. Sprag assembly

4b. Neutral clutch

5. Forward drive in reverse

5a. Manual linkage

5b. Neutral clutch

6. **Reverse drive in neutral**
    6a. Reverse cone clutch
7. **Drive in 3rd and 4th only**
    7a. Control valve assembly
8. **Drive in 1st, 2nd, and 4th only (might be reported as 2-3 slip)**
    8a. Control valve assembly
    8b. Coupling
9. **Drive in 1st, 2nd, and 3rd only**
    9a. Governor (G-2)
    9b. Control valve assembly
10. **Slipping 2-3 shift (can be reported as 2-4 only)**
    10a. Front clutch
    10b. Control valve assembly
    10c. Accumulator
    10d. Compensator body assembly
    10e. Low oil pressure
    10f. TV linkage
    10g. 2-3 oil passages
11. **Slipping 3-4**
    11a. Coupling
    11b. Control valve assembly
    11c. Front clutch
12. **Slipping all ranges**
    12a. Low oil pressure
13. **Rough 2-3 shift**
    13a. Accumulator
    13b. Compensator body assembly
    13c. Front clutch
    13d. Front clutch passage
    13e. Control valve assembly
    13f. TV linkage
    13g. Coupling
14. **Erratic shifts**
    14a. Governor assembly
    14b. Control valve assembly
15. **High or low upshifts**
    15a. TV linkage (short—high upshifts; long—low upshifts)
    15b. Control valve assembly
    15c. Governor
    15d. TV lever
    15e. Governor oil passage
    15f. TV pressure
    15g. Line pressure
16. **No engine braking intermediate or low range**
    16a. Overrun band
    16b. Overrun servo
17. **No part throttle or detent downshifts**
    17a. TV linkage
    17b. Control valve assembly
    17c. Accelerator travel
    17d. Governor

ROTO HYDRA-MATIC SHIFT POINTS

UPSHIFTS

Shift	Left-Drive Range		Right-Drive Range		Lo Range	
	Minimum Throttle	Full Throttle	Minimum Throttle	Full Throttle	Minimum Throttle	Full Throttle
2-3	14-18	33-40	14-18	33-40	No Shift Possible	
3-4	18-23	76-89	—	76-89	—	76-89

DOWNSHIFTS

Shift	Left-Drive Range		Lo Range		Right-Drive Range	
	Closed Throttle	Full Throttle Forced	Closed Throttle	Full Throttle Forced	Closed Throttle	Full Throttle Forced
4-3	20-15	84-68	84-72	84-72	84-72	84-72
3-2	16-13	29-25	16-13	29-25	52-46	52-46

18. **Selector lever will not go into reverse**
    18a. Manual linkage
    18b. Reverse blocker valve
    18c. Governor
19. **Selector lever will not go into park**
    19a. Parking linkage
    19b. Manual linkage
20. **Noise sources**
    20a. Oil pump: moan in all ranges, more pronounced with hot oil in 1st and 2nd gear at approximately 1000 rpm
    20b. Oil pump: whine during the 3-2 and/or 3-4 shift
    20c. Front unit gear set: 3rd and reverse gear noises at low rpm
    20d. Rear unit gear set: 1st, 2nd, 3rd, reverse, and neutral gear noises at high rpm, with the loudest noise during the 3-4 shift
    20e. Coupling fill: whine during the 3-4 shift, with hot oil at low rpm
    20f. Coupling: whine in all speeds, except 3rd
    20g. TV valves and governor: buzzing
    20h. Damper: rattle at light load in 4th gear

F-85 HYDRA-MATIC AUTOMATIC TRANSMISSION—1961-63

MAINLINE OIL PRESSURE SPECIFICATIONS

Engine Speed	Selector Lever Position	Pressure (Psi)
500 rpm	PRDSL or R	60-125 with not more than 10 psi difference between ranges

ROAD TEST

Shift	Selector Lever Position	Pressure (Psi)
1 & 2	D, S, L, or R	118-185
3rd	S (30 mph)	98-111
4th	D (o to 30 mph)	68-78

F-85 HYDRA-MATIC TROUBLESHOOTING CHART

Troubles & Causes

1. **No drive in drive range**
   1a. Low oil level
   1b. Low oil pressure
   1c. Manual linkage out of adjustment
   1d. Sticking valve in control valve assembly
   1e. Band not applying
   1f. Internal leak or passage restricted
   1g. Coupling not filling

2. **Missing all shifts**
   2a. Governor sticking
   2b. Sticking valve in the control valve assembly
   2c. Clutch not applying

3. **Drive in second and third speed only**
   3a. Sticking valve in the control valve assembly
   3b. Clutch locked up because of too many plates

4. **Drive in first and third only (might be reported as 1-2 slip)**
   4a. Sticking valve in the control valve assembly
   4b. Coupling not emptying

5. **Drive in first and second only**
   5a. G-2 governor valve sticking
   5b. Sticking valve in the control valve assembly

6. **Drive in third only**
   6a. Sticking valve in the control valve assembly
   6b. Band not applying
   6c. Governor valve sticking

7. **Drives in neutral**
   7a. Internal manual linkage engaging
   7b. Front clutch mispositioned
   7c. Reverse cone clutch not applying

8. **No reverse**
   8a. Internal manual linkage mispositioned
   8b. Low oil pressure
   8c. Reverse cone clutch not engaging
   8d. Restricted passageway
   8e. Band not releasing

9. **Rough 1-2 shift**
   9a. TV linkage out of adjustment
   9b. Sticking valve in control valve assembly
   9c. Sticking accumulator
   9d. Coupling not emptying fast enough
   9e. Front clutch slipping
   9f. 1-2 oil passageway restricted

10. **Rough 2-3 shift**
   10a. Band not releasing quickly
   10b. Sticking servo

11. **Slips in all ranges**
   11a. Low oil pressure

12. **Slips in 1-2 shift (might be reported as 1-3 only)**
   12a. TV linkage too long
   12b. Low oil pressure
   12c. Accumulator sticking
   12d. Sticking valve in the control valve assembly
   12e. Band slipping
   12f. Front clutch has too few plates
   12g. Restricted oil passageway

13. **Slips in 2-3**
   13a. Sticking valve in the control valve assembly
   13b. Coupling not filling fast enough
   13c. Front clutch slipping

DOWNSHIFT CHART

	Medium Throttle	Part Throttle	Detent
Drive Range:			
3-2	35 to 16	35 to 16	58 to 50
2-1	12 to 8	None	24 to 8
Super Range:			
3-2	58 to 50	58 to 50	58 to 50
2-1	12 to 8	None	22 to 8
Low Range:			
3-2	58 to 50	58 to 50	58 to 50
2-1	28 to 22	28 to 22	28 to 22

UPSHIFT CHART

	Minimum Throttle	Maximum Throttle
Drive Range:		
2-3	12 to 15	24 to 30
3-4	17 to 24	58 to 65
Super Range:		
1-2	12 to 15	24 to 30
2-3	60 to 68	60 to 68
Low Range:		
1-2	Not possible	Not possible
2-3	60 to 68	60 to 68

14. No engine braking in intermediate or low range

14a. Sticking valve in the control valve assembly

14b. Slipping band

14c. Servo not applying

15. No downshifts

15a. TV linkage too long

15b. Sticking valve in the control valve assembly

15c. Accelerator travel too short

15d. Governor valve sticking

16. Selector will not go into reverse

16a. Internal manual linkage mispositioned

16b. Reverse blocker valve stuck open

16c. G-2 governor valve sticking

17. Forward drive in reverse

17a. Internal manual linkage improperly assembled or distorted

18. High upshifts

18a. TV linkage too short

18b. Sticking valve in the control valve assembly

18c. Sticking governor valve

18d. TV lever bent

18e. TV pressure too high

18f. Line pressure too high

18g. Governor oil passageway restricted

19. Low upshifts

19a. TV linkage too long

19b. Sticking valve in the control valve assembly

19c. Sticking governor valve

19d. TV lever bent

19e. TV pressure too low

19f. Line pressure too low

19g. Governor passageway restricted

JETAWAY TWO-SPEED AUTOMATIC TRANSMISSION—1964-69

MAINLINE PRESSURE

Mainline pressure will vary, but the following statements apply in general. The line pressure should increase as engine manifold vacuum decreases (at a constant engine speed). Mainline pressure should decrease as car speed increases (at a constant intake manifold vacuum). For example, you should register about 13 psi about 40-60 mph. Reverse pressure should be about 85 psi at idle and over 200 psi at WOT, with the brakes applied. **CAUTION: Don't operate the engine at WOT longer than necessary to obtain a gauge reading, or you will burn out the transmission.**

MAXIMUM LINE PRESSURE

Maximum line pressure checks should be made with the vacuum line disconnected and plugged, and with engine speed adjusted to 1000 rpm. The pressures should agree with the accompanying chart.

MINIMUM LINE PRESSURE

Minimum line pressure checks are to be made while road testing the car with the vacuum modulator line connected. In PARK, NEUTRAL, and DRIVE, the minimum pressure should be 56 ± 2 psi. In LOW, the pressure should be 92 ± 4 psi while decelerating from 40-20 mph with your foot off the throttle. In REVERSE, the pressure should be 84 ± 4 psi during deceleration.

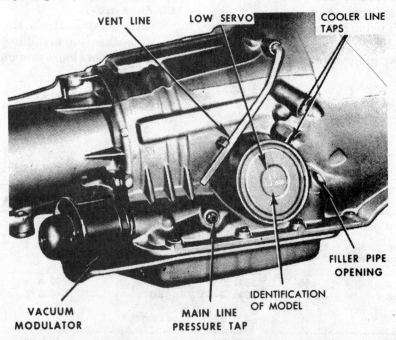

Transmission pressure checks for the Jetaway two-speed automatic transmission used in 1964-69.

TURBO HYDRA-MATIC AUTOMATIC TRANSMISSION (FSC)—1965-68

TROUBLESHOOTING CHART

Troubles & Causes

1. No drive in drive range
  1a. Low oil level
  1b. Manual linkage out of adjustment
  1c. Low oil pressure caused by a defect in the strainer or oil pump assembly
  1d. Manual valve disconnected from the manual lever pin
  1e. Forward clutch does not apply
  1f. Low sprag assembly assembled backwards

2. 1-2 shift on full throttle only
  2a. Defective detent switch
  2b. Defective detent solenoid
  2c. Control valve defects: leaking gasket, detent valve train assembled incorrectly, or 3-2 valve stuck

3. No 1-2 shift—first speed only
  3a. Governor valve sticking
  3b. Control valve 1-2 shift valve stuck closed
  3c. Valve body gasket leaking
  3d. Intermediate clutch case plug leaking or blown out
  3e. Governor feed channel blocked
  3f. Intermediate clutch problems: case center support oil ring broken or clutch piston seal cut

4. No 2-3 shift—first and second speed only
  4a. Detent solenoid stuck open
  4b. Detent switch defective
  4c. 2-3 valve train stuck or valve body gasket leaking
  4d. Direct clutch problems: case center support oil ring broken or clutch seal defective

5. Drive in neutral
  5a. Manual linkage out of adjustment
  5b. Forward clutch does not release

6. No drive in reverse
  6a. Low oil level
  6b. Manual linkage out of adjustment
  6c. Low oil pressure: vacuum modulator defective or sticking, restricted oil strainer, or regulator valve sticking in the oil pump
  6d. Control valve problems: leaking gasket, missing low-reverse ball check, 2-3 valve stuck open, or reverse feed passage missing
  6e. Rear servo and accumulator problems: servo piston seal damaged or band apply pin too short
  6f. Burned lining, apply pin or anchor pins not engaged, or the reverse or low band broken
  6g. Direct clutch problems: outer seal damaged or clutch plates burned
  6h. Forward clutch does not release

7. Slips in all ranges
  7a. Low oil level
  7b. Oil pressure problems: vacuum modulator defective or the valve is sticking, strainer assembly plugged, pump assembly valves sticking, or pump gasket damaged
  7c. Forward clutch slipping
  7d. Low sprag assembled backwards

8. Slips during 1-2 shift
  8a. Oil level low
  8b. Oil pressure problems: vacuum modulator defective or sticking or oil pump pressure regulator valve stuck

TURBO HYDRA-MATIC TRANSMISSION (FSC) TEST PRESSURES—1965-68

MAXIMUM TEST PRESSURES*

RANGE	PNDSL	REVERSE
RPM	1000	1000
PRESSURE	135-155	225 min.

*With the modulator vacuum line disconnected and the end plugged. The pressures will be 3 to 4 psi less per 1000' elevation.

MINIMUM TEST PRESSURES*

RANGE	PARK/NEUTRAL	DRIVE	SUPER/LOW	REVERSE
RPM	1000	750	750	750
PRESSURE	65-75	65 min.	135-155	100 min.

*With the modulator vacuum line connected. Elevation does not affect minimum pressures.

8c. Oil ring damaged on the front accumulator
8d. 1-2 accumulator valve train defective, may be called out as a slip/bump shift
8e. Oil ring broken on the rear accumulator
8f. Pump-to-case gasket damaged
8g. Intermediate clutch case plug leaking
8h. Lip seal damaged or the clutch plates burned on the intermediate clutch
8i. Case center support leaking

9. Rough 1-2 shift
9a. Oil pressure problems: vacuum modulator loose, restriction in the line, or the modulator defective; modulator valve stuck; pump regulator valve stuck; or the pump-to-case gasket damaged
9b. Control valve problems: 1-2 accumulator valve train stuck, valve body bolts loose, or the gasket damaged
9c. Intermediate clutch ball missing or not sealing properly
9d. Rear servo accumulator assembly problems: oil ring damaged, piston stuck, broken spring, or bore damaged

10. Slips in 2-3 shift
10a. Oil level too low
10b. Oil pressure too low: modulator assembly, modulator valve, pump pressure regulator valve or boost valve, or case-to-pump gasket
10c. Accumulator piston pin leaking at the swedged end
10d. Direct clutch piston seal leaking
10e. Case center support seal damaged

11. Rough 2-3 shift
11a. Oil pressure too high
11b. Front servo accumulator spring broken or the piston stuck

12. No engine braking in super range—2nd gear
12a. Front servo or accumulator oil ring broken
12b. Front band broken
12c. Front band not engaged on anchor pin or servo pin

13. No engine braking in low range—first gear
13a. Low-reverse check ball missing
13b. Rear servo oil seal ring leaking
13c. Short rear band apply pin or improperly assembled
13d. Rear band broken or not engaged on anchor pin or servo pin

14. No part-throttle downshifts
14a. Low oil pressure
14b. 3-2 valve stuck or spring broken

15. No detent downshifts
15a. Detent switch out of adjustment or defective
15b. Detent solenoid inoperative
15c. Detent valve train in control valve assembly

16. Shift points too high or too low
16a. Oil pressure problems: vacuum modulator, pump pressure, or regulator valve
16b. Governor valve sticking or feed holes plugged
16c. Detent solenoid stuck open will cause late shifts
16d. Control valve problems: detent valve train, 3-2 valve train, 1-2 shift valve train, or spacer plate gaskets

OIL PRESSURE CHECK – (WITH CAR STATIONARY)

TRANSMISSION OIL PRESSURE GAUGE AND ENGINE TACHOMETER SHOULD BE CONNECTED AND THE OIL PRESSURES SHOULD CHECK AS FOLLOWS:

Approximate Altitude (Ft. above sea level)	D,N,P	S or L	R
0	150	150	244
2,000	150	150	233
4,000	145	150	222
6,000	138	150	212
8,000	132	150	203
10,000	126	150	194
12,000	121	150	186
14,000	116	150	178

Turbo Hydra-Matic transmission test pressures for the full-sized car from 1965-68.

TURBO HYDRA-MATIC 350 & 400 AUTOMATIC TRANSMISSIONS

Both of these three-speed automatic transmissions use a three-element torque converter and a compound planetary gearset to provide the three speeds. The 350 unit contains four multiple-disc clutches, two sprag clutches, and one band, while the 400 model has three multiple-disc clutches, two sprag clutches, and two bands.

Both transmissions use a vacuum modulator to sense engine power demands, sending this signal to the pressure regulator for controlling the line pressure so that the shifts occur at the proper time. Some early models of the 400 transmission have a detent solenoid, which is activated by an electric switch at the carburetor to force a downshift at road speeds below 70 mph.

The 350 is a lighter unit used with the smaller engines, while the 400 model is used with the larger and high-performance engines. Because both of these transmissions are similar in action and have many parts in common, the troubleshooting procedures are grouped together as follows. Note, however, that the oil pressure checking procedures differ, and these are given in the specifications charts that accompany this section.

TROUBLESHOOTING PROCEDURES

Check the oil pressure with the vehicle stationary and the engine running at 1000 rpm with the modulator vacuum line connected and at 1200 rpm with the

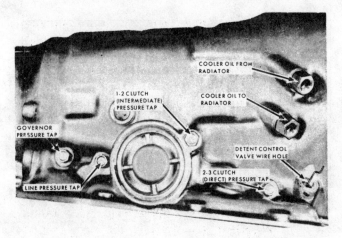

Pressure checking points on the right side of a Turbo Hydra-Matic 350 automatic transmission.

vacuum line disconnected on the 350 model. The pressures should agree with those in the accompanying charts.

Make a road test with the pressure and vacuum gauges connected and check the pressure against specifications with the modulator vacuum line connected.

VACUUM MODULATOR

A defective vacuum modulator can cause one or more of the following conditions: (1) harsh up and downshifts, (2) delayed upshifts, (3) soft up and downshifts, (4) delayed engagement of the low band on a downshift, (5) slipping in all gears, (6) overheating, and (7) engine burning transmission oil. If any of these are noted, the modulator should be checked as follows:

VACUUM LEAK CHECK

Turn the modulator so that the vacuum line stem

CAR STATIONARY - Parking Brake Applied, Wheels Blocked.		
RANGE	1000 RPM VAC. LINE CONNECTED (MIN. PSI)	1200 RPM VAC. LINE DISCONNECTED (MAX. PSI)
Park/Neutral	67	170
Reverse	92	250
Drive	67	170
Super	92	170
Low	92	170
ROAD TEST - Vacuum Line and Pressure Gauge Installed.		
Drive - 1st (0 to WOT)	67	170
- 2nd (0 to WOT)	67	170
- 3rd (Coast @ 30 mph)	67	--
Reverse (0 to WOT)	92	250
Low (Coast @ 30 mph)	92	--
Super (Coast @ 30 mph)	92	--

Oil pressure specifications for the Turbo Hydra-Matic 350 automatic transmission at 1000 and 1200 rpm (above) and on a road test under the stated condition.

Approximate Altitude of Check (Ft. Above Sea Level)	350 V-8			400 V-8		
	Drive Neutral Park	L1 or L2	Reverse	Drive Neutral Park	L1 or L2	Reverse
0	162	162	254	162	162	262
2000	157	158	240	162	162	248
4000	147	151	226	150	153	235
6000	135	142	213	143	148	222
8000	126	135	202	132	140	210

NOTE: Pressures (psi) are at O output speed with modulator tube disconnected and with engine at 1200 rpm.

Oil pressure specifications for the Turbo Hydra-Matic 350 automatic transmission at 1200 rpm with the modulator tube disconnected.

Approximate Altitude of Check (Ft. Above Sea Level)	Absolute Manifold Pressure ("Hg.)	Relative Engine Vacuum ("Hg.)	350 V-8			400 V-8		
			Drive Neutral Park	L1 or L2	Reverse	Drive Neutral Park	L1 or L2	Reverse
0	16	13.92		106	129		110	138
2000	16	11.83	88	108	134	93	112	142
4000	16	9.86	90	110	138	95	114	147
6000	16	7.96	92	112	142	97	116	151
8000	16	6.23	95	114	146	100	118	155

NOTE: Pressures (psi) are at O output speed with vacuum modulator tube connected and with sufficient engine speed to maintain 16 inches HG absolute manifold pressure.

Oil pressure specifications for the Turbo Hydra-Matic 350 automatic transmission with sufficient engine speed to maintain the 16″ Hg vacuum.

points down. If transmission oil comes out, the diaphragm is leaking and the unit must be replaced. *NOTE: Gas and water vapors may form in the vacuum side of the unit, and this does no damage.* Check the solution to see if it feels oily to determine the content.

ATMOSPHERIC LEAK CHECK

Apply a liberal coating of soap bubbles to the pipe seam and the crimped upper-to-lower housing seam. Use a piece of rubber tubing to apply oral pressure to the unit to check for leaks. **CAUTION: Don't use any method other than human lung power as pressures over 6 psi can destroy the modulator.**

BELLOWS COMPARISON CHECK

Use a new modulator and a gauge, which can be made as shown in the accompanying illustration, to compare the load of the new modulator with the one to be tested. Install both modulators on opposite ends of the gauge, as shown. Holding the modulators in a horizontal position, bring them together until either

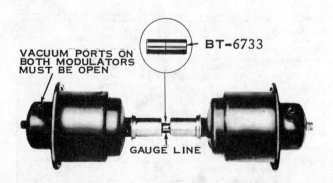

VACUUM PORTS ON BOTH MODULATORS MUST BE OPEN

BT-6733

GAUGE LINE

Details of mounting two vacuum modulators for the test discussed in the text. Tool BT-6733 can be made as shown in the next drawing.

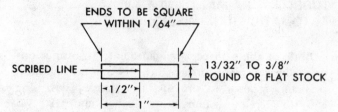

ENDS TO BE SQUARE WITHIN 1/64″

SCRIBED LINE

13/32″ TO 3/8″ ROUND OR FLAT STOCK

1/2″

1″

Details of the vacuum modulator comparison gauge, which can be substituted for tool BT-6733.

modulator sleeve end just touches the line in the center of the gauge. The gap between the opposite modulator sleeve end and the gauge line should be 1/16″ or less. If it is greater, the modulator under test must be replaced.

SLEEVE ALIGNMENT CHECK

Roll the main body of the modulator on a flat surface and observe the sleeve for concentricity to the can. If the sleeve is concentric and the plunger is free, the modulator is acceptable.

TRANSMISSION MOUNT CHECK

Raise the vehicle on a hoist. Push up and pull down on the transmission tailshaft, while observing the transmission mount. If the rubber separates from the metal plate, or if the tailshaft moves up but not down, the mount is bottoming out and must be replaced. If there is relative movement between the metal plate of the mount and its attaching point, tighten the nuts and bolts holding it to the transmission and/or crossmember.

TURBO-HYDRAMATIC TROUBLESHOOTING CHART

Troubles & Causes
1. **No drive in DRIVE range**
   1a. Low oil level
   1b. Leaking vacuum modulator diaphragm
   1c. Manual linkage out of adjustment
   1d. Low oil pressure
   1e. Filter leaking or plugged
   1f. Oil pump or pressure regulator damaged
   1g. Forward clutch does not apply
   1h. Damaged roller clutch
2. **Normal 1-2 shift on full throttle only**
   2a. Detent switch sticking (400 model only). This can be checked by pulling off the connector at the transmission, and you should obtain normal upshifts.

Super Range		Minimum	Maximum
2nd Gear – Steady road load at approximately 25 mph		145 psi	155 psi
Gear	Selector Lever Position	Minimum	Maximum
1st			
2nd	Drive (Zero to full throttle)	60	150
3rd			
3rd	Drive (Zero Throttle at 30 mph)	60	
Reverse	Reverse (Zero to full throttle).	95	260

Oil pressure specifications for the Turbo Hydra-Matic 400 automatic transmission under normal road test conditions.

2b. Detent solenoid loose or sticking
2c. Control valve damaged or stuck

3. Normal 1st speed only—no 1-2 shift
3a. Governor malfunction
3b. 1-2 shift valve stuck
3c. Governor oil passageway blocked or leaking
3d. Valve body gasket leaking or incorrectly installed
3e. Intermediate clutch malfunction; oil ring broken, orifice plug missing, piston seal cut

4. Normal 1st and 2nd speeds only—no 2-3 shift
4a. Defective detent solenoid or switch
4b. Control valve defects: 2-3 valve stuck; valve body gasket leaking
4c. Direct clutch malfunction: center support oil ring broken, clutch piston seal leaking, or piston ball check stuck

5. Vehicle moves forward in NEUTRAL
5a. Manual linkage out of adjustment
5b. Forward clutch not releasing. This will also cause a no-reverse condition.

6. No drive in REVERSE
6a. Low fluid level
6b. Manual linkage out of adjustment
6c. Oil pressure too low: vacuum modulator defective, modulator valve sticking, plugged oil filter, leak at intake pipe, defective pump or regulator
6d. Control valve defects: valve body gasket leaking or improperly installed, low-reverse ball check missing from case, 2-3 valve train stuck open, reverse feed passageway plugged
6e. Rear servo and accumulator defects: servo piston seal damaged or a short band-apply pin used in assembly
6f. Reverse or low band burned, lining loose, apply pin not properly engaged, or band broken
6g. Direct clutch defects: outer seal damaged or clutch plates burned. This may be caused by a stuck ball check in the piston.
6h. Forward clutch does not release

Approximate Altitude (Ft. above sea level)	D,N,P	S or L	R
0	150	150	244
2,000	150	150	233
4,000	145	150	222
6,000	138	150	212
8,000	132	150	203
10,000	126	150	194
12,000	121	150	186
14,000	116	150	178

Pressure specifications for the Turbo Hydra-Matic 400 automatic transmission, with the vacuum hose disconnected and the car stationary.

7. **Slips in all ranges**
   7a. Fluid level low or high
   7b. Oil pressure too high or too low: vacuum modulator defective, modulator valve sticking, filter plugged, O-ring damaged, oil pump defective, pump regulator sticking, or oil pump gasket leaking
   7c. Forward and direct clutches slipping

8. **Slips on 1-2 shift**
   8a. Fluid level incorrect
   8b. Oil pressure incorrect: vacuum modulator defective, modulator valve sticking, or pressure regulator valve stuck
   8c. Front accumulator oil ring damaged
   8d. Control valve defects: 1-2 accumulator valve train, porosity in valve body or case, or valve body bolts not properly torqued
   8e. Rear accumulator oil ring damaged
   8f. Oil pump gasket leaking
   8g. Intermediate clutch defects: lip seal damaged, clutch plates burned, center support oil leak

caused by bushing wear or damage to the oil rings, orifice bleed hole in center support blocked, too many waved steel plates used

9. **Rough 1-2 shift**
   9a. Oil pressure problems
   9b. Control valve defective
   9c. Rear survo accumulator defective
   9d. Too many waved steel plates used

10. **Slips in 2-3 shift**
    10a. Fluid level incorrect
    10b. Oil pressure too low
    10c. Control valve leaking at the accumulator piston pin
    10d. Direct clutch seals leaking or ball check stuck
    10e. Center support seal rings damaged
    10f. Extra waved plate installed

11. **Rough 2-3 shift**
    11a. Oil pressure too high
    11b. Front servo spring broken or piston stuck
    11c. Extra waved steel plate used

12. **No engine braking in 2nd gear**

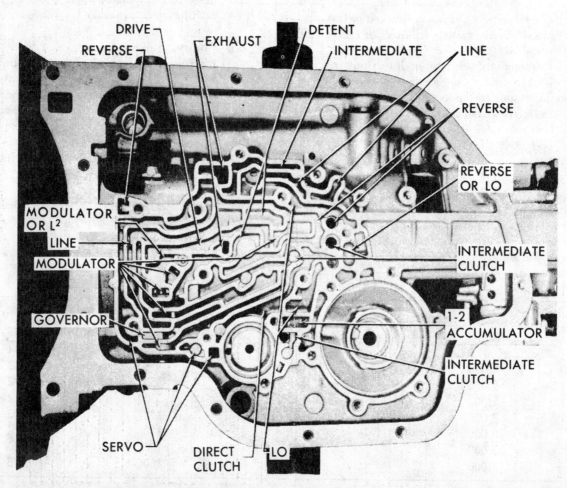

Case passageways on the **Turbo Hydra-Matic 400** automatic transmission, with the oil pan and the valve body removed for introducing compressed air to check the operation of the various control units.

PROBLEM

CAR ROAD TEST

LEGEND
X—PROBLEM AREA V.S. CAUSE
*—@ "O" VACUUM ONLY
O—BALLS #2/3/4 ONLY
L—LOCKED
S—STUCK

POSSIBLE CAUSE

Problem columns (car road test):

- ALL RANGES—SLIPS
- LINE PRESSURE—ALL LOW
- LINE PRESSURE—ALL HIGH
- 1-2 INTERM. CL. PRES. HIGH
- 2-3 INTERM. CL. PRES. LOW
- NO 1-2 DIRECT CL. PRES. LOW
- 2-3 DIRECT CL. PRES. HIGH
- 1-2 U.S. EARLY/LATE
- SLIPS—1-2 UPSHIFT @ W.O.T.
- ROUGH—1-2 UPSHIFT
- NO 2-3 UPSHIFT
- 2-3 U.S. EARLY/LATE
- SLIPS—2-3 UPSHIFT
- ROUGH—2-3 UPSHIFT
- NO WOT—1:2 UPSHIFT
- NO—PART TH. DOWN SHIFT
- NO—FULL TH. DOWN SHIFT
- 2-3 HARSH—DOWN SHIFT W.O.T. ONLY
- L1 RANGE—DOWN SHIFT
- L2 RANGE—NO ENG. BRAKING
- L1 RANGE—NO ENG. BRAKING
- NEUTRAL—DRIVES IN NEUTRAL
- REVERSE—NO REVERSE
- SLIPS IN REVERSE
- PARK—NO PARK—RATCHETS
- NOISY—ALL RANGES
- 1-2 2-3 SHIFT NOISY
- REV. & D, L1 & L2 NOISY
- LOW COOLER—FLOW
- SPEWS OIL OUT BREATHER

Possible cause rows:

- LOW OIL LEVEL/WATER IN OIL
- VACUUM LEAK
- MODULATOR & / OR VALVE
- STRAINER & / OR GASKET
- GOVERNOR—VALVE/SCREEN
- VALVE BODY—GASKET/PLATE
- PRES. REG. &, / OR BOOST VALVE
- BALL (#1) SHY
- 1-2 SHIFT VALVE
- 2-3 SHIFT VALVE
- MANUAL LOW CONT'L VALVE
- DETENT VALVE & LINKAGE
- DETENT REG. VALVE
- 2-3 ACCUMULATOR
- MANUAL VALVE/LINKAGE
- POROSITY/CROSS LEAK
- PUMP—GEARS
- PRIMING VALVE SHY
- COOLER VALVE LEAK
- CLUTCH SEAL RINGS
- POROUS/CROSS LEAK
- GASKET SCREEN—PRESSURE
- BAND—INTERM. O.R.
- CASE—POROUS/X LEAK
- 1-2 ACCUMULATOR
- INTERMED. SERVO
- FORWARD CLUTCH ASS'Y
- DIRECT CLUTCH ASS'Y
- INTERMED. CL. ASS'Y
- L & REV. CL. ASS'Y
- INT. ROLLER CL. ASS'Y
- L. & R. ROLLER CL. ASS'Y
- PARK PAWL/LINKAGE
- CONVERTER ASS'Y
- GEAR SET & BEARINGS

Turbo Hydra-Matic 350 automatic transmission diagnosis chart.

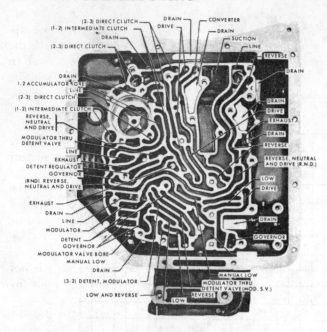

Case passageways on the Turbo Hydra-Matic 350 automatic transmission with the oil pan and valve body removed for introducing compressed air to check the operation of the various control units.

12a. Front servo accumulator oil ring broken or servo piston stuck

12b. Front band broken or burned

12c. Front band not engaged on anchor and/or servo pin

13. No engine braking in 1st gear

13a. Low-reverse ball check missing from case

13b. Rear servo defects: oil seal ring or piston damaged, leaks, rear band apply pin too short or improperly assembled, rear band broken or not engaged on anchor pin

14. No part-throttle downshift

14a. Oil pressure not correct

14b. Vacuum modulator valve and pressure regulator valve defects

14c. Control valve 3-2 valve stuck; spring missing or broken

15. No detent downshifts

15a. Detent switch out of adjustment

15b. Inoperative solenoid

15c. Control valve detent valve train sticking

16. Low or high shift points

16a. Oil pressure not correct

16b. Vacuum modulator not functioning properly

16c. Governor valve sticking or pipes leaking

16d. Feed line screen plugged

16e. Detent solenoid stuck open

16f. Control valve defects: detent valve train stuck, 3-2 valve train stuck, 1-2 shift valve train stuck, 1-2 regulator valve stuck, spacer plate gasket mispositioned or torn, intermediate plug leaking

17. Noisy transmission

17a. Pump noise from incorrect fluid level or water in fluid, cavitation due to plugged filter or O-ring damage, pump gears assembled in reverse or damaged

17b. Gear noise in planetary gear sets

17c. Clutch noise during application

REAR AXLE

The most common axle or driveline complaint is noise. Excessive rear axle or driveline noise may indicate a malfunction. However, it must be noted that axle gears inherently make some noise and an absolutely quiet unit is seldom found. When evaluating the rear axle, make sure that the noise is not caused by the road surface, by a grounding exhaust system, by the engine, tires, transmission, or wheel bearings, or by some other external component of the car.

ROAD TEST

Before a road test of the car is performed, make sure that there is sufficient lubricant of the specified type in the rear axle housing. Drive the car far enough to warm the lubricant to normal operating temperature before testing. A car should be tested for axle noise by being operated in high gear under the following four driving conditions:

1. DRIVE: Higher than normal road load power where the speed gradually increases on level road acceleration.

2. CRUISE: Constant speed operation at normal road speeds.

3. FLOAT: Using only enough throttle to keep the car from driving the engine. In float, the car will slow down with very little load on the rear axle gears.

4. COAST: Throttle closed—engine is braking the car. Load is on the coast side of the gear set.

When a rear axle is noisy, the following tests are to be performed to pinpoint the problem and eliminate the possibility that the noise is of external origin.

ROAD NOISE

Road surfaces, such as those of brick or rough-surfaced concrete, may cause a noise condition which may be mistaken for tire or rear axle noise. Driving on a smooth asphalt surface will quickly show whether the road surface is the cause of the noise. A road noise usually has the same pitch on DRIVE or COAST.

TIRE NOISE

Tire noise may easily be mistaken for rear axle noise, even though the noisy tires may be located on the front wheels. Sounds and vibrations are caused by unevenly worn tire surfaces or ply separations. Also, some designs of non-skid treads on low-pressure tires, snow tires, and other assorted types cause vibrations. *NOTE: Temporarily inflate all tires to approximately 40 pounds pressure for test purposes only.* This will alter any noise caused by tires but will not affect noise caused by the rear axle. Excessive rear axle noise usually diminishes or ceases during COAST at speeds under 30 miles per hour. However, tire noise continues, but with a lower tone as the car speed is reduced. Rear axle noise usually changes when comparing DRIVE and COAST. However, tire noise remains about the same.

FRONT WHEEL BEARING NOISE

Loose or rough front wheel bearing noises may be confused with rear axle noise. However, front wheel bearing noise does not change when comparing DRIVE and COAST. Drive the car through a series of left and right turns, which will put a load on the wheel bearings and emphasize a noisy condition, if it exists. A light application of the brake while holding the car speed steady will often cause wheel bearing noise to diminish. This action takes some weight off the bearings. If front wheel bearing noise is suspected, you can easily check it by jacking up the front wheels and spinning them while feeling and listening for roughness. Also, shake the wheels to determine if the bearings are loose.

BODY NOISES

The car body and/or one of the attached components may have a wind noise condition that sounds like a noisy rear axle. Items such as the grille, radio antenna, and hood may cause the condition which must be isolated. In some cases, loose body hold-down bolts or brackets may be a source of noise.

REAR AXLE NOISE

Sometimes a noise which seems to originate in the rear axle is actually caused by the engine, exhaust, transmission, or power steering. To determine which unit is actually causing the noise, observe the approximate car speeds and conditions under which the noise is most pronounced, and then stop the car in a quiet place to avoid interfering noises. With the transmission in neutral, run the engine slowly up and down through engine speeds corresponding to the car speed at which the noise was most pronounced. If a similar noise is produced with the car standing still, it is caused by components other than the rear axle or driveline assemblies.

If a careful road test of the car shows that the noise is not caused by the road surface or by components previously described, it is reasonable to assume that the noise is caused by the rear axle or driveline units. The rear axle should be tested on a smooth level road to avoid road noise. **CAUTION: It is not advisable to test the rear axle assembly for noise by running it with the rear wheels jacked up.**

Noises in the rear axle assembly may be caused by faulty rear wheel bearings; loss of pinion pre-load; faulty differential or pinion shaft bearings; worn differential side gears and pinions; or by a mismatched, improperly adjusted, or scored ring and pinion gear set. It is sometimes impossible to determine from a test exactly which internal repairs are required to

STETHOSCOPE

Wind noises can be traced by using a stethoscope with the indicating end removed. Close all windows and air vents and turn the ventilating fan to HIGH SPEED. Move the hose along the edges of all openings to trace wind noises caused by leaking seals. Some mechanics paint suspected areas with a soapy water solution and check for bubbles.

correct a noisy axle unit. The needed repairs can best be determined by a careful inspection of wear on the individual parts when the unit is disassembled.

REAR WHEEL BEARING NOISE

A rough rear wheel bearing produces a heavy grinding or "growling" noise in DRIVE and CRUISE which will continue when the transmission is positioned in neutral with the car coasting. A brinelled rear wheel bearing causes a knock or click approximately every two revolutions of the rear wheel, since the bearing rollers do not travel at the same speed as the rear axle shaft and wheel. To accentuate the noise of a suspected bearing, drive the car in a series of right and left turns to put a load on the bearings. Sometimes the bearings can be tested with the rear wheels jacked up. Spin the rear wheels by hand while listening at the hubs for evidence of rough or brinelled wheel bearings.

DIFFERENTIAL SIDE GEARS AND PINION NOISE

Differential side gears and pinions seldom cause noise since their movement is relatively small on straight-ahead driving. Noise produced by these gears will be most pronounced on turns. As a rule, the noise heard will be a "chuckling" sound, similar to the sound given by two steel balls when rattled together. The noise can be attributed to excessively worn or loosely fitted differential side gears.

PINION BEARING NOISE

Rough or brinelled pinion bearings produce a continuous "whine" that starts at a relatively low speed. The noise is most pronounced on FLOAT between 20 and 35 mph. In most instances, pinion bearing noise can be pinpointed by raising the rear axle on a hoist and running it with the transmission in high gear. If the pinion bearing is bad, the noise will be obvious.

RING AND PINION GEAR NOISE

Noise produced by the ring and pinion gear set generally shows up as DRIVE, COAST, or FLOAT noise. As the gears become worn or out of adjustment, a "heavy humming" sound will be noticed. The noise in DRIVE, COAST, and FLOAT will be very rough or irregular if the differential pinion shaft bearings are rough, worn, or loose, and will vary in tone with speed. As a rule, DRIVE noise is caused by a heavy

heel contact, and a COAST noise is caused by heavy toe contact. Heavy face contact is usually the trouble when the rear axle is noisy in FLOAT or CRUISE.

BACKLASH

Excessive backlash ("clunk noise") may be caused by worn axle shaft splines; loose axle shaft flange nuts; worn, broken, or loose universal joint flange or slip yoke mountings; excessive play between the drive pinion and ring gear; excessive backlash in the differential gears; bearings worn or out of adjustment; throttle linkage out of adjustment; or the engine idle rpm is too high.

VIBRATION

Excessive noise or vibration may be caused by a lack of lubrication in the driveshaft bearings, worn universal joint bearings, a bind between the universal joint and the rear axle companion flange (universal joint not seated properly), a sprung or damaged driveshaft, or a missing driveshaft balance weight. **CAUTION: Undercoating carelessly applied to the driveshaft can destroy the balance and cause vibration.**

Vibration or shudder, which is noticeable either on fast acceleration in DRIVE or when in COAST, may be caused by the rear axle housing being loose on the rear springs or by an excessive driveline angle.

TROUBLESHOOTING THE RUNNING GEAR

When troubleshooting a front suspension problem, it is important to follow a pattern before and during a road test that will isolate the area or item that is causing the trouble. This is because several of the problems attributable to front suspension components are also common to steering gear and linkage, rear suspension, and wheel or tire problems. For example, wrong or uneven tire pressures can cause steering problems. Also, a misaligned rear suspension, a binding steering linkage, or improperly aligned front suspension components have a similar effect on the steering ability of a car.

QUICK CHECKS

Check the attitude of the car for an unbalanced load condition or sagging springs. Jounce the front and rear of the vehicle to check for noisy, weak, loose, or damaged spring and shock absorbers. After it has settled, check the front and rear of the car for obviously improper front or rear spring riding heights.

If the vehicle looks uneven, measure the riding heights at the same places on each side. Although sagging may be apparent at one or more wheels, the action of all four shock absorbers and springs must be checked. One or more binding shock absorbers or springs may hold other corners of the car abnormally high or low, causing uneven weight distribution, with resulting abnormal tire wear.

Check the air pressure in each tire and the tires for uniformity in size. Also, observe the tread wear pattern for signs of misalignment. Rotate the front and rear wheels to make sure that they turn freely without brake or bearing bind. Check the front wheel bearings for noise, looseness, wear, or improper adjustment. Spin the wheels again to check the tires for runout, ply separation, or an unbalanced condition.

Inspect the steering column, steering gear and linkage, and stabilizer for loose mountings, wear, or damaged parts. Check the engine and transmission mounts for looseness or damage. Inspect the front and rear springs, shock absorbers, and suspension components for loose mountings, excessive wear, cracks, or damaged parts.

ROAD TEST

Perform a short road test over a smooth and level surface, rough surfaces, and a roadway with a series of small dips. On the level road, check the car for steering bind, side-to-side wander, looseness in the steering gear, shimmy, wheel tramp, pulling to one side, noisy conditions, excessive front-end vibration, and steering wheel vibration.

Drive the car over a surface that has roughness or dips and check for wander, rough ride, noisy conditions, excessive vibration at the steering wheel, weak or bottoming springs, and defective shock absorbers. Perform a series of quick stops in both forward and reverse gears and check for excessive dipping action, bounce, or bottoming, any of which is attributable to weak or damaged springs or shock absorbers. Perform a series of slow turns to the right and left and check the steering mechanism for excessive play, hard steering, and poor steering recovery. Check for excessive body sway, which can be attributed to weak springs, a weak shock absorber, or a loose stabilizer.

From a given point in a wide roadway, turn the steering wheel fully to the left. Then drive the car in a complete circle and observe the diameter of the turn. Perform a similar turn to the right. If the diameter is not the same on both turns, the steering mechanism is out of adjustment or the steering linkage or suspension arms are bent, worn, or damaged.

If misalignment or dog tracking of the front and rear suspension is suspected, drive the car straight ahead on a section of pavement, part of which is wet, and then stop about ten feet beyond the wet area. If alignment is correct, the rear tire imprints will overlap the front equally. If misalignment exists, it can be attributed to an improperly or loosely mounted rear axle or to rear suspension components.

If the vehicle pulls to one side, the condition may be caused by faulty front-end alignment, defective wheel bearings, steering gear defects, or chassis misalignment. Specific defects which can cause the car to pull to one side are the steering gear off the center position, brakes out of adjustment, contaminated brake linings, drums out of round, damaged or worn interior brake components, restricted hydraulic line to one cylinder, or worn wheel bearings.

Abnormal tire tread wear indicates a front-end alignment problem. To check this out, drive the car on a fairly level road in a straight-ahead direction, and then momentarily release the steering wheel to observe if the car pulls to one side. Make a few normal stops to determine how much the steering or front-end alignment problem is related to the amount or direction that the car pulls when the brakes are applied.

Vehicle Leads to One Side

Rear suspension misalignment is usually the cause of the vehicle leading to one side, and generally the trouble is the result either of bent parts or of a rear spring not being centered in a locating hole. To determine whether this condition exists, measure the distance between a locating hole at the rear of the spring mounting bracket common to both side rails and the forward edge of the axle. The dimension must be the same on both sides of the vehicle. Other causes of the vehicle leading to one side are front-end misalignment, uneven tire pressure, non-uniformity of tire sizes, a dragging brake or wheel bearing, the steering gear out of adjustment, or binding of the steering linkage.

Vibration or Shimmy

This common complaint is generally due to an unbalanced condition of the front wheels. Low-speed vibration results from a static unbalanced condition, while high-speed problems are always caused by dynamic imbalance. Shimmy results from a combination of an unbalanced condition and worn front-end parts. To check for an unbalanced condition during a road test, hold the steering wheel lightly and note the amount of vibration during various speeds.

Before balancing a tire, all foreign matter must be removed from the tread and bead. Check the wheels and tires for lateral and radial runout, the total of which must not exceed 0.080", with a tolerance of 0.060" even more desirable. **CAUTION: Adding balance weights cannot counteract for wheel and tire runout.** *NOTE: If excessive weight is required to balance a front tire, replace it with a new one or the spare.*

Other conditions which could cause vibration are damaged springs, inoperative shock absorbers, loose engine supports, worn universal joints, or a driveshaft that is loosely mounted or out of balance.

POWER STEERING

Power steering gear troubles generally include the following conditions: excess or loss of steering effort, partial steering assist or assist in only one direction, poor returnability, or leaks. Because the internal parts of the power gear assembly are always under high hydraulic pressure, lubrication and wear problems do not occur. However, because of the high pressures, seal problems and leaks are quite general.

Preliminary checks must include the drive belt condition and tension. Check the fluid level in the reservoir and add fluid if necessary. Start the engine and turn the steering wheel back and forth. Shut off the engine and recheck the fluid level. If the level is low, add fluid, but do not overfill.

A pressure check should be made on the pump, with and without the rest of the system, in order to isolate the trouble. This can be done by closing a shut-off valve between the pump and the power steering gear unit. If the pressure builds up to specifications with the shut-off valve closed, then the pump is OK, and the pressure loss must be in the power steering gear assembly. If the pump does not build up to the specified pressure, then the pump is defective. *NOTE: The pitman arm must be disconnected from the sector shaft in order to perform steering gear checks and/or adjustments.*

Some of the conditions that could cause a loss of power assist are drive belt loose, worn, broken, or slipping; fluid level low or air in the system; fluid leaking or damage to the lines; pump pressure too low; and control valve and/or power steering gear assembly defective.

If there is a partial assist or an assist in only one direction, the condition causing this trouble could be control valve out of adjustment; fluid level too low; air in system; drive belt loose, worn, or slipping; pump pressure too low; control valve defective; or power steering gear assembly defective.

Excessive steering effort and/or poor returnability can be caused by front-end misalignment, tire pressures too low, tires oversize, steering gear fluid low, steering gear out of adjustment, or steering linkage binding or bent.

IRREGULAR TIRE WEAR

Loose, worn, or bent front suspension parts and/or steering linkage can cause irregular tire wear.

CONDITION	RAPID WEAR AT SHOULDERS	RAPID WEAR AT CENTER	CRACKED TREADS	WEAR ON ONE SIDE	FEATHERED EDGE	BALD SPOTS
CAUSE	UNDER INFLATION	OVER INFLATION	UNDER-INFLATION OR EXCESSIVE SPEED	EXCESSIVE CAMBER	INCORRECT TOE	WHEEL UNBALANCED
CORRECTION		ADJUST PRESSURE TO SPECIFICATIONS WHEN TIRES ARE COOL		ADJUST CAMBER TO SPECIFICATIONS	ADJUST FOR TOE-IN 1/8 INCH	DYNAMIC OR STATIC BALANCE WHEELS

Uneven and excessive tire wear, causes, and corrections. The conditions are discussed in the text.

Underinflation Wear

Tires are designed so that under a given load and with the proper air pressure the tire will make a full pattern across the entire width of the tread, thereby distributing the wear evenly over the entire surface. When a tire is run underinflated, the side walls and the shoulders of the tread carry the load, while, due to the low internal air pressure, the center section folds in, or compresses. With the shoulders thus taking most of the driving and braking loads, they wear much faster than the center section.

Overinflation Wear

When a tire is overinflated, the outside or shoulder sections of the tread are lifted away from the road surface. The center section of the tread then receives most of the driving and braking loads, and this causes it to wear much faster than the shoulder sections.

Scuffing Wear

When the front wheels have an excessive amount of either toe-in or toe-out, the tires are actually dragged sideways when they travel straight down the road and a cross-wear or scraping action takes place, rapidly wearing away the tread. This scuffing action will produce a feather-edge on the ribs of the tread. In many instances, this can be detected by rubbing your hand across the face of the tire. If the feather-edges are on the inside of the tire ribs, too much toe-in is indicated. If the feather-edges are on the outside of the ribs, it indicates that the tires are being run with a toe-out condition.

Camber Wear

Excessive wheel camber causes the tire to run at a slight angle to the road surface, resulting in more wear on one side of the tread than on the other. With too much positive camber, the outside of the tread will show the most wear. Too much negative camber will show a similar wear pattern on the inside of the tread.

Cornering Wear

Cornering wear can be identified by a rough, diagonal wear pattern across the face of the tread. This pattern is the result of the driver making high-speed turns, resulting in an abrasive action caused by tire slippage.

Cup-and-Flat Spot Wear

Cups and flat spots generally are the result of road tramp, caused by wheels and tires being out of balance. Wheel misalignment, along with the unbalanced condition, can cause unusually severe tire cupping. Cupped or spotty tread wear on a front tire cannot be corrected by wheel alignment or balancing. A cupped tire, if transferred to a rear wheel, will true itself up to a certain degree by absorbing the driving and braking loads.

SERVICE BRAKES

The function of the hydraulic system is to deliver equal pressure to each of the four wheel cylinders. This pressure must cause each of the wheel cylinder pistons to move outward to apply the brake shoe linings against the braking surface of each brake drum with equal force. It is also important to remember the effect of the tire treads; each tire must be capable of creating equal friction at the road surface. Another fact to remember is that power brakes do not stop a vehicle better than manual brakes; they only reduce the amount of effort needed to depress the brake pedal.

Some typical problems with service brakes are grabbing, dragging, fading, and noise. Problems associated with brake pedal action are low pedal, soft or spongy pedal, and hard pedal action.

Grabbing Brakes

When one wheel brake grabs, the condition is caused by too much braking friction between the brake linings and brake drum of one wheel or unequal friction between the tread of one tire and the road surface. When all the brakes grab, the problem is at all four wheel brake assemblies.

If all four brakes grab, check the master cylinder piston for partially restricted movement. Check the push rod length adjustment if the car has power brakes. Also, check the internal parts of the power brake that could cause the problem; it could result from a sticking poppet valve, leaking reaction diaphragm, restricted diaphragm passage, or sticking actuating valve assembly.

Remove the brake drums and check the brake linings for defects or the wrong type of material. Wheel cylinder leakage and consequent lining contamination caused by improper overhaul or defective parts can also create a grabbing condition. Make sure that all of the internal brake parts are properly lubricated at the friction areas.

DRAGGING BRAKES

If the brakes are dragging at one wheel only, the trouble may be one wheel brake out of adjustment, a restriction in the hydraulic line, a front wheel bearing damaged or out of adjustment, weak return springs, or improper assembly of the brake shoes, causing their return to be restricted or the friction areas to be rusted or corroded. *NOTE: Rotate the defective wheel to determine just how much drag exists at the wheel, and then release the bleeder screw to determine if excessive hydraulic pressure is causing the shoes to be held against the drum.*

If a rear wheel brake is dragging, the trouble could be as described in the material just covered. In addition, check the parking brake adjustment and the operating linkage. If the brakes are dragging on all four wheels, the trouble could result from any of the following: restricted pedal return, a push rod of too great length, a defective residual check valve, a plugged compensator port, or a stuck piston or swollen rubber parts in the master cylinder.

If the vehicle is equipped with a power brake unit, see that all parts are free and allow the unit to return to the fully released position. Some of the following can cause trouble: a leak at the diaphragm assembly, sticking or unseated atmospheric check valve, sticking valve plunger, broken piston return spring, or a faulty check valve.

FADING BRAKES

Fading is generally due to an overheated drum expanding away from the brake linings after many hard stops. Fading is nonexistent with disc brakes, because the expansion of the rotor is against the friction pads. Any condition which causes overheating of the brake system can contribute to fading: riding the brake pedal, repeated panic stops, incorrect brake linings, glazed brake linings, thin brake drums, and weak brake shoe return springs.

NOISY BRAKES

Brake noises take several forms, one of the most annoying of which is squeal. This condition is caused by vibration due to loose parts or to misalignment of the brake shoes, which prevents the proper shoe contact with the drum.

When checking out other noises, rotate each wheel. Noise related to defective or loose wheel bearings or incorrectly assembled and rubbing internal brake parts should be evident. Rotate the wheel again and have someone depress the brake pedal lightly so that the noise level can be determined with the linings contacting the drums. Check the drum surfaces for evidence of threads cut during a drum-turning process; cut threads could cause the linings to shift to the side and then snap back during a brake application.

CHATTER

The problem of brake chatter is caused by the brake lining's failure to maintain constant pressure on the braking surface of the drum. Make a road test: apply and release the brakes while checking for any clicking or other unusual noises that may be audible at the four wheels. A noise indicates loose internal parts or parts that may not have been assembled correctly. Check to see if one particular wheel is causing the problem.

Brake chatter can be caused by loose backing plate retaining bolts; loose brake linings; oil, grease, or hydraulic fluid on the brake linings, causing unequal friction when the linings contact the drum; bent or distorted brake shoes; loose retaining springs; or distorted or out-of-round brake drums.

LOW PEDAL ACTION

With a low pedal, the brakes may be capable of stopping the car under normal conditions, but there may not be enough reserve left in case of emergency. Also, the depressed pedal height does not position the leverage at its most advantageous point.

A low pedal is generally caused by excessive brake shoe travel in relation to the distance that the brake pedal has to be depressed. Check for the following troubles: air in the hydraulic lines, low fluid level, or improper adjustment of the brake shoes.

If the car has self-adjusting brakes, first try a few firm reverse stops to see if the brakes will adjust themselves. If they won't, try adjusting the brakes by hand. You can determine which wheel is giving the trouble by the amount of adjustment required. If the trouble is a loose adjustment at one wheel, check the self-adjuster mechanism to see if the cable and springs are properly installed and if the adjusting lever and wheel are free from burrs.

A low fluid level in the master cylinder indicates possible fluid leakage. Add fluid and then check the complete system for improper assembly or defective parts. If the trouble is in the master cylinder, remove and disassemble it. Check the valve, valve seat, springs, cups, pistons, and cylinder bore for excessive wear or damage.

If the pedal action remains soft or spongy, check the complete brake system for leakage. Start at the master cylinder and then check the brake lines and connections to each wheel. Check the backing plate and the wheel area for evidence of wheel cylinder leakage. A fluid leak can cause inconsistency in building up pressure in the brake lines.

SOFT OR SPONGY PEDAL ACTION

Soft pedal action is generally due to air in the hydraulic lines. If the brake shoes are out of adjustment or if the shoes are bent or out of alignment, the entire face of the lining may not make full contact with the brake drum. Use of an improper lining, one that is too soft, can also cause this type of trouble.

HARD PEDAL ACTION

Hard brake pedal action can be caused by any mechanical restriction in either the brake pedal linkage or the brake shoe assembly parts. Or it can be caused by a restriction in the hydraulic system.

Remove the brake drums and examine the brake shoes for restrictions in travel. **CAUTION: Don't move the shoes out too far or you will pop out the wheel cylinder cups.** Make sure that the return and hold-down springs are properly installed. Lubricate all friction points. Tighten the backing plate bolts, as a loose backing plate will allow the shoes to be out of position in relationship to the braking surface of the drum. Brake linings that have hard or glazed surfaces will cause hard pedal action, because the cushioning effect between the face of the lining and the braking surface of the drum has been lost.

Check the hydraulic system for a restriction which could cause difficulty in moving the hydraulic fluid. Check the vent in the master cylinder cover and the compensating port for restrictions.

DISC BRAKES

The caliper-type disc brake saddles a rotating disc, often called a rotor. Frictional pads compress against the sides of the rotor. It is important to note the following advantages of a disc brake system: (1) Heat radiation is very efficient, making brake application very effective without fading. (2) Due to heat expansion, the rotor does expand radially, but the thickness does not alter, thus the pedal stroke does not change. (3) Pad replacement and system maintenance are relatively easy as compared with drum-type brakes. (4) Brake effectiveness-recovery from water occurs

quickly due to dispersion by centrifugal force. (5) Disc brakes are self-adjusting. As the pads wear, the piston is returned by the stretch of the piston seal within the cylinder.

TROUBLESHOOTING THE DISC BRAKE SYSTEM

WARNING LAMP

The brake warning lamp and the parking brake lamp utilize the same bulb, which may be tested by depressing the brake pedal with the ignition switch turned ON. If it doesn't light, replace the bulb or check for an open circuit.

After checking the warning lamp as discussed above, test the switch assembly by raising the car and loosening one of the wheel cylinder bleeder screws. Slowly depress the brake pedal with the ignition switch turned ON. The pressure differential should activate the switch and light the warning lamp. If the lamp does not light, replace the safety switch. To recenter the safety switch piston, tighten the bleeder screw, and then apply light brake pedal pressure. The piston will center itself automatically.

PROPORTIONING VALVE

A proportioning valve (brake pressure control valve) is connected into the rear brake hydraulic line, where it controls the rear brake line pressure on a fast, hard brake application in order to minimize rear wheel lockup.

A rough test can be made by making a hard brake application at about 40 mph. If the rear wheels lock up (skid), the trouble can be a defective proportioning valve.

BRAKE ROTOR

A disc brake rotor should be inspected visually for scoring, rust, hard spots, and ridges. A slight scoring of the rotor face is normal and does not lessen the effectiveness of the brake system. Rust can form on the face of the rotor when the vehicle is stored for a period of time and this can cause erratic braking.

A ridge build-up can also form at the outer and inner edges of the rotor from normal wear. The old pads wear to conform to these ridges. If new pads are installed without removing these ridges, erratic brake action generally results.

Brake rotors will sometimes show evidence of hard spots. They are very similar to the hard spots developed in a brake drum. Poor pad contact may then occur, resulting in brake squeal and fade. The hard spots can be removed by grinding or machine-turning the rotor on a brake lathe.

ROTOR RUN-OUT

It is first necessary to remove all wheel bearing end play. Do this by tightening the adjusting nut. Make sure that the bearing is loose enough so the rotor can be turned by hand. Mount a dial indicator so that it contacts the rotor approximately one inch from the edge; turn the rotor and check the run-out, which should be less than 0.005". If the rotor run-out is within limits, but the rotor has slight surface scores, it should be resurfaced on a drum lathe.

CALIPER ASSEMBLY

Check the caliper seals and piston dust boots for evidence of leaks or damage. If any brake fluid leakage is evident, it is necessary to disassemble the caliper and install a new seal kit as described in Chapter 8. Replace the brake pads when the lining is 1/16" thick.

DISC BRAKE TROUBLESHOOTING CHART

Symptoms & Causes
1. **Insufficient braking action**
   - 1a. Fluid leaking
   - 1b. Pad wear excessive
   - 1c. Pad contact surfaces wet with water or oil deposits
   - 1d. Rotor worn
   - 1e. Proportioning valve defective
2. **Noisy brakes**
   - 2a. Deposits on pad surfaces
   - 2b. Improper pad seating
   - 2c. Front wheel bearing adjustment loose
   - 2d. Lining material glazed
   - 2e. Backing plate bolts loose
3. **Car pulls to one side**
   - 3a. Pads wet with water or oil deposits
   - 3b. Tire inflation incorrect
   - 3c. Front end misaligned
   - 3d. Backing plate bolts loose
   - 3e. Wheel bearings loose
4. **Excessive pedal travel**
   - 4a. Air in hydraulic system
   - 4b. Excessive play at master cylinder push rod
   - 4c. Fluid leaking
5. **Rear wheel lockup**
   - 5a. Defective proportioning valve

POWER BRAKES

HARD PEDAL ACTION

If there is insufficient or no vacuum to the power brake unit, or if the push rod is incorrectly adjusted, the normal assist may be partially or totally missing. To find out if the trouble is in the power brake unit or in the service brakes, first remove all vacuum from the unit by depressing the brake pedal several times with the engine turned off. Hold the brake pedal down and then start the engine. If the pedal moves forward slightly, the power brake unit is functioning properly, and the problem is in the service brakes. If the pedal does not move forward, the vacuum operation of the power brake unit should be checked. With the engine running, remove the vacuum hose from the power brake unit. Place one finger over the open end of the hose to check for vacuum. If there is no vacuum, check all the vacuum lines, hoses, and connections for leakage or kinking.

2 tuning for performance

This chapter will cover the common tuning procedures that can be used on all engines, both emission-controlled and non-controlled, for restoring performance and fuel economy. Chapter 3 discusses the emission-control systems, and these must be checked out during each tune-up inasmuch as they affect engine performance to a marked degree.

TUNING FOR PERFORMANCE

Remove the spark plug wires by grasping, twisting, and then pulling on the molded cap only. **CAUTION: Don't pull on the wire, or the connection inside of the cap may become separated or the boot may be damaged.** Remove the spark plugs. **CAUTION: Don't tilt the spark plug socket, or you will crack the spark plug insulator.** Check the spark plugs against the illustrations in this chapter to determine the operating conditions of the engine. Clean and gap the spark plugs, and then place them on the bench for later installation. Test the compression by cranking the engine with a gauge inserted in each spark plug hole in turn. The actual reading is not as important as is a variation between cylinders which, if over 20 psi, indicates ring or valve trouble. Insert a teaspoonful of oil on top of the piston of a cylinder that reads abnorm-

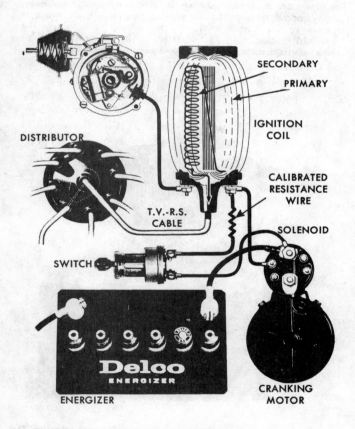

SECONDARY
PRIMARY
IGNITION COIL
CALIBRATED RESISTANCE WIRE
SOLENOID
DISTRIBUTOR
T.V.-R.S. CABLE
SWITCH
Delco ENERGIZER
ENERGIZER
CRANKING MOTOR

Typical ignition system

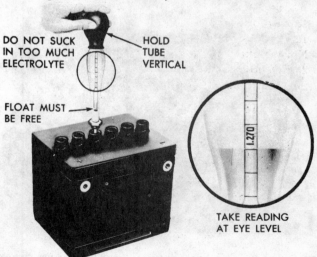

DO NOT SUCK IN TOO MUCH ELECTROLYTE
HOLD TUBE VERTICAL
FLOAT MUST BE FREE
1.270
TAKE READING AT EYE LEVEL

One of the first tune-up checks is to see that the battery is fully charged. Do this by using a hydrometer. A reading of 1.300 indicates a fully charged battery, while one of 1.150 means that the battery is discharged. Such a battery will make starting the engine difficult.

Check the fan belt tension every tune-up, and adjust to specifications.

Whenever tuning an engine, make sure that the manifold heat control valve is free by turning the counterweight. If necessary, apply special solvent to both ends of the valve shaft where it rotates in its bushings. Apply the solvent only when the manifold is cold. CAUTION: Don't apply lubricating oil, or the heat will cause it to carbonize and worsen the condition.

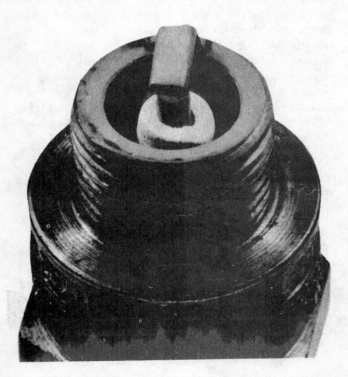

Check the spark plugs for abnormal conditions as you remove them from the engine. Spark plugs tell the story of engine operation and can be used as an important troubleshooting technique. This is how a normally operating spark plug should look. The compression is good and the carburetor air-fuel mixture is properly adjusted, as indicated by the light coloring of the tip. This lightness means that the tip was operating hot enough to burn off excess carbon.

This wet insulator is an indication of a nonfiring spark plug. The trouble can be either with the compression or the ignition. Better check this cylinder out before proceeding further.

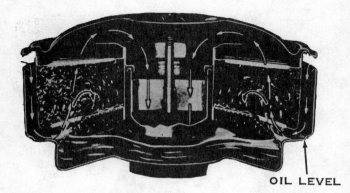

OIL LEVEL

The oil-bath type air cleaner should be cleaned in solvent every tune-up and the oil replaced at that time. Fill to the level mark, never above it.

ally low, and then crank the engine a few times to distribute the oil. Recheck the compression to see if the oil changed the reading. If the pressure increases, then the compression loss is past the piston rings; if not, the loss is past a burned valve.

IGNITION SYSTEM

Turn the crankshaft until the rotor points to the

The polyurethane element should be immersed in clean solvent and squeezed dry. Re-immerse the element in clean engine oil, and then squeeze out almost all of the oil. CAUTION: Don't shake or wring the element dry or you may tear it.

front of the engine; mark the position of the rotor on the edge of the distributor housing, and then remove the distributor. CAUTION: You cannot do a good job of reconditioning or replacing the contact points

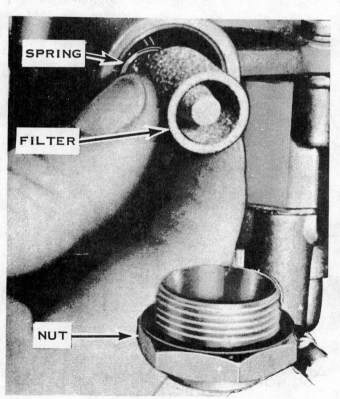

SPRING

FILTER

NUT

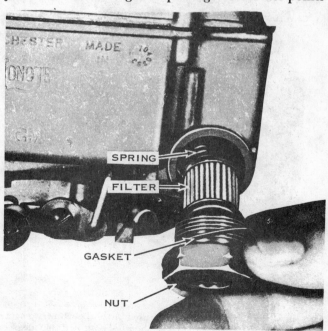

SPRING

FILTER

GASKET

NUT

To replace the fuel filter, disconnect the fuel line at the carburetor fuel inlet nut. The sintered bronze element (left) can be cleaned in solvent every tune-up, but should be replaced every 12,000 miles. The paper element (right) must be replaced every 12,000 miles. In-line fuel filter elements must be replaced every 24,000 miles.

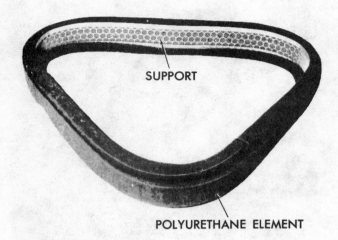

SUPPORT

POLYURETHANE ELEMENT

Some late-model engines use this type of polyurethane air filter element over a support screen. When replacing the element, care must be taken to see that the lower lip is properly positioned in the assembly and that the filter material is not creased to cause an imperfect seal.

with the distributor in the engine. Replace the contact points rather than filing them. It is seldom necessary to replace the condenser. Adjust the point gap to specifications. **CAUTION: Use only a cleaned feeler**

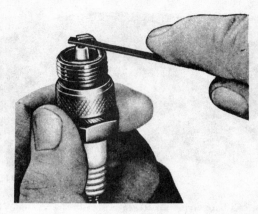

One of the most important service procedures is the filing of spark plug electrodes. These elements corrode and form a high-resistance path for the spark to jump across, resulting in engine misfiring on acceleration.

gauge blade; otherwise, you will coat the contact points with a film of oil, which will cause trouble when it oxidizes. When making the gap adjustment of a new set of contact points, add 0.003″ to the clearance specification to compensate for initial rubbing block wear. *NOTE: It is helpful to keep the contact point retaining screw snug during the adjustment so that*

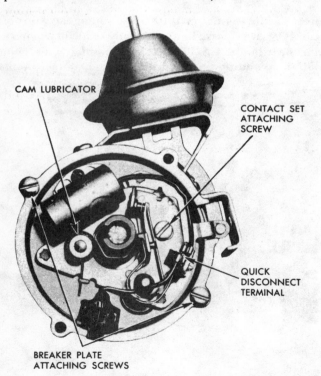

CAM LUBRICATOR

CONTACT SET
ATTACHING
SCREW

QUICK
DISCONNECT
TERMINAL

BREAKER PLATE
ATTACHING SCREWS

Details of the contact point set used in a six-cylinder engine distributor. The cam lubricator should be turned 180 degrees every 12,000 miles and replaced every 24,000 miles. Don't use engine oil on the cam lubricator, or it may get on the contact points and cause burning. Breaker point tension should be 19-23 ozs, and it can be adjusted by bending the spring.

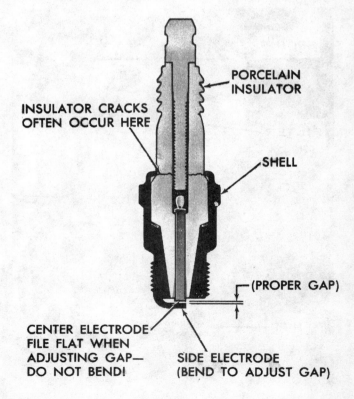

PORCELAIN
INSULATOR

INSULATOR CRACKS
OFTEN OCCUR HERE

SHELL

(PROPER GAP)

CENTER ELECTRODE
FILE FLAT WHEN
ADJUSTING GAP—
DO NOT BEND!

SIDE ELECTRODE
(BEND TO ADJUST GAP)

Details of the spark plug. Note that you must bend the side electrode to adjust the gap. Never bend the center electrode, or you will crack the porcelain, and the engine will misfire.

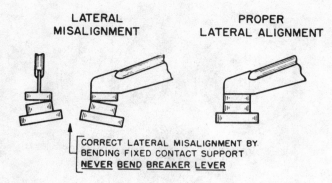

LATERAL MISALIGNMENT   **PROPER LATERAL ALIGNMENT**

CORRECT LATERAL MISALIGNMENT BY BENDING FIXED CONTACT SUPPORT
NEVER BEND BREAKER LEVER

The contact points must be aligned before being spaced. Correct misalignment by bending the fixed point support.

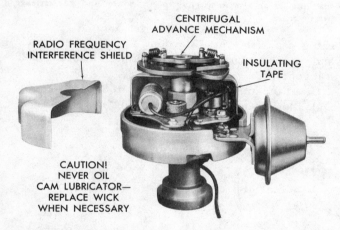

RADIO FREQUENCY INTERFERENCE SHIELD

CENTRIFUGAL ADVANCE MECHANISM

INSULATING TAPE

CAUTION! NEVER OIL CAM LUBRICATOR— REPLACE WICK WHEN NECESSARY

Details of the radio-frequency shield used on late-model distributors. This shield must be taken off before you can remove the contact points.

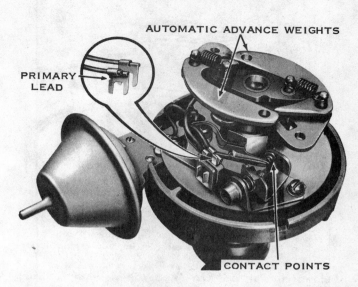

AUTOMATIC ADVANCE WEIGHTS

PRIMARY LEAD

CONTACT POINTS

Details of the primary and condenser leads of a distributor used on the V8 engine.

the gap does not change when tightening it. After making the gap adjustment, apply a *light* layer of heavy grease to coat the distributor cam. Turn the distributor shaft in the normal direction of rotation so that the lubricant is wiped off against the back of the rubbing block, where it remains as a reservoir to supply lubricant as the rubbing block wears. Wipe off the excess lubricant, leaving only the grease stored behind the rubbing block. Replace the distributor in the engine, with the rotor pointing toward the front and aligned with the mark you made on the housing edge

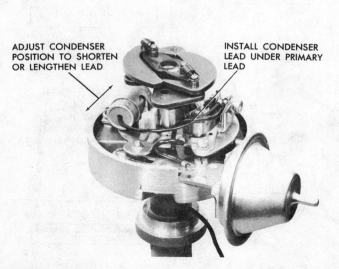

ADJUST CONDENSER POSITION TO SHORTEN OR LENGTHEN LEAD

INSTALL CONDENSER LEAD UNDER PRIMARY LEAD

When installing a replacement condenser in a late-model distributor, slide the condenser in its attaching bracket so that the primary lead does not rub on the shaft or rotor.

When installing the radio-frequency shield, make sure that the lead clips are not contacting the shield, or the engine won't run. Make sure that the second half of the shield mating flange rests on the outside of the first half before tightening the screw.

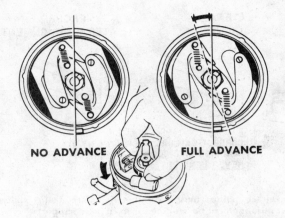

NO ADVANCE   **FULL ADVANCE**

If the primary wire lugs are not firmly pressed into place, they may be high enough to cause arcing and engine misfire.

before removal. *NOTE: The ignition timing will be adjusted after the engine is running.*

Tighten the cylinder head and the intake manifold bolts to the correct torque specified in the torque table in the appendix. Be sure to tighten the bolts in the sequence detailed by the illustrations in the chapter on Engine Service. **CAUTION: Uneven tight-**

Check the automatic advance weights for freedom of action by twisting the rotor, which must feel springy in one direction and solid in the other. If the weights don't move, the spark will not advance with engine speed; power and gas mileage will decrease.

ening can result in distortion. Replace the cleaned and gapped spark plugs, tightening them to 15-20 ft-lbs of torque.

Clean the air filter and reinstall it. Start the engine and allow it to warm to operating temperature.

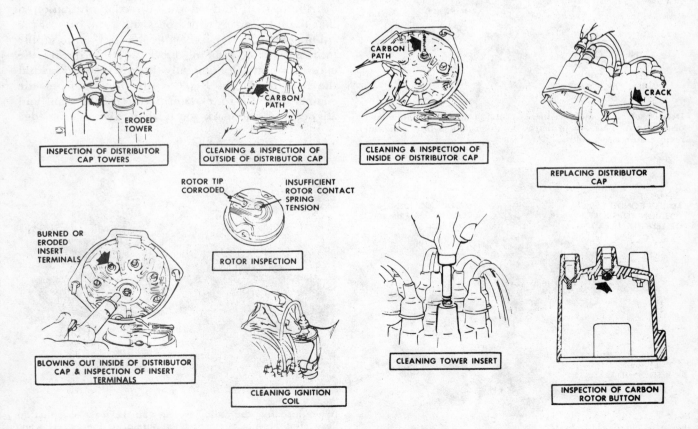

INSPECTION OF DISTRIBUTOR CAP TOWERS

CLEANING & INSPECTION OF OUTSIDE OF DISTRIBUTOR CAP

CLEANING & INSPECTION OF INSIDE OF DISTRIBUTOR CAP

REPLACING DISTRIBUTOR CAP

ROTOR INSPECTION

BLOWING OUT INSIDE OF DISTRIBUTOR CAP & INSPECTION OF INSERT TERMINALS

CLEANING IGNITION COIL

CLEANING TOWER INSERT

INSPECTION OF CARBON ROTOR BUTTON

Always inspect the distributor cap for evidence of carbon paths, which indicates a high-voltage leak to cause hard starting and misfiring on acceleration. Clean the distributor cap towers of all corrosion which causes high-resistance connections.

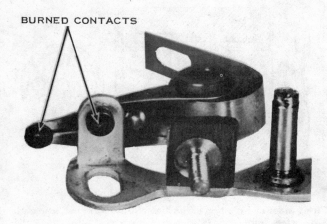

Details of a burned set of contact points, possibly caused by getting oil on the contact surfaces.

IGNITION TIMING

Disconnect the vacuum hose at the distributor and plug the end. If the air cleaner is removed, it will be necessary to plug the vacuum hose fitting with tape. Connect a tachometer and adjust the engine speed to specifications. Connect a power timing light to No. 1

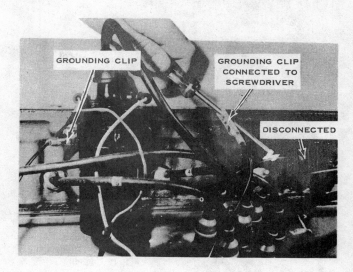

To check for leaking high-tension wires, use a jumper wire with one end grounded. Disconnect the high-tension cable to the spark plug to cause increased voltage in the cable and make the test more effective. Replace the high-tension wires every 2 years in any event to minimize hard-starting problems.

spark plug (left front). **CAUTION: Use an adaptor. Never puncture the wire or boot as this could start a high-voltage leak.**

Start the engine and check the dwell. If an adjustment is required on a V-8 engine, raise the adjusting screw window and insert an Allen wrench into the socket of the adjusting screw, which can be turned to

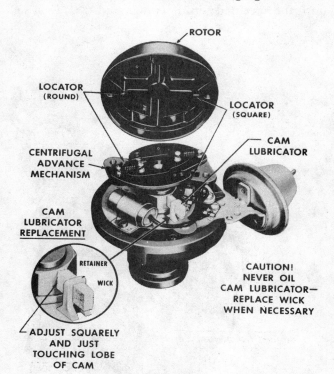

Details of the V-8 distributor and cam lubricator. Replace the wick every 24,000 miles. Never oil it, or the excess will get on the contact point surfaces where it will burn and cause high resistance, which will result in hard starting.

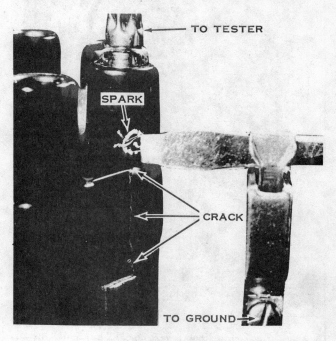

If a spark plug tester is available, connect its cable to a suspected distributor cap, and then use the grounded screwdriver blade as a probe to obtain this result when a distributor cap is cracked.

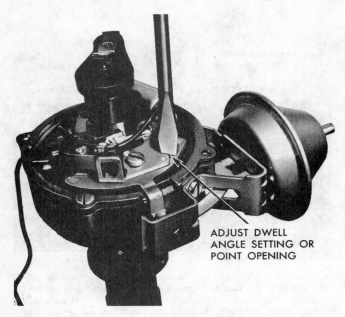

ADJUST DWELL ANGLE SETTING OR POINT OPENING

Use a screwdriver to adjust the point gap on a six-cylinder engine distributor.

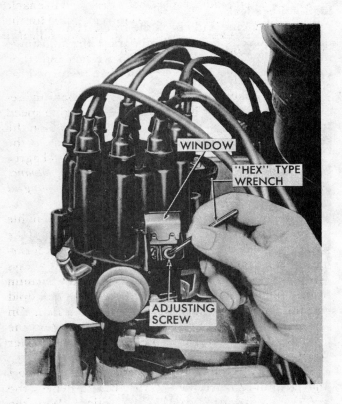

WINDOW

"HEX" TYPE WRENCH

ADJUSTING SCREW

To adjust the contact point gap on a V-8 engine, lift the window and use an Allen wrench to turn the adjusting screw. CAUTION: After making the adjustment, be sure to push the window fully down to prevent the entrance of dust and moisture which would cause many problems.

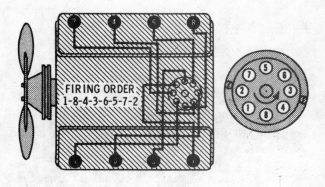

FIRING ORDER 1-8-4-3-6-5-7-2

Firing order and position of the high-tension wires in Oldsmobile V-8 engines from 1968–72.

obtain the specified 30±2° dwell. With a new set of points, adjust the dwell to 28° to allow for wearing in of the rubbing block.

To adjust the ignition timing, run the engine at the specified speed. **CAUTION: Many Oldsmobile engines are timed at speeds above idle.** Use a timing light to set the timing to specifications by loosening the distributor clamp bolt and rotating the distributor until the specified setting is obtained. *NOTE: A saw*

FRONT OF ENGINE

Diagram showing the high-tension wires and firing order for the 1970–72 Oldsmobile V-8 engine.

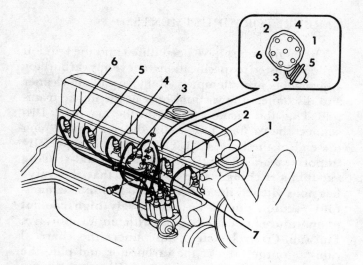

Placement of the high-tension wires for the 250 CID six-cylinder engine through 1974.

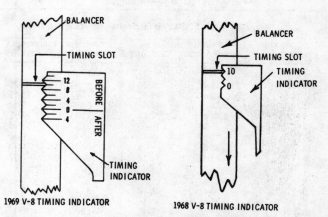

1969 V-8 TIMING INDICATOR   1968 V-8 TIMING INDICATOR

Details of the two timing indicators discussed in the text.

slot on the balancer indicates TDC. The six-cylinder engine timing indicator is marked in 2° increments, while the V-8 engine has four V-slots, each one representing 4°.

If the engine detonates with this setting, it can be caused by low octane fuel or an excessive carbon build-up in the combustion chambers. The timing can be retarded 2° from specifications if necessary to correct such detonation.

Tighten the clamp bolt and recheck the timing to be sure that it didn't move. Stop the engine and remove the timing light.

1969 Timing Indicator Change

The timing indicator used for the 1969 V-8 engines is different than the 1968 V-8 engine timing indicator. The 1969 indicator has four "V" slots; each slot represents 4°. The 1968 indicator has three "V" slots;

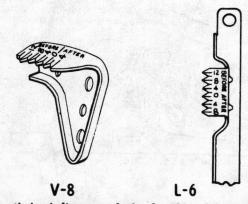

V-8   **L-6**

Ignition timing indicator marks for the Oldsmobile V-8 and L-6 engines.

each slot represents 5°. The 1969 indicator is marked in increments of 2°, ranging from 14° BTDC to 4° ATDC, whereas the 1968 indicator is marked in increments of 5°, ranging from 10° BTDC to 0° TDC. This new timing indicator has been designed to enable the technicians to obtain precise ignition timing for the 1969 engines. The 1969 L-6 engine timing indicator remains the same as the one used in 1968.

Distributor Advance

To check the distributor advance mechanism, reconnect the vacuum hose and increase engine speed to 2,500 rpm. Turn the advance control knob on the timing light until the ignition timing returns to the initial setting. The reading on the meter should agree with specifications. *NOTE: To obtain vacuum advance on 1970-72 models, disconnect the electrical coupling at the top of the solenoid.*

To obtain vacuum advance on a 1973-74 V-8 engine with a 4V carburetor, hold the throttle steady until the vacuum builds up. On 1973-74 engines with a 2V carburetor, nothing has to be done as vacuum is always present in the system. However, note that the vacuum values will be about 3"Hg lower than intake manifold vacuum because of the VRV valve in the system. On the six-cylinder engine, it is necessary to ground the cold terminal wire on the temperature switch in order to energize the CEC solenoid.

If the total advance is not as specified, disconnect the vacuum-advance hose so that you can check the centrifugal advance against specifications. With the hose disconnected, engine speed should decrease to reflect the loss of vacuum advance, therefore it will be necessary to return engine speed to 2,500 rpm for checking against specifications.

DISTRIBUTOR ADVANCE SPECIFICATIONS — OLDSMOBILE

ENGINE CID (CARB.)	IGNITION ADVANCE (Engine Degrees @ 2,500 rpm)			
	Manual Transmission		Automatic Transmission	
	Cent. & Vac.	Cent. Only	Cent. & Vac.	Cent. Only
1968:				
350 (2V)	40-44	16-20	40-44	16-20
350 (4V)	43-47	15-19	43-47	15-19
400 (2V)	34-28	10-14	34-38	10-14
400 (4V)	41-45	17-22	41-45	17-22
400 (4V) ①	31-36	15-20	31-36	15-20
455 (2V)	33-37	9-13	33-37	9-13
455 (4V)	33-37	9-13	33-37	9-13
455 (4V) ①	37-41	13-17	37-41	13-17
1969:				
350 (2V)	39-45	16-20	39-45	16-20
350 (4V)	32-38	15-19	32-38	15-19
350 (4V) ①	32-38	15-19	32-38	15-19
400 (4V)	41-48	17-22	30-37	15-20
400 (4V) ①	41-48	17-22	30-37	15-20
455 (2V)	37-43	14-18	37-43	14-18
455 (4V)	26-32	9-13	26-32	9-13
455 (4V) ①	36-42	13-17	36-42	13-17
1970:				
350 (2V)	36-43	13-15	36-43	13-15
350 (4V)	26-34	10-12	26-34	10-12
455 (2V)	32-40	10-12	32-40	10-12
455 (4V)	27-39	12-14	23-30	6-8
455 (4V) ①	32-47	17-22	35-45	19-21
1971:				
350 (2V)	44-53	23-27	44-53	23-27
350 (4V)	44-53	23-27	39-49	17-23
455 (2V)	34-43	14-18	34-43	14-18
455 (4V)	34-43	14-18	34-43	14-18
455 (4V) ①	38-47	17-21	33-42	21-25
455 (4V) ②	—	—	28-35	7-10
1972:				
350 (2V)	43-51	19-23	43-51	19-23
350 (4V)	43-51	19-23	42-51	18-23
455 (4V)	—	—	36-44	13-17
455 (4V) ①	41-49	17-21	45-53	21-25
455 (4V) ③	35-44	12-17	33-43	10-16
1973:				
250 (1V)	34-42	13-16	34-42	13-16
350 (2V)	37-45	19-23	37-45	19-23
350 (4V)	33-41	19-23	33-41	19-23
350 (4V) ④	—	—	39-47	25-29
455 (4V)	—	—	29-37	13-17
455 (4V) ②	—	—	26-34	10-14
1974:				
250 (1V)	25-29	13-17	25-29	13-17
350 (2V)	—	—	38-43	18-23
350 (4V) ⑦	—	—	34-38	18-22
350 (4V) ⑤	38-42	18-22	38-42	18-22
350 (4V) ⑥	—	—	40-45	24-29
455 (2V)	—	—	30-35	12-17
455 (4V)	32-37	12-17	32-37	12-17
455 (4V) ②⑥	—	—	33-38	9-14
455 (4V) ②⑤	—	—	27-32	9-14

① With Ram-Air Induction
② Toronado
③ Toronado and 442
④ Station Wagon
⑤ California only
⑥ 49 states
⑦ Cutlass and Omega

CARBURETOR ADJUSTMENTS

The engine must have been tuned and the ignition timing adjusted to specifications before any carburetor adjustments are attempted. Remove the air cleaner and disconnect the vacuum hose at the intake manifold. Plug the vacuum fitting on the manifold. Disconnect the vacuum hose at the distributor and plug the end of the hose. **CAUTION: This is especially important on an engine with a thermal-sensing vacuum-switching valve to insure that the valve has not switched the distributor to full intake manifold vacuum due to an excessively high coolant temperature.** On an engine with an Evaporative Emission-Control system, disconnect the charcoal canister purge hose at the carburetor and plug the opening. On an engine with an EGR valve, disconnect and plug the hose leading to the valve. Close the hot-idle compensator valve on four-barrel carburetors by depressing the plunger with your finger. On two-barrel carburetors, close the hot-idle compensator valve bleed hole inside of the air horn with your finger.

With the engine at normal operating temperature, shift the selector lever into DRIVE. With the air conditioner OFF, the choke valve fully open, and the fast-idle cam follower in the clearance section of the cam, adjust the idle speed and mixture as discussed below:

1968 Throttle-Stop Solenoid Adjustments

The two-barrel carburetors have a throttle-stop solenoid, which is activated by turning ON the ignition switch. When the ignition switch is turned OFF, the solenoid allows the throttle blades to close farther so the engine does not run after it is shut off. To adjust the solenoid, move it in its bracket so that the lower shoulder is flush with the bracket or protrudes

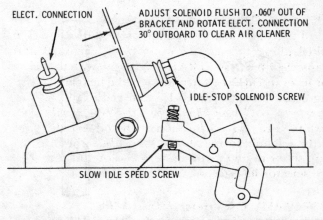

ELECT. CONNECTION

ADJUST SOLENOID FLUSH TO .060" OUT OF BRACKET AND ROTATE ELECT. CONNECTION 30° OUTBOARD TO CLEAR AIR CLEANER

IDLE-STOP SOLENOID SCREW

SLOW IDLE SPEED SCREW

The throttle-stop solenoid used on the 1968 Oldsmobile engine is adjusted in this manner.

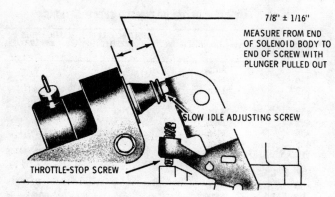

7/8" ± 1/16"

MEASURE FROM END
OF SOLENOID BODY TO
END OF SCREW WITH
PLUNGER PULLED OUT

SLOW IDLE ADJUSTING SCREW

THROTTLE-STOP SCREW

The throttle-stop solenoid used on the 1969 Oldsmobile 2V engines is adjusted in this manner.

from it up to 0.060″. Rotate the electrical connection 30° outboard in order to clear the air cleaner.

The 4MV carburetors have no solenoid, and the idle speed adjustment should be made with the throttle-stop screw in a conventional manner.

1969 Throttle-Stop Solenoid Adjustments

The throttle-stop solenoid of the two-barrel carburetor is positioned differently from the 1968 models discussed above, in that the throttle-stop screw is turned to obtain 575 rpm with the engine idling, and then the distance is measured from the edge of the clamp to the head of the screw with the plunger pulled out. Adjust the position of the solenoid body in the clamp to obtain 7/8″, as shown. Turn the electrical connector 90° outboard for clearance, and then tighten the clamp. Now, turn the throttle-stop screw out so that the throttle valves are just seated and ready for the final idle speed adjustments.

The 4MV carburetors have no solenoid, and the idle speed adjustment is made with the throttle-stop screw in a conventional manner.

1968-69 2GC Carburetor Adjustments

Adjust the solenoid plunger screw to obtain an initial idling speed of 675 rpm with a manual-shift transmission in NEUTRAL or 575 rpm with the selector lever in DRIVE. Turn in each idle mixture adjusting screw to obtain a 10-15 rpm reduction. *NOTE: The total reduction should be 20-30 rpm with both mixture screws adjusted as above.* Disconnect the wire to the solenoid terminal, and then adjust the throttle-stop screw to obtain an idling speed of 400 rpm with the selector lever in NEUTRAL.

1968-69 4MV Carburetor Adjustments

Adjust the throttle-stop screw and the idle mixture

screws alternately to obtain the best initial idle at 725 rpm with a manual-shift transmission in NEUTRAL (400 cu. in. engine), 675 rpm with a manual-shift transmission in NEUTRAL (350 and 455 cu. in. engines), or 575 rpm with an automatic transmission in DRIVE.

Turn the idle mixture screws in (lean) to obtain a 10-15 rpm reduction with each screw. *NOTE: The total reduction should be 20-30 rpm with both screws adjusted as above.* Now, turn each idle mixture adjusting screw out (richer) 1/4 turn.

1970 2GC Carburetor Adjustments

The idle mixture adjusting screws are preset and should not be disturbed unless a satisfactory idle cannot be obtained. Generally, all that is required is to adjust the throttle-stop screw to obtain the specified final idle speed.

If a satisfactory idle cannot be obtained and there are no vacuum leaks, turn each idle mixture adjusting screw gently into its seat, and then back it out 6 turns. Adjust the throttle-stop screw to obtain an initial idle speed of 620 rpm for all engines with an automatic transmission in DRIVE. Adjust the initial idle speed on engines with a manual transmission in NEUTRAL to 800 rpm for the 350 CID and to 720 rpm for the 455 CID engines. Turn each mixture adjusting screw in evenly (in 1/4 turn increments) until the final idle speed drops to 575 rpm for all engines with an automatic transmission in DRIVE. Adjust the final idle speed on engines with a manual transmission to 750 rpm for the 350 CID or to 675 rpm for the 455 CID engines. Note that the final idle speed represents about a 50 rpm drop from the best operating condition, and this means a 25 rpm drop for each mixture adjusting needle.

1970 4MV Carburetor Adjustments

The idle mixture adjusting screws are preset and should not be disturbed unless a satisfactory idle cannot be obtained. Generally, all that is required is to adjust the throttle-stop screw to obtain the specified final idle speed.

If a satisfactory idle cannot be obtained and there are no vacuum leaks, turn each idle mixture adjusting screw gently into its seat, and then back it out 6 turns (4 turns for the 350 CID engine in an "A" body). Adjust the initial idle speed to the specifications below, and then turn each mixture adjusting screw in evenly (in 1/4 turn increments) until the final idle speed drops to that specified below. Note that the final idle speed represents a 50-100 rpm drop from the best operating condition.

1971 Carburetor Adjustments

Adjust the throttle-stop screw to obtain 750 rpm with the shift lever in NEUTRAL, or to 600 rpm with the selector lever in DRIVE. The plastic limiter caps prevent making overrich mixture adjustments. If the carburetor has been overhauled and an air-fuel analyzer is available, the plastic limiter caps may be cut off and the idle mixture screw adjusted for a maximum reading of 0.6% CO for the 2GC carburetors or 0.3% for the 4MV carburetors. Install new service (colored) plastic limiter caps to prevent unauthorized adjustments.

Reconnect the distributor vacuum hose and the canister hose. Replace the air cleaner.

1972-74 2GC Carburetor Adjustments

A throttle-stop solenoid is used on these carburetors. The curb-idle speed should be adjusted to 650 rpm in DRIVE or to 750 rpm in NEUTRAL with the solenoid energized. Disconnect the solenoid wire and adjust the throttle-stop screw to obtain a slow-idle speed of 550 rpm in NEUTRAL or PARK.

The idle mixture adjusting screws have plastic caps and these should not be removed.

1972-74 4MV Carburetor Adjustments

With the antidieseling solenoid activated, adjust the idling speed to 650 rpm in DRIVE or to 750 rpm in NEUTRAL. Disconnect the solenoid wire and adjust the slow-idle speed of 550 rpm in NEUTRAL or PARK.

The idle mixture adjusting screws have plastic caps and these should not be removed.

Connect the throttle-stop solenoid wire. Connect the distributor vacuum hose and the carburetor hose to the charcoal canister. Install the air cleaner.

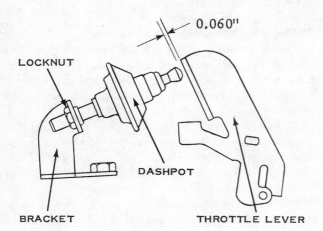

The Oldsmobile dashpot, where used, should be adjusted by turning the screw in the bracket to obtain 0.060″ clearance, as shown.

1970 4MV CARBURETOR IDLE SPEED SPECIFICATIONS

ENGINE CID "A" BODY	TRANSMISSION	INITIAL IDLE SPEED	FINAL IDLE SPEED
350	Auto.	625	575
350	Man.	725	650
350 [1]	Man.	[2]	750
350 [1]	Auto.	[2]	625
455	Auto.	700	600
455 [1]	Auto.	675	650
455	Man.	[2]	750
455 [1]	Man.	[2]	750
VISTA CRUISER	Auto.	650	575
"B" & "C" BODIES			
455	Auto.	625	600
TORONADO	Auto.	675	600

[1] Ram Air System
[2] Adjust to final idle speed

② TURN 1/8″ HEX SCREW TO ADJUST LOW IDLE (SOLENOID NOT ENERGIZED)

① SET IDLE R.P.M. TO SPECIFICATIONS (TURN ASSEMBLY IN OR OUT TO ADJUST SOLENOID ENERGIZED)

1. ENGINE AT NORMAL OPERATING TEMPERATURE AND CHOKE OPEN. SET PARKING BRAKE AND BLOCK DRIVE WHEELS.
2. DISCONNECT AND PLUG CARBURETOR HOSES FROM VAPOR CANISTER, E.G.R. VALVE AND DISTRIBUTOR VACUUM ADVANCE.
3. SET DWELL AND TIMING AT SPECIFIED R.P.M.
4. ADJUST IDLE STOP SOLENOID TO OBTAIN SLOW IDLE RPM (SOLENOID ENERGIZED)   M.T. 700 RPM (N)   A.T. 600 RPM (DRIVE)
5. ADJUST 1/8″ HEX SCREW OF IDLE STOP SOLENOID TO OBTAIN LOW (SHUT-OFF) IDLE (SOLENOID DE-ENERGIZED)   M.T. 450 RPM (N)   A.T. 450 RPM (PARK)
6. RECONNECT DISTRIBUTOR. CANISTER AND E.G.R. VALVE HOSES.

1973-74 Omega Carburetor Adjustments

3   emission-control systems

All Oldsmobile engines are equipped with a PCV valve for limiting crankcase emissions.

A Controlled-Combustion System (CCS) is designed into all Oldsmobile engines to minimize HC and CO emissions; it consists of engine, carburetor, and ignition modifications.

Since 1970, a Transmission-Controlled Spark (TCS) system has been used for the control of NOx. The TCS valve and the vacuum-switching valve were combined into a single unit for all 1971-72 models. The six-cylinder engine with a manual transmission used to power the Omega was the only one using a TCS system in 1973, and this was the Combined Emission-Control (CEC) valve. The 1974 six-cylinder engine with a manual transmission uses a different TCS system.

Since 1973, all Oldsmobile engines use Exhaust-Gas Recirculation (EGR) to reduce NOx emissions. A Thermal Check-and-Delay Valve (TCDV) is used on many 4V engines for 1973-74. A Vacuum-Reducer Valve (VRV) is used on some 1973 2V engines to prevent detonation when the coolant is above 226°F.

Since 1966, many Oldsmobile engines are equipped with an Air Injection Reaction (AIR) system for reducing HC and CO emissions in the exhaust manifold.

All 1975 engines will be equipped with a catalytic converter to reduce exhaust emissions.

An Evaporative-Emission-Control (EEC) system uses a charcoal canister for storing the gas tank and fuel bowl vapors until they can be drawn into the combustion chambers through a purge valve and line attached to the carburetor.

POSITIVE CRANKCASE VENTILATION

Uncontrolled crankcase emissions, consisting of blowby gases, make up about 25% of the total unburned hydrocarbons allowed to escape into the atmosphere. Blow-by gases are the small portion of the air-fuel mixture inside the combustion chamber that is forced past the piston rings into the crankcase. This happens just before and just after combustion occurs. Laboratory tests have established that blow-by amounts to about 0.14 cubic inch per cylinder for each complete combustion. The composition of these gases is about 80% unburned air-fuel mixture and about 20% combustion products including water, carbon dioxide, and carbon monoxide.

These blow-by gases always have been a problem to automotive engineers. If the gases are allowed to remain in the crankcase, they condense to form varnish deposits, acids, and sludge, all of which lessen engine life and performance. Before 1960 these blow-

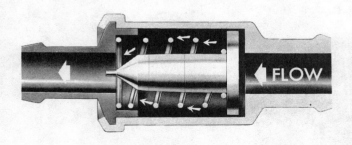

The PCV valve regulates the flow of blowby gases from the crankcase to the intake manifold.

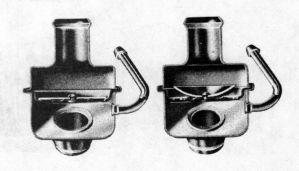

The crankcase ventilation valve used on early Oldsmobile engines had a diaphragm valve. The diaphragm valve is closed at idle (left) and opened at higher speeds.

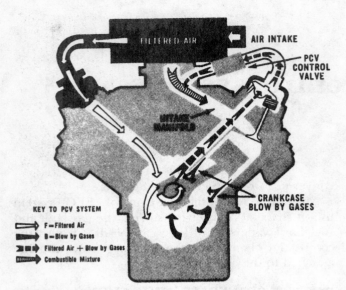

Diagram of a closed crankcase ventilation system using a positive crankcase ventilation (PCV) valve to control the flow of blow-by gases from the crankcase into the combustion chamber for burning.

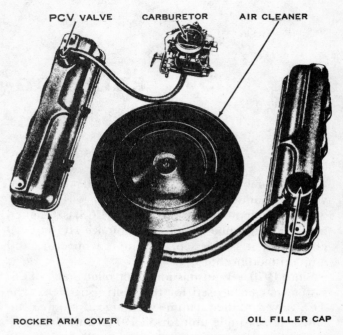

The closed system, sometimes called the California system, includes a hose from the oil filler cap to the air cleaner to take care of the excess blow-by generated during severe acceleration or by worn engines.

by gases were vented only into the atmosphere. Since that time, positive crankcase ventilation (PCV) systems have been installed on all automobile engines. These devices route the blow-by gases back to the combustion chamber, where they are consumed in the normal combustion process.

In older engines and during certain periods of operation, the amount of blow-by can exceed the

flow-rate of the control valve. If this occurs, some of the blow-by gases will escape to the atmosphere through the breather vent. This condition also occurs when the PCV valve becomes clogged. To minimize this source

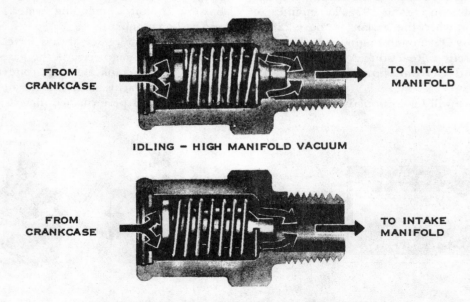

The PCV valve allows some air to bleed from the crankcase to the intake manifold during all engine operating conditions. When the engine is accelerated, spring pressure overrides the pull of the low intake manifold vacuum to allow the valve to open wider and thereby pass a greater volume of blow-by gases into the intake manifold.

of air pollution, engineers now are locating the breather vent inside the air cleaner so that air entering the induction system will carry with it any excess blow-by. This type of installation is called a closed system.

SERVICING THE CRANKCASE EMISSION-CONTROL SYSTEM

PCV difficulties usually are related to deposit formations on critical engine parts. With manifold return devices, plugging of the orifice or flow-control valve is the most common and troublesome problem. Partial plugging of the valve reduces the blowby-removing capacity of the system and may cause rough engine idle or stalling. Complete plugging results in more serious consequences—all ventilation is lost, blowby gases escape to the atmosphere, and engine sludging, rusting, and wear tend to increase dramatically. In severe cases, oil may be forced out of the breather, the dipstick tube, or even the crankshaft seals.

Moisture and oily products from the blowby fumes may also collect in the carburetor air-filter element, reducing its effective life. And in cool weather, condensation products from the blowby gases in the relatively long and large-diameter vent tube may drip back into the crankcase, adding to oil contamination.

Vehicle manufacturers recommend that crankcase control devices be checked and serviced every oil change or at intervals based on time or mileage, but not exceeding one year or 12,000 miles. Every 24,000 miles, the PCV valve should be replaced. These recommendations should be considered the minimum requirements for a satisfactory maintenance program. More frequent attention may be needed as operating severity is increased. Low ambient temperatures, frequent starts and stops, long idling periods, high blowby rates, and use of marginal-quality fuels and

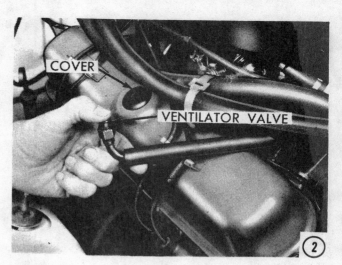

lubricants tend to increase the maintenance requirements.

Routine inspection of a PCV system usually involves checking the flow-control valve for proper flow and noting any evidence of malfunction of the system: outflow of blowby fumes, odor complaints, or oil on the outside of the engine. In vehicles using combination or air-cleaner return systems, the air-cleaner filter element or flame-arrester mesh will require periodic replacement or cleaning. With all types of systems, it is important to clean connecting hoses and fittings. Deposits left in these parts can later migrate to other parts of the system, causing premature clogging of the control valve and air-cleaner element. Breather caps also should be washed frequently in solvent to assure an unrestricted flow of ventilation air to the crankcase in "open" systems. Use of the correct replacement parts—particularly flow-control valves—is also of paramount importance. Failure to use the proper valve for a particular engine application will result in faulty engine operation or inadequate ventilation. Similarly, the correct type of breather cap must be used. Some systems are designed to work only with a conventional open-type cap, while others require a restricted or closed cap.

TESTING THE SYSTEM

① Remove the PCV valve from the rocker arm cover and shake it. You should hear a clicking noise if the valve is free. If not, replace the valve. **CAUTION: Don't attempt to clean the valve. Also, make sure that you replace it with one having the correct part number, as each has a different calibration.**

② Start the engine and a hissing noise should be heard as air passes through the valve. A strong vacuum should be felt when you place your finger over the valve inlet.

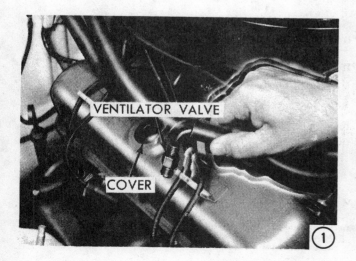

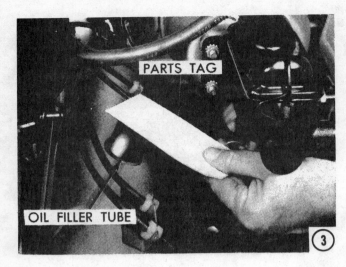

③ Reinstall the valve, and then remove the oil filler cap. Start the engine and hold a piece of cardboard over the opening in the rocker arm cover. If the system is functioning properly, the cardboard will be sucked against the opening with a noticeable force. If the cardboard is not sucked against the opening with a new PCV valve, it is necessary to clean the hoses, vent tube, and passageway in the lower part of the carburetor.

AIR INJECTOR REACTOR (AIR) SYSTEM— SINCE 1966

Combustion in the modern emission-controlled engine has been greatly improved by changes in the carburetor, distributor, and combustion chambers. However, on some engine-transmission combinations,

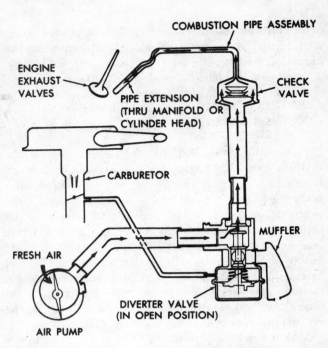

This flow diagram shows the current model of AIR system with its two-vane pump and a muffler on the by-pass (diverter) valve to silence the pump output during deceleration.

it is necessary to add oxygen to the very hot and highly flammable gases released by the exhaust valves. The added oxygen causes the remaining unburned hydrocarbons to ignite, changing them into harmless gases, which are the products of nearly complete combustion.

The AIR system is composed of an air pump, diverter valve, check valve(s), air manifold(s), and connecting hoses. In a typical V-8 engine installation, two air manifolds are used to route the compressed air into the exhaust manifolds.

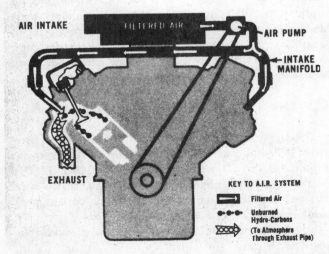

The Air Injection Reactor (AIR) system uses a pump to force air into the exhaust manifold to consume the unburned hydrocarbons as they leave the combustion chamber.

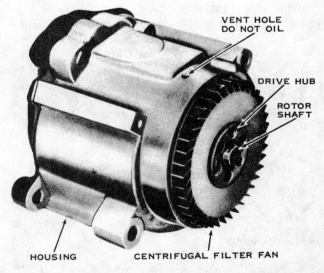

Details of the air pump which has a centrifugal-type filter fan on the drive pulley.

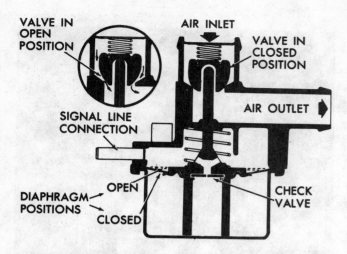

The air-gulp type of backfire-suppressor valve, used on Oldsmobile engines through 1967, dumps a slug of fresh air into the intake manifold during deceleration to compensate for the over-rich mixture.

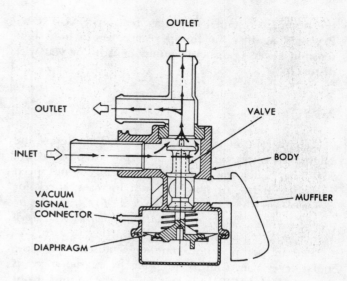

This new style by-pass valve has its own muffler to silence the sound of the discharged air during deceleration.

SERVICING THE AIR SYSTEM

Only a properly tuned engine can provide full power and performance and full value from the AIR system for the control of exhaust emissions. Therefore, it is essential for a good tune-up to be performed each 10,000 miles and a functional check of the AIR system made at the same time.

DRIVE BELT

Inspect the belt for wear, cracks, or deterioration;

replace the belt if necessary. Check the belt tension using a strain tension gauge; adjust if necessary. The belt setting may vary slightly with different applications, but a typical setting for a used belt is 55 lbs. and 75 lbs. for a new one. *NOTE: A belt that has been operated for over 10 minutes is considered a used belt.* If an adjustment is necessary, loosen the air pump mounting and adjusting bolts, and then move

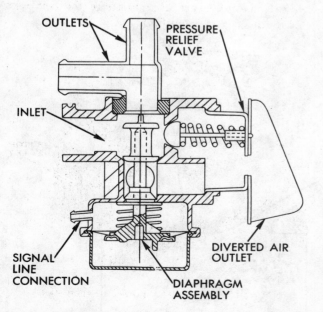

Some late-model AIR systems have the pressure-relief valve incorporated in the diverter valve.

A very important step in checking for trouble in an AIR system is to be sure that the air pump drive belt is tensioned properly.

the pump to obtain the proper tension. **CAUTION: Pry only against the pump rear cover to hold belt tension, never against the pump housing or you will distort it.**

Air Pump

Remove one of the outlet hoses and accelerate the engine to approximately 1,500 rpm to observe the air flow. The flow must increase as engine speed increases. If the air flow does not increase, check for a leaky pressure relief valve. *NOTE: Air may be heard leaking out of a normal valve with the pump operating at maximum pressure.*

The air pump is not completely noiseless, and the noise level rises slightly in pitch as engine speed is increased. **CAUTION: Don't oil the pump front bearing vent hole as this will lead to pump failure.** Before replacing a pump for excessive noise, remove the drive belt and operate the engine without the pump.

Diverter Valve

Check the routing and condition of all hoses, especially the vacuum signal line. All hoses must be secure, without crimps, and not leaking. Disconnect the signal line at the valve and hold your finger over the open end of the hose. You should feel vacuum with the engine idling. Reconnect the vacuum hose.

With the engine stabilized at idle, no air should

Check for leaks with a soapy water solution. Bubbles indicate the presence of a leak.

escape through the muffler. Open and close the throttle quickly, and a momentary blast of air should discharge through the muffler vents for at least one second. A defective diverter valve cannot be serviced and must be replaced. **CAUTION: These valves differ in specifications and you must install the correct one for efficient operation of the system.**

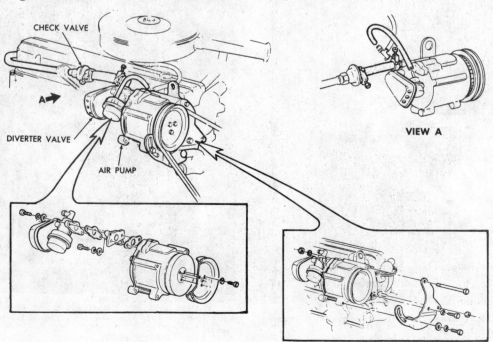

Location of the parts making up the AIR system on an Omega six-cylinder engine.

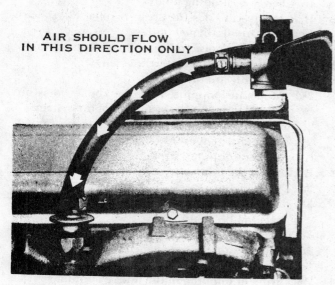

AIR SHOULD FLOW
IN THIS DIRECTION ONLY

This is the direction that air must flow in the system. If the check valve is leaking, exhaust gases will pass back to the air pump and destroy it.

Check to see that a vacuum signal is reaching the diverter valve with the engine idling.

Check Valve

The check valve(s) should be inspected whenever the hose is disconnected. An inoperative pump or a hose that shows evidence of exhaust gases indicates a check valve failure. Orally blow through the check valve toward the air manifold, and then attempt to suck back. The flow should be in one direction only—toward the air manifold.

A good way to check the efficiency of an AIR system is to close off the air supply to the injectors while the engine is idling. The needles of an HC/CO meter will deflect at least 5% to the rich side, if the system is functioning properly.

Air Manifold and Hoses

Inspect all hoses for deterioration, cracks, or holes. Check the air manifold for cracks or holes. Inspect all hose and manifold connections for tightness. If a leak is suspected on the pressure side of the system, check the component with a soapy water solution. **CAUTION: Keep the water away from the centrifugal filter of a two-vane air pump, or you will ruin it.** If you have to replace a hose, make sure that it is made of the special high-temperature material for that purpose. Other hose material will melt under the elevated operating temperatures.

Air Injector Nozzles

There is no periodic service or inspection needed, except when the cylinder heads are removed from the engine. At that time, remove any carbon build-up with a wire brush and replace warped or burned tubes.

AIR SYSTEM TROUBLESHOOTING CHART

Troubles & Causes
1. **Pump noisy**
   1a. Hose disconnected or leaking
   1b. Pivot bolt tightened too much
   1c. Chirping noise. This may be normal on a new pump until it is broken in
   1d. Improper belt tension
   1e. Seized or binding pump
   1f. Incorrect or missing pressure relief valve
   1g. Bent or misaligned pulleys
   1h. Knocking noise indicates broken pump vanes
2. **Popping in the exhaust system**
   2a. Rich idle mixture
   2b. Moderate popping with the choke on is an inherent design characteristic of the system
   2c. Popping during acceleration may be caused by retarded ignition timing or an incorrect accelerator pump stroke adjustment
3. **Backfire in the exhaust system**
   3a. Rich fuel mixture
   3b. Inoperative or incorrectly adjusted carburetor vacuum-break unit
   3c. Overchoking with a manual choke
   3d. Clogged air cleaner element
   3e. Clogged PCV valve
4. **Backfiring or popping in the intake manifold**
   4a. Intake manifold leaking air
   4b. Incorrect ignition timing
5. **Off-idle hesitation and rough hot idle**
   5a. Vacuum hose leak
   5b. Hot-idle compensator not closing properly or opening prematurely
   5c. Intake manifold or carburetor flange gasket leaking air
   5d. Insufficient fuel discharge from the carburetor acceleration pump
   5e. Carburetor fuel bowl level too low
   5f. Incorrect ignition timing

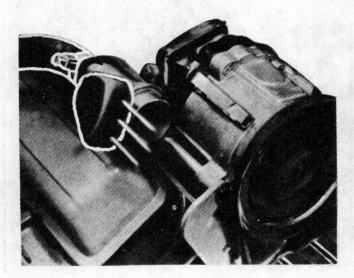

There should be a momentary blast of air through the diverter valve during deceleration.

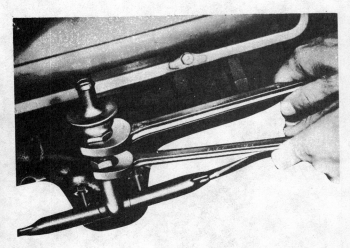

Always use two wrenches to remove the check valve: this will keep you from twisting the pipes.

6. **Rough idle or surge**
    6a. Incorrect idle mixture adjustment
    6b. Vacuum leak in signal line to diverter valve
    6c. Vacuum leak in hose to distributor vacuum-advance unit
    6d. Intake manifold or carburetor leaking air
    6e. Incorrect ignition timing
7. **Engine idle speed too fast**
    7a. Idle speed adjusted incorrectly
    7b. Throttle linkage sticking
8. **Afterrunning**
    8a. Idle speed too high
    8b. Fuel too volatile
    8c. Throttle-stop solenoid improperly adjusted
9. **Exhaust system overheats**
    9a. Retarded ignition timing
    9b. Fuel mixture too lean
    9c. Incorrect pressure relief valve in air pump
10. **Charred air supply hose**
    10a. Defective check valve

CONTROLLED-COMBUSTION SYSTEM (CCS)— SINCE 1967

In 1967 a breakthrough occurred in providing heated air to the carburetor induction system. A sheet metal stove is attached to the exhaust manifold where underhood air is heated as it passes over the hot exhaust manifold. The heated air is conducted from

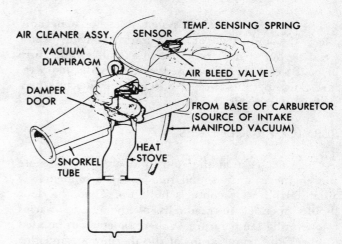

Details of the thermostatically-controlled air cleaner. Heated air from around the exhaust manifold is blended with underhood air to maintain an inlet air temperature of about 105°F.

the stove to the air cleaner through a flexible duct. The air cleaner is designed to control the inducted air temperature at approximately 100°F through about 70 mph road-load conditions. At speeds above 70 mph, decreasing intake manifold vacuum and an increasing differential pressure across the temperature-controlled door cause the door to open gradually until an intake manifold vacuum of about 5.5″ Hg is reached; at this time the heat-control door will be in the heat-off position, and the inducted air temperature will be the same as underhood air temperatures.

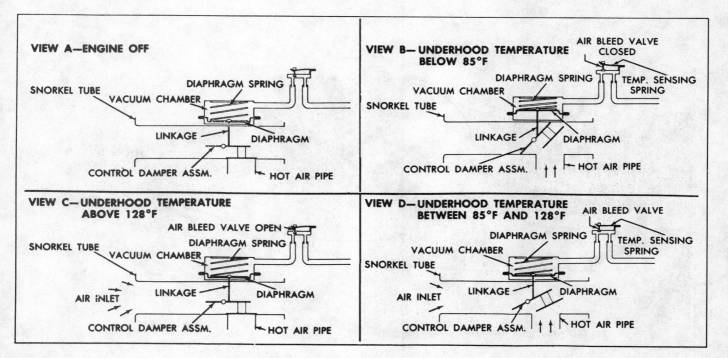

Air cleaner operation.

The use of a heated-air system does not materially affect the inducted air temperature during warm weather, but it does raise the intake air temperature in cold weather. A decreased spread in the temperature range permits the use of leaner air-fuel mixtures with satisfactory driveability.

SERVICE PROCEDURES

Check to see that the cold-air door is open before the engine is started, and that it closes immediately after starting as vacuum is built up. Then the door should open again gradually as the engine warms to operating temperature. A thermometer can be used to check the temperature of the thermostat, and this should begin to control the vacuum motor for starting to close the heated-air door at about 105°F.

TRANSMISSION-CONTROLLED SPARK (TCS)—1971-72

Since 1970, all Oldsmobile engines have used a Transmission-Controlled Spark (TCS) system for reducing oxides of nitrogen. In low gears, all vacuum is cut off from the distributor vacuum-advance unit to prevent spark advance during acceleration and deceleration. Vacuum spark advance occurs only in high gear to provide optimum performance and good cruising economy.

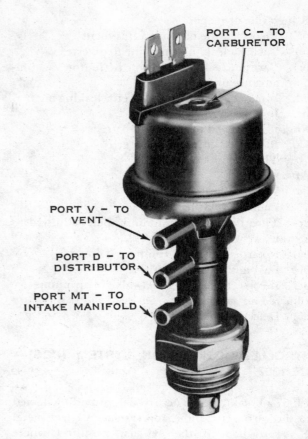

This is the combined thermal-sensing and vacuum-switching valve used on 1971-72 Oldsmobile V-8 engines for the control of NOx and overheating at idle speeds.

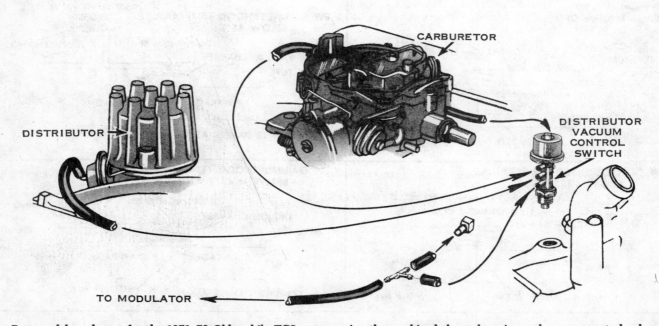

Parts and hose layout for the 1971–72 Oldsmobile TCS system using the combined thermal-sensing and vacuum-control valve.

The solenoid vacuum switch is energized in low gears by a transmission grounding switch to shut off the vacuum source to the distributor. At the same time, the solenoid opens a vent line to the distributor vacuum-advance unit to keep it from being locked in.

Temperature override for full vacuum advance in all gears is supplied with a cold engine. A temperature-sensing valve in the cooling system signals a relay when the engine is hot enough for the solenoid to cut off the vacuum supply to the distributor. Some vehicles have a hot override switch (thermal-sensing, distributor-control valve) for restoring full manifold vacuum to the distributor whenever the engine overheats. The extra spark advance increases idling speed and, thereby, coolant circulation to reduce engine temperatures to a safe level.

In 1971, Oldsmobile combined the TCS solenoid vacuum-control valve with the thermal-sensing, vacuum-control valve in the coolant chamber. This lessens the number of vacuum hoses, thus minimizing leaks and service problems.

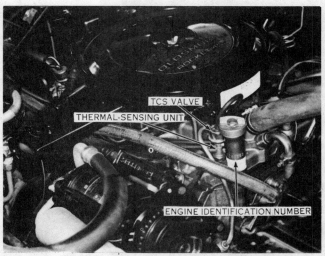

1971–72 Oldsmobile engines used a combined thermal-sensing and vacuum-control valve for the TCS system.

OPERATION:

The solenoid coil is energized in first and second cutting off ported vacuum to distributor vacuum advance. In third or high, solenoid is de-energized and the spring opens the solenoid valve to allow ported vacuum to the distributor vacuum advance.

If engine overheats, copper oxide paste senses high temperature from engine block and begins to expand. Expansion pushes pin up to unseat ball check valve. Engine vacuum is directed to the distributor to advance engine timing to assist engine cool down.

TO TEST SOLENOID:

1. Disconnect hoses and electrical connector.
2. Connect a hose to the port on top of the solenoid and blow through hose. Air should come out center port.
3. Plugging center port should shut off air flow through solenoid if valve is O.K.
4. Connect one electrical terminal to a 12 volt source and ground other terminal with a jumper.
5. Remove hose from port on top of solenoid and connect to center port on side of valve.
6. Blow through hose. Air should come out the top port on the side of the valve. If it does not, replace the valve.
7. Plug the top port on the side of the valve and blow into hose. Air should be blocked off. If air comes out the bottom port or the port on top of the solenoid, the valve should be replaced.

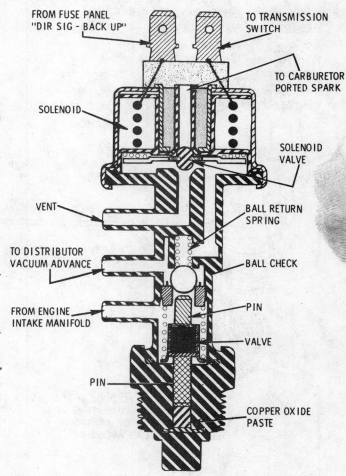

Troubleshooting chart and sectioned view through the combined distributor vacuum-control valve and TCS solenoid used in 1971–72.

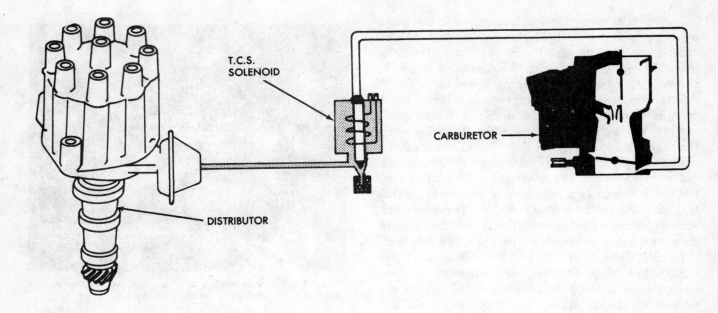

1 T.C.S. SOLENOID ENERGIZED, PROVIDING NO VACUUM ADVANCE IN ALL TRANSMISSION
RANGES BUT HIGH GEAR DURING NORMAL OPERATING TEMPERATURE.
(BETWEEN 85°F AND 220°F)

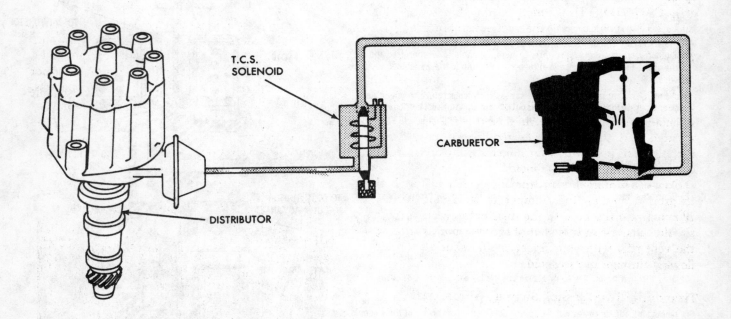

2 T.C.S. SOLENOID DE-ENERGIZED, ALLOWING FULL VACUUM ADVANCE IN HIGH GEAR
DURING NORMAL OPERATING TEMPERATURE AND ALL MODES OF TRANSMISSION OPERATION
DURING PERIODS OF ABNORMAL ENGINE OPERATING TEMPERATURE.
(BELOW 85°F AND ABOVE 220°F)

Operational diagram of the Transmission-Controlled Spark (TCS) system used on Oldsmobile V-8 engines from 1970–72.

SERVICE PROCEDURES

A failure in the TCS system could result in either of two troubles: (1) continuous vacuum advance in first and second gears, which would prevent the vehicle from passing the federal emissions standards, or (2) no vacuum advance in third gear, which would result in loss of power and lower gas mileage.

The following checks should be made as part of each engine tune-up: Secure the parking brake and block one wheel in front and back. Hook up a tachometer and timing light. Start the engine and move the transmission selector lever into DRIVE. Increase engine speed to approximately 1,000 rpm by positioning the fast-idle cam. Check the timing mark and there must be no vacuum advance. Shift into REVERSE and there should be full vacuum advance.

QUICK TEST

A quick test of the hoses and solenoid can be made by disconnecting the wires from the top of the coolant temperature-sensing valve with the engine idling. The ignition timing should advance about 5° and engine speed will increase if the system is functioning properly. **CAUTION: This action is not immediate, but takes a few seconds until the vacuum stabilizes.**

TESTING THE SOLENOID

Disconnect the hoses and the electrical connector. Connect a hose to the distributor vacuum port on the solenoid and blow into it. Air should come out of the vacuum port that was connected to the carburetor. Plugging this port with your finger should shut off the air flowing through the solenoid.

Connect a jumper wire from one solenoid terminal to ground and another jumper to a 12-volt source. Blowing into the hose to the distributor vacuum port should cause air to come out of the vent port. Plugging the vent port with your finger should shut off the air flowing through the solenoid.

TESTING THE TRANSMISSION SWITCH (AUTOMATIC)

Disconnect the electrical connector from the switch on the side of the transmission. Connect a test lamp (with a #1893 bulb) between the switch contact and a 12-volt source. **CAUTION: The bulb current must not exceed 0.8 amp, or you will burn the switch contacts.** The test lamp should light when the transmission is in drive with the engine running at about 1,500 rpm and go out when the selector lever is moved into reverse.

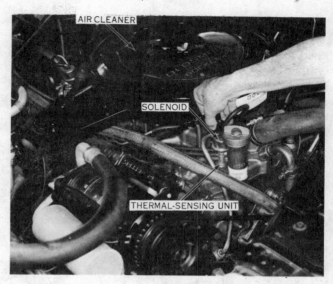

The control solenoid of the TCS system used on the 1971–72 Oldsmobile engine is part of the thermal-sensing, distributor-control valve. To test the function of the valve, pull off the connector with the engine idling. If the valve is operating properly, ignition timing should advance about 10°, and engine speed should increase slightly to reflect the added ignition advance.

TESTING THE TRANSMISSION SWITCH (MANUAL)

Disconnect the electrical connector from the switch on the side of the transmission. Connect a test lamp (with a #1893 bulb) between the switch contact and a 12-volt source. **CAUTION: The bulb current must not exceed 0.8 amp, or you will burn the switch contacts.** The test lamp should light in all gears, except high.

Details of the CEC valve used on the 1973 Omega with a six-cylinder engine.

Manual

Disconnect the electrical connector from the switch on the side of the transmission. Connect a test lamp (with a No. 1893 bulb) between the switch contact and a 12-volt source. **CAUTION: The bulb current must not exceed 0.8 amp, or you will burn the switch contacts.** The test lamp should light in all gears, except high.

TRANSMISSION-CONTROLLED SPARK (TCS) SIX-CYLINDER ENGINE—1971-73

The 1971-73 six-cylinder engine with a manual transmission is equipped with a Combination Emission-Control CEC valve on the carburetor. This valve acts as a TCS solenoid, an anti-dieseling solenoid, and a throttle-return check valve.

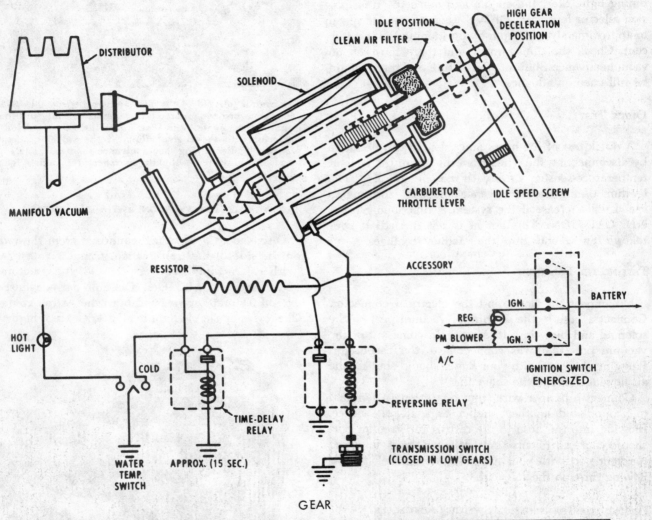

Transmission	Park	Neutral	Reverse	1st.	2nd.	3rd.	4th.
3 Speed	-	-	-	-	-	Vac.	-
4 Speed	-	-	-	-	-	Vac.	Vac.

Schematic wiring diagram of the Combined Emission-Control (CEC) valve and associated switches as used on the 1971-73 six-cylinder engine with a manual transmission. Vacuum advance is supplied only in high gear so as to minimize the formation of NOx. Six-cylinder engines with an automatic transmission use ported EGR for NOx control.

When the CEC valve is in the non-energized position, vacuum to the distributor vacuum-advance unit is shut off, and the distributor is vented to the atmosphere through a filter at the opposite end of the solenoid. Air passage through the solenoid is provided by grooves molded in the spool and by the clearance between the adjusting screw and the plunger stop. When the solenoid is energized, the vacuum port is uncovered, and the plunger is seated at the opposite end, shutting off the clean air vent. Curb-idle speed and the high gear deceleration throttle blade setting must be performed with the solenoid in the non-energized position. With the vacuum line removed at the distributor and plugged, and with the electrical connection also removed, the curb-idle speed is set with the carburetor idle-speed adjusting screw. The throttle-stop adjustment screw on the CEC valve is then pulled out to its fully extended position and adjusted to the specified rpm to provide the desired high-gear deceleration throttle blade opening. Thus, two separate throttle settings are now possible—one for curb idle and one for deceleration hydrocarbon control.

The CEC valve is controlled by two switches and a time-delay relay. The solenoid is energized in the high forward gears and reverse on Hydra-matic by a transmission-operated switch. Due to a design consideration, a reversing relay is required to reverse the function of the transmission switch. A thermostatic

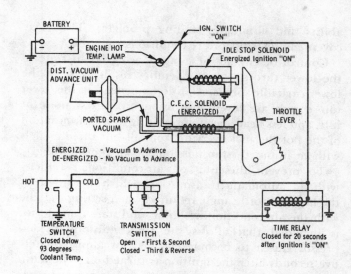

Schematic diagram of the 1973 Omega emission-control system, with the engine running and the transmission in high gear.

water temperature switch is used to provide thermal override below 82°F. The time-delay relay is incorporated in the circuit to energize the CEC valve for 20 seconds after the ignition key is turned on. Full vacuum to the distributor, independent of engine temperature for this time interval, improves drive-

Location of the thermal-override switch used on the Omega.

Location of the transmission switch, which activates the TCS or CEC valve on the Omega.

ability and eliminates stalling problems. This relay covers engine temperature conditions above 82°F.

Control of engine dieseling is achieved in spite of the lower throttle blade openings resulting from the lower curb-idle speeds. Additional benefits of the lower idle speeds are less transmission creep, less noise at idle, and less heat rejection resulting in the elimination of the hot thermal override from all but three models with an automatic transmission and air conditioning.

To prevent dieseling on air-conditioned vehicles with an automatic transmission, which is caused by the larger throttle angle required when setting the idle with the air conditioning on, a solid-state time device is included that allows the air conditioning compressor clutch to become engaged for approximately five seconds after the ignition is turned off. The additional load the compressor places on the engine brings it to a stop sooner, thereby effectively reducing the tendency to diesel.

TESTING THE CEC VALVE

Check the CEC valve for proper operation during each engine tune-up. Secure the parking brake and block one wheel at the front and back. Hook up a tachometer and timing light. Start the engine and there should be no vacuum advance at a fast-idle speed when checked with the timing light. Shift into REVERSE with a Turbo Hydra-Matic transmission and there should be full vacuum advance; engine speed should increase to reflect the added ignition advance.

The transmission switch is actuated by oil pressure in the direct clutch circuit of the transmission and it normally does not open until the transmission shifts into high gear. However, there is always oil pressure in the direct clutch circuit in REVERSE gear of a Turbo Hydra-Matic transmission so that this becomes a handy tool for checking the system.

With a manually shifted transmission, depress the clutch pedal and shift into and out of high gear with the engine at a fast idle to activate the switch. You should have vacuum advance in only third and fourth gears.

Check the throttle-return function of the valve by shifting into DRIVE. Jack up a rear wheel, accelerate the engine, and then allow it to coast back down to idle speed. The CEC valve plunger should extend,

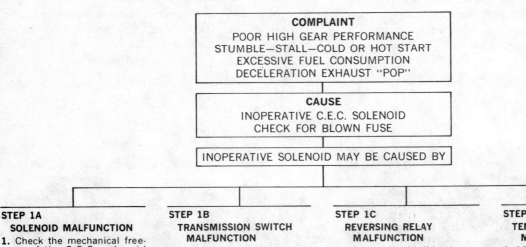

Troubleshooting roadmap for checking the six-cylinder TCS system if the complaint is due to an inoperative CEC solenoid.

causing the engine to run at a fast idle for a few seconds, and then the plunger should retract to allow a normal curb-idle speed.

A quick check of the throttle-return function of the CEC valve can be made by manually extending the plunger with the engine idling. Shut off the ignition key, and the plunger should retract.

SERVICE NOTE

The 1971 system operates opposite to that of the 1970 TCS system in that vacuum is cut off to the distributor when the solenoid is in the non-energized position for the 1971 system instead of the energized position as in 1970.

ADJUSTING THE CEC VALVE

This adjustment should be made only after (1) replacing the solenoid, (2) overhauling the carburetor, or (3) after replacing the throttle body. **CAUTION: The CEC valve adjustment must be made only after having completed all other tune-up settings.**

Make sure that the air conditioning system is OFF. Remove and plug the distributor vacuum hose. Dis-

connect the fuel tank hose from the charcoal canister. Start the engine and shift into DRIVE. Manually extend the CEC valve plunger to contact the throttle lever, and then adjust the plunger length to obtain 850 rpm idling speed. **CAUTION: If the CEC valve solenoid plunger adjustment is used to set the curb-idle speed, a decrease in engine braking may result.**

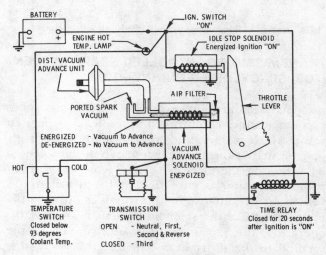

Wiring diagram for the 1974 Omega six-cylinder engine with a manual transmission. Note that the CEC solenoid has been replaced by the conventional TCS solenoid.

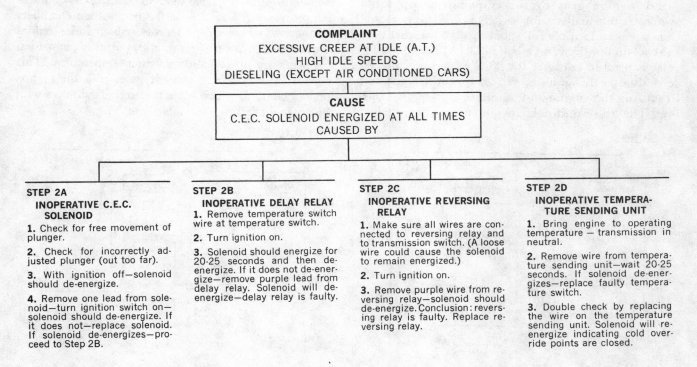

Troubleshooting roadmap for checking the six-cylinder TCS system if the complaint is due to a CEC solenoid which remains energized at all times.

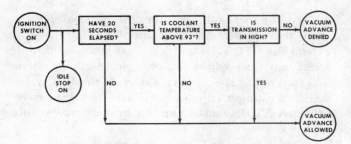

1974 Omega TCS vacuum-advance troubleshooting chart.

TRANSMISSION-CONTROLLED SPARK SYSTEM (TCS) SIX-CYLINDER ENGINE—1974

On six-cylinder engines with a manual transmission, vacuum advance is controlled by a solenoid-operated valve, which is energized by grounding a normally open switch at the transmission. When the solenoid is in the non-energized position, vacuum to the distributor actuator is cut off, and the distributor is vented to the atmosphere through a filter at the opposite end of the solenoid. When the solenoid is energized, the vacuum port is uncovered allowing vacuum to the distributor actuator; the solenoid is seated at the opposite end to shut off the clean-air vent.

The vacuum-advance (TCS) solenoid is controlled by two switches and a time relay. The solenoid is energized in high gear by the transmission-operated switch. A thermal-sensing switch is used to override the system and supply full vacuum advance whenever the coolant temperature is below 93°F. The time-delay relay is used to energize the TCS relay for about 20 seconds after the ignition switch is turned ON to assist in starting the engine and minimize cold-engine stalling. The 20-second delay begins when the switch is

turned ON, but the solenoid remains energized as long as coolant temperature is below 93°F. If for some reason, the engine is not started within the 20 seconds, vacuum advance is denied until the relay has cooled. In other words, once the relay has run its cycle, it must cool down before it can be re-activated.

A throttle-stop solenoid is used to prevent dieseling tendencies.

SERVICE PROCEDURES

Use the vacuum-advance troubleshooting chart to determine when vacuum advance is allowed or denied. Use the accompanying troubleshooting charts to pinpoint troubles.

EXHAUST-GAS RECIRCULATION (EGR)—SINCE 1973

The Exhaust-Gas Recirculation (EGR) system is used on all V-8 engines to reduce oxides of nitrogen emissions from the engine exhaust. It is also used on the Omega six-cylinder engine with an automatic transmission.

During the combustion process, nitrogen, which makes up 80 percent of the air, tends to mix with oxygen at temperatures above 2,500 degrees. During the combustion process, temperatures in the combustion chambers will go well above 2,500 degrees, which forms oxides of nitrogen. To lower the formations of nitrogen oxides, it is necessary to reduce combustion temperatures. This is done by introducing exhaust gases into the engine intake manifold, which enter the engine cylinders with the air-fuel mixture for combustion.

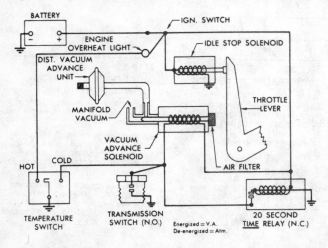

Circuit diagram of the 1974 TCS system in the low-gear operating mode.

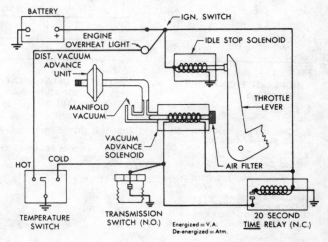

Circuit diagram of the TCS system used on the 1974 engine in the high-gear operating mode.

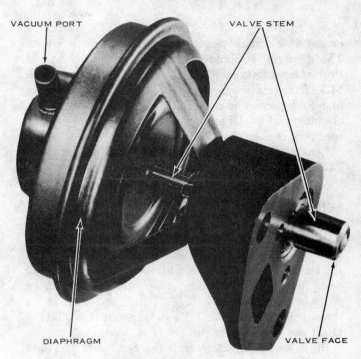

EGR valve details.

OPERATION

The EGR valve is operated by ported vacuum. It is fully closed with vacuum less than 2 inches and starts opening between 2 inches and 8.5 inches; it is fully open with more than 8.5 inches of vacuum. At idle and wide-open throttle, ported vacuum is low, the valve is closed, and recirculation does not occur. At part throttle, ported vacuum is high, the valve is open, and exhaust gas recirculation is at maximum.

EGR Control Valve

All engines use a temperature-sensitive control valve in the vacuum signal line to the EGR valve. The valve is closed below 55 degrees underhood temperature, blocking vacuum to the EGR valve, thus giving better driveaway when the engine is cold. The EGR control valve is open above 55 degrees underhood temperature, allowing EGR ported vacuum to be directed to the EGR valve.

FUNCTIONAL CHECK

Remove the air cleaner assembly and plug the manifold vacuum fitting. Remove the vacuum hose from the distributor and plug the end. Install a tachometer. Remove the hose from EGR valve and plug the hose end.

With the A/C off, drive wheels blocked, transmission in park, start the engine and bring it to operating temperature. Put the cam follower on the second step of the fast-idle cam and note engine speed.

Attach a vacuum hose between the air cleaner vacuum port on the intake manifold and the EGR valve,

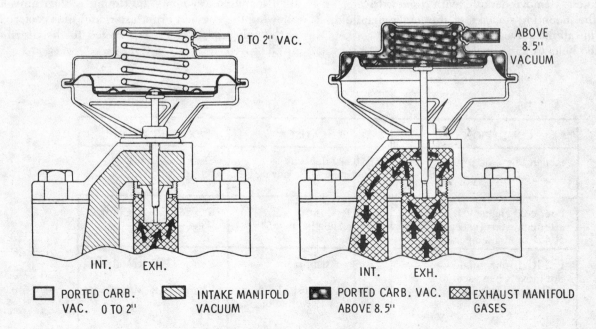

Operation of the EGR valve under varying vacuum conditions.

or use an external vacuum source of at least 9 inches. The diaphragm should rise and engine speed should drop at least 250 rpm with A.T. or at least 100 rpm with M.T. If engine speed does not drop, clean the intake manifold ports and the EGR valve assembly. After cleaning, recheck. If engine speed still does not drop as specified, replace the EGR valve assembly.

Remove the tachometer, connect the distributor and EGR vacuum hoses, and install the air cleaner.

SERVICE PROCEDURES

To clean the EGR valve and ports, remove the valve from the intake manifold and discard the gasket. Tape the round hole in the manifold on the EGR mounting pad. Remove the deposits under the primary valve ports by hand, using a 13/32″ drill, and then use a screwdriver to clean the holes and chamfer. **CAUTION: Don't use an electric drill.**

Brush small particles down the two ports and into the EGR passageways. Plug the right port and blow through the left port. Plug the left port and blow through the right port.

To clean the EGR valve, tap it lightly on the sides and end of the valve with a plastic hammer to remove the exhaust deposits from the valve seat. Empty the particles. **CAUTION: Don't hold the valve in a vise.** Use a wire brush to remove the exhaust deposits from the mounting surfaces and around the valve. Depress the valve diaphragm and check the valve seating area for cleanliness. Remove deposits with a screwdriver.

Clean the mounting surfaces of the intake manifold, and then install the valve assembly, using a new gasket. Tighten the bolts to 25 ft-lbs of torque.

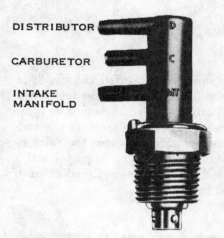

DISTRIBUTOR

CARBURETOR

INTAKE MANIFOLD

Details of the vacuum-switching valve used on many Oldsmobile engines to change the distributor vacuum advance source from a ported one at the carburetor to a direct intake manifold tap for greater ignition advance when an idling engine overheats.

THERMAL-VACUUM SWITCH (TVS)—SINCE 1969

All V-8 engines use a Thermal-Vacuum Switch (TVS) to advance the ignition timing at idle when the coolant temperature is high. At 226 degrees, a valve within the TVS moves and, if equipped with a 4 Bbl. carburetor, full manifold vacuum is directed to the distributor vacuum advance. The 350 CID 2 Bbl. engine has a vacuum reducer, so the vacuum supplied will be 3 inches less than manifold vacuum. The timing is then advanced, allowing the engine to run faster, and thus cooler. This is the only time vacuum is directed to the distributor at idle speed.

CONDITION	CAUSE	CORRECTION
Rough Idle	Exhaust deposits holding E.G.R. valve open.	Clean E.G.R. valve
Poor cold engine "Driveaway" after cold start (except L-6) at 45° or less temperature.	E.G.R. Control Valve not sealing below 55°	Replace E.G.R. Control Valve
E.G.R. diaphragm does not move when vacuum is applied and released	Broken diaphragm Exhaust deposits holding E.G.R. Valve open or closed.	Replace E.G.R. Valve. Clean E.G.R. Valve.

EGR system troubleshooting chart.

FUNCTIONAL CHECK

To test switch function, disconnect the distributor vacuum hose at port D of the TVS switch, connect a vacuum gauge, and check for vacuum with the engine idling at normal operating temperature. If more than 5 inches of vacuum is present, and the hoses are connected to the proper ports, replace the switch.

VACUUM HOSE ROUTING TO TVS

4 Bbl. Engines

Port "D"   Vacuum hose to the distributor vacuum advance.

Port "C"   Vacuum hose to the carburetor ported spark port. The distributor Thermal Check-and-Delay Valve is "in-line" in this hose.

Port "MT"   Vacuum hose to intake manifold elbow.

350 Cu. In. 2 Bbl.

Port "D"   Vacuum hose to the distributor vacuum advance.

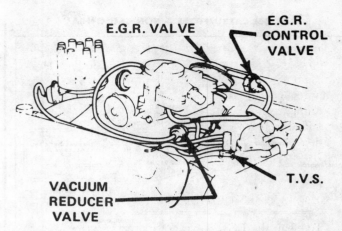

Vacuum hose routing for a 1973 Oldsmobile V-8 engine with a two-barrel carburetor.

Port "C"   Vacuum hose to a tee at the carburetor EGR port.

Port "MT"   Vacuum line to elbow at intake manifold. The Vacuum-Reducer Valve is "in-line" in this hose.

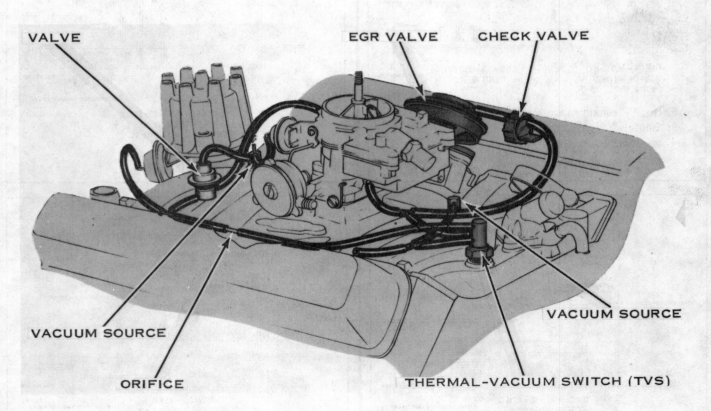

Details of the 1973 Oldsmobile V-8 engine exhaust emission-control system.

ALL 4 BBL CARBURETORS — NON CALIFORNIA

ALL 4 BBL CARBURETORS — CALIFORNIA

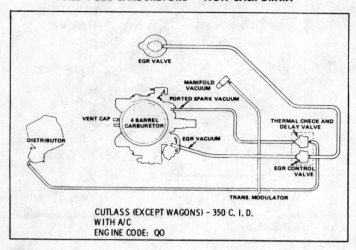

CUTLASS (EXCEPT WAGONS) - 350 C. I. D.
WITH A/C
ENGINE CODE: QO

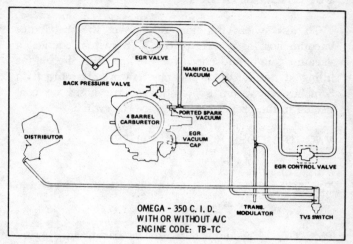

OMEGA - 350 C. I. D.
WITH OR WITHOUT A/C
ENGINE CODE: TB-TC

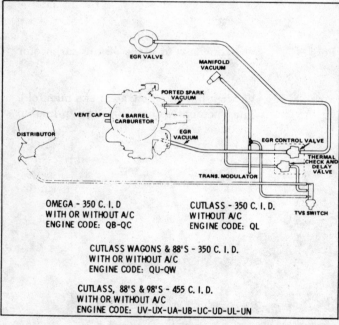

OMEGA - 350 C. I. D
WITH OR WITHOUT A/C
ENGINE CODE: QB-QC

CUTLASS - 350 C. I. D.
WITHOUT A/C
ENGINE CODE: QL

CUTLASS WAGONS & 88'S - 350 C. I. D.
WITH OR WITHOUT A/C
ENGINE CODE: QU-QW

CUTLASS, 88'S & 98'S - 455 C. I. D.
WITH OR WITHOUT A/C
ENGINE CODE: UV-UX-UA-UB-UC-UD-UL-UN

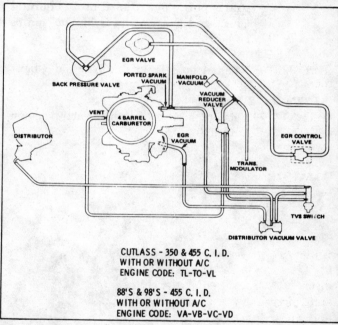

CUTLASS - 350 & 455 C. I. D.
WITH OR WITHOUT A/C
ENGINE CODE: TL-TO-VL

88'S & 98'S - 455 C. I. D.
WITH OR WITHOUT A/C
ENGINE CODE: VA-VB-VC-VD

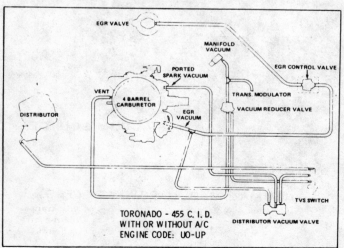

TORONADO - 455 C. I. D.
WITH OR WITHOUT A/C
ENGINE CODE: UO-UP

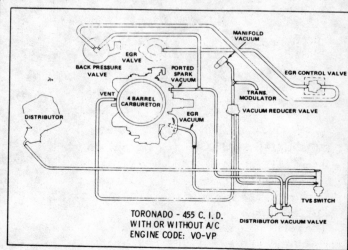

TORONADO - 455 C. I. D.
WITH OR WITHOUT A/C
ENGINE CODE: VO-VP

1974 Oldsmobile engine vacuum hose routings.

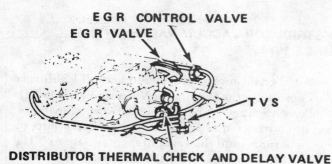

Vacuum hose routing for a 1973 Oldsmobile engine with a four-barrel carburetor, except Toronado.

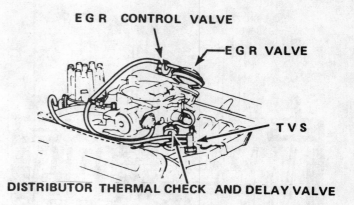

Vacuum hose routing for the 1973 Toronado.

THERMAL CHECK-AND-DELAY VALVE— SINCE 1973

A Thermal Check-and-Delay Valve is in the vacuum-advance circuit on 4 Bbl. engines, located in the vacuum hose between the carburetor ported vacuum hole and the TVS "C" port.

Below 50 degrees underhood temperature, the valve is open and the vacuum advance receives full distributor ported vacuum from the carburetor. Above 50 degrees underhood temperature, the valve is in the restricting position. Distributor ported vacuum is then metered through a 0.005" orifice in the valve. It takes up to 40 seconds for full vacuum advance after distributor ported vacuum has dropped to zero.

When the valve is in the restricting position and ported vacuum drops, there is a pressure differential within the valve; the valve momentarily opens, equalizing the vacuum between the vacuum advance and the distributor, retarding the distributor timing. When vacuum increases at the carburetor port, the valve goes to the restricting position so vacuum to the advance will be metered to increase the distributor vacuum advance.

The valve is bypassed above 226 degrees coolant temperature when the TVS valve switches. Vacuum for the advance then comes from the elbow on the intake manifold.

VACUUM-REDUCER VALVE (VRV)—SINCE 1973

A Vacuum-Reducer Valve (VRV) is used on 350 CID 2 Bbl. engines between the intake manifold elbow and the "MT" port of the TVS. The VRV reduces intake manifold vacuum 3 inches, which helps prevent detonation when the coolant is above 226 degrees and the TVS "MT" port is open to distributor advance.

The valve has one port on the manifold side and two ports on the TVS side of the valve; the center port is open to vent at the carburetor air horn, the outboard port to the "MT" port of the TVS.

BACK-PRESSURE TRANSDUCER VALVE (BPV)—SINCE 1974

This valve has a probe in the exhaust gas passageway to sense exhaust gas pressure. When engine load is high, a diaphragm is moved against spring pressure to seal the air bleed, allowing maximum EGR. When engine load decreases, the exhaust gas pressure decreases. The spring then pushes the diaphragm down. Vacuum to the EGR valve is then bled through the air bleed, reducing vacuum to the EGR valve and thus reducing Exhaust-Gas Recirculation (EGR). The vacuum source to this valve is ported so there is no EGR at idle or at WOT conditions.

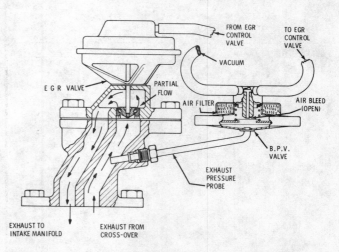

All 1974 California V-8 engines use this back-pressure transducer valve (BPV) to sense exhaust pressures. It seals the air bleed when the engine load is high, thus providing maximum EGR.

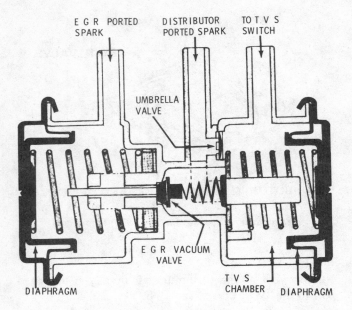

The Distributor Vacuum Valve (DVV) is used on all 1974 Toronado and California V-8 engines. The DVV valve allows vacuum to be directed to the distributor actuator from the ported spark port of the carburetor until the vacuum increases to 8"Hg (7"Hg for Calif. engines), and then the valve switches the vacuum source to the EGR port on the carburetor.

DISTRIBUTOR VACUUM VALVE (DVV)— SINCE 1974

All 1974 Oldsmobile Toronado and all California V-8 engines use the Distributor Vacuum Valve (DVV). It allows vacuum to be directed to the distributor vacuum advance unit from the ported spark port of the carburetor until the vacuum increases up to 8"Hg (7"Hg for California). The valve then switches so that vacuum is directed from the carburetor EGR port to the distributor actuator, and this is done to increase the driveability.

TESTING THE VALVE

Remove the air cleaner and plug the manifold vacuum fitting. With the air conditioner OFF, drive wheels blocked, transmission in PARK, start the engine and bring it to operating temperature. Remove the hose from the thermal vacuum-switching valve (TVS) "D" port, and then connect a vacuum gauge to the valve port. Use a T-fitting to connect a second vacuum gauge to the hose at the carburetor EGR port.

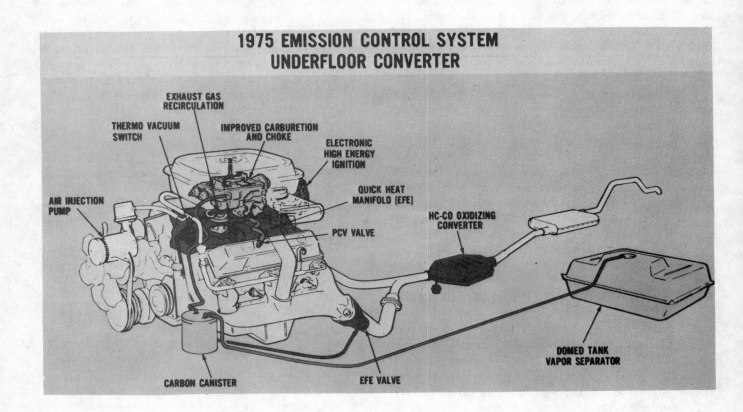

1975 Emission-control system using a catalytic converter for oxiding HC and CO emissions.

Gradually open the throttle until the first gauge rises to 8″Hg (7″Hg for California). Level off engine speed until the second gauge reaches 8″Hg (7″Hg for California), and then both gauges should read the same as the throttle is advanced. If not, replace the DDV unit. Remove the vacuum gauges, connect the hoses, and replace the air cleaner.

CATALYTIC CONVERTERS—SINCE 1975

A catalytic converter system provides for one or more containers filled with granular chemical compound through which the exhaust gases are passed as they move out of the engine. The granular compound of pellets is plated with noble metals, platinum and palladium, both rare and expensive.

A catalytic material, when added to a chemical reaction, has the ability to change the speed of the reaction. While a catalyst may undergo some temporary change, it is present in the same quantity and state at the end of the chemical reaction as at the beginning.

THERMAL PROTECTION

Misfiring spark plugs and carburetor adjustments that are abnormally rich provide additional fuel, and heat, to the converter so that some means of thermal protection must be provided to prevent destroying the unit. Normally, a catalytic converter operates at about 1400-1500°F., and this temperature will rise to about 2000°F. if two spark plugs are shorted out at 30 mph. Total ignition failure at 30 mph will cause the temperature to rise to about 2800°F. With the melting point of the pellets about 2000°F., it is quite evident that some form of thermal protection is needed. A thermal sensor is used to control the output of the AIR pump during warmup, and this controls the oxidation process and, therefore, the operating temperature.

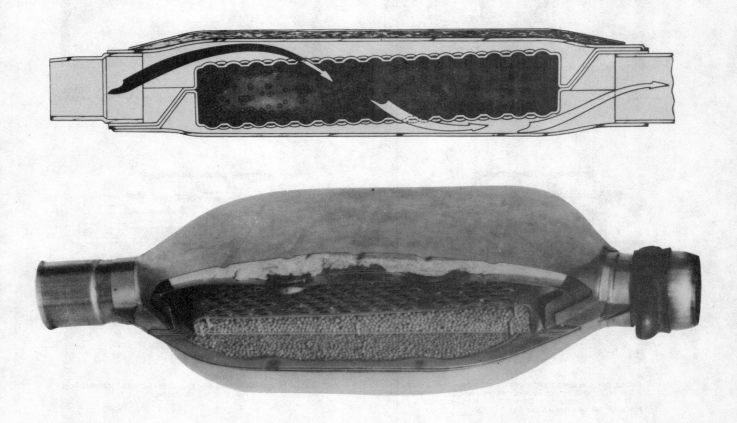

View through the AC catalytic converter used on 1975 models. The top view shows the passage of exhaust gases, while the bottom cutaway view shows the position of the pellets.

SERVICE PROCEDURES

Every 50,000 miles the pellets must be changed, and this can be done on the GM converter by removing a plug at the base of the unit and applying a special tool which vibrates the converter while applying suction to draw out all of the spent pellets.

The equipment is designed to insert a fresh charge, and then the plug is installed.

EVAPORATIVE EMISSION-CONTROL SYSTEM

Beginning in 1971 (1970 California), all vehicles imported into or manufactured in the United States had to be equipped with an approved method of controlling emissions from carburetor float bowls and fuel tanks. These emissions represent 10%-15% of all hydrocarbon emissions from vehicles.

Previously gas tanks and carburetors were vented to

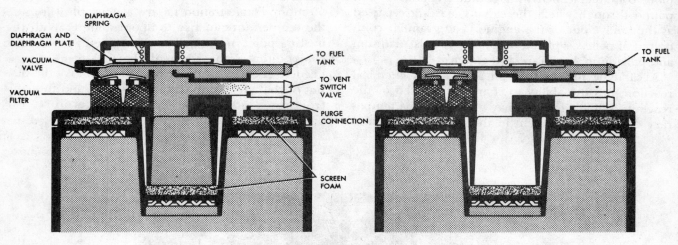

1. ENGINE OFF—TANK TEMPERATURE INCREASING—DIAPHRAGM OPENS TO PERMIT FUEL TANK VAPORS UNDER PRESSURE TO ESCAPE INTO CANISTER.

2. ENGINE OFF—TANK TEMPERATURE DECREASING—VACUUM VALVE OPENS TO PERMIT OUTSIDE AIR TO ENTER TANK DURING PERIOD OF NEGATIVE FUEL TANK PRESSURE.

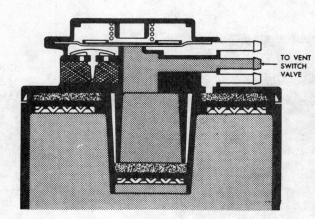

3. ENGINE OFF—CARBURETOR TO CANISTER VENT OPEN—THE CARBURETOR FLOAT BOWL AND INTAKE MANIFOLD VENT DIRECTLY THROUGH CANISTER TO ATMOSPHERE. THIS CONNECTION ALSO PROVIDES A SLIGHT PURGE OF THE CANISTER AT IDLE.

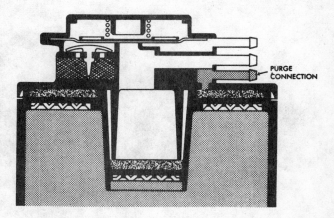

4. ENGINE RUNNING—DURING OFF IDLE OPERATION THIS CONNECTION ALLOWS COMPLETE PURGE OF THE CANNISTER.

This series of drawings shows the charcoal canister and valve assembly during four different engine operating conditions.

the outside air to allow pressures to equalize and to make use of atmospheric pressure in carburetor design. Unfortunately this design permits fuel vapors to leave the vehicle during two conditions: (1) fuel vapors left the carburetor vent during the "soak" period which follows hot engine shut off. Engine heat can cause the temperature of the fuel bowl to rise to as high as 200°F. At this temperature fuel will vaporize at a rate of from 2 to 28 grams per soak period; (2) fuel vapors leave the fuel tank during the daily temperature rise or when the vehicle is parked on a heat reflective surface.

SERVICING THE EVAPORATIVE EMISSION-CONTROL SYSTEM

TESTING THE PURGE CONTROL VALVE

Insert a vacuum gauge into the purge hose, using a T-fitting. Operate the engine at idle speed and check the vacuum gauge, which should read manifold vacuum. Increase engine speed to approximately 1,500 rpm, and the vacuum gauge should drop to a somewhat lower value, indicating that the purge control system is operating.

If the vacuum gauge does not drop to a lower value, it indicates that the purge control valve is not operating or the vacuum signal is not getting to the valve.

TESTING THE GAS TANK FILLER CAP

All vehicles use a sealed fuel tank, and the cap must have a pressure-vacuum relief valve which functions only under abnormal conditions. The valves work on very low pressures, usually under one psi. Testing of the filler cap can be done by applying oral vacuum and pressure to see that the valves seat one way and release the other.

SERVICING THE CHARCOAL CANISTER

Normally, the only service specified for the canister-type system used on General Motors products is to replace the filter located in the bottom of the canister

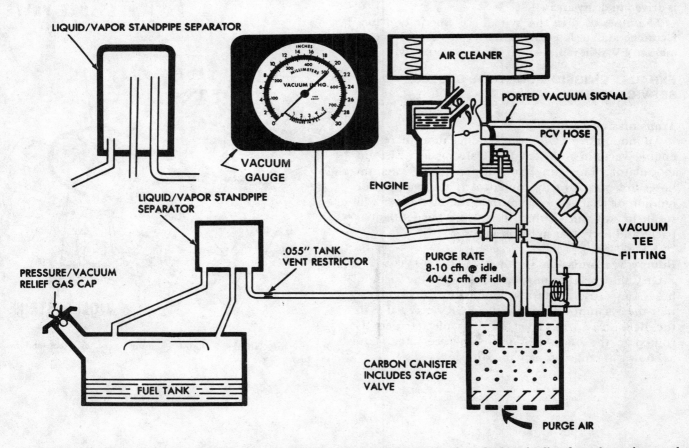

To test the staged-purge evaporative emission-control system, connect a vacuum gauge into the hose leading from the canister to the vacuum (unported) tap on the carburetor, as shown. The gauge reading should drop when the ported vacuum signal tap is uncovered by the advancing throttle valve; its function is to signal the purge valve that the engine is ready to receive the gas-laden vapors from the canister.

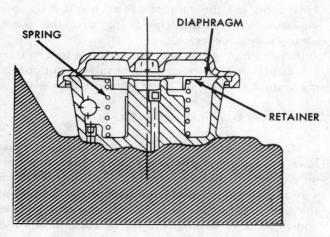

To service the purge valve, disconnect the lines. Snap off the valve cap, and then remove the diaphragm, spring retainer, and spring. CAUTION: The cap is under spring tension. Replace the valve or damaged parts as needed.

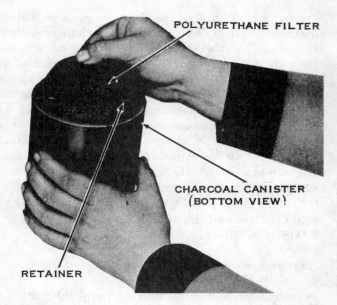

The foam-type filter element under the charcoal canister should be replaced every 12,000 miles.

each 24 months or 24,000 miles. More frequent replacement of the filter element may be required if the vehicle is driven in dusty areas.

The hoses used in this system are especially manufactured, and it is essential that you use only hoses marked EVAP if replacement becomes necessary.

EXHAUST EMISSION-CONTROL SYSTEM SERVICE NOTES

Transmission Failures

An inoperative EGR valve system causes increased engine vacuum to reach the transmission vacuum modulator. This can also happen if the vacuum hoses are not correctly routed. Any interruption of ignition or changes in vacuum to the modulator will result in soft shifts, which can cause burned clutch packs and early transmission failure.

Bumpy Transmission Shifting

On California cars, improper routing of the vacuum hoses can cause a shifting complaint. Check to see that the vacuum hose from the EGR delay valve to the Back-Pressure Valve (BPV) (violet striped) is routed to the outside of the crankcase filter vent, as shown in an accompanying drawing.

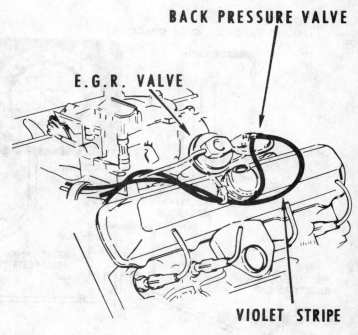

Routing of California engine vacuum hoses, as discussed in the text.

4 fuel system service

The fuel system consists of the fuel tank, fuel pump, fuel filters, carburetor, and connecting lines. In addition, late-model engines have thermostatically controlled air intake systems. Preventive maintenance includes replacing the fuel filter and cleaning the air cleaner periodically.

Overhauling the carburetor or replacing the fuel pump becomes necessary if the engine does not perform satisfactorily or if the gas mileage decreases below expectations.

FUEL FILTERS

An in-line fuel filter is used on some engines and it must be replaced every 24,000 miles, or sooner if it becomes clogged. To replace the filter element, remove the air cleaner, and then loosen the retaining clamps holding the hoses to the fuel filter. Disconnect the fuel filter from the hoses and discard the retaining clamps.

Install new clamps on the hoses and connect the hoses to the new filter. Tighten the filter. Position the fuel line hose clamps and crimp them securely. Start the engine and check for fuel leaks.

A filter element is located in the carburetor inlet on most engines, and this should be replaced every 12,000 miles.

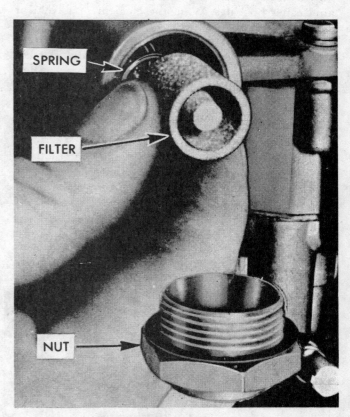

Some high-performance engines have an in-line fuel filter and a fuel-return line. This type of filter element must be replaced every 24,000 miles.

Early model carburetors had a sintered bronze fuel filter element in the inlet fitting, which could be cleaned in gasoline every 12,000 miles.

This mesh-type filter element has been used inside of the gas tank for the past several years. If you get moisture in the tank, this filter element will get soft and restrict the flow of fuel to limit top speed.

AIR CLEANERS

OIL-BATH TYPE

The oil-bath type air cleaners used on early models should be emptied of old oil and cleaned every 12,000 miles. Use SAE 30 weight oil to fill the unit to the level line.

POLYURETHANE TYPE

Check the element for tears or rips every 12,000 miles. Clean all accumulated dirt and grime from the air cleaner housings. Wash the element in solvent or kerosene, and then squeeze out the excess. Dip the element in light engine oil and squeeze out the excess. **CAUTION: Never shake or wring out the element as this can tear the material.** Always use a new gasket when installing the element.

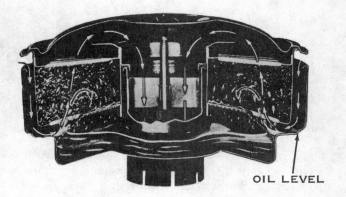

OIL LEVEL

The oil-bath type air cleaner must be cleaned every 12,000 miles.

OIL-WETTED PAPER ELEMENT TYPE

The element should be removed for cleaning every 12,000 miles and replaced every 24,000 miles. Inspect the element for punctures or splits by looking through it toward a light bulb.

The element should be cleaned by tapping it against a hard surface. **CAUTION: Don't tap it hard enough to deform the element.** The element can be cleaned with compressed air if the nozzle is held some distance away. If the nozzle is too close to the air cleaner, the high pressure can blow it apart. **CAU-**

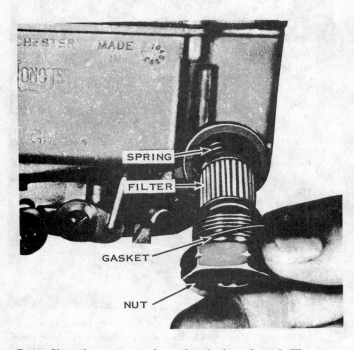

SPRING

FILTER

GASKET

NUT

Paper filter elements must be replaced when clogged. They can be checked by blowing and sucking through them to determine the condition.

The Polyurethane-type filter element should be rinsed in clean solvent and squeezed dry. **CAUTION: Never shake or wring out the element, or you will tear it.**

TION: Don't immerse the element in cleaning solvent. When the element is cleaned, wipe out the air cleaner body and the cover with a rag saturated in cleaning solvent, then wipe it dry.

When replacing the element, rotate it 180° from the originally installed position. If there is a crankcase ventilation filter element in the air cleaner shell, it must be replaced every 24,000 miles.

FUEL PUMP

Incorrect fuel pump pressure and inadequate volume are the two most likely fuel pump troubles. Low pressure will cause a low fuel level in the float bowl, a lean mixture, and fuel starvation at high speeds; excessive pressure will cause a high fuel level in the float bowl, a rich mixture, and flooding. Low volume will cause fuel starvation at high speeds. Service instructions, therefore, consist of testing the fuel pump to check it out as a source of trouble.

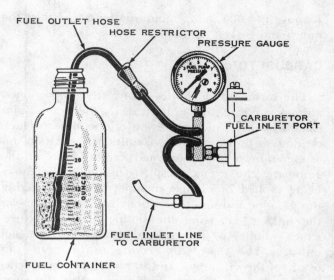

Method of hooking up a gauge and container to test fuel pump pressure and volume.

Most fuel pumps on late-model engines are of the sealed type and cannot be repaired. Even if the fuel pump is not sealed, it is usually more feasible to replace it than to repair it, as the cost of a new pump is nominal.

PRESSURE TEST

Remove the air cleaner and disconnect the fuel line at the carburetor. **CAUTION: Don't spill gasoline on the hot engine, or it may catch on fire.** Connect a pressure gauge, restrictor, container, and flexible hose between the fuel filter and the carburetor. With the engine idling, vent the outlet hose into the container by opening the hose restrictor momentarily. Close the hose restrictor and allow the pressure to stabilize, which should be 3.5-5.5 psi.

VOLUME TEST

If the fuel pump pressure is within specifications, test the volume by opening the hose restrictor with the engine idling and allowing fuel to discharge into the graduated container. A pint of fuel should be collected in 30 seconds for a six-cylinder engine and in 20 seconds for a V-8 engine.

REMOVING

Disconnect the fuel inlet and outlet pipes at the fuel pump. **CAUTION: Whenever disconnecting or connecting a fuel pump outlet pipe fitting, always use two wrenches to avoid damaging the fuel pump.**

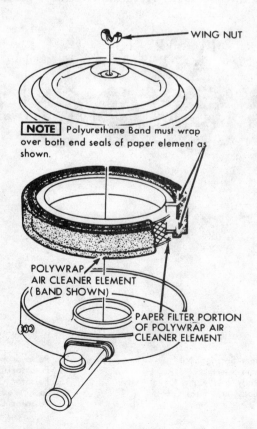

The dry paper filter element must not be cleaned with compressed air or dipped in solvent. Turn the element 180° every 12,000 miles and replace it every 24,000 miles. The Polyurethane band can be cleaned in solvent as shown in a previous illustration.

Remove the fuel pump mounting bolts and then the pump and gasket.

CARBURETORS

The carburetor furnishes a correctly proportioned air-fuel mixture to be burned in the combustion chambers. Dirt and gum restrict the flow of fuel, causing a lean operating condition; hesitation on acceleration results. Gum and carbon form in the automatic choke mechanism, resulting in the choke being applied for a longer than normal time, lowering the gasoline mileage proportionally. Wear occurs in the linkage, changing the timing of the mixture, which results in poor operation and lowered fuel mileage. The remedy, of course, is to clean and overhaul the carburetor and to make the adjustments which will restore it to its former operating efficiency.

SERVICE PROCEDURES

This section contains step-by-step illustrated instructions for overhauling all of the current carburetors.

Older models are covered by exploded views and the bench adjustments, which are essential in making the carburetor perform to its designed potential. On-the-car instructions are covered in Chapter 2.

ROCHESTER MODEL M CARBURETOR

This single-barrel carburetor has been used since 1968. It comes in two versions: Models M and MV. Model M designates a manual-choke model, while the MV unit is used with an automatic choke.

The Monojet carburetor is a single-bore downdraft carburetor with a triple venturi, coupled with a refined metering system which results in a unit of superior fuel mixture control and performance.

A plain-tube nozzle is used in conjunction with the multiple venturi. Fuel flow through the main metering system is controlled by a mechanically and vacuum-operated variable orifice jet. This consists of a specially tapered rod which operates in the fixed orifice main metering jet and is connected directly by linkage to the main throttle shaft. A vacuum-operated enrichment

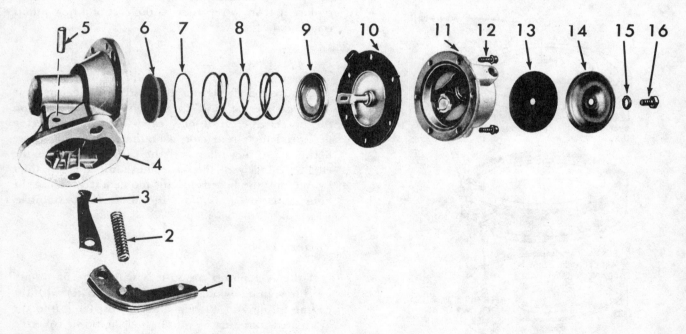

1. Rocker Arm
2. Rocker Arm Return Spring
3. Actuating Lever
4. Pump Body
5. Arm and Lever Pivot Pin
6. Oil Seal
7. Oil Seal Retainer
8. Diaphragm and Seal Retainer Spring
9. Diaphragm Spring Seat
10. Diaphragm Assembly
11. Valve Body and Pump Cover Assy.
12. Valve Body and Fuel Cover Screws
13. Pulsator Diaphragm
14. Pulsator Cover
15. Pulsator Cover Lock Washer
16. Pulsator Cover Bolt

Exploded view of the fuel pump used through 1966. CAUTION: Push the rocker arm to its fully depressed position before tightening the pump cover retaining screws, or the diaphragm will fail in a short time. Later-model pumps cannot be serviced; they must be replaced.

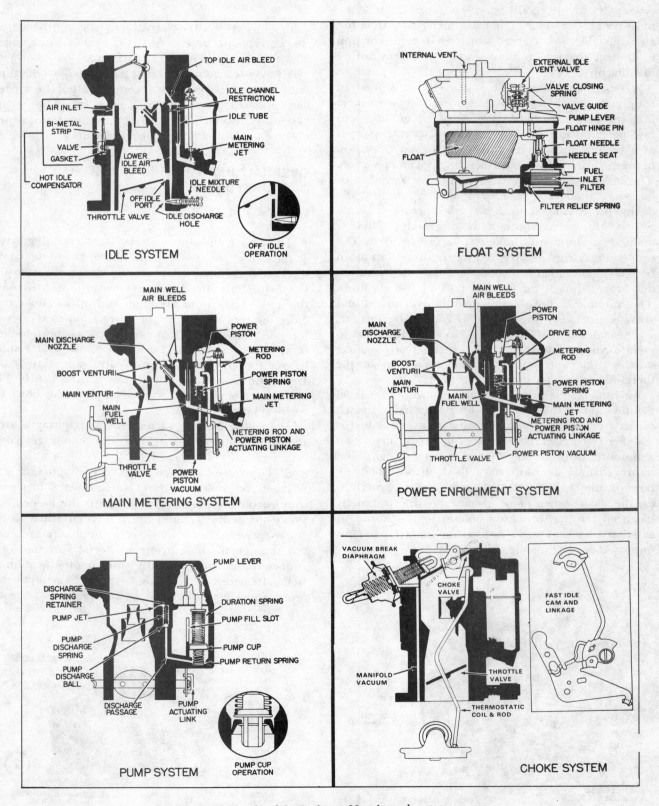

Operating circuits of the Rochester Monojet carburetor.

system is used in conjunction with the main metering system to provide good performance during moderate to heavy accelerations. The main metering system has an adjustable flow feature which enables production to control the fuel mixture more accurately during manufacture.

A separate and adjustable idle system is used in conjunction with the main metering system to meet fuel mixture requirements during engine idle and low-speed operation. The off-idle discharge port is of a vertical slot design, which gives good transition between curb idle and main metering system operation. The idle system incorporates a hot-idle compensator on some models to maintain smooth engine idle during periods of extreme hot-engine operation.

The Monojet carburetor is designed so that a manual or automatic choke system can be used. The conventional choke valve is located in the air horn bore. On automatic choke models, the vacuum-diaphragm unit is an integral part of the air horn. The automatic choke coil is manifold mounted and actuates the choke valve shaft by connecting linkage.

The choke system has a feature to give added enrichment during a cold start. This feature greatly reduces starting time and yet allows the use of low-torque thermostatic coils for increased economy.

An integral fuel filter is mounted in the fuel bowl behind the fuel inlet nut. The fiber filter has increased capacity to give maximum filtration of incoming fuel.

Other features of the Monojet carburetor include an aluminum throttle body for decreased weight and improved heat distribution, a thick throttle body-to-bowl insulator gasket to minimize engine heat flow to the float bowl. The carburetor has internally balanced venting through a hole in the air horn. An external idle vent valve is used on some models for improved hot-engine idle and starting.

SERVICE INSTRUCTIONS

Step-by-step illustrated instructions are provided for this current carburetor. Also included is an exploded view to show the placement of all parts.

Always use a complete kit of parts when overhauling one of these carburetors as it contains all of the needed and updated parts, as well as a complete set of gaskets. It also includes the latest specifications, which must be used for making the adjustments.

OVERHAULING A ROCHESTER MONOJET CARBURETOR

DISASSEMBLING

① Remove the upper choke lever retaining screw at the end of the choke shaft. Then remove the choke lever from the shaft. Remove the choke rod from the slot in the fast-idle cam by rotating the rod. Remove the upper lever from the other end of the choke rod. Note the position of the rod in relation to the levers for ease in assembly. Remove the six air horn-to-float bowl attaching screws. There are 3 long and 3 short screws. Remove the air horn by lifting it straight up. Invert the air horn and place it on a clean bench. The air horn-to-bowl gasket can remain on the bowl for removal later.

② Remove the two vacuum-break diaphragm cover screws. Then carefully remove the diaphragm cover retainer.

③ To remove the vacuum-break diaphragm and plunger rod, hold the choke valve open. Then push upward on the diaphragm rod until the looped end slides out of the vacuum break lever attached to the choke valve. Then remove the diaphragm plunger rod through the hole in the air horn. To remove the rubber diaphragm, carefully slide it off the plunger stem. If necessary, the choke valve, vacuum-break lever, and choke shaft can be removed from the air

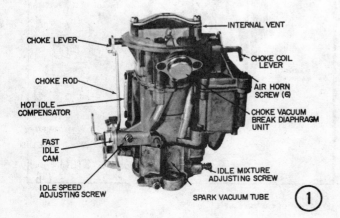

CHOKE LEVER
INTERNAL VENT
CHOKE COIL LEVER
CHOKE ROD
AIR HORN SCREW (6)
HOT IDLE COMPENSATOR
CHOKE VACUUM BREAK DIAPHRAGM UNIT
FAST IDLE CAM
IDLE MIXTURE ADJUSTING SCREW
IDLE SPEED ADJUSTING SCREW
SPARK VACUUM TUBE
①

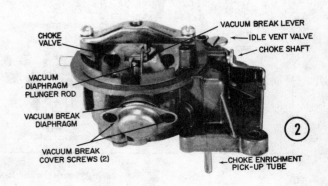

CHOKE VALVE
VACUUM BREAK LEVER
IDLE VENT VALVE
CHOKE SHAFT
VACUUM DIAPHRAGM PLUNGER ROD
VACUUM BREAK DIAPHRAGM
VACUUM BREAK COVER SCREWS (2)
CHOKE ENRICHMENT PICK-UP TUBE
②

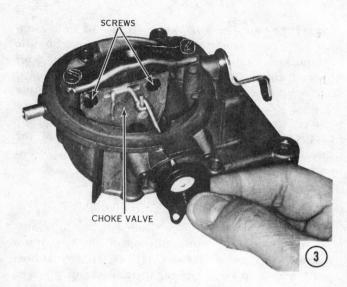

SCREWS

CHOKE VALVE

③

T-PUMP DISCHARGE GUIDE

IDLE TUBE

POWER PISTON

METERING ROD

SEAT

FLOAT NEEDLE

MAIN METERING JET   FUEL INLET NUT   ⑤

horn by removing the 2 choke valve screws. Staking on the screws should be filed off before removing so as not to ruin the threads and distort the choke shaft. No further disassembly of the air horn is necessary. The idle vent valve can be removed by turning the screw head out of the plastic guide. A repair kit is available if replacement parts are needed. **CAUTION: The cranking-enrichment valve is not removable. Make sure after cleaning that all solution**

is completely removed from the valve cavity, and that the bleed hole in the valve retainer is open.

④ Remove the air horn-to-float bowl gasket. The gasket is slit next to the metering rod lever so that it can be slid over the lever for removal. Remove the float assembly from the float bowl by lifting upward on the float hinge pin. Remove the hinge pin from the float arm.

⑤ Remove the float needle, and then remove the float needle seat and the gasket. To prevent damage

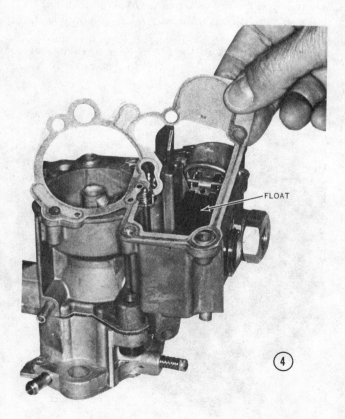

FLOAT

④

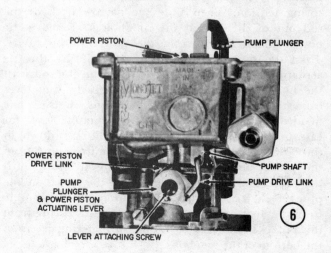

POWER PISTON   PUMP PLUNGER

POWER PISTON DRIVE LINK

PUMP SHAFT

PUMP PLUNGER & POWER PISTON ACTUATING LEVER

PUMP DRIVE LINK

LEVER ATTACHING SCREW   ⑥

SCREW

INSULATOR GASKET

⑦

to the needle seat, use seat removal tool BT-3006. Remove the fuel inlet nut and gasket, and then take out the filter element and the pressure relief spring. Using long-nosed pliers, remove the T-pump discharge guide. The pump discharge spring and ball can be removed by inverting the bowl. The idle tube can be removed at the same time while the bowl is inverted.

⑥ To remove the accelerating pump plunger-and-power piston metering rod assemblies, remove the actuating lever on the throttle shaft by taking out the attaching screw in the end of the shaft. Hold the power piston assembly down in the float bowl, and then remove the power piston drive link by sliding it out of the hole in the power piston drive rod. The power piston metering rod assembly can now be removed from the float bowl. The metering rod can be removed from the holder on the power piston by pushing downward on the end of the rod against spring tension. Then slide the narrow neck of the rod out of the slot in the rod holder. Remove the power piston spring from the power piston cavity. Take the power piston drive link off the throttle actuating lever by aligning the squirt on the rod with the notch in the lever. Remove the actuating lever from the accelerator pump drive link in the same manner. Note the position of the actuating lever for ease in assembly. Hold the pump plunger down in the bowl cavity, and then remove the drive link from the pump plunger shaft by rotating the link until the squirt on the link aligns with the notch in the plunger shaft. Remove the pump plunger assembly from the float bowl. Lift the pump return spring from the pump well. Remove the main metering jet from the bottom of the fuel bowl.

⑦ Take out the two screws from the idle compensator cover and then remove the cover, hot-idle compensator, and seal from the recess in the bowl beneath the compensator. Invert the carburetor bowl and remove the two throttle body-to-bowl attaching screws. Take off the throttle body and the insulator gasket. Remove the idle mixture needle and spring. **CAUTION: Due to the close tolerance fit of the throttle valve in the bore of the throttle body, do not remove the throttle valve or shaft.**

CLEANING AND INSPECTING

The carburetor should be cleaned in a cold immersion-type cleaner. Thoroughly clean the carburetor castings and metal parts. **CAUTION: Any rubber parts, plastic parts, diaphragms, and pump plunger, should not be immersed in carburetor cleaner.** However, the air horn which has the plastic vent valve guide and cranking enrichment valve will withstand normal cleaning in a carburetor cleaner. Make sure all of the cleaner is thoroughly removed from the choke enrichment valve cavity.

Blow out all passages in the castings with compressed air. Do not pass drills through jets or passages.

Inspect the idle mixture needle for damage.

Examine the float needle-and-seat assembly for wear. Install a new factory matched set to avoid leaks.

Inspect the upper and lower casting sealing surfaces for damage.

Inspect the holes in the levers for excessive wear or any out-of-round condition. If the levers or rods are worn, they should be replaced.

⑧

Examine the fast-idle cam for excessive wear or damage.

Check the throttle and choke levers and valve plates for binding and other damage.

Replace the filter element.

Check all springs for distortion or loss of tension.

Always use a complete repair kit of parts, which contains all the gaskets, wearing parts, and specifications needed to do a good job.

ASSEMBLING

⑧ Invert the float bowl and install a new throttle body-to-bowl insulator gasket, making sure all holes in the gasket align with the holes in the float bowl. Install the throttle body on the bowl gasket so that all holes in the throttle body align with the holes in the gasket. Install two throttle body-to-bowl attaching screws. Tighten them evenly and securely to 12-15 ft-lbs of torque. Install the idle mixture needle and spring until it is lightly seated. Back it out 1-1/2 to 2 turns as a preliminary adjustment.

⑨ Install the fast-idle cam to the boss on the float bowl, securing it with the fast-idle cam screw. The part number on the cam must face outward. Tighten the screw securely. Replace the seal in the recess in the idle compensator cavity of the float bowl, and then install the hot-idle compensator assembly. Install the idle compensator cover, securing it with 2 attaching screws. Tighten them securely.

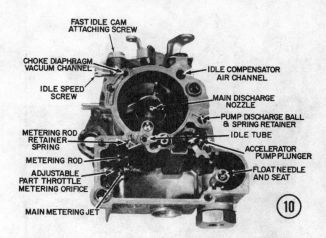

FAST IDLE CAM ATTACHING SCREW
CHOKE DIAPHRAGM VACUUM CHANNEL
IDLE SPEED SCREW
IDLE COMPENSATOR AIR CHANNEL
MAIN DISCHARGE NOZZLE
PUMP DISCHARGE BALL & SPRING RETAINER
METERING ROD RETAINER SPRING
IDLE TUBE
METERING ROD
ACCELERATOR PUMP PLUNGER
ADJUSTABLE PART THROTTLE METERING ORIFICE
FLOAT NEEDLE AND SEAT
MAIN METERING JET
⑩

⑩ Install the main metering jet into the bottom of the fuel bowl. Tighten it securely. Install the pump return spring into the pump well. Make sure the spring is properly seated in the bottom of the well. Install the pump plunger assembly into the pump well, with the actuating shaft protruding through the bottom of the bowl casting. Push down on the pump plunger, and then slide the pump drive link into the hole in the lower end of the plunger shaft. The ends of the drive link must point toward the carburetor bore. The bend in the link must face toward the fuel inlet. The squirt on the end of the link retains it to the

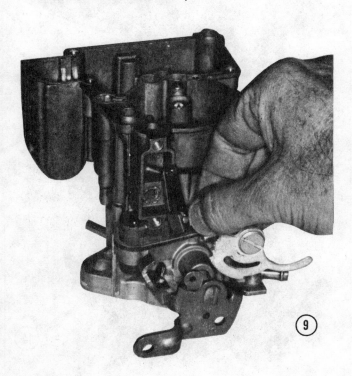

⑨

⑪

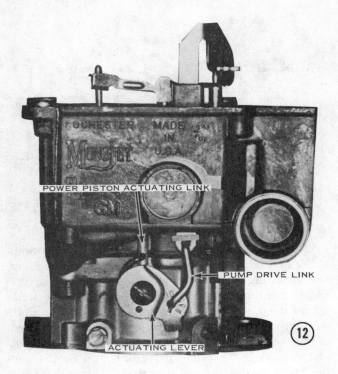

pump shaft. Install the pump-actuating lever to the lower end of the pump drive link by aligning the squirt on the rod with the notch in the lever. The projection on the actuating lever must point downward. Install the power piston drive link into the opposite end of the actuating lever. The lower end of the link has the retaining squirt and must face outward (away from the throttle bore).

⑪ Slip the power piston spring into the power piston cavity. Install the end of the power piston drive rod into the groove on the side of the power piston. Then slide the power piston metering rod assembly and drive rod into the float bowl. **CAUTION: The end of the metering rod must enter the jet orifice.**

⑫ Hold the complete assembly down in the bowl, and then slide the power piston drive link into the hole in the lower end of the power piston drive rod (beneath the bowl). Align the D-hole in the actuating lever with the flats on the throttle shaft, and then install the lever on the end of the throttle shaft. Insert the retaining screw in the end of the throttle shaft and tighten it securely.

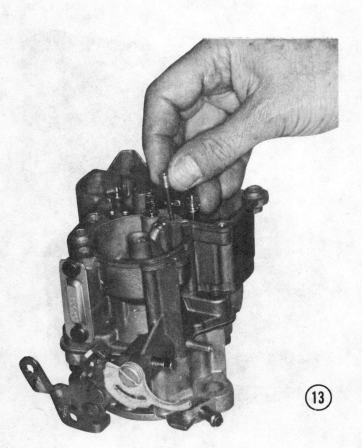

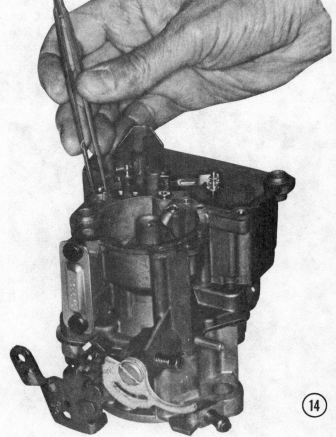

⑬ Slide the idle tube into its cavity in the float bowl.

⑭ Install the pump discharge ball in the bowl casting.

⑮ Install the spring and spring retainer. Make sure the spring retainer is flush with the top of the bowl casting.

⑯ Install the fuel filter relief spring, filter, nut, and gasket. **CAUTION: The open end of the filter must face the hole in the fuel inlet nut.** Tighten the nut securely.

⑰ Install the float needle seat and the gasket. Tighten it securely, using installation tool BT-3006. Install the float needle valve into the needle seat. Insert the float hinge pin into the float arm, and then slip the float and hinge pin into the float bowl.

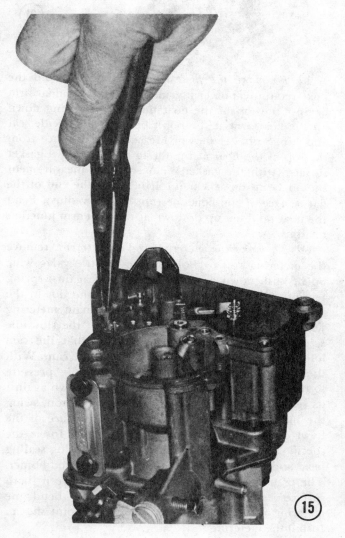

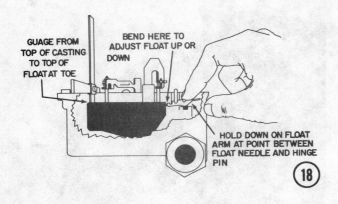

GUAGE FROM TOP OF CASTING TO TOP OF FLOAT AT TOE

BEND HERE TO ADJUST FLOAT UP OR DOWN

HOLD DOWN ON FLOAT ARM AT POINT BETWEEN FLOAT NEEDLE AND HINGE PIN

18

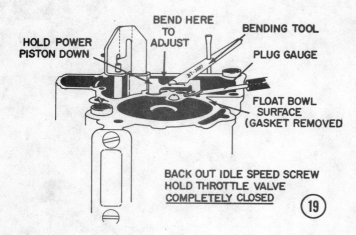

HOLD POWER PISTON DOWN

BEND HERE TO ADJUST

BENDING TOOL

PLUG GAUGE

FLOAT BOWL SURFACE (GASKET REMOVED

BACK OUT IDLE SPEED SCREW HOLD THROTTLE VALVE COMPLETELY CLOSED

19

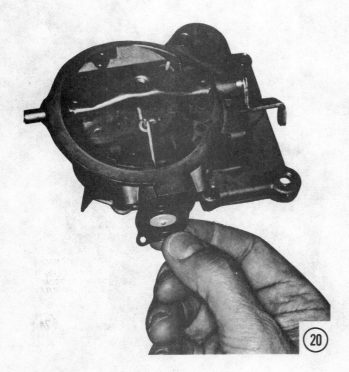

20

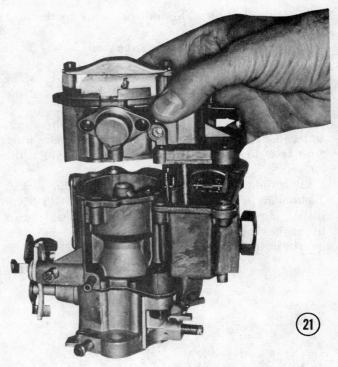

21

⑱ *To make the float level adjustment,* hold the float retaining pin firmly in place and the float arm against the top of the float needle by pushing down on the float arm at the point between the needle seat and hinge pin, as shown. Measure the distance from the top of the float at the toe to the float bowl gasket surface (with the gasket removed). The measurement should be made at a point 1/16″ from the end of the flat surface at the float toe (not on the radius). Bend the float pontoon up or down at the float arm junction to adjust.

⑲ *To make the metering rod adjustment,* remove the metering rod by holding the throttle valve wide open. Push down on the metering rod against spring tension. Slide the metering rod out of the slot in the holder, and then remove it from the main metering jet. To check the adjustment, back out the slow-idle screw and rotate the fast-idle cam so that the cam follower is not contacting any steps on the cam. With the throttle valve completely closed, apply pressure to the top of the power piston to hold it down against its stop. Holding pressure on the power piston, swing the metering rod holder over the flat surface of the bowl casting next to the carburetor bore. Insert the specified plug gauge between the bowl casting sealing bead and the lower surface of the metering rod holder. The gauge should have a slip fit between both surfaces, as shown. To adjust, carefully bend the metering rod holder up or down at the point shown. Install the metering rod.

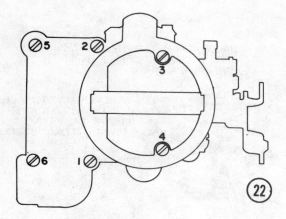

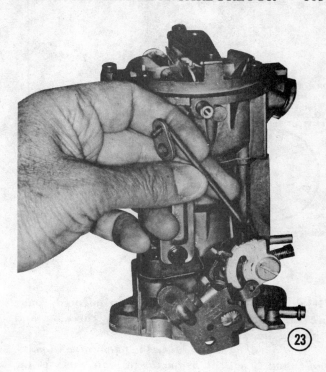

⓴ Install the idle vent valve assembly. Replace the choke shaft, choke valve plate, and vacuum-break lever. Align the choke valve, tighten the two retaining screws, and stake them securely. Install the vacuum-break rubber diaphragm on the plunger stem. *NOTE: The convolute of the diaphragm fits around the head of the plunger.* Install the plunger assembly into its cavity at the side of the air horn. With the choke valve in the open position, slide the eyelet of the plunger rod over the end of the vacuum-break lever on the choke valve. Seat the vacuum-break diaphragm over the sealing bead on the air horn casting. With the diaphragm held in place, carefully install the diaphragm cover and two retaining screws. Tighten the screws securely.

⓴ Install the air-horn gasket on the float bowl by sliding the slit portion of the gasket over the metering rod holder. Then align the gasket with the dowels on the top of the bowl casting; press the gasket firmly into place. Slide the air horn on the float bowl. Lower it carefully until it is seated.

⓴ Install 3 long and 3 short air horn-to-float bowl attaching screws. Tighten them securely using the sequence shown.

⓴ Assemble the choke rod to the choke shaft lever. The end of the rod will point away from the air-horn casting when installed properly. The lower end of the rod has the 45° bend and the part number on the lever must face outward. Install the lower end of the choke rod into the curved slot in the fast-idle cam. The steps on the cam should face the idle tang on the throttle lever. Install the upper choke lever to the choke shaft. The end of the lever must face toward the vacuum-break diaphragm. Install the choke lever screw and tighten it securely.

BENCH ADJUSTMENTS

All adjustments must be made in the order which follows. Use the specification in the repair kit.

⓴ *To make the idle vent adjustment*, set engine idle speed to specifications. Hold the choke valve wide open so that the fast-idle cam follower is not hitting the fast-idle cam. With the throttle lever held against the idle-stop screw, the idle vent valve should be open as specified. To measure, insert a plug gauge between the top of the air horn casting and the bottom surface of the vent valve. To adjust, turn the slotted vent valve head with a screwdriver clockwise (inward) to decrease the clearance as needed. **CAU-**

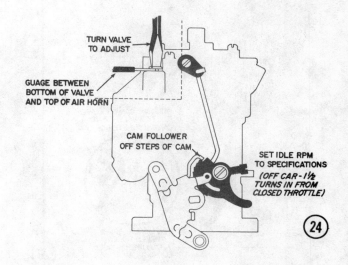

TURN VALVE TO ADJUST

GUAGE BETWEEN BOTTOM OF VALVE AND TOP OF AIR HORN

CAM FOLLOWER OFF STEPS OF CAM

SET IDLE RPM TO SPECIFICATIONS (OFF CAR—1½ TURNS IN FROM CLOSED THROTTLE)

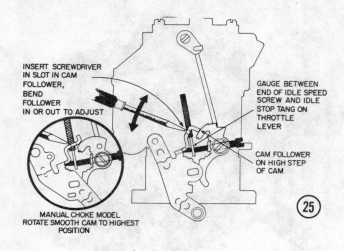

INSERT SCREWDRIVER IN SLOT IN CAM FOLLOWER, BEND FOLLOWER IN OR OUT TO ADJUST

GAUGE BETWEEN END OF IDLE SPEED SCREW AND IDLE STOP TANG ON THROTTLE LEVER

CAM FOLLOWER ON HIGH STEP OF CAM

MANUAL CHOKE MODEL ROTATE SMOOTH CAM TO HIGHEST POSITION

25

TION: On models with an idle-stop solenoid, make sure the solenoid is activated when checking and adjusting the idle vent valve.

25 *To make the fast-idle adjustment on automatic choke models with steps on the fast-idle cam,* set the normal engine idle speed to specifications. *NOTE: The setting off the car is 1-1/2 turns on the idle-speed screw from the closed throttle valve position.* Place the fast-idle cam follower tang on the highest step of the cam. With the tang held against the cam, check the clearance between the end of the slow-idle screw and the idle-stop tang on the throttle lever. It should be as specified.. To adjust, insert the end of a screwdriver into the slot provided in the fast-idle cam follower tang, and bend as needed to obtain the specified dimension. On manual choke models with a smooth contour cam surface, use the same procedure by rotating the fast-idle cam clockwise to its farthest up position.

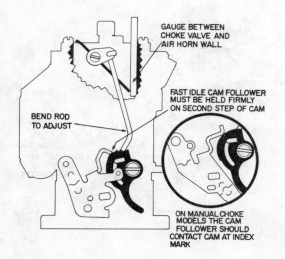

GAUGE BETWEEN CHOKE VALVE AND AIR HORN WALL

BEND ROD TO ADJUST

FAST IDLE CAM FOLLOWER MUST BE HELD FIRMLY ON SECOND STEP OF CAM

ON MANUAL CHOKE MODELS THE CAM FOLLOWER SHOULD CONTACT CAM AT INDEX MARK

26

4 GAUGE BETWEEN LOWER EDGE OF CHOKE VALVE AND AIR HORN WALL

5 BEND TANG TO ADJUST

2 ROTATE CHOKE VALVE TOWARDS CLOSED POSITION (USE RUBBER BAND OR SPRING TO KEEP CHOKE VALVE TOWARD CLOSED POSITION)

1 OPEN THROTTLE VALVE - SO CAM FOLLOWER ON THROTTLE LEVER CLEARS FAST IDLE CAM

3 SEAT DIAPHRAGM BY PUSHING PLUNGER IN WITH NEEDLE NOSED PLIERS

27

26 *To make the choke rod adjustment on automatic choke models with steps on the fast-idle cam,* place the fast-idle cam follower on the second step of the fast-idle cam and hold it firmly against the shoulder of the high step. Rotate the choke valve toward the direction of closed choke by applying force to the choke coil lever. Bend the choke rod at the point shown to give the specified opening between the lower edge of the choke valve (at the center of the valve) and the inside air-horn wall. On manual choke models with a smooth contour cam, use the same procedure except that there are no steps on the manual choke cam, therefore, the index line on the side of the cam should be lined up with the contact point of the fast-idle cam follower tang.

27 *To make the vacuum-break adjustment on models through 1971,* open the throttle valve so that the cam follower on the throttle lever clears the highest step on the fast-idle cam. Rotate the choke valve to the closed position. If the thermostatic coil is warm, hold the choke valve closed with a rubber

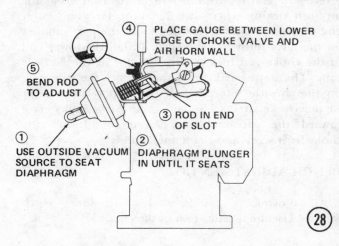

4 PLACE GAUGE BETWEEN LOWER EDGE OF CHOKE VALVE AND AIR HORN WALL

5 BEND ROD TO ADJUST

3 ROD IN END OF SLOT

1 USE OUTSIDE VACUUM SOURCE TO SEAT DIAPHRAGM

2 DIAPHRAGM PLUNGER IN UNTIL IT SEATS

28

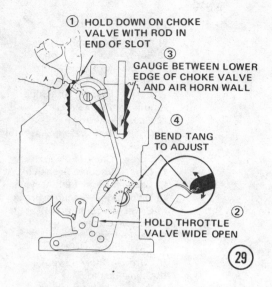

① HOLD DOWN ON CHOKE VALVE WITH ROD IN END OF SLOT

③ GAUGE BETWEEN LOWER EDGE OF CHOKE VALVE AND AIR HORN WALL

④ BEND TANG TO ADJUST

② HOLD THROTTLE VALVE WIDE OPEN

㉙

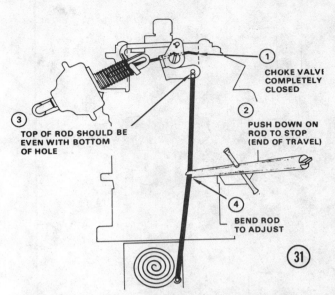

① CHOKE VALVE COMPLETELY CLOSED

② PUSH DOWN ON ROD TO STOP (END OF TRAVEL)

③ TOP OF ROD SHOULD BE EVEN WITH BOTTOM OF HOLE

④ BEND ROD TO ADJUST

㉛

band attached between the choke shaft lever and a stationary part of the carburetor. Grasp the vacuum-break plunger rod with needle-nosed pliers and push straight inward until the diaphragm seats. With the specified plug gauge, measure the clearance between the lower edge of the choke valve and the inside air-horn wall at the center of the valve, as shown. Bend the end of the vacuum-break lever at the point shown to adjust.

㉘ *To make the vacuum-break adjustment on models since 1972,* use an auxiliary vacuum source to seat the diaphragm. **CAUTION: Make sure the bucking spring is fully compressed.** Push the choke valve toward the closed position, and then insert the specified gauge between the lower edge of the choke valve and the wall of the air horn. If necessary, bend the vacuum-break rod at the point shown.

㉙ *To make the unloader adjustment,* hold the

choke valve in the closed position by applying a light force to the choke coil lever. Rotate the throttle lever to the wide-open position. Bend the unloader tang on the throttle lever to obtain the specified dimension between the lower edge of the choke valve (at the center) and the air-horn wall.

㉚ *To make the choke coil adjustment on models through 1971,* hold the choke valve closed. Pull upward on the coil rod to the end of its travel. The bottom of the rod end which slides into the hole in the choke lever should be even with the top of the hole. Bend the choke coil rod at the point shown to adjust. Connect the coil rod to the choke lever, and then install the retaining clip.

㉛ *To make the choke coil adjustment on models since 1972,* hold the choke valve completely closed and push down on the rod to the end of its travel; the top of the rod must be even with the bottom of the hole. If necessary, bend the rod where shown.

㉜ *To make the CEC valve adjustment,* it is neces-

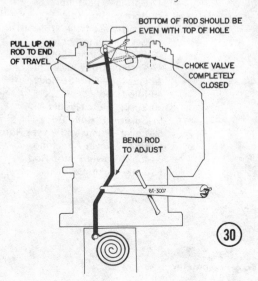

BOTTOM OF ROD SHOULD BE EVEN WITH TOP OF HOLE

PULL UP ON ROD TO END OF TRAVEL

CHOKE VALVE COMPLETELY CLOSED

BEND ROD TO ADJUST

BT-3007

㉚

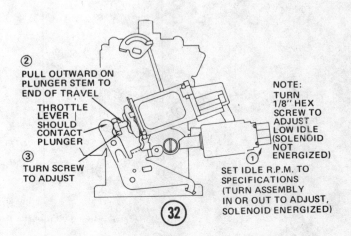

② PULL OUTWARD ON PLUNGER STEM TO END OF TRAVEL

THROTTLE LEVER SHOULD CONTACT PLUNGER

③ TURN SCREW TO ADJUST

NOTE: TURN 1/8" HEX SCREW TO ADJUST LOW IDLE (SOLENOID NOT ENERGIZED)

① SET IDLE R.P.M. TO SPECIFICATIONS (TURN ASSEMBLY IN OR OUT TO ADJUST, SOLENOID ENERGIZED)

㉜

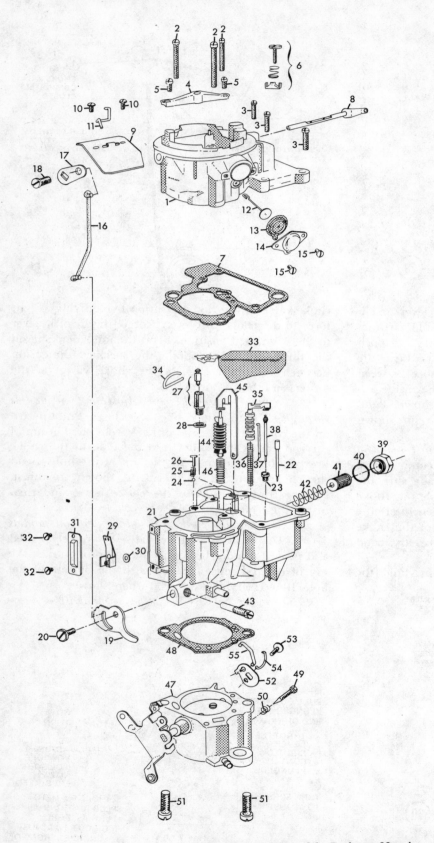

1-Air Horn Assembly
2-Screw—Air Horn—Long
3-Screw—Air Horn—Short
4-Bracket—Air Cleaner Stud
5-Screw—Bracket Attaching
6-Idle Vent Valve Kit
7-Gasket—Air Horn
8-Choke Shaft & Lever Assembly
9-Choke Valve
10-Screw—Choke Valve
11-Lever—Vacuum Break Link
12-Vacuum Break Link Assy.
13-Diaphragm—Vacuum Break
14-Cover—Vacuum Break
15-Screw—Cover
16-Choke Rod
17-Choke Lever
18-Screw—Choke Lever
19-Cam—Fast Idle
20-Screw—Cam Attaching
21-Float Bowl Assembly
22-Idle Tube Assembly
23-Jet—Main Metering
24-Ball—Pump Discharge
25-Spring—Pump Discharge
26-Guide—Pump Discharge
27-Needle and Seat Assy.
28-Gasket—Needle Seat
29-Idle Compensator Assembly
30-Gasket—Idle Compensator
31-Cover—Idle Compensator
32-Screw—Cover
33-Float Assembly
34-Hinge Pin—Float
35-Power Piston Assembly
36-Spring—Power Power Piston
37-Rod—Power Piston
38-Metering Rod & Spring Assembly
39-Filter Nut—Fuel Inlet
40-Gasket—Filter Nut
41-Filter—Fuel Inlet
42-Spring—Fuel Filter
43-Screw—Slow Idle
44-Pump Assembly
45-Lever—Pump Actuating
46-Spring—Pump Return
47-Throttle Body Assembly
48-Gasket—Throttle Body
49-Idle Needle
50-Spring—Idle Needle
51-Screw—Throttle Body
52-Lever—Pump and Power Rods
53-Screw-Lever Attaching
54-Link—Power-Piston Rod
55-Link—Pump Lever

Exploded view of the Rochester Monojet carburetor.

sary to have the engine running, the transmission in NEUTRAL or DRIVE, the air conditioner OFF, the distributor vacuum hose removed and the end plugged, and the fuel tank hose from the vapor canister disconnected. **CAUTION: This adjustment is to be made only after having replaced the CEC solenoid, overhauled the carburetor, or replaced the throttle body. CAUTION: Before making this adjustment, the engine curb-idle speed must have been properly adjusted either at the throttle-stop screw or at the idle-stop solenoid. CAUTION: Don't use the CEC valve to adjust the curb-idle speed or a serious loss of engine braking will result.** To make the CEC valve adjustment, manually extend the CEC valve plunger to contact the throttle lever. Pull outward on the plunger stem to the end of its travel. Turn the plunger screw to adjust engine speed to 850 rpm in NEUTRAL, or to 650 rpm in DRIVE.

MONOJET CARBURETOR SERVICE NOTES

REVISED CHOKE SHAFT REPLACEMENT KIT

On later models, the upper choke lever is slotted for free movement of the choke rod, and the fast-idle cam has a standard hole. On these models, a choke shaft-and-lever kit, Part No. 7036973, must be used to replace the upper choke rod slotted lever or the choke shaft-and-coil lever assembly. The new kit contains a choke shaft, with the slotted choke lever spun on one end and a separate choke coil rod lever with an attaching screw.

USE OF LOCTITE

Loctite should be applied to the two bridge screws and the three long air horn-to-float bowl attaching screws to prevent their loosening in service.

COLD-ENGINE LOADING

Vehicles equipped with the MV carburetor may experience a loading condition during cold-engine operation if the cranking enrichment valve sticks in the open position. This valve is located on the air horn and opens when the choke closes and pushes down on the valve stem. The valve is intended to allow fuel from the cranking valve channel (which leads directly from the bottom of the fuel bowl) to supplement that supplied by the idle circuit and main discharge nozzle during cold cranking. The valve may stick in the open position after the choke has moved to an open position and cause the loading condition described above.

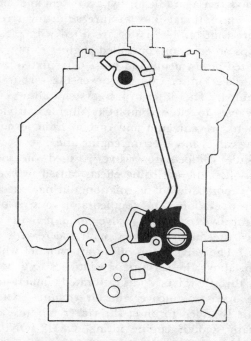

On late-model Monojet carburetors, the upper choke lever is slotted for free movement of the choke rod. A service kit is available for service, as discussed in the text.

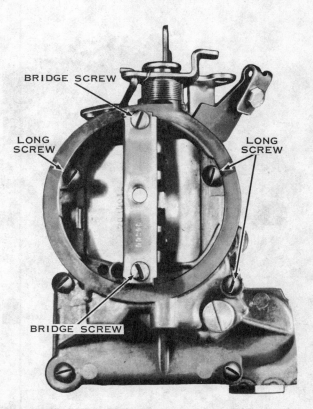

Locktite should be applied to the screws shown to prevent their coming loose in service.

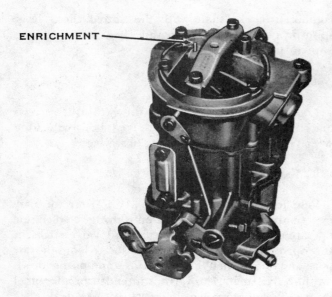

ENRICHMENT

If the cranking-enrichment valve sticks in the open position, the engine will load during cold-engine operation, as discussed in the text.

It has been found that cold-starting performance will not be adversely affected if this system is made inoperative. Use a pair of needle-nosed pliers to pull upward on the valve stem to assure that the valve is

LOW-IDLE
ADJUSTMENT SCREW

Since 1972, the low-idle speed adjustment is made at the Allen-headed screw located in the end of the idle-stop solenoid, as discussed in the text.

fully closed, and then remove the stem by bending it back and forth with the pliers until it breaks off. Fully removing the valve stem in this manner will place the valve out of contact with the choke valve, thus making the system inoperative.

Low-Idle Speed Adjustment — Since 1972

After making a curb-idle speed adjustment, the low-idle speed adjustment is made at the Allen-headed screw located in the end of the idle-stop solenoid. **CAUTION: When making the low-idle adjustment, clockwise rotation of the screw should never be continued after the screw is bottomed against the armature. Increased rotation will result in raising the solenoid cover up through the staked housing.**

ROCHESTER MODEL 2G CARBURETOR

This current two-barrel carburetor comes in three different models: 2G, 2GC, and 2GV. Model 2G is the basic carburetor with a manual choke. Model 2GC has an automatic choke as an integral part of the carburetor, while Model 2GV has an automatic choke with the thermostatic coil located on the engine manifold and connected to the choke valve by linkage. This model has a vacuum-break diaphragm on the carburetor in place of the conventional choke housing on the air horn.

Some models use an idle air bypass system and some have two conventional idle mixture adjusting screws for mixture control. The latter are fitted with plastic limiter caps on emission-controlled engines to prevent unauthorized adjustments and must be replaced with colored service limiter caps whenever the carburetor is overhauled. The idle bypass system allows the throttle valves to close completely during curb-idle operation to prevent gum and carbon from forming around the valves and affecting engine idle.

A hot-idle compensator valve is used on some models to offset the enriching effects caused by excessive fuel vapors due to percolation during extreme hot-engine operation. The compensator consists of a thermostatically controlled valve mounted in the area above the main ventures or at the rear of the float bowl. The valve closes off an air channel which leads from above the carburetor ventures to a point below the throttle valves. At its calibrated temperature, the valve opens to uncover the air channel so that enough air is added to offset the richer mixture and so maintain smooth engine idling. **CAUTION: In order to insure correct idle mixture adjustments, this valve must be manually held closed during the adjusting process.**

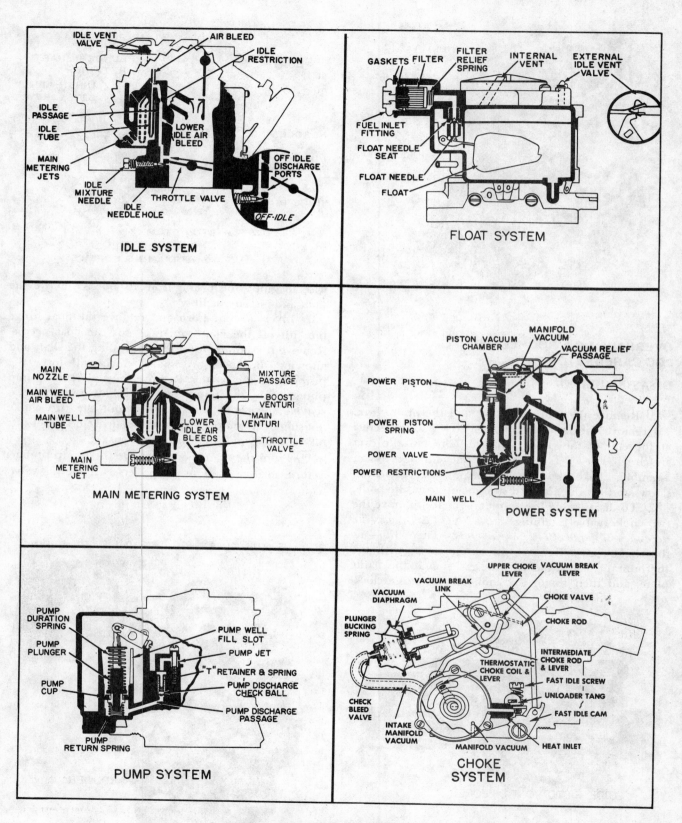

Operating circuits of the Rochester 2G carburetor.

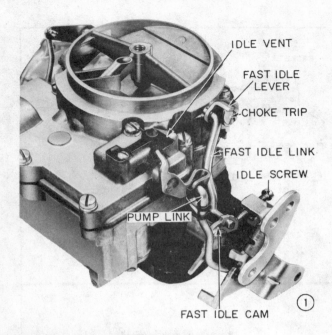

OVERHAULING A ROCHESTER 2GC CARBURETOR

DISASSEMBLING

① Remove the idle vent valve and the pump link. To remove the fast-idle linkage, take out the screw at the end of the choke shaft and the fast-idle cam attaching screw. Then remove the linkage as an assembly. Take out the eight air horn attaching screws and lift the air horn straight up from the body.

② To disassemble the automatic choke, remove the two choke valve retaining screws. *NOTE: It may be necessary to file the staked ends.* Then lift out the choke valve. Remove the choke cover, with the thermostatic coil attached, the gasket and the baffle plate, and then rotate the choke shaft counterclock-

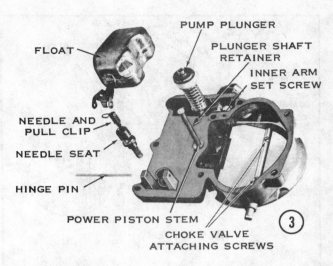

wise to guide the piston from its bore. Remove the shaft-and-piston assembly.

③ Invert the air horn and remove the float hinge pin, lift off the float, and take out the float needle. Remove the power piston by depressing the shaft and allowing the spring to snap, which will force the piston from the casting. Remove the accelerator pump plunger and the pump lever-and-shaft assembly. To remove the choke housing, take out the two choke housing-to-air horn attaching screws, and then lift off the choke housing. Discard the gasket.

④ From the main body, remove the pump plunger return spring, main metering jets, and power valve.

Many Oldsmobile carburetors have the choke mounted on the throttle body.

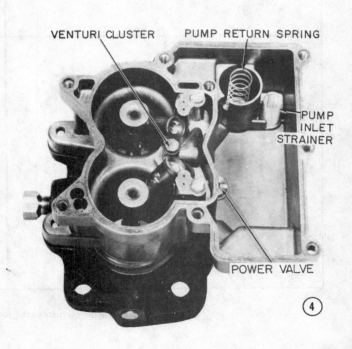

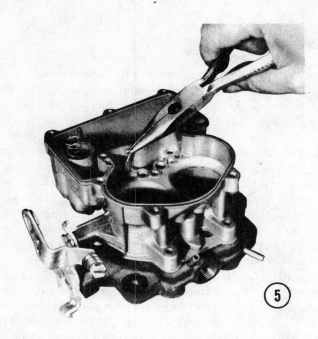

Some models have an aluminum inlet ball in the bottom of the pump well which drops out by inverting the carburetor. To take out the venturi cluster, remove the three attaching screws.

⑤ Use a pair of long-nosed pliers to remove the discharge ball spring T-shaped retainer. Then take out the pump discharge spring and the steel discharge ball. Invert the carburetor and remove the three throttle body-to-bowl attaching screws. Then lift off the throttle body. Do not disassemble the throttle body as parts are not available for service because of the close relationship that exists between the throttle plates and the idle ports.

CLEANING AND INSPECTING

Clean all parts in carburetor cleaner. Follow with a solvent bath and blow dry. Diaphragms, parts containing leather, the choke thermostatic cover, and the idle vent valve should be cleaned only in solvent—never in carburetor cleaner. Blow compressed air through all passageways and jets to make sure that they are open.

Move the throttle shaft back and forth to check for wear. If the shaft appears to be excessively loose, replace the entire throttle body as parts are not available for service.

Inspect the main body, air horn, and venturi cluster gasket surfaces for cracks and burrs which might cause leaking.

Shake the float to check for leaks. Replace the float if it has liquid in it. Check the float arm needle contacting surface and replace the float if this surface is grooved.

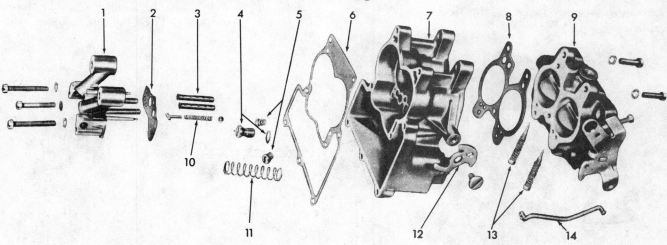

1. Cluster Assembly
2. Gasket
3. Splash Shield--Main Well
4. Power Valve Assembly
5. Main Jets
6. Air Horn Gasket
7. Bowl Assembly
8. Throttle Body to Bowl Gasket
9. Throttle Body Assembly
10. Pump Discharge Check Assembly
11. Accelerator Pump Spring
12. Fast Idle Cam
13. Idle Mixture Screws
14. Choke Rod

Exploded view of a Rochester 2G carburetor.

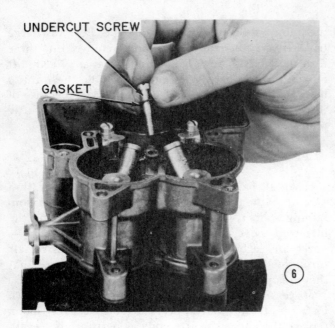

Check the idle adjusting needles; replace any that has a groove in its tapered section.

A carburetor kit should be purchased for each carburetor overhaul. It contains new parts to replace those which wear the most, plus a complete set of gaskets. Each kit also contains a matched fuel inlet needle and seat which should be replaced each time the carburetor is taken apart; otherwise, leaking may result.

ASSEMBLING

⑥ Screw the idle mixture adjusting needles and springs into the throttle body finger-tight, and then back the screws out 1-1/2 turns for a preliminary adjustment. Assemble the throttle body to the bowl, using a new gasket. Drop the pump discharge check steel ball, spring, and T-shaped retainer into the top of the main body. Replace the venturi cluster, using a new gasket. Make sure that the undercut screw has a gasket and is placed in the center hole. Replace the main metering jets and the power valve, using a new power valve gasket. Install the pump return spring in the pump well and the pump inlet screen in the bottom of the bowl.

⑦ Place a new choke housing gasket in position and install the choke housing (7), retaining it with the two attaching screws. Assemble the choke piston to the choke shaft and link (8). The piston pin and flat section on the side of the choke piston should face outward toward the air horn. Push the choke shaft into the air horn, rotating the shaft until the piston enters the housing bore. Place the choke valve (4) on the choke shaft with the letters RP facing up. Install the two choke valve retaining screws finger-tight. Place the choke rod lever (3) and the trip lever (1) on the end of the choke shaft. Center the choke valve to establish 0.020" clearance between the choke lever and the air horn casting. Then tighten and stake the

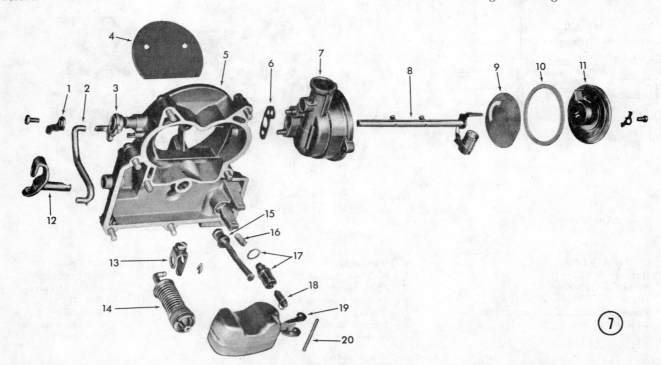

Many Oldsmobile 2G carburetors have the choke mounted on the throttle body instead of the air horn, as shown here.

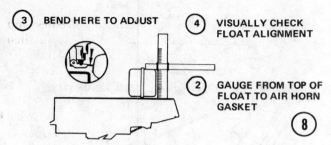

① INVERT AIR HORN WITH GASKET IN PLACE.

③ BEND HERE TO ADJUST

④ VISUALLY CHECK FLOAT ALIGNMENT

② GAUGE FROM TOP OF FLOAT TO AIR HORN GASKET

⑧

choke valve retaining screws. Replace the baffle plate (9), gasket (10), and thermostatic cover (11). Rotate the cover until the index marks align according to specifications. Then install and tighten the three cover retaining screws. Install the outer pump lever (12) in the air horn. Assemble the inner pump arm (13) and tighten the screw. Attach the pump plunger (14) to the inner arm (13), with the pump shaft pointing inward. Then install the horseshoe retainer. Place the screen (16) on the float needle seat (17) and screw the assembly into the air horn. Install the power piston (15) into the vacuum cavity. The piston must move freely. Stake the retainer lightly to hold it in place. Install the air horn gasket, attach the needle (18) to the float (19), and carefully insert the needle into the float needle seat while guiding the float between the bosses. Insert the hinge pin (20) to complete the air horn assembly. The two float adjustments which must now be made are float level and float drop.

⑧ *To check the float level on models with a vertical seam in the float,* measure from the top of the float to the air horn, with the gasket in place. To adjust, bend the float arm at the rear of the float, as shown in the inset.

⑨ *To check the float level on models with a horizontal seam in the float,* measure from the lower edge of the seam to the air horn, with the gasket in place.

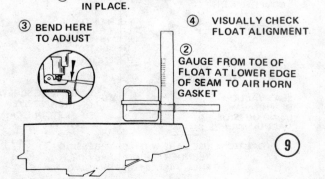

① INVERT AIR HORN WITH GASKET IN PLACE.

③ BEND HERE TO ADJUST

④ VISUALLY CHECK FLOAT ALIGNMENT

② GAUGE FROM TOE OF FLOAT AT LOWER EDGE OF SEAM TO AIR HORN GASKET

⑨

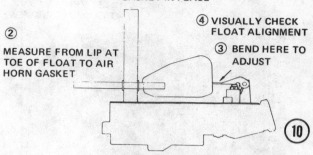

① INVERT AIR HORN WITH GASKET IN PLACE

② MEASURE FROM LIP AT TOE OF FLOAT TO AIR HORN GASKET

④ VISUALLY CHECK FLOAT ALIGNMENT

③ BEND HERE TO ADJUST

⑩

To adjust, bend the float arm at the rear of the float, as shown in the inset.

⑩ *To check the float level on models with a Nitrophyl-type float,* measure from the lip at the toe of the float to the air horn, with the gasket in place. To adjust, bend the float arm at the rear of the float, as shown.

⑪ *To check the float drop adjustment,* turn the air horn right side up to allow the float to move to the wide-open position, and then measure from the air-horn gasket to the bottom of the float. To adjust, bend the float tang, as shown in the inset.

⑫ *To check the float drop adjustment on a Nitrophyl-type float,* measure from the air-horn gasket

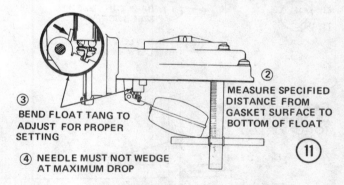

① AIR HORN RIGHT SIDE UP TO ALLOW FLOAT TO HANG FREE (GASKET IN PLACE)

② MEASURE SPECIFIED DISTANCE FROM GASKET SURFACE TO BOTTOM OF FLOAT

③ BEND FLOAT TANG TO ADJUST FOR PROPER SETTING

④ NEEDLE MUST NOT WEDGE AT MAXIMUM DROP

⑪

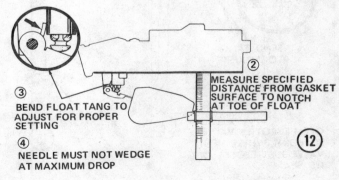

① AIR HORN RIGHT SIDE UP TO ALLOW FLOAT TO HANG FREE (GASKET IN PLACE)

② MEASURE SPECIFIED DISTANCE FROM GASKET SURFACE TO NOTCH AT TOE OF FLOAT

③ BEND FLOAT TANG TO ADJUST FOR PROPER SETTING

④ NEEDLE MUST NOT WEDGE AT MAXIMUM DROP

⑫

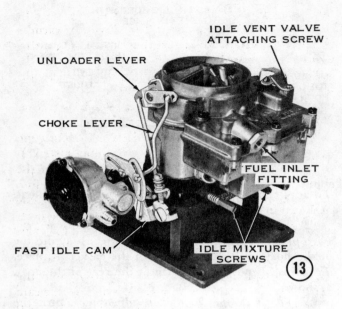

UNLOADER LEVER

IDLE VENT VALVE
ATTACHING SCREW

CHOKE LEVER

FUEL INLET
FITTING

FAST IDLE CAM

IDLE MIXTURE
SCREWS

⑬

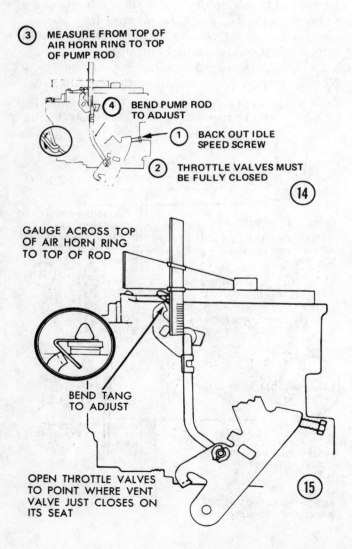

③ MEASURE FROM TOP OF
AIR HORN RING TO TOP
OF PUMP ROD

④ BEND PUMP ROD
TO ADJUST

① BACK OUT IDLE
SPEED SCREW

② THROTTLE VALVES MUST
BE FULLY CLOSED

⑭

GAUGE ACROSS TOP
OF AIR HORN RING
TO TOP OF ROD

BEND TANG
TO ADJUST

OPEN THROTTLE VALVES
TO POINT WHERE VENT
VALVE JUST CLOSES ON
ITS SEAT

⑮

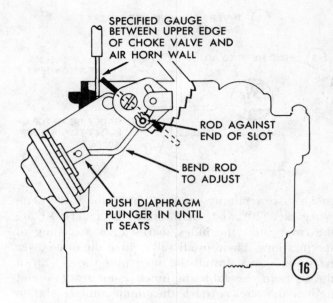

SPECIFIED GAUGE
BETWEEN UPPER EDGE
OF CHOKE VALVE AND
AIR HORN WALL

ROD AGAINST
END OF SLOT

BEND ROD
TO ADJUST

PUSH DIAPHRAGM
PLUNGER IN UNTIL
IT SEATS

⑯

to the notch at the toe of the float, as shown. To
adjust, bend the float tang, as shown in the inset.

⑬ Replace the assembled air horn on the bowl,
guiding the accelerator pump plunger into its well.
Install and tighten the cover screws. Replace the idle
vent valve, pump rod, fast-idle rod, and fast-idle cam.

BENCH ADJUSTMENTS

Use the specifications in the repair kit as they have
been updated to reflect the latest information. **CAU-
TION: These adjustments must be made in the order
given below.**

⑭ *To measure the pump arm position,* use the
specified gauge. With the throttle plates seated in
their bores (idle speed screws backed out fully), the
top surface of the pump rod should be the specified
distance from the top of the air horn ring. Bend the
pump rod as required.

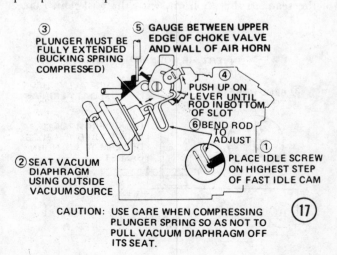

③ PLUNGER MUST BE
FULLY EXTENDED
(BUCKING SPRING
COMPRESSED)

⑤ GAUGE BETWEEN UPPER
EDGE OF CHOKE VALVE
AND WALL OF AIR HORN

④ PUSH UP ON
LEVER UNTIL
ROD IN BOTTOM
OF SLOT

⑥ BEND ROD
TO ADJUST

① PLACE IDLE SCREW
ON HIGHEST STEP
OF FAST IDLE CAM

② SEAT VACUUM
DIAPHRAGM
USING OUTSIDE
VACUUM SOURCE

CAUTION: USE CARE WHEN COMPRESSING
PLUNGER SPRING SO AS NOT TO
PULL VACUUM DIAPHRAGM OFF
ITS SEAT.

⑰

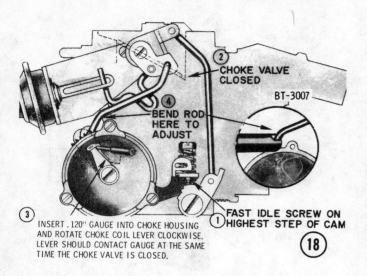

INSERT .120" GAUGE INTO CHOKE HOUSING AND ROTATE CHOKE COIL LEVER CLOCKWISE. LEVER SHOULD CONTACT GAUGE AT THE SAME TIME THE CHOKE VALVE IS CLOSED.

(18)

(15) *To check the idle vent adjustment on models through 1967,* open the throttle slowly to observe the point where the idle vent just closes. Use the specified gauge to check this position. Bend the tang on the pump lever as required.

(16) *To check the vacuum-break adjustment on models through 1970,* apply vacuum from an auxiliary source. Install a rubber band to the lever in such a manner as to close the choke blade. Insert the specified gauge between the air horn and the choke blade to measure the clearance. Bend the rod as shown to adjust.

(17) *To check the vacuum-break adjustment on models with a bucking spring (since 1971),* position the idle screw on the highest step of the fast-idle cam. Seat the diaphragm with an auxiliary vacuum source. **CAUTION: Make sure that the bucking spring is fully compressed.** Push up on the lever until the rod is bottomed in the slot, and then insert the specified gauge between the upper edge of the choke valve and the wall of the air horn. Bend the rod as shown to adjust.

(18) *To make the intermediate choke rod adjustment,* position the fast-idle screw on the highest step of the fast-idle cam. **CAUTION: Make sure that the choke valve is closed completely.** Insert a gauge into the choke housing as shown, and then rotate the coil lever clockwise until the choke valve closes. The lever must contact the gauge at the same time that the valve closes. If an adjustment is needed, bend the intermediate choke rod in the bent section, as shown.

(19) *To make the fast-idle cam adjustment,* hold the fast-idle screw on the second step of the fast-idle cam and against the highest step. Insert the specified gauge between the upper edge of the choke valve and the air horn wall. Bend the fast-idle actuating rod in the bent section, as shown.

(20) *To make the unloader adjustment,* hold the throttle valves wide open and the choke valve toward the closed position. The specified gauge should fit between the upper edge of the choke valve and the air horn wall. If it doesn't, bend the tang on the throttle lever to adjust the choke valve opening.

(21) *To make the choke setting,* loosen the retaining screws and then turn the cover to align the index marks as specified. Tighten the cover retaining screws securely.

(19) (2) GAUGE BETWEEN UPPER EDGE OF CHOKE VALVE AND AIR HORN WALL / (3) BEND ROD TO ADJUST / (1) HOLD FAST IDLE SCREW ON SECOND STEP OF CAM AGAINST HIGHEST STEP

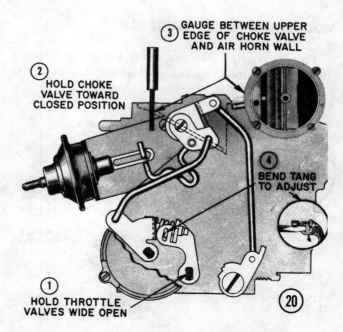

(3) GAUGE BETWEEN UPPER EDGE OF CHOKE VALVE AND AIR HORN WALL / (2) HOLD CHOKE VALVE TOWARD CLOSED POSITION / (4) BEND TANG TO ADJUST / (1) HOLD THROTTLE VALVES WIDE OPEN / (20)

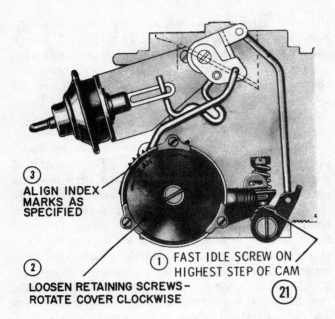

③ ALIGN INDEX MARKS AS SPECIFIED

② LOOSEN RETAINING SCREWS—ROTATE COVER CLOCKWISE

① FAST IDLE SCREW ON HIGHEST STEP OF CAM

㉑

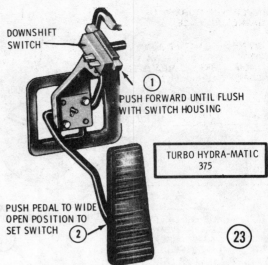

DOWNSHIFT SWITCH

① PUSH FORWARD UNTIL FLUSH WITH SWITCH HOUSING

TURBO HYDRA-MATIC 375

PUSH PEDAL TO WIDE OPEN POSITION TO SET SWITCH

②

㉓

1. PUSH PLUNGER OF DOWNSHIFT SWITCH FORWARD UNTIL FLUSH WITH SWITCH HOUSING.
2. PUSH ACCELERATOR PEDAL TO WIDE OPEN POSITION TO SET SWITCH.
3. ENERGIZING OF DOWNSHIFT SWITCH CIRCUIT CAN BE CHECKED WITH A TEST LIGHT.

㉒ *To make the throttle check (dashpot) adjustment,* position the fast-idle screw on the high step of the fat-idle cam, and then adjust the length of the plunger screw so that it just contacts the throttle lever. Use a wrench to hold the dashpot to keep it from twisting off and damaging the diaphragm.

㉓ *To make the downshift throttle switch adjustment on vehicles with a Turbo Hydra-Matic 375/400 automatic transmission,* push the plunger of the downshift switch forward until it is flush with the switch housing, and then push the accelerator pedal to the wide-open position to set the switch.

ROCHESTER 4GC CARBURETOR

This carburetor was used on V-8 engines through 1966. The instructions that follow for this outdated

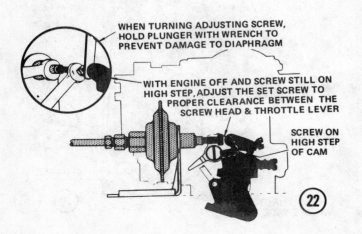

WHEN TURNING ADJUSTING SCREW, HOLD PLUNGER WITH WRENCH TO PREVENT DAMAGE TO DIAPHRAGM

WITH ENGINE OFF AND SCREW STILL ON HIGH STEP, ADJUST THE SET SCREW TO PROPER CLEARANCE BETWEEN THE SCREW HEAD & THROTTLE LEVER

SCREW ON HIGH STEP OF CAM

㉒

carburetor include an exploded view to show the placement of all parts and step-by-step adjustment procedures.

Always use a complete kit of parts when overhauling these carburetors as it contains all of the needed and updated parts, as well as a complete set of gaskets. It also includes the latest specifications, which are needed for making the following adjustments.

CARBURETOR ADJUSTMENTS

The adjustments must be made in the following order: (1) primary and secondary float level, (2) vacuum-assist spring, (3) float drop, (4) intermediate choke rod, (5) fast-idle cam rod, (6) secondary throttle lockout, (7) secondary throttle contour clearance, (8) pump rod, (9) idle vent, (10) unloader, and (11) throttle-return check (dashpot).

① *To measure the float level setting on models with D-type floats,* insert the specified gauge at the heel end of the float, with the tang of the gauge resting against the casting. The floats must touch the horizontal part of the gauge. Bend the float arms as required.

② *To measure the primary float level setting on models with pontoon-type floats,* insert the specified gauge over the heels of the secondary floats. The highest points of the floats must just touch the horizontal parts of the gauge. Bend the float arms to adjust.

① INVERT AIR HORN WITH GASKET IN PLACE

② ON MODELS WITH ROUND OR "D" TYPE FLOATS – GAUGE FROM GASKET SURFACE TO TOP OF EACH FLOAT

③ BEND FLOAT ARM TO ADJUST

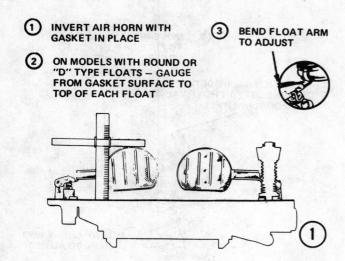

① HOLD POWER PISTON IN FULL UP POSITION (LIGHTLY MOVE FLOAT ASSEMBLY TO BE SURE THERE IS NO BIND)

③ BEND TANG TO ADJUST ④

② MEASURE FROM GASKET TO CENTER OF FLOAT DIMPLE

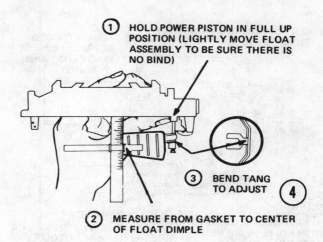

③ *To check the secondary float toe adjustment,* measure the distance between the dimple on the side of each float at the toe end and the bowl cover gasket, using the specified gauge. If an adjustment is necessary, bend the float at the soldered joint while holding the float arm stationary.

④ *To make the vacuum-assist spring adjustment,* hold the bowl cover so that the floats hang down. Use your thumb nail to push the brass portion of the

power piston to its highest point. Bounce the floats lightly to make sure that the cup retainer spring is not binding. The distance from the gasket to the center of the dimple on the side of the primary float should be as specified. To adjust, bend the slotted tang in the center of the float arm.

① INVERT AIR HORN WITH GASKET IN PLACE

② GAUGE FROM GASKET SURFACE TO TOP HEEL OF EACH FLOAT

③ BEND FLOAT ARM TO ADJUST

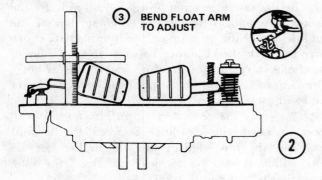

① INVERT AIR HORN WITH GASKET IN PLACE

③ BEND PONTOON LIGHTLY TO ADJUST

② MEASURE FROM GASKET SURFACE TO CENTER OF DIMPLE

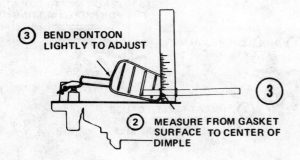

① AIR HORN RIGHT SIDE UP TO ALLOW FLOAT TO HANG FREE (GASKET IN PLACE)

④ NEEDLE MUST NOT WEDGE AT MAXIMUM DROP

③ BEND FLOAT TANG TO ADJUST

PRIMARY   SECONDARY

② MEASURE FROM GASKET TO CENTER OF DIMPLE ON SIDE OF EACH FLOAT TOE

PONTOON-TYPE FLOATS

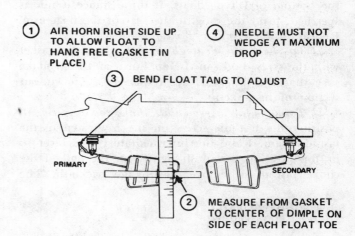

① AIR HORN RIGHT SIDE UP TO ALLOW FLOAT TO HANG FREE (GASKET IN PLACE)

④ NEEDLE MUST NOT WEDGE AT MAXIMUM DROP

③ BEND FLOAT TANG TO ADJUST

SECONDARY

PRIMARY   ② MEASURE FROM GASKET SURFACE TO BOTTOM OF FLOAT

D-TYPE FLOATS ⑤

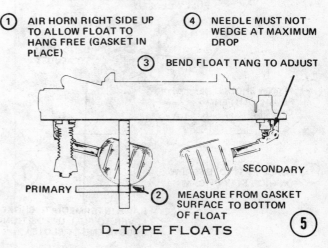

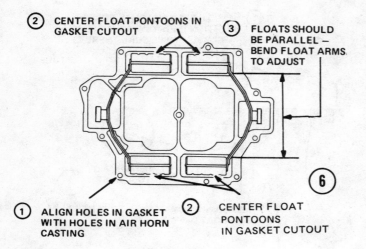

② CENTER FLOAT PONTOONS IN GASKET CUTOUT

③ FLOATS SHOULD BE PARALLEL — BEND FLOAT ARMS TO ADJUST

⑥

① ALIGN HOLES IN GASKET WITH HOLES IN AIR HORN CASTING

② CENTER FLOAT PONTOONS IN GASKET CUTOUT

② MOVE INTERMEDIATE LEVER TO FULL UP POSITION TO TAKE UP LASH IN SLOTS

③ SPECIFIED GAUGE BETWEEN UPPER EDGE OF CHOKE VALVE AND DIVIDING WALL

④ BEND CHOKE ROD HERE TO ADJUST

① PLACE FAST IDLE SCREW ON 2ND STEP AGAINST HIGH STEP

⑧

⑤ *To make the primary and secondary float drop adjustments,* hold the bowl cover so that the floats hang down. Release the power piston and measure the distance from the gasket to the center of the dimple on the toe end of the primary pontoon-type floats or to the bottom of D-type floats. If the distance is not as specified, bend the tang at the rear of the float arm. Repeat for the secondary float.

⑥ *To check the float alignment,* align the gasket with the screw holes in the air horn, and then make sure that the pontoons are centered in the cut-out sections of the gasket.

⑦ *To make the intermediate choke rod adjustment,* position the fast-idle screw on the high step of the fast-idle cam. Raise the intermediate choke lever to its top position and push lightly on the end of the choke piston to remove all linkage backlash. The

choke piston should be flush with the edge of its bore. Bend the intermediate choke rod for correction. Replace the baffle, the cover gasket, and the thermostatic coil and cover assembly. Rotate the cover counterclockwise until the coil picks up the tang on the piston linkage. Continue until the scribed line on the cover indexes with the specified mark on the casting. Install the three cover attaching screws and retainers.

⑧ *To make the fast-idle cam rod adjustment,* turn in the fast idle screw until it just contacts the second step and is against the highest step of the fast-idle cam. Now push up on the intermediate choke lever to check the clearance between the top edge of the choke valve and the dividing wall of the air horn. The clearance should be as specified. Bend the lower rod to adjust.

⑨ *To make the secondary throttle lockout adjustment,* measure the clearance between the lockout tang and the top edge of the slot in the fast-idle cam, which should be as specified. Bend the tang to obtain the required clearance.

⑤ BEND INTERMEDIATE CHOKE ROD TO ADJUST

③ CHOKE VALVE FULLY CLOSED

BEND HERE TO ADJUST

④ PISTON SHOULD BE FLUSH WITH END OF BORE

① PLACE FAST IDLE SCREW ON HIGH STEP OF CAM

⑦

② RAISE INTERMEDIATE CHOKE LEVER TO FULL UP POSITION— RODS IN END OF SLOTS

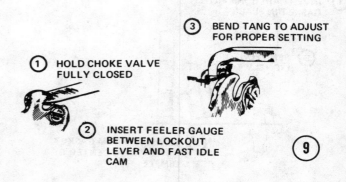

③ BEND TANG TO ADJUST FOR PROPER SETTING

① HOLD CHOKE VALVE FULLY CLOSED

② INSERT FEELER GAUGE BETWEEN LOCKOUT LEVER AND FAST IDLE CAM

⑨

① HOLD CHOKE VALVE WIDE OPEN

② INSERT FEELER GAUGE BETWEEN LOCKOUT LEVER AND FAST IDLE CAM

③ BEND TANG TO ADJUST

⑩

③ GAUGE FROM TOP OF AIR HORN TO BOTTOM OF PUMP SHAFT

② VENT VALVE JUST CLOSED

④ BEND TANG TO ADJUST

⑫

① OPEN THROTTLE VALVES TO WHERE VENT VALVE JUST CLOSES

③ BEND TANG ON FAST IDLE CAM TO ADJUST. NOTE: ON SOME MODELS, BEND UNLOADER TANG ON PUMP LEVER

② PLACE SPECIFIED GAUGE BETWEEN UPPER EDGE OF CHOKE VALVE AND DIVIDING WALL OF AIR HORN

① OPEN THROTTLE VALVES WIDE OPEN

⑬

⑩ *To make the secondary throttle contour clearance adjustment,* hold the throttle and choke in the wide-open position so that the secondary lockout tang is positioned over the fast-idle cam. Measure the clearance between the tang and the cam. Bend the tang as required to give the specified clearance.

⑪ *To make the pump rod adjustment,* back out the idle speed screw until the throttle valves seat. Then measure the clearance between the top of the air horn casting and the bottom edge of the pump plunger shaft. Bend the pump rod as required.

⑫ *To make the atmospheric idle vent adjustment,* open the throttle valves to the point where the idle vent valve just closes. The distance between the top of the air horn casting and the bottom of the pump plunger should be as specified. Bend the idle vent tang on the pump lever to adjust.

⑬ *To make the unloader adjustment,* hold the throttle lever in the wide-open position and check the clearance between the top edge of the choke valve and the dividing wall. Bend the small tang on the pump lever to adjust.

⑭ *To make the throttle return check (dashpot) adjustment,* rotate the fast-idle cam so that the fast-idle screw rests on the highest step of the cam. Measure

the clearance between the screw head and the contact arm on the throttle lever, which should be as specified. Use two wrenches to adjust the contact screw.

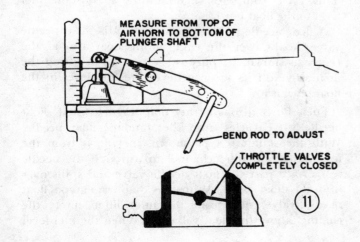

MEASURE FROM TOP OF AIR HORN TO BOTTOM OF PLUNGER SHAFT

BEND ROD TO ADJUST

THROTTLE VALVES COMPLETELY CLOSED

⑪

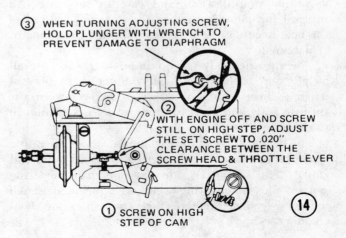

③ WHEN TURNING ADJUSTING SCREW, HOLD PLUNGER WITH WRENCH TO PREVENT DAMAGE TO DIAPHRAGM

② WITH ENGINE OFF AND SCREW STILL ON HIGH STEP, ADJUST THE SET SCREW TO .020" CLEARANCE BETWEEN THE SCREW HEAD & THROTTLE LEVER

① SCREW ON HIGH STEP OF CAM

⑭

ROCHESTER 4M CARBURETOR

This current Rochester carburetor is a four-barrel (Quadrajet) unit with a secondary-side air valve and tapered metering rods for controlling the air-fuel mixture. The carburetor is made in two versions, 4MV and 4MC. The 4MV model has the choke thermostatic unit in a well of the intake manifold, while the 4MC model has the thermostatic unit on the carburetor itself. This carburetor has been used on V-8 engines since 1965.

The Quadrajet carburetor has two stages. The primary (fuel inlet) side has small 1-3/8" bores with a triple venturi set-up equipped with plain-tube nozzles. Operation is similar to most carburetors using the venturi principle. The triple venturi, plus the small primary bores, result in more stable and finer fuel control during idle and part-throttle operation. During part-throttle operation, fuel metering is accomplished with tapered metering rods, positioned by a vacuum-responsive piston, and operating in specially designed jets.

The secondary side has two large (2-1/4") bores. These, added to the primary, give enough air capacity to meet most engine requirements. The air valve is used in the secondary side for metering control and supplements the primary bores to meet air and fuel requirements of the engine.

The secondary air valve mechanically operates tapered metering rods, which move in orifice plates, thereby controlling fuel flow from the secondary nozzles in direct proportion to air flowing through the secondary bores.

The float bowl is centrally located to avoid problems of fuel spillage causing engine turn cutout and delayed fuel flow. The float bowl reservoir is smaller in design than most four-barrel carburetors to reduce fuel evaporation during hot engine shut-down.

The float system has a single pontoon float and fuel valve for simplification and ease in servicing. An integral fuel filter located in the float bowl ahead of the float needle valve is easily removed for cleaning or replacement.

The throttle body is aluminum to reduce overall weight and to improve heat conduction to prevent icing. A heat insulator gasket is used between the throttle body and bowl to prevent fuel percolation in the float bowl.

The primary side of the carburetor has six operating systems: float, idle, main metering, power, pump, and choke. The secondary side has one main metering system, plus accelerating wells on some models. All metering systems receive fuel from the one float chamber.

FLOAT SYSTEM

The Quadrajet carburetor is unique in that it has a centrally located fuel bowl, which is between the primary bores and is adjacent to the secondary bores. This design assures an adequate fuel supply to all carburetor bores, which results in excellent performance with respect to car inclination or severity of turns. The float pontoon is solid and is made of a light plastic material, which gives added buoyancy and allows the use of a single float to maintain a constant fuel level.

There are two types of float needle valves used. One type is diaphragm assisted and the other is the standard needle and brass seat. The diaphragm-assisted float needle is primarily used with a smaller float and on engines with high-pressure fuel pumps. The needle seat is a brass insert and is pressed into the bowl fuel inlet channel below the diaphragm needle tip. The seat is not removable. The needle valve tip is of a material which makes seat wear negligible. Care should be used during servicing so that the seat is not nicked, scored, or moved. The float valve is factory staked and tested and should not be re-staked in the field.

The float system consists of a fuel chamber (float bowl), a single pontoon float, float hinge pin-and-retainer combination, float valve and seat, and a float valve pull clip. A plastic filler block is located in the top of the float chamber over the float valve to prevent fuel slosh into this area.

The float system operates in the following manner: Fuel enters the carburetor fuel inlet passage. It passes through the filter element, fuel inlet valve, and on into the float bowl chamber. As the incoming fuel fills the float bowl to the prescribed level, the float pontoon rises and forces the fuel inlet valve closed, shutting off fuel flow. As fuel is used from the float bowl, the float drops to allow the float needle valve to open, allowing more fuel to enter and fill the bowl. This cycle continues, maintaining a constant fuel level in the float bowl.

A float needle pull clip, fastened to the float needle valve, hooks over the edge of the float arm at the center as shown. Its purpose is to assist in lifting the float valve off its seat whenever the fuel level in the float bowl is low.

Fuel flow through the diaphragm-assisted float needle valve varies from the standard float needle. With the standard type shown, fuel flows from the inlet filter and inlet channel up through the needle seat orifice past the float needle valve and spills over into the float bowl. With the diaphragm-type float needle valve, fuel from the inlet filter enters the channel above the float valve tip. When the fuel level

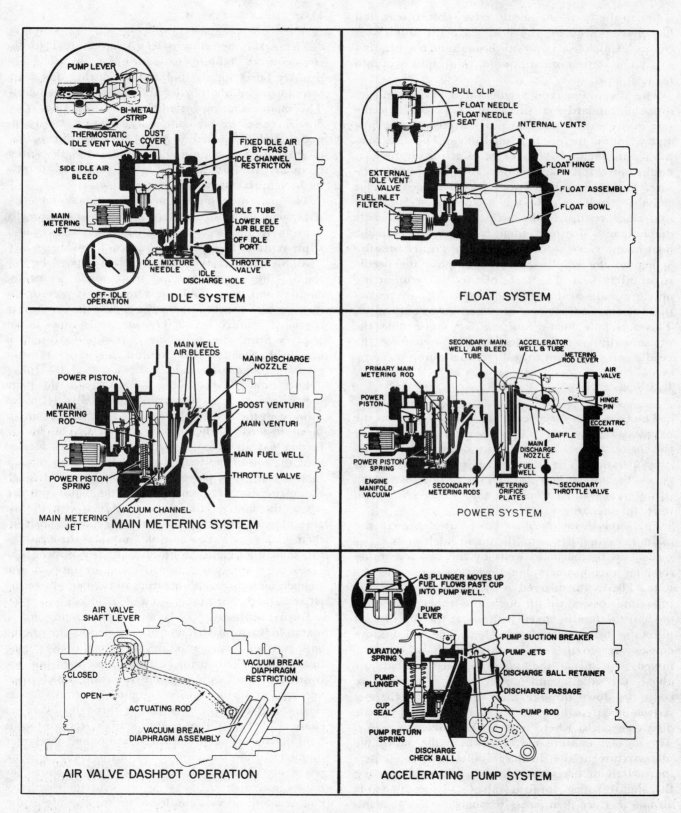

Operating circuits of the Rochester 4M carburetor.

is low in the bowl, the needle valve is off its seat, and fuel flows down past the float valve tip into a fuel channel, which leads upward through the bowl casting to a point above normal liquid level to spill over into the float bowl.

The diaphragm-type needle valve has advantages over the standard float needle in that a larger needle seat orifice can be used to provide greater fuel flow and yet allow the use of a small float. This is accomplished through a balance of forces acting on the float needle valve and diaphragm, against fuel pump pressure. Fuel pressure entering the float needle valve chamber tends to close the needle valve. However, the same pressure is also acting on the float needle diaphragm, which has a slightly larger area than the float needle valve head; therefore, the greater pressure acting on the diaphragm tends to push the needle valve off its seat. The force of the float arm, acting on the needle stem as the float bowl fills, overcomes this pressure difference and closes the needle valve. Therefore, the float's function is to overcome the pressure difference and does not have to force the needle valve closed against direct fuel pump pressure.

Idle System

The Quadrajet carburetor has an idle system on the primary side (fuel inlet side) of the carburetor to supply the correct air-fuel mixture ratios during idle and off-idle operation. The idle system is used during this period because air flow through the carburetor venturi is not great enough to obtain efficient metering from the main discharge nozzles.

Fuel flows from the float bowl down through the main metering jets into the main fuel wells. It is picked up in the main wells by the two idle tubes (one for each primary bore) which extend into the wells. The fuel is metered at the lower tip of the idle tube and passes up through the tubes. On some models, the fuel is mixed with air at the top of each idle tube through an idle air bleed. The fuel mixture crosses over to the idle-down channels, where it is mixed with air at the side idle bleed located just above the idle channel restriction. The mixture continues down through the calibrated idle channel restrictions, past the lower idle air bleeds and off-idle discharge ports, where it is further mixed with air. The air-fuel mixture moves down to the adjustable idle mixture needle discharge holes, where it enters the carburetor bores and blends with the air passing the slightly open throttle valves. The combustible air-fuel mixture then passes through the intake manifold to the engine cylinders.

Main Metering System

The main metering system supplies fuel to the engine from off-idle to wide-open throttle. The primary bores supply fuel and air during this range through plain-tube nozzles and the venturi principle. The main metering system begins to operate as air flow increases through the venturi system, and additional fuel is needed to supply the correct air-fuel mixture to the engine. Fuel from the idle system gradually diminishes as the lower pressures are now in the venturi system.

The main metering system consists of main metering jets, vacuum-operated metering rods, main fuel wells, main well air bleeds, fuel discharge nozzles, and a triple venturi. The system operates as follows.

As the primary throttle valves are opened beyond the off-idle range, allowing more air to enter the engine intake manifold, air velocity increases in the carburetor venturi. This causes a drop in pressure in the large venturi, which increases many times in the boost venturi. Since the low pressure (vacuum) is now in the smallest boost venturi, fuel flows from the main discharge nozzle as follows.

Fuel from the float bowl flows through the main metering jets into the main fuel wells. It passes upward in the main well and is fed with air by an air bleed located at the top of the well. The fuel is further fed air through calibrated air bleeds located near the top of the well in the carburetor bores. The fuel mixture then passes from the main well through the main discharge nozzles into the boost venturi, where the fuel mixture then combines with the air entering the engine through the carburetor bores. It then passes as a combustible mixture through the intake manifold and on into the engine cylinders. The main metering system is calibrated by tapered and stepped metering rods operating in the main metering jet and also through the main well air bleeds.

During cruising speeds and light engine loads, manifold vacuum is high. In this period the engine will run on leaner mixtures than required during heavy loads. The primary main metering rods are connected to a vacuum-responsive piston, which operates against spring tension. Engine manifold vacuum is supplied to the power piston through a vacuum channel. When the vacuum is high, the piston is held downward against spring tension, and the larger diameter of the metering rod is in the main metering jet orifice. This results in leaner fuel mixtures for economical operation. As engine load increases and engine manifold vacuum drops, spring pressure acting on the power piston overcomes the vacuum pull and gradually lifts the metering rods partially out of the main metering jets. This enriches the fuel mixture enough to give the desired power required to overcome the added load.

Emission-controlled carburetors have an adjustable part-throttle feature to maintain a very close tolerance of fuel mixtures during part-throttle operation. This includes a new type power piston and primary main metering rods. The new piston has a pin pressed into its base which protrudes through the float bowl and gasket and contacts an adjustable link in the throttle body. The metering rods are tapered at the upper metering end so that fuel flow through the main metering jets is controlled by the depth of the taper in the main metering jet orifice. During production, the adjustable part-throttle screw is turned in or out to place the taper at the exact point in the jet orifice to obtain the desired air-fuel mixture ratio. Once set, the adjustment screw is capped and no attempt should be made to readjust it in the field.

POWER SYSTEM

The power system provides extra mixture enrichment to meet power requirements under heavy engine loads and high-speed operation. The richer mixtures are supplied through the main metering systems in the primary and secondary sides of the carburetor.

The fuel mixture is enriched in the two primary bores through the power system, which consists of a vacuum-operated power piston and a spring located in a cylinder connected by a passage to intake manifold vacuum. The spring under the power piston pushes the piston upward against manifold vacuum.

During part throttle and cruising ranges, manifold vacuums are sufficient to hold the power piston down against spring tension so that the larger diameter of the metering rod tip is held in the main metering jet orifice. However, as engine load is increased to a point where extra mixture enrichment is required, the power piston spring overcomes the vacuum pull on the power piston, and the tapered tips of the metering rods move upward in the main metering jet orifices. The smaller diameter of the metering rod tip allows more fuel to pass through the main metering jet and enriches the fuel mixture to meet the added power requirements. As engine load decreases, the manifold vacuum rises and extra mixture enrichment is no longer needed. The higher vacuum pulls the power piston down against spring tension, which moves the larger diameter of the metering rod into the metering jet orifice, returning the fuel mixture to normal economy ranges.

The primary side of the carburetor provides adequate air and fuel for low-speed operation. However, at higher speeds, more air and fuel are needed to meet engine demands. The secondary side of the carburetor is used to provide the extra air and fuel.

The secondary section of the Quadrajet has a separate and independent metering system. It consists of two large throttle valves connected by a shaft and linkage to the primary throttle shaft. Fuel metering is controlled by spring-loaded air valves, metering orifice plates, secondary metering rods, main fuel wells with bleed tubes, fuel-discharge nozzles, accelerating wells and tubes. The secondary metering system supplements fuel flow from the primary side and operates as follows.

When the engine reaches a point where the primary bores cannot meet engine air and fuel demands, a lever on the primary throttle shaft, through a connecting link to the secondary throttle shaft, begins to open the secondary throttle valves. As the valves are opened, engine manifold vacuum (low pressure) is applied directly beneath the air valves. Atmospheric pressure on top of the air valves forces them open against spring tension and allows metered air to pass through the secondary bores of the carburetor.

On most models, accelerating wells are used to supply fuel immediately to the secondary bores. This prevents a momentary leanness until fuel begins to feed from the secondary discharge nozzles. When the air valves begin to open, the upper edge of each valve passes the accelerating well ports (one for each bore), which exposes them to manifold vacuum and then immediately feed fuel from the accelerating wells located on each side of the float bowl chamber. The accelerating ports will feed fuel until the fuel in the accelerating well is depleted. Each accelerating well has a calibrated orifice which meters the fuel supplied to the well from the float chamber.

The secondary main discharge nozzles (one for each bore) are located just below the center of the air valves, above the secondary throttle valves. The nozzles being located in a low-pressure area feed fuel as follows. As the secondary throttle valves are opened, atmospheric pressure opens the air valves. This rotates a plastic cam attached to the center of the air-valve shaft, which lifts the secondary metering rods out of the secondary orifice plates through the metering rod lever, which follows rotation of the eccentric cam.

Fuel flows from the float chamber through the secondary metering orifice plates into the secondary main wells where it is mixed with air from the secondary main well tubes. The air-emulsified fuel mixture travels from the main wells through the secondary discharge nozzles, where it sprays into the secondary bores. Here the fuel is mixed with air traveling through the secondary bores to supplement the air-fuel mixture delivered from the primary bores and goes on into the engine as a combustible mixture.

As the throttle valves are opened farther and engine speeds increase, air flow through the secondary side increases and opens the air valve to a greater degree which, in turn, lifts the secondary metering rods farther out of the orifice plates. The metering rods are tapered so that fuel flow through the secondary metering orifice plates is directly proportional to air flow through the secondary carburetor bores. In this manner, correct air-fuel mixtures through the secondary bores are controlled by the depth of the metering rods in the orifice plates.

The depth of the metering rods in the orifice plates in relation to air valve position is factory adjusted to meet air-fuel requirements for each specific engine. A service setting is released should field adjustment become necessary due to parts replacement.

Accelerating System

During acceleration when the throttle is opened rapidly, the air flow and manifold vacuum change almost instantaneously. The fuel, which is heavier, tends to lag behind causing a momentary leanness. The accelerator pump is used to provide the extra fuel necessary for smooth operation during this time.

The accelerating pump system is located in the primary side of the carburetor. It consists of a spring-loaded pump plunger and pump return spring, operating in a fuel well. The pump plunger is operated by a pump lever on the air horn, which is connected directly to the throttle lever by a pump rod.

When the pump plunger moves upward in the pump well, as happens during throttle closing, fuel from the float bowl enters the pump well through a slot in the top of the pump well. It flows past the synthetic pump cup seal into the bottom of the pump well. The pump cup is a floating type which moves up and down on the pump plunger head. When the pump plunger is moved upward, the flat on the top of the cup unseats from the flat on the plunger head and allows free movement of fuel through the inside of the cup into the bottom of the pump well. This also vents any vapors which may be in the bottom of the pump well so that a solid charge of fuel can be maintained in the fuel well beneath the plunger head.

When the primary throttle valves are opened, the connecting linkage forces the pump plunger down-

ward. The pump cup seats instantly, and fuel is forced through the pump discharge passage, where it unseats the pump discharge check ball and passes on through the passage to the pump jets located in the air horn, where it sprays into the venturi area of each primary bore.

It should be noted that the pump plunger is spring-loaded. The upper duration spring is balanced with the bottom pump return spring so that a smooth sustained charge of fuel is delivered during acceleration.

The pump discharge check ball seats in the pump discharge passage during upward motion of the pump plunger so that air cannot be drawn into the passage; otherwise, a momentary acceleration lag could result.

During high-speed operation, a vacuum exists at the pump jets. A cavity just beyond the pump jets is vented to the top of the air horn, outside the carburetor bores. This acts as a suction breaker so that when the pump is not in operation, fuel cannot be pulled out of the pump jets into the venturi area. This insures a full pump stream when needed and prevents any fuel "pull over" from the pump discharge passage.

Choke System

The Quadrajet choke valve is located in the primary side of the carburetor. It provides the correct air-fuel mixture enrichment for quick cold-engine starting and during the warm-up period. The air valve is locked closed until the engine is thoroughly warm and the choke valve is wide open.

The choke system consists of a choke valve located in the primary air horn bore, vacuum diaphragm unit, fast-idle cam, connecting linkage, air valve or secondary throttle valve lockout lever, and thermostatic coil that is connected by a rod to the intermediate choke shaft and lever assembly. Choke operation is controlled by the combination of intake manifold vacuum, the off-set choke valve, temperature, and throttle position.

During engine cranking, the choke valve is held closed by the tension of the thermostatic coil. This restricts air flow through the carburetor to provide a richer starting mixture. Some models use a cranking-enrichment system. Two fuel feed holes located just beneath the choke valve supply add fuel for cold enrichment during the cranking period. The extra fuel is supplied through channels which lead to the secondary well bleed tubes and allow fuel to be drawn from the secondary main wells.

When the engine starts, manifold vacuum applied to the vacuum diaphragm unit opens the choke valve to a point where the engine runs without loading or stalling. Also at this point, the cold-enrichment feed holes are no longer in a low-pressure area so they cease to feed fuel. From this point on they will be used as secondary main well air bleeds. At the same time, the fast-idle cam follower lever on the end of the primary throttle shaft drops from the highest step on the fast-idle cam to a lower step when the throttle is opened. This gives the engine sufficient fast idle and a correct fuel mixture for running until the engine begins to warm up and heat the thermostatic coil, which relaxes its tension and allows the choke valve to open farther because of intake air pushing on the off-set choke valve. Choke valve opening continues until the thermostatic coil is completely relaxed, at which point the choke valve is wide open.

OVERHAULING A ROCHESTER 4MV CARBURETOR

DISASSEMBLING

① Place the carburetor on a holding fixture. Remove the idle vent valve attaching screw, and then take out the idle vent valve assembly. Remove the clips from the upper end of the choke rod, disconnect the choke rod from the upper choke shaft lever, and then remove the choke rod from the bowl. Detach the spring clip from the upper end of the pump rod, and then disconnect the pump rod from the pump lever. Remove the nine air horn-to-bowl attaching screws. *NOTE: Two attaching screws are located next to the*

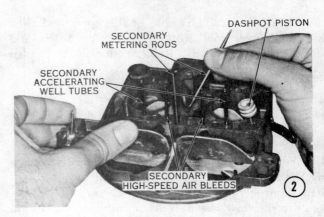

IDLE VENT VALVE   CHOKE ROD   AIR HORN

PUMP ROD   ①

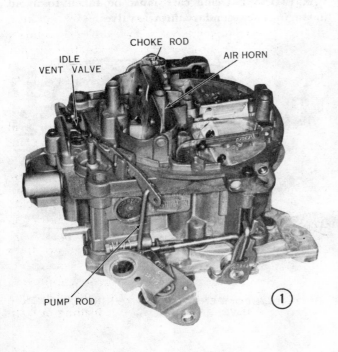

DASHPOT PISTON
SECONDARY METERING RODS
SECONDARY ACCELERATING WELL TUBES
SECONDARY HIGH-SPEED AIR BLEEDS   ②

primary venturi. Remove the air horn by lifting it straight up. **CAUTION: Care must be taken not to bend the accelerating well and air bleed tubes protruding from the air horn.**

② Remove the secondary metering rods by holding the air valve wide open and then tilting and sliding the rods from the holes in the hanger. Remove the dashpot piston from the air-valve link by rotating the bend through the hole, and then remove the dashpot from the air horn by rotating the bend through the air horn. *NOTE: Further disassembly of the air horn is not required.* **CAUTION: The air valves, air valve shaft, and secondary metering rod hangers are calibrated and must not be removed. CAUTION: The secondary high-speed air bleeds and accelerating well tubes are pressed in and must not be removed.**

③ Remove the accelerating pump piston from the pump well. Release the air-horn gasket from the

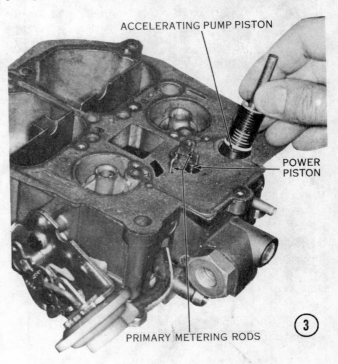

ACCELERATING PUMP PISTON
POWER PISTON
PRIMARY METERING RODS   ③

dowels on the secondary side of the bowl, and then pry the gasket from around the power piston and primary metering rods. Remove the pump return spring from the pump well.

④ Take out the plastic filler over the float valve. Remove the power piston and primary metering rods, using needle-nosed pliers to pull straight up on the metering rod hanger directly over the power piston. Remove the power piston spring from the well. Remove the metering rods from the power piston by disconnecting the tension spring from the top of each rod and then rotating the rod to remove it from the hanger. Remove the float assembly by pulling up slightly on the hinge pin until the pin can be removed by sliding it toward the pump well. After the pin is removed, slide the float assembly toward the front of the bowl to disengage the needle valve pull clip. **CAUTION: Be careful not to distort the pull clip.**

⑤ Remove the two screws from the float needle retainer, and then lift out the retainer and needle assembly. **CAUTION: The needle seat is factory staked and tested. Do not attempt to remove or restake it. If damaged, replace the float bowl assembly.** Remove both primary metering rod jets. Remove the

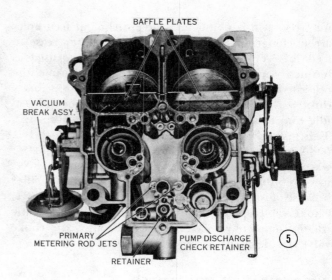

pump discharge check ball retainer and the check ball. Remove the baffle plates from the secondary side of the bowl. Disconnect the vacuum hose from the vacuum-break assembly and from the tube connection on the bowl. Remove the retaining screw, and then lift the assembly from the float bowl.

⑥ Remove the two screws from the hot-idle compensator cover, and then lift the hot-idle compensator and O-ring from the float bowl. Remove the fuel inlet filter retaining nut, gasket, filter, and spring. Remove the throttle body by taking out the throttle body-to-bowl attaching screws, and then lift off the insulator gasket. Remove the idle mixture screws and springs. **CAUTION: Extreme care must be taken to avoid damaging the secondary throttle valves.**

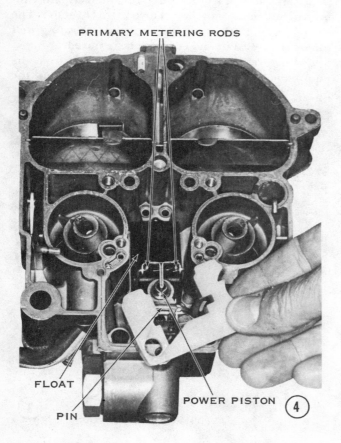

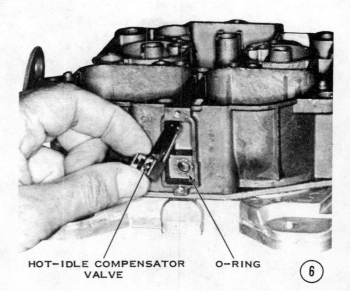

CLEANING AND INSPECTING

Thoroughly clean the carburetor castings and metal parts in an approved carburetor cleaner. **CAUTION: Rubber and plastic parts, diaphragms, pump plungers, and the vacuum-break assembly must not be immersed in carburetor cleaner.** Blow out all passages with compressed air. **CAUTION: Don't pass drills through jets or passages or you will destroy the calibration of the carburetor.**

Inspect the idle mixture needles for damage. Examine the float needle and diaphragm for wear. Inspect the upper and lower surfaces of the carburetor castings for damage. Inspect the holes in the levers for excessive wear or an out-of-round condition. Examine the fast-idle cam for wear or damage. Check the air valve for binding. If the air valve is damaged, the entire air horn assembly must be replaced. Check all throttle levers and valves for binding or damage.

Always use a complete kit of parts when overhauling these carburetors as it contains all of the needed and updated parts, as well as a complete set of gaskets. It also includes the latest specifications, which are needed for making the bench adjustments.

ASSEMBLING

⑦ Turn in the idle mixture adjusting screws until seated, and then back them out two turns for a preliminary adjustment. Install the pump rod in the lower hole of the throttle lever by rotating the rod. Position a new insulator gasket on the bowl, making certain that the gasket is properly located over the

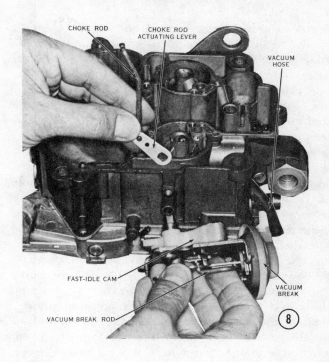

⑧

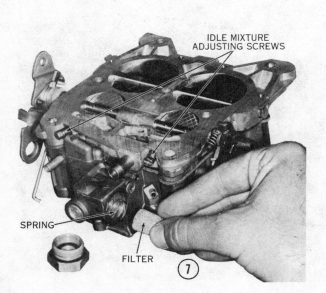

⑦

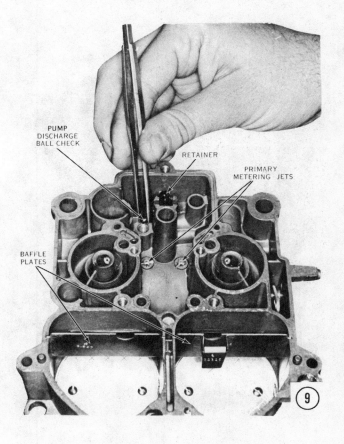

⑨

two dowels. Install the throttle body, making certain that it is properly located over the dowels on the float bowl. Install the throttle body-to-bowl screws; tighten them evenly and securely. Install the fuel inlet filter spring, filter, new gasket, and the inlet nut. Tighten the nut securely. Place a new hot-idle compensator O-ring seal in the recess in the bowl, and then install the hot-idle compensator.

⑧ Install the vacuum-break rod (U-bend end) in the diaphragm link, with the end toward the bracket, and then slide the grooved end of the rod into the hole of the actuating lever. Retain it to the vacuum-break lever with the spring clip. Install the fast-idle cam on the vacuum break or choke housing assembly. Be sure that the fast-idle cam actuating pin on the intermediate choke shaft is located in the cut-out area of the fast-idle cam. Connect the choke rod to the choke rod actuating lever (plain end) and then, holding the choke rod with the grooved end pointing inward, position the choke rod actuating lever in the well of the float bowl. Then install the choke assembly, engaging the shaft with the hole in the actuating lever. Install the retaining screw, and then tighten it securely. Remove the choke rod from the lever for later installation. Install and connect the vacuum hose.

⑨ Install the baffle plates in the secondary side

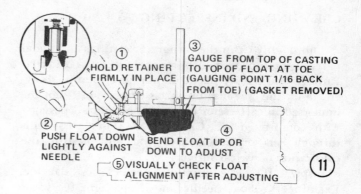

① HOLD RETAINER FIRMLY IN PLACE

② PUSH FLOAT DOWN LIGHTLY AGAINST NEEDLE

③ GAUGE FROM TOP OF CASTING TO TOP OF FLOAT AT TOE (GAUGING POINT 1/16 BACK FROM TOE) (GASKET REMOVED)

④ BEND FLOAT UP OR DOWN TO ADJUST

⑤ VISUALLY CHECK FLOAT ALIGNMENT AFTER ADJUSTING

⑪

of the bowl, with the notches facing up. Install the primary main metering jets. Install a new float needle and diaphragm assembly. Make certain that the diaphragm is properly positioned, and then install the retainer and two screws, tightening them securely. Install the pump discharge ball check and retainer in the passage next to the pump well.

⑩ Use needle-nosed pliers to install the pull clip on the needle. *NOTE: The pull clip is properly positioned with the open end toward the front of the bowl.* Install the float by sliding the float lever under the pull clip, from the front to the back. With the float lever in the pull clip, hold the float assembly by the toe, and then install the retaining pin from the pump-well side. **CAUTION: Be careful not to distort the pull clip.**

⑪ *To adjust the float level,* measure from the top of the float bowl gasket surface (with the gasket re-

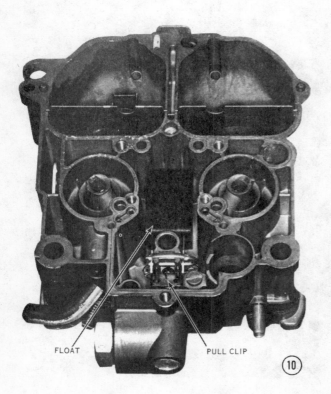

FLOAT   PULL CLIP   ⑩

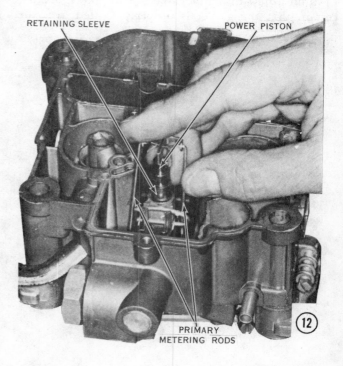

RETAINING SLEEVE   POWER PISTON

PRIMARY METERING RODS   ⑫

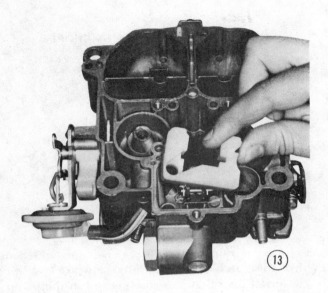

moved) to the top of the float at the toe end. **CAUTION: Make sure the retaining pin is held firmly in place and that the tang of the float is seated on the float needle.** Bend the float up or down to adjust.

⑫ Install the power piston spring in the power-piston well. If the primary main metering rods were removed from the hanger, reinstall them, making sure that the tension spring is connected to the top of each metering rod. Install the power-piston assembly in the well, with the metering rods properly located in the metering jets. Press down on the power piston to insure engagement of the retaining pin with the hole in the throttle body gasket on early models. A sleeve around the piston holds the later model pistons in place during assembly.

⑬ Install the plastic filler over the float needle, pressing down firmly until seated.

⑭ Position the pump return spring in the pump well. Install the air-horn gasket around the primary metering rods and piston. Position the gasket over the two dowels on the secondary side of the bowl. Install the accelerating pump plunger in the pump well.

⑮ Install the secondary metering rods. With the air valve held wide open, the rods should be positioned with their upper ends through the hanger holes and pointing toward each other.

⑯ Place the air-horn assembly on the bowl, carefully locating the secondary metering rods, high-speed

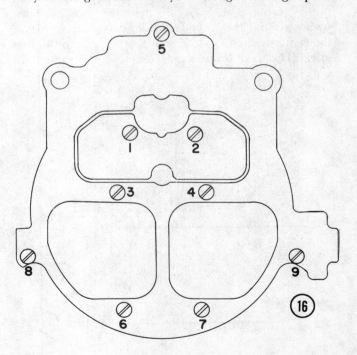

PUMP LEVER

⑰

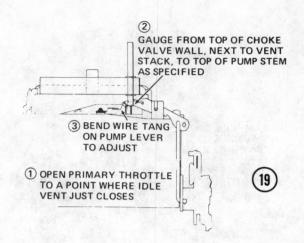

② GAUGE FROM TOP OF CHOKE VALVE WALL, NEXT TO VENT STACK, TO TOP OF PUMP STEM AS SPECIFIED

③ BEND WIRE TANG ON PUMP LEVER TO ADJUST

① OPEN PRIMARY THROTTLE TO A POINT WHERE IDLE VENT JUST CLOSES

⑲

air bleeds, and accelerating well tubes through the holes of the air-horn gasket. Make sure that the dash-pot and pump plunger are positioned properly through the holes in the air horn. **CAUTION: Do not force the air-horn assembly onto the float bowl as distortion of the secondary metering plates will result.** A slight sideward movement will center the metering rods in the metering plates. Install the four long air-horn screws around the secondary side, two short screws in the center section, and one short screw above the fuel inlet. The two counter-sunk screws are installed in

the primary venturi area. All screws must be tightened evenly and securely in the illustrated sequence.

⑰ Install the idle vent actuating rod in the pump lever. Connect the pump rod in the inner hole of the pump lever and retain it with a spring clip. Connect the choke rod in the lower choke lever and retain it with a spring clip. Install the idle vent valve, engaging the actuating rod, and then tighten the attaching screw.

BENCH ADJUSTMENTS

The following bench adjustments must be made in the order below. Use the specifications included in the repair kit for making the adjustments.

⑱ *To make the pump rod adjustment,* measure from the top of the choke valve wall, next to the vent stack, to the top of the pump stem, with the throttle valves completely closed and the pump rod in the inner hole of the pump lever. Bend the pump lever to adjust.

⑲ *To make the idle vent adjustment,* open the

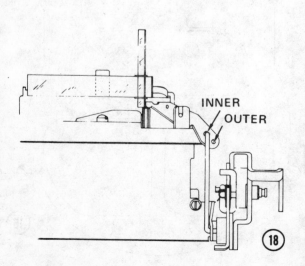

INNER
OUTER

⑱

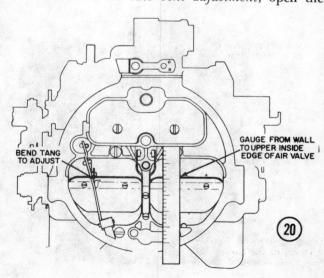

BEND TANG TO ADJUST

GAUGE FROM WALL TO UPPER INSIDE EDGE OF AIR VALVE

⑳

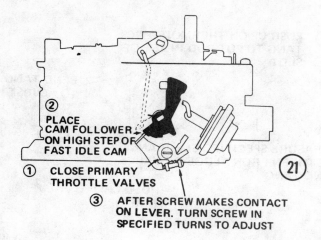

② PLACE CAM FOLLOWER ON HIGH STEP OF FAST IDLE CAM

① CLOSE PRIMARY THROTTLE VALVES

③ AFTER SCREW MAKES CONTACT ON LEVER. TURN SCREW IN SPECIFIED TURNS TO ADJUST

㉑

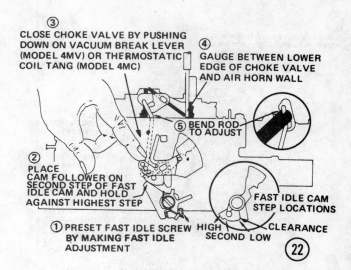

③ CLOSE CHOKE VALVE BY PUSHING DOWN ON VACUUM BREAK LEVER (MODEL 4MV) OR THERMOSTATIC COIL TANG (MODEL 4MC)

④ GAUGE BETWEEN LOWER EDGE OF CHOKE VALVE AND AIR HORN WALL

⑤ BEND ROD TO ADJUST

② PLACE CAM FOLLOWER ON SECOND STEP OF FAST IDLE CAM AND HOLD AGAINST HIGHEST STEP

① PRESET FAST IDLE SCREW BY MAKING FAST IDLE ADJUSTMENT

FAST IDLE CAM STEP LOCATIONS

HIGH SECOND LOW CLEARANCE

㉒

primary throttle to a point where the idle vent just closes. Measure the distance from the top of the choke valve wall, next to the vent stack, to the top of the pump plunger stem. Bend the wire tang on the pump lever to adjust.

⑳ *To make the air valve adjustment on early models,* measure the distance between the upper inside edge of the air valve and the back of the choke valve wall, at the torsion spring end. Bend the stop tang

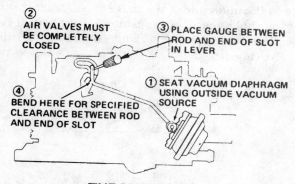

② AIR VALVES MUST BE COMPLETELY CLOSED

③ PLACE GAUGE BETWEEN ROD AND END OF SLOT IN LEVER

① SEAT VACUUM DIAPHRAGM USING OUTSIDE VACUUM SOURCE

④ BEND HERE FOR SPECIFIED CLEARANCE BETWEEN ROD AND END OF SLOT

THROUGH 1971

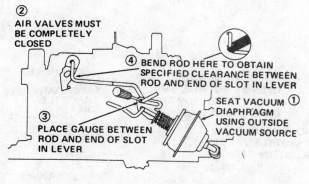

② AIR VALVES MUST BE COMPLETELY CLOSED

④ BEND ROD HERE TO OBTAIN SPECIFIED CLEARANCE BETWEEN ROD AND END OF SLOT IN LEVER

① SEAT VACUUM DIAPHRAGM USING OUTSIDE VACUUM SOURCE

③ PLACE GAUGE BETWEEN ROD AND END OF SLOT IN LEVER

SINCE 1972

On later models, the air-valve dashpot is adjusted by inserting a gauge in the slot in the choke lever or dashpot lever depending on the model.

on the dashpot lever to adjust. See the accompanying illustrations for making this adjustment on later models.

㉑ *To make the fast-idle adjustment,* turn the fast-idle screw in 3 turns after the screw makes contact with the lever, with the primary throttle valves completely closed and the cam follower over the high step of the fast-idle cam.

㉒ *To make the choke rod adjustment,* rotate the choke valve toward the closed position by pushing down on the vacuum-break lever. With the cam follower on the second step of the fast-idle cam, and against the high step, the dimension between the lower edge of the choke valve and the air horn wall should be as specified. Bend the choke rod to adjust.

㉓ *To make the vacuum-break adjustment on models through 1971,* hold the choke valve in the closed position using a rubber band on the vacuum-break lever. Hold the vacuum-break diaphragm stem against its seat so that the vacuum link is at the end of the slot. The dimension between the lower edge of

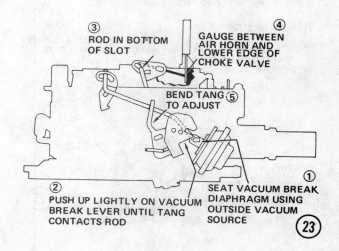

③ ROD IN BOTTOM OF SLOT

④ GAUGE BETWEEN AIR HORN AND LOWER EDGE OF CHOKE VALVE

⑤ BEND TANG TO ADJUST

② PUSH UP LIGHTLY ON VACUUM BREAK LEVER UNTIL TANG CONTACTS ROD

① SEAT VACUUM BREAK DIAPHRAGM USING OUTSIDE VACUUM SOURCE

㉓

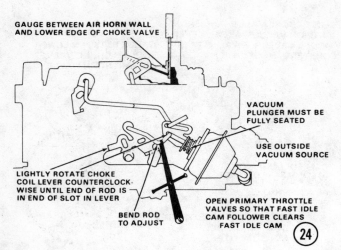

GAUGE BETWEEN AIR HORN WALL AND LOWER EDGE OF CHOKE VALVE

VACUUM PLUNGER MUST BE FULLY SEATED

USE OUTSIDE VACUUM SOURCE

LIGHTLY ROTATE CHOKE COIL LEVER COUNTERCLOCKWISE UNTIL END OF ROD IS IN END OF SLOT IN LEVER

BEND ROD TO ADJUST

OPEN PRIMARY THROTTLE VALVES SO THAT FAST IDLE CAM FOLLOWER CLEARS FAST IDLE CAM

24

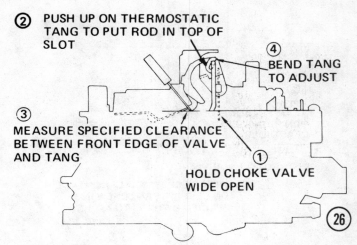

② PUSH UP ON THERMOSTATIC TANG TO PUT ROD IN TOP OF SLOT

④ BEND TANG TO ADJUST

③ MEASURE SPECIFIED CLEARANCE BETWEEN FRONT EDGE OF VALVE AND TANG

① HOLD CHOKE VALVE WIDE OPEN

26

the choke valve and the air horn at the choke lever end should be as specified. Bend the vacuum link or tang to adjust.

㉔ *To make the vacuum-break adjustment on models since 1972 (with a bucking spring)*, seat the vacuum-break diaphragm with an auxiliary vacuum source. Open the throttle slightly so that the cam follower clears the steps of the fast-idle cam, and then rotate the vacuum-break lever counterclockwise (toward a closed-choke position). Use a rubber band to hold it in place. The end of the vacuum-break rod must also be in the outer end of the slot in the vacuum-break diaphragm plunger. Measure the distance between the lower edge of the choke valve and the inside of the air horn. Bend the link where shown to make the adjustment.

㉕ *To make the unloader adjustment*, hold the choke valve in the closed position with a rubber band on the vacuum-break lever, and then open the primary throttle to the wide-open position. The dimension between the lower edge of the choke valve and the air horn wall should be as specified. Bend the tang on the fast-idle lever to adjust.

㉖ *To make the air-valve lockout adjustment*, apply sufficient force to the thermostatic spring tang to move the choke rod to the top of the slot in the choke lever with the choke valve wide open. Move the air valve toward the open position. Bend the upper end of the air valve lockout lever tang to provide the specified opening between the lockout tang and the front edge of the air valve as shown. Now, open the choke valve to its wide-open position by applying force to the underside of the choke valve. Making sure that the choke rod is in the bottom of the slot in the choke lever, the air valve lockout tang must hold the air valve closed.

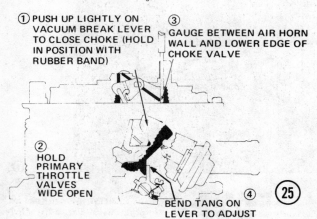

① PUSH UP LIGHTLY ON VACUUM BREAK LEVER TO CLOSE CHOKE (HOLD IN POSITION WITH RUBBER BAND)

③ GAUGE BETWEEN AIR HORN WALL AND LOWER EDGE OF CHOKE VALVE

② HOLD PRIMARY THROTTLE VALVES WIDE OPEN

④ BEND TANG ON LEVER TO ADJUST

25

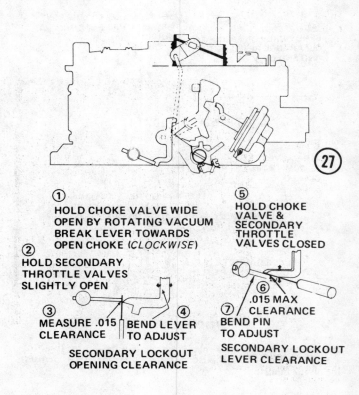

27

① HOLD CHOKE VALVE WIDE OPEN BY ROTATING VACUUM BREAK LEVER TOWARDS OPEN CHOKE (*CLOCKWISE*)

② HOLD SECONDARY THROTTLE VALVES SLIGHTLY OPEN

③ MEASURE .015 CLEARANCE

④ BEND LEVER TO ADJUST

SECONDARY LOCKOUT OPENING CLEARANCE

⑤ HOLD CHOKE VALVE & SECONDARY THROTTLE VALVES CLOSED

⑥ .015 MAX CLEARANCE

⑦ BEND PIN TO ADJUST

SECONDARY LOCKOUT LEVER CLEARANCE

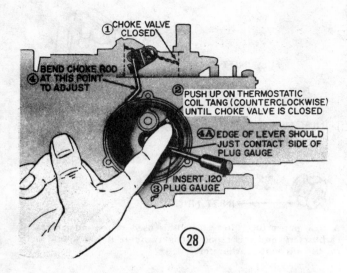

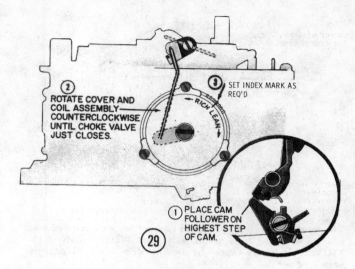

27 *To make the secondary lockout clearance adjustment,* hold the choke valve and both primary and secondary throttle valves fully closed. The lockout lever should not contact the lockout pin, but the clearance must not exceed 0.015″ as shown in the left-hand insert. Bend the lockout pin to adjust. Hold the choke valve and primary throttle valves in the wide-open position and the secondary throttle valves fully closed. The lockout pin should have a minimum of 75% contact on the lockout lever, as shown in the right-hand insert. To adjust, bend the lockout lever.

28 *To make the choke coil lever adjustment,* hold the choke valve closed. Push up on the thermostatic coil tang (counterclockwise) until the choke valve is completely closed. Insert a gauge at the point shown,

and the edge of the lever should just contact the side of the gauge. If an adjustment is required, bend the choke rod where shown.

29 *To make the choke coil adjustment,* position the cam follower on the highest step of the fast-idle cam. Loosen the three cover retaining screws, and then turn the cover counterclockwise until the choke valve just closes (engine at room temperature). Set the index mark as required.

4MV CARBURETOR SERVICE NOTES

SECOND DESIGN QUADRAJET CARBURETOR

A second version of this carburetor has been released for some engines during the 1967 model year; it is

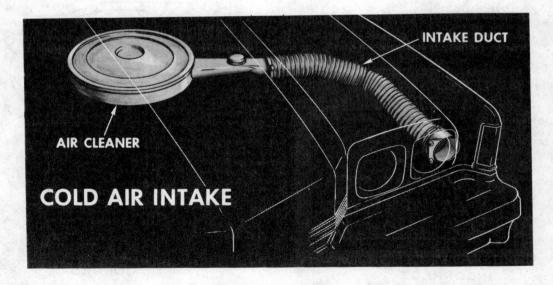

A cold-air induction system is used on many late-model engines to increase volumetric efficiency. The flexible duct brings cold air to the induction system, and this is heavier than the heated underhood air, thus packing more oxygen into the engine for more efficient combustion.

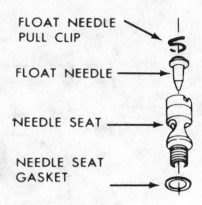

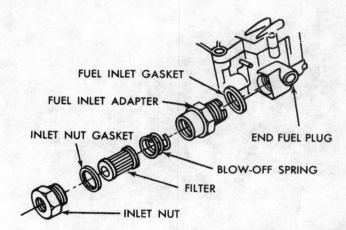

The second-generation Quadrajet carburetors are equipped with this conventional type needle valve and seat assembly. CAUTION: This needle cannot be used in place of the diaphragm-assist type needle.

A new paper fuel filter element is used on second-generation carburetors, and this repair kit is available if you should strip the threads on the carburetor.

serviced in the same manner as the previous model, with the following exceptions.

FUEL INLET NEEDLE

All second design carburetors use a conventional float needle valve and seat assembly to replace the diaphragm-assist type used on the first model. **CAUTION: The conventional needle cannot be used in place of the diaphragm-assist type.**

FLOAT ASSEMBLY

A new Nitrophyl float is used in the second design carburetor.

FUEL FILTER

A new paper fuel filter replaces the sintered bronze filter element. The paper filter should be replaced every 12,000 miles. **CAUTION: No attempt should be made to clean this type of filter element.**

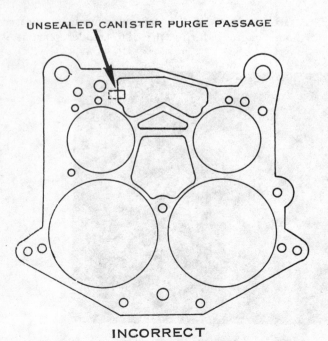

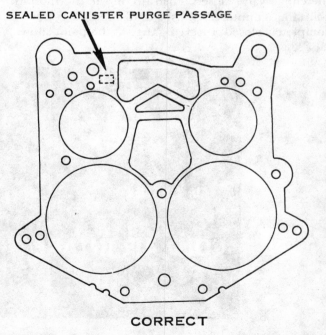

Since 1970, there has been a change in gaskets used between the float bowl and throttle body due to the addition of a charcoal canister purge port. When the wrong gasket is used on models since 1970, a vacuum leak occurs due to air by-passing the primary throttle valves through the canister purge passageway (left) and the engine idles roughly.

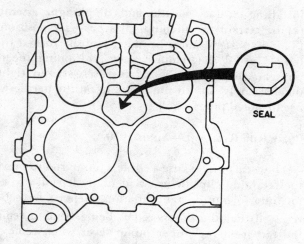

Some cases of fuel leakage past the secondary main well plugs have been reported on early model Quadrajet carburetors. If leakage does occur, it fills the secondary well cavity in the throttle body with fuel, which then seeps through the throttle body-to-bowl gasket and results in rough idling or hard starting when hot. This special Viton seal is available for service, and it should be installed in the bottom of the secondary well cavity in the throttle body, as shown.

THROTTLE VALVE SHAFTS AND LEVERS

The second design Quadrajet carburetors that are used on the larger engines have primary throttle valves that open faster than those in the first design units. The faster action results from a modification of the throttle lever-to-accelerator control rod attachment. Also, a longer accelerator control rod is used, and the bushing previously required in the throttle lever has been eliminated. In addition, the primary throttle shaft is coated with green-tinted teflon so as to retain the same pedal effort for the new accelerator control linkage.

The secondary throttle shaft is coated with teflon

to insure smooth operation. The secondary throttle opening and closing adjustment is the only service that is affected by the second design carburetor. This adjustment has been revised for both the first and second design carburetors. The procedures follow.

Secondary Opening Adjustment

In the first design carburetor, open the primary throttle valves until the actuating link contacts the extended tang on the secondary throttle lever. The bottom of the actuating link should be in the center of the secondary lever slot. If an adjustment is necessary, bend the extended tang on the secondary throttle lever as required.

In the second design carburetor, open the primary throttle valves until the secondary throttle actuating link just contacts the extended tang on the secondary throttle lever. While the throttle valves are in this position, the bottom of the secondary actuating link should be in the center of the secondary lever slot, and there should be 0.070″ clearance between the actuating link and the short tab on the secondary lever, as shown in the inset. If an adjustment is necessary, bend the extended tang on the secondary lever as required.

Secondary Closing Adjustment

In both designs of the carburetor, adjust the idle speed to obtain the recommended rpm. Be sure the fast-idle cam follower is not resting on the fast-idle cam. There should be 0.020″ clearance between the actuating link and the front of the slot in the secondary throttle lever, when the tang of the actuating lever on the primary shaft is against its mating tang on the primary actuating lever as shown. If an adjustment is necessary, bend the tang on the primary actuating lever as required.

Secondary throttle opening adjustments on the first and second design Quadrajet carburetors, as discussed in the text.

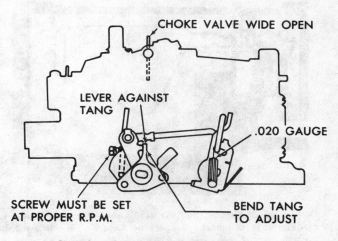

Secondary throttle closing adjustment.

Float Needle Pull Clip Installation

Reports have been received of incorrect installation of the float needle pull clip on the float arm during field replacement. If the clip is not installed as recommended, carburetor flooding can result. It is reported that the end of the pull clip is being installed through the holes in the top of the float arm above the needle. These are locating holes used for manufacture of the float arm and are not to be used for the pull clip.

Correct installation of the float needle pull clip is to hook the clip over the edge of the flat on the float arm facing the float pontoon, as shown. The only exception is when using the float needle modification kit, Part Number 7036775. This needle pull clip hooks over the opposite edge of the float arm, as shown on the instruction sheet in the kit.

Needle Valve and Diaphragm Installation

Investigation of some 1965, 1966, and early 1967 4MV carburetors returned from the field with complaints of flooding, hesitation, and/or surge, after having been overhauled and a new needle and diaphragm installed, revealed two causes of the problem. As can be seen, both result from improper installation. The diaphragm is not positioned properly on the needle, or the technician is trying to install the needle, diaphragm, and retainer at the same time.

The following sequence must be followed when installing a float needle and diaphragm assembly. (a) Be certain the diaphragm is properly positioned. (The diaphragm outer lip must be fully tucked in its bore.) Install the retainer after positioning the diaphragm. (b) Install the retainer screws and tighten them securely. Install the pull clip on the needle with needle-nosed pliers.

Pump Rod Removal—Since 1970

These carburetors use a clipless pump rod to prevent the retaining clips being accidentally left off or being lost due to improper installation. Reports have been received that the pump rod is being bent to remove the rod from the upper pump lever when removing the air horn from the float bowl. This is bad practice as the pump rod will be weakened and also may cause a bind due to its not being aligned properly after bending.

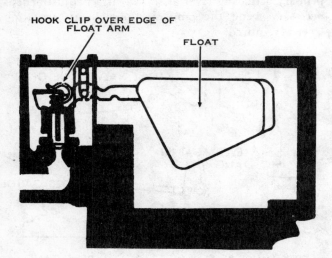

Correct installation of the float needle pull clip in a Quadrajet carburetor is important to prevent flooding, as discussed in the text.

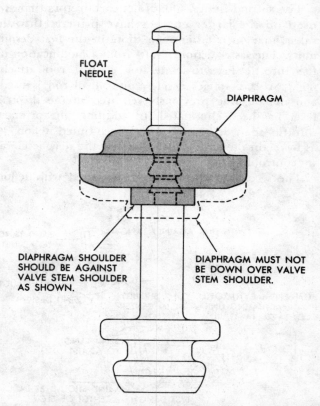

Proper installation of the needle diaphragm is important to prevent flooding in 1965-67 Quadrajet carburetors, as discussed in the text.

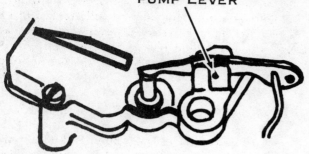

DRIVE PIN INWARD TO REMOVE PUMP LEVER

Correct removal of the clipless-type pump rod should be done by driving the small roll pin inward, as shown. **CAUTION: Don't bend the rod to remove it or you will cause it to bind after assembly.**

Correct removal of the pump rod should be done by driving the small roll pin retaining the upper pump lever inward (towards the air cleaner boss) until the lever can be removed from the boss on the air horn. Then remove the upper pump lever, pump rod, and air horn.

To install the pump rod after air horn installation, install the rod to the throttle lever and the upper end of the rod to the upper pump lever. Then insert the upper lever into the boss on the air horn and push the roll pin back through the hole in the pump lever until the outer end of the pin is flush with the boss on the air horn, as shown.

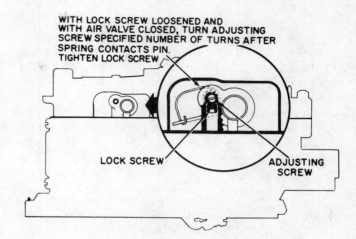

WITH LOCK SCREW LOOSENED AND WITH AIR VALVE CLOSED, TURN ADJUSTING SCREW SPECIFIED NUMBER OF TURNS AFTER SPRING CONTACTS PIN. TIGHTEN LOCK SCREW.

LOCK SCREW

ADJUSTING SCREW

To adjust the air-valve spring, loosen the Allen-headed lock-screw, and then turn the adjusting screw counterclockwise to remove all spring tension. With the air valve closed, turn the adjusting screw clockwise the specified part of a turn, as indicated on the accompanying chart, after the torsion spring contacts the pin on the shaft. Holding the adjusting screw in this position, tighten the lockscrew.

AIR VALVE WINDUP PROCEDURE

Loosen the lockscrew and close the air valve. Turn the adjusting screw the number of turns specified below after the spring contacts the pin. Tighten the lockscrew.

AIR VALVE SPRING WINDUP SPECIFICATIONS

Year	Carburetor Number	Turns
1966	7026250, 7026256, 7036250	3/4
1966	7026254, 7036254	1/2
1966	7026255	5/8
1967	7027156, 7027157	3/4
1967	7027153, 7027135, 7027036	1/2
1968	7028250	1/2
1968	7028251, 7028252, 7028255	3/4
1969	7029250	1/2
1969	7029251, 7029252, 7029253, 7029254, 7029255	3/4
1970	7040251, 704252, 7040253, 7040255, 7040256, 7040257	3/4
1970	7040258, 7040551, 7040552, 7040554, 7040555	3/4
1970	7040250, 7040550	1/2
1971	7041251, 7041252, 7041253, 7041257	3/4
1971	7041250	1/2
1972	7042251, 7042252, 7042951, 7042952, 7042953	3/4
1972	7042250, 7042950	1/2
1973-74	7043250, 7043255, 7043256, 7043257	1/2
1973-74	7043251, 7043252, 7043253, 7043254, 7043258, 7043259	3/4
1974	7044557, 7044558, 7044559	3/4

5 | engine service

All engines used in General Motors passenger cars operate on the four-stroke cycle principle. During this cycle, the piston travels the length of its stroke four times. As the piston travels up or down, the crankshaft is rotated halfway (180 degrees). To accomplish one cycle, the crankshaft rotates two complete turns; the camshaft, which controls the valves, is driven by the crankshaft at half crankshaft speed. Valve action, intake and exhaust, occurs once in each four-stroke cycle, and the piston acts as an air pump during the two remaining strokes.

INTAKE STROKE

The intake valve is opened as the piston moves down the cylinder, and this creates an area of pressure lower than that of the surrounding atmosphere. Atmospheric pressure will cause air to flow into this low-pressure area. By directing the air flow through the carburetor, a measured amount of vaporized fuel is added. When the piston reaches the bottom of the intake stroke, the cylinder is filled with air and vaporized fuel. The exhaust valve is closed during the intake stroke.

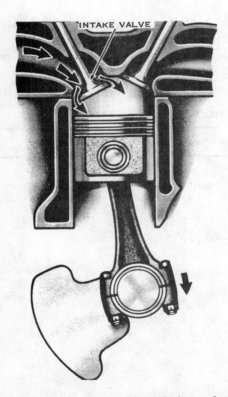

On the intake stroke of a four-stroke cycle internal-combustion engine, the piston moves down while the intake valve is open to draw in a combustible air-fuel mixture.

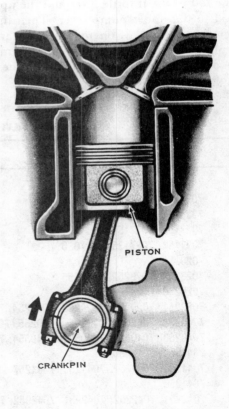

On the compression stroke, both valves are closed as the piston moves up to compress the air-fuel mixture.

140

COMPRESSION STROKE

When the piston starts to move upward, the compression stroke begins. The intake valve closes, trapping the air-fuel mixture in the cylinder. The upward movement of the piston compresses the mixture to a fraction of its original volume; exact pressure depends principally on the compression ratio of the engine.

POWER STROKE

The power stroke is produced by igniting the compressed air-fuel mixture. When the spark plug arcs, the mixture ignites and burns very rapidly during the power stroke. The resulting high temperature expands the gases, creating very high pressure on top of the piston, which drives the piston down. This downward motion of the piston is transmitted through the connecting rod and is converted into rotary motion by the crankshaft. Both the intake and exhaust valves are closed during the power stroke.

EXHAUST STROKE

The exhaust valve opens just before the piston completes the power stroke. Pressure in the cylinder at this time causes the exhaust gas to rush into the exhaust manifold (blowdown). The upward movement of the piston on its exhaust stroke expels most of the remaining exhaust gas.

As the piston pauses momentarily at the top of the exhaust stroke, the inertia of the exhausting gas tends to remove any remaining gas in the combustion chamber; however, a small amount always remains to dilute the incoming mixture. This unexpelled gas is captured in the clearance area between the piston and the cylinder head.

COMBUSTION

The power delivered from the piston to the crankshaft is the result of a pressure increase in the gas mixture above the piston. This pressure increase occurs

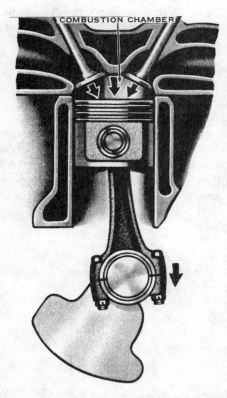

On the power stroke, the tightly compressed combustible mixture is ignited by the spark plug and the resulting burning of the fuel pushes the piston down the cylinder.

On the exhaust stroke, the exhaust valve is open, while the piston moves up to force the burned gases from the cylinder.

as the mixture is heated, first by compression, and then (on the down stroke) by burning. The burning fuel supplies heat that raises temperature and, at the same time, raises pressure. Actually, about 75 percent of the mixture in the cylinder is composed of nitrogen gas that does not burn but expands when heated by the burning of the combustible elements, and it is this expanding nitrogen that supplies most of the pressure on the piston.

The fuel and oxygen must burn smoothly within the combustion chamber to take full advantage of this heating effect. Maximum power would not be delivered to the piston if an explosion took place, because the entire force would be spent in one sharp hammer-like blow, occurring too fast for the piston to follow.

Instead, burning takes place evenly as the flame moves across the combustion chamber. Burning must be completed by the time the piston is about half-way down so that maximum pressure will be developed in the cylinder at the time the piston applies its greatest force to the crankshaft. This will be when the mechanical advantage of the connecting rod and crankshaft is at a maximum.

At the beginning of the power stroke (as the piston is driven down by the pressure), the volume above the piston increases, which would normally allow the pressure in the cylinder to drop. However, combustion is still in progress, and this continues to raise the temperature of the gases, expanding them and maintaining a continuous pressure on the piston as it travels downward. This provides a smooth application of power throughout the effective part of the power stroke to make the most efficient use of the energy released by the burning fuel.

VALVE TIMING

On the power stroke, the exhaust valve opens before bottom dead center in order to get the exhaust gases started out of the combustion chamber under the remaining pressure (blowdown). On the exhaust stroke, the intake valve opens before top dead center in order to start the air-fuel mixture moving into the combustion chamber. These processes are functions of camshaft design and valve timing.

Valves always open and close at the same time in the cycle; the timing is not variable with speed and load as is ignition timing. There is, however, one particular speed for each given engine at which the air-fuel mixture will pack itself into the combustion chambers most effectively. This is the speed at which the engine puts out its peak torque. At low engine speeds, compression is somewhat suppressed due to the slight reverse flow of gases through the valves just as they open or close when the mixture is not moving fast enough to take advantage of the time lag. At high speeds, the valve timing does not allow enough time during the valve opening and closing periods for effective packing of the air-fuel mixture into the cylinders.

ENGINE TYPES*

The Oldsmobile Division of General Motors has produced a variety of engines over the years, including an in-line and a V-6 engine. Most, however, were V-8 engines. Engines with strong similarities are grouped into families in this chapter for the purpose of discussing common service procedures. The following heads and the engine sizes that apply to that family are as follows:

V-8 Engines—Through 1964
    324, 371, and 394 CID engines

V-8 Engine—1961-63
    215 CID engine used in the F-85

V-6 Engine—1964-65
    225 CID engine used in the F-85

Six-Cylinder Engine—Since 1966
    250 CID engine

Engine application and identification charts are located in the Appendix.

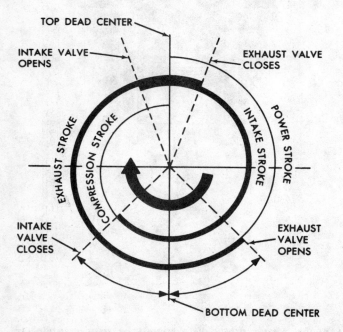

Typical valve timing diagram. Note that this represents two complete turns of the crankshaft (720°).

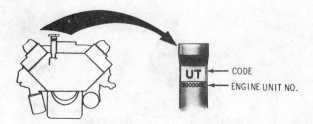

Oldsmobile V-8 engines can be identified by a code tape applied to the oil filler tube.

V-8 Engines—Since 1964

330, 350, 400, 425, and 455 CID engines

SERVICE PROCEDURES

The general service procedures that apply to all Oldsmobile engines will be discussed in the section that follows. This will be followed by the specific service instructions that apply to each of the engine families, in the order discussed above.

GENERAL SERVICE PROCEDURES

The following service procedures are common to all Oldsmobile engines. This section should be referred

Many of the late-model engines have the CID (Cubic Inch Displacement) on the air cleaner as well as being coded on the engine itself. In this case, the engine has a displacement of 400 cubic inches. See the Appendix for more detailed information on how to determine the engine size used in your vehicle.

A dial gauge can be used to determine the amount of taper and out-of-roundness of the cylinder bores.

to before doing any engine work and should be used in conjunction with the specific model instructions that follow these General Service Procedures.

It is necessary to remove the ring ridge before taking the pistons out; otherwise, you will break the piston when a ring jams under the ledge. When measuring the piston ring end gap, it is essential to position the piston ring near the bottom of the cylinder in the unworn area, so that there will be sufficient clearance at all times.

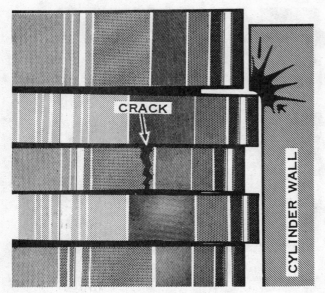

The ring ridge must be removed before the piston is pushed out of the top of the bore; otherwise, the top ring will strike it and break the piston ring land.

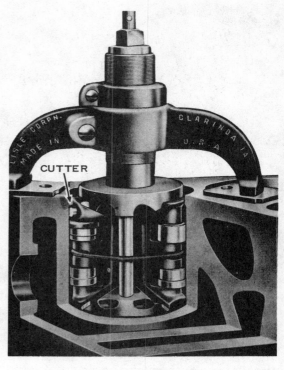

A ridge remover is needed to cut the ridge from the top of the cylinder walls. The stop under the blade keeps you from cutting into the walls too deeply. Don't cut more than 1/32″ below the bottom of the ridge.

CYLINDER BLOCK

The ring ridge must be removed before taking out the pistons; otherwise, the top ring will catch on the ledge and break a piston ring land. Inspect the cylinder walls for wear, scores, and evidence of scuffing. If the

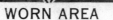

The cylinder walls wear the greatest amount at the top, due to the borderline lubrication conditions that exist. All measurements must be made in the worn area. This cylinder bore has been surfaced with a fine hone to remove the glaze for better piston ring seating.

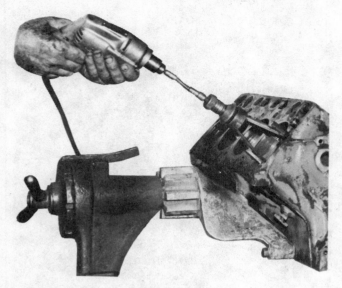

A flexible hone should be used to remove the cylinder wall glaze.

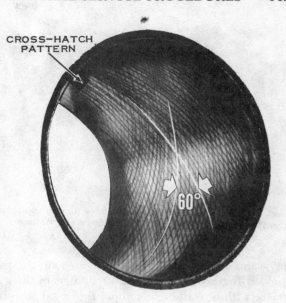

CROSS–HATCH PATTERN

60°

The cylinder walls should be honed to remove the glaze so that the new piston rings will seat quickly. The ideal cross-hatch pattern is 60°.

cylinder walls are worn over 0.012″, it will be necessary to recondition the cylinder bore to the next oversize and install new pistons. If the bore is not worn excessively, the cylinder walls should be honed to remove the glaze, which could prevent the new piston rings from seating quickly.

Cylinder Heads and Manifolds

Scrape all gasket materials from the manifolds and heads. Remove the deposits in the combustion chambers with a wire brush and scraper. **CAUTION: Be careful not to damage the gasket surfaces.** Clean the valve guides with a guide-cleaning brush. Apply some lacquer thinner to the revolving brush in order to dissolve the gum inside of the valve guides.

Check the gasket surface of the cylinder head for

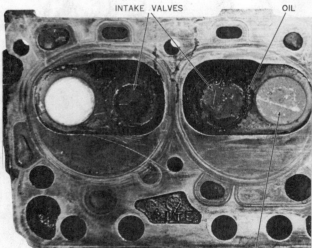

INTAKE VALVES   OIL

DARK EXHAUST VALVE

Note the relatively darker coloring of the exhaust valve in the right combustion chamber and the oil around the intake valve. This means that the compression in the right cylinder is lower than the compression in the left cylinder and that the intake valve guide and seal are defective and were allowing oil to leak into the combustion chamber.

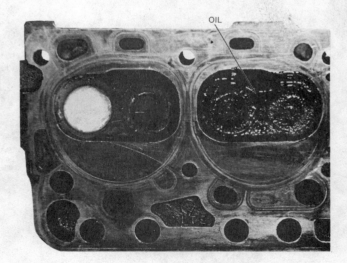

OIL

Always study the cylinder head when it is removed. The coloring of the valves tells a graphic story of the condition of the engine. In this case, the cylinder at the left was firing normally, as evidenced by the white (heated) exhaust valve. The cylinder at the right was pumping oil, possibly due to a scored cylinder wall or broken piston ring.

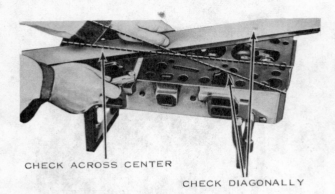

CHECK ACROSS CENTER

CHECK DIAGONALLY

Check the cylinder head gasket surface for uneven spots. Surface irregularities must not exceed 0.003″ in any six-inch space.

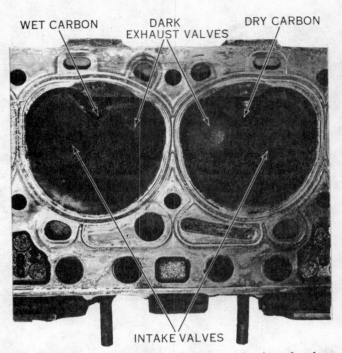

WET CARBON   DARK EXHAUST VALVES   DRY CARBON

INTAKE VALVES

The sooty black appearance of these combustion chambers indicates an excessively rich air-fuel mixture. Note the wet carbon in the left combustion chamber which indicates that piston ring trouble is starting there.

burrs and scratches, which could prevent the gasket from sealing properly. Check the flatness of the gasket surface with a straightedge and a feeler gauge. Surface irregularity must not exceed 0.003″ in any six-inch space, and the total must not exceed 0.007″ for the entire length of the head. If necessary, the cylinder head gasket surface can be machined. **CAUTION: Do not remove more than 0.010″ of stock.**

CRANKSHAFT

Clean the crankshaft with solvent and wipe the journals dry with a lint-free cloth. **CAUTION: Handle**

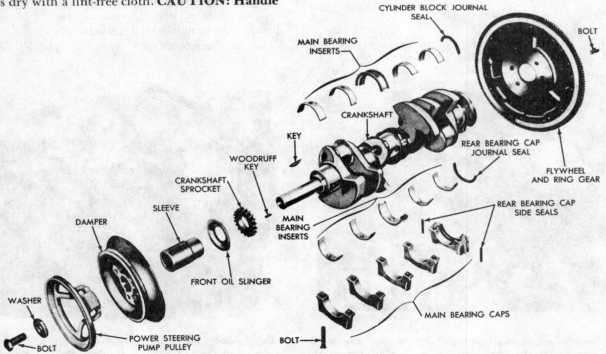

CYLINDER BLOCK JOURNAL SEAL

BOLT

MAIN BEARING INSERTS

CRANKSHAFT

KEY

REAR BEARING CAP JOURNAL SEAL

FLYWHEEL AND RING GEAR

WOODRUFF KEY

CRANKSHAFT SPROCKET

SLEEVE

DAMPER

MAIN BEARING INSERTS

REAR BEARING CAP SIDE SEALS

WASHER

FRONT OIL SLINGER

BOLT

MAIN BEARING CAPS

BOLT

POWER STEERING PUMP PULLEY

Exploded view of a typical eight-cylinder engine crankshaft and its associated parts.

the shaft carefully to avoid damaging the highly finished journal surfaces. Blow out all oil passages with compressed air. **CAUTION: Oil passageways lead from the rod to the main bearing journal. Be careful not to blow the dirt into the main bearing journal bore.**

Measure the diameter of each journal at four places to determine the out-of-round, taper, and wear. The out-of-round limit is 0.001″; the taper must not exceed 0.001″; and the wear limit is 0.0035″. If any of these limits is exceeded, the crankshaft must be reground to an undersize, and undersized bearing inserts must be installed.

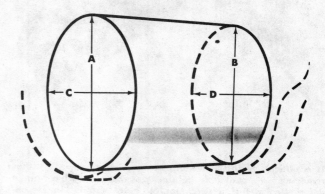

A VS B = VERTICAL TAPER
C VS D = HORIZONTAL TAPER
A VS C AND B VS D = OUT OF ROUND
CHECK FOR OUT-OF-ROUND AT EACH END OF JOURNAL

Measure the diameter of each journal at four places to determine the wear, taper, and out-of-round condition that exists.

0.002″–0.003″

0.004″–0.005″

PIT MARKS

0.005″–0.010″

The coloring of the insert is a good indication of the clearance that exists between the journal and the bearing insert. A normal bearing (top) will show a light gray indication. As the bearing wears and the oil clearance increases, the bearing insert darkens. And when the clearance is over 0.005″, pit marks occur in the surface.

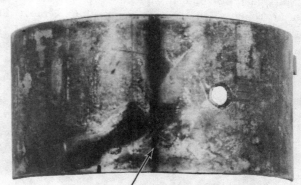

EVIDENCE OF FOREIGN PARTICLE

A foreign particle, such as a piece of dirt on the back of the insert, will keep the steel back from making the proper contact with the engine block, and this will lead to local overheating and loss of bearing materials, as shown in the bottom view.

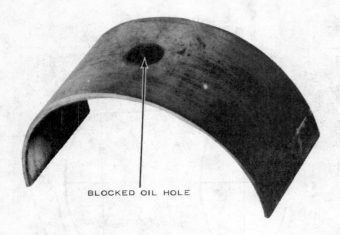

BLOCKED OIL HOLE

It is difficult to install a main bearing insert properly without removing the crankshaft because you can't see what you are doing. Be careful to check for oil holes and locking recesses before installing a new insert. A blocked oil hole will cause rapid destruction of the engine.

Main Bearings

Mark each bearing cap and the block so that the cap can be replaced in its proper position. Remove the main bearing cap and inspect the insert. If the upper half of the insert is to be removed, insert a bearing removal tool into the oil hole in the crankshaft, and then rotate the shaft in the direction of engine rotation to force the insert out of the block.

Clean the journal with solvent, and then wipe it dry with a lint-free cloth. If a new upper insert is to be installed, place the plain end over the shaft on the locking tang side and partially install it so that the inserting tool can be placed in the oil hole. Rotate the crankshaft in the direction opposite to engine rotation until the bearing is seated. Remove the tool.

Measuring the Oil Clearance

The clearance between the shaft and insert can be measured by using Plastigage. To check the clearance, support the crankshaft with a jack so that its weight will not compress the Plastigage and thereby provide an erroneous reading. Position the jack so that it bears against the counterweight adjoining the bearing to be checked.

Clean the journal thoroughly of all traces of oil, and then place a piece of Plastigage on the bearing surface, the full width of the cap. Install the cap and torque the retaining bolts to specifications. **CAUTION: Don't turn the crankshaft with the Plastigage in place or you will distort it.** Remove the cap. To determine the

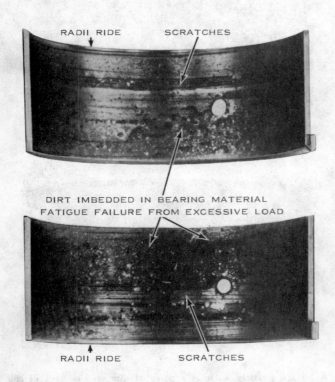

RADII RIDE   SCRATCHES

DIRT IMBEDDED IN BEARING MATERIAL
FATIGUE FAILURE FROM EXCESSIVE LOAD

RADII RIDE   SCRATCHES

Bearing defects caused by improper installation. Carefully wipe each insert before installing it and make sure that your hands are reasonably clean.

Plastigage can be placed on a main bearing journal for measuring the oil clearance.

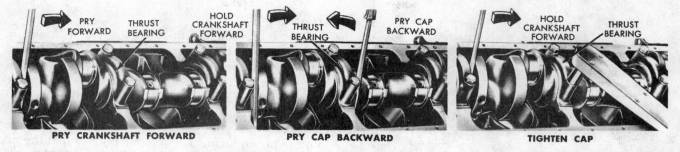

PRY CRANKSHAFT FORWARD   PRY CAP BACKWARD   TIGHTEN CAP

Before tightening the thrust bearing, it is essential to align it properly. This is done by prying the crankshaft forward and prying the main bearing cap backward, and then torquing the bolts to specifications.

clearance, use the scale on the package to check the width of the squeezed-out piece in the bearing insert. If the squeezed-out plastic strip is tapered, the journal is tapered. Measuring at the widest and narrowest points will determine the minimum and maximum clearances. If the clearance exceeds 0.0025", a new insert should be installed. If installing a new insert does not return the clearance to specifications, then an undersized insert should be used.

Connecting Rods

Remove the inserts from the rod and cap. Identify the inserts if they are to be used again. Clean the parts in solvent and blow dry.

Check the rod bolts and nuts for defects in the threads. Inspect the inside of the rod bearing bore for evidence of galling, which indicates that the insert is loose enough to move around. Check the parting cheeks to be sure that the cap or rod has not been filed. Replace any defective rods.

Whenever servicing the piston and rod assembly, it is generally advisable to install new piston pins, especially if the mileage is over 50,000. Loose piston pins, coupled with tight piston assemblies because of new piston rings, will cause piston pin noises, which may disappear as the engine loosens, but this is difficult to explain to a customer who has just paid the bill. Most mechanics have this work done by automotive machine shops, which have the necessary equipment for a precision job. At the same time, the connecting rods will be aligned so that the pistons and rings will run true with the cylinder walls.

You can measure the connecting rod bearing clearance in the manner described in the previous section on main bearings.

TOOL   BEARING   TOOL   BEARING

REMOVING   INSTALLING   ROD CAP

This illustration shows how to remove and install an upper main bearing insert. The round body of the tool is inserted in the oil hole in the main bearing journal, and then the crankshaft is rotated in a direction to unlock the retaining lip. The same tool can be used to install a new insert as shown at the right. Clean the insert and the shaft carefully to avoid getting dirt behind the insert.

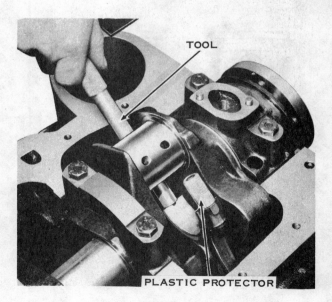

TOOL

PLASTIC PROTECTOR

Always use a piece of rubber hose to cover the rod bolt threads when removing the piston and rod assembly; otherwise, you may damage the bearing surface by scraping the threads over it.

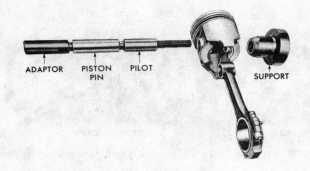

This illustration shows the method of assembling the parts of the special tool that is necessary to press out a piston pin that is an interference-fit in the rod.

PISTON PINS

Removing

Install the tool pilot on the main screw and the main screw through the piston pin. Install the anvil over the threaded end of the main screw, with the small end of the anvil against the piston boss. **CAUTION: Be sure the spring is removed from the anvil.** Install the nut loosely on the main screw, and then place the assembly on a press. Press the piston pin out of the connecting rod. **CAUTION: When the pin falls free from the connecting rod, stop the press to prevent damage to the bottom of the anvil.** Remove the tool from the piston.

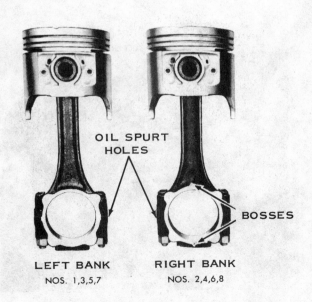

Correct assembly of the connecting rods to the pistons of a V-8 engine.

Installing

Test the piston pin fit in the piston. It should be a sliding fit in the piston at 70°F. Lubricate the piston pin holes in the piston and connecting rod. Install the spring inside the pilot, and then slide the spring and pilot into the anvil. Install the piston pin over the main screw.

Place the piston of a V-8 engine, with the F-mark on the piston facing up, over the pilot so that the pilot extends through the piston pin hole. Position the connecting rod over the pilot, which extends through the piston pin hole. Assemble the rods to the pistons so that the F-marks will face the front of the engine. The boss on the rods must face to the rear on the left bank and to the front on the right bank. The oil spurt holes must face up toward the camshaft on all rods.

For the V-8 and V-6 engines used in the F-85 model from 1961-65, the notch and F-mark on the piston must face the front on both banks. The spurt hole must face the camshaft and the rod identification marks must face toward the front on right-bank rods and toward the rear on left-bank rods.

On six-cylinder in-line engines, the notch in the top of the piston must face the front. Assemble the piston

Use a hydraulic press to force the pin out. CAUTION: Stop when the pin falls free from the rod to prevent damaging the bottom of the anvil.

to the rod so that the oil spurt holes and the numbered side of the rods face the camshaft (right) side of the engine.

Install the main screw and piston pin into the piston. Install the nut on the puller screw to hold the assembly together. Place the assembly on a press. Press the piston pin in until the piston pin "bottoms" on the pilot. This will position the pin properly in the connecting rod.

Remove the tool and arrange the tool parts and piston assembly in the same manner. Place the assembly in a vise. Attach a torque wrench to the nut and tighten it to 15 ft-lbs. If the connecting rod moves downward on the piston pin, reject this connecting rod and piston pin combination. Obtain a connecting rod with the proper small end bore diameter and repeat the installation and tightening procedures. If the connecting rod does not move under 15 ft-lbs, the piston pin and connecting rod interference fit is satisfactory. Remove the tool.

PISTONS

Remove deposits from the piston crown with a scraper. Clean the piston in solvent and blow dry.

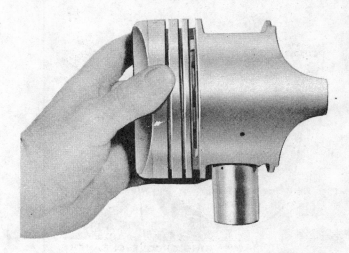

A properly fitted pin should support its own weight in either pin boss when coated with light engine oil at room temperature.

CAUTION: Don't soak the pistons in a caustic solution because it will corrode the aluminum. CAUTION: Don't buff the pistons on a wire brush because it will deform the soft metal. Clean the ring grooves with a ring groove cleaner or a piece of broken ring. CAUTION: Don't scrape or nick the sides of the grooves, or you will damage the sealing surfaces.

Inspect the piston for scuffed surfaces, cracks, and wear. Install a new compression ring in the top groove,

This scored piston is an indication of a tight piston pin. As the pin expands from the operating heat, it pushes the piston out of round in the boss area, causing this type of scuffing.

This melted piston crown was caused by preignition.

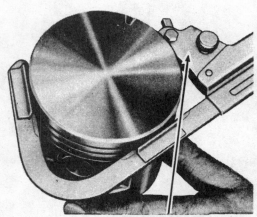

RING GROOVE CLEANER

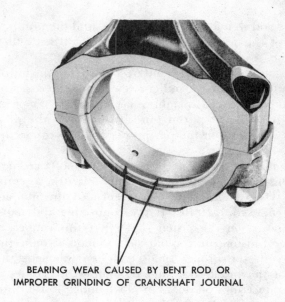

BEARING WEAR CAUSED BY BENT ROD OR
IMPROPER GRINDING OF CRANKSHAFT JOURNAL

Always clean the ring grooves so that the new rings can seat properly. Be careful not to nick the sealing surfaces, or the ring will leak compression.

A bent connecting rod will impart false bearing loads on the insert and cause this offset type of wear.

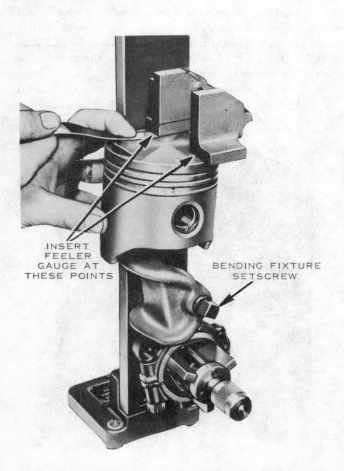

INSERT FEELER GAUGE AT THESE POINTS

BENDING FIXTURE SETSCREW

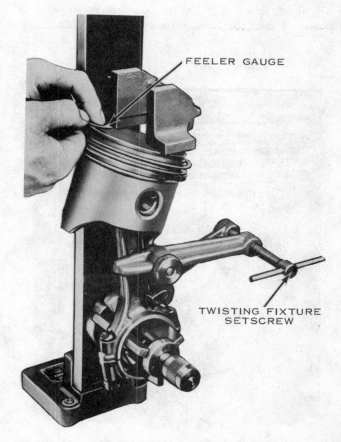

FEELER GAUGE

TWISTING FIXTURE SETSCREW

Showing the method of testing for, and correcting, a bent connecting rod.

To check a connecting rod for twist, turn the piston as far as possible on its wrist pin, and then measure the clearance, as shown. The twisting jig can be used to straighten the rod.

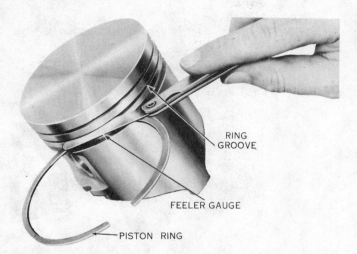

Measure the piston ring side clearance, which must not exceed 0.004".

and then insert a 0.006" feeler gauge to check for ring groove wear. If you can insert the feeler gauge over halfway into the top ring groove, it is worn, and the piston must be reconditioned by cutting the groove wide enough to accept a steel spacer.

Check the piston skirt-to-cylinder bore clearance by inserting the cleaned piston into the cylinder bore. If the cylinder walls have worn enough to form a ring ledge, the piston will be excessively loose. Generally, when installing new piston rings, it is considered good practice to have the pistons expanded in an automotive machine shop in order to compensate for this wear. The pistons can be expanded at the same time that the piston pins are fitted and the rods aligned.

RINGS

Always install a new set of piston rings when overhauling an engine. Order the ring set according to the amount of cylinder wall wear. If the wear is less than 0.005", a standard set of piston rings can be used. If the cylinder wall wear is between 0.006" and 0.012", a set of piston rings with a special oil ring and expanders will be required to keep the engine from pumping oil. If the cylinder bore is worn over 0.012", it should be reconditioned by boring or honing in order to straighten the cylinder walls so that the new piston rings will make a better seal.

Before installing a set of piston rings, the end gaps

A worn top piston ring groove must be reconditioned by machine work. The sealing surfaces of this worn groove will allow the fire to pass the ring and destroy the oil seal of the other rings.

Check the piston ring end gap by pushing the ring into the cylinder bore. The end gap must be 0.010"-0.020".

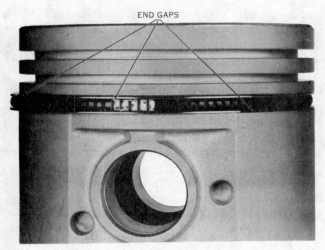

This picture shows how to space the rail gaps and the spacer gap on a compound oil ring.

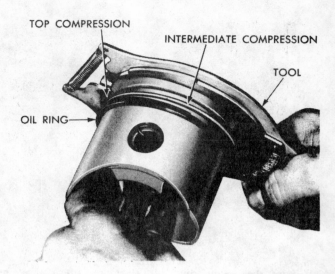

Always use a piston ring expanding tool to install the new piston rings. This tool avoids distorting a ring which could cause it to bind in the ring groove.

and the side clearance between the piston ring groove and the ring must be checked. The correct side clearance should be 0.002"-0.004", with a wear limit of 0.006". Generally, the side clearance of a new ring is not excessive unless the ring groove is worn. But a burr in the soft piston metal may cause the ring to bind. Rotate the back of each piston ring around the groove to make sure that it doesn't bind in any spot.

The end gaps must be checked by inserting each piston ring into its cylinder bore at the bottom, where very little wear exists, and then squaring up the ring

by inserting the piston upside down. Measure the end gap, which generally must be 0.010"-0.020", except for the steel rails of the oil rings, which must be 0.015"-0.030" unless specified differently in a specific engine family. If the end gap is too small, the ends of the ring can be filed to increase the gap.

When installing the rings on the piston, check the compression and scraper rings for the proper method of installation. Some rings have the word TOP stamped on the side that must face up. A compression ring with

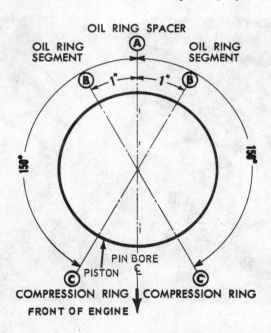

This diagram shows how to position the piston ring gaps for most efficient operation.

Oil the piston and rings, and then install the assembly with a compressor tool. Use the hammer handle to push the piston into the cylinder. Do not force it, because the edge of a ring may be caught on the top of the block. CAUTION: The side of the piston with the cast depression in the crown and the F-mark on the side must be facing the front of the engine.

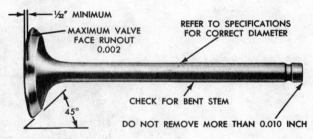

1/32" MINIMUM

MAXIMUM VALVE
FACE RUNOUT
0.002

REFER TO SPECIFICATIONS
FOR CORRECT DIAMETER

CHECK FOR BENT STEM

45°

DO NOT REMOVE MORE THAN 0.010 INCH

Critical valve tolerances.

a groove in its outer face must be installed with this groove facing down. If the groove is cut into the rear face of the ring, the groove must face up when installed. If a steel spacer is used in conjunction with a top compression ring in order to compensate for machine work on the groove, the steel spacer must be installed above the cast iron ring.

Valve Mechanism

Clean the valves, springs, spring retainers, locks, and sleeves in solvent, and then blow the parts dry. Inspect the valve face and the head for pits, grooves, and scores. Inspect the stem for wear and the end for grooves. The face must be trued on a valve grinding machine, which will remove minor pits and grooves. Valves with serious defects, or those having heads with a knife edge, must be replaced.

Use a wire brush to clean all carbon from the cylinder head.

This wet, oily condition of the valve head is caused by excessive lubricant leaking past the seal and valve guides.

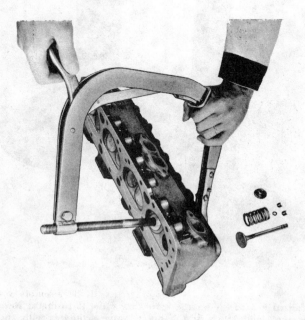

Use the illustrated tool to compress the valve spring, which will release the tapered keepers.

This exhaust valve face is severely burned. Note the gum on the neck of the valve stem, indicating that it was sticking in the guide. Be sure to clean the valve guide of all gum and carbon.

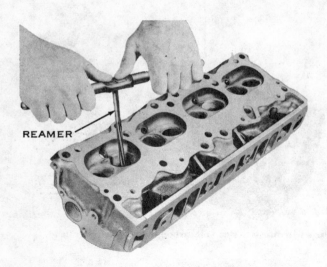

REAMER

To compensate for valve guide wear on late-model engines, ream the guide oversize and install a new valve with an oversize stem to match. Reamers are available in 0.003″, 0.005″, and 0.013″ oversizes.

VALVE GUIDES

Clean the inside of the valve guides with a wire brush and lacquer thinner to remove all gum and carbon deposits, since such deposits could prevent the valve from closing properly.

If the valve guide is worn excessively, it can be reamed to an oversize for new valves with oversize stems of 0.003″, 0.005″, and 0.013″. When going from a standard size to an oversize, always use the reamers in sequence. After reaming a valve guide, always break the sharp ID corner at the top of the guide to prevent galling the valve stem. **CAUTION: Always reface the valve seat after reaming a valve guide in order to true it up with the new guide hole.**

Using a grinding stone to reface the valve seat. The special driver must be lifted occasionally to allow the grinding particles to fly out, or the valve seat will be grooved.

Note the amount of carbon on the valve stem. This indicates that the valve guides are worn and leaking oil onto the top of the hot valve head, forming this type of carbon.

Localized heat areas on the valve face cause it to crack. Note how the small crack in the upper valve compares with the wider one in the lower valve face. This destructive process starts with a localized hot spot, possibly a piece of white-hot carbon on the seat.

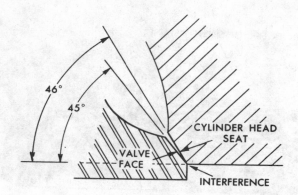

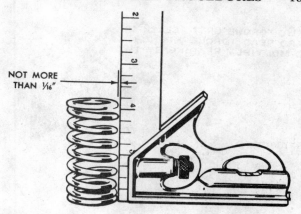

An interference angle of 1° should be ground into the valve or seat so that the seal is at the outer edge. This prevents carbon from being blown into the seating surfaces.

To check the valve stem-to-guide clearance, insert the valve and measure its sideways movement with a dial indicator. The clearance must not exceed 0.0025". If the play is excessive, repeat the measurement with a new valve to determine whether the wear is in the valve guide or on the valve stem.

Valve Springs

Check the valve springs for the correct tension against specifications. A quick check can be made by laying all of the springs on a flat surface and comparing the heights, which must be even. Also, the ends must be square or the spring will tend to cock the valve stem. Weak valve springs cause poor engine performance; therefore, if any spring is weak or out of square more than 1/16", replace it.

For a rough check on a valve spring, determine whether or not it is square with the end coils.

Valves

Grind the 45° valve face to a 44° angle for a 1° interference angle. Remove only enough stock to correct runout or to dress off the pits and grooves. If the edge of the valve head is less than 1/32" after grinding, replace the valve as it will run too hot in the engine. **CAUTION: Don't lap the valves together with grinding compound, or you will remove the interference angle.**

Valve Seats

The valve seat must be reground so that the pits and grooves are removed. Grind the seats to a 45° angle. Remove only enough stock to clean up the pits and grooves and to correct any runout of the seat and guide.

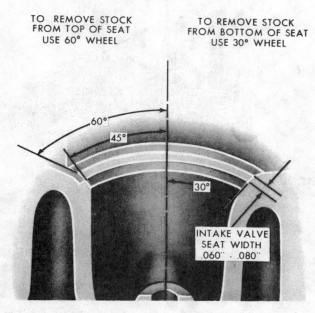

If it is necessary to narrow the valve seat, use a 60° grinding wheel to remove stock from the top.

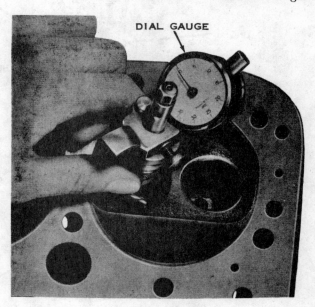

Use a dial gauge to see that the reground seat is concentric with the guide. The runout should not exceed 0.002".

APPLY TORQUE UNTIL CLICK IS
HEARD READ TORQUE WRENCH
AND MULTIPLY READING BY TWO
(2)

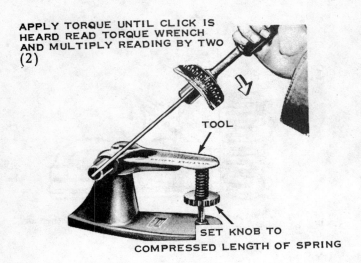

TOOL

SET KNOB TO
COMPRESSED LENGTH OF SPRING

Accurate equipment is available to measure spring pressure, as shown.

UNDER SIDE OF SPRING RETAINER

SURFACE OF SPRING PAD

Always measure the valve spring height and compare it with specifications. This measurement must be made from the underside of the retainer to the machined surface of the head. Spacers are available for adjusting the compressed height.

Measure the valve seat widths, which should be as specified. The seats can be narrowed by removing stock from the top and bottom edges by using a 30° stone and a 60° stone.

The finished seat should contact the approximate center of the valve face. To determine the position of the seat on the valve face, coat the seat with Prussian blue, and then rotate the valve in place with light pressure. The blue pattern on the valve face will show the position of the seat.

HYDRAULIC VALVE LIFTERS

Dirt, deposits of gum, and air bubbles in the lubricat-

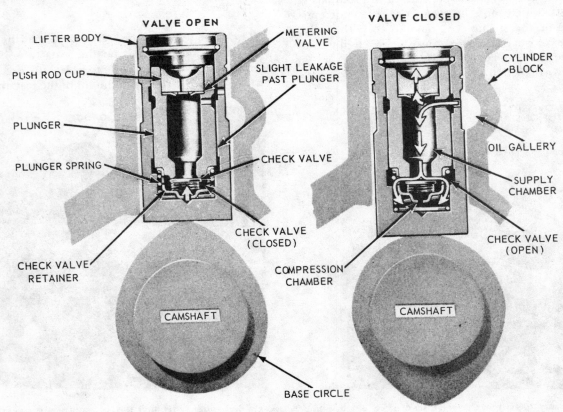

VALVE OPEN

LIFTER BODY
PUSH ROD CUP
PLUNGER
PLUNGER SPRING
CHECK VALVE RETAINER

METERING VALVE
SLIGHT LEAKAGE PAST PLUNGER
CHECK VALVE
CHECK VALVE (CLOSED)

CAMSHAFT

VALVE CLOSED

CYLINDER BLOCK
OIL GALLERY
SUPPLY CHAMBER
CHECK VALVE (OPEN)
COMPRESSION CHAMBER

CAMSHAFT

BASE CIRCLE

Operation of the hydraulic valve lifter.

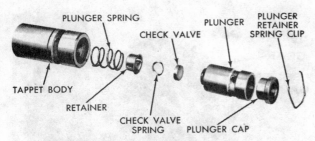

Exploded view of a hydraulic valve lifter.

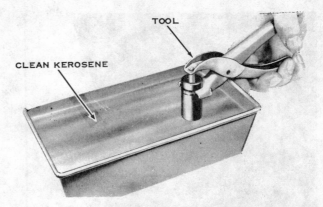

Testing a hydraulic tappet with a pair of special pliers. A good tappet will have considerable resistance to movement of the parts.

ing oil can cause the hydraulic lifters to wear enough to cause failure. The dirt and gum can keep a check valve from seating, which will cause the oil to return to the reservoir during the time that the push rod is being lifted. Excessive movement of the parts of the lifter causes wear, which soon destroys its effectiveness.

The valve lifter assemblies must be kept in the proper sequence so that they can be re-installed in their original position. Clean, inspect, and test each lifter separately so as not to intermix the internal parts. If any one part of a lifter needs to be replaced, replace the entire assembly.

To test a cleaned lifter, assemble the parts dry, and then quickly depress the plunger with your finger. The trapped air should partially return the plunger if the lifter is operating properly. If the lifter is worn, or if the check valve is not seating, the plunger will not return.

Install the assembled lifters in the engine dry. They will bleed to their correct operating position quicker than if you filled them with lubricating oil before installing.

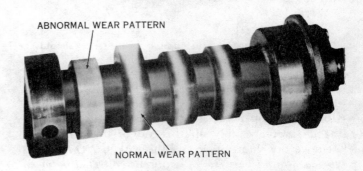

Typical wear patterns on the cam lobes of a camshaft.

Timing Chain, R&R

Drain the cooling system. Remove the radiator and

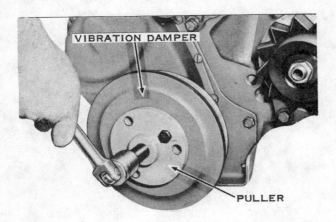

A special puller is available to remove the crankshaft vibration damper assembly, and this must be done before the timing case cover can be removed.

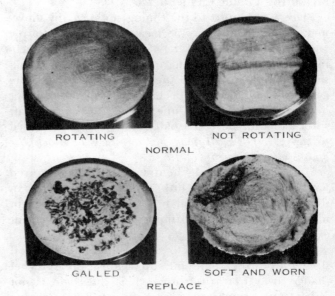

Details of the wear pattern to expect on the base of a tappet or hydraulic lifter.

The backlash between the timing gear teeth should be between 0.004-0.006″.

The in-line engine camshaft end play must not exceed 0.005″. Replace the camshaft thrust plate to establish the production limit of 0.001-0.005″.

the water pump assembly. Remove the crankshaft vibration damper attaching bolt. Install a tool to pull the damper assembly off the end of the crankshaft. Remove the chain cover and the gasket. *NOTE: It is normal to find particles of neoprene collected between the seal retainer and the crankshaft oil slinger after the seal has been in operation.* Slide the crankshaft oil slinger off the end of the crankshaft.

Measuring Timing Chain Stretch

Place a scale next to the timing chain so any movement of the chain may be measured. Place a torque wrench and socket over the camshaft sprocket attaching bolt and apply torque in the direction of crankshaft rotation to take up the slack; 30 ft-lbs with the cylinder heads installed or 15 ft-lbs with the cylinder heads removed. With torque applied to the camshaft sprocket bolt, the crankshaft must not be permitted to move. *NOTE: It may be necessary to block the crankshaft to prevent rotation.*

Holding a scale with the dimensional reading even with the edge of a chain link, apply the same torque in the reverse direction and note the amount of chain movement. Install a new timing chain if its movement exceeds 3/16″.

If the chain is satisfactory, slide the crankshaft oil slinger over the shaft and up against the sprocket (flange away from the sprocket). If the chain is not satisfactory, remove the camshaft sprocket attaching bolt and remove the timing chain with the crankshaft and camshaft sprockets.

Installing a New Timing Chain

Place the camshaft sprocket and the crankshaft sprocket on the bench, with the timing marks on the center line through both the camshaft and the crankshaft sprocket bores. Place the new timing chain around both sprockets.

Turn the crankshaft and camshaft to line up with the keyway location on the crankshaft sprocket and the dowel hole in the camshaft sprocket. Lift the sprockets and chain (keeping the sprockets tight against the chain) and slide both sprockets evenly over their respective shafts.

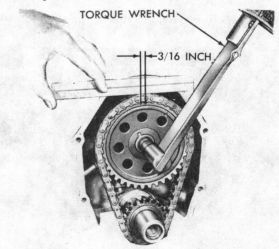

Measuring the timing chain stretch. With the crankshaft kept from rotating, tighten the sprocket attaching bolt to 15 ft-lbs of torque, and apply the same torque in a reverse direction. Replace the timing chain if its movement exceeds 3/16″.

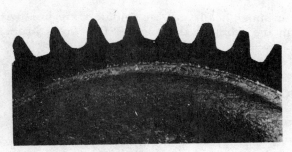

Timing gear wear is spotty. Note that the teeth at the right are fairly well formed, while those on the left are badly worn.

Timing sprocket wear caused by the teeth of the chain. This type of wear causes noise from the front of the engine.

Use a straightedge to measure the alignment of the timing marks. Install the camshaft sprocket bolt; tighten it to 20 ft-lbs. Check the end play of the camshaft on the small-bore engines, which should be 0.001" to 0.005", with a wear limit of 0.010". Slide the crankshaft oil slinger over the shaft and up against the sprocket (flange away from the sprocket).

Installing the Cover

Be sure the mating surfaces of the chain case cover and the cylinder block are clean and free from burrs. Using a new gasket, carefully install the chain case cover to avoid damaging the oil pan gasket. Tighten the chain case cover capscrews to 80 in-lbs first and then tighten the oil pan capscrews to specifications.

Position the damper hub slot on the key in the crankshaft, then slide the hub onto the crankshaft. Place the installing tool in position, and then press the damper hub onto the crankshaft. Slide the torsional damper over the shaft, then attach it with a bolt and lockwasher.

Install the water pump and housing assembly, using new gaskets. Tighten the bolts to 30 ft-lbs. Install the radiator, fan, belt, and hoses. Close the drains and fill the cooling system.

With the timing chain properly installed, the timing marks on the crankshaft and camshaft sprockets must be in alignment, as shown.

A worn timing chain can be bowed in this fashion, indicating wear in every link.

IN-LINE ENGINE

A new generation engine, that was developed for emission control, powers the Omega, Oldsmobile's smaller car. The six-cylinder engine has a capacity of 250 CID and has seven main bearings for smooth operation. The bore is 3.875″ and the stroke 3.53″. The block has a center-to-center bore spacing of 4.40″. The distributor is mounted at the front of the block.

The valves are arranged E-I-I-E-E-I-I-E-E-I-I-E in the cylinder head, and the cylinders are numbered from the front of the engine. The firing order is 1-5-3-6-2-4.

ENGINE, R&R

REMOVING

The engine and transmission are removed as a unit.

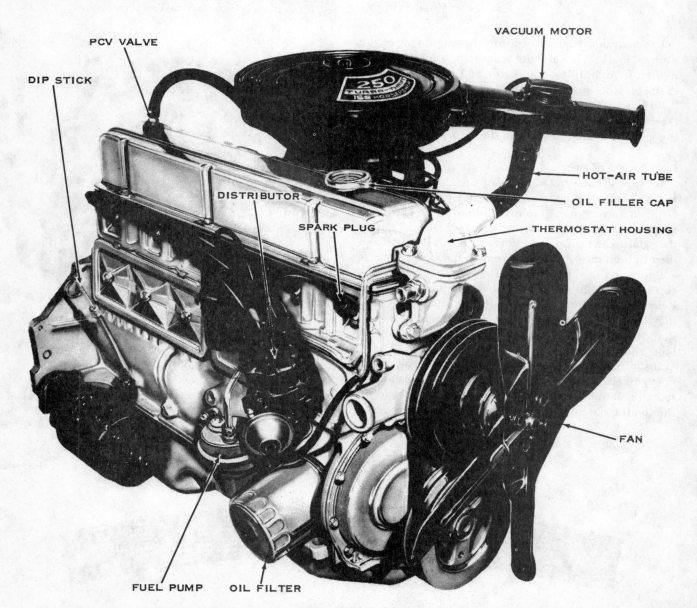

Side view of a modern 250 CID engine. Note that the air cleaner has a vacuum motor and hot-air tube to blend heated and underhood air to the carburetor for quicker warm-up to reduce emissions during this operating mode.

Scribe alignment marks around the hood hinges, and then remove the hood. Take off the air cleaner. Disconnect the battery cables at the battery. Remove the radiator and shroud. Take off the fan and pulley as an assembly.

Disconnect the wires to the CEC solenoid, starter solenoid, Delcotron, temperature switch, oil pressure switch, and coil.

Disconnect the accelerator linkage at the manifold bellcrank, exhaust pipe at the manifold flange, fuel line (from the tank) at the fuel pump, and vacuum line to the power brake unit at the manifold. Remove the power steering pump and lay it aside.

Raise the vehicle on a hoist. Drain the cooling system and engine oil. Remove the propeller shaft. *NOTE: If a plug for the propeller shaft opening in the transmission is not available, drain the transmission.*

Disconnect the transmission cooler lines, shift linkage, TCS switch, and speedometer cable at the transmission.

On synchromesh-equipped vehicles, disconnect the clutch linkage at the cross-shaft, and then remove the cross-shaft engine bracket; lower the vehicle. Connect a hoist to the engine lift bracket and raise the engine to take the weight off the front mounts. Remove the front mount through bolts. Remove the rear mount-to-crossmember bolts. Lift the engine-transmission assembly from the vehicle as a unit.

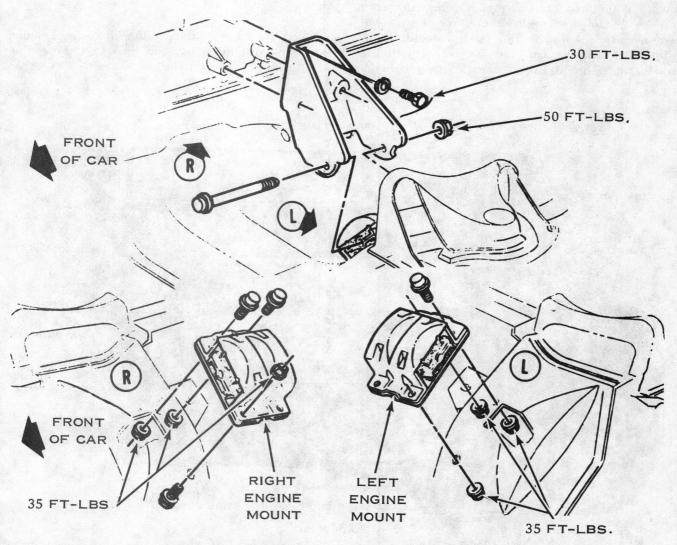

Engine mounts used on the Omega with a six-cylinder engine.

INSTALLING

Tilt and lower the engine and transmission assembly into the chassis as a unit, guiding the engine to align the front mounts with the frame supports. Install the front mount through bolts. Raise the engine enough to install the rear mount, and then lower the engine. Remove the lifting device. Torque all mount bolts to specifications.

On synchromesh-equipped vehicles, install the clutch cross-shaft engine bracket. Connect the speedometer cable, TCS switch, and shift linkage at the transmission. Install the propeller shaft. Lower the hoist.

Connect the power steering pump, vacuum line to the power brake unit, fuel line at the fuel pump, exhaust pipe at the manifold flange, and accelerator linkage at the manifold bellcrank. Connect the wires at the CEC solenoid, coil, oil pressure switch, temperature switch, Delcotron, and starter solenoid.

Install the pulley, fan, and fan belt. Install the radiator and shroud. Install and adjust the hood.

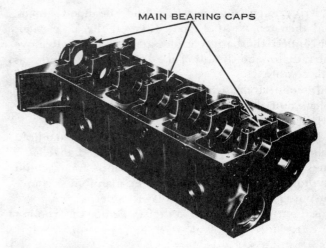

The new six-cylinder block has seven main bearings to support the crankshaft.

Connect the battery cables. Fill with coolant, engine oil, and transmission oil, and then start the engine to check for leaks. Install the air cleaner.

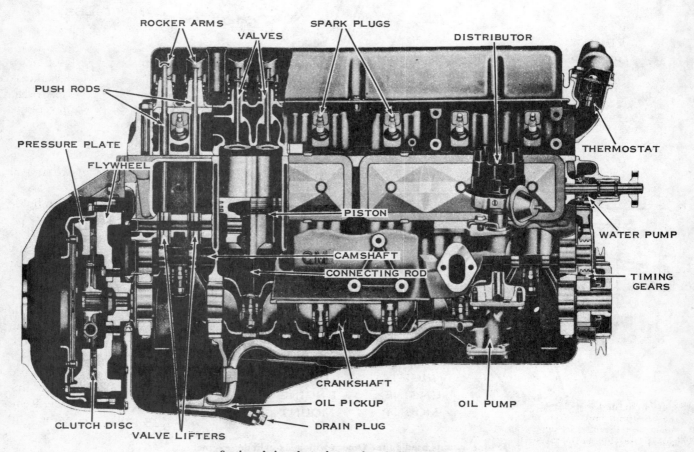

Sectioned view through a modern in-line engine.

OIL PAN, R&R

REMOVING

Disconnect the battery positive cable. Remove the radiator upper mounting panel or side mount bolts. Place a piece of heavy cardboard between the fan and radiator. Disconnect the fuel suction line at the fuel pump.

Raise the vehicle on a hoist and drain the engine oil. Disconnect and remove the starter. Remove either the flywheel underpan or the converter housing underpan and splash shield. Disconnect the steering rod at the idler lever, and then position the steering linkage to one side for oil pan clearance. Rotate the crankshaft until the timing mark on the damper is at the six o'clock position. Remove the bolts attaching the brake line to the front crossmember, and then move the brake line away from the crossmember. Remove the through bolts from the engine front mounts. Take out the oil pan bolts. Raise the engine until you can take out the motor mounts from the frame brackets. Remove the mounts. Continue rasing the engine until it is approximately three inches high.

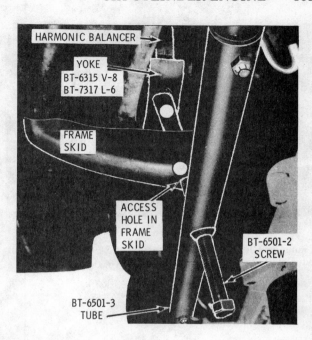

This lifting fixture is designed to support the front of the Omega engine so that wooden blocks are not needed when taking off the oil pan.

INSTALLING

Thoroughly clean all gasket sealing surfaces. From a new gasket set, install the rear seal in the rear main bearing cap. Install the front seal on the crankcase front cover, pressing the tips into the holes provided in the cover. Install the side gaskets to the engine block, using a gasket sealer with sufficient body to act as a retainer.

Install the oil pan, torquing the retaining bolts to 80 in-lbs. Raise the engine sufficiently to allow removal of the wood blocks. Install the engine mounts, lower the engine, and then install the mount through bolts. Tighten them securely.

Raise the engine sufficiently to allow removal of the wood blocks. Install the engine mounts, lower the engine, and install the mount through bolts. Tighten the bolts securely.

Reinstall the brake line to the front crossmember. Connect the steering rod at the idler lever. Install the flywheel underpan or the converter housing underpan and splash shield. Install and connect the starter. Install the radiator upper mounting panel or side mount bolts. Remove the cardboard from between the fan and radiator. Connect the fuel suction line at the fuel pump and the battery positive cable. Refill the crankcase with engine oil, start the engine, and check for leaks.

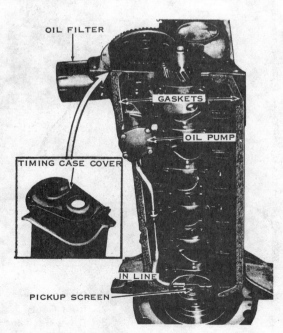

View from under the engine, showing the correct position of the oil pump and the oil pickup screen. The inset at the left shows how the oil pan must seat against the timing case cover gasket. Use sealer at the corners to avoid an oil leak.

On most models, it is necessary to raise the engine and install wooden blocks before the pan can be removed.

OIL PUMP, R&R

The oil pump consists of two gears and a pressure regulator valve, enclosed in a two-piece housing. The oil pump is driven by the distributor shaft, which is driven by a helical gear on the camshaft. A baffle is incorporated on the pickup screen to eliminate pressure loss due to sudden stops.

REMOVING

Remove the oil pan as outlined in the previous section. Take out the two flange mounting bolts and the pickup pipe bolt. Remove the pump and screen as an assembly.

INSTALLING

Align the oil pump driveshaft to match the distributor tang, and then push the pump into the block, positioning the flange over the distributor lower bushing. No gasket is needed. **CAUTION: The oil pump must slide into place with ease. If it doesn't, remove it and reposition the slit to align with the distributor tang properly.** Install the oil pan, using new gaskets as outlined in the previous section.

INTAKE AND EXHAUST MANIFOLDS, R&R

REMOVING

Remove the air cleaner wing nut and the air cleaner.

Disconnect both throttle rods at the bellcrank, and then take off the throttle return spring. Disconnect the fuel and vacuum lines from the carburetor and the crankcase ventilation hose at the rocker arm cover. On a 6-cylinder engine, remove the clean-air tube to the choke. Take off the carburetor. Disconnect the exhaust pipe at the manifold flange. Remove the manifold-to-head attaching bolts and clamps, and then take off the manifolds as an assembly.

INSTALLING

Position new gaskets over the manifold end studs and carefully install the manifold, making sure the gaskets remain in place. Install the bolts and clamps while holding the manifold in place with one hand. Tighten the center clamp bolts to 25-30 ft-lbs and the end bolts to 15-20 ft-lbs. Connect the exhaust pipe to the manifold, using a new packing seal.

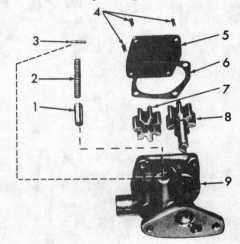

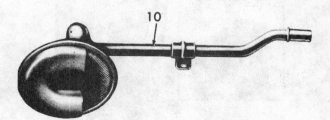

1. Pressure Regulator Valve
2. Pressure Regulator Spring
3. Retaining Pin
4. Screws
5. Pump Cover
6. Cover Gasket
7. Idler Gear
8. Drive Gear and Shaft
9. Pump Body
10. Pickup Screen and Pipe

Exploded view of the oil pump used on an in-line engine.

Installing the intake-and-exhaust manifold assembly. Tighten the center bolts to 25-30 ft-lbs and the end bolts to 15-20 ft-lbs of torque.

A broken heat-control valve housing is caused by someone hammering on it to free up the valve. Note that one crack was an old one, as shown by the darker coloring (arrow).

Replace the carburetor, clean-air tube, and the crankcase ventilation hose. Connect the throttle rods and replace the return spring. Replace the air cleaner.

CYLINDER HEAD SERVICE

REMOVING

Remove the air cleaner. Disconnect the crankcase ventilation hoses at the rocker arm cover, air injection pipe, and EGR valve. Disconnect all wires from the rocker arm cover clips. Remove the rocker arm cover.

Drain the coolant, disconnect the radiator hoses and the spark plug wires. Remove the spark plugs, being careful not to tilt the spark plug socket, which could crack the insulator. Remove the manifold assembly as previously discussed. Remove the rocker arm nuts, balls, rocker arms, and push rods. **CAUTION: Place all parts in a rack so that they can be reinstalled in the same way as removed.**

Disconnect the fuel and vacuum lines from the retaining clip at the water outlet, and then disconnect the wires from the temperature sending units. Disconnect the battery ground strap at the cylinder head, and the upper radiator hose at the water outlet housing. Remove the ignition coil. Loosen and remove the cylinder head bolts, take off the head, and discard the gasket.

CLEANING AND INSPECTING

Take off the valve rocker arm nuts, balls, and rocker arms. Keep all parts in their proper order for assembly purposes. Use a tool to compress the valve springs to remove the keys. Release the compressor, and then take off the spring caps, spring shields, springs, spring dampers, oil seals, and valve spring shims. Note the number of shims under each of the valve springs for assembly purposes. Remove the valves from the cylinder

A blown cylinder head gasket will cause a compression loss between cylinders.

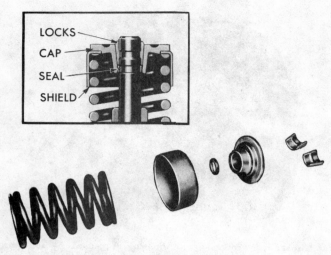

LOCKS
CAP
SEAL
SHIELD

Details of the parts of the valve mechanism.

The valve stem wear can be measured with a micrometer. However, a good indication is a wear lip as shown by the arrow.

head and place them in a rack in their proper sequence so that they can be installed in their original positions.

Clean all carbon from the combustion chambers and valve ports. Thoroughly clean the valve guides using lacquer thinner to cut the gum which causes sticky valves. Clean all carbon and sludge from the push rods, rocker arms, and push rod guides. Clean the valve stems and heads on a buffing wheel. Clean

all carbon deposits from the head gasket mating surface.

Inspect the cylinder head for cracks in the exhaust ports, combustion chambers, or external cracks to the water chamber. Inspect the valves for burned heads, cracked faces, or damaged stems. **CAUTION: Excessive valve stem-to-bore clearance will increase oil consumption and may cause valve breakage.** Insufficient clearance will result in noisy and sticky valves and also disturb engine smoothness.

Measure the valve stem clearance with a dial indicator clamped on one side of the cylinder head. Locate the indicator so that movement of the valve stem will cause a direct movement of the indicator stem. The indicator stem must contact the side of the valve stem just above the valve guide. With a new valve and the

To remove the valve locks, compress the spring, and then take off the locks, caps, springs, dampers, and oil seal. Push out the valve and keep it in a rack in its proper sequence.

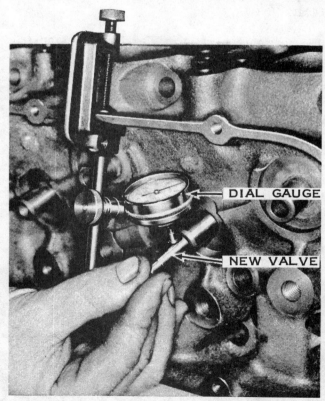

DIAL GAUGE

NEW VALVE

Valve guide wear can be measured by the deflection of a new valve stem. The wear limit is 0.001" for intake guides and 0.002" for exhaust guides.

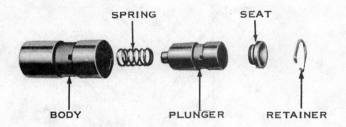

Exploded view of the hydraulic valve lifter

SPRING   SEAT

BODY   PLUNGER   RETAINER

head dropped about 1/16″ off the valve seat, move the stem of the valve from side to side, using light pressure to obtain a clearance reading. If the clearance exceeds 0.001″ for the intake or 0.002″ for the exhaust, it will be necessary to ream the valve guides for oversize valve stems.

Valves with oversize stems are available for inlet

and exhaust valves in the following sizes: 0.003″, 0.015″, and 0.030″. Use the 3/8″ diameter reamer sizes from Reamer Tool Set J-7049, which are: J-7049-7 Standard; J-7049-4, 0.003″ oversize; J-7049-5, 0.015″ oversize; and J-7049-6, 0.030″ oversize to ream the bores for new valves.

ROCKER ARM STUDS

Rocker arm studs that have damaged threads should be replaced with standard studs. If the studs are loose in the head, oversize studs are available in 0.003″ or 0.013″ oversize. They can be installed after reaming the holes with Tool J-5715 for 0.003″ oversize and Tool J-6036 for 0.013″ oversize as follows: Remove the old stud by placing Tool J-5802 over the stud. Install the nut and flat washer and remove the stud by turning the nut. Ream the hole for an oversize stud, using Tool J-5715 for 0.003″ oversize or Tool J-6036 for 0.013″ oversize. Coat the press-fit area of the stud with hypoid axle lubricant. Install a

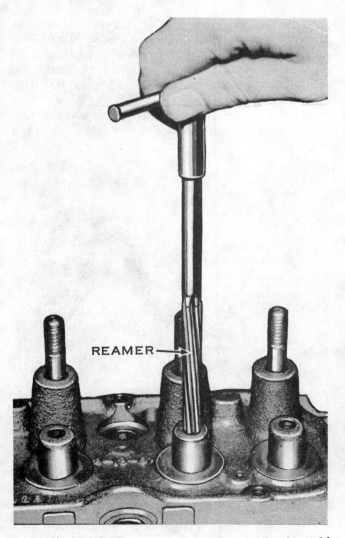

REAMER

Worn valve guides can be reamed oversize, and valves with oversize stems can be used to restore production clearances.

REMOVING TOOL

The pressed-in valve rocker arm studs can be pulled by using Tool No. J-5802.

Use hypoid axle lubricant on the parts, and then drive the new rocker arm stud into place with an installer tool, as shown.

new stud using Tool J-6880. The tool must bottom on the head.

Valve Seats

Reconditioning the valve seats is very important, because the seating of the valves must be perfect for the engine to deliver the power and performance

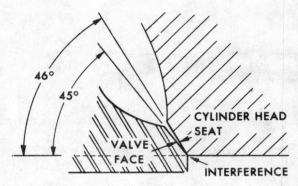

Valve seat angle for the in-line engine should be 46° to provide an interference angle of 1°.

built into it. Another important factor is the cooling of the valve heads. Good contact between each valve and its seat in the head is imperative to insure that the heat in the valve head will be properly carried away.

Regardless of what type of equipment is used, however, it is essential that valve guides be free from carbon, gum, or dirt to insure proper centering of the pilot in the guide. Use a 46° stone for the intake and exhaust valve seats. Narrow the seats to 1/32-1/16" for the intake and to 1/16-3/32" for the exhaust. Check the valve seat concentricity with a dial gauge, which should read within 0.002" total indicator reading.

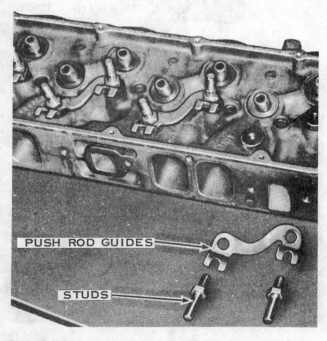

Details of the rocker arm studs and the push rod guides as the parts are to be assembled to the head.

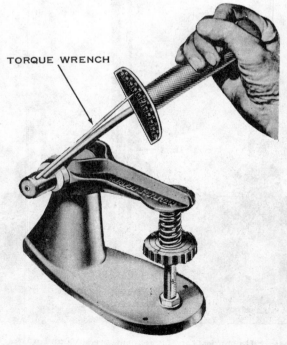

Check the valve spring tension with an accurate tester.

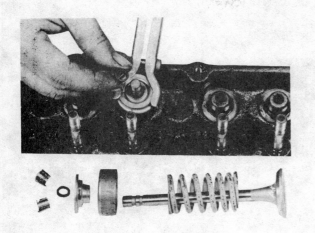

Assembling the valves to the cylinder head, with all of the parts shown in their correct placement.

VALVES

Valves that are pitted should be refaced to a 45° angle. Valve heads that are warped or have a knife edge will cause pre-ignition and should be replaced. If the edge of the valve head is less than 1/32" thick, replace the valve.

ASSEMBLING THE CYLINDER HEAD

Starting with No. 1 cylinder, place the well-lubricated exhaust valve in the port and the valve spring and cap in position. **CAUTION: The spring end with the closed coil must be against the cylinder head.** Place spring and rotator on the exhaust valves. Then compress the spring and install the oil seal and valve keys. **CAUTION: See that the seal is flat and not twisted in the valve stem groove and also that the keys seat properly.**

Assemble the remaining valves, valve springs, rotators, spring caps, oil seals, and valve keys in the cylinder head. Check the seals by placing a vacuum cup over the valve stem and cap; squeeze the vacuum cup to make sure there are no leaks past the oil seal.

Measure the valve spring compressed height, which should be 1-21/32 to 1-23/32". If necessary, shims can be placed between the lower end of the spring and the spring recess in the cylinder head to obtain this dimension.

INSTALLING THE CYLINDER HEAD

The gasket surfaces on both the head and the block must be clean of any foreign matter and free of nicks or heavy scratches. Bolt threads in the block

Measure the valve seat run-out with a dial indicator; it must not exceed 0.002".

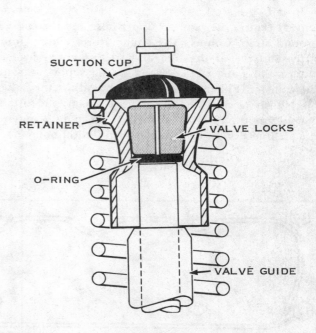

Use a suction cup to apply vacuum to the assembly to make sure that the O-ring seal is not leaking, or you will have an oil leak into the combustion chamber.

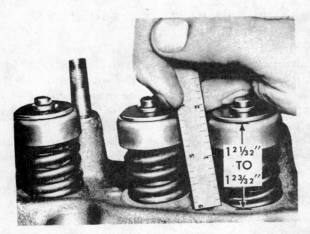

The installed valve spring height should be 1-21/32" to 1-23/32". If necessary, spring shims are available to correct if the measurement exceeds 1-23/32".

To make the valve lash adjustment, first loosen the rocker arm adjusting nut until the push rod can be turned easily. Now, turn down the adjusting nut slowly until you obtain zero lash, and then one additional turn to position the plunger in the center of the lifter travel.

and threads on the cylinder head bolts must be cleaned. (Dirt will affect bolt torque.) **CAUTION: Do not use gasket sealer on a composition steel-asbestos gasket.** Place the gasket in position over the dowel pins, with the bead up. Carefully guide the cylinder head into place over the dowel pins and gasket. Coat the threads of the cylinder head bolts with sealing compound and install them finger-tight. Tighten the cylinder head bolts a little at a time in the sequence shown until 95 ft-lbs of torque is reached. Install the push rods and rocker arms. Install the manifold assembly.

Install the coil, spark plugs, and high-tension wires. Connect the radiator upper hose and the engine ground strap. Connect the temperature sending unit wires and install the fuel and vacuum lines in the clip at the water outlet. Connect the vapor hoses at the canister. Fill the cooling system. Adjust the valve mechanism as discussed in the next paragraph. Install and torque the rocker arm cover to 45 in-lbs. Connect the air injection pipe, crankcase ventilation hoses, and EGR valve.

VALVE LASH

The valve lash can be made with the engine stationary or with it hot and idling. In either case, the adjustment is one turn down from the zero-lash position.

With the engine running, loosen the adjusting nut until the valve clatters, indicating a loose adjustment. Then, turn the push rod while you tighten the adjusting nut until all noise disappears and you feel

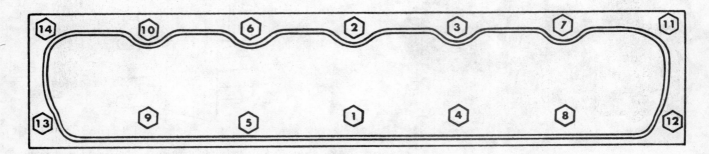

Cylinder head bolt tightening sequence for the six-cylinder engine.

resistance to turning the push rod. Now, turn the adjusting nut down exactly one complete turn to position the plunger in the center of its lifter travel. *NOTE: The engine may run rough until the lifter stabilizes itself, and then it should smooth out.* If it doesn't, replace the lifter, because it is sticky.

To make the valve lash with the engine not running, disconnect the spark plug wires, and then remove the spark plugs. Crank the engine until the distributor rotor points to number one cylinder position and the breaker points are open. The following valves can be adjusted with the engine in number one firing position:

Exhaust	Intake
1	1
3	2
5	4

Crank the engine until the distributor rotor points to number six position and the breaker points are open. The following valves can be adjusted with the engine in number six firing position:

Exhaust	Intake
2	3
4	5
6	6

PISTON AND RODS, R&R

REMOVING

With the oil pan, oil pump, and cylinder head off, use a ridge reamer to remove the ridge and deposits from the upper end of the cylinder bore. Before the ridge and/or deposits are removed, turn the crankshaft until the piston is at the bottom of its stroke and place a cloth on top of the piston to collect the cuttings. After the ridge is removed, turn the crankshaft until the piston is at the top of its stroke to remove the cloth and cuttings.

Scored crankshaft journals indicate the need for reconditioning. New inserts would soon be destroyed by this rough shaft.

Inspect the connecting rods and connecting rod caps for cylinder identification. If necessary, mark them. Remove the connecting rod cap nuts and install a thread-protecting tool on the studs. Push the connecting rod and piston assembly out of the top of the cylinder block. *NOTE: It will be necessary to turn the crankshaft slightly to disconnect some of the connecting rod and piston assemblies and push them out of the cylinders.*

CLEANING AND INSPECTING

CYLINDER BLOCK

Check the cylinder block for cracks in the cylinder walls, water jacket, and main bearing webs. Check the cylinder bores for taper, out-of-round, or excessive ridge wear at the top of the ring travel. This should be done with a dial indicator. Set the gauge so that the thrust pin is forced in about 1/4″ to enter the gauge in the cylinder bore. Center the gauge in the cylinder and turn the dial to "0". Carefully work the gauge up and down the cylinder to determine the amount of taper. Turn it to different points around the cylinder wall to determine the out-of-round condition. If the cylinders have more than 0.002″ out-of-round, boring will be necessary. If the cylinder bores are not worn excessively, use a 220-grit stone to remove the wall glaze so that the new rings will seat quickly. **CAUTION: Use a solution of soap and hot water to remove all traces of abrasives to prevent excessive engine wear.**

The coloring of the old bearing inserts tells a story. Note the light gray coloring of the upper bearing insert, which indicates that the bearing was operating with the proper clearance. The dark coloring of the lower insert indicates excessive bearing clearance.

Press-in piston pins must be removed with an arbor press and a special tool, as shown.

To measure the wear on a piston pin, it should be miked on an unworn section (center), and then on both ends for a comparative measurement.

PISTONS AND PINS

Wash the connecting rods in cleaning solvent and dry with compressed air. Check for twisted or bent rods and inspect for nicks or cracks. Replace any connecting rods that are damaged.

Clean varnish from the piston skirts and pins with a cleaning solvent. **CAUTION: Do not wire brush any part of the piston.** Clean the ring grooves with a groove cleaner and make sure the oil ring holes and slots are clean. Inspect the pistons for cracked ring lands, skirts, or pin bosses; wavy or worn ring lands; scuffed or damaged skirts; and eroded areas at the top of the pistons. Replace pistons that are damaged or show signs of excessive wear. Inspect the grooves for nicks or burrs that might cause the rings to hang up.

Measuring the cylinder wall taper and wear with a dial indicator.

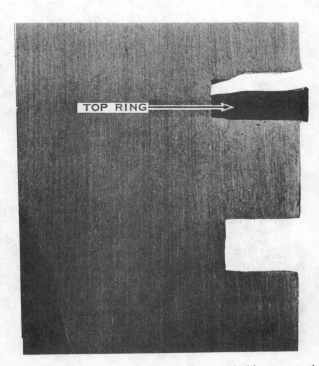

Top ring groove wear is commonplace, and this one requires that the groove be turned oversize and a steel spacer installed above the piston ring to restore production clearances.

Measure the piston skirt (across the center line of the piston pin) and check the clearance, which should not exceed 0.0025".

Inspect the piston pin bores and piston pins for wear. Piston pin bores and piston pins must be free of varnish or scuffing when being measured. The piston pin should be measured with a micrometer, and the piston pin bore should be measured with a dial bore gauge or an inside micrometer. If the clearance is in excess of 0.001", the piston and/or piston pin should be replaced.

Disassembling

Install the pilot of the piston pin removing and installing tool, J-6994, on the piston pin. Position the piston and rod assembly on a support and place the assembly in an arbor press as shown. Press the pin out of the connecting rod. Remove the assembly from the press, lift the piston pin from the support, and remove the tool from the piston and rod.

Assembling

Lubricate the piston pin holes in the piston and connecting rod to facilitate installation of the pin. Position the connecting rod in its respective piston so that the flange or heavy side of the rod at the bearing end will be toward the front of the piston (cast depression in the top of the piston head).

Install the piston pin on the installer and pilot spring and the pilot in the support. Install the piston and rod on the support, indexing the pilot through the piston and rod. Place the support on the arbor press, start the pin into the piston, and press on the installer until the pin pilot bottoms. Remove the installer-and-support assembly from the piston-and-connecting rod assembly. Check the piston pin for freedom of movement in the piston bores.

Piston Rings

Check the end gap of the two compression rings by inserting them into the proper cylinder bore and pushing them down with a piston held upside down. This squares the ring with the walls. Measure the end gaps, which should be between 0.010-0.020". The oil ring rail end gap should be 0.015-0.055".

Check the side clearance of each piston ring in its groove on the piston. The top ring side clearance is specified as 0.0012-0.0027", while that of the second ring is 0.0012-0.0032". The oil ring side clearance is 0.000-0.005".

All compression rings are marked on the upper side of the ring. When installing compression rings, make sure the marked side is toward the top of the piston. The top ring is chrome faced or treated with molybdenum for maximum life.

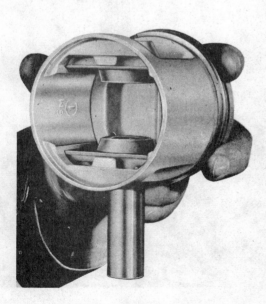

A correctly fitted and lightly oiled piston pin should just hold its own weight in either boss at room temperature.

Check the piston ring end gap with a feeler gauge, as shown.

This is the result of insufficient piston ring end gap. The ends of the rings butted at operating temperature and, having no place for expansion, broke and seized in the ring grooves.

Install the oil ring spacer in the groove with the gap in line with the piston pin hole. Hold the spacer ends butted, and then install the lower oil ring steel rail, with the gap located one inch to the left of the spacer gap. Install the upper oil ring steel rail, with the gap one inch to the right of the spacer gap. Install the second compression ring expander, and then the ring. Install the top compression ring. Adjust the location of the gaps of the two top rings so that each is 1/3 of the way around the piston and no gaps are aligned.

INSTALLING THE PISTON AND ROD ASSEMBLY

Lightly coat the piston, rings, and cylinder walls

250 CU. INCH

INSERT PISTONS WITH NOTCHES TOWARD FRONT OF ENGINES

← FRONT OF ENGINE

Piston markings and installation diagram for the 250 CID engine.

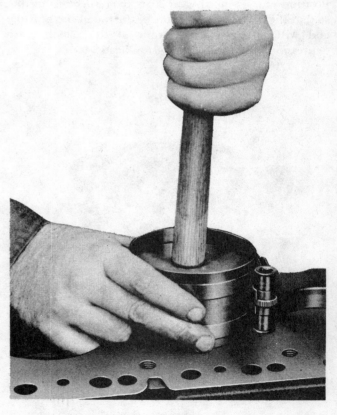

Install the well-lubricated piston and ring assembly into its proper cylinder. CAUTION: Don't hammer on the piston head, or you could break a piston ring that may have popped out of its groove.

Measure the ring side clearance of each ring in its groove, as shown.

The connecting rod side clearance must not exceed 0.014".

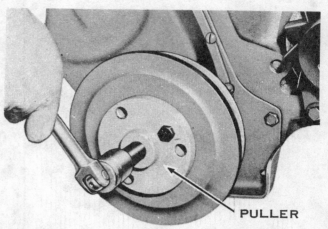

Attach a puller to remove the harmonic (torsional) balancer.

with light engine oil. With the bearing cap removed, install Tool J-5239 on the bearing cap bolts. Install each piston in its respective bore. The side of the piston with the cast depression in the head should be to the front of the cylinder block, and the oil hole on the connecting rod should face the camshaft side of the engine. Guide the connecting rod bearing into place on the crankshaft journal. Install the bearing cap and check the bearing clearance.

Install the oil pan gaskets, seals, and oil pan as previously described. Install the cylinder head gasket and head as previously described. Refill the crankcase and cooling system and check for leaks.

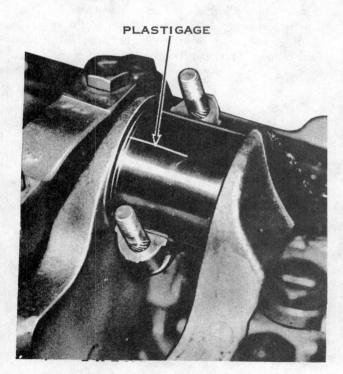

This shows a strip of Plastigage on the crankpin for measuring the oil clearance. CAUTION: Make sure there is no oil on the shaft, or the Plastigage will dissolve.

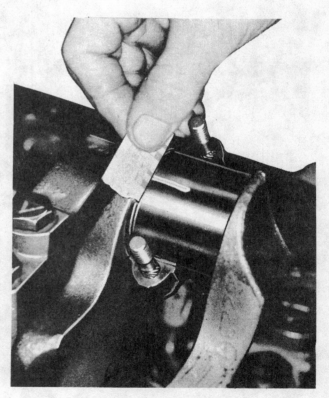

After tightening the connecting rod cap, the squeezed-out Plastigage can be compared with a scale on the side of the package to determine the clearance.

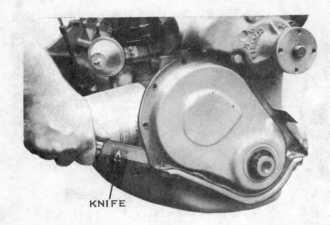

The ends of the oil pan gaskets must be cut with a knife to remove the crankcase front cover.

Oil pan front seal modifications, as discussed in the text.

A puller is required to take off the crankshaft gear.

Sealer must be applied to these points (arrows) in order to prevent an oil leak, after having cut the gaskets.

CRANKCASE FRONT COVER, R&R

REMOVING

Remove the radiator and front grille. Pull off the torsional damper. Remove the two oil pan-to-front cover screws, and then take out the front cover-to-block attaching screws. Pull the cover slightly forward.

Using a sharp knife, cut the oil pan front seal flush with the cylinder block at both sides of the cover, as shown. Remove the front cover and attached portion of the oil pan front seal. Remove the front cover gasket.

A new oil seal should be driven into the cover to prevent an oil leak at this point.

Apply sealer only to the shaded areas to prevent an oil leak at the rear main bearing.

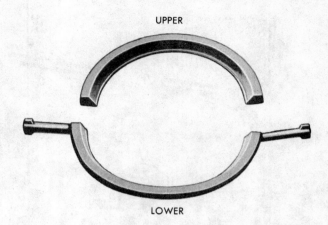

Details of the rear main bearing oil seal used on the in-line engine.

INSTALLING

Clean the gasket surfaces on the block and crankcase front cover. Cut the tabs from the new oil pan front seal, as shown in the accompanying illustration. Use a sharp instrument to ensure a clean cut. Install the seal on the front cover, pressing the tips into the holes provided in the cover. Coat the gasket with sealer and place it in position on the cover. Apply a 1/8″ bead of RTV (Part No. 105-1435) Silicone Rubber Seal to the joint at the oil pan and cylinder block as shown.

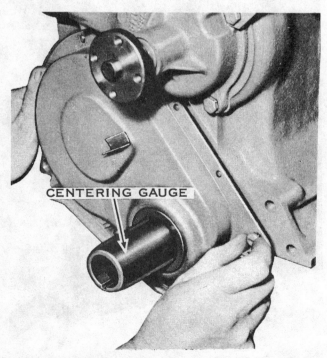

A centering gauge must be used to prevent an oil leak when installing the crankcase front cover.

Install the centering tool J-23042 into the crankcase front cover seal. **CAUTION: It is important for a centering tool to be used to align the crankcase front cover, so that the torsional damper installation will not damage the seal, and that the seal will be positioned evenly around the balancer.** Install the crankcase front cover to the block. Install, and partially tighten, the two oil pan-to-front cover screws. Install the front cover-to-block attaching screws. Remove the centering tool. Torque all cover attaching screws to 80 in-lbs. Install the torsional damper, radiator, and front grille.

ENGINE SERVICE SPECIFICATIONS

CRANKSHAFT

The crankshaft main bearing journals measure 2.2983-2.2993″, with a taper and out-of-round wear limit of 0.001″. The main bearing oil clearance should be 0.0003-0.0029″, with a wear limit of 0.002″ for the front main bearing and 0.0035″ for all others. The crankshaft end play should be 0.002-0.006″, and this is measured at the rear main bearing.

The crankpins should measure 1.999-2.000″, with a taper and out-of-round wear limit of 0.001″. The rod bearing clearance should be 0.0007-0.0027″, with a wear limit of 0.0035″. The connecting rod side clearance should be 0.0009-0.0014″.

CAMSHAFT

The camshaft, with journal sizes of 1.8682-1.8692″, is supported in four bearings. Timing gear backlash should be 0.004-0.006″, and the camshaft gear runout must not exceed 0.0015″. The lifter is a hydraulic type, with an adjustment of one turn down from the zero-lash position. The rocker arm ratio is 1.75:1.0.

Mounting a dial gauge to measure the cam lift.

Timing gear backlash must not exceed 0.006".

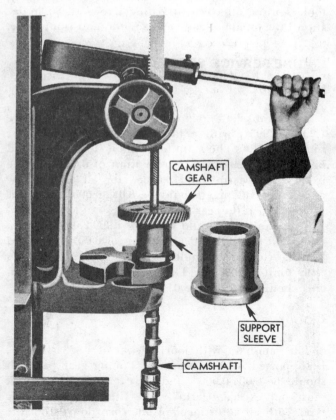

CAMSHAFT GEAR

SUPPORT SLEEVE

CAMSHAFT

The timing gear is a press-fit and must be removed in an arbor press.

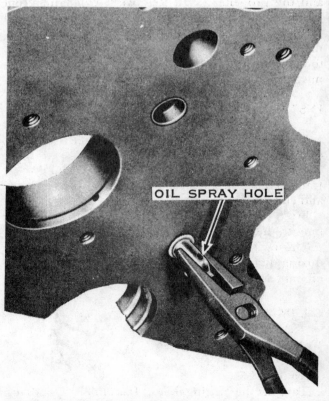

OIL SPRAY HOLE

The timing gear oil nozzle passageway must be clean and the nozzle aimed in this fashion to assure adequate lubrication for the timing gears.

324, 371 AND 394 CID V-8 ENGINES— THROUGH 1964

These V-8 engines are characterized by having the distributor located at the rear. The cylinder bore center-to-center spacing is 4.625″. The engines use a shaft for mounting the rocker arms, the piston pins are floating in both the rods and pistons, and the valve guides are replaceable. The valve arrangement is E-I-I-E-E-I-I-E on both banks, and the firing order is 1-8-7-3-6-5-4-2.

ENGINE, R&R

REMOVING

The engine and transmission must be removed as a unit.

Scribe lines around the hood hinges for alignment, and then take off the hood. Drain the cooling system and the oil pan. Disconnect the battery cables and the radiator hoses. Remove the radiator. Disconnect the wires, pipe lines, and vacuum hoses to the engine.

From under the car, disconnect the transmission oil cooler lines, clutch linkage, transmission linkage, and the propeller shaft. Remove both engine front mount bolts and attach a lifting device to support the weight of the engine. Remove the rear engine mounting bolts, and then raise the engine enough to drop the crossmember. Lift the engine and transmission from the frame.

INSTALLING

Lower the engine into place and attach the rear crossmember. Install the mounting bolts at front and rear. Attach the propeller shaft. Connect the transmission oil cooler lines, transmission linkage, and clutch linkage.

From the top, connect all wiring, hoses, and pipe lines to the engine. Replace the radiator and connect the hoses. Install the hood, aligning the marks made during disassembly. Refill the cooling system and the oil pan.

OIL PAN, R&R

REMOVING

Through 1958

Take off the starting motor. Disconnect the exhaust crossover pipe and the idler arm support. Drop the pan.

1959-60

Position No. 1 piston at the bottom of its stroke to move the crankshaft counterweight out of the way. Disconnect the battery cable, and then remove the exhaust crossover pipe. Disconnect the idler arm support. Remove the starting motor and take off the flywheel housing. Remove the oil pan. *NOTE: Four holes are provided in the front crossmember for access to the front oil pan retaining bolts.*

1961-64

Position No. 1 piston at the bottom of its stroke. This moves the crankshaft counterweights out of the way for clearance. Disconnect the battery cable.

On cars equipped with single exhaust system, remove the exhaust crossover pipe. Disconnect the idler arm support from the frame. Remove the attaching bolts and position the starter away from the engine. Remove the engine front mount-to-front crossmember attaching nuts, and then raise the front of the engine. This is necessary to provide clearance when removing the oil pan, front engine cover, or the exhaust manifold.

To raise the front of the engine, use Tool J-8568. Remove the threaded bolt of the tool from the support plate. Feed the support plate through the large opening in the underside of the front crossmember. Align the hole in the support plate with the center hole in the front crossmember. Attach a chain 18-24 inches long to the tool to aid in positioning it in and out of the front crossmember. Insert the threaded bolt into the support plate. Rotate the bolt until it

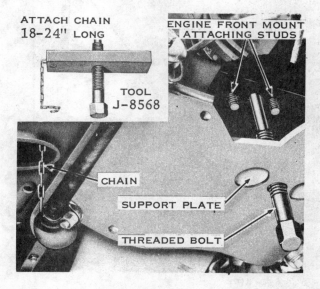

This attachment is used to support the front of the engine when removing the oil pan on any one of the larger V-8 engines through 1964.

contacts the engine front mount. Raise the engine until adequate clearance is obtained. **CAUTION: Do not allow the rear of the engine or engine components to contact the cowl.** Insert wood blocks between the exhaust manifolds and the front crossmember. Lower the engine onto the wood blocks. The threaded bolt can now be lowered away from the engine front mount.

Drain the oil from the pan; then remove the pan. *NOTE: Holes are provided in the frame crossmember for access to the front oil pan bolts.* Clean the oil pan. Use lacquer thinner to clean all old sealer from the pan rails.

INSTALLING

Apply sealer, Part No. 557622, to the bottom side of new fiber gaskets, and then install the gaskets on the pan. Install new front and rear synthetic rubber seals on the oil pan. Apply a light coating of sealer, Part No. 557622, to the exposed surfaces of the seals to insure that the seals do not hang up on the front cover and the rear main bearing cap sealing surfaces during oil pan installation. Apply cement, Part No. 557621, to both sides of the rear main bearing cap, and then install two new cork seals.

Install the oil pan, making sure that all seals are in position before the pan is tightened. Torque the oil pan bolts evenly to 10-15 ft-lbs. Lower the engine.

OIL PUMP, R&R

REMOVING

Remove the oil pan, as previously discussed. Take off the oil pump baffle. Remove the oil pump-to-rear main bearing cap bolts, and then take off the pump and driveshaft extension.

DISASSEMBLING

Remove the oil pump driveshaft extension. **CAUTION: Do not attempt to remove the washers from the driveshaft extension because the parts are serviced as an assembly.** Remove the intake pipe and screen assembly. Discard the gasket.

Remove the oil pump cover attaching screws, and then take off the cover. Remove the oil pump gears. Remove the oil pumps pressure regulator nut, spring, and valve.

CLEANING AND INSPECTING

Wash all parts in clean solvent and blow out the passages with compressed air.

Inspect all moving parts for scoring. Small imperfections can be cleaned up with crocus cloth.

Check the pressure relief valve clearance in bore, which should be 0.0025″ to 0.005″. Too much clear-

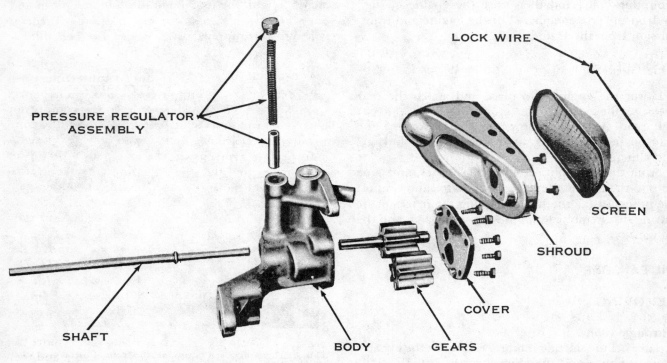

Exploded view of the oil pump used on the larger V-8 engines.

ance can affect the oil pressure at idle. (The oil pressure warning light on the instrument panel is calibrated to light when the oil pressure is less than 3 lbs.)

Check the end clearance of the gears, which should be 0.0025″ to 0.008″.

ASSEMBLING

Replace the oil pump pressure regulator valve, spring, and nut. Install the gears, and replace the cover.

Install the intake pipe and screen assembly, using a new gasket.

INSTALLING THE OIL PUMP

To install the oil pump, insert the driveshaft extension through the opening in the block until the shaft mates in the distributor drive gear. **CAUTION: When assembling the driveshaft extension to the driveshaft, the end of the extension nearest the special washers must be inserted into the driveshaft.** Position the pump onto the rear main bearing cap and torque the attaching bolts to 24-34 ft-lbs. Install the oil pump baffle, and then the oil pan.

INTAKE MANIFOLD, R&R

REMOVING

Drain the radiator, and then disconnect the radiator upper hose from the water outlet. Remove the air cleaner. Disconnect the spark plug wires and the throttle linkage.

Remove the fuel and vacuum lines from the carburetor. Disconnect the wiring from the coil.

If equipped with power steering, disconnect the power steering pump and bracket as an assembly. If equipped with air conditioning, disconnect the Delcotron, remove the attaching bolts, and tip the compressor and bracket rearward to obtain clearance.

Remove the intake manifold with the coil and carburetor attached.

INSTALLING

Clean the cylinder head and intake manifold machined surfaces. Use new graphite-coated metal gaskets between the head and the intake manifold. Apply No. 3 sealer on both sides of the gasket. Replace the manifold. Dip the threads of the bolts in C.P. No. 9 sealer; install and tighten the bolts and

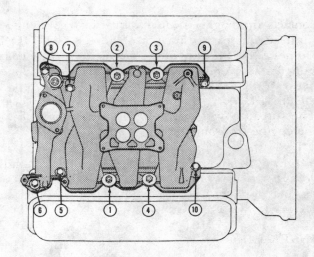

Intake manifold bolt tightening sequence.

nuts to 22-34 ft-lbs, in the sequence shown.

Replace the Delcotron, air conditioner compressor, and power steering pump. Connect the wires to the coil. Replace the fuel and vacuum lines. Connect the throttle linkage.

Connect the spark plug wires, install the air cleaner, and replace the radiator upper hose. Fill the radiator with coolant.

ROCKER ARM SHAFT ASSEMBLY

REMOVING

Remove the crankcase ventilation valve from the rocker arm cover, and then take off the rocker arm cover. If equipped with air conditioning, disconnect the battery cable, and then remove the compressor and Delcotron bracket attaching bolts. Tip the compressor and Delcotron rearward to remove the right-side rocker arm cover. If equipped with power steering, remove the pump mounting bracket attaching bolts and move the assembly to one side to gain access to the left side rocker arm cover.

Remove the rocker arm bracket bolts, and then take off the rocker arm shaft assembly.

To disassemble the rocker arms, remove the brackets and rocker arms from the shaft. *NOTE: One bracket is attached to the shaft by an anchor pin. It is not necessary to remove this bracket unless either the bracket, shaft, or pin has to be replaced. If it is necessary to remove it, insert a drift through the oil passage in the bracket and drive out the pin. If it is necessary to remove the rocker shaft plug, punch a hole in the plug, and then pry the plug from the end of the shaft.*

EXCESSIVE WEAR

OFF SQUARE

Worn parts like these should be replaced; otherwise, the valve mechanism will be noisy.

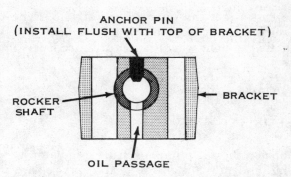

ANCHOR PIN
(INSTALL FLUSH WITH TOP OF BRACKET)

ROCKER SHAFT

BRACKET

OIL PASSAGE

One of the rocker arm support brackets is attached to the rocker arm shaft by means of this anchor pin, which must be flush with the top of the bracket, as shown.

Lubricate all frictional surfaces of the rocker arms, brackets, and shaft, and then assemble the rocker arm shaft assembly as shown in the accompanying illustration.

INSTALLING

Position the rocker arm shaft assembly on the cylinder head. Install and torque the large rocker arm bracket retaining bolts to 60-80 ft-lbs. and the small ones to 14-22 ft-lbs. Replace the rocker arm covers, air conditioning compressor, Delcotron bracket bolts, and power steering pump attaching bolts. Replace the crankcase ventilation valve in the rocker arm cover.

CYLINDER HEAD, R&R

REMOVING

Drain the radiator and cylinder block. Remove the

ASSEMBLING

If the shaft, pin, or pinned bracket was removed, install a new pin. Drive the pin flush with the bracket. **CAUTION: The rocker arm shaft oil ports must face down.** If the rocker shaft plug was removed, position a new plug in the end of the shaft, and then install the plug until its outer shoulder is 9/32″ into the end of the shaft. Stake the end of the shaft to retain the plug.

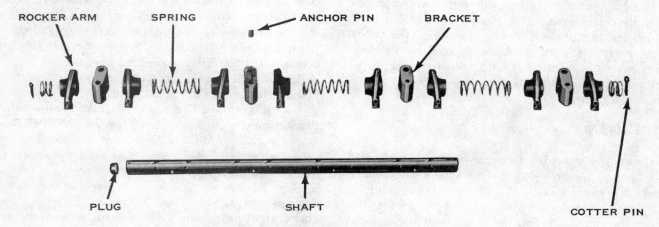

ROCKER ARM   SPRING   ANCHOR PIN   BRACKET

PLUG   SHAFT   COTTER PIN

Exploded view of the rocker arm shaft for the larger V-8 engines.

intake manifold and the Delcotron. Disconnect the exhaust pipes.

Remove the crankcase ventilation valve from the right-side rocker arm cover, and then take off the rocker arm cover. If equipped with air conditioning, remove the compressor and Delcotron bracket attaching bolts, and then tip the compressor rearward to remove the right-side rocker arm cover. If equipped with power steering, remove the pump mounting bracket attaching bolts and move the assembly to one side to gain access to the left-side rocker arm cover.

Remove the rocker arm shaft assembly. Disconnect the ground strap from the rear of the cylinder head. Remove the push rods. Keep the rods grouped so they can be installed in their original locations. Remove the cylinder head bolts, and then take off the cylinder head with the exhaust manifold attached.

DISASSEMBLING

Remove the spark plugs and the exhaust manifold.

Remove the valve keys by compressing the valve spring. Remove the valve spring retainer cups and springs.

Remove the oil deflectors from the valve stems. Invert the head and remove the valves. Keep the valves separated so they can be installed in their original locations. If it is necessary to remove the valve guides, support the head on wood blocks, and then drive out the old guides.

Worn valve guides can be driven out of the cylinder head with this tool.

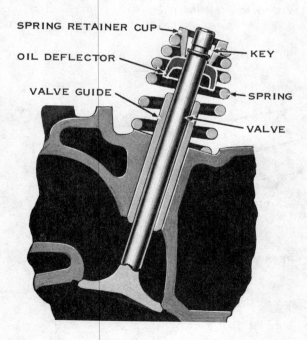

Details of the valve assembly.

When installing a new valve guide, the grooved end of the guide must be facing up. The installed valve guide must extend 25/32" above the face of the valve spring seat.

ASSEMBLING

To install new valve guides, lay Gauge Washer J-5158-3 on the valve spring seat. Install the guide into the cylinder head (with the grooved end of the guide up) by driving on Tool J-5158-2 until the tool seats against the gauge washer. This will allow each of the valve guides to extend 25/32" above the face of the valve spring seat.

When reconditioning valves and valve seats, only precision equipment should be used. Clean the carbon from the heads and also from the valve guides. Whenever valves are ground or new valves and guides are installed, the valve seats must be reconditioned. A grinding stone with a 45°-angle is required for reseating, and a snug-fitting solid pilot of the correct size should be used. New guides, if required, should be in place at the time seats are ground. **CAUTION: Service guides are Parco-Lubrited and finished to size, and should not be reamed.** Oversize guides of 0.010" can be identified by a groove on the O.D. of the guide. To insure satisfactory service, it is necessary that the valve seat width be 0.037" to 0.075". A 15°-cutter should be used to narrow the seat.

Install the well-oiled valves in their guides. Use a new oil deflector over each of the valve stems. Force the deflector down as far as possible on the valve stem. *NOTE: The deflectors will position themselves properly when the engine starts.* Position a valve spring over the valve stem, with the large-coil end down, install the valve lock retainer cups, compress the spring, and

Removing a hydraulic valve lifter.

then install the two valve stem keys. **CAUTION: Check each valve to be sure the keys are properly seated.**

Before assembling the exhaust manifold to the head, apply graphite grease, part No. 581823, to the sealing surfaces of the exhaust manifold center and end port flanges. *NOTE: Gaskets are not used between the cylinder head and the exhaust manifold.* If the manifold attaching studs show signs of coolant leakage, remove the studs and apply C.P. No. 9 sealer to the stud threads, and then reinstall the studs. Torque the manifold-to-head nuts to 19-25 ft-lbs. Set the spark plug gaps to 0.030", and then install the plugs, torquing them to 18-34 ft-lbs.

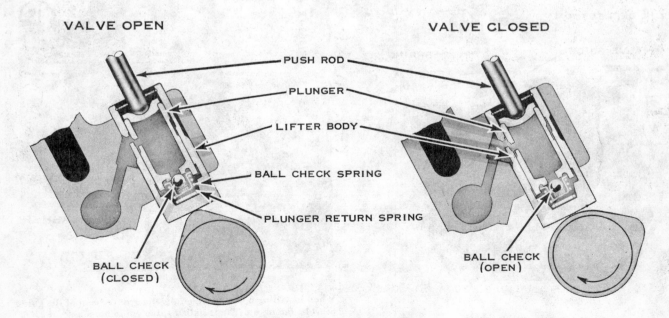

Sectioned view through the hydraulic lifters to show the action during its high (left) and low points.

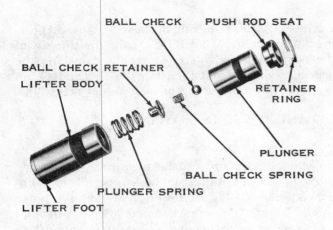

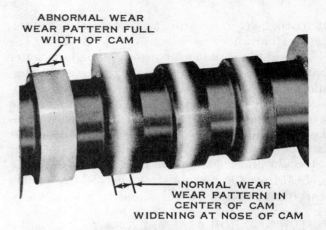

Exploded view of the valve lifter.

This shows normal and abnormal camshaft lobe wear patterns.

INSTALLING THE CYLINDER HEAD

Install cylinder-head guide studs, J-3455, into the cylinder head bolt holes at each end of the block. Apply sealer, Part No. 557622, to both sides of a new head gasket, and then position the gasket over the guide studs. Place the cylinder head in position. Apply a sealer, such as C.P. No. 9, to the head bolts. Install the center and lower row of attaching bolts finger-tight, after removing the guide studs.

Install the push rods and the rocker arm shaft assembly, making sure that the push rods are properly seated in the rocker arms and valve lifters. Tighten the rocker arm shaft bracket and cylinder head

A. TIGHTEN ALL BOLTS SNUG.
B. TIGHTEN NUMBERED BOLTS IN SEQUENCE SHOWN 50-60 FT. LBS.
C. TIGHTEN LETTERED BOLTS 14-22 FT. LBS.
D. RETIGHTEN NUMBERED BOLTS IN SEQUENCE SHOWN 60-80 FT. LBS.
E. RETIGHTEN LETTERED BOLTS 14-22 FT. LBS.

Cylinder head bolt tightening sequence for the larger V-8 engines.

attaching bolts in the sequence shown in the accompanying illustration.

Connect the ground strap to the rear of the cylinder head. Cement a new gasket to the rocker arm cover, and then install the cover. Install the crankcase ventilation valve and hoses on the right-side rocker arm cover. Connect the exhaust pipes to the exhaust manifold, using new gaskets. Install the Delcotron and air conditioner compressor. Adjust the belts. Apply sealer to the attaching bolts, and then install the intake manifold. Torque the nuts and bolts to 22-34 ft-lbs. Fill the radiator with coolant.

PISTON AND ROD ASSEMBLY, R&R

REMOVING

Take off both cylinder heads and the oil pan, as previously described. Before removing the rod nuts, the cylinder numbers must be stamped on the machined surfaces of the rod and cap, on the side opposite the oil spurt hole. **CAUTION: To prevent damage to the rods, the stamping operation must be performed while the rods are still attached to the crankshaft.**

Remove the ring ridge at the top of the cylinder bore before attempting to remove the piston and rod

Use this tool or a piece of rubber hose over the threads of the connecting rod bolt to protect the crankshaft journals when taking out a piston-and-rod assembly.

assemblies. After removing the bearing caps and bearings, place guide, Tool BT-22, over the threads of the connecting rod bolts to prevent damaging the bearing journals, and then tap the rod and piston assembly through the top of the cylinder bore.

CLEANING AND INSPECTING

CYLINDER BORE

Cylinder bore size can be measured with inside micrometers. Maximum allowable taper of the cylinder bore is 0.010″. Reconditioned cylinder bores should be held to not more than 0.001″ out of round and 0.001″ taper (larger at the bottom). It is important that reconditioned cylinder bores be thoroughly washed with a large brush and a soap-and-water solution to remove all traces of abrasive material to eliminate rapid wear after the engine is put back into service.

PISTONS

Clean the pistons by scraping the carbon off the top of the piston, and then immersing the pistons in a solvent. Deposits in the ring grooves can be removed by using a broken piston ring or a suitable groove-cleaning tool.

When measuring a piston for size or taper, the measurement must be made on the skirt 90° from the piston pin hole with the piston pin removed. When measuring the taper, the largest reading must be at the bottom of the skirt. Allowable taper is 0.000″ to 0.001″.

PISTON PINS

Piston pins are available in three sizes: standard, 0.001″, and 0.003″ oversizes. Honing of the piston pin hole for oversize pins is the most satisfactory method of sizing.

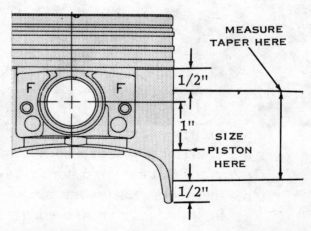

Cam-ground pistons must be measured at these points to determine the size.

The correct piston pin fit in the piston and in the connecting rod is 0.0003-0.0005″ loose. If the pin-to-piston clearance is to the high limit of 0.0005″, the pin can be inserted in the piston with very little hand pressure. The pin will fall through the piston by its own weight. If the pin-to-piston clearance is to the low limit, 0.0003″, very little hand pressure will be required to insert the pin into the piston. The pin will not slide through the piston by its own weight. It is important that both the pin and piston pin hole be clean and free of oil when checking the pin fit.

CONNECTING RODS

In rod bushing replacement, the bronze bushing, after having been pressed into the rod, should be burnished, and then finished to size with a hone. The fit of the piston pin in the connecting rod bushing should be 0.0003-0.0005″ loose.

After the connecting rods and pistons are separated, the rods should be checked for alignment. If a rod is twisted or bent, a new rod must be installed. No attempt should be made to straighten connecting rods. Lubricate the piston pin hole and the piston pin to facilitate installation, and then position the connecting rod, with its respective piston, as shown in the accompanying illustration. Install the piston pin and the pin retainers.

PISTON RINGS

The pistons have three rings (two compression rings and one oil ring). Production rings are supplied from two sources and are of similar design. On both types of rings, the outside diameter of the top compression ring is chrome plated; the second compression ring is of the step type and has a black finish. Both types of oil rings consist of 2 rails and an expander.

When installing new rings, the ring gap and side clearance should be checked as follows: Each ring and rail gap must be measured with the ring or rail positioned squarely and at the bottom of the ring-travel area of the bore. If the gap measurement is not within the specifications shown in the accompanying illustration, file the ends of the rings and rails until the minimum gap is obtained. The ends of the rings and rails must be filed squarely.

Each ring must be checked for side clearance in its respective piston groove by inserting a feeler gauge between the ring and its upper land. **CAUTION: The piston grooves must be cleaned before checking the ring for side clearance.**

ALLOWABLE SIDE CLEARANCE
Oil rings   0.0005-0.007″
Compression rings   0.001-0.004″

INSTALLING

When installing the piston and connecting rod assemblies, a connecting rod bolt guide, Tool BT-22, should be placed over the connecting rod bolt threads to protect the crankshaft bearing surfaces. Apply SAE No. 20 oil to the rings and piston, and then install each rod-and-piston assembly in its respective bore so the notch, cast in the top of each piston, will be toward the front of the engine after installation. The piston can be installed in the piston bore without danger of breaking the piston rings if a ring compressing tool is used.

Install the connecting rod caps with the bearing index notches in the rod and cap on the same side. The connecting rod cap attaching nuts should be tightened only enough to keep each rod in position

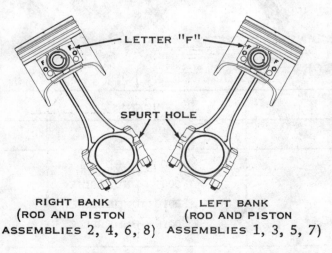

Piston-and-rod assembly details for the larger V-8 engines through 1964.

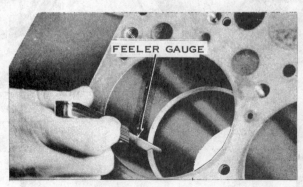

RING GAP

	COMPRESSION RING	OIL RAIL
ALL SERIES	0.013-0.023″	0.015-0.055″

Measuring a piston ring end gap.

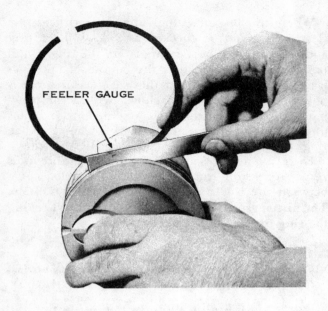

FEELER GAUGE

Measuring the piston ring side clearance. Generally, the top ring groove wears the most, and the clerance here must not exceed 0.006"; otherwise, the ring groove must be reconditioned.

until all of the piston and rod assemblies have been installed. This will facilitate installation of the remaining piston assemblies.

The clearance between adjacent rods on each crankpin should be from 0.002-0.011" when checked with a feeler gauge. Torque the rod bearing cap nuts to 38-48 ft-lbs.

Replace the oil pan and cylinder heads.

MAIN BEARINGS, R&R

Main bearing clearances should be within specifications of 0.0005-0.0021" for Nos. 1 and 2 bearings, 0.0008-0.0024" for Nos. 3 and 4 bearings, and 0.0020-0.0034" for No. 5 bearing. Excessive clearance must be corrected by the use of selective upper and lower shells. **CAUTION: Under no circumstances should shims be used behind the shells to compensate for wear. CAUTION: The upper and lower shells must be installed in pairs.**

NO. 5   NO. 4, 3 OR 2   NO. 1

IDENTIFICATION (ON SHELL TANG)		THICKNESS
NO. 1 THRU 4	NO. 5	
NONE	NONE	STANDARD
B	A	.0005" UNDERSIZE
C	B	.0010" UNDERSIZE
E	C	.0015" UNDERSIZE

Main bearing identification markings.

To install main bearing shells, remove the bearing cap and take out the lower shell. Insert a flattened cotter pin in the oil passage hole in the crankshaft, and then rotate the crankshaft in the direction opposite to cranking rotation. The cotter pin will contact the upper shell and force it out.

The main bearing journals should be checked for roughness and wear. Slight roughness can be removed with a fine-grit polishing cloth, saturated with engine oil. Burrs can be removed with a fine oil stone. If the journals are scored or ridged, the crankshaft must be replaced or reground. The maximum out-of-round condition of the crankshaft journals must not exceed 0.0015″.

INSTALLING

Clean the crankshaft journals and bearing caps thoroughly before installing new main bearings. On No. 5 bearing, apply special lubricant, Part No. 567196, to the thrust flanges of the bearing shells. Place the new upper shell on the crankshaft journal, with the locating tang in the correct position, and then rotate the shaft to turn it into place, using the cotter pin as during removal. Place a new lower shell in the bearing cap.

On No. 5 bearing, install a new asbestos oil seal in

These cork seals are used on the sides of the rear main bearings to keep the oil from leaking.

the rear main bearing cap. Install the bearing caps. Torque Nos. 1 through 4 bearing caps to 90-120 ft-lbs. and No. 5 bearing cap to 130-160 ft-lbs.

REAR MAIN BEARING OIL SEAL

The rear main bearing is sealed against oil leaks by a special asbestos-covered wiper seal. Special care must be exercised when installing this seal. Whenever the crankshaft is removed, a new seal, coated with graphite grease, should be installed in the engine block. Whenever the No. 5 bearing cap is removed, a new seal should be installed in the bearing cap. The

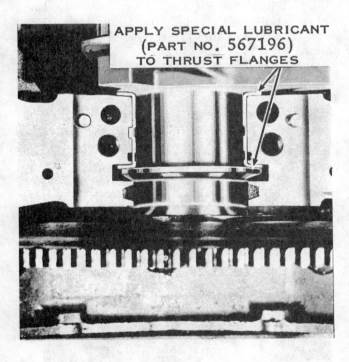

You must apply this special lubricant to the thrust flanges of No. 5 main bearing to keep it from wiping out when the engine is first started.

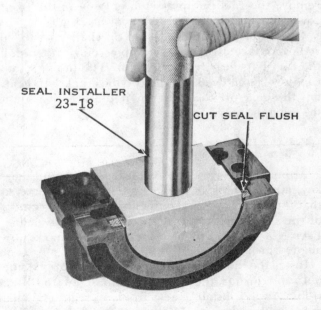

This main bearing seal-installing tool should be used to form the seal.

seal, to be installed properly, should be crowded into the groove in the bearing cap and block by hand, then driven tightly into the groove by tapping with a hammer and punch, as shown.

After the seal has been seated in the bearing cap and, while the tool is still resting in the bearing cap, the seal should be cut flush with the parting line between the upper and lower bearing. The ends of the seal must be cut clean so no frayed ends will be clamped between the block and cap, and the seal must fill the groove entirely. After the rear main bearing cap has been installed, DuPont Cement No. 5402 should be wiped into the grooves in the block on both sides of the bearing cap, and then two new cork seals pressed into place in the grooves, as shown in the accompanying illustration.

TIMING GEARS AND/OR CHAIN, R&R

REMOVING

Drain the cooling system. Disconnect the radiator lower hose and the heater hose from the front cover. Disconnect the Delcotron link.

Raise the front of the engine as outlined under oil pan removal. Remove the oil pan.

Take off the fan blades and pulley. Remove the crankshaft pulley. Remove the distributor cap. Install a jumper wire, crank the engine until the distributor rotor points to the front of the engine, and then remove the fuel pump assembly. Remove the front cover attaching bolts and front cover assembly.

Whenever the timing gears or chain are to be removed, take off the fuel pump eccentric, then pull the camshaft gear from the shaft. The timing chain can now be removed. To remove the crankshaft gear, tap the gear off the shaft or, if the gear is a tight fit, use a universal puller.

INSTALLING

Apply sealer, Part No. 557622, to the crankshaft key, and then install the gears and timing chain so that the marks are in alignment through the centers of the shafts, as shown. A special gauge is available, Part No. BT-11, to be sure that the marks are aligned properly.

Install the fuel pump eccentric, with the cupped side out, and torque the attaching cap screw to 14-22 ft-lbs. Always install a new front oil seal. The fuel pump rocker arm pad should be coated with lubricant, Part No. 567196. Install the fuel pump, with the

rocker arm of the pump resting on top of the fuel pump eccentric. The front cover attaching bolts should be dipped in sealer, Part No. 557622. Torque them to 24-40 ft-lbs. One side of the fuel and vacuum pump gasket should be coated with sealer, Part No. 557622.

Replace the distributor cap and the fan blades and pulley. Replace the oil pan, attach the Delcotron, and connect the radiator and heater hoses. Fill the cooling system.

ENGINE SERVICE SPECIFICATIONS

CRANKSHAFT

The crankshaft main bearing journals for 1955-56 engines should measure 2.6230-2.6240″ for the rear journal and 2.4980-2.4990″ for all others. In 1957-58, all main bearing journals should measure 2.7480-2.7490″. From 1959-64, all main bearing journals should measure 2.9990-3.000″; all of these dimensions are plus a wear limit of 0.002″.

The crankpins should measure 2.2490-2.2500″ through 1958 and 2.4992-2.5002″ since then. All dimensions are plus a wear limit of 0.002″.

The oil clearance should be 0.0005-0.0026″ for all connecting rod and main bearings, except for the rear main bearing, which should measure 0.002-0.0035″. The thrust is taken by No. 5 main bearing, and the crankshaft end play should be 0.004-0.008″ in all cases. All of these clearances are plus a wear limit of 0.002″.

When installing the timing chain, the timing marks should align through the center of the shafts, as shown. This special gauge has been designed to check the timing mark alignment.

215 CID V-8 ENGINE, F-85—1961-63

This smaller V-8 engine is used exclusively on the F-85 model. The engine has a bore of 3.5″ and a stroke of 2.8″, providing a displacement of 215 cubic inches. The cylinder bore center-to-center spacing is 4.24″. The cylinder block is cast aluminum with nonreplaceable cast iron cylinder liners cast integral with the block. A one-piece intake manifold gasket is used, which also serves as the engine top cover. The left bank of cylinders (as viewed from the drivers seat) are numbered (from front to rear) 1-3-5-7. Cylinders in the right bank are numbered (from front to rear) 2-4-6-8.

The cylinder heads are made of cast aluminum, with cast iron valve seat inserts and valve guides. Right and left cylinder heads are identical and interchangeable. The valve guides can be replaced. The valve arrangement is E-I-E-I-I-E-I-E on both banks, and the firing order is 1-8-4-3-6-5-7-2.

The oil pump and distributor are located in the front engine cover. The distributor is driven by a driving gear that is bolted to the end of the camshaft. The oil pump is driven by the distributor shaft.

ENGINE, R & R

REMOVING

When it is necessary to remove the engine assembly, the necessary items should be disconnected and the body raised off the engine and suspension assembly. To do this, remove the hood and place protective covers on the fenders. Disconnect the following: Battery cable from starter, ground cable, engine ground strap, accelerator linkage, oil pressure switch, ignition switch wire, temperature gauge, and fuel line. On 3147 models, disconnect the turbo-rocket fluid tank hoses and the performance vacuum line.

Drain the radiator and disconnect the radiator hoses and heater hoses. If equipped with air conditioning, remove the pressure hoses from the compressor and fan shroud. Remove the air cleaner and disconnect the front exhaust pipe from the rear exhaust pipe. On 3147 models, it will be necessary to remove the turbo-charger outlet pipe.

Disconnect the speedometer cable, front of propeller shaft, and shift linkage from the transmission. Disconnect the clutch and clutch equalizer on synchromesh-equipped cars, stabilizer brackets from the frame rail, front brake hoses, and steering shaft from the gear. Raise the steering shaft into the steering column. Place a block of wood between the front cross bar and the front of the engine oil pan. Remove the rear transmission mount crossmember and support the rear of the transmission with a stand.

With the front wheels on the floor, remove the three isolation mount bolts and carefully raise the body off the engine and suspension. Care must be taken not to let the suspension tip.

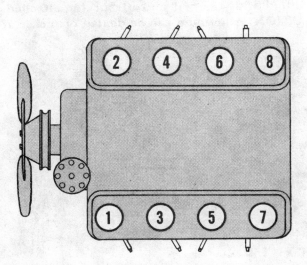

Cylinder numbering on the 215 CID V-8 engine used in the F-85 from 1961-63.

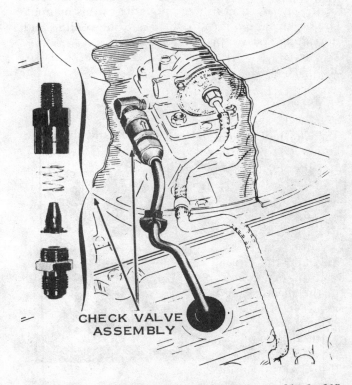

Details of the positive crankcase ventilator valve used in the 215 CID engine.

This engine support brace is designed to hold the engine up while removing the oil pan.

INSTALLING

When installing the assembly into the body, the torque specifications and adjustments can be found for the specific unit in the Appendix of this manual. The brake system must be bled and the cooling and lubricating systems properly serviced.

OIL PAN, R&R

REMOVING

Remove the dipstick. Hoist the car and drain the oil. Disconnect the idler arm from the relay rod.

Remove the cover on the front of the lower flywheel housing, and then remove the pan bolts. *NOTE: On some types of lifts, it may be necessary to drop the oil intake into the pan before removing it. The crankshaft should be positioned so the counterweights do not interfere with the pan removal.*

INSTALLING

Lubricate the pan bolts with engine oil, and then install the pan. Torque the bolts 6-15 ft-lbs. Attach the idler arm to the relay rod, and then install the flywheel cover.

INTAKE MANIFOLD, R&R

REMOVING

Drain the radiator, and then disconnect the upper radiator hose from the water outlet. Also, disconnect the heater hose at the rear of the manifold. On 3147 models, it will be necessary to remove the turbocharger.

Disconnect the spark plug wires and remove the air cleaner assembly. Disconnect the throttle linkage from the accelerator bellcrank. Disconnect the choke heat tubes and the lower throttle rod. Remove the fuel and vacuum lines from the carburetor. Disconnect the primary wiring and the secondary lead from the coil. Disconnect the temperature gauge wire. Slide the thermostat by-pass hose clamp back on the hose at the water pump.

Remove 12 intake manifold bolts. Then lift off the manifold with the coil and carburetor attached. **CAUTION: Aluminum can be dented or nicked if**

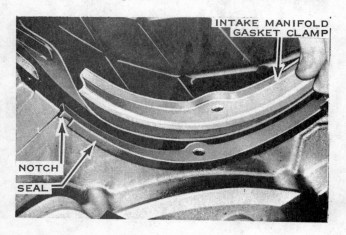

Details for installing the intake manifold gasket and clamp.

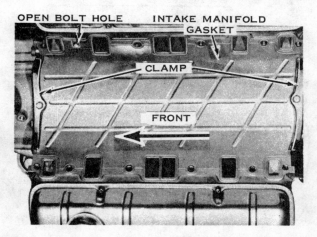

When tightening the clamp bolts, the intake manifold gasket must be positioned so that the manifold-to-head bolts will be open.

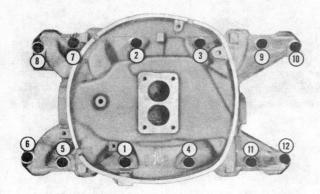

Intake manifold bolt tightening sequence.

ROCKER ARM SHAFT
BRACKET TO HEAD BOLTS

These four bolts hold the rocker arm shaft assembly to the cylinder head.

carelessly handled. Use particular care to protect gasket surfaces against damage. Remove 2 intake manifold gasket clamp bolts, clamps, seals, and gasket. Discard the seals and gasket.

Clean the machined surfaces of the cylinder head and intake manifold with a putty knife. Use extreme care not to gouge or scratch the machined surface.

INSTALLING

Coat both sides of the gasket sealing surface that seal the intake manifold to the head with POB #3 sealer and install a new intake manifold gasket. Install the end seals and clamps. Lubricate the bolts with engine oil. Install and torque the bolts to 10-15 ft-lbs. **CAUTION: When tightening the clamp bolts, the intake manifold gasket must be positioned so that the manifold-to-head bolt holes will be open, as shown in the accompanying picture.**

Position the intake manifold on the engine. Connect the thermostat by-pass hose to the water pump. Coat 12 intake manifold bolts with engine oil and install the bolts. Torque to 25-30 ft-lbs, as shown in the accompanying illustration.

Connect the temperature gauge wire and the primary wire and secondary lead to the coil. Install the fuel and vacuum lines. Connect the upper radiator hose, spark plug wires, heater hose, and carburetor linkage. Install the carburetor cover. On 3147 models, replace the turbo-charger. Fill the cooling system.

ROCKER ARMS AND SHAFTS

REMOVING

Remove the carburetor cover. Disconnect the heat tube from the carburetor and manifold on the right side. Disconnect the spark plug wires and move them away from the valve cover.

Remove the 5 valve cover-to-cylinder head screws,

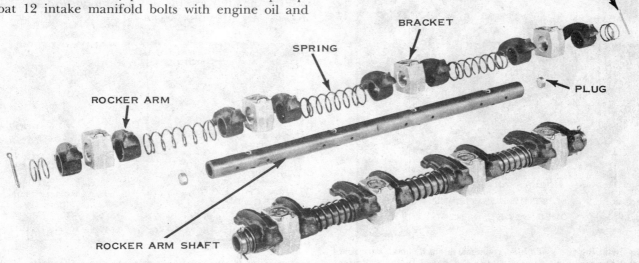

COTTER PIN

SPRING

BRACKET

PLUG

ROCKER ARM

ROCKER ARM SHAFT

Assembled and disassembled rocker arm shaft assembly used on the 215 CID V-8 engine.

and then rotate the cover off the breather pipe. Take off the cover.

Remove the 4 rocker arm shaft bracket-to-head bolts. Take off the heater-blower assembly to remove the right rocker arm assembly.

DISASSEMBLING

Remove the cotter pins from the ends of the shaft. *NOTE: Disassemble one shaft assembly at a time and place the assembled shaft on a bench so the parts can be assembled in their original place.* Remove the springs, arms, and brackets from the shaft. If it is necessary to remove the shaft end plug, punch a hole in the plug, and then pry the plug from the end of the shaft.

ASSEMBLING

If the shaft end plug was removed, drive a new plug into the shaft to clear the cotter pin hole. Lubricate the frictional surfaces of the rocker arms and shaft with engine oil and assemble as shown.

INSTALLING

Position the rocker arm shaft assembly on the cylinder head and align the brackets with the mounting bolts. The shaft goes on a dowel on the head. Coat the bolt threads with POB No. 4 Sealer, and then torque them to 45-55 ft-lbs. Check the rocker arm-to-valve stem contact for proper alignment. Install the valve cover with a new gasket. Connect the spark plug wires, heat tube, heat tube retainer, and the carburetor cover.

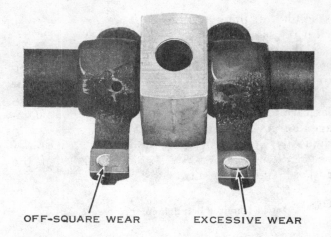

OFF-SQUARE WEAR   EXCESSIVE WEAR

This shows the type of rocker arm wear that calls for replacement of the worn parts.

CYLINDER HEAD, R&R

REMOVING

Drain the radiator and cylinder block. Remove the intake manifold. Disconnect the exhaust pipe. Disconnect the spark plug wires and remove the valve covers.

To remove the right cylinder head, take off the Delcotron rear mounting bracket bolt. Remove the ground straps at the front and rear of the cylinder head. If equipped with a heater, remove all head bolts, except the rear rocker arm shaft bracket bolt. (The blower motor case prevents this.) Loosen the rear rocker arm shaft bracket bolt, and then raise the shaft assembly from the head. Remove all push rods except No. 16. Lift No. 16 push rod to within 1″ of the blower case and tape it to the rocker shaft. Lift the head, rocker shaft assembly, and exhaust

ROCKER ARM SHAFT MUST BE POSITIONED OVER DOWEL IN HEAD

When installing the assembled rocker arm shaft, make sure that the end is positioned properly over the dowel in the cylinder head.

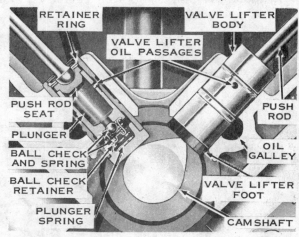

RETAINER RING   VALVE LIFTER BODY
VALVE LIFTER OIL PASSAGES
PUSH ROD SEAT
PLUNGER
BALL CHECK AND SPRING
BALL CHECK RETAINER
PLUNGER SPRING
PUSH ROD
OIL GALLEY
VALVE LIFTER FOOT
CAMSHAFT

Sectioned view through the engine to show the parts of the hydraulic lifter mechanism.

manifold off the dowel pins and move it forward to clear the blower case.

To remove the left cylinder head, take off the power steering belt. Remove 2 power steering pump bracket-to-cylinder head bolts. **CAUTION: Aluminum can be dented or nicked if carelessly handled. Use particular care to protect the gasket surfaces against damage.** Remove the rocker arm shaft assembly, and then take out the push rods. Remove the cylinder head bolts and take off the cylinder head with the gasket manifold attached.

DISASSEMBLING THE HEAD

Remove the spark plugs and the exhaust manifold. Remove the valve keys by compressing the valve spring. Take off the valve spring retainers and springs. Remove the oil deflectors from the valve stems. Lift out the valves. Keep the valves separated so they can be installed in their original locations.

RECONDITIONING THE VALVES

When reconditioning the valves and valve seats, clean all carbon from the cylinder heads and valves, using extreme care not to gouge or scratch machined surfaces. A soft-wire brush is suitable for the purpose. Whenever valves are replaced or new valves and guides are installed, the valve seats must be reconditioned. New guides, if required, must be in place at the time the seats are reconditioned. Service guides are finished to size. **CAUTION: To assure** satisfactory service, it is necessary that the valve seat width of 1/16″ with a seat angle of 45° be maintained.

VALVE GUIDES

Valve guides are identified as follows:

Standard Guides	No grooves
0.001″ oversize	2 grooves
0.010″ oversize	1 groove
0.011″ oversize	3 grooves

Standard guides should be replaced with 0.001″ oversize guides, and 0.010″ guides should be replaced with 0.011″ oversize.

To install new guides, lubricate the guide bore with 10W-30 oil. Insert the valve guide with the outside bevelled end of the guide facing up. *NOTE: The inside bore of the guides are grooved for lubrication. The exhaust guide has grooves the full length of the bore. The intake guide has grooves to within 1/2″ of the bottom.* **CAUTION: The intake guides must be installed with the grooves up.**

Place guide installer, Tool BT-68-5B, over the new guide and tap it until the tool makes contact with the cylinder head. This will automatically position the guide properly.

This tool is designed to drive the old valve guide out of the cylinder head.

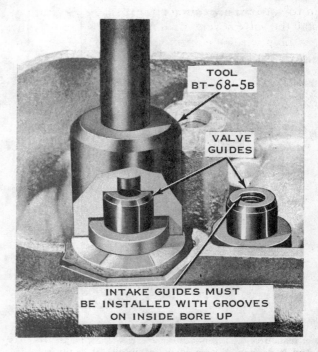

Installing new valve guides. The oil grooves on the inside must be facing up and the outside bevel must be at the top.

ASSEMBLING THE HEAD

Install the valves in their respective guides. Install a new oil deflector over each valve stem. Force the deflectors down as far as possible. The deflectors will correctly position themselves when the engine is started.

Position the valve springs over the valve stems, with the large diameter against the head. Install the valve spring retainers, and then compress the springs with a tool. Install the valve stem keys. Check the valve springs and keys to make sure they are properly seated.

Install the exhaust manifolds. Torque the bolts and nuts to 18-24 ft-lbs. Set the spark plug gap to 0.030" for all except the Jetfire and the 4 Bbl. carburetor engine with synchromesh transmission, which should be set to 0.025". Lubricate the plug threads with a drop of 10W-30 oil and install the plugs. Torque them to 12-17 ft-lbs.

INSTALLING THE CYLINDER HEAD

All cylinder head bolt threads must be coated with P.O.B. No. 4 Sealer. The head gaskets should be coated on both sides with P.O.B. No. 4 Sealer before installation. Torque the head bolts to 45-55 ft-lbs and the exhaust manifold-to-head bolts 18-24 ft-lbs in the sequence shown.

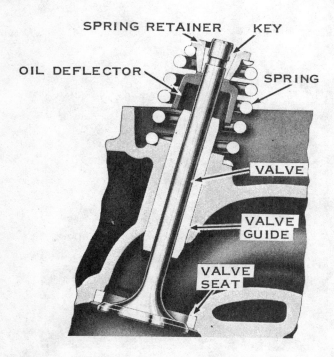

Sectioned view through the valve assembly to show the parts making up the mechanism.

Cylinder head bolt tightening sequence.

Replace the power steering pump and belt on the left cylinder head. On the right side, remove the tape and lower No. 16 push rod. Install the rocker arm shaft assembly on both heads. Replace the ground straps and the Delcotron.

Replace the valve covers and connect the spark plug wires. Connect the exhaust pipe, replace the intake manifold, and fill the radiator.

PISTON AND ROD, R&R

REMOVING

Remove the intake manifold, heads, and oil pan. **CAUTION: Stamp the cylinder number on the machined surfaces of the bolt bosses of the connecting rod and cap for identification when installing. If the pistons are to be removed from the connecting rod, mark the cylinder number on each piston with a silver pencil or quick-drying paint.** The right bank is numbered 2-4-6-8, left bank 1-3-5-7.

Examine the cylinder bores above the ring travel for a ridge. Remove the ridges with a ridge reamer before attempting to remove the piston and rod assembly.

Remove the rod bearing cap and bearing. Install guide Tool BT-8822 over the threads of the rod bolts to prevent damage to the bearing journal and rod bolt threads.

Remove the rod and piston assembly through the top of the cylinder bore. Remove the other rod and piston assemblies in the same manner.

CLEANING AND INSPECTING

CYLINDER BORES

If the cylinder bores are worn excessively, they must be bored to the next oversize. Pistons and rings are available in 0.010", 0.020", 0.030", and 0.040" oversizes. If the cylinder bores are not worn too much, the glazed surfaces must be removed by honing with a 220-grit stone. **CAUTION: Clean all** traces of abrasives with soap and hot water to prevent excessive wear after the engine is placed back in service.

PISTON PINS

The piston pins are locked in the rod by an interference fit, and the pins turn in the pistons. New pins are available in 0.0015", 0.003", 0.005", and 0.010" oversizes.

To remove a piston pin, install the illustrated tool, and then push the piston pin out. Remove the connecting rod from the piston.

To assemble a fitted piston pin to its rod, lubricate the piston pin holes in the piston and connecting rod to facilitate installation. Position the connecting rod in its respective piston so that the notch in the piston crown and the letter "F" will face the front of the engine. The oil spurt hole must face the camshaft on both banks, while the rod identification marks for the left-bank rods will face to the rear of the engine. The rod identification marks for right-bank rods must face to the front of the engine.

Install the piston pin on the installer and the spring and pilot into the support. Install the piston and rod

Install this tool, or a piece of rubber hose, over the bolt threads to prevent damage to the bearing journal.

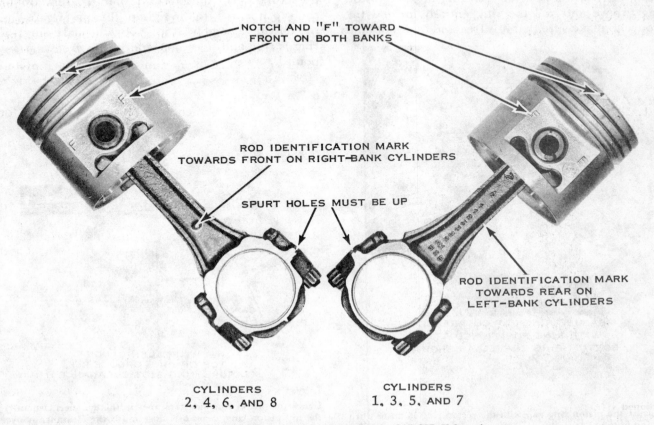

NOTCH AND "F" TOWARD FRONT ON BOTH BANKS

ROD IDENTIFICATION MARK TOWARDS FRONT ON RIGHT-BANK CYLINDERS

SPURT HOLES MUST BE UP

ROD IDENTIFICATION MARK TOWARDS REAR ON LEFT-BANK CYLINDERS

CYLINDERS 2, 4, 6, AND 8

CYLINDERS 1, 3, 5, AND 7

Details of the piston-and-rod assembly for the 215 CID V-8 engine.

on the support, indexing the pilot through the piston and rod. Place the assembly on an arbor press, start the pin into the piston, and press on the installer until the pilot bottoms. Remove the installer-and-support assembly from the piston-and-connecting rod assembly. Check the piston pin for freedom of movement in the piston bores.

PISTON RINGS

The top compression ring is chrome plated. The second compression ring is the deep-section twist type. This type of compression ring takes its name from its installed position, which is cocked or twisted. It assumes and maintains this position for life because the lower edge of the ring is chamfered, making the rings unbalanced in cross section. All compression rings are marked on the upper side of the ring. When installing compression rings, make sure the marked side faces the top of the piston.

The oil-control rings consist of two segments (rails) and a spacer. Piston rings are furnished in standard sizes as well as 0.020", 0.030", and 0.040" oversizes.

Check the space or gap between the ends of the compression rings with a feeler gauge, which should be 0.010-0.020" for both rings. The oil ring rail gap should be 0.015-0.055".

Slip the outer surface of each ring into the piston ring groove and roll the ring entirely around the groove to make sure that it is free and does not bind

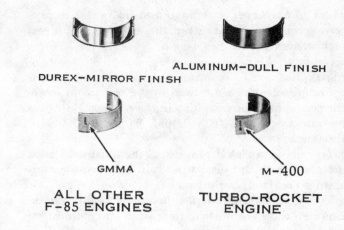

Details of the types of connecting rod bearing inserts used on the 215 CID engine.

in the groove at any point. The compression ring side clearance should be 0.003-0.005". The assembled oil ring side clearance should be 0.0005-0.0065".

Install the oil ring spacer in the oil ring groove and position the gap in line with the piston pin hole. Hold the spacer ends butted, and then install a steel rail on the top side of the spacer. Position the gap at least 1" to the left of the spacer gap, and then install the second rail on the lower side of the spacer. Position the gap at least 1" to the right of the spacer gap. Flex the oil ring assembly in its groove to make sure the ring is free and does not bind in the groove at any point.

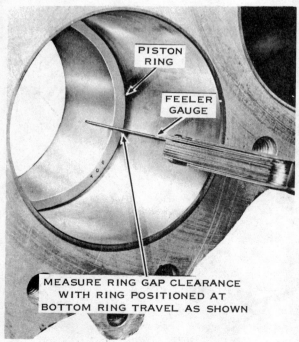

Measure the piston ring gap with the piston ring in an unworn section of the bore.

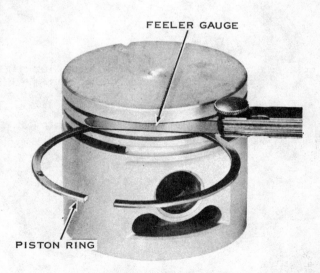

Check the piston ring side clearance in this manner. Generally, the top piston ring wears the most and if the clearance is over 0.006", the piston must be reconditioned, or replaced.

INSTALLING

The rods should be installed in the same cylinder from which they were removed and with the piston marks facing the front. Lubricate the pistons and cylinder bores, remove the bearing caps, and install the piston and rod assembly into its proper bore. Use a compressor to hold the rings in place. Lubricate the crankpin and pull the connecting rod down onto it. Install the cap and nuts; torque them to 30-35 ft-lbs.

Replace the oil pump. Install new oil pan gaskets and end corks. Carefully place the oil pan in position and tighten the oil pan bolts to 6-15 ft-lbs of torque. Lower the engine and connect all parts. Replace the intake manifold and cylinder heads.

TIMING GEAR AND/OR CHAIN, R&R

REMOVING

Drain the cooling system. Disconnect the heater hose, by-pass hose, and both radiator hoses. Disconnect the oil pressure switch wire.

Remove the crankshaft pulley, fan, fan pulley, and all belts. Take off the distributor cap, vacuum hose, Delcotron, and mounting bracket. Remove the distributor. Remove the fuel pump hoses and the fuel pump. Take off the oil pan. Remove nine (9) front cover-to-block attaching bolts and then remove the cover.

Remove the distributor drive gear bolt, washer, and gear from the end of the camshaft. Take off the fuel pump eccentric. Remove the crankshaft gear, chain, and cam gear together.

INSTALLING

Install the camshaft gear, crankshaft gear, and timing chain together, aligning the timing marks through the centers of the shafts, as shown. Install the fuel pump eccentric, with the flat side to the rear. Replace the distributor drive gear, washer, and bolt. Torque the bolt to 40-45 ft-lbs. Install the oil slinger.

Apply P.O.B. No. 2 Sealer to the front cover, apply a new gasket, and then install the front cover. **CAUTION: Whenever the front timing chain cover is removed, it will be necessary to remove the oil pump cover and pack the space around the oil pump gears completely full of petrolatum. This step is very important as the oil pump may lose its prime when the cover is removed. If the pump is not packed, it may not pump oil as soon as the engine starts.** Apply 10W-30 oil to the bolts and install them. Torque the bolts evenly to 20-25 ft-lbs.

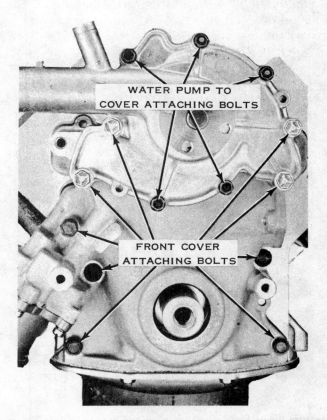

Use a ring compressor when installing the assembled piston and rings to prevent damaging them.

These nine (9) bolts hold the engine front cover to the block. Don't confuse them with the water pump retaining bolts.

FUEL PUMP ECCENTRIC

OIL GROOVE

CAMSHAFT

DISTRIBUTOR DRIVE GEAR

Installing the distributor drive gear.

Apply seal lubricant on the pulley seal surface. Install the pulley and pulley bolt, torquing it to 140-160 ft-lbs.

ALIGN TIMING MARKS

When installing the timing gears and chain, align the timing marks through the center of the gears, as shown.

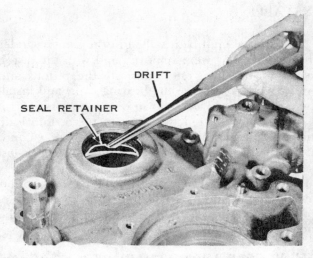

DRIFT

SEAL RETAINER

Always install a new oil seal in the front cover to minimize the chances of an oil leak. This shows how the old seal can be removed.

Connect the oil pressure switch. Install the Delcotron, mounting bracket, and adjusting link. Install a new fuel pump gasket using P.O.B. No. 2 Sealer. Apply special seal lubricant to the fuel pump arm. Apply 10W-30 oil to the two fuel pump attaching bolts, and torque them to 20-25 ft-lbs. Connect the fuel lines.

Install the distributor, timing it to No. 1 cylinder. Connect the distributor vacuum advance hose and primary lead. Install the distributor cap and wires.

Connect the heater hose, by-pass hose, and both

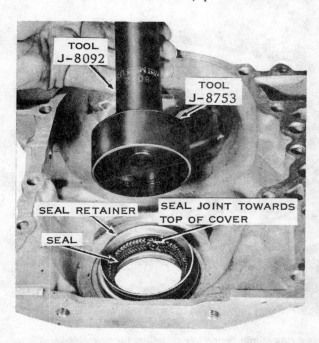

TOOL J-8092

TOOL J-8753

SEAL RETAINER

SEAL JOINT TOWARDS TOP OF COVER

SEAL

This tool is designed to drive in the new seal without distorting it.

radiator hoses. Install the fan pulley, fan, and four attaching bolts. Torque the bolts 15-20 ft-lbs. Install the belts and adjust the tension.

Install the oil pan. Fill the radiator and crankcase.

OIL PUMP, R&R

REMOVING

Disconnect the pressure switch wire. Clean all dirt away from the pump-to-front cover joint, also around the oil filter joint. Remove the oil filter.

Remove six pump cover-to-front cover attaching screws. Remove the cover carefully as the idler gear may fall out. Slide out the idler and oil pump drive gears.

DISASSEMBLING

Remove the oil filter by-pass valve cap, with the pressure switch. Remove the oil filter by-pass spring and the valve. Remove the oil pressure valve cap and the spring. Remove the pressure regulator valve by tapping the housing in the palm of your hand.

CLEANING AND INSPECTING

Wash all parts in clean solvent and blow out all passages with compressed air. Inspect all parts for

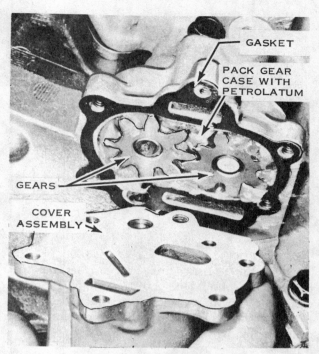

Always pack the oil pump with petrolatum, otherwise the pump may not pick up oil during the initial start and burn up the engine.

scoring. Small imperfections can be cleaned with crocus cloth. **CAUTION: Do not break the sharp edges of the valve with the crocus cloth.**

Check the cover bore for cracks, nicks, or warping.

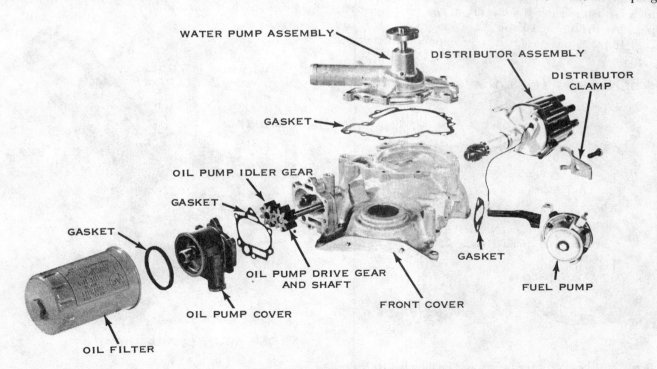

Exploded view of the parts of the engine front cover.

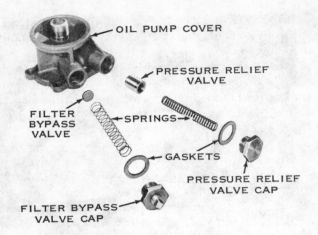

OIL PUMP COVER

PRESSURE RELIEF VALVE

FILTER BYPASS VALVE

SPRINGS

GASKETS

PRESSURE RELIEF VALVE CAP

FILTER BYPASS VALVE CAP

Details of the oil pump cover.

Check the pressure relief valve clearance in the bore, which should be 0.0015-0.0035". Too much clearance can affect oil pressure at idle. (The oil pressure warning light on the instrument panel is calibrated to light when the oil pressure is less than 3 lbs.)

Check the end clearance of the gears, which should be 0.0015-0.0075".

ASSEMBLING

Install the filter by-pass valve into the output passage bore (this is the passage with the inside diameter ribs), seating it squarely in the bottom of the passage. Install the spring (light weight), gasket, and cap. Replace the gasket if it is damaged. Install the pressure regulator valve (flat end first), pressure regulator spring, gasket, and oil pressure regulator cap. Torque the cap to 30-35 ft-lbs.

INSTALLING

Install the pump drive gear and the idler gear. Position a new gasket on the pump cover. Fill the gear cavity with petrolatum and force it into every cavity of the gear pocket; also between the teeth of the gears. **CAUTION: This step is very important to assist in instant priming when the engine is started. Unless the pump is packed with petrolatum, it may not prime itself when the engine starts.**

Replace the cover, install a new oil filter, and connect the pressure switch wire.

REAR MAIN BEARING AND/OR OIL SEALS, R&R

REMOVING

Remove the oil pan, as previously discussed. Remove the rear main bearing cap; take out the bearing insert and old seals. Clean the bearing cap and seal grooves. Inspect for cracks.

To remove the upper bearing shell, insert a flattened cotter pin in the oil passage hole in the crankshaft, and then rotate the crankshaft in a direction opposite to cranking rotation. The pin will contact the upper shell and roll it out.

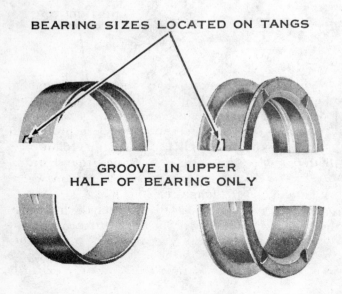

BEARING SIZES LOCATED ON TANGS

GROOVE IN UPPER HALF OF BEARING ONLY

Details of the main bearing inserts used on the 215 CID engine. Note the oil groove in the upper half of the bearing only.

TOOL J-8807

REAR MAIN OIL SEAL

CUT SEAL HERE

REAR MAIN BEARING CAP

This tool should be used to form a new rear main bearing oil seal.

The main bearing journals should be checked for roughness and wear. Slight roughness can be removed with a fine-grit polishing cloth saturated with 10W-30 oil. Burrs can be removed with a fine oil stone. If the journals are scored or ridged, the crankshaft must be replaced or reground. The journals can be measured for out-of-round with the crankshaft installed by using a crankshaft caliper and inside micrometer or a main bearing micrometer. The upper bearing shell must be removed when measuring the crankshaft journals. Maximum out-of-round of the crankshaft journals must not exceed 0.0015".

Clean the crankshaft journals and bearing caps thoroughly before installing new main bearing inserts.

INSTALLING

Place a new upper shell on the crankshaft journal, with the locating tang in the correct position. Rotate the shaft to turn it into place, using a cotter pin as during removal.

Install a new seal into the bearing cap, packing it by hand. Using Seal Installer J-8807, hammer the seal into its groove. To check if the seal is fully seated in the bearing cap, slide Tool J-8807 away from the seal. Now, slide the tool against the seal. If the undercut area of the tool slides over the seal, the seal is fully seated. If the tool butts against the seal, the seal must be driven farther into the seal groove. Rotate the tool before cutting off excess seal packing.

Holding the tool tightly against the seal, cut 1/16" from the bearing surface. Taper the end of the seal into a point. With a screwdriver, pack all seal fibers towards the center, away from the edges. Rotate the seal installer to cut the seal between the notch and handle. Install the two new side bearing cap seals, leaving the seal extended on each side of the cap.

Coat the back of the new bearing insert with light oil, and then install it in the bearing cap. Clean the crankshaft bearing journal and seal contact areas. Install bearing cap guide pins. Force the bearing cap into place by tapping it with a block of wood. Remove the guide pins. Apply lubricant Part No. 980131 to the cap bolts. Torque the bolts to 65-70 ft-lbs. **CAUTION: Do not trim the ends of the side seals.**

Install the pan with a new gasket. Install the lower flywheel cover.

ENGINE SERVICE SPECIFICATIONS

CRANKSHAFT

The crankshaft main bearing journals should all measure 2.2980-2.2990". The crankpins should measure 1.999-2.000", and the crankshaft end play should be 0.004-0.008".

The oil clearance should be 0.0008-0.0024" for all main bearings and 0.0002-0.0022" for the connecting rods, both of these dimensions have an additional wear limit of 0.002".

VALVES

The faces of the intake and exhaust valves and seats should be 45°, with a seat width of 0.037-0.075" for each. The intake valve stem should measure 0.3427-0.3432", with a valve stem-to-guide clearance of 0.0010-0.0025". The exhaust valve stem should measure 0.3422-0.3427", with a stem-to-guide clearance of 0.0015-0.0030".

225 CID V-6 ENGINE—1964-65

This V-6 engine used only in the F-85 models was characterized by having the distributor mounted in the front of the engine. The cylinder bore center-to-center spacing is 4.24". The unusual valve arrangement for the left bank is E-I-E-I-I-E and for the right bank E-I-I-E-I-E, both stated from the front to the rear of the engine, and the firing order is 1-6-5-4-3-2. The cylinders in the left bank are numbered 1-3-5 and the ones in the right bank are numbered 2-4-6.

The piston pins are a press-fit in the upper end of the connecting rods and are a sliding fit in the pistons. Cylinder heads are cast iron, with the valve stem guides cast in place. Right and left cylinder heads are interchangeable.

ENGINE, R&R

REMOVING

When it is necessary to remove the engine assembly, the necessary items should be disconnected and the body raised off the engine and suspension assembly. To do this, remove the hood and place protective covers on the fenders. Disconnect the following: Battery cable, ground cable, engine ground strap, accelerator linkage, oil pressure switch, ignition switch wire, temperature gauge, and fuel line.

Drain the radiator and disconnect the radiator hoses and heater hoses. If equipped with air conditioning, remove the pressure hoses from the compressor and fan shroud. Remove the air cleaner and disconnect the front exhaust pipe from the rear exhaust pipe.

Disconnect the speedometer cable, front of the propeller shaft, and shift linkage from the transmission. Disconnect the clutch and clutch equalizer on synchromesh-equipped cars, stabilizer brackets from the frame rail, front brake hoses, and steering shaft from the gear. Raise the steering shaft into the steering column. Place a block of wood between the front cross bar and the front of the engine oil pan. Remove the rear transmission mount crossmember and support the rear of the transmission with a stand.

With the front wheels on the floor, remove the three isolation mount bolts and carefully raise the body off the engine and suspension. **CAUTION: Care must be taken not to let the suspension tip.**

INSTALLING

When installing the assembly into the body, the torque specifications and adjustments can be found for the specific unit in the Appendix of this manual. The brake system must be bled and the cooling and lubricating system properly serviced.

OIL PAN, R&R

REMOVING

Raise the car and support it on stands. Drain the oil. Remove the lower flywheel housing bolts and the housing.

Remove the oil pan bolts and lower the oil pan enough to remove the oil pump pipe and screen-to-cylinder block bolts. *NOTE: On synchromesh models, it will be necessary to raise the engine.* Rotate the crank-

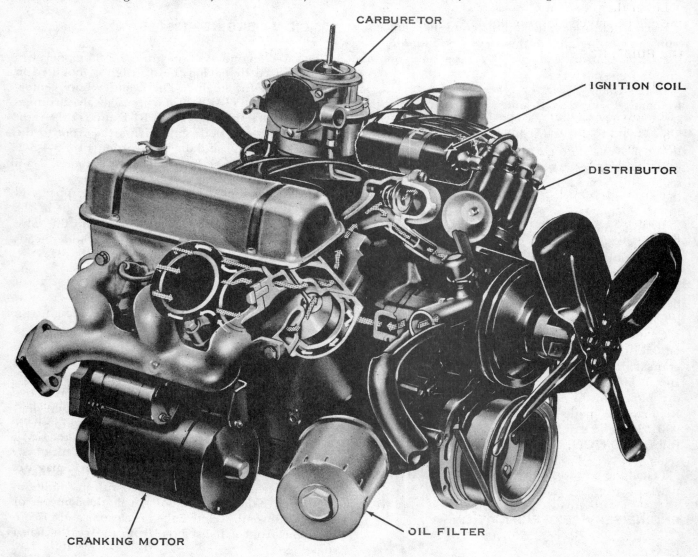

CARBURETOR

IGNITION COIL

DISTRIBUTOR

CRANKING MOTOR

OIL FILTER

Sectioned view of the V-6 engine to show the main parts and the flow of coolant.

shaft to provide maximum clearance at the forward end of the oil pan. Move the front of the pan to the right, and then lower it.

Clean the oil pan. Pry the screen out of the housing to examine it for evidence of clogging. Clean the screen and housing thoroughly in solvent and blow dry with an air stream. Snap the screen into the housing.

INSTALLING

Move the oil pan into position, and then install the oil pump pipe and screen-to-cylinder block bolts. Install and tighten the oil pan bolts to 15 ft-lbs of torque. **CAUTION: Tighten the bolts evenly, but do not overtighten.** Replace the lower flywheel housing.

Lower the vehicle and replace the engine oil. Start the engine and check for oil leaks.

OIL PUMP, R&R

REMOVING

Remove the oil filter. Take out the screws attaching the oil pump cover assembly to the timing chain cover. Remove the cover assembly and slide out the oil pump gears.

CLEANING AND INSPECTING

Wash off the gears and inspect for wear and scores. Replace any unsatisfactory gears.

Remove the oil pressure relief valve cap, spring, and valve. The oil filter bypass valve and spring are staked in place and must not be removed.

Wash the parts thoroughly and inspect the relief valve for wear or scores. Check the relief valve spring to see that it is not worn on its side or collapsed. Replace any relief valve spring that is questionable.

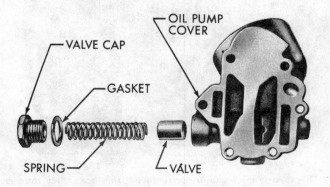

Exploded view of the oil pump cover.

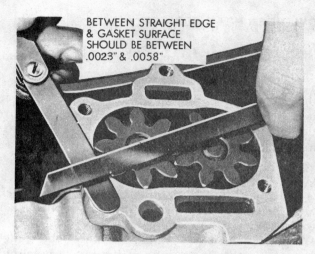

BETWEEN STRAIGHT EDGE & GASKET SURFACE SHOULD BE BETWEEN .0023" & .0058"

Measuring the oil pump gear end clearance.

Thoroughly clean the screen staked in the cover.

Check the relief valve in its bore in the cover. The valve should have no more clearance than an easy slip fit. If any perceptible side shake can be felt, the valve and/or the cover should be replaced.

Check the filter bypass valve for cracks, nicks, or warping. The valve should be flat and free of nicks or scratches.

ASSEMBLING

Lubricate and install the pressure relief valve and spring into the bore of the oil pump cover. Install the cap and gasket. Torque the cap to 25-35 ft-lbs. with a reliable torque wrench. **CAUTION: Do not overtighten.**

Install the oil pump gears and shaft into the oil pump body section of the timing chain cover to check the gear end clearance. Place a straightedge over the gears, and then measure the clearance between the straightedge and the gasket surface, which should be between 0.0023" and 0.0058". If the clearance is less than 0.0023", check the timing chain cover gear pocket for evidence of wear.

If the gear end clearance is satisfactory, remove the gears and pack the gear pocket full of petroleum jelly. **CAUTION: Do not use chassis lube. CAUTION: This step is very important. Unless the pump is packed with petroleum jelly, it may not prime itself when the engine is started.** Install the gears so the petroleum jelly is forced into every cavity of the gear pocket and between the teeth of the gears.

Place a new gasket in position. Install the cover assembly screws. Tighten them alternately and evenly to a torque of 8-12 ft-lbs. Install the filter on the nipple.

CYLINDER HEAD SERVICE

REMOVING THE CYLINDER HEAD

Drain the radiator and cylinder block. Disconnect the battery cables. Remove the air cleaner. Disconnect all pipes and hoses from the carburetor. Remove the ignition coil. Disconnect the water temperature indicator wire from the switch. Disconnect the accelerator linkage, throttle return spring, and positive crankcase ventilator hose.

Slide the front thermostat bypass hose clamp back, and then disconnect the hose at the timing chain cover to allow the coolant to drain from the manifold. Disconnect the upper radiator hose at the outlet. Disconnect the heater hose at the intake manifold.

Remove the bolts holding the intake manifold to the cylinder heads. Remove the intake manifold and carburetor as an assembly. Discard the intake manifold gasket and seals.

Pull the spark plug wire retainers from the brackets on the rocker arm cover. Disconnect the spark plug wires at the plugs and swing the wires and retainer out of the way. Remove the screws attaching the rocker arm cover to the cylinder head. On the right side,

remove the positive crankcase ventilator valve, rocker arm cover, and gasket. Remove the rocker arm shaft bracket-to-cylinder head attaching bolts. Remove the rocker arm and shaft assembly. The oil baffle is mounted under the rear bolts on the right rocker arm-and-shaft assembly.

Remove the push rods. If the lifters are to be serviced, remove them. Otherwise, protect the lifters and camshaft from dirt by covering the area with clean cloths.

Remove the Delcotron mounting bracket and brace attaching bolts. Position the Delcotron out of the way. Remove the power steering pump rear bracket-to-cylinder head attaching bolts. If equipped with a Jetaway transmission, remove the filler tube support-to-exhaust manifold bolt. Remove the exhaust manifold-to-exhaust pipe bolts and take out the cylinder head bolts. Lift off the cylinder head with the exhaust manifold attached.

RECONDITIONING THE VALVES AND GUIDES

Place the cylinder head on a clean, smooth surface. Using a suitable tool, compress the valve spring and remove the cap retainers. Release the tool and remove the spring and cap. Repeat for the other valves. Remove the valves. **CAUTION: The valves should be set in a rack so they can be reinstalled in their original locations.**

Remove the carbon from the combustion chambers,

Details of the valve mechanism of the V-6 engine.

The valve guides cannot be removed; therefore, they must be reamed oversize if worn, and a valve with an oversize stem used to obtain the specified clearance.

using care to avoid scratching the head or the valve seats. Clean all carbon and gum deposits from the valve guide bores. Clean the valves. Inspect the valve faces and seats for pits, burned spots, or evidence of poor seating.

Grind or replace valves as necessary. If a valve head must be ground to a knife edge to obtain a true face, the valve should be replaced; as a sharp edge will run too hot. 45° is the correct angle for valve faces.

Valve stem guides are non-replaceable. If a valve stem has excessive clearance, the guide must be reamed 0.003″ oversize, using Reamer J-5830-1. Valves with 0.003″ oversize stems are available for service.

True up the valve seats to 45°. Cutting a valve seat results in lowering the valve spring pressure and increases the width of the seat. The nominal width of the valve seat is 1/16″. If a valve seat is over 5/64″ wide after truing, it should be narrowed to the specified width by using 20° and 70° stones.

Improper hydraulic valve lifter operation will result if the valve and seat are refinished to the extent that the valve stem is raised more than 0.050″ above its normal height. In this case, it is necessary to replace the worn parts. The normal height of the valve stem above the valve spring seat surface of the head is 1.825″.

Lightly lap the valves into their seats with fine grounding compound. The refacing and reseating operations should leave the refinished surfaces smooth and true so that a minimum of lapping is required. Excessive lapping will groove the valve face, preventing a good seat when hot.

Test each valve for concentricity with its seat and for tight seating. The usual test is to coat the valve face lightly with Prussian blue and turn the valve against the seat. If the valve seat is concentric with the valve guide, a mark will be made all around the seat. If the seat is not concentric with the guide, a mark will be made on only one side of the seat. Next, coat the valve seat lightly with Prussian blue. Rotate the valve against the seat to determine if the valve face is concentric with the valve stem, and if the valve is seating all the way around. Both of these tests are necessary to prove that a proper seat has been obtained.

Lube the stems and tips with engine oil and re-install the valves, springs, caps, and cap retainers. **CAUTION: Install the valve spring, with the closely wound coils toward the cylinder head.**

REPLACING ROCKER ARMS

Remove the rocker arm-and-shaft assembly. Take out the cotter pin, plain washer, and spring washer from each end of the rocker arm shaft. Remove the bracket bolts. Slide the rocker arms and brackets off the shaft.

Clean and inspect all parts, taking particular care to clean out all oil holes. Replace parts that are excessively worn.

Assemble the springs, rocker arms, and brackets on the shaft. Take care that the assembly for the right side has the notch in the shaft facing forward and the left side has the notch to the rear. Install the spring washer, flat washer, and cotter pin on each end of the shaft in the order named.

Install the bolts, with plain washers, through the brackets and shaft so the notch in the right assembly is facing up and to the front, and the notch in the left assembly is facing up and to the rear.

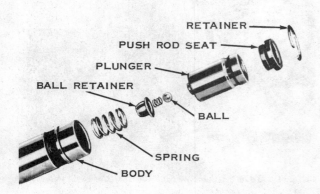

RETAINER
PUSH ROD SEAT
PLUNGER
BALL RETAINER
BALL
SPRING
BODY

Exploded view of a hydraulic valve lifter.

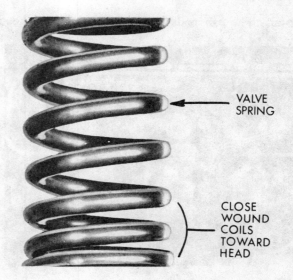

VALVE SPRING

CLOSE WOUND COILS TOWARD HEAD

The valve springs must be installed with the close-wound coils against the cylinder head.

INSTALLING THE CYLINDER HEAD

Wipe off the engine block gasket surface and be certain no foreign material has fallen into the cylinder bores, bolt holes, or valve lifter area. It is good practice to clean out all bolt holes with compressed air.

Install a new head gasket on the cylinder block. Dowels in the block hold the gasket in position. Always handle gaskets carefully to avoid kinking or damaging the surface treatment. **CAUTION: Do not use any type of sealing material on head gaskets. The gaskets are coated with a special lacquer to provide a good seal, once the parts have warmed to operating temperature.**

Assemble the exhaust manifold to each cylinder head. Torque the bolts to 10-15 ft-lbs. The Jetaway transmission filler tube bracket fastens to the rear bolt on the right side.

Clean the gasket surface of the cylinder head and carefully set it in place on the engine block, locating the holes in the dowel pins. Clean and coat the head bolts with sealer. Install the bolts as shown. Tighten the head bolts a little at a time, about three times around, in the sequence shown. Torque the bolts in the same sequence to 65-70 ft-lbs. **CAUTION: Use an accurate torque wrench when installing head bolts and do not overtighten. Uneven tightening of the cylinder head bolts can distort the cylinder bores, causing compression loss and excessive oil consumption.**

INSTALLING THE ROCKER ARM-AND-SHAFT ASSEMBLY

Install the push rods through the cylinder head

Cylinder head bolt tightening sequence for the V-6 engine.

openings so the rods are correctly positioned on the lifter plungers. Clean the bases of the rocker arm shaft brackets and bracket bosses on the cylinder head. Check the notch on one end of the rocker arm shaft to be sure it is positioned correctly.

Tilt the rocker arms toward the push rods and locate the top of each push rod in its rocker arm seat. Draw down the rocker arm and shaft assembly by tightening the bracket bolts a little at a time. Use a reliable torque wrench to torque the bracket bolts to 25-35 ft-lbs. **CAUTION: Do not overtighten.**

Install the rocker arm cover and gasket. On the right side, connect the positive crankcase ventilation system. Connect the spark plug wires and set the wire retainers in position on the brackets.

The cylinder head bolts are of three different lengths, and this illustration shows where each should be installed.

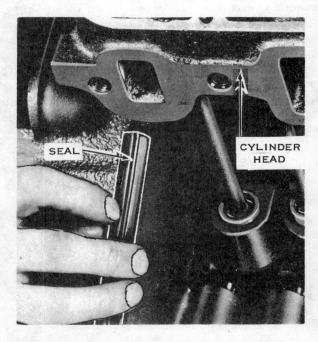

Installing the front seal on the rail of the cylinder block.

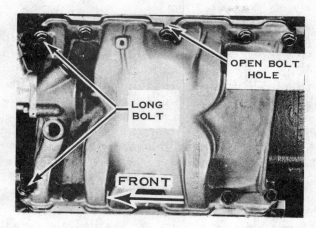

The open bolt hole is held to close tolerances so that the bolt in this location serves to locate the manifold perfectly.

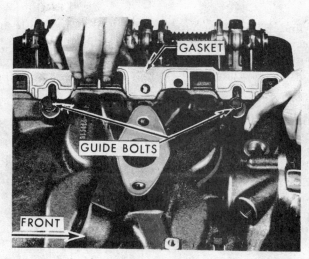

Lift the intake manifold slightly, and then install the gasket, which is notched to go over the guide bolts.

INSTALLING THE INTAKE MANIFOLD

Place new rubber manifold seals in position at the front and rear rails of the cylinder block. **CAUTION: Be sure the pointed ends of the seal fit snugly against the block and head.**

Set the intake manifold in place carefully and start two guide bolts on each side. Lift the manifold slightly and slip the gaskets into position as shown. Take care to see that the gasket is installed with the three intake manifold ports aligned with the head and manifold. The gasket should be installed as shown for the left side and reversed for right-side installation.

Install a manifold attaching bolt in the open bolt hole as shown. *NOTE: The open bolt hole is held to close tolerances and the bolt in this location serves to locate the manifold perfectly fore-and-aft.* Install the remaining manifold-to-cylinder head bolts with the longer bolts at the forward location. Torque the bolts alternately and evenly to 35 ft-lbs.

PISTON AND ROD, R&R

REMOVING

Remove the cylinder heads. Examine the cylinder bores above the ring travel. If the bores are worn so a shoulder or ridge exists at this point, remove the ridges with a ridge reamer to avoid damaging the rings or cracking the ring lands during removal.

Use a silver pencil or quick drying paint to mark the cylinder number on all pistons, connecting rods, and caps. Starting at the front end of the crankcase, the cylinders in the right bank are numbered 2-4-6 and in the left bank they are numbered 1-3-5.

Remove the cap and bearing shell from No. 1 connecting rod. Install a connecting rod bolt guide hose on the bolts to hold the upper half of the bearing shell in place. Push the piston and rod assembly up and out of the cylinder. Then remove the guides and install the bearing shells and caps on the rod.

Remove the other rod-and-piston assemblies in the same manner.

Remove the compression rings with an expander. Remove the oil ring by removing the two rails and the spacer-expander, which are separate pieces in each piston's third groove.

To remove the piston pin, set up Tool BT-6408 and Adapter BT-6408-5, as shown.

CLEANING AND INSPECTING

CYLINDER BORES

Inspect the cylinder walls for scoring, roughness, or ridges which indicate excessive wear. Check the

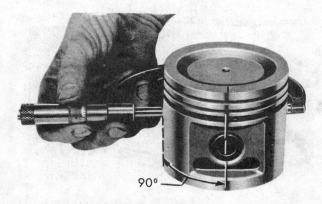

Measuring the piston skirt to determine the amount of wear.

cylinder bores for taper and out-of-round with an accurate cylinder gauge at the top, middle, and bottom of the bore, both parallel and at right angles to the centerline of the engine.

A cylinder bore which is tapered 0.005″ or more, or is out-of-round 0.003″. or more, must be reconditioned.

PISTONS

Clean the carbon from the piston surfaces and the under side of the piston heads. Clean all carbon from the ring grooves with a suitable tool and remove all gum or varnish from the piston skirts with a suitable solvent.

Carefully examine the pistons for rough or scored bearing surfaces, cracks in the skirt or head, cracked or broken ring lands, and chipping or uneven wear, which would cause the rings to seat improperly or to have excessive clearance in the ring grooves. Damaged or faulty pistons must be replaced.

The pistons are cam-ground, which means that the diameter at a right angle to the piston pin is greater than the diameter parallel to the piston pin. When a piston is checked for size, it must be measured with micrometers applied to the skirt at points 90° to the piston pin. The piston should be measured (for fitting purposes) 1/4″ below the bottom of the oil ring groove.

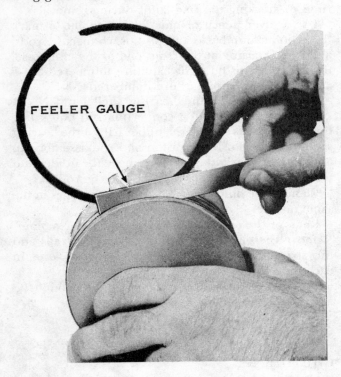

Checking the piston ring side clearance.

PISTON PINS

Inspect the bearing surfaces of the piston pins. Check for wear by measuring the worn and unworn surfaces with micrometers. Rough or worn pins must be replaced. Test the fit of the piston pins in the piston bosses. If the piston bosses are worn out-of-round or oversize, the piston and pin assembly must be replaced. Oversize pins are not practical due to the pin being a press-fit in the connecting rod. Piston pins must fit the piston with an easy finger push at 70°F (0.0003″ to 0.0005″ clearance).

PISTON RINGS

When new piston rings are installed, the glazed cylinder walls should be slightly dulled, but without increasing the bore diameter, by means of the finest grade of stones in a cylinder hone. New piston rings must be checked for clearance in piston grooves and for end gap in the cylinder bores; however, the flexible oil rings are not checked for end gap. The cylinder bores and piston grooves must be clean, dry, and free of carbon and burrs.

To check the end gap of compression rings, place the ring in the cylinder in which it will be used, square it in the bore using the upper end of a piston, and then measure the gap with a feeler gauge. Piston rings should have not less than 0.010″ gap when placed in the cylinder bores. If the gap is less than 0.010″, file the ends of the rings carefully with a smooth file to obtain the proper gap.

With the rings installed on the piston, check the clearance in the grooves by inserting a feeler gauge between each ring and its lower land. Any wear that occurs forms a step at the inner portion of the lower land. If the piston grooves have worn to the extent that relatively high steps exist on the lower lands, the piston should be replaced because the steps will inter-

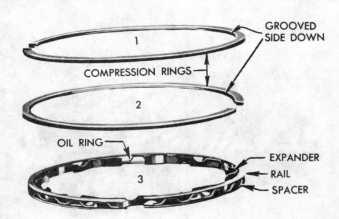

Details for installing the piston rings in the V-6 engine.

fere with the operation of new rings and the ring clearance will be excessive.

When fitting new rings to new pistons, the side clearance of the compression rings should be 0.003″ to 0.005″, and the side clearance of the oil ring should be 0.0035″ to 0.0095″.

INSTALLING

To assemble the piston, pin and connecting rod, set up Tool BT-6408 and Adapter BT-6408-4 as shown. The piston and rod assembly must be mated as shown for right and left bank rods. Assemble the piston and rod on the spring-loaded guide pin. Lubricate the piston pin to avoid damage when pressing it through the connecting rod. Install the drive pin in the upper end of the piston pin. Press on the drive pin until the piston pin bottoms. Remove the piston and rod assembly from the press. Rotate the piston on the pin to be sure the pin was not damaged during the pressing operation.

Install the piston rings as shown. Position the expander ends over the piston pin. Install the oil ring rail spacer and oil ring rails. Position the gaps in the rails on the same side of the piston as the oil spit hole in the connecting rod. Install the compression rings in the upper two grooves. If a single chrome-plated compression ring is used, it must be installed in the top groove. *NOTE: All compression rings are marked with a dimple, a letter "T", a letter "O", or the word TOP to identify the side of the ring which must be assembled toward the top of the piston.*

Make sure the cylinder bores, pistons, connecting rod bearings, and crankshaft journals are absolutely clean, and then coat all bearing surfaces with engine oil. Position the crankpin straight down. Remove the connecting rod cap and, with the bearing upper shell seated in the rod, install the connecting rod guides

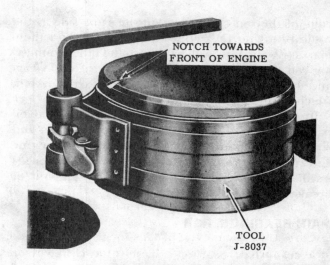

A ring clamp should be used when pushing an assembled piston into the cylinder bore to keep from breaking the rings.

to hold the upper bearing shell in place and prevent damage to the crankpin.

Make sure the gap in the oil ring rails is toward the center of the engine and the gaps of the compression rings are not in line with each other or with the gaps in the oil ring rails. Be certain the ends of the oil ring spacer-expander are butted together, not lapped over.

Lubricate the piston and rings and install the assembly in its bore by compressing the rings with a compressor. Use the wooden end of a hammer handle to push the piston down. **CAUTION: Don't hammer on the piston because a ring may be caught and you could snap it.** Install the cap with a new lower bearing shell and tighten both nuts to 30-35 ft-lbs. of torque.

Install the other piston-and-rod assemblies in the same manner. When the piston-and-rod assemblies are properly installed, the oil spit holes in the connecting rods will be facing the camshaft, the rib on the

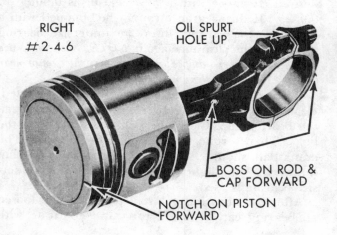

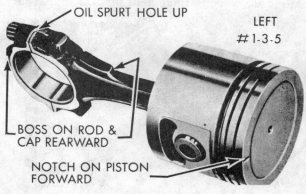

Details of the piston-and-rod assembly for the V-6 engine.

edge of the rod cap will be on the same side as the conical boss on the connecting rod web, and these marks (rib and boss) will be toward the other connecting rod on the same crankpin. Check the end clearance between the connecting rods on each crankpin, which should be between 0.005″ and 0.012″.

Installing the cylinder heads, oil screen, and oil pan. **CAUTION: After installing new pistons and rings, care should be used in starting the engine and running it for the first hour. Avoid high speeds until the parts have had a reasonable amount of break-in to avoid scuffing.**

MAIN BEARINGS, R&R

A crankshaft bearing consists of two halves or shells which are not interchangeable in the cap and crankcase. The upper (crankcase) half of the bearing is grooved to supply oil to the connecting rod bearings, while the lower (bearing cap) half of the shell is not grooved. All crankshaft bearings, except the thrust bearing, are identical. The thrust bearing is longer and flanged to take end thrust. When the shells are placed in the crankcase and bearing cap, the ends extend slightly beyond the parting surfaces so that when the cap bolts are tightened, the shells will be clamped tightly in place to insure positive seating and to prevent turning. The ends of the shells must never be filed flush with the parting surface of the crankcase or bearing cap.

REMOVING

Remove the oil pan, oil pump pipe, and oil screen. Inspect each main bearing in turn so that the crankshaft is well supported by other bearings. Since any service conditions which affect the crankshaft bearings also affect the connecting rod bearings, it is advisable to inspect the connecting rod bearings first. If the crankpins are worn to the extent that the crankshaft

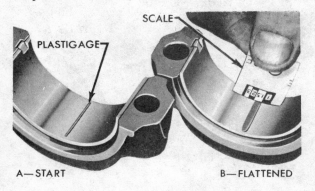

A—START   B—FLATTENED

Checking the rod bearing insert oil clearance with Plastigage.

must be replaced, the engine must be removed from the frame.

Remove one bearing cap, then clean and inspect the lower bearing shell and the crankshaft journal. If the journal surface is scored or ridged, the crankshaft must be replaced. Slight roughness can be polished out with fine-grit polishing cloth thoroughly wetted with engine oil; burrs can be honed off with a fine stone.

If the condition of the lower bearing shell and crankshaft journal is satisfactory, check the bearing clearance with Plastigage. Turn the crankshaft so that the oil hole is up to avoid dripping oil on the Plastigage, which would dissolve the material. Place paper shims in the lower halves of the adjacent bearings and tighten the cap bolts to take the weight of the crankshaft off the lower shell of the bearing being checked. If the clearance exceeds 0.003″, it is advisable to install a new bearing.

INSTALLING

To replace the inserts, loosen all crankshaft bearing cap bolts 1/2 turn, and remove the cap of the bearing to be replaced. Remove the upper bearing shell.

Before installing new bearing shells, make sure that the crankshaft journal and the bearing seats in the crankcase and cap are thoroughly cleaned. Coat the inside surface of the upper bearing shell with engine oil and place the shell against the crankshaft journal so that the tang on the shell will engage the notch in the crankcase when the shell is rotated into place. **CAUTION: The upper bearing shells have an oil groove in their center, while the lower shells are plain. They must not be interchanged.** Rotate the bearing shell into place.

Place the lower bearing shell into the bearing cap, and then check the clearance with Plastigage. The desired clearance with a new bearing is 0.0005″ to 0.0025″. If this clearance cannot be obtained with a standard size bearing, insert an undersize bearing and check the clearance again. *NOTE: Each undersize shell has a number stamped on the outer surface on or near the tang to indicate the amount of undersize.*

When the proper size bearing has been selected, clean out all Plastigage, oil the lower shell, and reinstall the bearing cap. Clean the bolt holes and lube the bolts. Then torque the cap bolts to 70 ft-lbs. The crankshaft should turn freely at the flywheel rim; however, a very slight drag is permissible if an undersize bearing is used.

After each bearing is installed and tested, loosen all bearing cap bolts 1/2 turn and continue with the other bearings. When all the bearings have been installed and tested, tighten all bearing cap bolts to 70 ft-lbs of torque. If the thrust bearing shell is replaced, it is necessary to line up the thrust surfaces of the bearing shell before the cap bolts are tightened. To do this, move the crankshaft fore and aft the limit of its travel several times with the thrust bearing cap bolts finger-tight.

REAR BEARING OIL SEAL, R&R

The rear bearing oil seal should be replaced every time the main bearings are serviced. Braided fabric seals are pressed into grooves formed in the crankcase and rear bearing cap to the rear of the oil-collecting groove to seal against leakage of oil around the crankshaft. Neoprene composition seals are placed in grooves in the sides of the bearing cap to seal against leakage in the joints between the cap and crankcase. The neoprene composition swells in the presence of oil and heat. They are undersize when newly installed and may even leak for a short time until they have had time to swell and seal the opening.

The braided fabric seal can be installed in the crankcase only when the crankshaft is removed; however, the seal can be replaced in the cap whenever the cap is removed. Remove the old seal and place a new seal in the groove, with both ends projecting above the parting surface of the cap. Force the seal into the groove, using Tool J-8753-1, until the seal projects above the groove not more than 1/16". Cut the ends off flush with the surface of the cap, using a sharp knife or razor blade. Lube the seal with heavy engine oil just before installation.

The neoprene composition seals are slightly longer than the grooves in the bearing cap. The seals must not be cut to length. Just before installing the bearing cap in the crankcase, lightly lubricate the seals and install them in the bearing cap with the upper end protruding approximately 1/16". After the cap is installed, force the seals up into the cap with a blunt instrument to be sure of a good seal at the upper parting line between the cap and case. **CAUTION: The engine must be operated at slow speed when first started after a new braided seal has been installed.**

TIMING CHAIN, R&R

REMOVING THE COVER

Drain the radiator and block. Disconnect the upper radiator hose and heater return hose at the water pump. Disconnect the lower radiator hose. Remove the attaching bolts and brackets and take out the radiator core.

Remove the fan, fan pulleys, and belts. Take off the crankshaft pulley and pulley reinforcement. Remove the harmonic balancer-to-crankshaft bolt and washer. Pull off the harmonic balancer. It may be necessary to tap the balancer with a plastic mallet to start it off the crankshaft. If the car is equipped with power steering, remove the steering pump bracket bolts attached to the timing chain cover and loosen or remove the other bolts to allow the brackets and pump to be moved out of the way.

Disconnect the fuel lines and remove the fuel pump. Take off the Delcotron and brackets. Remove the distributor cap and pull the spark plug wire re-

This special tool is designed to force the harmonic balancer from the crankshaft.

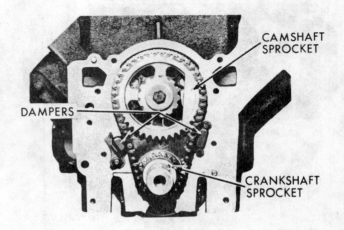

Details of the timing chain and the two dampers used on the V-6 engine.

tainers off the brackets on the rocker arm cover. Swing the distributor cap, with wires attached, out of the way. Disconnect the distributor primary lead. Remove the distributor. If the timing chain and sprockets are not going to be disturbed, note the position of the distributor rotor for installation in the same position.

Loosen and slide the front clamp on the thermostat bypass hose rearward. Remove the bolts attaching the timing chain cover to the cylinder block. Remove the two oil pan-to-timing chain cover bolts. Take off the timing chain cover assembly and gasket. Thoroughly clean the cover, taking care to avoid damaging the gasket surfaces.

REMOVING THE TIMING CHAIN

With the timing chain cover removed, temporarily install the harmonic balancer bolt and washer in the end of the crankshaft. Turn the crankshaft so the sprockets are positioned as shown. Doing so will make it easier to install parts. Remove the harmonic balancer bolt and washer using a sharp rap on the wrench handle to start the bolt out without changing the position of the sprockets. *NOTE: It is not necessary to remove the timing chain dampers unless they are worn or damaged and require replacement.*

Remove the front crankshaft oil slinger. Remove the bolt and special washer retaining the camshaft distributor drive gear and fuel pump eccentric to the camshaft forward end. Slide the gear and eccentric off the camshaft. Use two large screwdrivers alternately to pry the camshaft sprocket and then the crankshaft sprocket forward, until the camshaft sprocket is free, and then remove the camshaft

sprocket and chain while you finish working the crankshaft sprocket off the crankshaft.

Thoroughly clean the timing chain, sprockets, distributor drive gear, fuel pump eccentric, and crankshaft oil slinger.

INSTALLING THE TIMING CHAIN

Turn the crankshaft so No. 1 piston is at top dead center. Turn the camshaft so that, with the sprocket temporarily installed, the timing mark is straight down, as shown. Remove the sprocket.

Assemble the timing chain on the sprockets, and then slide the sprocket-and-chain assembly on the shafts, with the timing marks in their closest together position and in line with the sprocket hubs. *NOTE: It will be necessary to hold the spring-loaded timing chain damper out of the way while sliding the chain and sprockets into position.*

Assemble the slinger on the crankshaft with the ID against the sprocket. *NOTE: The concave side must be toward the front of the engine.* Slide the fuel pump eccentric on the camshaft and key, with the oil groove facing forward. Install the distributor drive gear, eccentric, bolt, and retaining washer. Torque it to 40-45 ft-lbs.

Install the timing chain cover, using a new gasket. Pay particular attention to the following. Remove the oil pump cover and pack the space around the oil pump gears completely full of petroleum jelly. **CAUTION: There must be no air space left inside the pump.** Install the cover, using a new gasket. This step is very important as the oil pump may lose its prime whenever the pump, pump cover, or timing

When installing a new timing chain, align the timing marks through the centers of the shafts.

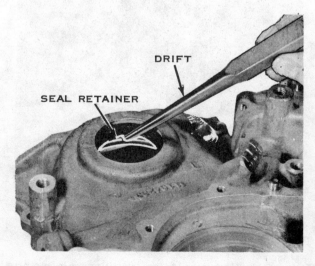

The oil seal in the front cover can be forced out with a drift.

chain cover is disturbed. If the pump is not packed, it may not begin to pump oil as soon as the engine is started.

The gasket surface of the block and timing chain cover must be smooth and clean. Use a new gasket and be certain it is positioned correctly. Position the timing chain cover against the block and make certain the dowel pins engage the dowel pin holes before starting the bolts. Lube the bolt threads before installation.

If the car is equipped with power steering, the front steering pump bracket should be installed at this time. Lube the OD of the harmonic balancer before installation to prevent damage to the seal during installation and when the engine is first started.

ENGINE SERVICE SPECIFICATIONS

CRANKSHAFT

The crankshaft main bearing journals should measure 2.2992" and the crankpins 2.000". No. 2 main bearing takes the end thrust. The end play should be 0.004-0.008", all dimensions with a wear limit of 0.002".

PISTON AND CLINDER BORE

The cylinder bore should measure 3.750", and the piston nominal diameter should be 3.7498". Piston clearance in the cylinder bore should be 0.0002-0.0023". The wrist pins should measure 0.8747".

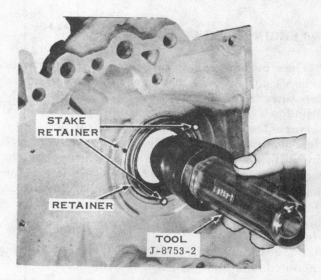

This tapered tool is designed to form the front cover oil seal.

VALVES

The valve face angle should be 45°. The intake valve stem should measure 0.3412" at the top and 0.3407" at the bottom. The exhaust valve stem should measure 0.3407" at the top and 0.3402" at the bottom. The intake valve stem-to-guide clearance should be 0.001-0.003" at the top and 0.0015-0.0035" at the bottom. The exhaust valve stem-to-guide clearance should be 0.0015-0.0035" at the top and 0.002-0.004" at the bottom. The valve springs should show 168 lbs. at a compressed height of 1.260".

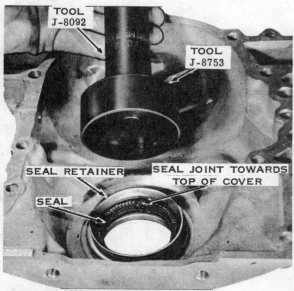

STAKE RETAINER AFTER INSTALLING

This special tool is designed to drive in a new oil seal without distorting it.

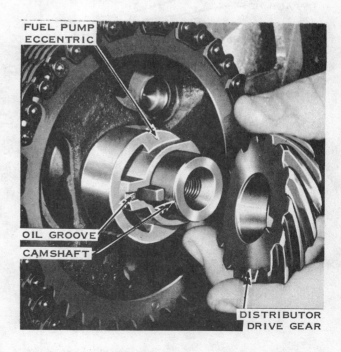

Assembling the distributor timing gear to the camshaft.

V-8 ENGINES—SINCE 1964

The same basic engine has been used in Oldsmobile vehicles since 1964. It has been produced in several capacities: 330, 350, 400, 425, and 455 CID. The cylinder block is cast iron, and the intake manifold serves as the engine top cover. The left bank of cylinders (as viewed from the driver's seat) are numbered from front to rear: 1-3-5-7. The cylinders in the right bank are numbered 2-4-6-8. There are five main bearings, with No. 3 taking the end thrust. The oil pump is mounted to the rear main bearing inside of the crankcase and is driven by a shaft from the distributor.

In 1964, the 330 CID engine had the rocker arms mounted on a shaft, while all V-8 engines since 1965

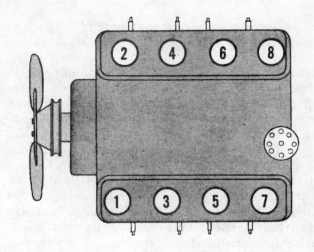

Cylinder numbering system for the standard V-8 engine.

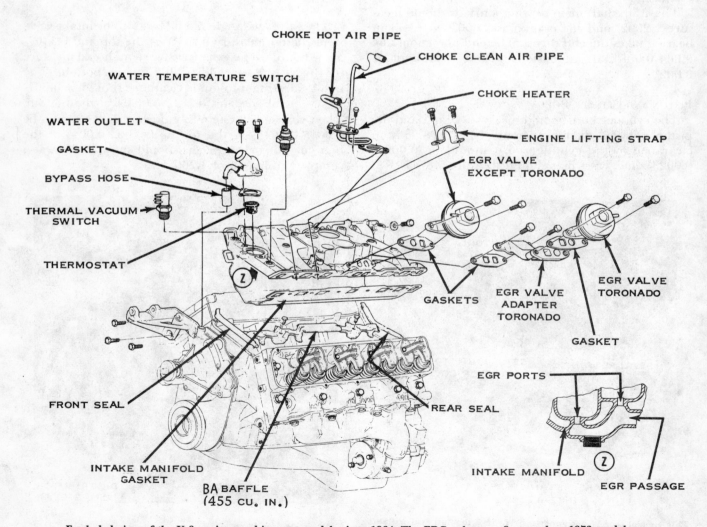

Exploded view of the V-8 engine used in most models since 1964. The ERG valve was first used on 1973 models.

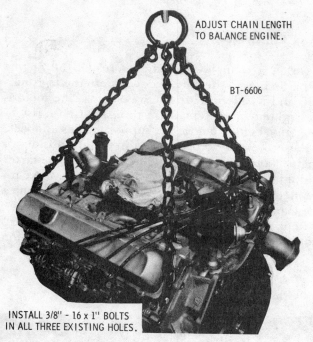

ADJUST CHAIN LENGTH
TO BALANCE ENGINE.

BT-6606

INSTALL 3/8" - 16 x 1" BOLTS
IN ALL THREE EXISTING HOLES.

Lifting the engine from the frame.

have the rocker arms mounted on individual pivots.

The front-wheel drive Toronado used the 425 CID engine in 1966-67 and a 455 CID engine since that time. These engines have the automatic transmission mounted at the left side and a modified oil pan to allow one of the driveshafts to pass under it.

ENGINE, R&R—EXCEPT TORONADO

REMOVING

Drain the cooling system. Remove the air cleaner and hot-air pipe. Remove the hood from its hinges, after marking the hood hinges for assembly.

Disconnect the battery negative cable at the battery and the ground wire at the inner fender panel. Disconnect the engine ground strap from the right head to the cowl. Disconnect the radiator hoses, automatic transmission cooler lines, heater hoses, vacuum hoses, power steering pump with hoses attached, power steering hose bracket from the engine air conditioning

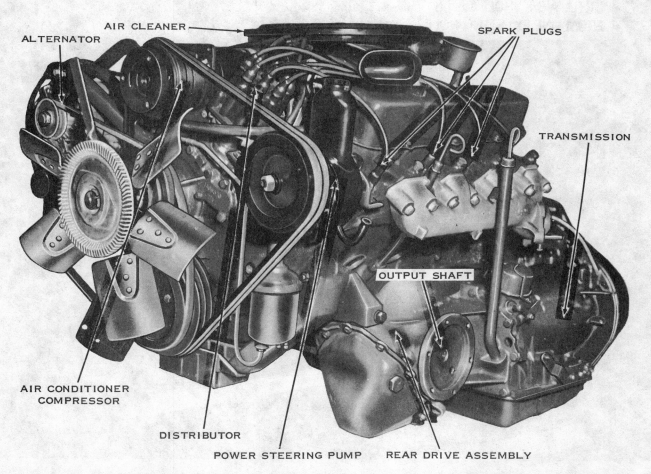

ALTERNATOR

AIR CLEANER

SPARK PLUGS

TRANSMISSION

OUTPUT SHAFT

AIR CONDITIONER COMPRESSOR

DISTRIBUTOR

POWER STEERING PUMP

REAR DRIVE ASSEMBLY

The automatic transmission and rear drive assembly of the Toronado are mounted alongside of the left side of the engine.

compressor with brackets and hoses attached, fuel hose from the fuel line, wiring, and throttle cable. Remove the upper radiator support and radiator.

Raise the car. Disconnect the exhaust pipes at the manifold. Remove the torque converter cover and the three bolts holding the converter to the flywheel. Remove the engine mount bolts or nuts. Remove three bolts, transmission-to-engine, on the right side. Remove the starter with wires attached and secure it to the frame to support it. Lower the car. Secure a lift chain to the engine.

Place a board on top of a jack and slightly raise the transmission. Remove three left transmission-to-engine bolts, and then lift out the engine.

INSTALLING

Fasten a chain to the engine. Install the engine in place. Locate the engine dowels into the transmission and position the through bolts into the mounts and tighten them. Replace the three left transmission-to-engine bolts. Remove the support chains and jack.

Raise the car. Replace the three transmission-to-engine bolts on the right side. Replace the starter and attaching bolts. Replace the three converter-to-flywheel and torque converter cover bolts. Connect the exhaust pipes and lower the car.

Replace the radiator and upper radiator support. Connect the radiator hoses, automatic transmission

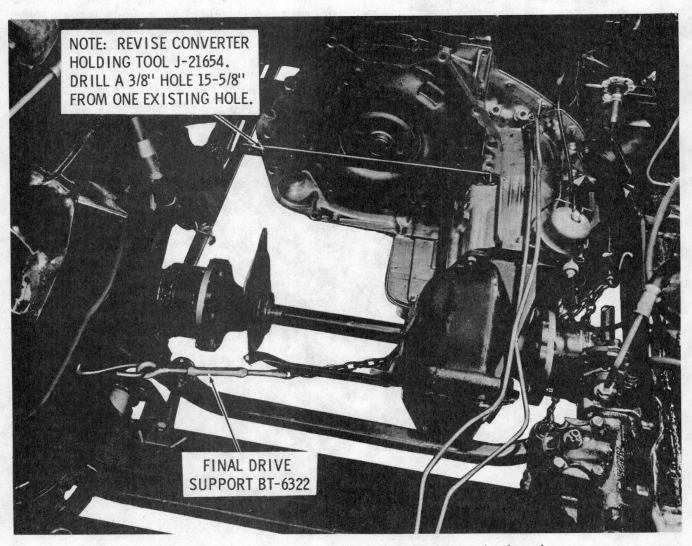

NOTE: REVISE CONVERTER HOLDING TOOL J-21654. DRILL A 3/8" HOLE 15-5/8" FROM ONE EXISTING HOLE.

FINAL DRIVE SUPPORT BT-6322

The final drive supporting tool installed in the Toronado for removing the engine.

cooler lines, heater hoses, vacuum hoses, power steering pump hoses, power steering hose bracket, air conditioning compressor, fuel hose, wiring, and accelerator linkage.

Replace the air cleaner and hot-air pipe. Replace and align the hood with the scribe marks. Connect the battery cable and ground wires. Add engine oil and coolant. Adjust the carburetor idle speed if necessary.

ENGINE, R&R—TORONADO

REMOVING

Disconnect the battery. Drain the cooling system. If equipped with a venturi shroud, unhook the strap, remove the clips securing the seal to the venturi ring and move the seal towards the radiator to gain clearance. Remove the air cleaner and hot-air pipe. Scribe the hood hinge location, and then remove the hood.

Disconnect the engine ground strap. Disconnect the upper and lower radiator hoses at the engine. Disconnect the transmission oil cooler lines at the radiator. Disconnect the heater hose at the water pump and water control valve.

Remove the upper radiator baffle, and then take off the radiator. Remove the radiator fan shroud and venturi parts, if so equipped.

Remove the power steering pump bracket from the engine. *NOTE: Do not disconnect the oil lines. Position the pump to the side to gain access.* Remove the air conditioning compressor bracket from the engine. *NOTE:*

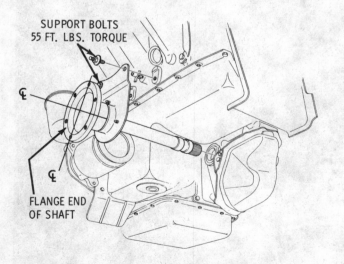

SUPPORT BOLTS
55 FT. LBS. TORQUE

℄

℄

FLANGE END
OF SHAFT

When attaching the right-hand output shaft to the Toronado, don't let the shaft hang. Assemble the support bolts loosely and, by moving the flange end of the shaft up and down and back and forth, you can find the center location. Holding the shaft in this position, torque the support bolts to 55 ft-lbs.

Do not disconnect the lines. Compressor and brackets can be positioned to the side to gain access.

Disconnect the fuel line and fuel-return line at the fuel pump. Disconnect the throttle cable, vacuum hoses, and electrical connections. Disconnect the left-hand exhaust pipe from the manifold. Hoist the car.

Loosen, but do not remove the upper left-hand bolt holding the flywheel cover. *NOTE: The bolt can be loosened using two 3/8" drive, 12" extensions and one 6" extension, with a 7/16" socket.* Disconnect the right-hand exhaust pipe at the manifold. Disconnect the starter wiring and remove the starter. Remove the remaining three bolts securing the flywheel cover and pivot cover out of the upper left-hand bolt slot. Remove the three converter-to-flywheel bolts. *NOTE: Mark or scribe the converter to the flywheel for correct assembly.*

Remove the engine front mounting attaching nuts. Remove the two bolts securing the right-hand output shaft support brackets. *NOTE: Using a sharp awl, scribe as far around the washers as possible. This will assure original alignment when replacing the bracket.* On the left side, remove the through bolt and bracket securing the final drive to the engine. Remove the lower right-hand transmission-to-engine attaching bolts. *NOTE: The bolt also retains the modulator line clip.*

Attach final drive support chain, BT-6322, as shown. Lower the car and attach a lifting chain to the engine. Remove the five remaining transmission-to-engine bolts. *NOTE: It may be necessary to raise or lower the transmission using a floor jack with a wood block between the jack and transmission.* Raise the engine from the engine compartment and place it on an engine support stand.

OIL PAN, EXCEPT TORONADO, R&R

REMOVING

Remove the distributor cap and align the rotor in the No. 1 firing position. Disconnect the battery cable. Remove the dip stick. Remove the upper radiator support and fan shroud attaching screws on Models 88 and 98.

Hoist the car and drain the oil. Remove the flywheel cover. Remove the starter assembly. Disconnect the exhaust pipes and crossover pipe.

Disconnect the engine mounts and jack up the front of the engine as far as possible, using Engine Support Tool BT-6501. Remove the oil pan attaching bolts and take off the oil pan.

INSTALLING

Apply 1050026 Sealer or equivalent to both sides of the pan gaskets and install it on the block. Install the front and rear seal (rubber). Use lube, #1050169, or equivalent on the seal area, and then install the pan. Torque the bolts to 10 ft-lbs. Lower the engine and connect the engine mounts.

Connect the exhaust pipe(s), replace the starter, and install the flywheel cover. Replace the upper radiator support and fan shroud attaching screws. Connect the battery cable, replace the distributor cap, and fill the crankcase.

OIL PAN, TORONADO, R&R

It is necessary to take the engine out of the frame to remove the oil pan.

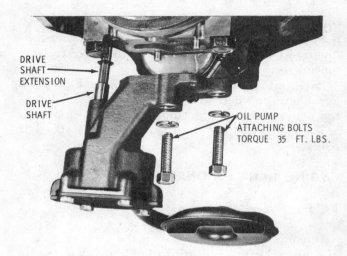

Details of the oil pump mounting.

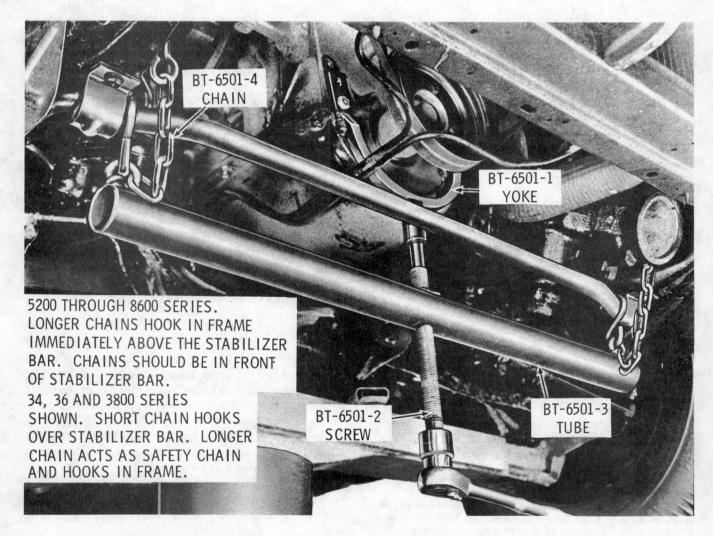

5200 THROUGH 8600 SERIES. LONGER CHAINS HOOK IN FRAME IMMEDIATELY ABOVE THE STABILIZER BAR. CHAINS SHOULD BE IN FRONT OF STABILIZER BAR.
34, 36 AND 3800 SERIES SHOWN. SHORT CHAIN HOOKS OVER STABILIZER BAR. LONGER CHAIN ACTS AS SAFETY CHAIN AND HOOKS IN FRAME.

This engine support tool is used to hold the front of the engine up, while you drop the oil pan.

OIL PUMP, R&R

REMOVING

Remove the oil pan. Take off the oil pump-to-rear main bearing cap attaching bolts, and then remove the pump and driveshaft extension. *NOTE: On Toronado and 455 CID S.M. engines, remove the rear oil deflector.*

DISASSEMBLING

Remove the oil pump driveshaft extension. **CAUTION: Do not attempt to remove the washers from the driveshaft extension. The extension and washers are serviced as an assembly.**

Remove the cotter pin, spring, and pressure regulator valve. **CAUTION: Position your thumb over the pressure regulator bore before removing the cotter pin, as the spring is under pressure.**

Remove the oil pump cover attaching screws, and then take off the oil pump cover and gasket. Remove the drive gear and idler gear from the pump body.

CLEANING AND INSPECTING

Check the gears for scoring or other damage. If they are damaged, new gears should be installed. During assembly, the gear end clearance should be gauged; the clearance is 0.0025″ to 0.0065″. Also check the pressure regulator valve, valve spring, and bore for damage. Proper valve-to-bore clearance is 0.0025″ to 0.0050″.

ASSEMBLING

Install the drive gear into the pump, with the hex ID of the driveshaft toward the oil pump mounting pad, and then install the idler gear. Position a new gasket on the pump body, and then install the oil pump cover. Tighten the cover screws to 8 ft-lbs.

Position the pressure regulator valve into the pump cover, closed end first, and then install the spring and retaining pin. **CAUTION: When assembling the driveshaft extension to the driveshaft, the end of the extension nearest the washers must be inserted into the driveshaft.**

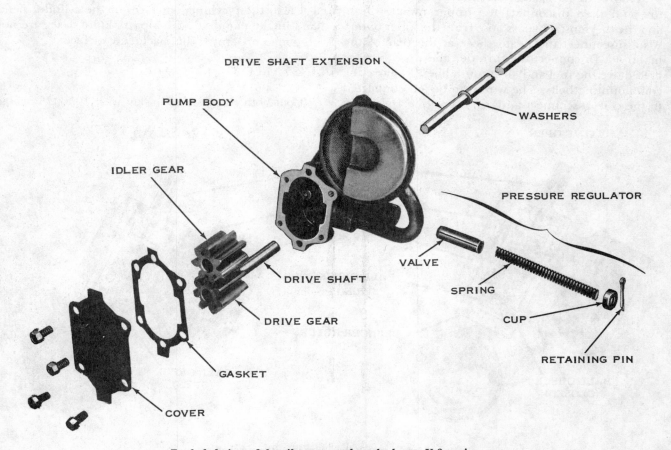

Exploded view of the oil pump used on the larger V-8 engine.

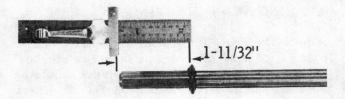

**The washer on the oil pump driveshaft must be located 1-11/32"
from the end.**

INSTALLING

Insert the driveshaft extension through the opening in the main bearing cap and block until the shaft
slides into the distributor drive gear. Position the
pump onto the rear main bearing cap, and then
install the attaching bolts. Torque the bolts to 35
ft-lbs. On Toronado and 455 CID S.M. engines,
replace the rear oil deflector. Install the oil pan.

INTAKE MANIFOLD, R&R

REMOVING

Remove the air cleaner assembly. Drain the radiator, and then disconnect the upper radiator hose
and the thermostat bypass hose from the water outlet.
Also, disconnect the heater hose at the rear of the
manifold. Disconnect the throttle cable.

Remove the fuel and all vacuum lines. Remove the
coil mounting bolts. The wires can be left connected
to the coil. Disconnect and/or remove the Delcotron

**Make sure that the baffle is in place before installing the intake
manifold.**

and air conditioning compressor brackets. Disconnect
the temperature gauge wire.

Remove the intake manifold bolts; then remove
the manifold with the carburetor attached. *NOTE:
It will be necessary to remove the oil filler tube on 455 CID
engines to provide clearance.*

Clean the machined surfaces of the cylinder head
and intake manifold with a putty knife. Use care not
to gouge or scratch the machined surface.

INSTALLING

Coat both sides of the gasket with 1050026 Sealer

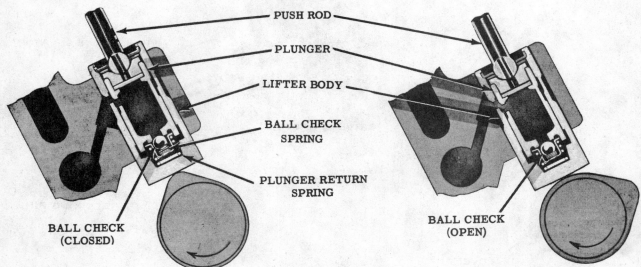

Sectioned view through the hydraulic lifter mechanism

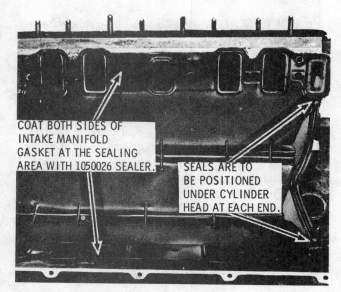

COAT BOTH SIDES OF INTAKE MANIFOLD GASKET AT THE SEALING AREA WITH 1050026 SEALER.

SEALS ARE TO BE POSITIONED UNDER CYLINDER HEAD AT EACH END.

The end seals should be positioned under the cylinder head at each end.

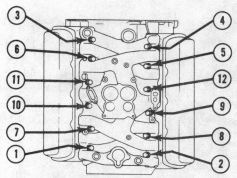

1. LUBRICATE ENTIRE BOLT IN ENGINE OIL.
2. TORQUE ALL BOLTS IN SEQUENCE SHOWN TO 15 FT. LBS.
3. RE-TORQUE IN SEQUENCE SHOWN TO 40 FT. LBS,

Intake bolt tightening sequence.

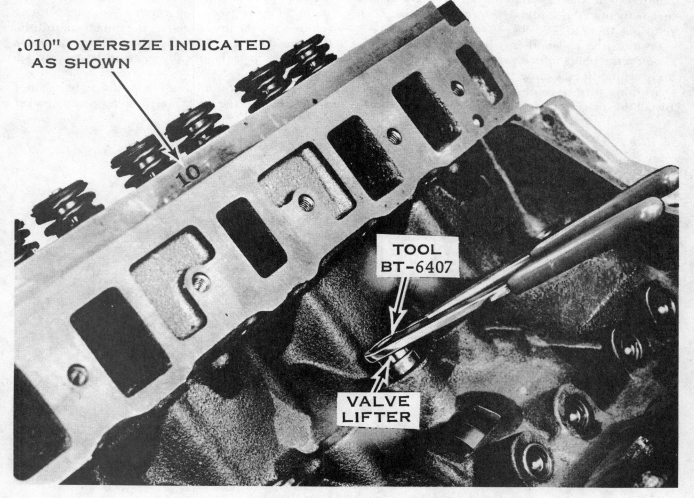

.010" OVERSIZE INDICATED AS SHOWN

TOOL BT-6407

VALVE LIFTER

This tool is useful to remove stuck hydraulic valve lifters.

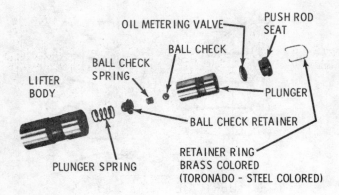

Exploded view of a hydraulic valve lifter.

and position the intake manifold gasket against the head. Install the end seals, making sure that the ends are positioned under the cylinder heads, as shown.

Position the intake manifold on the engine and connect the thermostat bypass hose to the water pump. Dip the intake manifold bolts in engine oil and torque them in the sequence shown to 15 ft-lbs. Then re-torque them to 40 ft-lbs.

Position the coil and install the mounting bolt. Connect the temperature gauge wire. Install the fuel and vacuum lines. Connect the upper radiator hose, spark plug wires, heater hose, and throttle linkage. Install the air cleaner and fill the cooling system.

CYLINDER HEAD SERVICE

Before removing the heads, check the valve rotators on late-model engines. The action can be checked by applying a daub of paint across the top of the body and down the collar. Run the engine at approximately 1500 rpm. There should appear to be motion between the body and collar; the body will appear to "walk" around the collar. Rotator action can be either clockwise or counterclockwise. Sometimes on removal and installation, the direction of rotation will change, but this does not matter so long as it rotates.

Anytime the valves are removed for service, the tips should be inspected for an improper pattern, which could indicate valve rotator malfunction. The rotators cannot be disassembled. They require replacement when they fail to rotate the valve.

REMOVING THE HEAD

Drain the radiator. By raising the rear wheels about 24", the block will drain enough coolant to remove the heads. Remove the intake manifold. Remove the exhaust manifolds. Remove the valve cover. Loosen or remove any accessory brackets which interfere.

Remove the ground strap from the right cylinder head. Remove the rocker arm bolts, pivots, rocker

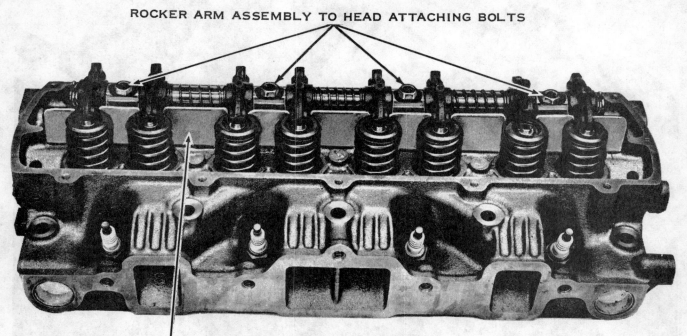

ROCKER ARM ASSEMBLY TO HEAD ATTACHING BOLTS

NOTE: BAFFLE USED ON EARLY PRODUCTION ENGINES

Rocker arm attaching bolts used on early 330 CID engines.

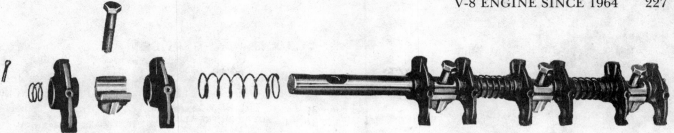

Details of the rocker arm shaft assembly used on the 1964 330 CID engine.

arms, and push rods. **CAUTION: Scribe marks on the pivots. Keep the rocker arms apart so they can be installed in their original locations.** Remove the cylinder head bolts, and then take off the cylinder head.

DISASSEMBLING THE HEAD

Remove the spark plugs. Remove the valve keys by compressing each valve spring with a tool. Remove the valve spring rotators or retainers and the springs.

Remove the oil seals from the valve stems. Remove the valves. Keep them separated so they can be installed in their original locations.

RECONDITIONING THE PARTS

When reconditioning valves and valve seats, clean all carbon from the cylinder heads and valves, using care not to gouge or scratch machined surfaces. A soft wire brush is suitable for this purpose. Whenever valves are replaced or new valves installed, the valve seats must be reconditioned. **CAUTION: Ex-**

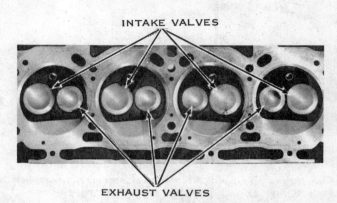

Intake and exhaust valve location in the cylinder head.

haust valve seats are hardened and must be ground.

If the valve guide bores are worn excessively, they can be reamed oversize. This will require replacement of the valves with oversize valve stems. The guide bores should be reamed before grinding the valve seats. The valve clearance in each guide bore should be 0.001″ to 0.004″.

If a standard valve guide bore is being reamed, use the 0.003″ or 0.005″ oversize reamer. For the

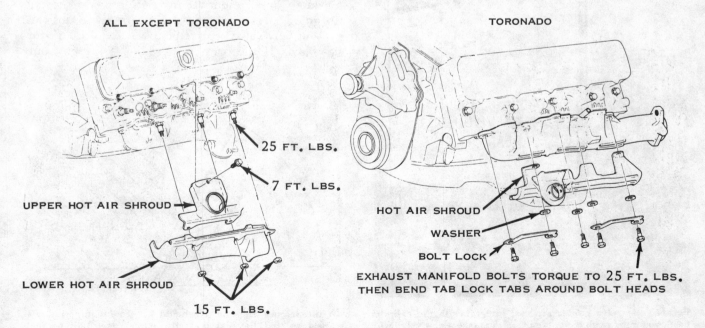

Exploded view of the hot-air shrouds around the exhaust manifold.

Cleaning the valve guides. A few drops of lacquer thinner applied to the revolving cleaning tool will assist in removing all gum.

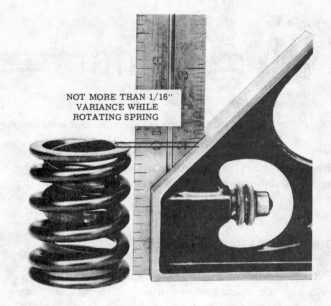

The valve springs should be checked by rotating them against a square. There must not be more than 1/16″ variation.

0.010″ oversize valve guide bore, use the 0.013″ oversize reamer. **CAUTION: If too large a reamer is used and the spiraling is removed, it is possible that the valve will not receive the proper lubrication.**

Occasionally a valve guide bore will be oversize when manufactured. These are marked on the inboard side of the cylinder heads on the machined surface just above the intake manifold surface, as shown. These markings are visible without removing any parts other than the air cleaner assembly. Before removing the cylinder heads to perform service to either the valves or valve guide bores, the cylinder heads should be inspected to determine if these markings are present. If no markings are present, the guide bores are standard. If oversize markings are present, any valve replacement will require an oversize valve. If the oversize marking is present, only

Because the valve guides are cast integral with the cylinder head, you must ream the guide oversize to take a new valve with an oversize stem to restore the specified clearance.

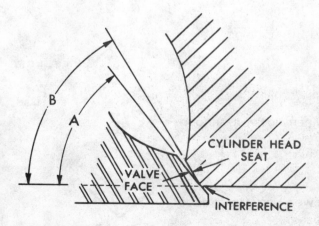

An interference angle of 1° should be ground into the valve or seat so that the seal is at the outer edge. This prevents carbon from being blown into the seating surfaces.

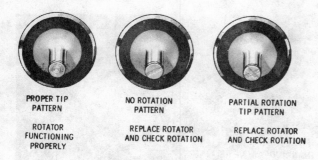

PROPER TIP PATTERN
ROTATOR FUNCTIONING PROPERLY

NO ROTATION PATTERN
REPLACE ROTATOR AND CHECK ROTATION

PARTIAL ROTATION TIP PATTERN
REPLACE ROTATOR AND CHECK ROTATION

These three valve face patterns indicate the condition of the valve rotator.

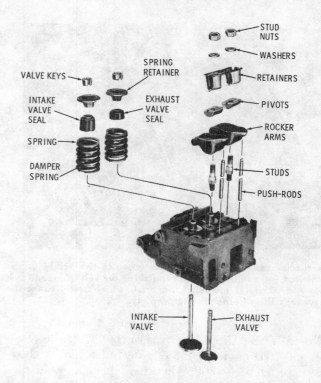

STUD NUTS
WASHERS
RETAINERS
PIVOTS
ROCKER ARMS
STUDS
PUSH-RODS

VALVE KEYS
SPRING RETAINER
INTAKE VALVE SEAL
EXHAUST VALVE SEAL
SPRING
DAMPER SPRING

INTAKE VALVE
EXHAUST VALVE

Details of the cylinder head assembly. Note the paired rocker arm retainers.

that particular bore would be oversize. Service valves are available in five different stem diameters: standard, 0.003″ oversize, 0.005″ oversize, 0.010″ oversize, and 0.013″ oversize.

ASSEMBLING THE CYLINDER HEAD

Install the well-oiled valves into their respective guides. Use Tool BT-6804 to install new oil seals. Position the seals down as far as possible on the valve stem. The seals will position themselves properly when the engine is started. **CAUTION: Check each of the seals for cracks caused by installation.** Position the valve springs over the valve stems, and then install the valve rotators (only on late-model engines). Compress each valve spring and install the valve stem keys. **CAUTION: Check the valve springs and keys to be sure that they are properly seated.**

MEASURING THE VALVE STEM HEIGHT

Whenever a new valve is installed, or after grinding the valves, it is necessary to measure the valve stem height as follows: Install Gauge BT-6428 as

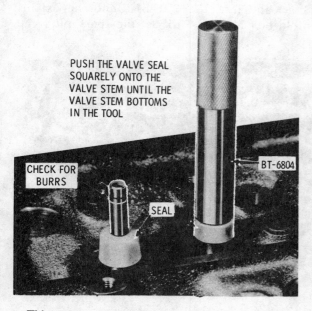

PUSH THE VALVE SEAL SQUARELY ONTO THE VALVE STEM UNTIL THE VALVE STEM BOTTOMS IN THE TOOL

BT-6804

CHECK FOR BURRS

SEAL

This tool is useful in installing new valve seals.

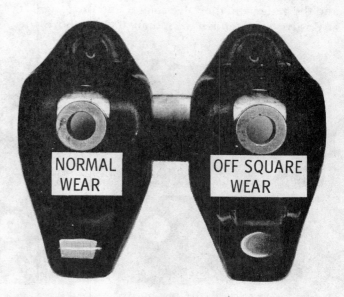

NORMAL WEAR

OFF SQUARE WEAR

Rocker arm wear patterns. Replace any showing off-square wear patterns.

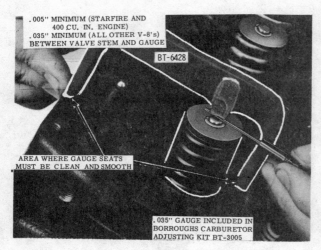

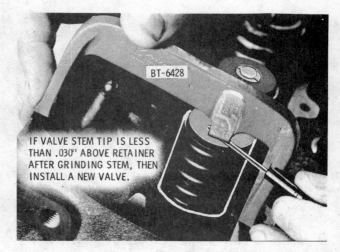

A special gauge must be used to measure the height of the installed valve to be sure that refinishing the valve face and seat has not taken off too much material, which could cause the hydraulic lifter to function improperly.

This gauge is used to measure the height of the valve after the retainer is installed.

shown. There should be at least 0.035″ clearance on all 350 CID engines. 455 engines must have a clearance of at least 0.005″ between the gauge surface and end of the valve stem. If the clearance is less than specifications, remove the valve and grind the tip of the stem as required on a valve refacing machine, using the V-block attachment to insure a smooth 90° end. Also, be certain to break the sharp edge on the ground valve tip.

After all the valve keys have been installed, tap each valve stem end with a hammer to seat the valve rotators, retainers, and keys. Using Gauge BT-6428 as shown, regauge all valves between the valve stem and the gauge and the valve rotator and the gauge. If any valve stem end is less than 0.005″ above the

rotator or 0.030″ above the retainer, the valve is too short and a new valve must be installed.

Example

Valve rotator-to-gauge clearance	0.038″
Minus valve stem-to-gauge clearance	0.035″
	0.003″

This is less than 0.005″, and a new valve should be installed.

INSTALLING THE CYLINDER HEAD

Install the exhaust manifold and shroud. Torque the bolts and nuts to 25 ft-lbs. Bend the exhaust manifold bolt lock tabs up. Set the spark plug gap.

Cylinder head bolt tightening sequence.

Lubricate the plug threads with one drop of engine oil and re-install the plugs. Torque them to 35 ft-lbs.

The head gasket should be coated on both sides with No. 1050026 Sealer, or equivalent, before installation. Clean and dip the cylinder head bolts in engine oil, torque the bolts to 60 ft-lbs. in the sequence shown, and then re-torque them in sequence to 85 ft-lbs.

Install the push rods and rocker arms in their original locations, as marked during disassembly. Replace the ground strap at the right cylinder head. Replace the valve cover and the intake manifold. Refill the cooling system. Start the engine and check for leaks.

PISTON-AND-ROD ASSEMBLY, R&R

REMOVING

Remove the intake manifold and cylinder heads. Remove the oil pan and the oil pump assembly.

Stamp the cylinder number on the machined surfaces of the bolt bosses of the connecting rod and cap for identification when installing. If the pistons are to be removed from the connecting rod, mark the cylinder number on the piston with a silver pencil or quick-drying paint for proper cylinder identification and cap-to-rod location. The right bank is numbered 2-4-6-8; left bank 1-3-5-7. Examine the cylinder bore above the ring travel. If a ridge exists, remove it with a ridge reamer before attempting to remove the piston-and-rod assembly.

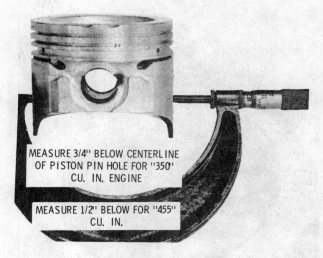

Measuring a cam-ground piston for wear.

Remove the rod bearing cap and bearing. Install a guide hose over the threads of the rod bolts. This is to prevent damage to the bearing journal and the rod bolt threads. Remove the rod-and-piston assembly through the top of the cylinder bore. Remove other assemblies in the same manner.

CLEANING AND INSPECTING

CYLINDER BORES

Reconditioned cylinder bores should be held to not more than 0.001″ out-of-round and 0.001″ taper. If the cylinder bores are smooth, the cylinder walls

Always use a short piece of hose over the connecting rod bolt threads to keep from scratching the crankshaft journal.

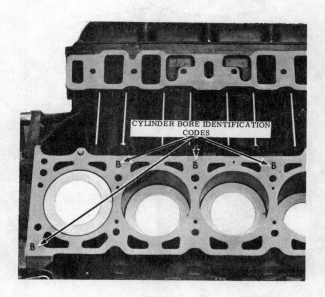

The cylinder bore identification codes are stamped in these locations.

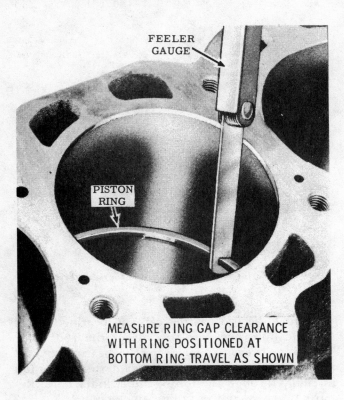

FEELER
GAUGE

PISTON
RING

MEASURE RING GAP CLEARANCE
WITH RING POSITIONED AT
BOTTOM RING TRAVEL AS SHOWN

Measuring a piston ring end gap.

should not be deglazed. If the cylinder walls are glazed, the walls may have to be honed before installing new rings. It is important that reconditioned cylinder bores be thoroughly washed with a soap and water solution to remove all traces of abrasive material to eliminate premature wear.

PISTONS

Clean the pistons by scraping the carbon off the top. Deposits in the ring grooves should be removed with a suitable ring-groove cleaning tool. It is important that the ring grooves be completely free of deposits.

RINGS

The pistons have three rings (two compression rings and one oil ring). The oil ring consists of two rails and an expander.

When installing new rings, the ring gap and side clearance should be checked as follows: Each ring and rail gap must be measured with the ring or rail positioned squarely and at the bottom of the ring-travel area of the bore. The gap measurement should be 0.013" to 0.023" for compression rings and 0.015" to 0.055" for oil rings.

Each ring must be checked for side clearance in its respective piston groove by inserting a feeler gauge between the ring and its upper land. The grooves must be clean before checking a ring for side clearance.

ALLOWABLE SIDE CLEARANCE

Compression Rings	0.002" to 0.004"
Oil Ring	0.001" to 0.005"

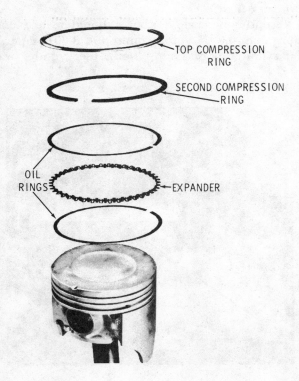

TOP COMPRESSION
RING

SECOND COMPRESSION
RING

OIL
RINGS

EXPANDER

Details of the piston rings used in a V-8 engine.

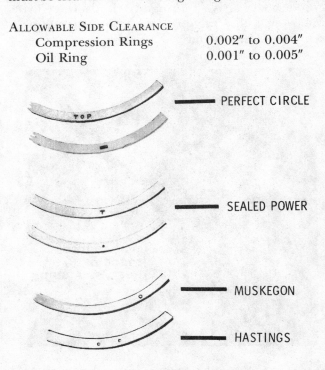

PERFECT CIRCLE

SEALED POWER

MUSKEGON

HASTINGS

Piston ring identification codes.

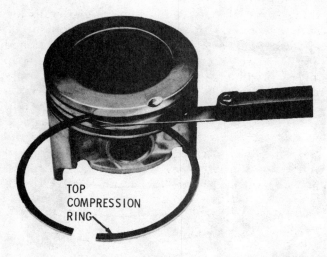

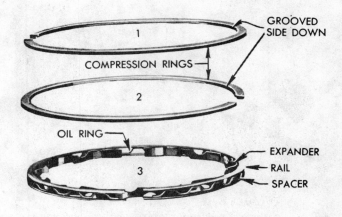

Method of assembling the piston rings on the piston.

Measuring the piston ring side clearance. Generally, the top groove wears the most and if the clearance in this groove is over 0.006″, the ring land must be reconditioned, or the piston replaced.

PISTON PINS

The correct piston pin fit in the piston is 0.0003″ to 0.0005″ loose. If the pin-to-piston clearance is to the high limit, the pin can be inserted into the piston with very little hand pressure and will fall through the piston by its own weight. If the clearance is 0.0003″, the pin will not fall through. It is important that the piston pin hole be clean and free of oil when checking the pin fit. The pin is a press-fit in the connecting rod.

To remove a piston pin, place Tool BT-6802-1 on Tool BT-6408-1. Place the piston on the piston pin remover, Tool BT-6802-1, with the letter "F" on the piston facing up. Place the Remover Tool, BT-6408-3, in the piston pin as shown, and press the pin out.

To install a new piston pin, place Tool BT-6802-1 on Tool BT-6408-1. Place the piston on Tool BT-6802-1, with the letter "F" facing up. Coat the piston with engine oil and, using the tools as shown, press in the pin until it contacts the stop tool. The piston pin-to-connecting rod fit is 0.0008″ to 0.0018″ *tight*.

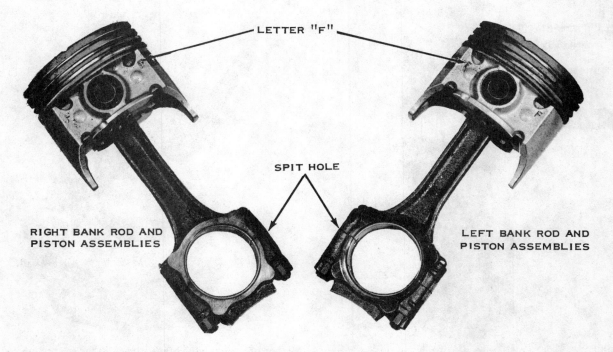

Piston and rod assembly details for the V-8 engine used since 1964.

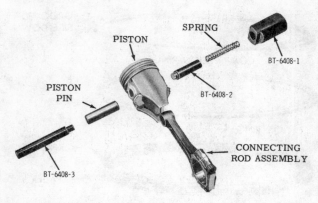

Details of the tool needed for pressing out the piston pin.

INSTALLING THE PISTON-AND-ROD ASSEMBLY

Install the piston rings on the pistons, and then stagger the end gaps so that none are in line. Install connecting rod bolt guide hoses over the rod bolt threads. Apply engine oil to the rings and piston,

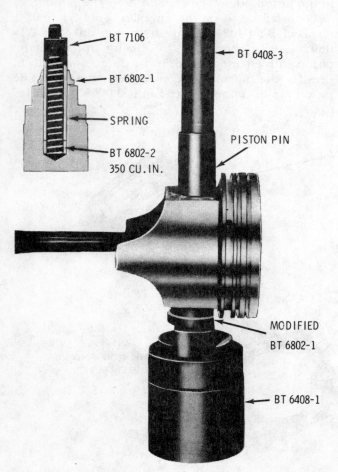

Pressing in a new piston pin.

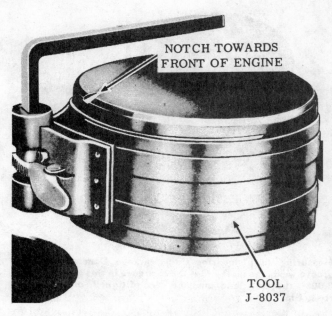

Always use a piston ring compressor to keep from breaking a ring when installing the assembly into the cylinder bore.

and then install a piston ring compressing tool on the piston. Insert the assembly into its respective cylinder bore so the notch cast in the top of the piston is towards the front of the engine. Lubricate the crankshaft journal with engine oil, and then install the connecting rod bearing and cap, with the bearing index tang in the rod and cap on the same side. When more than one rod-and-piston assembly is being

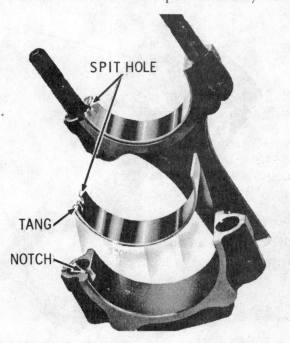

Method of retaining the bearing insert in the connecting rod and cap.

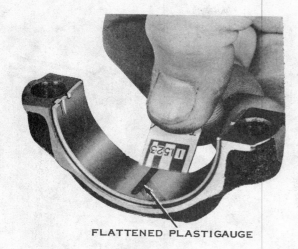

FLATTENED PLASTIGAUGE

Using Plastigage for measuring the oil clearance.

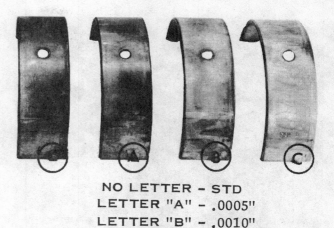

NO LETTER – STD
LETTER "A" – .0005"
LETTER "B" – .0010"
LETTER "C" – .0015"

Method of marking the main bearing inserts.

installed, the connecting rod cap attaching nuts should be tightened only enough to keep each rod in position until all have been installed. This will facilitate installation of the remaining piston assemblies.

The clearance between adjacent rods, when checked with a feeler gauge on each crankpin, should be from 0.006" to 0.020".

Torque the rod bolt nuts to 42 ft-lbs.

Replace the oil pan and fill it with lubricating oil.

SPREAD RODS WITH A SCREWDRIVER, CHECK CLEARANCE WITH A FEELER GAUGE. CLEARANCE SHOULD BE .006–.013".

The side clearance between connecting rod pairs should be 0.006-0.013".

MAIN BEARINGS, R&R

REMOVING

Take off the oil pan. Remove the bearing cap and take out the lower shell. Insert a flattened cotter pin or roll-out pin into the oil passage hole in the crankshaft, and then rotate the crankshaft in the direction opposite to cranking rotation. The pin will contact the upper shell and roll it out.

The main bearing journals should be checked for roughness and wear. Slight roughness can be removed with a fine-grit polishing cloth saturated with engine oil. Burrs can be removed with a fine oil stone. If the journals are scored or ridged, the crankshaft must be replaced. The journals can be measured for out-of-round with the crankshaft installed by using a crankshaft caliper and inside micrometer or a main bearing micrometer. The upper bearing shell must be removed when measuring the crankshaft journals. Maximum out-of-round of the journals must not exceed 0.0015".

INSTALLING

Clean the crankshaft journals and bearing caps thoroughly before installing new main bearings. Apply special lubricant, No. 1050169 or equivalent, to the thrust flanges of the bearing shells on No. 3 bearing. Place a new upper shell on the crankshaft journal, with the locating tang in the correct position, and then rotate the shaft to turn it into place using a cotter pin or roll-out pin as during removal.

Place a new bearing shell in the bearing cap. On No. 5 bearing, install a new asbestos oil seal in the rear main bearing cap. Install sealer on the cap as

CENTER MAIN BEARING
THRUST FLANGES

WOOD
BLOCK

BUMP SHAFT IN EACH
DIRECTION TO ALIGN THRUST
FLANGES OF CENTER MAIN BEARING

Before tightening the center main bearing cap, align the thrust faces of the bearing by bumping the crankshaft in each direction.

shown. Install the bearing caps, lubricate the bolt threads with No. 1050125 Lubricant, or equivalent, and then install them. Torque Nos. 1 through 4 to 80 ft-lbs. and No. 5 to 120 ft-lbs. for the 350 Cu. In. engine. Torque Nos. 1 through 5 to 120 ft-lbs. for the 455 Cu. In. engines.

Replace the oil pan and fill the crankcase with oil.

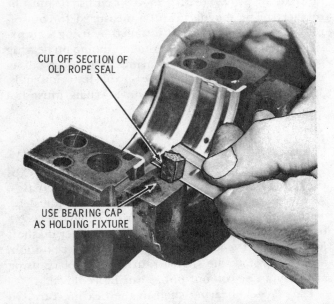

CUT OFF SECTION OF
OLD ROPE SEAL

USE BEARING CAP
AS HOLDING FIXTURE

Cutting off the protruding ends of the oil seal after forming it in the cap.

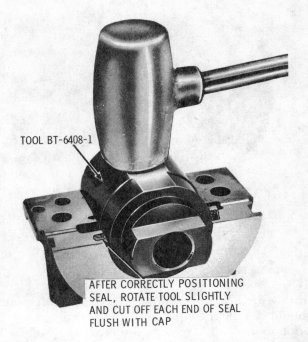

TOOL BT-6408-1

AFTER CORRECTLY POSITIONING
SEAL, ROTATE TOOL SLIGHTLY
AND CUT OFF EACH END OF SEAL
FLUSH WITH CAP

Installing and forming the oil seal in a 330 CID engine rear main bearing cap.

REAR MAIN BEARING OIL SEAL, R&R

REMOVING

Tools have been released to provide a means of correcting engine rear main bearing upper seal leaks without the necessity of removing the crankshaft. The procedure for a seal leak correction is as follows.

Drain the oil and remove the oil pan and the rear main bearing cap. Insert Packing Tool BT-6433 against one end of the seal in the cylinder block and drive the old seal gently into the groove until it is packed tight. This varies from 1/4″ to 3/4″, depending on the amount of pack required. Repeat this on

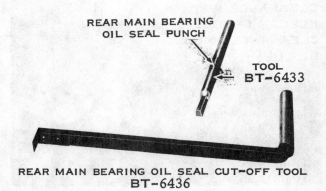

REAR MAIN BEARING
OIL SEAL PUNCH

TOOL
BT-6433

REAR MAIN BEARING OIL SEAL CUT-OFF TOOL
BT-6436

These tools are helpful in packing the oil seal into the upper groove.

the other end of the seal in the cylinder block. Measure the amount the seal was driven up on one side, plus 1/16″, and then cut this length from the old seal removed from the main bearing cap with a single edge razor blade. Add 1/16″ and cut another length from the old seal. Use a main bearing cap as a holding fixture when cutting the seal, as shown.

Place a drop of 1050026 Sealer, or equivalent, on each end of the seal and cap as indicated. Work these two pieces of seal into the cylinder block (one piece on each side) with two small screwdrivers. Using the Packing Tool, pack these short pieces up into the block. Use Seal Trimming Tool BT-6436 to trim the seal flush with the block, as shown. **CAUTION: Place a piece of shim stock between the seal and crankshaft to protect the bearing surface before trimming.**

Form a new rope seal in the rear main bearing cap. Assemble the cap to the block and torque it to specifications. Replace the oil pan and crankcase oil.

TIMING CHAIN, R&R

REMOVING

Drain the cooling system. Disconnect the radiator hoses, heater hose, and the bypass hose. Remove the radiator upper support and the radiator. Remove all belts, fan and fan pulley, and crankshaft pulley.

Drain the oil and remove the oil pan. On Toronado models, it will be necessary to remove the engine.

Remove the harmonic balancer hub bolt and washer. Using a puller, remove the balancer, as shown.

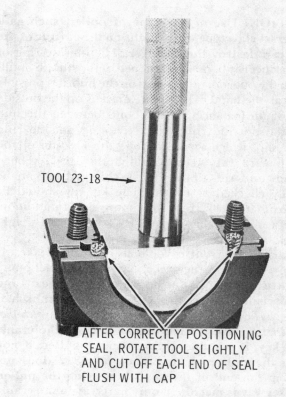

Installing and forming the oil seal in a 425/455 CID rear main bearing cap.

You have to pack a new oil seal into the upper part of the oil seal groove as shown.

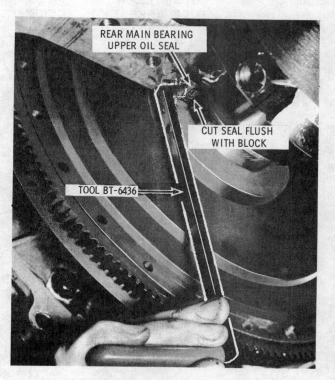

Tool BT 6436 can be used to cut off the protruding end of the seal. CAUTION: Protect the crankshaft journal with a piece of brass.

CAUTION: Use of any type of puller, such as a universal claw type which pulls on the outside of the hub, can destroy the balancer. The outside ring of the balancer is bonded in rubber to the hub; by pulling on the outside, rather than on the hub, it is possible to break the bond. The timing mark is on the outside ring of the balancer; if the bond between the hub and the outside ring is broken, the outside ring could slip, which would change the location of the timing mark. If it is suspected that the bond has been broken and the timing mark changed, it can be visually checked as shown. The keyway should be approximately 16° from the timing slot. In addition, there are chisel aligning marks between the weight and hub; the marks should be together.

Remove the front cover bolts, and then take off the cover. Discard the gasket. Remove the fuel pump eccentric. Take off the oil slinger, cam gear, and timing chain. Remove the key and then the crankshaft gear. *NOTE: The gear-to-crankshaft fit may be such that a puller is necessary.* **CAUTION: Remove the crankshaft key, if possible, before using a puller; if not, align the puller so that Tool BT-6812 does not overlap the end of the key when using the puller. The keyway is machined only part way in the crankshaft gear and breakage would occur.**

When installing a new timing chain, align the timing marks through the centers of the shafts.

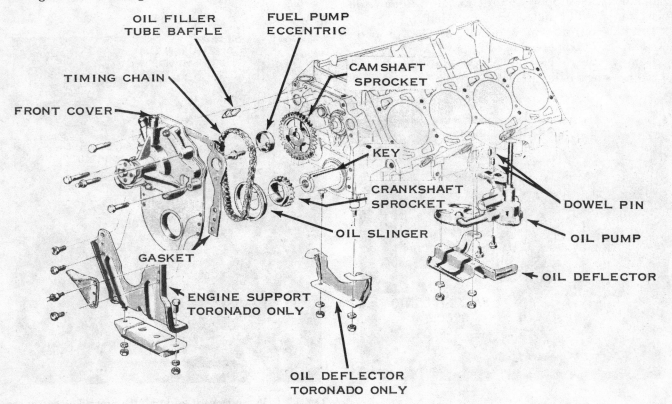

Exploded view of the front engine cover and mounts.

INSTALLING

Install the camshaft gear, crankshaft gear, and timing chain together, with the timing marks aligned.

Install the fuel pump eccentric, with the flat side rearward. Drive the key in with a brass hammer until it bottoms in the gear. Install the oil slinger.

Install a new cover gasket. Apply #1050026 Sealer, or equivalent, to the gasket around the water holes, and then place it on the block. Install the front cover, timing indicator, and water pump. Apply engine oil to the bolt threads and heads, and install them. Torque the bolts evenly. Apply lubricant #1050169, or equivalent, on the pulley hub seal surface.

Install the oil pan. Install the pulley hub and pulley hub bolt. Torque it to 160 ft-lbs. minimum.

Connect the heater hose, bypass hose, and radiator hoses. Install the crankshaft pulley and four attaching bolts. Torque them to 10 ft-lbs. Install the fan pulley, fan, and four attaching bolts. Torque the bolts to 20 ft-lbs. Install the belts and adjust the tension. Fill the radiator and crankcase.

330 CID ENGINE SERVICE SPECIFICATIONS

CRANKSHAFT

The main bearing journals should measure 2.4983-

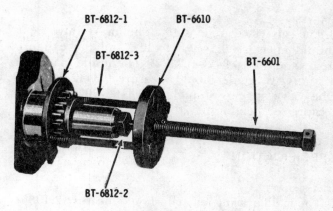

Pulling the crankshaft timing gear.

2.4993″. The crankpin diameters should be 2.1238-2.1248″. The end play is 0.004-0.008″, and all dimensions have a wear limit of 0.002″.

PISTON AND CYLINDER BORE

The cylinder bore dimensions should be 3.9385″ and the piston nominal diameter should measure 3.9375″. The clearance at the piston thrust surface should be 0.00075-0.00125″. The wrist pin should measure 0.9803-0.9807″.

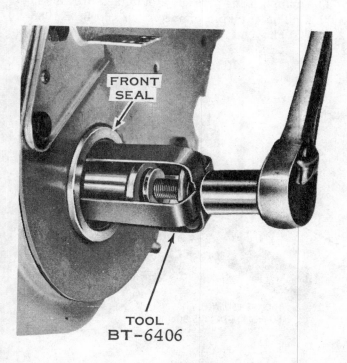

Pulling out the oil seal from the front cover.

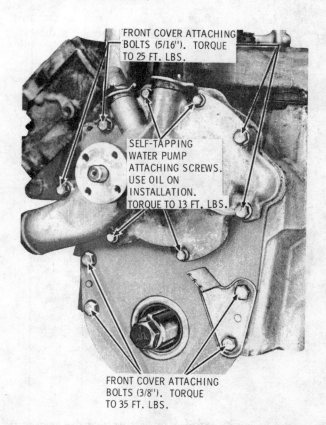

Engine front cover attaching bolts and tightening torques.

VALVES

The valve face angle is 45°. The intake valve stem should measure 0.3425-0.3432″, and the exhaust stem should be 0.3420-0.3427″. The inside diameter of the valve guide should measure 0.3442-0.3452″. The valve springs should show 193-207 lbs. at a compressed height of 1.20″.

350 CID ENGINE SERVICE SPECIFICATIONS

CRANKSHAFT

The main bearing journals should measure 2.4985-2.4995″ for Nos. 2, 3, 4, and 5. No. 1 journal should measure 2.4988-2.4998″. The crankpin diameters should be 2.1238-2.1248″. The end play is 0.004-0.008″, and all dimensions have a wear limit of 0.002″.

PISTON AND CYLINDER BORE

The cylinder bore dimension should be 4.057″, and the nominal piston diameter should measure 4.055-4.056″. The clearance at the piston thrust surface should be 0.001-0.002″. The wrist pin should measure 0.9803-0.9807″.

VALVES

The intake valve face angle is 30° and the exhaust 45°. The intake valve stem should measure 0.3425-

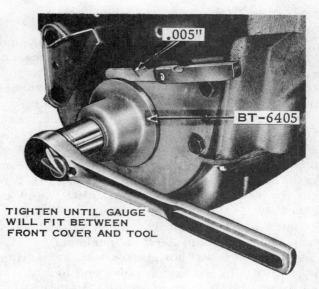

TIGHTEN UNTIL GAUGE WILL FIT BETWEEN FRONT COVER AND TOOL

Installing the front cover oil seal.

0.3432″ and the exhaust stem should be 0.3420-0.3427″. The intake valve stem-to-guide clearance should be 0.0010-0.0027″ and that for the exhaust 0.0015-0.0032″. The valve springs should show 180-194 lbs. at a compressed height of 1.27″.

400 CID ENGINE SPECIFICATIONS

CRANKSHAFT

The main bearing journals should measure 2.9993-3.0003″. The crankpin diameters should be 2.4988-2.5003″. The end thrust is taken by No. 3 main

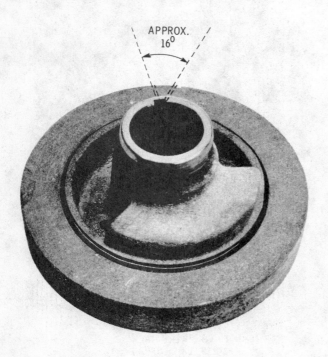

APPROX. 16°

Check the harmonic balancer to be sure that the keyway is approximately 16° away from the TDC mark.

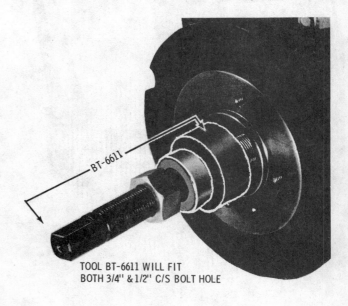

BT-6611

TOOL BT-6611 WILL FIT BOTH 3/4″ & 1/2″ C/S BOLT HOLE

Using tool BT-6611 to install the harmonic balancer.

bearing, and the end play is 0.004-0.008″; all of these dimensions have a wear limit of 0.002″.

PISTON AND CYLINDER BORE

The cylinder bore should measure 4.000″, and the piston nominal diameter should be 3.999″. The clearance at the piston thrust surface should be 0.00075-0.00125″. The wrist pin should measure 0.9803-0.9807″.

VALVES

The intake valve angle is 30° and the exhaust 45°. The intake valve stem should measure 0.3425-0.3432″, and the exhaust stem should be 0.3420-0.3427″. The stem-to-guide clearance should be 0.001-0.003″ for both valves. The valve springs should show 180-194 lbs. at a compressed height of 1.27″.

425 CID ENGINE SPECIFICATIONS

CRANKSHAFT

The main bearing journals should measure 2.9993-3.0003″. The crankpin diameters should be 2.4988-2.5003″. The end thrust is taken by No. 3 main bearing, and the end play is 0.004-0.008″; all of these dimensions have a wear limit of 0.002″.

PISTON AND CYLINDER BORE

The cylinder bore should measure 4.126″, and the piston nominal diameter should be 4.125″. The clearance at the piston thrust surface should be 0.00075-0.00125″. The wrist pin should measure 0.9803-0.9807″.

VALVES

The valve face angle is 45°. The intake valve stem should measure 0.3425-0.3432″, and the exhaust stem should be 0.3420-0.3427″. The stem-to-guide clearance should be 0.001-0.003″ for both valves. The valve springs should show 180-194 lbs. at a compressed height of 1.27″.

455 CID ENGINE SPECIFICATIONS

CRANKSHAFT

The main bearing journals should measure 2.9993-3.0003″. The crankpin diameters should be 2.4988-2.4998″. The end play is 0.004-0.008″, and all of these dimensions have a wear limit of 0.002″.

PISTON AND CYLINDER BORE

The cylinder bore dimensions should be 4.126″, and the piston nominal diameter should measure 4.1245″. The clearance at the piston thrust surface should be 0.001-0.002″. The wrist pin should measure 0.9803-0.9807″.

VALVES

The valve face angle is 45° for both valves, except on the H.O. engines, in which case the intake valve face angle is 30°. The intake valve stem should measure 0.3425-0.3432″, and the exhaust stem should be 0.3420-0.3427″. The intake valve stem-to-guide clearance should be 0.0010-0.0027″ and that for the exhaust 0.0015-0.0032″. The valve springs should show 180-194 lbs. at a compressed height of 1.27″.

6 | driveline service

The driveline consists of a clutch, transmission, driveshaft, and rear axle.

CLUTCH

A mechanical clutch is used only in vehicles with a standard-shift transmission. Vehicles with an automatic transmission have a torque converter in place of the conventional clutch.

The clutch is a diaphragm type, with a single dry disc. The assembly consists of a clutch disc, pressure plate, and clutch release bearing. The engine flywheel is the driving part of the clutch assembly.

When the clutch pedal is in the engaged position (not depressed), the clutch disc facings are clamped between the engine flywheel and the clutch pressure plate, thereby connecting the engine mechanically to the transmission. Depressing the clutch pedal actuates the clutch release lever, which moves the clutch release bearing against the clutch pressure plate fingers.

This, in turn, moves the pressure plate away from the flywheel to release the clutch disc, thereby disconnecting engine power from the transmission.

CLUTCH, R&R

Raise the vehicle on a hoist. Remove the driveshaft. To remove the transmission, disconnect the speedometer cable, back-up lamp switch, TCS switch, and the gear shift rods. Support the engine with a jack, and then remove the nuts holding the transmission rear support to the crossmember. Raise the rear of the engine with the jack, and then remove the nuts, washers, and the bolts holding the crossmember to the frame supports. Remove the crossmember.

Remove the bolts that hold the transmission to the flywheel housing, and then pull the transmission rearward until the input shaft clears the housing. **CAUTION: Don't let the transmission hang while**

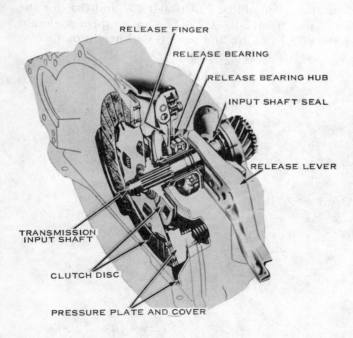

RELEASE FINGER
RELEASE BEARING
RELEASE BEARING HUB
INPUT SHAFT SEAL
RELEASE LEVER
TRANSMISSION INPUT SHAFT
CLUTCH DISC
PRESSURE PLATE AND COVER

Phantom view of the clutch.

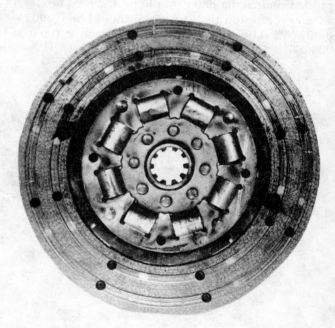

Scored clutch facings indicate that the pressure plate is likewise scored.

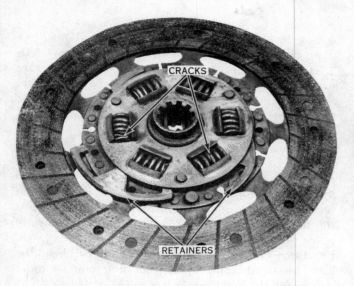

Note the broken retainer, which will cause noisy operation.

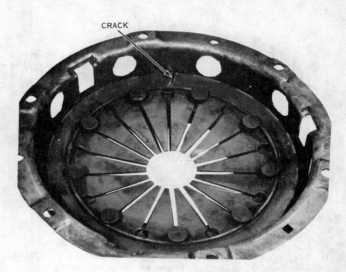

The pressure plate cracks in this fashion.

the end of the clutch shaft is still in the hub of the clutch disc, or you will bend the disc.

Remove the flywheel housing. Slide the clutch fork from the ball stud, and then remove the fork from the dust boot. If the ball stud is worn, it can be screwed out of the housing and a new one installed.

To remove the clutch, install an alignment tool to support the weight of the disc. Mark the cover and the flywheel so that the pressure plate can be installed in the same position in order to maintain balance. Loosen the six pressure plate cover attaching bolts evenly to release the spring tension. **CAUTION: Unless the bolts are released one turn at a time, the pressure plate cover will bend.** Remove the pressure plate assembly and the clutch disc.

INSTALLING

Coat the pilot bushing bore in the crankshaft with

FLYWHEEL

DRIVEN PLATE ASSEMBLY

PRESSURE PLATE AND COVER ASSEMBLY

THROWOUT BEARING

CLUTCH HOUSING COVER

CLUTCH FORK

CLUTCH HOUSING

CLUTCH FORK BALL STUD

Exploded view of a diaphragm-type clutch.

If the release bearing surface is scored, replace the bearing, but also check the diaphragm fingers for similar damage.

a small quantity of wheel bearing lubricant. **CAUTION: Avoid using too much, or it will be thrown onto the clutch disc when the assembly revolves.** Hold a new clutch disc and reconditioned pressure plate in position on the flywheel. **CAUTION: Avoid contaminating the linings with greasy hands.** Start the cover attaching bolts to hold the pieces in place, but do not tighten them. Align the clutch disc with an arbor or an old clutch shaft, and then torque the six pressure plate cover attaching bolts evenly to 12-20 ft-lbs. Remove the arbor tool.

Make sure that the release bearing is in good condition and that the hub is properly installed on the

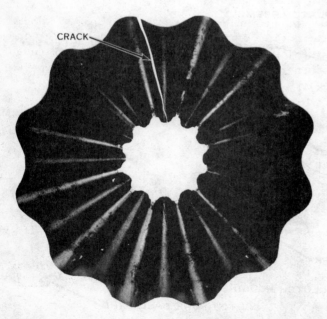

Note the cracked and worn fingers on this diaphragm spring.

release lever. Coat the bearing retainer OD with a light film of a grease that contains graphite. **CAUTION: Don't lubricate the bearing hub.** Make sure that the flywheel housing mounting surfaces are clean, and then install the housing. Seat the clutch release rod in the release lever socket, and then install the return spring.

To install the transmission, first make sure that the mounting surfaces are free of dirt, paint, and burrs. Install two guide pins in the lower bolt holes of the flywheel housing, and then slide the transmission forward on the guide pins until it is positioned against the flywheel housing. **CAUTION: In the absence of guide pins, don't allow the transmission to hang with the clutch shaft in the clutch disc, or you will bend the disc.** Install the two upper retaining bolts, remove the guide pins, and then replace the lower bolts.

Raise the rear of the engine enough to permit replacing the crossmember. Remove the jack. Connect the gear shift rods, back-up light switch, and TCS switch. Replace the driveshaft, and then adjust the clutch pedal free play.

ADJUSTING THE CLUTCH PEDAL FREE PLAY

The clutch pedal must have free travel before the throwout bearing engages the clutch diaphragm spring levers. Play is required to prevent clutch slippage, which would occur if the bearing were held against the fingers. It is also required to keep the bearing from running continuously, which would make it fail.

To adjust the play, disconnect the push rod and the return spring at the clutch fork. Rotate the clutch lever-and-shaft assembly until the clutch pedal is firmly against the rubber bumper on the dash brace.

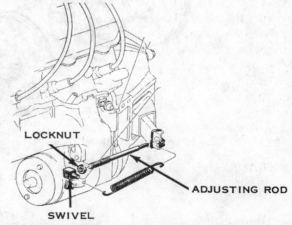

The clutch adjustment is made by loosening the locknut on the adjusting rod and then removing the swivel retainer. Adjust the swivel to obtain a clutch pedal free travel of 3/4" to 1". CAUTION: Install the retainer in the swivel before checking the free travel.

1-R GEAR

CLUTCH GEAR

EXTENSION HOUSING

①

Push the outer end of the clutch fork rearward until the throwout bearing lightly contacts the pressure plate fingers. Loosen the locknut on the adjusting rod, and then remove the swivel retainer. Take out the swivel and adjust its position on the rod to obtain a clutch pedal free travel of 3/4″ to 1″. **CAUTION: Install the retainer in the swivel before checking the free travel.**

SYNCHROMESH TRANSMISSIONS

Six different transmissions have been used on Oldsmobile vehicles: A G.M. transmission through 1965 and a heavy duty Dearborn through 1968. A Detroit transmission was used on the full-sized cars from 1961-64. All three of these are synchronized only between and third speeds. Since 1966, three-speed, fully synchronized Saginaw and Muncie transmissions have been used as well as a heavy duty Dearborn unit on some models since 1969. Two types of four-speed transmissions have been used as optional equipment on various models.

Service procedures for all of these transmissions will be covered by step-by-step illustrated instructions.

G.M. TRANSMISSION—THROUGH 1965

DISASSEMBLING

① Remove the bolts holding the side cover in place, and then take off the cover. Discard the gasket. Remove the extension-to-transmission case bolts. Pull the extension and mainshaft assembly out of the case. Rotate the mainshaft and second-speed gear slowly to

COUNTERGEAR ②

obtain alignment of the synchronizing clutch teeth and splines on the mainshaft. Slide the first-and-reverse gear from the second-and-third speed clutch. Then remove them separately through the opening

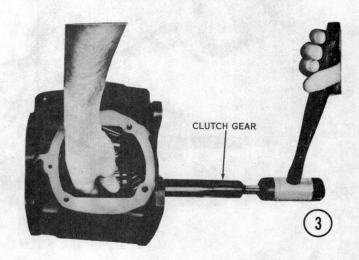

CLUTCH GEAR

③

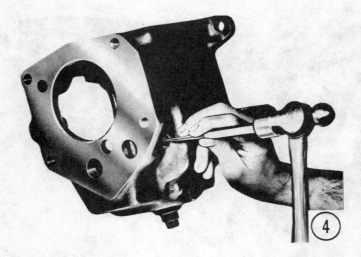

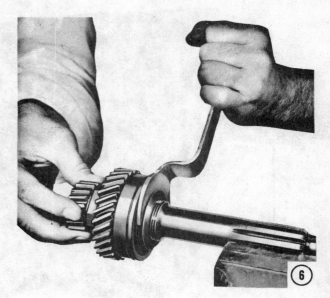

in the case. Remove the pilot bearing rollers from inside the clutch gear.

② Remove the front bearing retainer bolts and the retainer. Drive the countershaft from the front of the case. Lower the countergear to the bottom of the case to obtain sufficient clearance in order to remove the clutch gear and bearing.

③ Remove the clutch gear bearing snap ring. Tap the end of the shaft to push the gear and bearing assembly into the case for removal through the side. Remove the countergear and thrust washers from the case.

④ Drive the reverse idler shaft lock pin into the shaft, and then remove both of them. Use a hammer and drift punch on the rear of the reverse idler shaft to drive out the retainer plug. Remove the reverse

idler gear, front thrust washer, radial roller thrust bearing, and rear thrust washer.

⑤ To remove the mainshaft from the extension housing, take out the speedometer driven gear. Expand the bearing snap ring, and then tap the rear of the shaft with a soft hammer to force the assembly forward and out of the extension housing.

⑥ If it is necessary to replace the mainshaft bearing, press the speedometer drive gear off the mainshaft. Remove the bearing-to-mainshaft snap ring and press the bearing off the shaft. Remove the second-speed gear thrust washer and second-speed gear. If the clutch gear

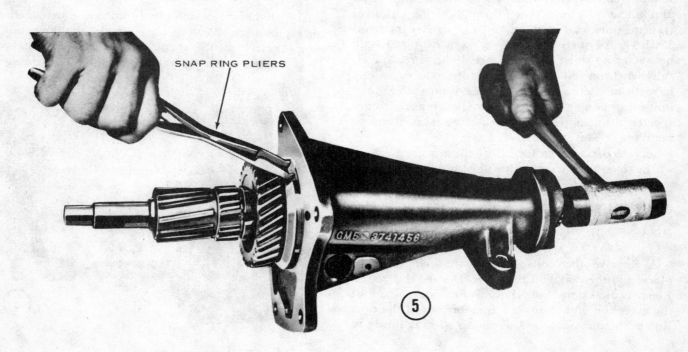

SNAP RING PLIERS

bearing needs replacement, hold the clutch gear shaft in a vise with soft jaws. Remove the bearing retainer nut, which has a left-hand thread and is locked in place by being staked into a hole in the clutch gear shaft. Temporarily replace the clutch gear and bearing assembly in the transmission case in order to press the clutch gear shaft from the bearing. Tap the bearing from the case.

⑦ To disassemble the clutch sleeve and synchronizer rings, remove the first-and-reverse sliding gear. Turn one synchronizing ring in the clutch sleeve until the ends of the snap ring retainer can be seen through the slot in the clutch. Expand the snap ring retainer, and then withdraw the synchronizing ring. Remove the other synchronizing ring in the same manner.

CLEANING AND INSPECTING

Wash the bearings in cleaning solvent. Blow them dry with compressed air. **CAUTION: Do not spin the bearings with compressed air; otherwise, they will be damaged.** After a thorough cleaning, lubricate the bearings with light engine oil to prevent rusting. Turn the lubricated bearings slowly through your fingers to feel for roughness and excessive play. Inspect the needle bearings for pits.

Wash the transmission case and extension with cleaning solvent. Inspect the case for cracks or burrs, which might hinder the seating of a snap ring. Dress off any burrs with a fine-cut mill file.

Clean the gears thoroughly and replace any that are worn or damaged.

Check the bushings in the case for excessive wear. The proper clearance between the shaft and bushings is 0.002"-0.004".

The thrust washers should be closely examined for wear or damage. They should be replaced if worn because they control the end play of the countergear and reverse idler gear.

Check the synchronizer cones for wear or for looseness in the second-and-third speed clutch. If the cones are damaged in any way, it will be necessary to replace

⑦

PITTED TEETH

Pitted gear teeth will cause noisy operation.

the clutch assembly and both synchronizing rings. Inspect the synchronizer rings for smoothness. Place the rings in the synchronizer cones and check with your thumbs to see that the rings do not rock; otherwise, there will be improper synchronization during shifting.

ASSEMBLING

⑧ To install the reverse idler gear, coat the thrust washers and the radial roller thrust bearing with lubricant. Position them on the idler gear, with the

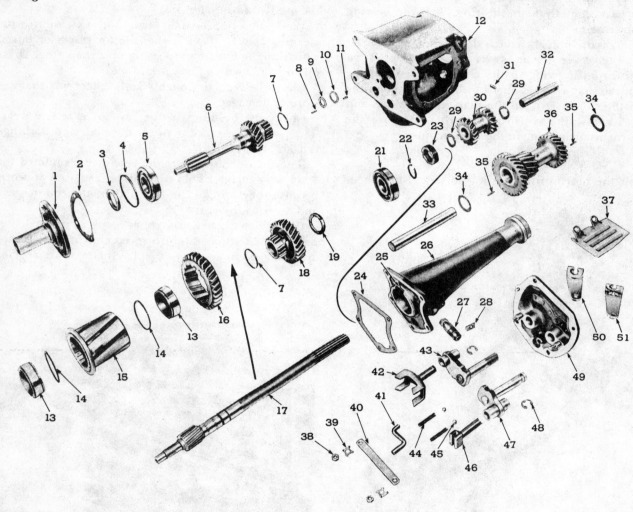

1. Clutch Gear Bearing Retainer
2. Bearing Retainer Gasket
3. Bearing Nut and Oil Slinger
4. Bearing Snap Ring
5. Clutch Gear Bearing
6. Clutch Gear
7. Energizing Spring
8. Front Pilot Bearing Roller
9. Thrust Washer
10. Thrust Washer
11. Rear Pilot Bearing Rollers
12. Transmission Case
13. Synchronizer Ring
14. Snap Ring
15. Second and Third Speed Clutch
16. First and Reverse Sliding Gear
17. Mainshaft

18. Second Speed Gear
19. Thrust Washer
21. Mainshaft Rear Bearing
22. Snap Ring
23. Speedometer Drive Gear
24. Case Extension Gasket
25. Rear Bearing Snap Ring
26. Case Extension
27. Speedometer Driven Gear and Fitting
28. Lock Plate
29. Thrust Washer
30. Reverse Idler Gear
31. Reverse Idler Shaft Pin
32. Reverse Idler Shaft
33. Countershaft
34. Countergear Thrust Washers

35. Bearing Roller
36. Countergear
37. Collector
38. Shifter Interlock Retainer Stud Nut
39. Shifter Interlock Retainer Stud Nut Lock
40. Shifter Interlock Retainer
41. Shifter Interlock Shaft
42. First and Reverse Shifter Fork
43. First and Reverse Shifter Lever (Inner)
44. Shifter Fork Detent Spring
45. Shifter Fork Detent Ball
46. Second and Third Shifter Fork
47. Second and Third Shifter Lever (Inner)
48. Shifter Fork Retainer
49. Side Cover
50. First and Reverse Shifter Lever (Outer)
51. Second and Third Shifter Lever (Outer)

Exploded view of the three-speed transmission used through 1964.

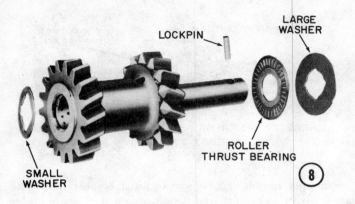

LOCKPIN

LARGE WASHER

SMALL WASHER

ROLLER THRUST BEARING

8

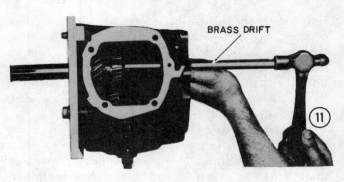

BRASS DRIFT

11

DUMMY SHAFT

9

radial roller thrust bearing against the end with the chamfered gear teeth. The large washer must be against the bearing and the small washer at the opposite end of the gear. Install the gear assembly, with the radial roller thrust bearing toward the rear of the case. Install the idler shaft, aligning the lock pin hole in the shaft with the hole in the case. Coat a new idler shaft lock pin with Permatex and drive it in approximately 1/16" past the edges of the case hole. Peen the hole slightly to lock the pin and prevent oil leaks. Install a new idler shaft expansion plug in the case.

⑨ To install the countergear needle bearings, apply cup grease to the roller bearing areas at each end of the countergear. Insert a dummy shaft, and then install the rollers in each end. The cup grease will hold the rollers in place while you are installing the assembly in the case.

⑩ Apply cup grease to the bearing thrust washers and countergear thrust washers. Place one of each at each end of the countergear. Install the assembled countergear in the case and rest it on the bottom.

⑪ Wipe the mainshaft pilot hole in the clutch gear with cup grease and install the roller bearings. Insert the clutch gear and bearing assembly from

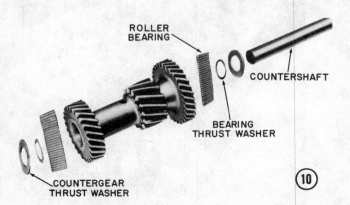

ROLLER BEARING

COUNTERSHAFT

BEARING THRUST WASHER

COUNTERGEAR THRUST WASHER

10

DUMMY SHAFT

COUNTERSHAFT

12

inside the case. Using a brass drift, tap the outer race of the clutch gear bearing until the bearing-locating ring groove is outside the case. Install a snap ring on the bearing, and then tap the clutch gear rearward until the snap ring rests firmly against the case. Install the clutch gear bearing retainer, using a new gasket. Tighten the bolts to 10-12 ft-lbs of torque.

⑫ Start the countershaft into the case from the rear. Tap the shaft through, pushing the dummy shaft out through the front of the case. Turn the countershaft so that the flat on the end of the shaft is horizontal and toward the bottom of the case to permit installation of the case extension. Ease the shaft through the hole in the front of the case, and then drive it into position until the flat is flush with the rear face of the case. The countershaft end play should be 0.010-0.024".

⑬ Check the synchronizer energizing springs in the second-speed gear. Notice that one of the ends is slightly offset. Each spring must be assembled in its groove in the clutch gear and the second-speed gear with the offset locking end between the third and fourth teeth on either of the two banks of teeth, thus keeping the spring from turning in its groove. Under normal conditions, it is not necessary to replace the energizing springs; however, should one be removed

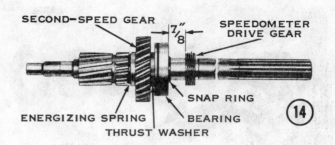

for any reason, a new spring must be installed. The spring may be removed by slipping a thin blade under it to raise the spring sufficiently to slide it over the clutch teeth. In replacing a spring, be careful to avoid distortion caused by expanding it too much.

⑭ To assemble the mainshaft, slide the second-speed gear on, and then install the thrust washer with the oil grooves toward the gear. Replace the rear bearing. Be sure that the snap ring groove is toward the second-speed gear. Install the thickest snap ring that will enter the groove to keep the end play to a maximum of 0.004". Start the speedometer drive gear on the shaft, with the chamfered ID of the gear toward the bearing. Press the gear onto the shaft until it is 7/8" from the bearing.

⑮ Install the assembled mainshaft into the transmission case extension and secure it with the snap ring in the bearing, which should be toward the front of the extension housing. Install a new gasket. Align the clutch splines on the mainshaft with the clutch splines on the second-speed gear so as to receive the inner splines of the second-and-third speed clutch. Then mark them with red lead for identification.

LOCATE THE OFFSET END OF EACH SPRING BETWEEN THE 3RD AND 4TH TEETH OF EITHER BANK

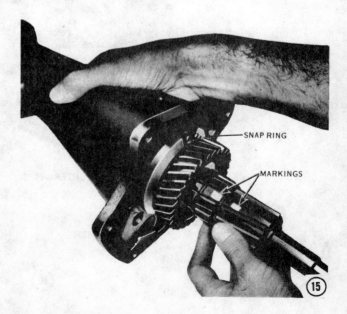

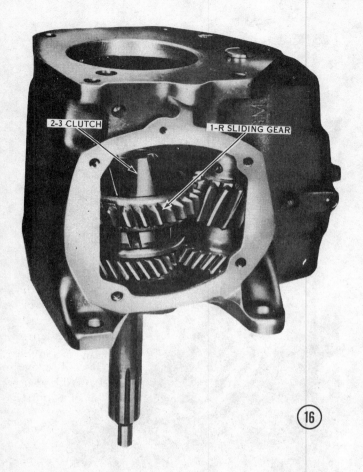

2-3 CLUTCH   1-R SLIDING GEAR

⑯ Install the synchronizing snap ring retainers into the counterbores at each end of the second-and-third speed clutch. Expand the retainer in the counterbore, lubricate the synchronizer ring with light oil, and install it in the clutch. Make sure that the retainer seats fully in its groove and is free-turning. Install the other synchronizer ring in the same manner. Insert the first-and-reverse sliding gear into the case, with the chamfer on the teeth facing toward the front of the case. Insert the synchronizing clutch assembly through the side opening, and then slide the first-and-reverse sliding gear onto the clutch.

⑰ Lower the mainshaft and extension housing assembly into the rear of the transmission so that the splines of the second-and-third speed clutch engage the splines of the mainshaft and second-speed gear. Rotate the extension housing to line up with the case. Insert the housing-to-case bolts and washers, and then tighten them finger-tight. Set the case assembly on the bench, top side up. Maneuver the synchronizing drum of the second-and-third speed clutch until the extension housing fits flush against the transmission case. Now, tighten the housing-to-case bolts. Install the speedometer fitting in the extension housing.

⑱ With the transmission gears and the shifter forks in neutral, install the cover. **CAUTION: The hump on the first-and-reverse shifter fork must face toward the rear of the transmission.**

⑯

EXTENSION HOUSING

ALIGNMENT MARKS

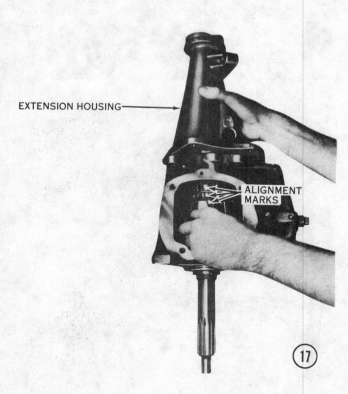

⑰

1-R SHIFTER FORK

⑱

COVER AND GASKET

RETURN SPRING   SPRING CLIP

SPRING EXTENSION

①

DETROIT TRANSMISSION—1961-64

This heavy duty three-speed transmission was synchronized only between second and high gears.

DISASSEMBLING

① Remove the return spring, spring extension, spring clip, cover, and cover gasket. Remove the speedometer driven gear, rear bearing retainer, and gasket. Take out the setscrews from the two shifter yokes.

② Pull the mainshaft rearward until the rear bearing clears the case. If the bearing is tight, it may be necessary to tap the second-speed gear with a hammer and block of wood, as shown.

③ Remove the synchronizer clutch from the mainshaft, as shown.

④ Remove the snap ring holding the second-speed gear on the mainshaft. Take off the keyed thrust washer, second-speed gear, and rear thrust washer from the mainshaft.

⑤ Remove the low-and-reverse gear snap ring, and then slide the gear off the mainshaft. Pull the

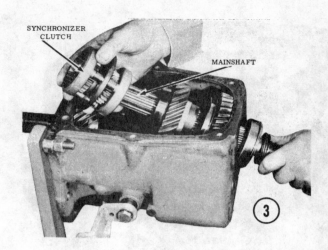

SYNCHRONIZER CLUTCH

MAINSHAFT

③

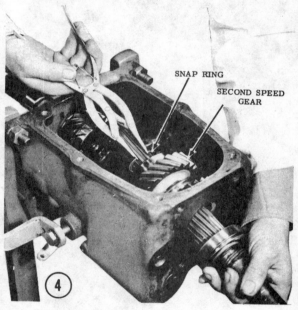

SNAP RING

SECOND SPEED GEAR

④

SECOND SPEED GEAR

②

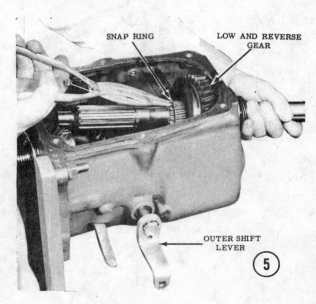

SNAP RING   LOW AND REVERSE GEAR

OUTER SHIFT LEVER

⑤

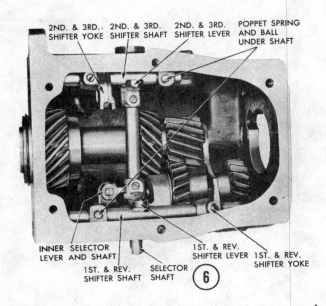

2ND. & 3RD. SHIFTER YOKE | 2ND. & 3RD. SHIFTER SHAFT | 2ND. & 3RD. SHIFTER LEVER | POPPET SPRING AND BALL UNDER SHAFT

INNER SELECTOR LEVER AND SHAFT | 1ST. & REV. SHIFTER SHAFT | SELECTOR SHAFT | 1ST. & REV. SHIFTER LEVER | 1ST. & REV. SHIFTER YOKE

⑥

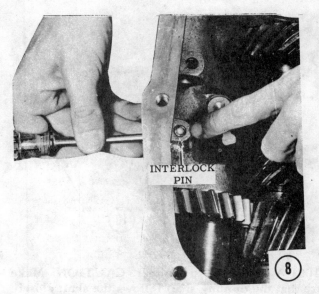

INTERLOCK PIN

⑧

mainshaft out of the rear of the case. Loosen the outer shaft lever bolt. Position the lever so that the inner shift levers are vertical, and then remove the outer shift lever.

⑥ Remove the setscrews from the inner shift lever.

⑦ Pull the selector shaft away from the second- and third-speed shifter shaft, and then remove the interlock retainer. Drive the selector shaft out through the right side of the case. *NOTE: The welch plug will be driven out by the shaft.* **CAUTION: Don't allow the levers of the interlock to drop into the case. CAUTION: If the selector shaft is removed from the left side of the case, the seal will be damaged.**

⑧ Push the 1-R shifter shaft through the rear of the case, taking care that the poppet spring and ball do not fly out. Remove the 1-R shifter yoke, ball, and spring. Push the 2-3 shifter shaft through the front of the case, taking care to keep the poppet ball and spring from flying out. Remove the 2-3 shifter yoke, ball, and spring. Remove the 1-R interlock pin from the case near the selector shaft seal. Remove the retaining ring from the main drive gear bearing outer race, and then tap the drive gear and bearing assembly toward the rear of the case. Remove the main drive gear assembly from the front of the case.

⑨ Drive the counter gear shaft lock pin into the shaft.

⑩ Drive the counter gear shaft out through the rear end of the case, using a dummy shaft or Tool No.

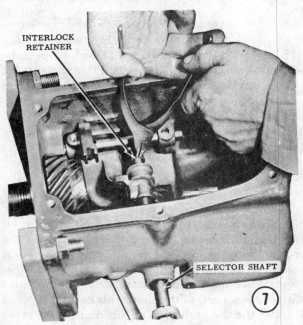

INTERLOCK RETAINER

SELECTOR SHAFT

⑦

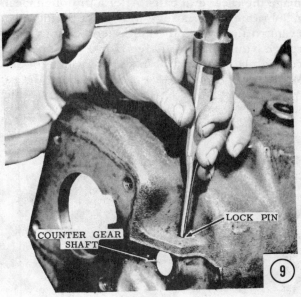

COUNTER GEAR SHAFT | LOCK PIN

⑨

LOADING TOOL
J-1001-A

COUNTER GEAR
SHAFT

(10)

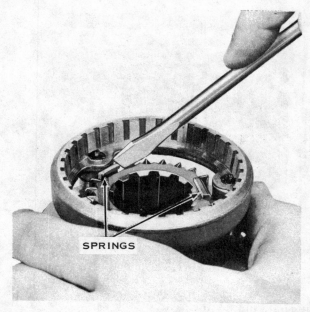

SPRINGS

The synchronizer clutch springs can be removed by prying each one loose with a screwdriver. New springs can be installed by pushing them into position in the grooves.

J-1001-A and a brass hammer. **CAUTION: Make sure that the dummy shaft follows the shaft closely so that the bearings and thrust washers do not drop.** Lift the counter gear assembly from the case. Remove the transmission outer selector lever nut, lockwasher, and lever, and then take out the inner selector shaft-and-lever assembly.

⑪ Drive the reverse idler gear shaft lock pin into the shaft. Drive the reverse idler gear shaft out through the rear of the case with a 1/2″ × 8″ brass drift. Remove the reverse idler gear and thrust washer. Drive the lock pin out of the reverse idler gear shaft.

CLEANING AND INSPECTING

Wash the bearings in clean solvent and blow them dry with compress air. **CAUTION: Don't spin the dry bearings with compressed air; otherwise, you will damage the races and balls.** After a thorough cleaning, lubricate the bearings with light engine oil to prevent rusting. Turn the lubricated bearings slowly through your fingers to feel for roughness and excessive play. Inspect the needle bearings for pits.

Wash the transmission case and extension with clean solvent. Inspect the case for cracks or burrs, which

might hinder the seating of a snap ring. Dress off any burrs with a fine-cut mill file.

Clean the gears thoroughly and replace any that are worn or damaged.

Check the bushings in the case for excessive wear. The proper clearance between a shaft and bushing is 0.002-0.004″. The thrust washers must be closely examined for wear or damage. They should be replaced if worn or grooved, because they control the end play of the counter gear and reverse idler gear.

Check the synchronizer cones for wear or for looseness on the clutches. If the cones are worn or damaged in any way, they should be replaced. Inspect the synchronizer rings for smoothness. Place the rings in the cones and check with your thumbs to see that the rings do not rock; otherwise, improper synchronizing during shifting will occur.

Always replace all gaskets and seals to minimize leaks.

ASSEMBLING

⑫ Position the reverse idler gear and bronze thrust washers into the case, with the chamfered teeth facing the rear of the case, as shown. Install the idler gear, with the slotted end out, until the front of the shaft picks up the front thrust washer and just starts into the inner support in the case. Coat the protruding end (slotted) of the shaft with Permatex No. 2 sealer. Use the slot in the end of the idler gear shaft to

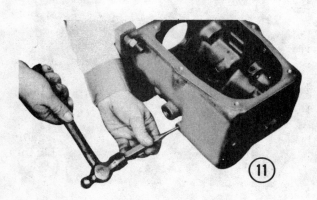

(11)

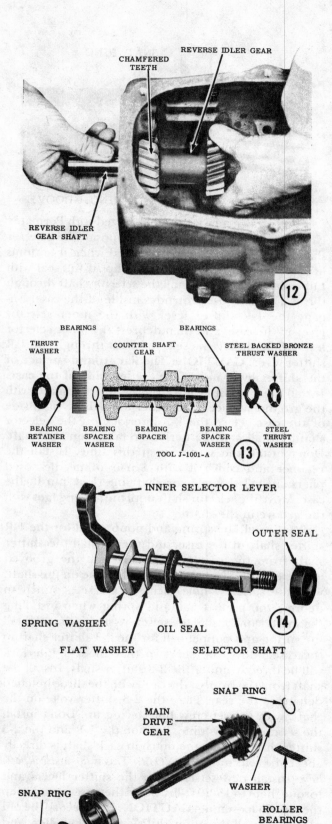

CHAMFERED TEETH

REVERSE IDLER GEAR

REVERSE IDLER GEAR SHAFT

⑫

THRUST WASHER

BEARINGS

COUNTER SHAFT GEAR

BEARINGS

STEEL BACKED BRONZE THRUST WASHER

BEARING RETAINER WASHER

BEARING SPACER WASHER

BEARING SPACER

BEARING SPACER WASHER

STEEL THRUST WASHER

TOOL J-1001-A

⑬

INNER SELECTOR LEVER

OUTER SEAL

SPRING WASHER

OIL SEAL

FLAT WASHER

SELECTOR SHAFT

⑭

SNAP RING

MAIN DRIVE GEAR

WASHER

ROLLER BEARINGS

SNAP RING

BEARING

WASHER

⑮

align the lock pin hole in the shaft and case, and then drive the shaft into the case with a brass drift and hammer. Coat a new lockpin with Permatex No. 2 sealer, and then drive the lockpin 1″ below the surface of the boss on the case.

⑬ Assemble the counter gear by installing the bearing spacer and the spacer washers on the dummy shaft or loading tool No. J-1001-A, and then inset the tool into the counter gear. Install 26 needle bearings in each end of the gear around the loader tool. Position the first bearing under the tool so that it is centered in the bore of the gear. Install the bearing retainer washer and large perforated thrust washer on the loader tool at the large end of the counter gear. Use petrolatum to hold the washers in place. Install the steel thrust washer on the loader tool at the small end of the counter gear, indexing the four tangs with the four slots in the gear. Install the bronze and steel thrust washers on the tool, holding them with petrolatum. **CAUTION: The steel side of the thrust washer must be toward the case.** Position the counter gear assembly in the case, with the large bronze thrust washer toward the front of the case. Align the counter gear assembly with the counter gear shaft holes in the case. **CAUTION: The tang of the combination steel-and-bronze thrust washer must index with the case.** Install the counter gear shaft, with the small end first, from the rear of the case until the front end of the shaft just enters the bore in the front wall of the case. **CAUTION: Make sure that the shaft closely follows the bearing loading tool to keep the bearings and thrust washers in place.** Line up the lockpin hole in the shaft with the hole in the case, and then coat the protruding end of the shaft with Permatex No. 2 sealer. Use a brass drift and hammer to drive the shaft into place. Coat a new lockpin with Permatex No. 2 sealer, and then drive the pin in flush with the case.

⑭ Apply Lubriplate to the inner selector shaft, insert the shaft into the case, and then install the outer selector lever, washer, and nut so that the bend of the lever faces down.

⑮ To assemble the main drive (clutch) gear, hold the shaft vertically, and then install the 14 needle bearings in the bore of the gear, holding them with petrolatum. Install the retaining washer and lock ring.

⑯ Install the main drive gear bearing on the shaft, with the shielded side facing the gear. Install the washer, with the dished side toward the bearing, and then install the retaining ring on the shaft, against the washer. Insert the main drive gear assembly into the front of the case and retain it with the bearing lock ring.

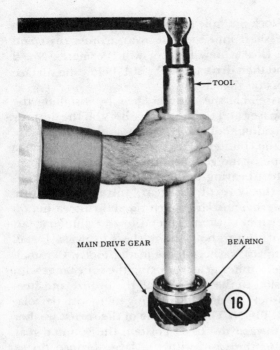

MAIN DRIVE GEAR   BEARING

⑯

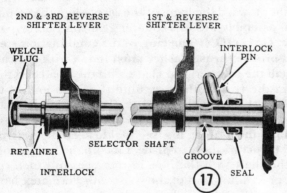

2ND & 3RD REVERSE
SHIFTER LEVER

1ST & REVERSE
SHIFTER LEVER

WELCH
PLUG

INTERLOCK
PIN

RETAINER   SELECTOR SHAFT

INTERLOCK

GROOVE

SEAL

⑰

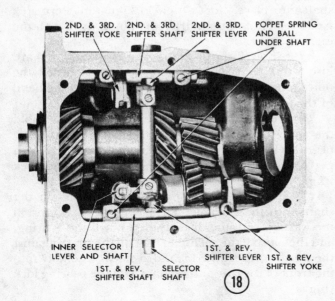

2ND. & 3RD.
SHIFTER YOKE

2ND. & 3RD.
SHIFTER SHAFT

2ND. & 3RD.
SHIFTER LEVER

POPPET SPRING
AND BALL
UNDER SHAFT

INNER SELECTOR
LEVER AND SHAFT

1ST. & REV.
SHIFTER SHAFT

SELECTOR
SHAFT

1ST. & REV.
SHIFTER LEVER

1ST. & REV.
SHIFTER YOKE

⑱

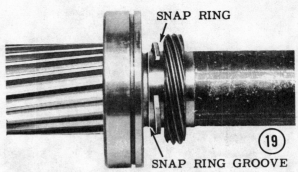

SNAP RING

⑲

SNAP RING GROOVE

⑰ Install a new welch plug coated with Permatex No. 2 into the side of the case opposite the selector shaft seal. The welch plug is seated when it bottoms in the bore of the case. Coat the lip of the seal with Lubriplate, and then install the selector shaft through the seal until it just protrudes inside of the case. Engage the 1-R shifter lever with the inner selector lever in the case, and then depress the inner selector lever while sliding the selector shaft through the 1-R shifter lever. **CAUTION: The flat ground surface of the shifter lever must face the left side of the case.** Install the 2-3 shifter lever on the selector shaft, with the ground surface of the lever toward the right side of the case. Place the 2-3 interlock on the selector shaft. Install a new interlock retainer on the shaft. Don't install the setscrews at this time. Install the retainer and clinch it with a pair of needle-nosed pliers. Install the selector shaft interlock pin in the case. Move the selector shaft until the pin engages with the groove in the shaft.

⑱ Install the spring and poppet ball for the 1-R shifter shaft in the case, and then install the shifter shaft from the rear of the case, with the grooved end rearward. Place the 1-R shifter yoke on the shaft, with the setscrew hole facing up. Use a punch to depress the poppet ball and spring when installing the shaft. Don't install the setscrews at this time. Install the spring and poppet ball for the 2-3 shifter shaft in the case. Move the shaft so that the 2-3 interlock will be directly under the 2-3 shifter shaft. Install the shaft from the front of the case, with the three notched detents to the rear. Place the 2-3 shifter yoke on the shaft, with the setscrew hole facing up. Don't install the setscrew at this time. Position the 1-R and the 2-3 shifter shafts so that the notch in each shaft is directly above the selector shaft. *NOTE: This is the neutral position.* Install new setscrews in the shifter levers and torque them to 15-20 ft-lbs. Stake the setscrews to keep them from loosening. **CAUTION: Don't reuse the old screws.** Install the outer shift lever, lockwasher, and bolt on the selector shaft.

⑲ To assemble the mainshaft, install the bearing, with the shielded side facing the shoulder of the

WIRE SPACER RING

THRUST WASHER GROOVE

⑳

splines. Install the snap ring against the inner race of the bearing, and then slide on a new speedometer gear spacer. Drive the speedometer gear onto the mainshaft against the spacer.

⑳ Slide the mainshaft through the bore in the rear of the case, and then install the 1-R gear, with the flat side of the gear to the rear. Install the wire spacer ring and line up the gap with the machined thrust washer keyway groove on the 2nd-speed gear bearing surface. **CAUTION: There are two grooves machined the full length of the 2nd-speed gear bearing surface of the mainshaft.** The shallow-angle

groove is for lubrication purposes only and must not be obstructed. The deep groove, similar to a spline, is designed to receive the tangs of the two 2nd-speed gear thrust washers.

㉑ Install the 2nd-speed gear inner thrust washer, indexing the tang with the proper groove on the mainshaft. Slide the 2nd-speed gear onto the mainshaft, with the cone clutch surface facing forward. Install the outer thrust washer and retain it with a new snap ring. **CAUTION: Use a new snap ring to prevent breakage during use.**

㉒ Install the synchronizing drum on the mainshaft, with the counter-bored end facing the 2nd-speed gear. Engage the synchronizing drum with the 2-3 shifter yoke, and then index the 1-R shifter yoke. Now, tap the mainshaft forward until it pilots in the main drive gear and the rear bearing pilots in the case. Install the rear bearing retaining ring. Install new setscrews in the shifter yokes and torque them to 15-20 ft-lbs. Stake the setscrews to prevent them from loosening. *NOTE: The screws are deformed at the slotted end to provide a self-locking feature, and this would be lost if the screws were reused.* Coat the rear bearing retainer bushing with gear lubricant, position a new gasket on the case, and then install the rear bearing retainer to the case. Apply Permatex No. 2 to the rear bearing retainer screws, install them, and torque them to 28-33 ft-lbs. Coat the sealing lip of the rear bearing retainer oil seal with Special Lubricant, Part No. 567196. Coat the outer diameter of the seal with Permatex No. 3, and then install the seal with Tool No. J-5154. Position a new gasket on the top of the case, and then install the cover, spring clip, attaching screws, and lockwashers. Install the toggle spring and spring extension between the spring clip and the outer shift lever.

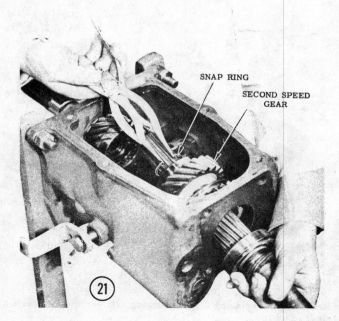

SNAP RING

SECOND SPEED GEAR

㉑

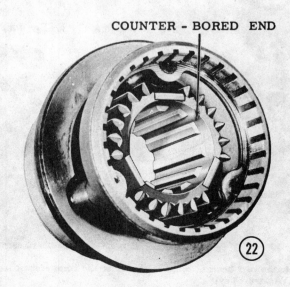

COUNTER - BORED END

㉒

DEARBORN HEAVY DUTY SYNCHROMESH TRANSMISSION—THROUGH 1968

This three-speed transmission was synchronized between second and third gears. It is used on the heavy duty chassis for police and taxi cabs as well as optional equipment with some high-performance engines.

DISASSEMBLING

Place the transmission assembly on a bench or a suitable repair stand, and then remove the nine cap screws and lockwashers securing the side cover to the transmission case. Remove the side cover assembly and gasket. Do not disassemble the cover unless parts need replacing.

Lock the transmission in two gears so that the mainshaft cannot be turned, and then remove the hex head bolt and special washer securing the universal joint yoke to the mainshaft. Remove the yoke and speedometer drive gear as an assembly. Slide the spacer from the mainshaft.

Remove the four cap screws securing the mainshaft rear bearing retainer to the case, move the retainer away from the case approximately one-half inch, and then rotate the retainer to expose the countershaft and lock key. Use a dummy shaft to drive the countershaft to the rear. When the lock key clears the transmission case, remove the key to permit the countershaft to clear the rear bearing retainer. Drive the countershaft all the way out and leave the dummy shaft in the countershaft gear to retain the bearings.

Drop the countershaft gear into the transmission case, and then remove the rear bearing retainer, gasket, and mainshaft assembly from the case.

Remove 14 mainshaft front roller bearings from inside the main drive gear, and then remove the bearing spacing washer from the front end of the mainshaft. Remove the four cap screws securing the main drive gear bearing retainer to the case, and then take off the bearing retainer and gasket.

Remove the main drive gear snap ring and washer from the main drive gear at the front side of the main drive gear bearing using snap ring pliers. Place the transmission case on end on an arbor press bed, and then press the main drive gear out of the bearing. Remove the oil retaining washer from the main drive gear.

Tap the main drive gear bearing out through the front of the case. Drive the reverse idler gear shaft to the rear of the case, and then remove the lock key, shaft, and reverse idler gear. Lift the countershaft gear assembly and thrust washers from the

Rotate the rear bearing retainer to expose the countershaft lock key (Woodruff key).

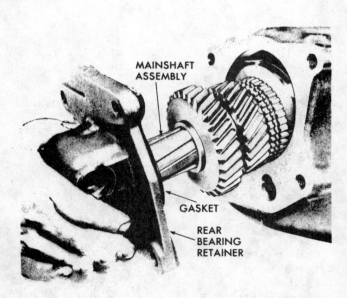

Removing or replacing the rear bearing retainer with the mainshaft attached.

transmission case. Remove the tool from the counter-shaft gear. Remove 80 roller bearings, four bearing retaining washers, and the bearing spacer from inside the gear.

Remove the synchronizing cone from the front side of the 2nd-and-3rd speed clutch sleeve. Remove the clutch hub retaining snap ring from the front end of the mainshaft. If the relationship of the 2nd-and-3rd speed clutch sleeve and 2nd-and-3rd speed clutch hub are not marked, mark them for assembly purposes. Remove the 2nd-and-3rd speed clutch sleeve from the clutch hub and the clutch hub from the main-shaft. Remove two clutch key springs and three clutch keys from the clutch hub.

Remove the synchronizing cone and 2nd-speed gear from the mainshaft. Remove the first-and-reverse sliding gear from the mainshaft. Remove the main-shaft rear bearing front snap ring from the rear bearing retainer, and then tap the mainshaft and rear bearing out of the retainer. Remove the mainshaft rear bearing rear snap ring from the retainer. Remove the rear bearing from the mainshaft, using the second-speed gear as a slide hammer. Drive the oil seal out of the rear bearing retainer.

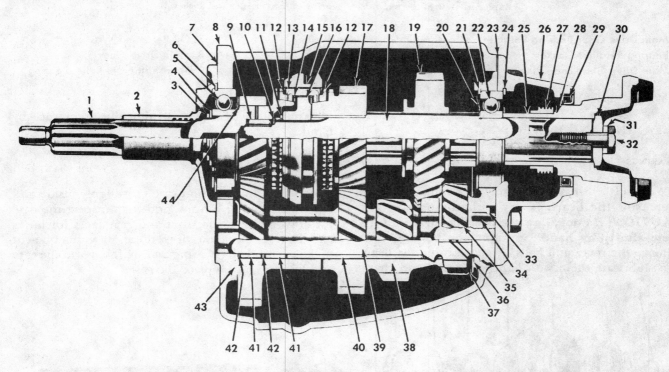

Cross-sectioned view through the Dearborn transmission used through 1968.

1. Main Drive Gear	16. 2nd and 3rd Speed Clutch Hub
2. Main Drive Gear Bearing Retainer	17. 2nd Speed Gear
3. Main Drive Gear Snap Ring	18. Mainshaft
4. Main Drive Gear Washer	19. 1st and Reverse Sliding Gear
5. Main Drive Gear Bearing	21. Mainshaft Rear Bearing Front Snap Ring
6. Main Drive Gear Bearing Snap Ring	22. Mainshaft Rear Bearing
7. Bearing Retainer Gaskets	23. Rear Bearing Retainer Gasket
8. Transmission Case	24. Mainshaft Rear Bearing Rear Snap Ring
9. Mainshaft Front Roller Bearings	25. Spacer
10. Bearing Spacing Washer	26. Mainshaft Rear Bearing Retainer
11. Clutch Hub Retaining Snap Ring	27. Speedometer Drive Gear
12. Synchronizing Cones	28. Universal Joint Yoke
13. Clutch Key	29. Rear Bearing Retainer Oil Seal
14. Clutch Key Springs	30. Special Washer
15. 2nd and 3rd Speed Clutch Sleeve	31. Lock Washer

32. Universal Joint Flange Retaining Bolt
33. Reverse Idler Gear Shaft Lock Key
34. Reverse Idler Gear Shaft
35. Reverse Idler Gear
36. Countershaft Gear Rear Thrust Washer (Steel)
37. Countershaft Gear Rear Thrust Washer (Bronze)
38. Countershaft Gear
39. Countershaft
40. Countershaft Bearing Spacer
41. Countershaft Roller Bearings
42. Countershaft Bearing Retainer Washers
43. Countershaft Gear Front Thrust Washer (Bronze)
44. Oil Retaining Washer

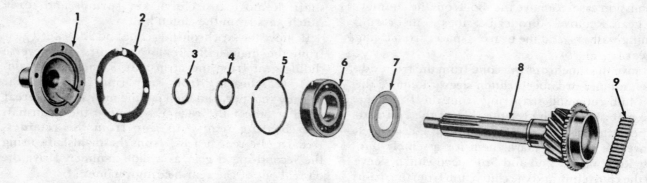

Exploded view of the main drive gear, with the retainer and gasket.

1. Main Drive Gear Bearing Retainer
2. Bearing Retainer Gasket
3. Main Drive Gear Snap Ring
4. Main Drive Gear Washer
5. Main Drive Gear Bearing Snap Ring
6. Main Drive Gear Bearing
7. Oil Retaining Washer
8. Main Drive Gear
9. Mainshaft Front Roller Bearings

CLEANING AND INSPECTING

BEARINGS

Wash all bearings thoroughly in cleaning solvent, then blow the bearings dry with compressed air. **CAUTION: Do not allow the bearings to spin; turn them slowly by hand.** Spinning the bearings will damage the races and balls. After cleaning the bearings, lubricate them with light engine oil and check for roughness by slowly turning the outer race by hand.

TRANSMISSION CASE

Wash the transmission case thoroughly inside and out with cleaning solvent, and then inspect the case for cracks. Check the front and rear faces for burrs and, if any are evident, dress them off with a fine-cut mill file. Check the bearing and shaft bores in the case and, if damaged, replace the case.

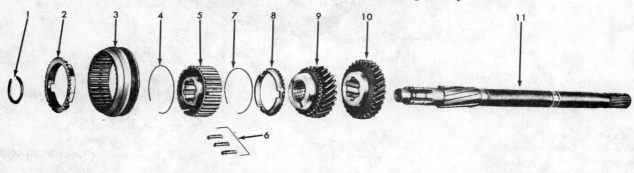

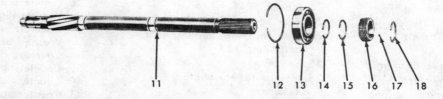

Exploded view of the mainshaft. (1) Snap ring, (2) front synchronizer ring, (3) 2-3 speed clutch sleeve, (4) clutch key spring, (5) clutch hub, (6) keys, (7) spring, (8) rear synchronizer ring, (9) 2nd-speed gear, (10) 1-R sliding gear, (11) mainshaft, (12) rear bearing front snap ring, (13) mainshaft rear bearing, (14) rear snap ring, (15) speedometer drive gear front snap ring, (16) speedometer drive gear, (17) detent ball, (18) rear snap ring.

GEARS

Inspect all gears for excessive wear, chips, or cracks, and replace any that are not in good condition. Inspect the bushings in the second-speed gear and reverse idler gear for wear or damage. If either bushing is worn or damaged, replace the complete gear assembly. Bushings are not serviced separately.

Check the first-and-reverse sliding gear for freedom of movement on the mainshaft. Check the 2nd-and-3rd speed clutch sleeve to see that it slides freely on the clutch hub.

Inspect the speedometer drive gear on the universal joint yoke. If worn or damaged, press the yoke or flange out of the gear, and then press a new gear into place.

ASSEMBLING

Press the rear bearing onto the mainshaft. Install the mainshaft rear bearing rear snap ring into the groove in the rear bearing retainer. Install the mainshaft and rear bearing in the rear bearing retainer,

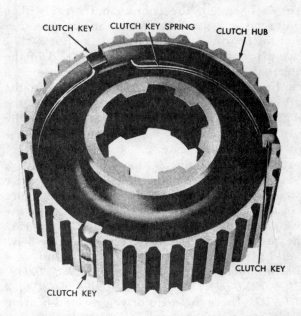

Details of the clutch keys and synchronizer springs installed on the clutch hub.

and secure it by installing the mainshaft rear bearing front snap ring. *NOTE: Front snap rings are available in thicknesses of 0.088", 0.091", 0.094", 0.097", and 0.100"; select the proper size snap ring to prevent bearing end play.* Press a new oil seal into the rear end of the rear bearing retainer, using oil seal replacer J-5154-A. Coat the lip of the oil seal with transmission lubricant.

Install the spacer on the rear end of the mainshaft. Install the universal joint yoke on the mainshaft and secure it with the special flat washer, lockwasher, and hex-head bolt. The cap screws will be tightened later. Place the first-and-reverse sliding gear and the 2nd-speed gear over the front end of the mainshaft.

Assemble the clutch key springs in the 2nd-and-3rd speed clutch hub, with one end of each spring in the same slot and the other end free, and then place three clutch keys in the slots in the hub. Install the 2nd-and-3rd speed clutch sleeve on the clutch hub, with the marks made at disassembly aligned. Place the synchronizing cone in each side of the sleeve-and-hub assembly, making sure the slots in the cones are aligned with the clutch keys. Install the sleeve, hub, and synchronizing cone assembly on the mainshaft, and secure it with a clutch hub retaining snap ring. Make sure the synchronizing cones turn freely.

Install the bearing spacing washer on the pilot on the front end of the mainshaft. Place the countershaft bearing spacer and countershaft bearing loader tool J-5589 (or a dummy shaft) inside the countershaft gear. Install two rows of 20 roller bearings over the

Removing or replacing the mainshaft snap ring.

tool in each end of the countershaft gear with a bearing retainer between each row and at the outer ends of the bearing.

Place a bronze thrust washer at each end of the countershaft gear. Place the transmission case on a bench. Install the countershaft gear assembly into the case through the side cover opening, inserting the large gear end first. Place a steel thrust washer at the rear of the countershaft gear between the bronze thrust washer and the case.

Install the oil retaining washer on the main drive gear and install the bearing. Install the main drive gear washer against the bearing inner race and secure it by installing the main drive gear snap ring into the groove provided in the drive gear. Select a snap ring of the proper thickness to prevent all main drive gear end play in the bearing. *NOTE: Snap rings are available in the following thicknesses: 0.086-0.088", 0.089-0.091", 0.092-0.094", 0.095-0.097", 0.098-0.100", and 0.101-0.103".* Drive the main drive gear-and-bearing assembly into the case from the front until the proper position is obtained for installation of a snap ring. Install the snap ring into the groove in the main drive gear bearing.

Position the reverse idler gear in the rear of the case. Insert the idler gear shaft through the case and gear, place the lock key in the notch in the shaft, then drive the shaft into the case until the lock key seats against the cutout in the case.

Place 14 roller bearings in the bore in the rear end of the main drive gear. Coat the bearings with lubricant to hold them in place. Place the rear bearing retainer gasket on the rear end of the case. Carefully

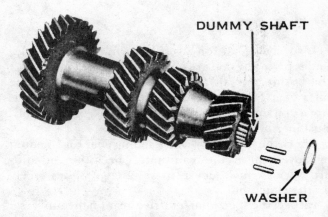

Countershaft bearings being loaded on dummy shaft.

install the mainshaft-and-gear assembly through the opening in the rear of the case, making sure the front end of the mainshaft enters the roller bearings in the main drive gear. **CAUTION: Be sure all roller bearings are in place and are not forced into the lubricant opening in the drive gear.**

Position the main drive gear bearing retainer over the main drive gear, against the drive gear bearing outer race. Check the clearance between the bearing retainer bolting flange and the transmission case with a feeler gauge to determine the thickness of gaskets required to form a seal. Gaskets are available in thicknesses of 0.010" and 0.015". Remove the bearing

Exploded view of the mainshaft and gears.

1. Snap Ring
2. Synchronizer Ring
3. Clutch Sleeve
4. Clutch Key Spring

5. Clutch Hub
6. Clutch Key
7. Clutch Key Spring

8. Synchronizer Ring
9. 2nd Speed Gear
10. 1st and Reverse Sliding Gear
11. Mainshaft

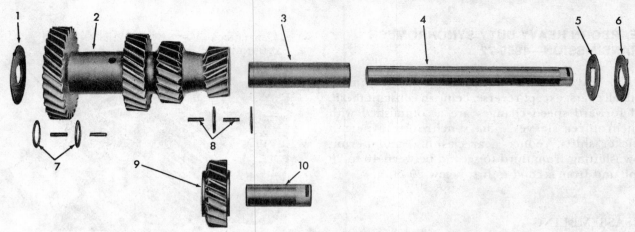

Exploded view of the countershaft gear, with the reverse idler gear and shaft.

retainer, select a gasket combination of the proper thickness, and then install the gaskets and bearing retainer. Attach the bearing retainer to the case with four cap screws and lockwashers. Tighten them securely.

Turn the transmission over on the repair stand to assist in aligning the countershaft gear with the shaft openings in the case. Insert the countershaft through the opening in the rear of the case, making sure it passes through the two thrust washers before it enters the countershaft gear. Drive the countershaft into the gear, forcing out tool J-5589 from the front of the case. *NOTE: It is necessary to rotate the rear bearing*

retainer away from the case approximately one-half inch, as shown, to uncover the countershaft bore.

Before the countershaft is driven fully into place, install the lock key in the notch in the shaft, and then drive the shaft in until the lock key seats against the cutout in the case.

Align the mainshaft rear bearing retainer and gasket with the case, install four attaching cap screws, and tighten securely. Lock the transmission in two gears to prevent the mainshaft from turning, then tighten the universal joint yoke retaining bolt.

Install the side cover assembly on the transmission case.

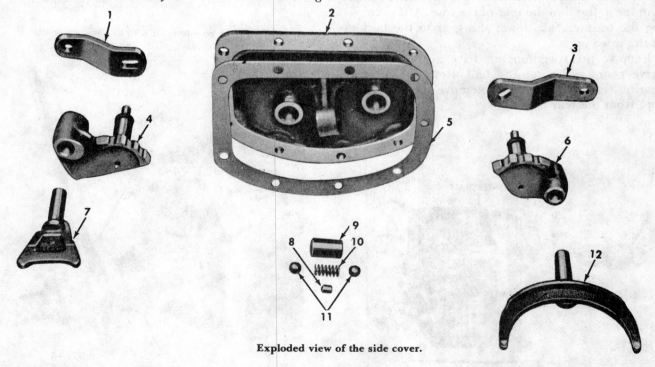

Exploded view of the side cover.

1. 1st and Reverse Control Lever
2. Side Cover
3. 2nd and 3rd Control Lever
4. 1st and Reverse Shifter Lever
5. Gasket
6. 2nd and 3rd Shifter Lever
7. 1st and Reverse Shift Fork
8. Interlock Pin
9. Interlock Sleeve
10. Poppet Spring
11. Poppet Balls
12. 2nd and 3rd Shift Fork

DEARBORN HEAVY DUTY SYNCHROMESH TRANSMISSION—1969-72

This heavy duty transmission is fully synchronized, with all gears, except reverse, being in constant mesh. All forward speed changes are accomplished with synchronizer sleeves. The synchronizers permit quicker shifts, reduce gear clashing, and permit downshifting from third to second between 40 to 20 mph and from second to first below 20 mph.

DISASSEMBLING

Remove the front bearing retainer and gasket. Take off the case cover and gasket. Remove the speedometer driven gear extension and gasket.

Remove the filler plug from the right side of the case and, through the filler plug hole, drive out the countershaft retaining pin.

Remove the interlock spring and rod pin, using a small magnet. With the transmission in neutral, remove both shift fork-to-rail set screws. Push the first-and-reverse shifter rail out of the rear of the case.

Using Tool J-3049, rotate the 2nd-and-3rd shifter rail 90°. Using a brass drift, drive the 2nd-and-3rd shifter rail and the welch plug out of the front of the case. Using a dummy shaft, Tool J-21775-01, drive the countershaft out of the rear of the case. After removing the countershaft, lower the gear to the bottom of the case.

Remove the speedometer drive gear snap ring, drive gear, and retaining ball. Remove the rear bearing retaining snap ring. Remove the large snap ring from the rear bearing.

Rotating the 2nd-and-3rd shifter rail, as discussed in the text.

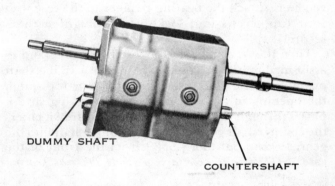

Removing the countershaft with the dummy shaft.

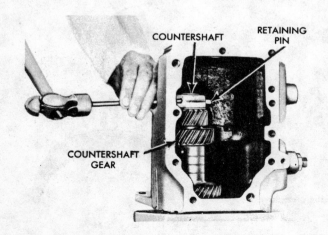

Removing the countershaft retaining pin.

Removing the rear bearing.

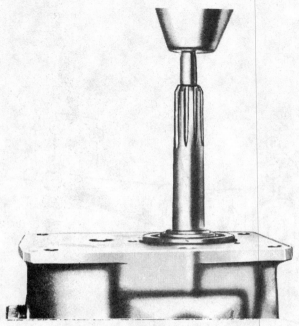

Pressing the input shaft out of the bearing.

Removing the reverse idler shaft.

Slide Tool J-21774-1 over the bearing and install the snap ring (in tool) into the snap ring groove in the bearing. Install the speedometer drive gear snap ring on the mainshaft. Slide Tool J-21774-2 onto the mainshaft and thread it into J-21774-1. While holding Tool J-21774-1 from turning, thread J-21774-2 into J-21774-1 with Handle J-8614-1 until the bearing pulls free of the mainshaft. Remove the bearing, snap ring, and tools.

Slide the input shaft forward until the main drive gear rests against the case. Remove the shift forks. Remove the mainshaft through the top of the case. Remove the large snap ring from the bearing, and then lift the input shaft out through the top of the case.

Remove the countershaft gear and thrust washers. Using a brass drift, drive the reverse idler gear shaft out of the rear of the case, and then lift the gear and thrust washers from the case. Remove the interlock spring and rod pins.

DISASSEMBLING THE MAINSHAFT

Remove the front blocking ring. Remove the synchronizer insert retainer spring. Mark the clutch hub and clutch hub sleeve so they can be matched on assembly, and then remove the 2nd-and-3rd gear synchronizer clutch hub sleeve.

Remove the synchronizer hub-to-shaft snap ring, clutch hub, blocking ring, retainer spring, and clutch hub inserts. Remove the second-speed gear. Remove the first-speed gear thrust washer-to-shaft snap ring, thrust washer, first-speed gear, and blocking ring.

Remove the first-and-reverse synchronizer hub-to-shaft snap ring. Mark the hub and gear so they can be matched on assembly and, using an arbor press, remove the first-and-reverse synchronizer hub-and-sliding gear.

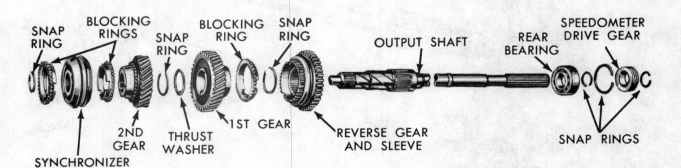

Fig. 7A-15 Exploded View of Mainshaft

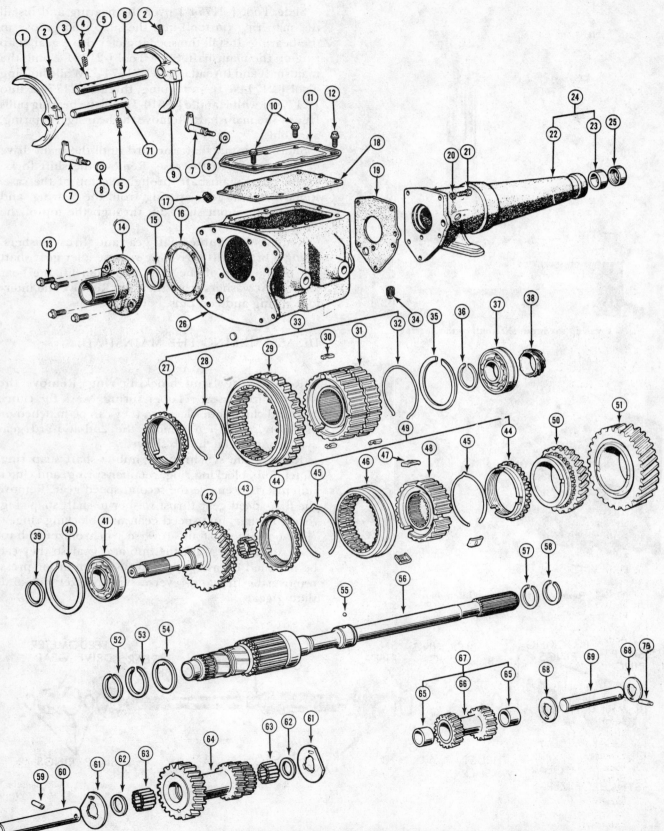

Exploded view of the Dearborn heavy duty transmission used on some vehicles from 1969-72.

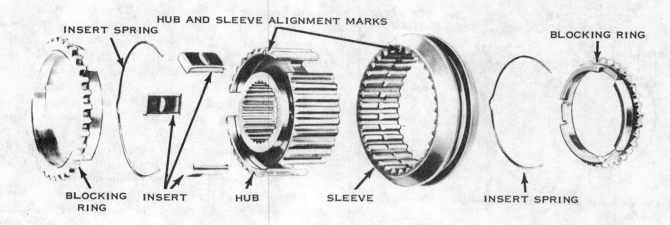

Exploded view of the 2nd-and-3rd synchronizing unit.

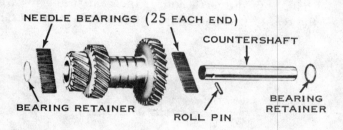

Exploded view of the countershaft gear and countershaft.

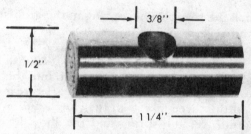

Details of the detent pin installer mentioned in the text.

1. Second and Third Gear Shifter Fork
2. Shifter Fork to Rail Set Screw
3. Shift Rail Inter-lock Pin
4. Shift Rail Inter-lock Pin Spring Set Screw
5. Shift Rail Inter-lock Spring
6. First and Reverse Shift Rail
7. Shift Lever
8. Shift Lever Oil Seal
9. First and Reverse Shifter Fork
10. Access Cover Screw
11. Access Cover
12. Access Cover Screw
13. Drive Gear Bearing Retainer Bolt
14. Drive Gear Bearing Retainer
15. Input Shaft Oil Seal
16. Main Drive Gear Bearing Retainer Gasket
17. Filler Plug
18. Access Cover Gasket
19. Extension Housing Gasket
20. Lock Washer
21. Extension Housing Bolt
22. Extension Housing
23. Extension Housing Bushing
24. Extension Housing Assembly
25. Extension Housing Seal
26. Case

27. Synchronizer Blocking Ring
28. First and Reverse Synchronizer Spring (Front)
29. First and Reverse Sliding Gear
30. Synchronizer Hub Insert
31. First and Reverse Synchronizer Hub
32. First and Reverse Synchronizer Spring (Rear)
33. First and Reverse Synchronizer Assembly
34. Drain Plug
35. Drive Gear Rear Bearing Retaining Snap Ring
36. Drive Gear Rear Bearing to Shaft Snap Ring
37. Drive Gear Rear Bearing
38. Speedometer Drive Gear
39. Front Bearing to Shaft Snap Ring
40. Front Bearing Retaining Snap Ring
41. Front Bearing
42. Input Shaft
43. Input Shaft Roller Bearing
44. Second and Third Synchronizer Blocking Ring
45. Second and Third Synchronizer Spring
46. Second and Third Synchronizer Sleeve
47. Second and Third Synchronizer Insert

48. Second and Third Synchronizer Hub
49. Second and Third Synchronizer Assembly
50. Second Gear
51. First Gear
52. Second and Third Synchronizer Hub to Shaft Snap Ring
53. Synchronizer Blocking Ring to Shaft Snap Ring
54. Low Gear Thrust Washer
55. Speedometer Drive Gear Retaining Ball
56. Output Shaft
57. Main Drive Gear Bearing to Shaft Snap Ring
58. Speedometer Drive Gear to Shaft Snap Ring
59. Countershaft Retaining Pin
60. Countershaft
61. Countershaft Gear Thrust Washer
62. Countershaft Washer
63. Countershaft Gear Roller Bearing
64. Countershaft Gear
65. Reverse Idler Gear Bushing
66. Reverse Idler Gear
67. Reverse Idler Gear Assembly
68. Reverse Idler Gear Thrust Washer
69. Reverse Idler Gear Shaft
70. Reverse Idler Gear Retainer Pin
71. Second and Third Shift Rail

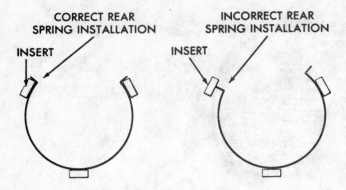

CORRECT REAR SPRING INSTALLATION

INSERT

INCORRECT REAR SPRING INSTALLATION

INSERT

Correct installation of the synchronizer retainer springs and inserts.

ASSEMBLING THE MAINSHAFT

Install the rear retainer spring in the groove in the first-and-reverse synchronizer clutch hub. Make sure the spring covers all insert grooves. *NOTE: If the tip of the rear retainer spring is less than 0.120" in length, replace the spring.* Start the clutch hub into the sliding sleeve, making sure the alignment marks are indexed. Position the three inserts in the clutch hub, with the small end over the spring and the shoulder on the inside of the hub. Slip the sliding gear onto the clutch hub until the detent is engaged. Install the front retainer spring in the clutch hub. Install one retainer spring into the groove of the 2nd-and-3rd speed synchronizer clutch hub, making sure that all three insert slots are fully covered. With the marks on the clutch hub and sleeve aligned, start the hub into the sleeve. Place the three inserts on top of the retainer spring and push the assembly together. Install the remaining retainer spring so that the spring ends cover the same slots as does the other spring. **CAUTION: Do not stagger the springs.**

Place a synchronizer blocking ring on each end of the synchronizer sleeve. Lubricate the mainshaft splines and machined surfaces with transmission lubricant. Using an arbor press, install the first-and-reverse gear synchronizer assembly onto the mainshaft, with the teeth end of the gear facing toward the rear of the shaft. When pressed into place, install the snap ring.

Installing the 1st-and-reverse synchronizer assembly.

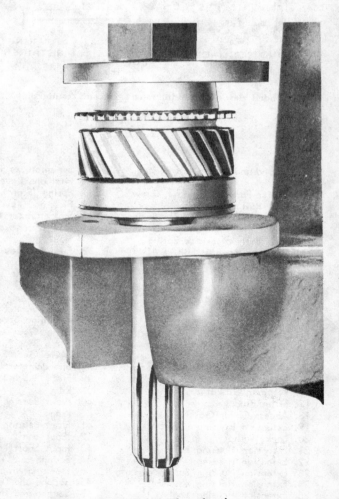

Installing the front bearing.

Coat the tapered machined surface of the first-speed gear with grease. Place the blocking ring on the greased surface. Slide the first gear onto the mainshaft, with the blocking ring toward the rear of the shaft. Rotate the gear as necessary to engage the three notches in the blocking ring with the synchronizer inserts. Secure the first-speed gear with a thrust washer and snap ring.

Coat the tapered machined surface of the second-speed gear with grease, and then slide the blocking ring onto it. Slide the second-speed gear, with the blocking ring and the 2nd-and-3rd synchronizer assembly, onto the mainshaft. The tapered machined surface of the second-speed gear must be toward the front of the shaft. Make sure the notches in the blocking ring engage the synchronizer inserts. Secure the synchronizer with a snap ring.

ASSEMBLING THE TRANSMISSION

Install the reverse idler gear, with a thrust washer on each end, into the case. Make sure the lock pin is seated in the slot in the back face of the case.

Assemble the countershaft gear, countershaft alignment tool (dummy shaft), roller bearings, and thrust washers. Place it in the bottom of the case. *NOTE: The*

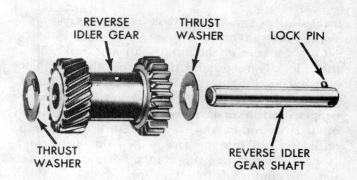

Exploded view of the reverse idler gear and shaft.

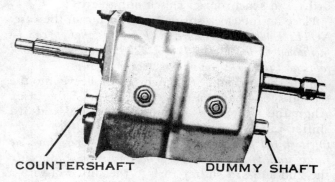

Installing the countershaft.

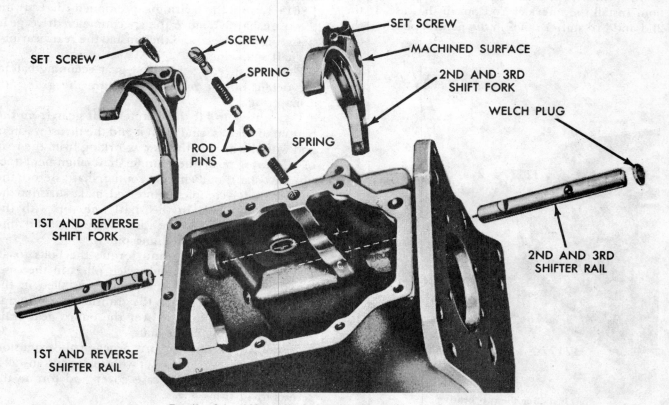

Details of the shifter rails, forks, rod pins, and interlock springs.

countershaft gear must remain there until the main and input shafts have been installed.

Coat the bore of the input shaft and gear with a thin film of grease, and then install the 15 roller bearings in the bore. **CAUTION: A thick film of grease will plug the lubricant holes and prevent proper lubrication of the roller bearings.** Install the input shaft-and-bearing assembly through the top of the case and into the bore in the front of the case. Install the large snap ring on the bearing, and then slide the input shaft fully forward.

Position the mainshaft assembly in the case. Install the 2nd-and-3rd speed shift fork on the 2nd-and-3rd speed synchronizer clutch hub sleeve.

Place an interlock spring and rod pin in the case. *NOTE: Interlock rod pin and spring installation can be facilitated by the use of Tool J-22239 or a similar tool fabricated from 1/2" round bar stock, as shown.*

Slide the 2nd-and-3rd synchronizer sleeve into the second-speed position (toward the rear of the case). Align the shift fork and install the 2nd-and-3rd shifter rail. *NOTE: It will be necessary to depress the interlock rod pin to install the rail in the bore. Move the rail in until the rod pin engages the forward notch.* Secure the 2nd-and-3rd shifter fork to the shift rail with a set screw.

Move the synchronizer sleeve to the neutral position. Install the interlock rod pin in the case. If the 2nd-and-3rd shifter rail is in the neutral position, the top of the interlock rod pin will be slightly lower than the surface of the first-and-reverse shift rail bore.

Move the first-and-reverse sliding gear forward, and then place the first-and-reverse shift fork in the groove of the synchronizer sliding gear. Align the shift fork and install the first-and-reverse shift rail. Move the rail in until the center notch is aligned with the rod pin bore. Install the remaining interlock rod pin and spring. Secure the first-and-reverse shift fork to the shifter rail with a set screw. Install a new shifter rail expansion plug into the front of the case.

While holding the input shaft and blocking ring in position, move the mainshaft forward to seat the mainshaft pilot in the roller bearings of the input shaft. Tap the front bearing into place in the case while holding the mainshaft to prevent the roller bearings from dropping out. Install the front bearing retainer and a new gasket, making sure the oil return slot is toward the bottom of the case. Torque the attaching bolts to 22 ft-lbs.

Install the large snap ring on the rear bearing. Position the bearing on the mainshaft, with the snap ring toward the rear of the shaft. Thread Tool J-21774-2 all the way into J-21774-1 and place the tools on the mainshaft next to the bearing. Install the speedometer drive gear snap ring on the mainshaft. Back Tool J-21774-2 out of J-21774-1, using Handle J-8614-1, until the bearing is positioned correctly on the mainshaft. Remove the speedometer drive gear snap ring and tools, and then install the rear bearing-to-shaft snap ring.

Place the speedometer drive gear retaining ball in the detent on the mainshaft. Secure the gear with a snap ring.

Use a hook to lift the countershaft gear from the bottom of the case and align it and the thrust washers and with the bore in the case. Working from the rear of the case, push the countershaft alignment tool (dummy shaft) out with the countershaft. Before the countershaft is completely inserted, make sure that the retaining pin hole in the shaft lines up with the retaining pin hole in the case. Drive the shaft into place and insert the retaining pin.

Install the extension and torque the bolts to 46 ft-lbs. Install the filler and welch plugs in the case, making sure the magnetic plug is installed in the bottom of the case. Shift the transmission into any gear and pour lubricant over the entire gear train while rotating the input shaft.

Install the speedometer driven gear in the extension. Coat a new case cover gasket with sealer and install it on the case. Install the case cover and torque the screws to 17 ft-lbs.

Installing the rear bearing.

MUNCIE/SAGINAW THREE-SPEED TRANSMISSIONS—SINCE 1965

Both Muncie and Saginaw three-speed transmissions have been used on various models since 1965. Both of them are fully synchronized in all forward gears and are basically alike, differing only in minor details. For instance, the Saginaw transmission uses 27 roller bearings at each end of the countergear, while the Muncie has 29. The Saginaw transmission uses 14 roller bearings in the clutch gear, while the Muncie has 16. Another difference is in the use of an E-clip to hold the reverse idler shaft in the Saginaw transmission case, while it is held in position by the extension housing on the Muncie transmission.

The following service procedures contain step-by-step illustrated instructions for overhauling a Saginaw three-speed transmission and they can be used equally well for the Muncie unit. To assist, an exploded view of both mainshafts is shown.

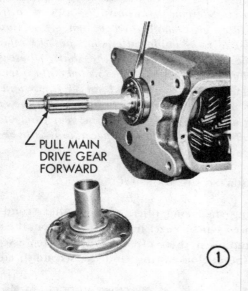

PULL MAIN DRIVE GEAR FORWARD

①

REVERSE IDLER GEAR E-CLIP

SCREWDRIVER

②

REAR BEARING RETAINER AND MAINSHAFT ASSEMBLY

③

OVERHAULING A SAGINAW THREE-SPEED TRANSMISSION

DISASSEMBLING

① Remove the side cover attaching screws, and then take off the side cover and shift forks as an assembly. Remove the clutch gear bearing retainer. Remove the clutch gear bearing-to-gear stem snap ring, and then take out the drive gear bearing by pulling outward on the gear until a screwdriver can be inserted between the bearing large snap ring and case to remove it. The clutch gear bearing is a slip fit on the gear and in the case bore to provide clearance for removal of the clutch gear and mainshaft as an assembly.

② Remove the reverse idler shaft E-ring. *NOTE: This ring is not used in the Muncie transmission.*

③ Remove the extension-to-case attaching bolts. Pull out the clutch gear, mainshaft, and extension housing as an assembly through the rear case opening.

④

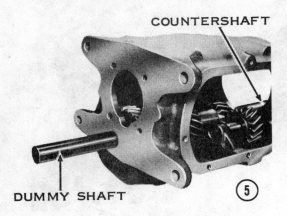

Remove the clutch gear, needle bearings, and synchronizer ring from the mainshaft.

④ Using snap ring pliers, expand the snap ring in the extension which holds the mainshaft rear bearing, and then remove the extension.

⑤ Using a dummy shaft, drive the countershaft and its Woodruff key out the rear of the case. The dummy shaft will hold the roller bearings in position within the countergear bore. Remove the gear, bearings, and thrust washers.

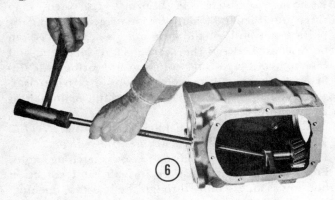

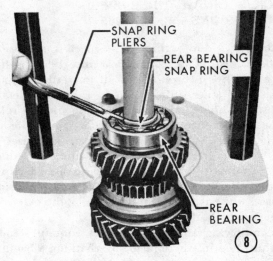

⑥ Use a long punch through the front bearing case bore to drive the reverse idler shaft and Woodruff key through the rear of the case. *NOTE: The truck three-speed Saginaw transmission uses a different reverse idler gear shaft than passenger car models. The passenger car model idler shaft has the retaining ring groove at the center of the shaft, whereas the truck shaft has the groove located off-center and farther away from the gear. A spacer is used in conjunction with the truck shaft to fit between the retaining ring and idler gear to keep the gear from moving axially. The truck shaft and spacer unit will be used to service all models.*

Disassembling the Mainshaft

⑦ Using snap ring pliers, remove the second- and third-speed synchronizer hub snap ring from the mainshaft, and then press off the synchronizer assembly, second-speed blocker ring, and the second-speed gear

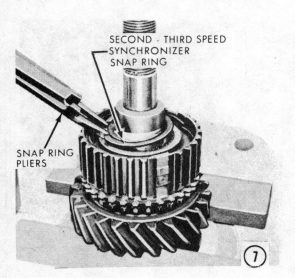

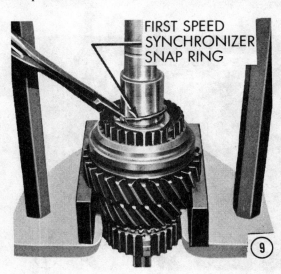

from the front of the mainshaft.

⑧ Depress the speedometer retaining clip, and then slide the gear off the rear of the mainshaft. Remove the rear bearing snap ring from its mainshaft groove. Support the reverse gear with plates, and then press on the rear of the mainshaft to remove the reverse gear,

thrust washer, spring washer, rear bearing, and snap ring from the rear of the mainshaft.

⑨ Remove the first-and-Reverse synchronizer hub snap ring from the mainshaft, and then slide off the synchronizer assembly, first-speed blocker ring, and first-speed gear from the rear of the mainshaft.

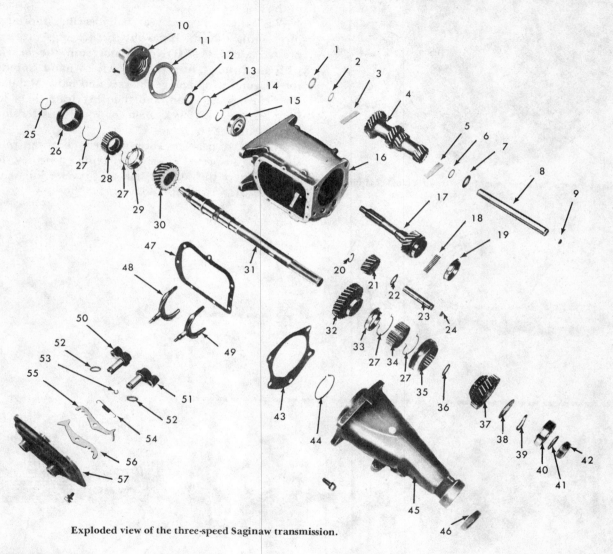

Exploded view of the three-speed Saginaw transmission.

1. Thrust Washer – Front	15. Clutch Gear Bearing	30. 2nd Speed Gear	44. Snap Ring – Rear Bearing to Extension
2. Bearing Washer	16. Case	31. Mainshaft	45. Extension
3. Needle Bearings	17. Clutch Gear	32. 1st Speed Gear	46. Oil Seal
4. Countergear	18. Pilot Bearings	33. 1st Speed Blocker Ring	47. Gasket
5. Needle Bearings	19. 3rd Speed Blocker Ring	34. 1-2 Synchronizer Hub Assembly	48. 2-3 Shift Fork
6. Bearing Washer	20. Retainer "E" Ring	35. 1-2 Synchronizer Sleeve	49. 1st and Reverse Shift Fork
7. Thrust Washer – Rear	21. Reverse Idler Gear	36. Snap Ring – Hub to Shaft	50. 2-3 Shifter Shaft Assembly
8. Counter Shaft	22. Thrust Washer (Tanged)	37. Reverse Gear	51. 1st and Reverse Shifter Shaft Assembly
9. Woodruff Key	23. Reverse Idler Shaft	38. Thrust Washer	52. "O" Ring Seal
10. Bearing Retainer	24. Woodruff Key	39. Spring Washer	53. "E" Ring
11. Gasket	25. Snap Ring – Hub to Shaft	40. Rear Bearing	54. Spring
12. Oil Seal	26. 2-3 Synchronizer Sleeve	41. Snap Ring – Bearing to Shaft	55. 2nd and 3rd Detent Cam
13. Snap Ring – Bearing to Case	27. Synchronizer Key Spring	42. Speedometer Drive Gear	56. 1st and Reverse Detent Cam
14. Snap Ring – Bearing to Gear	28. 2-3 Synchronizer Hub Assembly	43. Gasket	57. Side Cover
	29. 2nd Speed Blocker Ring		

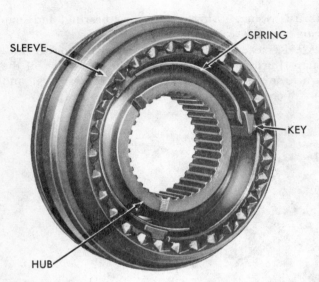

Details of the synchronizer assembly without a blocker ring.

CLEANING AND INSPECTING

Wash the transmission thoroughly inside and out with cleaning solvent, and then inspect the case for cracks. Check the front and rear faces for burrs; dress them off with a fine mill file. Check the bearing bores in the case for damage.

Wash the front and rear ball bearings thoroughly in cleaning solvent. Blow out the bearings with compressed air. **CAUTION: Do not spin the bearings with air. Instead, turn them slowly by hand. Spinning the bearings will damage the race and balls.** Make sure the bearings are clean, and then lubricate them with light engine oil. Check them for roughness by slowly turning the race by hand.

All clutch gear and countergear bearing rollers should be inspected closely and replaced if they show wear. Inspect the countershaft and reverse idler shaft. Replace all worn shafts and washers.

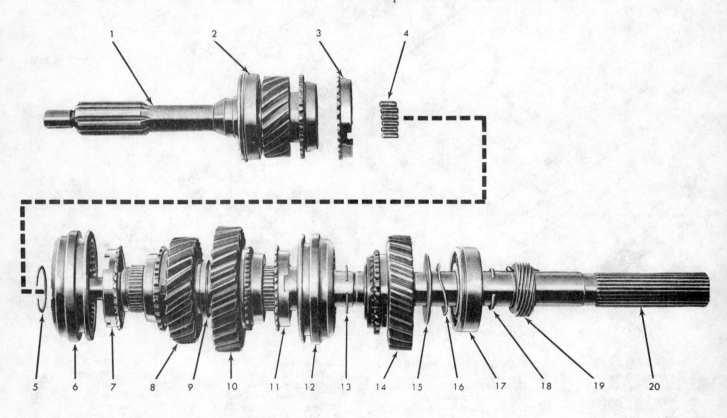

1. Clutch Gear
2. Clutch Gear Bearing
3. 3rd Speed Blocker Ring
4. Mainshaft Pilot Bearings (14)
5. Snap Ring
6. 2-3 Synchronizer Assembly
7. 2nd Speed Blocker Ring
8. 2nd Speed Gear
9. Shoulder (Part of Main Shaft)
10. 1st Speed Gear
11. 1st Speed Blocker Ring
12. 1st Speed Synchronizer Assembly
13. Snap Ring
14. Reverse Gear
15. Reverse Gear Thrust Washer
16. Spring Washer
17. Rear Bearing
18. Snap Ring
19. Speedo Drive Gear and Clip
20. Mainshaft

Details of the clutch gear and mainshaft used in the three-speed Saginaw transmission.

Inspect all gears for excessive wear, chips, or cracks and replace any that are worn or damaged. Inspect the reverse gear bushing. If it is worn or damaged, replace the entire gear. Check both clutch sleeves to see that they slide freely on their hubs.

The bushing used in the idler gear is pressed into the gear and finish-bored in place to insure positive alignment of the bushing and shaft as well as proper meshing of the gears. Because of the high degree of accuracy to which these parts are machined, the bushing is not serviced separately.

Inspect the countershaft anti-rattle plate teeth for wear or other damage. The plate and two damper springs are retained to the countergear by three rivets. Disassembly is not recommended.

The synchronizer hubs and sliding sleeves are a selected assembly and should be kept together as originally assembled, but the keys and two springs may be replaced if they are worn or broken. To disassemble

Ball bearings with gall marks will cause noisy operation and must be replaced when overhauling a transmission.

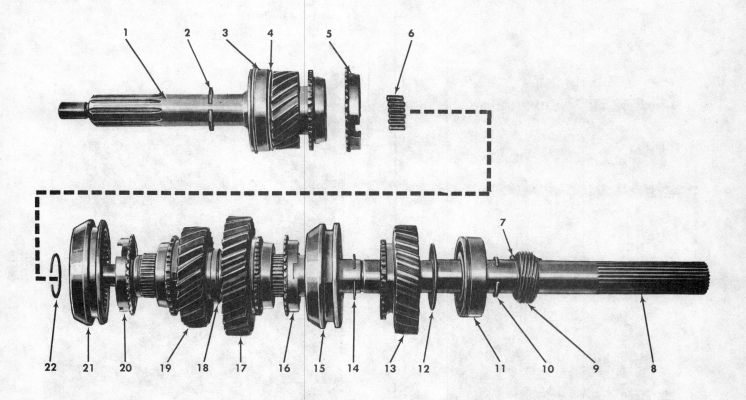

1. Clutch Gear	7. Retaining Clip	13. Reverse Gear	18. Shoulder (Part of Mainshaft)
2. Snap Ring	8. Mainshaft	14. Snap Ring	19. 2nd Speed Gear
3. Clutch Gear Bearing	9. Speedo Drive Gear	15. 1st Speed Synchronizer Assembly	20. 2nd Speed Blocker Ring
4. Oil Slinger	10. Snap Ring	16. 1st Speed Blocker Ring	21. 2-3 Synchronizer Assembly
5. 3rd Speed Blocker Ring	11. Rear Bearing	17. 1st Speed Gear	22. Snap Ring
6. Mainshaft Pilot Bearings (16)	12. Reverse Gear Thrust Washer		

Details of the clutch gear and mainshaft used in the three-speed Muncie transmission. Note the reversed direction of the chamfer in the first-speed synchronizer (15).

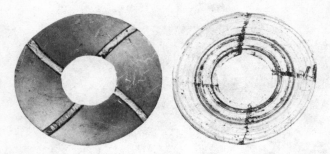

New cluster gear thrust washer (left) is shown for comparison with a worn one. This washer controls the end play of the cluster gear.

a synchronizer unit, mark the hub and sleeve so they can be matched on assembly. Push the hub from the sliding sleeve. The keys and the springs can then be removed.

To assemble a synchronizer unit, place the three

A piece of broken tooth was forced between two teeth, causing one to snap. Note the indentation in the top tooth, a graphic indication of the terrific pressure.

Rough balls and rollers can be felt by slowly turning the bearings through your fingers.

The 3rd-speed clutch teeth generally wear in this fashion.

keys and two springs in position (one on each side of the hub) so all three keys are engaged by both springs. The tanged end of each synchronizer spring should be installed into different key cavities on either side. Slide the sleeve onto the hub, aligning the marks made before disassembly. *NOTE: A groove around the outside of the synchronizer hub identifies the end that must be opposite the fork slot in the sleeve when assembled. This groove indicates the end of the hub with a 0.070" greater recess depth.*

If the bushing in the rear of the extension requires replacement, remove the seal and use Tool J-5778 to drive the bushing into the extension housing. Using the same tool, drive a new bushing in from the rear. Coat the ID of the bushing and seal with transmission lubricant, and then install a new oil seal.

If the lip seal in the retainer needs replacement, pry the old seal out and replace it with a new seal, using Tool J-7785 until the seal seats in its bore.

ASSEMBLING

Mainshaft

⑩ Turn the front of the mainshaft upward and install the second-speed gear, with the clutching teeth upward; the rear face of the gear will butt against the flange on the mainshaft. Install a blocking ring, with the clutching teeth downward over the synchronizing

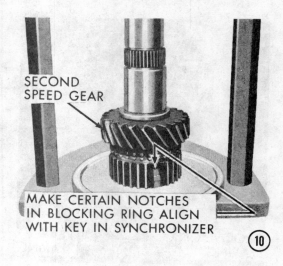

SECOND SPEED GEAR

MAKE CERTAIN NOTCHES IN BLOCKING RING ALIGN WITH KEY IN SYNCHRONIZER

⑩

surface of the second-speed gear. *NOTE: All three blocker rings used in this transmission are identical.* Install the second-and-third synchronizer assembly, with the fork slot downward; press it onto the splines on the mainshaft until it bottoms. *NOTE: Both synchronizer assemblies used in this transmission are identical.* **CAUTION: Be sure the notches of the blocker ring align with the keys of the synchronizer assembly.** Install the snap ring holding the synchronizer hub to the mainshaft. *NOTE: Both synchronizer snap rings are identical.*

⑪ Turn the rear of the mainshaft upward, and then install the first-speed gear, with the clutching teeth upward; the front face of the gear will butt against the flange on the mainshaft. Slide on a blocker ring, with the clutching teeth downward, over the synchronizing surface of the first-speed gear. Install the first-gear synchronizer assembly, with the fork slot downward; push it onto the splines on the mainshaft.

Sometimes the snap ring groove shoulder in the extension housing breaks out (arrow), and this causes excessive backlash in the mainshaft.

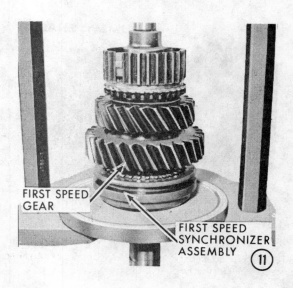

FIRST SPEED GEAR

FIRST SPEED SYNCHRONIZER ASSEMBLY

⑪

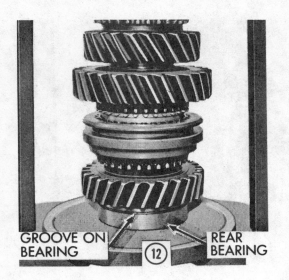

GROOVE ON BEARING ⑫ REAR BEARING

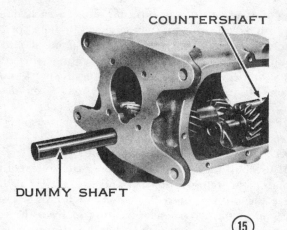

COUNTERSHAFT

DUMMY SHAFT

⑮

CAUTION: Be sure the notches of the blocker ring align with the keys of the synchronizer assembly. Install the synchronizer hub-to-mainshaft snap ring. Slide on the reverse gear, with the clutching teeth downward. Install the reverse gear thrust washer (steel) and the spring washer.

⑫ Replace the rear ball bearing, with the snap ring slot as shown, and then press it onto the mainshaft. Install the rear bearing-to-mainshaft snap ring.

⑬ Press on the speedometer drive gear and retaining clip.

ASSEMBLING THE TRANSMISSION

⑭ Using a dummy shaft in the countergear, load a row of roller bearings (27) and a bearing thrust washer at each end of the gear. Use heavy grease to hold them in place.

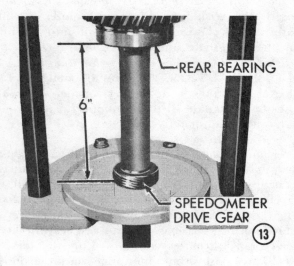

REAR BEARING

6"

SPEEDOMETER DRIVE GEAR

⑬

DUMMY SHAFT

⑭

⑯

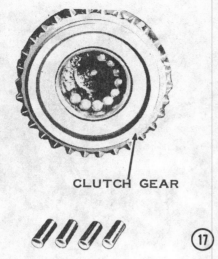

CLUTCH GEAR

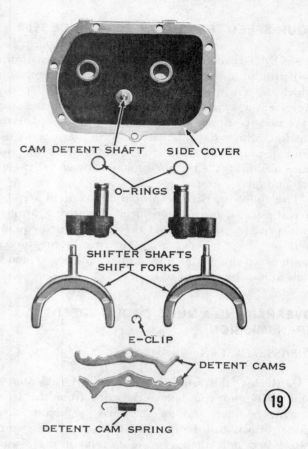

CAM DETENT SHAFT   SIDE COVER

O-RINGS

SHIFTER SHAFTS
SHIFT FORKS

E-CLIP

DETENT CAMS

⑲

DETENT CAM SPRING

⑰

⑮ Slide the countergear assembly through the case rear opening, along with a tanged thrust washer (tang away from the gear) at each end, and then drive in the countergear shaft and Woodruff key from the rear of the case. **CAUTION: Be sure the countershaft picks up both thrust washers and that the tangs are aligned with their notches in the case.** Install the reverse idler gear and shaft, with its Woodruff key, from the rear of case. Do not install the idler shaft E-ring at this time.

⑯ Using snap ring pliers, expand the snap ring in the extension housing, and then assemble the extension housing over the rear of the mainshaft and onto the rear bearing. Seat the snap ring in the rear bearing groove.

⑰ Load the mainshaft pilot bearings (14) into the clutch gear cavity, and then slide the 3rd-speed blocker

ring onto the clutch gear clutching surface, with its teeth toward the gear. Pilot the clutch gear, pilot bearings, and 3rd-speed blocker ring assembly over the front of the mainshaft. Do not assemble the bearing on the gear at this time. **CAUTION: Be sure the notches in the blocker ring align with the keys in the 2-3 synchronizer assembly.**

⑱ Place the extension-to-case gasket at the rear of the case, holding it in place with grease and, from the rear of the case, slide the clutch gear, mainshaft, and extension into the case as an assembly. **CAUTION: Be sure the clutch gear engages the countergear anti-lash plate.** Install the extension-to-case retaining bolts. Install the front bearing outer snap ring, and then position the bearing over the stem of the clutch gear and into the front case bore. Install the snap ring-to-clutch gear stem, and then replace the clutch gear bearing retainer and gasket. **CAUTION: The retainer oil return hole must be at the bottom.** Install the reverse idler gear retainer E-ring.

⑲ Shift the synchronizer sleeves to neutral positions, and then install the cover, gasket, and fork assembly to the case. Be sure the forks align with their synchronizer sleeve grooves. Tighten all bolts. Rotate the clutch gear shaft and shift the transmission into each gear to be sure there is free rotation.

REAR BEARING
RETAINER AND
MAINSHAFT ASSEMBLY   ⑱

FOUR-SPEED TRANSMISSIONS—SINCE 1963

Since 1963, many of these vehicles have been equipped with an optional Muncie four-speed transmission, which is synchronized in all four forward speeds. Reverse is not synchronized. Since 1966, many vehicles have been equipped with a Saginaw four-speed transmission, which has a great many similarities to the Muncie unit. The main difference between the two transmissions is the method of mounting and engaging first and reverse gears.

The following service procedures contain step-by-step illustrated instructions for overhauling a Muncie four-speed transmission and they can be used equally well for the Saginaw unit. To assist, some special Saginaw service notes, illustrations, and an exploded view follow the Muncie section.

OVERHAULING A MUNCIE FOUR-SPEED TRANSMISSION

DISASSEMBLING

① Remove the transmission side cover. Take out the four bolts and two bolt lock strips from the front bearing retainer, and then remove the retainer and gasket. Lock up the transmission by shifting into two gears, and then remove the main drive gear retaining nut.

② With the transmission gears in neutral, drive the lock pin from the reverse shifter lever boss, and then pull the shifter shaft out about 1/8″. This disengages the reverse shift fork from the reverse gear.

③ Remove the six bolts attaching the extension to the case. Tap the extension with a soft hammer in a rearward direction to start it. When the reverse idler

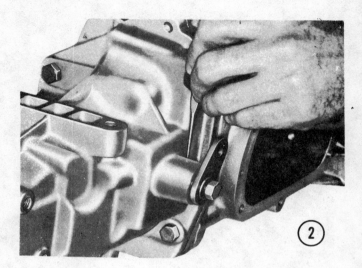

shaft is out as far as it will go, move the extension to the left so the reverse fork clears the reverse gear, and then remove the extension and gasket. Take off the rear reverse idler gear, flat thrust washer, shaft, and roll spring pin. Remove the speedometer gear and the reverse gear, using Tool J-5814.

④ Slide the 3-4 synchronizer clutch sleeve forward to the 4th-speed gear position. Carefully remove the

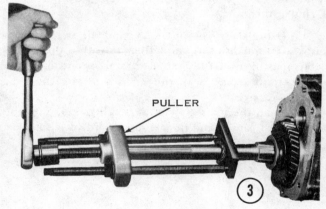

PULLER

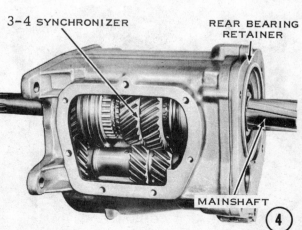

3-4 SYNCHRONIZER   REAR BEARING RETAINER

MAINSHAFT

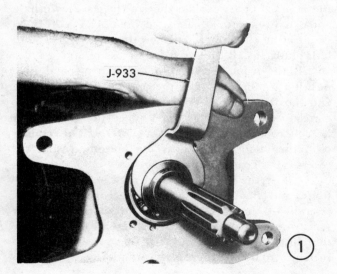

J-933

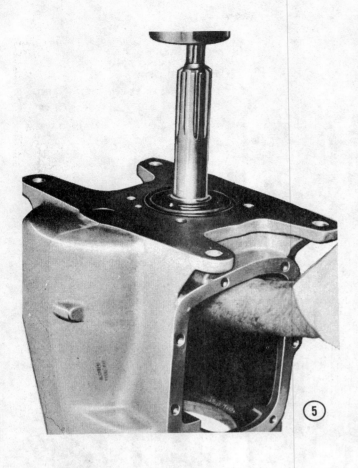

⑤

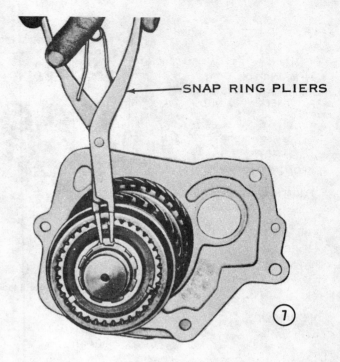

SNAP RING PLIERS

⑦

rear bearing retainer-and-mainshaft assembly from the case by tapping the bearing retainer with a soft hammer. Unload 17 bearing rollers from the main drive (clutch) gear, and then remove the 4th speed synchronizer blocker ring. Lift the front half of the reverse idler gear and its tanged thrust washer from the case.

⑤ Press the main drive gear down from the front bearing. From inside of the case, tap out the front bearing and snap ring.

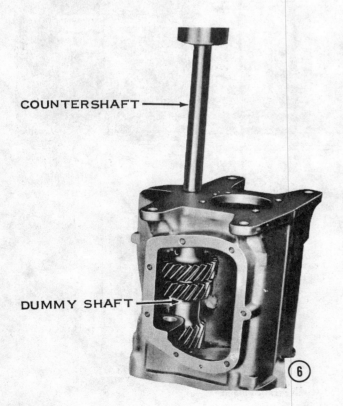

COUNTERSHAFT

DUMMY SHAFT

⑥

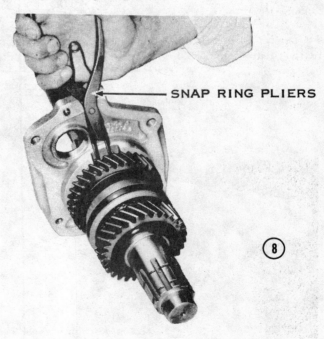

SNAP RING PLIERS

⑧

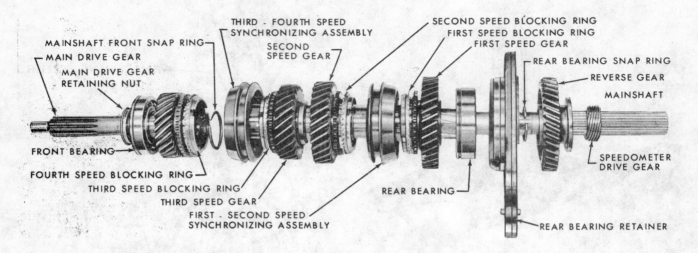

MAINSHAFT FRONT SNAP RING
MAIN DRIVE GEAR
MAIN DRIVE GEAR
RETAINING NUT

THIRD - FOURTH SPEED
SYNCHRONIZING ASSEMBLY

SECOND
SPEED GEAR

SECOND SPEED BLOCKING RING
FIRST SPEED BLOCKING RING
FIRST SPEED GEAR

REAR BEARING SNAP RING
REVERSE GEAR
MAINSHAFT

FRONT BEARING

FOURTH SPEED BLOCKING RING
THIRD SPEED BLOCKING RING
THIRD SPEED GEAR
FIRST - SECOND SPEED
SYNCHRONIZING ASSEMBLY

REAR BEARING

SPEEDOMETER
DRIVE GEAR

REAR BEARING RETAINER

Details of the main drive (clutch) gear and mainshaft assembly used on the Muncie transmission.

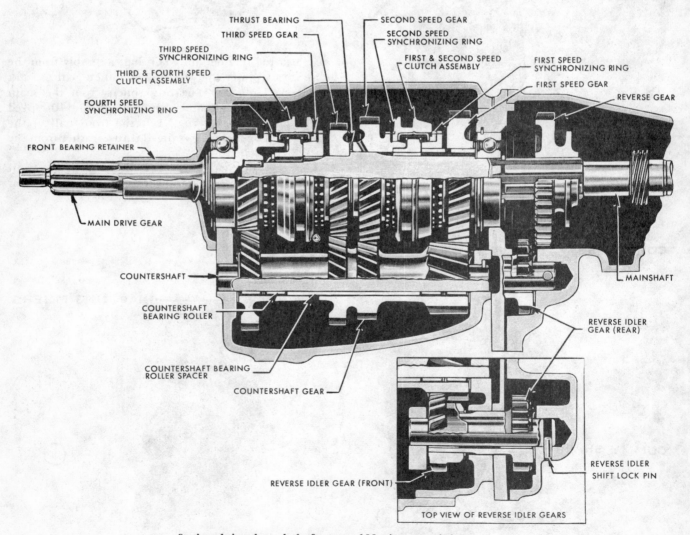

THRUST BEARING
THIRD SPEED GEAR

THIRD SPEED
SYNCHRONIZING RING

THIRD & FOURTH SPEED
CLUTCH ASSEMBLY

FOURTH SPEED
SYNCHRONIZING RING

SECOND SPEED GEAR

SECOND SPEED
SYNCHRONIZING RING

FIRST & SECOND SPEED
CLUTCH ASSEMBLY

FIRST SPEED
SYNCHRONIZING RING

FIRST SPEED GEAR

REVERSE GEAR

FRONT BEARING RETAINER

MAIN DRIVE GEAR

COUNTERSHAFT

COUNTERSHAFT
BEARING ROLLER

COUNTERSHAFT BEARING
ROLLER SPACER

COUNTERSHAFT GEAR

MAINSHAFT

REVERSE IDLER
GEAR (REAR)

REVERSE IDLER GEAR (FRONT)

REVERSE IDLER
SHIFT LOCK PIN

TOP VIEW OF REVERSE IDLER GEARS

Sectioned view through the four -speed Munice transmission.

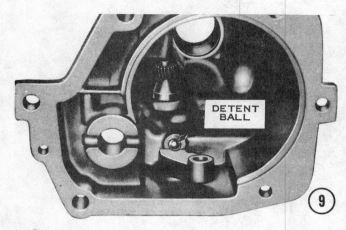

⑥ From the front of the case, press out the counter-shaft, using Tool J-22246, or a dummy shaft. Then remove the countergear and both tanged washers. Remove the 112 rollers, six 0.070" spacers, and the roller spacer from the countergear.

⑦ Remove the mainshaft front snap ring, as shown, and then slide the 3-4 speed clutch assembly, 3rd-speed gear, and synchronizing ring from the front of the mainshaft.

⑧ Spread the rear bearing retainer snap ring, and then press the mainshaft out of the retainer. Remove the mainshaft rear snap ring. Support the 2nd-speed gear, and then press on the rear of the mainshaft to remove the rear bearing, 1st-speed gear and sleeve, 1st-speed synchronizing ring, 1-2 speed synchronizer clutch assembly, 2nd-speed synchronizer ring, and 2nd-speed gear.

⑨ If the reverse shifter shaft or seal is damaged, drive the shifter shaft into the case extension, allowing the ball detent to drop into the case.

CLEANING AND INSPECTING

Wash the transmission case inside and out with cleaning solvent; inspect for cracks. Inspect the front face which fits against the clutch housing for burrs and dress any off with a fine-cut mill file. **CAUTION: Be sure the cleaning solvent does not loosen the case magnet.**

Wash the front and rear bearings thoroughly in cleaning solvent. Blow out the bearings with compressed air. **CAUTION: Do not allow the bearings to spin or you will damage the races and balls.** Make sure the bearings are clean, and then lubricate them with light engine oil. Check them for roughness, which can be determined by slowly turning the outer race by hand. **CAUTION: Bearings must be lubricated with light oil before checking for roughness.**

All main drive (clutch) gear and countergear bearing rollers should be inspected closely and replaced if they show wear. Inspect the countershaft at the same time and replace it if it is worn. Replace all worn spacers.

Inspect all gears and replace any that are defective or damaged. Inspect for a loose damper plate on the countergear.

The bushings used in the idler gear are pressed

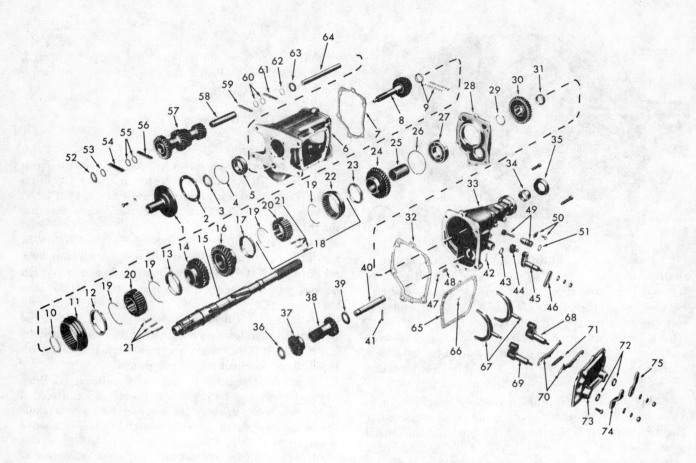

1. Bearing Retainer
2. Gasket
3. Bearing Retaining Nut
4. Bearing Snap Ring
5. Main Drive
   Gear Bearing
6. Transmission Case
7. Rear Bearing
   Retainer Gasket
8. Main Drive Gear
9. Bearing Rollers (17)
   and Cage
10. Snap Ring
11. Third and Fourth
    Speed Clutch
    Sliding Sleeve
12. Fourth Speed Gear
    Synchronizing Ring
13. Third Speed
    Synchronizing Ring
14. Third Speed Gear
15. Mainshaft
16. Second Speed Gear
17. Second Speed Gear
    Synchronizing Ring
18. First and Second Speed
    Clutch Assembly

19. Clutch Key Spring
20. Clutch Hub
21. Clutch Keys
22. First and Second Speed
    Clutch Sliding Sleeve
23. First Speed Gear
    Synchronizing Ring
24. First Speed Gear
25. Sleeve
26. Rear Bearing
    Snap Ring
27. Rear Bearing
28. Rear Bearing Retainer
29. Selective Fit Snap Ring
30. Reverse Gear
31. Speedometer
    Drive Gear
32. Rear Bearing Retainer to
    Case Extension Gasket
33. Case Extension
34. Extension Bushing
35. Rear Oil Seal
36. Reverse Idler
    Front Thrust
    Washer (Tanged)
37. Reverse Idler
    Gear (Front)

38. Reverse Idler
    Gear (Rear)
39. Flat Thrust Washer
40. Reverse Idler Shaft
41. Reverse Idler Shaft
    Roll Pin
42. Reverse Shifter
    Shaft Lock Pin
43. Reverse Shifter
    Shaft Lip Seal
44. Reverse Shift Fork
45. Reverse Shifter Shaft
    and Detent Plate
46. Reverse Shifter Lever
47. Reverse Shifter Shaft Ball
48. Reverse Shifter Shaft
    Ball Detent Spring
49. Speedometer Driven
    Gear and Fitting
50. Retainer and Bolt
51. "O" Ring Seal
52. Tanged Washer
53. Spacer (.050")
54. Bearing Rollers (20)
55. Spacers (2-.050")
56. Bearing Rollers (20)
57. Countergear

58. Countergear
    Roller Spacer
59. Bearing Rollers (20)
60. Spacers (2-.050")
61. Bearing Rollers (20)
62. Spacer (.050")
63. Tanged Washer
64. Countershaft
65. Gasket
66. Detent Cams
    Retainer Ring
67. Forward Speed
    Shift Forks
68. First and Second Speed
    Gear Shifter Shaft and
    Detent Plate
69. Third and Fourth Speed
    Gear Shifter Shaft and
    Detent Plate
70. Detent Cams
71. Detent Cam Spring
72. Lip Seals
73. Transmission Side Cover
74. Third and Fourth Speed
    Shifter Lever
75. First and Second Speed
    Shifter Lever

Exploded view of the four-speed Muncie transmission.

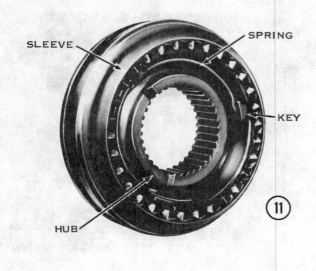

SLEEVE

SPRING

KEY

HUB

⑪

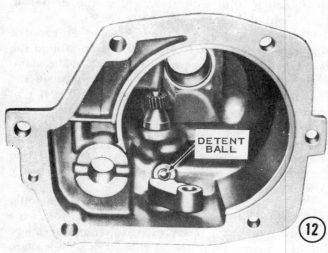

DETENT
BALL

⑫

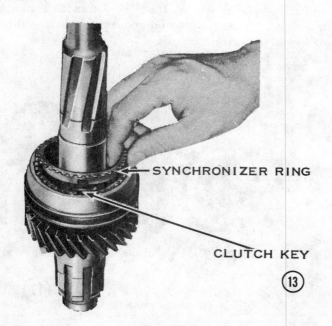

SYNCHRONIZER RING

CLUTCH KEY

⑬

into the gear and then peened into the holes in the bores. Then they are bored in place to insure positive alignment of the bushings and their shafts, as well as proper meshing of gears. Because of the high degree of accuracy to which these parts are machined, the bushings are not serviced separately. Check the bushings for wear by using a narrow feeler gauge between the shaft and the bushing. The proper clearance should be from 0.003″ to 0.005″.

ASSEMBLING

⑩ The synchronizer hubs and sliding sleeves are a select-fit assembly and should be kept together as originally assembled, but the three keys and two springs can be replaced if worn or broken. Push the hub from the sliding sleeve, and the keys will fall free. Remove the springs.

⑪ To assemble the synchronizer unit, place the two springs in position (one on each side of the hub) so all three keys are engaged by both springs. Place the keys in position and, holding them in place, slide the hub into the sleeve. *NOTE: The sleeve with the large square edge opposite the fork groove identifies the 3-4 synchronizer sleeve.*

⑫ To replace the reverse shifter shaft or seal, place the ball detent spring into the detent spring hole, and then, from inside the extension, install the shifter shaft fully into its opening until the detent plate is butted against the inside of the extension housing. Place the detent ball on the spring and, holding the ball down with your thumb, push the shifter shaft back in, away from the case, until it is directly over the ball, and then turn it until the ball drops into the detent on the shaft detent plate. Install the shift fork. *NOTE: Do not drive the shifter shaft lock pin into place until the extension has been installed on the transmission case.*

⑬ To assemble the mainshaft, slide the 2nd-speed gear (with the hub of the gear toward the rear of the shaft). Install the 1-2 synchronizer clutch assembly onto the mainshaft (sliding clutch sleeve taper toward the rear; hub to the front), together with a synchronizing ring on each side of the clutch assembly so their keyways line up with the clutch keys. Press the 1st-gear sleeve onto the mainshaft, using a 1-3/4″ ID pipe, cut to a convenient length.

⑭ Install the 1st-speed gear (with the hub toward the front) and, using 1-5/8″ ID pipe, cut to a suitable length, press on the rear bearing. Choose the correct selective-fit snap ring (0.087″, 0.090″, 0.093″, or 0.096″), and then install it in the groove in the mainshaft behind the rear bearing. With the proper ring, the maximum clearance between the snap ring and the rear face of

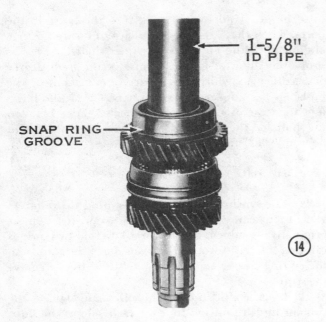

1-5/8"
ID PIPE

SNAP RING
GROOVE

(14)

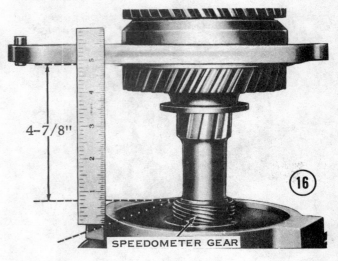

4-7/8"

(16)

SPEEDOMETER GEAR

the bearing will be from zero to 0.005". **CAUTION: Always use new snap rings when assembling a transmission and do not expand a snap ring farther than necessary.** Install the 3rd-speed gear (hub to the front of the transmission) and the 3rd-speed gear synchronizing ring (notches to the front of the transmission). Install the 3-4 speed gear clutch hub and sliding sleeve, with the sleeve taper toward the front, making sure the keys in the hub correspond to the notches in the 3rd-speed gear synchronizing ring. Install the snap ring in the groove of the mainshaft in front of the 3-4

speed clutch hub, with the ends of the snap ring seated behind the spline teeth.

⑮ Install the rear bearing retainer. Spread the snap ring in the plate to allow it to drop around the rear bearing, and then press on the end of the mainshaft until the snap ring engages the groove in the rear bearing. Install the reverse gear (shift collar to the rear) and two anti-rattle springs.

⑯ Install the retaining clip and speedometer gear. On models using the metal gear, press the gear onto the mainshaft to obtain a measurement of 4-7/8" from the forward side of the gear to the flat surface of the rear bearing retainer.

⑰ To assemble the countergear, install the roller spacer tube into the countergear and then insert the dummy shaft. Using heavy grease to retain the rollers, install a spacer, 28 rollers, a spacer, 28 more rollers, and then another spacer. Install a spacer, 28 rollers, a spacer, 28 more rollers, and another spacer into the other end of the countergear.

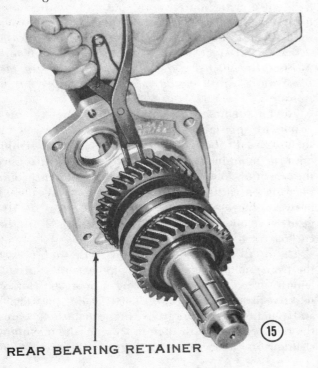

(15)

REAR BEARING RETAINER

(17)

DUMMY SHAFT

BOTTOM OF CASE ➡

(18)

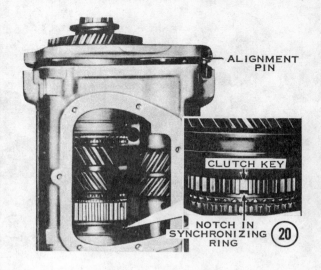

ALIGNMENT PIN

CLUTCH KEY

NOTCH IN SYNCHRONIZING RING

(20)

⑱ Rest the transmission case on its side, with the side cover opening facing you. Put the countergear tanged thrust washers in place, retaining them with heavy grease. **CAUTION: Make sure the tangs are resting in the notches of the case.** Lay the countergear assembly in place in the bottom of the transmission case, making sure that the tanged thrust washers are not dislodged. Position the transmission case so it rests on its front face. Lubricate and insert the counter-shaft into the rear of the case. Turn the countershaft so the flat on the end of the shaft is horizontal and facing the bottom of the case. Align the countergear with the shaft, and then press the countershaft into the case (pushing the dummy assembly tool out of the front of the case) until the flat on the shaft is flush with the rear of the case. **CAUTION: Make sure the thrust washers remain in place.**

⑲ Attach a dial indicator and check the end play of the countergear. If the end play is greater than 0.025", new thrust washers must be installed. Install the cage and the seventeen roller bearings into the main drive (clutch) gear, using heavy grease to hold the bearings in place. Install the oil slinger on the main drive gear, with the concave side toward the gear.

⑳ Install the main drive gear and pilot bearings through the side cover opening and into position in the front bore of the transmission. Place a gasket on the front face of the rear bearing retainer. Install the 4th-speed synchronizing ring on the main drive gear, with the notches toward the rear of the transmission. Position the reverse idler gear thrust washer (tanged) on the machined face of the ear cast in the case for the reverse idler shaft; hold it with heavy grease. Position the front reverse idler gear next to the thrust washer, with the hub facing toward the rear of the case. Lower the mainshaft assembly into the case, making certain the notches on the 4th-speed synchronizing ring correspond to the keys in the clutch assembly. **CAUTION: Before attempting to slide the mainshaft assembly into the case, slide the 3-4 synchronizing clutch sleeve forward into the 4th-speed detent position. CAUTION: Be sure the main drive gear engages both the countergear and the anti-lash plate on standard-ratio models.** With the guide pin in the rear bearing retainer aligned with the hole in the rear of the case, tap the rear bearing retainer into position with a soft hammer.

㉑ From the rear of the case, insert the rear reverse idler gear, engaging the splines with the portion of the front gear inside the case. Using heavy grease, place a gasket on the rear face of the rear bearing retainer. Install the remaining flat thrust washer on

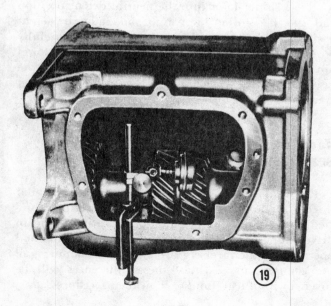

(19)

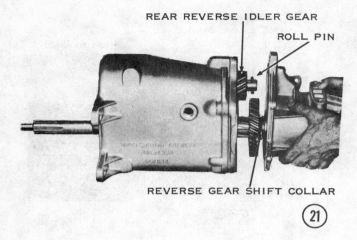

REAR REVERSE IDLER GEAR

ROLL PIN

REVERSE GEAR SHIFT COLLAR

㉑

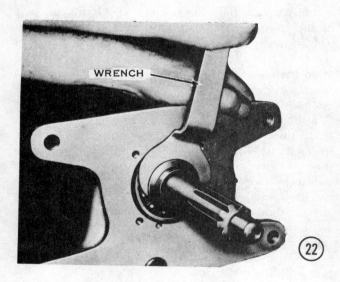

WRENCH

㉒

1-2 SLIDING CLUTCH SLEEVE

㉓

3-4 SLIDING CLUTCH SLEEVE

the reverse idler shaft. Install the reverse idler shaft, roll pin, and thrust washer into the gears and front boss of the case. **CAUTION: Make sure to pick up the front tanged thrust washer. CAUTION: The roll pin must be in a vertical position.** Pull the reverse shifter shaft to the left side of the extension, and then rotate the shaft to bring the reverse shift fork forward in the extension to the reverse detent position. Start the extension onto the transmission case, while slowly pushing in on the shifter shaft to engage the shift fork with the reverse gear shift collar. Then pilot the reverse idler shaft into the extension housing, permitting the extension to slide onto the transmission case. Install and tighten the six extension and retainer-to-case attaching bolts. Push or pull the reverse shifter shaft to line up the groove in the shaft with the holes in the boss, and then drive in the lock pin. Install the shifter lever.

㉒ Press the bearing onto the main drive gear (snap ring groove to the front) and into the case until several main drive gear retaining nut threads are exposed. Lock the transmission up by shifting into two gears. Install the main drive gear retaining nut on the gear shaft and draw it up tight, using Tool J-933. Be sure the bearing seats fully against the shoulder on the gear. Torque the retaining nut to 40 ft-lbs, and then lock it in place by staking it securely into the main drive gear shaft hole with a center punch. Care must be used to avoid damaging the threads on the shaft. Install and tighten the main drive gear bearing retainer, gasket, four attaching bolts and two strip bolt lock retainers, using sealer on the bolts.

㉓ Shift the mainshaft 3-4 sliding clutch sleeve into neutral position and the 1-2 sliding clutch sleeve into the 2nd-gear (forward) detent position. Shift the side cover 3-4 shifter lever into the neutral detent position and the 1-2 shifter lever into the 2nd-gear detent position. Install the side cover gasket and carefully position the side cover into place. There is a dowel pin in the cover to assure proper alignment with the case. Install the attaching bolts and tighten them evenly to avoid distortion.

SAGINAW FOUR-SPEED TRANSMISSION SERVICE NOTES

The Saginaw four-speed transmission is quite similar in construction and in service procedures to the Muncie unit, except for the method of mounting the main drive (clutch) gear, the difference in construction and operation of the reverse gearing, and the mounting of the countershaft. Each of these differences will be covered with illustrations to show the procedures.

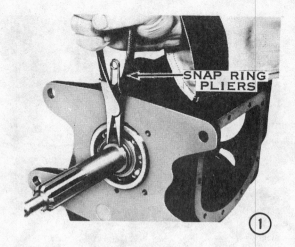

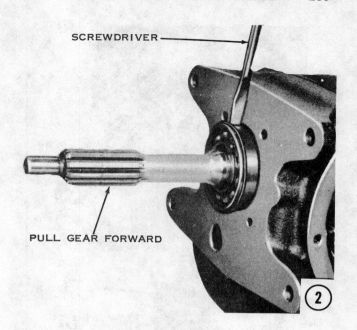

DISASSEMBLING

① The ball bearing is secured to the main drive (clutch) gear by a lock ring, instead of a locknut. The lock ring must be removed before the bearing can be

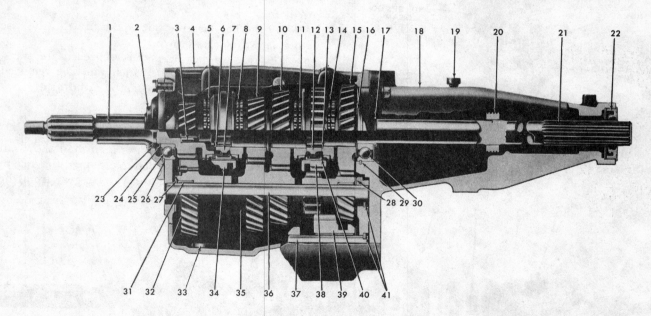

Sectioned view through the four-speed Saginaw transmission.

1. Main Drive Gear
2. Front Bearing Retainer
3. Bearing Roller
4. Case
5. Fourth Speed Blocking Ring
6. Third and Fourth Synchronizer Snap Ring
7. Third and Fourth Synchronizer Hub
8. Blocking Ring
9. Third Speed Gear
10. Second Speed Gear
11. Blocking Ring
12. First and Second Synchronizer Hub
13. First and Second Synchronizer Snap Ring
14. First Speed Blocking Ring
15. First Gear
16. Reverse Gear Thrust and Spring Washers
17. Bearing To Mainshaft Snap Ring
18. Case Extension
19. Vent
20. Speedometer Drive Gear
21. Mainshaft
22. Rear Oil Seal
23. Bearing Retainer Oil Seal
24. Bearing To Gear Snap Ring
25. Front Bearing
26. Bearing To Case Snap Ring
27. Thrust Washer (Front)
28. Thrust Washer (Rear)
29. Bearing To Extension Snap Ring
30. Rear Bearing
31. Countergear Bearing Rollers
32. Anti-Rattle Plate Assy.
33. Magnet
34. Third and Fourth Synchronizer Sleeve (Sliding)
35. Countergear Assy.
36. Countershaft
37. Reverse Idler Shaft
38. First and Second Speed Synchronizer Sleeve and Reverse Gear
39. Reverse Idler Gear
40. Clutch Keys
41. Woodruff Key

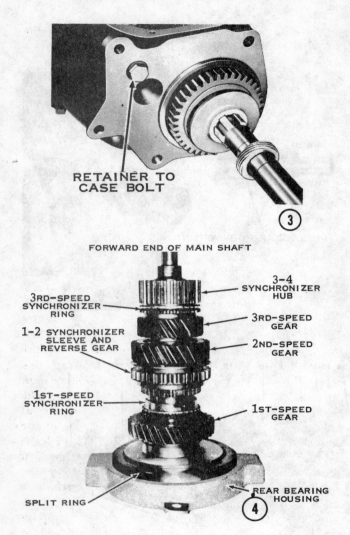

RETAINER TO CASE BOLT

③

FORWARD END OF MAIN SHAFT

3-4 SYNCHRONIZER HUB

3RD-SPEED SYNCHRONIZER RING

3RD-SPEED GEAR

1-2 SYNCHRONIZER SLEEVE AND REVERSE GEAR

2ND-SPEED GEAR

1ST-SPEED SYNCHRONIZER RING

1ST-SPEED GEAR

SPLIT RING

REAR BEARING HOUSING

④

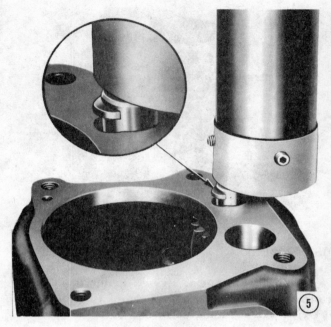

⑤

pried out of the case recess.

② Pry the ball bearing out of the front of the case with a screwdriver, as shown.

③ The rear bearing support is secured to the transmission case with one bolt, which must be removed before the mainshaft assembly can be withdrawn.

ASSEMBLING

④ This assembled view of the mainshaft shows all of the parts properly assembled. Note the difference in the 1-2 synchronizer sleeve and reverse gear from the

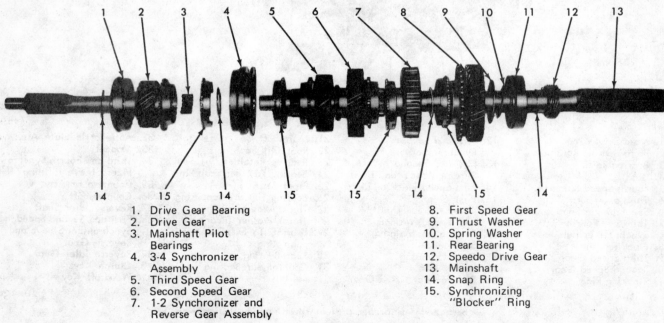

1. Drive Gear Bearing
2. Drive Gear
3. Mainshaft Pilot Bearings
4. 3-4 Synchronizer Assembly
5. Third Speed Gear
6. Second Speed Gear
7. 1-2 Synchronizer and Reverse Gear Assembly
8. First Speed Gear
9. Thrust Washer
10. Spring Washer
11. Rear Bearing
12. Speedo Drive Gear
13. Mainshaft
14. Snap Ring
15. Synchronizing "Blocker" Ring

Details of the clutch and mainshaft used on the four-speed Saginaw transmission.

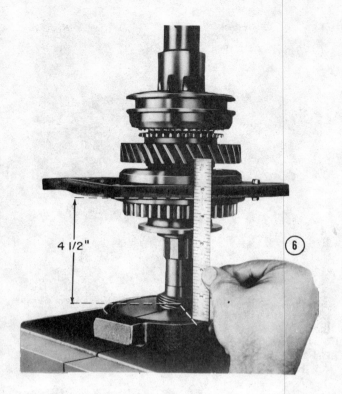

4 1/2"

⑥

Muncie transmission previously overhauled.

⑤ The countershaft is held in place by means of a half-round washer, which must be aligned in the case recess, as shown.

⑥ The speedometer gear should be pressed on until it is 4-1/2" from the face of the bearing retainer.

AUTOMATIC TRANSMISSIONS

Six types of transmissions have been used: (1) Dual-coupling through 1960, (2) Roto Hydra-Matic from 1961-64, (3) Jetaway two-speed from 1964-69, (4) Turbo Hydra-Matic from 1965-68, (5) Turbo Hydra-Matic 350/400 since 1969, and (6) a special version of the THM 400 for the Toronado.

GENERAL TESTING

When diagnosing an automatic transmission problem, first refer to the diagnosis guide in the trouble-shooting chapter for detailed information on items that could be causing the problem. The following preliminary checks must be made before proceeding with the other diagnosis checks.

Fluid Level

If the level of the fluid is too high, it will become aerated, which will cause low control pressure. If the

level is too low, it may affect the operation of the transmission. Also, a low fluid level indicates that there are leaks, which may result in transmission damage.

To check the fluid level, make sure that the vehicle is level, and then firmly apply the parking brakes. Run the engine at normal idle speed (with a warm engine), shift the selector lever through all positions, and then position it in PARK. Pull the dipstick out of the tube, wipe it clean, and then push it all the way back into the tube. Pull out the dipstick again and check the fluid level, which must be between the full mark and 1/4" below it, but never higher than the full mark.

Stall Test

A stall test is made in DRIVE position at full throttle to check engine performance; converter clutch operation; and the holding ability of the clutches and bands. To make a stall test, apply both the parking and service brakes. Connect a tachometer. Start the engine (thoroughly warmed), shift into DRIVE, and then open the accelerator wide. **CAUTION: While making this severe test, don't hold the throttle open for more than five seconds at a time.** After each test, move the selector lever to NEUTRAL and run the engine at about 1000 rpm for 20 seconds in order to cool the converter before making the next test. **CAUTION: If the engine speeds exceeds the maximum specified limit, release the accelerator immediately because clutch or band slippage is indicated.** Additional abuse may destroy the slipping unit.

If the stall speed is too high, band or clutch slippage is indicated and the transmission must be removed for service. When the stall test speeds are too low, the engine needs tuning.

Road Tests

The transmission should shift automatically at approximately the speeds shown in the charts in Chapter 1. The shifts may occur at somewhat different speeds due to production tolerances and rear axle ratios, but this is not as important as the quality of the shifts, which must be smooth, responsive, and made with little noticeable engine speed-up.

AUTOMATIC TRANSMISSION SERVICE PROCEDURES

Because of the complexity of the service procedures, only the external adjustments are discussed in this section: shift linkage adjustments, detent linkage adjustments, and band adjustments.

ROTO HYDRA-MATIC AUTOMATIC TRANSMISSION —1961-64

Two different types of transmissions were used interchangeably on the smaller models (F-85) and on the full-sized cars (FSC). Some of them were three-speed units and some four. While the FSC used these units in 1961-64, the F-85 models used them only through 1963. The throttle linkage adjustments for both cars are the same, but a band adjustment is possible only on the transmission used for the F-85.

BAND ADJUSTMENT—F-85

The band must be adjusted every 26,000 miles. To do this, remove the oil pan and cleaner. Loosen the adjusting screw locknut. Torque the adjusting screw to 100 in-lbs, and then back it off (loosen) the screw exactly 2-1/4 turns. Tighten the locknut. Replace the oil cleaner and the oil pan. Refill the transmission.

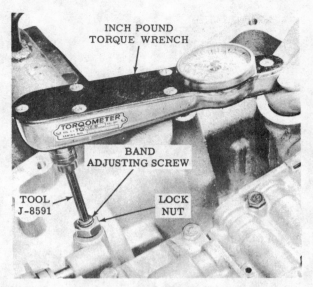

Adjusting the band on the Roto Hydra-Matic automatic transmission used on the F-85 from 1961-63.

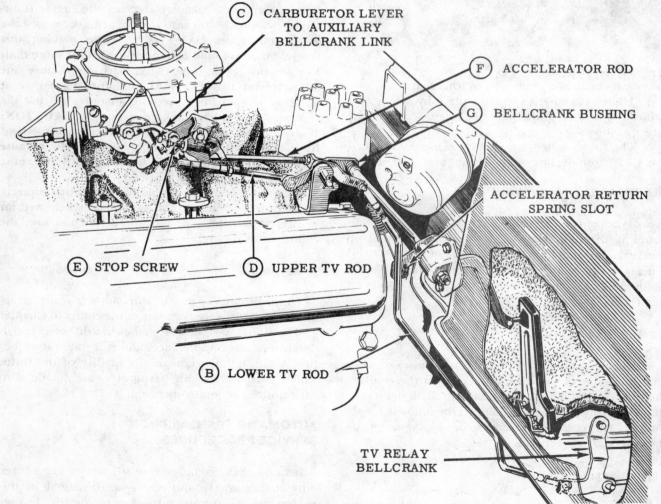

Throttle linkage adjustments for the Roto Hydra-Matic automatic transmission used from 1961-64.

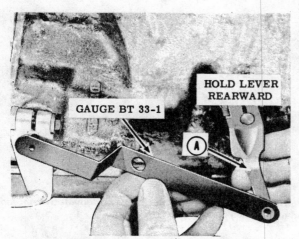

BEND THROTTLE LEVER UNTIL HOLE IN LEVER IS VISIBLE WITHIN HOLE IN GAUGE BT 33-1, NOT NECESSARILY CENTERED.

Using Gauge BT-33-1 to check the TV lever adjustment, as discussed in the text. Use Gauge BT-33-7 for the F-85 models.

THROTTLE LINKAGE ADJUSTMENTS—ALL MODELS

The throttle linkage adjustments must be made in the following order: (1) TV lever at the side of the transmission, (2) lower TV rod, (3) carburetor lever-to-auxiliary bellcrank link, (4) upper TV rod, and (5) throttle downshift stop screw.

TV LEVER AT THE SIDE OF THE TRANSMISSION

Raise the car and remove the lower TV rod from the lever at the right side of the transmission. Place the short end of the TV lever gauge into the manual lever shaft. Holding the TV lever at the end of its rearward travel, the TV lever hole must be visible within the hole in the guage, as shown. If necessary, bend the lever and then recheck the adjustment with the gauge.

LOWER TV ROD

The carburetor throttle valves must be completely closed. For this adjustment, start the engine, remove the air cleaner, and block the intermediate choke lever at the choke housing to release the fast-idle cam. Install a dashpot holding tool to keep the throttle-return check plunger away from the throttle lever. Turn off the ignition switch, and then back out the curb-idle adjusting screw until the throttle valves are fully seated. In a true closed-bore position, there must be clearance at the end of the fast-idle screw, curb-idle screw, and throttle return-check plungers.

Now, loosen the jam nut on the lower TV rod B, and then remove both rods from the TV bellcrank. *NOTE: The upper TV rod has socket-and-ball stud connections which can be snapped off.* Hold the TV bellcrank and the transmission lower TV rod B against their rearward stops, and then adjust the lower TV rod clevis so that the pin enters the holes in the clevis and TV bellcrank freely.

CARBURETOR LEVER-TO-AUXILIARY BELLCRANK LINK

Measure the clearance between the auxiliary bellcrank and its bracket, which must be 0.020-0.040″. If necessary, remove the carburetor lever-to-auxiliary bellcrank link and change the shape at the bent section to obtain the specified clearance. *NOTE: The link can be installed with the bent section up or down.*

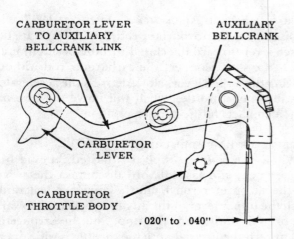

Checking the carburetor linkage, as discussed in the text.

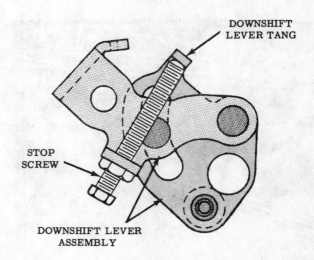

Downshift stop screw adjustment.

UPPER TV ROD

Adjust the TV rod slightly short, and then snap it onto the ball stud. While holding the TV bellcrank against the stop, lengthen the TV rod until the swivel turns freely and feels sloppy. Continue to lengthen the rod until a very slight resistance is felt. *NOTE: At this point, the upper TV rod is properly adjusted.* Tighten the locknut while holding the swivel.

THROTTLE DOWNSHIFT STOP SCREW

Loosen the jam nut and back out the stop screw several turns. Push rearward on the accelerator pedal lever until the throttle valves are wide open. Hold the throttle lever at WOT with your left hand and rotate the TV bellcrank counterclockwise with your right hand to the point of maximum transmission lever travel. **CAUTION: This point is a matter of feel so don't bend or stretch the linkage beyond this point.** Adjust the stop screw so that it just touches the tang on the downshift lever. Allow the throttle valves to return to idle, and then turn the stop screw in 1-1/2 to 2 turns. Tighten the jam nut.

JETAWAY AUTOMATIC TRANSMISSION— 1964-69

This two-speed automatic transmission is used on F-85 models and the Jetsar 88. It contained a variable-pitch stator on V-8 engine models through 1968 and a fixed-pitch unit since then. The stator pitch is actuated electrically by a switch on the throttle linkage. Since 1968, an electric switch on the firewall activates a detent solenoid to cause the transmission to downshift on wide-open throttle acceleration.

The low band can be adjusted externally. The carburetor rod and throttle switch (through 1967)

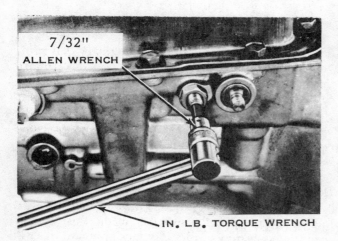

Making the Jetaway automatic transmission low-band adjustment, as discussed in the text.

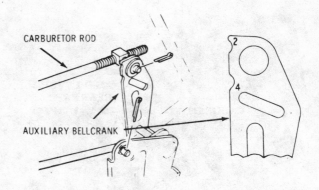

Carburetor rod adjustment for the Jetaway automatic transmission used on the F-85 from 1968-69.

must be adjusted in this order. Since 1968, a downshift throttle switch must be adjusted.

LOW BAND ADJUSTMENT

Remove the low-speed band adjusting screw protective cap. Use a 7/32" Allen wrench to tighten the screw to 40 in-lbs of torque. Back off the band adjusting screw exactly four (4) turns and tighten the locknut. Replace the protective cap.

THROTTLE LINKAGE ADJUSTMENTS

CARBURETOR ROD ADJUSTMENT—THROUGH 1967

With the curb-idle speed adjusted properly and the engine shut off, check to see that a test lamp across the switch terminals are ON (stator in high-pitch position for maximum acceleration). Lengthen the carburetor rod until the test lamp goes out. Now, slowly shorten the rod until the test lamp just lights, and then shorten it an additional two (2) turns. Tighten the locknut.

THROTTLE SWITCH ADJUSTMENT—THROUGH 1967

Disconnect the carburetor rod, and then rotate the switch lever (toward the closed-throttle position) until it hits the stop. Connect the carburetor rod without moving the switch lever. Now, depress the accelerator to wide-open throttle, which will move the internal switch contacts to the proper position.

CARBURETOR ROD ADJUSTMENT—1968-69

With the curb-idle properly adjusted, engine off, choke open, and fast idle off, disconnect the swivel on the carburetor rod from the auxiliary bellcrank. Push the upper lever of the auxiliary bellcrank toward the firewall until it hits the stop. Pull the carburetor rod toward the firewall until the throttle is wide open. Now, adjust the swivel until the swivel pin enters the

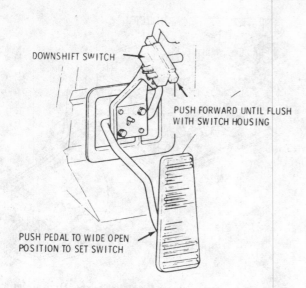

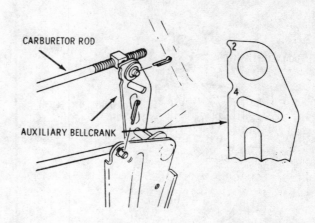

Carburetor rod adjustment for the Turbo Hyra-Matic automatic transmission used on the full-sized car from 1965-68.

Downshift throttle switch adjustment for the Jetaway automatic transmission used on the F-85 from 1968-69.

THROTTLE LINKAGE ADJUSTMENTS

CARBURETOR ROD ADJUSTMENT—THROUGH 1967

With the curb-idle speed adjusted properly and the engine shut off, check to see that a test lamp across the switch terminals are ON (stator in high-pitch position). Lengthen the carburetor rod until the test lamp goes out. Now, slowly shorten the rod until the test lamp just lights, and then shorten it an additional two (2) turns. Tighten the locknut.

No. 2 notch for a two-barrel carburetor, or the No. 4 notch for a four-barrel carburetor. Connect the carburetor rod to the auxiliary bellcrank.

DOWNSHIFT THROTTLE SWITCH ADJUSTMENT—1968-69

Push the plunger of the downshift switch forward until it is flush with the switch housing. Push the accelerator pedal to its wide-open position, and this will set the switch. Check the energizing contacts of the switch with a testlight.

THROTTLE SWITCH ADJUSTMENT—THROUGH 1967

Disconnect the carburetor rod, and then rotate the switch lever forward (toward the closed-throttle position) until it hits the stop. Connect the carburetor rod without moving the switch lever. Now, depress the accelerator to wide-open throttle, which will move the internal switch contacts to the proper position.

TURBO HYDRA-MATIC AUTOMATIC TRANSMISSION (FSC)—1965-68

This three-speed automatic transmission had a variable-pitch stator through 1967. The stator pitch-control solenoid is activated by a signal from a switch on the carburetor linkage (at the firewall) at engine idle, which changes the stator blade angle from low to high. It is also energized at throttle blade angles over 40°. This VP stator was changed to a fixed-pitch unit in 1968.

An electric switch on the carburetor linkage activates a detent solenoid, causing the transmission to downshift at speeds below 70 mph, whenever the throttle is opened fully.

The carburetor rod and throttle switch must be adjusted in this order. There is no external band adjustment because this must be done during overhaul by selecting one of three apply pins by means of a special gauge.

CARBURETOR ROD ADJUSTMENT—1968

With the curb-idle properly adjusted, engine off, choke open, and fast idle off, disconnect the swivel on the carburetor rod from the auxiliary bellcrank. Push the upper lever of the auxiliary bellcrank toward the firewall until it hits the stop. Pull the carburetor rod toward the firewall until the throttle is wide open. Now, adjust the swivel until the swivel pin enters the No. 2 notch for a two-barrel carburetor, or the No. 4 notch for a four-barrel carburetor. Connect the carburetor rod to the auxiliary bellcrank.

DOWNSHIFT THROTTLE SWITCH ADJUSTMENT—1968

Push the plunger of the downshift switch forward until it is flush with the switch housing. Push the accelerator pedal to its wide-open position, and this will set the switch. Check the energizing contacts of the switch with a testlight.

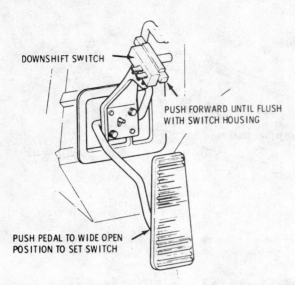

Downshift throttle switch adjustment for the Turbo Hydra-Matic automatic transmission used on the full-sized car from 1965-68.

TURBO HYDRA-MATIC AUTOMATIC TRANSMISSION—SINCE 1969

Three different Turbo Hydra-Matic transmissions have been used on Oldsmobile engines: THM 350, THM 375/400/425, and THM 400 as used on the Toronado (since 1966). There is no external band adjustment on any of these transmissions. The THM 400 automatic transmission used on the Toronado from 1966-67 had a variable-pitch stator, which was actuated by a switch on the throttle linkage.

THM 350 has a detent cable, which must be adjusted for proper downshifting. The other models have an

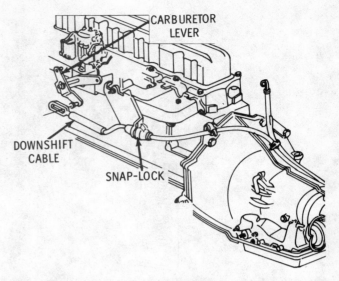

Downshift cable adjustment used on the Turbo Hydra-Matic 350 automatic transmission for the Omega with a six-cylinder engine.

electric switch on the accelerator pedal linkage, which must be adjusted to obtain proper downshifting.

Variable-Pitch Stator Adjustments—
Toronado 1966-67

There are two adjustments, a carburetor rod and a throttle switch, and both of these are adjusted like the Turbo Hydra-Matic automatic transmission used on the FSC from 1965-67. Refer to this section for the needed procedures.

Detent Cable Adjustment for the Full-Sized Cars

Position the downshift cable clip at the initial adjustment, which is 0.010-0.030″ from the groove end, as

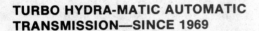

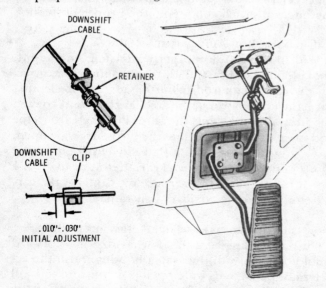

Downshift throttle switch adjustment for the Turbo Hydra-Matic 350 automatic transmission used on the full-sized car since 1969.

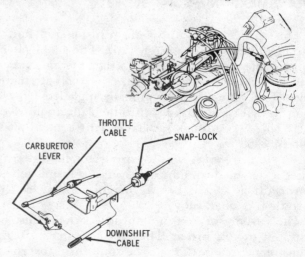

Downshift cable adjustment used on the Turbo Hydra-Matic 350 automatic transmission for the Omega with a V-8 engine.

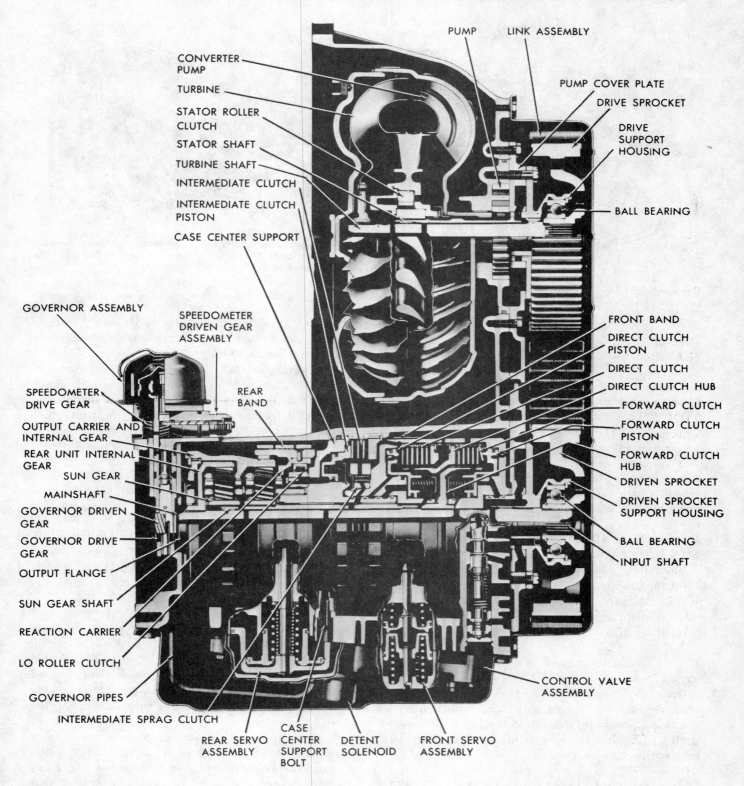

Cutaway through the Turbo Hydra-Matic automatic transmission used on the Toronado.

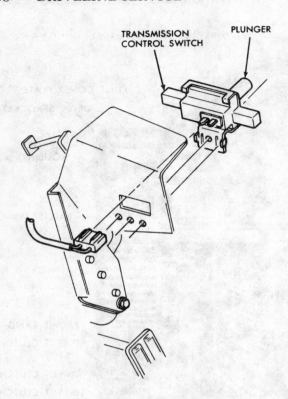

Detent switch adjustment for the Turbo Hydra-Matic 375/400/425 automatic transmission since 1969.

A link belt connects the flywheel of the engine (drive sprocket) to the converter drive plate (driven sprocket) of the automatic transmission of the Toronado.

shown at the left. Now push the accelerator pedal to WOT, which will position the clip properly. No other adjustment is needed.

DETENT CABLE ADJUSTMENT FOR THE OMEGA WITH A SIX-CYLINDER ENGINE

Raise the "Snap-Lock" with a small screwdriver. With the engine shut off, move the throttle lever to WOT. Push the "Snap-Lock" downward until it is flush with the rest of the cable, and then release the throttle lever.

DETENT CABLE ADJUSTMENT FOR THE OMEGA WITH A V-8 ENGINE

Raise the "Snap-Lock" with a small screwdriver. With the engine shut off, move the throttle lever to the WOT position. Push the "Snap-Lock" downward until it is flush with the rest of the cable, and then release the throttle lever.

DETENT SWITCH ADJUSTMENT FOR THM 375/400/425

The downshift on these transmissions is obtained by an electric switch on the accelerator pedal linkage actuating a solenoid control valve inside of the transmission. When the throttle is fully opened, the switch on the accelerator linkage is closed to activate the detent solenoid and cause the transmission to downshift at any speed below 70 mph.

The switch needs to be adjusted only when a new one is installed, and this is done by pressing the switch plunger as far forward as possible. This presets the switch for the adjustment. Now make a WOT application, and the switch will adjust itself.

SHIFT LINKAGE ADJUSTMENTS

The shift tube-and-lever assembly must be free in the mast jacket before any checks or adjustments can be made. Lift the transmission selector lever towards the steering wheel, and then position it in the DRIVE detent. **CAUTION: Don't use the indicator pointer as a reference, because this is adjusted last.** With the selector lever released, it may be inhibited from entering LOW unless the lever is lifted.

Lift the selector lever and allow it to be positioned in NEUTRAL by the transmission detent. Release the lever, and it must be inhibited from engaging REVERSE unless it is lifted. A properly adjusted linkage will prevent the lever from moving beyond both the neutral detent and the drive detent unless the lever is lifted to pass over the mechanical stops in the steering column.

If an adjustment is required, position the selector lever in DRIVE as determined by the transmission detent. Loosen the adjustment swivel at the cross-shaft, and then rotate the transmission lever so that it contacts the drive stop in the steering column. Tighten the swivel and recheck the adjustment.

Adjust the indicator needle, if necessary, to agree with the transmission detent positions, as discussed above. Adjust the neutral safety switch, if necessary, to provide the correct relationship to the transmission detent positions.

BACK-DRIVE ADJUSTMENT

Since 1969, all G.M. vehicles are equipped with a transmission-and-steering wheel locking system. On these vehicles, it is essential that the "back-drive" linkage be adjusted when any change has been made to the manual-shift linkage. **CAUTION: This adjustment must be made exactly as described; otherwise, the transmission may be operating in other than in the full detent positions, which will cause reduced oil pressures and subsequent failure.**

To check the back-drive adjustment, first make sure that the linkage has been adjusted properly as described above so that the transmission is in its full detent position in each of the selector positions. With the ignition key in the RUN position and the selector lever in REVERSE, you should not be able to withdraw the key and the steering wheel should not be locked. With the key in the LOCKED position and the transmission in PARK, you should be able to

remove the key and the steering wheel must be locked.

To make the back-drive adjustment, position the shift lever in PARK, turn the key to the LOCK position, loosen the rod retaining clamp nut at the cross-shaft, remove all column lash by rotating the shift lever downward, and then secure the rod by tightening the clamp nut. Recheck the adjustment as described above.

DRIVESHAFT

The driveshaft receives the power from the engine, through the clutch and transmission, and transfers it to the differential in the rear axle, and then to the rear wheels. The driveshaft incorporates two universal joints and a slip yoke. The splines in the yoke and those on the transmission output shaft permit the driveshaft to move forward and rearward as the axle moves up and down. All driveshafts are balanced. If the vehicle is to be undercoated, cover the driveshaft and the universal joints to protect them from the undercoating material.

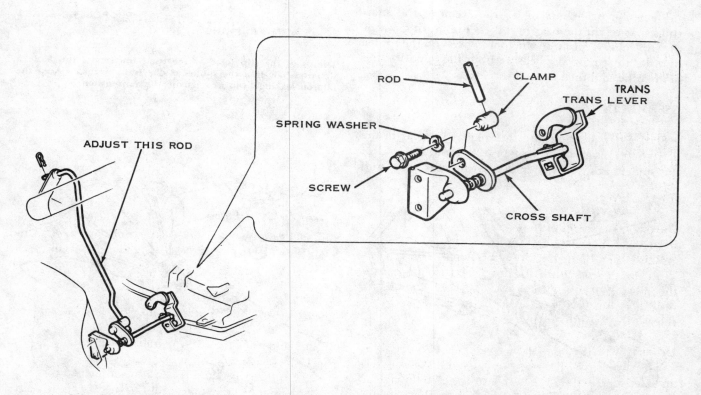

Steering-column type shift linkage showing the rod for making the back-drive adjustment, as discussed in the text.

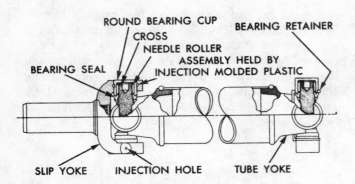

Typical propeller shaft assembly and parts nomenclature.

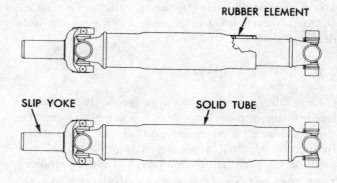

Construction of a typical propeller shaft. The lower view shows a solid-tube type shaft used on some high-performance vehicles.

REMOVING

Whenever a driveshaft is to be removed, be sure to mark it for correct assembly in order to preserve the balance. Disconnect the rear universal joint from the axle drive pinion flange. Wrap tape around the loose bearing caps to keep them from falling off. Pull the driveshaft toward the rear of the vehicle until the slip yoke clears the transmission extension housing and the seal.

UNIVERSAL JOINT REPLACEMENT

Place the driveshaft in a vise. Remove the snap rings that retain the bearings. Press the bearing out of the slip yoke. Reposition the tool to press on the spider in order to remove the bearing from the opposite side of the yoke, and then take off the yoke.

ASSEMBLING

Start a new bearing into the yoke at the rear of the driveshaft. Insert the thrust bearings into the end of the spider. Position the spider in the rear yoke, and

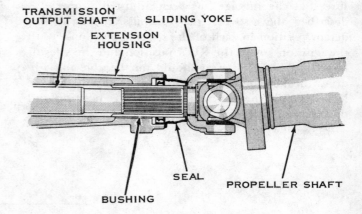

Details of the slip joint at the front universal joint. Slide a dummy shaft into the splines of the transmission to keep the oil from leaking if you are removing the transmission.

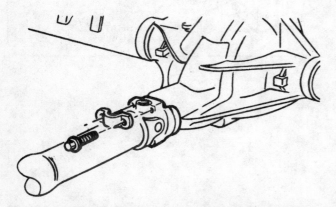

The propeller shaft rear universal joint can be secured to the pinion flange by means of straps, as shown here.

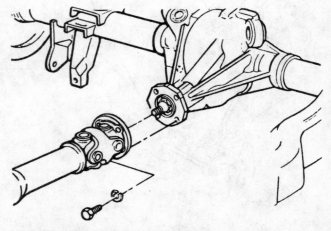

Flange-type propeller shaft attachment.

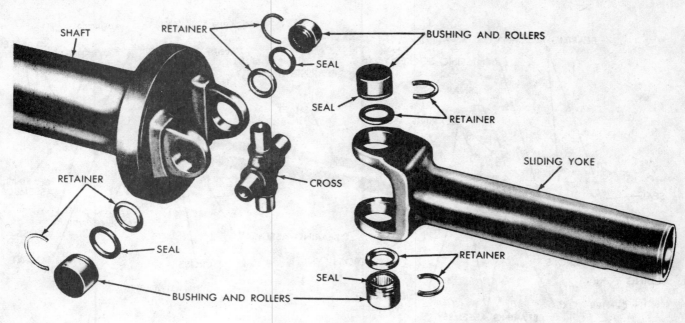

Exploded view of a typical front universal joint.

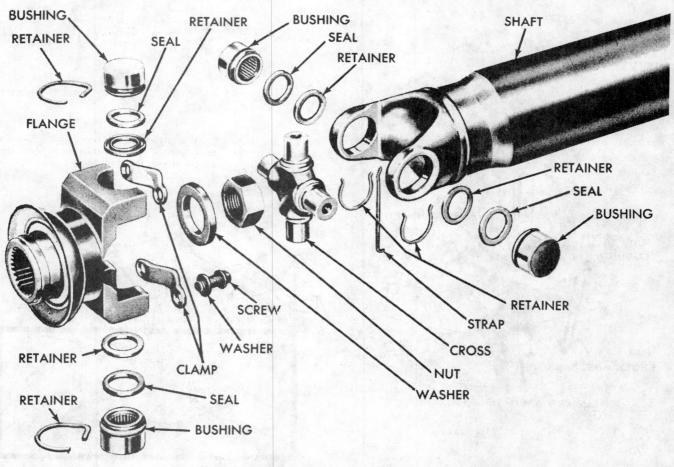

Exploded view of a typical rear universal joint.

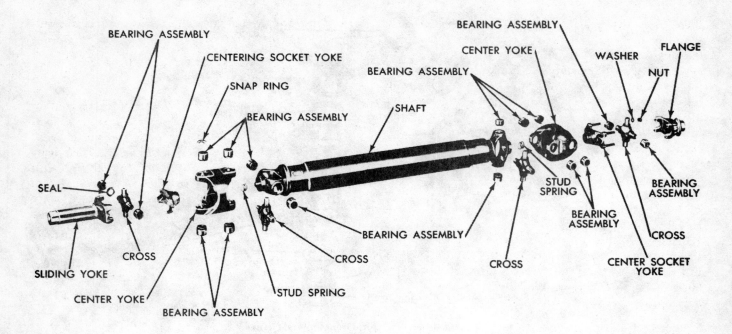

Details of a propeller shaft with a constant-velocity type universal joint.

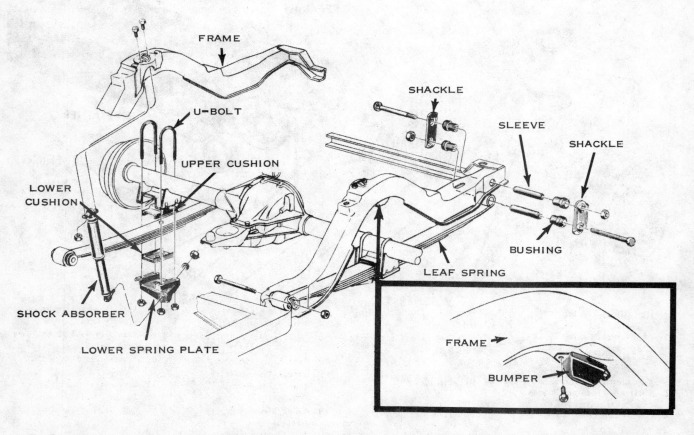

Leaf-type spring suspension used on early models as well as the current Custom Cruiser (Station Wagon) and the Toronado.

then press the bearing in 1/4" below the surface. Remove the tool and install a new snap ring. Insert the thrust bearings into the end of the spider. Start a new bearing into the opposite side of the yoke. Install the tool and press on the bearing until the opposite bearing contacts the snap ring. Remove the tool and install a new snap ring. *NOTE: It may be necessary to dress off the surface of the snap ring to permit easy entry.*

Reposition the driveshaft and install the new spider, thrust bearings, and the two new bearings in the same manner as the rear yoke. Position the slip yoke on the spider, and then install the thrust bearings and two new bearings and snap rings.

Check the joint for free movement. If it binds, a sharp rap on the yokes with a brass hammer will seat the bearing needles and free the joint. **CAUTION: Support the shaft end during this operation to prevent damage to the driveshaft. CAUTION: Don't install the driveshaft assembly in the vehicle unless the universal joints move freely.**

REAR AXLE SUSPENSION

Some early models had the rear axle supported on two leaf-type springs, while most models use coil springs at all four wheels, except for the current Custom Cruiser and Toronado, which still use leaf-type springs. To maintain alignment on models with coil springs in the rear, a link-type suspension system is used. Two rubber-bushed lower control arms are mounted between the axle assembly and the frame to maintain the fore-and-aft relationship of the axle. Two rubber-bushed upper control arms, angularly mounted with respect to the centerline of the car, control driving and braking torque as well as sideway movements of the axle assembly.

REAR AXLES

Two types of rear axles are used on these vehicles: Spicer and a removable-carrier type. Either one may be equipped with a Sure Grip differential. The Spicer rear axle has a cover on the rear of the differential housing, which can be used for servicing the differential assembly. In the removable-carrier type, the differential assembly is bolted to the front of a banjo-type axle housing; the entire assembly must be removed for service.

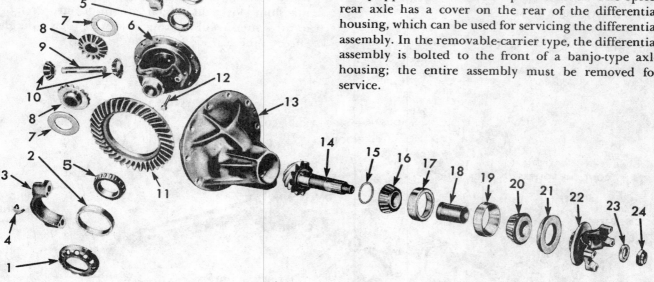

1. Differential Bearing Adjusting Nut
2. Differential Bearing Outer Race
3. Differential Bearing Caps
4. Differential Bearing Adjusting Nut Lock
5. Differential Bearing Cone and Roller Assembly
6. Differential Case
7. Differential Side Gear Thrust Washer
8. Differential Side Gear
9. Differential Pinion Gear Shaft
10. Differential Pinion Gear
11. Ring Gear
12. Differential Pinion Gear Shaft Lock
13. Differential Carrier
14. Drive Pinion Gear
15. Pinion Depth Adjusting Shim
16. Rear Pinion Bearing Cone and Roller Assembly
17. Rear Pinion Bearing Outer Race
18. Pinion Bearing Spacer
19. Front Pinion Bearing Outer Race
20. Front Pinion Bearing Cone and Roller Assembly
21. Companion Flange Oil Seal
22. Companion Flange
23. Special Washer
24. Self Locking Nut

Exploded view of a removable-carrier type differential unit.

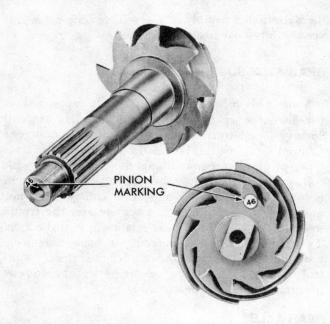

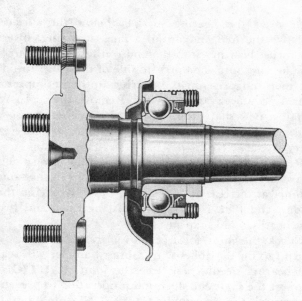

Cross-sectioned view through a rear axle mounting.

Method of marking the pinion to determine the pinion-positioning shim to be used, as discussed in the text.

Pinion-Positioning Shim

The pinion-positioning shim is installed just behind the pinion gear, between it and the cone of the rear roller bearing, in all units. Changing the thickness of this shim moves the pinion gear in or out in relation to the centerline of the ring gear, which has a decided effect on the gear tooth pattern.

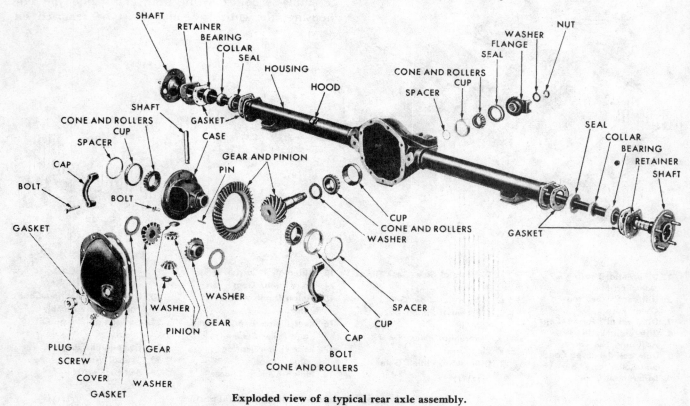

Exploded view of a typical rear axle assembly.

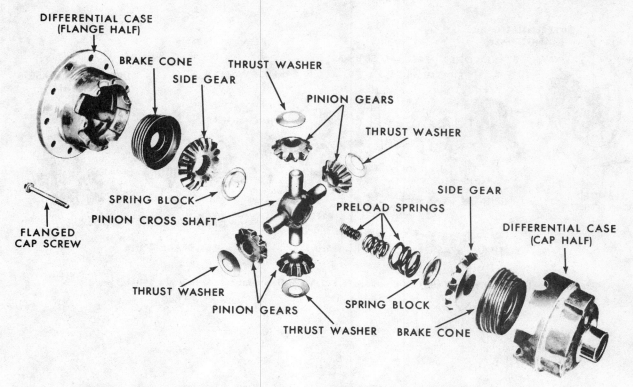

Exploded view of the four-pinion type Safe-T-Track differential case with brake cones.

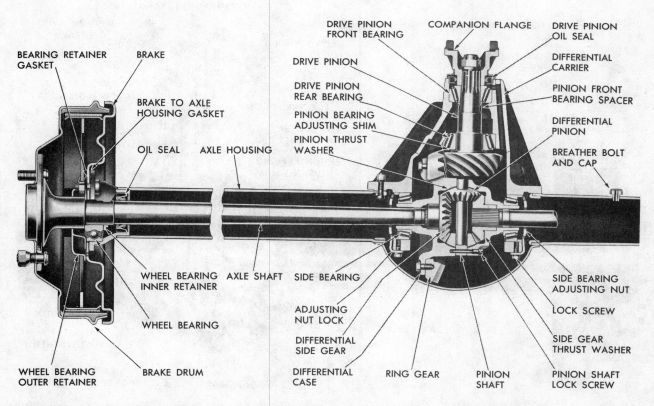

Cross-sectioned view through the rear axle used on these vehicles through 1964. Note that the side bearings are adjusted by a large nut on each side.

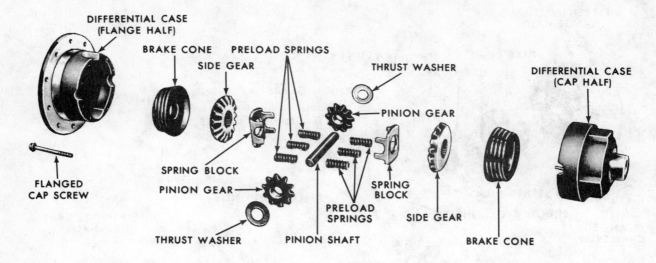

Exploded view of the two-pinion Safe-T-Track differential case with brake cones.

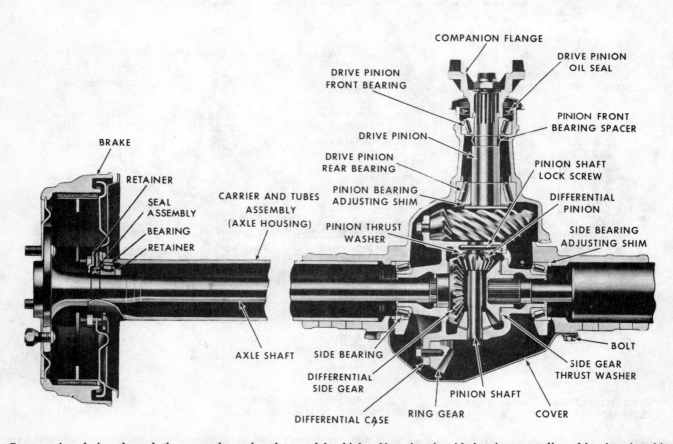

Cross-sectioned view through the rear axle used on late-model vehicles. Note that the side bearings are adjusted by changing shims.

PATTERN CLOSE TO CENTER

TOE END

HEEL END—DRIVE SIDE (CONVEX)   HEEL END—COAST SIDE (CONCAVE)

This is the desired ring gear tooth contact pattern under light loading.

Generally, it requires special tools to determine the correct pinion-positioning shim when starting from scratch. However, the marks on the heads of the old and the replacement pinion gears can be used for selecting the correct shim. If the mark on the replace-

ment pinion gear head is the same as on the one it is to replace, use the original shim. If the mark is more positive (i.e., if it changes from +1 to +4), use a 0.003″ thinner shim. If the mark is more negative (i.e., changes from +1 to −1), use a 0.002″ thicker shim.

PINION BEARING PRELOAD ADJUSTMENT

The pinion bearing preload adjustment is made by means of selective shims in both types of drive units. Use a thinner shim to increase the preload and a thicker shim to decrease it.

DIFFERENTIAL BEARING PRELOAD ADJUSTMENT

The differential side bearing preload adjustment is made by adding or removing shims between the side bearings and the case in the Spicer-type rear axle assembly. It is made by means of two differential case bearing adjuster nuts in the integral-carrier type.

INDENTATIONS

SURFACE DEPRESSIONS ON RACE AND ROLLERS CAUSED BY HARD PARTICLES OF FOREIGN MATERIAL.

CLEAN ALL PARTS AND HOUSINGS. CHECK SEALS AND REPLACE BEARINGS IF ROUGH OR NOISY.

CAGE WEAR

WEAR AROUND OUTSIDE DIAMETER OF CAGE AND ROLLER POCKETS CAUSED BY ABRASIVE MATERIAL AND INEFFICIENT LUBRICATION.

CLEAN RELATED PARTS AND HOUSINGS. CHECK SEALS AND REPLACE BEARINGS.

MISALIGNMENT

OUTER RACE MISALIGNMENT

CLEAN RELATED PARTS AND REPLACE BEARING. MAKE SURE RACES ARE PROPERLY SEATED.

Types of roller bearing failures.

PATTERN MOVES TOWARD CENTER AND DOWN

TOE END

HEEL END—DRIVE SIDE (CONVEX)   HEEL END—COAST SIDE (CONCAVE)

PATTERN MOVES INWARD AND UP

TOE END

HEEL END—DRIVE SIDE (CONVEX)   HEEL END— COAST SIDE (CONCAVE)

The figure at the left shows the effect of increasing the thickness of the pinion-positioning shim. The pattern at the right shows the effect on the tooth contact pattern as the shim thickness is decreased.

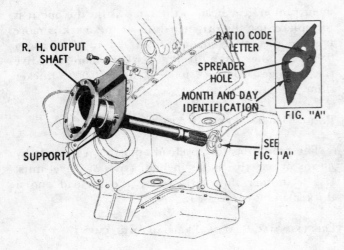

Details of the right-hand drive axle assembly.

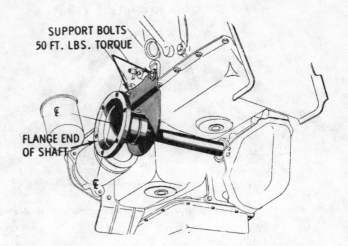

When attaching the right-hand output shaft to the engine, don't let the shaft hang. Align it as discussed in the text.

TORONADO FRONT-WHEEL DRIVE

The front-wheel drive of the Toronado is unique in American automotive design in that the automatic transmission is mounted at the left side of the engine and is driven by means of a link-type drive belt. The final drive unit (differential) is mounted directly to the forward end of the transmission case and drives the front wheels through two output shafts (live-type axles) with a constant-velocity joint at each end. The right-side shaft is longer than the left and it passes under the engine to drive the right-front wheel.

RIGHT-HAND DRIVE AXLE, R&R

REMOVING

Hoist the car under the control arms, and then remove the drive axle cotter pin, nut, and washer. Remove the oil filter element. Take out the inner constant-velocity (CV) joint attaching bolts, and then push the inner CV joint outward enough to disengage it from the final drive output shaft and move it rearward.

Remove the right-hand output shaft support bolts to the engine and final drive. Remove the right-hand output shaft, and then take out the drive axle assembly. **CAUTION: Care must be exercised that the CV joints do not turn to their full extremes and that the seals are not damaged against the shock absorber or stabilizer bar.**

INSTALLING

Carefully place the drive axle assembly into the lower control arm and enter the outer race splines into the knuckle. Lubricate the final drive output shaft seal with Seal Lubricant No. 1050169. Install the output shaft into the final drive, and then attach the support bolts to the engine. **CAUTION: Don't let the shaft hang.** Assemble the bracket bolts loosely and, by moving the flange end of the shaft up and down and

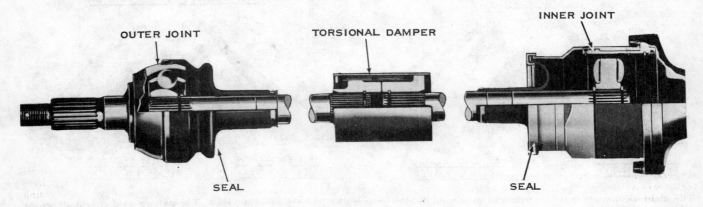

Right-hand output shaft attachment.

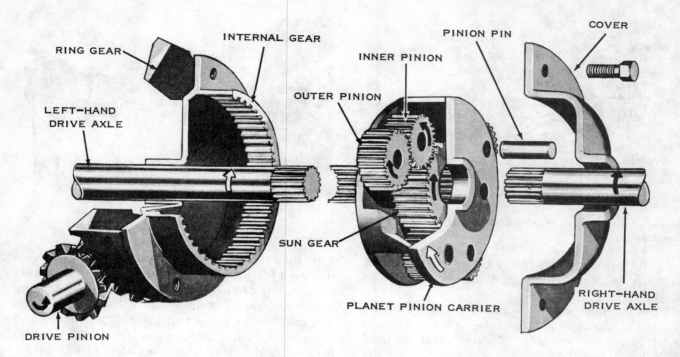

Details of the gear train during a left turn, with the right wheel turning faster than the left. The black arrows indicate the parts which are turning faster.

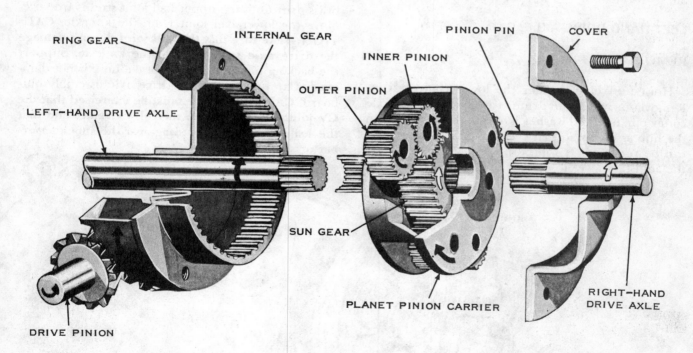

Details of the gear train during a right turn, with the left wheel turning faster than the right. In this case, the torque is transmitted to the ring gear, which is bolted to the internal gear. The integral internal gear drives the three outer pinions, which are in mesh with and drive the three inner pinions. These mesh with the sun gear, which is turning at wheel speed. The planet pinion carrier is prevented from turning at the right wheel speed because of the left tire friction with the ground. With the left wheel turning slower than the right, the planet pinion carrier "walks" around the internal gear.

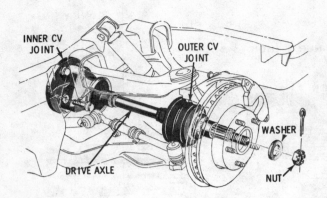

Details of the left-hand drive axle in the front-wheel drive Toronado.

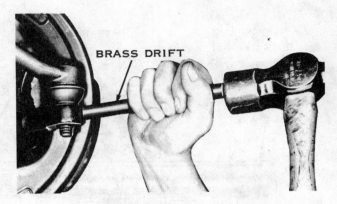

Removing the tie rod end.

back and forth, find the center location. Hold the shaft in this position, and then torque the bolts to 50 ft-lbs on the support.

Move the right-hand drive axle assembly toward the front of the car and align it with the right-hand output shaft. Install the attaching bolts and torque them to 65 ft-lbs. Install the oil filter element. Install the washer and nut on the drive axle and torque it to 150 ft-lbs. Insert the cotter pin and crimp the end. Remove the floor stands and lower the hoist. Check the engine oil.

LEFT-HAND DRIVE AXLE, R&R

REMOVING

Hoist the vehicle under the lower control arms. Remove the wheel and drum. Take out the drive axle cotter pin, nut, and washer. Position the access slot in the hub assembly so that each of the attaching bolts can be removed. It will be necessary to push aside the adjusting lever to remove one of the bolts.

Position the spacers of Tool J-22237, and then install Tool J-21579 and slide hammer J-2619 to pull off the hub. It will be necessary to push aside the adjusting lever for clearance. Remove the tie rod end cotter pin and nut. Drive on the knuckle with a hammer and brass drift until the tie rod end stud is free. Remove the bolts from the drive axle assembly and left output shaft.

Remove the upper control arm ball joint cotter pin and nut. Detach the brake hose clip from the ball joint stud. Drive on the knuckle with a hammer and brass drift until the upper ball joint stud is free. Remove the lower ball joint from the knuckle. **CAUTION: Take care that the ball joint doesn't damage the drive axle seal.** Remove the knuckle. Support the backing plate so that the brake hose is not damaged. Carefully guide the drive axle assembly outboard. **CAUTION: Care must be exercised that the CV joints do not turn to the full extremes and that the seals are not damaged against the shock absorber or stabilizer bar.**

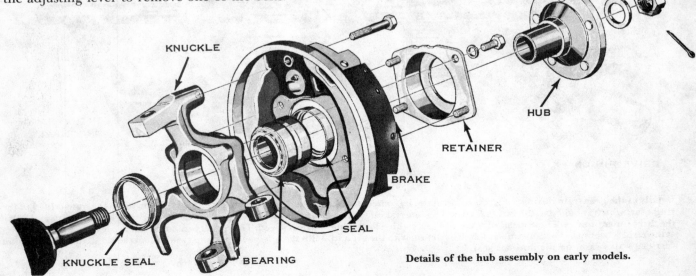

Details of the hub assembly on early models.

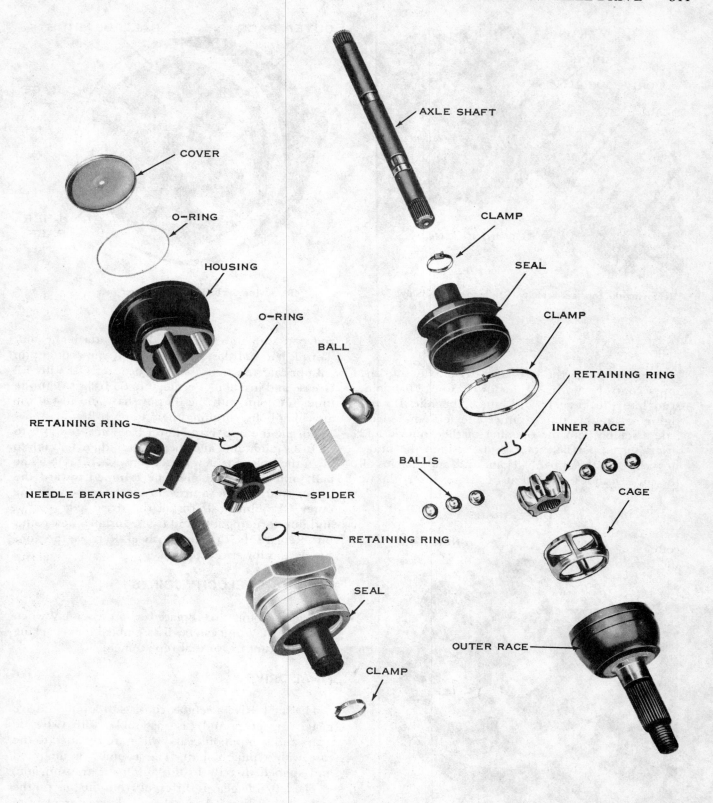

COVER

O-RING

HOUSING

O-RING

RETAINING RING

NEEDLE BEARINGS

BALL

SPIDER

RETAINING RING

SEAL

CLAMP

AXLE SHAFT

CLAMP

SEAL

CLAMP

RETAINING RING

INNER RACE

BALLS

CAGE

OUTER RACE

Exploded view of the left-hand drive axle assembly.

Removing the constant-velocity (CV) housing assembly.

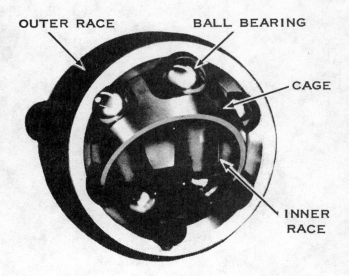

Removing the balls from the outer race.

INSTALLING

Carefully guide the left-hand drive axle onto the lower control arm. Insert the lower control ball joint stud into the knuckle and attach the nut. Do not tighten it at this time. Center the left-hand drive axle assembly into the opening of the knuckle and insert the upper ball joint stud. Position the brake hose clip over the upper ball joint stud, and then install the nut. Do not tighten it at this time. Insert the tie

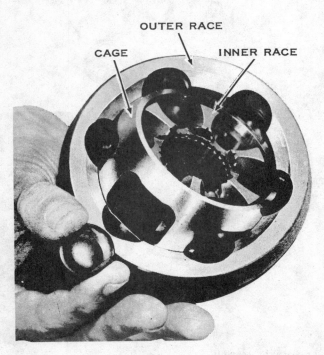

To install the balls in the outer race, it is necessary to tip the cage.

rod end stud into the knuckle and attach the nut. Torque it to 50 ft-lbs, and then install a new cotter pin.

Lubricate the hub assembly bearing OD with EP Grease and install it. Torque it to 65 ft-lbs. Align the inner CV joint with the output shaft and install the attaching bolts, torquing them to 65 ft-lbs.

Torque the upper and lower ball joint stud nuts to 85 ft-lbs minimum, and then tighten them enough to align the holes for new cotter pins. **CAUTION: The ball joint cotter pin must be crimped toward the upper control arm to prevent interference with the outer CV joint seal.** Install the drive axle washer and nut, torquing it to 150 ft-lbs. Install a new cotter pin. Replace the drum and wheel. Remove the floor stands and lower the vehicle.

CONSTANT-VELOCITY JOINTS

Velocity joints are replaced as an assembly when worn. The CV unit can be disassembled for repacking with lubricant or for seal replacement.

FINAL DRIVE

The final drive assembly consists of a pinion drive gear, ring gear, and case assembly, with two side gears and two pinion gears which are retained to the case with a pinion shaft. The assembly is mounted and splined directly to the automatic transmission.

The left-side gear is different from the one on the right side in that it has a threaded retainer plate to which the left output shaft bolts. The carrier is similar in construction and adjustments to a conventional differential assembly.

FINAL DRIVE, R&R

REMOVING

Disconnect the battery. Remove bolts A, B, C, and nut D, as shown in the accompanying illustration. Nut D must be removed with a special wrench, such as S-147. *NOTE: It may be necessary to remove the transmission filler tube for clearance.* Hoist the car and use floor stands at the front frame rails.

Disconnect the right- and left-drive axles from the output shafts. Remove the engine oil filter element. Disconnect the right-hand output shaft support from the engine. Move the right-hand drive axle rearward until the output shaft can be taken out of the final drive. Remove bolt X and loosen bolts Y and Z in the accompanying drawing. Remove the final drive cover and allow the lubricant to drain.

Position a transmission lift for the final drive, as shown, and then install an anchor bolt through the final drive housing and lift pad. Remove bolts E, F, and G, as well as nut H, as shown in the accompanying illustration. Move the transmission lift toward the front of the car to disengage the final drive splines from the transmission. *NOTE: Provide a container to catch the transmission fluid which will drain.* Lower the lift and remove the final drive. Use a 9/16" socket to remove the left output shaft retainer bolt, and then pull the output shaft from the final drive.

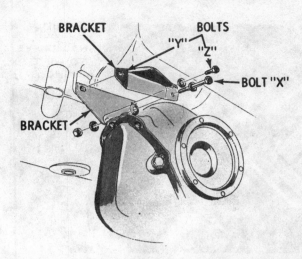

Disconnecting the·final drive from the engine, as discussed in the text.

INSTALLING

Apply Seal Lubricant, 1050169, to the two output shaft seals. Install the left output shaft into the final drive. Retain it with the bolt torqued to 40 ft-lbs. Position the final drive on the transmission lift pad

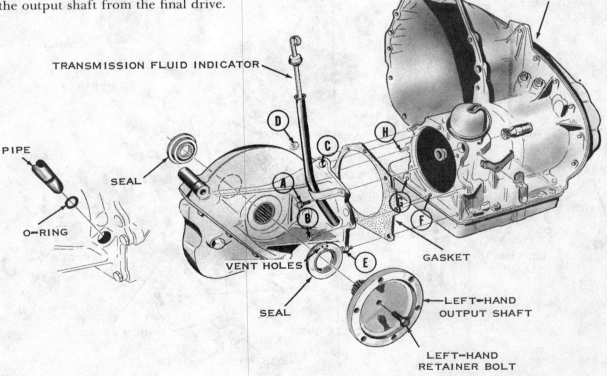

Details of the final drive attachment. The circled letters from A through H are discussed in the text.

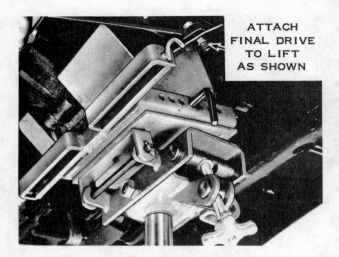

ATTACH
FINAL DRIVE
TO LIFT
AS SHOWN

Connecting the lift to the final drive.

drive, and then move the final drive unit until it mates with the transmission. **CAUTION: It may be necessary to rotate the left output shaft for the splines to engage, but be careful to keep the gasket in position while you do this.**

Install bolts E, F, and G, as well as nut H. Install bolts A, B, and C, as well as nut D. Torque all final drive-to-transmission bolts to 25 ft-lbs. Install bolt X and torque it to 105 ft-lbs. Tighten and torque bolts Y and Z to 50 ft-lbs. Loosen and remove the transmission lift.

Position a new gasket on the final drive, and then install the cover, torquing the bolts to 25 ft-lbs. Install the right output shaft into the final drive, indexing the splines of the output shaft with the splines of the side gear. Install the support bolts. **CAUTION: When attaching the right-hand output shaft to the engine, do not let the shaft hang.** Assemble the support bolts loosely and, by moving the flange end of the shaft up and down and back and forth, find the center location. Hold the shaft in this position and then torque the bolts on the support to 50 ft-lbs. Connect the drive axles to the output shafts and torque the bolts to 65 ft-lbs. Install the engine oil filter element, raise the

and secure it with an anchor bolt through the housing and lift pad. Apply a thin film of Seal Lubricant on the transmission side of a new final drive-to-transmission gasket, and then place the gasket on the transmission. Raise the lift, align the two bolt studs D and H on the transmission with their mating holes in the final

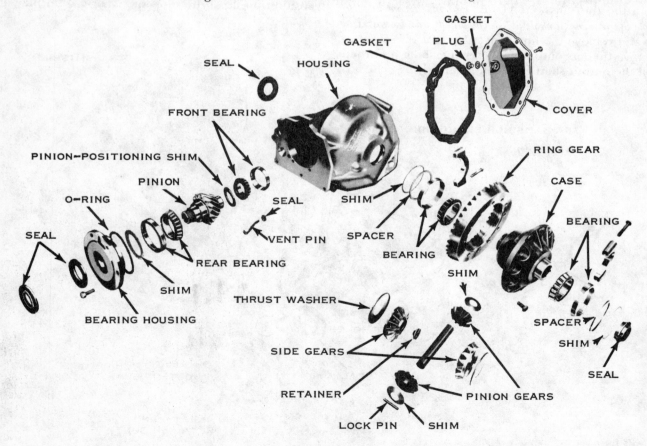

Exploded view of the final drive used on the Toronado.

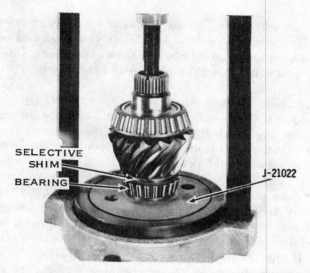

The pinion-positioning shim is between the front bearing and the pinion gear.

Checking the pinion gear bearing pre-load.

hoist, remove the floor stands, and lower the car. Install the oil filler tube, using a new O-ring. Connect the battery. Fill the final drive with 4-1/2 pints of Lubricant 1050081. The fluid level must be 1/2″ below the filler plug hole. Check the engine oil level, start the engine, and check the transmission fluid level.

FINAL DRIVE ADJUSTMENTS

Pinion Positioning Shim Adjustment

The final drive adjustments are similar to those described for the conventional differential assembly. The pinion-positioning shim is placed between the pinion gear and the front bearing. Add shims to obtain a bearing pre-load of 2-5 in-lbs with used bearings, or 2-15 in-lbs with new bearings. Adjustment shims are available in increments of 0.002″ from 0.036-0.070″.

Side Bearing Pre-Load Adjustment

Differential side bearing pre-load is adjusted by means of shims between the side bearings and housing. Shims are used on both sides and are available in increments of 0.002″ from 0.038-0.074″. A spacer of 0.140″ is used on each side. The pre-load adjustment

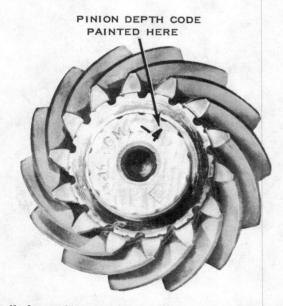

Details for marking the pinion depth code. In many cases, the code is etched on the edge of the ring gear.

This type of spreader is used to allow insertion of the adjusting shims between the case and side bearing, as discussed in the text.

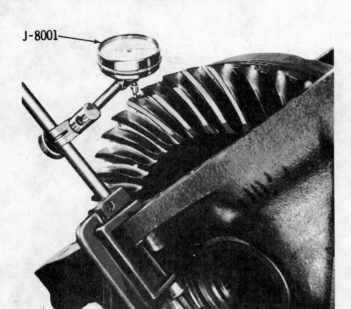

J-8001

Mounting a dial gauge to measure ring gear backlash.

is made by adding or taking out an equal number of shims from each side. **CAUTION: You must add or subtract an equal number of shims from each side, or you will change the backlash of the gears.**

Backlash Adjustment

Mount a dial indicator as shown, with the button contacting the heal end of a tooth. Set the indicator so that the stem is in line, as nearly as possible, with gear rotation and perpendicular to the tooth angle for an accurate reading. Check the backlash at three or four points, and it must not vary over 0.002″ or there are burrs between the ring gear and housing, or the case is distorted. The backlash at the point of minimum lash should be 0.005-0.009″.

If the backlash is not within specifications, it is necessary to correct by decreasing the thickness of shims between one differential case side bearing and the case and adding a like amount of shims to the other side. For each 0.001″ change in backlash that must be corrected, transfer 0.002″ of shims from one side to the other. **CAUTION: Don't change the total thickness of shims for both sides, or you will be changing the side bearing pre-load.**

7 | running gear service

WHEEL SUSPENSION

The front wheels are suspended on coil springs, which are attached to a long-and-short arm type suspension system. The front end incorporates ball joints, which allow the front wheels to move up and down with changes in the road surface. A direct-action shock absorber is bolted to the arm and to the top of the spring housing on each side.

The front wheels of the Toronado are mounted to the long-and-short arm suspension by means of torsion bars.

Some early models had the rear axle supported on two leaf-type springs, while most models use coil springs at all four wheels. The Station Wagon and Toronado still use leaf-type rear springs. To maintain alignment on models with coil springs in the rear, a link-type suspension system is used. Two rubber-bushed lower control arms are mounted between the axle assembly and the frame in order to maintain the fore-and-aft relationship of the axle. Two rubber-bushed upper control arms, angularly mounted with respect to the centerline of the car, control driving and braking torque, as well as sideway movements of the axle assembly.

FRONT WHEEL BEARINGS

Early models had the front wheels mounted on ball bearings, while later models use tapered roller bearings. The proper adjustment of front wheel bearings is one of the important service operations that has a definite bearing on safety. A car with improperly adjusted front wheel bearings lacks steering stability, has a tendency to wander or shimmy, and wears tires excessively.

ADJUSTING FRONT HUB BALL BEARINGS

Jack up the front of the vehicle. Remove the wheel

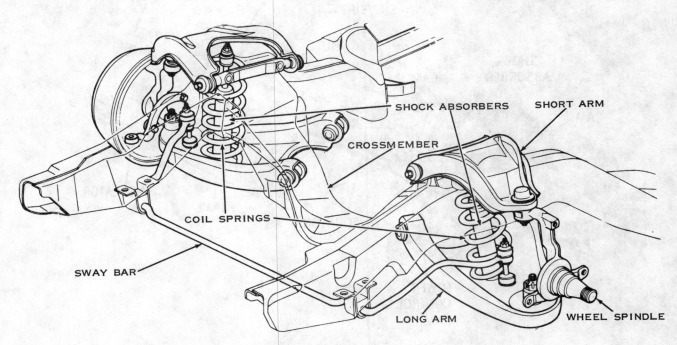

Front suspension used on most models.

317

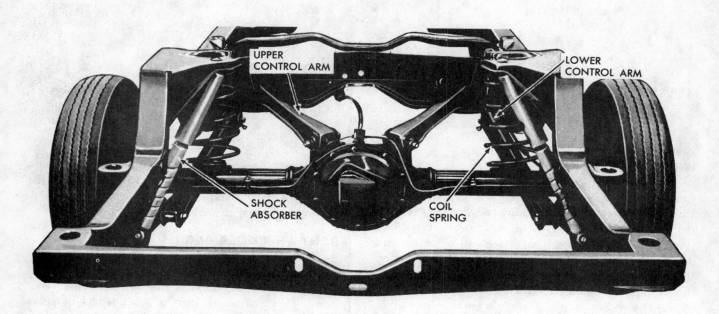

Details of a typical rear suspension. Note the angular mounting of the upper control arms and the cover plate over the differential gears, which signifies that it is the removable-carrier type.

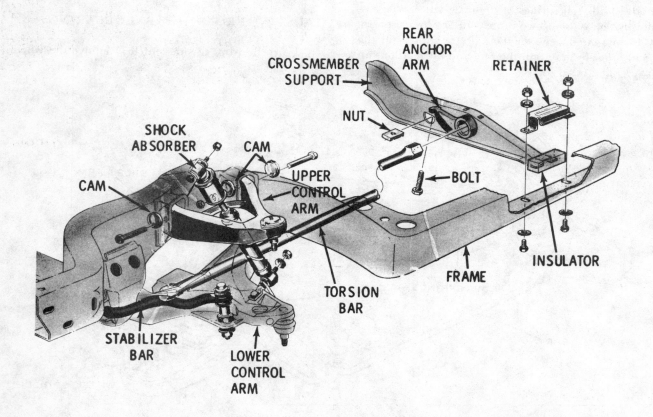

Front suspension used on the Toronado. Note the torsion bar and shock absorber placement compared with the coil springs of the conventional front end.

cover and dust cap. Take out the cotter pin, and then tighten the spindle nut to 28 ft-lbs of torque while rotating the wheel to seat the bearings.

Back off the adjusting nut until the wheel is loose, and then retorque it to 12 ft-lbs. Check the location of a slot in the nut with reference to a hole in the spindle. If a slot in the nut lines up with either the vertical or horizontal holes in the spindle, insert a new cotter pin. If the slot in the nut has passed a hole in the spindle, back off the nut to line up the next slot, and then insert a new cotter pin. Install the dust cap and wheel cover, and then remove the jack.

ADJUSTING FRONT HUB TAPERED ROLLER BEARINGS

Jack up the front of the vehicle. Remove the wheel cover and dust cap. Take out the cotter pin, and then tighten the spindle nut to seat the bearings fully while you spin the wheel.

Back off the adjusting nut 1/4-1/2 turn until it is just loose, and then hand-snug the nut. Loosen the nut until either hole in the spindle lines up with the slot in the nut, and then insert a new cotter pin. When the bearing is properly adjusted, there must be 0.001-0.008″ end play. **CAUTION: Under no circumstances should the bearing adjustment be even finger-tight, or you will burn out the bearings.**

WHEEL ALIGNMENT

Front wheel alignment is the proper adjustment of all the interrelated suspension angles affecting the running and steering of the front wheels of the vehicle. The importance of wheel alignment and wheel balancing is considered essential in order to maintain ease of steering and good directional stability and to prevent abnormal tire wear.

1. HAND SPIN WHEEL

2. "SNUG-UP" THE NUT TO FULLY SEAT BEARINGS—THIS OVERCOMES ANY BURRS ON THREADS.

3. BACK OFF NUT UNTIL JUST LOOSE (1/4—1/2 TURN)

4. HAND "SNUG-UP" THE NUT

5. LOOSEN NUT UNTIL EITHER HOLE IN THE SPINDLE LINES UP WITH A SLOT IN THE NUT—THEN INSERT COTTER PIN.

NOTE: UNDER NO CIRCUMSTANCES IS THE BEARING TO BE EVEN FINGER TIGHT.

6. WHEN THE BEARING IS PROPERLY ADJUSTED THERE WILL BE FROM .001—.008 INCHES END-PLAY (LOOSENESS).

Making a front wheel bearing adjustment on late-model cars.

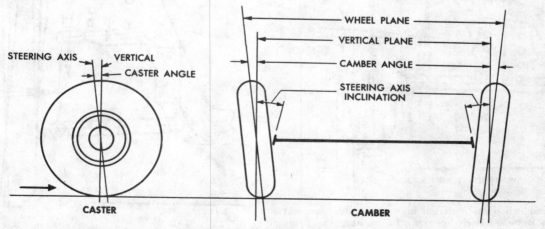

STEERING AXIS
VERTICAL
CASTER ANGLE
CASTER

WHEEL PLANE
VERTICAL PLANE
CAMBER ANGLE
STEERING AXIS INCLINATION
CAMBER

Caster and camber angles of the front suspension.

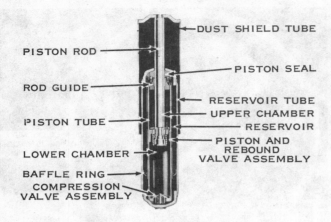

Details of a shock absorber.

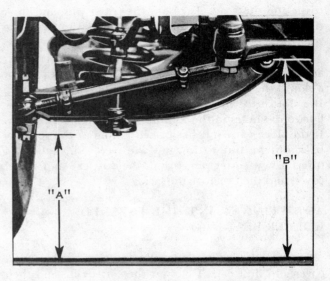

Checking the riding height is important before testing front end alignment. If one spring is sagged, it should be replaced to restore the designed spring height; otherwise, the front end angles will be adversely affected.

The six basic factors which are the foundation of front wheel alignment are: height, caster, camber, toe-in, steering axis inclination, and turning radius. All of the angles, except steering axis inclination and turning radius, are adjustable. The two unadjustable angles are valuable in determining if parts are bent, especially so when the other angles cannot be adjusted to specifications.

HEIGHT

The front suspension height must be held to specifi-

cations for a satisfactory ride, correct appearance, proper front wheel alignment, and reduced tire wear. The heights must be measured only after the vehicle has the recommended tire pressures, a full tank of fuel, no passengers, no luggage, and is on a level floor.

Jounce the vehicle several times and release it on a downward motion. Measure the distance from the lowest point on one adjusting blade to the floor to obtain measurement "A" and from the lowest point

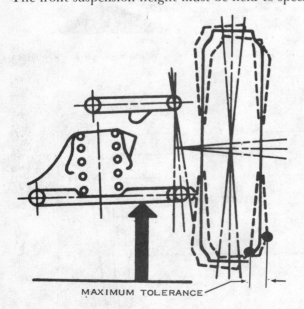

The front end ball joints must not be worn, or the front end alignment will be adversely affected. To measure the lower ball joint radial play, support the front end under the lower suspension arm, as indicated by the black arrow.

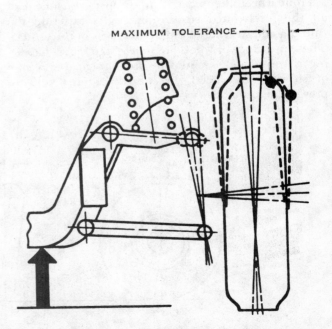

To measure the upper ball joint wear radial play, support the vehicle at the frame, as indicated by the black arrow.

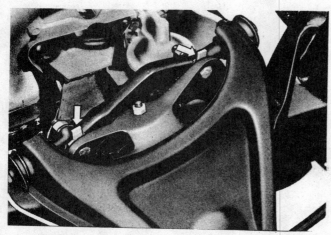

Most Oldsmobile model front suspensions are designed to adjust the caster and camber angles by changing the number of shims (arrows) between the control arm and its support bracket. Shims can be changed at either the front of the shaft or the rear to change caster, or equally at both points to change camber. A 1/32" shim will change camber about 1/6°.

of the steering knuckle arm to the floor to obtain measurement "B." The difference between measurements "A" and "B" is the front suspension height, and the maximum allowable difference between sides is 1/8". Replace the front springs, if necessary, to establish the correct heights.

CASTER AND CAMBER

Caster is the forward (negative) or rearward (positive) tilt of the top of the wheel spindle. Camber is the amount that the front wheels are tilted outward (positive) or inward (negative) at the top. The maximum difference between the front wheel caster angles or the front wheel camber angles should not exceed 1/2°.

Caster and camber adjustments are made on the older cars by the use of 1/16" and 1/32" shims placed between the upper control arm support brackets and the frame sub side rails. Shims may be changed at either the front or rear bracket to change the caster setting. Shims changed equally at both brackets change the camber.

Removal of shims at the rear bracket or the addition of shims at the front bracket will decrease caster. *NOTE: One 1/16" shim will change the caster approximately 3/8°.* The addition of shims at both the front and rear support brackets will decrease positive camber. *NOTE: One 1/16" shim at each bracket will change the camber 5/16°.*

On some late-model vehicles eccentric cams on the end of the control arms are used for making the adjustments. Changing the position of both cams an equal amount affects camber only. Changing one cam.

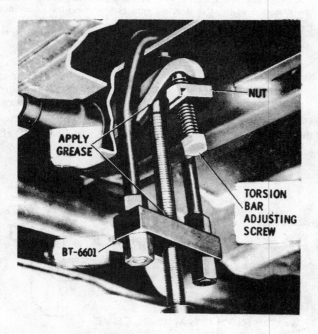

This torsion bar screw should be used to adjust and even the front end of the Toronado.

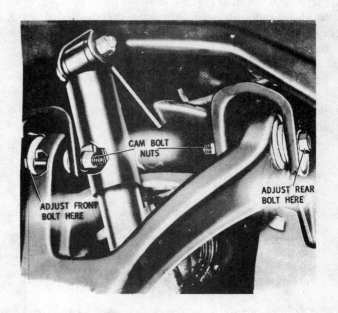

These eccentric cams are used to adjust the caster and camber on Toronado models.

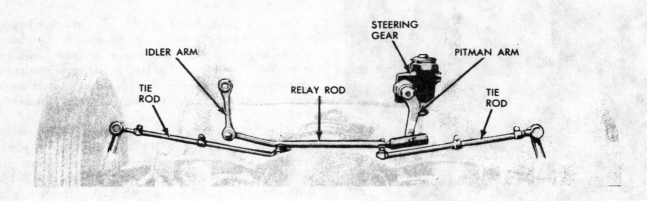

Details of a conventional steering linkage.

or both cams in different directions, affects caster.

On some late-model vehicles, the caster angle is adjusted by turning the two nuts which are on the front of the lower control arm strut rod. The camber angle is adjusted by loosening the lower control arm pivot bolt and then rotating the cam located on the pivot. The eccentric cam action moves the lower control arm in or out.

TOE-IN

Toe-in is the difference between the distance at the extreme front and rear of both front wheels. It must be measured only after you have corrected the caster and camber angles, as these angles affect the toe-in reading.

Check the steering wheel spoke position when the front wheels are pointed straight ahead. If the spokes are not correctly positioned, they can be adjusted at the same time that the toe-in is being adjusted. To adjust toe-in, if the steering wheel spokes are correctly positioned, loosen the two clamp bolts on each spindle

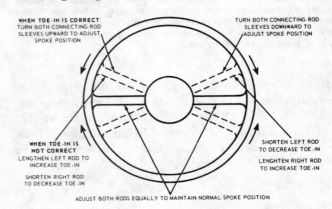

The steering wheel must be aligned in the straight-ahead position; otherwise, the steering gear box over-center adjustment will not be positioned properly, and a binding condition may result on a turn. This diagram shows how the connecting rod sleeves should be turned to make this adjustment.

connecting rod sleeve and lengthen or shorten both rods equally. If the spokes are not correctly positioned, make the necessary rod adjustments as indicated in the accompanying illustration.

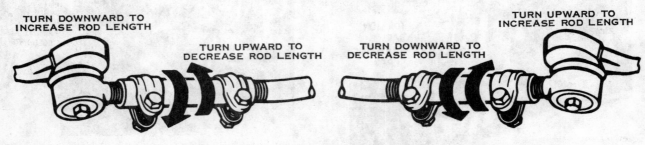

To make the toe-in adjustment, turn the connecting rod sleeves as shown.

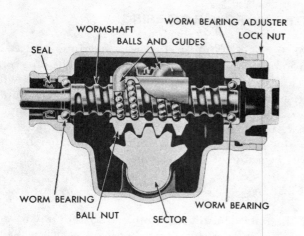

WORM BEARING ADJUSTER
LOCK NUT
WORMSHAFT
BALLS AND GUIDES
SEAL
WORM BEARING
BALL NUT
SECTOR
WORM BEARING

Sectioned view through a conventional steering gear housing.

When the correct alignment is obtained, tighten the clamp bolts on both connecting rod sleeves. **CAUTION: The sleeve clamp bolts must be at the bottom.**

TURNING RADIUS

When the front wheels are turned so that the inside wheel on a curve is turned 20°, the outside wheel should turn 18-3/4°. This angle is not adjustable, but it is affected by the other three front-end alignment angles. If the front-end is in alignment, except for the turning radius angle, it is an indication of a bent spindle or a damaged suspension part.

STEERING GEAR

The standard steering gear is of the worm-and-recirculating ball type. The worm bearing preload is controlled by the large bearing adjuster which is threaded into the housing. The sector shaft mesh load is controlled by an adjusting screw located in the housing cover. To make the worm bearing preload adjustment, tighten the bearing adjuster until it takes 4-5 in-lbs torque to turn the input shaft at approximately 1-1/2 turns either side of center, with the steering gear out of the vehicle (or with the pitman arm disconnected).

To make the mesh adjustment, turn the adjusting screw in the housing cover until the total load (mesh and bearing preload) that is required to rotate the worm past the center high spot is 9-10 in-lbs torque. **CAUTION: No perceptible slack is permissible at 30° either side of center.**

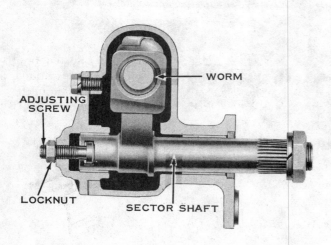

WORM
ADJUSTING SCREW
LOCKNUT
SECTOR SHAFT

End view of the steering gear housing to show the sector shaft end play adjusting screw. The sector gear is mounted slightly off-center, and moving it closer to the center of the worn gear takes out excessive steering wheel play.

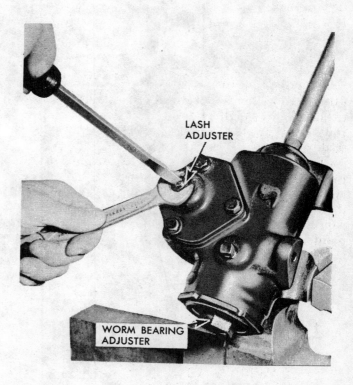

LASH ADJUSTER
WORM BEARING ADJUSTER

The worm bearing adjuster nut should be tightened to remove all end play of the worm, but not tight enough to cause it to bind. The lash adjuster should be turned to obtain just a trace of steering wheel play.

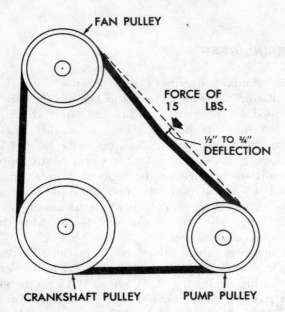

The power steering pump drive belt should deflect 1/2-3/4" under a force of 15 lbs.

INTEGRAL POWER STEERING

The Saginaw integral power steering unit is a torsion-bar type, hydraulic-assist system. The unit consists of a worm-and-rack piston, which is meshed with the gear teeth on the steering sector shaft. The unit also contains a hydraulic valve, valve actuator, input shaft, and a torsion-bar assembly, which are mounted on the end of the worm shaft and operated by the twisting action of the torsion bar.

STEERING GEAR ADJUSTMENT

The only adjustment possible with the unit in the vehicle is the over-center position load, which is made to eliminate excessive lash between the sector and rack teeth.

To make this adjustment, disconnect the pitman arm from the sector shaft and the fluid line at the reservoir. Cap the reservoir return line pipe. Place

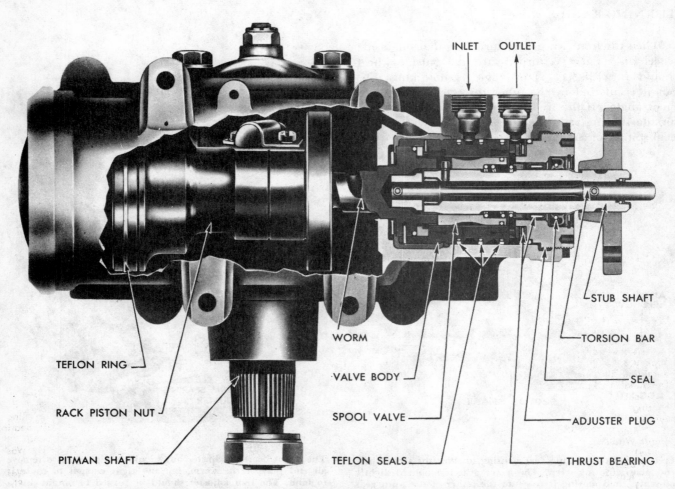

Sectioned view through a Saginaw integral power steering unit used on many models.

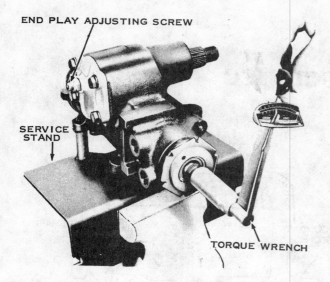

END PLAY ADJUSTING SCREW

SERVICE STAND

TORQUE WRENCH

Checking the pitman shaft preload by means of a torque wrench, as discussed in the text.

the end of the return line in a clean container and cycle the steering wheel in both directions to discharge the fluid from the gear housing.

Remove the ornamental cover from the steering wheel hub, and then turn the steering wheel to 45° from the left stop. Use a torque wrench on the steering wheel nut to determine the effort required to rotate the shaft slowly through a 1/8th turn from the 45° position. Turn the steering wheel back to center, and then determine the torque required to rotate the shaft back and forth across the center position. Loosen the adjuster nut, and then turn the adjuster screw in until the reading is 3-6 in-lbs greater in the center position than 45° from the stop. Tighten the locknut while holding the adjuster screw. Recheck the readings.

Replace the pitman arm and the steering wheel hub cover. Connect the fluid return line to the reservoir and fill the reservoir with fluid to the proper level.

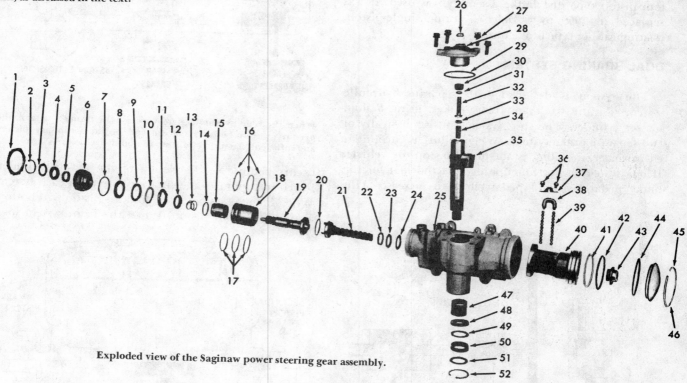

Exploded view of the Saginaw power steering gear assembly.

1. Locknut
2. Retaining Ring
3. Dust Seal
4. Oil Seal
5. Bearing
6. Adjuster Plug
7. "O" Ring
8. Thrust Washer (Large)
9. Thrust Bearing
10. Thrust Washer (Small)
11. Spacer
12. Retainer
13. Spool Valve Spring
14. "O" Ring
15. Spool Valve
16. Teflon Oil Rings
17. "O" Rings
18. Valve Body
19. Stud Shaft
20. "O" Ring
21. Worm Shaft
22. Thrust Washer
23. Thrust Bearing
24. Thrust Washer
25. Housing
26. Locknut
27. Attaching Bolts and Washers
28. Side Cover
29. "O" Ring
30. Adjuster Retainer
31. Shim
32. Adjuster Screw
33. Thrust Washer
34. Spring
35. Pitman Shaft
36. Screws and Lock Washers
37. Clamp
38. Ball Return Guide
39. Balls
40. Rack-Piston
41. Teflon Oil Seal
42. "O" Ring
43. Plug
44. "O" Ring
45. Housing End Cover
46. Retainer Ring
47. Needle Bearing
48. Oil Seal
49. Back Up Washer
50. Oil Seal
51. Back Up Washer
52. Retaining Ring

8 | brake service

All General Motors vehicles are equipped with Bendix Duo-Servo, drum-type brakes; self-adjusting devices were added in 1963. Since 1968, all vehicles have been equipped with a split braking system, using a dual master cylinder with two sections; one for the front wheel brakes and the other for the rear wheels.

Disc brakes have been used on the front wheels of many models since 1967. Initially, a Delco Moraine four-piston type disc brake assembly was used. It was replaced in 1969 by a Delco Moraine single-piston, floating-caliper type brake unit.

DUAL BRAKING SYSTEM

The system is designed with separate hydraulic systems for the front and rear brakes, using a dual master cylinder. The split system consists basically of two separate brake systems. When failure is encountered in either, the other is adequate to stop the vehicle. If one system is not functioning, it is normal for the brake pedal lash and pedal effort to increase. This

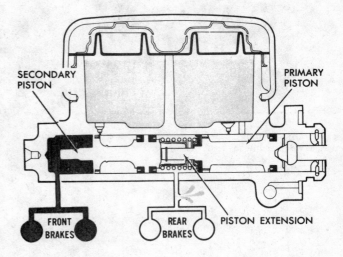

When the rear hydraulic system loses fluid through a leak, the primary piston bottoms on the end of the secondary piston, and sufficient pressure is built up to stop the vehicle.

occurs because of the design of the master cylinder, which incorporates an actuating piston for each system. When the rear system loses fluid, its piston will bottom against the front piston. When the front system loses

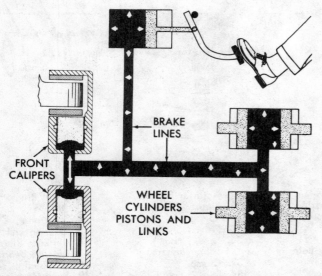

Hydraulic pressure is distributed equally to the hydraulic cylinders at all four wheels.

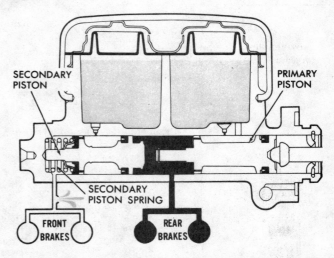

When the front system loses hydraulic pressure, the secondary piston bottoms in the end of the master cylinder, and then the primary piston develops sufficient pressure to stop the vehicle.

326

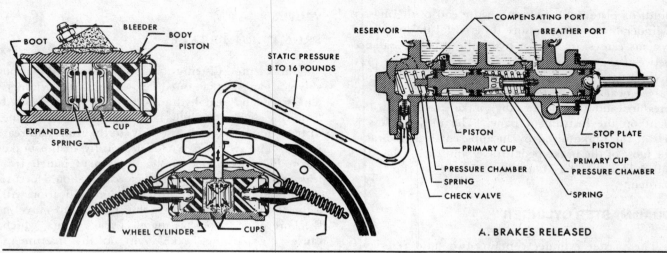

BOOT | BLEEDER | BODY | PISTON

EXPANDER | SPRING | CUP

STATIC PRESSURE 8 TO 16 POUNDS

WHEEL CYLINDER | CUPS

RESERVOIR | COMPENSATING PORT | BREATHER PORT

PISTON | PRIMARY CUP | PRESSURE CHAMBER | SPRING | CHECK VALVE

STOP PLATE | PISTON | PRIMARY CUP | PRESSURE CHAMBER | SPRING

A. BRAKES RELEASED

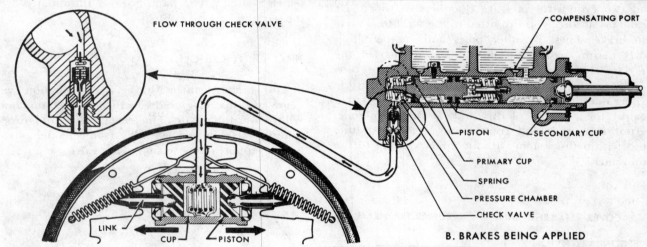

FLOW THROUGH CHECK VALVE

COMPENSATING PORT

LINK | CUP | PISTON

PISTON | SECONDARY CUP | PRIMARY CUP | SPRING | PRESSURE CHAMBER | CHECK VALVE

B. BRAKES BEING APPLIED

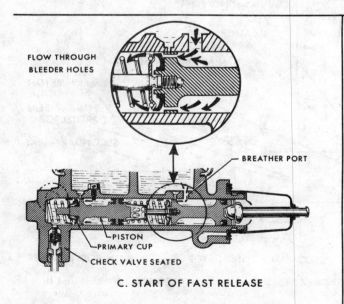

FLOW THROUGH BLEEDER HOLES

BREATHER PORT

PISTON | PRIMARY CUP | CHECK VALVE SEATED

C. START OF FAST RELEASE

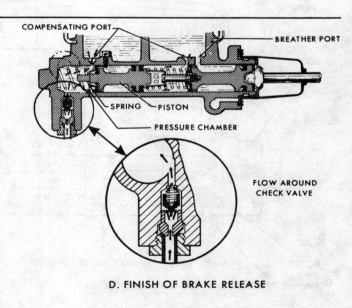

COMPENSATING PORT | BREATHER PORT

SPRING | PISTON | PRESSURE CHAMBER

FLOW AROUND CHECK VALVE

D. FINISH OF BRAKE RELEASE

Action of the various parts of the hydraulic system under different operating conditions.

fluid, its piston will bottom on the end of the master cylinder body. The pressure differential in one of the systems causes an uneven hydraulic pressure balance between the front and rear systems. The brake pipe distribution and switch assembly, or combination valve, near the master cylinder detects the loss of pressure and illuminates the brake alarm indicator light on the instrument panel. The pressure loss is felt at the brake pedal by an apparent lack of brakes for most of the brake pedal travel and then, when the failed chamber has bottomed, the pedal effort will harden.

DUAL MASTER CYLINDER

The master cylinder contains two fluid reservoirs and two cylindrical pressure chambers in which the brake pedal force is transmitted to the fluid to actuate the brake shoes. Breather ports and compensating ports permit passage of fluid between each of the pressure chambers and its fluid reservoir during certain operating conditions. A vented cover and flexible rubber diaphragm at the top seal the hydraulic system against the entrance of dirt and, at the same time, permit expansion and contraction of the hydraulic fluid within the system without direct venting to the atmosphere.

VALVES
FRONT DRUM BRAKES

A brake pipe distribution-and-switch (combination valve) assembly is mounted below the master cylinder. The front and rear hydraulic brake lines are routed from the master cylinder, through the brake pipe distribution-and-switch assembly, to the front and rear brakes. The switch is wired electrically to the brake alarm indicator light on the instrument panel. If a leak in either the front or rear system should occur, the pressure differential during brake application will cause the piston to compress the springs and move in the bore until it touches the electrical contact, which causes the parking brake lamp on the instrument panel to light. This lamp is also illuminated when the parking brake is applied.

FRONT DISC BRAKES

Disc brake vehicles have a combination valve below the master cylinder, which houses the brake-failure warning switch, metering valve, and proportioning valve in one assembly (some models do not have a proportioning section of the valve).

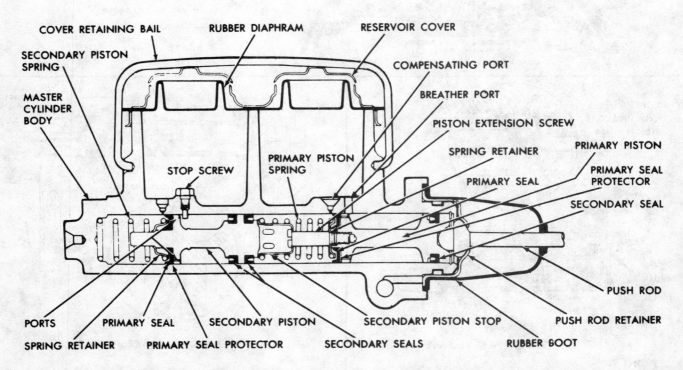

The dual master cylinder used with modern braking systems has two reservoirs and two pistons to develop pressure in each of the braking systems. A vented cover and flexible rubber diaphragm at the top of the reservoirs seal the system from contamination.

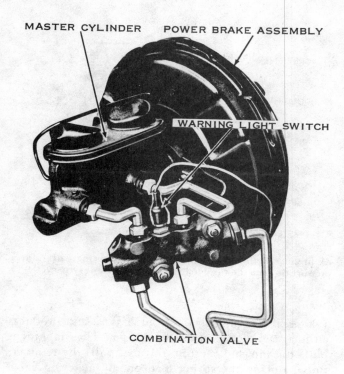

MASTER CYLINDER   POWER BRAKE ASSEMBLY

WARNING LIGHT SWITCH

COMBINATION VALVE

A brake distribution-and-switch (combination valve) assembly is mounted below the master cylinder.

COMBINATION VALVE

The combination valve contains a metering valve, failure-warning switch, and proportioner valve combined into an assembly which also serves as the front junction block. This valve is used on all disc brake applications. The input-output characteristics of the valve vary with vehicle usage.

METERING VALVE

This valve delays front disc brake application until the shoes of the rear drum brakes contact the drum. The action is needed because of the return springs on the rear wheel brake shoes. Disc brake shoes have no return springs.

Brakes Not Applied

The metering valve allows free flow of brake fluid through the valve when the brakes are not applied. This allows the fluid to expand and contract with temperature changes.

Shut-Off Point (Initial Brake Apply)

The metering valve stem moves to the left and, at

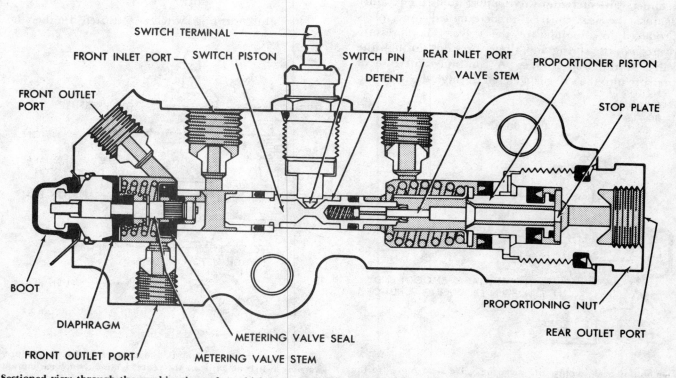

SWITCH TERMINAL

FRONT INLET PORT   SWITCH PISTON   SWITCH PIN   REAR INLET PORT   PROPORTIONER PISTON
                                          DETENT   VALVE STEM

FRONT OUTLET
PORT   STOP PLATE

BOOT

                                                                              PROPORTIONING NUT

DIAPHRAGM   REAR OUTLET PORT

FRONT OUTLET PORT   METERING VALVE SEAL
                     METERING VALVE STEM

Sectioned view through the combination valve, which houses the brake-failure warning switch, metering valve, and proportioning valve.

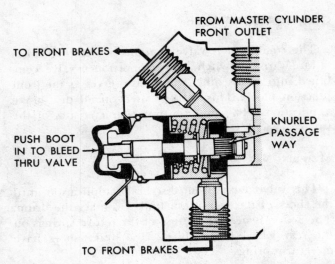

The metering valve keeps the disc brake pads from operating until the shoes of the rear drum brake contact the drum. In this non-applied position, free passage of brake fluid is allowed through the knurled passageway.

4 to 30 psi, the smooth end of the stem is in a sealing position with the metering valve seal lip, and this is the shut-off point.

Hold-Off Bend Pressure

The metering valve stem continues to the left on initial brake apply and stops on the knurl at the metal retainer. The metering valve spring holds the retainer against the seal until a predetermined pressure is produced at the inlet of the valve. This pressure overcomes the spring and allows pressure through the valve to the front brakes. A continued increase of pressure into the valve is metered through the metering

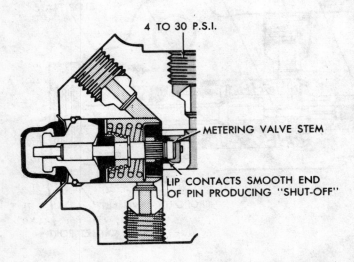

On initial brake apply, the metering valve stem moves to the left and shuts off hydraulic pressure to the front disc brakes.

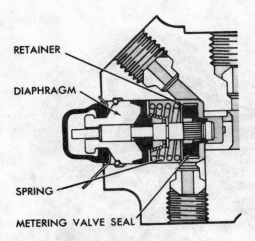

As pressure builds up in the system, the metering valve allows pressure through the valve to the front disc braking system.

valve seal (through to the front brakes) and produces an increasing force on the diaphragm. The diaphragm pulls the pin and the pin, in turn, pulls the retainer, thus reducing the spring load on the metering valve seal. Eventually, the pressure reaches a point where the spring is completely pulled away by the diaphragm pin and retainer, leaving the metering valve seal free to pass unrestricted pressure through the valve.

FAILURE-WARNING SWITCH

The failure-warning switch is activated if either the

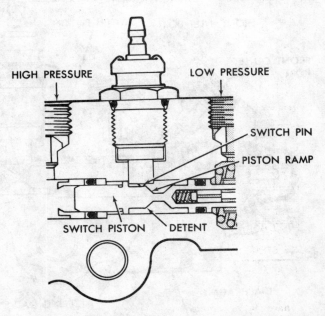

In the combination valve used on late models, the failure-warning switch action is in the center section, and this diagram shows a rear-wheel braking system failure.

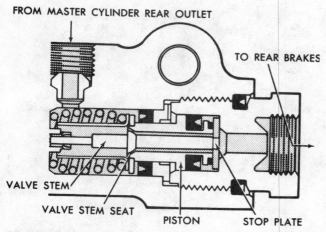

FROM MASTER CYLINDER REAR OUTLET

TO REAR BRAKES

VALVE STEM

VALVE STEM SEAT

PISTON   STOP PLATE

The combination valve has a proportioner valve at the right end to improve front-to-rear brake balance during sudden stops. This valve is necessary to prevent rear-wheel lock-up and skids during emergency stops. During normal stops, fluid flows through the space between the piston center hole and the valve stem, and the valve has no effect on brake operation.

front or rear brake system fails and, when activated, completes a circuit to the dash warning lamp. If the rear hydraulic system fails, the pressure of the good front system forces the switch piston to the right. The switch pin is forced up into the switch by the piston ramp and completes the electrical circuit, lighting the dash lamp; it is held in this position by the piston. When repairs are made and pressure is returned to the rear system by bleeding, the piston moves to the left and resets the switch to the OFF position. The detent on the piston typically requires 100 to 450 psi

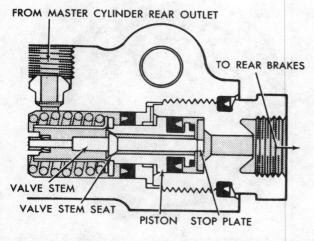

FROM MASTER CYLINDER REAR OUTLET

TO REAR BRAKES

VALVE STEM

VALVE STEM SEAT

PISTON   STOP PLATE

On a hard brake application, pressure pushes against the large end of the piston, and when sufficient to overcome the spring load, moves the piston to the left so that pressure flow through the valve is restricted.

FAILURE-WARNING SWITCH

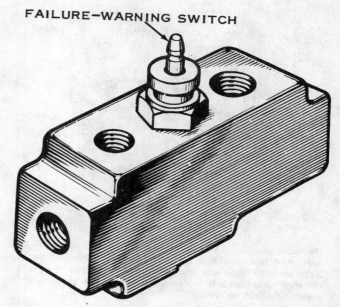

Since the split hydraulic brake system was introduced in 1968, this brake failure-warning switch was used in the pipe distribution block of early models. Loss of hydraulic pressure in either system activates the switch to light a warning lamp on the dash.

pressure before allowing full reset (centering) of the piston. The same condition exists if the front hydraulic system fails, except the piston moves to the left.

PROPORTIONER

The rear brake proportioner improves front-to-rear brake balance at high deceleration. During quick stops, a percentage of the rear weight is transferred to the front wheels. Compensation must be made for the resultant loss of weight to the rear wheels to avoid early rear wheel skid. The proportioner part of the combination valve reduces the rear brake pressure and so delays a rear wheel skid. The proportioner is not repairable; it must be replaced if defective.

Normal Brake Stops

The proportioner does not operate during normal brake stops. Fluid normally flows into the proportioner through the space between the piston center hole and valve stem, through the stop plate, and out to the rear brakes. The spring loads the piston so that it rests against the stop plate during normal brake pressures.

Proportioning Action

Pressure developed within the valve pushes against

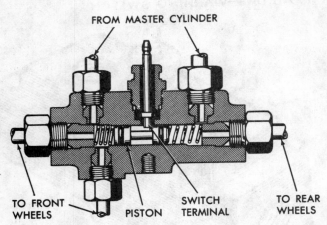

FROM MASTER CYLINDER

TO FRONT WHEELS   PISTON   SWITCH TERMINAL   TO REAR WHEELS

On early models, the brake distribution switch was a separate unit, and this sectioned view shows it in a "failed" position. Note how the right-side contact has moved forward to contact the stem of the switch terminal because of low pressure in the front-wheel braking system.

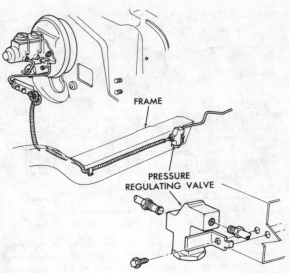

FRAME

PRESSURE REGULATING VALVE

In early models, the brake pressure regulating valve was mounted somewhere in the hydraulic line to the rear brakes.

the large end of the piston and, when sufficient to overcome the spring load, moves the piston to the left. The piston contacts the spherical stem seat and starts proportioning by restricting pressure through the valve.

BRAKE DISTRIBUTION SWITCH

This switch assembly is used on all front drum-type braking systems since 1968. It is a pressure-differential type, designed to light a brake-warning lamp on the instrument panel if either the front or rear hydraulic system fails. The lamp provides the driver a visible warning that part of the car's brake system has failed.

When hydraulic pressure is equal in both the front and rear hydraulic systems, the switch piston remains centered and does not contact the terminal in the switch cylinder bore. The switch includes a spring on each side of the piston to hold the piston in the centered position. If pressure fails in one of the systems, hydraulic pressure moves the piston toward the inoperative side. The shoulder of the piston then contacts the switch terminal to provide a ground for the warning lamp circuit and lights the warning lamp.

This switch is a non-adjustable, non-serviceable component. If defective, it must be replaced. **CAUTION: The brake warning light will come on when the brakes are applied in a defective system. It must not remain on when the brakes are released.**

DRUM-TYPE BRAKES

The brakes are the Duo-Servo, single-anchor pin type, which utilize the momentum of the vehicle to assist in the brake application. The self-energizing force is applied to both brake shoes at each wheel in both forward and reverse directions.

Wheel cylinders are the double-piston type. To keep out dust and moisture, both ends are sealed with a rubber boot. The wheel cylinders have no adjustments.

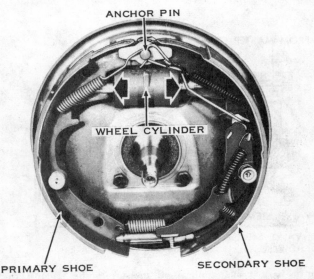

ANCHOR PIN

WHEEL CYLINDER

PRIMARY SHOE   SECONDARY SHOE

The front-wheel braking mechanism is mounted on the brake flange plate, which is bolted directly to the front wheel steering knuckle.

All parking brakes have a foot-operated, ratchet-type pedal, mounted to the left of the steering column. A cable assembly connects the pedal to an intermediate cable by means of an equalizer, where the adjustment for the parking brake is incorporated. The intermediate cable attaches to the two rear cables, which operate the rear service brakes.

FRONT WHEEL BRAKES

The wheel brake mechanism is mounted on the brake flange plate, which is bolted directly to the front wheel steering knuckle. The anchor pin is the upper pivot point of the brake shoes, and it is located above the wheel cylinder. Two brake shoes are used, a primary shoe toward the front of the car and a secondary shoe toward the rear. The primary shoe lining is always shorter than the secondary. The two brake shoes are held to the anchor pin at the top by color-coded retracting springs.

SELF-ENERGIZING ACTION

When the driver applies pressure to the brake pedal, fluid pressure is applied to the two pistons at each of the four wheel cylinders. This action forces the shoes outward at the top, causing the shoes to expand, pivoting on the adjusting screw. As they contact the drum, friction forces them to rotate with it. The primary shoe (front one) moves away from the anchor pin and exerts a rearward force on the adjusting screw, and this forces the secondary shoe upward, tightly against the anchor pin, so that the force applied to the secondary shoe is the sum of the original appli-

cation force and the rotational force applied by the primary shoe.

When the brakes are applied while the vehicle is reversing, the rear shoe becomes, in effect, the primary shoe, applying its forces in like manner to the front shoe.

SELF-ADJUSTING ACTION

A self-adjusting actuating lever is mounted on the secondary shoe; it is attached to the shoe by the hold-down spring pin-and-spring assembly, which allows the lever to pivot about this point.

During a forward stop, the shoes contact the drum and rotate with it until the secondary shoe contacts the anchor pin; it moves only far enough to place the lining in contact with the drum. The small amount of movement does not activate the adjusting mechanism.

During a reverse stop, the shoes contact the drum and rotate with it until the primary shoe contacts the anchor pin. If there is excessive clearance because of brake lining wear, secondary shoe movement is enough to activate the adjusting mechanism by pulling the top of the actuating lever inward. As the lever pivots on the hold-down spring-and-pin assembly, the pawl end rocks down on the star wheel and turns it one notch to increase the length of the adjusting screw and so makes a take-up adjustment.

When the brakes are released, the retracting springs return the brake shoes to their normal positions, and the actuating lever return spring raises the pawl end of the activating lever to return it to its normal position. The pawl slips back over the teeth of the star wheel and takes a new "bite" on another tooth.

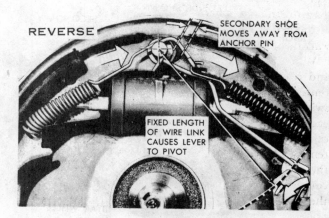

FORWARD

PRIMARY SHOE MOVES AWAY FROM ANCHOR PIN

During forward stops, friction between the brake lining and drum causes the primary shoe to move away from the anchor pin, and this exerts a rearward force on the adjusting screw to force the secondary shoe into tighter contact with the drum.

REVERSE

SECONDARY SHOE MOVES AWAY FROM ANCHOR PIN

FIXED LENGTH OF WIRE LINK CAUSES LEVER TO PIVOT

During a reverse stop, the secondary shoe moves away from the anchor pin, and the action is reversed. If there is excessive clearance because of brake lining wear, secondary shoe movement is enough to activate the adjusting mechanism by pulling the top of the actuating lever inward (arrow).

When there is only a slight clearance between the shoes and drum, such as might occur when the brake linings are near their proper adjustment, the brake shoes rotate only a small amount before they contact the anchor pin, and this is not enough movement to cause the actuating lever to advance the star wheel.

REAR WHEEL BRAKES

The rear wheel brake mechanism is the same as the front, except for the additional parking brake activating mechanism, which consists of an operating lever located in back of the secondary shoe and attached to the shoe by a pivot at the upper end. A strut rod, located a few inches below the pivot point, extends forward from this lever to the primary shoe.

The parking brake cable is connected to the lower end of the operating lever. When the parking brake is applied, the cable pulls the lower end of the operating lever forward, causing the strut rod to push the primary shoe forward. At the same time, the upper end of the lever pushes the secondary shoe rearward. The combined action of the lever and the strut rod drives the primary and secondary shoes apart and into contact with the drums.

SINGLE-PISTON TYPE DISC BRAKES

When pressure is applied to a hydraulic system, it acts equally in all directions. In the single-piston mechanism, the pressure acts on two surfaces. The first is the piston. The second is in the opposite direction, against the bottom of the bore of the caliper housing.

Since the area of the piston and bottom of the caliper bore are equal, equal forces are developed.

Hydraulic force in the caliper bore is exerted against the piston which is transmitted to the inner brake shoe and lining assembly and to the inner surface of the disc. This tends to pull the caliper assembly inboard, sliding on the four rubber bushings. The outer lining, which rests on the caliper housing, then applies a force on the outer surface of the disc and together the two linings slow the car. Since an equal hydraulic force is applied both to the caliper housing and the piston, the force created against the outer surface of the disc is the same as the inner. Since there are equal forces on the linings, no flexing or distortion of the disc occurs regardless of the severity or length of application, and lining wear tends to be equal.

As the brake linings wear, the caliper assembly moves inboard and fluid fills the area behind the piston, so that there is no pedal travel increase. As the driver releases the brake pedal, the piston and caliper merely relax into the released position, and braking effort is removed.

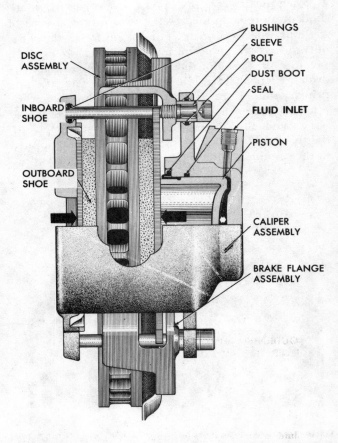

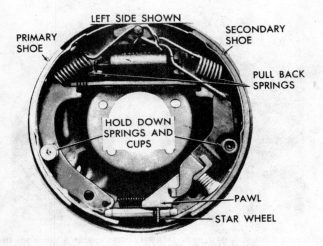

The rear-wheel brake mechanism is the same as the front, except for the parking brake actuating strut rod between the shoes, located just under the hydraulic cylinder.

Sectioned view through the single-piston type caliper disc brake assembly.

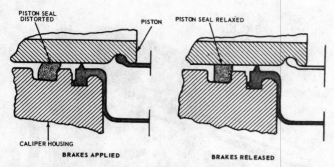

BRAKES APPLIED   BRAKES RELEASED

The piston seals distort when the brakes are applied, and this forces the piston back slightly from the rotor for running clearance when brake pedal pressure is released. As the linings wear, the seals slip in the bore to take up a new position so that the adjustment is automatically made.

An important thing about disc brakes is that the lining is in constant contact with the disc, giving the advantages of improved brake response, reduced pedal travel, and faster generation of line pressure. The shoe, being at zero clearance, also wipes the disc free of foreign matter.

FOUR-PISTON TYPE DISC BRAKES

The caliper contains two pairs of directly-opposed

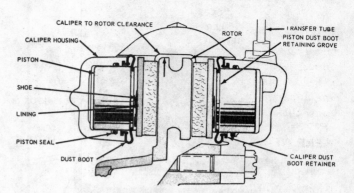

Sectioned view through the caliper assembly to show how the pistons force the linings into contact with the rotor, which is secured to the hub.

pistons. When installed on the vehicle, the caliper straddles the disc so that, on application, the pistons, through the shoes and linings, clamp the disc an equal amount on each side. The caliper housing consists of an inboard and outboard half that is bolted together. The outboard half has the extension that straddles the disc. The caliper is of nodular iron and is machined to receive two pistons in each half.

The two piston bores in each half are connected

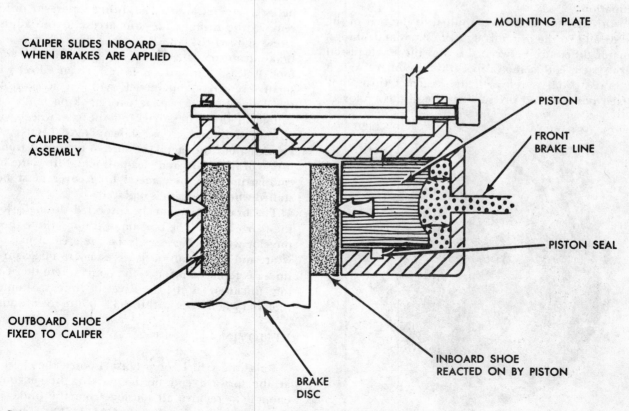

When fluid is contained in a closed system and pressure is applied, it is exerted equally in all directions and, in the single-piston assembly, it acts on two surfaces: (1) the piston, and (2) in the opposite direction against the caliper housing, which pulls the housing inboard, sliding on the four rubber bushings.

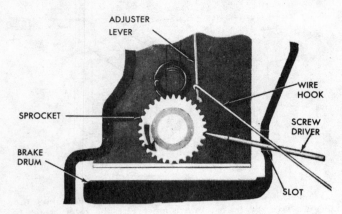

Some brake drums have a lanced area which can be knocked out in order to insert a screwdriver for retracting the star wheel adjuster.

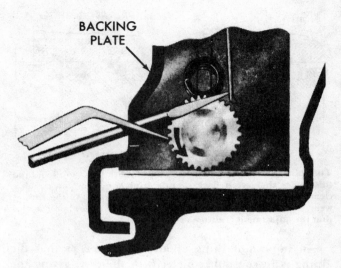

On most models, it is possible to pry out the rubber cover in the backing plate to gain access to the star adjusting wheel.

hydraulically by internal passages. The two halves are connected hydraulically by means of a crossover passage. Each piston bore has a groove that accepts the outer lip of a dust boot. Each piston has two grooves. The inner groove is tapered slightly and accepts the hydraulic seal. The outer groove accepts the inner lip of the dust boot, so that the caliper bore and piston are completely sealed from external contamination.

In this system, pressure is applied to the rear of the pistons and to the disc through the shoes and linings. A major difference between this and the single-piston brake system is that the caliper stays stationary. When the brake pedal is released, the system returns to a relaxed position and pressure on the disc is removed.

DRUM-TYPE BRAKE SERVICE PROCEDURES

RELINING

If the brake drums are worn severely, it may be necessary to retract the adjusting screws in order to remove the drums. To gain access to the adjusting screw star wheel, knock out the lanced area in the brake drum or flange plate, using a chisel or similar tool. Release the actuator from the star wheel with a small screwdriver on models with an access hole in the flange plate or with a wire hook on models with a hole in the drum. Back off the star wheel with a second screwdriver, as shown. **CAUTION: After knocking out the metal, be sure to remove it from the inside of the drum and clean all metal from the brake compartment. A new metal hole cover must be installed when the drum is replaced.**

The brake lining can be inspected through slots in the flange plate. The portion of lining visible through the slot will not necessarily be the area of maximum wear, and extra caution is necessary to make sure the lining is replaced prior to the point where the remaining thickness is 1/16″. Riveted linings should be replaced when worn within 1/32″ of the rivet heads.

REMOVING

Raise the vehicle on a hoist. Loosen the check nuts at the forward end of the parking brake equalizer enough to remove all tension from the brake cable. Remove the brake drums. **CAUTION: The brake pedal must not be depressed while the drums are removed.**

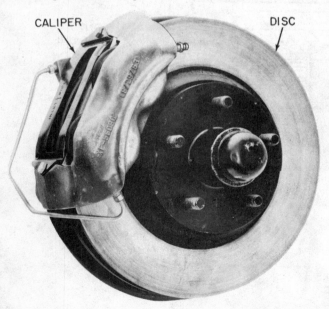

The four-piston caliper straddles the disc, and four pistons apply pressure equally to both sides of the rotor when the brakes are applied.

Unhook the brake shoe retracting springs from the anchor pin and link end. Remove the actuator return spring. Disengage the link end from the anchor pin and then from the secondary shoe. Remove the hold-down pins and springs.

Remove the actuator assembly. The actuator, pivot, and override spring are an assembly and should not be disassembled for service, unless they are broken. It is much easier to assemble the brakes by leaving them intact. Separate the brake shoes by removing the adjusting screw and spring. **CAUTION: Mark the shoe and lining positions if they are to be reinstalled.** Remove the parking brake lever from the secondary brake shoe.

INSPECTING

Clean all dirt out of the brake drum. Inspect the drums for roughness, scoring, or out-of-round. Replace or recondition the drums as necessary.

Carefully pull the lower edges of the wheel cylinder boots away from the cylinders and note whether the interior is wet with brake fluid. Excessive fluid at this point indicates leakage past piston cups, requiring an overhaul of the wheel cylinder. *NOTE: A slight amount of fluid is nearly always present to act as lubricant for the piston.* **CAUTION: If one wheel cylinder is leaking, all hydraulic cylinders should be overhauled at the same time because all have had** equal wear and will be leaking in a short time if not repaired.

Inspect the flange plate for oil leakage past the axle shaft oil seals. Install new seals if necessary.

Check all brake flange plate attaching bolts to make sure they are tight. Clean all rust and dirt from the shoe contact faces on the flange plate, using fine emery cloth.

INSTALLING

Inspect the new linings and make sure there are no nicks, burrs, or bonding material on the shoe edges where contact is made with the brake flange plate or on any of the contact surfaces. **CAUTION: Keep your hands clean while handling brake shoes. Do not permit oil or grease to come in contact with linings.** Lubricate the parking brake cable with Delco Brake Lube No. 5450032. Lubricate the fulcrum end of the parking brake lever and the bolt, and then attach the lever to the secondary shoe with a bolt, spring washer, lockwasher, and nut. Make sure that the lever moves freely.

Put a light coat of lube on the pads, flange plate, and threads of the adjusting screw. **CAUTION: A loose adjustment can occur from an adjusting screw that is not properly operating. CAUTION: Be careful**

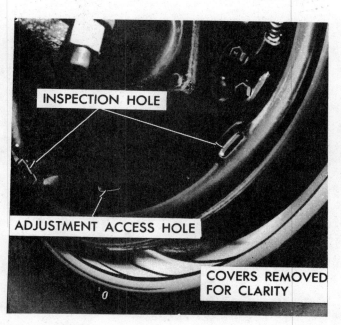

Inspection holes in the backing plate provide means to determine the brake lining thickness without removing the wheel and drum.

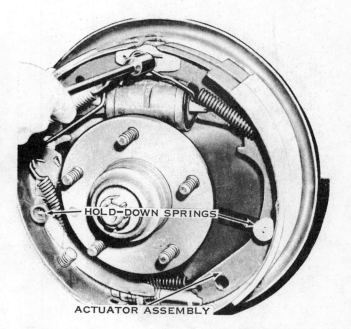

Unhook the brake shoe retracting spring from the anchor pin with this tool, and then depress each of the hold-down spring retainers to disengage them. Take off the actuator assembly, and then remove both brake shoes.

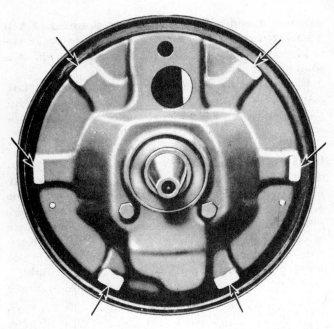

Lightly lubricate the brake shoe support surfaces (arrows) on the backing plate. CAUTION: Don't get any lubricant on the brake linings, or they will grab.

to keep lubricant off the brake linings.

Connect the brake shoes together with the adjusting screw spring, and then place the adjusting screw, socket, and nut in position. CAUTION: Make sure

Install the brake shoes, and then insert the hold-down springs and retainers. Pull the retracting springs over the anchor pin with the illustrated tool.

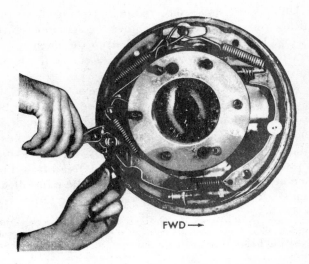

On rear-wheel brakes, connect the parking brake strut, and then secure the brake shoes with the hold-down pin and spring. Connect the return springs to the anchor bolt at the top of the backing plate.

the proper adjusting screw is used ("L" for the left side of the vehicle, "R" for the right side). The star wheel should be installed with the wheel nearest the secondary shoe and the adjusting screw spring inserted to prevent interference with the star wheel. Make sure the right-hand thread adjusting screw is on the left side of the car and the left-hand thread adjusting screw is on the right side of the car. Make certain the star wheel lines up with the adjusting hole in the flange plate.

A special brake drum gauge is available to measure the inside diameter of the drum.

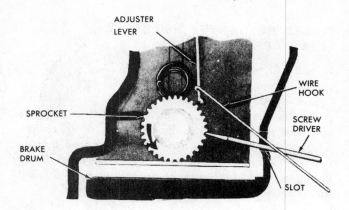

This diagram shows how a wire hook can be used to keep the adjuster lever from interfering with the brake adjusting tool when the adjustment is made through the slot in the brake drum.

On rear wheels, connect the parking brake cable to the lever. Secure the primary brake shoe (short lining —faces forward) first, with the hold-down pin and spring. At the same time, engage the shoes with the wheel cylinder connecting links. Install and secure the actuator assembly and secondary brake shoe with the hold-down pin and spring. On rear wheels, position the parking brake strut and strut spring. Install the guide plate over the anchor pin. Install the wire link. **CAUTION: Do not hook the wire link over the anchor pin stud with a regular spring hook tool or you will stretch it. Fasten the wire link to the actuator assembly first, then place it over the anchor pin stud by hand, while holding the adjuster assembly in the full-down**

position. **Install the actuator return spring. CAUTION: Do not pry on the actuator lever to install the return spring. Ease it into place, using the end of a screwdriver.**

If the old brake retracting springs are nicked, distorted, or if their strength is doubtful, install new ones. Hook the springs into the shoes by installing the primary spring from the shoe over the anchor pin and then the spring from the secondary shoe over the wire link end. **CAUTION: Make certain the actuator lever functions easily by hand, operating the self-adjusting feature.** Adjust the service brake and parking brake. Install the drum and the wheel. Lower the vehicle to the floor.

ADJUSTING DRUM-TYPE BRAKES

After installing new brake linings, it is necessary to make an adjustment to the star wheel in order to be able to install the brake drums. A special drum-to-brake shoe clearance gauge is available to check the diameter of the brake drum, and then the tool is reversed to straddle the brake shoes. To make a preliminary adjustment, turn the star wheel until the gauge just goes over the brake shoes, and then install the brake drum.

Alternatively, the star wheel can be backed off enough to install the drums, and then a preliminary adjustment can be made by holding the ratchet off the

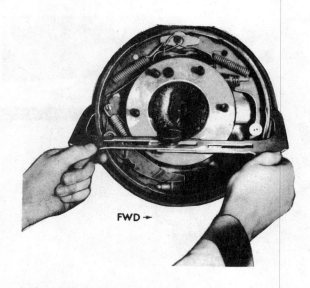

Note how the gauge is reversed in this diagram to set the brake shoes to the diameter of the drum.

When making a brake shoe adjustment from the backing plate side, a pointed tool can be used to hold the adjuster lever away from the star adjusting wheel, which can then be turned with a screwdriver.

When properly adjusted, the brake pedal should have about 1/4" free play.

star wheel with a thin-bladed screwdriver through the access hole in the backing plate while you make the adjustment.

The final adjustment must be made by making numerous forward and reverse stops, spplying the brakes with firm pedal effort until a satisfactory pedal height results. **CAUTION: Frequent shifting of an automatic transmission into the forward range to halt reverse vehicle motion can prevent the automatic adjusters from functioning properly, thereby inducing a low pedal height.**

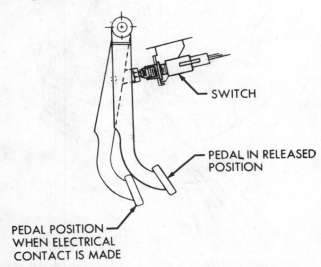

The stop light switch can be adjusted by rotating it in its bracket. The lamp should light when the pedal is depressed about 1/2".

SINGLE-PISTON TYPE DISC BRAKE SERVICE PROCEDURES

INSPECTING

Jack up the front end of the vehicle to inspect the pads. Remove the wheels and check both ends of the outboard shoe by looking in at each end of the caliper. This is the point at which the highest rate of wear normally occurs. At the same time, check the lining thickness on the inboard shoe by looking down through the inspection hole in the top of the caliper.

The outboard shoes have ears near the outer edge, which are bent over at right angles to the shoe. The top ends of the shoe have looped ears with holes in them, which the caliper retaining bolts fit through. The large tab at the bottom of the shoe is bent over at a right angle and fits in the cut-out in the outboard section of the caliper. The inboard shoe and lining has ears on the top ends, which fit over the caliper retaining bolts. A special spring inside the hollow piston supports the bottom edge of the inboard shoe. *NOTE: Outboard shoes (with formed ears) are designed for original installation only and are fitted to the caliper. The shoes should never be relined or reconditioned.*

REMOVING THE BRAKE SHOES

Remove the master cylinder cover and observe the brake fluid level in the reservoirs. If a reservoir is more than 1/3 full, siphon the necessary amount out.

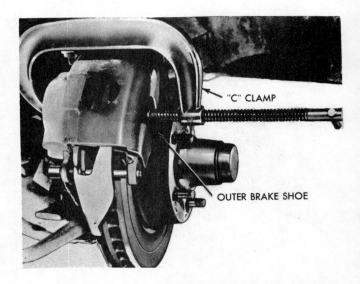

Use a C-clamp to push the piston into its bore to assist in removing the caliper. **CAUTION: The master cylinder reservoir must not be more than 1/3 full, or the excess will overflow.**

CAUTION: This step is taken to avoid reservoir overflow when the caliper piston is pushed back into its bore. Discard the brake fluid you removed. **CAUTION: Never reuse brake fluid.**

Push the piston back into its bore. This can be accomplished by using a C-clamp, as shown. Remove the two mounting bolts which attach the caliper to the support. Lift the caliper off the disc. Remove the inboard shoe, dislodge the outboard shoe, and position the caliper on the front suspension arm so that the brake hose does not support the weight of the caliper. **CAUTION: Mark the shoe positions if they are to be reinstalled.**

Remove the shoe support spring from the piston, the two sleeves from the inboard ears of the caliper, and the four rubber bushings from the grooves in each of the caliper ears.

CLEANING AND INSPECTING

The shoes should be replaced when the lining is worn to approximately 1/32" thickness over the rivet heads. **CAUTION: Always replace the shoes** in axle sets.

Thoroughly clean the holes and the bushing grooves in the caliper ears and wipe any dirt from the mounting bolts. **CAUTION: Do not use abrasives on the bolts, since this can damage the plating. If the bolts are damaged or corroded, they should be replaced.**

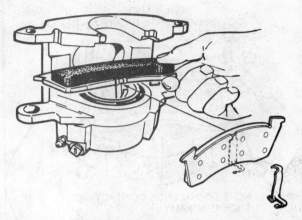

Installing the shoe support spring and the inboard shoe in the center of the piston cavity.

Examine the inside of the caliper for evidence of fluid leakage. If leakage is noted, the caliper should be overhauled. Wipe the inside of the caliper clean, including the exterior of the dust boot. Check the boot for cuts, cracks, or other damage. **CAUTION: Do not use compressed air to clean the inside of the caliper. This can unseat the dust boot.**

INSTALLING

Lubricate new sleeves, new rubber bushings, the bushing grooves, and the end of the mounting bolts with Delco Silicone Lube No. 5459912. **CAUTION: It is essential that new sleeves and rubber bushings**

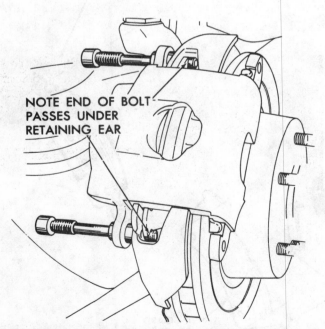

NOTE END OF BOLT PASSES UNDER RETAINING EAR

Removing the two mounting bolts which hold the caliper to the support.

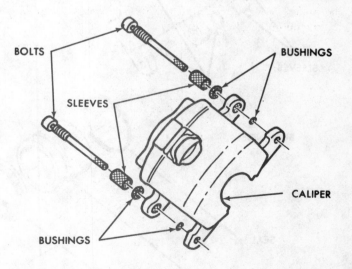

BOLTS

BUSHINGS

SLEEVES

CALIPER

BUSHINGS

▒▒▒▒ LUBRICATE AREAS INDICATED

Lubricate these parts with Silicone Lube No. 5459912. **CAUTION: Never use mineral oil on any parts of the brake system, or the rubber parts will swell.**

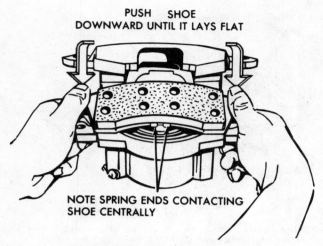

PUSH SHOE
DOWNWARD UNTIL IT LAYS FLAT

NOTE SPRING ENDS CONTACTING
SHOE CENTRALLY

Installing the inboard brake shoe.

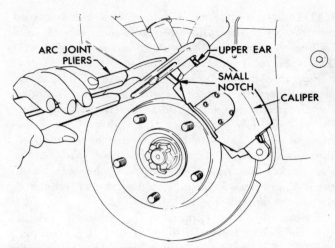

ARC JOINT PLIERS

UPPER EAR

SMALL NOTCH

CALIPER

Use arc-joint pliers to bend both upper ears of the outboard shoe until all radial clearance is removed, as discussed in the text.

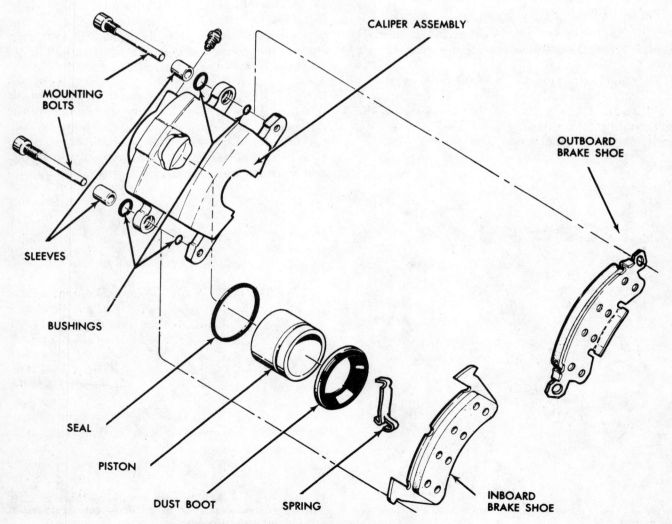

CALIPER ASSEMBLY

MOUNTING BOLTS

OUTBOARD BRAKE SHOE

SLEEVES

BUSHINGS

SEAL

PISTON

DUST BOOT

SPRING

INBOARD BRAKE SHOE

Exploded view of the single-piston caliper assembly.

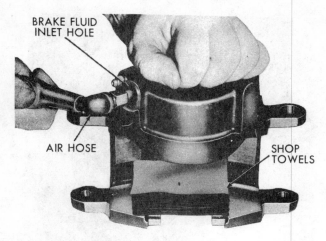

If the piston needs to be removed from the caliper, use air pressure to force it out.

Installing a new dust boot on the piston.

be used and that lubrication instructions be followed in order to ensure the proper functioning of the sliding caliper design. Install the new rubber bushings in the caliper ears. Install the new sleeves to the inboard ears of the caliper. *NOTE: Position the sleeve so that the end toward the shoe-and-lining assembly is flush with the machined surface of the ear.*

Install the shoe support spring and the inboard shoe in the center of the piston cavity, as shown. **CAUTION: If the original shoes are being reinstalled, they must be replaced in the original positions (as marked at removal).** Push down until the shoe lies

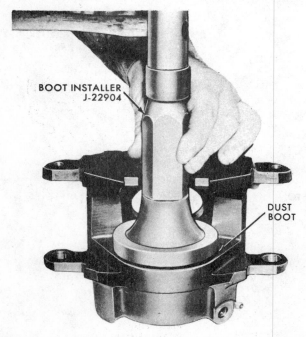

Driving the piston into the caliper. Use the illustrated tool to make sure that the dust boot seats properly.

flat against the caliper. Position the outboard shoe in the caliper, with the ears at the top of the shoe over the caliper ears and the tab at the bottom of the shoe engaged in the caliper cut-out.

With both shoes installed, lift up the caliper assembly and rest the bottom edge of the outboard lining on the outer edge of the brake disc to make sure there is no clearance between the tab at the bottom of the outboard shoe and the caliper abutment. Position the caliper over the brake disc, lining up the hole in the caliper ears with the holes in the mounting bracket. **CAUTION: Make sure that the brake hose is not twisted or kinked.** Start the caliper-to-mounting bracket bolts through the sleeves in the inboard caliper ears and through the mounting bracket, making sure that the ends of the bolts pass under the retaining ears on the inboard shoe. Push the mounting bolts through to engage the holes in the outboard shoes and the outboard caliper ears, threading the mounting bolts into the mounting bracket. Torque the mounting bolts to 35 ft-lbs.

Pump the brake pedal to seat the linings against the rotors. Using arc-joint pliers, as shown, bend both upper ears of the outboard shoe until no radial clearance exists between the shoe and the caliper housing. Locate the pliers on the small notch of the caliper housing during the clinching procedure. **CAUTION: If radial clearance exists after the initial clinching, repeat the process.**

Reinstall the front wheel and lower the vehicle. Add brake fluid to the master cylinder reservoir to bring the fluid level up to within 1/4″ of the top. **CAUTION: Before moving the vehicle, pump the brake pedal several times to make sure that it is firm. Do not move the vehicle until a firm pedal is obtained. Check the master cylinder fluid level again after pumping the brake pedal.**

FOUR-PISTON TYPE DISC BRAKE SERVICE PROCEDURES

INSPECTING

Jack up the front of the vehicle and remove the wheel. Shoes with bonded linings should be replaced when the lining is worn to approximately 1/16" thickness. Shoes with linings retained by rivets should be replaced when the lining is worn to approximately 1/32" thickness over the rivet heads.

REMOVING THE BRAKE SHOES

Syphon 2/3 of the brake fluid from the master cylinder reservoirs to prevent the fluid from overflowing when the thicker linings are installed. **CAUTION: Do not drain the reservoirs completely or air will be sucked into the system.** Remove and discard the cotter pin from the inboard end of the shoe retaining pin, and then slide out the retaining pin. Remove the inboard shoe by pulling it up. **CAUTION: If the shoes are to be reused, identify their location.**

INSTALLING NEW SHOES

Insert the new shoe and lining into position. Use two screwdrivers to push the pistons back as the shoe is inserted. Replace the outboard shoe in the same

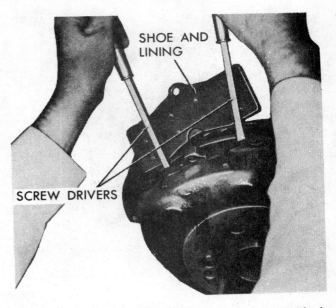

To install new brake shoes, use two screwdrivers to push the pistons back as the shoe is inserted. CAUTION: Make sure that the master cylinder reservoir is not over 1/3 full, or the excess will overflow.

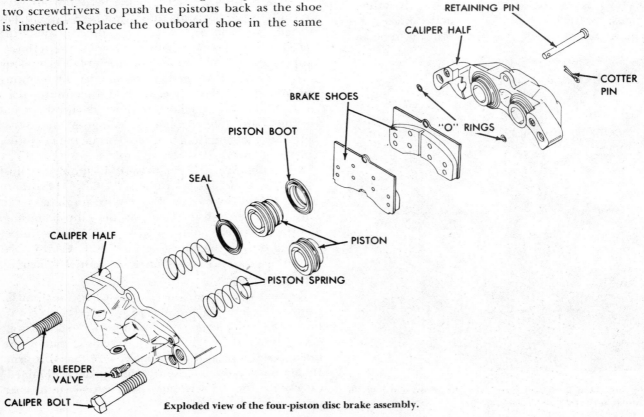

Exploded view of the four-piston disc brake assembly.

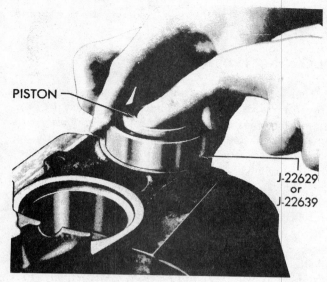

PISTON

J-22629
or
J-22639

Installing the piston in the caliper with the aid of a special tool.

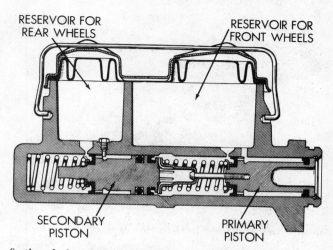

RESERVOIR FOR REAR WHEELS

RESERVOIR FOR FRONT WHEELS

SECONDARY PISTON

PRIMARY PISTON

Sectioned view through the Bendix master cylinder used in the split braking system. Note that the front wheel reservoir is at the rear of the master cylinder. Also note the stop bolt in the bottom of the front reservoir to keep the secondary piston from moving back too far.

manner. When both shoes have been replaced, install the shoe-retaining pin through the outboard caliper half, outboard shoe, inboard shoe, and inboard caliper half. Insert a new 3/32 × 5/8″ plated cotter pin through the retaining pin, and then bend back the ends of the cotter pin.

Refill the master cylinder fluid level to within 1/4″ of the top. If necessary, bleed the brake system. Install the wheels and lower the vehicle. **CAUTION: Do not move the car until a firm pedal is obtained.**

MASTER CYLINDER SERVICE PROCEDURES

REMOVING

Wipe the master cylinder and lines clean with a clean cloth. Place dry cloths below the master cylinder area to absorb any fluid spillage. Disconnect the hydraulic lines at the master cylinder. Cover the line ends with clean lint-free material to prevent foreign matter from entering the system.

Disconnect the push rod from the brake pedal. Unbolt and remove the master cylinder from the dash panel or power brake booster.

J-22628
OR
J-22638

Use the illustrated tool to seat a new boot seal in the caliper.

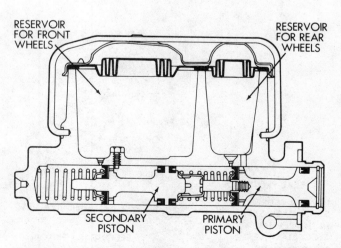

RESERVOIR FOR FRONT WHEELS

RESERVOIR FOR REAR WHEELS

SECONDARY PISTON

PRIMARY PISTON

Sectioned view through the Delco-Moraine master cylinder. Note the reversal of the reservoirs from the Bendix. Also note the stop bolt in the bottom of the front reservoir to keep the secondary piston from moving back too far.

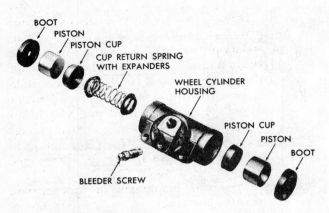

Exploded view of a wheel cylinder used with drum-type brakes.

DISASSEMBLING

Remove the small secondary piston stop screw from the bottom of the front fluid reservoir of the master cylinder. Place the master cylinder in the vise so that the lock ring can be removed from the small groove in the I.D. of the bore. Remove the lock ring-and-primary piston assembly. Remove the secondary piston, secondary piston spring, and retainer by blowing air through the stop screw hole. Remove the primary seal, primary seal protector, and secondary seals from the secondary piston.

The brass tube fitting insert should not be removed unless visual inspection indicates the insert is damaged. To replace a defective insert, thread a No. 6=32 x 5|8" self-tapping screw into the tube-fitting insert. Using

the claw end of a hammer, remove the screw and insert.

CLEANING AND INSPECTING

Remove the casting from the vise and inspect the bore for corrosion, pits, and foreign matter. Be sure the outlet ports are clean. Inspect the fluid reservoirs for foreign matter. Check the bypass and compensating ports to the master cylinder bore to determine if they are unrestricted.

Use clean brake fluid to clean all reusable brake parts thoroughly. Immerse them in the cleaning fluid and brush metal parts to remove all foreign matter. Blow out all passages, orifices, and valve holes. Place cleaned parts on clean paper or lint-free clean cloth. If slight rust is found inside of either the front or rear half housing assemblies, polish with crocus cloth or fine emery paper, washing clean afterwards. **CAUTION: Be sure to keep parts clean until assembly. Rewash if there is any doubt of cleanliness. If there is any suspicion of contamination or any evidence of corrosion, completely flush the entire hydraulic brake system. Failure to clean the hydraulic brake system can result in early repetition of trouble. Use of gasoline, kerosene, anti-freeze, alcohol, or any other cleaner, with even a trace of mineral oil, will damage rubber parts.**

Always replace all rubber parts.

ASSEMBLING

If the brass tube inserts were removed, place the

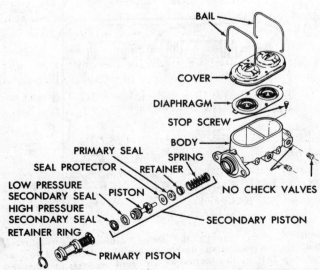

Exploded view of the split-braking system master cylinder.

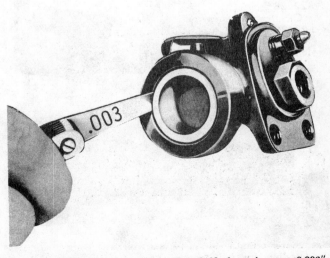

The wheel cylinder must be replaced if there is over 0.003" clearance between the piston and cylinder bore.

master cylinder in a vise so that the outlet holes are facing up. Position the new brass tube inserts in the outlet holes, making sure they are not cocked. Thread a spare brake line tube nut into each outlet and turn the nuts down until the insert bottoms. Remove the tube nut and check the outlet hole for loose brass burrs, which might have been turned up when the insert was pressed into position.

Place new secondary seals in the two grooves in the flat end of the secondary piston assembly. The seal which is nearest the flat end must have its lip facing toward this flat end. On Delco units, the seal in the second groove should have its lip facing toward the end of the secondary piston which contains the small compensating holes. On Bendix units, the seal in the second groove is an O-ring seal. Assemble a new primary seal and primary seal protector over the end of the secondary piston, opposite the secondary seals, so that the flat side of the seal seats against the flange of the piston which contains the small compensating holes.

In order to ensure a correct assembly of the primary piston assembly, a complete primary piston assembly is included in the repair kit.

Coat the bore of the master cylinder and the primary and secondary seals on the secondary piston with clean brake fluid. Insert the secondary piston spring retainer into the secondary piston spring. Place the retainer and spring down over the end of the secondary piston so that the retainer locates inside the lips of the primary seal. Holding the master cylinder with the open end of the bore up, push the secondary piston into the bore so that the spring seats against the closed end of the bore. Use a small wooden rod to push the secondary piston into its seat.

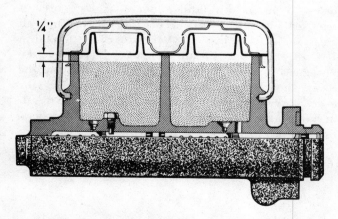

The master cylinder should be kept full of brake fluid during the bleeding process. The correct level is 1/4" below the top of the reservoir.

Coat the primary and secondary seals on the primary piston with clean brake fluid. Push the primary piston (secondary piston stop first) into the bore. Hold the piston down and snap the lock ring into position in the small groove in the I.D. of the bore. Continue to hold the primary piston down, which will also move the secondary piston forward and will insure that the secondary piston will be forward far enough to clear the stop screw hole, which is in the bottom of the front fluid reservoir. Install the stop screw and tighten it to a torque of 33 in-lbs.

Install the reservoir diaphragm in the reservoir cover and position the cover on the master cylinder. Assemble the bail wires into position to retain the reservoir cover. The master cylinder is now ready for "bench bleeding."

BENCH BLEEDING

Install plastic plugs in both outlet ports. Clamp the master cylinder in a bench vise, with the front end tilted down slightly. **CAUTION: Tighten the vise only enough to hold the reservoir securely; too much pressure will damage the master cylinder.** Fill both reservoirs with clean brake fluid.

Insert a rod with a smooth round end into the primary piston, and then press in to compress the piston return spring. Release pressure on the rod. Watch for air bubbles in the reservoir fluid. Repeat as long as bubbles appear.

INSTALLING

Assemble the push rod through the push rod retainer, if it has been disassembled. Push the retainer over the end of the master cylinder. Assemble a new boot over the push rod and press it down over the push rod retainer. Slide a new mounting gasket into position.

Secure the master cylinder to the dash panel with the mounting bolts. Connect the push rod clevis to the brake pedal with a pin and retainer. Connect the brake lines to the master cylinder.

BLEEDING THE HYDRAULIC SYSTEM

The hydraulic brake system must be bled whenever any line has been disconnected or air has entered the system. Bleeding of the brake system may be performed by one of two methods—either pressure or manual. Bleeder valves are provided at the calipers, wheel cylinders, and on some master cylinders.

It is advisable to bleed one valve at a time to avoid

allowing the fluid level in the reservoir to become dangerously low. The correct sequence is to bleed the valve (either front or rear system) nearest the master cylinder first. This sequence expels air from the lines and calipers or wheel cylinders nearest the master cylinder first and eliminates the possibility that air in a line close to the master cylinder may enter a line farther away after it has been bled.

To bleed the system, clean all dirt from the top of the master cylinder, and then remove the cylinder cover and rubber diaphragm. If pressure-bleeding equipment is to be used, install the brake bleeder adaptor on the master cylinder. *NOTE: Pressure-bleeding equipment must be of the diaphragm type. That is, it must have a rubber diaphragm between the air ...pply and the brake fluid to prevent air, moisture, ..., and dirt from entering the hydraulic system.* Connect a hose from the bleeder equipment to the bleeder adaptor, and then open the release valve on the bleeder equipment. On disc-brake cars, a combination metering, proportioning, and failure-warning switch is in the hydraulic system. It is mounted either on the frame rail or under the master cylinder. **CAUTION: This valve must be held in the open position**

This illustration shows pressure-bleeding equipment in place and use of the tool J-23709 to hold the metering valve depressed during the bleeding operation.

while bleeding. This can be accomplished by installing Tool J-23709, with the open slot under the mounting bolt and pushing in on the pin in the end of the valve, as shown.

Install a bleeder wrench on the caliper bleeder valve nearest the master cylinder, and then install one end of a bleeder hose on the bleeder valve. *NOTE: If the master cylinder is equipped with bleeder valves, bleed these first.* Pour enough brake fluid into a transparent container to ensure that the end of the bleeder hose will remain submerged. Place the loose end of the hose in the container. **CAUTION: Make sure the hose end is always submerged in fluid.**

Open the bleeder valve approximately 3/4 of a turn and observe the flow of fluid at the end of the bleeder hose. To assist in the bleeding operation, a rawhide mallet can be used to tap the caliper while fluid is flowing. Close the bleeder valve tight as soon as bubbles stop, and the brake fluid flows in a solid stream from the bleeder hose.

If you are not using pressure-bleeding equipment, have a helper depress the brake pedal. Just before the brake pedal reaches the end of its travel, close the bleeder valve tightly and allow the brake pedal to return slowly to the released position. Repeat until the expelled brake fluid flows in a solid stream, without air bubbles, and then close the bleeder valve tightly. **CAUTION: Carefully monitor the fluid level in the master cylinder. Do not allow the level to drop enough to expose the ports, which would allow air to enter the system.** Remove the wrench and hose from the bleeder valve. Repeat on the remaining bleeder valves.

Disconnect the bleeder equipment from the brake bleeder adaptor. **CAUTION: The master cylinder on some models is tilted. When removing the bleeder adaptor on these models, place a clean, dry cloth below it to absorb fluid spillage as the cover is removed.** Remove the bleeder adaptor. Wipe all areas dry. Fill the master cylinder reservoirs to within 1/4" of the rims. Install the master cylinder diaphragm and cover. **CAUTION: When installing the cover, the retaining bail must be slipped over the lower cover bosses. Incorrect installation could result in bail tension loss and fluid leakage.** Test the operation of the brake pedal before moving the vehicle.

9 | electrical system service

The service procedures covered in this chapter are: battery, charging, cranking, ignition, and lighting systems. A great deal of ignition system service procedures can be found in Chapter 2, with detailed ignition system troubleshooting tests in Chapter 1. The sections will be covered in the above order.

BATTERY

The battery is made up of a number of separate elements, each located in an individual cell in a hard-rubber case. Each element consists of an assembly of positive plates and negative plates containing dissimilar active materials and kept apart by separators. The elements are immersed in an electrolyte composed of dilute sulfuric acid. Plate straps, located on the top of each element, connect all the positive plates and all the negative plates into groups. The elements are connected in series electrically by connectors that pass directly through the case partitions between the

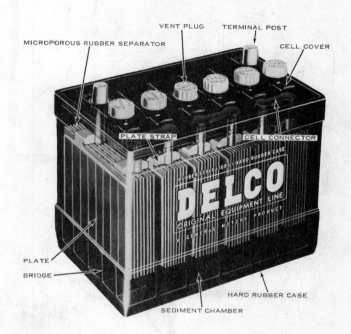

Parts of the battery.

Details of the battery (energizer) with side terminals used on late-model vehicles.

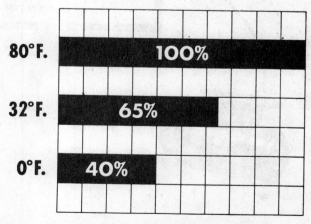

The capacity of a battery falls off rapidly with lower temperatures. At 0°F, a battery has only 40% of its 80°-capacity.

cells. The top is a one-piece cover. The cell connectors, passing through the cell partitions, connect the elements along the shortest practical path. With the length of the electrical circuit inside the battery reduced to a minimum, the internal voltage drop is decreased, resulting in improved performance, particularly during engine cranking at low temperatures.

A battery has two classifications of ratings: (1) a 20-hour rating at 80°F and, (2) a cold rating at 0°F which indicates the cranking load capacity. The ampere-hour

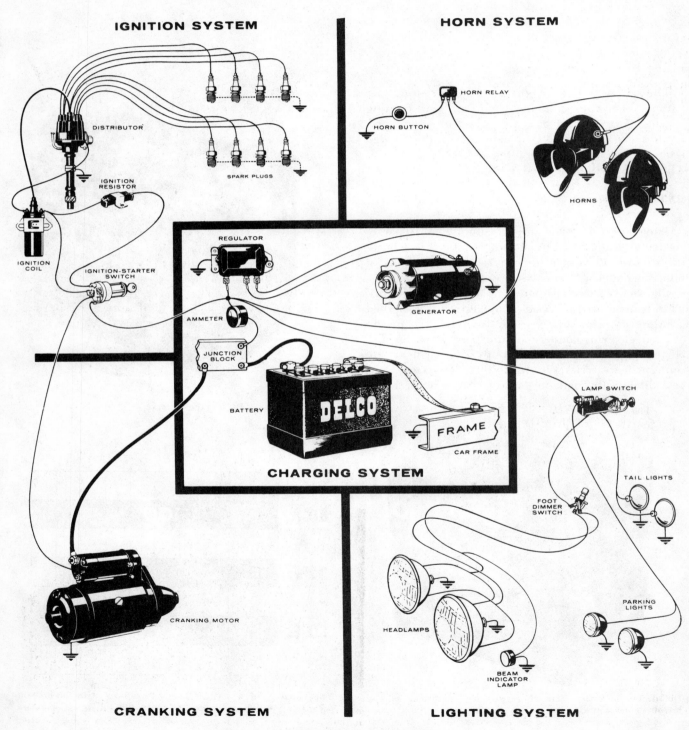

Typical electrical system of an automobile.

rating found on older batteries was based on the 20-hour rating. That is, a battery capable of furnishing three amperes for 20 hours, while maintaining a specified average individual cell voltage, would be classified as a 60-ampere hour battery (e.g., 3 amperes × 20 hours = 60 A.H.). A Peak Watt Rating (PWR) has been developed as a measure of the battery's cold-cranking ability. The numerical rating is embossed on each case at the base. This value is determined by multiplying the maximum current by the maximum voltage. The PWR should not be confused with the ampere-hour rating since two batteries with the same ampere-hour rating can have quite different PWR ratings. For battery replacement, a unit of at least equal power rating must be selected.

BATTERY SERVICE

Since the battery is a perishable item which requires periodic servicing, a good maintenance program will insure the longest possible life. If the unit tests good but fails to perform satisfactorily in service for no apparent reason, the following are some of the more important factors that may point to the cause of the trouble. (1) Vehicle accessories inadvertently left on overnight to cause a discharged condition. (2) Slow speed driving of short duration to cause an

A battery cell group consists of a set of positive plates, nestled together with a set of negative plates and kept apart by separators, which are porous to allow a free flow of electrolyte through them.

undercharged condition. (3) The vehicle electrical load exceeding the generator capacity. (4) A defect in the charging system such as high resistance, slipping fan belt, faulty generator, or voltage regulator. (5)

One of the greatest difficulties in the electric system is the maintenance of the correct operating voltage, and this, in turn, is dependent on minimizing resistance between connections in the charging circuit. One of the most important service procedures is the cleaning of the battery terminal posts and cable connections.

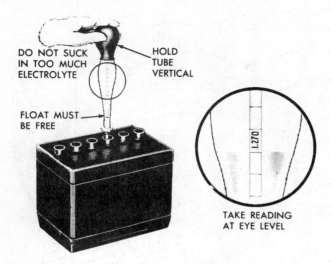

DO NOT SUCK IN TOO MUCH ELECTROLYTE

HOLD TUBE VERTICAL

FLOAT MUST BE FREE

1.270

TAKE READING AT EYE LEVEL

Checking the specific gravity with a hydrometer, as discussed in the text.

Battery abuse, including failure to keep the battery top clean, cable ends clean and tight, and improper addition of water to the cells.

ELECTROLYTE LEVEL

Late-model batteries feature an electrolyte-level indicator, which is a specially designed vent plug with a transparent rod extending through the center. When the electrolyte is at the proper level, the lower tip of the rod is immersed, and the exposed top of the rod appears very dark; when the level falls below the tip of the rod, the top glows. The level indicator is used only on the second cell cap from the positive terminal because, when the electrolyte level is low in one cell, it is generally low in all cells.

An alternate method of checking the electrolyte level is to remove the vent plug and visually observe the electrolyte level in the vent well. The bottom of the vent well features a split vent, which causes the surface of the electrolyte to appear distorted when it makes contact. The electrolyte level is correct when the distortion first appears at the bottom of the split vent.

The electrolyte level should be checked regularly. In hot weather, particularly during trip driving, checking should be more frequent because of more rapid loss of water. If the electrolyte level is found to be low, then colorless, odorless, drinking water should be added to each cell until the liquid level rises to the split vent located in the bottom of the vent well. **CAUTION: Do not overfill because this will cause loss of electrolyte, which will result in poor performance, short life, and excessive corrosion. CAUTION: Only water should be added to the battery, never electrolyte.**

The liquid level in the cells should never be allowed to drop below the top of the plates, as the portion of the plates exposed to air may be permanently damaged with a resulting loss in performance. Excessive usage

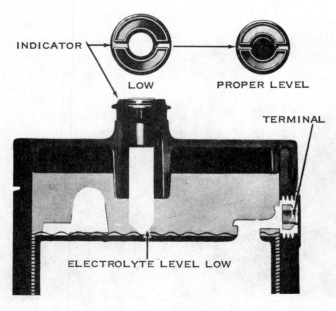

INDICATOR

LOW   PROPER LEVEL

TERMINAL

ELECTROLYTE LEVEL LOW

Late-model batteries have an indicator which tells the level of the electrolyte. When it is low, the indicator will glow white. A satisfactory level is shown in the inset to the right.

Sulfation results from a low water level. The top plate area is removed from active service by the insulating sulfated coating, cutting the battery capacity in half. This process cannot be reversed.

of water indicates the battery is being overcharged. The most common causes of overcharge are high battery operating temperatures, too high a voltage regulator setting, or a poor regulator ground wire connection. Normal battery water usage is approximately one to two ounces per month per battery.

CLEANING

The external condition of the battery should be checked periodically for damage or for the presence of dirt and corrosion. The battery should be kept clean. An accumulation of acid film and dirt can permit current to flow between the terminals, which will slowly discharge the battery. For best results when cleaning a battery, wash it first with a diluted ammonia or a soda solution to neutralize any acid present, then flush it with clean water. Care must be taken to keep the vent plugs tight so that the neutralizing solution does not enter the cells.

Clean the battery posts by scraping with a sharp-bladed tool or with a wire brush. Clean the inside of the cable clamps to make sure that they do not cause resistance. This is very important since a poor contact at the terminals adds resistance to the charging circuit and causes the voltage regulator to be "looking" at a

The results of overcharging are bent plates, crushed separators, and powered out tops of the positive plates.

fully charged battery; therefore, it calls for a reduced generator output to compound a battery problem.

TESTING

A hydrometer can be used to measure the specific gravity of the electrolyte in each cell. It measures the percentage of sulfuric acid in the battery electrolyte in terms of specific gravity. As a battery drops from a charged to a discharged condition, the acid leaves the solution and enters the plates, causing a decrease in specific gravity of the electrolyte.

When using a hydrometer, observe the following points: (1) The hydrometer must be clean, inside and out, to insure an accurate reading. (2) Hydrometer readings must never be taken immediately after water has been added. The water must be thoroughly mixed with the electrolyte by charging for at least 15 minutes at a rate high enough to cause vigorous gassing. (3) If the hydrometer has a built-in thermometer, draw liquid into it several times to insure correct temperature before taking a reading. (4) Hold the hydrometer vertically and draw in just enough liquid so that the float is free floating. (5) Hold the hydrometer at eye level so that the float is vertical and free of the outer tube, then take a reading at the surface of the liquid. Disregard the curvature where the liquid rises against the float stem due to surface tension. (6) Avoid dropping battery fluid on the car or your clothing as it is extremely corrosive. Any fluid that drops should be washed off immediately with water and neutralized with a baking soda solution.

The specific gravity of the electrolyte varies with the percentage of acid in the liquid and also with temperature. As temperature increases, the electrolyte expands so that the specific gravity is reduced. Unless these variations in specific gravity are taken into account, the specific gravity obtained by the hydrometer may not give a true indication of the concentration of acid in the electrolyte. A fully charged battery will have a specific gravity reading of approximately 1.270 at an electrolyte temperature of 80°F. If the electrolyte temperature is above or below 80°F., additions or subtractions must be made in order to obtain a hydrometer reading corrected to the 80°F. standard. For every 10° above 80°F., add four specific gravity points (0.004) to the hydrometer reading. Example: A hydrometer reading of 1.260 at 110°F. would be 1.272 corrected to 80°F., indicating a fully charged battery. For every 10° below 80°F., subtract four points (0.004) from the reading. Example: A hydrometer reading of 1.272 at 0°F. would be 1.240 corrected to 80°F., indicating a partially charged battery.

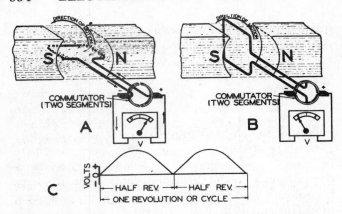

Generation of pulsating DC current, as discussed in the text.

rotates, one side of the loop passes a *north* magnetic pole. During the second half of the rotating cycle, it passes a *south* magnetic pole.

The direction of current flow in the loop is reversed at each half turn. If the current is taken from the rotating loop by means of slip rings, the generator produces AC current; if it is removed by a commutator, it produces DC current.

Generators are designed to produce DC current. This is accomplished by using a commutator to which the rotating loops are connected. A pair of diametrically opposed brushes picks up the current generated in the rotating loops in the form of pulsating DC current. The commutator is composed of a series of insulated brass strips to which the armature loops are connected. It operates by connecting each brush first to one end of a revolving loop, and then to the other, just as the voltage is reversing in the loop. Therefore, the current delivered to the external circuit is always in the same direction. The commutator is, in effect, a reversing switch.

CHARGING SYSTEM

Through 1962, all G.M. products used a generator to develop electrical energy for the ignition and lighting system, as well as for the accessories. The excess was used to charge the battery. Since then an alternator (Delcotron) has been used, and this has been improved in 1969 with the 10SI Series unit, which has a solid-state regulator mounted inside of the alternator.

GENERATORS

A generator produces electricity because a coil of wire is moved across a magnetic field. The coil is in the armature and the field is produced by the pole pieces located in the generator housing. As the coil

GENERATOR REGULATORS

Shunt-type generators have no control of their output. The faster they are driven, the more the output. Unless externally controlled, they would soon burn up. The current produced by the generator is dependent on the number of turns of wire that are wound around each armature coil, the strength of the magnetic field, and the speed of rotation. To control the output of the generator, the strength of the magnetic field is varied by a regulator.

To control the externally grounded type of generator used on all G.M. vehicles, a resistance is inserted or shorted out of the field circuit by a vibrating relay. When the resistance is in the circuit, the magnetic

By increasing the number of rotating loops, the voltage variations can be minimized.

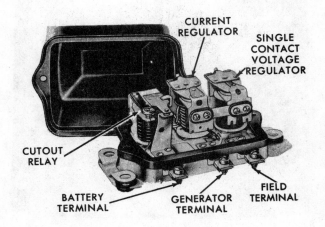

Single-contact type regulator.

flux of the field is relatively weak, causing the generator output to drop. When the resistance is shorted out of the circuit, the magnetic flux of the field is increased and the generator charges at a maximum rate. In operation, the relay vibrates, varying the energy in the field circuit according to the needs of the battery.

As a battery becomes charged, its resistance increases. To overcome this added resistance in the charging circuit, the generator output rises. When the output voltage reaches the calibrated setting of the voltage regulator, it begins to vibrate and limits the field strength, and thus the generator output. Whenever the system voltage rises high enough to cause the unit to operate, the regulator holds the voltage constant at the calibrated value.

In addition to voltage control, a current-limiting relay is used to keep the output of the generator to a safe value. It is also of the vibrating type and its contact points similarly short out or insert a resistance in the generator field circuit. Because the current regulator's core is wound with a few turns of heavy wire, it is designed to be sensitive to current variations, operating when the current reaches a predetermined value.

In addition to the two vibrating controls, all regulators contain a circuit breaker to connect the generator into the charging circuit when the generator is producing electricity and to disconnect it when the generator stops rotating. If this were not done, the battery current would reverse itself and flow into the generator during the time that the engine is stopped. This would soon discharge the battery.

GENERATOR SERVICE PROCEDURES

Generally, the carbon brushes wear and should be replaced before they become too short, causing intermittent contact with the commutator. This causes arcing, which will result in increased operating voltage to burn out the generator. High-resistance connections in the charging circuit also cause higher operating voltages, leading to generator destruction.

An exploded view of a Delco Remy generator is provided for servicing these units. However, most are replaced with a rebuilt generator. After installing a rebuilt generator, it is essential to polarize the unit before the engine is started. This can be done by momentarily connecting a jumper lead between the GEN and BAT terminals of the regulator. **CAUTION: Failure to do this will result in damage to the regulator.**

REGULATOR SERVICE PROCEDURES

Generally, defective regulators are replaced as the cost is nominal. Anytime the generator fails because

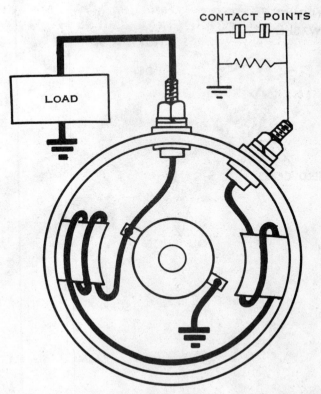

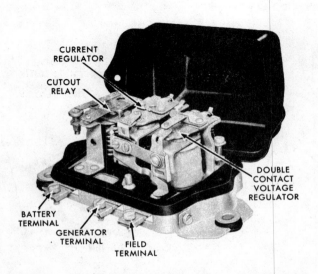

CURRENT REGULATOR

CUTOUT RELAY

DOUBLE CONTACT VOLTAGE REGULATOR

BATTERY TERMINAL

GENERATOR TERMINAL

FIELD TERMINAL

Double-contact type regulator used on heavy-duty equipment.

CONTACT POINTS

LOAD

In its basic form, the regulator grounds one end of the field circuit to energize the generator. The voltage and current regulator points are wired in series, so that the field strength is reduced whenever either one vibrates to insert resistance into the field circuit.

This arcing is caused by sticky brushes, and this soon leads to the destruction of the generator.

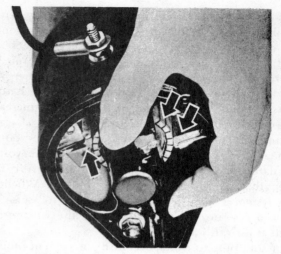

An important generator service is to inspect the brushes. If they are worn or sticky, the charging system voltage will increase and cause other electrical units to burn out.

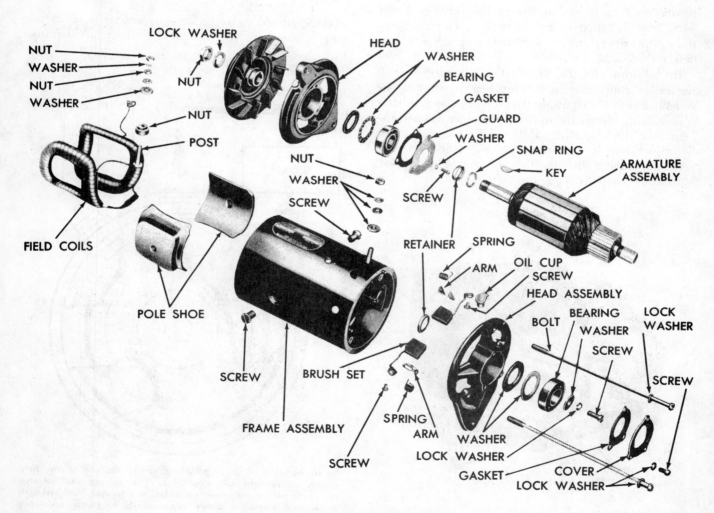

Parts of a typical generator.

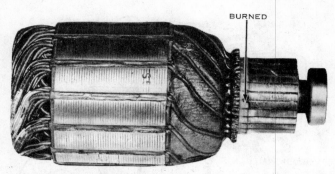

Note how one commutator segment is burned. This is caused by the solder melting out at that winding by overloading (high voltage due to high resistance connections).

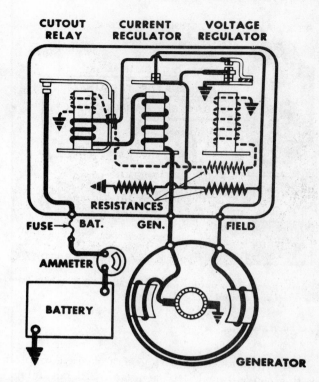

Actual schematic wiring diagram of a heavy-duty, double-contact regulator and generator.

of overheating, it is advisable to replace the regulator with it because it failed to control the output. **CAUTION: Anytime the generator fails in this manner, it is essential that you locate and repair the high-resistance connection in the charging circuit which is causing the trouble.**

To determine whether a charging system defect is in the generator or regulator, disconnect the field lead from the F-terminal of a single-contact type regulator and ground it to the regulator base. If the output increases more than 2 amperes, oxidized regulator contact points are indicated. If the output does not increase, the generator is at fault and must be replaced. Oxidized regulator points can be cleaned and the voltage adjusted, but frequently the regulator is replaced with a new one.

In charging circuits where a voltage regulator having two sets of contacts is used, it is quite important never to ground the generator or regulator field terminal when these units are connected or operating together. To do so, will result in burning up the upper set of voltage regulator contacts. It is necessary to test such a regulator with proper test equipment.

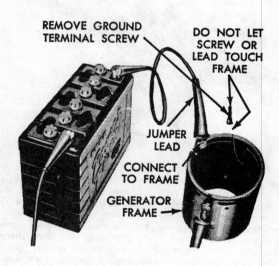

The field windings must not be grounded, and the test can be made in this manner.

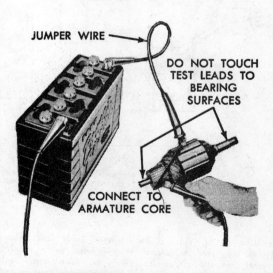

The armature commutator must not be grounded, and the test can be made in this manner.

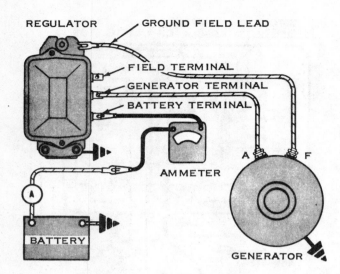

To make a generator output test with a single-contact regulator, disconnect and ground the field, as discussed in the text.

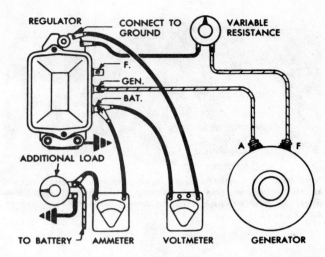

Generator output check with a double-contact type regulator. CAUTION: You cannot ground the field in this type of circuit without burning up the double-contact point set.

ALTERNATORS

The alternator is an AC generator used in place of the conventional DC generator. Its advantages include a higher charging rate, lower cut-in charging speed, lighter weight, and longer trouble-free service. The alternator differs from the conventional generator in that the armature is the stationary member, called the stator, while the field is the rotating member, called the rotor. An advantage of this type of construction is that the higher current values carried by the stator are conducted to the external circuit through fixed leads, rather than through a rotating commutator and brushes, as must be done in the DC generator. The relatively small current supplied to the fields

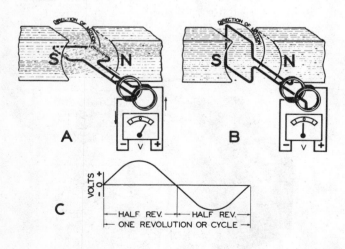

Generation of AC voltage. In its most basic form, the stator is a coil of wire, which is shown here as a single loop. (Naturally, in the alternator, there are many such coils.) As the magnetic field from the spinning rotor cuts across this wire, an electrical voltage is produced in the loop. The faster the rotor turns, the greater will be the generated voltage.

The rotor of an alternator consists of the field winding, two iron segments with interlacing fingers called poles, the shaft, and two slip rings. The slip rings, on which the brushes ride, are connected to the leads from the field coil. When the ignition switch is first closed, current from the battery passes through one brush, through the slip ring, and then through the field coil; from whence it returns to the battery through the other slip ring, brush, and ground circuit. This flow of current forms a north magnetic pole at each pole of one rotor segment and a south magnetic pole at each pole of the other segment. As the rotor turns, a spinning magnetic field is produced.

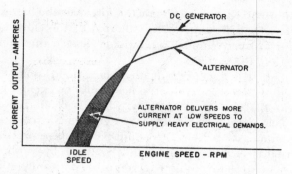

Alternator output curve as compared with that of a conventional DC generator. Note the improved output of the alternator at low speeds.

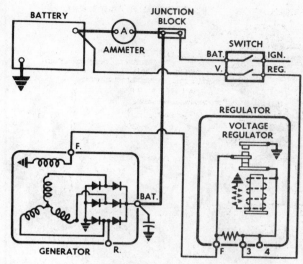

can be conducted through small brushes and rotating slip rings with trouble-free ease.

The alternator charging circuit consists of the battery, alternator, voltage regulator, ignition switch, ammeter, and charging circuit wiring, with the return through the vehicle frame. Many models use a charge indicator lamp in place of the ammeter, in which case a charge indicator light relay is required in the regulator.

The alternator employs a three-phase stator winding in which the windings are phased electrically 120° apart. The rotor consists of a field coil encased between two four- or six-pole, interleaved sections, producing an eight- or twelve-pole magnetic field with alternate north and south poles. The rotation of the rotor inside the stator induces an alternating current (AC) in the stator windings, which is rectified (changed into DC) by six silicon diodes and brought out to the output terminal of the alternator.

To control the alternator's output, a vibrating-type voltage regulator is connected into the field circuit in a manner similar to that of the conventional shunt-type DC generator. No current regulator is required as the alternator is basically a self-regulating type machine. No cut-out relay is required because the diodes, that are connected in the battery circuit, pass current in only one direction. This circuit is typical of many G.M. products, in which a single unit controls the generator and an ammeter is used to indicate the output. Alternator regulators will be discussed more thoroughly in the next section of the book.

The silicon diode rectifiers act as electrical one-way valves. Three are polarized one way and are pressed into an aluminum heat sink (to carry away the heat), which is grounded to the slip ring end head. The other three diodes are polarized the opposite way and are pressed into a similar heat sink, which is insulated from the end head and connected to the alternator output terminal. Since a diode has high

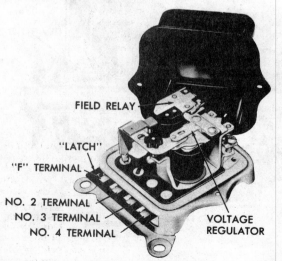

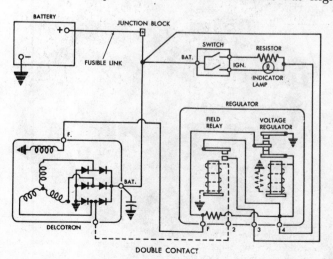

Double-contact type regulator and its schematic wiring diagram used with the 1D Delcotron.

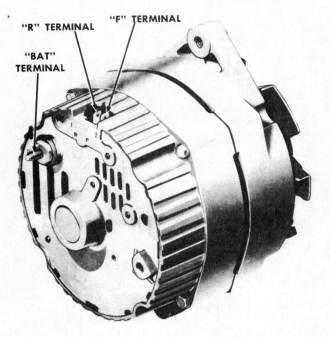

"R" TERMINAL

"F" TERMINAL

"BAT" TERMINAL

In 1972, a 10DN Series Delcotron was used on many engines to replace the 1D series type. Note that the relay and field terminals are taken out of the top. This unit uses the same double-contact vibrating regulator as the earlier model Delcotron.

resistance to the flow of electricity in one direction and passes current with very little resistance in the opposite direction, it is connected in a manner which allows current to flow from the alternator to the battery in the low-resistance direction. The high resistance in the opposite direction prevents the battery current from flowing to the alternator, therefore no circuit breaker (cutout) is required between the alternator and the battery.

Residual magnetism in the rotor field poles is negligible and, therefore, the field must be excited by an external source, the battery, which is connected to the field winding through the ignition switch and regulator. As in the DC shunt-type generator, the alternator charging voltage is regulated by varying the field strength. This is accomplished through the use of a voltage regulator unit. No current regulator is required since the alternator has self-limiting current characteristics.

DELCOTRON 10-SI SERIES

This series is similar to past models, but it has a solid-state regulator built right in the end frame. The stator windings are assembled on the inside of a laminated core that forms part of the generator frame. A rectifier bridge is connected to the stator windings; it contains six diodes (three positive and three negative) molded into an assembly which is connected to the stator windings. The rectifier bridge changes the stator AC voltages into DC voltages, which appear at the output terminal. The blocking action of the diodes prevent battery discharge back through the Delcotron. Because of this action, there is no need for a cutout relay in the charging circuit.

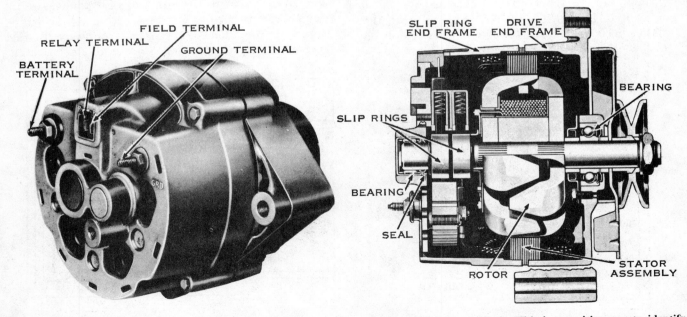

FIELD TERMINAL

RELAY TERMINAL

GROUND TERMINAL

BATTERY TERMINAL

SLIP RING END FRAME

DRIVE END FRAME

BEARING

SLIP RINGS

BEARING

SEAL

ROTOR

STATOR ASSEMBLY

Parts of the 1D Delcotron. Note the terminal in the rear plate for the relay and field terminals. This is a positive way to identify this early model.

THEORY OF OPERATION

When the switch is closed, current from the energizer flows to the generator No. 1 terminal, through resistor R1, diode D1, and the base-emitter of transistor TR1 to ground, and then back to the battery. This turns on transistor TR1, and current flows through the generator field coil and TR1 back to the energizer. The indicator lamp then turns on. The resistor in parallel with the indicator lamp reduces total circuit resistance to provide higher field current for initial voltage build-up when the engine starts.

With the generator operating, AC voltage is generated in the stator windings, and the stator supplies DC field current through the diode trio, the field, TR1, and then through the grounded diodes in the rectifier bridge back to the stator. Also, the six diodes in the rectifier bridge change the stator AC voltages to a DC voltage which appears between ground and the generator "BAT" terminal. As generator speed increases, current is provided for charging the energizer and operating electrical accessories. Also, with the generator operating, the same voltage appears at the "BAT" and No. 1 terminals, and the indicator lamp goes out to indicate the generator is producing voltage.

The No. 2 terminal on the generator is always connected to the energizer, but the discharge current is limited to a negligible value by the high resistances of R2 and R3. As the generator speed and voltage increase, the voltage between R2 and R3 increases to the point where Zener diode D2 conducts. Transistor TR2 then turns on and TR1 turns off. With TR1 off, the field current and system voltage decrease and D2

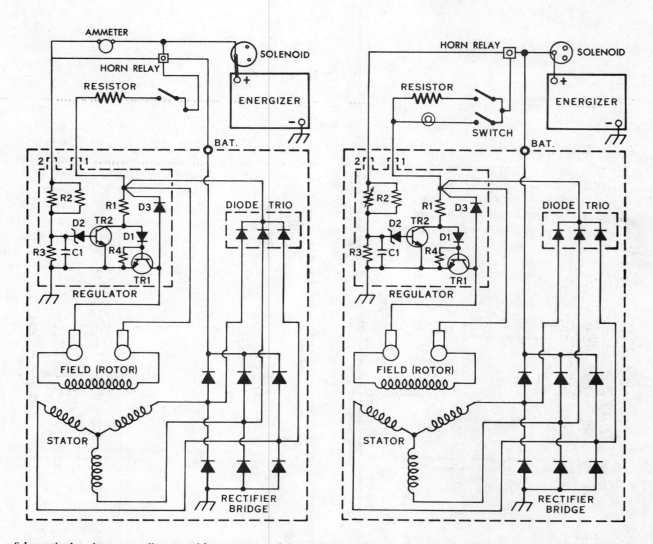

Schematic charging system diagram with an ammeter (left) and indicator lamp (right) as used on the 1973 10SI Series Delcotron.

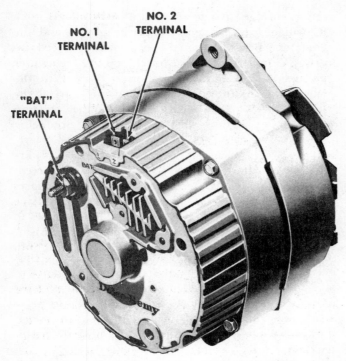

"BAT" TERMINAL

NO. 1 TERMINAL

NO. 2 TERMINAL

In 1973, a 10SI Series Delcotron was introduced for many models. It has a solid-state regulator built into the end frame. Note how the No. 1 and No. 2 terminal contacts differ from the 10DN Series unit.

then blocks current flow, causing TR1 to turn back on. The field current and system voltage increase, and this cycle then repeats many times per second to limit the generator voltage to a preset value.

Capacitor C1 smooths out the voltage across R3, resistor R4 prevents excessive current through TR1 at high temperatures, and diode D3 prevents high-induced voltages in the field windings when TR1 turns off.

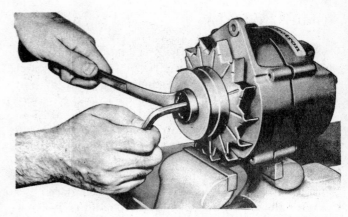

To remove the pulley on a Delcotron, place a 15/16" box wrench on the retaining nut. Insert a 5/16" Allen wrench into the shaft to hold it while you remove the nut. When installing the nut, tighten it to 50 ft-lbs of torque.

SERVICE PROCEDURES

Service Precautions

(1) Reversed battery connections will damage the diodes. Battery polarity must be checked with a voltmeter before any connections are made to make sure that the connections correspond to the vehicle battery ground polarity. (2) The field circuit between the alternator and the regulator must never be grounded; otherwise, the regulator will be damaged. (3) Grounding the alternator output terminal will damage the alternator and/or wiring. This is true even when the engine is not in operation since no circuit breaker is used, and battery current is applied to the alternator output terminal at all times. (4) The alternator must not be operated on an open circuit with the field

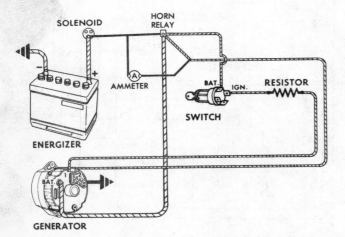

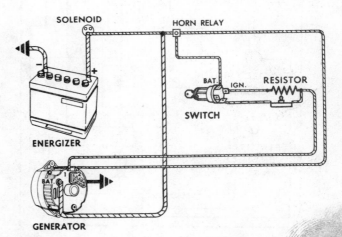

Basic wiring diagrams with an ammeter (left) and indicator lamp (right) as used with the 1973 10SI Series Delcotron.

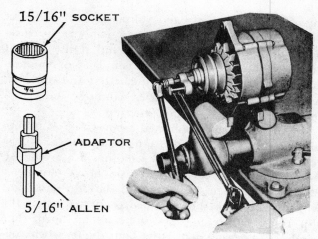

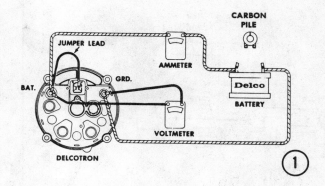

To remove a double-groove pulley, use an adaptor, J-21501, and a box wrench on the retaining nut. Insert a 5/16″ Allen wrench through the adaptor to hold the shaft while you remove the nut. When installing the nut, tighten it to 50 ft-lbs of torque.

winding energized, or the unit will be damaged. (5) Do not attempt to polarize the alternator as it is never required. Any attempt to do so will result in damage to the alternator, regulator, or wiring. (6) Do not short the bending tool to the regulator base when adjusting the voltage, or the unit will be damaged. The bending tool should be insulated by tape, or an

insulating plastic sleeve. (7) If booster batteries are to be used for starting, they must be connected properly to prevent damage to the diodes. The negative (−) cable from the booster battery must be connected to the negative terminal of the vehicle battery, and the positive (+) booster cable to the positive terminal. Always disconnect the battery ground strap before replacing an alternator or connecting any meter to it. (8) When a fast charger is to be used to charge the battery, the vehicle battery cables must be disconnected. The fast charger must never be used as a booster for starting the engine. Failure to observe these precautions will result in damage to the diodes.

SERVICING THE DELCOTRON

Output Test

① To check a Delcotron generator for output, connect a jumper lead from the generator output or "BAT" terminal to the field or "F" terminal, a voltmeter from the "BAT" terminal to ground, and an ammeter in the circuit at the "BAT" terminal. If two

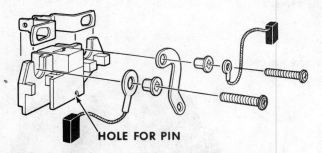

Exploded view of the brush holder of the Delcotron.

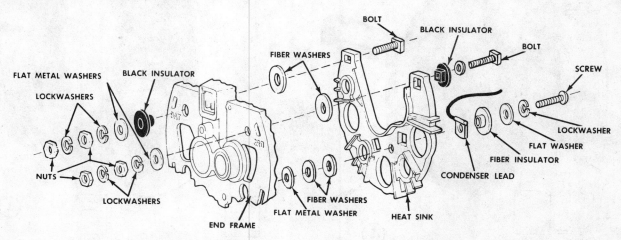

Exploded view of the heat sink used on early Delcotrons.

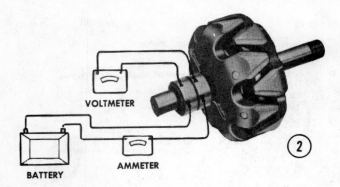

VOLTMETER

BATTERY

AMMETER

②

terminals are present, ground the other field terminal with a jumper lead. Operate the generator at the specified speed, adjust the variable load connected across the battery to obtain the specified voltage, and observe the current output. If the output does not meet specifications, disassemble the generator for checks of the rotor. stator, and diodes.

When measuring the Delcotron output on late-model vehicles, all accessories should be turned off and the heater-A/C blower motor lead disconnected. If this is not done, part of the Delcotron output goes to the blower motor and is not recorded on the am-meter, which only senses current going through the battery post adaptor. This will be most noticeable on automatic A/C cars because the blower draws 10 amperes in the low position.

Rotor

② The rotor windings may be checked by connect-

ing a battery, ammeter and voltmeter to the edge of the slip rings. If the current draw is above specifica-tions, the windings are shorted, and if the current draw is low, excessive resistance is indicated. An ohm-meter may be used in place of the battery and ammeter. A low resistance indiates shorted windings, and a high resistance an open or poor connection.

③ An ohmmeter connected from either slip ring to the shaft should show a high resistance. A low resistance indicates the field windings are grounded. A test light may be used in place of an ohmmeter to check for opens and grounds, but the test light will not check for shorts. When connected across the slip rings, failure to light indicates an open. The windings are grounded if the lamp lights when con-nected from either slip ring to the shaft.

Stator

④ Checks on the stator should be made with all diodes disconnected from the stator. It is not practical to check the stator for shorts due to the very low resistance of the windings. Also, it is not practical to check the delta stator for opens because the windings are connected in parallel. To check the Y-connected stator for open circuits, connect an ohmmeter or test light across any two pairs of terminals. A high ohm-meter reading, or no light, will reveal an open

(CHECK FOR GROUNDS)
OHMMETER

③

OHMMETER
(CHECK FOR SHORTS AND OPENS)

(CHECK FOR OPENS)
OHMMETER

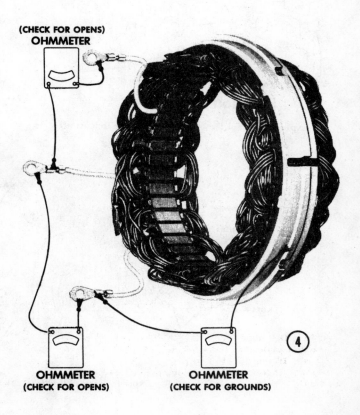

④

OHMMETER
(CHECK FOR OPENS)

OHMMETER
(CHECK FOR GROUNDS)

winding. Either type of stator winding may be checked for grounds by connecting an ohmmeter or test light from either terminal to the stator frame. The windings are grounded if the ohmmeter reads low, or if the lamp lights. If all checks are satisfactory, including the diode tests listed below, but the generator fails to provide rated output, a shorted Y-connected or delta stator winding, or an open delta winding, can be suspected.

Diodes

⑤ Diodes, when disconnected from the stator, can be checked for defects with an ohmmeter having a 1-1/2 volt cell. Using the lowest range scale, connect the ohmmeter leads to the diode case and the diode stem, and then reverse the connections. On push-in type diodes, if both readings are very low, the diode is shorted. If both readings are very high, the diode is open circuited. On threaded-type diodes, if both readings are below 300 ohms, or if both readings are above 300 ohms, the diode is defective. The 300 ohm value should be near mid-scale for accuracy. A good

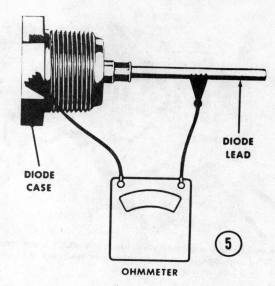

diode will give one very low and one very high reading. **CAUTION: Do not use high voltage such as a 110 volt test light to check diodes, or you will burn them out.**

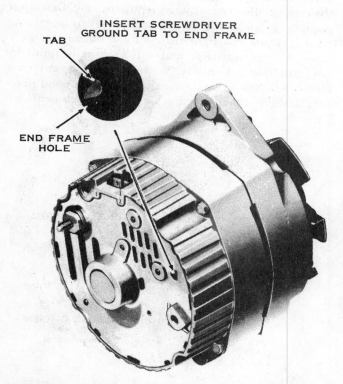

The 10S1 Delcotron has a field-shorting tab located in a hole of the end plate for grounding the field in order to check the regulator. If shorting the field to ground with a screwdriver causes the Delcotron to function, then the integral regulator is at fault.

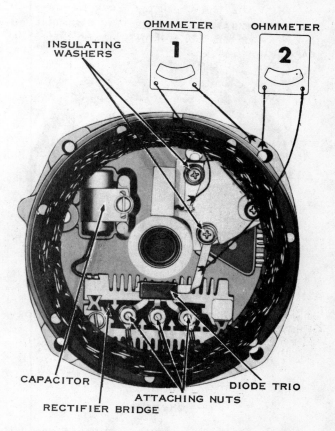

Checking the brush lead clips for continuity on the 10S1 Delcotron.

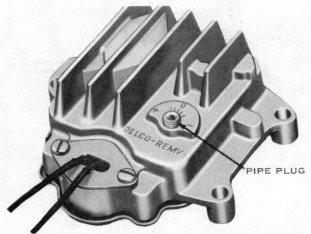

The transistorized regulator used sometime ago has no moving parts. The adjustment screw for raising or lowering the operating voltage is located under the pipe plug.

ALTERNATOR REGULATORS

All alternators have the field excitation current supplied through the ignition switch, through the voltage regulator relay winding, and thence to the field, which is grounded internally. The alternator field strength is controlled by the vibrating voltage regulator points and this, in turn, varies the output of the charging system in accordance with the needs of the electrical system.

Because of the low cost involved, regulators are often replaced rather than serviced. Late-model systems have solid-state regulators which are not adjustable.

Voltage Regulator Buzz

Complaints of a buzzing voltage regulator on GM cars equipped with a side-terminal battery have been traced to a loose battery cable at the battery terminal. The loose connection results in an unstable voltage. This, in turn, sets up a vibration of the regulator armature. Due to the plastic insulators at the battery connections, the cables may appear to be tight. Insure good connections with a torque wrench and tighten the cable bolts to approximately 90 in-lbs of torque.

Loose Delcotron Lead

When diagnosing electrical failures, such as a dead battery or defective voltage regulator, the Delcotron battery terminal nut should be checked to determine that it is properly tightened. A loose nut may cause a noisy voltage regulator and will eventually result in an undercharged battery. When performing any type of work in the engine compartment, it is a good practice to check this connection for proper attachment.

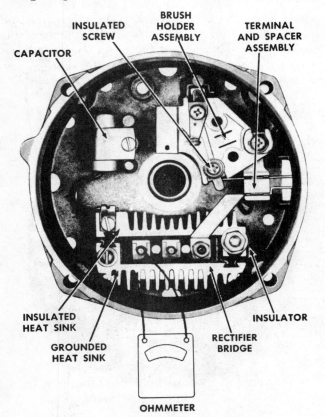

Checking the diodes on the 10DN type Delcotron, since 1972. These diodes are not serviced separately. **CAUTION: Do not ground No. 2 lead or you will burn up the regulator.**

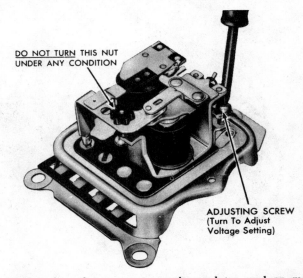

Adjusting the voltage on a two-unit regulator used on most alternator charging circuits, except the 10SI Delcotron, with an integral regulator. The voltage should be adjusted to 13.5-14.2 volts with the regulator at an operating temperature of 105°

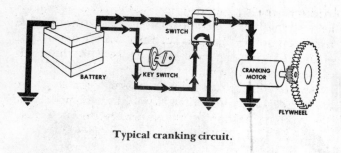

Typical cranking circuit.

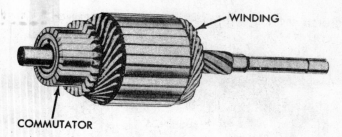

Details of the cranking motor armature. Note the copper ribbons, which are needed because of the large amount of current that must flow.

CRANKING SYSTEM

The cranking system includes the cranking motor and drive, battery, solenoid, ignition switch, and the necessary cables and wires to connect the components. Vehicles with an automatic transmission have a neutral-start switch which prevents operation of the starting motor unless the selector lever is in NEUTRAL or PARK. Vehicles with a standard transmission have a similar safety-start switch on the clutch pedal.

CONSTRUCTION

The cranking motor is made up of a set of field coils placed over pole pieces, which are attached to the inside of a heavy iron frame, an armature, an overrunning clutch drive mechanism, and a solenoid.

The armature consists of a stack of iron laminations placed over a steel shaft, a commutator, and the armature winding. The windings are heavy copper ribbon that are assembled into slots in the iron laminations. The winding ends are soldered or welded to the commutator bars, which are electrically insulated from each other and from the iron shaft.

The overrunning clutch drive contains a pinion which is made to move along the shaft by means of a shift lever to engage the engine ring gear for cranking. A gear reduction is provided between the pinion and ring gear to meet the cranking requirements of the engine. With this gear reduction, the motor operates to crank the engine at speeds required for starting.

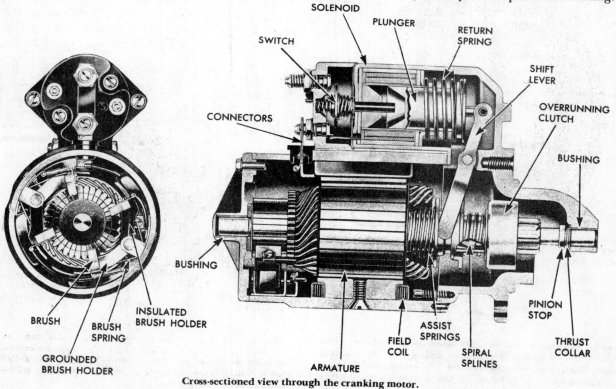

Cross-sectioned view through the cranking motor.

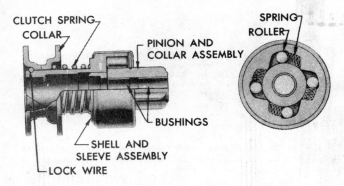

Details of the overrunning clutch assembly. CAUTION: Don't wash this part in solvent, or you will dissolve the lubricant and it will seize.

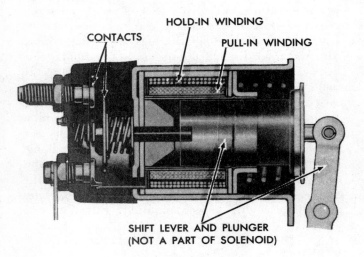

Cross-sectioned view through the solenoid.

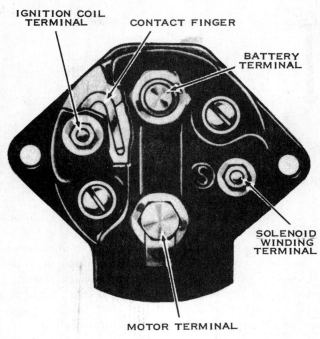

Sectioned view of the back end of the solenoid to show the contact finger which shorts out the resistance wire to the ignition coil during the cranking phase for higher voltages to the ignition system.

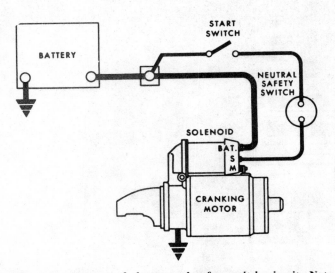

Schematic diagram of the neutral safety switch circuit. Note that the solenoid cannot get current unless the safety switch is closed. This switch is located on the clutch pedal on a manual-transmission vehicle, or in the selector linkage on a vehicle with an automatic transmission.

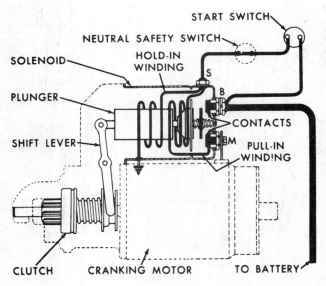

Solenoid windings, which are used to pull the overrunning clutch into position as well as to make contact between the battery and cranking motor.

The overrunning clutch drive has a shell and sleeve assembly, which is splined internally to match the spiral splines on the armature shaft. The pinion is located inside the shell along with spring-loaded rollers that are wedged against the pinion and a taper inside the shell. The springs may be either helical or accordion type. Four rollers are used. A collar and spring, located over the sleeve, are the other major clutch components.

When the shift lever is operated by the solenoid, it moves the collar endwise along the shaft. The spring pushes the pinion into mesh with the ring gear. If a tooth abutment occurs, the spring compresses until the switch is closed, at which time the armature rotates and the tooth abutment is cleared. The compressed spring then pushes the pinion into mesh and cranking begins. Torque is transmitted from the shell to the pinion by the rollers, which are wedged tightly between the pinion and the taper cut into the shell.

When the engine starts, the ring gear drives the pinion faster than the armature, and the rollers move away from the taper, allowing the pinion to overrun the shell. The start switch should be opened immediately when the engine starts to avoid prolonged overrun. When the shift lever is moved back by the return spring, the pinion moves out of mesh and the cranking cycle is completed.

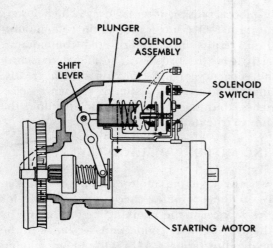

DISENGAGED

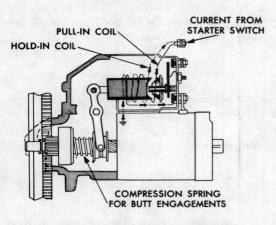

PINION PARTIALLY ENGAGED

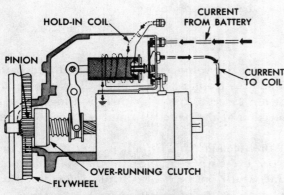

PINION FULLY ENGAGED AND STARTING MOTOR CRANKING

Action of the cranking motor solenoid during the three operating phases.

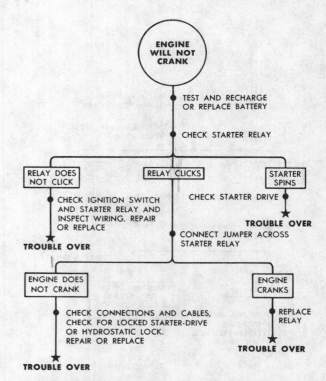

Roadmap for troubleshooting a cranking motor that does not crank the engine.

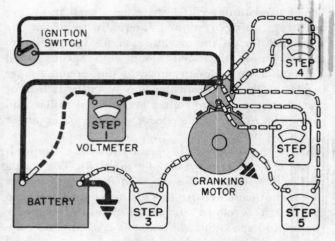

Cranking motor voltage test that are discussed in the text.

CRANKING MOTOR SERVICE PROCEDURES

Because the cranking motor drive-end bushing is inaccessible, it receives no lubrication while the commutator-end bushing sometimes receives too much. The result is that the drive-end bushing wears, allowing the armature to drop down and rub against the field pole pieces, causing internal drag which lowers the output torque. Overlubrication of the commutator-end bushing results in an oil-covered commutator, insulating it from the brushes. The added resistance lowers the efficiency of the cranking system greatly.

Cranking motor service consists of replacing defective switches, bushings, brushes, and turning the commutator to true it up.

CRANKING MOTOR VOLTAGE TESTS

Although the cranking motor cannot be checked accurately on the engine, a check can be made for excessive resistance in the cranking motor circuit by making the five voltmeter connections as shown in the accompanying illustration. **CAUTION: Before making these checks, ground the primary lead to the distributor to keep the engine from starting.** Then measure the voltage drop across each part of the circuit with the engine being cranked as follows:

STEP 1

Connect the voltmeter across the insulated battery post and the solenoid battery terminal. The voltage (loss) must not exceed 0.2 volt, or there is a high-resistance connection at the battery terminal or the cable is too thin.

STEP 2

Connect the voltmeter across the solenoid battery terminal and the solenoid motor terminal. The voltage (loss) must not exceed 0.2 volt, or the solenoid contacts have high resistance.

STEP 3

Connect the voltmeter across the grounded battery post and the cranking motor frame. The voltage (loss) must not exceed 0.2 volt, or there is a high-resistance connection at the battery ground terminal or ground strap.

If the solenoid fails to pull in, the trouble can be due to excessive resistance in the solenoid-control circuit, which can be checked with two addition tests, as follows:

STEP 4

Connect the voltmeter across the solenoid battery terminal and the solenoid switch terminal. The voltage (loss) must not exceed 2.4 volts on a 12-volt system

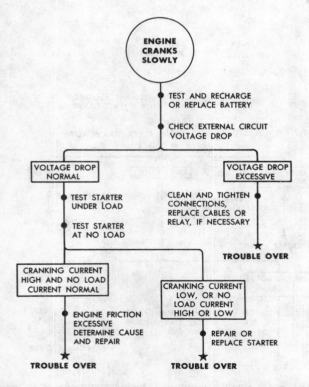

Roadmap for troubleshooting a cranking motor that cranks the engine too slowly.

or 0.75 volt on a 6-volt system, or excessive resistance is indicated in the solenoid-control circuit.

STEP 5

If the voltage loss in the previous test did not exceed 2.5 volts and the solenoid did not pull in, connect the voltmeter across the solenoid switch terminal and ground. The solenoid should pull in if the voltmeter reading is 7.7 volts or more; if it doesn't, replace the solenoid.

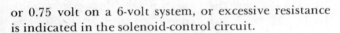

CRANKING MOTOR SERVICE

OVERHAULING A CRANKING MOTOR

Use the exploded view as a guide to disassemble and assemble the cranking motor. The following step-by-step illustrated instructions are provided as a guide for testing the various parts of the cranking motor.

① Test the field on units containing a shunt winding by disconnecting the field from the connector bar and then test the circuit; there must be continuity.

② Test the field on units containing a series winding by touching one test prod to the case and the other to the main terminal. There must be continuity.

③ Test the series field winding for ground by touching one test prod to the case and the other to the main terminal; the test lamp must not light.

④ Always replace the drive-end bushing.

BUSHING

DRIVE-END HOUSING

HACKSAW BLADE

(5)

⑤ True the commutator in a lathe. Don't undercut the mica because the brushes are harder than the insulation. Test the armature on a growler. The hacksaw blade must not vibrate, or there is a shorted winding coil. Test the armature for grounded windings.

⑥ Wash the brush holder in solvent, blow it dry, and then use a continuity tester to see that two of the brush holders are grounded and two are insulated.

⑦ The overrunning clutch is secured to the armature by a snap ring, which can be removed if the clutch needs to be replaced. **CAUTION: Never wash an overrunning clutch in solvent, or you will dissolve the lubricant, and it will soon fail.** When it does, the engine will drive the cranking motor armature at a high rate of speed, and the windings will be thrown out by centrifugal force.

⑧ Measure the pinion clearance by energizing the solenoid coil with a 6-volt battery. **CAUTION: Don't use a 12-volt battery or the armature will turn.** With the solenoid energized, push the pinion back to take up the slack, and the clearance must be between 0.010-0.140″. If it is not, the solenoid is not properly installed, or the linkage is worn.

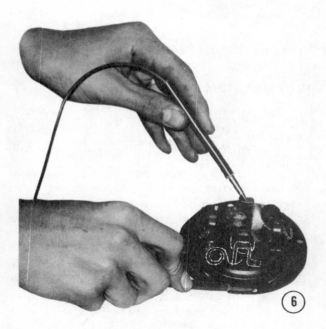

(6)

(7)

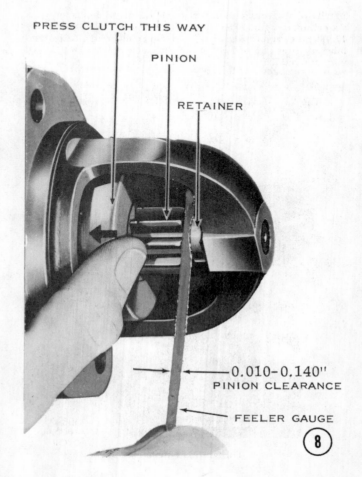

PRESS CLUTCH THIS WAY

PINION

RETAINER

0.010-0.140″
PINION CLEARANCE

FEELER GAUGE

(8)

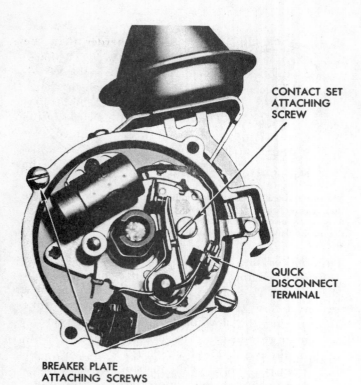

CONTACT SET ATTACHING SCREW

QUICK DISCONNECT TERMINAL

BREAKER PLATE ATTACHING SCREWS

Details of the contact point plate of the distributor used on a six-cylinder engine. The cam lubricator must be rotated every 12,000 miles and replaced every 24,000 miles. CAUTION: Don't lubricate it or you will get oil on the contact points, which will burn and oxidize.

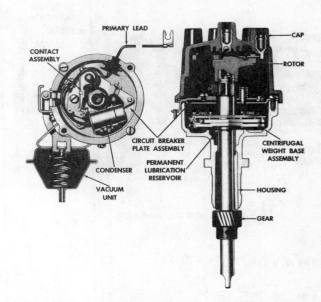

PRIMARY LEAD

CONTACT ASSEMBLY

CAP

ROTOR

CIRCUIT BREAKER PLATE ASSEMBLY

CONDENSER

PERMANENT LUBRICATION RESERVOIR

VACUUM UNIT

CENTRIFUGAL WEIGHT BASE ASSEMBLY

HOUSING

GEAR

Sectioned view through the distributor used on a six-cylinder engine.

IGNITION SYSTEM

Most of the ignition system service procedures will be found in Chapter 2, Tuning for Performance. Ignition system troubleshooting procedures are fully covered in Chapter 1.

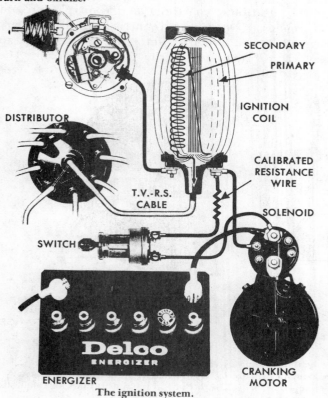

SECONDARY

PRIMARY

IGNITION COIL

CALIBRATED RESISTANCE WIRE

SOLENOID

DISTRIBUTOR

T.V.-R.S. CABLE

SWITCH

Deleo ENERGIZER

ENERGIZER

CRANKING MOTOR

The ignition system.

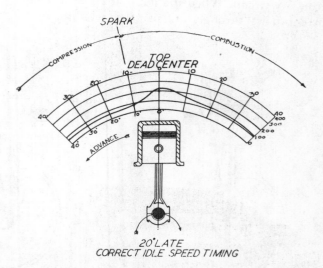

SPARK

COMPRESSION

COMBUSTION

TOP DEAD CENTER

ADVANCE

20° LATE
CORRECT IDLE SPEED TIMING

This graph shows the pressure rise in the combustion chamber during compression and after the air-fuel mixture is ignited. With the engine idling, ignition occurs at 10° BTDC, and maximum pressure is developed just as the piston passes TDC. The 10° timing advance compensates for the 1/350th of a second that it takes for combustion to be completed.

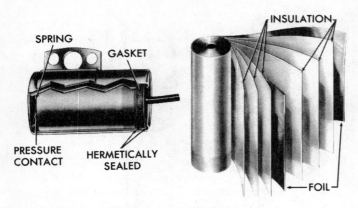

Details of the condenser.

NO ADVANCE

FULL ADVANCE

The mechanical-advance mechanism consists of two fly weights that are retained by springs. As rotational speed increases, the weights fly outward because of centrifugal force (right), causing the mechanism to advance ignition timing.

THEORY OF OPERATION

The ignition system produces high-voltage surges of up to 20,000 volts and delivers them to the spark plugs in "time" with the engine. Each high-voltage surge jumps across a spark plug gap and ignites the compressed air-fuel mixture. The ignition system is composed of two circuits: a low- and a high-voltage circuit. The primary circuit (low voltage) consists of a battery, ignition switch, distributor contact points, condenser, ignition coil primary winding and a resistor. The secondary circuit (high voltage) consists of an ignition coil secondary winding, a rotor, high-tension wiring, and spark plugs.

The primary circuit triggers the operation of the secondary circuit. When the ignition switch is closed, current flows through the primary winding of the ignition coil and through the closed contact points. When the engine turns, a cam, driven by the camshaft, opens the contact points at the exact instant a piston is close to the top of its compression stroke. Interrupting the flow of primary current causes a voltage surge to be generated in the secondary winding of the ignition coil. This high-tension surge is delivered to the center terminal of the distributor cap, where it is picked up by the rotor and directed to the proper spark plug.

DISTRIBUTOR

The distributor contains a set of contact points and a condenser which are connected in the primary circuit. It also contains a rotor and a distributor cap which are connected in the secondary circuit. The

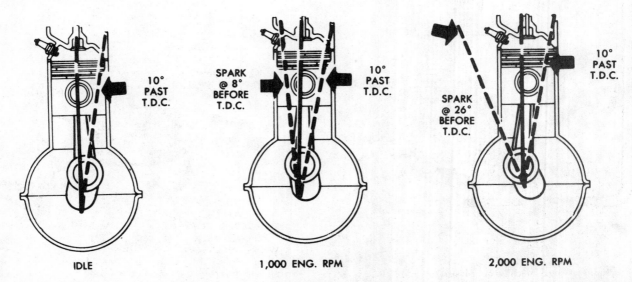

IDLE   1,000 ENG. RPM   2,000 ENG. RPM

The mechanical spark advance mechanism is designed to advance ignition timing as engine speed increases. At idle speeds (left), the spark must occur at TDC for the burning fuel to develop its maximum pressure by 10° ATDC. At 1,000 rpm, it is necessary to advance the ignition timing about 8° for maximum pressure to be developed by 10° ATDC because of the time it takes for combustion to occur. At 2,000 rpm, the spark must occur approximately 26° BTDC for maximum pressure to develop by 10° ATDC.

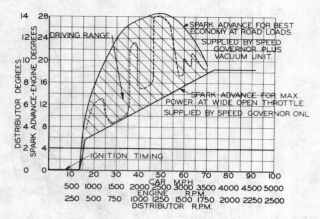

In operation, the ignition timing may be at any point in the shaded section of this graph, due to the action of the centrifugal advance, modified by the vacuum-advance.

distributor is driven by a gear on the camshaft in time with the engine. Because the timing of the spark varies according to the load and speed of the engine, an automatic spark advance mechanism, sensitive to

both speed and load, is incorporated in the distributor. A centrifugal governor advances the position of the cam according to the speed of the engine. A vacuum diaphragm controls the position of the breaker plate assembly according to the load on the engine.

CENTRIFUGAL-ADVANCE MECHANISM

When the engine is idling, the spark is timed to occur just before the piston reaches top dead center, so that combustion can be completed by the time the piston reaches a little past top dead center. At higher engine speeds, there is less time for the mixture to ignite, burn, and deliver its power to the piston. Consequently, at higher engine speeds, the spark must be delivered earlier in the cycle. This is accomplished by a centrifugal advance mechanism designed about two governor weights, which throw out against spring tension as engine speed increases. This motion is transmitted to the breaker cam, which is advanced with regard to the distributor driveshaft.

VACUUM-ADVANCE MECHANISM

Under light engine load conditions, there is a high vacuum in the intake manifold caused by the restriction of the partially closed throttle valve; consequently, there is a smaller amount of air-fuel mixture delivered to the combustion chambers. Because of the fewer particles, the mixture will not burn as rapidly; therefore, ignition must take place earlier in the cycle.

To provide additional spark advance control,

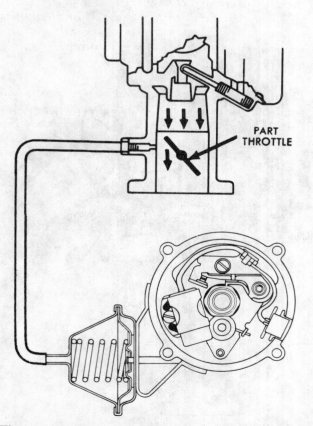

The vacuum-advance mechanism consists of a diaphragm unit which receives its vacuum supply from the manifold side of the throttle valve. Generally, this tap is above the throttle blade at idle speed so that there is no vacuum advance; this is especially true on emission-controlled engines.

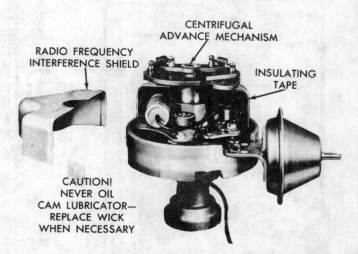

Late-model distributors used on V-8 engines have a radio-frequency interference shield over the breaker points to minimize interference in high-fidelity radios and TV sets while the engine is running.

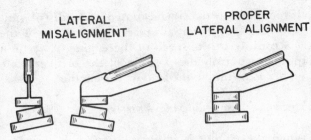

LATERAL MISALIGNMENT   PROPER LATERAL ALIGNMENT

New contact points must be aligned by bending the fixed contact support. CAUTION: Never bend the breaker lever.

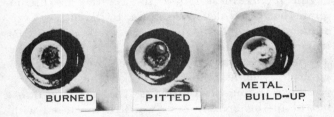

BURNED   PITTED   METAL BUILD-UP

CONTACT SUPPORT POINTS

BURNED   PITTED   WORN

BREAKER ARM POINTS

Defective contact points, which will cause hard starting.

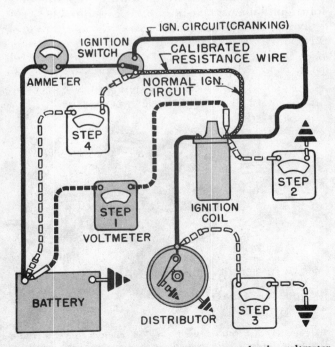

IGN. CIRCUIT (CRANKING)

IGNITION SWITCH   CALIBRATED RESISTANCE WIRE

AMMETER   NORMAL IGN. CIRCUIT

STEP 4

STEP 2

STEP 1   IGNITION COIL

VOLTMETER

BATTERY   DISTRIBUTOR   STEP 3

This diagram shows the four positions to apply the voltmeter prods for making voltage-loss tests in an ignition system which is giving trouble.

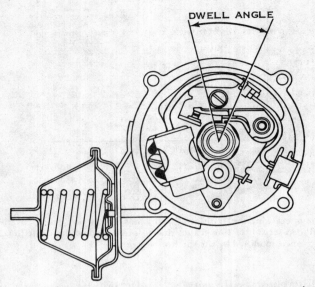

DWELL ANGLE

The dwell angle is the length of time that the contact points remain together, and this is more important than the distance they separate, because it affects the length of time that the primary of the ignition coil can build up.

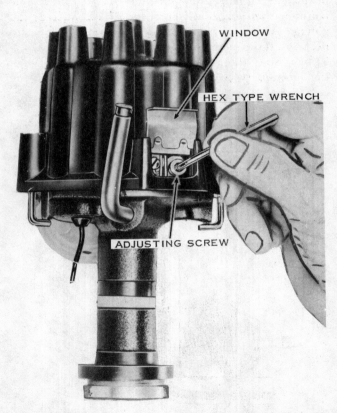

WINDOW

HEX TYPE WRENCH

ADJUSTING SCREW

The dwell can be adjusted on a V-8 engine by lifting the window and turning the hex-type adjusting screw while the engine is idling. CAUTION: Be sure to shut the window securely after making the adjustment to prevent the entrance of dust and moisture.

based on intake manifold pressures, a vacuum advance mechanism is incorporated in the distributor. It contains a spring-loaded diaphragm which rotates the breaker plate assembly. The diaphragm is connected to a vacuum passageway in the carburetor bore, located on the atmospheric side of the throttle valve when the engine is idling. In this position, no vacuum is applied to the diaphragm, and the breaker plate is retarded by spring pressure. As the throttle is opened, it swings past the vacuum port, applying vacuum to the diaphragm, moving it against spring pressure to advance the breaker plate.

When the engine is accelerated, intake manifold vacuum drops according to the degree of throttle advance, retarding the position of the breaker plate assembly accordingly.

IGNITION SERVICE NOTES

IGNITION SWITCH WIRING CHECK

Crank the engine until the contact points are closed, and then measure the voltage between the positive primary terminal of the ignition coil and ground. The voltmeter should show a reading of 5-7 volts. If the voltage is lower, the circuit has high-resistance connections. If the meter shows 12 volts, the ignition switch is bypassing the resistance wire connected between the ignition switch and the positive terminal of the coil.

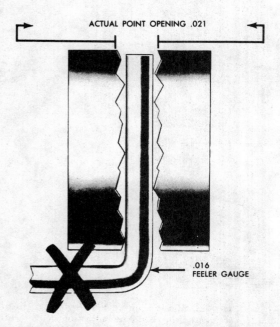

ACTUAL POINT OPENING .021

.016 FEELER GAUGE

Because contact points wear irregularly, a feeler gauge cannot be used to gap them accurately. Instead a dwell meter should be used.

UNIT DISTRIBUTOR

This high-energy ignition system is a self-contained unit, with the ignition coil attached to the distributor cap. No contact points are used; the advantage being less chance of engine misfire and no change in ignition timing, which always occurs when conventional contact points wear. The advantage of this system is better emission control.

A magnetic pickup assembly, located over the shaft, contains a permanent magnet, a pole piece with internal teeth, and a pickup coil. When the teeth of the timer core, rotating inside of the pole piece, line up with the teeth of the pole piece, an induced voltage in the pickup coil signals the all-electronic module to open the ignition coil primary circuit. As a result, the primary current decreases and a high voltage is induced in the ignition coil secondary winding. This voltage is directed through the rotor, distributor cap, and high-voltage leads to fire the spark plugs.

The magnetic pickup assembly is mounted over the main bearing on the distributor housing, and is made to rotate by the vacuum-control unit, thus providing vacuum advance. The timer coil is made to rotate about the shaft by conventional mechanical advance weights to provide centrifugal advance.

SERVICE PROCEDURES

No periodic lubrication is needed because engine oil lubricates the lower bushing, and an oil-filled reservoir provides lubrication for the upper bushing. **CAUTION: When making compression checks, disconnect the ignition switch connector from the Unit Ignition System, or high-voltage flashing will occur.**

Use the Troubleshooting Diagnosis Chart to locate any problem that might occur in the system.

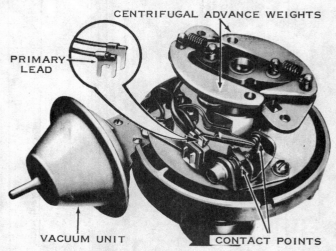

CENTRIFUGAL ADVANCE WEIGHTS

PRIMARY LEAD

VACUUM UNIT

CONTACT POINTS

V-8 engine distributor lead arrangement.

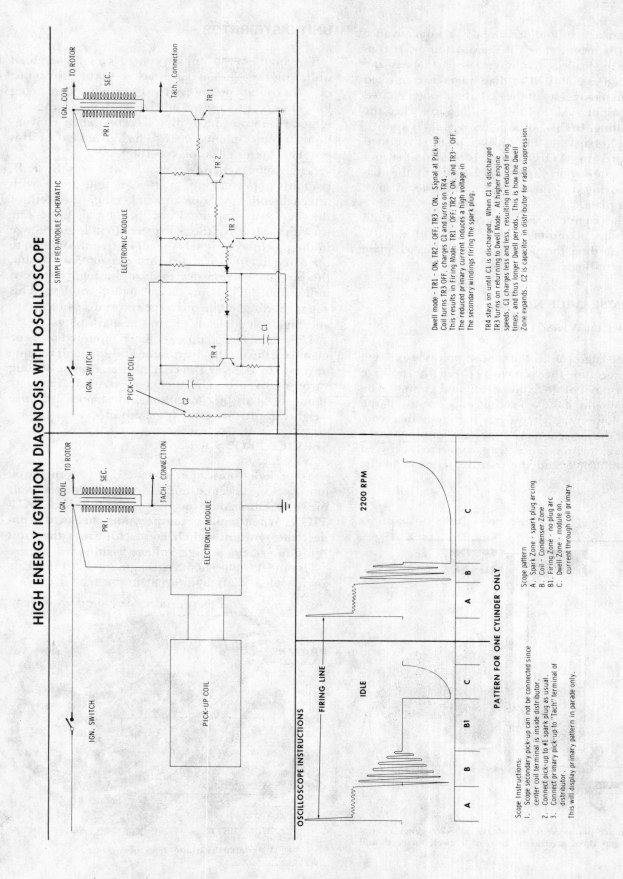

HIGH ENERGY IGNITION DIAGNOSIS WITH OSCILLOSCOPE

SIMPLIFIED MODULE SCHEMATIC

TO ROTOR

IGN. COIL

SEC.

TR 1

PRI.

Tach. Connection

IGN. SWITCH

ELECTRONIC MODULE

TR 2

TR 3

TR 4

PICK-UP COIL

C1

C2

Dwell mode - TR1 - ON: TR2 - OFF: TR3 - ON. Signal at Pick-up Coil turns TR3 OFF, charges C1 and turns on TR4.
This results in Firing Mode: TR1 - OFF: TR2 - ON, and TR3- OFF. The reduced primary current induces a high voltage in The secondary windings firing the spark plug.

TR4 stays on until C1 is discharged. When C1 is discharged TR3 turns on returning to Dwell Mode. At higher engine speeds, C1 charges less and less, resulting in reduced firing times, and thus longer Dwell periods. This is how the Dwell Zone expands. C2 is capacitor in distributor for radio supression.

TO ROTOR

IGN. COIL

SEC.

PRI.

TACH. CONNECTION

IGN. SWITCH

ELECTRONIC MODULE

PICK-UP COIL

OSCILLOSCOPE INSTRUCTIONS

FIRING LINE

IDLE

2200 RPM

A   B   BI   C

A   B   C

PATTERN FOR ONE CYLINDER ONLY

Scope pattern
A. Spark Zone - spark plug arcing
B. Coil - Condenser Zone
B1. Firing Zone - no plug arc
C. Dwell Zone - module on, current through coil primary

Scope instructions:
1. Scope secondary pick-up can not be connected since center coil terminal is inside distributor.
2. Connect pick-up to #1 spark plug as usual.
3. Connect primary pick-up to "Tach" terminal of distributor.
This will display primary pattern in parade only.

Oscilloscope patterns with the High-Energy Ignition system.

HIGH ENERGY IGNITION DIAGNOSIS

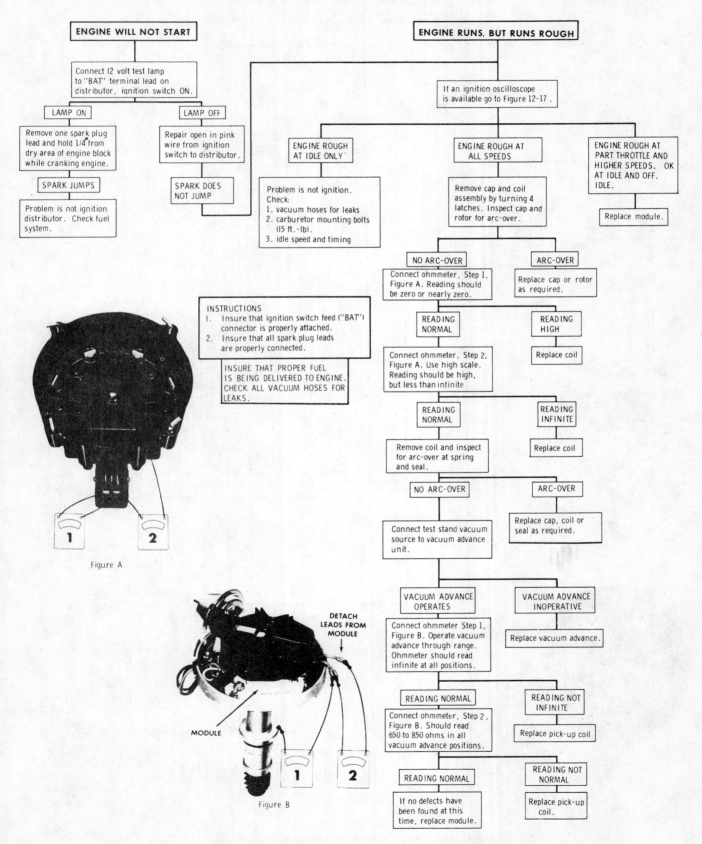

ENGINE WILL NOT START

Connect 12 volt test lamp to "BAT" terminal lead on distributor, ignition switch ON.

LAMP ON

Remove one spark plug lead and hold 1/4" from dry area of engine block while cranking engine.

SPARK JUMPS

Problem is not ignition distributor. Check fuel system.

LAMP OFF

Repair open in pink wire from ignition switch to distributor.

SPARK DOES NOT JUMP

INSTRUCTIONS
1. Insure that ignition switch feed ("BAT") connector is properly attached.
2. Insure that all spark plug leads are properly connected.

INSURE THAT PROPER FUEL IS BEING DELIVERED TO ENGINE. CHECK ALL VACUUM HOSES FOR LEAKS.

Figure A

DETACH LEADS FROM MODULE

MODULE

Figure B

ENGINE RUNS, BUT RUNS ROUGH

If an ignition oscilloscope is available go to Figure 12-17.

ENGINE ROUGH AT IDLE ONLY

Problem is not ignition. Check:
1. vacuum hoses for leaks
2. carburetor mounting bolts (15 ft.-lb)
3. idle speed and timing

ENGINE ROUGH AT ALL SPEEDS

Remove cap and coil assembly by turning 4 latches. Inspect cap and rotor for arc-over.

NO ARC-OVER

Connect ohmmeter, Step 1, Figure A. Reading should be zero or nearly zero.

READING NORMAL

Connect ohmmeter, Step 2, Figure A. Use high scale. Reading should be high, but less than infinite

READING NORMAL

Remove coil and inspect for arc-over at spring and seal.

NO ARC-OVER

Connect test stand vacuum source to vacuum advance unit.

VACUUM ADVANCE OPERATES

Connect ohmmeter Step 1, Figure B. Operate vacuum advance through range. Ohmmeter should read infinite at all positions.

READING NORMAL

Connect ohmmeter, Step 2, Figure B. Should read 650 to 850 ohms in all vacuum advance positions.

READING NORMAL

If no defects have been found at this time, replace module.

ARC-OVER

Replace cap or rotor as required.

READING HIGH

Replace coil

READING INFINITE

Replace coil

ARC-OVER

Replace cap, coil or seal as required.

VACUUM ADVANCE INOPERATIVE

Replace vacuum advance.

READING NOT INFINITE

Replace pick-up coil

READING NOT NORMAL

Replace pick-up coil.

ENGINE ROUGH AT PART THROTTLE AND HIGHER SPEEDS. OK AT IDLE AND OFF. IDLE.

Replace module.

High-Energy (Unit) Ignition system diagnosis—section one.

HIGH ENERGY IGNITION DIAGNOSIS WITH OSCILLOSCOPE

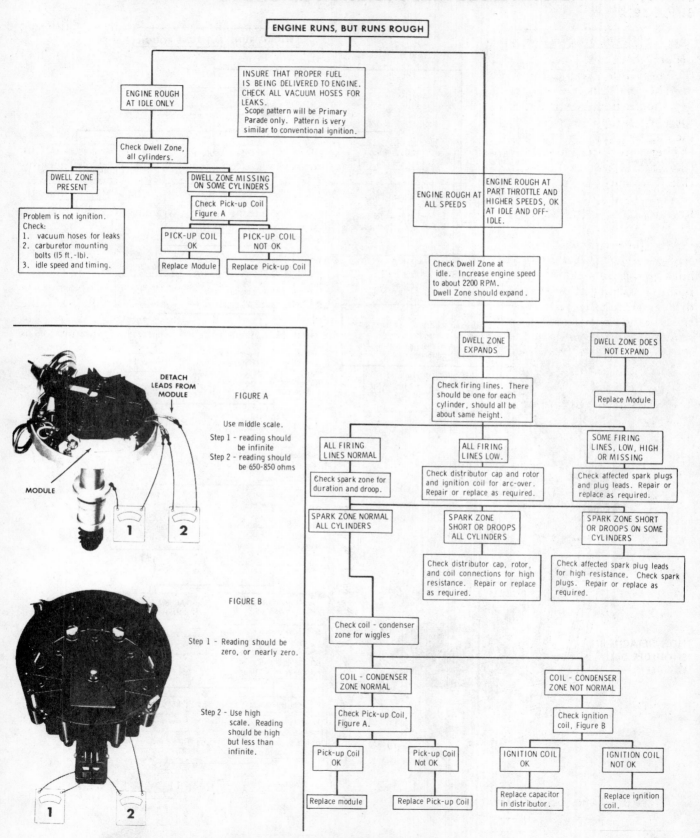

ENGINE RUNS, BUT RUNS ROUGH

ENGINE ROUGH AT IDLE ONLY

INSURE THAT PROPER FUEL IS BEING DELIVERED TO ENGINE. CHECK ALL VACUUM HOSES FOR LEAKS.
Scope pattern will be Primary Parade only. Pattern is very similar to conventional ignition.

Check Dwell Zone, all cylinders.

DWELL ZONE PRESENT

DWELL ZONE MISSING ON SOME CYLINDERS

Problem is not ignition. Check:
1. vacuum hoses for leaks
2. carburetor mounting bolts (15 ft.-lb).
3. idle speed and timing.

Check Pick-up Coil Figure A

PICK-UP COIL OK

PICK-UP COIL NOT OK

Replace Module

Replace Pick-up Coil

ENGINE ROUGH AT ALL SPEEDS

ENGINE ROUGH AT PART THROTTLE AND HIGHER SPEEDS, OK AT IDLE AND OFF-IDLE.

Check Dwell Zone at idle. Increase engine speed to about 2200 RPM. Dwell Zone should expand.

DWELL ZONE EXPANDS

DWELL ZONE DOES NOT EXPAND

Replace Module

Check firing lines. There should be one for each cylinder, should all be about same height.

ALL FIRING LINES NORMAL

Check spark zone for duration and droop.

ALL FIRING LINES LOW.

Check distributor cap and rotor and ignition coil for arc-over. Repair or replace as required.

SOME FIRING LINES, LOW, HIGH OR MISSING

Check affected spark plugs and plug leads. Repair or replace as required.

SPARK ZONE NORMAL ALL CYLINDERS

SPARK ZONE SHORT OR DROOPS ALL CYLINDERS

Check distributor cap, rotor, and coil connections for high resistance. Repair or replace as required.

SPARK ZONE SHORT OR DROOPS ON SOME CYLINDERS

Check affected spark plug leads for high resistance. Check spark plugs. Repair or replace as required.

Check coil - condenser zone for wiggles

COIL - CONDENSER ZONE NORMAL

Check Pick-up Coil, Figure A.

COIL - CONDENSER ZONE NOT NORMAL

Check ignition coil, Figure B

Pick-up Coil OK

Pick-up Coil Not OK

IGNITION COIL OK

IGNITION COIL NOT OK

Replace module

Replace Pick-up Coil

Replace capacitor in distributor.

Replace ignition coil.

DETACH LEADS FROM MODULE

FIGURE A

Use middle scale.
Step 1 - reading should be infinite
Step 2 - reading should be 650-850 ohms

MODULE

1   2

FIGURE B

Step 1 - Reading should be zero, or nearly zero.

Step 2 - Use high scale. Reading should be high but less than infinite.

1   2

High-Energy Ignition system diagnosis—section two.

SEAT BELT/STARTER INTERLOCK SYSTEM— SINCE 1974

This system prevents cranking the engine unless the proper three-step starting sequence is employed: (1) The driver and passenger must be in their seats. (2) The seat belts must be buckled. (3) The ignition key should now be turned to the START position for starting the engine. If this order is not followed, the engine cannot be cranked.

There are three other ways to obtain a START condition: (1) restart, (2) mechanic's start, and (3) override relay start.

RESTART AFTER STALL

After the engine has been started using the correct sequence, it can be restarted with the seat belts buckled or unbuckled at the occupied front-seat positions as long as the driver remains seated. If the driver vacates the seat, the restart provisions are terminated, and the correct three-step starting sequence must be instigated.

MECHANIC'S START

The engine can be started regardless of the seat belt condition as long as the front seat is unoccupied. That is, the engine can be started by reaching in and turning the key to the START position.

OVERRIDE RELAY START

In the event of a malfunction in the system, provision is made to start the engine by depressing the button on the override relay after turning the ignition key to the ON position. This activates the override relay to bypass the interlock system for one start so that the vehicle can be driven to a garage for service.

WARNING SYSTEM

The system contains a warning light and buzzer, which will be activated under either of the following conditions: (1) If the engine is started properly and the seat belt is unbuckled while the transmission is

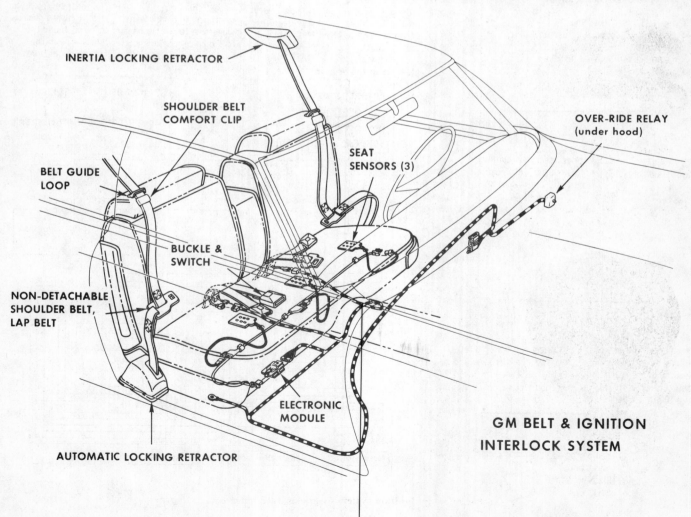

INERTIA LOCKING RETRACTOR

SHOULDER BELT COMFORT CLIP

BELT GUIDE LOOP

SEAT SENSORS (3)

OVER-RIDE RELAY (under hood)

BUCKLE & SWITCH

NON-DETACHABLE SHOULDER BELT, LAP BELT

ELECTRONIC MODULE

AUTOMATIC LOCKING RETRACTOR

GM BELT & IGNITION INTERLOCK SYSTEM

SEAT BELT SYSTEM DIAGNOSIS

ENGINE STARTS WHEN THREE WIRE CONNECTOR NEAR FUSE PANEL IS DISCONNECTED OR WHEN TURNING IGNITION TO START, SEAT BELTS UNFASTENED AND NO ONE SITTING ON SEATS.

NOTE: To remove Electronic Module connectors use Tool J-24388 or BT7402A.

Turn ignition to RUN, press and release each seating position (2) and listen for interlock relay. Should click when seat position is pressed and again when it is released. (Seat belts unfastened, three wire connector near fuse panel connected).

TWO CLICKS CAN BE HEARD AT EACH POSITION

1. Sit on seat, hold seat belt release button in and connect belt. Relay should click when belt is fastened. (Holding release button prevents snap lock from making more noise than the relay).
2. Perform the same test at the right hand seating position.
3. Determine which test does not cause interlock relay to click when seat belt is fastened. If relay does not click at any position, skip Steps 4, 5 & 6 and go to TEST LIGHT ON, Step 2.
4. Disconnect seat belt connector determined in previous test.
5. Connect self powered test light to the two terminals in belt side of connector.
6. Connect seat belt.

TEST LIGHT OFF

Replace buckle side of belt

TEST LIGHT ON

1. Connect seat belt connector.
2. Remove Electronic Module from seat frame and disconnect 10-wire connector (If Steps 4, 5 & 6 in previous test were not performed, skip Step 3 and go to TEST LIGHT ON.)
3. Connect self-powered test light to the 2 wires in the 10 pin connector or that connects to the seat belt connector.

TEST LIGHT OFF

Repair open circuit in one or both wires leading to the seat belt connector from the 10 pin connector.

TEST LIGHT ON

Connect self powered test light to a good ground and to the black wire in the 10 pin connector.

TEST LIGHT OFF

Repair ground connection. (Black wire to body).

TEST LIGHT ON

Replace Electronic Module

TWO CLICKS CAN BE HEARD BUT NOT AT BOTH POSITIONS

1. Disconnect seat sensor at seat position where two clicks cannot be heard.
2. Connect self powered test light to the two terminals in sensor side of connector. Press on seat position.

TEST LIGHT OFF

Replace seat sensor

TEST LIGHT ON

1. Connect seat sensor.
2. Remove Electronic Module from seat frame and disconnect 4-wire connector
3. Connect self-powered test light to the black wire in the 4-wire connector and to the other wire leading to the seat sensor determined above.
4. Press on seating position.

TEST LIGHT ON

Replace Electronic Module

TEST LIGHT OFF

Repair open circuit in one or both wires from 4 wire connector to seat sensor connector.

TWO CLICKS CANNOT BE HEARD AT ANY POSITION

1. Disconnect three wire connector near fuse panel.
2. Remove Electronic Module from seat frame and disconnect 10-wire connector
3. Connect self-powered test light to the dark green wire in the 10 pin connector and ground.

TEST LIGHT ON

Repair short circuit to ground in dark green wire from 10 pin connector to 3 wire connector near fuse panel.

TEST LIGHT OFF

Connect self powered test light to a good ground and to the black wire in the 10 pin connector.

TEST LIGHT OFF

Repair ground connection (Black wire to body)

TEST LIGHT ON

Replace Electronic Module

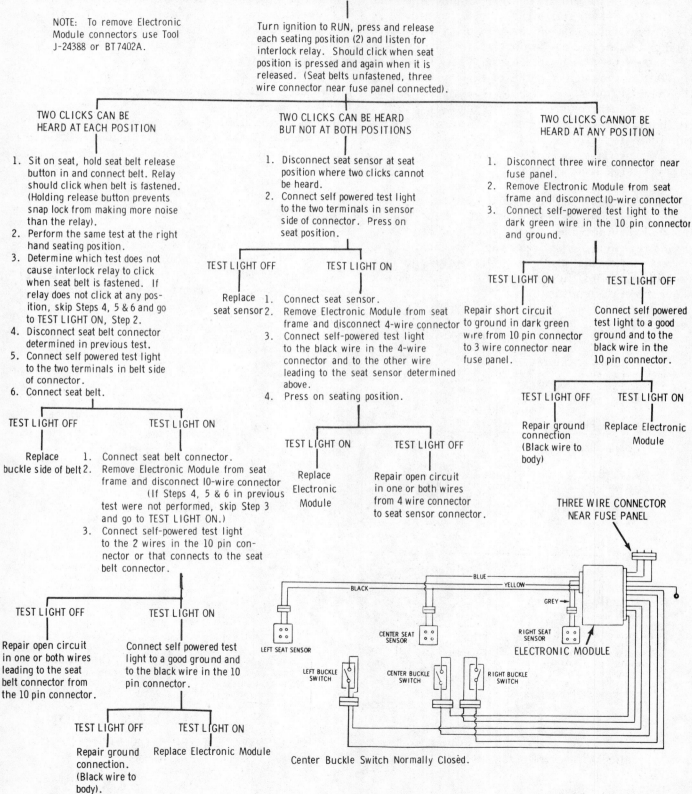

THREE WIRE CONNECTOR NEAR FUSE PANEL

BLUE
BLACK
YELLOW
GREY

LEFT SEAT SENSOR
CENTER SEAT SENSOR
RIGHT SEAT SENSOR
ELECTRONIC MODULE

LEFT BUCKLE SWITCH
CENTER BUCKLE SWITCH
RIGHT BUCKLE SWITCH

Center Buckle Switch Normally Closed.

SEAT BELT STARTER INTERLOCK SYSTEM DIAGNOSIS

STARTER WILL NOT CRANK
(Using correct starting procedure)

Check For Click in Starter Solenoid

SOLENOID CLICKS

Seat belt starter interlock system is OK. Refer to STARTING CIRCUIT DIAGNOSIS.

BATTERY AND/OR CABLE CONNECTIONS BAD

Repair as necessary

SOLENOID DOES NOT CLICK

Honk horn to make sure battery & cables are OK.

BATTERY & CABLES OK

1. Shift lever in PARK position and turn ignition switch to RUN.
2. Press & release override relay button in engine compartment.
3. Turn ignition to START (while seated).

STARTER CRANKS

Normal starter system is OK. Get out of car. Reach in and turn ignition to START. Do not apply pressure on seat. Leave seat belts unfastened.

STARTER CRANKS

Trouble is in body section. Proceed to SEAT SYSTEM DIAGNOSIS

STARTER DOES NOT CRANK

1. Turn ignition OFF.
2. Disconnect 3-wire connector near fuse block (yellow, orange and green).
3. Turn ignition to START.

STARTER CRANKS

Proceed to SEAT BELT SYSTEM DIAGNOSIS.

STARTER DOES NOT CRANK

1. Turn Ignition OFF.
2. Disconnect Interlock Relay (2 Screws).
3. Connect a test light to the GREEN/BLACK wire at the Interlock Relay and ground.
4. Turn Ignition to START.

TEST LIGHT ON

1. Turn ignition to RUN.
2. Check for shorts in green wire, interlock connector to 3-wire connector.
3. Turn ignition OFF.
4. Disconnect interlock relay connector from interlock relay.
5. Temporarily connect jumper wire to 12 volts and touch to purple wire in interlock relay connector.

TEST LIGHT OFF

Repair open in circuit between ignition switch, neutral start switch, and interlock relay. (Could be misadjusted neutral start switch.)

STARTER DOES NOT CRANK

Repair open circuit in purple wire, interlock relay to starter.

STARTER CRANKS

Replace interlock relay.

STARTER DOES NOT CRANK

1. Make sure neutral start switch is properly adjusted. (If manual trans. check clutch switch.)
2. Shift lever in PARK and turn ignition switch to RUN.
3. Disconnect override relay. (Push retaining tab down and pull override relay out.)
4. Temporarily connect jumper wire to 12 volts and touch to purple wire ("C" terminal) on override relay connector.

STARTER DOES NOT CRANK

Trouble is in starting circuit. Refer to STARTING CIRCUIT DIAGNOSIS.

STARTER CRANKS

1. Leave the ignition in RUN position.
2. With a 12 volt test light, check for 12 volts at the pink wire ("D" terminal) on override relay connector.

TEST LIGHT OFF

Repair open circuit in pink wire, override relay connector to ignition switch.

TEST LIGHT ON

1. Turn ignition OFF.
2. Connect one lead of a 12 volt test light to the green/black wire ("B" terminal) on the override relay connector and the other lead to ground.
3. Turn ignition to START.

TEST LIGHT OFF

1. Turn ignition OFF.
2. Repair open circuit in green/black wire, override relay connector to neutral start switch.

TEST LIGHT ON

Check black ground wire on the override relay connector for a good connection & good ground.

CONNECTION & GROUND BAD

Repair as necessary

CONNECTION & GROUND OK

Replace override relay

SEAT BELT STARTER INTERLOCK SYSTEM DIAGNOSIS (CONTINUED)

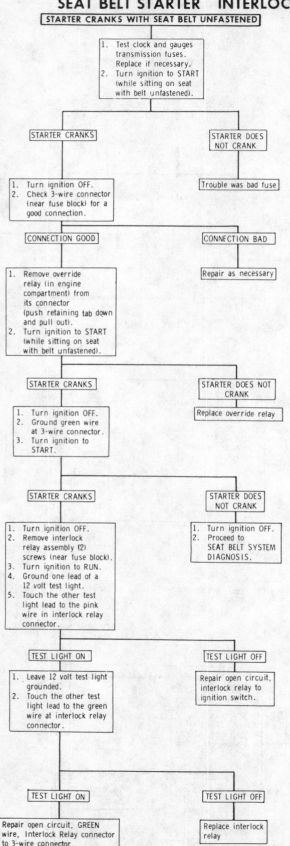

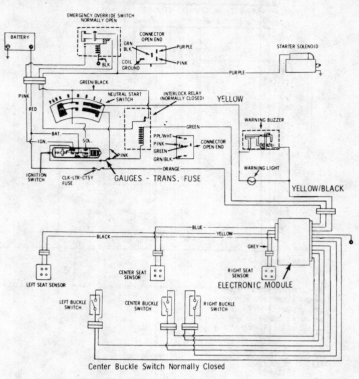

Center Buckle Switch Normally Closed

in gear. (2) If after a mechanic's start or an override relay start, the shift lever is moved into gear with an occupied front seat and an unbuckled seat belt.

BOUNCE FEATURE

The system incorporates a bounce feature that prevents out-of-sequence violations from being recorded under the following conditions. If a driver fastens his seat belt properly, and then lifts his hips to get the ignition key from his pocket, he may inadvertently deactivate the seat sensor momentarily. When the sensor is reactivated, the system would then be out of sequence, with the seat sensor being activated after the seat belt was buckled, and this would prevent a normal start. The bounce delay built into the system prevents deactivation of the seat sensor from being recorded for a few seconds to keep the system in a good start sequence.

PARTS OF THE SYSTEM

ELECTRONIC MODULE

This device receives signals from the seat sensor and buckle switches to monitor the proper belt-buckling sequence. If the proper sequence is followed, the module opens the interlock relay coil ground, and the contact points close to allow the engine to be cranked.

SEAT BELT WARNING SYSTEM DIAGNOSIS

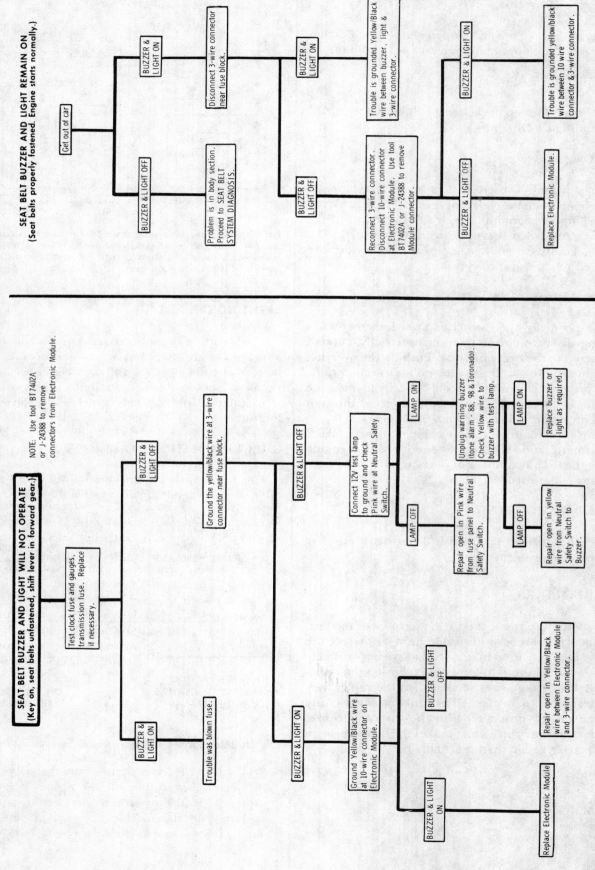

SEAT BELT BUZZER AND LIGHT REMAIN ON
(Seat belts properly fastened. Engine starts normally.)

Get out of car

BUZZER & LIGHT ON → Disconnect 3-wire connector near fuse block. → BUZZER & LIGHT ON → Trouble is grounded Yellow/Black wire between buzzer, light & 3-wire connector.

BUZZER & LIGHT OFF → Problem is in body section. Proceed to SEAT BELT SYSTEM DIAGNOSIS.

BUZZER & LIGHT OFF → Reconnect 3-wire connector. Disconnect 10-wire connector at Electronic Module. Use tool BT7402A or J-24388 to remove Module connector.

BUZZER & LIGHT ON → Trouble is grounded yellow/black wire between 10 wire connector & 3-wire connector.

BUZZER & LIGHT OFF → Replace Electronic Module.

NOTE: Use tool BT7402A or J-24388 to remove connectors from Electronic Module.

SEAT BELT BUZZER AND LIGHT WILL NOT OPERATE
(Key on, seat belts unfastened, shift lever in forward gear.)

Test clock fuse and gauges, transmission fuse. Replace if necessary.

BUZZER & LIGHT OFF → Ground the yellow/black wire at 3-wire connector near fuse block. → BUZZER & LIGHT OFF → Connect 12V test lamp to ground and check Pink wire at Neutral Safety Switch.

LAMP ON → Unplug warning buzzer (tone alarm - 88, 98 & Toronado). Check Yellow wire to buzzer with test lamp. → LAMP ON → Replace buzzer or light as required.

LAMP OFF → Repair open in yellow wire from Neutral Safety Switch to Buzzer.

LAMP OFF → Repair open in Pink wire from fuse panel to Neutral Safety Switch.

BUZZER & LIGHT ON → Trouble was blown fuse.

BUZZER & LIGHT ON → Ground Yellow/Black wire at 10-wire connector on Electronic Module.

BUZZER & LIGHT OFF → Repair open in Yellow/Black wire between Electronic Module and 3-wire connector.

BUZZER & LIGHT ON → Replace Electronic Module.

SEAT SENSOR SWITCHES

There are three normally-open seat sensor switches in the seat cushion, one under each seat position.

SEAT BELT BUCKLE SWITCHES

A switch is located in each seat belt buckle to record the condition of the buckle.

INTERLOCK RELAY

This normally-closed switch has contact points which open when the coil is energized. This is achieved by turning the ignition switch ON with the driver and/or outboard seat sensor switches activated. The contact points close when the seat belt buckles are fastened to allow a start condition.

OVERRIDE RELAY

This normally-open switch is used for emergency starting. By turning the ignition switch ON, current is directed to the override relay. Pushing the override relay button down closes the points mechanically. They are held closed by the coil. Now, by turning the ignition key to START, current is directed through the neutral start switch, through the override relay, to the starter solenoid so that the engine can be cranked. Once the override relay coil is energized, the engine can be started any number of times as long as the ignition key is not turned OFF.

TROUBLESHOOTING

Use the following troubleshooting maps for isolating the problem.

FUSIBLE LINKS

In addition to fuses, the wiring harness of modern cars incorporates several fusible links to protect the wiring. Links are used in circuits that are not normally fused, such as the ignition circuit. Fusible links are usually four gauge sizes smaller than the cables they are designed to protect. The links are generally marked on the insulation with the wire gauge size, because the heavy insulation makes the link appear to be a heavier gauge than it actually is.

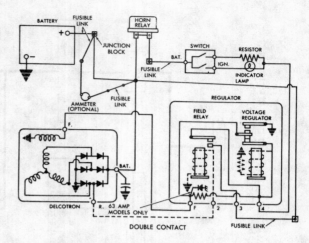

Fusible links have been used since 1967 in several circuits that are not protected by conventional fuses. When a fusible link burns out because of a short circuit, the insulation will appear quite bubbly because of the heat.

LIGHTING CIRCUIT

The lighting and accessory circuits of modern automobiles are exceedingly complex because of the maze of circuits, switches, and controls. However, most problems concern burned-out bulbs, which are easily replaceable. More difficult problems revolve about locating open and short circuits.

CHECKING A SHORT CIRCUIT

The first step is to disconnect the battery ground cable at the engine and connect a 12-volt test lamp

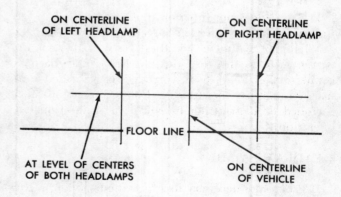

Headlamp screen aiming pattern discussed in the text.

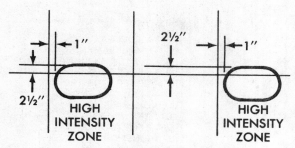

Low beam adjustment pattern.

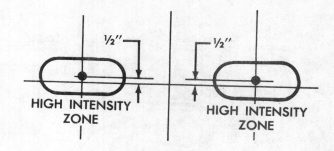

High beam adjustment pattern.

between the end of the disconnected cable and a good ground as shown. If there is a short circuit, the test lamp will glow with all accessories turned off. If the vehicle is equipped with an electric clock, make the battery connection for a few seconds to wind the clock so that you can have a two-minute test period before the clock runs down and needs to be energized again. **CAUTION: Make sure that all vehicle doors are closed so that the courtesy lights are not lit, which would cause the bulb to glow dimly in some cases.** It is not a good idea to use a voltmeter in place of the suggested test lamp because, in late-model vehicles with diodes in the charging circuit, some voltmeter reading will be obtained under normal conditions.

To check for a short, disconnect and reconnect each electrical circuit, one at a time. When a disconnect causes the test lamp to go out, you have found the shorted circuit and each section of it can be tested in a like manner.

CHECKING AN OPEN CIRCUIT

If a unit does not function, the first check is to see that the unit in question is getting current. Use a test lamp or voltmeter for these tests. If there is no current, check the fuse, fusible links, and harness connectors. A loose, bent, corroded, or damaged connector can cause this trouble. Loose connections and corroded or loose-fitting fuses can cause intermittent operation.

HEADLAMP AIMING

If it becomes necessary to adjust the headlamps, the following screen method will give accurate results. Position the vehicle on a level floor, 25′ from a light-colored wall. Make four lines on the wall, as shown in the accompanying drawing. (1) A horizontal line at the level of the centers of the headlights. (2) a center vertical line, which must be aligned with the vehicle center line. *NOTE: A good method of doing this is*

to sight through the rear window and align the center of the rear window molding through the mirror bracket or hood center line. (3) A vertical line aligned with the center line of the left headlamp. (4) A vertical line aligned with the center line of the right headlamp.

Adjust the low beam and high beam patterns as shown in the accompanying drawings.

FUEL GAUGES

These gauges work on a lowered voltage, and the voltage is dropped by a CV (constant voltage) regulator, which provides pulsating voltage at an average value of 5 volts. Care must be taken when working around the CV regulator because of the delicate nature of its contacts. Always disconnect the battery cable before doing any work in that area.

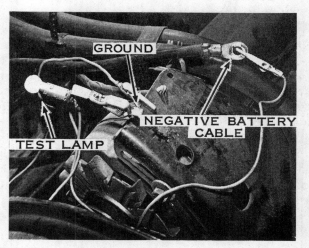

To check for a short circuit, connect a test lamp between the disconnected battery cable and a good ground, as discussed in the text.

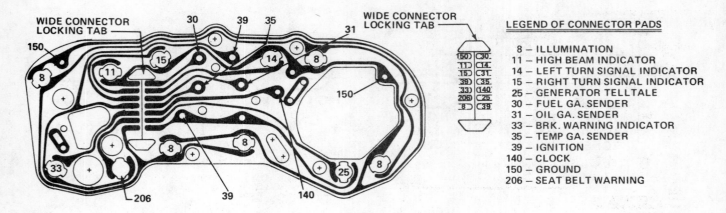

WIDE CONNECTOR LOCKING TAB

WIDE CONNECTOR LOCKING TAB

LEGEND OF CONNECTOR PADS

8 — ILLUMINATION
11 — HIGH BEAM INDICATOR
14 — LEFT TURN SIGNAL INDICATOR
15 — RIGHT TURN SIGNAL INDICATOR
25 — GENERATOR TELLTALE
30 — FUEL GA. SENDER
31 — OIL GA. SENDER
33 — BRK. WARNING INDICATOR
35 — TEMP GA. SENDER
39 — IGNITION
140 — CLOCK
150 — GROUND
206 — SEAT BELT WARNING

Fuel gauge problems can be caused by a poor ground connection, especially on printed-circuit dashes. Check the tightness of the gauge contact nuts.

FUEL GAUGE TROUBLESHOOTING CHART

The following checks of this circuit will assist you to determine quickly whether incorrect fuel gauge readings are the result of an improperly operating gauge, fuel tanking sending unit, or circuit wiring. Similar tests can be performed on the other gauge circuits in the event of a malfunction.

HORNS

Generally, a horn is serviced because it does not operate or because it is out of tune. An inoperative horn can usually be traced to an open circuit in the wiring or a defective relay. To check the relay and horn wiring, connect a jumper from the battery to the horn terminal. If the horn now operates, the trouble

---

ERRATIC FUEL GAUGE READINGS

Inspect all circuit wiring for damage to insulation and conductor, also carefully check to assure good electrical connections are provided at the following locations:

1. Ground connections at dash unit mounting.
2. Harness connector to dash unit.
3. Body harness connector to chassis harness.
4. Ground connection from tank unit to trunk floor pan.
5. Feed wire connection at tank unit.

GAUGE ALWAYS READS EMPTY
(With Ignition Switch On)

Disconnect tank unit feed wire and do not allow wire terminal to ground. Dash unit should now read full.

Gauge Reads Empty

1. Remotely connect a spare dash unit into the dash unit harness connector and provide ground for unit. If full reading shown, dash unit shorted. Replace.
2. If still reads empty, short in harness between tank unit and dash unit.

Gauge Now Reads Full

1. Connect a spare tank unit to tank feed wire and the ground lead.
2. Raise and lower float while observing dash unit. If dash unit follows float movement, replace tank unit.

GAUGE ALWAYS READS FULL
(With Ignition Switch On)

1. Check for proper electrical connections at the dash unit, the body harness connector to chassis harness connector or tank unit connector in the trunk.
2. Check ground wire from tank to trunk floor pan for continuity.
3. Connect a spare tank unit to the tank feed wire and the ground lead. Raise and lower float, observing dash unit. If dash unit follows arm movement, replace tank unit.

GAUGE NEEDLE NEVER REACHES FULL MARK

Disconnect feed wire to tank unit and connect the wire to ground thru a variable resistor in shop test equipment or thru a spare tank unit. The dash unit should read full when resistance is increased to approximately 90 ohms* (equivalent to fully raised float on tank unit). If the above check shows the dash unit to be operating properly, then the trouble is either that the tank unit rheostat is shorter or the float is binding or arm is bent, or the tank itself may even be deformed. Inspect and correct as necessary.

*Prior to 1967 Models, maximum resistance is approximately 29 to 32 ohms.

Fuel gauge troubleshooting chart.

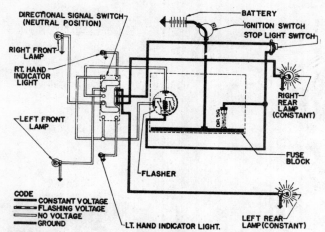

Directional signal lamp circuit. The stop lights are lit, but no turn is indicated.

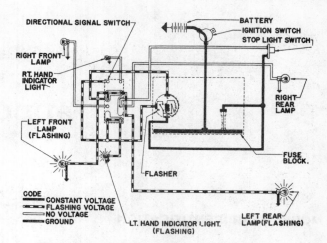

The stop lights are out, with a left turn indicated.

is in the relay or horn wiring; otherwise, the horn itself is defective. As a further check, connect a second jumper from the horn frame to a ground to check the ground connection.

The contact points should be cleaned with crocus cloth and carbon tetrachloride. Do not force the contacts apart or you will bend the contact spring and change the operating tension. Test the winding for open circuit, faulty insulation, and ground. Check the resistor with an ohmmeter, or test the condenser for capacity, ground, and leakage. Inspect the diaphragm for cracks and the horn parts for loose rivets.

To adjust the tone, it is necessary to loosen the locknut, and then turn the adjustment screw until the desired tone is obtained. On dual horns, disconnect one horn so that only one will blow at a time. A simple way to make the contact point adjustment is to insert a 0.007″ feeler gauge blade between the adjusting nut and the contact blade insulator. **CAUTION: Make sure that the gauge does not touch the metallic parts of the contact points, because it will short them out.** Loosen the locknut and turn the adjusting nut down until the horn does not blow. Then loosen the adjusting nut slowly until the horn barely blows. **CAUTION: The locknut must be tightened after each trial adjustment.** Without the feeler gauge in place, the horn will operate satisfactorily and the current draw will be within specifications.

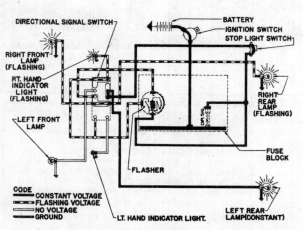

The stop lights are lit, with a right turn indicated. A dual-horn installation requires a relay to minimize the voltage loss of long wires.

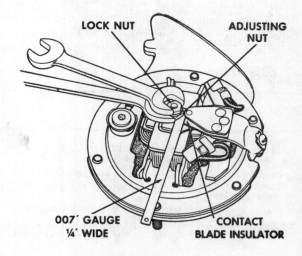

Using a 0.007″ feeler gauge to make an adjustment to the horn, as discussed in the text.

appendix

MODEL YEAR IDENTIFICATION

An identification plate is attached to the left-front door pillar on models through 1967 and to the left upper instrument panel, with the numbers visible from outside of the car, on models since that time. In all cases, the sixth digit, or the one just in front of the assembly plant letter, is the last number of the year of manufacture.

ENGINE IDENTIFICATION

All engines have a prefix to the engine number, which can be used to identify the engine size and year from the following codes. All V-8 engines used in the full-sized cars through 1964 had the engine number (and prefix) stamped at the top of the center exhaust port of the left cylinder head. The 215 CID V-8 engine used in the F-85 for the years of 1962-63 had the number stamped on the front of the right cylinder head, and the V-6 engine had the number stamped on the right cylinder block deck face. The V-8 engines used in the full-sized cars from 1964-67 had the number stamped on a machined pad at the front of the right cylinder head. Since 1968, all engines have the identification codes on a label affixed to the oil filler tube.

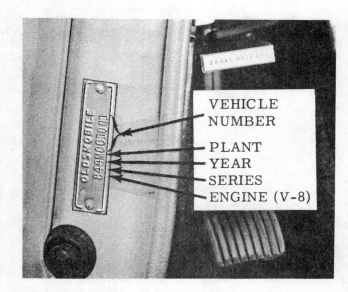

All models through 1967 had this type of vehicle identification number plate affixed to the left-front door pillar. The third digit indicates the year of manufacture which, in this case, is 1964.

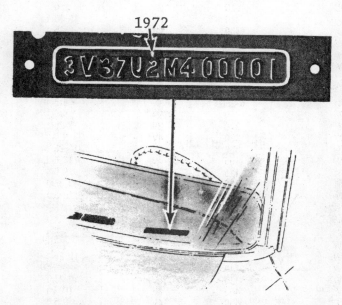

The vehicle identification number (VIN) can be used to determine the year of manufacture.

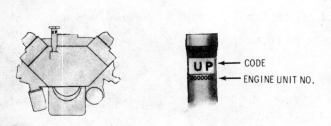

The Oldsmobile engine identification code letters are on a tape affixed to the oil filler tube at the front of the engine.

390

ENGINE IDENTIFICATION CODES

CODES	CID	CARBURETOR	COMPRESSION RATIO
1955-56:			
B	324	2V & 4V	9.25/1
1957-58:			
C	371	2V & 4V	9.75/1
1959-60:			
C	371	2V	8.75/1
D	394	4V	9.75/1
1961:			
S	215	2V	8.75/1
S	215	4V	10.25/1
F	394	2V	8.75/1
G	394	4V	10.0/1
1962:			
S	215	1V	8.75/1
S	215	1V	10.25/1
F	394	2V	8.75/1
G	394	4V	10.25/1
1963:			
S	215	1V	10.25/1
S	215	2V	8.75/1
S	215	4V	10.75/1
H	394	2V	8.75/1
H	394	2V	10.25/1
J	394	4V	10.5/1
1964:			
KH	V6-225	1V	9.0/1
T	330	2V	9.0/1
T	330	4V	10.25/1
H	394	4V	10.5/1
1965:			
LH	V6-225	1V	9.0
U	330	2V	9.0
U	330	2V	10.25/1
U	330	4V	10.25/1
W	400	4V	10.25/1
M	425	2V	10.25/1
M	425	4V	10.25/1
			10.5/1
1966:			
F	6-250	1V	8.5/1
X	330	2V	9.0/1
X	330	2V	10.25/1
X	330	4V	9.0/1
X	330	4V	10.25/1
V	400	4V	10.5/1
M	425	2V	9.0/1
M	425	2V	10.25/1
M	425	4V	10.5/1
1967:			
F	6-250	1V	8.5/1
W	330	2V	9.0/1
W	330	2V	10.25/1
W	330	4V	9.0/1
W	330	4V	10.25/1
V	400	2V	10.5/1
V	400	4V	10.5/1
P	425	2V	9.0/1
R	425	2V	10.25/1
R	425	4V	10.5/1

ENGINE IDENTIFICATION CODES

CODES	CID	CARBURETOR	COMPRESSION RATIO
1968:			
QA, QB, QI, TB, TD, TL	350	2V	9.0/1
QN, QP, QV	350	4V	10.5/1
QR, QS, QT	400	4V	10.5/1
UA, UB	425	2V	10.25/1
UN, UO	425	4V	10.25/1
US, UT, UV, UW	425	4V	10.5/1
1969:			
QA, QB, QI, TB, TC, TD, TL	350	2V	9.0/1
QN, QP, QV, QX*	350	4V	10.5/1
QR, QS, QT*, QU*, QW	400	4V	10.5/1
UC, UD, UJ	455	2V	9.0/1
UL, UN, UO, US, UT, UV, UW*	455	4V	10.25/1
1970:			
QA, QI, QJ, TC, TD, TL	350	2V	9.0/1
QD*, QN, QP, QV, QX*	350	4V	10.5/1
UC, UD, UJ	455	2V	9.0/1
TX, TY	455	2V	10.25/1
TP, TQ, TS*, TT*, TU, TV, TW	455	4V	10.5/1
UL*, UN, UO, US, UT, UV*, UW*	455	4V	10.25/1
1971:			
QA, QJ, TC, TD, TE	350	2V	8.5/1
QB, QN, QO, QP	350	4V	8.5/1
UC, UD, UE	455	2V	8.5/1
TA, TB*, TL*, TN, TP, TQ, TS*, TT*, TU, TV, TW	455	4V	8.5/1
UC, UD, UE, UN, UO, US, UT	455	4V	8.5/1
1972:			
QA, QB, QC, QN, QO	350	2V	8.5/1
QD, QE, QJ, QK, QP, QQ	350	4V	8.5/1
UA, UB, UD, UE, US, UT, UU, UV	455	4V	8.5/1
UL, UN, UO	455	4V*	8.5/1
1973:			
CCA, CCB, CCC, CCD	250	1V	8.5/1
QN, QO, QS, QT	350	2V	8.5/1
QA, QB, QD, QE, QJ, QK, QL	350	4V	8.5/1
UA, UB, UD, US, UT, UU, UV	455	4V	8.5/1
1974:			
CCA, CCB, CCC, CCD	250	1V	8.0/1
QS, QT	350	2V	8.5/1
QB, QC, QL, QO, QU, QW, TB, TC, TL, TO	350	4V	8.5/1
UU, UW	455	2V	8.5/1
UA, UB, UC, UD, UL, UN, UO, UP, UR, UV, UX	455	4V	8.5/1
VA, VB, VC, VD, VL, VO, VP	455 ①	4V	8.5/1

*Ram air induction
① California engines

TORQUE SPECIFICATIONS

NOTE: Specified torque is for installation of parts only. Checking of torque during inspection may be 15% below the specified minimum.

Application	Ft. Lbs.
CRANKSHAFT AND CONNECTING RODS	
Connecting Rod Bearing Cap Bolts	32 to 42
Crankshaft Bearing Cap Bolts (Nos. 1, 2, 3 & 4)	90 to 120
Crankshaft Bearing Cap Bolts (Rear)	130 to 160
Crankshaft Pulley Bolt	100 Min.
ENGINE MOUNTS	
Front Mount to Front Cover Bolts	40 to 60
Front Mount to Frame Nuts	45 to 50
Rear Mount to Flywheel Housing Bolts	50 to 60
Rear Mount to Cross Member	40 to 56
HEAD AND VALVE MECHANISM	
Rocker Arm Cover Bolts	4 to 7
Cylinder Head to Block Bolts	60 to 80
Rocker Shaft Bracket to Head	14 to 22
Spark Plugs	18 to 34
FLYWHEEL AND DAMPER PLATE	
Flywheel to Crankshaft Bolts	85 to 95
Clutch Pressure Plate to Flywheel Bolts	14 to 17
Damper Plate to Flywheel Bolts	17 to 22
FLYWHEEL AND CLUTCH HOUSING	
Flywheel Lower Housing Cover Bolts	4 to 7
Flywheel Lower Housing to Block Bolts	50 to 55
Flywheel Cover Housing to Block and Flywheel Housing	50 to 55
Clutch Housing to Block and Flywheel Housing Bolts	50 to 55
FRONT COVER AND WATER PUMP	
Cover to Block Bolts (3/8")	24 to 40
Water Pump to Front Cover (3/8")	24 to 40
Water Pump to Front Cover (1/4")	5 to 8
Water Outlet to Manifold	22 to 26
FUEL AND VACUUM PUMP	
Pump to Front Cover Bolts	35 to 40
Fuel Pump Eccentric	14 to 22
MANIFOLD	
Intake Manifold to Head Bolts	22 to 34
Exhaust Manifold to Head Bolts and Nuts	19 to 25
OIL PAN, PUMP AND FILTER	
Oil Pan Bolts	10 to 18
Oil Pan Drain Plug	35 to 45
Pump to Bearing Cap	24 to 34
Pump Cover Bolts	5 to 8
Pump Screen Bolts	4 to 7
Filter Assembly to Cylinder Block Bolts	28 to 38
Filter Housing	10 to 20
Oil Pressure Switch	10 to 15

Torque specifications for the full-sized car V-8 engine through 1964.

TORQUE SPECIFICATIONS

NOTE: Before threading bolts into aluminum, some must be coated with Part No. 980131 lubricant, some with engine oil and others with sealer. Consult the component part of the text for correct installation.

Application	Ft. Lbs.
CRANKSHAFT AND CONNECTING RODS	
Connecting Rod Bearing Cap Bolts	30 to 35
Crankshaft Bearing Cap Bolts (No. 1-2-3-4)	50 to 60
Crankshaft Bearing Cap Bolt (No. 5)	65 to 70
Crankshaft Balancer	140 to 160
Fan Driving Pulley to Balancer	15 to 20
Fan and Driven Pulley to Hub	15 to 20
ENGINE MOUNTS	
Front Mount to Block Bolts	50 to 55
Front Mount to Crossbar Nuts	55 to 65
Rear Mount to Transmission	30 to 40
Rear Mount to Cross Support	20 to 34
HEAD AND VALVE MECHANISM	
Valve Cover Bolts	3 to 5
Cylinder Head to Block Bolts	45 to 55
Rocker Shaft Bracket to Head	45 to 55
Spark Plugs (1 Drop of Engine Oil on Threads)	12 to 17
FLYWHEEL AND DAMPER	
Flywheel to Crankshaft Bolts	85 to 95
Clutch to Flywheel	14 to 17
Damper to Flywheel	17 to 22
CLUTCH HOUSING	
Clutch Lower Housing to Upper Housing Bolts	4 to 7
Clutch Housing to Block Bolts	30 to 35
Flywheel Cover to Housing Bolts	20 to 25
FRONT COVER AND WATER PUMP	
Cover to Block Bolts	20 to 25
Water Pump to Front Cover	6 to 8
Oil Pressure Switch to Filter Valve Cap	10 to 15
FUEL AND VACUUM PUMP	
Fuel Pump to Front Cover Bolts	20 to 35
Fuel Pump Eccentric to Camshaft	40 to 45
MANIFOLD	
Intake Manifold Gasket Clamp Bolts (2-5/16")	10 to 15
Intake Manifold to Head Bolts	25 to 30
Exhaust Manifold to Head Bolts and Nuts	18 to 24
Water Outlet to Intake Manifold	10 to 15
Carburetor to Intake Manifold	14 to 17

Torque specifications for the F-85 215 CID V-8 engine used in 1961-63.

TORQUE SPECIFICATIONS

Part	Application	Thread	Torque Ft. Lbs.
Plug	Spark	14mm	35
Plug	Crankcase drain	1/2 -20	35
Bolt	Water pump and timing chain cover to block	5/16-18	25
Bolt	Water pump cover to timing chain cover	1/4 -20	9
Bolt	Water outlet to intake manifold	5/16-18	25
Bolt	Intake manifold gasket clamp to block	5/16-18	15
Bolt	Intake manifold to cylinder head	3/8 -16	35
Bolt	Exhaust manifold to cylinder head	3/8 -16	35
Bolt	Carburetor to intake manifold	5/16-18	15
Bolt	Fuel pump to timing chain cover	5/16-18	25
Bolt	Camshaft Sprocket to camshaft	7/16-20	45
Bolt	Rocker arm shaft bracket to cylinder head	3/8 -16	35
Screw	Rocker arm cover to cylinder head	1/4 -20	5
Bolt	Cranking motor to cylinder block	3/8 -16	35
Bolt	Distributor clamp to timing chain cover	3/8 -16	17
Bolt	Crankshaft bearing cap to crankcase	1/2 -13	70
Plug	Cylinder block water drain	1/4 -18	20
Bolt	Cylinder head to block.	7/16-14	70
Bolt	Upper flywheel housing to cylinder block.	3/18-16	40
Bolt	Lower flywheel housing to block and upper flywheel housing	5/16-18	12
Bolt	Flywheel to crankshaft	7/16-20	60
Bolt	Harmonic balancer to crankshaft	5/8 -18	160
Nut	Connecting rod bolt	11/32-24	35
Bolt	Oil pan to block	5/16-18	15
Bolt	Oil screen housing pipe and flange assembly to block	1/4 -20	9
Bolt	Timing chain cover to block	5/16-18	25
Cap	Oil pressure relief valve		35
Screw	Oil pump cover assembly to timing chain cover	1/4 -20	12
Switch	Oil pressure.		10
Bolt	Fan and pulley to water pump hub	5/16-24	25
Bolt	Pulley and reinforcement to harmonic balancer	5/16-18	25
Bolt	Engine mount to cylinder block	7/16-14	55
Bolt	Engine mount to frame bracket	7/16-20	65

Torque specifications for the V-6 engine used in the F-85 for the years of 1964-65.

TORQUE SPECIFICATIONS

NOTE: Specified torque is for installation of parts only. Checking of torque during inspection may be 10% below specification.

Application	Ft. Lbs.
FUEL PUMP	
Fuel Pump to Block Bolt and Nut	25
Fuel Pump Eccentric to Camshaft	65
EXHAUST SYSTEM	15-20
ENGINE	
Crankshaft Bearing Cap Bolts (400 cu. in. and 425 cu. in. engines)	120
Crankshaft Bearing Cap Bolts Nos. 1, 2, 3 & 4 (330 cu. in. engine)	80
Crankshaft Bearing Cap No. 5 (330 cu. in. engine)	120
*Cylinder Head to Block	80
Connecting Rod Nuts	42
Oil Pump to Bearing Cap Bolts	35
Oil Pump Cover to Pump Bolts	8
Rocker Arm Studs to Head	35
Rocker Arm Nuts to Studs	25
Valve Cover Bolts	7
Oil Pan Bolts 5/16"	15
Oil Pan Bolts 1/4"	8
Oil Pan Drain Plug	50
Crankshaft Balancer or Hub to Crankshaft Bolt	50
Oil Filter Element to Base	20
Oil Filter Assembly to Cylinder Block Bolts	35
Front Cover to Cylinder Block Bolts 3/8"	35
Front Cover to Cylinder Block Bolts 5/16"	25
Fan Driven Pulley to Hub Bolts	20
Fan Driving Pulley to Hub or Balancer Bolts	20
Water Pump to Front Cover Bolts	13
Water Outlet to Manifold Bolts	20
*Intake Manifold to Cylinder Head Bolts	35
Intake Manifold Baffle to Cylinder Block Bolts	8
Exhaust Manifold to Cylinder Head Bolts	25
Carburetor to Intake Manifold Bolts	15
Tube and Plate to Intake Manifold Bolts	15
Air Cleaner to Carburetor Stud	5
Motor Mount to Cylinder Block Bolts	50
Starter to Cylinder Block Bolts	35
Starter Brace to Cylinder Block Bolt	25
Starter Brace to Starter Bolt	15
Distributor Clamp to Cylinder Block Bolt	14
Spark Plugs	35
Coil to Intake Manifold Bolt	15

*Clean and dip entire bolt in engine oil before tightening to avoid an erroneous torque reading.

Torque specifications for the 330, 400, and 425 CID engines used to power the full-sized cars since 1964.

TORQUE SPECIFICATIONS

NOTE: Specified torque is for installation of parts only. Checking of torque during inspection may be 10% below specification.

Application   Ft. Lbs.

FUEL PUMP
    Fuel Pump to Block Bolt and Nut 25
    Fuel Pump to Eccentric to Camshaft 65

EXHAUST SYSTEM 15-20

ENGINE
    Crankshaft Bearing Cap Bolts (455 Cu. In. Engines) 120
    Crankshaft Bearing Cap Bolts Nos. 1, 2, 3 & 4 (350 Cu. In. Engines) 80
    Crankshaft Bearing No. 5 (350 Cu. In. Engine) 120
    E.G.R. Valve to Intake Manifold 25
    Flywheel to Crankshaft (Automatic) 60
    Flywheel to Crankshaft (Synchromesh) 90
    Oil Pump to Bearing Cap Bolts 35
    Oil Deflector to Bearing Cap (Toronado) 35
    Oil Pump Cover to Pump Bolts 8
    Rocker Arm Pivot Bolt to Head 25
    Valve Cover Bolts 7
    Oil Pan Bolts 10
    Oil Pan Drain Plug 30
    Crankshaft Balancer or Hub to Crankshaft Bolt . . . . 160 Min.
    Oil Filter Element to Base 20
    Oil Filter Assembly to Cylinder Block Bolts 35
    Support/Front Cover to Cylinder Block Bolts 3/8" (Exc. Toronado) 35
    Support/Front Cover Block (Toronado) 50
    Fan Driven Pulley to Hub Bolts 20
    Fan Driving Pulley to Balancer Bolts 20
    Water Pump to Front Cover Bolts 13
    Water Outlet to Manifold Bolts 20
    *Intake Manifold to Cylinder Head Bolts 40
    Exhaust Manifold to Cylinder Head Bolts 25
    Carburetor to Intake Manifold Bolts 15
    Choke Tube and Plate to Intake Manifold Bolts 15
    Air Cleaner to Carburetor Stud 5
    Engine Mount to Cylinder Block Bolts 75
    Engine Mount to Frame Mount 50
    Starter to Cylinder Block Bolts 35
    Starter Brace to Cylinder Block Bolts 25
    Starter Brace to Starter Bolt 15
    Starter Brace to Starter Stud 8
    Distributor Clamp to Cylinder Block Bolt 17
    Spark Plugs 35
    Coil to Intake Manifold Bolt 15
    *Cylinder Head Bolts 85
    Connecting Rod Nuts 42

*Clean and dip entire bolt in engine oil before tightening to obtain a correct torque reading.

Torque specifications for the 350 and 455 CID engines used to power the full-sized cars since 1968.

TUNE-UP SPECIFICATIONS—THROUGH 1967

YEAR & MODEL	SPARK PLUGS Type (AC)	Gap (In.)	DISTRIBUTOR Point Gap (In.)	Cam Angle (Deg.)	TIMING (Degrees) B = Before Top Dead Center	IDLE SPEED N = Neutral D = Drive A = Air Cond. T = Air Injection System	FUEL PUMP PRESSURE (Psi)	VALVE CLEARANCE (Inches)
1955-56	44	.030	.016	30	5B	400N	4-5-1/2	Hyd.
1957	44	.030	.016	30	5B	460D	5-6	Hyd.
1958	44	.030	.016	30	5B	460D	5-6	Hyd.
1959	44	.030	.016	30	5B ⑥	460D, 520A	5-6	Hyd.
1960	45 ①	.030	.016	30	5B ⑥	460D, 520A	5-6	Hyd.
1961								
32	45	.030	.016	30	5B ⑥	460D, 520A	5-6	Hyd.
35, 38	44	.030	.016	30	5B ⑥	460D, 520A	5-6	Hyd.
F85	46FFX ③	.040	.016	30	5B ⑥	550N, 500D, 550A	5-6	Hyd.
1962-63								
32	44	.030	.016	30	5B ②, ⑥	550N, 500D, 550A	6-8	Hyd.
35, 38	44	.030	.016	30	5B ⑥	550N, 500D, 550A	6-8	Hyd.
F85	46FFX ③	.030	.016	30	5B ④, ⑥	550N, 500D, 550A	6-8	Hyd.
1964								
V6-F85	45S	.030	.016	30	5B	550N, 550D, 600A	4-1/2-5-3/4	Hyd.
V8-330, Jet Star 88	44S	.030	.016	30	7-1/2B ⑥	600N, 500D, 600A	7-3/4-9	Hyd.
V8-394	44	.030	.016	30	5B ⑤, ⑥	500N, 500D, 550A	5-6	Hyd.
1965								
F85, V6	44S	.033	.016	30	5B	550N, 550D	4-1/4-5-3/4	Hyd.
F85, V8	45S	.030	.016	30	7-1/2B ⑥	600N, 600D	7-3/4-9	Hyd.
Cutlass	44S	.030	.016	30	7-1/2B ⑥	600N, 600D	7-3/4-9	Hyd.
Jetstar and Starfire	44S	.030	.016	30	7-1/2B ⑥	600N, 600D	7-3/4-9	Hyd.
88 and 98	44S	.030	.016	30	5B ⑥	550N, 550D	7-3/4-9	Hyd.
1966-67								
L-6	46N	.035	.019	33	6B ⑦	500N, 500D, 500NT, 650DT	3-1/4-4-1/2	Hyd. ⑧
V8; 330, 2-Bbl.	44S	.030	.016	30	7-1/2B ⑥	600N, 500D, 650NT, 550DT	7-3/4-9	Hyd.
V8; 330, 4-Bbl.	44S	.030	.016	30	7-1/2B ⑥	600N, 500D, 650NT, 550DT	7-3/4-9	Hyd.
4-4-2; 400, 4-Bbl.	44S	.030	.016	30	7-1/2B ⑥	550N, 550D, 600A, 600DA	7-3/4-9	Hyd.
88 & 98; 425, 2-Bbl.	44S	.030	.016	30	5B ⑥	550N, 500D	7-3/4-9	Hyd.
Toronado	44S	.030	.016	30	7-1/2B ⑥	550N, 500D, 600NA, 550DA	7-3/4-9	Hyd.

① No. 44 spark plugs used in 9.75/1 CR engine.
② Set timing 2.5°B with low compression engine.
③ With 4 Bbl. carburetor, use 45FF spark plug.
④ Set timing to 7-1/2° BTDC with 4 Bbl. carburetor, or to 10° BTDC with Turbo-Rocket engine.
⑤ With standard transmission, set timing to 2-1/2°B.
⑥ At 850 rpm.
⑦ At 500 rpm.
⑧ One turn down from zero-lash position.

TUNE-UP SPECIFICATIONS—1968-74

ENGINE CID (Carbs.)	CODE ① LETTERS	SPARK PLUGS Type (AC)	Gap (Inches)	DISTRIBUTOR Point Gap (Inches)	Dwell (°±2)	IGNITION TIMING ② Degrees @ Rpm Auto. Trans.	Man. Trans.	IDLE SPEED Auto. Trans. (Drive) (Slow)	(Final)	Man. Trans. (Neutral) (Slow)	(Final)
1968:											
350 (2V)	—	45S	.030	.016	30	5B @ 850	5B @ 850	575	550	675	650
350 (4V)	—	44S	.030	.016	30	7.5B @ 850	7.5B @ 850	575	550	675	650
400 (2V)	—	45S	.030	.016	30	5B @ 850	5B @ 850	575	550	675	650
400 (4V)	—	44S	.030	.016	30	7.5B @ 850	2.5B @ 850	575	550	725	700
400 (4V) ③	—	44S	.030	.016	30	—	10B @ 1,250	575	550	725	700
455 (2V)	—	45S	.030	.016	30	5B @ 850	5B @ 850	575	550	675	650
455 (2V) HC	—	44S	.030	.016	30	7.5B @ 850	—	575	550	675	650
455 (4V)	—	44S	.030	.016	30	7.5B @ 850	7.5B @ 850	575	550	675	650
455 (4V) ③	—	44S	.030	.016	30	10B @ 850	10B @ 850	575	550	675	650
1969:											
350 (2V)	OT	R46S	.030	.016	30	6B @ 850	6B @ 850	575	550	675	650
350 (4V)	OU	R45S	.030	.016	30	8B @ 850	8B @ 850	575	550	675	650
350 (4V) ③	O3	R43S	.030	.016	30	—	12B @ 1,000	—	—	850	825
400 (4V)	OV	R44S	.030	.016	30	8B @ 850	8B @ 850	575	550	750	725
400 (4V)	O2	R44S	.030	.016	30	10B @ 850	10B @ 850	575	550	750	725
400 (4V)	OX	R44S	.030	.016	30	—	2B @ 850	—	—	750	725
400 (4V) ③	OY	R44S	.030	.016	30	14B @ 1,250	14B @ 1,250	—	650	—	850
455 (2V)	OW	R45S	.030	.016	30	6B @ 850	6B @ 850	575	550	675	650
455 (4V)	OV	R44S	.030	.016	30	8B @ 850	8B @ 850	575	550	675	650
455 (4V) ④	O2	R44S	.030	.016	30	10B @ 850	10B @ 850	575	550	—	—
1970:											
350 (2V)	OO	R46S	.030	.016	30	10B @ 1,100	—	620	575	—	—
350 (2V)	OG	R46S	.030	.016	30	—	10B @ 1,100	—	—	800	750
350 (4V)	OJ	R45S	.030	.016	30	10B @ 1,100	—	625	575	—	—
350 (4V)	OI	R43S	.030	.016	30	14B @ 1,100	14B @ 1,100	—	625	—	750
455 (2V)	ON/OT	R45S	.030	.016	30	8B @ 1,100	—	620	575	—	—
455 (2V)	OD	R46S	.030	.016	30	8B @ 1,100	8B @ 1,100	620	575	720	675
455 (4V)	OM	R44S	.030	.016	30	12B @ 1,100	—	700	600	—	—
455 (4V)	OE	R44S	.030	.016	30	—	12B @ 1,100	—	—	—	750
455 (4V) ③	OF/OP	R44S	.030	.016	30	10B @ 850	12B @ 850	675	650	—	750
455 (4V)	OA/OR	R45S	.030	.016	30	8B @ 1,100	—	650	575	—	—
455 (4V) ④	OK/OS	R45S	.030	.016	30	8B @ 1,100	—	675	600	—	—
455 (4V) ③④	OL	R44S	.030	.016	30	12B @ 1,100	—	675	600	—	—
1971:											
350 (4V)	OA	R46S	.040	.016	30	10B @ 1,100	10B @ 1,100	—	600	—	750
350 (4V)	OB	R45S	.040	.016	30	—	10B @ 1,100	—	—	—	750
455 (2V)	OF/OJ	R46S	.040	.016	30	8B @ 1,100	8B @ 1,100	—	600	—	750
455 (4V)	OD/OK	R45S	.040	.016	30	10B @ 1,100	10B @ 1,100	—	600	—	750
455 (4V)	OG	R46S	.040	.016	30	8B @ 1,100	—	—	600	—	—
455 (4V) ③	OE/OL	R45S	.040	.016	30	10B @ 850	12B @ 1,100	—	600	—	750
455 (4V) ④	OH	R46S	.040	.016	30	10B @ 1,100	—	—	600	—	—

① Code letters on tune-up decal.
② With the vacuum hose to the distributor removed and plugged.
③ Air-induction system.
④ Toronado.
⑤ 442 model.
⑥ In PARK.
⑦ California model.
⑧ Special spark plugs for the HEI system have longer side electrodes than regular spark plugs.

TUNE-UP SPECIFICATIONS—1968-74

ENGINE CID (Carbs.)	CODE ① LETTERS	SPARK PLUGS		DISTRIBUTOR		IGNITION TIMING ②		IDLE SPEED			
		Type (AC)	Gap (Inches)	Point Gap (Inches)	Dwell (°±2)	Degrees @ Rpm		Auto. Trans. (Drive)		Man. Trans.	(Neutral)
						Auto. Trans.	Man. Trans.	(Slow)	(Final)	(Slow)	(Final)
1972:											
350 (2V)	SA	R46S	.040	.016	30	8B @ 1,100	8B @ 1,100	—	650	—	750
350 (4V)	SD	R46S	.040	.016	30	12B @ 1,100	—	—	600	—	—
350 (4V)	SC	R45S	.040	.016	30	—	8B @ 1,100	—	—	—	550
455 (4V)	SH	R46S	.040	.016	30	8B @ 1,100	—	—	600	—	—
455 (4V) ③	SG	R45S	.040	.016	30	10B @ 850	10B @ 1,100	—	650	—	1,000
455 (4V) ④	SF	R46S	.040	.016	30	8B @ 1,100	—	—	650	—	—
455 (4V) ⑤	SF	R45S	.040	.016	30	—	10B @ 1,100	—	—	—	750
1973:											
250 (1V)	WB	R46TS	.035	.019	33	6B @ 700	6B @ 700	450 ⑥	600	450	700
350 (2V)	OA	R46S	.040	.016	30	14B @ 1,100	—	550 ⑥	650	—	—
350 (2V)	OB	R46S	.040	.016	30	12B @ 1,100	—	550 ⑥	700	—	—
350 (4V)	OC	R46S	.040	.016	30	12B @ 1,100	—	550 ⑥	650	—	—
350 (4V)	OH	R45S	.040	.016	30	—	12B @ 1,100	—	—	750	1,000
455 (4V)	OJ	R45S	.040	.016	30	—	10B @ 1,100	—	—	750	1,000
455 (4V)	OD	R46S	.040	.016	30	8B @ 1,100	—	550 ⑥	650	—	—
455 (4V) ④	OK	R46S	.040	.016	30	8B @ 1,100	—	550 ⑥	650	—	—
1974:											
250 (1V)	ZM	R46TS	.035	.019	33	8B @ 600	8B @ 600	450 ⑥	600	450	850
250 (1V) ⑦	ZN	R46TS	.035	.019	33	8B @ 600	8B @ 600	450 ⑥	600	450	850
350 (2V)	OA	R46S	.040	.016	30	14B @ 1,100	—	550 ⑥	700	—	—
350 (4V)	OB/OC	R46S	.040	.016	30	12B @ 1,100	—	550 ⑥	650	—	—
350 (4V) ⑦	OD/OS	R46S	.040	.016	30	12B @ 1,100	—	550 ⑥	650	—	—
455 (2V)	OF	R46S	.040	.016	30	8B @ 1,100	—	550 ⑥	700	—	—
455 (4V)	OR	R45S	.040	.016	30	14B @ 1,100	—	550 ⑥	650	—	—
455 (4V)	OH/OK	R46S	.040	.016	30	8B @ 1,100	—	550 ⑥	650	—	—
455 (4V)	OJ/OL	R46SX ⑧	.080	—	—	8B @ 1,100	—	550 ⑥	650	—	—
455 (4V)	OM/ON	R46S	.040	.016	30	10B @ 1,100	—	550 ⑥	650	—	—
455 (4V)	OP/OQ	R46SX ⑧	.080	—	—	10B @ 1,100	—	550 ⑥	650	—	—

① Code letters on tune-up decal.
② With the vacuum hose to the distributor removed and plugged.
③ Air-induction system.
④ Toronado.
⑤ 442 model.
⑥ In PARK.
⑦ California model.
⑧ Special spark plugs for the HEI system have longer side electrodes than regular spark plugs.

HIGH-ENERGY IGNITION (HEI) SYSTEM SPARK PLUG USAGE

Spark plugs used with the High-Energy Ignition (HEI) system are especially designed with a longer side electrode to allow for the 0.080″ gap. If regular spark plugs are gapped at 0.080″, the side electrode will be bent at an angle and this will result in unparallel side-to-center electrode alignment.

TUNE-UP SPECIFICATIONS

ENGINE AND CODE (Code is on Oil Filter Pipe V-8)	IGNITION TIMING L-6 33° DWELL V-8 30° DWELL	SPARK PLUG TYPE & GAP	SOLENOID SCREW † (RPM)	SLOW IDLE CARBURETOR SCREW (RPM)	FAST IDLE RPM ▲	CARBURETOR IDENTIFICATION 704	EMISSION CONTROL DEVICES	EGR VALVE MODEL	TUNE-UP LABEL CODE	SPARK DELAY DEVICE	DISTRIBUTOR MODEL	DISTRIBUTOR VACUUM MODEL	VACUUM ADVANCE @INCHES OF VACUUM (IN CRANK DEGREES)	MECHANICAL ADVANCE (CRANK DEGREES@ ENGINE RPM)
250 C.I.D. 1BBL. L-6 ENG. CODE (L-22) CCC, (CCD CALIF.) M.T. CCA, (CCB CALIF.) A.T. OMEGA	8° @ 850 M.T. / A.T. 8° @ 600	R46TS .035" GAP / R46TS .035" GAP	850 (N) / 600 (DR)	*450 (N) / •450 (PARK)	PRESET / PRESET	4017 (M.T.) (M.T.) Cal. / 4014 (A.T.) 4314 (A.T.) Cal.	T.C.S., C.C.S. P.C.V. / A.I.R.@, C.C.S. P.C.V., E.G.R. @CALIF.	7035170 / 7035169	ZM / ZN@	NO / NO	1110499	1973428	START 12° / 6-8 IN. HG. 14.5-15.5 IN. HG.	0° 2° 14° 24° — 930 RPM 1270 RPM 2300 RPM 4100 RPM
350 C.I.D. 2BBL. V-8 ENG. CODE (L-32 A.T.) QS, QT, OMEGA	14° @1100	R46S .040" GAP	700 (DR)	550 (PARK)	900 (PARK)	4158 (A.T.)	C.C.S., E.G.R. T.V.S., P.C.V.	7040497	OA	NO	1112226	1973468	START 20° 3.5-4.5 IN. HG. 12-13 IN. HG.	0°-4° 16°-20° 28°-32° — 800 RPM 2100 RPM 4000 RPM
350 C.I.D. 4BBL. V-8 ENG. CODES (L-34 EXC. WGN. A.T.) QB, QC, QI, QO OMEGA & CUTLASS	12° @1100	R46S .040" GAP	650 (DR)	550 (PARK)	1000 (PARK)	•3255 OMEGA •3250 CUTLASS	C.C.S., E.G.R. T.V.S.@ P.C.V. @EXC. A/C CUT.	7040452	OB OC* A/C Cut.	YES	1112195	1973453	START 16° 5-7 IN. HG. 10-12 IN. HG.	0°-4° 16°-20° 28°-32° — 800 RPM 2100 RPM 4000 RPM
350 C.I.D. 4BBL. V-8 (CALIF.) ENG. CODES (L-34 EXC. WGN. A.T.) TB, TC, TL, TO OMEGA & CUTLASS	12° @1100	R46S .040" GAP	650 (DR)	550 (PARK)	1000 (PARK)	•3255 OMEGA •3250 CUTLASS	C.C.S., E.G.R. B.P.V., D.V.V.@ T.V.S., P.C.V. @CUTLASS	7041437	OD OS* *Cut.	YES (OMEGA) NO (CUTLASS)	1112226 1112828	1973468	START 20° 3.5-4.5 IN. HG. 12-13 IN. HG.	0°-4° 16°-20° 28°-32° — 800 RPM 2100 RPM 4000 RPM
350 C.I.D. 4BBL. V-8 ENG. CODES (L-34 WGN. A.T.) QU, QW, CUTLASS & V.C.	12° @1100	R46S .040" GAP	650 (DR)	550 (PARK)	1000 (PARK)	•3256	C.C.S., E.G.R. T.V.S., P.C.V.	7040452	OB	YES	1112225	1973453	START 16° 5-7 IN. HG. 10-12 IN. HG.	0°-4° 10°-14° 22°-26° 34°-38° — 760 RPM 1100 RPM 2100 RPM 4000 RPM
455 C.I.D. 4BBL. V-8 ENG. CODES (L-76) UV, UX CUTLASS (G-37)	14° @1100	R45S .040" GAP	650 (DR)	550 (PARK)	1000 (PARK)	•4559	C.C.S., E.G.R. T.V.S., P.C.V.		OR	YES	1112550	1973427	START 16° 12 IN. HG. 18 IN. HG.	0° 14° 26° — 750 RPM 1200 RPM 3000 RPM
350 C.I.D. 4BBL. V-8 ENG. CODES (L-35) QU, QW, 88	12° @1100	R46S .040" GAP	650 (DR)	550 (PARK)	1000 (PARK)	•3256	C.C.S., E.G.R. T.V.S., P.C.V.	7040452	OB	YES	1112225	1973453	START 16° 5-7 IN. HG. 10-12 IN. HG.	0°-4° 10°-14° 22°-26° 34°-38° — 760 RPM 1100 RPM 2100 RPM 4000 RPM
455 C.I.D. 2BBL. V-8 ENG. CODE (L-72 A.T.) UU, UW, 88	8° @1100	R46S .040" GAP	700 (DR)	550 (PARK)	900 (PARK)	•4152	C.C.S., E.G.R. T.V.S., P.C.V.	7040497	OF	NO	1112197	1973232	START 18° 7-9 IN. HG. 15-16.6 IN. HG.	0°-4° 10°-14° 18°-22° — 1080 RPM 2000 RPM 3600 RPM
455 C.I.D. 4BBL. V-8 ENG. CODES (L-74&L-75 A.T.) UL, UA, UC, CUTLASS, WGNS., 88&98	8° @1100	R46S .040" GAP	650 (DR)	550 (PARK)	1000 (PARK)	•3251	C.C.S., E.G.R. T.V.S., P.C.V.	7040452	OH	YES	1112197	1116232	START 18° 7-9 IN. HG. 15-16.6 IN. HG.	0°-4° 10°-14° 18°-22° — 1080 RPM 2000 RPM 3600 RPM
455 C.I.D. 4BBL. V-8 (CALIF.) ENG. CODES (L-74&L-75 A.T.) VL, VA, VC, CUTLASS, WGNS., 88&98	8° @1100	R46S .040" GAP	650 (DR)	550 (DR)	1000 (PARK)	•4558	C.C.S., E.G.R. B.P.V., D.V.V. T.V.S., P.C.V.	7041437	OK	NO	1112531	1973496	START 18° 6 IN. HG. 10 IN. HG.	0°-4° 10°-14° 18°-22° — 1080 RPM 2000 RPM 3600 RPM
455 C.I.D. 4BBL. V-8 W/K-86 ENG. CODES (L-74) UB, UD, 88&98	8° @1100	R46SX .080" GAP	650 (DR)	550 (PARK)	1000 (PARK)	•3251	C.C.S., E.G.R. T.V.S., P.C.V.	7040452	OJ	YES	1112506	1973474	START 18° 7-9 IN. HG. 15-16.6 IN. HG.	0°-4° 10°-14° 18°-22° — 1080 RPM 2000 RPM 3600 RPM
455 C.I.D. 4BBL. V-8 W/K-86 (CALIF.) ENG. CODES (L-74) VB, VD, 88&98	8° @1100	R46SX .080" GAP	650 (DR)	550 (PARK)	1000 (PARK)	•3251	C.C.S., E.G.R. B.P.V., D.V.V. T.V.S., P.C.V.	7041437	OL	NO	1112532	1973499	START 20° 4 IN. HG. 13 IN. HG.	0°-4° 10°-14° 18°-22° — 1080 RPM 2000 RPM 3600 RPM
455 C.I.D. 4BBL. V-8 ENG. CODE (L-78 A.T.) UO, TORONADO	10° @1100	R46S .040" GAP	650 (DR)	550 (PARK)	1000 (PARK)	•3252	C.C.S., E.G.R. D.V.V. T.V.S., P.C.V.	7048215	OM	NO	1112827	1973497	START 24° 7 IN. HG. 17 IN. HG.	0°-4° 7°-11° 14°-18° — 1150 RPM 2000 RPM 3400 RPM
455 C.I.D. 4BBL. V-8 (CALIF.) ENG. CODE (L-78 A.T.) VO, TORONADO	10° @1100	R46S .040" GAP	650 (DR)	550 (PARK)	1000 (PARK)	☆4557	C.C.S., E.G.R. D.V.V., B.P.V. T.V.S., P.C.V.	7041437	ON	NO	1112825	1973496	START 18° 6 IN. HG. 10 IN. HG.	0°-4° 7°-11° 14°-18° — 1150 RPM 2000 RPM 3400 RPM
455 C.I.D. 4BBL. V-8 W/K-86 ENG. CODE (L-78 A.T.) UP, TORONADO	10° @1100	R46SX .080" GAP	650 (DR)	550 (PARK)	1000 (PARK)	•3252	C.C.S., E.G.R. D.V.V. T.V.S., P.C.V.	7048215	OP	NO	1112830	1973500	START 24° 7 IN. HG. 17 IN. HG.	0°-4° 7°-11° 14°-18° — 1150 RPM 2000 RPM 3400 RPM
455 C.I.D. 4BBL. V-8 W/K-86 (CALIF.) ENG. CODE (L-78 A.T.) VP, TORONADO	10° @1100	R46SX .080" GAP	650 (DR)	550 (PARK)	1000 (PARK)	☆4557	C.C.S., E.G.R. D.V.V., B.P.V. T.V.S., P.C.V.	7041437	OQ	NO	1112829	1973499	START 20° 4 IN. HG. 13 IN. HG.	0°-4° 7°-11° 14°-18° — 1150 RPM 2000 RPM 3400 RPM

† Turn Idle Stop Solenoid In or Out To Adjust Slow Idle RPM (Solenoid Energized)
* Turn 1/8" Hex Screw To Adjust Low (Shutoff) Idle (Solenoid De-Energized)
▲ With E.G.R. Vacuum Hose Removed and Plugged-Low Step of Fast Idle Cam
♦ Solenoid De-Energized
☆ Choke Set At Index
• Choke Set One Notch Rich

C.E.C. = Combined Emission Control Valve
A.I.R. = Air Injection Reactor
E.G.R. = Exhaust Gas Recirculation
C.C.S. = Controlled Combustion System
T.V.S. = Thermal Vacuum Switch
P.C.V. = Positive Crankcase Ventilation
D.V.V. = Distributor Vacuum Valve
B.P.V. = Back Pressure Transducer Valve

1974 Oldsmobile tune-up and distributor specifications.

Wiley 11th Hour Guide for
2019 Level I CFA Exam

Thousands of candidates from more than 100 countries have relied on these Study Guides to pass the CFA® Exam. Covering every Learning Outcome Statement (LOS) on the exam, these review materials are an invaluable tool for anyone who wants a deep-dive review of all the concepts, formulas, and topics required to pass.

Wiley study materials are produced by expert CFA charterholders, CFA Institute members, and investment professionals from around the globe. For more information, contact us at info@efficientlearning.com.

Wiley 11th Hour Guide for 2019 Level I CFA Exam

WILEY

Contents

Derivatives
Alternative Investments

Foreword

Wiley 11th Hour Guide for 2019 Level I CFA Exam is a concise and easy-to-understand review book that is meant to supplement your review for the CFA Level I exam. It becomes extremely difficult to go through the entire curriculum in the last few weeks leading up to the exam, so we have condensed the material for you. You must remember, though, that this book is not meant to be a primary study tool for the exam. It is designed to help you review the material in an efficient and effective manner so that you can be confident on exam day.

About the Authors

Wiley's Study Guides are written by a team of highly qualified CFA charterholders and leading CFA instructors from around the globe. Our team of CFA experts work collaboratively to produce the best study materials for CFA candidates available today.

Wiley's expert team of contributing authors and instructors is led by Content Director Basit Shajani, CFA. Basit founded online education start-up Élan Guides in 2009 to help address CFA candidates' need for better study materials. As lead writer, lecturer, and curriculum developer, Basit's unique ability to break down complex topics helped the company grow organically to be a leading global provider of CFA Exam prep materials. In January 2014, Élan Guides was acquired by John Wiley & Sons, Inc., where Basit continues his work as Director of CFA Content. Basit graduated magna cum laude from the Wharton School of Business at the University of Pennsylvania with majors in finance and legal studies. He went on to obtain his CFA charter in 2006, passing all three levels on the first attempt. Prior to Élan Guides, Basit ran his own private wealth management business. He is a past president of the Pakistani CFA Society.

There are many more expert CFA charterholders who contribute to the creation of Wiley materials. We are thankful for their invaluable expertise and diligent work. To learn more about Wiley's team of subject matter experts, please visit: www.efficientlearning.com/cfa/why-wiley/.

STUDY SESSION 1: ETHICAL AND PROFESSIONAL STANDARDS

ETHICS AND TRUST IN THE INVESTMENT PROFESSION
Cross-Reference to CFA Institute Assigned Reading #1

Ethics describes a system of principles, beliefs, and values that guide (or society believes should guide) our behavior. Principles are fundamental truths that form the basis for a chain of reasoning leading to beliefs about cause and effect and the way things should and shouldn't be.

Standards of conduct serve as benchmarks for the minimally acceptable behavior required of members of a group. They serve to clarify the organization's code of ethics, which lays out its beliefs regarding obligatory and forbidden conduct.

Professionals use specialized knowledge and skills in service to others. A profession's code of ethics publicly communicates the shared principles and expected behaviors of a profession's members. It helps foster confidence in members of the profession.

Challenges to Ethical Behavior

- Overconfidence bias: People being more likely to overestimate the morality of their own behavior, particularly in situations that they have not faced before.
- Situational influences: External factors, such as environmental or cultural elements, that shape a person's thinking, decision making, and behavior such as the bystander effect (where people are less likely to intervene in an emergency when others are present).
- Focusing on the immediate rather than long-term outcomes or consequences of a decision.

Some ethical behavior may be illegal. New laws designed to reduce or eliminate conduct that adversely affects the markets can create opportunities for different, but similarly problematic, conduct.

Ethically sound decisions are almost always better than law from an equity standpoint, but almost always require good judgment and active consideration of stakeholders' interests from the stakeholder perspective.

Ethical Decision-Making Frameworks

An ethical decision-making framework is a tool for analyzing the potential alternative actions and consequences of a decision. It raises awareness of different perspectives, improves decision-making, and helps avoid unanticipated ethical consequences.

A general ethical decision-making framework is shown below:

- Identify: Facts of the situation, ethical/legal obligations to stakeholders, and potential conflicts of interest.
- Consider: Potential alternatives, situational influences, and guidance external to the situation.
- Decide and act.
- Reflect: Why did or why didn't the decision yield the expected result?

CODE OF ETHICS AND STANDARDS OF PROFESSIONAL CONDUCT; GUIDANCE FOR STANDARDS I–VII
Cross-Reference to CFA Institute Assigned Readings #2 & #3

All CFA Institute members and candidates enrolled in the CFA Program are required to comply with the Code of Ethics and the Standards of Professional Conduct (Code and Standards). The CFA Institute Bylaws and Rules of Procedure for Proceedings Related to Professional Conduct (Rules of Procedure) form the basic structure for enforcing the Code and Standards.

The Rules of Procedure are based on the following two principles:

1. Fair process.
2. Maintaining confidentiality of process.

The CFA Institute Board of Governors is responsible for implementing the Professional Conduct Program (PCP) through the Disciplinary Review Committee (DRC).

The CFA Institute Designated Officer, through the Professional Conduct staff, carries out professional conduct inquiries. Circumstances which can initiate an inquiry include:

- Information disclosed on the annual Professional Conduct Statement.
- Written complaints received by Professional Conduct staff.
- Questionable conduct as publicized by the media or any other source.
- A violation report submitted by a CFA examination proctor.

Once an inquiry is initiated, the Professional Conduct staff undertakes an investigation which can include:

- Requesting a written explanation.
- Interviewing related person(s).
- Collecting any supporting documents.

The information collected is reviewed by the Designated Officer, who may conclude that:

1. No disciplinary action is needed
2. A cautionary letter needs to be issued
3. Proceedings need to be continued

If it is concluded that there has been a violation of the Code and Standards, the Designated Officer can propose a disciplinary sanction. The member or candidate has the right to accept or reject the decision. A rejection would require the matter to be referred to a hearing by a panel of CFA Institute members. Sanctions by CFA Institute may include condemnation by peers, consequences for current or future employment or suspension from the CFA program.

The adherence of investment professionals to ethical practices benefits all market participants.

- Clients are reassured that investment professionals they hire prioritize their interests.
- Investment professionals benefit from the more efficient and transparent operation of the market that promotes integrity.

Sound ethics is fundamental to capital markets and the investment profession as it increases investors' confidence in global financial markets. Ethics is also of paramount importance because of the interconnectedness of global financial markets, which gives rise to the issue of market sustainability. It is imperative that top management foster a strong culture of ethics not just among CFA charter holders and candidates but among all staff members who are involved directly or indirectly with client relations, the investment process, record keeping, and beyond.

However, new challenges continually arise for members and candidates in applying the Code and Standards. This is because ethical dilemmas are not unambiguously right or wrong and require a bit of judgment.

The CFA Institute Code of Ethics plays an integral role in maintaining the integrity of CFA Institute members and upholding professional excellence. All CFA Institute members and CFA candidates must abide by this code and are encouraged to notify their employers of any violations. Violations may result in disciplinary sanctions by CFA Institute, which may include revocation of membership, candidacy in the CFA program and the right to use the CFA designation.

The Code of Ethics requires all members and candidates to:

- Act with integrity, competence, diligence, respect, and in an ethical manner with the public, clients, prospective clients, employers, employees, colleagues in the investment profession, and other participants in the global capital markets.
- Place the integrity of the investment profession and the interests of clients above their own personal interests.
- Use reasonable care and exercise independent professional judgment when conducting investment analysis, making investment recommendations, taking investment actions, and engaging in other professional activities.
- Practice and encourage others to practice in a professional and ethical manner that will reflect credit on themselves and the profession.
- Promote the integrity of, and uphold the rules governing, capital markets.
- Maintain and improve their professional competence and strive to maintain and improve the competence of other investment professionals.

Standards of Professional Conduct:

I. Professionalism
    A. Knowledge of the Law
    B. Independence and Objectivity
    C. Misrepresentation
    D. Misconduct

II. Integrity of Capital Markets
   A. Material Nonpublic Information
   B. Market Manipulation

III. Duties to Clients
   A. Loyalty, Prudence, and Care
   B. Fair Dealing
   C. Suitability
   D. Performance Presentation
   E. Preservation of Confidentiality

IV. Duties to Employers
   A. Loyalty
   B. Additional Compensation Arrangements
   C. Responsibilities of Supervisors

V. Investment Analysis, Recommendations, and Actions
   A. Diligence and Reasonable Basis
   B. Communication with Clients and Prospective Clients
   C. Record Retention

VI. Conflicts of Interest
   A. Disclosure of Conflicts
   B. Priority of Transactions
   C. Referral Fees

VII. Responsibilities as a CFA Institute Member or CFA Candidate
   A. Conduct as Participants in CFA Institute Programs
   B. Reference to CFA Institute, the CFA Designation, and the CFA Program

The best way to prepare for Ethics is to thoroughly read the Standards themselves, along with related guidance and examples.

INTRODUCTION TO THE GLOBAL INVESTMENT PERFORMANCE STANDARDS (GIPS®)
Cross-Reference to CFA Institute Assigned Reading #4

Individual and institutional investors typically use past investment performance to gauge a fund manager's ability and to make investment decisions. Questions relating to the accuracy and credibility of the data used to present investment performance make comparisons difficult.

The GIPS standards aim to provide clients and prospective clients with comparable and representative investment performance data. They establish an industry-wide, standard approach for calculation and presentation of investment performance. This forces complying firms to avoid misrepresentation and to communicate all relevant information that prospective clients should know to make informed investment decisions. Compliance with GIPS standards for any firm is *voluntary* and not required by any legal or regulatory authorities. However, only investment management firms that actually manage assets can claim compliance. Plan sponsors and consultants cannot claim to comply with GIPS if they do not manage any assets. They can only endorse the standards or require their investment managers to comply with them. Further, compliance is a firm-wide process that cannot be achieved on a single product or composite. In order to claim compliance, the firm needs to comply with all requirements of GIPS standards; there is no such thing as partial compliance to GIPS.

The GIPS standards benefit two main groups—investment management firms and prospective clients.

The GIPS standards require the use of composites. A composite is formed by combining discretionary portfolios into one group that represents a particular investment objective or strategy. A composite representing a particular strategy, must include **all** discretionary portfolios managed according to that strategy.

To ensure that the firm does not include only its best performing funds when presenting its investment performance, the GIPS standards require that the criteria for classifying portfolios into composites be decided before performance is known (i.e., on an ex-ante basis), not after the fact.

Firms that claim compliance with GIPS standards are responsible for ensuring that they really are compliant and that they maintain their compliant status going forward. After claiming compliance, firms may hire an independent third party to verify that they are compliant to add credibility to their claim.

Verification assures that the investment manager is compliant with GIPS standards on a firm-wide basis. Verification needs to be performed on the entire firm rather than specific composites. Verification tests:

- Whether the investment firm has complied with all the composite construction requirements on a firm-wide basis; and
- Whether the firm's processes and procedures calculate and present performance information according to GIPS standards.

Verification is optional, and it cannot be performed by the firm itself.

Objectives of GIPS

- To establish investment industry's best practices for calculating and presenting investment performance that promote investor interests and instill investor confidence.
- To obtain worldwide acceptance of a single standard for the calculation and presentation of investment performance based on the principles of fair representation and full disclosure.
- To promote the use of accurate and consistent investment performance data.
- To encourage fair, global competition among investment firms without creating barriers to entry.
- To foster the notion of industry "self-regulation" on a global basis.

Overview

GIPS standards have the following key features:

- GIPS standards are ethical standards to ensure full disclosure and fair representation of investment performance. In order to claim compliance, firms must adhere to all the requirements of the GIPS standards.
- Apart from adhering to the minimum requirements of the GIPS standards, firms should try to adhere to the recommendations of the GIPS standards to achieve best practice in the calculation and presentation of performance.
- Firms should include all actual, discretionary, and fee-paying portfolios in at least one composite defined by investment mandate, objective, or strategy in order to prevent firms from cherry-picking their best performance.
- The accuracy of performance presentation is dependent on the accuracy of input data. The underlying valuations of portfolio holdings drive the portfolio's performance. Therefore, it is essential for these and other inputs to be accurate. The GIPS standards require firms to adhere to certain calculation methodologies and to make specific disclosures along with the firm's performance.
- Firms must comply with all requirements of the GIPS standards, including any updates, Guidance Statements, interpretations, Questions & Answers, and clarifications published by CFA Institute and the GIPS Executive Committee, which are available on the GIPS website as well as in the GIPS Handbook.

The GIPS standards do not address every aspect of performance measurement or cover unique characteristics of each asset class. However, they will continue to evolve over time to address additional areas of investment performance.

Fundamentals of Compliance

The fundamentals of compliance include both recommendations and requirements.

Requirements

- Firms must comply with all the requirements of the GIPS standards, including any updates, Guidance Statements, interpretations, Questions & Answers, and clarifications published by CFA Institute and the GIPS Executive Committee, which are available on the GIPS website as well as in the GIPS Handbook.
- Firms must comply with all applicable laws and regulations regarding the calculation and presentation of performance.
- Firms must not present performance or performance-related information that is false or misleading.
- The GIPS standards must be applied on a firm-wide basis.
- Firms must document their policies and procedures used in establishing and maintaining compliance with the GIPS standards, including ensuring the existence and ownership of client assets, and must apply them consistently.
- If the firm does not meet all the requirements of the GIPS standards, it must not represent or state that it is "in compliance with the Global Investment Performance Standards except for…" or make any other statements that may indicate partial compliance with the GIPS standards.
- Statements referring to the calculation methodology as being "in accordance," "in compliance," or "consistent with" the GIPS standards, or similar statements, are prohibited.
- Statements referring to the performance of a single, existing client portfolio as being "calculated in accordance with the GIPS standards" are prohibited, except when a GIPS-compliant firm reports the performance of an individual client's portfolio to that particular client.
- Firms must make every reasonable effort to provide a compliant presentation to all prospective clients. Firms must not choose whom they present a compliant presentation to. As long as a prospective client has received a compliant presentation within the previous 12 months, the firm has met this requirement.
- Firms must provide a complete list of composite descriptions to any prospective client that makes such a request. They must include terminated composites on their list of composite descriptions for at least five years after the composite termination date.
- Firms must provide a compliant presentation for any composite listed on their list of composite descriptions to any prospective client that makes such a request.
- Firms must be defined as an investment firm, subsidiary, or division held out to clients or prospective clients as a distinct business entity.
- For periods beginning on, or after 1 January 2011, total firm assets must be aggregate fair value of all discretionary and non-discretionary assets managed by the firm. This includes both fee-paying and non-fee-paying portfolios.
- Total firm assets must include assets assigned to a sub-advisor provided that the firm has discretion over the selection of the sub-advisor.

- Changes in a firm's organization must not lead to alteration of historical composite performance.
- When the firm jointly markets with other firms, the firm claiming compliance with the GIPS standards must ensure that it is clearly defined and separate from the other firms being marketed, and that it is clear which firm is claiming compliance.

Recommendations

- Firms should comply with the recommendations of the GIPS standards, including recommendations in any updates, Guidance Statements, interpretations, Questions & Answers, and clarifications published by CFA Institute and the GIPS Executive Committee, which will be made available on the GIPS website as well as in the GIPS Handbook.
- Firms should be verified.
- Firms should adopt the broadest, most meaningful definition of the firm, encompassing all geographical offices operating under the same brand name regardless of the actual name of the individual investment management company.
- Firms should provide to each existing client, on an annual basis, a compliant presentation of the composite in which the client's portfolio is included.

Historical Performance Record

Firms are required to present a minimum of five years of GIPS-compliant historical investment performance. If the firm or composite has been in existence for less than five years, the presentation should include performance since inception. After initiating compliance with GIPS standards, the firm must add one year of compliant performance each year, so that the firm eventually presents a (minimum) performance record of 10 years.

Firms may link non-GIPS-compliant performance records to their compliant history as long as the non-compliant record is not for data after January 1, 2000. In such a case the firm must disclose the period of non-compliant data and disclose how the performance presentation differs from GIPS standards.

Firms that manage private equity, real estate, and/or wrap fee/separately managed account (SMA) portfolios must also comply with Sections 6, 7, and 8, respectively, of the Provisions of the GIPS standards that became effective as of 1 January 2006.

The effective date for the 2010 edition of the GIPS standards is 1 January 2011. Compliant presentations that include performance for periods that begin on or after 1 January 2011 must be prepared in accordance with the 2010 edition of the GIPS standards. Prior editions of the GIPS standards may be found on the GIPS website.

Implementation of GIPS Standards

In countries where laws and regulations regarding performance presentation do exist, firms are encouraged to adhere to GIPS in addition to their local laws. In case of a conflict, local laws are applicable and firms are required to disclose the conflict.

Nine Major Sections of the GIPS Standards

The nine major sections of the GIPS standards are:

0. Fundamentals of compliance which discusses issues pertaining to definition of a firm, documentation of policies and procedures, maintaining compliance with any updates and ensuring proper reference to claim of compliance with GIPS and references to verification of GIPS.
1. Input data which specifies standards for input data to be used to calculate investment performance. For periods beginning on or after 1 January 2011, all portfolios must be valued in accordance with the definition of fair value and the GIPS Valuation Principles.
2. Calculation methodology includes definitions of specific methods for return calculations of portfolios and composites.
3. Composite construction: Composites should be constructed to achieve consistency and fair presentation. Details were discussed in LOS 3b.
4. Disclosures Requirements for disclosure of information pertaining to a firm's policies and performance presentation.
5. Presentation and reporting: Performance presentation must be according to GIPS requirements.
6. Real estate standards must be applied to present performance relating to real estate investments.
7. Private equity: GIPS Private Equity Valuation Principals must be used to value private equity investments, except for open-end and evergreen funds.
8. Wrap Fee/Separately Managed Account (SMA) Portfolios: Firms must include the performance record of all wrap fee/SMA portfolios in appropriate composites in accordance with the firm's established portfolio inclusion policies.

STUDY SESSION 2:
QUANTITATIVE METHODS (1)

THE TIME VALUE OF MONEY
Cross-Reference to CFA Institute Assigned Reading #6

Interest rates can be thought of in three ways:

- The minimum rate of return that you require to accept a payment at a later date.
- The discount rate that must be applied to a future cash flow to determine its present value.
- The opportunity cost of receiving money today as opposed to saving it for a certain period and earning a return on it.

Interest rates are composed of the real risk-free rate plus compensation for bearing various risks.

- The real risk-free rate is the single-period return on a risk-free security assuming zero inflation. With no inflation, every dollar holds on to its purchasing power, so this rate purely reflects individuals' preferences for current versus future consumption.
- The inflation premium is added to the real risk-free rate to reflect the expected loss in purchasing power over the term of a loan. The real risk-free rate plus the inflation premium equals the nominal risk-free rate.
- The default risk premium compensates investors for the risk that the borrower might fail to make her payments on time in full.
- The liquidity premium compensates investors for any difficulty they might face in converting their holdings readily into cash at close to the most recent market price. Securities that trade infrequently or with low volumes require a higher liquidity premium than those that trade frequently with high volumes.
- The maturity premium compensates investors for the higher sensitivity of the market values of longer term debt instruments to changes in interest rates.

Present Value versus Future Value

- Present value (PV) is the current worth of sum of money or stream of cash flows that will be received in the future, given the interest rate.
  - For a given discount rate, the *longer* the time period till the future amount is received, the *lower* the present value.
  - For a given time period, the *higher* the discount rate, the *lower* the present value of an amount.
- Future value (FV) is the value of a sum of money at a specified date in the future.
  - For a given interest rate, the future value *increases* as the number of periods *increases*.
  - For a given number of periods, the future value *increases* as the interest rate *increases*.

Since PV and FV are separated in time, remember the following that we can add sums of money only if they are being valued at exactly the same point in time.

Annuities

- An annuity is a series of recurring periodic level payments.
- An ordinary annuity is an annuity where the cash flows occur at the end of each compounding period.
- An annuity due is an annuity where cash flows occur at the beginning of every period. Problems relating to annuities due can either be solved in [BGN] mode or by converting the value of an ordinary annuity to that of an annuity due.

$$PV_{\text{Annuity Due}} = PV_{\text{Ordinary Annuity}} \times (1 + r)$$
$$FV_{\text{Annuity Due}} = FV_{\text{Ordinary Annuity}} \times (1 + r)$$

Perpetuities

A perpetuity is a never ending series of level payments, where the first cash flow occurs one period from now (at t = 1).

$$PV = \frac{PMT}{I/Y}$$

The Effects of Compounding Frequency

- As the number of compounding periods *increases*, the future value of the investment *increases*.
- As the number of compounding periods *increases*, the present value of the investment *decreases*.
- The effective annual rate *rises* as compounding frequency *increases*.

Loan Payments and Amortization Schedules

Loan amortization is the process of retiring a loan obligation through predetermined equal monthly payments. Each of these payments includes an interest component, which is calculated on the principal outstanding at the beginning of the period, and a principal repayment component. The principal component increases with the passage of time, and the interest component declines over time in line with the decreasing amount of principal outstanding.

The principal outstanding at any payment date equals the present value of the remaining payments discounted at the periodic discount rate.

The Cash Flow Additivity Principle

The additivity principle states that the present value of any stream of cash flows equals the sum of the present values of the individual cash flows. If we have two streams of cash flows, the sum of the present values of the two streams at any point in time is the same as the present value of the two series combined by adding cash flows that occur at the same point in time. The cash flow stream can also be divided in any desired manner, and the present value of the pieces will equal the present value of the series.

DISCOUNTED CASH FLOW APPLICATIONS
Cross-Reference to CFA Institute Assigned Reading #7

Net Present Value

The net present value (NPV) of an investment equals the present value of all expected inflows from the project minus the present value of all expected outflows. The rate used to discount all cash flows is the appropriate cost of capital, which reflects the opportunity cost of undertaking the particular investment, and compensates investors for various risks inherent in the project.

- Positive NPV projects increase shareholder wealth and should be accepted.
- Negative NPV projects decrease shareholder wealth and should be rejected.
- For mutually exclusive projects (where only one project can be chosen from several options) the project with the highest, positive NPV should be chosen as it would add the most value to the firm.

Internal Rate of Return (IRR)

The internal rate of return (IRR) of a project is the discount rate that equates the project's NPV to zero. Effectively, it is the discount rate that equates the present value of all inflows from a project to the present value of all project-related outflows. Calculating IRR only requires forecasts of cash flows in the future; there is no need for externally generated market data to determine appropriate discount rates. An important thing to remember regarding IRR is that it assumes that all cash flows from the project will be reinvested at the IRR.

- Projects for which the IRR *exceeds* the required rate of return should be accepted.
- Projects for which the IRR is *lower* than the required rate of return should be rejected.

NPV versus IRR

In deciding whether a single project should be undertaken, IRR and NPV will offer the same recommendation.

- If IRR is *greater* than the required rate of return, NPV is *positive*.
- If IRR is *less* than the required rate of return, NPV is *negative*.

When only one of two or more projects can be accepted, the projects are said to be mutually exclusive. For mutually exclusive projects, NPV and IRR may offer conflicting conclusions. This can happen in two scenarios:

- When the projects' initial cash outlays are different.
- When there is a difference in timing of the cash flows across the projects.

NPV assumes that interim cash flows from the project will be reinvested at the required rate of return, whereas IRR assumes that they will be reinvested at the IRR. When choosing between mutually exclusive projects, use the NPV rule if the recommendations of the NPV and IRR rules conflict.

Measures of Portfolio Return

- The holding period yield (HPY), also known as holding period return, is simply the return earned on an investment over the entire investment horizon.
- The money-weighted rate of return is simply the internal rate of return of an investment.
- The time-weighted rate of return measures the compounded rate of growth of an investment over the stated measurement period.
  - It is not affected by cash withdrawals or contributions to the portfolio.
  - It is basically the geometric mean of subperiod returns.
  - The time-weighted rate of return is preferred because it is not affected by the timing and amount of cash inflows and outflows.
  - Decisions regarding contributions and withdrawals from a portfolio are usually made by clients. Since these decisions are not typically in invest-ment managers' hands, it would be inappropriate to evaluate their perfor-mance based on money-weighted returns. If a manager does have discretion over withdrawals and contributions of funds in a portfolio, money-weighted return might be a more appropriate measure of portfolio performance.

Money-Weighted versus Time-Weighted Rates of Return

- If funds are deposited to the investment portfolio prior to a period of superior performance, the money-weighted return will be *higher* than the time-weighted return.
- If funds are deposited into the investment portfolio just before a period of relatively poor performance, the money-weighted return will be *lower* than the time-weighted return.

Market Yields

The bank discount yield is a quoting convention used primarily for quoting Treasury bills. It annualizes the discount on the instrument as a percentage of *par or face value* over a *360-day* period.

$$r_{BD} = \frac{D}{F} \times \frac{360}{t}$$

Yields presented on a bank discount basis do not hold much meaning to investors for the following reasons:

- Investors want to evaluate returns on the amount invested to purchase the instrument; BDY calculates returns based on par value.
- Returns are based on a 360-day year; not a 365-day year.

- BDY assumes simple interest. In doing so, it ignores interest earned on interest (compound interest).

The holding period yield equals the return realized on an investment over the entire horizon that it is held (which can either be till maturity or sale). It is an *unannualized* return measure.

$$HPY = \frac{P_1 - P_0 + D_1}{P_0} = \frac{P_1 + D_1 - 1}{P_0}$$

The effective annual yield is an *annualized* return measure that accounts for *compounding* over a *365-day* period.

$$EAY = (1 + HPY)^{365/t} - 1$$

We can also convert an EAY to HPY using the following formula:

$$HPY = (1 + EAY)^{t/365} - 1$$

The money-market yield is the holding period yield annualized on a *360-day* year. Further, it does *not* consider the effects of compounding. It is different from the bank discount yield as it is based on the *purchase price*, not par value.

$$R_{MM} = \frac{360 \times r_{BD}}{360 - (t \times r_{BD})}$$

And, more conveniently:

$$R_{MM} = HPY \times (360/t)$$

A relatively simple way to get through problems on market yields is to first calculate the HPY and then convert it into the required return measure.

- The HPY is the actual unannualized return an investor realizes over the investment period.
- The EAY is the HPY annualized on a *365-day* year *with* compounding.
- The money-market yield is the HPY annualized on a *360-day* year *without* compounding.

The bond equivalent yield (BEY) is simply the semiannual discount rate multiplied by two. This convention comes from the U.S. where bonds are quoted at twice the semiannual rate because coupon payments are made semiannually.

STATISTICAL CONCEPTS AND MARKET RETURNS
Cross-Reference to CFA Institute Assigned Reading #8

A **population** includes *all* the members of a particular group. It is usually very costly and time consuming to obtain measurements for each member of the population. Therefore, information about a small subset of the population, called a **sample**, is collected and conclusions about the population are drawn from the information obtained from the sample.

Types of Scales

- Nominal scales categorize or count data but do not rank them.
- Ordinal scales sort data into categories that are ranked according to certain characteristics. However, they tell us nothing about the magnitude of the difference between categories.
- Interval scales rank observations such that the difference between scale values is equal so that values can be added and subtracted meaningfully.
- Ratio scales have all the characteristics of interval scales and have a true zero point as the origin. Therefore, meaningful ratios can also be computed with ratio scales.

Methods of Presenting Data

- A frequency distribution is a tabular illustration of data categorized into a relatively small number of intervals or classes.
- The relative frequency for an interval is the proportion or fraction of total observations that are represented by a particular interval.
- The cumulative absolute frequency or cumulative frequency for an interval is the number of observations that are less than the upper bound of the interval. Alternatively, it is the sum of the frequencies of all intervals less than and including the said interval.
- The cumulative relative frequency for an interval is the proportion of total observations that are less than the upper bound of the interval.
- A histogram is used graphically to represent the data contained in a frequency distribution.
- A frequency polygon also graphically illustrates the information in a frequency distribution. The coordinates or points of a frequency polygon are the frequency of each interval plotted against the midpoint of the interval.

Measures of Central Tendency

The arithmetic mean is the sum of all the observations in a data set divided by the total number of observations. The arithmetic mean of a sample is the best estimate of the value of the next observation.

- All observations are used in the computation of the arithmetic mean.
- All interval and ratio data sets have an arithmetic mean.

- The sum of the deviations from the arithmetic mean always equals zero.
- An arithmetic mean is unique—a data set only has one arithmetic mean.

The median is the value of the middle item of a data set once it has been sorted into an ascending or descending order. The advantage of using the median is that, unlike the mean, it is not sensitive to extreme values. However, the median does not use all the information about the size and magnitude of the observations and only focuses on their relative positions.

The mode of a data set is simply its most frequently occurring value. A data set that has one mode is said to be unimodal, while one that has two modes is said to be bimodal. It is also possible for a data set to have no mode, where all values are different and no value occurs more frequently than others. For grouped data, the **modal interval** is the interval with the highest frequency. The mode is the only measure of central tendency that can be used with nominal data.

The weighted mean is calculated by assigning different weights to observations in the data set to account for the disproportionate effect of certain observations on the arithmetic mean. The arithmetic mean assigns equal weights to every observation in the data set, which makes it very sensitive to extreme values.

The geometric mean is used to average rates of change over time or to calculate the growth rate of a variable over a period. In order to calculate the geometric mean for returns data, we must add 1 to each return observation (expressed as a decimal) and then subtract 1 from the result.

$$R_G = \left[\sqrt[n]{(1+R_1) \times (1+R_2) \times \ldots \times (1+R_n)} \right] - 1$$

Important Relationships Between the Arithmetic Mean and Geometric Mean

- The geometric mean is always less than or equal to the arithmetic mean.
- The geometric mean equals the arithmetic mean only when all the observations are identical.
- The difference between the geometric and arithmetic mean increases as the dispersion in observed values increases.

The harmonic mean is used in the investment management arena to determine the average cost of shares purchased over time. It may be viewed as a special type of weighted mean where the weight of an observation is inversely proportional to its magnitude.

$$\text{Harmonic mean}: \bar{X}_H = \frac{N}{\sum_{i=1}^{N} \frac{1}{x_i}}$$

Mathematically, unless all the observations in the data set are identical (equal in value), the harmonic mean will always be less than the geometric mean, which itself will be less than the arithmetic mean.

Quantiles

A quantile is a value at, or below which a stated proportion of the observations in a data set lie. Examples of quantiles include:

- quartiles, which divide the distribution in quarters or four equal parts.
- quintiles, which divide the distribution into fifths.
- deciles, which divide the data into tenths.
- percentiles, which divide the distribution into hundredths.

Measures of Dispersion

Dispersion is the variability or spread of a random variable around its central tendency.

The range is one of the most basic measures of variability of data. It is simply the difference between the highest and lowest values in a data set.

$$\text{Range} = \text{Maximum value} - \text{Minimum value}$$

The mean absolute deviation (MAD) is the average of the *absolute* values of deviations of observations in a data set from their mean.

$$MAD = \frac{\sum_{i=1}^{n} |X_i - \bar{X}|}{n}$$

The variance is the average of the squared deviations around the mean. The standard deviation is the positive square root of the variance. While the variance has no units, the standard deviation has the same units as the random variable.

Population Variance and Standard Deviation

$$\sigma^2 = \frac{\sum_{i=1}^{n} (X_i - \mu)^2}{n}$$

$$\sigma = \sqrt{\frac{\sum_{i=1}^{n} (X_i - \mu)^2}{n}}$$

Sample Variance and Standard Deviation

$$s^2 = \frac{\sum\limits_{i=1}^{n}(X_i - \bar{X})^2}{n-1}$$

$$s = \sqrt{\frac{\sum\limits_{i=1}^{n}(X_i - \bar{X})^2}{n-1}}$$

The mean absolute deviation (MAD) will always be less than or equal to the standard deviation. This is because, by squaring all deviations from the mean, the standard deviation attaches a greater weight to larger deviations from the mean.

The semivariance is the average of squared deviations *below* the mean, while the semideviation is the positive square root of the semivariance. The target semivariance refers to the sum of the squared deviations from a specific target return and its square root.

Chebyshev's Inequality

Chebyshev's inequality gives an approximate value for the proportion of observations in a data set that fall within k standard deviations from the mean.

$$\text{Proportion of observations within k standard deviations from mean} = 1 - 1/k^2$$

The advantage of Chebyshev's inequality is that it holds for samples and populations and for discrete and continuous data regardless of the shape of the distribution.

Coefficient of Variation

The coefficient of variation, which is the ratio of the standard deviation of the data set to its mean, is used to compare the relative dispersions of data sets. A lower coefficient of variation is better.

$$CV = \frac{s}{X}$$

Remember: The CV measures risk per unit of return.

Sharpe Ratio

The Sharpe ratio is the ratio of excess return over the risk-free rate from an investment to its standard deviation. It basically measures excess return per unit of risk. Portfolios with higher Sharpe ratios are more attractive.

> The Sharpe ratio measures excess return per unit of risk.

$$\text{Sharpe ratio} = \frac{\overline{r}_p - r_f}{\sigma_p}$$

Issues with the Sharpe Ratio

All other factors remaining the same:

- For portfolios with positive Sharpe ratios, the Sharpe ratio decreases if we increase risk. A portfolio with a higher positive Sharpe ratio offers a better risk-adjusted return.
- For portfolios with negative Sharpe ratios, the ratio increases (to a negative number closer to zero) if we increase risk. With negative Sharpe ratios we cannot always assume that the portfolio with the higher Sharpe ratio (closer to zero) offers a better risk-adjusted performance. If the standard deviation of two portfolios with negative Sharpe ratios is the same, the one with the higher ratio offers the better risk-adjusted performance.

The standard deviation (which is used in the Sharpe ratio as a measure of risk) is an appropriate measure or risk only for investments and strategies that have approximately symmetric distributions. Use of the Sharpe ratio to evaluate the performance of hedge funds and option strategies (that have an asymmetric returns distribution) would give inaccurate results.

Symmetrical versus Nonsymmetrical Distributions

A distribution is said to be **symmetrical** about its mean when each side of the distribution is a mirror image of the other. Loss and gain intervals exhibit the same frequencies for a symmetrical distribution (e.g., the frequency of a loss between 2% and 5% is identical to the frequency of a gain between 2% and 5%). For a symmetrical distribution, the mean, median and mode are equal.

When a distribution is not symmetrical, it is said to be skewed. Skewness can be negative or positive.

- A distribution that is positively skewed (or skewed to the right) has a long tail on the right side. It contains some observations that are much larger in value than most of the observations in the data set. For positively skewed distributions, the mode is less than the median, which is less than the mean. The mean is affected the most by the extreme values (outliers) in the tail on the right side, and is "pulled" towards them.

- A negatively skewed distribution (skewed to the left) has a long tail on the left side. It contains outliers that are much smaller in value than the majority of observations in the distribution. For a negatively skewed distribution, the mode is greater than the median, which is greater than the mean. The mean is "pulled" lower by the outliers in the tail on the left side of the distribution.

Sample Skewness

$$S_K \approx \frac{1}{n} \frac{\sum_{i=1}^{n}(X_i - \bar{X})^3}{s^3}$$

where:

s = sample standard deviation

Some researchers believe that, all other factors remaining the same, investors should prefer positive skewness i.e., portfolios that have a higher probability of earning relatively large profits.

QM

- When the distribution is positively (right) skewed, sample skewness is positive because the numerator of the formula above is a positive number (the average of deviations above the mean is larger than that of deviations below the mean).
- When the distribution is negatively (left) skewed, sample skewness is negative because the numerator of the formula above is a negative number (the average of deviations below the mean is larger than that of deviations above the mean).
- Sample skewness of zero indicates that the data set follows a symmetrical distribution.
- Absolute values of skewness greater than 0.5 suggest that the data set is significantly skewed.

Kurtosis

Kurtosis measures the combined weight of the tails of a distribution relative to the rest of the distribution, or the proportion of the total probability that lies in the tails. A normal distribution has a kurtosis of 3. Excess kurtosis equals the kurtosis of the distribution minus the kurtosis of the normal distribution (3).

- A *leptokurtic* distribution has *fatter* tails than a normal distribution and has an excess kurtosis greater than zero. A leptokurtic distribution has the same mean, standard deviation, and skewness as a normal distribution. However, it generates more-frequent extremely large deviations from the mean (and more-frequent observations that are near the mean).
- A *platykurtic* distribution has *thinner* tails than a normal distribution. Its excess kurtosis is less than zero.
- A *mesokurtic* distribution has the same relative weight in the tails as a normal distribution and has an excess kurtosis of zero.

Sample Kurtosis uses standard deviations to the fourth power, and is calculated as:

$$K_E \approx \frac{1}{n} \frac{\sum\limits_{i=1}^{n}(X_i - \bar{X})^4}{s^4} - 3$$

where:
s = sample standard deviation

For a sample size greater than 100, a sample excess kurtosis of greater than 1.0 would be considered unusually high.

Geometric versus Arithmetic Mean

For reporting historical returns, the geometric mean is more appropriate because it equals the rate of growth an investor would have to earn each year to match the actual cumulative investment performance. The geometric mean is an excellent measure of past performance. The arithmetic mean can distort evaluation of past performance.

- If we want to gauge performance over a single period, the arithmetic mean should be used because the arithmetic mean is the average of one-period returns.
- If we want to estimate returns over more than one period, we should use the geometric mean as it measures how investment returns are linked over time.

To calculate expected equity risk premiums (in a forward-looking context) use of the arithmetic mean is more appropriate.

- Uncertainty in cash flows or returns causes the arithmetic mean to be larger than the geometric mean. The more the uncertainty, the greater the divergence between the two.

Studies have shown that the geometric mean return approximately equals the arithmetic mean minus half the variance of returns.

PROBABILITY CONCEPTS
Cross-Reference to CFA Institute Assigned Reading #9

- A random variable is one whose possible values or results are *uncertain*.
- An outcome is the observed value of a random variable.
- An event could be a single outcome or a set of outcomes.
- Mutually exclusive events are events that cannot happen simultaneously. The occurrence of one precludes the occurrence of the other.
- Exhaustive events cover the range of *all possible outcomes* of an event.

A probability is a number between 0 and 1 that reflects the chance of a certain event occurring. A probability of zero means that it is impossible for the event to occur, while a probability of 1 means that an event will definitely occur and the outcome is not random.

There are two basic defining principles of probability:

1. The probability of any event, E, is a number between 0 and 1.
2. The sum of the probabilities of mutually exclusive and exhaustive events equals 1.

Methods of Estimating Probabilities

An empirical probability estimates the probability of an event based on its frequency of occurrence in the past.

A subjective probability draws on subjective reasoning and personal judgment to estimate the probability of an event.

An a priori probability is based on formal analysis and reasoning.

Probabilities Stated as Odds

The odds *for* an event are stated as the probability of the event occurring to the probability of the event not occurring. Odds for an event, E, are stated as P(E) to [1 – P(E)].

If the odds *for* are given as "a to b" then:

$$P(E) = \frac{a}{(a + b)}$$

The odds *against* an event are stated as the probability of an event not occurring to the probability of the event occurring. Odds *against* an event, E, are stated in the form of [1 – P(E)] to P(E).

If the odds *against* are given as "a to b" then:

$$P(E) = \frac{b}{(a + b)}$$

- Given the odds for an outcome, the odds against the outcome are simply the *reciprocal* of the odds for.
- Given the odds against an outcome, the odds for the outcome are simply the *reciprocal* of the odds against.

The Dutch Book Theorem states that if the probabilities reflected in the stock prices are not consistent, they give rise to profit opportunities. As investors take positions to take advantage of such opportunities, the inconsistency is eventually eliminated.

Conditional versus Unconditional Probabilities

Unconditional or marginal probabilities estimate the probability of an event irrespective of the occurrence of other events. They can be thought of as stand-alone probabilities and answer questions like "What is the probability of a return on a stock above 10%?" or "What are the chances of getting a 3 on a roll of a die?"

Conditional probabilities express the probability of an event occurring *given* that another event has occurred. The questions answered are like "What is the probability of the return on a stock being more than 10%, *given* that the return is above the risk free rate?" or "What is the probability of rolling a 3, *given* that an odd number is rolled." Conditional probabilities are computed using joint probabilities.

- A *joint probability*, P(AB), answers questions like, "What is the probability of *both* A **and** B happening?"
  - If A and B are mutually exclusive events, the joint probability P(AB) equals zero. This is because mutually exclusive events cannot occur simultaneously.
  - If A is contained within the set of possible outcomes for B, P(AB) = P(A)

Mathematically, conditional probability is expressed as:

$$P(A|B) = \frac{P(AB)}{P(B)} \text{ given that } P(B) \neq 0$$

The multiplication rule for probability calculates joint probabilities using a conditional probability.

$$P(AB) = P(A \mid B) \times P(B)$$

The addition rule for probabilities is used to calculate the probability of A or B occurring.

$$P(A \text{ or } B) = P(A) + P(B) - P(AB)$$

Given that A and B share some outcomes, if we simply add P(B) to P(A) we would be double counting the shared outcomes. Therefore, we subtract the joint probability from the sum of the probabilities of A and B.

If the events are mutually exclusive, the joint probability of A and B, P(AB), equals zero, so P(A or B) would simply equal P(A) + P(B).

Dependent versus Independent Events

With two dependent events, the occurrence of one is related to the occurrence of the other. For example, the probability of doing well on an exam is related to the probability of preparing well for it.

Two events are independent if the occurrence of one does *not* have any bearing on the occurrence of the other. For example, the probability of doing well on an exam is unrelated to the probability of there being 5 trees in the park nearby.

When two events are independent:

$$P(A|B) = P(A) \text{ or equivalently, } P(B|A) = P(B)$$

- With independent events, the word *and* implies multiplication, and the word *or* implies addition.

$$P(A \text{ or } B) = P(A) + P(B) - P(AB)$$

$$P(A \text{ and } B) = P(A) \times P(B)$$

The Total Probability Rule for Unconditional Probabilities

The total probability rule expresses the unconditional probability of an event in terms of conditional probabilities for mutually exclusive and exhaustive events.

$$P(A) = P(AS) + P(AS^C)$$

$$P(A) = P(A|S) \times P(S) + P(A|S^c) \times P(S^c)$$

The probability of Event A, P(A), is expressed as a weighted average in the total probability rule. The weights applied to the conditional probabilities are the probabilities of the scenarios. For example, the weight attached to the conditional probability, P(A|S), is the probability of scenario S, P(S).

Expected Value

The expected value of a random variable is the probability-weighted average of all possible outcomes for the random variable.

$$E(X) = \sum_{i=1}^{n} P(X_i)X_i$$

$$E(X) = P(X_1)X_1 + P(X_2)X_2 + \ldots P(X_n)X_n$$

Variance

If variance is zero, there is no dispersion in the distribution. In this case, the outcome is certain, and the variable is not a random variable.

$$\sigma^2(X) = E\left\{[X - E(X)]^2\right\}$$

$$\sigma^2(X) = \sum_{i=1}^{n} P(X_i)[X_i - E(X)]^2$$

Standard deviation is the positive square root of the variance. The variance has no units while the standard deviation is expressed in the same unit as the expected value and the random variable itself.

Total Probability Rule for Expected Value

Similar to the total probability rule for stating unconditional probabilities in terms of conditional probabilities, the total probability rule for expected value states (unconditional) expected values in terms of conditional expected values.

$$E(X) = E(X|S)P(S) + E(X|S^c)P(S^c)$$

$$E(X) = E(X|S_1) \times P(S_1) + E(X|S_2) \times P(S_2) + \ldots + E(X|S_n) \times P(S_n)$$

Covariance Vol 1, pg 434

Covariance is a measure of the extent to which two random variables move together.

$$\text{Cov}(R_i, R_j) = E\left\{[R_i - E(R_i)][R_j - E(R_j)]\right\}$$

The covariance between the returns on Asset I and Asset J can also be calculated as:

$$\text{Cov}(R_i R_j) = \sigma(R_i)\sigma(R_j)\rho(R_i, R_j)$$

Properties of Covariance

- Covariance is a similar concept to variance. The difference lies in the fact that variance measures how a random variable varies with itself, while covariance measures how a particular random variable varies with another.
- Covariance is symmetric, i.e., $\text{Cov}(X,Y) = \text{Cov}(Y,X)$.
- Covariance may range from positive infinity to negative infinity. Variance on the other hand, is always positive.
- The covariance of X with itself, $\text{Cov}(X,X)$ equals the variance of X, $\text{Var}(X)$.

Interpretation of Covariance

- When the covariance of returns of two assets is *negative*, it means that when the return on one asset is above its expected value, the return on the other tends to be below its expected value. There is an *inverse* relationship between the two variables.
- When the covariance of returns of two assets is *positive*, it means that when the return on one asset is above its expected value, the return on the other also tends to be above its expected value.
- Covariance of returns is zero if the returns are unrelated.

Limitations of Covariance

- Because the unit that covariance is expressed in depends on the unit that the data is presented in, it is difficult to compare covariance across data sets that have different scales.
- In practice, it is difficult to interpret covariance as it can take on extreme large values.
- Covariance does not tell us anything about the strength of the relationship between the two variables.

Correlation Coefficient

The correlation coefficient measures the strength and direction of a linear relationship between two random variables. It is obtained by dividing the covariance between two random variables by the product of their standard deviations.

$$\text{Corr}(R_A, R_B) = \rho(R_A, R_B) = \frac{\text{Cov}(R_A, R_B)}{(\sigma_A)(\sigma_B)}$$

Properties of the Correlation Coefficient

- It measures the strength of the relationship between two random variables.
- It has no unit.
- It lies between −1 and +1.

Interpretation of the Correlation Coefficient

- A correlation coefficient of +1 indicates a perfectly positive correlation between two random variables.
- A correlation coefficient of −1 indicates a perfectly negative correlation between two random variables.
- A correlation coefficient of zero indicates no linear relationship between two random variables.

A shortcoming of the correlation coefficient is the fact that it does not specify which factor or variable *causes* the linear relationship between the two variables.

Expected Return of a Portfolio

$$E(R_p) = \sum_{i=1}^{N} w_i E(R_i) = w_1 E(R_1) + w_2 E(R_2) + \ldots + w_N E(R_N)$$

Variance of a 2-Asset Portfolio

$$Var(R_p) = w_A^2 \sigma^2(R_A) + w_B^2 \sigma^2(R_B) + 2w_A w_B Cov(R_A, R_B)$$

$$Var(R_p) = w_A^2 \sigma^2(R_A) + w_B^2 \sigma^2(R_B) + 2w_A w_B \rho(R_A, R_B)\sigma(R_A)\sigma(R_B)$$

Variance of a 3-Asset Portfolio

$$Var(R_p) = w_A^2 \sigma^2(R_A) + w_B^2 \sigma^2(R_B) + w_C^2 \sigma^2(R_C)$$
$$+ 2w_A w_B Cov(R_A, R_B) + 2w_B w_C Cov(R_B, R_C) + 2w_C w_A Cov(R_C, R_A)$$

To calculate the variance for a portfolio containing *n* different assets we would require *n(n-1)/2* unique covariances.

Finally, the expected value of the products of uncorrelated random variables equals the product of their expected values.

$E(XY) = E(X)E(Y)$ if X and Y are uncorrelated.

Bayes' Formula

By using Bayes' formula, we can reverse the "given that probability" P(A|B) and convert it into P(B|A) using P(A) and P(B). Bear in mind that you will probably have to use the total probability rule to calculate P(B).

$$P(B \mid A) = \frac{P(A \mid B) \times P(B)}{P(A)}$$

$$P(\text{Event} \mid \text{Information}) = \frac{P(\text{Information} \mid \text{Event}) \times P(\text{Event})}{P(\text{Information})}$$

Counting Problems

- **Factorials** are used when there is only one group and we are simply arranging a given set or group of n items. Given n items, there are n! ways of arranging them.
- **The labeling formula** is used for three or more groups of predetermined sizes. Each item must be labeled as a member of one of the groups.
- **The combination formula** is used when there are only two groups of predetermined sizes and crucially, the order or rank of labeling is NOT important.
- **The permutation formula** is used when there are only two groups of predetermined sizes and the order or ranking IS important.

STUDY SESSION 3:
QUANTITATIVE METHODS (2)

COMMON PROBABILITY DISTRIBUTIONS
Cross-Reference to CFA Institute Assigned Reading #10

Discrete versus Continuous Random Variables

- A *discrete random variable* is one that can take on a countable number of values. Each outcome has a specific probability of occurring, which can be measured.
- A *continuous random variable* is one for which the number of possible outcomes cannot be counted (there are infinite possible outcomes) and therefore, probabilities cannot be attached to specific outcomes.

The **probability distribution** of a random variable identifies the probability of each of the possible outcomes of a random variable.

A **probability function p(x),** expresses the probability that "X," the random variable takes on a specific value of "x." A probability function can also be stated as $P(X = x)$.

A **probability density function (pdf),** which is denoted by $f(x)$, is used to determine the probability that the outcome lies within a specified range of possible values. It is used to interpret the probability structure of continuous random variables.

A **cumulative distribution function (cdf),** or distribution function, expresses the probability that a random variable, X, takes on a value *less than or equal to* a specific value, x. It is the sum of the probabilities of all outcomes that are less than or equal to the specified value, x. A cdf is denoted by $F(x) = P(X \leq x)$.

The Discrete Uniform Distribution

A discrete uniform distribution is one in which the probability of each of the possible outcomes is identical. The best example of a uniform distribution is the probability distribution of the outcomes from the roll of a fair die, for which the probability of each outcome is 1/6.

The Continuous Uniform Distribution

A continuous uniform distribution is described by a lower limit, *a*, and an upper limit, *b*. These limits serve as the parameters of the distribution. The probability of any outcome or range of outcomes outside this interval is 0. Being a continuous distribution, individual outcomes also have a probability of 0. The distribution is often denoted as U(*a,b*).

The probability that the random variable will take a value that falls between x_1 and x_2, that both lie within the range, *a* to *b*, is the proportion of the total area taken up by the range, x_1 to x_2.

$$P(x_1 \leq X \leq x_2) = \frac{x_2 - x_1}{b - a}$$

Remember that $P(X \geq x)$ is the same as $P(X > x)$ or this distribution because it is a continuous distribution where $P(X = x)$ equals zero.

The Binomial Distribution

A binomial random variable is the number of successes (X) from a Bernoulli trial that is carried out "n" times. A Bernoulli experiment is an experiment that has only 2 possible outcomes which are labeled "success" and "failure." Further, these two outcomes are mutually exclusive and collectively exhaustive.

The probability of x successes in n trials is given by:

$$P(X = x) = {_n}C_x (p)^x (1-p)^{n-x}$$

- The **expected value** of a binomial random variable (X) is given by:

$$E(x) = n \times p$$

- The **variance** of a binomial random variable is given by:

$$\sigma^2 = n \times p \times (1-p)$$

Binomial Trees

Binomial trees may be drawn to illustrate possible stock price movements. Binomial stock price models are extensively used in option pricing.

The Normal Distribution

- It is completely described by its mean and variance.
- It is symmetric about the mean (skewness = 0).
- Kurtosis = 3.
- Any linear combination of jointly, normally distributed random variables is also normally distributed.

Skewness and the Binomial Distribution

- If the probability of success is 0.50, the binomial distribution is symmetric.
- If the probability of success is less than 0.50, the binomial distribution is skewed to the right.
- If the probability of success is more than 0.50, the binomial distribution is skewed to the left.

Tracking Objectives, Tracking Errors, and Portfolio Risk

Tracking error is a measure of how closely a portfolio's returns match the returns of the index to which it is benchmarked. It is the difference between the total return on the portfolio (before deducting fees) and the total return on the benchmark index.

> Tracking error = Gross return on portfolio – Total return on benchmark index

Calculating Probabilities Using the Standard Normal Distribution

This standard normal distribution is a normal distribution that has been standardized so that it has a mean of zero and a standard deviation of 1. To standardize an observation from a normal distribution, its standardized value or *z-score* must be calculated. This is done by subtracting the mean of the population from the observed value of the random variable, and dividing the result by the standard deviation.

> z-score = (observed value – population mean) / standard deviation = $(x - \mu) / \sigma$

Essentially the z-value represents the number of standard deviations away from the population mean, an observed value of a random variable lies.

Confidence Intervals

A confidence interval represents the range of values within which a certain population parameter is expected to lie in a specified percentage of the time.

Shortfall Risk and Safety-First Ratio

Shortfall risk is the probability that a portfolio's value or return, $E(R_P)$, will fall below a particular target return (R_T) over a given period.

Roy's safety-first criterion states that an optimal portfolio minimizes the probability that the actual portfolio return, RP, will fall below the target return, R_T.

The safety-first ratio (SF Ratio) is similar to the Sharpe Ratio. The Sharpe Ratio is a special case of the SF Ratio, where the threshold level is the risk-free rate.

> Shortfall ratio (SF Ratio) or z-score $= \dfrac{E(R_p) - R_T}{\sigma_p}$

Portfolios with *higher* SF Ratios are *preferred* to those that have a *lower* SF ratio; *higher* SF Ratio portfolios have a *lower* probability of not meeting their target returns.

The Lognormal Distribution

A random variable, Y, follows the lognormal distribution if its natural logarithm (ln Y) is normally distributed. Three important features differentiate the lognormal distribution from the normal distribution:

1. It is bounded by zero on the lower end.
2. The upper end of its range is unbounded.
3. It is skewed to the right (positively skewed).

The lognormal distribution is frequently used to model the distribution of asset prices because it is bounded on the left by zero.

Discretely compounded returns are based on discrete or defined compounding periods, such as 12 months or 6 months. As the compounding periods get shorter and shorter, the effective annual rate (EAR) rises. With continuous compounding, the effective annual rate is given as:

$$EAR = e^{r_{cc}} - 1 \qquad r_{cc} = \text{continuously compounded annual rate}$$

The expression for calculating the continuously compounded rate, r_{cc}, is given as:

$$r_{cc} = \ln(EAR + 1)$$

Simulation

Monte Carlo simulation generates random numbers and operator inputs to synthetically create probability distributions for variables. It is used to calculate expected values and dispersion measures for random variables, which are then used for statistical inferences.

Investment Applications

- To experiment with a proposed policy before actually implementing it.
- To provide a probability distribution to estimate investment risk.
- To provide expected values of investments that can be difficult to price.
- To test models and investment tools and strategies.

Limitations

- Answers are as good as the assumptions and model used.
- Does not provide cause-and-effect relationships.

Historical simulation assumes that the distribution of the random variable going forward depends on its distribution in the past. This method of forecasting has an advantage, in that the distribution of risk factors does not need to be estimated. However, it faces the following limitations:

- A risk factor that was not represented in historical data will not be considered in the simulation.
- It does not facilitate "what if" analysis if the "if" factor has not occurred in the past. Monte Carlo simulation can be used for "what if" analysis.
- It assumes that the future will be similar to the past.
- It does not provide any cause-and-effect relationship information.

- In a simple random sample, each member of the population has the same likelihood of being included in the sample.
- In systematic sampling, every kth member in the population is selected until the desired sample size is reached.
- Stratified random sampling: Stratification is the process of grouping members of the population into relatively homogeneous subgroups, or strata, before drawing samples. The strata should be mutually exclusive and collectively exhaustive. Random sampling is applied within each stratum and the size of the sample from each stratum is based on the size of the stratum relative to the population. This often improves the *representativeness* of the sample by reducing sampling error.

Sampling error is the difference between a sample statistic and the corresponding population parameter.

$$\text{Sampling error of the mean} = \text{sample mean} - \text{population mean} = \bar{x} - \mu$$

Time-Series versus Cross-Sectional Data

- Time-series data consists of observations measured over a period of time, spaced at uniform intervals. The monthly returns on a particular stock over the last 5 years are an example of time-series data.
- Cross-sectional data refers to data collected by observing many subjects (such as individuals, firms or countries/regions) at the same point in time. The returns of individual stocks over the last years are examples of cross-sectional data.

Longitudinal versus Panel Data

- Longitudinal data refers to data collected over time about multiple characteristics of the same observational unit. The various economic indicators—unemployment levels, inflation, and GDP growth rates (multiple characteristics) of a particular country (observational unit) over a decade (period of time) are examples of longitudinal data.
- Panel data refers to data collected over a time about a single characteristic of multiple observational units. The unemployment rate (single characteristic) of a number of countries (multiple observational units) over a time are examples of panel data.

The Central Limit Theorem

The important properties of the central limit theorem are:

- Given a population with *any* probability distribution, with mean, μ, and variance, σ^2, the sampling distribution of the sample mean x, computed from sample size n

will approximately be *normal* with mean, μ (the population mean), and variance, σ^2/n (population variance divided by sample size), when the sample size is greater than or equal to 30.

- No matter what the distribution of the population, for a sample whose size is greater than or equal to 30, the sample mean will be normally distributed.

$$\bar{x} \sim N\left(\mu, \frac{\sigma^2}{n}\right)$$

- The mean of the population (m) and the mean of the distribution of sample means are equal.
- The variance of the distribution of sample means equals σ^2/n, or population variance divided by sample size.

Standard Error of Sample Mean

The standard deviation of the distribution of sample means is known as the standard error of the statistic (σ_x).

When the population variance is known, the standard error of sample mean is calculated as:

$$\sigma_{\bar{x}} = \sigma \Big/ \sqrt{n}$$

Practically speaking, population variances are almost never known, so we estimate the standard error of the sample mean using the sample's standard deviation.

$$s_{\bar{x}} = \frac{s}{\sqrt{n}}$$

Point Estimates versus Confidence Intervals

A point estimate involves the use of sample data to calculate a single value that serves as an approximation for an unknown population parameter. For example, the sample mean, x, is a point estimate of the population mean, μ.

A confidence interval uses sample data to calculate a range of possible (or probable) values that an unknown population parameter can take, with a given probability of (1-α). α is called the level of significance, and (1-α) refers to the degree of confidence that the relevant parameter will lie in the computed interval. For example, a calculated interval between 100 and 150, at the 5% significance level, implies that we can be 95% confident that the population parameter lies between 100 and 150.

A (1-α)% confidence interval has the following structure:

$$\text{Point estimate} \pm (\text{reliability factor} \times \text{standard error})$$

Desirable Properties of an Estimator

- Unbiasedness.
- Efficiency.
- Consistency.

Characteristics of Student's t-Distribution

- It is symmetrical.
- It is defined by a single parameter, the degrees of freedom, (df), where degrees of freedom equal sample size minus one (n − 1).
- It has a lower peak than the normal curve, but fatter tails.
- As the degrees of freedom increase, the shape of the t-distribution approaches the shape of the standard normal curve.

As the degrees of freedom increase, the t-distribution curve becomes more peaked and its tails become thinner (bringing it closer to a normal curve). Therefore, the confidence interval for a random variable that follows the t-distribution will become narrower when the degrees of freedom increase for a given significance level.

The t-distribution is used in the following scenarios:

- It is used to construct confidence intervals of a normally (or approximately normally) distributed population whose variance is *unknown* when the sample size is small (n < 30).
- It may also be used for a non-normally distributed population whose variance is unknown if the sample size is large (n ≥ 30).

When the population is *normally* distributed we:

- Use the z-statistic when the population variance is known.
- Use the t-statistic when the population variance is not known.

When the distribution of the population is *nonnormal* the construction of an appropriate confidence interval depends on the size of the sample:

- If the population variance is known and the sample size is large we use the z-statistic. This is because the central limit theorem tells us that the distribution of the sample mean is approximately normal when sample size is large.
- If the population variance is not known and sample size is large, we can use the z-statistic or the t-statistic. However, in this scenario the use of the t-statistic is encouraged because it results in a more conservative measure.
- This implies that we cannot construct confidence intervals for nonnormal distributions if sample size is less than 30.

When Sampling from a:	Small Sample $n < 30$	Large Sample $n > 30$
Normal distribution with known variance	z-statistic	z-statistic
Normal distribution with unknown variance	t-statistic	t-statistic*
Non-normal distribution with known variance	not available	z-statistic
Non-normal distribution with unknown variance	not available	t-statistic*

Use of z-statistic is also acceptable

Sample Biases

Data-Mining Bias

Data mining is the practice of extensively searching through a data set for statistically significant relationships till a pattern "that works" is discovered. In the process of data mining, large numbers of hypotheses about a single data set are tested in a very short time by searching for combinations of variables that might show a correlation.

Warning signs that data mining bias might exist are:

- Too much digging warning sign.
- No story, no future warning sign.

The best way to avoid data-mining bias is to test the "apparently statistically significant relationships" on "out-of-sample" data to check whether they hold.

Sample Selection Bias

Sample selection bias results from the exclusion of certain assets from a study due to the unavailability of data.

Some databases use historical information and may suffer from a type of sample selection bias known as **survivorship bias**. Databases that only list companies or funds currently in existence suffer from this bias.

Look-Ahead Bias

An analyst may not have complete information at the time of testing. Look-ahead bias arises if the analyst uses an assumed figure instead. The actual figure may be different from the one used in the study.

Time-Period Bias

Time-period bias arises if the sample data is drawn from a certain time period. The results obtained from the study of such a data set will be time-specific.

HYPOTHESIS TESTING
Cross-Reference to CFA Institute Assigned Reading #12

Steps in Hypothesis Testing

- State the hypothesis.
- Select the appropriate test-statistic.
- Specify the level of significance.
- State the decision rules.
- Calculate the sample statistic.
- Make a decision regarding the validity of the hypothesis.

Null versus Alternative Hypotheses

- The null hypothesis (H_0) generally represents the status quo, and is the hypothesis that we are interested in rejecting. This hypothesis will not be rejected unless the sample data provides sufficient evidence to suggest otherwise.
- The alternate hypothesis (H_A) is the statement that will only be accepted if the sample data provides convincing evidence of its truth. It is the conclusion of the test if the null hypothesis is rejected. *The alternate hypothesis is essentially the statement whose validity we are tying to evaluate.*

One-Tailed versus Two-Tailed Tests

Under one-tailed tests, we assess whether the value of the population parameter is either *greater than, or less than* a given hypothesized value. Hypotheses for one-tailed hypotheses tests are structured as:

- $H_0 : \mu \leq \mu_0$ versus $H_a : \mu > \mu_0$; when determining whether the population mean is *greater* than a hypothesized value.
- $H_0 : \mu \geq \mu_0$ versus $H_a : \mu < \mu_0$; when determining whether the population mean is *less* than a hypothesized value.

The following rejection rules apply when we are trying to determine whether the population mean is *greater* than the hypothesized value.

When we want to ascertain whether the population mean is *greater* than the hypothesized mean, we compare the test statistic to the *positive* critical value.

- Reject H_0 when:
  Test statistic > Positive critical value

- Fail to reject H_0 when:
  Test statistic ≤ Positive critical value

The following rejection rules apply when we are trying to determine whether the population mean is *lower* than the hypothesized value.

- Reject H_0 when:
  Test statistic < Negative critical value

- Fail to reject H_0 when:
  Test statistic ≥ Negative critical value

Under two-tailed tests, we assess whether the value of the population parameter is *simply different from* a given hypothesized value. Hypotheses for two-tailed hypotheses tests are structured as:

$$H_0 : \mu = \mu_0$$
$$H_a : \mu \neq \mu_0$$

The following rejection rules apply for two-tailed hypothesis test

- Reject H_0 when:
  Test statistic < Lower critical value
  Test statistic > Upper critical value

- Fail to reject H_0 when:
  Lower critical value ≤ Test statistic ≤ Upper critical value

> When we want to ascertain whether the population mean is *less* than the hypothesized mean, we compare the test statistic to the *negative* critical value.

Type I versus Type II Errors

- Type I error: Rejecting the null when it is actually true.
- Type II error: Not rejecting the null when it is actually false.

The significance level (α) represents the probability of making a Type I error. A significance level of 5% means that there is a 5% chance of rejecting the null when it is actually true.

If we were to fail to reject the null hypothesis given the lack of overwhelming evidence in favor of the alternate, we risk a Type II error—*failing to reject the null hypothesis when it is false*.

Sample size and the choice of significance level (probability of Type I error) together determine the probability of a Type II error.

The power of a test is the probability of *correctly* rejecting the null hypothesis when it is false.

Power of a test = 1 – P(Type II error)

Errors in Hypothesis Testing

Decision	H_0 is true	H_0 is false
Do not reject H_0	Correct decision	Incorrect decision **Type II error**
Reject H_0	Incorrect decision **Type I error** Significance level (α)	Correct decision Power of the test $= 1 - P(\text{Type II error})$

- The *higher* the power of the test, the *better* is it for purposes of hypothesis testing.
- An *increase* in the power of a test comes at the cost of *increasing* the probability of a Type I error.
- The only way to *decrease* the probability of a Type II error given the significance level is to *increase the sample size*.

Confidence Intervals versus Hypothesis Tests

- In a confidence interval we state that the population parameter lies within the interval, which represents the "fail-to-reject-the-null region" with a $(1 - \alpha)$ level of confidence.
- In a hypothesis test, we examine whether the population parameter lies in the rejection region, or outside the interval, at the α level of significance.

P-Values and Hypothesis Tests

The p-value is the smallest level of significance at which the null hypothesis can be rejected. It is the probability of obtaining a critical value that would lead to the rejection of the null hypothesis.

- If the p-value is *less* than the required level of significance, we can *reject* the null hypothesis.
- If the p-value is *greater* then the required level of significance, we *fail to reject* the null hypothesis.

Hypothesis Tests Concerning a Single Mean

The t-test is used when the variance of the population is unknown *and* either of the conditions below hold:

- The sample size is large.
- The sample is small, but the underlying population is normally distributed or approximately normally distributed.

Summary of Hypothesis Tests on the Mean of a Single Population

Type of test	Null hypothesis	Alternate hypothesis	Reject null if	Fail to reject null if	P-value represents
One-tailed (upper tail)	$H_0 : \mu \leq \mu_0$	$H_a : \mu > \mu_0$	Test statistic > Critical value	Test statistic $\leq$ Critical value	Probability that lies above the computed test statistic.
One-tailed (lower tail)	$H_0 : \mu \geq \mu_0$	$H_a : \mu < \mu_0$	Test statistic < Critical value	Test statistic $\geq$ Critical value	Probability that lies below the computed test statistic.
Two-tailed	$H_0 : \mu = \mu_0$	$H_a : \mu \neq \mu_0$	Test statistic < Lower critical value Test statistic > Upper critical value	Lower critical value $\leq$ Test statistic $\leq$ Upper critical value	Probability that lies above the positive value of the computed test statistic *plus* the probability that lies below the negative value of the computed test statistic.

The t-statistic for hypothesis test concerning the mean of a single population is:

$$\text{t-stat} = \frac{\overline{x} - \mu_0}{s / \sqrt{n}}$$

In a t-test, the sample's t-statistic is compared to the critical t-value with degrees of freedom (n-1) at the desired level of significance.

The z-test is used to conduct hypothesis tests of the population mean when the population is normally distributed and its variance is known.

$$\text{z-stat} = \frac{\overline{x} - \mu_0}{\sigma / \sqrt{n}}$$

The z-test can also be used when the population's variance is unknown, but the sample size is large.

$$\text{z-stat} = \frac{\overline{x} - \mu_0}{s / \sqrt{n}}$$

In a z-test, the z-statistic is compared to the critical z-value at the given level of significance.

Hypothesis Tests Concerning the Mean of Two Populations

Population distribution	Relationship between samples	Assumption regarding variance	Type of test
Normal	Independent	Equal	t-test with pooled variance
Normal	Independent	Unequal	t-test with variance not pooled
Normal	Dependent	N/A	t-test with paired comparisons

Hypothesis Tests Concerning the Variance

Hypothesis tests for the variance of a normally distributed population involve the use of the chi-square distribution where the test statistic is denoted as χ^2. Three important features of the chi-square distribution are:

- It is asymmetrical.
- It is bounded by zero. Chi-square values cannot be negative.
- It approaches the normal distribution in shape as degrees of freedom increase.

The chi-square test statistic with n − 1 degrees of freedom is calculated as:

$$\chi^2 = \frac{(n-1)s^2}{\sigma_0^2}$$

Hypotheses related to the equality of the variance of two populations are tested with an F-test. This test is used under the assumptions that:

- The populations from which samples are drawn are normally distributed.
- The samples are independent.

The test statistic for the F-test is given by:

$$F = \frac{s_1^2}{s_2^2}$$

Features of the F-distribution:

- It is skewed to the right.
- It is bounded by zero on the left.
- It is defined by two separate degrees of freedom.

The rejection region for any F-test, whether it be one-tailed or two-tailed, always lies in the right tail. This unique feature makes the F-test different from other hypothesis tests.

Hypothesis Test Concerning	Appropriate test statistic
Variance of a single, normally distributed population	Chi-square stat
Equality of variance of two independent, normally distributed populations	F-stat

Parametric versus Nonparametric Tests

A parametric test has at least one of the following two characteristics:

- It is concerned with parameters, or defining features, of a distribution.
- It makes a definite set of assumptions.

A non-parametric test is not concerned with a parameter, and makes only a minimal set of assumptions regarding the population. Non-parametric tests are used when:

- The researcher is concerned about quantities other than the parameters of the distribution.
- The assumptions made by parametric tests cannot be supported.
- When the data available is ranked. For example, non-parametric methods are widely used for studying populations such as movie reviews that receive one to five stars based on people's preferences.

The Spearman rank correlation coefficient is calculated on the ranks of two variables within their respective samples.

Statistically versus Economically Meaningful Results

Even though a trading strategy that is being studied provides a statistically significant return of greater than zero (based on the hypothesis test) it does not guarantee that trading on this strategy would result in economically meaningful returns. The returns may not be economically significant after accounting for taxes, transaction costs and risks inherent in the strategy.

TECHNICAL ANALYSIS
Cross-Reference to CFA Institute Assigned Reading #13

Technical analysis is a security analysis technique that involves the examination of past market trends (using data such as prices and trading volumes) to predict the future behavior of the overall market and of individual securities.

Technical analysis is based on the following:

- Supply and demand determine prices in real time.
- Changes in supply and demand cause changes in prices.
- Prices can be projected with charts and other technical tools.

Principles and Assumptions

- Technicians suggest that market trends and patterns reflect irrational human behavior.
- Technicians believe that the market reflects collective investor knowledge and sentiment.
- Technical analysis is the only tool available to investors to forecast future prices for assets that do not have underlying financial statements or associated income streams.
- Technicians believe that security price movements occur before fundamental developments occur or are reported.

Technical versus Fundamental Analysis

- Technical analysis uses only trading data, which includes market price and volume information. Fundamental analysis uses external information (e.g., financial reports, industry and macroeconomic analysis) and also incorporates social and political variables.
- The data used by technical analysts is more concrete and reliable. The financial statements used by fundamental analysts are subject to manipulation by management.
- Fundamental analysis is more conceptual as it aims to determine the theoretical long-term (intrinsic) value of a security. Technical analysis is more practical as it studies actual trading patterns to evaluate the market price of a security.
- Technical analysis has been in use for a longer period in investment decision-making. Fundamental analysis is a relatively new field.

Drawbacks of Technical Analysis

- Technicians only study market movements and trends, which can change without warning. Further, it may take some time for a clear, identifiable trend to emerge.
- Technicians expect trends to repeat themselves so a change in investor psychology may be missed by them.

- Application of technical analysis is limited in markets that are subject to significant outside manipulation and in illiquid markets.

Construction and Interpretation of Technical Analysis Charts

Charts

Charts are used to illustrate historical price information, which is used by technicians to infer future price behavior. The choice of charts is governed by the purpose of the analysis.

Line Charts

- A line chart is a simple graphical display of prices over time.
- Charts plot closing prices as data points, and have a line connecting these points.
- Time is plotted on the horizontal axis and prices are plotted on the vertical axis.
- Line charts provide a broad overview of investor sentiment, and the information they provide can be analyzed quickly.

Bar Charts

- A bar chart presents four pieces of information-opening price, highest and lowest prices, and the closing price for each time interval.
- A short bar indicates low price volatility, while a longer bar indicates high price volatility.
- For each time interval, the top of the line shows the highest price, while the bottom of the line shows the lowest price. The cross-hatch to the left indicates the opening price, while the cross-hatch to the right indicates the closing price.

Candlestick Charts

- A candlestick chart provides the opening and closing prices, and highs and lows during the period.
- Further, it also clearly illustrates whether the market closed up or down.
- The body of the candle is shaded if the closing price was lower than the opening price, and the body is clear if the closing price was higher than the opening price.

Point and Figure Chart

To construct a point and figure chart, a box size and a reversal size must first be determined.

- The box size refers to the minimum change in price that will be represented by a box on the chart.
- The reversal size determines when a new column will be created on the chart.
- The vertical axis measures discrete movements in price.
- Box and figure charts are useful as they highlight the prices at which trends change (when the columns change), as well as price levels at which the security most frequently trades (congestion areas).

Scale

The vertical axis on a charts can be constructed with a linear (arithmetic) scale or a logarithmic scale.

- A linear scale is more appropriate when the data fluctuate within a narrow range.
- In a logarithmic scale, percentage changes are plotted on the vertical axis. They are more appropriate when the range of data is larger.
- Time is plotted on the horizontal axis.

Volume

Volume is used by technicians as a barometer of the strength of a trend.

- If a security's price is increasing with increasing volumes, it shows that more and more investors are purchasing the stock at higher prices. This indicates that the trend is expected to continue as the two indicators "confirm" each other.
- If a security's price is rising with declining volumes (the two indicators are diverging), it suggests that the trend is losing momentum as fewer investors are willing to buy at higher prices.

Time Intervals

Short term investors may create charts with intervals less than a minute long, while longer term investors may use charts with intervals as long as one year.

Relative Strength Analysis

Relative strength analysis is used to evaluate the relative performance of a security compared to a stated benchmark by plotting the ratio of the security's price to the benchmark index over time.

- An upward-sloping line indicates outperformance.
- A downward-sloping line suggests underperformance.

Trend, Support, Resistance Lines, and Changes in Polarity

Trend analysis assumes that investors tend to behave in herds and that trends usually continue for an extended period of time.

An uptrend occurs when a security's price makes higher highs and higher lows.

- Higher highs occur when each high lies above the previous high, and when the price declines (there is a retracement) each subsequent low is higher than the prior low.
- To illustrate an uptrend, the technician connects all the lows on the price chart with a straight line.
- Major retracements (that drag the security's price significantly below the trend line) indicate that the uptrend is over and that the price may decline further.

- There are more ready buyers for a security than there are sellers and traders are willing to pay a higher price for the security over time.

A downtrend is indicated by lower highs and lower lows on the price chart.

- A technician connects all the highs on the chart to illustrate the downtrend.
- Major breakouts above the trend line may indicate that the downtrend is over and that the security's price could rise further.
- In a downtrend, sellers are willing to accept lower and lower prices for the security, which indicates negative investor sentiment regarding the asset.

During a sideways trend, there is a relative balance between demand and supply.

- Typically, options positions are more profitable than long or short positions on the security itself during a sideways trend.

Trend analysis involves the use of support and resistance levels.

- A support level is defined as the price at which there is sufficient buying interest in the stock to arrest the price decline.
- A resistance level is the price at which enough selling activity is generated to prevent any further increase in price.

Support and resistance levels may be horizontal or sloped lines.

The change in polarity principle asserts that once the price rises above the resistance level, it becomes the new support level. Similarly, once the price falls below a support level, it becomes the new resistance level.

Chart Patterns

Chart patterns are formations on price charts that look like recognizable shapes. Recurring chart patterns can be used to predict future prices because these patterns essentially represent collective investor sentiment over a given time period.

Reversal Patterns

Reversal patterns indicate the end of a prevailing trend.

Head and Shoulders

A head and shoulders pattern follows an uptrend in the price of a security. It is composed of three parts:

Left shoulder: The left shoulder consists of a strong rally with high volumes.
Head: The price starts to rise again, and this time records a higher high than the one reached in the left shoulder. However, volumes in this rally are lower.
Right shoulder: The right shoulder is similar to the left shoulder, but with lower volumes.

Note that the neckline may not always be a perfectly horizontal line.

Volume is very important in analyzing head and shoulders patterns. The fact that the high of the "head" is higher than the "high" of the left shoulder, but has lower volumes indicates that investor interest is waning.

When one indicator is bullish (rising price) while another is bearish (lower volumes) it is known as a **divergence**.

- Once a head and shoulders pattern has formed, prices are expected to decline (the uptrend that preceded the head and shoulders pattern is expected to reverse).
- Once the price falls below the neckline (which previously acted as a support level), it becomes the new resistance level (change in polarity principle).

Inverse Head and Shoulders

- A downtrend in prices precedes an inverse head and shoulders pattern.
- The price characteristics of each of the three segments of the head and shoulders pattern are reversed in an inverse head and shoulders pattern, but the volume characteristics are the same.

Setting Price Targets with Head and Shoulders Patterns

Once the neckline has been breached in the head and shoulders pattern, the price is expected to decline by an amount equal to the distance between the top of the head and the neckline.

$$\text{Price target} = \text{Neckline} - (\text{Head} - \text{Neckline})$$

Typically, the stronger the rally preceding the head and shoulders pattern, the more pronounced the expected reversal.

Setting Price Targets for Inverse Head and Shoulders Patterns

Inverse head and shoulders patterns are preceded by a downtrend. Therefore, prices are expected to rise or break out above the neckline after the right shoulder has been formed.

$$\text{Price target} = \text{Neckline} + (\text{Neckline} - \text{Head})$$

Double Tops and Bottoms

A double top occurs when an uptrend in prices reverses twice at approximately the same price level (two highs are recorded at roughly the same level). Usually, the first top has a higher volume.

For a double top, the price target (where the reversal will end) is established at a level that is lower than the valley (the low recorded between the two tops) by an amount that equals the distance between the tops and the valley.

The more significant the sell-off after the first top (deeper the valley) and the longer the time period between the two tops, the more significant the formation is considered to be.

A double bottom indicates the reversal of a downtrend. It occurs when, following a recent downtrend, prices fall to a certain level, rise for a bit, then fall back to the same level and rise again.

For double bottoms, the price is expected to rise above the peak between the two bottoms by approximately an amount equal to the distance between the bottoms and the peak.

Triple Tops and Bottoms

A triple top consists of three peaks at roughly the same level, while a triple bottom occurs when three troughs are formed at roughly the same price level.

- Triple tops and bottoms are rare, but when they occur, they indicate more significant reversals than double tops and double bottoms.
- Generally speaking, the greater the number of times the price reverses at a given price level, and the longer the period over which the pattern is formed, the more significant the expected reversal.

Continuation Patterns

A continuation pattern is used to confirm the resumption of the current market trend.

Triangle Patterns

A triangle pattern is formed when the range between highs and lows over a period narrows down on the price chart. The line connecting the highs over the period eventually meets the line connecting the lows, forming a triangle.

An ascending triangle is formed when the trend line connecting the highs is horizontal while the trend line connecting the lows is upward-sloping.

- Ascending triangles form during an uptrend.
- Eventually the share price is expected to rise.

A descending triangle suggests that the stock price will continue to decline.

- The line connecting the highs is downward-sloping, while the line connecting the lows is horizontal.

In a symmetrical triangle, the line connecting the highs is downward-sloping, while the line connecting the lows is upward-sloping.

- Such a formation suggests that buyers are becoming more bullish as they continue to buy at higher prices than before, but sellers are becoming increasingly bearish as they sell at successively lower prices.
- After the formation, the trend ends up in the same direction as the trend that preceded the triangle formation.

More about Triangle Patterns

- The height of the triangle (also known as **measuring implication**) equals the distance between the two trend lines at the start of the formation.
- Once the price breaks through one of the trend lines, analysts expect the price to move further by roughly the measuring implication.
- Usually, the breakout from the triangle occurs between halfway and three-fourths of the way into the pattern; not at the end of the pattern.
- The longer the triangle pattern, the more significant and volatile the subsequent price movement is expected to be.

Rectangle Patterns

When the two trend lines (one that connects the highs and the other that connects the lows) are both horizontal, a rectangle pattern is formed. Once a breakout occurs, the trend in prices is the same as the trend that preceded the rectangle formation.

Flags and Pennants

Flags and pennants form over a much shorter time interval (usually on a daily price chart over a week) compared to triangles and rectangle patterns.

A flag is formed when two trend lines are parallel to each other (similar to country flags or parallelograms).

- Typically, the slope of the trend lines is opposite to that of the prevailing trend.

A pennant is basically a triangle that is formed over a relatively short span of time (typically over a week).

- For both flags and pennants, the expectation is that the trend that preceded the formation will continue after the pattern.
- The breakout beyond the trend line is expected to roughly equal the distance between the start of the trend and the flag or the pennant.

Common Technical Analysis Indicators

Price-Based Indicators

Price-based technical indicators incorporate current and historical market price information.

Moving Average

A moving average is the average of the closing price over a given number of periods. Moving averages smooth out short term price fluctuations and therefore, give a clearer picture of a market trend.

- A simple moving average uses the arithmetic mean, weighing each price equally in computing the average.
- An exponential moving average attaches a greater weight to recent prices in computing the average.

Applications of Moving Averages

- Generally, a stock that is in a downtrend tends to trade below its moving average, while one in an upward trend will typically trade above its moving average.
- Moving average trend lines can also act as support or resistance levels.
- When the short-term moving average intersects the long-term moving average from below, the formation is referred to as a *golden cross* and is a bullish sign.
- When the short-term moving average intersects the long-term moving average from above, it forms a *dead cross* which is a bearish signal.

Bollinger Bands

Bollinger bands consist of a simple moving average plus upper and lower bands that are calculated by adding and subtracting a specific number of standard deviations from the moving average.

Applications of Bollinger Bands

- A contrarian technical strategy based on Bollinger bands aims to sell the security when it reaches the upper band and purchase the security when it touches the lower band. The assumption here is that the security will continue to trade within the bands.
- A long-term investor may purchase the security once it has broken out significantly above the upper band, or short the security once it has fallen significantly below the lower band.

Momentum Oscillators

Momentum oscillators are used to identify changes in market sentiment. They are calculated in such a manner that they either fluctuate within a range (usually between 0 and 100) or hover around a number (such as 0 or 100).

- It is easy to identify extreme highs and lows on oscillators, and these extremes indicate that market buying/selling activity is more aggressive than historical levels.
- Technicians focus on whether oscillators and price data are moving in the same direction (convergence) or in different directions (divergence).

QM

- When the price forms a new low, but the momentum oscillator is not at its lowest, the formation is a divergence. It implies that the downtrend is weakening and is expected to end soon.

Applications of Momentum Oscillators

- The oscillator range for a security can be used to determine the strength of a trend. Oversold conditions suggest that bearish market sentiment will end soon, while overbought conditions signal that the bullish market sentiment may soon change.
- They may signal a trend reversal when they reach historical highs or lows.
- They can be used to make short-term trading decisions in non-trending markets.

Momentum or Rate of Change Oscillator

A momentum oscillator (rate of change (ROC) oscillator) is calculated as follows:

$$M = (V - Vx) \times 100$$

where:
 M = momentum oscillator value
 V = last closing price
 Vx = closing price x days ago, typically 10 days

- When the momentum oscillator value crosses zero into positive territory in an uptrend (when prices are also rising) it is a bullish signal.
- When it crosses zero into negative territory in a downtrend (when prices are falling), it is a bearish signal.
- Crossovers that occur in the opposite direction of the trend are ignored because technicians who use oscillators first consider the general trend when making trading decisions.

The base value for an oscillator can also be set at 100. In this case, the oscillator is calculated as:

$$M = \frac{V}{Vx} \times 100$$

Relative Strength Index

A relative strength index (RSI) compares a security's gains with its losses over a given time period.

$$RSI = 100 - \frac{100}{1 + RS}$$

$$\text{where } RS = \frac{\Sigma \ (\text{Up changes for the period under consideration})}{\Sigma \ (|\text{Down changes for the period under consideration}|)}$$

- The RSI lies between the 0 and 100.
- A value above 70 typically represents an overbought situation, while a value below 30 usually indicates an oversold situation.
- Less volatile stocks may trade in a narrower range.
- The RSI range for any stock does not need to be symmetrical around 50.

Stochastic Oscillator

A stochastic oscillator is based on the assumption that in an uptrend, the stock price tends to close near the high of its recent range, while in a downtrend it tends to close around its recent low.

The stochastic oscillator lies between 0 and 100 and is usually calculated using 14-day price data. It is composed of two lines, %K and %D.

$$\%K = 100\left(\frac{C - L14}{H14 - L14}\right)$$

where:
   C = last closing price
L14 = lowest price in last 14 days
H14 = highest price in last 14 days

%D (signal line) = Average of the last three %K values calculated daily.

Applications of Stochastic Oscillators

- Generally speaking, when the stochastic oscillator is greater than 80, it usually indicates that the security is overbought and should be sold. A value lower than 20 indicates that the security is oversold and should be purchased. However, analysts should consider the absolute level of the two lines in light of their historical range.
- Crossovers between the two lines can also give trading signals similar to crossovers of moving average lines. When the %K (smoothed line) crosses %D from below, it is a short-term bullish signal, and if it crosses %D from above, it is a bearish signal.

Moving Average Convergence/Divergence Oscillator

The moving average convergence/divergence oscillator (MACD) is the difference between the short term and long term moving average of a security's price. The MACD is composed of two lines:

- The MACD line, which is the difference between two exponentially smoothed moving average lines (typically over 12 and 26 days).
- The signal line, which is the exponentially smoothed moving average of the MACD line (typically over 9 days).

The MACD is compared with its historical levels to determine whether market sentiment regarding the security is different from what it usually is. The indicator itself moves around 0 and has no limits.

Applications of the MACD Oscillator

- Crossovers of the MACD line and the signal line may indicate a change in trend (similar to crossovers of moving averages and the stochastic oscillator).
- When MACD line moves outside its historical range, it indicates a weakening in the current trend.
- Convergence (which suggests that the trend will continue) occurs when the MACD and price move in the same direction, while divergence (which suggests that the trend will reverse) occurs when the MACD and price move in opposite directions.

Sentiment Indicators

Sentiment indicators evaluate investor activity looking for signs of bullishness or bearishness.

Opinion Polls

A number of companies conduct regular polls of investors and investment professionals to gauge market sentiment. Technicians compare the data (which is also presented graphically) with recent market highs, lows and inflection points to establish relationships that might be useful in predicting future market direction.

Calculated Statistical Indices

- A high **put-call ratio** indicates that the market is bearish, while a low ratio suggests that the market is bullish.
- The **VIX** rises when investors fear a market decline.
- **Margin debt levels** are very strongly correlated with the movement in the market.
- The **short interest ratio** may be interpreted in two ways. A high ratio may suggest that:
  - There is overall a negative outlook on the security and one should expect the price to decline.
  - The effect of short sales has already been factored into the current market price. When these short sellers cover their positions, the price of the stock will rise.

Flow of Funds Indicators

Technicians also look at the potential demand and supply for securities in making trading decisions.

Arms Index

$$\text{Arms Index} = \frac{\text{Number of advancing issues} / \text{Number of declining issues}}{\text{Volume of advancing issues} / \text{Volume of declining issues}}$$

- When the market is in balance, the arms index is close to 1.
- Values above 1 indicate that there is more activity in declining stocks, and that the market is in a selling mood.
- Values below 1 indicate that there is more activity in advancing stocks and that market sentiment is currently bullish.

Margin Debt

Margin loans may increase stock purchases, while declining margin balances may force the selling of stocks.

Mutual Fund Cash Positions

- Contrarians buy when mutual funds' cash positions are high and sell when their cash positions are low.
- The average cash percentage of mutual funds has historically hovered around 6.8%.

New Equity Issuance

When the new equity issuance indicator is high, the market is usually near its peak and is likely to decline in the future.

Secondary Offerings

While these offerings do not increase the number of shares outstanding, they do increase the number of shares available for trading (the free float). Therefore, secondary offerings affect the supply of shares just like IPOs.

Cycles

Over time, technicians have observed recurring cycles in the markets, only some of which can be logically explained. By identifying different cycles, technicians look to predict the market's future direction.

Kondratieff Waves

Nikolai Kondratieff suggested that economies went through a 54-year economic cycle. His theory was mainly derived from economic cycles and commodity prices, but similar cycles have also been seen in equity prices during the time of his work.

QM

18-year cycle

The 18-year cycle is usually mentioned in real estate markets though it can also be observed in equities and other markets.

Decennial Pattern

The decennial pattern traces the average annual stock returns (based on the DJIA) according to the last digit of the year. The DJIA has historically performed poorly in years ending with a 0, while the best ones have been years that end with a 5.

Presidential Cycle

Historically, it has been observed that the third year (of the four-year U.S. Presidential term) boasts the best stock market performance. The stock market has done reasonably well in the fourth year as well. One explanation for this is that politicians up for re-election inject stimuli into the economy to increase their popularity.

Elliott Wave Theory and Fibonacci numbers

Elliott Wave Theory

In 1938, R. N. Elliott proposed that the market moves in regular cycles or waves.

- In a bull market, the market moves up in five waves (called **impulse waves**) in the following pattern: 1 = up, 2 = down, 3 = up, 4 = down and 5 = up.
- The impulse wave is followed by a corrective wave that has three components: a = down, b = up and c = down.
- The same pattern is reversed in a bear market.
- Each wave can be broken into smaller waves. Starting with the largest "grand supercycle" which takes place over centuries, waves can be broken down into supercycles, cycles, and subcycles which take place over shorter and shorter intervals.

The **Fibonacci Sequence** starts with the numbers 0, 1, 1, and then each subsequent number in the sequence is the sum of the two preceding numbers: 0, 1, 1, 2, 3, 5, 8, 13, . . .

Elliott discovered that market waves followed patterns that were ratios of numbers in a **Fibonacci sequence**.

- Positive price movements would take prices up by a factor equal to the ratio of a Fibonacci number to its preceding number.
- Negative price movements would reverse prices by a factor of a Fibonacci number to the next number.
- Elliott wave theory is used along with Dow Theory, trend analysis, pattern analysis and oscillator analysis to forecast market movements.
- Its biggest advantage is that it can be applied in short-term trading as well as long-term economic analysis.

Intermarket Analysis

Intermarket analysis refers to the technique of combining analysis of different markets to identify trends and reversals of trends. It is based on the principle that markets for different categories of securities (stocks, bonds, currencies, commodities, etc.) are interrelated and influence each other, and asserts that these relationships are strengthening with increasing globalization. Some of the relationships that have been observed between different asset classes are:

- Stock prices and bond prices tend to move in the same direction. Therefore, rising bond prices are a positive for stocks.
- Declining bond prices are a signal of commodities prices possibly rising.
- A strong dollar usually results in lower commodity prices.

Applications of Intermarket Analysis

- Technicians often use relative strength analysis to identify **inflection points** in a particular market and then look for a change in trend in a related market.
- Given technical observations regarding the business cycle at any time, relative strength analysis can be used to identify potentially lucrative investments from within the equity market.
- Intermarket analysis can also be used to identify which countries one should invest in.

QM

STUDY SESSION 4:
ECONOMICS (1)

TOPICS IN DEMAND AND SUPPLY ANALYSIS
Cross-Reference to CFA Institute Assigned Reading #14

Demand Concepts

Demand is defined as the willingness and ability of consumers to purchase a given amount of a good or a service at a particular price.

The law of demand states that as the price of a product increases, consumers will be willing and able to purchase less of it, and as the price decreases, they will be willing and able to purchase more of it (i.e., price and quantity demanded are inversely related).

The **demand function** uses quantity demanded as the dependent variable in capturing the relationship between own-price and quantity demanded. The **inverse demand function** makes price the dependent variable in capturing the relationship between own-price and quantity demanded. The **demand curve** is based on the inverse demand function.

The slope of the demand curve equals the coefficient on quantity demanded in the inverse demand function. The slope of the demand curve is also the reciprocal of the coefficient on own-price in the demand function.

Changes in Demand versus Movements along the Demand Curve

- When own-price changes, there is a **movement along the demand curve** or a **change in quantity demanded**.
- When there is a change in anything else that affects demand (i.e., a change in any of the factors assumed constant in the demand function), there is a **shift in the demand curve** (because the intercept term in the inverse demand function changes) or a **change in demand**.

Demand Elasticities

The own-price elasticity of demand is calculated as:

$$ED_{Px} = \frac{\%\Delta QD_x}{\%\Delta P_x}$$

$$ED_{Px} = \frac{\%\Delta QD_x}{\%\Delta P_x} = \frac{\Delta QD_x / QD_x}{\Delta P_x / P_x} = \left(\frac{\Delta QD_x}{\Delta P_x}\right)\left(\frac{P_x}{QD_x}\right)$$

Slope of demand function

Coefficient on own-price in market demand function

We look at the absolute value of own-price elasticity of demand when classifying how sensitive quantity demanded is to changes in price:

- If own-price elasticity of demand equals 1, demand is said to be unit elastic.
- If own-price elasticity of demand equals 0, demand is said to be perfectly inelastic.
- If own-price elasticity of demand equals ∞, demand is said to be perfectly elastic.
- If the absolute value of price elasticity of demand lies between 0 and 1, demand is said to be relatively inelastic.
- If the absolute value of price elasticity of demand is greater than 1, demand is said to be relatively elastic.

While the slope of the demand curve remains constant along a downward-sloping linear demand curve, the ratio of price to quantity is different at each point along the demand curve (unless the demand curve is perfectly elastic or perfectly inelastic).

- At relatively low prices (relatively high quantities), the ratio of price to quantity is relatively low so own-price elasticity of demand (absolute value of ED_P) is low and demand is relatively inelastic.
- At relatively high prices (relatively low quantities), the ratio of price to quantity is relatively high so own-price elasticity of demand (absolute value of ED_P) is high and demand is relatively elastic.
- Demand is unit elastic at the midpoint of the demand curve, relatively elastic above the midpoint, and relatively inelastic below the midpoint.

Factors That Affect Price Elasticity of Demand

Availability of close substitutes: If a consumer can *easily* switch away from a good, her ability to respond to a price increase (by reducing consumption of the good) is *high*, and demand for that product would be *relatively elastic*.

Proportion of income spent on the good: If a relatively *small* proportion of a consumer's income is spent on a good (e.g., soap), she will not significantly cut down on consumption if prices increase. Demand for such a good will be *relatively inelastic*.

Time elapsed since price change: The *longer* the time that has elapsed since the price change, the *more elastic* demand will be.

The extent to which the good is viewed as necessary or optional: The *more* the good is seen as being necessary, the *less elastic* its demand is likely to be.

Own-Price Elasticity of Demand and Total Expenditure/Total Revenue

- If demand is relatively elastic, a decrease in price will result in an increase in total expenditure, and an increase in price will result in a decrease in total expenditure.
- If demand is relatively inelastic, a decrease in price will result in a decrease in total expenditure, and an increase in price will result in an increase in total expenditure.

- If demand is unit elastic, a decrease or an increase in price will result in no change in total expenditure.

Total Expenditure/Revenue Test

- If the price cut *increases* total revenue, demand is relatively elastic.
- If the price cut *decreases* total revenue, demand is relatively inelastic.
- If the price cut *does not change* total revenue, demand is unit elastic.

Total Revenue and Price Elasticity

- If the demand curve facing a producer is relatively elastic, an *increase* in price will *decrease* total revenue.
- If the demand curve facing a producer is relatively inelastic, an *increase* in price will *increase* total revenue.
- If the demand curve facing a producer is unit elastic, an *increase* in price will *not change* total revenue.

Note that no producer would knowingly set a price that falls in the inelastic region of the demand curve.

Income Elasticity of Demand

Income elasticity of demand measures the responsiveness of demand for a particular good to a change in income, holding all other things constant.

$$ED_1 = \frac{\%\Delta QD_x}{\%\Delta I} = \frac{\Delta QD_x / QD_x}{\Delta I / I} = \left(\frac{\Delta QD_x}{\Delta I}\right)\left(\frac{I}{QD_x}\right)$$

$$E_1 = \frac{\%\,change\ in\ quantity\ demanded}{\%\,change\ in\ income}$$

If income elasticity is *greater* than 1, demand is income elastic, and the product is classified as a *normal good*.

- As income *rises*, the percentage increase in demand *exceeds* the percentage change in income.
- As income *increases*, a consumer spends a *higher proportion* of her income on the product.

If income elasticity lies *between* zero and 1, demand is income inelastic, but the product is still classified as a *normal good*.

- As income *rises*, the percentage increase in demand is *less* than the percentage increase in income.
- As income *increases*, a consumer spends a *lower proportion* of her income on the product.

EC

If income elasticity is *less* than zero (negative), the product is classified as an *inferior good*.

- As income *rises*, there is a *negative* change in demand.
- As income *increases*, the amount spent on the good *decreases*.

When income changes, there is a shift in the demand curve (change in demand).

Cross-Price Elasticity of Demand

Cross elasticity of demand measures the responsiveness of demand for a particular good to a change in price of *another* good, holding all other things constant.

$$ED_{Py} = \frac{\%\Delta QD_x}{\%\Delta P_y} = \frac{\Delta QD_x / QD_x}{\Delta P_y / P_y} = \left(\frac{\Delta QD_x}{\Delta P_y}\right)\left(\frac{P_y}{QD_x}\right)$$

$$E_C = \frac{\% \text{ change in quantity demanded}}{\% \text{ change in price of substitute or complement}}$$

For **substitutes**, the numerator and denominator of the cross elasticity formula head in the *same* direction. Therefore, cross elasticity of demand for substitutes is *positive*.

- *A high* value for cross elasticity indicates that the two products are very *close* substitutes.
- For substitutes, an increase in the price of another good results in an increase in demand (shift in demand to the right).

For **complements**, the numerator and denominator of the cross elasticity formula head in *opposite* directions. If the price of one good increases, demand for the other falls. Therefore, the cross elasticity of demand for complements is *negative*.

- *A high* absolute value for cross elasticity indicates that the two products are very *close* complements.
- For complements, an increase in price of another good results in a decrease in demand (shift in demand to the left).

Substitution and Income Effects

The law of demand states that when the price of a good falls, quantity demanded increases, and when the price rises, quantity demanded decreases. There are two main reasons for this:

The substitution effect: If the good becomes cheaper compared to other goods, more of the good gets substituted for other goods in the consumer's consumption basket. The substitution effect always goes in the opposite direction of the price change.

The income effect: If the consumer's real income increases (in terms of the quantity of goods and services that can be purchased with the same dollar income), then, if the good is a normal good (which most goods are), the increase in real income (due to the decrease in its price) leads to an increase in quantity purchased.

Normal Goods

For **normal goods** (e.g., restaurant meals, which most people tend to buy more of when their incomes rise), the substitution and the income effects reinforce one another.

Inferior Goods

If a good is an **inferior good**:

- The substitution effect of a change in price will be the same as for a normal good (i.e., a decrease in price of the good will cause the consumer to buy more of the good).
- However, the income effect will be the opposite of what it is for a normal good. For an inferior good, the increase in real income resulting from a decline in the good's price will cause the consumer to buy less of this good.

Overall, for an inferior good (e.g., margarine, which most people buy less of as their incomes rise), the income effect mitigates the substitution effect of a price change.

Note that:

- The substitution effect of a change in the price will always go in the direction opposite to that of the price change. If the price increases, less will be consumed, and if the price decreases, more will be consumed.
- The income effect of that same price change, however, depends on whether the good is normal or inferior.
  - For a normal good, the income effect reinforces the substitution effect, both leading to a negatively sloped demand curve.
  - For an inferior good, the income effect and the substitution effect work in opposite directions.

Giffen and Veblen Goods

For Giffen goods and Veblen goods, the demand curve is actually upward sloping.

A **Giffen good** is a special case of an inferior good where the negative income effect of a decrease in price of the good is so strong that it outweighs the positive substitution effect. Therefore, for a Giffen good, quantity demanded actually falls when there is a decrease in price, which makes the demand curve upward sloping.

Note the following:

- All Giffen goods are inferior goods because the income effect and substitution effect work in opposite directions.

- However, not all inferior goods are Giffen goods.
  - For inferior goods, the income effect partially mitigates or offsets the substitution effect.
  - For Giffen goods, the income effect outweighs the substitution effect.

With status goods such as expensive jewelry, the high price itself adds to the utility from the good, such that the consumer values the item more if it has a higher price. Such goods are known as Veblen goods.

Giffen Goods versus Veblen Goods

- Giffen goods **are inferior goods**. They are not status goods. An increase in income would reduce demand for them (due to negative income elasticity of demand).
- Veblen goods **are not inferior goods**. An increase in income would not lead to a decrease in demand.

Supply Analysis: The Firm

Short Run versus Long Run

- In the short run, at least one factor of production is fixed. Usually we assume that labor is the only variable factor of production in the short run.
- In the long run, quantities of all factors of production can be varied.

Total, Average, and Marginal Product of Labor

Total product (TP) is the maximum output that a given quantity of labor can produce when working with a fixed quantity of capital units.

- TP provides insight into the company's size relative to the overall industry.
- It does not show how efficient the firm is in producing its output.
- In the initial stages, total product *increases at an increasing rate*. Later, as more units of labor are employed to work with the fixed quantity of capital, total output *increases at a decreasing rate*, and the slope of the TP curve becomes *flatter*.

Marginal product (MP) (also known as marginal return) equals the increase in total product brought about by hiring one more unit of labor, while holding quantities of all other factors of production constant.

- MP measures the productivity of the individual additional unit of labor.

Average product (AP) equals the total product of labor divided by the quantity of labor units employed.

- AP is a measure of overall labor productivity.
- The lower a firm's AP, the more efficient it is.

Relationship between MP and AP

- MP intersects AP from *above* through the *maximum point* of AP.
- When MP is *above* AP, AP *rises*, and when MP is *below* AP, AP *falls*.

Note the following:

- Total product is simply an indication of a firm's output volume and potential market share.
- Average product and marginal product are better measures of productivity, as they can reveal competitive advantage through production efficiency.
- Average product is the preferred measure of productivity when workers perform tasks collectively, as in that case individual worker productivity is not easily measurable.

Breakeven and Shutdown Analysis

Accounting Profit versus Economic Profit

Accounting profit (also known as **net profit**, **net income**, and **net earnings**) equals revenue less all accounting (or explicit) costs. Accounting costs are payments to nonowner parties for goods and services supplied to the firm, and do not necessarily require a cash outlay.

$$\text{Accounting profit (loss)} = \text{Total revenue} - \text{Total accounting costs}$$

Economic profit (also known as **abnormal profit** or **supernormal profit**) is calculated as revenue less all economic costs (economic costs include explicit and implicit costs). Alternatively, economic profit can be calculated as accounting profit less all implicit opportunity costs that are not included in total accounting costs.

$$\text{Economic profit} = \text{Total revenue} - \text{Total economic costs}$$

$$\text{Economic profit} = \text{Total revenue} - (\text{Explicit costs} + \text{Implicit costs})$$

$$\text{Economic profit} = \text{Accounting profit} - \text{Total implicit opportunity costs}$$

Normal profit is the level of accounting profit that is required to cover the implicit opportunity costs that are not included in accounting costs.

$$\text{Accounting profit} = \text{Economic profit} + \text{Normal profit}$$

Note that:

- When accounting profit equals normal profit, economic profit equals 0.
- When accounting profit is greater than normal profit, economic profit is positive.
- When accounting profit is less than normal profit, economic profit is negative.

Total, Average, and Marginal Revenue

Revenue	Calculation
Total revenue (TR)	Price times quantity (P × Q), or the sum of individual units sold times their respective prices; $\Sigma(Pi \times Qi)$
Average revenue (AR)	Total revenue divided by quantity; (TR/Q)
Marginal revenue (MR)	Change in total revenue divided by change in quantity; ($\Delta TR/\Delta Q$)

The Demand Curve in Perfect and Imperfect Competition

- In **perfect competition**, each individual firm faces a perfectly elastic demand curve (i.e., it can sell as many units of output as it desires at the given market price).
- In **imperfect competition**, the firm has at least some control over the price at which it sells its output. The demand curve facing the firm is downward sloping, so in order to increase units sold the firm must lower its price.

Total, Average, and Marginal Revenue under Perfect Competition

- MR always equals AR, and they both equal market price.
- If there is an increase in market demand, the market price increases, which results in both MR and AR shifting up and TR pivoting upward as well.

Total, Average, and Marginal Revenue under Imperfect Competition

- As quantity increases, the rate of increase in TR (as measured by MR) decreases.
- AR equals price at each output level.
- MR is also downward sloping, with a slope that is steeper than that of AR (demand).
- TR reaches its maximum point when MR equals 0.

Note that MR equals price plus Q multiplied by the slope of the demand curve.

$$MR = P + Q(\Delta P / \Delta Q) \text{ or } MR = P + Q * \text{Slope of demand curve}$$

- Under perfect competition, the slope of the demand curve is zero. Therefore, MR = P
- Under imperfect competition, the slope of the demand curve is negative. As a result, MR is less than price.

Total, Average, Marginal, Fixed, and Variable Costs

Cost	Calculation
Total fixed cost (TFC)	Sum of all fixed expenses, here defined to include all opportunity costs
Total variable cost (TVC)	Sum of all variable expenses, or per unit variable cost times quantity; (per unit VC × Q)
Total cost (TC)	Total fixed cost plus total variable cost; (TFC + TVC)
Average fixed cost (AFC)	Total fixed cost divided by quantity; (TFC/Q)
Average variable cost (AVC)	Total variable cost divided by quantity; (TVC/Q)
Average total cost (ATC)	Total cost divided by quantity; (TC/Q) or (AFC + AVC)
Marginal cost (MC)	Change in total cost divided by change in quantity; (ΔTC/ΔQ)

Characteristics of Total Cost Curves

- TC and TVC increase at a decreasing rate at low levels of output, and increase at an increasing rate at higher levels of output.
- The difference between TC and TVC equals TFC.

Characteristics of Average Cost Curves

- As output levels rise, AFC continues to fall at a decreasing rate as total fixed costs are spread over more and more units.
- The ATC curve is U-shaped. It falls initially as fixed costs are spread over an increasing number of units. Later, however, the effect of a falling AFC is offset by diminishing marginal returns (increasing AVC) so ATC starts rising.
- The vertical distance between the AVC and ATC curves equals AFC. The vertical distance between the AVC and ATC curves gets smaller as output increases.

Average Cost and Marginal Cost Curves

- MC intersects ATC and AVC from *below* at their respective *minimum* points.
- When MC lies below AVC, AVC falls, and when MC lies above AVC, AVC rises.
- When MC lies below ATC, ATC falls, and when MC lies above ATC, ATC rises.

Short-Run Marginal Cost (SMC) versus Long-Run Marginal Cost (LMC)

- SMC is the additional cost of the variable input (labor) that must be incurred to increase the level of output by one unit.
- LMC is the additional cost of all inputs necessary to increase the level of output, allowing the firm the flexibility of changing both labor and capital inputs in a way that maximizes efficiency.

Marginal Product and Marginal Cost Curves

- A firm's MP curve is linked to its MC curve. Initially, as more labor is hired, MP rises and MC falls.
- At the point where MP reaches its maximum, MC stands at its minimum.
- As output expands further, MP falls and MC rises.

Average Product and Average Variable Cost Curves

- A firm's AP curve is linked to its AVC curve. Initially, as the firm hires more labor, AP rises and AVC falls.
- At the point where AP reaches its maximum, AVC is at its minimum.
- As the firm increases output further, AP falls and AVC rises.

Costs are directly related to input prices and inversely related to productivity.

- If the wage rate were to rise, costs would also rise, but if labor productivity were to improve, costs would fall. This relationship can be captured by the expression: $MC = w/MP_L$.
- Similarly, if wages rise, AVC also rises, but if labor productivity were to improve, AVC would fall. Therefore, $AVC = w/AP_L$.
- As the firm benefits from increasing marginal returns, MP_L increases and MC declines. However, as more and more labor is added to a fixed amount of capital, diminishing marginal returns set in and MP_L falls, causing MC to rise.

Marginal Revenue, Marginal Cost, and Profit Maximization

Profits are maximized when the difference between TR and TC is at its highest. The level of output at which this occurs is the point where (1) marginal revenue equals marginal cost (MC = MR), and (2) MC is not falling.

- When MR > MC, the firm should increase production, as the last unit produced added more to revenue that it did to costs.
- When MR < MC, the firm should reduce production, as the last unit produced added more to costs than it did to revenue.
- Recall that $MC = w/MP_L$, so if MC is falling, MP would be rising. If an additional unit of labor causes MC to fall, the firm would want to add that unit of labor until MC is upward sloping.

Perfect Competition

- The firm's profit-maximizing quantity is the output level where MR (which equals P and AR) equals MC while MC is rising. If P is greater than ATC, the firm makes economic profits. Economic profits are possible in perfect competition only in the short run. In the long run, more firms will enter the industry, taking market prices down to a level where they equal ATC.

Monopoly

- A monopoly faces a downward-sloping demand curve. As a result, the MR and demand curves are not identical. The profit-maximizing level of output occurs at the point where MC equals MR while MC is rising. Once the profit-maximizing level of output has been determined, the optimal price is obtained from the demand curve. If P is greater than ATC, the monopolist earns positive economic profits, and these can continue in the long run due to high barriers to entry.

Breakeven Analysis

A firm is said to break even if its TR equals its TC. At the breakeven quantity of production, price (or AR) equals ATC. This is true under both perfect and imperfect competition. Breaking even implies that the firm is covering all its economic costs (total accounting costs and implicit opportunity costs), so, while it is not earning positive economic profits, the firm is at least covering the opportunity cost of all its factors of production, including capital. In other words, the firm is earning normal profit.

The Shutdown Decision

- At price levels below AVC, the firm will not be willing to produce, as continued production would only extend losses beyond simply total fixed costs.
- When price lies between AVC and ATC, the firm will remain in production in the short run, as it meets all variable costs and covers a portion of its fixed costs.
- To remain in business in the long run, the firm must break even or cover all costs (revenues should meet total costs).
- Once prices exceed ATC, the firm makes economic profits.

Short-Run and Long-Run Operating Decisions

Revenue-Cost Relationship	Short-Run Decision	Long-Run Decision
TR = TC	Continue to operate	Continue to operate
TR = TVC but TR < TC	Continue to operate	Exit market
TR < TVC	Shut down	Exit market

Economies and Diseconomies of Scale

A company's production function shows how different quantities of labor and capital affect total product.

- Short-run ATC curves are U-shaped.
- The larger the plant, the greater the output at which short-run ATC is at its minimum.

The **long-run average cost (LRAC)** curve illustrates the relationship between average total cost and output when all factors of production are variable. The LRAC curve is also known as a *planning curve* because it shows the expected per-unit cost of producing various levels of output using different combinations of factors of production.

- **Economies of scale** occur in the downward-sloping region of the LRAC curve. They result from mass production and specialization of labor.
- **Diseconomies of scale** occur in the upward-sloping region of the LRAC curve. They result from bureaucratic inefficiencies as effective management, supervision, and communication become difficult.
- In the horizontal portion of the LRAC curve, when an increase in production does not result in any change in average costs, a firm realizes **constant returns to scale**.

Also, note that:

- The **minimum efficient scale** is the smallest quantity of output at which long-run average cost reaches its lowest level.
- In the long run, all firms in perfect competition operate at their minimum efficient scale, as price equals minimum average cost.

THE FIRM AND MARKET STRUCTURES
Cross-Reference to CFA Institute Assigned Reading #15

PERFECT COMPETITION

Characteristics

- There are a large number of buyers and sellers.
- Each seller offers an identical product for sale.
- There are minimal barriers to entry.
- Sellers have no pricing power.
- There is no non-price competition in the market.

Demand in a Perfectly Competitive Market

- The market demand curve is downward sloping.
- The relationship between MR and price elasticity can be expressed as:

$$MR = P[1 - (1 / E_P)]$$

Optimal Price and Output in Perfectly Competitive Markets

Each firm in perfect competition is very small compared to the size of the overall market. The actions of any firm do not impact market equilibrium. Each firm can sell as much output as it desires at the equilibrium market price.

- Therefore, the demand curve faced by an individual firm is perfectly elastic (horizontal).

Average revenue equals price and marginal revenue. AR = P = MR

The law of diminishing marginal returns dictates the "U" shape of SR cost curves.

Firms always maximize profits at the point where MC equals MR.

- Total revenue equals price times quantity sold.
- Total cost equals AC times quantity sold.
- The positive (negative) difference between the two equals economic profit (loss).
- If the two are equal, the firm only makes normal profit.

In the short run, a firm in perfect competition can make economic profits, economic losses or normal profit.

- In each scenario the firm produces the output level at which MC equals MR.
- Whether it makes a profit or a loss depends on the position of the demand curve relative to its average cost at the profit-maximizing quantity.

- If P > AC ⇒ Economic profit
- If P = AC ⇒ Normal profit
- If P < AC ⇒ Economic loss

In the long run, all firms in perfect competition will only make normal profit.

- In the LR, MC = MR = P = AR = min AC

Schumpeter's Take on Perfect Competition

Joseph Schumpeter suggested that perfect competition is more of a long-run type of market structure. In the short run, companies develop new products or processes that give them an edge over competitors but in the long run, as competitors adopt those new products, perfect competition prevails.

MONOPOLY

Characteristics

- There is a single seller of a highly differentiated product, which has no close substitutes.
- There are high barriers to entry.
- The firm has considerable pricing power.
- The product is differentiated through non-price strategies (e.g., advertising).

Factors that Give Rise to Monopolies

- Control over critical sources of production
- Patents or copyrights
- Non-price differentiation leading to pricing-power
- Network effects, which result from synergies related to increasing market penetration
- Government-controlled authorization

Demand Analysis in Monopoly Markets

The demand curve faced by the monopoly is effectively the industry demand curve. It is downward-sloping.

- The AR curve is the same as the demand curve.
- The MR curve and the demand curve have the same y-intercept.
- The slope of the MR curve is two times the slope of the demand curve.
- The x-intercept of the MR curve is half of that of the demand curve.
- The MR curve is the derivative of the TR curve with respect to quantity sold.

Supply Analysis in Monopoly Markets

- The monopolist does not have a well-defined supply function that determines optimal price and output.

- The profit-maximizing output level occurs at the point where MR = MC.
- The price is determined from the demand curve (based on the profit-maximizing quantity).

Optimal Price and Output in Monopoly Markets

The profit-maximizing output level equals the quantity at which:

- MC = MR; and
- Profit is unaffected by changes in quantity: $\Delta\pi/\Delta Q_D = 0$

The profit-maximizing level of output always occurs in the relatively elastic portion of the demand curve. Given its cost structure and price elasticity of demand, a monopoly can use the following equation to determine the profit maximizing price.

$$P[1 - (1/E_P)] = MC$$

Natural Monopolies

A natural monopoly is an industry where the supplier's average cost is still falling even when it satisfies total market demand entirely on its own.

Regulation of Natural Monopolies

- Marginal cost pricing forces a monopoly to charge a price that equals its marginal cost of production. Under marginal cost pricing, the monopoly makes an economic loss, which the government must subsidize. Alternatively the government may allow the monopoly to discriminate on prices or to engage in two-part pricing to offset losses. Marginal cost pricing is also known as efficient regulation.
- Average cost pricing forces a monopoly to charge a price that equals its average cost of production. This allows the monopoly to earn normal profits.

Price Discrimination and Consumer Surplus

First-degree price discrimination occurs when a monopolist is able to charge each individual consumer the highest price that she is willing and able to pay.

Under perfect price discrimination:

- The MR curve equals the demand curve.
- The profit maximizing level of output increases.
- The entire consumer surplus is eaten up by the producer.
- There is no dead weight loss.
- The more perfectly a monopolist can price discriminate, the more "efficient" the outcome.

In **second-degree price discrimination**, the monopolist offers a variety of quantity-based pricing options that induce customers to self-select based on how highly they value the product (e.g., volume discounts, product bundling).

Third-degree price discrimination can occur when customers can be separated by geographical or other traits. One set of customers is charged a higher price, while the other is charged a lower price (e.g., airlines charge higher fares on one day roundtrip tickets as they are more likely to be purchased by business people).

Factors Affecting Long-Run Equilibrium in Monopoly Markets

An unregulated monopoly can earn economic profits in the long run as it is protected by substantial barriers to entry.

For regulated monopolies, such as natural monopolies there are various solutions:

- A marginal cost pricing structure. However, the firm must be provided a subsidy in this scenario.
- An average cost pricing structure.
- National ownership of the monopoly.
- Franchising the monopoly via a bidding war (e.g., selling retail space at railway stations and airports).

MONOPOLISTIC COMPETITION

Characteristics

- There are a large number of buyers and sellers.
- The products offered by each seller are similar, but not identical. They serve as close substitutes to each other.
- Firms try to differentiate their product from the competition through advertising and other non-price strategies.
- There are low barriers to entry and exit.
- Firms have some degree of pricing power.

Demand and Supply Analysis in Monopolistically Competitive Markets

Demand:

- Each firm faces a downward sloping demand curve.
- Demand is relatively elastic at higher prices and relatively inelastic at lower prices.

Supply:

- There is no well-defined supply function.
- Neither the MC nor the AC curve represent the firm's supply curve.
- The firm will always produce at the output level where MC = MR.
- The price that is charged is derived from the market demand curve.

Short-Run versus Long-Run Equilibrium

- In the short run, a firm in monopolistic competition produces the output level where MC equals MR, and charges the maximum possible price that buyers are willing to pay for its product (determined by the demand curve).
- In the long run, firms in the industry make normal profits, there is no incentive for new firms to enter, or for existing firms to exit the industry.

Monopolistic Competition versus Perfect Competition

- A firm in monopolistic competition generally produces *lower* output and charges a *higher* price than in perfect competition. In perfect competition, price *equals* marginal cost, while in monopolistic competition, price *exceeds* marginal cost. This excess of price over marginal cost is known as *markup*.
- For a firm in monopolistic competition, in the long run, the profit maximizing output level occurs at a point where demand is tangent to the average cost curve, but at a stage where average costs are *still falling*. In perfect competition in the long run, each firm produces an output level where average cost is at its *minimum*, or at its efficient scale of production. Firms under monopolistic competition therefore, have *excess capacity*.

However, monopolistic competition enjoys some support because it offers consumers options to choose from. Product innovation, advertising and brand building are crucial to a firm's success in monopolistic competition.

OLIGOPOLY

Characteristics

- There are a small number of sellers.
- The products offered by sellers are close substitutes for each other. Products may be differentiated by brand (e.g., Coke® and Pepsi®) or be homogenous (e.g., oil).
- There are high costs of entry and significant barriers to competition.
- Firms enjoy substantial pricing power.
- Products are often differentiated on the basis of quality, features, marketing, and other non-price strategies.

Demand Analysis and Pricing Strategies in Oligopoly Markets

Pricing interdependence (kinked demand curve model): The demand curve has two contrasting shapes. It is relatively elastic above current prices, and relatively inelastic below current prices. This results in a kink in the firm's demand curve and a break in its marginal revenue curve. This break in the MR curve implies that it would take a significant change in costs of production to change the firm's profit-maximizing output level.

The Cournot assumption asserts that each firm determines its profit-maximizing level assuming that other firms' output will not change. In equilibrium, no firm has an incentive to change output. In the long run, prices and output are stable (i.e., there is no possible change in output or price that would make any firm better off).

Game theory: Nash equilibrium is achieved when none of the firms in an oligopoly market can increase profits by unilaterally changing its price. Each firm tries to maximize its own profits given the responses of its rivals. Each firm anticipates how its rival will respond to a change in its strategy and tries to maximize its profits under the forecasted scenario. As a result, the firms in the market are interdependent, but their actions are non-cooperative: Firms do not collude to maximize profits.

The Stackelberg model (also known as the dominant firm model) assumes that decision-making is sequential. The leader or dominant firm determines its profit-maximizing level of output, the price is determined from the demand curve for its product (the dominant firm is the price-maker) and then each of the follower firms determine their quantities based on the given market price (they are price-takers).

Factors Affecting Chances of Successful Collusion

- There are fewer firms in the industry or if one firm is dominant. Collusion becomes difficult as competition between firms in the industry increases.
- The firms produce similar products.
- The firms have similar cost structures.
- Order size is small and orders are received more frequently.
- There is minimal threat of retaliation from other firms in the industry.
- There is minimal external competition.

Supply Analysis in Oligopoly Markets

- The supply function for a firm in an oligopoly is not well-defined because optimal quantity and price depend on the actions of rival firms.
- The firm produces where MC = MR.
- Equilibrium price comes from the demand curve.

Optimal Price and Output in Oligopoly Markets

There is no single optimal price and output that fits all oligopoly market situations.

- In the kinked demand curve model, the optimal price is the prevailing price (at which the demand curve kinks).
- In the dominant firm model, the leader produces an output level where MC = MR. Followers have little or no power to influence price.
- In the Cournot assumption, each firm assumes that rivals will have no response to any actions on their part. Each firm produces where MC = MR.
- In Nash equilibrium, firms continue to respond to changing circumstances with the aim of maximizing their own profit. Since there is significant interdependence between firms, there is no certainty regarding an individual firm's price and output.

Identification of Market Structure

Econometric Approaches: Estimate the price elasticity of market demand based on time series analysis or cross sectional regression analysis.

N-firm concentration ratio: Computes the aggregate market share of the N largest firms in the industry.

- It does not quantify market power.
- It is unaffected by mergers in the top tier.

Herfindahl-Hirschman Index (HHI): Adds up the squares of the market shares of each of the largest N companies in the market.

- The HHI equals 1 for a monopoly.
- If there are M firms in the industry with equal market shares, the HHI will equal $1/M$.
- Does not account for the possibility of entry, nor does it consider the elasticity of demand. However, it is more useful than the concentration ratio.

EC

AGGREGATE OUTPUT, PRICE, AND ECONOMIC GROWTH
Cross-Reference to CFA Institute Assigned Reading #16

Aggregate output refers to the total value of all the goods and services produced in an economy over a period of time.

Aggregate income refers to the total value of all payments earned by the suppliers of factors of production in an economy over a period of time.

Aggregate expenditure refers to the total amount spent on the goods and services produced in the domestic economy over a period of time.

Gross Domestic Product (GDP)

- Output definition: GDP is the market value of all final goods and services produced within an economy over a period of time.
- Income definition: GDP is the aggregate income earned by all households, companies, and the government in an economy over a period of time.

Criteria for Inclusion in GDP

- Only goods and services produced *during* the measurement period are included.
  - Transfer payments and income from capital gains are excluded.
- Only goods and services whose value can be determined by being sold in the market are included.
  - The value of labor used in activities that are not sold in the market is excluded.
  - By-products of production processes which have no explicit market value are not included.
  - Activities in the underground economy are not included.
  - Barter transactions are not included.
- Only the value of *final* goods and services is included in the calculation of GDP. The value of intermediate goods (that are resold to produce another good) is excluded because the entire value added during the production process is reflected in the selling price of the final good produced (**value-of-final-output**). GDP can also be measured by summing the value added at each stage of the production and distribution processes (**sum-of-value-added**).

Nominal versus Real GDP

> Nominal GDP = Quantity produced in Year t × Prices in Year t

> Real GDP = Quantity produced in Year t × Base-year prices

GDP Deflator

The GDP deflator broadly measures the aggregate change in prices across the overall economy. Changes in the GDP deflator provide a useful measure of inflation.

$$\text{GDP deflator} = \frac{\text{Value of current year output at current year prices}}{\text{Value of current year output at base year prices}} \times 100$$

$$\text{GDP deflator} = \frac{\text{Nominal GDP}}{\text{Real GDP}} \times 100$$

The Components of GDP

$$\text{GDP} = C + I + G + (X - M)$$

Expenditure Approach

$$
\begin{aligned}
\text{GDP} = {} & \text{Consumer spending on goods and services} \\
& + \text{Business gross fixed investment} \\
& + \text{Change in inventories} \\
& + \text{Government spending on goods and services} \\
& + \text{Government gross fixed investment} \\
& + \text{Exports} - \text{Imports} \\
& + \text{Statistical discrepancy}
\end{aligned}
$$

Income Approach

$$
\begin{aligned}
\text{GDP} = {} & \text{National income} + \text{Capital consumption allowance} \\
& + \text{Statistical discrepancy}
\end{aligned}
$$

GDP-Related Measures

National income equals the sum of incomes received by all factors of production used to generate final output. It includes:

- Employee compensation
- Corporate and government enterprise profits before taxes
  - Dividends paid to households
  - Corporate profits retained by businesses
  - Corporate taxes paid to the government
- Interest income
- Rent and unincorporated business net income (proprietor's income)
- Indirect business taxes less subsidies

The **capital consumption allowance (CCA)** accounts for the wear and tear or depreciation that occurs in capital stock during the production process. It represents the amount that must be reinvested by the company in the business to maintain current productivity levels. You should think of profits + CCA as the amount earned by capital.

Personal income measures the ability of households to make purchases and includes all income received by households, regardless of whether it is **earned** or **unearned**. It differs from national income in the following respects:

- National income includes income that goes to businesses and the government (e.g., indirect business taxes, corporate income taxes and retained earnings), which personal income does not.
- National income does not include household income that is not earned (e.g., transfer payments).

> Personal income = National income
>   − Indirect business taxes
>   − Corporate income taxes
>   − Undistributed corporate profits
>   + Transfer payments

Personal disposable income measures the amount of income that households have left to spend or to save after paying taxes.

> Personal disposable income = Personal income − Personal taxes

> Personal disposable income = Household consumption + Household saving

> Household saving = Personal disposable income
>   − Consumption expenditures
>   − Interest paid by consumers to businesses
>   − Personal transfer payments to foreigners

> Business sector saving = Undistributed corporate profits
>   + Capital consumption allowance

The Equality of Expenditure and Income

$$S = I + (G - T) + (X - M)$$

Based on this equation we can say that domestic private saving can be used for:

- Investment spending (I);
- Financing government deficits (G − T); and/or

- Building up financial claims against overseas economies by financing their trade deficits (lending the domestic economy's trade surplus, X − M).
- If an economy has a negative trade balance, foreign savings will supplement domestic savings and foreigners will build up financial claims against the domestic economy.
- If the government runs a fiscal surplus, the surplus will add to domestic savings.

$$(G - T) = (S - I) - (X - M)$$

A fiscal deficit occurs when government expenditures exceed net taxes (i.e., G − T > 0). In order to finance a fiscal deficit:

- The private sector must save more than it invests (S > I); and/or
- The country's imports must exceed its exports (M > X ⇒ trade deficit) with a corresponding inflow of foreign saving.

Generating the Aggregate Demand Curve

The **aggregate demand (AD)** curve shows the combinations of aggregate income and price level at which the following conditions are satisfied:

- Planned expenditures equal actual (or realized) income/output.
- There is equilibrium in the money market.

The first condition gives rise to the **IS curve**, while the second gives rise to the LM curve. By combining the IS and LM curves, we obtain the **aggregate demand curve**.

Deriving the IS Curve: Relationship between Income and the Real Interest Rate

- Consumption varies positively with income, but negatively with taxes.
- Investment expenditure varies positively with income, and negatively with real interest rates.
- Government expenditure does not vary with income. Taxes vary positively with income. Therefore, the government's fiscal balance varies negatively with income.
- Net exports vary negatively with income, and negatively with domestic price levels.

$$S - I = (G - T) + (X - M)$$

- The fiscal balance (G − T) and the trade balance (X − M) **decline** as income rises.
- The saving-investment differential (S − I), **increases** as income increases.

The point of intersection between these two lines defines the point where aggregate expenditure and aggregate income are equal.

Changes in the level of real interest rates (r) cause shifts in the line representing the saving-investment differential. If the real interest rate falls (rises) the point of intersection between the $(S - I)$ and the $(G - T) + (X - M)$ curves occurs at a higher (lower) level of income.

This **inverse relationship between income and the real interest rate** is referred to as the IS curve.

The LM Curve

The LM curve shows the combinations of interest rates and real income for which the money market is in equilibrium. Equilibrium in the money market requires that real money demand (M_D/P) equals real money supply (M/P).

Demand for real money $(RM_D$ or $M_D/P)$ is a positive function of real income and a negative function of interest rates. Given the real money supply, an **increase** in real income (which would lead to an increase in real money demand) must be accompanied by an **increase** in interest rates (which would lead to a decrease in real money demand) so that demand for real money remains the same and equilibrium in the money market is maintained.

Therefore, if real money supply is held constant, we can infer a positive relationship between real income (Y) and the real interest rate (r). This **positive** relationship between real income and the real interest rate is illustrated by the LM curve.

Changes in real money supply cause shifts in the LM curve. If real money supply increases (decreases), the LM curve would shift to the right (left).

The Aggregate Demand Curve

If money supply is held constant, the only variable that affects real money supply is price. A **decrease** (increase) in the price level leads to an increase (decrease) in real money supply. The increase (decrease) in real money supply leads to a rightward (leftward) shift in the LM curve so the point of intersection of the IS and LM curves now occurs at a **higher** (lower) level of income.

The inverse relationship between the price level (P) and real income (Y) is captured by the aggregate demand curve. IS-LM analysis also suggests a positive relationship between the price level and real interest rates.

Slope of the AD Curve

The steepness of the slope of the AD curve depends on the relative sensitivities of investment, saving, and money demand to income and real interest rates. The AD curve will be flatter (small changes in price cause relatively large changes in quantity demanded) if:

- Investment expenditure is highly sensitive to the interest rate.
- Saving is insensitive to income.

- Money demand is insensitive to interest rates.
- Money demand is insensitive to income.

Interest Rates and Aggregate Demand

- If the increase in aggregate demand is caused by an increase in money supply, interest rates fall.
- If the increase in aggregate demand is caused by any other factor (with real money supply, M constant) interest rates will rise.

Aggregate Supply

Aggregate supply (AS) represents the quantities of goods and services that domestic producers are willing and able to supply at various price levels.

- The very short-run aggregate supply curve is horizontal.
- The short-run aggregate supply curve is upward-sloping.
- The long-run aggregate supply curve is vertical.

In the long run, wages, prices and expectations can adjust but capital and technology remain fixed. This condition is relaxed in the very long run.

The LRAS curve basically defines the potential output of the economy. The potential output of any economy does not vary with the price level. When an economy operates at its potential output level, all its resources are fully employed and it is said to be working at full employment. At this output level, unemployment is at its natural rate.

- Structural unemployment results from structural changes in the economy, which make some skills obsolete and leave previously employed people jobless.
- Cyclical unemployment is the unemployment generated as an economy goes through the phases of a business cycle.

Short-Run versus Long-Run Equilibrium

- The point of intersection of the AD curve and the LRAS curve defines the economy's long-run equilibrium position. At this point, actual real GDP equals potential GDP.
- The point of intersection of the AD curve and the SRAS curve defines the economy's short-run equilibrium position. Short-run fluctuations in equilibrium of real GDP may occur due to shifts in either or both the AD and SRAS curves. Short run equilibrium may be established at, below, or above potential output. Deviations of short-run equilibrium from potential output result in business cycles.
  - In an expansion, real GDP is increasing, the unemployment rate is falling and capacity utilization is rising. Further, inflation tends to rise during an expansion.
  - In a contraction, real GDP is decreasing, the unemployment rate is rising and capacity utilization is falling. Further, inflation tends to fall during a contraction.

EC

Shift in Aggregate Demand

An Increase in the Following Factors	Shifts the AD Curve	Reason
Stock prices	Rightward: Increase in AD	Higher consumption
Housing prices	Rightward: Increase in AD	Higher consumption
Consumer confidence	Rightward: Increase in AD	Higher consumption
Business confidence	Rightward: Increase in AD	Higher investment
Capacity utilization	Rightward: Increase in AD	Higher investment
Government spending	Rightward: Increase in AD	Government spending a component of AD
Taxes	Leftward: Decrease in AD	Lower consumption and investment
Bank reserves	Rightward: Increase in AD	Lower interest rate, higher investment and possibly higher consumption
Exchange rate (foreign currency per unit domestic currency)	Leftward: Decrease in AD	Lower exports and higher imports
Global growth	Rightward: Increase in AD	Higher exports

Shift in Aggregate Supply

An Increase in	Shifts SRAS	Shifts LRAS	Reason
Supply of labor	Rightward	Rightward	Increases resource base
Supply of natural resources	Rightward	Rightward	Increases resource base
Supply of human capital	Rightward	Rightward	Increases resource base
Supply of physical capital	Rightward	Rightward	Increases resource base
Productivity and technology	Rightward	Rightward	Improves efficiency of inputs
Nominal wages	Leftward	No impact	Increases labor cost
Input prices (e.g., energy)	Leftward	No impact	Increases cost of production
Expectation of future prices	Rightward	No impact	Anticipation of higher costs and/or perception of improved pricing power
Business taxes	Leftward	No impact	Increases cost of production
Subsidy	Rightward	No impact	Lowers cost of production
Exchange rate	Rightward	No impact	Lowers cost of production

EC

Business Cycles

Fluctuations in aggregate demand and aggregate supply in the short-run explain why short run real GDP deviates from potential GDP. These deviations of actual GDP from full-employment GDP form phases of the business cycle.

Investment Applications of an Increase in AD Resulting in an Inflationary Gap

If economic data suggest that the economy is undergoing an expansion caused by an increase in AD, going forward:

- Corporate profits will be expected to rise.
- Commodity prices will be expected to increase.
- Interest rates will be expected to rise.
- Inflationary pressures will build in the economy.

Therefore, investors should:

- Increase investments in cyclical companies as their earnings would rise significantly in this scenario.
- Increase investments in commodities and/or commodity oriented companies. Reduce investments in defensive companies as their profits would not rise as significantly as those of cyclical companies.
- Reduce investments in fixed-income securities (especially those with longer maturities) as their values would fall when interest rates go up.
- Increase investments in junk bonds as default risk (already factored into their prices) should fall in an expansion (and result in an increase in their prices).

Investment Applications of a Decrease in AD Resulting in a Deflationary Gap

If economic data suggest that the economy is undergoing a recession caused by a decrease in AD, going forward:

- Corporate profits will be expected to fall.
- Commodity prices will be expected to decline.
- Interest rates will be expected to fall.
- Demand for credit will decrease.

Therefore, investors should:

- Reduce investments in cyclical companies.
- Reduce investments in commodities and/or commodity oriented companies.
- Increase investments in defensive companies as their profits would decline modestly compared to cyclical companies.
- Increase investments in investment-grade or government-issued fixed-income securities as their values (particularly of those with longer maturities) will rise if interest rates go down.
- Decrease investments in junk bonds as default risk should rise in a recession (and result in a decrease in their prices).

Stagflation

Shifts in the SRAS curve (due to any of the factors discussed earlier in the reading) cause structural fluctuations in real GDP. A decrease in SRAS causes stagflation (high unemployment and higher inflation), while an increase in SRAS brings about economic growth and low inflation.

Investment Applications of a Shift in SRAS

If the SRAS curve shifts to the left (SRAS declines), investors may want to:

- Reduce investments in fixed-income securities because increasing output prices (inflation) may put an upward pressure on nominal interest rates (which would decrease the value of fixed-income instruments).
- Reduce exposure to equities in anticipation of a decline in output and profit margins coming under pressure.
- Increase investments in commodities and/or commodity-oriented companies because their prices and profits are likely to rise (due to higher prices).

Conclusions on AD and AS

	Real GDP	Unemployment Rate	Aggregate Level of Prices
An increase in AD	Increases	Falls	Increases
A decrease in AD	Falls	Increases	Falls
An increase in AS	Increases	Falls	Falls
A decrease in AS	Falls	Increases	Increases

Effect of Combined Changes in AS and AD

Change in AS	Change in AD	Effect on Real GDP	Effect on Aggregate Price Level
Increase	Increase	Increase	Uncertain
Decrease	Decrease	Decrease	Uncertain
Increase	Decrease	Uncertain	Decrease
Decrease	Increase	Uncertain	Increase

Economic Growth

Economic growth may be calculated as:

- The annual percentage change in real GDP, which tells us how rapidly the economy is expanding as a whole; or
- The annual change in real per capita GDP. Real GDP per capita is calculated as total real GDP divided by total population. It is a useful indicator of the standard of living in a country.

The Production Function and Potential GDP

The production function asserts that an increase in an economy's potential GDP can be caused by:

- An increase in the quantity of inputs used in the production process (e.g., capital and labor).
- An increase in the productivity of these inputs with the application of better technology. Improving technology enables an economy to produce more output using the same quantity of inputs.

Because of diminishing marginal returns to labor and capital, the only way to "sustain" growth in potential GDP is growth in total factor productivity.

The Growth Accounting Equation

$$\text{Growth in potential GDP} = \text{Growth in technology} + W_L(\text{Growth in labor}) + W_K(\text{Growth in capital})$$

$$\text{Growth in per capital potential GDP} = \text{Growth in technology} + W_K(\text{Growth in capital-labor ratio})$$

Takeaway: Advances in technology have a more significant impact on an economy's standard of living compared to capital.

Sources of Economic Growth

- Growth in labor supply
- Improvements in quality of human capital
- Growth in physical capital stock
- Improvements in technology
- Availability of natural resources

Measures of Sustainable Growth

Labor productivity refers to the quantity of goods and services (real GDP) that a worker can produce in one hour of work.

> Labor productivity = Real GDP/ Aggregate hours

Labor productivity depends on:

- Physical capital per worker (K/L) or the mix of inputs (which is easily calculated based on input data)
- Total factor productivity or technology (A). This is a scale factor and can be estimated based on output and input data.

Labor productivity is much easier to measure directly than growth in potential GDP. Labor productivity can explain differences in living standards and long term sustainable growth rates across countries.

Measuring Sustainable Growth

Potential GDP is a combination of aggregate hours and productivity of labor:

> Potential GDP = Aggregate hours × Labor productivity

> Potential GDP growth rate = Long-term growth rate of labor force
> + Long-term labor productivity growth rate

UNDERSTANDING BUSINESS CYCLES
Cross-Reference to CFA Institute Assigned Reading #17

Overview of Business Cycles

- Business cycles usually occur in economies that mainly rely on business enterprises (as opposed to agricultural or centrally planned economies).
- There is a sequence of distinct phases that comprise a business cycle. *(See table.)*
- Almost all sectors of the economy undergo the phases of the business cycle at about the same time. Phases of the business cycle are not restricted to certain sectors.
- Business cycles are recurrent (they occur again and again), but they are not periodic (they do not always have the same intensity and/or duration).
- Business cycles typically last between 1 and 12 years.

Phases of the Business Cycle

- The trough is the lowest point of a business cycle as the economy comes out of a recession towards an expansion.
- An expansion occurs after the trough and before the peak. It is a period during which aggregate economic activity is increasing.
- The peak is the highest point of a business cycle as the expansion slows down and the economy moves towards a recession.
- A contraction (or recession) occurs after the peak. It is a period during which aggregate economic activity is declining. A particularly severe recession is known as a depression.

Describing Phases of the Business Cycle

	Early Expansion (Recovery)	Late Expansion	Peak	Contraction (Recession)
Economic Activity	Gross domestic (GDP), industrial production, and other measures of economic activity stabilize and then begin to increase.	Activity measures show an accelerating rate of growth.	Activity measures show decelerating rate of growth.	Activity measures show outright declines.
Employment	Layoffs slow but new hiring does not yet occur and the unemployment rate remains high. Business turns to overtime and temporary employees to meet rising product demands.	Business begins full time rehiring as overtime hours rise. The unemployment rate falls.	Business slows its rate of hiring. The unemployment rate continues to fall but at a decreasing rate.	Business first cuts hours and freezes hiring, followed by outright layoffs. The unemployment rate rises.
Consumer and Business Spending	Upturn in spending is often most pronounced in housing, durable consumer items, and orders for light producer equipment.	Upturn becomes more broad-based. Business begins to order heavy equipment and engage in construction.	Capital spending expands rapidly, but the growth rate of spending starts to slow down.	Decreased spending is most evident in industrial production, housing, consumer durable items, and orders for new business equipment.
Inflation	Inflation remains moderate and may continue to fall.	Inflation picks up modestly.	Inflation further accelerates.	Inflation decelerates but with a lag.

Fluctuations in Capital Spending over the Business Cycle

Changes in capital spending affect business cycles in three stages or phases:

Stage 1: Spending on equipment falls off abruptly at the onset of an economic slowdown.

Stage 2: In the initial stages of an economic recovery, orders begin to pick up (despite low capacity utilization levels).

Stage 3: Eventually, after an extended expansion, businesses are unable to meet consumer demand with existing capacity and therefore, look to expand.

Fluctuations in Inventory Levels over the Business Cycle

Stage 1: Typically, businesses are slow to cut back on production when the economy starts to slow down. This results in an involuntary build-up of inventories, and combined with a drop in sales, results in a sharp increase in the inventory-sales ratio.

Stage 2: As businesses continue to cut back on production (to get rid of excess inventories), the inventory-sales ratio approaches normal levels. However, businesses soon start to raise production (even though there is no apparent growth in sales) just to arrest the decline in inventory levels.

Stage 3: During the upturn, as sales rise, businesses struggle to keep production on pace with sales growth, which leads to declining inventory levels. The rapidly-falling inventory-sales ratio stimulates businesses to increase production.

Consumer Behavior and the Business Cycle

Spending on Durable Goods

- A decrease in spending on durable goods relative to non-durable goods and services is an early indication of economic weakness.
- An increase in spending on durable goods (to catch up for the delay in spending on them) relative to non-durables and services suggests that a recovery may be on the way.

Permanent Income

Permanent income adjusts for temporary unsustainable sources of income and estimates the income that households can rely on. Spending on durables tends to fluctuate with changes in temporary or unsustainable sources of income, which are excluded from the calculation of permanent income. Basic consumption expenditure is related to permanent income.

The Savings Rate

- Fluctuations in the savings rate capture changes in consumers' willingness to reduce spending out of current income.
- The savings rate is also a good indicator of consumers' expectations regarding future income. A rise in the savings rate may indicate that consumers are uncertain about future income, suggesting that the economy is weakening. Note that a very high savings rate contributes to future spending and therefore, can help revive the economy even before incomes start to rise.

Housing Sector Behavior and the Business Cycle

Although the housing sector forms a relatively small part of the economy, fluctuations in the sector occur so rapidly that it makes a significant contribution to overall economic movements.

- Since most home sales are usually financed by mortgage loans, housing sector activity is particularly sensitive to the level of interest rates. A rise (fall) in interest rates leads to a decline (an increase) in home purchasing and construction.
- Home sales are also affected by income levels relative to housing prices. Low housing prices relative to income, coupled with low costs of supporting an average house (when mortgage rates are low), increase demand for housing units.

External Trade Sector Behavior and the Business Cycle

- An increase in domestic GDP leads to an increase in demand for imports. Domestic exports usually tend to rise with an increase in GDP of major trading partners even if the domestic economy is weak. Therefore, patterns of external trade balances are not directly linked to domestic economic cycles.
- An appreciation of the domestic currency makes imports cheaper and, at the same time, makes domestic goods more expensive for trading partners, reducing net exports.
- GDP growth differentials have a more immediate and straightforward impact on the external trade balance.
- Currency movements have a more complex and gradual impact on the trade balance.

THEORIES OF THE BUSINESS CYCLE

Neoclassical School of Thought

- The "invisible hand" will lead the market towards general equilibrium. Fluctuations in aggregate economic activity are short-lived as the economy will quickly readjust (e.g., via lower interest rates and lower wages if aggregate demand falls).
- Resources are allocated efficiently when MC equals MR, and there is no voluntary unemployment of labor and capital.
- All that is produced will be sold as supply creates its own demand (Say's Law). When something is produced, factors of production are compensated for their services. This creates purchasing power and stimulates demand.

Austrian School of Thought

- Shares some views with the neoclassical school, but focuses more on money and government.
- Money was not important in the neoclassical school (as barter could be used to achieve equilibrium), while the role of the government was limited to upholding the law and securing borders.
- The Austrian school argues that when governments try to increase employment and GDP through expansionary monetary policies, interest rates fall below their

natural rate, which leads to overinvestment (an inflationary gap). Once companies realize that they have gone overboard, they cut back spending drastically, which reduces aggregate demand and causes a recession. The government only causes a "boom-and-bust" cycle. To restore equilibrium, the economy must be left alone and all prices (including wages) must decrease.

- The theory explicitly identifies "misguided government intervention" as the cause of business cycles.

Keynesian School of Thought

- The general price and wage reduction (required under the Austrian and neoclassical schools to bring the economy out of a recession) are hard to attain.
- Even if nominal wages were reduced, lower salary expectations would only result in a further decline in aggregate demand and actually exacerbate a recession (the domino effect).
- Lower interest rates will not necessarily reignite growth due to weak business confidence.
- The economy's self-correcting mechanism may work in the long run, but definitely should not be relied upon in the short run. It is the short run that really matters.
- The government should step in during a recession and stimulate aggregate demand (via larger fiscal deficits) to keep labor and capital employed.
- Note that Keynes did not encourage the government to be ever-present in fine-tuning the economy.

Monetarist School of Thought

- Money supply is supremely important. The government should maintain a steady growth rate of money supply.
- If money supply grows too fast, there will be an unsustainable boom and inflation. If it grows too slow, there will be a recession.
- The government's expansionary fiscal actions may take effect once the recession is over and actually do more harm than good.
- The government should play a very limited role in the economy. Fiscal and monetary policy should be clear and consistent over time.
- Business cycles can be caused by exogenous shocks or government actions. During a recession it would be better to let the economy restore equilibrium on its own than to risk worsening the situation.

The New Classical School (RBC Theory)

- Business cycles have real causes (e.g., changes in technology). Monetary variables (such as inflation) are assumed to have no impact on GDP and unemployment.
- The government should not intervene in the economy (through fiscal or monetary policy).
- Unemployment (apart from frictional unemployment) is only short term. A person would only be unemployed if she is asking for wages that are too high.
- Aggregate supply plays a more prominent role (than in other theories) in bringing about business cycles.

Neo-Keynesian or New Keynesian Theory

- Like the New Classical School, this theory seeks to draw macroeconomic conclusions based on microeconomic (utility-maximizing) reasoning.
- Markets do not self-adjust seamlessly if they find themselves in disequilibrium. This is because:
  - Prices and wages are "downward sticky" (in contrast to the new classical view).
  - It is costly for companies to constantly update prices to clear markets (menu costs).
  - Companies need time to reorganize production in response to economic shocks.
- Therefore, government intervention is useful in eliminating unemployment and restoring macroeconomic equilibrium.

Measuring Unemployment

- Employed: Number of people with a job. This excludes those working in the informal sector (e.g., unlicensed cab drivers, illegal workers, etc.).
- Labor force: Number of people who either have a job, or are actively looking for one. This excludes people who are not employed and are not actively seeking employment (e.g., retirees, children, stay-at-home parents, fulltime students, etc.).
- Unemployed: People who are currently without a job, but are actively looking for one.
  - Long-term unemployed: People who have been out of work for a long time (more than 3-4 months) and are still looking for a job.
  - Frictionally unemployed: People who have just left a job and are about to start another one i.e., they already have a job waiting for them, which they have not started yet.
- Activity (or participation) ratio: Ratio of the labor force to total working age population (usually those between 16 and 64 years of age).
- Underemployed: People who currently have jobs, but have the qualifications to do significantly higher-paying jobs. They are not considered unemployed.
- Discouraged worker: A person who has stopped looking for a job. These people are excluded from the labor force and therefore, not accounted for in the official unemployment rate.
- Voluntarily unemployed: These are people who choose to remain outside the labor force (e.g., workers who retire early, or those who are unwilling to take up a vacancy because the wage offered is lower than their threshold).

The Unemployment Rate

The unemployment rate equals the ratio of the number of people who are unemployed to the total labor force. Although unemployment measures provide useful insights into the current state of an economy, they are not very useful in predicting an economy's cyclical direction as they are lagging economic indicators. This is because:

- The size of the labor force responds to changes in economic conditions.
- Businesses are reluctant to lay off workers at the first sign of economic weakness and are slow to rehire previously laid-off workers in the early stages of a recovery.

Overall Payroll Employment and Productivity Indicators

- **Size of payrolls:** This measure is not biased by the number of discouraged workers. Generally speaking, payrolls tend to shrink when the economy slides into a recession, and rise when a recovery is underway.
- The number of hours worked (especially overtime), and the use of temporary workers, tend to increase at the first signs of a recovery, and decrease at the first signs of economic weakness.
- An economy's productivity is measured by dividing total output by the number of hours worked. It measures the intensity of workflow of existing employees. Productivity measures (if available promptly) can identify an economy's cyclical direction even before a change in the number of hours worked is noticed. Productivity increases during an expansion (as output rises) and decreases during a recession (as output falls).

Inflation, Disinflation, and Deflation

Inflation: Generally speaking, inflation is procyclical (i.e., it goes up and down with the business cycle), but with a lag of around one year. Inflation is defined as a persistent increase in the overall level of prices (aggregate price level) in an economy over a period of time. The **inflation rate** measures the speed of overall price movements by calculating the rate of change in a price index. Both investors and policy-makers watch the inflation rate very closely.

Deflation: Deflation is defined as a persistent decrease in the aggregate level of prices in an economy over a period of time. The value of money actually rises in a deflationary environment. Since most debt contracts are written in fixed monetary amounts, the liability (in real terms) of the borrower rises during deflation.

Hyperinflation: Hyperinflation refers to a situation when the inflation rate is extremely high. It typically occurs when, instead of being backed by real tax revenue, large-scale government spending is supported by an increase in money supply.

Disinflation: Disinflation is defined as a fall in the inflation rate (e.g., from 15% to 5%). Disinflation is very different from deflation in the sense that deflation refers to a situation when the inflation rate is negative (aggregate price level is decreasing), while disinflation refers to a situation when the inflation rate falls, but remains positive (the aggregate price level continues to increase, but at a slower rate).

Price Indices

A price index that holds quantities of goods in the consumption basket constant is called a Laspeyres index. Most price indices around the world are Laspeyres indices, and consumption baskets are only updated after a certain number of years (typically 5). Using a fixed basket of goods and services to measure the cost of living gives rise to three biases:

- **Substitution bias:** Changes in the relative prices of goods motivate consumers to replace expensive goods with cheaper substitutes. Use of a fixed basket results in an upward bias in the computed inflation rate. Use of chained price index formulas (e.g., the Fisher index) can mitigate this bias.

- Quality bias: Improvements in product quality sometimes come at the cost of higher prices. If price indices are not adjusted for quality improvements, there will be an upward bias in the measured inflation rate. Prices can be adjusted for quality improvements through a practice known as hedonic pricing.
- New product bias: Recently introduced products are not included in the price index if the consumption basket is fixed. This usually creates an upward bias in the measured inflation rate. In order to mitigate this bias, new products can be introduced into the basket more regularly.

A Paasche Index is based on the current composition of the basket.

A Fisher Index is calculated as the geometric mean of the Laspeyres index and the Paasche index.

Cost-Push Inflation

Cost-push inflation occurs when rising costs compel businesses to raise prices. Costs of production may rise because of an increase in money wage rates, or an increase in the price of raw materials.

The effect of labor market constraints on wage rates is usually observed relative to the natural rate of unemployment (NARU). It is at the natural rate of unemployment (not at 0% unemployment) that the economy begins to experience bottlenecks in the labor market and feel wage-push inflationary pressures. It is preferred to combine trends in labor costs with productivity measures to evaluate the state of the labor market.

Labor productivity (output per hour) is important because it determines the number of units across which businesses can spread their labor costs. Unit labor cost (ULC) is calculated as:

$$ULC = W / O$$

- If wage rates grow at a faster rate than labor productivity, business's costs per unit of output (ULC) increase. Businesses then look to increase output prices to protect profit margins so the end result is cost-push inflation.
- If wage rates increase at a slower rate than labor productivity, ULC falls. This eases inflationary pressures.

Demand-Pull Inflation

Demand-pull inflation is caused by increasing demand, which causes higher prices and eventually results in higher wages to compensate for the rise in cost of living. Demand-pull inflation may be analysed based on the economy's capacity utilization levels:

- As the economy's actual GDP approaches its potential GDP (capacity utilization increases), there is an increase in the probability of shortages and bottlenecks occurring, so prices tend to rise.

- The further the economy operates below its potential output, the greater the probability of a slowdown in inflation (or even outright deflation).

Monetarists' Views on Inflation

Monetarists believe that inflation occurs when the growth rate of money supply in the economy outpaces growth in GDP. They explicitly place the blame for demand-pull inflation on excess money growth.

- If money growth exceeds nominal GDP growth, there is a possibility of inflation.
- If money growth is slower than nominal GDP growth, there could be disinflationary or deflationary pressures in the economy.

Inflation Expectations

Inflation expectations also play an important role in policy-making. Once economic agents start expecting prices to continue to rise going forward, they change their actions in line with those expectations. This can lead to higher inflation and cause it to persist in the economy even after its real underlying cause is no longer present.

Economic Indicators

An economic indicator is a variable that provides information on the state of the broader economy.

- Leading economic indicators have turning points that usually **precede** the turning points of the broader economy. Economists use them to predict the economy's **future state**.
- Coincident economic indicators have turning points that usually occur **close to** the turning points of the broader economy. Economists use them to identify the **current state** of the economy.
- Lagging economic indicators have turning points that usually occur after the turning points of the broader economy. Economists use them to identify the economy's **past condition**.

More About Economic Indicators

- Practitioners take an aggregate perspective when interpreting various economic indicators. Typically aggregate measures are combined into composites known to lead the cycle, coincide with the cycle or lag the cycle.
- Composites for different countries are usually composed of different indicators based on their own historical experiences.
- The timing record of various composite indices has varied considerably.
- The relationship between an indicator and the business cycle can be quite uncertain.
  - This is why analysts combine different indicators with common factors among them when constructing indicator indices, and why diffusion indices are used.

EC

U.S. Economic Indicators[1]

Indicator and Description

Leading	Reason
1. Average weekly hours, manufacturing	Because businesses will cut overtime before laying off workers in a downturn and increase it before rehiring in a cyclical upturn, these measures move up and down before the general economy.
2. Average weekly initial claims for unemployment insurance	This measure offers a very sensitive test of initial layoffs and rehiring.
3. Manufacturers' new orders for consumer goods and materials	Because businesses cannot wait too long to meet demands for consumer goods or materials without ordering, these gauges tend to lead at upturns and downturns. Indirectly, they capture changes in business sentiment as well, which also often leads the cycle.
4. ISM new order index[a]	This index is a diffusion index that refects the month-to-month change in new orders for final sales. The weakening of demand, which can lead to a recession, is usually first refected in the decline of new orders.
5. Manufacturers' new orders for non-defense capital goods excluding aircraft	In addition to offering a first signal of movement, up or down, in an important economic sector, movement in this area also indirectly captures business expectations.
6. Building permits for new private housing units	Because most localities require permits before new building can begin, this gauge foretells new construction activity.
7. S&P 500 Index	Because stock prices anticipate economic turning points, both up and down, their movements offer a useful early signal on economic cycles.
8. Leading Credit Index	This index aggregates the information from six leading fnancial indicators, which refect the strength of the fnancial system to endure stress. A vulnerable fnancial system can amplify and propagate the effects of negative shocks, resulting in a widespread recession for the whole economy.
9. Interest-rate spread between 10-year Treasury yields and overnight borrowing rates (federal funds rate)	Because long-term yields express market expectations about the direction of short-term interest rates, and rates ultimately follow the economic cycle up and down, a wider spread, by anticipating short rate increases, also anticipates an economic upswing. Conversely, a narrower spread, by anticipating short rate decreases, also anticipates an economic downturn.
10. Average consumer expectations for business and economic conditions	If consumers are optimistic about future business and economic conditions, they tend to increase spending. Because consumption is economic conditions about two-thirds of the U.S. economy, its future movements offer early insight into the direction ahead for the whole economy.

[1] Exhibit 5, Volume 2, CFA Program Curriculum 2018

Coincident	Reason
1. Employees on non-agricultural payrolls	Once recession or recovery is clear, businesses adjust their full-time payrolls.
2. Aggregate real personal income (less transfer payments)	By measuring the income fow from non-corporate profts and wages, this measure captures the current state of the economy.
3. Industrial Production Index	Measures industrial output, thus capturing the behavior of the most volatile part of the economy. The service sector tends to be more stable.
4. Manufacturing and trade sales	In the same way as aggregate personal income and the industrial production index, this aggregate offers a measure of the current state of business activity.

Lagging	Reason
1. Average duration of unemployment	Because businesses wait until downturns look genuine to lay off, and wait until recoveries look secure to rehire, this measure is important because it lags the cycle on both the way down and the way up.
2. Inventory-to-sales ratio	Because inventories accumulate as sales initially decline and then, once a business adjusts its ordering, become depleted as sales pick up, this ratio tends to lag the cycle.
3. Change in unit labor costs	Because businesses are slow to fire workers, these costs tend to rise into the early stages of recession as the existing labor force is used less intensely. Late in the recovery when the labor market gets tight, upward pressure on wages can also raise such costs. In both cases, there is a clear lag at cyclical turns.
4. Average bank prime lending rate	Because this is a bank-administered rate, it tends to lag other rates that move either before cyclical turns or with them.
5. Commercial and industrial loans outstanding	Because these loans frequently support inventory building, they lag the cycle for much the same reason that the inventory-sales ratio does.
6. Ratio of consumer installment debt to income	Because consumers only borrow heavily when confident, this measure lags the cyclical upturn, but debt also overstays cyclical downturns because households have trouble adjusting to income losses, causing it to lag in the downturn.
7. Change in consumer price index for services	Inflation generally adjusts to the cycle late, especially in the more stable services area.

[a] A diffusion index usually measures the percentage of components in a series that are rising in the same period. It indicates how widespread a particular movement in the trend is among the individual components.

EC

STUDY SESSION 5:
ECONOMICS (2)

MONETARY AND FISCAL POLICY
Cross-Reference to CFA Institute Assigned Reading #18

Monetary Policy

- Monetary policy refers to the government's or central bank's manipulation of money supply to influence the quantity of money and credit in the economy.

The Functions of Money

- Medium of exchange
- Store of value
- Unit of account

Paper Money and the Money Creation Process

Required reserve ratio = Required reserves / Total deposits

Money multiplier = 1/ (Reserve requirement) = 1/(0.2) = 5

The banking system as a whole that goes through the following cycle and increases the quantity of money:

1. Banks have excess reserves.
2. They lend the excess reserves.
3. Bank deposits increase.
4. Quantity of money increases.
5. Deposits in the banking system increase.
6. These deposits in turn create excess reserves which are loaned out.

Definitions of Money

- Narrow money refers to notes and coins in circulation plus other highly liquid deposits.
- Broad money includes narrow money plus the entire range of liquid assets that can be used to make purchases.

Checking account balances are included in measures of money. Checks make this transfer possible but this does not make the check itself money. Credit cards are not money either.

The Quantity Theory of Money

The quantity theory of money expresses the relationship between money and the price level. The quantity equation of exchange states that:

$$M \times V = P \times Y$$

Money neutrality says that an increase in money supply will not result in an increase in real output (Y). Therefore, an increase in money supply will cause the aggregate price level (P) to rise. The assertions of the quantity theory of money are in line with the consequences of money neutrality (as velocity is assumed constant).

Monetarists use the quantity theory of money to support their belief that inflation can be controlled by manipulating the money supply growth rate.

The Demand for Money

Transactions-related demand for money arises from the need to use money to finance transactions. Generally speaking, transactions-related demand for money is positively related to average transaction size and overall GDP.

Precautionary money balances are held for use in unforeseen circumstances. Precautionary balances are positively related to average transactions size, total volume of transactions, and therefore to overall GDP as well.

Speculative or portfolio demand for money is related to perceived opportunities and risks of holding other financial instruments (such as bonds). Speculative demand for money is inversely related to the returns available on other financial assets. At the same time, it is positively related to the perceived risk in these financial assets.

Supply and Demand for Money

Money supply is assumed fixed so it is represented by a vertical line. Money demand is inversely related to interest rates (speculative money demand increases as interest rates fall). Therefore, money demand is represented by a downward-sloping line. The point of intersection between the money demand and supply curves determines short run equilibrium nominal interest rates.

The Fisher Effect

The Fisher effect is directly related to the concept of money neutrality. It states that the nominal interest rate (R_N) reflects the real interest rate (R_R) and the expected rate of inflation (Π^e).

$$R_N = R_R + \Pi^e$$

The Fisher effect does not consider uncertainty. The greater the uncertainty, the higher the required risk premium.

The Roles of the Central Bank

- Monopoly supplier of currency.
- Banker to the government (and to other banks) and lender of last resort.
- Supervise the banking system.
- Oversee, regulate, and set the standards for a country's payments system.

- Manage the country's foreign currency and gold reserves.
- Conducting monetary policy.

Objectives of Monetary Policy

- Maximum employment.
- Stable prices (this is the overarching objective of most central banks).
- Moderate long-term interest rates.

Costs of Inflation

Expected inflation is the inflation rate that economic agents expect to see in the economy in the future. Expected inflation gives rise to menu costs and shoe leather costs. Expected or anticipated inflation is reflected in all long-term contracts. People accept this level of inflation, and budget for it.

Unexpected inflation is the level of inflation that comes as a surprise to economic agents. It is arguably more costly than expected inflation. In addition to the costs of expected inflation, unexpected inflation also leads to:

- Inequitable transfers of wealth between borrowers and lenders.
  - If actual inflation is less than expected inflation (which is built into nominal interest rates) lenders benefit and borrowers lose out as the real value of payments on debts rises.
  - If actual inflation is greater than expected inflation, borrowers benefit and lenders lose out as the real value of payments on debts falls.
- Higher risk premia in borrowing rates: Higher uncertainty associated with future inflation leads to lenders demanding a higher risk premium, which inflates the nominal interest rate and hurts economic activity.
- A reduction in the information content of market prices: Businesses may attribute an increase in prices of their products to an increase in demand (or decrease in supply) when in fact, the price increase may be in line with the overall level of inflation in the economy. Businesses would increase production only to find that they are struggling to sell their output, and involuntarily build up inventories. As a result, they would cut back production drastically, which would hurt the economy.

Monetary Policy Tools

Required reserve ratio: An increase in the required reserve ratio results in a decrease in money supply.

The central bank's policy rate: Generally speaking, the higher the policy rate, the higher the penalty that banks will have to pay the central bank if they run short of liquidity. This would make them more conservative in lending, reducing broad money supply.

Open market operations: An open-market sale (purchase) directly reduces (increases) banks' reserves.

The Transmission Mechanism

If the central bank increases its official policy rate:

- Banks respond to the increase in the official interest rate by increasing their base rates (the reference rates on which they base lending rates to customers). As a result, individuals and businesses borrow less.
- Asset prices and values of capital projects tend to fall as present values of expected future cash flows decline.
- Economic agents' expectations regarding the economy are dampened as they associate higher interest rates with slower future economic growth and reduced profits.
- The domestic currency appreciates in value (as hot money flows in). This makes domestic goods and services more pricey (less competitive) in the international market, leading to a decline in exports.
- If the increase in interest rates is widely expected to be followed by further rate hikes, economic agents will change their behavior to reflect these revised expectations.
- Overall, the decline in consumption, borrowing, and asset prices will reduce aggregate demand.
- Weaker demand will reduce domestic prices. This, along with lower import prices, (due to appreciation of the domestic currency) will put a downward pressure on actual inflation.

Monetary Policy Strategies

Inflation targeting: Under this strategy, the central bank makes a public commitment to achieving an explicit inflation target, and to explaining how its actions will achieve that target. The argument here is that inflationary expectations must be managed, and, when everyone is aware (and believes) that the central bank will move to contain inflation within an acceptable range, spending and investing decisions will be made wisely.

Exchange rate targeting: The central bank supports a target exchange rate by buying and selling the domestic currency in the foreign exchange market. Basically, the aim here is to "import" the inflation experience of an economy with a good track record on inflation, by tying the domestic currency to the currency of that economy.

Qualities of Effective Central Banks

The central bank should be independent and not come under political pressures when formulating policy. There are two aspects of central bank independence:

- Operational independence is when the central bank decides the level of interest rates.
- Target independence is when the central bank determines the inflation rate that is targeted and the horizon over which this target is to be achieved.

The public should have confidence in the central bank i.e., it must have credibility. If economic agents believe that the central bank will hit its inflation target, the belief itself could become self-fulfilling.

There should be transparency in the central bank's decision-making. Transparency comes from the central bank clearly explaining its views on the economy and communicating its views on various economic indicators to economic agents on a regular basis.

Finally (if the central bank follows an inflation targeting strategy), the central bank must have a realistic, forward-looking inflation target.

Contractionary and Expansionary Monetary Policies

- When the central bank believes that the current growth rate of economic activity will lead to inflation, it will look to reduce money supply and increase interest rates. Such actions are known as contractionary measures as they are meant to rein in an overheating economy.
- When the central bank believes that the current level of economic growth is too slow and inflation is weakening, it will look to increase money supply and reduce interest rates. Such actions are known as expansionary measures as they are meant to stimulate a receding economy.

The Neutral Rate of Interest

The neutral rate is the rate of interest that neither slows down, nor spurs growth in the underlying economy. When the policy rate is below (above) the neutral rate, monetary policy is expansionary (contractionary). However, economists' estimates of the neutral rate for a given economy typically vary. What they do agree on, is that the neutral rate has two components:

1. Real trend of growth in the underlying economy: This corresponds to the rate of economic growth that gives rise to stable inflation in the long run.
2. Long run expected inflation.

Limitations of Monetary Policy

- Central banks cannot control the amount of money that households and businesses choose to save.
- While central banks can influence the ability of banks to extend loans and create credit, they cannot easily control the willingness of banks to do so.
- If the central bank lacks credibility, there is a lower chance of its "policy message" being successfully transmitted through the economy.

FISCAL POLICY

Roles and Objectives of Fiscal Policy

The main aim of fiscal policy is to regulate the economy's real GDP by influencing aggregate demand.

Fiscal policy is an important tool for economic stabilization through its impact on output.

- In a recession, governments can increase spending and/or reduce taxes (expansionary fiscal policy) to try to raise employment and output.
- In an expansion, governments can reduce spending and/or increase taxes (contractionary fiscal policy) to try to control inflation.

The budget surplus/deficit equals the difference between the government's revenue and expenditure over a period of time. Analysts look at the change in the budgetary position to determine whether fiscal policy is getting tighter or looser:

- An increase (decrease) in a budget surplus is contractionary (expansionary).
- An increase (decrease) in a budget deficit is expansionary (contractionary).

Automatic stabilizers work in the absence of explicit action by the government to bring the economy towards full employment. There are two automatic stabilizers embedded in fiscal policy.

- Induced taxes
- Needs-tested spending

Discretionary fiscal actions are enacted by the government, and involve changing tax rates or the level of government spending. Basically, these actions are up to the government's discretion as opposed to automatic stabilizers, which act on their own to bring the economy towards full employment.

Deficits and National Debt

Reasons to be concerned about national debt relative to GDP:

- High debt levels may lead to high tax rates (to service the debt) going forward. Higher expected future tax rates may serve as a disincentive for labor and entrepreneurial activity.
- If markets lose confidence in the government, the central bank may have to print money to finance the deficit. This would lead to high inflation (e.g., Zimbabwe in 2008–2009).
- Government spending may crowd out private investment. Higher demand for borrowing (to finance the deficit) by the government would raise interest rates, reducing private sector investment.

Reasons not to be concerned about national debt relative to GDP:

- The problem is not really a major issue if debt is owed to the country's own citizens. In this case the government can just print money to retire the debt. However, note that this strategy comes with the risk of high inflation.
- Some of the borrowed funds may have been used for capital investment projects, which would raise the economy's productive capacity (and tax revenues) going forward.
- The private sector may adjust to offset fiscal deficits by increasing savings in anticipation of future tax increases (to finance the deficit). This is known as Ricardian equivalence: The increase in government spending (or reduction in taxes) meant to stimulate aggregate demand will have no impact on economic activity as economic agents will save more because they expect the government to finance the deficit by increasing taxes in the future.
- If there is widespread unemployment in the economy, fiscal deficits will not be diverting any resources away from productive uses so total output will increase.
- Large fiscal deficits require tax changes, which may correct the distortions created by the current tax structure.

Fiscal Policy Tools and the Macroeconomy

Government spending takes the following forms:

- Transfer payments
- Current government spending
- Capital expenditure

Justifications for Government Spending

- The government provides services such as defense that benefit all citizens equally.
- Infrastructure spending helps the country's economic growth.
- Helps redistribute wealth in society.
- Can be used as a tool to control inflation unemployment, and growth.
- Can be used to subsidize the development of innovative and high-risk new products (e.g., alternative energy).

Types of Taxes

- Direct taxes
- Indirect taxes

Taxes can be justified in terms of raising revenue to finance government expenditure and in terms of income and wealth redistribution.

Desirable Properties of Tax Policy

- Simplicity
- Efficiency

- Fairness
- Revenue sufficiency

Advantages and Disadvantages of Different Fiscal Policy Tools

Advantages:

- Indirect taxes can be adjusted very quickly. They are very effective in influencing spending behavior and in generating revenue at little cost to the government.
- Social objectives (e.g., reducing alcohol or cigarette consumption) can easily be met by raising indirect taxes.

Disadvantages:

- Direct taxes, and welfare and other social transfers are difficult to change without significant notice. However, they begin to have an impact on behavior soon after their announcement.
- Capital spending decisions are slow to plan, implement and execute.

In addition to their direct effects on the economy, the above-mentioned fiscal policy tools also have strong expectational effects on the economy.

- Direct government spending has a much bigger impact on aggregate spending and output than income tax cuts or transfer increases.
- However, if transfer increases target the poorest in society (whose marginal propensity to consume is highest), they can have a relatively strong impact on spending.

The Fiscal Multiplier

$$\frac{1}{[1 - MPC(l - t)]}$$

The Balanced Budget Multiplier

The balanced budget multiplier is positive. An increase in government spending combined with an equivalent dollar increase in taxes leads to a higher real GDP.

Issues in Fiscal Policy Implementation

Deficits and the Fiscal Stance

The size of a fiscal deficit cannot be used to determine whether fiscal policy is expansionary or contractionary.

- Automatic stabilizers for example lead to changes in the budgetary status that are unrelated to fiscal policy changes. Therefore, economists look at the structural or cyclically adjusted budget deficit as an indicator of the government's fiscal stance.

The structural deficit is the deficit that would exist were the economy working at full-employment.

- Government expenditure includes the cash amount of payments on debt, which inflates the actual deficit. This is because the real value of outstanding debt falls with inflation.

Difficulties in Executing Fiscal Policy

Recognition lag: This refers to the time that it takes the government to figure out that the economy is not functioning at its potential output.

Action lag: The government might have recognized the need for action, but its implementation may be delayed in obtaining the necessary approvals.

Impact lag: This refers to the time it takes for a fiscal stimulus to flow through the economy and generate the changes in spending patterns that are desired.

The Relationships between Monetary and Fiscal Policy

Easy fiscal policy/tight monetary policy: Results in higher output, higher interest rates and government expenditure would form a larger component of national income.

Tight fiscal policy/easy monetary policy: The private sector's share of overall GDP would rise (as a result of low interest rates), while the public sector's share would fall.

Easy fiscal policy/easy monetary policy: This would lead to a sharp increase in aggregate demand, lowering interest rates and growing private and public sectors.

Tight fiscal policy/tight monetary policy: This would lead to a sharp decrease in aggregate demand, higher interest rates and a decrease in demand from both private and public sectors.

Factors Influencing the Mix of Fiscal and Monetary Policy

- If the government is primarily concerned with growing the economy's potential output, it should aim to keep interest rates low and keep fiscal policy relatively tight to ensure that free resources are available in the growing economy.
- If the government's main concern is to build infrastructure and develop high quality human capital, it should focus on spending in those areas. If monetary policy is kept loose during this time, inflation may result.

INTERNATIONAL TRADE AND CAPITAL FLOWS
Cross-Reference to CFA Institute Assigned Reading #19

Gross Domestic Product (GDP) measures the market value of all **final** goods and services produced by factors of production (e.g., labor, capital, etc.) located **within** a country/economy during a period of time.

- GDP *includes* goods and services produced by foreigners within the country.
- GDP *excludes* goods and services produced by citizens outside the country.

Gross National Product (GNP) measures the market value of all final goods and services produced by factors of production (e.g., labor, capital, etc.) supplied by the citizens of the country, regardless of whether production takes place within or outside of the country.

- GNP *includes* goods and services produced by citizens outside the country.
- GNP *excludes* goods and services produced by foreigners within the country.

Terms of trade refer to the ratio of the price of exports to the price of imports.

FDI versus FPI

When a firm in the source country makes an investment in the productive assets of the host country, it is referred to as Foreign Direct Investment (FDI).

Foreign Portfolio Investment (FPI) refers to shorter-term investments in foreign financial instruments (e.g., foreign stocks, foreign government bonds, etc.).

Benefits of International Trade

- Countries gain from exchange and specialization.
- Efficient resource allocation.
- Domestic companies gain access to global markets and customers, which leads to increased exchange of ideas and greater awareness of changing consumer tastes and preferences.
- Capital intensive industries gain access to much larger markets, enabling them to reap the benefits of economies of scale.
- Domestic households are able to choose from a wider variety of goods and services.
- Increased foreign competition reduces monopoly power of domestic firms and forces them to continuously strive to become more efficient.
- Trade liberalization can lead to higher inflation-adjusted GDP as a result of a more efficient allocation of resources, learning by doing, knowledge spillovers and improved productivity.

Costs of International Trade

- Companies that are less efficient than international firms may go out of business if foreign firms are allowed to enter the market. This will lead to higher (structural) unemployment.

- The counter argument is that despite the short and medium term costs and unemployment, these resources will eventually be reemployed in more efficient industries.

Comparative versus Absolute Advantage

Absolute advantage refers to a country's ability to produce a good at a **lower cost** or using fewer resources than its trading partners.

Comparative advantage refers to a country's ability to produce a particular good at a **lower opportunity cost** than its trading partners.

Even if a country does not have an absolute advantage in the production of a good or service, it (and its trading partners) can still gain from trade if it produces and exports goods in which it has a comparative advantage.

Trade Models and Sources of Comparative Advantage

Ricardian Model

- Assumes that labor is the only variable factor of production.
- A country gains a comparative advantage in the production of a good based on differences in labor productivity, which reflect underlying differences in technology.
- Differences in technology are the key source of comparative advantage.
- Even if the country is very small compared to the size of its trading partner, it will continue to produce the good that it holds a comparative advantage in, and trade some of it to obtain other goods.
- Technological gaps between countries can decrease over time, leading to shifts in comparative advantage.

Heckscher-Ohlin Model (also referred to as the factor-proportions theory)

- Assumes that both capital and labor are variable factors of production, so a good can be produced with varying combinations of the two.
- Technology is the same in each industry across countries, but it varies across different industries.
- Differences in factor endowments are the primary source of comparative advantage.
- A country has a comparative advantage in a good whose production requires intensive use of a factor with which it is relatively abundantly endowed.
- Allows for redistribution of income through trade as it assumes that more than one factor of production is variable.
- Theoretically, free trade should eventually result in equal prices of goods and services and equal prices of factors of production across countries.
  - However, in the real world trade only results in a tendency for factor prices to converge in the long run.

Arguments for Trade Restrictions

- Protection of established domestic industries from foreign competition.
- Protection of new (infant) industries from foreign competition until they mature.
- Protection of employment in the country.
- Generation of revenue from tariffs.
- Retaliation against trade restrictions imposed by trading partners.

Tariffs

When the government imposes a tariff on imports, the price effectively rises, domestic demand falls, domestic supply rises and the volume of imports falls.

- The government manages to lower the trade deficit (by decreasing imports) and also manages to earn some revenue for itself (Region C).
- There is an increase in producer surplus (Region A).
- Consumer surplus falls (Regions B, C, and D).
- The overall effect is a net decrease in welfare (Regions B and D).

Quotas

Quotas are restrictions on the quantity of a good that can be imported into a country for a specified period. When a quota is in place, each importing firm receives an import license, which specifies the quantity that it can import.

The main difference between tariffs and quotas is that the government earns direct revenue through tariffs, but this is not the case with quotas. With a quota, foreign producers may raise their prices to earn higher profits than they would in the absence of the quota. These profits are known as quota rents.

- Region C (previously government revenue from the tariff) is now more likely to be captured by foreign producers (quota rents), increasing the welfare loss for the importing country to Regions B+C+D (relative to just Regions B+D under a tariff).
- If the importing country can generate an amount equal to Area C by auctioning import licenses for a fee, then its welfare loss can be limited to just Regions B+D (as is the case with tariffs).
- Quota rents arising from a quota can be captured by the exporting country or the importing country.

Voluntary Export Restraints

Voluntary Export Restraints (VERs) are restrictions on the quantity of a good that can be exported. While quotas are imposed by the importing country, VERs are imposed by the exporting country. Under VERs, the exporting country captures the quota rent (Region C) but the welfare loss to the importing country equals Regions B, C and D.

Export Subsidies

Export subsidies refer to payments made by the government to domestic exporters of certain goods. While they aim to stimulate exports, export subsidies interfere with the free market mechanism and may result in trade patterns that diverge from those dictated by comparative advantage. Further, domestic producers would be more inclined to export their output rather than selling it in the domestic market.

Effects of Alternative Trade Policies

Panel A: Effects of Alternative Trade Policies

	Tariff	Import Quota	Export Subsidy	VER
Impact on	Importing country	Importing country	Exporting country	Importing country
Producer surplus	Increases	Increases	Increases	Increases
Consumer surplus	Decreases	Decreases	Decreases	Decreases
Government revenue	Increases	Mixed (depends on whether the quota rents are captured by the importing country through sale of licenses or by the exporters)	Falls (government spending rises)	No change (rent to foreigners)
National welfare	Decreases in small country Could increase in large country	Decreases in small country Could increase in large country	Decreases	Decreases

Panel B: Effects of Alternative Trade Policies on Price, Production, Consumption, and Trade

	Tariff	Import Quota	Export Subsidy	VER
Impact on	Importing country	Importing country	Exporting country	Importing country
Price	Increases	Increases	Increases	Increases
Domestic consumption	Decreases	Decreases	Decreases	Decreases
Domestic production	Increases	Increases	Increases	Increases
Trade	Imports decrease	Imports decrease	Exports increase	Imports decrease

CAPITAL RESTRICTIONS

Capital restrictions are defined as controls placed on foreigners' ability to own domestic assets and/or domestic citizens' ability to own foreign assets.

Common Objectives

- The government may place restrictions on inward investment by foreigners relating to how much can be invested, and in which industries.
  - The government may impose ownership restrictions on strategic industries such as defense and telecommunications.
  - The government may forbid foreign investment into certain industries to protect domestic companies from foreign competition, and to protect jobs.
- The government may place restrictions on outflow of capital from repatriation of capital, interest, profits, royalty payments, and license fees, and on foreign investments by its citizens in order to conserve scarce foreign exchange reserves.
- Capital restrictions are often used in conjunction with other policy instruments, such as fixed exchange rate targets to achieve policy objectives in times of macroeconomic crises.
  - Capital controls are used to control the economy's external balance, while other, more traditional policy tools are used to pursue other objectives.

Forms of Capital Controls

- Taxes
- Price controls
- Quantity controls
- Outright prohibitions on international trade in assets

Benefits of Free Movement of Financial Capital

- Allows capital to be invested wherever it will earn the highest return.
- The economy's productive capacity can grow at a higher rate than possible based on domestic savings alone.
- Foreign firms may enter domestic industries, bringing competition to local firms, which may:
  - Encourage local firms to improve the quality of their goods and services.
  - Lead to better prices.
  - Bring new technologies into the country.

Effectiveness of Capital Controls

An IMF study found that:

- Effective controls on capital inflows entail significant administrative costs.
- Imposition of controls on capital outflows during times of financial crisis have produced mixed results:
  - They have only provided temporary relief to some countries, but offered others (e.g., Malaysia in 1997) enough time to restructure their economies.

○ If the government is wary of capital leaving the country, capital controls (when combined with fixed exchange rates) afford the central bank a degree of monetary policy independence that would not be possible without capital controls.

Costs of Capital Controls

- Administrative costs.
- Controls may give rise to negative market perceptions and make it more costly for the country to raise foreign funds.
- Protection of domestic financial markets may delay necessary policy adjustments or impede private-sector adaptation to changing international circumstances.

Trade Blocs

Members of a regional trading agreement (RTA) agree to eliminate barriers to trade and movement of factors of production among the members of the bloc.

Members of a free trade area (FTA), for example NAFTA, eliminate almost all barriers to free trade with each other. However, each member still maintains its own policies regarding trade with non-member countries.

A customs union (e.g., Benelux) is very similar to an FTA, but all member countries have similar policies regarding trade with non-member countries.

A common market (e.g., MERCOSUR) incorporates all the provisions of a customs union, and also allows free movement of factors of production among the member countries.

An economic union (e.g., EU) incorporates all the aspects of a common market and also requires common economic institutions and coordination of economic policies among member countries. If the members of the economic union decide to adopt a common currency, it is also referred to as a monetary union.

Trade Creation versus Trade Diversion

Only if trade creation is larger than trade diversion, is there a positive net effect on welfare from forming the trade bloc.

- Trade creation occurs when higher-cost domestic production is replaced with lower-cost imports from fellow members of a trade bloc.
- Trade diversion occurs when lower-cost imports from non-member countries are replaced with higher-cost imports from member countries (because tariffs are imposed on imports from non-member countries but not on imports from member countries).

Advantages of Trade Blocs

All the benefits of free trade (greater specialization, reduction in monopoly power due to competition, economies of scale, learning by doing, knowledge spillovers, technology transfers, better quality intermediate inputs, etc.) apply to trade blocs as well. Further, trade blocs:

- Reduce the potential for conflict among members.
- Give members greater bargaining power in the global economy as they form a united front.
- Offer new opportunities for trade and investment.
- Typically, growth in a member country tends to spill over into other members as well.

Challenges in the Formation of an RTA

- Cultural differences and historical conflicts may complicate the process of integration.
- Free trade and mobility of labor limit the extent to which member countries can pursue independent economic and social policies.

The Balance of Payments

The **balance of payments (BOP)** is a double entry bookkeeping system that summarizes a country's economic transactions with the rest of the world over a period of time.

Balance of Payment Components

The current account can be decomposed into the following sub-accounts:

- Merchandise trade consists of all commodities and manufactured goods bought, sold or given away.
- Services include tourism, transportation, engineering and business services.
- Income receipts include income from ownership of foreign assets (e.g., interest and dividends).
- Unilateral transfers represent one-way transfers of assets (e.g., worker remittances, foreign aid and gifts).

The capital account can be decomposed into the following sub-accounts:

- Capital transfers include debt forgiveness and migrants' transfers. They also include:
  - Transfer of ownership of fixed assets
  - Transfer of funds received for the sale or acquisition of fixed assets
  - Gift and inheritance taxes
  - Death duties
  - Uninsured damage to fixed assets
- Sales and purchases of non-produced, non-financial assets such as rights to natural resources, intangible assets (e.g., patents, copyrights, etc.)

The financial account can be decomposed into the following sub-accounts:

- Financial assets abroad are composed of:
  - Official reserve assets
  - Government assets
  - Private assets
- Foreign owned financial assets in the reporting country are composed of:
  - Official assets
  - Other foreign assets

National Economic Accounts and the Balance of Payments

$$Y = C + I + G + X - M$$

- A current account deficit must be financed by foreign direct investment, loans by foreign banks, or the sale of domestic debt and equity securities to foreign investors.
- A current account surplus is used to finance the current account deficit of trading partners (through loans and investments in real and financial assets).

$$CA = X - M = Y - (C + I + G)$$

- A country can have a current account deficit and consume more than it produces (C + I + G greater than Y) if it borrows the shortfall from foreigners.
- A country can have a current account surplus and consume less than it produces (C + I + G less than Y) if it lends the shortfall to foreigners.

$$S_P + S_G = I + CA$$

- In a closed economy, savings can only be used for domestic investment.
- In an open economy, savings can be used for domestic and foreign investment.

$$S_P = I + CA - S_G$$

This equation clearly shows that an economy's private savings can be used for:

- Domestic investment.
- Foreign investment (purchasing assets from foreigners).
- Purchasing government debt.

$$CA = S_P + S_G - I$$

A current account deficit results from:

- Low private savings
- A government deficit
- High private investment

If a country running a trade deficit mainly borrows to finance consumption, then eventually it must reduce consumption to repay its debts. If the borrowings are mainly used to finance investment, then future economic growth is likely to provide the means to repay its liabilities.

World Bank Group

The World Bank's main objective is to fight poverty and enhance environmentally sound economic growth. The World Bank and its affiliated entities:

- Provide cheap loans and grants to countries that have limited or no access to international financial markets.
- Provide analysis, advice and information to countries to encourage social and economic development.
- Share knowledge and promote dialogue to increase the capabilities of their partners and members.
- Help members create the basic economic infrastructure that is essential for the development of domestic financial markets.

World Trade Organization (WTO)

The WTO's primary objective is to enhance and liberalize international trade.

- The WTO's important functions include the implementation, administration, and operation of individual agreements, providing a platform for negotiations and settling trade disputes.
- It also provides technical cooperation and training to developing, under developed and poor countries to bring them in compliance with WTO rules.
- It reviews members' trade policies on a regular basis and ensures coherence and transparency of trade policies through surveillance.
- It is a major source of economic research and analysis.
- Its framework of global trade rules provides a major institutional and regulatory base, without which large multinationals would not be able to operate on such a large scale.

International Monetary Fund

The main objective of the IMF is to ensure the stability of the international monetary system, the system of exchange rates and international payments that enables countries to participate in international trade. More specifically, the IMF:

- Provides a forum for cooperation on international monetary problems.
- Facilitates the growth of international trade, thereby promoting job creation, economic growth, and poverty reduction.
- Promotes exchange rate stability and an open system of international payments.
- Lends foreign exchange to member countries when needed, on a temporary basis and under adequate safeguards, to help them address balance of payments problems.

In the aftermath of the global financial crisis of 2007–2009, the IMF has redefined its operations by:

- Enhancing its lending facilities.
- Strengthening the monitoring of global, regional, and country economies.
- Helping resolve global economic imbalances.
- Analysing capital market developments.
- Assessing financial sector vulnerabilities.
- Working to cut poverty.

From an investment perspective the IMF helps to keep country-specific market risk and global systematic risk under control.

CURRENCY EXCHANGE RATES
Cross-Reference to CFA Institute Assigned Reading #20

An exchange rate represents the price of one currency in terms of another currency. It is stated in terms of the number of units of a particular currency (price currency) required to purchase a unit of another currency (base currency). Stated differently, it is the cost of one unit of the base currency in terms of the price currency.

In this reading, we will refer to exchange rates using the convention "A/B," i.e. the number of units of Currency A (price currency) required to purchase one unit of Currency B (base currency). For example, suppose that the USD/GBP exchange rate is currently 1.5125. From this exchange rate quote we can infer that:

- The GBP is the base currency and USD is the price currency.
- It will take 1.5125 USD to purchase 1 GBP.
- 1 GBP will buy 1.5125 USD or 1 GBP costs 1.5125 USD.
- A decrease in this exchange rate (e.g., to 1.5120) means that 1 GBP will be able to purchase fewer USD.
- Alternatively, less USD will now be required to purchase 1 GBP (the cost of a GBP has fallen).
- This decrease in the exchange rate means that the GBP has depreciated (lost value) against the USD, or equivalently, the USD has appreciated (gained value) against the GBP.
- It would help you to think of exchange rates in the following manner: An increase in the quoted exchange rate (price/base) means an increase (appreciation) in the value of the currency in the denominator (base currency) and a decrease (depreciation) in the value of the currency in the numerator (price currency).
- The numerical value of the exchange rate and the value of the base currency are positively related.
- The numerical value of the exchange rate and the value of the price currency are negatively related.

Nominal versus Real Exchange Rates

- When the value of a currency is stated in terms of units of another currency (as in the example above), it is referred to as a nominal exchange rate.
- On the other hand, real exchange rates measure changes in the relative purchasing power of one currency compared with another.

Purchasing power parity (PPP) asserts that nominal exchange rates adjust to ensure that identical goods (or baskets of goods) have the same price in different countries.

- The nominal exchange rate and relative purchasing power are **inversely** related.
- The price level in the foreign country (or foreign inflation) and relative purchasing power are **inversely** related.

Just like the price of any product, an exchange rate reflects the price of the currency in the denominator. For example, a price of $5/bag of chips reflects the price of a bag of chips (base or denominator) in terms of the price currency (USD). Similarly, a price (exchange rate) of $2/GBP is the price of GBP (base currency) in terms of USD (price currency). An increase in the price of chips (e.g., to $6/bag) means that the value of a bag of chips (the item in the denominator) in terms of USD has risen. Similarly, an increase in the exchange rate to $3/GBP implies an increase in the value of GBP (currency in the denominator).

- The price level in the home country (or domestic inflation) and relative purchasing power are **positively** related.

Determining the Real Exchange Rate

An increase in purchasing power implies a decrease in the real exchange rate (in terms of DC/FC), i.e. purchasing power and the real exchange rate are **inversely** related. Therefore, we can say that the real exchange rate is:

- An increasing function of the nominal exchange rate (in terms of DC/FC).
- An increasing function of the foreign price level.
- A decreasing function of the domestic price level.

The real exchange rate may be calculated as:

$$\text{Real exchange rate}_{DC/FC} = S_{DC/FC} \times (P_{FC} / P_{DC})$$

Spot versus Forward Exchange Rates

Spot exchange rates (S) are quotes for transactions that call for immediate delivery. For most currencies, immediate delivery means "T + 2" delivery i.e., the transaction is actually settled 2 days after the trade is agreed upon by the parties.

Forward exchange rates (F) are quotes for transactions that are contracted (agreed upon) today, but settled at a pre-specified date in the future (settlement occurs after a longer period than the two days for spot transactions).

Types of Contracts Used for Trading Currencies

- Futures contracts
- FX swaps
- FX options

Functions of the Foreign Exchange Market

- Facilitate international trade
- Allow investors to convert between currencies in order to move funds into (or out of) foreign assets.
- Enable market participants who face exchange rate risk to hedge their risks.
- Allow investors to speculate on currency values.

EC

Market Participants

Sell Side

- The very largest dealing banks
- All other regional and local banks

Buy Side

- Corporate accounts
- Real money accounts
- Leveraged accounts
- Retail accounts
- Governments
- Central banks
- Sovereign wealth funds (SWFs)

Market Size and Composition

- Investment pools and professional traders account for a large (and growing) proportion of FX market volumes. Portfolio flows and speculative activities dominate FX market volumes.
- High frequency algorithmic traders are accounting for a growing proportion of FX market volumes.
- Purchases and sales of foreign goods and services by individuals and corporations form a relatively small proportion of FX market volumes.
- London, New York, and Tokyo account for the highest FX market volumes.
- The majority of FX market transactions occur in the FX swap market.

Direct versus Indirect Quotes

- In a **direct currency quote (DC/FC)**, the *domestic* currency is stated as the *price* currency and *foreign* currency is stated as the *base* currency.
- In an **indirect currency quote (FC/DC)**, the *foreign* currency is stated as the *price* currency and *domestic* currency is stated as the *base* currency.

Direct and indirect quotes are just the inverse (reciprocal) of each other.

Exchange Rate Quote Conventions

FX Rate Quote Convention	Name Convention	Actual Ratio (Price currency/Base currency)
EUR	Euro	USD/EUR
JPY	Dollar–yen	JPY/USD
GBP	Sterling	USD/GBP
CAD	Dollar–Canada	CAD/USD
AUD	Aussie	USD/AUD
NZD	Kiwi	USD/NZD
CHF	Swiss franc	CHF/USD
EURJPY	Euro–yen	JPY/EUR
EURGBP	Euro–sterling	GBP/EUR
EURCHF	Euro–Swiss	CHF/EUR
GBPJPY	Sterling–yen	JPY/GBP
EURCAD	Euro–Canada	CAD/EUR
CADJPY	Canada–yen	JPY/CAD

EC

Understanding Exchange Rate Quotes

When both currencies are mentioned in the code or the name convention, the first currency is the base currency and the second currency is the price currency. For example, dollar-yen refers to the exchange rate of JPY/USD i.e., USD is the base currency and JPY is the price currency. Note that dollar-yen (quote: JPY) may also be written as USDJPY, USD:JPY or USD-JPY. They all mean the same thing i.e., JPY/USD.

In professional FX markets, an exchange rate is usually quoted as a two-sided price. Dealers usually quote a bid-price (the price at which they are willing to buy), and an ask-price or offer price (the price at which they are willing to sell). Bid-ask prices are always quoted in terms of buying and selling the *base* currency. For example, a EUR:USD (or USD/EUR) quote of 1.3802–1.3806 means that the dealer is willing to buy EUR for 1.3802 USD and is willing to sell EUR for 1.3806 USD. From the client's perspective, she will receive 1.3802 USD for selling 1 EUR, but will have to pay 1.3806 USD to purchase 1 EUR.

Suppose that the JPY/USD exchange rate increases from 77.58 to 78.45. An increase in the JPY/USD exchange rate means that USD has now become more costly in terms of JPY (it now takes more units of JPY to purchase 1 unit of USD). Stated differently, USD has appreciated against JPY, and JPY has depreciated against USD. The unannualized percentage increase in the value of the USD against JPY can be calculated as:

$$(78.45 / 77.58) - 1 = 1.12\%$$

The percentage increase in the value of the USD against JPY does not equal the percentage decrease in the value of JPY against USD. In order to determine the percentage decrease in the value of JPY against USD, we must make JPY the *base* currency in the exchange rates that we use in the calculation.

Cross Rates

A cross rate is an exchange rate between two currencies that is derived from each currency's relationship with a third currency. For example, using the EUR (which represents USD/EUR) and JPY (which represents JPY/USD) exchange rates, we can calculate the cross rate between the euro and the yen (EURJPY or JPY/EUR) as follows:

$$\frac{JPY}{EUR} = \frac{\cancel{USD}}{EUR} \times \frac{JPY}{\cancel{USD}}$$

The given exchange rates should be multiplied such that the third currency (common currency) disappears (or mathematically cancels out as it forms the numerator of one quote and the denominator of the other).

In order to cancel out the third currency, you might sometimes need to invert one of the exchange rate quotes. For example, consider the EUR (which represents USD/EUR) and GBP (which represents USD/GBP) exchange rates. A trader who wants to calculate the cross rate between the Euro and the British pound cannot do so by simply multiplying these two exchange rates in their presented forms (because the USD will not cancel out). One of the exchange rates must be inverted. The Euro-sterling exchange rate (which represents GBP/EUR) can be calculated as:

$$\frac{GBP}{EUR} = \frac{USD}{EUR} \times \left(\frac{USD}{GBP}\right)^{-1} = \frac{USD}{EUR} \times \frac{GBP}{USD}$$

Forward Rate Quotes

In professional FX markets, forward exchange rates are quoted in terms of points (pips), which simply represent the difference between the forward rate and the spot rate. Note that these points (pips) are scaled so that they can be related to the last digit in the spot quote (usually the fourth decimal place).

- If the forward rate is higher than the spot rate, the points are positive and the base currency is said to be trading at a forward premium because it is expected to appreciate in the future. At the same time, the price currency would be trading at a forward discount, which means it is expected to depreciate.
- If the forward rate is lower than the spot rate, the points are negative and the base currency is trading at a forward discount as it is expected to depreciate. At the same time, the price currency would be trading at a forward premium and is expected to appreciate.

For example, assume that a trader is quoted a spot CAD/USD exchange rate of 1.0155 and a one-year forward CAD/USD exchange rate of 1.0183. The forward rate is higher than the spot rate which means that the USD (base currency) is trading at a forward premium and is expected to appreciate. The one-year forward points will be quoted as 28, calculated as follows:

$$\text{Forward points} : (1.0183 - 1.0155) \times 10,000 = 28 \text{ points}$$

Dealers typically quote forward rates in terms of the number of forward points. Forward point quotes may be converted into forward rates by dividing the number of points by 10,000 and adding the result to the spot rate quote (assuming that the quote has 4 decimal places). Continuing with our CAD/USD example, the one-year forward rate may be computed based on forward points as:

$$1.0155 + (28 / 10,000) = 1.0155 + 0.0028 = 1.0183$$

Sometimes forward rates or points may be quoted as a percentage of the spot rate rather than in terms of an absolute number of points. Continuing with our CAD/USD example, the one year forward rate for the USD can be quoted as:

$$[(1.0155 + 0.0028) / 1.0155] - 1 = (1.0183 / 1.0155) - 1 = 0.2757\%$$

The base currency (USD) is said to be trading at a forward premium of 0.2757%.

When the forward premium is presented in terms of a percentage, the forward rate may be calculated by multiplying the spot rate by one plus (minus) the percentage premium (discount). Continuing with the CAD/USD example, the forward premium of 0.2757% can be used to calculate the forward rate as:

$$1.0155 \times (1 + 0.002757) = 1.0183$$

If the number of points were −28 (if the base currency were trading at a forward discount), the forward rate would be expressed in terms of a percentage as:

$$[(1.0155 - 0.0028) / 1.0155] - 1 = -0.2757\%$$

In this case, the forward exchange rate would be calculated as:

$$1.0155 \times (1 - 0.002757) = 1.0127; \text{ or}$$
$$1.0155 - 0.0028 = 1.0127$$

Forward Rates, Spot Rates and Interest Rates

Forward exchange rates are calculated in a manner that ensures that traders are not able to earn arbitrage profits. This means that a trader with a specific amount of domestic currency should be able to earn the exact same amount from both the following investment options:

- **Option 1:** She invests the funds at the domestic risk-free rate (r_{DC}) for a particular period of time.
- **Option 2:** She converts the funds into a foreign currency (at the current spot rate, $S_{FC/DC}$), invests them at the foreign risk-free rate (r_{FC}) for the same period of time (as in Option 1), and then converts them back to the domestic currency at the forward exchange rate ($F_{DC/FC}$) which she locks in today.

Both these investment options are risk-free because they require the money to be invested at risk-free interest rates. Further, the exchange rate risk in the second option is eliminated (hedged) by locking in the forward rate at the time of investment. Since these two investments have identical risk characteristics, it follows that they must have the same return (to preclude arbitrage profits), leading to the following equality:

The CFA Program curriculum presents this equation in the following form:

$$(1+i_d) = S_{f/d}(1+i_f)\frac{1}{F_{f/d}}$$

We believe that our approach is easier and more intuitive. Both the formulas will of course give you the same answer.

$$(1+r_{DC}) = S_{FC/DC}\ (1+r_{FC})\ F_{DC/FC}$$

The above equality can be used to derive the formula for the forward rate:

$$F_{DC/FC} = \frac{1}{S_{FC/DC}} \times \frac{(1+r_{DC})}{(1+r_{FC})} \text{ or } F_{DC/FC} = S_{DC/FC} \times \frac{(1+r_{DC})}{(1+r_{FC})}$$

This version of the formula is perhaps easiest to remember because it contains the DC term in numerator for all three components: $F_{DC/FC}$, $S_{DC/FC}$ and $(1 + r_{DC})$

Forward rates are sometimes interpreted as expected future spot rates.

$$F_t = S_{t+1}$$

$$\frac{(S_{t+1})}{S} - 1 = \Delta\%S(DC/FC)_{t+1} = \frac{(r_{DC} - r_{FC})}{(1+r_{FC})}$$

Under this interpretation, the expected percentage change in the spot rate is proportional to the interest rate differential ($r_{DC} - r_{FC}$). However, such an interpretation should be used cautiously. Forward rates are unbiased predictors of future spot rates, but this does not make them accurate predictors of future spot rates:

- The direction of the predicted change in spot rates is counterintuitive.
- Historical data show that forward rates are poor predictors of future spot rates. Aside from interest rate differentials, exchange rates are influenced by several other factors.

Important Takeaways

- Given the same interest rate differential, the longer the term to maturity, the higher the absolute number of forward points.
  - However, note that the number of forward points is not exactly proportional to the horizon of the forward contract.
- Given the same term to maturity, the higher the interest rate differential, the higher the absolute number of forward points.
  - The number of forward points is exactly proportional to the interest rate differential.

Exchange Rate Regimes

Desirable Properties

- The exchange rate between any two currencies should be credibly fixed.
- All currencies should be fully convertible to ensure unrestricted flow of capital.
- Each country should be able to undertake fully independent monetary policy.

Generally speaking, the more freely the currency is allowed to float and the more tightly convertibility is controlled, the greater the effectiveness of monetary policy.

Types of Exchange Rate Regimes

Arrangements with No Separate Legal Tender

- Dollarization: A country uses the currency of another nation (usually the U.S. dollar) as its medium of exchange and unit of account.
- Monetary union: Member countries share the same legal tender (e.g., the European Economic and Monetary Union (EMU) whose members use the Euro as their currency).

Currency Board System

- The central bank holds foreign currency reserves to cover, at the fixed parity, the entire monetary base of a country (e.g., Hong Kong).
- Expansion and contraction of the monetary base are directly linked to trade and capital flows.
- The exchange rate is essentially fixed, but it is allowed to fluctuate within a narrow band.
- The central bank cannot act as the lender of last resort, but can provide short term liquidity.
- The monetary authority can earn a profit by paying little or no interest on its liabilities (the monetary base), and earning a market rate on its assets (foreign currency reserves). This profit is referred to as seigniorage. Under dollarization, seigniorage goes to the country whose currency is used.

EC

Fixed Parity

- The exchange rate is either pegged to a single currency or to a basket of currencies of major trading partners. The monetary authority stands ready to buy or sell foreign currency reserves to maintain the exchange rate within a narrow band.
- Although monetary independence is limited, the central bank can act as a lender of last resort.
- The success of this system depends on both the country's willingness as well as its ability to maintain the fixed exchange rate.

Target Zone

- Similar to a fixed-rate system.
- The only difference is that the monetary authority aims to maintain the exchange rate within a slightly broader range.
    - This gives the central bank greater ability to conduct discretionary policy.

Active and Passive Crawling Pegs

- Under a passive crawling peg system, the exchange rate is adjusted frequently in line with the rate of inflation.
- Under an active crawling peg system, the exchange rate is pre-announced for the coming weeks and changes are made in small steps.

Fixed Parity with Crawling Bands

- The country initially fixes its exchange rate to a foreign currency, but gradually moves towards a more flexible system by pre-announcing the widening of bands around the central parity. This allows the country greater flexibility in determining its monetary policy.

Managed Float

- The country does not explicitly state its exchange rate target, but intervenes in the FX markets to meet its policy objectives (regarding balance of trade, price stability or unemployment).
- Such intervention (also called dirty floating) typically also causes the country's trading partners to retaliate in a similar fashion and leads to instability in FX markets as a whole.

Independently Floating Rates

- The central bank rarely intervenes in the determination of its exchange rate, which is left to be determined by market supply and demand factors.
- Enables the central bank to engage in independent monetary policy aimed at achieving price stability and full employment.
- Also allows it to act as a lender of last resort to troubled institutions.

Relating the Trade Balance to Savings

$$(X - M) = (S - I) + (T - G)$$

Trade surplus = Government saving + Private saving – Investment

- A trade surplus means that the economy as whole (government saving and private saving combined) saves enough to fund its investment needs. The excess saving is used to accumulate financial claims against the rest of the world.
- A trade deficit means that the country must borrow from the rest of the word to meet its investment needs.

Exchange Rates and the Trade Balance

The Elasticities Approach

A devaluation or depreciation of the domestic currency makes domestic goods relatively cheaper for foreigners (reduces the price of domestic goods). At the same time it implies an appreciation of foreign currencies, which makes foreign goods relatively more expensive for domestic citizens (increases the price of foreign goods).

The ideal combination for a country that wants to reduce its trade deficit and expects its currency to depreciate is that its imports and exports both be relatively elastic. This is the basic idea behind the Marshall-Lerner condition. Demand for imports and exports must be sufficiently price sensitive such that increasing the price of imports increases the difference between export revenue and import expenditures.

Marshall-Lerner condition: $\omega_X \varepsilon_X + \omega_M (\varepsilon_M - 1) > 0$

Where:
ω_X = Share of exports in total trade
ω_M = Share of imports in total trade
ε_X = Price elasticity of demand for exports
ε_M = Price elasticity of demand for imports

If this condition is satisfied, devaluation/depreciation in the domestic currency will lead the trade balance towards a surplus.

Note that the elasticity of demand for imports becomes more important (and export elasticity less important) as the trade deficit gets larger.

Generally speaking, exchange rates will be more effective in adjusting trade imbalances if the countries' imports and exports are composed of items that have relatively elastic demand.

Finally, note that the impact of exchange rates on the trade balance may not always be immediate due to the fact that there is a time lag between the initial depreciation and the eventual impact on quantities of imports and exports. The increase in import prices will lead to an increase in total expenditure on imports over the short run (leading to a deepening of the deficit). However, as the currency stabilizes at the new (lower) levels, economic agents adapt and eventually the trade balance improves (towards a surplus). Overall, the trade deficits makes a "*J*-like" formation.

The Absorption Approach

Devaluation of the exchange rate can direct the trade balance towards a surplus if it increases:

- National income relative to expenditure; or equivalently
- National saving relative to investment in physical capital

If an economy is operating below full employment, then, by diverting demand towards domestically produced goods, devaluation can increase income/output.

If the economy is operating at full employment, output/income cannot be increased further. As a result, expenditure must decline for there to be an improvement in the trade balance.

STUDY SESSION 6:
FINANCIAL REPORTING AND ANALYSIS (1)

FRA

FINANCIAL STATEMENT ANALYSIS: AN INTRODUCTION
Cross-Reference to CFA Institute Assigned Reading #21

The **role of financial statement reporting** is to provide information about a company's financial performance, financial position and changes in financial position.

The **role of financial statement analysis** is to assess a company's past performance and evaluate its future prospects using financial reports along with other relevant company information.

- *Liquidity* refers to a company's ability to meet its short term obligations.
- *Solvency* refers to a company's ability to meet its long term obligations.

Footnotes contain important details about accounting methods, estimates and assumptions that have been used by the company in preparing its financial statements. For example, information about the choice of revenue recognition method and assumptions made to calculate depreciation expense are found in the footnotes. The availability of such information allows comparisons between companies that prepare their financial statements in accordance with different accounting standards (IFRS versus U.S. GAAP).

The management discussion and analysis section (required under **U.S. GAAP**) highlights important trends and events that affect a company's liquidity, capital resources and operations. Management also discusses prospects for the upcoming year with respect to inflation, future goals, material events and uncertainties. The section must also discuss critical accounting policies that require management to make subjective judgments and have a material impact on the financial statements. Although it contains important information, analysts should bear in mind that the MD&A section is not audited.

IFRS provides a framework that offers guidance rather than requirements in a standard. According to the framework, "decision-useful" management commentary includes:

- The nature of the business
- Management objectives and strategies
- The company's significant resources, risks and relationships
- Results of operations
- Critical performance measures

Auditor's Reports

Under International Standards for Auditing, objectives of an auditor are:

1. To obtain reasonable assurance about whether the financial statements as a whole are free from material misstatement, whether due to fraud or error, thereby enabling the auditor to express an opinion on whether the financial statements are prepared, in all material respects, in accordance with an applicable financial reporting framework; and
2. To report on the financial statements, and communicate as required by the ISAs, in accordance with the auditor's findings.

Types of Audit Opinions

- An unqualified opinion states that the financial statements have been fairly presented in accordance with applicable accounting standards.
- A qualified opinion states that the financial statements have been prepared fairly, but do contain exception(s) to the accounting standards. The audit report provides further details and explanations relating to the exception(s).
- An adverse opinion states that the financial statements have not been presented fairly, and significantly deviate from acceptable accounting standards.
- A disclaimer of opinion is issued when the auditor, for whatever reason, is not able to issue an opinion on the financial statements.

Other Sources of Company-Related Information

- **Interim reports** are prepared either semiannually or quarterly. They contain the four financial statements and footnotes but are *not audited*.
- **Proxy statements** are distributed to shareholders to decide on matters that require a shareholder vote. They provide information about management and director compensation, company stock performance and potential conflicts of interest between management, the board of directors and shareholders.
- **Press releases**, in addition to company websites and conference calls, provide current information about companies.
- **External sources** provide information about the economy, the industry that the company operates in, and the company's competitors. Examples of external sources include trade journals and government agencies.

Steps in the Financial Statement Analysis Framework

- Define the context and purpose of analysis.
- Collect data.
- Process data.
- Analyze/interpret the processed data.
- Develop and communicate conclusions.
- Follow up.

FRA

FINANCIAL REPORTING STANDARDS
Cross-Reference to CFA Institute Assigned Reading #22

Financial statements are not designed only to facilitate asset valuation; they provide information to a host of users (e.g., creditors, employees and customers). At the same time, they do provide important inputs for the asset valuation process. For analysts, it is extremely important to understand how, and when judgments and subjective estimates affect the financial statements. Such an understanding is important to evaluate the wisdom of business decisions, and to make comparisons between companies.

Standard-Setting Bodies versus Regulatory Bodies

- Standard-setting bodies, such as the International Accounting Standards Board (IASB) and U.S. Financial Accounting Standards Board (FASB), are private sector organizations, of accountants and auditors, who develop financial reporting rules, regulations and accounting standards.
- Regulatory authorities like the Securities and Exchange Commission (SEC) in the United States, and FSA in the United Kingdom, have legal authority to enforce financial reporting requirements, and can overrule private-sector standard-setting bodies.

Standard-Setting Bodies

The IASB is the independent standard-setting body of the IFRS Foundation, which is an independent, not-for-profit private sector organization.

The FASB standards are contained in the FASB Accounting Standard Codification™ (Codification). The Codification is the source of all authoritative U.S. generally accepted accounting principles (U.S. GAAP) for non-governmental entities.

Desirable Attributes of an Accounting Standards Board

- The responsibilities of all parties involved in the standard-setting process should be clearly defined.
- All parties involved in the standard-setting process should observe high professional and ethical standards, including standards of confidentiality.
- The organization should have adequate authority, resources, and competencies.
- There should be clear and consistent processes to guide the organization and formation of standards.
- There should be a well-articulated framework with a clearly stated objective to guide the board.
- The board should seek and consider input from all stakeholders. However, it should operate independently and make decisions that are in line with the stated objective of the framework.
- The board should not succumb to pressure from external forces.
- Final decisions should be in public interest, and should lead to a set of high-quality standards that will be recognized and adopted by regulatory authorities.

FRA

Regulatory Authorities

Regulatory authorities are governmental entities that have the legal authority to enforce the financial reporting requirements set forth by the standard-setting bodies, and to exert control over entities that participate in capital markets within their jurisdiction.

IOSCO (International Organization of Securities Commission) is not a regulatory authority, but its members regulate a large portion of the world's financial capital markets.

Any company issuing securities in the U.S., or otherwise involved in U.S. capital markets is subject to the rules of the **Securities and Exchange Commission (SEC)**. The SEC requires companies to submit numerous forms periodically. These filings, which are available on the SEC website (www.sec.gov), are a key source of information for analysis of listed firms.

Convergence of Global Financial Reporting Standards

The move toward developing one set of universally accepted financial reporting standards is impeded by two factors:

- Standard-setting bodies and regulators have different opinions regarding appropriate accounting treatments due to differences in institutional, regulatory, business and cultural environments.
- Powerful lobbyists and business groups, whose reported financial performance would be affected adversely by changes in reporting standards, exert pressure against the adoption of unfavorable standards.

Objective of Financial Statements

Under the Conceptual Framework, the objective of general purpose financial reporting is to provide financial information that is useful in making decisions about providing resources to the entity to existing and potential providers of resources (e.g., investors, lenders and creditors) to the entity.

Qualitative Characteristics

Fundamental qualitative characteristics that make financial information useful:

- Relevance
- Faithful representation

Faithful representation requires that the information presented is:

- Complete
- Neutral
- Free from error

Supplementary qualitative characteristics that increase the usefulness of relevant and faithfully represented financial information.

- Comparability
- Verifiability
- Timeliness
- Understandability

Constraints on Financial Statements

While it would be ideal for financial statements to exhibit all the desirable characteristics listed earlier, there are several constraints to achieving this goal:

- There may be a trade-off between certain desirable characteristics.
- There is a cost of providing useful financial information. The benefits from information should exceed the costs of providing it.
- Intangible aspects (e.g., company reputation, brand name, customer loyalty and corporate culture) cannot be quantified and reflected in financial statements.

Reporting Elements

The elements of financial statements that are related to the measurement of financial position are:

- Assets
- Liabilities
- Equity

Elements related to the measurement of financial performance are:

- Income
- Expenses

Underlying Assumptions in Financial Statements

- Accrual basis accounting requires that transactions should be recorded on the financial statements (other than on the cash flow statement) when they actually occur, irrespective of when the related exchange of cash occurs.
- Going concern refers to the assumption that the company will continue operating for the foreseeable future. If this is not the case, fair representation would require all assets to be written down to their liquidation values.

Recognition and Measurement of Financial Statement Elements

An element should be recognized on the financial statements if the future benefit from the item (flowing into or out of the firm) is probable, and if its value/cost can be estimated with reliability.

FRA

Measurement Bases

- Historical cost: For an asset historical cost refers to the amount that it was originally purchased for. For liabilities, it refers to the amount of proceeds that were received initially in exchange for the obligation.
- Amortised cost: Historical cost adjusted for amortisation, depreciation, or depletion and/or impairment.
- Current cost: For an asset, current cost refers to the amount that the asset can be purchased for today. For liabilities, it refers to the total undiscounted amount of cash that would be required to settle the obligation today.
- Realizable (settlement) value: In reference to assets, realizable value refers to the amount that the asset can be sold for in an ordinary disposal today. For liabilities, it refers to the undiscounted amount of cash expected to be paid to settle the liability in the normal course of business.
- Present value: For assets, present value refers to the discounted value of future net cash flows expected from the asset. For liabilities, it refers to the present discounted value of future net cash outflows that are expected to be required to settle the liability.
- Fair value: Fair value is defined in IFRS and U.S. GAAP as an exit price, the price that would be received to sell an asset, or paid to transfer a liability, in an orderly transaction between market participants at the measurement date. This may involve either market measures or present value measures, depending on the availability of information.

Required Financial Statements

- Statement of financial position (balance sheet).
- Statement of comprehensive income (in a single statement or in two separate statements i.e., the income statement + statement of comprehensive income).
- Statement of changes in equity.
- Statement of cash flows.
- Significant accounting policies and explanatory notes to facilitate the understanding of financial statements.
- In certain cases, a statement of financial position from earliest comparative period.

General Features of Financial Statements

- Fair presentation: This requires faithful representation of transactions, in compliance with the definitions and recognition criteria for reporting elements (assets, liabilities, equity, income and expenses) set out in the Conceptual Framework.
- Going concern: Financial statements should be prepared on a going concern basis unless management has plans to liquidate the company.
- Accrual basis: All financial statements, except the cash flow statement, should be prepared on an accrual basis.
- Materiality and aggregation: Financial statements should be free from omissions and misrepresentations that could influence decisions taken by users. Similar items should be grouped and presented as a material class. Dissimilar items, unless immaterial, should be presented separately.

- No offsetting: Assets and liabilities, and income and expenses should not be used to offset each other, unless a standard requires or allows it.
- Frequency of reporting: Financial statements must be prepared at least annually.
- Comparative information: Comparative amounts should be presented for prior periods unless a specific standard permits otherwise.
- Consistency: Items should be presented and classified in the same manner every period.

Structure and Content Requirements

- Classified statement of financial position: Current and noncurrent assets and current and noncurrent liabilities should be shown separately on the balance sheet.
- Minimum information on the face of financial statements: Certain items must be explicitly disclosed on the face of the financial statements.
- Minimum information in the notes (or on the face of financial statements): Disclosures relating to certain items must be in the notes to the financial statements (e.g., measurement bases used).
- Comparative information: Comparative amounts should be presented for prior periods unless a specific standard permits otherwise.

Comparison of Key Concepts of Financial Reporting Standards

- FASB, in addition to the financial performance elements recognized under the IASB Framework (revenues and expenses), also identifies gains, losses and comprehensive income.
- Reporting elements relating to financial position are defined differently. Under FASB, assets are the "future economic benefits" rather than "resources" from which future economic benefits are expected to flow under IASB.
- Under FASB, the word "probable" is not discussed in its revenue recognition criteria, while under IASB it is required that its is probable that a future economic benefit flow to/from the entity. FASB also has a separate recognition criterion of relevance.
- Regarding measurement of financial elements, both frameworks are broadly consistent. However, FASB does not allow upward revaluation of assets except for certain categories of financial instruments that must be reported at fair value.

Characteristics of an Effective Financial Reporting Framework

- Transparency: A transparent reporting framework should reflect the underlying economics of the business. Full disclosure and fair representation create transparency.
- Comprehensiveness: A comprehensive reporting framework is one that is based on universal principles that provide guidance for recording all kinds of financial transactions—those already in existence, and others that emerge with time.
- Consistency: Financial transactions of a similar nature should be measured and reported in a similar manner, irrespective of industry type, geography, and time period.

FRA

Barriers to Creating a Single Coherent Framework

- **Valuation:** When choosing a measurement base, it is important to remember the tradeoff between reliability and relevance. Historical cost is a more reliable measure of value but fair value is more relevant over time.
- **Standard-setting approach:** Reporting standards can be based on one of the following approaches:
  - ○ A principles-based approach provides a broad financial reporting framework with limited guidance on how to report specific transactions.
  - ○ A rules-based approach provides strict rules for classifying elements and transactions.
  - ○ An objectives-oriented approach is a combination of a principles-based and rules-based approach.

  IFRS has a principles-based approach. FASB has historically followed a rules-based approach, but recently explicitly stated that it is moving towards an objectives-oriented approach.
- **Measurement:** Reporting of financial statement elements can be based on the asset/liability approach (where the elements are properly valued at a point in time) or the revenue/expense approach (where changes in the elements are properly valued over a period of time).

Monitoring Developments in Financial Reporting Standards

It is important for analysts to keep track of developments in financial reporting standards and assess their implications for security analysis and valuation. Analysts must pay careful attention to:

- New products and transactions in capital markets.
- Actions of standard-setting bodies.
- Company disclosures including the footnotes and the MD&A section.

STUDY SESSION 7:
FINANCIAL REPORTING AND ANALYSIS (2)

UNDERSTANDING INCOME STATEMENTS
Cross-Reference to CFA Institute Assigned Reading #23

Under **IFRS**, the income statement may be presented as:

- A section of a single statement of comprehensive income; or
- A separate statement (showing all revenues and expenses) followed by a statement of comprehensive income that begins with net income.

Under **U.S. GAAP**, the income statement may be presented as:

- A section of a single statement of comprehensive income.
- A separate statement followed by a statement of comprehensive income that begins with net income.
- A separate statement with the components of other comprehensive income presented in the statement of changes in shareholders' equity.

Revenues versus Gains

Income includes revenues and gains. Revenues arise from ordinary, core business activities, whereas gains arise from non-core or peripheral activities. For example, for a software development company, the sale of software to customers will be classified as revenue, but profit on the sale of some old office furniture will be classified as a gain.

Income Statement Formats

A company may prepare its income statement using a single-step or multi-step format. When an income statement explicitly calculates gross profit, it uses a multi-step format.

For nonfinancial firms, operating profit refers to earnings *before* financing costs (interest expense) and income taxes. For financial firms, interest expense is usually considered an operating expense. Their operating profit is calculated *after* accounting for interest expense.

If a company has a subsidiary in which it enjoys majority ownership, the subsidiary's accounts are consolidated with its own. Consolidation requires the parent company to combine all the revenues and expenses of the subsidiary with its own and present the combined results on its income statement. If the subsidiary is not wholly-owned, minority interest is deducted from total income as it represents the proportionate share of the subsidiary's minority share holders in the subsidiary's net income.

The IASB framework defines income as "an increase in economic benefits during the accounting period in the form of inflows or enhancements of assets, or reduction in values of liabilities that result in increases in equity, other than those relating to contributions from equity participants."

FRA

Revenue Recognition

Up until January 1, 2018, under IFRS (IAS 18), revenue is recognized for a sale of goods when:

1. Significant risks and rewards of ownership are transferred to the buyer.
2. There is no managerial involvement or effective control over the goods sold.
3. Revenue can be measured reliably.
4. It is probable that the economic benefits from the transaction will flow to the entity.
5. Costs incurred, or to be incurred for the transaction can be measured reliably.

Under FASB, revenue is recognized on the income statement when it is "realized or realizable" and "earned."

The SEC provides specific guidelines under which these two conditions are met:

1. There is evidence of an arrangement between buyer and seller.
2. The product has been delivered, or the service has been rendered.
3. The price is determined, or determinable.
4. The seller is reasonably sure of collecting money.

Specific Revenue Recognition Applications

There are certain special circumstances in which revenue may be recognized *prior* to the sale of a good/service or even *after* the sale.

1. Long-term contracts

Long-term contracts are contracts that extend over more than one accounting period, such as construction projects. In long-term contracts, questions arise as to how revenues and expenses should be allocated to each accounting period. The treatment of these items depends on how reliably the outcome of the project can be measured.

> **FRA**
>
> Under U.S. GAAP, the completed contract method is also appropriate when the contract is not a long-term contract. Note however, that when a contract is started and completed in the same period, there is no difference between the percentage-of-completion and completed contract methods.

- If the outcome of the contract can be measured *reliably*, the percentage of completion revenue recognition method is used under both the original IFRS standards (IAS 18 and IAS 11) and U.S. GAAP. Under this method, revenues, costs and profits are allocated to each accounting period in proportion to the percentage of the contract completed during the given period.
- If the outcome *cannot be measured reliably*:
  - The completed-contract method is used under U.S. GAAP. Under this method, no revenues or costs are recognized on the income statement until the entire project is completed.
  - Under IFRS, revenue is recognized on the income statement to the extent of costs incurred during the period. No profits are recognized until completion of the project.

The percentage of completion method is a more aggressive (less conservative) approach to revenue recognition. It is also more subjective as it depends on management estimates and judgement relating to reliability of estimates.

The percentage of completion method matches revenues with costs over time and provides smoother, less volatile earnings. Remember that cash flows are exactly the same under both the methods.

Under IFRS and U.S. GAAP, if a loss is expected on the contract, it must be recognized immediately, regardless of the revenue recognition method used.

2. Installment Sales

An **installment sale** occurs when a firm finances a customer's purchase of its products. Customers make payments (installments) to the company over an extended period.

Under **IFRS**, installment sales are separated into selling price (discounted present value of installment payments) and an interest component. Revenue attributable to the sale price is recognized at the date of sale, while the interest component is recognized over time.

Under **U.S. GAAP**, a sale of real estate is reported at the time of sale using the normal revenue recognition conditions if the seller:

- Has completed the significant activities in the earnings process; and
- Is either assured of collecting the selling price, or able to estimate amounts that will not be collected.

When these two conditions are not fully met, some of the profit must be deferred and one of the following two methods may be used:

- The installment method is used when collectability of revenues cannot be reasonably estimated. Under this method, profits are recognized as cash is received. The percentage of profit recognized in each period equals the proportion of total cash received in the period.
- The cost-recovery method is used when collectability is highly uncertain. Under this method, profits are only recognized once total cash collections exceed total costs incurred.

3. Barter Transactions

In barter transactions, goods are exchanged between two parties and there is no exchange of cash. One form of barter transactions is a *round-trip* transaction, in which a good is sold by one party in exchange for the purchase of an identical good. The issue with these transactions is whether revenue should be recognized.

- Under IFRS, revenue from barter transactions can be reported on the income statement based on the fair value of revenues from similar *non-barter* transactions with *unrelated parties*.
- Under U.S. GAAP, revenue from barter transactions can be reported on the income statement at fair value only if the company has a history of making or receiving cash payments for such goods and services and hence, can use its historical experience to determine fair value. Otherwise, revenue should be reported at the carrying amount of the asset surrendered.

4. Gross versus Net Reporting

- Under gross revenue reporting, sales and cost of sales are reported separately.
- Under net reporting, only the difference between sales and costs of sales is reported on the income statement.

Under U.S. GAAP, only if the following conditions are met can the company recognize revenue based on gross reporting:

- The company is the primary obligor under the contract.
- The company bears inventory and credit risk.
- The company can choose its suppliers.
- The company has reasonable latitude to establish price.

Revenue Recognition Accounting Standards Issued in May 2014

In May 2014, IFRS and FASB issued a set of converged standards to make comparisons between companies operating in different jurisdictions easier. Under **IFRS**, these converged standards are effective for reporting periods beginning after January 1, 2018, while under **US GAAP**, they are effective for reporting periods beginning after December 15, 2017.

The converged standards provide a principles-based approach to revenue recognition that can be applied to different types of revenue-generating activities.

Core Principle

The core principle of the converged standards is that revenue should be recognized in order to "depict the transfer of promised goods or services to customers in an amount that reflects the consideration to which the entity expects to be entitled in an exchange for those goods or services." In order to attain this core principle, the standards describe five steps in recognizing revenue:

1. Identify the contract(s) with a customer.
2. Identify the separate or distinct performance obligations in the contract.
3. Determine the transaction price.
4. Allocate the transaction price to the performance obligations in the contract.
5. Recognize revenue when (or as) the entity satisfies a performance obligation.

A contract is an agreement and commitment, with commercial substance, between the contacting parties. It establishes each party's obligations and rights, including payment terms. In addition, a contract exists only if collectability is probable. While IFRS and US GAAP use the same word (probable), they apply a different threshold for probable collectability. Under **IFRS**, probable means more likely than not, while under **US GAAP**, it means likely to occur. This subtle difference can result in economically similar contracts being treated differently under the two standards.

Performance obligations represent promises to transfer **distinct** good(s) or service(s). A good or service is distinct if (1) the customer can benefit from it on its own or in combination with readily available resources and (2) the promise to transfer it can be separated from other promises in the contract. Each identified performance obligation is accounted for separately.

The **transaction price** is the amount that the seller estimates it will receive in exchange for transferring the good(s) or service(s) identified in the contract to the buyer. The transaction price is then allocated to each identified performance obligation. The amount recognized reflects expectations about collectability and (if applicable) an allocation to multiple obligations within the same contract. Revenue is recognized when the obligation-satisfying transfer is made.

Accounting Treatment

- When revenue is recognized, a **contract asset** is presented on the balance sheet.
- If all performance obligations have been satisfied, but payment has not been received, a **receivable** appears on the seller's balance sheet.
- If payment is received in advance of transferring good(s) or service(s), the seller presents a **contract liability**.

For complex contracts, **variable consideration** may only be recognized as revenue if the company can conclude that it will not have to reverse the cumulative revenue in the future. The converged standards also provide guidance on whether a change in a contract is a **new contract or just a modification** of an existing contract.

- In order to be considered a new contract, the change would need to involve goods and services that are distinct from the goods and services already transferred.
- If the changes do not meet the criteria for a new contract then they are treated as contract modifications. The company must reflect the impact on a **cumulative catch-up basis** by updating the transaction price and measure of progress.

The converged standards also lay down specific accounting treatments for certain related costs and also require extensive disclosures. The impact of converged standards will be felt more by industries where bundled sales are common, such as telecommunications and software.

Expense Recognition

The IASB framework defines expenses as "decreases in economic benefits during the accounting period in the form of outflows or depletions of assets or incurrence of liabilities that result in decreases in equity, other than those relating to distributions to equity participants."

Expenses also include losses, which result from non-operating activities of the business. The most important principle of expense recognition is the **matching principle**, which requires that expenses be matched with associated revenues when recognizing them in the income statement. If goods bought in the current year remain unsold at the end of the year, their cost is not included in the cost of goods sold for the current year. Instead, the cost of these goods will be deducted from next period's revenues once they are sold.

Certain expenses, such as administrative costs, cannot be directly linked to the generation of revenues. These expenses are called period costs and are expensed in the period in which they are incurred.

Issues in Expense Recognition

- Doubtful accounts.
- Warranties.
- Depreciation and amortization

Operating versus Nonoperating Components of the Income Statement

IFRS does not define operating activities. Therefore, companies that choose to report operating income or the results of operating activities need to ensure that such activities would normally be regarded as operating.

On the other hand, U.S. GAAP defines operating activities as those that generally involve producing and delivering goods and providing services, and include all transactions and other events that are not defined as investing or financing activities.

Discontinued Operations

Under both IFRS and U.S. GAAP, the income statement must report an operation separately as a "discontinued operation" when the company disposes of, or is expected to dispose of a component that is operationally and physically separable from the rest of the firm.

- Discontinued operations are reported *net of tax* as a *separate* line item *after* income from continuing operations (this treatment is permitted under IFRS and U.S. GAAP).
- As the disposed operation will not earn revenue for the company going forward, it will not be taken into account in forecasting the company's future profits.

Extraordinary Items

IFRS does not allow any items to be classified as extraordinary. U.S. GAAP defines extraordinary items as being **both** unusual in nature **and** infrequent in occurrence. A significant degree of judgment is involved in classifying an item as extraordinary. For example, losses caused by Hurricane Katrina in the Unites States were not classified as extraordinary items because natural disasters can reasonably be expected to reoccur.

- Extraordinary items are reported *net of tax* and as a *separate* line item *after* income from continuing operations (below discontinued operations).

- Analysts should eliminate extraordinary items from expectations about a company's future financial performance unless there are indications that these extraordinary items may reoccur.
- For fiscal periods beginning after December 15, 2015, U.S. GAAP will no longer include the concept of extraordinary items. Under the new guidance, items will simply be classified as unusual, infrequent, or unusual and infrequent.

Unusual or Infrequent Items

These items are **either** unusual in nature **or** infrequent in occurrence. Examples of such items include restructuring charges and gains and losses arising from selling an asset for a price other than its carrying value.

- These items are listed as separate line items on the income statement but are *included* in income from continuing operations and hence, reported *before-tax.*
- Analysts should not ignore all unusual or infrequent items. They should assess whether these items are likely to reoccur when forecasting future operations.

Accounting Changes

- A change in accounting principle can occur if it is required by standard setters or because of a management decision (e.g., changing from LIFO to FIFO method of inventory valuation). The change is applied retrospectively, which means that financial data for all periods is presented according to the new principal. This retrospective change facilitates comparisons across reporting periods. A description of, and justification for the change are provided in the footnotes to the financial statements.
- A change in an accounting estimate (e.g., a change in the residual value of an asset) is applied prospectively and only affects financial statements for current and future periods. Significant changes in accounting estimates must be disclosed in the footnotes.
- A correction of prior-period errors is made by restating all prior-period financial statements presented in the financial report. In addition, disclosure about the error is required in the footnotes. Analysts should carefully assess these disclosures as they may point to weaknesses in a company's accounting system or financial controls.

Earnings Per Share

A firm may have a simple capital structure or a complex capital structure. A company has a simple capital structure when it does not have any securities outstanding that can be converted into common stock. Firms with simple capital structures are required to report basic earnings per share (EPS) only.

$$\text{Basic EPS} = \frac{\text{Net income} - \text{Preferred dividends}}{\text{Weighted average number of shares outstanding}}$$

If a company declares a stock split or a stock dividend during the year, the calculation of the weighted average number of issued shares outstanding is based on the assumption that the additional (newly issued) shares have been outstanding since the date that the original shares were outstanding from.

A complex capital structure includes securities that can be converted into common stock (e.g., convertible bonds, convertible preferred stock, warrants and options). These securities are *potentially dilutive* so companies with complex capital structures are required to report basic and diluted EPS. A dilutive security is one whose conversion into shares of common stock would result in a reduction in EPS. EPS calculated after taking into account all dilutive securities in the capital structure is known as diluted EPS.

In determining which potentially dilutive securities should be included in the calculation of diluted EPS, each of the securities must be evaluated individually and independently to determine whether they are dilutive. Any anti-dilutive securities must be ignored from the diluted EPS calculation.

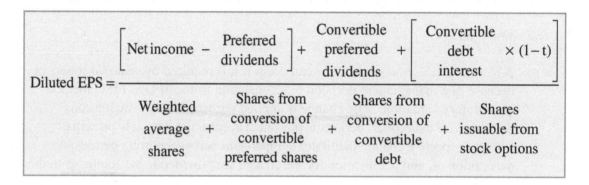

$$\text{Diluted EPS} = \frac{\left[\text{Net income} - \frac{\text{Preferred}}{\text{dividends}}\right] + \frac{\text{Convertible}}{\text{preferred}} + \left[\frac{\text{Convertible}}{\text{debt}} \times (1-t)\right]}{\frac{\text{Weighted}}{\text{average}} + \frac{\text{Shares from}}{\text{conversion of}} + \frac{\text{Shares from}}{\text{conversion of}} + \frac{\text{Shares}}{\text{issuable from}}}$$

Both U.S. GAAP and IFRS require the presentation of EPS (basic EPS and their diluted EPS) on the face of the income statement.

Treasury Stock Method

In the calculation of diluted EPS, stock options and warrants are accounted for by using the treasury stock method (required under U.S. GAAP). The treasury stock method assumes that all the funds received by the company from the exercise of options and warrants are used by the company to repurchase shares at the average market price. The resulting net increase in the number of shares equals the increase in shares from exercise of options and warrants minus the decrease in the number of outstanding shares from repurchases.

Common-size income statements

present each item on the income statement as a percentage of *sales*. They facilitate financial statement analysis as the data can be used to conduct time-series (across time periods) and cross-sectional (across companies) analysis.

FRA

> IFRS requires the use of a similar method, but does not refer to it as the Treasury stock method. The proceeds of option exercise are assumed to be used to repurchase shares at the average market price and these shares are known as inferred shares. The excess of new issued shares over inferred shares is added to the weighted average number of shares outstanding.

Comprehensive Income

IFRS defines total comprehensive income as "the change in equity during a period resulting from transactions and other events, other than those changes resulting from transactions with owners in their capacity as owners."

Under U.S. GAAP, comprehensive income is defined as "the change in equity (net assets) of a business enterprise during a period from transactions and other events and circumstances from nonowner sources. It includes all changes in equity during a period except those resulting from investments by owners and distributions to owners."

Under U.S. GAAP, there are four major types of items that are classified as other comprehensive income:

- Foreign currency translation adjustments.
- Minimum pension liability adjustments.
- Unrealized gains or losses on derivatives contracts, those considered as hedges.
- Unrealized holding gains and losses on available-for-sale securities.

> Net income + Other comprehensive income = Comprehensive income

Under IFRS, certain changes in the value of long-lived assets that are measured using the revaluation model (as opposed to the cost model) are also included in other comprehensive income.

The "available-for-sale" classification no longer appears in IFRS with the issuance of IFRS 9 (*Financial Instruments*) as of January 1, 2018. Although the available-for-sale category will not exist, IFRS still permits certain equity investments to be measured at fair value with any unrealized holding gains or losses recognized in other comprehensive income.

FRA

UNDERSTANDING BALANCE SHEETS
Cross-Reference to CFA Institute Assigned Reading #24

Limitations of the Balance Sheet

- Under current accounting standards, measurement bases of different assets and liabilities may vary considerably, which can have a significant impact on reported figures.
- The value of items reported on the balance sheet reflects their value at the end of the reporting period, which may not necessarily remain "current" at a later date.
- The balance sheet does not include qualitative factors (e.g., reputation, management skills, etc.) that have an important impact on the company's future cash-generating ability and therefore, its overall value.

Alternative Formats of Balance Sheet Presentation

- Report format: Assets, liabilities and equity are presented in a single column. This format is the most commonly-used balance sheet presentation format.
- Account format: Assets are presented on the left hand side of the balance sheet, with liabilities and equity on the right side.
- Classified balance sheet: Different types of assets and liabilities are grouped into subcategories to give a more effective overview of the company's financial position. Classifications typically group assets and liabilities into their current and non-current portions.
- Liquidity-based presentation: **IFRS** allows the preparation of a balance sheet using a liquidity-based presentation format (rather than a current/non-current format), if such a format provides more reliable and relevant information. In a liquidity-based presentation, all assets and liabilities are broadly presented in order of liquidity. This format is typically used by banks.

IFRS and U.S. GAAP Balance Sheet Presentation

Both **IFRS** and **U.S. GAAP** require that assets and liabilities be grouped separately into their current and non-current portions, which makes it easier for analysts to examine the company's liquidity position as of the balance sheet date. However, it is not required that current assets be presented before noncurrent assets, or that current liabilities be presented before noncurrent liabilities. Further, under **IFRS**, the current/non-current classifications are not required if a liquidity-based presentation provides more relevant and reliable information.

Measurement Bases of Various Financial Assets

Measured at Fair Value	Measured at Cost or Amortized Cost
Financial Assets	**Financial Assets**
Financial assets held for trading (stocks and bonds).	Unlisted instruments.
Available-for-sale financial assets (stocks and bonds).	Held-to-maturity investments.
Derivatives.	Loans and receivables.
Non-derivative instruments with face value exposures hedged by derivatives.	

Accounting for Gains and Losses on Marketable Securities

	Held-to-Maturity Securities	Available-for-sale Securities	Trading Securities
Balance Sheet	Reported at cost or amortized cost.	Reported at fair value. Unrealized gains or losses due to changes in market value are reported in other comprehensive income.	Reported at fair value.
Items Recognized on the Income Statement	Interest income Realized gains and losses.	Dividend income. Interest income. Realized gains and losses.	Dividend income. Interest income. Realized gains and losses. Unrealized gains and losses due to changes in market value.

Measurement Bases of Various Financial Liabilities

Measured at Fair Value	Measured at Cost or Amortized Cost
Financial Liabilities	**Financial Liabilities**
Derivatives.	All other liabilities (bonds payable and notes payable).
Financial liabilities held for trading.	
Non-derivative instruments with face value exposures hedged by derivatives.	

FRA

The Components of Shareholders' Equity

- Capital contributed by owners (common stock or issued capital).
  - Authorized shares are the maximum number of shares that can be sold under the company's Articles of Incorporation.
  - Issued shares are the total number of shares that have been sold to shareholders.
  - Outstanding shares equal the number of shares that were issued less the number of shares repurchased (treasury stock).
- Preferred shares
- Treasury shares
- Retained earnings
- Accumulated other comprehensive income
- Noncontrolling interest (minority interest)

Statement of Changes in Owners' Equity

This statement presents the effects of all transactions that increase or decrease company's equity over the period. Under **IFRS**, the following information should be included in the statement of changes in equity:

- Total comprehensive income for the period.
- The effects of any accounting changes that have been retrospectively applied to previous periods.
- Capital transactions with owners and distributions to owners; and
- Reconciliation of the carrying amounts of each component of equity at the beginning and end of the year.

Under U.S. GAAP, companies are required to provide an analysis of changes in each component of stockholders' equity that is shown in the balance sheet.

Uses and Analysis of Balance Sheets

Analysts can gain information regarding a company's liquidity, solvency, and the economic resources controlled by the company by examining its balance sheet.

- Liquidity refers to a company's ability to meet its short-term financial obligations.
- Solvency refers to a company's ability to meet its long-term financial obligations.

Two of the techniques that may be used to analyze a company's balance sheet are common-size analysis and ratio analysis.

Common-Size Balance Sheets

A vertical common-size balance sheet expresses each balance sheet item as a percentage of total assets. This allows an analyst to perform historical analysis (time-series analysis) and cross-sectional analysis across firms within the same industry.

Balance Sheet Ratios

These are ratios that have balance sheet items in the numerator and the denominator. The two main categories of balance sheet ratios are liquidity ratios, which measure a company's ability to settle short-term obligations and solvency ratios, which evaluate a company's ability to settle long-term obligations.

The *higher* a company's liquidity ratios, the *greater* the likelihood that the company will be able to meet its short-term obligations.

Liquidity ratios

	Numerator	Denominator
Current ratio	Current assets	Current liabilities
Quick ratio (acid test ratio)	Cash + marketable securities + receivables	Current liabilities
Cash ratio	Cash + marketable securities	Current liabilities

Higher solvency ratios, on the other hand, are *undesirable* and indicate that the company is highly leveraged and risky.

Solvency Ratios

	Numerator	Denominator
Long-term debt-to-equity ratio	Total long-term debt	Total equity
Debt-to-equity ratio	Total debt	Total equity
Total debt ratio	Total debt	Total assets
Financial leverage ratio	Total assets	Total equity

FRA

UNDERSTANDING CASH FLOW STATEMENTS
Cross-Reference to CFA Institute Assigned Reading #25

Under both IFRS and U.S. GAAP, cash flows are classified into the following categories:

Cash Flows from Operating Activities (CFO) are inflows and outflows of cash generated from a firm's day-to-day business activities.

Cash Flows from Investing Activities (CFI) are inflows and outflows of cash generated from purchase and disposal of long-term investments. Long-term investments include plant, machinery, equipment, intangible assets, and non-trading debt and equity securities.

All securities that are considered highly liquid (cash equivalents) are not included in investing activities and neither are securities held for trading. Cash flows associated with the purchase and sale of highly liquid cash equivalents, and of securities for trading purposes are classified as cash flows from operating activities.

Cash Flows from Financing Activities (CFF) are cash inflows and outflows generated from issuance and repayment of capital (long-term debt and equity).

Indirect short term borrowings from suppliers that are classified as accounts payable and receivables from customers are not financing activities; they are classified as operating activities.

Cash Flow Classification

CFO

Inflows	Outflows
Cash collected from customers.	Cash paid to employees.
Interest and dividends received.	Cash paid to suppliers.
Proceeds from sale of securities held for trading.	Cash paid for other expenses.
	Cash used to purchase trading securities.
	Interest paid.
	Taxes paid.

CFI

Inflows	Outflows
Sale proceeds from fixed assets.	Purchase of fixed assets.
Sale proceeds from long-term investments.	Cash used to acquire LT investment securities.

CFF

Inflows	Outflows
Proceeds from debt issuance.	Repayment of LT debt.
Proceeds from issuance of equity instruments.	Payments made to repurchase stock.
	Dividends payments.

FRA

Cash Flow Presentation Formats

Under both IFRS and U.S. GAAP, there are two acceptable formats for presenting the cash flow statement—the direct method and the indirect method. These methods differ only in the *presentation* of the *CFO* section of the cash flow statement; calculated values for CFO are the same under both. Further, the presentation of financing and investing activities is exactly the same.

Direct Method versus Indirect Method

- The direct method explicitly lists the actual sources of operating cash inflows and outflows, whereas indirect method only provides net results for these inflows and outflows. The information provided under the direct method is very useful in evaluating past performance and making projections of future cash flows.
- The indirect method provides a list of items that are responsible for the difference between net income and operating cash flows. The differences can then be used to estimate future operating cash flows. The indirect method facilitates forecasting of future cash flows since forecasts of future net income simply have to be adjusted for changes in working capital accounts.

Sources and Uses of Cash

- *Increases* in current assets are *uses* of cash, and *decreases* in current assets are *sources* of cash. Changes in asset balances and cash are *negatively* related.
- *Increases* in current liabilities are *sources* of cash, while *decreases* in current liabilities are *uses* of cash. Changes in liability balances and cash are *positively* related.

The Direct Method

Step 1: Start with sales on the income statement.

Step 2: Go through each income statement account and adjust it for changes in all relevant working capital accounts on the balance sheet. This serves to remove the effects of the timing difference between the recognition of revenues or expenses, and the actual receipt or payment of cash.

Step 3: Check whether changes in these working capital accounts indicate a source or use of cash. Make sure you put the right sign in front of the income statement item. Sales are an inflow item so they have a positive effect on cash flow, while COGS, wages, taxes, and interest expense are all outflow items that have negative effects on cash flow.

Step 4: Ignore all nonoperating items (e.g., gain/loss on sale of plant and equipment) and noncash charges (e.g., depreciation and amortization).

FRA

The Indirect Method

Step 1: Start with net income.

Step 2: Go up the income statement and remove the effect of all noncash expenses and gains from net income. For example, the negative effect of depreciation is removed from net income by adding depreciation back to net income. Cash net income will be higher than accrual-based net income by the amount of noncash expenses.

Step 3: Remove the effects of all nonoperating activities from net income. For example the positive effect of a gain on sale of fixed assets on net income is removed by subtracting the gain from net income.

Step 4: Make adjustments for changes in all working capital accounts. Add all sources of cash (increases in current liabilities and decreases in current assets) and subtract all uses of cash (decreases in current liabilities and increases in current assets).

Cash Flows Statements under IFRS and U.S. GAAP

	IFRS	U.S. GAAP
Classification of Cash Flows		
Interest and dividends received	CFO or CFI	CFO
Interest paid	CFO or CFF	CFO
Dividend paid	CFO or CFF	CFF
Dividends received	CFO or CFI	CFO
Taxes paid	CFO, but part of the tax can be categorized as CFI or CFF if it is clear that the tax arose from investing or financing activities.	CFO
Bank overdrafts	Included as a part of cash equivalents.	Not considered a part of cash equivalents and included in CFF.
Presentation Format		
CFO (No difference in CFI and CFF presentation)	Direct or indirect method. The former is preferred.	Direct or indirect method. The former is preferred. However, if the direct method is used, a reconciliation of net income and CFO must be included.
Disclosures		
	Taxes paid should be presented separately on the cash flow statement.	If taxes and interest paid are not explicitly stated on the cash flow statement, details can be provided in footnotes.

FRA

Cash Flow Analysis

Major sources and uses of cash	Sources and uses of cash depend on the company's stage of growth.

- Companies in the early stages of growth may have negative operating cash flows as cash is used to finance inventory and receivables. These negative operating cash flows are supported by financing inflows from issuance of debt or equity.
- Inflows of cash from financing activities are not sustainable. Over the long-term, a company must generate positive cash flows from operating activities that exceed capital expenditures and payments to providers of debt and equity capital.
- Companies in the mature stage of growth usually have positive cash flows from operating activities. These inflows can be used for debt repayment and stock repurchases. They can also be used by the company to expand its scale of operations (investing activities).

Operating cash flows	Changes in relevant asset and liability accounts should be used to determine whether business operations are a source or use of cash.

- Operating cash flow should be compared to net income. If high net income is not being translated into high operating cash flows, the company might be using aggressive revenue recognition policies.
- Companies should ideally have operating cash flows that are greater than net income.
- The variability of operating cash flows and net income is an important determinant of the overall risk inherent in the company.

Investing cash flows	Changes in long-term asset and investment accounts are used to determine sources and uses of investing cash flows.

- Increasing outflows may imply capital expenditures. Analysts should then evaluate how the company plans to finance these investments (i.e., with excess operating cash flows or by undertaking financing activities).

Financing cash flows	Changes in long-term debt and equity are used to determine sources and uses of financing cash flows.

- If debt issuance contributes significantly to financing cash flows, the repayment schedule must be considered.
- Increasing use of cash to repay debt, repurchase stock and make dividend payments might indicate a lack of lucrative investment opportunities for the company.

FRA

Free Cash Flow

Free cash flow is the excess of a company's operating cash flows over capital expenditure undertaken during the year. Free cash flow to the *firm* and free cash flow to *equity* are more precise measures of free cash flow as they identify specifically whom the cash is available to.

Free cash flow to the firm (FCFF) is cash available to equity and debt holders after the company has met all its operating expenses, and satisfied its capital expenditure and working capital requirements.

$$FCFF = NI + NCC + [Int \times (1 - tax\ rate)] - FCInv - WCInv$$
$$FCFF = CFO + [Int \times (1 - tax\ rate)] - FCInv$$

Free cash flow to equity (FCFE) is the cash that is available only to common shareholders.

$$FCFE = CFO - FCInv + Net\ borrowing - Net\ debt\ repayment$$

FINANCIAL ANALYSIS TECHNIQUES
Cross-Reference to CFA Institute Assigned Reading #26

Limitations of Ratio Analysis

- Companies may have divisions that operate in different industries. This can make it difficult to find relevant industry ratios for comparison purposes.
- There are no set ranges within which particular ratios for a company must lie. An analyst must use her own judgment to evaluate the implications of a given value for a ratio. This usually involves examining the entire operations of a company, the external industry and economic scenario.
- Firms enjoy significant latitude in the choice of accounting methods that are acceptable given the jurisdiction that they operate in. For example, under U.S. GAAP, companies can:
  - Choose from a variety of inventory cost flow assumptions (e.g., FIFO, AVCO or LIFO).
  - Choose from a variety of depreciation methods (e.g., MACRS and straight-line).
- Comparing ratios of firms across international borders is even more difficult, in that several countries use IFRS. Despite the growing convergence between IFRS and U.S. GAAP, significant differences remain.

Common Ratios Used in Financial Analysis

Activity ratios measure how productive a company is in using its assets and how efficiently it performs its everyday operations.

$$\text{Inventory turnover} = \frac{\text{Cost of goods sold}}{\text{Average inventory}}$$

$$\text{Days of inventory on hand (DOH)} = \frac{365}{\text{Inventory turnover}}$$

$$\text{Receivables turnover} = \frac{\text{Revenue}}{\text{Average receivables}}$$

$$\text{Days of sales outstanding (DSO)} = \frac{365}{\text{Receivables turnover}}$$

$$\text{Payables turnover} = \frac{\text{Purchases}}{\text{Average trade payables}}$$

FRA

$$\text{Number of days of payables} = \frac{365}{\text{Payables turnover}}$$

$$\text{Working capital turnover} = \frac{\text{Revenue}}{\text{Average working capital}}$$

$$\text{Fixed asset turnover} = \frac{\text{Revenue}}{\text{Average fixed assets}}$$

$$\text{Total Asset Turnover} = \frac{\text{Revenue}}{\text{Average total assets}}$$

Liquidity ratios measure the company's ability to meet its short-term cash requirements.

$$\text{Current ratio} = \frac{\text{Current assets}}{\text{Current liabilities}}$$

$$\text{Quick ratio} = \frac{\text{Cash} + \text{Short-term marketable investments} + \text{Receivables}}{\text{Current liabilities}}$$

$$\text{Cash ratio} = \frac{\text{Cash} + \text{Short-term marketable investments}}{\text{Current liabilities}}$$

$$\text{Defensive interval ratio} = \frac{\text{Cash} + \text{Short-term marketable investments} + \text{Receivables}}{\text{Daily cash expenditures}}$$

$$\text{Cash conversion cycle} = \text{DSO} + \text{DOH} - \text{Number of days of payables}$$

Solvency ratios measure a company's ability to meet its long-term obligations.

$$\text{Debt-to-assets ratio} = \frac{\text{Total debt}}{\text{Total assets}}$$

$$\text{Debt-to-capital ratio} = \frac{\text{Total debt}}{\text{Total debt} + \text{Shareholders' equity}}$$

$$\text{Debt-to-equity ratio} = \frac{\text{Total debt}}{\text{Shareholders' equity}}$$

$$\text{Financial leverage ratio} = \frac{\text{Average total assets}}{\text{Average total equity}}$$

$$\text{Interest coverage ratio} = \frac{\text{EBIT}}{\text{Interest payments}}$$

$$\text{Fixed charge coverage ratio} = \frac{\text{EBIT} + \text{Lease payments}}{\text{Interest payments} + \text{Lease payments}}$$

Profitability ratios measure a company's ability to generate an adequate return on invested capital.

$$\text{Gross profit margin} = \frac{\text{Gross profit}}{\text{Revenue}}$$

$$\text{Operating profit margin} = \frac{\text{Operating profit}}{\text{Revenue}}$$

$$\text{Pretax margin} = \frac{\text{EBT (earnings before tax, but after interest)}}{\text{Revenue}}$$

$$\text{Net profit margin} = \frac{\text{Net profit}}{\text{Revenue}}$$

$$\text{ROA} = \frac{\text{Net income}}{\text{Average total assets}}$$

$$\text{Adjusted ROA} = \frac{\text{Net income} + \text{Interest expense} \, (1 - \text{Tax rate})}{\text{Average total assets}}$$

$$\text{Operating ROA} = \frac{\text{Operating income or EBIT}}{\text{Average total assets}}$$

$$\text{Return on total capital} = \frac{\text{EBIT}}{\text{Short-term debt} + \text{Long-term debt} + \text{Equity}}$$

FRA

$$\text{Return on equity} = \frac{\text{Net income}}{\text{Average total equity}}$$

$$\text{Return on common equity} = \frac{\text{Net income} - \text{Preferred dividends}}{\text{Average common equity}}$$

Interpretation and Context

- Actual ratios should be compared to the company's stated objectives. This helps in determining whether the company's operations are moving in line with its strategy.
- A company's ratios should be compared with those of others in the industry. When comparing ratios across firms from the same industry, analysts must be careful because:
  - Not all ratios are important to every industry.
  - Companies can have several lines of business, which can cause aggregate financial ratios to be distorted. In such a situation, analysts should evaluate ratios for each segment of the business in relation to the relevant industry average.
  - Companies might be using different accounting methods.
  - Companies could be at different stages of growth, or may have different strategies. This can result in different values for various ratios for firms in the same industry.
- Ratios should be studied in light of the current phase of the business cycle.

DuPont Analysis: The Decomposition of ROE

ROE measures the return a company generates on its equity capital. Decomposing ROE into its components through DuPont analysis has the following uses:

- It facilitates a meaningful evaluation of the different aspects of the company's performance that affect reported ROE.
- It helps in determining the reasons for changes in ROE over time for a given company. It also helps us understand the reasons for differences in ROE for different companies over a given time period.
- It can direct management to areas that it should focus on to improve ROE.
- It shows the relationship between the various categories of ratios and how they all influence the return that owners realize on their investment.

$$\text{ROE} = \frac{\text{Net income}}{\text{Average shareholders' equity}}$$

$$\text{ROE} = \frac{\text{Net income}}{\text{Average total assets}} \times \frac{\text{Average total assets}}{\text{Average shareholder's equity}}$$

FRA

$$\text{ROE} = \frac{\text{Net income}}{\text{Revenue}} \times \frac{\text{Revenue}}{\text{Average total assets}} \times \frac{\text{Average total assets}}{\text{Average shareholders' equity}}$$

$$\text{ROE} = \frac{\text{Net income}}{\text{EBT}} \times \frac{\text{EBT}}{\text{EBIT}} \times \frac{\text{EBIT}}{\text{Revenue}} \times \frac{\text{Revenue}}{\text{Average total assets}} \times \frac{\text{Average total assets}}{\text{Avg. shareholders' equity}}$$

Valuation ratios measure the quantity of an asset or flow (for e.g., earnings) associated with ownership of a specific claim (for e.g., common stock).

$$\text{P/E} = \frac{\text{Price per share}}{\text{Earnings per share}}$$

$$\text{P/CF} = \frac{\text{Price per share}}{\text{Cash flow per share}}$$

$$\text{P/S} = \frac{\text{Price per share}}{\text{Sales per share}}$$

$$\text{P/BV} = \frac{\text{Price per share}}{\text{Book value per share}}$$

$$\text{Cash flow per share} = \frac{\text{Cash flow from operations}}{\text{Average number of shares outstanding}}$$

$$\text{EBITDA per share} = \frac{\text{EBITDA}}{\text{Average number of shares outstanding}}$$

$$\text{Dividends per share} = \frac{\text{Common dividends declared}}{\text{Weighted average number of ordinary shares}}$$

$$\text{Dividend payout ratio} = \frac{\text{Common share dividends}}{\text{Net income attributable to common shares}}$$

$$\text{Retention Rate} = \frac{\text{Net income attributable to common shares} - \text{Common share dividends}}{\text{Net income attributable to common shares}}$$

$$\text{Sustainable growth rate} = \text{Retention rate} \times \text{ROE} \quad \Longleftarrow$$

FRA

Credit Analysis

Credit Ratio	Numerator	Denominator
EBIT interest coverage	EBIT	Gross interest
EBITDA interest coverage	EBITDA	Gross interest
Free operating cash flow to total debt	CFO	Total debt
Return on capital	EBIT	Capital = Average Equity
Total debt to total debt plus equity	Total debt	Total debt plus equity

Industry Specific Ratios

Ratios	Numerator	Denominator
Business Risk		
Coefficient of variation of operating income	Standard deviation of operating income	Average operating income
Coefficient of variation of net income	Standard deviation of net income	Average net income
Coefficient of variation of revenues	Standard deviation of revenues	Average revenue
Financial Sector Ratios		
Capital adequacy—Banks	Various components of capital	Risk weighted assets, market risk exposure, and level of operational risk assumed
Monetary reserve requirement	Reserves held at central bank	Specified deposit liabilities
Liquid asset requirement	Approved "readily marketable securities"	Specified deposit liabilities
Net interest margin	Net interest income	Total interest-earning assets
Retail Ratios		
Same store sales	Average revenue growth year on year for stores open in both periods	Not applicable
Sales per square foot (meter)	Revenue	Total retail space in feet or meters
Service Companies		
Revenue per employee	Revenue	Total number of employees
Net income per employee	Net income	Total number of employees
Hotels		
Average daily rate	Room revenue	Number of rooms sold
Occupancy rate	Number of rooms sold	Number of rooms available

Segment Analysis

Segment Ratios	Numerator	Denominator	Measures
Segment margin	Segment profit (loss)	Segment revenue	Operating profitability relative to sales.
Segment turnover	Segment revenue	Segment assets	Overall efficiency- how much revenue is generated per dollar of assets.
Segment ROA	Segment profit (loss)	Segment assets	Operating profitability relative to assets.
Segment debt ratio	Segment liabilities	Segment assets	Solvency of the segment.

Model Building and Forecasting

Sensitivity analysis shows the range of possible outcomes as underlying assumptions are altered.

Scenario analysis shows the changes in key financial quantities that result from events such as a loss of supply of raw materials or a reduction in demand for the firm's products.

Simulations are computer generated sensitivity or scenario analyses that are based on probability models for the factors that drive outcomes.

FRA

STUDY SESSION 8:
FINANCIAL REPORTING AND ANALYSIS (3)

FRA

INVENTORIES
Cross-Reference to CFA Institute Assigned Reading #27

Cost of Inventories

IFRS and U.S. GAAP suggest a similar treatment of various expenses in the determination of inventory cost. The following items are capitalized inventory costs, which are included in the cost of inventories.

- Costs of purchase.
- Costs of conversion.

Capitalization of these costs results in a build-up of asset balances, and delays recognition of costs until inventory is sold.

The following items are not capitalized as inventory costs; they are expensed on the income statement as incurred:

- Abnormal costs from material wastage.
- Storage costs that are not a part of normal production processes.
- Administrative expenses.
- Selling and marketing costs.

Capitalization of costs that should be expensed results in overstatement of net income due to the delay in recognition of costs, and an overstatement of inventory value on the balance sheet.

Inventory Valuation Methods

FIFO
- Older units are the first ones sold.
- Units that are purchased recently are included in EI.
- COGS is composed of units valued at older prices.
- EI is composed of units valued at recent prices.

LIFO
- Recently acquired units are the first ones to be sold.
- Oldest units are included in EI.
- COGS is composed of units valued at recent prices.
- Ending inventory is composed of units valued at older prices.

AVCO (weighted-average cost)
- COGS is composed of units valued at average prices.
- Ending inventory is also composed of units that are valued at average prices.

FIFO will always give a better reflection of the current economic value of inventory because the units currently in stock are valued at the most *recent* prices.

- If prices are *rising* LIFO and AVCO will *understate* ending inventory value.
- If prices are *falling*, LIFO and AVCO will *overstate* ending inventory value.
- When prices are stable, the three methods will value inventory at the same level.

LIFO will always offer a closer reflection of replacement costs in COGS because it allocates *recent* costs to COGS. LIFO is the most economically accurate method for income statement purposes because it provides a better measure of current income and future profitability.

- If prices are *rising*, FIFO and AVCO will *understate* replacement costs in COGS and *overstate* profits.
- If prices are *falling*, FIFO and AVCO will *overstate* replacements costs in COGS and *understate* profits.
- When prices are stable, the three methods will value COGS at same level.

When prices are *rising* during the year and inventory levels are stable or rising:

- $COGS_{LIFO} > COGS_{AVCO} > COGS_{FIFO}$
- $EI_{FIFO} > EI_{AVCO} > EI_{LIFO}$

When prices are *falling* during the year and inventory levels are stable or rising:

- $COGS_{FIFO} > COGS_{AVCO} > COGS_{LIFO}$
- $EI_{LIFO} > EI_{AVCO} > EI_{FIFO}$

LIFO versus FIFO when Prices Are Rising

	LIFO	FIFO
COGS	Higher	Lower
Income before taxes	Lower	Higher
Income taxes	Lower	Higher
Net income	Lower	Higher
Cash flow	Higher	Lower
EI	Lower	Higher
Working capital	Lower	Higher

Periodic versus Perpetual Inventory Systems

Periodic inventory system: Under this system, the quantity of inventory on hand is calculated periodically. The cost of goods available for sale during the period is calculated as beginning inventory plus purchases over the period. The ending inventory amount is then deducted from cost of goods available for sale to determine COGS.

Perpetual inventory system: Under this system, changes in the inventory account are updated continuously. Purchases and sales are recorded directly in the inventory account as they occur.

Under the **LIFO** cost flow assumption, in a period of rising prices, use of the periodic system for inventory results in a:

- *Lower* value of ending inventory.
- *Higher* value for COGS.

Therefore, gross profit would be *lower* under the periodic system.

Other important takeaways:

- The value of sales and cost of goods available for sale are the same under the two systems in the first year of operations.
- In subsequent years, the amounts of cost of goods available for sale can be different under the two systems due to different values of opening inventory (previous periods' ending inventory).
- If a company uses FIFO, COGS and EI is the same under the periodic and perpetual inventory systems.
- If a company uses separate identification, COGS and EI is the same under the periodic and perpetual inventory systems.
- If a company uses AVCO:
    - COGS and EI are the same as under FIFO and AVCO under the perpetual inventory system.
    - COGS and EI are different from their value under FIFO under the periodic inventory system.

Generally speaking, analysts do not make adjustments when comparing financial statements of a company that uses AVCO to one that uses FIFO. This is because:

- The perpetual inventory system is more common (the values of COGS and EI are similar under FIFO and AVCO if the perpetual system is used).
- There is a general dearth of relevant disclosures in this area.

Assuming rising prices and stable or increasing inventory quantities, use of the LIFO method generally results in higher COGS, lower EI, lower GP, and lower NP than with the FIFO method, under both periodic and perpetual inventory systems.

FRA

LIFO to FIFO Conversion

$$EI_{FIFO} = EI_{LIFO} + LIFO\ reserve$$
$$COGS_{FIFO} = COGS - (LR_{Ending} - LR_{Beginning})$$

During a period of rising prices and stable or rising inventory quantities:

- Net income after tax under FIFO will be greater than LIFO net income after tax by:
  - Change in LIFO reserve × (1 − tax rate)
- Equity (retained earnings) under FIFO will be greater by:
  - LIFO reserve × (1− tax rate)
- Liabilities (deferred taxes) under FIFO will be greater by:
  - LIFO reserve × (tax rate)
- Current assets (inventory) under FIFO will be greater by:
  - LIFO reserve

Increase in LIFO Reserve

In every period during which prices are rising and inventory quantities are stable or rising, the LIFO reserve will increase as the excess of FIFO ending inventory over LIFO ending inventory increases.

Decline in LIFO Reserve

There can be two reasons for a decline in LIFO reserve:

1. LIFO liquidation.
2. Declining prices.

LIFO Liquidation

LIFO liquidation occurs when, during an inflationary period, a firm that uses LIFO sells more units during a given period than it purchases over the period. This causes year-end inventory levels to be lower than beginning-of-year inventory levels.

When a LIFO firm sells more units than it purchases, some of the goods sold are units that were included in beginning inventory. LIFO allocates the oldest prices to inventory, and in some cases these older prices could be outdated by many years. When a company includes older, cheaper stock in its COGS, it severely understates its COGS, and LIFO COGS no longer reflect recent, current prices. Consequently a firm with LIFO liquidation overstates net income. The higher profits are unsustainable because eventually, the firm will run out of cheaper, older stock to liquidate. The higher net income also comes at the cost of higher taxes that reduce operating cash flow. To postpone these taxes on holding gains on old units of inventory, a LIFO firm must always purchase as many as, if not more units, than it sells.

LIFO liquidation can result from strikes, recessions, or a decline in demand for the firm's product. The irony is that when there is LIFO liquidation, the firm reports surprisingly high profits (due to the realization of holding gains) in hard times when production cuts result in the liquidation of lower cost LIFO inventory.

Analysts should be aware that management can inflate their company's reported gross profits and net income by intentionally reducing inventory quantities and liquidating older (cheaper) units of stock. Therefore, it is important to analyse the LIFO reserve footnote disclosures to determine if LIFO liquidation has occurred. If it is found that LIFO liquidation has occurred, analysts must exclude the increase in earnings due to LIFO liquidation from their analysis. COGS must be adjusted upwards for the decline in LIFO reserve, and net income must be lowered.

LIFO liquidations are more likely to occur with firms that break inventory down into numerous categories. When the different types of inventory are pooled into only a few broad categories, decreases in quantities of certain items are usually offset by increases in quantities of others.

Declining Prices

When prices of the firm's products fall over a given period, the firm will see a decline in its LIFO reserve. If the change in LIFO reserve is negative, $COGS_{FIFO}$ will be greater than $COGS_{LIFO}$. FIFO would continue to reflect the latest (and in this case lower) prices in inventory, and will provide the most economically accurate measure of inventory value, while LIFO would continue to reflect current replacement costs in COGS. When the reduction in LIFO reserve is caused by declining prices, no analytical adjustments are necessary.

Inventory Method Changes

Consistency in the inventory costing method used is required under U.S. GAAP and IFRS.

Under **IFRS**, a change in policy is acceptable only if the change results in the provision of more reliable and relevant information in the financial statements.

- Changes in inventory accounting policy are applied retrospectively.
- Information for all periods presented in the financial report is restated.
- Adjustments for periods prior to the earliest year presented in the financial report are reflected in the beginning balance of retained earnings for the earliest year presented in the report.

FRA

U.S. GAAP has a similar requirement for changes in inventory accounting policies.

- However, a company must thoroughly explain how the newly-adopted inventory accounting method is superior and preferable to the old one.
- The company may be required to seek permission from the Internal Revenue Service (IRS) before making any changes.
- If inventory-related accounting policies are modified, changes to the financial statements must be made retrospectively, unless the LIFO method is being adopted (which is applied prospectively).

Inventory Adjustments

Under **IFRS**, inventory must be stated at the lower of cost or net realizable value (NRV). **NRV** is the estimated selling price in the ordinary course of business less the estimated costs necessary to make the sale and estimated costs to get the inventory in condition for sale. If the NRV of inventory falls below the cost recorded on the balance sheet, inventory must be written down, and a loss must be recognized (as a part of COGS or separately) on the income statement. A subsequent increase in NRV would require a reversal of the previous write-down, which would reduce COGS in the period that the increase in value occurs. However, the increase in value that can be recognized is limited to the total write-down that had previously been recorded. Effectively, inventory value can never exceed the amount originally recognized.

U.S. GAAP used to require the application of the lower of cost or market (LCM) principle to value inventory. For fiscal years beginning after December 15, 2016, inventories measured using other than LIFO and retail inventory methods are measured at the lower of cost or net realizable value. This is broadly consistent with IFRS, with one major difference: that U.S. GAAP prohibits the reversal of write-downs.

When the LCM principle must be applied under U.S. GAAP (for inventories measured using LIFO and retail inventory methods), market value is defined as replacement cost, where replacement cost must lie within a range of values from NRV minus normal profit margin to NRV. If replacement cost is higher than NRV, it must be brought down to NRV, and if replacement cost is lower than NRV minus normal profit margin, it must be brought up to NRV minus normal profit margin. This adjusted replacement cost is then compared to carrying value (cost), and the lower of the two is used to value inventory. Any write-down of inventory reduces the value of inventory and increases COGS.

An inventory write-down reduces both profit and the carrying amount of inventory on the balance sheet and thus has a negative effect on profitability, liquidity, and solvency ratios. However, activity ratios such as inventory turnover will be positively affected. Due to overall negative financial impact, some companies may be reluctant to record inventory write-downs unless the decline in value is believed to be permanent. This is especially true under U.S. GAAP where reversal of a write-down is prohibited.

Companies that use separate identification, AVCO, or FIFO inventory methods are more likely to incur inventory write-downs than companies that use LIFO. This is because LIFO values units of inventory at the oldest prices, which, given that prices are generally on the rise, results in lower carrying values for inventory. Since LIFO inventory is based on oldest and lowest costs, there is a lower chance of an inventory write-down, and if there is a write-down, it will likely be of a lesser magnitude.

In certain industries like agriculture, forest products, and mining, both U.S. GAAP and IFRS allow companies to value inventory at NRV even when it exceeds historical cost. If an active market exists for the product, quoted market prices are used as NRV; otherwise the price of the most recent market transaction is used. Unrealized gains and losses on inventory resulting from fluctuating market prices are recognized on the income statement.

The impact of an inventory write-down on a company's reported financial position can be substantial. Therefore, analysts should careful evaluate the potential for any inventory write-downs and gauge their impact on financial ratios, especially if debt covenants entail financial ratio requirements. The potential for inventory write-downs tends to be higher in industries where technological obsolescence of inventories is a significant risk.

Inventory write-downs raise concerns regarding management's ability to anticipate how much and what type of inventory is required. Further, they affect a company's future reported earnings.

Impact of an Inventory Write-Down on Various Financial Ratios

Type of Ratio	Effect on Numerator	Effect on Denominator	Effect on Ratio
Profitability ratios			
NP and GP margins	COGS increases so profits fall	Sales remain the same	Lower (worsens)
Solvency ratios			
Debt-to-equity and debt ratio	Debt levels remain the same	Equity decreases (due to lower profits) and current assets decrease (due to lower inventory)	Higher (worsens)
Liquidity ratios			
Current ratio	Current assets decrease (due to lower inventory)	Current liabilities remain the same	Lower (worsens)
Activity ratios			
Inventory turnover	COGS increases	Average inventory decreases	Higher (improves)
Total asset turnover	Sales remain the same	Total assets decrease	Higher (improves)

FRA

Presentation and Disclosure

IFRS requires companies to make the following disclosures relating to inventory:

1. The accounting policies used to value inventory.
2. The cost formula used for inventory valuation.
3. The total carrying value of inventories, and the carrying value of different classifications (e.g., merchandise, raw materials, work-in-progress, finished goods).
4. The value of inventories carried at fair value less selling costs.
5. Amount of inventory-related expenses for the period (cost of sales).
6. The amount of any write-downs recognized during the period.
7. The amount of reversal recognized on any previous write-down.
8. Description of the circumstances that led to the reversal.
9. The carrying amount of inventories pledged as collateral for liabilities.**U.S. GAAP** does not permit the reversal of prior-year inventory write-downs. U.S. GAAP also requires disclosure of significant estimates applicable to inventories and of any material amount of income resulting from the liquidation of LIFO inventory.

Inventory Ratios

$$\text{Inventory turnover} = \frac{\text{COGS}}{\text{Average inventory}}$$

$$\text{No. of days of inventory} = \frac{365}{\text{Inventory turnover}}$$

$$\text{Gross profit margin} = \frac{\text{Gross profit}}{\text{Sales revenue}}$$

If a company has a *higher* inventory turnover ratio and a *lower* number of days of inventory than the industry average, it could mean one of two things:

- It could indicate that the company is more efficient in inventory management as less resources are tied up in inventory at any given point in time.
- It could also suggest that the company does not carry enough inventory at any point in time, which might be hurting sales.

To determine which explanation holds true, analysts should compare the firm's revenue growth with that of the industry. A low sales growth compared to the industry would imply that the company is losing out on sales by holding low inventory quantities. A sales growth rate similar to, or higher than industry sales growth would suggest that the company manages inventory more efficiently than its peers.

A firm whose inventory turnover is *lower* and number of days of inventory is *higher* than industry average could have a problem with slow moving or obsolete inventory.

FRA

The gross profit margin indicates the percentage of sales that is contributing to net income as opposed to covering the cost of sales.

- Firms in relatively competitive industries have lower gross profit margins.
- Firms selling luxury products tend to have lower volumes and higher gross profit margins.
- Firms selling luxury products are likely to have lower inventory turnover ratios.

Remember that inventory ratios are directly affected by the cost flow assumption used by the firm. When making comparisons across firms, analysts must understand the differences that arise from the use of different cost flow assumptions.

LIFO versus FIFO Ratio Comparisons when Prices are Rising

Type of Ratio	Effect on Numerator	Effect on Denominator	Effect on Ratio
NP and GP margins	Income is lower under LIFO because COGS is higher.	Sales are the same under both	Lower under LIFO
Debt to equity	Same debt levels	Lower equity under LIFO	Higher under LIFO
Current ratio	Current assets are lower under LIFO because EI is lower.	Current liabilities are the same	Lower under LIFO
Quick ratio	Assets are higher as a result of lower taxes paid	Current liabilities are the same	Higher under LIFO
Inventory turnover	COGS is higher under LIFO	Average inventory is lower under LIFO	Higher under LIFO
Total asset turnover	Sales are the same	Lower total assets under LIFO	Higher under LIFO

Financial Statement Analysis Issues

- A significant increase in unit volumes of raw materials and/or WIP inventory may suggest that the company expects an increase in demand for its products.
- An increase in finished goods inventory with declining raw materials and WIP inventory may signal decrease in demand for the company's products.
- If growth in inventories is greater than the growth in sales, it could indicate a decrease in demand.
- To obtain additional information about a company's inventory and its future sales, analysts should examine the MD&A section, industry-related news and publications, and industry data.

FRA

Example

- A superficial comparison between inventory-related ratios of two companies (let's say ABC and XYZ) may show that ABC has a lower percentage of assets ties up in inventory, suggesting that ABC is using its working capital more efficiently. However, if ABC were using LIFO and XYZ were using FIFO in an inflationary environment with stable or rising inventory quantities, ABC's lower ratio could be explained by its use of the LIFO cost flow assumption (inventory is carried at a lower value under LIFO in an inflationary environment), not by relative efficiency in inventory management.

- Further, growth in inventory may exceed growth in sales for both ABC and XYZ, suggesting that both companies may be accumulating excess inventory. A superficial comparison of the ratio of inventory growth to sales growth for the companies may indicate that ABC's growth rate in finished goods compared to growth rate in sales is lower than XYZ's (indicating that XYZ in more danger of being left with too much inventory). However, if ABC were using LIFO and XYZ were using FIFO in an inflationary environment with stable or rising inventory quantities, the analyst would be able to conclude that ABC's growth rate in finished goods to growth rate in sales is relatively lower (at least partially) due to its use of LIFO (which carries ending inventory at a lower value than FIFO in an inflationary environment).

FRA

LONG-LIVED ASSETS
Cross-Reference to CFA Institute Assigned Reading #28

Long-lived assets are expected to provide economic benefits to a company over an extended period of time, typically longer than one year. There are three types of long-lived assets:

- Tangible assets have physical substance, (e.g., land, plant, and equipment).
- Intangible assets do not have physical substance (e.g., patents and trademarks).
- Financial assets include securities issued by other companies.

The cost of most long-lived assets is allocated over the period of time that they are expected to provide economic benefits. The two types of long-lived assets whose costs are not expensed over time are **land** and **intangible assets with indefinite useful lives**.

LONG-LIVED TANGIBLE ASSETS: PROPERTY PLANT & EQUIPMENT (PP&E)

Capitalization versus Expensing

Effects of Capitalization

	Effects on Financial statements
Initially when the cost is capitalized	- Noncurrent assets *increase*. - Cash flow from investing activities *decreases*.
In future periods when the asset is depreciated or amortized	- Noncurrent assets *decrease*. - Net income *decreases*. - Retained earnings *decrease*. - Equity *decreases*.

Effects of Expensing

	Effects on Financial statements
When the item is expensed	- Net income *decreases* by the entire after-tax amount of the cost. - No related asset is recorded on the balance sheet and therefore no depreciation or amortization expense is charged in future periods. - Operating cash flow *decreases*. - Expensed costs have no financial statement impact in future years.

Impact on Financial Statements and Ratios

Financial Statement Effects of Capitalizing versus Expensing

	Capitalizing	Expensing
Net income (first year)	Higher	Lower
Net income (future years)	Lower	Higher
Total assets	Higher	Lower
Shareholders' equity	Higher	Lower
Cash flow from operations activities	Higher	Lower
Cash flow from investing activities	Lower	Higher
Income variability	Lower	Higher
Debt-to-equity ratio	Lower	Higher

All other factors remaining the same, the decision to expense an item as opposed to capitalizing it would give the impression of *greater earnings growth*. Further, expensing allows companies to report lower taxable income in the current period and pay out *lower taxes* (conserving cash).

On the other hand, the decision to capitalize an item as opposed to expensing may make it easier for a company to *achieve earnings targets* for a particular period. Further, capitalization allows companies to report *higher operating cash flow*, which is an important valuation metric.

Therefore, when making comparisons across companies, it is important to account for differences in the companies' expenditure capitalizing policies. Analysts should be wary of companies that:

- Inflate reported cash flow from operations by capitalizing expenditures that should be expensed.
- Inflate profits to meet earnings targets by capitalizing costs that should be expensed.
- Depress current period income by expensing costs that should be capitalized, in order to be able to exhibit impressive profitability growth going forward without any real improvement in operating performance.

If a company continues to purchase comparable or increasing amounts of fixed assets every year, capitalization will result in higher profits over an extended period. This would continue to be the case until the value of fixed assets purchased in a given year (amount expensed by the expensing firm) is lower than depreciation charged on capitalized assets by the capitalizing firm.

Acquisition of Long-Lived Tangible Assets Acquired through an Exchange

- If an asset is acquired in a **nonmonetary exchange**, the amount recognized on the balance sheet typically equals the fair value of the asset acquired.

- In accounting for such exchanges the carrying amount of the asset given up is removed from noncurrent assets on the balance sheet, the fair value of the asset acquired is added, and any difference between the two values is recognized on the income statement as a gain or a loss.
- If the fair value of the asset acquired is greater (lower) than the value of the asset given up, a gain (loss) is recorded on the income statement.
- In rare cases, if the fair value of the acquired asset cannot be determined, the amount recognized on the balance sheet equals the carrying amount of the asset given up. In this case, no gain or loss is recognized.

Acquisition of Long-Lived Tangible Assets Acquired through a Purchase

When a long-lived asset is purchased, expenses other than the purchase price may be incurred.

- These costs are also capitalized and included in the value of the asset on the balance sheet.
- Subsequent expenses related to the long-lived asset may be capitalized if they are expected to provide economic benefits beyond one year, or expensed if they are not expected to provide economic benefits beyond one year.
- Expenditures that extend an asset's useful life are usually capitalized.

Capitalization of Interest Costs

Companies must capitalize interest costs associated with financing the acquisition or construction of an asset that requires a long period of time to ready for its intended use. For example, if a company constructs a building for its own use, interest expense incurred to finance construction must be capitalized along with the costs of constructing the building. The interest rate used to determine the amount of interest capitalized depends on the company's existing borrowings or, if applicable, on borrowings specifically incurred to finance the cost of the asset.

- Under **IFRS**, but not **U.S. GAAP**, income earned from temporarily investing borrowed funds that were acquired to finance the cost of the asset must be subtracted from interest expense on the borrowed funds to determine the amount that can be capitalized.
- If a company is constructing the asset for its own use, capitalized interest is included in the cost of the asset and appears on the balance sheet as a part of property, plant, and equipment. Once the asset is brought into use, the entire cost of the asset, inclusive of capitalized interest, is depreciated over time, so capitalized interest is then a part of depreciation expense, not interest expense. As a result of this accounting treatment, a company's interest costs can appear on the balance sheet (when capitalized) or on the income statement (when expensed).
- If construction and sale of buildings is the core business activity of the firm, and a building is constructed with the intention of selling it, capitalized interest costs are included along with costs of construction in inventory as a part of current assets. The capitalized interest is expenses as a part of COGS in the period that the building is sold.
- Interest payments made prior to completion of construction that are **capitalized** are classified under cash flow from *investing activities*.

FRA

- Interest payments that are **expensed** may be classified as *operating* or *financing* cash outflows under **IFRS**, and are classified as *operating* cash outflows under **U.S. GAAP**.

Analytical Issues Relating to Capitalization of Interest Costs

- Capitalized interest costs reduce investing cash flow, while expensed interest costs reduce operating cash flow. Therefore, analysts may want to examine the impact of classification on reported cash flows.
- To provide a true picture of a company's interest coverage ratio, the entire amount of interest expense for the period, whether capitalized or expensed, should be used in the denominator. If the company is depreciating interest that was capitalized in previous years, net income should be adjusted to remove the effect of depreciation of capitalized interest.

> Interest coverage ratio = (EBIT/Interest expense)

The interest coverage ratio measures the number of times that a company's operating profits (EBIT) cover its interest expense. A higher ratio indicates that the company can comfortably service its debt through operating earnings.

- Any interest costs capitalized in the current period should be treated as interest expense. Net income should be reduced by the amount of interest capitalized in the current period.

INTANGIBLE ASSETS

Intangible assets lack physical substance and include items that involve exclusive rights such as patents, copyrights, and trademarks. Some intangible assets have finite lives, while others have indefinite lives.

- The cost of an intangible assets with a **finite life** (e.g., patent) is amortized over its useful life.
- The cost of an intangible asset with an **indefinite life** (e.g., goodwill) is not amortized; instead, the asset is tested (at least annually) for impairment. If deemed impaired, the asset's balance sheet value is reduced and a loss is recognized on the income statement.

Intangible assets can also be classified as **identifiable** or **unidentifiable** intangible assets.

Under **IFRS**, identifiable intangible assets must meet three definitional criteria and two recognition criteria.

Definitional criteria:

- They must be identifiable. This means that they should either be separable from the entity or must arise from legal rights.
- They must be under the company's control.
- They must be expected to earn future economic benefits.

Recognition criteria:

- It is probable that their expected future economic benefits will flow to the entity.
- The cost of the asset can be reliably measured.

An **unidentifiable intangible asset** is one that cannot be purchased separately and may have an indefinite life. The best example of such an asset is goodwill, which arises when one company purchases another and the acquisition price exceeds the fair value of the identifiable (tangible and intangible) assets acquired.

Accounting for an intangible asset depends on the manner of its acquisition.

Intangible Assets Acquired in Situations Other than Business Combinations (e.g., Buying a Patent)

These assets are recorded at their **fair value** when acquired, where the fair value is assumed to equal the purchase price. They are recognized on the balance sheet, and costs of acquisition are classified as *investing* activities on the cash flow statement. If several intangible assets are acquired as a group, the purchase price is allocated to each individual asset based on its fair value.

Companies use a significant degree of judgment to determine fair values of individual intangible assets purchased. Therefore, analysts focus more on the types of intangible assets purchased as opposed to the value assigned to each individual asset. Understanding the types of intangible assets the company is acquiring can offer valuable insight into the company's overall strategy and future potential.

Intangible Assets Developed Internally

These are generally expensed when incurred, but may be capitalized in certain situations. Due to the differences in requirements regarding expensing/capitalizing when it comes to intangible assets developed internally versus those acquired, a company's strategy (developing versus acquiring intangible assets) can significantly impact reported financial ratios.

- A company that develops intangible assets internally will expense costs of development and recognize no related assets, while a firm that acquires intangible assets will recognize them as assets.
- A company that develops intangible assets internally will classify development-related cash outflows under *operating* activities on the cash flow statement, while an acquiring firm will classify these costs under *investing* activities.

Research and Development Costs (R&D)

IFRS requires that expenditures on *research* or during the *research phase* of an internal project be **expensed** rather than capitalized as an intangible asset.

IFRS allows companies to recognize an intangible asset arising from *development* or the *development phase* of an internal project if certain criteria are met, including a demonstration of the technical feasibility of completing the intangible asset and the intent to use or sell the asset.

FRA

Generally speaking, **U.S. GAAP** requires that R&D costs be **expensed** when incurred. However, it does require that certain costs related to *software development* be **capitalized**.

- Costs incurred to develop software for sale are expensed until the product's technological feasibility has been established. Once feasibility has been established, associated development costs are capitalized.
- Costs related directly to the development of software for internal use are also expensed until it is probable that the project will be completed and that the software will be used as intended. After that, related development costs are capitalized.

Note the following:

- The probability of "the project being completed" is easier to establish than "technological feasibility".
- The involvement of subjective judgment in determining technological feasibility means that capitalization practices vary to a significant extent across companies.
- Capitalized costs related directly to developing software for sale of internal use include the cost of employees who help build and test the software.
- The treatment of software development costs under **U.S. GAAP** is similar to the treatment of all costs of internally developed intangible assets under **IFRS**.

Expensing rather than capitalizing development costs results in:

- *Lower* net income in the current period.
- *Lower* operating cash flow and higher investing cash flow in the current period.

Note that if current period software development costs exceed amortization of prior periods' capitalized development costs, net income would be *lower* under expensing. If, however, software development expenditures were to slow down such that current year expenses are lower than amortization of prior periods' capitalized costs, net income would be *higher* under expensing.

Intangible Assets Acquired in a Business Combination

When a company acquires another company, the transaction is accounted for using the acquisition method (under both **IFRS** and **U.S. GAAP**). Under this method, if the purchase price paid by the acquirer to buy a company exceeds the fair value of its net assets, the excess is recorded as **goodwill**.

Goodwill is an intangible asset that cannot be identified separately from the business as a whole.

- Only goodwill created in a business acquisition can be recognized on the balance sheet; internally generated goodwill cannot be capitalized.

Under **IFRS**, acquired intangible assets are classified as identifiable intangible assets if they meet the definitional and recognition criteria that we listed earlier. If an item acquired does not meet these criteria and cannot be recognized as a tangible asset, it is recognized as a part of goodwill.

Under **U.S. GAAP**, an intangible asset acquired in a business combination should be recognized separately from goodwill if:

- The asset arises from legal or contractual rights; or
- The item can be separated from the acquired company.

Examples of intangible assets treated separately from goodwill include intangible assets like patents, copyrights, franchises, licenses and internet domain names.

Analyst Adjustments for Variation in Capitalization Practices Across Companies

Adjustments must be made to compare the financial performance of a company that expenses software development costs with that of a peer company that capitalizes these costs. For the company that capitalizes software development costs, an analyst should make the following adjustments:

- The income statement for the current period should include related software development costs as an expense and exclude amortization of development costs capitalized in prior periods.
- The capitalized asset should be removed from the balance sheet (decrease assets and equity).
- Operating cash flow should be reduced and investing cash flow should be increased by the amount of development costs that have been capitalized in the current period.
- Ratios that include income, long-lived assets, or cash flow from operations should be recalculated using adjusted values.

DEPRECIATION METHODS AND CALCULATION OF DEPRECIATION EXPENSE

The Cost Model

The **cost model** is required under **U.S. GAAP** and permitted under **IFRS**. Under this model, the cost of long-lived tangible assets (except land) and intangible assets with finite useful lives is allocated over their useful lives as depreciation and amortization expense. Under the cost model, an asset's carrying value equals its historical cost minus accumulated depreciation/amortization (as long as the asset has not been impaired).

Straight line depreciation expense

$$\text{Depreciation expense} = \frac{\text{Original cost} - \text{Salvage value}}{\text{Depreciable life}}$$

Double declining balance depreciation

$$\text{DDB depreciation in Year X} = \frac{2}{\text{Depreciable life}} \times \text{BV at the beginning of Year X}$$

Straight Line versus Accelerated Depreciation

All other factors remaining the same, a company that uses the straight-line method to depreciate its assets will report:

- A lower asset turnover ratio during the early years of the asset's use because a lower depreciation charge results in higher net assets.
- Higher operating profit margin in the early years of the asset's use because lower depreciation expense results in higher operating income.
- Higher operating return on assets (ROA) in the early years of the asset's use (due to lower depreciation expense) and lower ROA in later years.

Further, a company that uses an accelerated depreciation method will report an improving asset turnover ratio, operating profit margin, and ROA over time.

Estimates Used for Calculating Depreciation

Assumptions of a *longer* useful life and a *higher* expected residual value result in *lower* annual depreciation expense compared to assumptions of a shorter useful life and a lower salvage value. The subjective nature of these assumptions allows management to manipulate earnings.

Management could significantly write-down the value of long-lived assets and recognize a hefty charge against net income in the current period. While this would depress earnings in the current year, it would allow management to recognize lower annual depreciation expense going forward, inflate profits, and report impressive growth in profitability.

Management could also overstate the useful life and the salvage value of an asset to show impressive profits over the near term, and recognize a significant loss at a later point in time when the asset is eventually retired.

Additional assumptions are required to allocate depreciation expense between cost of goods sold (COGS) and selling, general, and administrative expenses (SG&A). Including a higher proportion of total depreciation expense in COGS lowers the gross profit margin and lowers operation expenses. However, it does not affect the net profit margin.

There are no significant differences between IFRS and U.S. GAAP regarding the definition of depreciation and acceptable depreciation methods. However, **IFRS** requires companies to use the component method of depreciation. Under this method, companies depreciate different components of assets separately (using estimates for each component). Under **U.S. GAAP**, this method is allowed but not widely used.

The Revaluation Model

IFRS allows companies to use the revaluation model or the cost model to report the carrying amounts of noncurrent assets on the balance sheet. Revaluation results in the carrying amount of an asset reflecting its fair value (as long as it can be measured reliably). Under **U.S. GAAP**, only use of the cost model is permitted.

A key difference between the revaluation and the cost model is that revaluation allows for the reported value of the asset to be higher than its historical cost. Under the cost model on the other hand, the reported value of an asset can never exceed its historical cost.

IFRS allows the revaluation model to be used for certain classes of assets and for the cost model to be used for others as long as:

1. The company applies the same model to assets in a particular class (e.g., land and buildings, machinery, factory equipment etc.)
2. Whenever a revaluation is performed, all assets in the particular class must be revalued (to avoid selective revaluation).

The revaluation model may also be used to value intangible assets, but only if an active market for the asset exists where its fair value can be determined.

Under the revaluation model, whether a revaluation affects earnings (net income) depends on whether the revaluation initially increases or decreases the carrying amount of the asset class.

- If a revaluation initially *decreases* the carrying amount of an asset:
  - The decrease in value is recognized as a loss on the income statement.
  - Later, if the value of the asset class increases:
    - The increase is recognized as a gain on the income statement to the extent that it reverses a revaluation loss previously recognized on the income statement against the same asset class.
    - Any increase in value beyond the reversal amount will not be recognized on the income statement, but adjusted directly to equity through the revaluation surplus account.
- If a revaluation initially *increases* the carrying amount of an asset:
  - The increase in value bypasses the income statement and goes directly to equity through the revaluation surplus account.
  - Later, if the value of the asset class decreases:
    - The decrease reduces the revaluation surplus to the extent of the gain previously recognized in the revaluation surplus against the same asset class.
    - Any decrease in value beyond the reversal amount will be recognized as a loss on the income statement.

If an asset is sold or disposed of, any associated revaluation surplus recognized in other comprehensive income is transferred directly to retained earnings.

Considerations for Financial Analysis

Asset revaluations require many considerations for financial statement analysis.

- An increase in the carrying value of depreciable long-lived assets increases total assets and shareholders' equity. Hence, revaluation of assets can be used to reduce reported leverage

FRA

- Asset revaluations that decrease the value of an asset also decrease net income in the year of revaluation. In the year of revaluation, return on assets and return on equity decline. In future years however, the lower values of assets and equity may result in higher ROA and ROE. Further, reversals of downward revaluations also go through income. Managers can then opportunistically time the reversals to manage earnings and increase income.
- If the carrying value of the asset is increased in a revaluation, assets and equity increase, and annual depreciation expense also increases. As a result, performance measures such as ROA and ROE may decline in the future. This is ironic given that an upward revaluation is usually associated with an improvement in the operating capacity of the asset and is beneficial for the company.
- Analysts should also look into who performs asset value appraisals and how often revaluations are recognized.

AMORTIZATION METHODS AND CALCULATION OF AMORTIZATION EXPENSE

Intangible Assets with Finite Lives

Intangible assets with finite useful lives are amortized over their useful lives. This results in the cost of these assets being "matched" with the benefits that accrue from them. Acceptable amortization methods are the same as acceptable depreciation methods. The estimates required to calculate yearly amortization expense for an intangible fixed asset with a finite life are:

- The original value of the intangible asset.
- The residual value at the end of its useful life.
- The length of its useful life.

IMPAIRMENT OF ASSETS

An **impairment** charge is made to reflect the unexpected decline in the fair value of an asset. Impairment recognition has the following effects on a company's financial statements:

- The carrying value of the asset decreases.
- The impairment charge reduces net income.
- Impairment does not affect cash flows because it is a noncash charge.

Impairment of Property, Plant, and Equipment

Companies are required to assess whether there are indications of impairment of property, plant, and equipment at the end of each reporting period. If there are no suggestions of impairment, the asset is not tested for impairment. However, if there are indications of impairment, the recoverable amount of the asset must be measured in order to test the asset for impairment. Indications of impairment include evidence of obsolescence, decrease in demand for the asset's output, and technological advancements.

Under **IFRS**, an asset is considered impaired when its carrying amount exceeds its recoverable amount. The recoverable amount equals the higher of "fair value less costs to sell" and "value in use," where value in use refers to the discounted value of future cash flows expected from the asset. The impairment loss that must be recognized equals the carrying amount minus the recoverable amount.

Under **U.S. GAAP**, determining whether an asset is impaired is different from measuring the impairment loss. An asset is considered impaired when its carrying value exceeds the total value of its undiscounted expected future cash flows (recoverable amount). Once the carrying value is determined to be unrecoverable, the impairment loss is measured as the difference between the asset's carrying amount and its fair value (or the discounted value of future cash flows, if fair value is not known).

Impairment of Intangible Assets with a Finite Life

Intangible assets with finite lives are amortized. These assets are not tested for impairment annually (unlike intangible assets with indefinite lives); they are only tested for impairment upon the occurrence of significant adverse events (e.g., a significant decrease in market price or adverse changes in legal and economic factors). Accounting for impairment of these assets is essentially the same as accounting for impairment of property, plant, and equipment.

Impairment of Intangibles with Indefinite Lives

Goodwill and other intangible assets with indefinite lives are not amortized. They are carried on the balance sheet at historical cost and tested at least annually for impairment. Impairment must be recognized when carrying value exceeds fair value.

Impairment of Long-Lived Assets Held for Sale

A long-lived asset is reclassified (from being an asset "held-for-use") to an asset "held-for-sale" when it is no longer in use and management intends to sell it. These assets are tested for impairment when they are categorized as held-for-sale. If it is found that the carrying value exceeds their fair value less selling costs, an impairment loss is recorded and their carrying value is brought down to fair value less selling costs. Once classified as held-for-sale, these assets are no longer depreciated or amortized by the company.

Reversals of Impairments of Long-Lived Assets

Under **U.S. GAAP**, once an impairment loss is recorded for assets held-for-use, it cannot be reversed. However, for assets held-for-sale, if the fair value of the asset increases subsequent to impairment recognition, the loss can be reversed and the asset's value can be revised upward.

IFRS allows reversal of impairment losses if the value of the asset increases regardless of classification of the asset. Reversal of a previously recognized impairment charge increases reported profits. Note that IFRS only allows reversals of impairment losses. It does not allow the value of the asset to be written up to a value greater than the previous

FRA

carrying amount even if the new recoverable amount is greater than the previous carrying value.

DERECOGNITION

A company **derecognizes** or removes an asset from its financial statements when the asset is disposed of or is not expected to provide any future economic benefits from use or disposal.

Sale of Long-Lived Assets

Gain (loss) on asset disposal = Selling price − Carrying/book value of asset

Carrying/book value = Historical cost − Accumulated depreciation

A gain or loss on the sale of a fixed asset is disclosed on the income statement either as a component of other gains and losses (if the amount is insignificant) or as a separate line item (if the amount is significant). Gains and losses on disposal of fixed assets can also be found on the cash flow statement if prepared using the indirect method. A company may disclose further details about the sale of long-lived assets in the management discussion and analysis (MD&A) section and/or financial statement footnotes.

Long-Lived Assets Disposed of Other than by a Sale

Long-lived assets intended to be disposed of other than by a sale (e.g., abandoned, exchanged for another asset, or distributed to owners in a spin-off) are classified as held for use until disposal. Just like other noncurrent assets held by the company, they continue to be depreciated and tested for impairment until actual disposal.

When an asset is **retired or abandoned**, the company does not receive any cash for it. Assets are reduced by the carrying value of the asset at the time of retirement or abandonment, and a loss equal to the asset's carrying amount is recorded on the income statement.

When an asset is **exchanged** for another asset, the carrying amount of the asset given up is removed from the company's balance sheet, and replaced by the fair value for the asset acquired. Any difference between the carrying amount and the fair value is recognized as a gain or loss on the income statement. Note that the fair value used is the fair value of the asset given up unless the fair value of the asset acquired is more clearly evident. If no reliable measure of fair value exists, the acquired asset is measured at the carrying amount of the asset given up.

In a **spin-off** an entire cash-generating unit of a company is separated into a new entity, with shareholders of the parent company receiving a proportional number of shares in the new company. All the assets of the new entity are removed from the balance sheet of the parent at the time of the spin-off.

PRESENTATION AND DISCLOSURES

Disclosures: Tangible Assets

IFRS

The measurement bases used.

- The depreciation method used.
- Useful lives (or depreciation rate).
- Accumulated depreciation at the beginning and end of the period.
- Restrictions on title.
- Pledges of property as security.
- Contractual agreements to acquire PP&E.
- If the revaluation model is used, the company must disclose:
  - The date of revaluation.
  - Details of fair value determination.
  - The carrying amount under the cost model.
  - Amount of revaluation surplus.

U.S. GAAP

- Depreciation expense for the period.
- The balances of major classes of depreciable assets.
- Accumulated depreciation by major classes or in total.
- General description of depreciation methods used for major classes of depreciable assets.

FRA

Disclosures: Intangible Assets

IFRS

- For each class of intangible assets whether they have a finite or indefinite life.
  - If finite, for each class disclose:
    - The useful life (or amortization rate).
    - The amortization methods used.
    - The gross carrying amount.
    - Accumulated amortization at the beginning and end of the period.
    - Where amortization is included on the income statement.
    - Reconciliation of carrying amounts at the beginning and end of the period.
  - If indefinite:
    - Carrying amount of the asset.
    - Why it is considered to have an indefinite life.
- Restrictions on title.
- Pledges as security.
- Contractual agreement to purchase any intangible assets.
- If the revaluation model is used, the company must disclose:
  - The date of revaluation.
  - Details of fair value determination.
  - The carrying amount under the cost model.
  - Amount of revaluation surplus.

U.S. GAAP

- Gross carrying amounts in total and by major classes of intangible assets.
- Accumulated amortization in total and by major classes of intangible assets.
- Aggregate amortization expense for the period.
- Estimated amortization expense for the next 5 fiscal years.

Disclosures: Impairment

IFRS

- The amounts of impairment losses and reversal of impairment losses recognized in the period.
- Where these impairment losses and reversals are recognized on the financial statements.
- Main classes of assets affected by impairment losses and reversals.
- Events and circumstances that led to these impairment losses and reversals.

U.S. GAAP

- Description of the impaired asset.
- Circumstances that led to impairment.
- The method of fair value determination.
- The amount of impairment loss.
- Where the loss is recognized on the financial statements.

Disclosures about long-lived assets appear throughout the financial statements:

- The balance sheet reports the carrying value of the asset.
- On the income statement, depreciation expense may or may not appear as a separate line item.
- On the cash flow statement:
  - Acquisitions and disposals of fixed assets are found in the investing section.
  - Further, if prepared using the indirect method, depreciation and amortization are shown as separate line item adjustments to net income in the computation of cash flow from operating activities.
- The notes to the financial statements describe the company's accounting methods, estimated useful lives, historical cost by categories of fixed asset, accumulated depreciation, and annual depreciation expense.

Evaluating a Company's Fixed Assets

The higher the fixed asset turnover ratio, the higher the amount of sales a company is able to generate with a given amount of investment in fixed assets, suggesting that the company is operating more efficiently.

Estimated useful life = Gross investment in fixed assets/Annual depreciation expense

Average age of asset = Accumulated depreciation/Annual depreciation expense

Remaining useful life = Net investment in fixed assets/Annual depreciation expense

Asset age ratios help identify older, obsolete assets that might make the firm's operations less efficient. Further, they help forecast future cash flows from investing activities and identify major capital expenditures that the company might need to raise cash for in the future. If the calculated average depreciable life of a company's assets is in line with that of other firms in the industry that use similar equipment, we can conclude that management is not tweaking useful life and salvage value assumptions to manipulate reported profits.

Another popular method for making comparisons across companies is calculating annual capital expenditure as a percentage of depreciation expense.

- A company for whom this ratio is significantly lower than 100% is currently replacing its fixed assets at a rate that is slower than the rate at which they are being depreciated. This might indicate the need for hefty capital expenditure in the future and that further examination of the company's capital expenditure policies is required.
- A company for whom this ratio is close to 100% is replacing its fixed assets at a rate similar to that of their use.

INVESTMENT PROPERTY

IFRS defines investment property as property that is owned (or leased under a finance lease) for the purpose of earning rentals or capital appreciation or both. Investment property differs from long-lived tangible assets (e.g., PP&E) in that investment property is not owner occupied, nor is used for producing the company's products and services.

FRA

Under IFRS, investment property may be valued using either the cost model or the fair value model.

Cost model: This is identical to the cost model used for property, plant, and equipment.

Fair value model: This differs from the revaluation model used for PP&E in the way net income is affected.

- Under the revaluation model, the impact of the revaluation on net income depends on a previously recognized increase or decrease in the carrying amount of the asset.
- Under the fair value model, all changes in the fair value of an asset have an impact on net income.

Further, note that:

- A company is required to use one model (either cost or fair value) for all its investment properties.
- The fair value model may be used only if the company is able to reliably estimate the property's fair value on a continuing basis.
- If a company chooses the fair value model, it must continue to do so until it disposes of the property or changes its use such that it is no longer classified as investment property.

Valuation Issues

- If investment property is valued using the cost model, a move to owner-occupied property or inventory will not lead to a change in the carrying amount of the property.
- If investment property is valued using the fair value model, a move to owner-occupied property or inventory will be made at fair value. The property's fair value will become its new cost for the purpose of ongoing accounting for the property.
- If owner-occupied property is reclassified as investment property (and the owner prefers to use the fair value model), the change in the value from depreciated cost to fair value at the time of transfer is treated like a revaluation.
- If inventory is reclassified as investment property (and the owner prefers to use the fair value model), the difference between the carrying amount and fair value at the time of transfer is recognized as a profit or loss.

Investment property is reported as a separate line item on the balance sheet. Further, companies must disclose which model they have used (cost or fair value) to value the property.

U.S. GAAP does not specifically define investment property. U.S. companies that hold investment property use the historical cost model.

LEASING

A lease is a contract between the owner of the asset (lessor) and another party that wants to use the asset (lessee). The lessee gains the right to use the asset for a period of time in return for periodic lease payments.

Leasing an asset holds the following advantages over purchasing the asset:

- Leases often have fixed interest rates.
- They require no down payment so they conserve cash.
- At the end of the lease the asset can be returned to the lessor so the lessee escapes the risk of obsolescence and is not burdened with having to find a buyer for the asset.
- Operating leases do not require recognition of an asset or a liability on the balance sheet so they improve reported performance and leverage ratios.
- In the U.S., leases can be structured as synthetic leases where the company can gain tax benefits of ownership, while not reflecting the asset on its financial statements.

Leases can be classified as finance or operating leases. A finance lease is similar to purchasing an asset with a loan, while an operating lease is similar to renting the asset for a period of time.

Under **previous international accounting standards**, if substantially all the risks and rewards incidental to ownership are transferred to the lessee, the **lessee** can classify the lease as a finance lease. Otherwise, the lease was reported as an operating lease.

However, under the **new international accounting standard (IFRS 16)**, the **lessee** is required to recognize leases with a term longer than 12 months (other than small asset leases) on the balance sheet, and the lessee can no longer classify a lease as an operating lease. Essentially, both operating and finance leases must be accounted for as finance leases by the lessee.

It is important to note that the **lessor** continues to classify its leases as operating or finance leases under IFRS 16.

Under **previous U.S. GAAP standards**, a lease that meets any one of four specific requirements is classified as a finance lease.

1. The lease transfers ownership of the asset to the lessee at the end of the term.
2. A bargain purchase option exists.
3. The lease term is greater than 75% of the asset's useful economic life.
4. The present value of the lease payments at inception exceeds 90% of the fair value of the leased asset.

However, the **proposed new accounting standard** (ASC Topic 842) requires the lessee to recognize a liability for its lease obligation (initially measured at the present value of the future lease payments not yet paid over the lease term), and an asset for its right to use the underlying asset equal to the lease liability, adjusted for lease payments made at or before lease commencement, lease incentives, and any initial direct costs.

LESSEE'S PERSPECTIVE

Operating Lease

The accounting treatment for an operating lease is similar to that of renting an asset for a period of time. The asset is not purchased; instead annual payments are made for using it.

Under an operating lease, no lease-related entries are made on the balance sheet. The firm has not purchased the asset so there is no addition to fixed assets, and it has not borrowed any money to finance the purchase, so there is no related liability.

Accounting entries at inception

Balance sheet: None because no asset or liability is recognized.

Income statement: None because the asset has not been used yet.

Statement of cash flows: None because there has been no cash transaction.

Accounting entries every year during the lease term

Balance sheet: None because there are no lease-related assets and liabilities.

Income statement: Leasehold (rental) expense is charged every year.

Statement of cash flows: The lease-related expense is classified as a cash outflow from operating activities.

Capital or Finance Lease

A finance lease requires the company to recognize a lease-related asset and liability at inception. The accounting treatment for a finance lease is similar to that of purchasing an asset and financing the purchase with a long-term loan.

Accounting entries at inception

Balance sheet: The present value of lease payments is recognized as a long-lived asset. The same amount is also recognized as a long-term liability.

Income statement: None because the asset has not been used yet.

Statement of cash flows: None because no cash transaction has occurred. Disclosure of lease inception is reported as a "significant noncash financing and investing activity."

Accounting entries every year during the term of the lease

Balance sheet: The value of the asset falls every year as it is depreciated. Interest is charged on the liability (discount rate multiplied by the beginning-of-period liability). The excess of the lease payment over the year's interest expense reduces the liability.

Income statement: Depreciation expense (against the asset) and interest expense (on the liability) are charged every year.

Statement of cash flows: The portion of the lease payment attributable to interest expense is deducted from CFO, while the remainder that serves to reduce the liability is subtracted from CFF.

Finance versus operating Lease: Lessee's perspective

Income Statement Item	Finance Lease	Operating Lease
Operating expenses	Lower	Higher
Non-operating expenses	Higher	Lower
EBIT (operating income)	Higher	Lower
Total expenses—early years	Higher	Lower
Total expenses—later years	Lower	Higher
Net income—early years	Lower	Higher
Net income—later years	Higher	Lower

Balance Sheet Item	Capital Lease	Operating Lease
Assets	Higher	Lower
Current liabilities	Higher	Lower
Long term liabilities	Higher	Lower
Total cash	Same	Same

CF Item	Capital Lease	Operating Lease
CFO	Higher	Lower
CFF	Lower	Higher
Total cash flow	Same	Same

Ratio	Numerator under Finance Lease	Denominator under Finance Lease	Effect on Ratio	Ratio Better or Worse under Finance Lease
Asset turnover	Sales—same	Assets—higher	Lower	Worse
Return on assets*	Net income—lower	Assets—higher	Lower	Worse
Current ratio	Current assets—same	Current liabilities—higher	Lower	Worse
Leverage ratios (D/E and D/A**)	Debt—higher	Equity—same Assets—higher	Higher	Worse
Return on equity*	Net income—lower	Equity—same	Lower	Worse

*In early years of the lease agreement.

Note: Lower ROE under a finance lease is due to lower net income (numerator effect), while lower ROA is primarily due to higher assets (denominator effect).

FRA

LESSOR'S PERSPECTIVE

Lessors are required to recognize finance leases when any one of the four previously defined criteria for recognizing finance leases by lessees hold, and the following two criteria also hold:

1. Collectability of the lease payments is predictable.
2. There are no significant uncertainties regarding the amount of costs still to be incurred by the lessor under the provisions of the lease agreement.

Leases not meeting the above criteria must be classified as operating leases because the earnings process is not complete, or the risks and benefits of the leased assets have not been transferred.

- If the lessor classifies the lease as an operating lease, it records lease revenue when earned, continues to list the asset on its balance sheet, and depreciates it every year on its income statement. In this case, the lessee does not record a lease-related long-lived asset on its balance sheet.
- If the lessor classifies the lease as a finance lease, it records a receivable equal to the present value of lease payments on its balance sheet, and removes the asset from long-lived assets in its books. In this case, the lessee records a lease-related long-lived asset.

Direct Financing Leases

Financial institutions and leasing companies offer financial leases that generate interest income only. These are known as direct financing leases, where the present value of lease payments equals the carrying value of the asset. In direct financing leases, no gross profits are recognized.

Direct Financing versus operating Leases: Lessor's perspective

	Financing Lease	Operating Lease
Total net income	Same	Same
Taxes (early years)	Higher	Lower
Total CFO	Lower	Higher
Total CFI	Higher	Lower

Sales type Leases

Some manufacturers offer their customers financing options to purchase their products. These sales-type leases include a gross profit (the normal selling price of the product minus the carrying value), which is recognized at inception of the lease, and interest income as payments are received over a period of time. In a sales-type lease, the present value of lease payments equals the selling price of the asset, which is higher than the cost or carrying value of asset.

FRA

Disclosures

Under **U.S. GAAP**, lease disclosures require a company to list the lease obligations of the firm for the next five years under all operating and finance leases. These disclosures allow analysts to evaluate the extent of off-balance sheet financing used by the company. They can also be used to determine the effects on the financial statements if all the operating leases were capitalized and brought "on to" the balance sheet.

Under IFRS, future payments are disclosed for the first year, in aggregate for years two through five, and then aggregate for all subsequent years.

Summary of Financial Statement Impact of Leases on the Lessee and Lessor

Lessee	Balance Sheet	Income Statement	Statement of cash Flows
Operating Lease	No effect	Reports rent expense	Rent payment is an operating cash outflow
Finance Lease under IFRS (capital lease under U.S. GAAP)	Recognizes leased asset and lease liability	Reports depreciation expense on leased asset	Reduction of leased liability is a financing cash outflow

Lessor			
Operating Lease	Retains asset on balance sheet	Reports rent income	Rent payments received are an operating cash inflow
Finance Lease*			
When present value of lease payments equals the carrying amount of the leased asset (called a direct financing lease in U.S. GAAP)	Removes asset from balance sheet. Recognizes lease receivable.	Reports interest revenue on lease receivable	Interest position of lease payment received is either an operating or investing cash inflow under IFRS and an operating cash inflow under U.S. GAAP. Receipt of lease principal is an investing cash inflow.**
When present value of lease payments exceeds the carrying amount of the leased asset (called a sales-type lease in U.S. GAAP)	Removes asset. Recognizes lease receivable.	Reports profit on sale. Reports interest revenue on lease receivable.	Interest position of lease payment received is either an operating or investing cash inflow under IFRS and an operating cash inflow under U.S. GAAP. Receipt of lease principal is an investing cash inflow.**

*U.S GAAP distinguishes between a direct finance lease and a sales-type lease, but IFRS does not. The accounting is the same for IFRS and U.S. GAAP despite this additional classification under U.S. GAAP.

**If providing leases is part of a company's normal business activity, the cash flows related to the leases are classified as operating cash.

INCOME TAXES
Cross-Reference to CFA Institute Assigned Reading #29

The tax return is prepared to calculate taxes payable to the authorities. Taxes payable result in an outflow of cash from the firm, so firms try to minimize taxes payable and retain cash. This objective is achieved by recognizing *higher* expenses on the tax return, which leads to *lower* taxable income and consequently, *lower* taxes payable.

Financial statements are prepared to report the company's operating performance over the year to shareholders, financial institutions and other stakeholders. For financial reporting purposes, companies try to show healthy performance and profitability. This objective is achieved by recognizing *lower* expenses on the income statement, which leads to *higher* pretax income, and (despite *higher* income tax expense) *higher* net income than on the tax return.

- The **tax base** of an asset or liability is the amount that is recognized on the balance sheet for tax purposes.
- The **carrying value** is the amount recognized on the balance sheet for financial reporting.

Determining the Tax Base of an Asset

An asset's tax base is the amount that will be expensed on the income statement in the future as the economic benefits are realized from the asset. For example, if the historical cost of the asset is $10,000, and $4,000 worth of accumulated depreciation has already been charged against it on *tax returns* over previous years, the asset's tax base equals $6,000. This amount will be depreciated in future periods (expensed on the tax return) as the asset is utilized over its remaining life (economic benefits of the asset are realized).

The carrying value of the asset is simply the historical cost of the asset minus the accumulated depreciation charged against over previous years on the company's *financial statements*.

Determining the Tax Base of a Liability

Two types of liabilities can result from accrual accounting; unearned revenues and accrued expenses. The *carrying value* of these liabilities is the amount recognized on the balance sheet in the financial statements. The rules for calculating the *tax base* of liabilities are given below:

1. Tax base of accrued *expense* liability = Carrying amount of the liability on the balance sheet (financial reporting) minus amounts that have **not** been expensed for tax purposes yet; but **can** be expensed (are tax-deductible) in the future.
2. The tax base of unearned *revenue* liability = Carrying value of the liability minus the amount of revenue that **has already been taxed**, and therefore, will **not** be taxed in the future.

Deferred Tax Liabilities

A deferred tax liability usually arises when:

- *Higher* expenses are charged on the tax return as compared to the financial statements.
- Taxable income is *lower* than pretax or accounting profit.
- Taxes payable are *lower* than income tax expense.
- An asset's tax base is *lower* than its carrying value.

Accounting Entries for an Increase in Deferred Tax Liabilities

- Any *increase* in deferred tax liabilities **increases total liabilities** on the balance sheet.
- The increase in deferred tax liabilities is added to taxes payable in the calculation of income tax expense, so it decreases net income, retained earnings and **reduces owners' equity**.

Deferred Tax Assets

A deferred tax asset usually arises when:

- *Higher* expenses are charged on the financial statements than on the tax return.
- Taxable income is *higher* than pretax or accounting profit.
- Taxes payable are *higher* than income tax expense.
- A liability's tax base is *lower* than its carrying value.

Accounting Entries for an Increase in Deferred Tax Assets

- Any *increase* in deferred tax assets **increases total assets** on the balance sheet.
- The increase in deferred tax assets is subtracted from taxes payable in the calculation of income tax expense, so it **increases net income, retained earnings and equity**

Effects of Changes in Tax Rates

When tax rates *rise*, the balances of both deferred tax assets and liabilities *rise*. When tax rates *fall*, the balances of both deferred tax assets and liabilities fall.

$$\boxed{\text{Income tax expense} = \text{Taxes payable} + \text{Change in DTL} - \text{Change in DTA}}$$

- If a company has a net DTL (excess of DTL over DTA), a reduction in tax rates would *reduce* liabilities, *reduce* income tax expense, and *increase* equity.
- If the company has a net DTA (excess of DTA over DTL), a reduction in tax rates will *reduce* assets, *increase* income tax expense, and *decrease* equity.
- If a company has a net DTL, an increase in tax rates would *increase* liabilities, *increase* income tax expense, and *reduce* equity.
- If the company has a net DTA, an increase in tax rates will *increase* assets, *decrease* income tax expense, and *increase* equity.

FRA

Temporary versus Permanent Differences

- Temporary differences arise because of differences between the tax base and carrying amounts of assets and liabilities.
- Permanent differences are differences between tax and financial reporting of revenues and expenses that *will not* reverse at any point in the future. Examples of the items that give rise to permanent differences include:

1. Revenue items that are not taxable.
2. Expense items that are not tax deductible.
3. Tax credits for some expenses that directly reduce taxes.

The important thing to remember is that permanent differences do not result in deferred taxes. They result in a difference between effective and statutory tax rates and should be considered in the analysis of effective tax rates. A firm's reported effective tax rate is given by:

$$\text{Effective tax rate} = \frac{\text{Income tax expense}}{\text{Pretax income}}$$

Temporary differences can be divided into two categories:

Taxable temporary differences

Taxable temporary differences result in deferred tax liabilities. They are expected to result in future taxable income. Deferred tax liabilities arise when:

- The carrying amount of an asset *exceeds* its tax base; or
- The carrying amount of a liability is *less* than its tax base.

Deductible temporary differences

Deductible temporary differences result in deferred tax assets. They are expected to provide tax deductions in the future. Deferred tax assets arise when:

- The tax base of an asset *exceeds* its carrying amount; or
- The tax base of a liability is *less* than its carrying amount.

Treatment of Temporary Differences

Balance Sheet Item	Carrying Value vs. Tax Base	Results in...
Asset	Carrying amount is greater.	DTL
Asset	Tax base is greater.	DTA
Liability	Carrying amount is greater.	DTA
Liability	Tax base is greater.	DTL

Temporary Differences at Initial Recognition of Assets and Liabilities

In some situations, the carrying value and tax base of certain assets and liabilities may not be equal at initial recognition. In such circumstances (even though the tax base and the carrying amount of the item are different) a company cannot recognize deferred tax assets or liabilities.

In a business combination, if the fair value of acquired intangible assets (including goodwill) is different from their carrying amounts, deferred taxes can be recognized.

With regards to investments in subsidiaries, branches, associates and interests in joint ventures, deferred tax liabilities can be recognized unless:

- The parent is in a position to control the timing of the future reversal of the temporary difference, and
- It is probable that the temporary difference will not reverse in the future.

While deferred tax assets will only be recognized if:

- The temporary difference will reverse in the future, and
- Sufficient taxable profits exist against which the temporary difference can be used.

Unused Losses and Tax Credits

Under IFRS, unused tax losses and credits may only be recognized to the extent of probable future taxable income against which these can be applied. On the other hand, under U.S. GAAP, deferred tax assets are recognized in full and then reduced through a valuation allowance if they are unlikely to be realized. A company that has a history of tax losses may be unlikely to earn taxable profits in the future against which it can apply deferred tax assets.

Recognition and Measurement of Current and Deferred Tax

Current taxes are based on the tax rates applicable at the balance sheet date. Deferred taxes on the other hand, are measured at the rate that is expected to apply when they are realized (when the temporary differences that gave rise to them reverse).

FRA

Even though deferred tax assets and liabilities arise from temporary differences that are expected to reverse at some point in the future, present values are not used in determining the amounts to be recognized. Deferred taxes should always be recognized unless they pertain to:

- Taxes or deferred taxes charged directly to equity.
- A possible provision for deferred taxes relates to a business combination.

Even if there has been no change in temporary differences during the current period, the carrying amount of DTA and DTL may change due to:

- Changes in tax rates.
- Reassessments of recoverability of DTA.
- Change in expectations as to how the DTA or DTL will be realized.

Valuation Allowance

Deferred tax assets must be evaluated at each balance sheet date to ensure that they will be recovered. If there are any doubts regarding their realization, their carrying value should be reduced to the expected recoverable amount. Doubts regarding realization of deferred tax assets may stem from the expectation of insufficient future taxable income to recover the tax assets (prepaid taxes).

DTA are reduced by creating a contra-asset account known as the valuation allowance. An increase in the valuation allowance reduces deferred tax assets. The negative change in deferred tax assets causes an increase in income tax expense. Higher income tax expense translates into lower net income, retained earnings and equity. Subsequently, if the likelihood of realizing deferred tax assets increases, the previous reduction in DTA is reversed by reducing the valuation allowance.

Recognition of Current and Deferred Tax Charged Directly to Equity

Under both IFRS and U.S. GAAP, deferred tax assets and liabilities should generally have the same accounting treatment as the assets and liabilities that give rise to them. If the item that gave rise to the deferred tax asset/liability be taken directly to equity, the resulting deferred tax item should also be taken directly to equity.

A deferred tax liability should be reduced if it is not expected to reverse. The amount by which it is reduced should be taken directly to equity.

Comparison of IFRS and U.S. GAAP

	IFRS	U.S. GAAP
ISSUE SPECIFIC TREATMENTS		
Revaluation of fixed assets and intangible assets.	Recognized in equity as deferred taxes.	Revaluation is prohibited.
Treatment of undistributed profit from investment in subsidiaries.	Recognized as deferred taxes except when the parent company is able to control the distribution of profits and it is probable that temporary differences will not reverse in future.	No recognition of deferred taxes for foreign subsidiaries that fulfill indefinite reversal criteria. No recognition of deferred taxes for domestic subsidiaries when amounts are tax-free.
Treatment of undistributed profit from investments in joint ventures.	Recognized as deferred taxes except when the investor controls the sharing of profits and it is probable that there will be no reversal of temporary differences in future.	No recognition of deferred taxes for foreign corporate joint ventures that fulfill indefinite reversal criteria.
Treatment of undistributed profit from investments in associates.	Recognized as deferred taxes except when the investor controls the sharing of profits and it is probable that there will be no reversal of temporary differences in future.	Deferred taxes are recognized from temporary differences.
DEFERRED TAX MEASUREMENT		
Tax rates.	Tax rates and tax laws enacted or substantively enacted.	Only enacted tax rates and tax laws are used.
Deferred tax asset recognition.	Recognized if it is probable that sufficient taxable profit will be available in the future.	Deferred tax assets are recognized in full and then reduced by a valuation allowance if it is likely that they will not be realized.
DEFERRED TAX PRESENTATION		
Offsetting of deferred tax assets and liabilities.	Offsetting allowed only if the entity has right to legally enforce it and the balance is related to a tax levied by the same authority.	Same as in IFRS.
Balance sheet classification.	Classified on balance sheet as net noncurrent with supplementary disclosures.	Classified as either current or noncurrent based on classification of underlying asset and liability.

FRA

NON-CURRENT (LONG-TERM) LIABILITIES
Cross-Reference to CFA Institute Assigned Reading #30

A bond is a contract between a borrower and a lender that obligates the borrower to make payments to the lender over the term of the bond. Two types of payments are usually involved-periodic interest payments and principal repayments.

Accounting for Financing Liabilities

The effective interest method results in a constant rate of interest over the life of the bond. It is required under IFRS and preferred under U.S. GAAP. Under this method, the market interest rate at issuance is applied to the carrying amount of the bonds to determine periodic interest expense. Further, the difference between interest expense and the actual coupon payment equals the amount of discount/premium amortized over the period.

The straight-line method, which is also permitted under U.S. GAAP, evenly amortizes the premium or discount over the life of the bond (similar to straight-line depreciation).

The par or face value is the amount that the borrower has to pay back at the maturity of the bond. It does not necessarily equal the amount that the issuer receives upon issuing debt.

The coupon rate is multiplied by the par value of the bond to compute the periodic coupon payment.

Market interest rates are used to value bonds. These rates incorporate various types of risks inherent in the bond, and must not be confused with coupon rates. Market interest rates change frequently.

- To value a company's debt obligations at a particular point in time, we discount the remaining payments at current market interest rates.
- For accounting purposes, under the effective interest method, the book value of the liability recognized on a firm's balance sheet upon debt issuance equals the present value of its obligations discounted at *market interest rates at issuance*.
- Market interest rates at issuance determine how much the company receives in bond proceeds.
    - If market interest rates equal the bond's coupon rate, the bond will be issued at par.
    - If the market interest rate is *greater* than the coupon rate, the bond will be issued at a *discount*.
    - If the market interest rate is *lower* than the coupon rate, the bond will be issued at *a premium*.

Interest Expense versus Coupon Payment

- Interest expense (under the effective interest method) for a given period is calculated as the book value of the liability at the beginning of the period multiplied by market interest rates at issuance. Interest expense is charged every year on the *income statement*.

- Coupon payments are calculated as the coupon rate times the par value of the bonds. Coupon payments are classified as outflows from operating activities on the *cash flow statement*.

Effects of Issuing a Par Bond on Financial Statements

Balance sheet: The year end value of the liability is listed on the balance sheet. For bonds issued at par, the liability balance remains at par throughout the life of the bond.

Income statement: Interest expense is deducted from operating profits. For bonds issued at par, interest expense equals the coupon payment, and is constant over the life of the bond.

Statement of cash flows:

- At issuance, the bond proceeds are reported as inflows from financing activities.
- During the term of the bond, coupon payments (not interest expense) are deducted from CFO.
- At maturity, cash used to repay the principal amount (par value) is deducted from CFF.

For bonds issued at par the inflows recorded at issuance under CFF equal the outflows at maturity from CFF. Coupon payments are deducted from CFO every year.

Effects of Issuing a Discount Bond on Financial Statements

Balance sheet: The liability increases over the life of the bond as the discount is amortized over the term of the bond. The value of the liability at bond maturity equals par.

Income statement: Interest expense rises each year in line with the increasing balance of the liability.

Statement of cash flows: Inflows recorded at issuance under CFF are lower than outflows at maturity from CFF. Coupon payments are deducted from CFO every year.

Effect of Issuing a Premium Bond on Financial Statements

Balance sheet: The liability decreases over the life of the bond as the premium is amortized over the term of the bond. The value of the liability at maturity equals par.

Income statement: Interest expense declines every year in line with the decreasing balance of the liability.

Statement of cash flows: Inflows recorded at issuance under CFF are greater than the outflows at maturity from CFF. Coupon payments are deducted from CFO every year.

Important Shortcuts

- Interest expense over the term of the bond can also be calculated as all the issuer's outflows over the life of the bond (coupon payments plus principal repayment) minus the inflows received at issuance (bond proceeds).

FRA

- To determine the book value of the liability at any point in time simply compute the present value of the bond's remaining cash flows discounting them at market interest rates at issuance.

IFRS versus U.S. GAAP

- The **effective interest** method is *required* under IFRS and *preferred* under U.S. GAAP because it accurately reflects the economics of the transaction. U.S. GAAP also permits use of the **straight-line method** of amortization, which evenly amortizes the premium or discount over the life of the bond.
- Printing costs, legal fees and other charges are incurred when debt is issued. Under IFRS, these costs are included in the measurement of the liability. Under U.S. GAAP, companies used to capitalize these costs and write them off over the bond's term on a straight-line basis. However, U.S. GAAP now requires that debt issuance costs be deducted from the related debt liability. Debt issuance costs for lines of credit may still be treated as an asset.
- U.S. GAAP requires interest payments on bonds to be classified under cash flows from operations. IFRS allows more flexibility in that classification of interest payments as CFO or CFF is permitted.
- Amortization of the bond discount/premium is a non-cash item so it has no effect on cash flows (aside from the effect on taxable income). In the reconciliation of net income to operating cash flow, amortization of a discount (premium) is added back to (deducted from) net income.

Fair Value Reporting Option

When a company uses the effective interest method to amortize bond discounts and premiums, the book value of debt is based on market interest rates at issuance. Over the life of the bonds, as market interest rates fluctuate, the actual value of the firm's debt deviates from its reported book value. For example, if interest rates rise, the current market value of debt would fall. The reported book value of debt (based on the market interest rates at issuance) would be *higher* than the true economic value of the firm's obligations. In this case, using the book value will *overstate* leverage levels as the firm is actually better off than its financial statements indicate.

Recently, companies have been allowed to report financing liabilities at fair value. Companies that choose to report their financing liabilities at fair value report gains (losses) when market interest rates increase (decrease) as the carrying value of their obligations (liabilities) falls (rises).

If fair values are not explicitly reported on the financial statements, IFRS and U.S. GAAP both require companies to disclose the fair value of their financing liabilities. An analysis of a company could be materially affected if the company's reported carrying amount of debt (based on amortized cost) is significantly different from the fair value of its liabilities.

Derecognition of Debt

A company may leave the bonds that it issues outstanding until maturity or retire them prior to maturity by either purchasing them from the open market or calling them (if a call provision exists). If the company leaves the bonds outstanding until maturity, it pays investors the par value of the bonds at maturity.

However, if the company decides to retire the bonds prior to maturity, the book value of the liability is reduced to zero and a gain or loss on extinguishment is computed by subtracting the amount paid to retire the bonds from their book value.

- Under **U.S. GAAP**, because issuance costs are capitalized, any unamortized issuance costs must also be subtracted from gains on extinguishment.
- Under **IFRS**, issuance costs are included in the book value of the liability so there is no need to adjust the gain on extinguishment for these expenses.

Financial Statement Presentation of and Disclosures Relating to Debt

On the balance sheet, long-term liabilities are listed as one aggregate figure for all liabilities due after one year. Liabilities due within one year are included in short-term liabilities (current liabilities). Financial statement footnotes usually include:

- Stated and effective interest rates.
- Maturity dates.
- Restrictions imposed by creditors (covenants).
- Pledged collateral.
- Scheduled repayments over the next five years.

More information regarding a firm's debt and off balance-sheet financing sources can be found in the MD&A section.

Leases

A lease is a contract between the owner of the asset (lessor) and another party that wants to use the asset (lessee). The lessee gains the right to use the asset for a period of time in return for periodic lease payments.

Leasing an asset holds the following advantages over purchasing the asset:

- Leases often have fixed interest rates.
- They require no down payment so they conserve cash.
- At the end of the lease the asset can be returned to the lessor so the lessee escapes the risk of obsolescence and is not burdened with having to find a buyer for the asset.
- Operating leases do not require recognition of an asset or a liability on the balance sheet so they improve reported performance and leverage ratios.
- In the U.S., leases can be structured as synthetic leases where the company can gain tax benefits of ownership, while not reflecting the asset on its financial statements.

Finance or Capital Lease versus Operating Lease

Leases may be classified as finance leases (or capital leases) and operating leases. The classification of the lease has important implications for the financial statements of both the lessee and lessor. In essence:

- A finance (capital) lease is equivalent to a transaction where the lessee purchases an asset from the lessor with the lessor directly financing the transaction.
- An operating lease equivalent to the lessee renting the asset for a period of time from the lessor.

Under the existing IFRS standard (IAS 17), the classification of a lease depends on the transfer of the risks and rewards incidental to ownership of the leased asset.

- If substantially all the risks and rewards are transferred to the **lessee**, the lessee classifies the lease as a finance lease, where it reports a leased asset and lease obligation on its balance sheet. Otherwise, the lease is reported as an operating lease, in which case the lessee reports neither an asset nor a liability, only a periodic lease expense.
- Similarly, if the **lessor** transfers substantially all the risks and rewards, the lessor classifies the lease as a finance lease, where it reports a lease receivable on its balance sheet and removes the leased asset from its balance sheet. Otherwise, the lease is reported as an operating lease, where the lessor keeps the leased asset on its balance sheet.

A new IFRS standard for accounting for leases (IFRS 16) is applicable for financial years beginning 1 January 2019. IFRS 16 defines a lease as "a contract, or part of a contract, that conveys the right to use an asset (the underlying asset) for a period of time in exchange for consideration." In essence, IFRS 16 requires lessees to record both finance and operating leases as finance leases with assets and associated liabilities on the lessee's balance sheet.

U.S. GAAP is guided by a similar principle of the transfer of benefits and risks, and is more prescriptive in its criteria for classifying capital and operating leases. Under U.S. GAAP, a **lessee** may recognize a lease as a capital lease when any one of the following criteria hold:

1. Ownership of the leased asset transfers to the lessee at the end of the lease.
2. The lease contains an option for the lessee to purchase the leased asset cheaply (bargain purchase option).
3. The lease term is 75% or more of the useful life of the leased asset.
4. The present value of lease payments is 90% or more of the fair value of the leased asset.

On the **lessor** side, satisfying at least one of these four criteria plus meeting revenue recognition requirements (cash collection is reasonably assured and the lessor has performed substantially under the lease) allow recognition of a capital lease.

LESSEE's PERSPECTIVE

Operating Lease

The accounting treatment for an operating lease is similar to that of renting an asset for a period of time. The asset is not purchased; instead annual payments are made for using it.

Under an operating lease, no lease-related entries are made on the balance sheet. The firm has not purchased the asset so there is no addition to fixed assets, and it has not borrowed any money to finance the purchase, so there is no related liability.

Following the introduction of IFRS 16, all contracts meeting the criteria of a lease are classified as finance leases by the lessee, whereas the lessor continues to classify leases as either financial or operating.

FRA

Accounting entries at inception

Balance sheet: None because no asset or liability is recognized.

Income statement: None because the asset has not been used yet.

Statement of cash flows: None because there has been no cash transaction.

Accounting entries every year during the lease term

Balance sheet: None because there are no lease-related assets and liabilities.

Income statement: Leasehold (rental) expense is charged every year.

Statement of cash flows: The lease-related expense is classified as a cash outflow from operating activities.

Capital or Finance Lease

A finance lease requires the company to recognize a lease-related asset and liability at inception. The accounting treatment for a finance lease is similar to that of purchasing an asset and financing the purchase with a long-term loan.

Accounting entries at inception

Balance sheet: The present value of lease payments is recognized as a long-lived asset. The same amount is also recognized as a long-term liability.

Income statement: None because the asset has not been used yet.

Statement of cash flows: None because no cash transaction has occurred. Disclosure of lease inception is reported as a "significant noncash financing and investing activity."

Accounting entries every year during the term of the lease

Balance sheet: The value of the asset falls every year as it is depreciated. Interest is charged on the liability (discount rate multiplied by the beginning-of-period liability). The excess of the lease payment over the year's interest expense reduces the liability.

Income statement: Depreciation expense (against the asset) and interest expense (on the liability) are charged every year.

Statement of cash flows: The portion of the lease payment attributable to interest expense is deducted from CFO, while the remainder that serves to reduce the liability is subtracted from CFF.

FRA

Finance versus Operating Lease: Lessee's Perspective

Income Statement Item	Finance Lease	Operating Lease
Operating expenses	Lower	Higher
Nonoperating expenses	Higher	Lower
EBIT (operating income)	Higher	Lower
Total expenses—early years	Higher	Lower
Total expenses—later years	Lower	Higher
Net income—early years	Lower	Higher
Net income—later years	Higher	Lower

Balance Sheet Item	Capital Lease	Operating Lease
Assets	Higher	Lower
Current liabilities	Higher	Lower
Long term liabilities	Higher	Lower
Total cash	Same	Same

CF Item	Capital Lease	Operating Lease
CFO	Higher	Lower
CFF	Lower	Higher
Total cash flow	Same	Same

Ratio	Numerator under Finance Lease	Denominator under Finance Lease	Effect on Ratio	Ratio Better or Worse under Finance Lease
Asset turnover	Sales—same	Assets—higher	Lower	Worse
Return on assets*	Net income lower in early years	Assets—higher	Lower	Worse
Current ratio	Current assets-same	Current Liabilities—higher	Lower	Worse
Leverage ratios (D/E and D/A)	Debt—higher	Equity same Assets higher	Higher	Worse
Return on equity*	Net income lower in early years	Equity same	Lower	Worse

* In early years of the lease agreement.

LESSOR's PERSPECTIVE

Lessors are required to recognize finance leases when any one of the four previously defined criteria for recognizing finance leases by lessees hold, and the following two criteria also hold:

1. Collectability of the lease payments is predictable.
2. There are no significant uncertainties regarding the amount of costs still to be incurred by the lessor under the provisions of the lease agreement.

Leases not meeting the above criteria must be classified as operating leases because the earnings process is not complete, or the risks and benefits of the leased assets have not been transferred.

- If the lessor classifies the lease as an operating lease, it records lease revenue when earned, continues to list the asset on its balance sheet, and depreciates it every year on its income statement. In this case, the lessee does not record a lease-related long-lived asset on its balance sheet.
- If the lessor classifies the lease as a finance lease, it records a receivable equal to the present value of lease payments on its balance sheet, and removes the asset from long-lived assets in its books. In this case, the lessee records a lease-related long-lived asset.

Direct Financing Leases

Financial institutions and leasing companies offer financial leases that generate interest income only. These are known as *direct financing leases*, where the present value of lease payments equals the *carrying value* of the asset. In direct financing leases no gross profits are recognized.

Direct Financing versus Operating Leases: Lessor's Perspective

	Direct Financing Lease	Operating Lease
Total net income	Same	Same
Taxes (early years)	Higher	Lower
Total CFO	Lower	Higher
Total CFI	Higher	Lower

Sales Type Leases

Some manufacturers offer their customers financing options to purchase their products. These *sales-type* leases include a gross profit (the normal selling price of the product minus the carrying value), which is recognized at inception of the lease, and interest income as payments are received over a period of time. In a sales-type lease the present value of lease payments equals the *selling price* of the asset, which is *higher* than the cost or carrying value of asset.

Under IFRS, if a lessor enters into a finance lease, the lessor reports a receivable at an amount equal to the net investment in the lease (calculated as the present value of the minimum lease payments receivable plus the present value of the estimated salvage value). The leased asset is derecognized—assets are reduced by the carrying amount of the leased asset. The lease payment is treated as repayment of principal (reduces lease receivable) and finance income. The recognition of finance income should reflect a constant periodic rate of return on the lessor's net investment in the lease. Remember that under the new IFRS on lease accounting (IFRS 16), lessors continue to recognize leases as either finance or operating leases in a similar manner to current standards.

FRA

Summary of Financial Statement Impact of Leases on the Lessee and Lessor

Lessee	Balance Sheet	Income Statement	Statement of Cash Flows
Operating Lease	No effect	Reports rent expense	Rent payment is an operating cash outflow
Finance Lease under IFRS (capital lease under U.S. GAAP)	Recognizes leased asset and lease liability	Reports depreciation expense on leased asset. Reports interest expense on lease liability	Reduction of lease liability is a financing cash outflow. Interest portion of lease payment is either an operating, or financing cash outflow under IFRS and an operating cash outflow under U.S. GAAP.

Lessor			
Operating Lease	Retains asset on balance sheet	Reports rent income. Reports depreciation expense on leased asset	Rent payments received are an operating cash inflow.
Finance Lease[a]			
When present value of lease payments equals the carrying amount of the leased asset (called a direct financing lease in U.S. GAAP)	Removes asset from balance sheet. Recognizes lease receivable	Reports interest revenue on lease receivable	Interest portion of lease payment received is either an operating or investing cash inflow under IFRS and an operating cash inflow under U.S. GAAP. Receipt of lease principal is an investing cash inflow.[b]
When present value of lease payments exceeds the carrying amount of the leased asset (called a sales-type lease in U.S. GAAP)	Removes asset Recognizes lease receivable	Reports profit on sale. Reports interest revenue on lease receivable	Interest portion of lease payment received is either an operating, or investing cash inflow under IFRS and an operating cash inflow under U.S. GAAP. Receipt of lease principal is an investing cash inflow.[b]

[a]U.S. GAAP distinguishes between a direct financing lease and a sales-type lease, but IFRS does not. The accounting is the same for IFRS and U.S. GAAP despite this additional classification under U.S. GAAP.
[b]If providing leases is part of a company's normal business activity, the cash flows related to the leases are classified as operating cash.

Pensions

Defined contribution plans are pension plans in which the company contributes a certain amount of funds into the plan. Accounting for defined contribution plans is quite straightforward.

- On the income statement, the company recognizes the amount it is required to contribute into the plan as pension expense for the period.
- On the balance sheet, the company records a decrease in cash. If the agreed upon amount is not deposited into the plan during a particular period, the outstanding amount is recognized as a liability.
- On the cash flow statement, the outflow is treated as an operating cash flow.

Under a **defined benefit plan**, the company promises to make future payments to the employee during retirement. For example, a company could promise an employee annual pension payments equal to 60% of her final salary at retirement until death. A number of assumptions are made to determine the total amount that must be paid to the employee during retirement, including:

- Expected salary at date of retirement
- Number of years of retirement

The company estimates the amount of benefits it will pay out to an employee during retirement and then allocates the present value of these payments (known as pension obligation) over the employment term of the employee as a part of pension expense.

1. The service cost for an employee over a period refers to the present value of the increase in pension benefits earned by the employee over the year (as a result of her service to the company).
2. Interest costs are added to pension expense because the company does not pay out service costs earned by the employee over the year until her retirement. The company owes these benefits to the employee so interest accrues on the amount of benefits outstanding.
3. Companies make pension payments into a pension trust fund. The assets in this fund are invested until funds are required to make payments. The expected return on these investments is subtracted from other pension costs to determine pension expense for a particular period. In order to reduce the volatility in reported pension expense, companies are allowed to use the expected return on plan assets instead of the actual return on plan assets in the calculation of pension expense for the period. However, if the difference between expected return and actual return is significant, companies are required to amortize a portion of the difference into pension expense.
4. Actuarial gains and losses arise due to changes in the assumptions used for calculating pension expense (e.g., employee turnover, mortality rates, and compensation increases).
5. Prior service costs arise due to changes in promised benefits.

FRA

Evaluating Solvency Ratios

Solvency refers to the ability of a company to satisfy its long term debt obligation (both principal and interest payments). Ratio analysis is frequently used to evaluate a company's solvency levels relative to its competitors. The two main types of solvency ratios used are leverage ratios and coverage ratios.

Leverage ratios are derived from balance sheet numbers and measure the extent to which a company uses debt rather than equity to finance its assets. Higher leverage ratios indicate weaker solvency.

Coverage ratios focus more on income statement and cash flow numbers to measure the company's ability to service its debt. Higher coverage ratios indicate stronger solvency.

Solvency Ratios	Description	Numerator	Denominator
Leverage Ratios			
Debt-to-assets ratio	Expresses the percentage of total assets financed by debt	Total debt	Total assets
Debt-to-capital ratio	Measures the percentage of a company's total capital (debt + equity) financed by debt	Total debt	Total debt + Total shareholders' equity
Debt-to-equity ratio	Measures the amount of debt financing relative to equity financing	Total debt	Total shareholders' equity
Financial leverage ratio	Measures the amount of total assets supported by one money unit of equity	Average total assets	Average shareholders' equity
Coverage Ratios			
Interest coverage ratio	Measures the number of times a company's EBIT could cover its interest payments	EBIT	Interest payments
Fixed charge coverage ratio	Measures the number of times a company's earnings (before interest, taxes and lease payments) can cover the company's interest and lease payments	EBIT + Lease payments	Interest payments + Lease payments

FRA

STUDY SESSION 9:
FINANCIAL REPORTING AND ANALYSIS (4)

FINANCIAL REPORTING QUALITY
Cross-Reference to CFA Institute Assigned Reading #31

Financial reporting quality refers to the usefulness of information contained in the financial reports, including disclosures in notes.

- High-quality reporting provides information that is useful in investment decision-making in that it is relevant and faithfully represents the company's performance and position.

Earnings quality (or quality of reported results) pertains to the earnings and cash generated by the company's core economic activities and its resulting financial condition.

- High-quality earnings (1) come from activities that the company will be able to sustain in the future and (2) provide an adequate return on the company's investment.
- Note that the term, earnings quality, encompasses quality of earnings, cash flow, and balance sheet items.

Relationship between Financial Reporting Quality and Earnings Quality

		Financial Reporting Quality	
		Low	**High**
Earnings (Results) Quality	High	LOW financial reporting quality impedes assessment of earnings quality and impedes valuation.	HIGH financial reporting quality enables assessment. HIGH earnings quality increases company value.
	Low		HIGH financial reporting quality enables assessment. LOW earnings quality decreases company value.

QUALITY SPECTRUM OF FINANCIAL REPORTS

GAAP, decision-useful, sustainable, and adequate returns: These are high-quality reports that provide useful information about high-quality earnings.

GAAP, decision-useful, but sustainable? This level refers to a situation where reporting is of high quality, but earnings are either inadequate or unsustainable.

Within GAAP, but biased accounting choices: Biased choices result in financial reports that do not faithfully represent the company's true economic situation.

- Management can make aggressive or conservative accounting choices, both of which go against the concept of neutrality as **unbiased** financial reporting is the ideal.

FRA

- Earnings smoothing results from employing conservative assumptions to understate performance when the company is actually doing well and then using aggressive assumptions when the company is not doing as well.
- Biases can also creep into the way information is presented. A company may choose to present information in a manner that obscures unfavorable information and/or highlights favorable information.

Within GAAP, but "earnings management": Earnings can be managed by taking real actions or through accounting choices. Note that it is typically very difficult to determine intent so there is a very fine line between earnings management and biased accounting choices.

Departures from GAAP Non-Compliant Accounting: Financial information that deviates from GAAP is obviously of low quality. Further, such financial information cannot be used to assess earnings quality as comparisons with other entities or earlier periods cannot be made.

Departures from GAAP Fictitious Transactions: Companies may use fictitious transactions to (1) fraudulently obtain investments by inflating company performance, or (2) to obscure fraudulent misappropriation of company assets.

Conservative versus Aggressive Accounting

When it comes to financial reporting, the ideal situation would be if financial reporting were unbiased, i.e., neither conservative nor aggressive.

- Aggressive choices can (1) increase reported revenues, (2) increase reported earnings, (3) increase reported operating cash flow, (4) decrease reported expenses, and/or (5) decrease reported debt in the current period.
  - Aggressive accounting choices in the current period may create a sustainability issue.
- Conservative choices can (1) decrease reported revenues, (2) decrease reported earnings, (3) decrease reported operating cash flow, (4) increase reported expenses, and/or (5) increase reported debt in the current period.
  - Conservative accounting choices do not give rise to a sustainability issue.

Conservatism in Accounting Standards

Despite efforts to encourage neutrality in financial reporting, some conservatively biased standards remain. Further, different sets of accounting standards may have different degrees of conservatism embedded in them.

Bias in the Application of Accounting Standards

In order to characterize the application of an accounting standard as conservative or aggressive, we must look at *intent* (rather than at a definition). Intent can be inferred from a careful analysis of disclosures, facts, and circumstances. Examples of biased accounting disguised as conservatism include:

- Big bath behavior: **This refers to the strategy of manipulating a company's income statement to make poor results look even worse. The big bath is often implemented in a bad year with a view to inflating subsequent period earnings. New management teams sometime use the big bath so that poor current performance can be blamed on previous management, while they take credit for the impressive growth that follows in subsequent periods.**
- Cookie jar reserve accounting: **This refers to the practice of creating a liability when a company incurs an expense that cannot be directly linked to a specific accounting period. Companies may recognize such expenses in periods during which profits are high as they can afford to take the hit to income, with a view to reducing the liability (the reserve) in future periods during which the company may struggle. The practice results in smoothing of income over time.**

CONTEXT FOR ASSESSING FINANCIAL REPORTING QUALITY

In assessing financial reporting quality, it is important to consider (1) whether a company's management may be motivated to issue financial reports that are not of high quality, and (2) whether the reporting environment is conducive to misreporting.

Motivations for Issuing Low-Quality Financial Reports

- To mask poor performance.
- To meet or beat analyst's forecasts or management's own forecasts.
  - Equity market effects **refer to management trying to build credibility with market participants and to positively impact the company's stock price.**
  - Trade effects **refer to management trying to improve the company's reputation with customers and suppliers.**
- To address managers' concerns regarding their careers.
- To avoid debt covenant violations.

Conditions Conducive to Issuing Low-Quality Financial Reports

- Opportunity: **Poor internal controls, an ineffective board of directors, or accounting standards that allow divergent choices and/or provide minimal consequences for inappropriate choices can give rise to opportunities for management to issue low-quality financial reports.**
- Motivation: **Motivation to issue low-quality financial reports can come from personal reasons (e.g., increasing bonus payments) or corporate reasons (e.g., alleviating concerns about being able to raise funds in the future).**
- Rationalization: **This is important because individuals need to justify their choices to themselves.**

MECHANISMS THAT DISCIPLINE FINANCIAL REPORTING QUALITY

- Markets
- Regulatory authorities
- Registration requirements
  - Disclosure requirements
  - Auditing requirements
  - Management commentaries
  - Responsibility statements
  - Regulatory review of filings
  - Enforcement mechanisms
- Auditors
- Private contracting

DETECTION OF FINANCIAL REPORTING QUALITY ISSUES

Presentation Choices

- Under the pretext of assisting investors in evaluating operating performance, struggling companies may (conveniently) exclude restructuring charges in pro forma measures of financial performance.
- Due to investors' focus on EBITDA, companies may come up with their own definitions of EBITDA (sometimes referring to it as adjusted EBITDA) which may exclude certain expenses.
- Companies may use non-GAAP measures to distract users from GAAP measures. US GAAP and IFRS have both moved to pacify these concerns.

Accounting Choices and Estimates

Revenue Recognition

- Sometimes management may be pushing shipments out the door (channel stuffing) under FOB shipping point arrangements in order to maximize revenue recognized in the current accounting period.
  - If the ratio of accounts receivable to revenues is abnormally high relative to the company's history or its peers, there is a chance that channel stuffing has occurred.
- At other times, for shipments towards the end of the reporting period, management may set shipping terms as FOB destination. Management may engage in this practice if there was an overabundance of orders during the current period, and it does not want investors/analysts to get too optimistic.
- A company can reduce its allowance for sales returns as a proportion of sales to reduce expenses and increase profits.
  - Analysts should examine whether the company's actual collection experience has tended to be different from historical provisioning in order to assess the accuracy of the company's provisioning policies.

- If a company participates in "bill-and-hold" transactions, it is possible that it is recognizing fictitious sales by reclassifying end-of-period inventory as "sold but held" through minimal effort and fake documentation.
- If the company uses rebates as part of its marketing approach, changes in estimates of rebate fulfillment can be used to manipulate reported revenues and profitability (similar to allowance for sales returns).
- Companies can use changes in depreciation estimates (useful life and salvage value) and depreciation methods to manipulate reported earnings and profits.
  - If the company has recorded significant asset write-downs in the recent past, it may suggest that the company's policies relating to asset lives need to be examined.
- Management may try to capitalize costs that ought to be recorded as expenses to increase reported income.
  - Management may use low fair value estimates for assets acquired in an acquisition in order to depress future depreciation expense and inflate future profitability.
  - In order to determine the fair value of goodwill, forecasts of future financial performance must be made, and these projections may be biased upward to avoid a goodwill write-down.
  - Analysts should also examine how the company's capitalization policies compare with the competition, and determine whether its amortization policies are reasonable.
- Analysts should determine how a company's inventory methods compare with others in its industry.
  - If the company uses reserves for obsolescence in its inventory valuation, unusual fluctuations in this reserve might suggest that the company is manipulating them to attain a desired level of earnings.
  - If a company uses LIFO in an inflationary environment, it can temporarily increase reported profits through LIFO liquidation.
- Analysts must evaluate whether the company's estimate of the valuation allowance (against deferred tax assets) is reasonable given its current operating environment and future prospects. Specifically they should:
  - Determine whether there are contradictions between the management commentary and the allowance level, or the tax note and the allowance level.
  - Look for changes in the tax asset valuation account.
- Analysts should examine whether warranty reserves have been manipulated to meet earnings targets. Further, the trend in actual costs relative to amounts allocated to reserves should be assessed as it can offer insight into the quality of products sold.
- If the company engages in extensive dealings with related parties, those entities could be used to absorb losses (e.g., through supply arrangements that are unfavorable to the non-public company) in order to improve the public company's reported performance.

FRA

Choices that Affect the Cash Flow Statement

- Management may try to delay payments to creditors (stretch out payables) until after the balance sheet date, so that the increase in accounts payable over the period (source of cash) results in an increase in cash generated from operations. In order to detect this issue, analysts could:
  - Examine changes in working capital to look for unusual patterns that may indicate manipulation of cash provided from operations.
  - Compare the company's cash generation with the cash operating performance of its competitors.
  - Compare the relationship between cash generated from operations and net income. Analysts should be concerned if cash generated from operations is less than net income, as it may suggest that accounting estimates are being used to inflate net income.
- A company may misclassify uses of operating cash flow into the investing or financing section of the cash flow statement to inflate cash generated from operating activities.
- In certain areas where investors may not even be aware that choices exist (e.g., amortization of discount/premium on capitalized interest), accounting standards offer companies the flexibility to manage cash generated from operations to a certain extent.

ACCOUNTING WARNING SIGNS

Warning Signs Related to Revenue

Analysts should:

- Determine whether company policies make it easy to prematurely recognize revenue by allowing use of FOB shipping point shipping terms and bill-and-hold arrangements.
- Determine whether a significant portion of revenues come from barter transactions (which are difficult to value properly).
- Evaluate the impact of estimates relating to the company's rebate programs on revenue recognition.
- Look for sufficient clarity regarding revenue recognition practices relating to each item or service delivered under multiple-deliverable arrangements of goods and services.
- Determine whether the company's revenue growth is in line with its competitors, the industry, and the overall economy.
- Determine whether receivables are increasing as a percentage of sales. This may suggest channel-stuffing activities or even recognition of fictitious sales.
- Determine whether there are any unusual changes in the trend in receivables turnover and seek an explanation for any changes.
- Compare the company's receivables turnover (or DSO) with competitors and look out for suggestions that revenues have been recognized prematurely, or that the provision for doubtful accounts is insufficient.
- Examine asset turnover.

- If post-acquisition revenue generation is weak, management may try to play with estimates to increase reported revenue in order to be able to justify their strategic choices.
- If asset turnover is trending lower, or if it lags the asset turnover of competitors, it may signal future asset write-downs by the company.

Warning Signs Related to Inventories

Analysts should:

- Compare growth in inventories with competitors and industry benchmarks. If inventory levels are increasing with no accompanying increase in sales, it could suggest (1) poor inventory management or (2) inventory obsolescence. In case of the latter, current profitability and inventory value would be overstated.
- Compute the inventory turnover ratio. Declining inventory turnover could also suggest inventory obsolescence.
- Check for inflated profits through LIFO liquidations (only applicable for firms using LIFO).

Warning Signs Related to Capitalization Policies and Deferred Costs

- Analysts should examine the company's accounting policy notes for its capitalization policy for long-term assets (including interest costs) and for its handling of other deferred costs and compare those policies with industry practice.

Warning Signs Related to the Relationship between Cash Flow and Income

If a company's net income is persistently higher than cash provided by operations, it raises the possibility that aggressive accrual accounting policies have been used to shift current expenses to later periods.

- Analysts may consider constructing a time series of cash generated by operations divided by net income. If the ratio is consistently below 1.0, or has declined consistently, there may be problems in the company's accrual accounts.

Other Potential Warning Signs

- Depreciation methods and useful life estimates that are inconsistent with peer companies.
- Fourth-quarter surprises.
- Presence of related-party transactions.
- Non-operating income and one-time sales included in revenue.
- Classification of an expense as non-recurring.
- Gross/operating margins out of line with competitors or industry.
- Younger companies with an unblemished record of meeting growth projections.
- Management has adopted a minimalist approach to disclosure.
- Management fixation on earnings reports.
- Significant restructuring and/or impairment charges.
- Management has a merger and acquisition orientation.

FRA

FINANCIAL STATEMENT ANALYSIS: APPLICATIONS
Cross-Reference to CFA Institute Assigned Reading #32

Evaluating Past Financial Performance

Analysts should focus on:

- Important changes that have occurred in corporate measures of profitability, efficiency, liquidity and solvency and the reasons behind these changes.
- Comparisons of ratios with firms from the same industry, and the reasons behind any differences.
- Examination of performance aspects that are critical for a company to successfully compete in the industry, and a comparison of the company's performance on these fronts with that of competitors.
- The company's business model and strategy, and how it influences operating performance.

Projecting Performance

The **top-down approach** that is typically used to forecast sales involves the following steps:

- Attain forecasts for the economy's expected GDP growth rate.
- Use regression models to determine the historical relationship between the economy's growth rate and the industry's growth rate.
- Undertake market share analysis to evaluate whether the firm being analyzed is expected to gain, lose or retain its market share over the forecasting horizon.

Once a forecast for sales has been established, earnings and cash flows can be estimated.

- Estimate gross profit margins over the forecasting horizon. Net profit margins are affected by leverage ratios and tax rates, so historical data provides a more reliable measure for gross profit margins. This model tends to be simpler and works well for mature companies that operate in non-volatile markets.
- Make separate forecasts for individual expense items, aggregate them, and subtract the total from sales to calculate net income. This is a very subjective exercise as each expense item must be projected based on a relationship with sales or some other relevant variable.

The most important things that an analyst needs to consider when forecasting cash flows are:

- Required increases in working capital.
- Capital expenditures on new fixed assets.
- Repayment and issuance of debt.
- Repurchase and issuance of stock (equity).

Assessing Credit Risk

Credit analysis involves evaluation of the 4 "C's" of a company.

- Character refers to the quality of management.
- Capacity deals with the ability of the issuer to fulfill its obligations.
- Collateral refers to the assets pledged to secure a loan.
- Covenants are limitations and restrictions on the activities of issuers.

The four general categories of items considered in credit analysis are:

- Scale and diversification of the business.
- Operational efficiency.
- Stability and sustainability of profit margins.
- Degree of financial leverage.

Screening is the process of filtering a set of potential investments into a smaller set by applying a set of criteria. Ratios computed from the information in financial statements and market data are used to screen potential equity investments.

Growth versus Value Investors

Growth investors invest in those companies that are expected to see higher earnings growth in the future. A growth investor would set screens like high price-to-cash flow ratios, and sales growth exceeding 20% over the last three years.

Value investors try to pay a low price relative to a company's net asset value or earning prowess. A value investor might set screens like a higher-than-average ROE, and a lower-than-average P/E ratio to shortlist equity investments that suit her style.

Back-Testing

Analysts evaluate how a portfolio based on particular screens would have performed historically through the process of *back-testing*. This method applies the portfolio selection rules to historical data and calculates returns that would have been realized had particular screens been used. Back-testing has its limitations in that it suffers from:

- Survivorship bias.
- Look-ahead bias.
- Data-snooping bias.

Analyst Adjustments to Reported Financials

Adjustments related to investments: Investments in securities issued by other companies can be classified under different categories. Unrealized gains and losses on securities classified as "available-for-sale" are not recorded on the income statement. Changes in their values are reflected in "other comprehensive income" as a part of equity on the balance sheet. Changes in the value of "trading" securities are recorded on the income statement and have an impact on reported profits. If an analyst is comparing two firms with significant differences in the classification of investments, adjustments for the different financial statement impact of the classifications will be necessary.

Adjustments related to inventory: A LIFO company's financial statements need to be adjusted before comparisons with FIFO firms can be undertaken. Important accounts affected by conversion from LIFO to FIFO are net income, retained earnings, inventory, COGS and deferred taxes.

FIFO to LIFO Conversions

$$EI_{FIFO} = EI_{LIFO} + LIFO\ reserve$$

$$COGS_{FIFO} = COGS_{LIFO} - (LR_{ending} - LR_{beginning})$$

During a period of rising prices:

- Net income after tax under FIFO will be greater than LIFO net income after tax by:
  Change in LIFO reserve × (1 − tax rate)

- Equity (retained earnings) under FIFO will greater by:
  LIFO reserve × (1 − tax rate)

- Liabilities (deferred taxes) under FIFO will be greater by:
  LIFO reserve × (tax rate)

- Current assets (inventory) under FIFO will be greater by:
  LIFO reserve

The calculations of estimated useful life, average age, and remaining useful life are important because:

- They help identify older, obsolete assets that might make the firm's operations less efficient.
- They help forecast future cash flows from investing activities and identify major capital expenditures that the company might need to raise cash for in the future.

Adjustments related to property, plant and equipment: A company that uses accelerated depreciation methods and shorter estimated life assumptions for long-lived assets will report lower net income than a firm that employs longer useful life assumptions and uses straight-line depreciation. Depreciation and net fixed asset values must be assessed and necessary adjustments must be made to bring sets of financial statements on the same footing before making comparisons.

$$Estimated\ useful\ life = \frac{Gross\ investment\ in\ fixed\ assets}{Annual\ depreciation\ expense}$$

$$Average\ age\ of\ asset = \frac{Accumulated\ depreciation}{Annual\ depreciation\ expense}$$

$$\text{Remaining useful life} = \frac{\text{Net investment in fixed assets}}{\text{Annual depreciation expense}}$$

Adjustments related to goodwill: Goodwill is recognized when the price paid for an acquisition exceeds the fair value of its net assets. A company that grows via acquisitions will have higher reported assets and a greater book value than a company that grows internally. Analysts must remove the inflating effect of goodwill on book values and rely on the price-to-tangible book value ratio to make comparisons.

Adjustments related to off-balance sheet financing: Bringing off-balance sheet items "on to" the balance sheet decreases return on assets and increases leverage ratios.

FRA

STUDY SESSION 10:
CORPORATE FINANCE (1)

CORPORATE GOVERNANCE AND ESG: AN INTRODUCTION
Cross-Reference to CFA Institute Assigned Reading #33

Corporate governance is defined as the system of internal controls and procedures through which individual companies are managed. It aims to minimize and manage conflicts of interest between those within the company and stakeholders. A **stakeholder** is any person or group that has an interest in the company. Not all stakeholders' interests are aligned in the same manner, and they often conflict with each other.

Key Stakeholders

- **Shareholders** own shares of stock in a corporation and are entitled to certain rights, such as the right to receive dividends and the right to vote on certain corporate issues. They are typically focused on those efforts that support growing the profitability of the company and maximizing its value.
- **Creditors** have little influence on the company, other than covenants and restrictions they can put in place as its banks or bondholders.
- **Employees** have a significant stake in the company's operation, as they are paid salaries and wages as well as other incentives and perquisites for their work.
- The **board of directors** acts in the best interests of the shareholders who elect them.
- **Customers** would like a product that is a good value for the price and is safe to operate.
- Company **suppliers** have a goal of being paid for their services and materials.
- The **government and regulators** wish to protect the economy and the interests of the general public.

Key Relationships in Corporate Governance

Shareholder and manager/director relationships. Although they are agents of shareholders, managers and directors may take advantage of information asymmetries to take more risk than warranted to maximize personal benefit.

Controlling and minority shareholders. Controlling groups may behave in a manner that does not maximize value for minority shareholders (e.g., during voting on takeover offers, during related-party transactions, etc.).

Manager and board relationships. If management provides only limited information to the directors, the board's ability to effectively monitor the business is reduced.

Shareholder versus creditor interests. Shareholders may look for additional risk for greater return, while creditors look for stability and lower risk.

Other stakeholder conflicts. Conflicts may arise between customers and shareholders (e.g., product safety), between customers and suppliers (e.g., when the company extends lenient terms of credit to customers), and between the government and shareholders (e.g., if the government raises company taxes).

CF

Stakeholder Management

The foundations of stakeholder management frameworks are constructed from the various legal, contractual, organizational, and governmental components that define the rights, responsibilities, and powers of each group.

- The legal infrastructure lays out the framework of rights established by law as well as the ease or availability of legal recourse.
- The contractual infrastructure is the means used to secure the rights of both parties through contractual agreements between the company and its stakeholders.
- The way the company manages its stakeholder relationships through its governance procedures, internal systems, and practices is the organizational infrastructure.
- The regulations imposed on the company are considered the governmental infrastructure.

Mechanisms to Manage Stakeholder Relationships and Mitigate Associated Risks

- General meetings
- Board of directors
- Audit function
- Reporting and transparency
- Remuneration policies
- Say on pay
- Contractual agreements with creditors
- Employee laws and contracts
- Contractual agreements with customers and suppliers
- Laws and regulations

The Board of Directors

The board of directors monitors management and the strategic direction of the company while reporting to shareholders.

The board plays an active role in managing the company through managers, who are given the responsibility for day-to-day operations of the company. The board establishes milestones for the company based on the strategic direction it oversees. In monitoring progress, the board selects, appoints, and terminates the employment of senior management.

The board also establishes committees to aid in the oversight of key functions. Common committees are the following:

- Audit committee
- Governance committee
- Remuneration committee
- Nomination committee
- Risk committee
- Investment committee

Factors That Affect the Stakeholder Relationship and Corporate Governance

Market Factors

- Shareholder engagement. The transparency and information sharing from frequent engagement with shareholders tend to increase support for management and to reduce the potential for efforts by shareholders to more actively pursue other means to influence outcomes.
- Shareholder activism. Activism by shareholders involves more forceful paths to increase shareholder value. Examples include lawsuits, raising public awareness, and proxy battles.
- Competition and takeovers. Corporate takeovers can take the form of proxy contests, tender offers, or hostile takeovers.

Non-Market Factors

- The legal environment. Generally speaking, around the world, creditors enjoy better-protected positions compared to shareholders.
- Media. Increasingly, the media (especially social media) can influence stakeholder relationships.
- The corporate governance industry. External corporate governance services increasingly exert significant influence. Thus, corporations pay attention to their ratings and change their behavior if necessary.

Risks of Poor Corporate Governance and Stakeholder Management

- Weak control systems
- Ineffective decision-making
- Legal, regulatory, and reputational risks
- Default and bankruptcy risks

Benefits of Effective Governance

- Operational efficiency
- Improved control
- Better operating and financial performance
- Lower default risk and cost of debt

Analysis of Corporate Governance and Stakeholder Management

Key areas of interest are:

- Economic ownership and voting control. Dual-class companies tend to trade at a discount to their peers.
- Board of directors representation. Generally speaking, well-diversified, diverse, and skilled boards are desirable.
- Remuneration and company performance. It is important that compensation programs align with shareholders.

- Investors in the company. Concentrated holdings can dictate how the company is run. Further, a significant number of activist investors may force the company to focus on the short term.
- Strength of shareholders' rights. Ideally, shareholders would like the power to remove board members and convene special stockholder meetings.
- Managing long-term risks. It is desirable for the company to have healthy stakeholder relations and for management to be able to deal effectively with long-term risks.

Environmental and Social Considerations in Investment Analysis

Environmental, social, and governance (ESG) integration refers to the use of environmental and social factors alongside corporate governance in the investment process. Both sustainable investing (SI) and responsible investing (RI) utilize ESG in their investment processes.

Socially responsible investing (SRI) limits investments in companies whose products are contrary to the ethical and moral values of an investor, such as weapons and tobacco. Impact investing seeks to meet specific social and environmental goals with identifiable financial returns.

ESG Factors in Investment Analysis

Environmental issues have various financial risks for companies. Stranded assets (also referred to as carbon assets) face the risk of no longer being economically viable because of changes in regulations or investor sentiment. Material events that impact the environment can be costly in terms of legal and regulatory issues, such as fines and litigation. They very well may include clean-up costs as well as reputational costs.

Societal issues can be very broad, including issues within the workplace, human rights, and welfare. They can also include the impact on the community.

Implementation of ESG Mandates

Negative screening is used to exclude certain sectors as defined by the investor, such as fossil fuels, companies with human rights or environmental issues, or companies that do not align with religious or personal beliefs.

Positive screening and best-in-class approaches focus on including investments with favorable ESG aspects.

Thematic investing is utilized when a strategy is implemented using only one factor to evaluate companies relative to ESG criteria.

CAPITAL BUDGETING
Cross-Reference to CFA Institute Assigned Reading #34

Capital budgeting is used to determine whether long-term investments such as acquiring new machinery, replacing current machinery, launching new products, and spending on research and development, are worth pursuing.

Steps in Capital Budgeting

- Generating ideas.
- Analyzing individual proposals.
- Planning the capital budgeting.
- Monitoring and post-auditing.

Categories of Capital Projects

- Replacement projects.
- Expansion projects.
- New products and services.
- Regulatory/safety and environmental projects.
- Other projects.

Important Definitions

Sunk costs are those costs that cannot be recovered once they have been incurred. Capital budgeting ignores sunk costs as it is based only on current and future cash flows. Example of sunk costs are the market research costs incurred by the company to evaluate whether a new product should be launched.

Opportunity cost is the value of the next best alternative that is *foregone* in making the decision to pursue a particular project. Opportunity costs should be *included* in project costs.

An incremental cash flow is the additional cash flow realized as a result of a decision. Incremental cash flow equals cash flow with a decision minus cash flow without the decision.

An externality is the effect of an investment decision on things other than the investment itself. Externalities can be positive or negative and, if possible, externalities should be considered in investment decision-making. An example of a negative externality is *cannibalization* as new products reduce sales of existing products of the company.

A conventional cash flow stream is a cash flow stream that consists of an initial outflow followed by a series of inflows. The sign of the cash flows changes only once. For a nonconventional cash flow pattern, the initial outflow is not followed by inflows only, but the direction of the cash flows can change from positive to negative again.

Basic Principles of Capital Budgeting

1. **Decisions are based on actual cash flows:** Only incremental cash flows are relevant to the capital budgeting process, while sunk costs are completely ignored. Analysts must also attempt to incorporate the effects of both positive and negative externalities into their analysis.
2. **Timing of cash flows is crucial:** Analysts try to predict exactly when cash flows will occur, as cash flows received earlier in the life of the project are worth more than cash flows received later.
3. **Cash flows are based on opportunity costs:** Projects are evaluated on the incremental cash flows they bring in over and above the amount that they would generate in their next best alternative use (opportunity cost).
4. **Cash flows are analyzed on an after-tax basis.**
5. **Financing costs are ignored from calculations of operating cash flows.** Financing costs are reflected in the required rate of return from an investment project, so cash flows are not adjusted for these costs.
6. **Accounting net income is not used as cash flows for capital budgeting** because accounting net income is subject to noncash charges (e.g., depreciation) and financing charges (e.g., interest expense).

Interactions between Projects

- **Independent versus mutually exclusive projects:** Independent projects are those whose cash flows are unrelated. Mutually exclusive projects compete directly with each other for acceptance.
- **Project sequencing:** Sometimes projects may only be undertaken in a certain order, so investing in one project creates the opportunity to invest in other projects in the future.
- **Unlimited funds versus capital rationing:** If the capital required to invest in all profitable projects exceeds resources available, the company must allocate funds to only the most lucrative projects to ensure that shareholder wealth is maximized.

INVESTMENT DECISION CRITERIA

Net Present Value (NPV)

A project's NPV equals the present value of all expected inflows minus the present value of all expected outflows. The rate used to discount each cash flow is the project's cost of capital.

- A project should be undertaken if its NPV is greater than zero. Positive NPV projects increase shareholder wealth.
- Projects with a negative NPV decrease shareholder wealth and should not be undertaken.
- A project with an NPV of zero has no impact on shareholder wealth.

Internal Rate of Return (IRR)

For an investment project that requires only one investment outlay that is made at inception, IRR is the discount rate that equates the sum of the present values of future after-tax cash flows to the initial investment outlay. Alternatively, IRR is the discount rate that equates the sum of present values of all after-tax cash flows for a project (inflows and outflows) to zero. Therefore, IRR is the discount rate at which NPV equals zero.

- A company should invest in a project if its IRR is *greater* than the required rate of return. When the IRR is greater than the required return, NPV is positive.
- A company should not invest in a project if its IRR is *less* than the required rate of return. When the IRR is lower than the required return, NPV is negative.

Payback Period

A project's payback period equals the time it takes for the initial investment for the project to be recovered through after-tax cash flows from the project. All other things being equal, the best investment is the one with the shortest payback period.

Advantages

- It is simple to calculate and explain.
- It can also be used as an indicator of *liquidity*. A project with a shorter payback period may be more liquid than one that has a longer payback period.

Drawbacks

- It ignores the time value of money and the risk of the project. Cash flows are *not* discounted at the project's required rate of return.
- It ignores cash flows that occur after the payback period is reached.
- It is not a measure of profitability so it cannot be used in isolation to evaluate capital investment projects. The payback period should be used along with the NPV or IRR to ensure that decisions reflect the overall profitability of the project being considered.

Discounted Payback Period

The discounted payback period equals the number of years it takes for cumulative *discounted* cash flows from the project to equal the initial outlay. A project's discounted payback period will always be *greater* than its payback period because the payback period does not discount the cash flows.

Advantage

- It accounts for the time value of money and risks associated with the project's cash flows.

Drawback

- It ignores cash flows that occur after the payback period is reached. Therefore, it does not consider the overall profitability of the project.

Average Accounting Rate of Return (AAR)

The AAR is the ratio of the project's average net income to its average book value.

Advantage

- It is easy to understand and easy to calculate.

Drawbacks

- It is based on accounting numbers and not cash flows. Accounting numbers are more susceptible to manipulation than cash flows.
- It does not account for time value of money.
- It does not differentiate between profitable and unprofitable investments accurately as there are no benchmarks for acceptable AARs.

Profitability Index

The profitability index (PI) of an investment equals the present value (PV) of a project's future cash flows divided by the initial investment. Therefore, the PI is the *ratio* of future discounted cash flows to the initial investment. NPV is the *difference* between future discounted cash flows and the initial investment. The PI indicates the value that a company receives in exchange for one unit of currency invested. It is also known as the "benefit-cost" ratio.

- A company should invest in a project if its PI is *greater* than 1. The PI is greater than 1 when NPV is positive.
- A company should not invest in a project if its PI is *less* than 1. The PI is less than 1 when NPV is negative.

NPV Profiles

An NPV profile is a graphical illustration of a project's NPV at different discount rates. NPV profiles are downward-sloping because as the cost of capital increases, the NPV of an investment falls.

- The discount rate at which the NPVs of two projects are the same (their NPV profiles intersect) is called the *crossover* rate.
- A project's NPV profile intersects the x-axis at its IRR.

CF

NPV versus IRR

For independent projects, the NPV and IRR criteria for acceptance lead to the same result:

- Accept the project if NPV is greater than zero.
- Accept the project if IRR is greater than the cost of capital.

For mutually exclusive projects, NPV and IRR may offer different recommendations. In such a situation, a company should select the project with the *higher NPV*. NPV is a better criterion because of its more realistic reinvestment rate assumption.

- IRR assumes that interim cash flows received during the project are reinvested at the IRR. This assumption is sometimes rather inappropriate—especially for projects with high IRRs.
- NPV makes a more realistic assumption that interim cash flows are reinvested at the required rate of return.

NPV and IRR may give conflicting project rankings because of *differences in project size* and *cash flow timing differences*.

Problems with the IRR

It is possible for a project's cash flow stream to have no IRR or even multiple IRRs. This may occur even though the project has a positive NPV.

Popularity of Capital Budgeting Techniques

- The payback method is very popular in European countries.
- Larger companies prefer the NPV and IRR methods over the payback method.
- Private corporations use the payback period more often than the public companies.
- Companies headed by MBAs have a preference for discounted cash flow techniques.

NPV, Company Value, and Stock Price

If a company invests in a positive NPV project, the expected addition to shareholder wealth should lead to an increase in the company's stock price.

However, the effect of a project's NPV on share prices is not so simple. The value of a company is determined by valuing its existing investments and adding the expected NPV of its future investments. The impact of the decision to undertake a particular project on a company's stock price depends on how the actual profitability of the investment differs from its expected profitability. Expected profitability is usually already factored into current market prices.

If the profitability of a positive NPV project that the company is about to undertake is below expectations, stock prices may fall. On the other hand, certain capital projects undertaken by the company may signal that there are other potentially lucrative projects to follow. Taking on a project that brings with it the expectation of even greater future profits from subsequent opportunities may increase stock prices beyond the actual addition to the company value from the said project alone.

Capital budgeting processes tell us two things about company management:

- The extent to which management pursues the goal of shareholder wealth maximization.
- Management's effectiveness in pursuit of this goal.

COST OF CAPITAL
Cross-Reference to CFA Institute Assigned Reading #35

The weighted average cost of capital (WACC) is the expected rate of return that investors demand for financing an average risk investment of a company.

$$WACC = (w_d)(r_d)(1-t) + (w_p)(r_p) + (w_e)(r_e)$$

- Interest payments result in tax savings for the company. Therefore, the after-tax cost of debt is used in the WACC formula.
- Payments to holders of preferred and common stock do not result in tax savings.

Methods of Determining Weights of Components of Capital

- Use the weights of each component in the *target capital structure* that the company aims to maintain.
- Use the weights of each component in the company's *current capital structure* based on *market* values.
- Examine trends in the company's capital structure over time and statements made by management regarding the company's capital structure policy to estimate the target capital structure.
- Use average weights of components in comparable companies' capital structures to estimate the target capital structure for the company.

The Optimal Capital Budget

A company's marginal cost of capital (MCC) *increases* as it raises additional capital. This is because most firms are required to pay a higher cost to obtain increasing amounts of capital.

The profitability of a company's investment opportunities *decreases* as the company makes additional investments. The company prioritizes investments in projects with the highest IRRs. As more resources are invested in the most rewarding projects, remaining opportunities offer lower and lower IRRs. This fact is represented by an investment opportunity schedule (IOS), that is downward-sloping.

The optimal capital budget occurs at the point where the marginal cost of capital intersects the investment opportunity schedule.

The WACC and Capital Budgeting

The WACC is the discount rate that reflects the average risk of the company. When we choose the WACC to evaluate a particular investment project, we assume that:

- The project under consideration is an average-risk project.
- The project will have a constant capital structure throughout its life, which will be the same as the company's target capital structure.

If the project being evaluated has *a higher* risk than the average risk of the firm's existing projects, the WACC is adjusted *upwards*. If the project has *less* risk than the average risk of the firm's existing projects, the WACC is adjusted *downwards*.

Estimating Cost of Debt

Yield-to-Maturity Approach

The bond's yield to maturity (YTM) is the IRR of an investment in the bond, assuming that it is purchased at the current market price and held till maturity. It is the yield that equates the present value of a bond's expected future cash flows to its current market price.

Debt Rating Approach

When a reliable current market price for the company's debt is not available, the before-tax cost of debt can be estimated by using the yield on similarly-rated bonds that have terms to maturity that are similar to the company's existing debt.

Issues in Estimating Cost of Debt

- *Fixed-rate versus floating-rate debt:* The cost of floating-rate debt is reset periodically based on a reference rate (usually LIBOR) and is therefore, more difficult to estimate than the cost of fixed-rate debt.
- *Debt with option-like features:* If option-like features are expected to be removed from future debt issues, an analyst must adjust the yield to maturity on existing bonds for their option features, and use the adjusted rate as the company's cost of debt.
- *Nonrated debt:* If a company does not have any debt outstanding (to be rated) or yields on existing debt are not available (due to lack of current price information), an analyst may not be able to use the yield on similarly-rated bonds or the yield to maturity approach to estimate the company's cost of debt.
- *Leases:* If a company uses leases as a source of finance, the cost of these leases should be included in its cost of capital.

Estimating Cost of Preferred Stock

$$r_p = D_p / V_p$$

Estimating Cost of Equity

1. Capital Asset Pricing Model (CAPM)

The capital asset pricing model (CAPM) states that the expected rate of return from a stock equals the risk-free interest rate plus a premium for bearing risk.

$$r_e = R_F + B_i[E(R_M) - R_F]$$

2. Dividend Discount Model (DDM)

The dividend discount model asserts that the value of a stock equals the present value of its expected future dividends.

$$r_e = \frac{D_1}{P_0} + g$$

3. Bond Yield plus Risk Premium Approach

The bond yield plus risk premium approach is based on the basic assumption that the cost of capital for riskier cash flows is higher than that of less risky cash flows. Therefore, we calculate the return on equity by adding a risk premium to the before-tax cost of debt.

$$r_e = r_d + \text{Risk premium}$$

Estimating Betas

- Beta can be calculated by regressing the company's stock returns against market returns over a given period of time.
- Analysts use the **pure-play** method to estimate the beta of a particular project or of a company that is not publicly traded. This method involves the adjustment of a comparable publicly-listed company's beta for differences in financial leverage.
    - First find a comparable company that faces similar business risks as the company or project under study and estimate the equity beta of that company.
    - To remove all elements of financial risk from the comparable's beta "unlever" the beta. The unlevered beta reflects only the business risk of the comparable and is known as *asset beta*.
    - Finally, adjust the unlevered beta of the comparable for the level of financial risk (leverage) in the project or company under study.

Business Risk versus Financial Risk

Business risk comprises of sales risk and operating risk. Sales risk refers to the unpredictability of revenues and operating risk refers to the company's operating cost structure.

Financial risk refers to the uncertainty of profits and cash flows because of the use of fixed-cost financing sources such as debt and leases. The greater the use of debt financing, the greater the financial risk of the firm.

Country Risk Premium

Studies have shown that a stock's beta captures the country risk of a stock accurately only in developed markets. Beta does not effectively capture country risk in developing nations. To deal with this problem, the CAPM equation for stocks in developing countries is modified to add a country spread, or the country equity premium (CRP) to the market risk premium.

$$k_e = R_F + \beta \, [E(R_M) - R_F + CRP]$$

Country risk premium	= Sovereign yield spread	× $\dfrac{\text{Annualized standard deviation of equity index of developing country}}{\text{Annualized standard deviation of sovereign bond market in terms of the developed market currency}}$

MCC Schedules and Break Points

A company's marginal cost of capital (MCC) increases as additional capital is raised. This is because of the following reasons:

- The company may have existing *debt covenants* that restrict the company from issuing debt with similar seniority. Subsequent rounds of debt will be subordinated to the senior issue so they will obviously carry more risk, and therefore, entail a higher cost.
- Due to economies of scale in raising significant amounts of a component (debt or equity) of capital in one go, a company may deviate from its target (optimal) capital structure over the short-term. These deviations may cause the marginal cost of capital to rise.

The amount of capital at which the WACC changes is referred to as a break point.

$$\text{Break point} = \frac{\text{Amount of capital at which the component's cost of capital changes}}{\text{Proportion of new capital raised from the component}}$$

Flotation Costs

Flotation costs refer to the fee charged by investment bankers to assist a company in raising new capital. In the case of debt and preferred stock, we do not usually incorporate flotation costs in the estimated cost of capital because the amount of these costs is quite small. However, for equity issues, flotation costs are usually quite significant.

Accounting for Flotation Costs in Capital Budgeting

- Incorporate flotation costs into the cost of capital. This approach is theoretically incorrect.
- Adjust the cash flows used in the valuation by adding the estimated dollar amount of flotation costs to the initial cost of the project.

STUDY SESSION 11:
CORPORATE FINANCE (2)

CF

MEASURES OF LEVERAGE
Cross-Reference to CFA Institute Assigned Reading #36

Leverage refers to a company's use of fixed costs in conducting business. Fixed costs include:

- Operating costs (e.g., rent and depreciation)
- Financial costs (e.g., interest expense)

Importance of Leverage

- Leverage increases the volatility of a company's earnings and cash flows, thereby increasing the risk borne by investors in the company.
- The more significant the use of leverage by the company, the more risky it is and therefore, the higher the discount rate that must be used to value the company.
- A company that is highly leveraged risks significant losses during economic downturns.

Leverage is affected by a company's cost structure. Generally companies incur two types of costs.

- Variable costs vary with the level of production and sales (e.g., raw materials costs and sales commissions).
- Fixed costs remain the same irrespective of the level of production and sales (e.g., depreciation and interest expense).

The higher the proportion of fixed costs (both operating and financial) in a company's cost structure (higher leverage) the greater the company's earnings volatility.

The greater the degree of leverage for a company, the steeper the slope of the line representing net income.

Business Risk

Business risk refers to the risk associated with a company's operating earnings. Operating earnings are risky because total revenues and costs of sales are both uncertain. Therefore, business risk can be broken down into sales risk and operating risk.

Sales risk: The uncertainty associated with total revenue is referred to as sales risk. Revenue is affected by economic conditions, industry dynamics, government regulation, and demographics.

The higher the standard deviation of price and units sold, the wider the distribution of operating profit.

Operating risk: The risk associated with a company's operating cost structure is referred to as operating risk. A company that has a greater proportion of fixed costs in its cost structure has greater operating risk.

CF

In order to examine a company's sensitivity of operating income to changes in unit sales, we use the **degree of operating leverage (DOL)**. DOL is the ratio of the percentage change in operating income to the percentage change in units sold.

$$DOL = \frac{\text{Percentage change in operating income}}{\text{Percentage change in units sold}}$$

$$DOL = \frac{Q \times (P - V)}{Q \times (P - V) - F}$$

DOL is different at different levels of sales. If the company is making operating profits, the sensitivity of operating income to changes in units sold decreases at higher sales volumes (in units).

- DOL is negative when operating income (the denominator in the DOL equation) is negative, and is positive when the company earns operating profits.
- Operating income is most sensitive to changes in sales around the point where the company makes zero operating income.
- DOL is undefined when operating income is zero.
- The lower the proportion of fixed costs in a company's cost structure, the less sensitive its operating income is to changes in units sold and therefore, lower is the company's operating risk.

Business risk is composed of operating and sales risk, both of which are largely determined by the industry in which the company operates.

A company has more control over operating risk than sales risk.

Financial Risk

Financial risk refers to the risk associated with how a company chooses to finance its operations. The higher the amount of fixed financial costs taken on by a company, the greater is its financial risk.

Financial risk can be measured as the sensitivity of cash flows available to owners to changes in operating income. This measure is known as the **degree of financial leverage (DFL)**.

$$DFL = \frac{\text{Percentage change in net income}}{\text{Percentage change in operating income}}$$

$$DFL = \frac{[Q(P - V) - F](1 - t)}{[Q(P - V) - F - C](1 - t)} = \frac{[Q(P - V) - F]}{[Q(P - V) - F - C]}$$

The higher the use of fixed financing sources by a company, the greater the sensitivity of net income to changes in operating income and therefore, the higher the financial risk of the company.

The degree of financial leverage is also different at different levels of operating income. The degree of financial leverage is usually determined by the company's management. Companies with relatively high ratios of tangible assets to total assets or those with revenues that have below-average business cycle sensitivity are able to use more financial leverage.

Total Leverage

The degree of total leverage (DTL) looks at the combined effect of operating and financial leverage i.e., it measures the sensitivity of net income to changes in units produced and sold.

$$DTL = \frac{\text{Percentage change in net income}}{\text{Percentage change in the number of units sold}}$$

$$DTL = DOL \times DFL$$

$$DTL = \frac{Q \times (P - V)}{[Q(P - V) - F - C]}$$

DTL is also different at different numbers of units produced and sold. This is because DOL is different at different levels of units produced and sold, while DFL is different at different levels of operating earnings. DTL combines the effects of DOL and DFL.

Breakeven Points and Operating Breakeven Points

A company's breakeven point occurs at the number of units produced and sold at which its net income equals zero. It is the point at which a company's revenues equal its total costs and the company goes from making losses to making profits.

The breakeven point for a company occurs when:

$$PQ = VQ + F + C$$

The breakeven number of units can be calculated as:

$$Q_{BE} = \frac{F + C}{P - V}$$

While greater leverage entails higher risk, it also raises the company's potential for profit.

CF

A breakeven point can also be specified in terms of operating profit, in which case it is known as the operating breakeven point. At this point, revenues equal operating costs. The expression for operating breakeven point is given as:

$$PQ_{OBE} = VQ_{OBE} + F$$

$$Q_{OBE} = \frac{F}{P - V}$$

The farther unit sales are from the breakeven point for high-leverage companies, the greater the magnifying effect of leverage.

The Risks of Creditors and Owners

Creditor claims on the assets of the company are senior to those of equity holders. In return for lending money to the company, creditors demand timely interest and principal payments. Payments to creditors must be made irrespective of whether the company is profitable. Inability to make these payments may lead to the company having to declare bankruptcy. Returns for creditors are predefined; even if the company does very well, they do not see any of the upside.

Owners only have a claim on what is left over after all the financial obligations of the company have been met. In return for the lower priority in claims, equity holders enjoy decision-making power in the company, and participate in the upside if the company does well.

Legal codes in most countries are provided for companies to file for bankruptcy protection. There are two main types of bankruptcy protection.

- Reorganization (Chapter 11), which provides the company temporary protection from creditors so that it can reorganize its capital structure and emerge from bankruptcy as a going concern.
- Liquidation (Chapter 7), which allows for an orderly settlement of the creditors' claims. In this category of bankruptcy, the original business ceases to exist.

Companies with high operating leverage have less flexibility in making changes to their operating structures so bankruptcy protection does little to help reduce operating costs. On the other hand, companies with high financial leverage can use Chapter 11 protection to change their capital structure and, once the restructuring is complete, emerge as ongoing concerns.

Under both Chapter 7 and Chapter 11, providers of equity capital generally lose out. On the other hand, debt holders typically receive at least a portion of their capital, but only after the period of bankruptcy protection ends.

CF

WORKING CAPITAL MANAGEMENT
Cross-Reference to CFA Institute Assigned Reading #37

Working capital management deals with the short-term aspects of corporate finance activities. Effective working capital management ensures that a company has adequate ready access to funds that are needed for day-to-day expenses, and at the same time invests its assets in the most productive manner.

Sources of Liquidity

- Primary sources are readily available resources such as cash balances and short-term funds.
- Secondary sources provide liquidity at a higher cost than primary sources. They include negotiating debt contracts, liquidating assets or filing, for bankruptcy protection.

Drags versus Pulls on Liquidity

A **drag on liquidity** occurs when there is a delay in cash coming into the company. Major drags on liquidity include:

- Uncollected receivables.
- Obsolete inventory.
- Tight credit.

Drags on liquidity can be dealt with by enforcing strict credit and collection policies.

A **pull on liquidity** occurs when cash leaves the company too quickly. Major pulls on payments include:

- Making payments early.
- Reduced credit limits.
- Limits on short-term lines of credit.
- Low existing levels of liquidity.

Evaluation of Liquidity Management

Current ratio

- A higher current ratio means that a company is better positioned to meet its short term obligations.
- A current ratio of less than one indicates negative working capital, which might imply that the company faces a liquidity crisis.

In order to gauge whether a given quick or current ratio is good or bad, we must look at the trend in ratios, how they compare with ratios of competitors, and available opportunities to invest in more profitable, longer-term investments.

CF

Accounts receivable turnover ratio

- It is desirable to have an accounts receivable turnover ratio close to the industry average.

Number of days of receivables

- A collection period that is too high might imply that customers are too slow in making payments and too much of the company's capital is tied up in accounts receivable.
- A collection period that is too low might suggest that the company's credit policy is too strict, which might hurt sales.

The number of days of receivables must be evaluated in light of the credit terms offered to customers, and the relation between sales and extension of credit.

Inventory turnover ratio

- An inventory TO ratio that is too high might indicate that the company has too little stock on hand at any given point in time, which might hurt sales.
- A low inventory TO ratio might suggest that the company has too much liquidity tied up in inventory, perhaps because the units held are obsolete.

Payables' turnover

- A high payables' turnover ratio might indicate that the company is not making full use of available credit facilities.
- A low ratio could suggest that the company has trouble making payments on time.

The **operating cycle** is a measure of the time needed to convert raw materials into cash from sales.

> **Operating cycle** = Number of days of inventory + Number of days of receivables

The **cash conversion cycle** or the **net operating cycle** equals the time period between paying suppliers for materials and collecting cash from sales to customers.

> **Net operating cycle** = Number of days of inventory + Number of days of receivables − Number of days of payables

Examples of Cash Inflows and Outflows

Inflows	Outflows
• Receipts from operations.	• Payables and payroll disbursements.
• Funds transfers from subsidiaries, joint ventures, and third parties.	• Funds transfers to subsidiaries.
	• Investments made.
• Maturing investments.	• Debt repayments.
• Debt proceeds (short and long term).	• Tax payments.
• Other income items (interest, etc.).	• Interest and dividend payments.
• Tax refunds.	

Components of a Cash Forecast

	Short Term	Medium Term	Long Term
Data Frequency	Daily/weekly for 4–6 weeks	Monthly for one year	Annually for 3–5 years
Format	Receipts and disbursements	Receipts and disbursements	Projected financial statements
Techniques	Simple projections	Projection models and averages	Statistical models
Accuracy	Very high	Moderate	Lowest
Reliability	Very high	Fairly high	Not as high
Uses	Daily cash management	Planning financial transactions	Long-range financial position

Predicting sales peaks caused by seasonality is very important if the company will have to borrow funds to cover its needs.

- If a company sets aside too much money, it will lose out in terms of investment income forgone (opportunity cost).
- If a company sets aside too little, it will incur higher costs to raise funds very quickly.

A company maintains a daily cash position to make sure that it has the necessary funds (the target balance) to carry on its day-to-day activities. If it keeps too much cash on hand, it loses out in terms of interest foregone. *Short-term investments* represent a temporary store for funds that are not needed for financing daily operations. Typical short-term investments that businesses invest their excess cash in are highly liquid and have low risk.

Yields on Short-Term Investments

$$\text{Money market yield} = \left(\frac{\text{Face value} - \text{price}}{\text{Price}}\right) \times \left(\frac{360}{\text{Days}}\right) = \text{Holding period yield} \times \left(\frac{360}{\text{Days}}\right)$$

$$\text{Bond equivalent yield} = \left(\frac{\text{Face value} - \text{price}}{\text{Price}}\right) \times \left(\frac{365}{\text{Days}}\right) = \text{Holding period yield} \times \left(\frac{365}{\text{Days}}\right)$$

$$\text{Discount basis yield} = \left(\frac{\text{Face value} - \text{price}}{\text{Face value}}\right) \times \left(\frac{360}{\text{Days}}\right) = \% \text{ discount} \times \left(\frac{360}{\text{Days}}\right)$$

CF

Cash Management Investment Strategies

- A passive strategy involves a limited number of transactions, and is based on very few rules for making daily investments. The focus is simply on reinvesting funds as they mature with little attention paid to yields.
- An active strategy involves constant monitoring to exploit profitable opportunities in a wider array of investments. Active strategies call for more involvement, more thorough study, evaluation, forecasts, and a flexible investment policy.

Cash Management Investment Policy

- The *purpose* of the investment policy states reasons for the existence of the portfolio and describes its general attributes, such as the investment strategy to be followed.
- It identifies the *authorities* who supervise the portfolio managers and details actions that must be undertaken if the policy is not followed.
- It describes the types of investments that should be considered for inclusion in the portfolio. The policy also contains *restrictions* on the maximum proportion of each type of security in the portfolio and the minimum credit rating of portfolio securities.

Evaluating Management of Accounts Receivable

- An *aging schedule* classifies accounts receivable according to the length of time that they have been outstanding.
- The *weighted average collection period* measures how long it takes to collect cash from the company's customers irrespective of the level of sales or changes in sales.

Evaluating Inventory Management

The main goal of inventory management is to maintain a level of inventory that ensures smooth delivery of sales without having more than necessary invested in stock.

- A high level of inventory is undesirable as it inflates storage costs, can result in losses from obsolescence or damage, and can squeeze liquidity from the firm.
- A shortage of inventory can hurt sales as the company loses out on potential customers.

Evaluating Management of Accounts Payable

Managing accounts payable is an important part of working capital management as accounts payable can be a source of working capital for the firm.

- If it pays too early, a company loses out on interest income.
- If it pays late, the company risks ruining its reputation and relationships with suppliers. Further, penalties and interest charges for late payment can be very significant.

Evaluating Trade Discounts

A company should review its evaluation of trade discounts periodically. An early payment discount must be availed if the savings from paying suppliers early are *greater* than the returns that could have been earned by investing the funds instead. The rate implicit in the discount must be compared to the return on the alternative short-term investment.

$$\text{Implicit rate} = \text{Cost of trade credit} = \left(1 + \frac{\text{Discount}}{1 - \text{Discount}}\right)^{\left(365 \Big/ \substack{\text{Number of days} \\ \text{beyond discount period}}\right)} - 1$$

Terms of "2/10 net 30" mean that a 2% discount is available if the amount owed is paid within 10 days; otherwise, the full amount is due by the 30th day.

Bank Sources of Finance

- *Uncommitted lines of credit* are the weakest and least reliable form of borrowing. Their advantage is that they do not require any compensation other than interest.
- *Regular lines of credit* (committed lines of credit) are stronger than uncommitted lines of credit as they require a formal commitment from the bank.
- *Revolving credit agreements* are the strongest form of short term borrowing.

Computing the Cost of Borrowing

$$\text{Line of credit cost} = \frac{\text{Interest} + \text{Commitment fee}}{\text{Loan amount}}$$

Cost of banker's acceptance and other sources whose costs are stated as "all inclusive":

$$= \frac{\text{Interest}}{\text{Net proceeds}} = \frac{\text{Interest}}{\text{Loan amount} - \text{Interest}}$$

Cost of sources with dealer's fees and backup fees that are quoted as "all inclusive":

$$= \frac{\text{Interest} + \text{Dealer's comission} + \text{Backup costs}}{\text{Loan amount} - \text{Interest}}$$

CF

STUDY SESSION 12:
PORTFOLIO MANAGEMENT (1)

PORTFOLIO MANAGEMENT: AN OVERVIEW
Cross-Reference to CFA Institute Assigned Reading #38

Importance of the Portfolio Perspective

- Portfolios of securities may offer equivalent expected returns with lower volatility of returns (lower risk) compared to individual securities.
- A simple measure of the value of diversification is the diversification ratio. It is the ratio of the standard deviation of an equal-weighted portfolio to the standard deviation of a randomly selected component of the portfolio. The lower the diversification ratio, the greater the risk reduction benefits of diversification, and the greater the portfolio effect.
- The composition of the portfolio (weight of each security held in the portfolio) is an important determinant of the overall level of risk inherent in the portfolio. By varying the weights of the individual securities, investors can arrive at a portfolio that offers the same return as an equally weighted portfolio, but with a lower standard deviation (risk).

Types of Investment Management Clients

Table 1: Summary of Investment Needs by Client Type

Client	Time Horizon	Risk Tolerance	Income Needs	Liquidity Needs
Individual investors	Varies by individual	Varies by individual	Varies by individual	Varies by individual
Defined benefit pension plans	Typically long-term	Typically quite high	High for mature funds; low for growing funds	Typically quite low
Endowments and foundations	Very long-term	Typically high	To meet spending commitments	Typically quite low
Banks	Short-term	Quite low	To pay interest on deposits and operations expenses	High to meet repayment of deposits
Insurance companies	Short-term for property and casualty; long-term for life insurance companies	Typically quite low	Typically low	High to meet claims
Investment companies	Varies by fund	Varies by fund	Varies by fund	High to meet redemptions

Steps in the Portfolio Management Process

Planning

The planning step involves understanding the client's needs and constraints and developing an investment policy statement (IPS). The IPS is a written document that describes the objectives and constraints of the investor.

Execution

Asset Allocation: The asset allocation of a portfolio refers to the distribution of investable funds between various asset classes (e.g., equities, fixed-income securities, alternative investments, etc.).

Security analysis: Analysts use their knowledge of various companies and the industry to identify investments that offer the most attractive risk return characteristics from within each asset class.

Portfolio construction: After determining the target asset allocation and conducting security analysis, the portfolio manager will construct the portfolio in line with the objectives outlined in the IPS.

Feedback

Portfolio monitoring and rebalancing: The portfolio must be regularly monitored. Changes in fundamental factors and client circumstances may require changes in the portfolio's composition. Rebalancing may be required when changes in security prices cause a significant change in weights of assets in the portfolio.

Performance measurement and reporting: This step involves measuring the performance of the portfolio relative to the benchmark stated in the IPS and reporting portfolio performance to the client.

Pooled Investments

Pooled investments are investments in securities issued by entities that represent ownership in the underlying assets held by those entities. These include:

- Mutual funds and exchange traded funds, in which investors can participate with a relatively small initial investment.
- Hedge funds and private equity funds, which may require a minimum investment of US$1 million or more.

Mutual Funds

Mutual funds pool money from several investors and invest these funds in a portfolio of securities.

- *Open-end funds* accept new investment funds and issue new shares at a value equal to the fund's net asset value per share at the time of investment. These funds also allow investors to redeem their investment in the fund at the prevailing net asset value per share.
- *Closed-end funds* accept no new investment money into fund. Shares in the fund are traded in the secondary market so new investors invest in the fund by purchasing shares in the market, and investors liquidate their holdings by selling the shares in the market. Unlike open-end funds, shares of closed-end funds can trade at a discount or premium to the net asset value per share, depending on the demand and supply of shares in the market.

The structure of open-end funds makes it easy for them to grow in size, but it does pose the following problems:

- The portfolio manager needs to manage cash inflows and outflows.
- An inflow of new investment requires the manager to find new investments.
- Funds need to keep cash for redemptions.

Closed-end funds do not face these problems, but as mentioned earlier, they cannot accept new investments.

Mutual funds may also be classified into:

- *Load funds* that charge a percentage fee for investing in the fund and/or for redemptions from the fund on top of an annual fee.
- *No-load funds* that only charge an annual fee based on a percentage of the fund's NAV.

Types of Mutual Funds

- *Money market funds:* These invest in high-quality, short-term debt instruments. Money-market mutual funds can be divided into tax-free and taxable funds.
- *Bond funds:* These invest in individual bonds and sometimes preference shares as well. Unlike money-market mutual funds, they usually invest in longer term instruments.
- *Stock funds:* These invest in equities and equity indices. Stock mutual funds can be actively or passively managed.
- *Hybrid or balanced funds:* These invest in both bonds and equities.

Other Investment Products Compared with Mutual Funds

Exchange Traded Funds (ETFs)

- Investors in index mutual funds purchase shares directly from the fund, while investors in an ETF purchase shares from other investors (just like buying or selling shares of stock). Investors are allowed to short ETF shares and even purchase them on margin.

- ETFs have lower costs, but unlike index mutual funds, investors do incur brokerage costs when trading ETFs.
- ETFs are constantly traded throughout the business day. Each trade occurs at the prevailing market price at that time. All purchases and redemptions for a mutual fund for a given day occur at the end of a trading day, at the same price.
- ETFs pay out dividends, while index mutual funds usually reinvest dividends.
- The minimum required investment is usually smaller for an ETF.
- ETFs are generally considered to have a tax advantage over index mutual funds.

Separately Managed Accounts (SMAs)

- Unlike investors in mutual funds, investors in SMAs directly own the shares and therefore, have control over which assets are bought and sold, and over the timing of transactions.
- Unlike mutual funds, in which no consideration is given to the tax position of the investor, transactions in SMAs take into account the specific tax needs of the investor.
- The required minimum investment for an SMA is usually much higher than for a mutual fund.

Hedge Funds

- Hedge funds differ from mutual funds in that most hedge funds are exempt from many of the reporting requirements for a typical public investment company.
- They require a minimum investment that is typically US$250,000 for new funds and US$1 million or more for well-established funds.
- They usually place restrictions on investors' ability to make withdrawals from the fund.
- Total management fee also has a performance-based component.

Buyout and Venture Capital Funds

- They take equity positions in companies and play a very active role in managing those companies.
- The eventual exit strategy is an important consideration when funds evaluate potential investments.

PORTFOLIO RISK AND RETURN: PART I
Cross-Reference to CFA Institute Assigned Reading #39

Measures of Return

Holding period return is simply the return earned on an investment over a single specified period of time.

$$R = \frac{P_T + D_T}{P_0} - 1$$

Holding period returns may also be calculated for more than one period by compounding single period returns:

$$R = [(1 + R_1) \times (1 + R_2) \times \ldots \times (1 + R_n)] - 1$$

The arithmetic or mean return is a simple average of all holding period returns.

- Arithmetic return is easy to calculate and has known statistical properties such as standard deviation, which is used to evaluate the dispersion of observed returns.
- The arithmetic mean return is biased upwards as it assumes that the amount invested at the beginning of each period is the same. This bias is particularly severe if holding period returns are a mix of both positive and negative returns.

$$R = \frac{R_{i1} + R_{i2} + \ldots + R_{iT}}{T} = \frac{1}{T} \sum_{t=1}^{T} R_{iT}$$

The geometric mean return accounts for compounding of returns, and does not assume that the amount invested in each period is the same.

- The geometric mean is lower than the arithmetic mean (due to the effects of compounding) unless there is no variation in returns, in which case they are equal.

$$R = \left\{ [(1 + R_1) \times (1 + R_2) \times \ldots \times (1 + R_n)]^{1/n} \right\} - 1$$

The money-weighted return accounts for the amount of money invested in each period and provides information on the return earned on the actual amount invested.

- The money-weighted return equals the internal rate of return of an investment.
- A drawback of the money-weighted return is that it does not allow for return comparisons between different individuals or different investment opportunities.

Annualized returns are calculated to make comparisons across investment instruments with different maturities.

- It is assumed that returns earned over short investment horizons can be replicated over the year.

$$r_{annual} = (1 + r_{period})^n - 1$$

The return on a portfolio is simply the weighted average of the returns on individual assets. For example, the return of a two-asset portfolio can be calculated as:

$$R_p = w_1 R_1 + w_2 R_2$$

Other Return Measures and Their Applications

Gross versus Net Returns

- Gross returns are calculated before deductions for management expenses, custodial fees, taxes and other expenses that are not directly linked to the generation of returns.
- Net returns deduct all managerial and administrative expenses that reduce an investor's return. Investors are primarily concerned with net returns.

Pre-Tax versus After-Tax Nominal Returns

- Pre-tax nominal returns do not adjust for taxes or inflation.
- After-tax nominal returns account for taxes. Most investors are concerned with returns on an after-tax basis.

Real versus Nominal Returns

- Nominal returns consist of the real risk-free rate of return, a premium for risk, and a premium for inflation.
- Investors calculate the real return because:
  - It is useful in comparing returns across time periods as inflation rates may vary over time.
  - It is useful in comparing returns among countries when returns are expressed in local currencies in which inflation rates vary between countries.
  - The after-tax real return is what an investor receives as compensation for postponing consumption and assuming risk after paying taxes on investment returns.

Leveraged Return

The leveraged return is computed when an investor uses leverage (by either borrowing money or using derivative contracts) to invest in a security. Leverage enhances returns, but also magnifies losses.

Variance and Covariance of Returns

The risk of an asset or a portfolio of assets can be measured by its standard deviation, which is the positive square root of variance.

Variance of a Single Asset

Variance equals the average squared deviation of observed values from their mean.

- A higher variance indicates higher volatility or dispersion of returns.

Standard Deviation of an Asset

The population and sample standard deviations are calculated as:

$$\sigma = \sqrt{\frac{\sum_{t=1}^{T}(R_t - \mu)^2}{T}} \qquad s = \sqrt{\frac{\sum_{t=1}^{T}(R_t - \bar{R})^2}{T-1}}$$

Variance of a Portfolio of Assets

The formula for the variance of a portfolio is:

$$\sigma_P^2 = \sum_{i,j=1}^{N} w_i w_j Cov(R_i, R_j)$$

$$\sigma_P^2 = \sum_{i=1}^{N} w_i^2 Var(R_i) + \sum_{i,j=1, i \neq j}^{N} w_i w_j Cov(R_i, R_j)$$

The standard deviation of a portfolio of two risky assets is calculated as:

$$\sigma_p = \sqrt{w_1^2 \sigma_1^2 + w_2^2 \sigma_2^2 + 2w_1 w_2 \sigma_1 \sigma_2 \rho_{1,2}} \text{ or } \sqrt{w_1^2 \sigma_1^2 + w_2^2 \sigma_2^2 + 2w_1 w_2 Cov_{1,2}}$$

Other Investment Characteristics

Distributional Characteristics

- Skewness refers to the asymmetry of a returns distribution.
    - When most of the distribution is concentrated on the left, it is referred to as right skewed or positively skewed.
    - When most of the distribution is concentrated to the right, it is referred to as left skewed or negatively skewed.

- Kurtosis refers to fat tails or higher than normal probabilities for extreme returns. This leads to an increase in an asset's risk that is not captured by the mean-variance framework.

Market Characteristics

Markets are not always *operationally efficient*. One limitation on operational efficiency in markets is liquidity. Liquidity has an impact on the bid-ask spread (illiquid stocks have a wider spread) and on the price impact of a trade (illiquid stocks suffer a greater price impact).

Informational efficiency is discussed in later readings on market efficiency.

The Concept of Risk Aversion

Risk-averse investors aim to maximize returns for a given level of risk, and minimize risk for a given level or return.

Risk-seeking investors get extra utility or satisfaction from the uncertainty associated with their investments.

Risk-neutral investors seek higher returns irrespective of the level of risk inherent in an investment.

Risk tolerance refers to the level of risk that an investor is willing to accept to achieve her investment goals.

- The lower the risk tolerance, the lower the level of risk acceptable to the investor.
- The lower the risk tolerance, the higher the risk aversion.

Utility Theory

In order to quantify the preferences for investment choices using risk and return, utility functions are used. An example of a utility function is:

$$U = E(R) - \frac{1}{2}A\sigma^2$$

"A" is a measure of risk aversion. It is higher for investors who are more risk averse as they require larger compensation for accepting more risk.

The utility function assumes the following:

- Investors are generally risk averse, but prefer more return to less return.
- Investors are able to rank different portfolios based on their preferences and these preferences are internally consistent.

We can draw the following conclusions from the utility function:

- Utility is unbounded on both sides- it can be highly negative or highly positive.
- Higher return results in higher utility.
- Higher risk results in lower utility.
- The higher the value of "A" the higher the negative effect of risk on utility.

Important Notes Regarding the Risk Aversion Coefficient, "A"

- "A" is positive for a risk-averse investor. Additional risk reduces total utility.
- It is negative for a risk seeking investor. Additional risk enhances total utility.
- It equals zero for a risk neutral investor. Additional risk has no impact on total utility.

Indifference Curves

The risk-return trade-off that an investor is willing to bear can be illustrated by an indifference curve. An investor realizes the same total utility or satisfaction from every point on a given indifference curve. Since each investor can have an infinite number of risk-return combinations that generate the same utility, indifference curves are continuous at all points.

1. They are *upward sloping*. This means that an investor will be indifferent between two investments with different expected returns only if the investment with the lower expected return entails a lower level of risk as well.
2. They are *curved*, and their slope becomes steeper as more risk is taken. The increase in return required for every unit of additional risk increases at an increasing rate because of the diminishing marginal utility of wealth.

The slope of an indifference curve represents the extra return required by the investor to accept an additional unit of risk.

- A risk-averse investor would have a relatively steep indifference curve (significant extra return required to take on more risk).
- A less risk-averse investor would have a flatter indifference curve (lower extra return required to take on more risk).
- A risk-seeking investor would have an indifference curve with a negative slope. Her utility increases with higher return and higher risk.
- A risk-neutral investor would have a perfectly horizontal indifference curve. Her utility does not vary with risk.

Application of Utility Theory to Portfolio Selection

Capital Allocation Line

$$E(R_p) = RFR + \sigma_{port} \frac{[E(R_i) - RFR]}{\sigma_i}$$

- The CAL has an intercept of RFR.
- The expression for the slope of the CAL is the extra return required for each additional unit of risk and is also known as the market price of risk.

The point of tangency between the CAL and an investor's indifference curve indicates the optimal risky asset portfolio that the investor should invest in.

Portfolio Risk

The formula for the standard deviation of a portfolio consisting of 2 risky assets is:

$$\sigma_p = \sqrt{w_1^2\sigma_1^2 + w_2^2\sigma_2^2 + 2w_1w_2\sigma_1\sigma_2\rho_{1,2}} \text{ or } \sqrt{w_1^2\sigma_1^2 + w_2^2\sigma_2^2 + 2w_1w_2 \, cov_{1,2}}$$

The first part of the formula for the 2-asset portfolio standard deviation $(w_1^2\sigma_1^2 + w_2^2\sigma_2^2)$ tells us that portfolio standard deviation is a *positive* function of the standard deviation and weights of the individual assets held in the portfolio. The second part $(2w_1w_2Cov_{1,2})$ shows us that portfolio standard deviation is also dependent on how the two assets move in relation to each other (covariance or correlation).

From the 2-asset portfolio standard deviation formula it is also important to understand that:

- The maximum value for portfolio standard deviation will be obtained when the correlation coefficient equals +1.
- Portfolio standard deviation will be minimized when the correlation coefficient equals –1.
- If the correlation coefficient equals zero, the second part of the formula will equal zero and portfolio standard deviation will lie somewhere in between.

Implications

- When asset returns are *negatively* correlated, the final term in the standard deviation formula is negative and serves to *reduce* portfolio standard deviation.
- If the correlation between assets equals zero, portfolio standard deviation is *greater* than when correlation is negative.
- When asset returns are positively correlated, the second part of the formula for portfolio standard deviation is also positive, and portfolio standard deviation is higher than when the correlation coefficient equals zero. With a correlation coefficient of +1 (perfect positive correlation) there are no diversification benefits.

- The risk (standard deviation) of a portfolio of risky assets depends on the asset weights and standard deviations, *and most importantly on the correlation of asset returns*. The *higher* the correlation between the individual assets, the *higher* the portfolio's standard deviation.
- A conservative investor can experience both a higher return and a lower risk by diversifying into a higher-risk, higher-return asset if the correlation between the assets is fairly low.
- When correlation equals +1, the risk-return combinations that result from altering the weights lie along a straight line between the two assets' risk-return profiles.
- As correlation falls, the curvature of this line increases.
- When correlation equals -1, the curve is represented by two straight lines that meet at the vertical axis. This point represents a zero-risk portfolio where portfolio return must equal the risk-free rate to prevent arbitrage.

Avenues for Diversification

- Investing in a variety of asset classes that are not highly correlated.
- Using index funds that minimize the costs of diversification and grant exposure to specific asset classes.
- Investing among countries that focus on different industries, are undergoing different stages of the business cycle and have different currencies.
- Choosing not to invest a significant portion of their wealth in employee stock plans as their human capital is already entirely invested in their employing companies.
- Only adding a security to the portfolio if its Sharpe ratio is greater than the Sharpe ratio of the portfolio times the correlation coefficient.
- Only adding a security to the portfolio if the benefit (additional expected return, reduced portfolio risk) is greater than the associated costs (trading costs and costs of tracking a larger portfolio).
- Adding insurance to the portfolio by purchasing put options or adding an asset class that has a negative correlation with the assets in the portfolio (e.g., commodities).

The Minimum-Variance and Efficient Frontiers, and the Global Minimum-Variance Portfolio

- Combining risky assets may result in a portfolio that has lower risk than any of the individual assets in the portfolio.
- As the number of assets available increases, they can be combined into a large number of different portfolios (each with different assets and weights), and we can create an opportunity set of investments.
- Combinations of these assets can be formed into portfolios that entail the lowest level of risk for each level of expected return. An envelope curve that plots the risk-return characteristics of the lowest risk portfolios is known as the minimum variance frontier.
  - No risk-averse investor would invest in any portfolio that lies to the right of the MVF as it would entail a higher level of risk than a portfolio that lies on the MVF for a given level of return.

- The global minimum-variance portfolio is the portfolio of risky securities that entails the lowest level of risk among all the risky asset portfolios on the minimum variance frontier.
- All portfolios on the MVF that lie above and to the right of the global minimum-variance portfolio dominate all portfolios on the MVF that lie below and to the right of the global minimum variance portfolio.
  - This dominant portion of the MVF (the one above and to the right of the global minimum variance portfolio) is known as the Markowitz efficient frontier. It contains all the possible portfolios that rational, risk-averse investors will consider investing in.

A Risk-Free Asset and Many Risky Assets

- The risk-free asset has zero risk (so it plots on the y-axis), an expected return of RFR, and zero correlation with risky assets.
- The risk-return characteristics of portfolios that combine the risk-free asset with a risky asset or a portfolio of risky assets lie along a straight line.

As the investor combines the risk-free asset with portfolios further up the efficient frontier, she keeps attaining better portfolio combinations. Each successive portfolio on the efficient frontier has a steeper line (higher slope) joining it to the risk-free asset. The slope of this line represents the additional return per unit of extra risk. The steeper the slope of the line, the better the risk-return trade-off the portfolio offers. The line with the steepest slope is the one that is drawn from the risk-free asset to Portfolio M (which occurs at the point of tangency between the efficient frontier and a straight line drawn from the risk-free rate). This particular line offers the best risk-return trade-off to the investor. Any combination of the risk-free asset and Portfolio M dominates all portfolios below CAL_M.

The Two-Fund Separation Theorem

The two-fund separation theorem states that regardless of risk and return preferences, all investors hold some combination of the risk-free asset and an optimal portfolio of risky assets. Therefore, the investment problem can be broken down into two steps:

1. The investing decision, where an investor identifies her optimal risky portfolio.
2. The financing decision, where she determines where exactly on the optimal CAL, she wants her portfolio to lie. Her risk preferences (as delineated by her indifference curves) determine whether her desired portfolio requires borrowing or lending at the risk-free rate.

Optimal Investor Portfolio

- The line CAL_M represents the best portfolios available to an investor. The portfolios along this line contain the risk-free asset and the optimal portfolio, Portfolio M, with varying weights.
- An individual's optimal portfolio depends on her risk-return preferences, which are incorporated into her indifference curves. The point where her indifference curve is tangent to CAL_M indicates her optimal investor portfolio.

PORTFOLIO RISK AND RETURN: PART II
Cross-Reference to CFA Institute Assigned Reading #40

Review

- Risky assets can be combined into portfolios that may have a lower risk than each of the individual assets in the portfolio if assets are not perfectly positively correlated.
- An investor's investment opportunity set includes all the individual risky assets and risky asset portfolios that she can invest in.
- The minimum variance frontier reduces the investment opportunity set to a curve that contains only those portfolios that entail the lowest level of risk for each level of expected return.
- The global minimum variance portfolio is the portfolio of risky assets that entails the lowest level of risk among all portfolios on the minimum variance frontier.
- Investors aim to maximize return for every level of risk. Therefore, all portfolios above and to the right of the global minimum variance portfolio dominate those that lie below and to the right of the global minimum variance portfolio.
- The section of the minimum variance frontier that lies above and to the right of the global minimum variance portfolio is referred to as the Markowitz efficient frontier.

A risk-free asset has an expected return of RFR, a standard deviation (risk) of zero, and a correlation with any risky asset of zero. Once the risk-free asset is introduced into the mix:

- Any portfolio that combines a risky asset portfolio that lies on the Markowitz efficient frontier and the risk-free asset has a risk return trade-off that is linear (CAL is represented by a straight line).
- The point at which a line drawn from the risk-free rate is tangent to the Markowitz efficient frontier defines the optimal risky asset portfolio. This line is known as the optimal CAL.
- Each investor will choose a portfolio (optimal investor portfolio) that contains some combination of the risk-free asset and the optimal risky portfolio. The weights of the risk-free asset and the optimal risky portfolio in the optimal investor portfolio depend on the investor's risk tolerance (indifference curve).
- The optimal investor portfolio is defined by the point where the investor's indifference curve is tangent to the optimal CAL.

The CAL and the CML

A capital allocation line (CAL) includes all combinations of the risk-free asset and **any risky asset portfolio**.

The capital market line (CML) is a special case of the capital allocation line where the risky asset portfolio that is combined with the risk-free asset is the **market portfolio**.

Graphically, the market portfolio occurs at the point where a line from the risk-free asset is tangent to the Markowitz efficient frontier. The market portfolio is the optimal risky asset portfolio given homogenous expectations. All portfolios that lie below the CML offer a lower return than portfolios that plot on the CML for each level of risk.

Equation of CML:

$$E(R_p) = R_f + \frac{E(R_m) - R_f}{\sigma_m} \times \sigma_p$$

Figure 12.1 illustrates the CML.

Figure 1: Capital Market Line

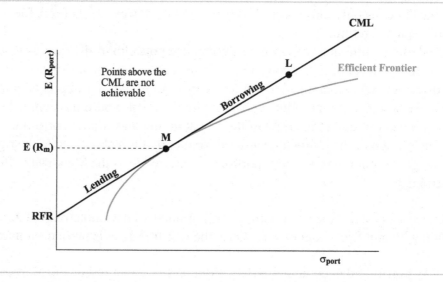

- At Point RFR, an investor has all her funds invested in the risk-free asset.
- At Point M, she has all of her funds invested in the market portfolio (which only contains risky securities).
- At any point between RFR and M, she holds both the market portfolio and the risk-free asset (i.e., she is lending some of her funds at the risk-free rate).

However, an investor may want to attain a higher expected return than available at Point M, where all her funds are invested in the market portfolio. Adding leverage to the portfolio by borrowing money at the RFR and investing it in the market portfolio will allow her to attain a risk-return profile beyond (to the right of, or above) Point M on the CML (e.g., Point L).

The particular point that an investor chooses on the CML depends on her utility function, which in turn is determined by her risk and return preferences.

Leveraged Positions with Different Lending and Borrowing Rates

Practically speaking, an investor's ability to repay is not as certain as that of the U.S. government, so the rate at which she would be able to borrow would be higher than the rate at which she would be able to lend. Given the disparity in borrowing and lending rates, the CML would no longer be a straight line.

- The slope of the CML to the left of Point M (when she invests a portion of her portfolio in the risk-free asset at R_f) would be:

$$\frac{E(R_m) - R_f}{\sigma_m}$$

- The slope CML to the right of Point M (where she is borrowing at R_b) would be:

$$\frac{E(R_m) - R_b}{\sigma_m}$$

Systematic and Nonsystematic Risk

When investors diversify across assets that are not perfectly positively correlated, the portfolio's risk is lower than the weighted average of the individual assets' risks. In the market portfolio, all the risk unique to individual assets comprising the portfolio has been diversified away.

- The risk that disappears due to diversification in the portfolio construction process is known as unsystematic risk (also known as unique, diversifiable or firm-specific risk).
- The risk inherent in all risky assets (caused by macro-economic variables) that cannot be eliminated by diversification is known as systematic risk (also known as non-diversifiable or market risk).

$$\text{Total Risk} = \text{Systematic risk} + \text{Unsystematic risk}$$

Complete diversification of a portfolio requires the elimination of all unsystematic or diversifiable risk. Once unsystematic risk has been eliminated and only systematic risk remains, a completely diversified portfolio would correlate perfectly with the market.

By adding assets to a portfolio that are not perfectly correlated with the assets already in the portfolio, we can reduce the overall standard deviation of the portfolio. However, we cannot eliminate the variability and uncertainty of macroeconomic factors that affect returns on all risky assets. We do not have to include all the assets in the market portfolio to diversify away unsystematic risk. Studies have shown that a portfolio consisting of 12–30 different stocks can diversify away 90% of unsystematic risk.

In capital market theory, taking on a higher degree of unsystematic risk will not be compensated with a higher return because unsystematic risk can be eliminated, without additional cost, through diversification. Only if an investor takes on a higher level of risk that cannot be easily diversified away (systematic risk) should she expect to be rewarded in the form of a higher return. Systematic risk is measured as the contribution of a security to the risk of a well diversified portfolio.

Return-Generating Models

A return generating model is a model that is used to forecast the return on a security given certain parameters. A multi-factor model uses more than one variable to estimate returns.

- Macroeconomic factor models use economic factors (e.g., economic growth rates, interest rates and inflation rates) that correlate with security returns to estimate returns.
- Fundamental factor models use relationships between security returns and underlying fundamentals (e.g., earnings, earnings growth and cash flow growth) to estimate returns.
- Statistical factor models use historical and cross-sectional returns data to identify factors that explain returns and use an asset's sensitivity to those factors to project future returns.

The Market Model

The market model is an example of a single-index return generation model. It is used to estimate beta risk and to compute abnormal returns. The market model is given as:

$$R_i = \alpha_i + \beta_i R_m + e_i$$

First, the intercept α_i and slope coefficient β_i are estimated using historical asset and market returns. These estimates are then used to predict returns in the future.

Calculation and Interpretation of Beta

Beta is a measure of the sensitivity of an asset's return to the market's return. It is computed as the covariance of the return on the asset and the return on the market divided by the variance of the market.

$$\beta_i = \frac{Cov(R_i, R_m)}{\sigma_m^2} = \frac{\rho_{i,m} \sigma_i \sigma_m}{\sigma_m^2} = \frac{\rho_{i,m} \sigma_i}{\sigma_m}$$

Important Points Regarding Beta

- Beta captures an asset's systematic or non-diversifiable risk.
- A positive beta suggests that the return on the asset follows the overall trend in the market.
- A negative beta indicates that the return on the asset generally follows a trend that is opposite to that of the current market trend.
- A beta of zero means that the return on the asset is uncorrelated with market movements.
- The market has a beta of 1. Therefore, the average beta of stocks in the market also equals 1.

The market model described previously can also be used to compute beta.

The Capital Asset Pricing Model

The capital asset pricing model (CAPM) is a single-index model that is widely used to estimate returns given security betas. The CAPM is expressed as:

$$E(R_i) = R_f + \beta_i[E(R_m) - R_f]$$

Assumptions of the CAPM

- Investors are utility maximizing, risk-averse, rational individuals.
- Markets are frictionless, and there are no transaction costs and taxes.
- All investors have the same single period investment horizon.
- Investors have homogenous expectations and therefore, arrive at the same valuation for any given asset.
- All investments are infinitely divisible.
- Investors are price-takers. No investor is large enough to influence security prices.

The Security Market Line

The SML illustrates the CAPM equation. Its y-intercept equals the risk-free rate and its slope equals the market risk premium ($R_m - R_f$).

Recall that the CAL and the CML only applied to efficient portfolios; not to individual assets or inefficient portfolios. They used total risk on the x-axis, and since only systematic risk is priced, they could only be used for efficient portfolios (those with no unsystematic risk and whose total risk therefore was the same as their systematic risk).

The SML and the CAPM on the other hand, apply to any security or portfolio, regardless of whether it is efficient. This is because they are based only on a security's systematic risk, not total risk.

The CAPM equation tells us that the expected (required) rate of return for a risky asset is determined by the risk-free rate plus a risk premium. The risk premium for an asset is determined by the systematic risk of the asset (β_i), and the prevailing market risk premium (Rm – Rf).

Portfolio Beta

The CAPM can also be applied to portfolios of assets.

- The beta of a portfolio equals the weighted average of the betas of the securities in the portfolio.
- The portfolio's expected return can be computed using the CAPM:

$$E(R_p) = R_f + \beta_p[E(R_m) - R_f]$$

Applications of the CAPM

Estimate of expected return: The expected rate of return computed from the CAPM is used by investors to value stocks, bonds, real estate and other assets. In capital budgeting, where the NPV is used to make investing decisions, the CAPM is used to compute the required rate of return, which is then used to discount expected future cash flows.

Portfolio Performance Evaluation

The *Sharpe ratio* is used to compute excess returns per unit of total risk. It is calculated as:

$$\text{Sharpe ratio} = \frac{R_p - R_f}{\sigma_p}$$

Notice that the Sharpe ratio basically equals the slope of the CAL. A portfolio with a higher Sharpe ratio is preferred to one with a lower Sharpe ratio given that the numerator of the portfolios being compared is positive. If the numerator is negative, the ratio will be closer to zero (less negative) for riskier portfolios, resulting in distorted rankings. Two drawbacks of the Sharpe ratio are that it uses total risk as a measure of risk even though only systematic risk is priced, and that the ratio itself is not informative.

The *Treynor ratio* basically replaces total risk in the Sharpe ratio with systematic risk (beta). It is calculated as:

$$\text{Treynor ratio} = \frac{R_p - R_f}{\beta_p}$$

For the Treynor ratio to offer meaningful results, both the numerator and the denominator must be positive. Neither the Sharpe nor the Treynor ratio offer any information about the significance of the differences between the ratios for portfolios.

M-squared (M²) is also based on total risk, not beta risk. It is calculated as:

$$M^2 = (R_p - R_f)\frac{\sigma_m}{\sigma_p} - (R_m - R_f)$$

M^2 offers rankings that are identical to those provided by the Sharpe ratio. However, these rankings are easier to interpret as they are in percentage terms. A portfolio that matches the market's performance will have an M^2 of zero, while one that outperforms the market will have a positive M^2. The M^2 also enables us to tell which portfolios beat the market on a risk-adjusted basis.

Jensen's alpha is based on systematic risk (like the Treynor ratio). It first estimates a portfolio's beta risk using the market model, and then uses the CAPM to determine the required return from the investment (given its beta risk). The difference between the portfolio's actual return and the required return (as predicted by the CAPM) is called Jensen's alpha. Jensen's alpha is calculated as:

$$\alpha_p = R_p - [R_f + \beta_p(R_m - R_f)]$$

Jensen's alpha for the market equals zero. The higher the Jensen's alpha for a portfolio, the better its risk adjusted performance.

Security Characteristic Line

The security characteristic line (SCL) plots the excess returns of a security against the excess returns on the market. The equation of the SCL is given as:

$$R_i - R_f = \alpha_i + \beta_i(R_m - R_f)$$

Note that Jensen's alpha is the y-intercept, and beta is the slope of the SCL.

Security Selection

- If the expected return using price and dividend forecasts is higher than the investor's required return given the systematic risk in the security, the security is undervalued and the investor should buy it.
- If the expected return using price and dividend forecasts is lower than the investor's required return given the systematic risk in the security, the security is overvalued and the investor should sell it.

Constructing a Portfolio

The CAPM tells us that investors should hold a portfolio that combines the risk-free asset with the market portfolio. Let's assume that we begin with the S&P 500 as our risky asset portfolio. The S&P 500 index only contains large-cap U.S. stocks, but does not encompass the entire global market. Therefore, we might want to consider a security not included in the S&P 500 for inclusion in the portfolio. The decision regarding whether the particular security should be included in our portfolio depends on the α_i of the security (based on the CAPM and the S&P 500 as the market portfolio). Positive α_i securities (even if they are correctly priced) should be added to the portfolio.

Further, within the set of securities included in the S&P 500, some may be undervalued (expected to generate positive alpha) and others may be overvalued (expected to generate negative alpha) based on investor expectations. The weight of undervalued securities should be increased and that of overvalued securities should be reduced.

PM

> The information ratio $\left(\dfrac{\alpha_i}{\sigma_{ei}}\right)$ measures the abnormal return per unit of risk added by the security to a well-diversified portfolio. The larger the information ratio is, the more valuable the security.

The weight of each nonmarket security in the portfolio should be proportional to:

$$\frac{\alpha_i}{\sigma_{ei}^2}$$

where:

α_i = Jensen's alpha

σ_{ei}^2 = Nonsystematic variance of the security

Beyond the CAPM

Limitations of the CAPM

Theoretical limitations

- The CAPM is a single-factor model; only systematic risk is priced in the CAPM.
- It is only a single period model.

Practical limitations

- A true market portfolio is unobservable as it would also include assets that are not investable (e.g., human capital).
- In the absence of a true market portfolio, the proxy for the market portfolio used varies across analysts, which leads to different return estimates for the same asset (not permissible in the CAPM world).

Extensions of the CAPM

Theoretical models like the arbitrage pricing theory (APT) expand the number of risk factors.

Practical models use extensive research to uncover risk factors that explain returns.

STUDY SESSION 13:
PORTFOLIO MANAGEMENT (2)

BASICS OF PORTFOLIO PLANNING AND CONSTRUCTION
Cross-Reference to CFA Institute Assigned Reading #41

The Investment Policy Statement

An investment policy statement is an invaluable planning tool that adds discipline to the investment process. Before developing an IPS, an investment manager must conduct a fact finding discussion with the client to learn about the client's risk tolerance and other specific circumstances.

The IPS can be thought of as a roadmap which serves the following purposes:

- It helps the investor decide on realistic investment goals after learning about financial markets and associated risks.
- It creates a standard according to which the portfolio manager's performance can be judged.
- It guides the actions of portfolio managers, who should refer to it from time to time to assess the suitability of particular investments for their clients.

Major Components of an IPS

- An introduction that describes the client.
- A statement of purpose.
- A statement of duties and responsibilities, which describes the duties and responsibilities of the client, the custodian of the client's assets, and the investment manager.
- Procedures that outline the steps required to keep the IPS updated and steps required to respond to various contingencies.
- The client's investment objectives.
- The client's investment constraints.
- Investment guidelines regarding how the policy should be executed (e.g., whether use of leverage and derivatives is permitted) and specific types of assets that must be excluded.
- Evaluation and review guidelines on obtaining feedback on investment results.
- Appendices that describe the strategic asset allocation and the rebalancing policy.

Risk Objectives

- An example of an absolute risk objective would be that the client does not want to lose more than 5% of her capital over a particular period.
- Relative risk objectives relate risk to a certain benchmark that represents an appropriate level of risk.

Risk tolerance is a function of both, a client's ability to take risk as well as her willingness to take risk. The ability to take risk is a function of several factors including time horizon, expected income, and net worth. Generally speaking, a client with a longer time horizon, high expected income and greater net worth has a greater ability to bear risk. A client's willingness to bear risk, on the other hand, is based on more subjective factors including her psychological makeup, and level of understanding of financial markets.

- When the client's ability to take risk is below average and her willingness to take risk is also below average, the investor's overall risk tolerance is below average.
- When the client's ability to take risk is above average and her willingness to take risk is also above average, the investor's overall risk tolerance is above average.
- When the client's ability to take risk is below average and her willingness to take risk is above average, the investor's overall risk tolerance is below average.
- When the client's ability to take risk is above average and her willingness to take risk is below average, the investment manager should explain the conflict and implications to the client.

When there is a mismatch between a client's ability and willingness to take risk, the prudent approach is to conclude that the client's tolerance for risk is the lower of the two factors. Further, any decisions made must be documented.

Return Objectives

- Absolute return objectives state the percentage return desired by the client. The return may be expressed on a real or nominal basis.
- Relative return objectives express the required return relative to a stated benchmark. A good benchmark should be investable i.e., an investor should be able to replicate it.

The return objective may be stated before or after fees and on a pre- or post-tax basis. Further, it could also be expressed in terms of a required return i.e., the amount an investor needs to earn over the investment horizon to meet a specified future goal.

The portfolio manager must ensure that the client's return objective is realistic in light of her tolerance for risk.

Investment Constraints

Liquidity refers to the ability to readily convert investments into cash at a price close to fair market value. Investors may require ready cash to meet unexpected needs and could be forced to sell their assets at unfavorable terms if the investment plan does not consider their liquidity needs.

Time Horizon refers to the time period between putting funds into an investment and requiring them for use. A close relationship exists between an investor's time horizon, liquidity needs and ability to take risk. The shorter the time horizon, the harder it would be for an investor to overcome losses.

Tax Concerns play a very important role in investment planning because, unlike tax-exempt investors, taxable investors are really only concerned with after-tax returns on their portfolios.

Legal and Regulatory Factors: Investors also need to be aware of legal and regulatory factors. For example, some countries impose a limit on the proportion of equity securities in a pension fund's portfolio.

Unique Circumstances: There may be a number of individual and unusual considerations that affect investors. For example, many investors may want to exclude certain investments from their portfolios based on personal or socially conscious reasons.

Portfolio Construction

Once the IPS has been compiled, the investment manager begins constructing the portfolio. How the portfolio funds are allocated across different asset classes is referred to as the portfolio's strategic asset allocation (SAA). A portfolio's SAA is important because it is a portfolio's allocation across various asset classes (not its allocation across securities within those asset classes) that is the primary determinant of portfolio returns.

Capital Market Expectations

Capital market expectations refer to a portfolio manager's expectations regarding the risk and return prospects of various asset classes. Capital market expectations are quantified in terms of expected returns, standard deviation of returns, and correlations among asset classes.

The Strategic Asset Allocation

The strategic asset allocation defines how the investor's funds are divided across different asset classes. Traditionally, cash, equities, bonds, and real estate were defined as the major asset classes. Recently, hedge funds, private equity and commodities have been added to the list. Further, each asset class can be subdivided into several sub-classes.

The risk return characteristics of the strategic asset allocation depend on the expected returns and risk of the individual asset classes, and on the correlations between the asset classes. Typically, risk-averse investors will place a higher weight on government bonds and cash in their SAA's, while those with a higher risk tolerance will have a higher weight invested in equities.

Steps Toward an Actual Portfolio

1. Risk budgeting: This is the process of subdividing the desired level of portfolio risk (which has been determined in the IPS) across the different sources of investment returns i.e., the strategic asset allocation, tactical asset allocation and security selection.
2. Tactical asset allocation: This refers to an allocation where the manager deliberately deviates from the strategic asset allocation for the short term.
3. Security selection: A manager may be able to outperform the asset class benchmark by investing in particular securities within the asset class that she expects to do well (better than the benchmark).

PM

4. Portfolio rebalancing: Changes in security prices will lead to changes in the weights of different asset classes in the portfolio and cause them to deviate or "drift" from policy weights. Therefore, the portfolio should be rebalanced periodically and brought in line with policy weights.

Additional Portfolio Organizing Principles

The top-down investment framework has two drawbacks:

- If several managers are hired to manage different subclasses within the same asset class it may result in underutilization of the risk budget.
- Each manager would trade within the portfolio under her management so the portfolio overall may not be efficient from a capital gains tax point of view.

In order to avoid this, managers invest most of their funds in passive investments and trade a minority of assets actively. This approach is known as the "core-satellite" approach.

RISK MANAGEMENT: AN INTRODUCTION
Cross-Reference to CFA Institute Assigned Reading #42

Risk encompasses all of the uncertain environmental variables that lead unpredictability of outcomes. Taking risk is an integral part of conducting business and managing investment portfolios. While risk is generally seen in an unfavorable light, the challenge for companies/investment managers lies in carefully choosing, understanding, and managing the risks entailed by their decisions.

RISK MANAGEMENT FRAMEWORK

A risk management framework refers to the infrastructure, process, and analytics required to support the risk management function in an organization.

Risk governance comes from the board. It is the top-down process and guidance, which directs risk management activities to align with the organization's goals and risk appetite.

Risk identification and measurement is an ongoing process that requires entails analyzing the business or portfolio to identify risk exposures, tracking changes in those risk exposures, calculating risk metrics to gauge the significance of those risks under various scenarios, as well as keeping an eye on the business environment for potential risk drivers.

- A risk driver refers to any fundamental underlying factor that gives rise to a risk that is relevant to the entity.

Risk infrastructure refers to the people, systems and technology required to track risk exposures and conduct quantitative risk analysis. It includes the process (known as risk capture) through which risk exposures are populated in the risk management system, as well as the databases, models, and skilled personnel needed to develop and maintain the risk framework.

Policies and processes translate risk governance into the organization's day-to-day operations and decision-making processes in order to ensure that risky activities kept in line with the entity's risk tolerance levels.

Risk monitoring, mitigation, and management requires pulling together risk governance, identification and measurement, infrastructure, and policies and processes and continually reviewing and reevaluating in the face of changing risk exposures and risk drivers. Further, it requires recognizing when the entity's risk exposure is not aligned with its predetermined risk tolerance, and then taking action to bring them back into alignment.

Communication of critical risk issues must happen continuously across all levels of the organization.

Note that:

- Risk management is not about minimizing risk. It is about actively understanding and embracing those risks that offer the best chance of achieving organization's goals with an acceptable chance of failure.
- Risk management is not even about predicting risks. It is about being prepared for (positive or negative) unpredictable events such that their impact would have already been quantified and considered in advance.

RISK GOVERNANCE

An Enterprise View of Risk

The governing body, or board, plays the following roles within the risk management framework:

- It determines the organization's goals and priorities, which form the basis of enterprise risk management.
- It determines the organization's risk appetite/tolerance i.e., defines which risks are acceptable, which risks must be mitigated and to what extent, and which risks are unacceptable.
- It is responsible for overseeing risk management to continually ensure that it is functioning properly, and is consistent with the goal of maximizing value.

Desirable Properties of Good Risk Governance

- Good risk governance should provide a sense of the worst loss that the organization can manage in various scenarios.
- It should provide clear guidance, but at the same time leave enough flexibility for management to execute strategy.
- The focus should be on enterprise risk management (that focuses on the objectives, health and value of the organization as a whole).
- It should provide a regular forum (e.g., a risk management committee) where the risk framework and key risk issues are discussed at management level.
- It should provide for the appointment of a chief risk officer (CRO) who is responsible for building and implementing the risk framework for the enterprise and managing all related activities. Further, the CRO's insight should be used in making key strategic decisions.

Risk Tolerance

Risk tolerance identifies the extent to which the entity is willing to experience losses or opportunity costs and to fail meeting its objectives. At the governance level, the idea is not really to select activities that will maximize value or produce the highest returns given an acceptable level of risk (this duty falls on management), but to define the entity's risk appetite.

Defining an organization's risk tolerance calls for answering the following questions:

- What shortfalls within the organization would cause it to fail to achieve critical goals? This questions looks to address internal risk factors.
- What uncertain forces is the organization exposed to? This question focusses on outside risk factors.

Factors that Affect a Company's Risk Tolerance

- The more dynamic a company in its ability to respond to adverse events, the higher its risk tolerance.
- The greater the loss a company can bear without impairing its status as a going concern, the higher its risk tolerance.
- The stronger the company's competitive position, the higher its risk tolerance.
- The overall competitive landscape in the industry and the regulatory landscape also influence a company's risk tolerance.

Risk Budgeting

Risk budgeting focuses on how risk is taken by quantifying and allocating tolerable risk to various activities/investments based on their characteristics.

Risk budgets can be complex/multi-dimensional or simple/one-dimensional.

- Single-dimension risk measures include standard deviation, beta, value at risk (VaR) and scenario loss.
- Multi-dimension risk approaches include one where portfolio risk is evaluated based on the risk profiles of underlying asset classes (equity, fixed income, etc.), and another risk-factor approach where exposure to various risk factors is used to capture associated risk premiums (value stocks versus growth stocks).

The benefit of risk budgeting lies in the fact that it forces the organization into thinking about risk trade-offs and fosters a culture where risk is an important consideration in all key decisions.

IDENTIFICATION OF RISKS

Financial Risks

- Market risk arises from changes in interest rates, stock prices, exchange rates and commodity prices.
  - Generally speaking, the underlying risk drivers of market risk are fundamental economic conditions or events in the overall economy, industry or the company itself.
- Credit risk (default risk or counterparty risk) is the risk of loss if one party fails to pay an amount owed on an obligation (e.g., bond or derivative).
  - Generally speaking, the underlying risk drivers of credit risk tend to be fundamental weakness in the economy, industry or in demand for a company's products.

- **Liquidity risk** (or **transaction cost risk**) is the risk of a substantial downward valuation adjustment when trying to sell an asset.
  - In several transactions, there is a bid-ask spread that is known at the time of purchase. This spread is simply a **transaction cost**. Liquidity risk would arise if this spread would widen when it the asset is being sold.
  - Generally speaking, the primary drivers of liquidity risk are (1) changes in market conditions or the market for the individual asset and (2) the size of the position i.e., large positions are typically more difficult and costly to offload.

Non-Financial Risks

- **Settlement risk** (also known as **Herstatt risk**) is related to default risk, but has more to do with settlement of payments just before a default.
- **Legal risk** is of two types. First, there is the risk of being sued for something the entity does or fails to do. Second, there is the risk of the terms of a contract not being upheld by the legal system.
- **Compliance risk** encompasses **regulatory risk**, **accounting risk** and **tax risk**. It refers to the risk of the organization incurring significant unexpected costs, back taxes, financial restatements and penalties.
- **Model risk** is the risk of a valuation error resulting from using an incorrectly specified model or improperly using a valid model.
  - **Tail risk** is related to model risk, and can even be viewed as a form of model risk. It refers to the risk of events captured by the tail of a distribution occurring more frequently than expected by the model.
- **Operational risk** is used to describe all internal risks that arise from the people and processes that work together in an organization to produce its output. Examples include the risk of hackers breaking into the company's computer systems, its computers becoming infected with a virus, and programming errors and bugs.
- **Solvency risk** is the risk that the entity runs out cash, and is therefore unable to survive or succeed, even if it is otherwise solvent.

Interactions between Risks

It is very important for organizations to recognize that risks interact, and that the interaction is more 'toxic' in stressed market conditions. When different sources of risk come together, the combined risk is almost always non-linear in that the total risk faced is much greater than the simple sum of the individual risks, and this makes the situation even worse. Unfortunately, most risk models and systems do not directly account for risk interactions.

MEASURING AND MODIFYING RISKS

Value at Risk (VaR)

Value at risk or **VaR** is a measure of the size of the tail of the distribution of profits on a portfolio or for an entity. A VaR measure is composed of (1) a currency amount, (2) a time period, and (3) a probability. If a bank states that its VaR is $4 million at 3% for one day, it means that bank expects to lose a minimum of $4 million in one day 3% of the time.

- VaR is a **minimum** extreme loss metric.
  - There is no ultimate maximum loss that is stated in the measure. However, the statistics used to compute VaR can be used to estimate average extreme losses.
    - **Conditional VaR** or **CVaR** is calculated as the weighted average of all loss outcomes in a statistical distribution that exceed the VaR loss.
    - **Expected loss given default** (which is used to measure credit risk) measures the average expected loss if the underlying company defaults.
- VaR can be measured in several different ways, which results in highly diverse estimates.
- VaR is subject to model risk as well.
  - VaR is based on a particular assumption about the probability distribution of returns or profits. If that assumption is incorrect, the VaR estimate will be incorrect.
  - VaR also requires certain inputs. If those inputs are incorrect, the VaR estimate will be incorrect.
- VaR can understate actual risk. Under the normal distribution, extreme negative returns are accounted for, but they are offset by extreme positive returns. However, actual historical returns have exhibited a tendency for more extreme negative returns than assumed by the normal distribution (tail risk). In response, statisticians have developed **extreme value theory** to help them gauge the likelihood of outcomes that exceed those that would normally be expected.

Due to its shortcomings, critics have argued that naive users of VaR can be lulled into a false sense of security. A presumably tolerable VaR can give the illusion that risk is under control, even when it is actually not. Nonetheless, VaR is accepted as a risk measure by most banking regulators and is approved for disclosure purposes in accounting standards.

Two measures in particular that are often used to complement VaR are **scenario analysis** and **stress testing**. Although scenario analysis and stress testing can provide useful information (and banks are required to perform them) they are also subject to model risk.

METHODS OF RISK MODIFICATION

Risk Prevention and Avoidance

In organizations, the board typically decides which business or investment activities are not worth pursuing based on the organization's goals and the perceived risk-return trade-off. Areas where the board believes management has a better chance of adding value are the ones whose risks are taken, but they are still managed via (1) self-insurance, (2) risk transfer, or (3) risk shifting.

Risk Acceptance: Self-Insurance and Diversification

- **Self-insurance** refers to retaining exposure to a risk that is considered undesirable but is too costly to eliminate by external means.
- **Diversification** is another form of accepting risk, but it does so in the most efficient manner possible. When it comes to portfolio risk management, diversification is the key to eliminating non-systematic risk, but other forms of risk management may be needed to mitigate other risks.

Risk Transfer is the process of passing on a risk to another party, usually in the form of an insurance policy.

Risk shifting refers to actions that change the distribution of risk outcomes. Risk shifting is associated with derivative contracts and risk modification vehicles. Risk shifting mechanism are used when the organization wants to modify the probability distribution of returns, or adjust the payoff diagram of its risk exposures.

How to Choose a Method for Modifying Risk

Generally speaking:

- For risks that lie outside the core competencies of the organization, management should try to avoid those risks. If the potential value added is too great to ignore, then management must at least take adequate precautions.
- Organizations that have large amounts of free cash flow should self-insure as much as possible because self-insurance reduces costs and enables the company to retain flexibility. At the same time, organizations should aim to diversify as much as possible.
- Insurance works best when risks can be pooled, but this is not the case for many types of risks, particularly those that can affect a large number of parties at the same time as premiums can be prohibitively high.
- For financial risks that exceed risk appetite, risk shifting is a very common choice. However, risk shifting tools such as derivatives may not be available for all types of risks.

FINTECH IN INVESTMENT MANAGEMENT
Cross-Reference to CFA Institute Assigned Reading #43

Fintech refers to the use of technology-based innovations that are changing the way financial services and products are being designed and delivered to clientele.

Big Data refers to the massive amounts of data produced by financial markets, businesses, governments, individuals, and sensor networks.

- Structured data can be stored in database tables.
- Unstructured data cannot be stored in tables.
- Semi-structured data can have both characteristics.

Artificial Intelligence(AI) is designed to perform cognitive or decision-making tasks in a comparable or superior manner to human intelligence.

Machine learning (ML) consists of computer programs that use algorithms to learn how to complete tasks over time so that greater experience translates into better performance.

Analysts must they to ensure that they select appropriate input data and appropriate data analysis techniques. They must always be wary of overfitting data (which occurs when the program learns inputs and targeted outputs too precisely) and underfitting data (which occurs when a program is too simplistic, precluding the ML program from identifying relationships and patterns when training with a dataset). Finally, they must be wary of their programs becoming "black box" approaches, which can create results that are inexplicable or hard to understand.

Types of Machine Learning

Supervised learning involves labeling or identifying inputs and outputs to the algorithm so that it can be trained to identify relationships for labeled data and work with other data sets.

Unsupervised learning does not involve giving programs labeled data, but instead requires algorithms to describe the data and its structure on its own.

Deep learning (or deep learning nets) is a technique that uses neural networks to perform multistage, nonlinear processing to identify patterns and relationships in data through a supervised or unsupervised approach.

Data Science

Data science is an interdisciplinary field that uses advances in computer science (including machine learning), statistics, and other disciplines for the purpose of extracting information from Big Data (or data in general). Data-processing methods include data capture, curation, storage, search, and transfer.

Data visualization refers to how the data will be formatted, displayed, and summarized in graphical form. Traditional structured data can be visualized using tables, charts, and trends, while non-traditional unstructured data require new techniques of data visualization. Some of these newer techniques that can be applied to textual data include tag clouds and mind maps.

Common programming languages used in data science include Python, R, Java, C/C++, and Excel VBA. Common databases include SQL, SQLite, and NoSQL.

Fintech Applications in Investment Management

- Text analytics is the use of programs to retrieve and analyze information from unrelated sources to conduct predictive analysis and find indicators of future performance.
- Natural language processing (NLP) is the analysis and interpretation of language using artificial intelligence, including translation, speech recognition, and text mining.
- Robo-advisory services aim to provide cost-effective and easily accessible investment solutions through the Internet without the interaction of human financial advisers.
- Risk analysis applications include stress-testing financial institutions, identifying adverse near-term market trends, detecting declining corporate earnings, analyzing real-time trading patterns, portfolio scenario analysis and back-testing, and assessing alternative data quality.
- Algorithmic trading involves computerized buying and selling based on prespecified rules and guidelines for lowering costs, improving execution speed, and providing anonymity for investment managers. High-frequency trading (HFT) is a form of algorithmic trading that uses real-time, granular market data to execute trades in fractions of a second through ultra-high-speed networks when certain conditions are met.

Distributed Ledger Technology

Distributed ledger technology (DLT) is a new form of financial recordkeeping that allows entities to share database information through networks. A DLT network consists of a digital ledger and a consensus mechanism that involves networked computers (or nodes) validating transactions and agreeing on updates to create unchangeable records that are easily accessible to participants on a near-real-time basis. To provide security for networks and database integrity, DLTs use cryptography (or algorithms) to encrypt data so that it is unusable to any unauthorized parties.

Blockchains are digital ledgers where information is sequentially recorded in "blocks" that are "chained" together using cryptography. This means transactions are grouped together into blocks that are linked to previous blocks through a secure link (or "hash").

- In permissioned networks, members might have restrictions on their activities and level of access to the ledger, such as adding transactions, viewing transactions, and seeing limited details of transactions.

- In a permissionless (or open) DLT network, all users can see every blockchain transaction and have the ability to perform all network functions.

Potential applications of DLT to investment management include cryptocurrencies, tokenization, post-trade clearing and settlement, and compliance.

Challenges to the Adoption of DLT by the Investment Industry

- Lack of DLT network standardization.
- Not be financially competitive with existing solutions.
- Substantial storage and power requirements.
- Accidental trades can only be undone by submitting offsetting trades (due to immutability of transactions).
- Regulatory approaches typically differ by jurisdiction.

STUDY SESSION 14:
EQUITY INVESTMENTS (1)

MARKET ORGANIZATION AND STRUCTURE
Cross-Reference to CFA Institute Assigned Reading #44

Functions of a Financial System

1. Help people achieve their purposes in using the financial system.
2. To facilitate the discovery of the rate of return where aggregate savings equal aggregate borrowings.
3. Allocating capital to its most efficient uses.

Classifications of Assets and Markets

Assets may be classified as financial or physical assets:

- Financial assets include securities, currencies and contracts.
- Physical assets include commodities and real assets.

Markets may be classified on the basis of:

- The timing of delivery.
- Who the seller is.
- The maturity of instruments that are traded.
- The types of securities.

Securities

Securities include bonds, notes, commercial paper, mortgages, common stock, preferred stock, warrants, mutual fund shares, unit trusts and depository receipts. They may be classified as:

- **Public securities** that trade in public markets (e.g., exchanges). Issuers of public securities are usually required to comply with strict rules and regulatory standards.
- **Private securities** that can typically only be purchased by qualified investors. Private securities are relatively illiquid.

Fixed Income Securities

Fixed income instruments are promises to repay borrowed money. Payments (which include interest and principal amounts) may be pre-specified or may vary according to a fixed formula based on a reference rate. Fixed income instruments may be classified as:

- *Notes*: Fixed income securities with maturities of 10 years or less.
- *Bonds*: Fixed income securities with maturities greater than 10 years.
- *Bills*: These are issued by governments and have maturities of one year or less.
- *Certificates of deposit*: These are issued by banks and usually mature within a year.
- *Commercial paper*: These are issued by corporations and usually mature within a year.

- *Repurchase agreements*: These are short-term lending instruments.
- *Money market instruments*: These are traded in the money market and have maturities of one year or less.

Equities

Equity owners have ownership rights in a company. Equity securities include:

- *Common shares*: Holders of common shares can participate in the company's decision-making process. They are entitled to receive dividends declared by the company, and if the company goes bankrupt, they have a claim on the company's assets after all other claims have been satisfied.
- *Preferred shares*: Preferred shareholders have a higher priority in claims on dividends and on the company's assets in case of liquidation. They are entitled to receive fixed dividends on a regular basis.
- *Warrants*: Holders of warrants have the right to purchase an entity's common stock at a pre-specified price at, or before the warrants' expiration date.

Pooled Investments

Pooled investment vehicles (e.g., mutual funds, depositories, and hedge funds) issue securities that represent shared ownership in the assets held by them. People invest in these vehicles to benefit from their investment management expertise and to diversify their portfolios.

- *Asset-backed securities*: Companies often use pools of loans or receivables (e.g., auto loans and leases, consumer loans, credit cards, etc.) as underlying assets to issue securities known as asset-backed securities. These securities then transfer any interest and principal payments from the underlying assets to their holders on a monthly basis.

Currencies

These are monies issued by national monetary authorities and primarily trade in the foreign currency market. Retail currency trades occur through ATM machines, credit cards and debit cards when transactions are executed in currencies different from the currency held in customers' accounts.

Contracts

Contracts are agreements between two or more parties to do something in the future. A contract's value depends on the value of its underlying, which may be a commodity, a security, an index, an interest rate or even another contract. Contracts may be settled in cash or may require physical delivery, and may be classified on the basis of:

- The nature of the underlying asset
- The timing of delivery

Forward Contracts

A forward is a contract between two parties, where one (the long position) has the obligation to buy, and the other (the short position) has an obligation to sell an underlying asset at a fixed price (established at the inception of the contract) at a future date. Market participants usually enter a forward contract to hedge a pre-existing risk.

Future Contracts

Futures contracts are similar to forward contracts in that they may also be deliverable or cash-settled, but there are also significant differences between the two. Unlike forward contracts:

- Futures contracts are standardized and trade on organized exchanges.
- A clearinghouse is the counterparty to all futures contracts.

Swap Contracts

A swap is an agreement between two parties to exchange a series of cash flows at periodic settlement dates over a certain period of time. A swap may also be looked upon as a series of forward contracts.

Option Contracts

Option contracts give their holders the right to buy or sell a security at a predetermined price (exercise price) some time in the future.

- **Call options** give their holders the right to purchase the underlying asset at some future date at the option's exercise price. Holders are likely to exercise their call options when the price of the underlying asset is greater than the exercise price.
- **Put options** give their holders the right to sell the underlying asset at some future date at the option's exercise price. Holders are likely to exercise their put options when the price of the underlying asset is lower than the exercise price.

Options that can only be exercised at their expiration dates are known as European options, while options that can be exercised anytime until, or at their expiration dates are known as American options.

Insurance Contracts

People often enter into insurance contracts to protect themselves from unexpected losses. Insurance contracts include credit default swaps (CDSs) that promise to pay their holders the amount of principal in case a company defaults on its bonds.

Commodities

Commodities include precious metals, energy products, industrial metals, agricultural products, and carbon credits. Commodities may trade in the spot market (for immediate delivery) or in the forward or futures market (for delivery in the future).

EI

Real Assets

Real assets include tangible properties such as real estate, airplanes, machinery and lumber stands. Institutional investors are increasingly adding them to their portfolios either directly (through direct ownership of the asset), or indirectly (through investments in securities of companies that invest in these assets). Real assets are attractive because:

- They may have low correlations with other assets in the investor's portfolio, thus providing diversification benefits.
- They offer income and tax benefits to investors.

Real asset valuation is very difficult due to the heterogeneous nature of each investment. Further, real assets tend to be relatively illiquid and entail high management costs.

FINANCIAL INTERMEDIARIES

Brokers, Exchanges, and Alternative Trading Systems

Brokers are agents who fulfill orders for their clients. They reduce costs of trading for their clients by finding counterparties for their trades.

- *Block brokers* provide brokerage services to large traders.
- *Investment banks* provide a variety of services to companies, including:
  - Arranging initial and seasoned security offerings.
  - Issuing securities to finance their business.
  - Identifying and acquiring other companies.

Exchanges provide a platform where traders can carry out their trades.

Alternative Trading Systems (ATSs) (also known as electronic communications networks, ECNs, and multilateral trading facilities, MTFs) are trading venues just like exchanges. However, they differ from exchanges in that they do not exercise regulatory authority over their members except with respect to the conduct of their trading in their trading networks. Many ATSs are known as "dark pools" because they do not display orders sent to them.

Dealers

Unlike brokers, dealers fulfil orders for their clients by actually taking positions as counterparties for their trades. Essentially, they indirectly connect two traders who arrive in the market at different points in time. By acting as counterparties to trades, dealers create liquidity in the market.

Dealers may also often act as brokers and vice-versa, so practitioners often use the term **broker-dealer** to refer to brokers and dealers.

Securitizers

Securitization is the process of buying assets, placing them in a pool, and issuing securities that represent ownership of the assets in the pool. Entities that undertake this process are known as securitizers. They create and sell securitized instruments and act as financial intermediaries by connecting borrowers and lenders.

Depository Institutions and Other Financial Corporations

Depository institutions include commercial banks, savings and loan banks, credit unions, and other institutions that gather funds from depositors and lend them to borrowers. Brokers also act as financial intermediaries when they lend funds deposited by their clients to other clients who wish to buy securities on margin. Such brokers are known as **prime brokers.**

Insurance Companies

Insurance companies create and sell contracts that protect buyers of these contracts from risks that they seek protection from. Insurance companies are financial intermediaries as they connect the buyers of insurance contracts with investors, creditors and reinsurers who are willing to bear the insured risks. Insurance buyers benefit as they are able to transfer risks to entities that are willing to assume them, while owners, creditors and reinsurers of the insurance company (who assume these risks) benefit from being able to sell their tolerance to risk without having to manage the contracts. Managing insurance contracts requires the insurance company to manage fraud, moral hazard and adverse selection.

- Fraud occurs when people deliberately report fake losses.
- Moral hazard occurs when people are less careful about avoiding losses as they are covered by insurance.
- Adverse selection occurs as only those who are most at risk usually buy insurance.

Arbitrageurs

Arbitrageurs, who buy and sell the same security in two different markets (at different prices), act as financial intermediaries as they effectively connect sellers in one market with buyers in another market. They also bring liquidity to markets.

Settlement and Custodial Services

Clearinghouses arrange for the final settlement of trades. They also serve as guarantors of performance in futures markets and as escrow agents in other markets. Banks and broker-dealers may offer custodial services for holding securities on behalf of their clients. This helps prevent the loss of securities through fraud or oversight.

A position in an asset refers to the quantity of the asset that an entity owns or owes.

- A person with a long position owns an assets or a contract. She benefits when there is an increase in the price of the asset or contract.
- A person with a short position has sold an asset that she does not own, or has written or sold a contract. She benefits when there is a decrease in the price of the asset or contract.

Positions on Forwards and Futures

The long position in a forward or a futures contract is the side that is obligated to take physical delivery of the asset or its cash equivalent at contract expiration. She will benefit from an increase in the price of the underlying asset.

The short position in a forward or a futures contract is the side that is obligated to make physical delivery of the asset or its cash equivalent at contract expiration. She will benefit from a decrease in the price of the underlying asset.

Positions on Options

The long position on an options contract is the party that holds the right to exercise the option. The short side refers to the writer of the option, who must satisfy any obligations arising from the contract.

- The long position on a call option will benefit when the underlying rises in value.
- The short position on a call option will benefit when the underlying falls in value.
- The long position on a put option will benefit when the underlying falls in value.
- The short position on a put option will benefit when the underlying rises in value.

Swap Contracts

The two parties in a swap contract simply agree to exchange contractually determined cash flows. There is no real buyer or seller, which makes it difficult to determine the long and short side of the contract. Usually, the party that benefits from an increase in the quoted price is referred to as the long.

Currency Contracts

A party that purchases one currency simultaneously sells another currency (the other currency in the price quote or exchange rate). Therefore, whenever we mention a long or a short position in a currency contract, we must mention the other currency as well. For example, we may state that a party is long on the dollar against the yen.

Short Positions

Short positions in contracts are created by selling contracts that the short seller does not own. The short seller is basically the issuer of the contract.

Short positions in securities are created by selling securities that the short seller does not own. In order to sell the securities, the short seller borrows the securities from long holders to deliver them to buyers. To unwind the position, the short seller then repurchases the security (hopefully at a lower price) from the market and returns it to the long holder.

The maximum profit for the holder of a long position on an asset is unlimited, while her losses are limited to the price she purchased the asset for. In contrast, the maximum profit for a short seller of an asset is limited to her selling price, while her losses are unlimited.

Levered Positions

Many markets allow investors to borrow funds from brokers to purchase securities. The investor borrows a portion of the price of the stock, contributes the rest of the funds herself and puts up the stock as collateral. The borrowed money is known as the margin loan and the interest rate paid on it is the call money rate.

Traders who purchase securities on margin face minimum margin requirements. The initial margin requirement refers to the proportion of the total cost of the asset that an investor must invest with her own equity. This requirement may be determined by the government, the exchange or the clearinghouse.

When traders borrow money to purchase securities, they are said to be leveraging their positions. The leverage ratio is the ratio of the value of the position to the value of the equity investment in it. The maximum leverage ratio for a position financed by a margin loan equals one divided by the minimum margin requirement.

Leverage enhances a trader's returns, but also magnifies losses.

In addition to the initial margin requirement, traders who invest on margin must also adhere to maintenance margin requirements. If the proportion of the value of the security financed by the investor's own equity (after adjusting for the price change) falls below the maintenance margin, the investor will receive a margin call, and she would have to deposit enough funds into her account to at least meet the maintenance margin level. If she fails to do so, her broker can sell the stock to pay off the margin loan.

The price at which an investor who goes long on a stock receives a margin call is calculated as:

$$P_0 \times \frac{(1 - \text{Initial margin})}{(1 - \text{Maintenance margin})}$$

Traders who sell securities short are also subject to margin requirements as they have borrowed securities to take their positions.

Execution, Validity, and Clearing Instructions

The prices at which dealers and other proprietary traders are willing to buy securities are called bid prices and those at which they are willing to sell are called ask (or offer) prices. The quantities that market participants are willing to trade at the bid and ask prices are called bid sizes and ask sizes respectively.

The highest bid in the market is the highest price that a dealer is willing to pay for the security and is known as the best bid. On the other hand, the lowest ask price is the best offer. The difference between the best bid and the best offer is the market bid-ask spread. Liquid markets with low transaction costs generally have small bid-ask spreads.

Execution Instructions

Execution instructions indicate how an order should be filled. They include:

- Market orders, which instruct brokers or the exchange to fill an order immediately at the best available price. Market orders generally execute immediately as long as there are traders willing to take the other side of the trade. However, they may be expensive to execute, especially when the order size is large relative to the normal trading activity in the market.
- Limit orders, which instruct the broker or the exchange to fill an order at a specified price or better. These specified prices (maximum price for a limit buy order and minimum price for a limit sell order) are referred to as limit prices. Limit orders prevent trades from executing at unacceptable prices. However, this also means that they may not execute at all if the limit price on a buy order is too low or the limit price on a sell order is too high.
  - A limit buy order is aggressively priced when the limit price is high relative to the market "bid" and "ask" prices.
  - A limit buy order placed above the best offer is likely to be at least partially executed immediately and is called a marketable limit order.
  - A limit buy order placed above the best bid but below the best offer is said to have created a new market by establishing the new best bid.
  - A limit buy order placed at the best bid is said to make market. This order will have to wait for all buy orders (that were placed earlier) at that price to execute first.
  - A limit buy order placed below the best bid is referred to as behind the market and will not execute unless market prices drop. These orders are known as standing limit orders.

Exposure Instructions

Exposure instructions specify whether, how and to whom orders may be exposed.

Hidden orders are exposed only to the brokers or exchanges that receive them. Other traders can discover hidden size only after submitting orders that will trade with that size. However, hidden orders may not execute at all as other traders do not know about them. Therefore, traders may sometimes indicate a specific display size (which is lower than the actual order size) with their orders to signal to other traders that someone is willing to trade at the displayed price. As most of the order size is hidden, these orders are also referred to as iceberg orders.

Validity Instructions

Validity instructions indicate when an order may be filled. They include:

- Day orders, which are only valid for the day on which they are submitted. These orders expire if not filled at the close of business.
- Good till-cancelled orders, which are valid until cancelled by the broker.
- Immediate or cancel orders, which may only be filled, completely or in part, immediately and are otherwise cancelled. These are also known as fill or kill orders.
- Good-on-close orders, which only execute at the close of trading and are also called market-on-close orders.
- Stop orders (often referred to as stop-loss orders), which are placed by investors to protect themselves from adverse price movements.

Clearing Instructions

Clearing instructions indicate how the final settlement of trades should be arranged. They include details of the entities responsible for clearing and settling the trade. Further, security sale orders must also indicate whether the sale is a long sale or a short sale.

Primary Markets

Primary markets are markets where issuers first sell their securities to investors. When a security is issued to the public for the first time, it is referred to as an initial public offering (IPO). On the other hand, when additional units of a previously issued security are sold, it is referred to as a seasoned offering (or a secondary offering) and the issue is called a seasoned issue.

Public Offerings

Companies generally issue securities to the public through an investment bank. The investment bank performs the following functions:

- Through a process called book building, it lines up subscribers who wish to purchase the security.
- It provides investment information about the issuer to its clients and to the public.

The issuer's arrangement with the investment bank may take one of the following forms:

- In an underwriting offer, the investment bank guarantees the sale of the issue at an offering price negotiated with the issuer. If the issue is not fully subscribed, the investment bank commits to purchasing the leftover securities at the offer price.
- In a best efforts offering, the investment bank merely acts as a broker. It tries its best to sell the securities at the negotiated price, but does not promise to purchase unsold securities.

Private Placements

In a private placement securities are not offered to the public. Companies sell securities directly to a group of qualified investors, usually through an investment bank. Qualified investors are generally those who understand associated risks and have sufficient wealth to withstand significant losses. Privately placements are typically cheaper than public offerings as they do not require as much public disclosure. However, since privately placed securities do not trade on organized secondary markets, investors require a higher rate of return from them.

Other Primary Market Transactions

- Companies that issue securities via a *shelf registration* make all the public disclosures that are required in a regular offering, but they do not need to issue all the shares at once. They can sell them directly in the secondary market over time, which offers them flexibility as they can raise capital when they need it.
- Companies that issue securities through *dividend reinvestment plans (DRPs)* allow shareholders to reinvest their dividends by purchasing shares of the company. These shares may be newly issued or purchased from the open market.
- Companies sometimes offer *rights* to existing shareholders to purchase additional shares of the company in proportion to their current holdings at a fixed price.

Secondary Markets

The secondary market is that part of the financial market where previously issued securities and financial instruments are traded. Secondary markets play a very important role in that they provide liquidity to investors who purchased their securities in the primary market. Investors will hesitate to participate in the primary market if they cannot subsequently sell their holdings in the secondary market.

Secondary markets are also important for seasoned security issuers as the prices of their new offerings are derived from the secondary market prices of currently outstanding securities that trade on the secondary market.

Trading Sessions

In a call market, all bid and ask prices for an asset are gathered to determine one price where the quantity offered for sale is close to the quantity demanded. All transactions take place at this single price. Call markets are popular in smaller markets. However, they are also used on larger exchanges to determine the opening price of a trading session.

In a continuous market, transactions can take place whenever the market is open. Prices are set either through an auction process or by dealer bid-ask quotes. Most global stock exchanges are continuous markets.

EI

of a call market is that it makes it easier for buyers and sellers to find each
ring all traders at the same place at the same time. In a continuous market,
seller (or their orders) are not present at the same time, they cannot trade.
e of a continuous market is that a willing buyer and seller can trade anytime
open. In a call market they would only be able to trade when the market is

echanisms

market (order-driven) is one where participants submit their bid and ask
ral location. Matching bids and offers are paired together and orders are
r-driven matching mechanisms are characterized by two sets of rules:

matching rules match buy orders to sell orders. They rank buy and sell
based on:
Price precedence: Highest priced buy orders and lowest priced sell orders
re ranked first.
isplay precedence: Displayed quantities have precedence over
displayed quantities at the same price.
me precedence: Orders that arrived first have precedence over orders that
rived later with the same price and with the same display status.
cing rules determine the prices at which matched trades take place. Prices
termined based on any of the following:
der a uniform pricing rule, the same price is used for all trades. This rule
sed by call markets where the market chooses the price that maximizes
l quantity traded.
der a discriminatory pricing rule, the limit price of the order or quote
arrived first (the standing order) determines the trade price. Continuous
ling markets use this rule.
erivative pricing rule uses the mid-point of the best bid and ask quotes
m another market. Crossing networks (which may themselves be
anized as call or continuous trading markets) use this pricing rule.

ote driven market or price-driven market) consists of individual
signed specific securities. These dealers create liquidity by purchasing
their own inventory of securities. Competition between dealers ensures
ces are available.

arket, brokers arrange trades among their clients. Brokers organize
ique items (e.g., real estate properties and fine art masterpieces) that only
ted number of people.

Market Information Systems

Markets may be structured based on the type and quantity of information th
to the public.

- Pre-trade transparent markets publish real time data about quotes an(
- Post-trade transparent markets publish data about trade prices soon a
  occur.

Characteristics of a Well-Functioning Financial System

- Timely and accurate information on the price and volume of recent
  If timely information is not available, a seller may not get the best p
  and a buyer may end up paying too high a price.
- Liquidity, which refers to the ability to buy or sell the asset quickly,
  close to that of a recent market transaction, assuming no new inforr
  received. To achieve price continuity, the market must be significa
- Internal efficiency in that there are low transaction costs, which in
  of reaching the market and brokerage costs.
- External or informational efficiency, which is achieved when mar
  all external available information about an asset. Prices should ra
  reflect any new information.

Objectives of Market Regulation

- Control fraud or deception of uninformed market participants.
- Control agency problems by setting minimum standards of com
  and by defining and enforcing minimum standards of practice.
- Promote fairness by creating a level playing field for market par
- Set mutually beneficial standards for financial reporting.
- Prevent undercapitalized financial firms from exploiting their in
  excessively risky investments; and
- Ensure that long-term liabilities are funded.

The advantage
other by gathe
if a buyer and
The advantage
the market is
called.

Execution M

A pure auction
prices to a cent
executed. Orde

- Order
  orders
  - a
  - D
    u
  - T
    ar
- Trade pri
  may be de
  - Un
    is u
    tota
  - Un
    tha
    trac
  - A d
    fro
    org

A dealer market (
dealers who are as
and selling against
that competitive pr

In a brokered m
markets for un
interest a limi

ey disseminate

d orders.
fter trades

transactions.
ossible price,

at a price
nation has been
ntly deep.
clude the costs

ket prices reflect
apidly adjust to

petence for agents

ticipants.

vestors by making

SECURITY MARKET INDEXES
oss-Reference to CFA Institute Assigned Reading #45

et index consists of individual securities (also called constituent
present a given security market, market segment, or asset class. Each
dex may have two versions depending on how returns are calculated:

turn index only reflects the prices of constituent securities.
urn index not only reflects prices, but also assumes reinvestment of all
ceived since inception.

h versions of an index are the same at inception. However, as time
turn index will be greater in value than the price return index by an

on

anaging a security market index involves:

et selection
ection
ting

on

Security Selection

ay be based on:

g., equities, fixed income, or real estate)
ion (e.g., Japan, South Africa or Europe)
n which the securities are traded (e.g., New York, London or

stics (e.g., economic sector, company size and investment style)

all the securities in the target market or just a representative
et.

ed index the weight of each constituent security is determined by
ce by the sum of the prices of all constituent securities:

$$= \frac{P_i}{\sum\limits_{i=1}^{N} P_i}$$

The value of a price-weighted index is computed by dividing the sum of th[e]
prices by the divisor. At inception, the divisor is typically set to the number
the index.

The advantage of a price-weighted index is its simplicity. One of the issue[s]
weighted index is that a stock split or stock dividend by one of the consti[tu]
changes the weights of all securities in the index. To prevent stock splits [and]
dividends from changing the value of the index, the divisor of a price-wei[ghted]
be adjusted.

Equal Weighting

In an equal-weighted index, each constituent security is given an identica[l]
index at inception. The weights are calculated as:

$$w_i^E = \frac{1}{N}$$

The number of shares of each security included in the index is calculate[d]
allotted to each constituent security divided by the price of the security.
weighted index, where the weights are arbitrarily determined by marke[t]
weights in an equal-weighted index are effectively determined by the i[ndex]
choosing the particular weighting mechanism).

Equal-weighted indices are also preferred because of their simplicity.
a few disadvantages:

- Assigning an equal weight to all securities under-represents (o[ver])
  those securities that constitute a relatively large (small) fracti[on]
  market.
- The index does not remain equally weighted once the price[s]
  securities change. Frequent adjustments must be made to m[aintain]
  weighting.

Market-Capitalization Weighting

A market-capitalization weighted (value weighted) index is based
value (current stock price times the total number of shares outstand[ing])
index. The proportion of each constituent security is determined by
capitalization by the total market capitalization of all the securities i[n]

$$w_i^M = \frac{Q_i P_i}{\sum_{j=1}^{N} Q_j P_j}$$

A **security mar**

securities) that re

security market i

- A price re
- A total re
  income re

The values of bot

passes, the total r

increasing amoun

Index Constructi

Constructing and m

- Target mark
- Security sel
- Index weigh
- Rebalancing
- Reconstituti

Target Market and

The **target market** m

- Asset class (e.
- Geographic reg
- The exchange
  Tokyo)
- Other characteri

An index may consist of

sample of the target mark

Index Weighting

Price Weighting

In a price-weigh

dividing its pri

$$w_i^P$$

e security

r of securities in

s with a price-

uent securities

and stock

ghted index must

l weight in the

ed as the value

Unlike a price-

t prices, the

ndex provider (in

However, they have

over-represents)

on of the target

s of the constituent

aintain equal

on the total market

ling) of all stocks in the

dividing its market

the index:

The initial market value is assigned a base number (e.g., 100) and a new market value is computed periodically. The change in the index is measured by comparing the new market value to the base market value.

Value-weighted indices automatically adjust for stock splits and stock dividends.

Float-Adjusted Market-Capitalization Weighting

In a float-adjusted market-capitalization weighted index, the proportion of each constituent security is determined by adjusting its market capitalization for its market float.

Market float generally refers to the number of shares of the constituent security that are available to the investing public. Shares held by controlling shareholders, other corporations and governments are subtracted from the total number of outstanding shares to determine the market float.

The float-adjusted market-capitalization weight of each constituent security is calculated as:

$$w_i^M = \frac{f_i Q_i P_i}{\sum_{j=1}^{N} f_j Q_j P_j}$$

The primary advantage of market capitalization weighting (and float-adjusted market capitalization weighting) is that securities are held in proportion to their value in the target market. A disadvantage is that stocks with larger market values have a larger impact on the index. Stocks that have seen their prices rise (fall) will see their relative weight in the index increase (decline). The effect of market value weighting is therefore similar to that of a momentum trading strategy.

Fundamental Weighting

Instead of using prices of constituent securities, a fundamental weighted index uses other measures of a company's size (that are independent of the stock price) such as book value, cash flow, revenues and earnings to determine weights of securities in the index. Some fundamental indices use a single measure to weight the constituent securities, while others combine weights from several measures to form a composite value that is used for weighting.

The fundamental weight on security i can be calculated as:

$$w_i^F = \frac{F_i}{\sum_{j=1}^{N} F_j}$$

In contrast to market-capitalization weighted indices, in which the weight of a stock in the index moves in the same direction as its price, fundamental weighted indices have a "contrarian" effect in that the portfolio weights move away from securities whose prices have risen.

Rebalancing

In order to keep the weights of constituent securities consistent with the index's weighting method security weights must be adjusted or rebalanced.

- In equal-weighted indices, the weights of securities that have witnessed price appreciation increase over time, and weights of securities that have underperformed decrease over time. Rebalancing an equal-weighted index would require reducing the weight of securities that have outperformed and increasing the weight of securities that have underperformed.
- Price-weighted indices do not need to be rebalanced as the weight of each constituent security is determined by its price.
- Market-capitalization weighted indices rebalance themselves to reflect changes in the market-capitalization of constituent securities. They only need to be rebalanced to reflect mergers, acquisitions, liquidations, etc.

Reconstitution

Constituent securities need to be examined on a regular basis to evaluate whether they still meet the criteria for inclusion in the index. If they no longer meet the criteria, they must be replaced with securities that do meet the criteria. Index reconstitution is performed in order to:

- Reflect changes in the target market as a result of bankruptcies, de-listings, mergers, etc.
- Reflect the judgement of the selection committee.

Uses of Security Market Indices

- To gauge market sentiment.
- As proxies for measuring and modeling returns, systematic risk, and risk-adjusted performance.
- As proxies for asset classes in asset allocation models.
- As benchmarks for actively managed portfolios.
- As the basis for the creation of numerous investment products.

Types of Equity Indices

Broad market indices: A broad equity market index contains securities representing more than 90% of the selected market.

Multi-market indices: Multi-market indices consist of security market indices from different countries and may represent multiple national markets, geographic regions, economic development groups or even the entire world.

Sector indices: Sector indices only include securities representing a particular economic sector (e.g., finance, health care, technology, etc.) where the economic sector may be classified on a national, regional or global basis.

Style indices: Financial firms like Dow Jones and Standard & Poor's have developed different indices based on specific investment strategies used by portfolio managers. These indices include those based on size (e.g., small-cap versus large-cap equities) and others based on style (e.g., growth versus value stocks). Style indices generally have much higher turnover than broad market indices.

Fixed-Income Indices

Creating bond-market indices presents the following challenges:

- There is a broader universe of bonds than of stocks.
- The universe of bonds is constantly changing as a result of new issues, calls, and maturities.
- The price volatility of a bond (as measured by duration) is constantly changing. Duration changes with a bond's maturity and market yields.
- Current and continuous transaction prices are not available for bonds.

Types of Fixed-Income Indices

Fixed-income securities can be classified along the following dimensions:

- Type of issuer (government, government agency, corporation).
- Type of financing (general obligation, collateralized).
- Currency of payments.
- Maturity.
- Credit quality (investment grade, high yield, credit agency ratings).
- Absence or presence of inflation protection.

Fixed-income indices can be categorized as follows:

- Aggregate or broad market indices.
- Market sector indices.
- Style indices.
- Economic sector indices.
- Specialized indices such as high-yield, inflation-linked, and emerging market indices.

Indices Representing Alternative Investments

Commodity indices: Commodity indices consist of futures contracts on one or more commodities and have the following characteristics:

- They do not have an obvious weighting method so index providers create their own weighting methods.

- Different weighting methods lead to different exposures to specific commodities, which result in very different risk and return profiles of commodity indices.
- The performance of commodity indices may differ from that of the underlying commodities because indices consist of futures contracts on commodities rather than the actual commodities.

Real estate investment trust indices: Real estate indices represent the market for real estate and real estate securities. They can be categorized as:

- Appraisal indices
- Repeat sales indices
- Real estate investment trust (REIT) indices

REIT indices consist of shares of publicly traded REITs (public or private organizations that combine individual investors' funds and provide them access to real estate investments). Shares issued by REITs trade on various exchanges around the world and are priced continuously.

Hedge fund indices: Hedge fund indices are designed to represent the performance of hedge funds (private investment vehicles that typically use leverage and long and short investment strategies) on a very broad, global level or the strategy level. Hedge fund indices have the following characteristics:

- They rely on voluntary disclosures from funds as it is not mandatory for hedge funds to disclose performance to any party other than investors.
- If they do decide to disclose performance, hedge funds have a choice regarding which index or indices they report their performance to. Therefore, rather than index providers determining the constituents, the constituents determine the index. Further, different hedge fund indices may reflect very different performance for the hedge fund industry over the same period of time based on the hedge funds represented in those indices.
- Poorly performing hedge funds may stop reporting their performance to hedge fund indices or may cease to exist altogether. This leads to survivorship bias and an upward bias in hedge fund performance as represented by these indices.

MARKET EFFICIENCY
Cross-Reference to CFA Institute Assigned Reading #46

An informationally efficient market (an efficient market) is one where security prices adjust rapidly to reflect any new information. It is a market where asset prices reflect all past and present information.

Investment managers and analysts are interested in market efficiency because it dictates how many profitable trading opportunities may abound in the market.

- In an efficient market, it is difficult to find inaccurately priced securities. Therefore, superior risk-adjusted returns cannot be attained in an efficient market, and it would be wise to pursue a passive investment strategy which entails lower costs.
- In an inefficient market, securities may be mispriced and trading in these securities can offer positive risk-adjusted returns. In such a market, an active investment strategy may outperform a passive strategy on a risk-adjusted basis.

In an efficient market, the time frame required for security prices to reflect any new information is very short. Further, prices only adjust to new or unexpected information (surprises).

Market Value versus Intrinsic Value

The market value or market price of the asset is the price at which the asset can currently be bought or sold. It is determined by the interaction of demand and supply for the security in the market. Intrinsic value or fundamental value is the value of the asset that reflects all its investment characteristics accurately. Intrinsic values are estimated in light of all the available information regarding the asset; they are not known for certain.

In an efficient market, investors widely believe that the market price reflects a security's intrinsic value. On the other hand, in an inefficient market, investors may try to develop their own estimates of intrinsic value in order to profit from any mispricing (difference between the market price and intrinsic value).

Factors Contributing to and Impeding a Market's Efficiency

Market participants: Generally speaking, the greater the number of active market participants (investors and financial analysts) that analyze an asset or security, the greater the degree of efficiency in the market.

Information availability and financial disclosure: The availability of accurate and timely information regarding trading activities and traded companies contributes to market efficiency.

Limits to trading: The activities of arbitrageurs, who seek opportunities to trade on mispricings in the market to earn arbitrage (riskless) profits, contribute to market efficiency.

Transactions costs and information acquisition costs: Investors should consider transaction costs and information-acquisition costs in evaluating the efficiency of a market.

Two securities that should trade for the exact same price in an efficient market may trade at different prices if the costs of trading on the mispricing (to make a profit) for the lowest cost traders are greater than the potential profit. In such cases, these prices are still "efficient" within the bounds of arbitrage. The bounds of arbitrage are relatively narrow in highly liquid markets (e.g., U.S. T-bills), but wider in relatively illiquid markets.

Further, there are always costs associated with gathering and analyzing information. Net of information acquisition costs, the return offered on a security should be commensurate with the security's level of risk. If superior returns can be earned after deducting information-acquisition costs, the market is relatively inefficient.

EFFICIENT MARKET HYPOTHESES

Weak-Form Efficient Market Hypothesis

Weak-form EMH assumes that current stock prices reflect *all security market information* including historical trends in prices, returns, volumes and other market-generated information such as block trades and trading by specialists. Under this hypothesis, because current stock market prices have essentially factored in all historical data, future returns on a stock should be independent of past returns or patterns.

Proponents of weak-form EMH assert that abnormal risk-adjusted returns cannot be earned by using trading rules and technical analysis, which make investing decisions based on historical security market data.

On the whole, various tests for weak-form EMH have backed the theory that current market prices reflect all available security market information and lead to the conclusion that the markets tend to be weak-form efficient. However, there is evidence that in countries with developing markets (e.g., China, Bangladesh and Turkey) opportunities to profit from technical analysis do exist.

Semi-Strong Form Efficient Market Hypothesis

Semi-strong form EMH assumes that current security prices fully reflect *all security market information* and other public information. It encompasses weak-form EMH and also includes non-market public information such as dividend announcements, various financial ratios, and economic and political news in the set of information that is already factored into market values.

Proponents of the hypothesis assert that investors cannot earn abnormal risk-adjusted returns if their investment decisions are based on important material information after it has been made public. They stress that security prices rapidly adjust to reflect all public information.

Overall, semi-strong form EMH has received considerable support from studies in developed markets. In these markets, it has been found that abnormal risk-adjusted returns cannot be earned based on public information because security prices adjust for the information very quickly. However, there is some evidence that developing countries may not have semi-strong form efficient markets.

Strong-Form Efficient Market Hypothesis

Strong form EMH contends that stock prices reflect *all public and private information*. It implies that no group of investors has sole access to any information that is relevant in price formation. Basically, there is no information out there that has not already been accounted for in current market prices.

Strong-form EMH encompasses weak-form and semi-strong form EMH and assumes perfect markets where information is cost free and available to all. Under strong-form EMH, no one can consistently achieve abnormal risk-adjusted returns, not even company insiders.

Studies have found that securities markets are not strong form efficient. Abnormal risk-adjusted returns can be earned if material non-public information is used.

Implications of Efficient Market Hypothesis

- Securities markets are weak-form efficient. Therefore, past trends in prices cannot be used to earn superior risk-adjusted returns.
- Securities markets are also semi-strong form efficient. Therefore, investors who analyze information should consider what information is already factored into a security's price, and how any new information may affect its value.
- Securities markets are not strong-form efficient. This is because insider trading is illegal.

Efficient Markets and Technical Analysis

Technical analysts utilize charts to identify price patterns, which are used to make investment decisions. If the market is weak-form efficient, prices already reflect all available security market public information, and technical trading systems that depend only on past trading and price data cannot hold much value. Since tests have predominantly confirmed weak-form efficiency of markets, technical trading rules should not generate abnormal risk adjusted-profits after accounting for risks and transaction costs.

Efficient Markets and Fundamental Analysis

Fundamental analysts are concerned with the company that underlies the stock. They evaluate a company's past performance and examine its financial statements. They compute many performance ratios that aid them in assessing the validity of the stock's current price. They believe that a company's stock price can differ from its true intrinsic value, and investors who recognize the discrepancy can profit from it.

Fundamental analysis is necessary in a well-functioning securities market as it helps market participants understand the implications of any new information. Further, fundamental analysis can help generate abnormal risk-adjusted returns if an analyst is superior to her peers in valuing securities.

Efficient Markets and Portfolio Management

If markets and weak and semi-strong form efficient, active management is not likely to earn superior risk-adjusted returns on a consistent basis. Therefore, passive portfolio management would outperform active management. Studies have shown that on a risk-adjusted basis, mutual funds perform as well as the market before considering fees and expenses, but underperform the market after considering these costs.

The implication here is that the role of the portfolio manager is not necessarily to beat the market, but to manage the portfolio in light on the investor's risk and return objectives.

Pricing Anomalies

An anomaly occurs when a change in the price of an asset cannot be explained by the release of new information into the market.

- If markets are efficient, trading strategies designed to exploit market anomalies will not generate superior risk-adjusted returns on a consistent basis.
- An exception to the notion of market efficiency (an anomaly) would occur if a mispricing can be used to earn superior risk adjusted returns consistently.

Observed anomalies can be placed into three categories.

1. Time-Series Anomalies

Calendar Anomalies

January effect: Studies have shown that since the 1980s, investors have earned significantly higher returns in the equity market during January compared to other months of the year. Recent evidence has suggested that the January effect is not persistent and does not produce superior returns on a risk-adjusted basis. Therefore, it is not a pricing anomaly.

Momentum and Overreaction Anomalies

Investors tend to inflate (depress) stock prices of companies that have released good (bad) news. Studies have shown that "losers" (stocks that have witnessed a recent price decline due to the release of bad news) have outperformed the market in subsequent periods, while winners have underperformed in subsequent periods. Other studies have also shown that securities that have outperformed in the short term continue to generate high returns in subsequent periods (carrying on price momentum).

The overreaction and momentum anomalies go against the assertions of weak-form efficiency in markets.

2. Cross-Sectional Anomalies

Size Effect

Studies conducted in the past showed that shares of smaller companies outperformed shares of larger companies on a risk-adjusted basis. However, recent studies have failed to reach the same conclusion.

Value Effect

Studies have found that low P/E stocks have experienced higher risk-adjusted returns than high P/E stocks. These results go against semi-strong form market efficiency. However, when the Fama and French three-factor model is used instead of the CAPM to predict stock returns, the value stock anomaly disappears.

Other Anomalies

Closed-End Investment Fund Discounts

Several studies have shown that closed-end funds tend to trade at a discount (sometimes exceeding 50%) to their per share NAVs. Theoretically, investors could purchase all the shares in the fund, liquidate the fund, and make a profit by selling the constituent securities at their market prices. However, after accounting for management fees, unrealized capital gains taxes, liquidity and transaction costs, any profit potential is eliminated.

Earnings Surprises

Several studies have shown that although earnings surprises are quickly reflected in stock prices most of the time, this is not always the case. Investors may be able to earn abnormal returns using publicly available earnings information by purchasing stocks of companies that have announced positive earnings surprises. However, recent evidence has suggested that abnormal returns observed after earnings surprises do not control for transaction costs and risk.

Initial Public Offerings (IPOs)

Evidence suggests that investors who are able to acquire the shares of a company in an IPO at the offer price may be able to earn abnormal profits. However, this has not always proven to be the case. Further, over the long run, performance of IPOs has generally been below average.

Predictability of Returns based on prior Information

Considerable research has suggested that equity returns are based on factors such as interest rates, inflation rates, stock volatility, etc. However, the fact that equity returns are related to economic fundamentals is not evidence of market inefficiency.

Implications for Investment Strategies

Although there is some evidence to support the existence of valid anomalies, it is difficult to consistently earn abnormal returns by trading on them. On average, markets are efficient. Further, it is possible that identified anomalies may not be violations of market efficiency, but the result of the statistical methodologies used to detect them.

BEHAVIORAL FINANCE

Behavioral finance looks at investor behavior to explain why individuals make the decisions that they do, whether these decisions are rational or irrational. It is based on the premise that individuals do not always make 'efficient' investment decisions, nor do they always act 'rationally' due to the presence of **behavioral biases**.

Behavioral Biases

Loss Aversion

Behavioral finance asserts that investors exhibit **loss aversion** i.e., they dislike losses more than they like comparable gains, which results in a strong preference for avoiding losses as opposed to achieving gains. Advocates of this bias argue that loss aversion is more important to investors than risk aversion, which is why the 'overreaction' anomaly is observed. While loss aversion can explain the overreaction anomaly, studies have shown that under reactions are just as common as overreactions, which counters the assertions of this bias.

Herding

Herding behavior is a behavioral bias that explains both under reactions and overreactions in financial markets. Herding occurs when investors ignore their own analysis, and instead make investment decisions in line with the direction of the market.

Overconfidence

Overconfidence bias asserts investors have an inflated view of their ability to process new information appropriately. Overconfident investors are inaccurate when it comes to valuing securities given new information, and therefore stocks will be mispriced if there is an adequate number of such investors in the market.

Evidence has suggested that overconfidence has led to mispricing in most major markets around the world, but the bias has been observed predominantly in higher-growth companies, whose prices are slow to factor in any new information.

Another aspect of this bias is that overconfident investors tend to maintain portfolios that are less-than-optimally diversified because they tend to overestimate their stock-picking abilities.

> Most asset-pricing models assume that markets are rational and that the intrinsic value of a security reflects the rationality. But market efficiency and asset-pricing models do not require that each individual is rational–rather, only that the market is rational.

EI

Information Cascades

An information cascade refers to the transfer of information from market participants who are the first to take investment action upon the release of new information, and whose decisions influence the decisions of others.

Information cascades can be rational. If informed traders act first and uninformed traders follow their lead, there will be an improvement in market efficiency as the cascade is helping the market correctly incorporate relevant information. Information cascades can also result in serial correlation in stock returns and to overreactions to information. Studies have shown that information cascades tend to be greater for stocks when reliable and relevant information about the underlying company is not easily available. They can actually improve the quality of information available to investors.

Other Behavioral Biases

- **Representativeness**, where investors assess probabilities of future outcomes based on how similar they are to the current state.
- **Mental accounting**, where investors keep track of gains and losses from different investments in separate mental accounts.
- **Conservatism**, where investors are slow to react to changes and continue to maintain their initial views.
- **Narrow framing**, where investors focus on issues in isolation.

Concluding Remarks

Whether investor behavior can explain market anomalies is a subject open to debate.

- If investors must be rational for the market to be efficient, then markets cannot be efficient.
- If markets are defined as being efficient, investors cannot earn superior risk-adjusted profits consistently, available evidence suggests that markets are efficient even though investors do exhibit irrational behavior, such as herding.

STUDY SESSION 15:
EQUITY INVESTMENTS (2)

EI

EI

OVERVIEW OF EQUITY SECURITIES
Cross-Reference to CFA Institute Assigned Reading #47

Importance of Equities in Global Financial Markets

- In 2008, on a global level, the equity market capitalization to GDP ratio was close to 100% (more than twice the long run average of 50%).
- Studies have shown that during 1900-2008, government bonds and bills earned annualized real returns of 1% to 2% on average, which is in line with the inflation rate. On the other hand, equity markets earned real returns in excess of 4% per year in most markets.
- In most developed countries, equity ownership as a percentage of the population was between 20% and 50%.

Types of Equity Securities

Common Shares

Investors in common shares have an ownership interest in the company. They share the operating performance of the company, participate in the governance process through voting rights, and have a residual claim on the company's net assets in case of liquidation.

- **Callable** common shares give the issuing company the right, but not the obligation, to buy back shares from investors at a later date at the call price (which is specified when the shares are originally issued). Companies are likely to buy back shares when their market price is higher than the call price. This is beneficial for the company as it is able to:
  - Buy shares at a lower price and resell them at the higher market price.
  - Save on dividend payments and preserve its capital.

Callable common shares are also beneficial for the investors as they get a guaranteed return on their investments when the shares are called.

- **Putable** common shares give investors the right, but not the obligation, to sell their shares back to the issuing company at the put price (which is specified when the shares are originally issued). Investors are likely to exercise this right when the market price of shares is lower than the put price. Putable common shares limit investor losses. As far as the company is concerned, they make it easier to raise capital as the put feature makes the shares more appealing to investors.

Preference Shares

Preference shares (also known as preferred stock) have the following characteristics:

- They do not give holders the right to participate in the operating performance of the company and they do not carry voting rights unless explicitly allowed for at issuance.

- They receive dividends before ordinary shareholders. Further, preferred dividends are fixed and are usually higher than dividends on common shares. However, the company is still not contractually obligated to make regular payments to holders of preferred stock.
- In case of liquidation, they have a higher priority in claims on the company's net assets than common shares. However, they still have a lower priority than bondholders.
- They can be perpetual (i.e., have no fixed maturity date), can pay dividends indefinitely, and can be callable or putable.

Preference shares can be classified into the following categories:

- **Cumulative:** Unpaid dividends on cumulative preference shares accrue over time and must be paid in full before dividends on common shares can be paid.
- **Non-cumulative:** Unpaid dividends for one or more periods are forfeited permanently and are not accrued over time to be paid at a later date.
- **Participating:** These are entitled to preferred dividends plus additional dividends if the company's profits exceed a pre-specified level. Further, investors in participating preferred shares might be entitled to an additional distribution of the company's assets upon liquidation above the par value of the preference shares. Participating preference shares are more common in smaller, riskier companies in which investors are concerned about the company's possible future liquidation.
- **Non-participating:** These are only entitled to a fixed preferred dividend and the par value of shares in the event of liquidation.
- **Convertible:** These are convertible into a specified number of common shares based on a conversion ratio that is determined at issuance. They have the following advantages:
  - They allow investors to earn a higher dividend than if they had invested in the company's common shares.
  - They offer investors the opportunity to share the profits of the company.
  - They allow investors to benefit from a rise in the price of common shares through the conversion option.
  - Their price is less volatile than the underlying common shares because their dividend payments are known and more stable.

Convertible preference shares are becoming increasingly common in venture capital and private equity transactions.

Private Equity Securities

Private securities are issued primarily to institutional investors via non-public offerings, such as private placements, and have the following characteristics:

- There is no active secondary market for them as they are not listed on public exchanges. Therefore, they do not have market-determined quoted prices.
- They are highly illiquid, and require negotiations between investors in order to be traded.

- The issuing companies are not required by regulatory authorities to publish financial statements and other important information regarding the company, which makes it difficult to determine fair values.

Types of Private Equity Investments

- Venture capital
- Leveraged Buyout (LBO)
- Private Investment in Public Equity

Advantages of Private Companies

- The longer investment horizons allow investors to focus on long-term value creation and to address any underlying operational issues facing the company. Publicly-traded companies feel pressured to focus on short term performance (e.g., to meet market expectations regarding earnings, growth, etc.).
- Certain costs that public companies must bear, such as those incurred to meet regulatory and stock exchange filing requirements, are avoided by private companies.

Advantages of Public Companies

- Public equity markets are much larger than private equity networks. Therefore, they provide more opportunities to companies for raising capital cheaply.
- Publicly traded companies are encouraged to be open about their policies, which ensures that they act in shareholder interest.

Non-Domestic Equity Securities

- An increasing number of companies have issued shares in markets outside of their home country.
- The number of companies whose shares are traded in markets outside of their home country has increased.
- An increasing number of companies are dual-listed i.e., their shares are simultaneously issued and traded in two or more markets.

Listing a company on an international exchange has the following benefits:

- It improves awareness about the company's products and services.
- It enhances the liquidity of the company's shares.
- It increases corporate transparency due to the additional market exposure and the need to meet a greater number of filing requirements.

Methods for Investing in Non-Domestic Equity Securities

Direct Investing

The most obvious way to invest in equity securities of foreign companies is to buy and sell securities directly in foreign markets. However, direct investing has the following implications:

- All transactions are in the company's, not the investor's domestic currency. Therefore, investors are also exposed to exchange rate risk.
- Investors must be familiar with the trading, clearing, and settlement regulations and procedures of the foreign market.
- Investing directly may lead to less transparency (due to the unavailability of audited financial statements on a regular basis) and increased volatility (due to limited liquidity).

Depository Receipts

A depository receipt (DR) is a security that trades like an ordinary share on a local exchange and represents an economic interest in a foreign company. It is created when a foreign company deposits its shares with a bank (the depository) in the country on whose exchange the shares will trade. The bank then issues a specific number of receipts representing the deposited shares based on a pre-determined ratio. Hence, one DR might represent one share, a number of shares or a fractional share of the underlying stock.

A DR can be sponsored or unsponsored.

- A sponsored DR is when the foreign company that deposits its shares with the depository has a direct involvement in the issuance of receipts.
- In an unsponsored DR, the foreign company that deposits its shares with the depository has no involvement in the issuance of receipts.

There are two types of depository receipts:

- *Global Depository Receipts (GDRs)*: GDRs are issued by the depository bank outside of the company's home country and outside of the U.S.
- *American Depository Receipts (ADRs)*: ADRs are denominated in U.S. dollars and trade like a common share on U.S. exchanges. They are basically GDRs that can be publicly traded in the U.S.

Global Registered Shares (GRS)

A GRS is an ordinary share that is quoted and traded in different currencies on different stock exchanges around the world. GRSs offer more flexibility than DRs as the shares represent actual ownership in the issuing company, they can be traded anywhere and currency conversions are not required to trade them.

Basket of Listed Depository Receipts (BLDR)

This is an exchange-traded fund (ETF) that represents a portfolio of DRs. Like all other ETFs, it trades throughout the day and can be bought, sold, or sold short just like an individual share. Further, it can be purchased on margin and used in hedging and arbitrage strategies.

Return Characteristics of Equity Securities

The two main sources of an equity security's total return are:

- Capital gains from price appreciation.
- Dividend income.

The total return on non-dividend paying stocks only consists of capital gains.

Investors in depository receipts and foreign shares also incur foreign exchange gains (or losses).

Another source of return arises from the compounding effects of reinvested dividends.

Risks of Equity Securities

- Preference shares are less risky than common shares.
- Putable common shares are less risky than callable or non-callable common shares.
- Callable common and preference shares are more risky than their non-callable counterparts.
- Cumulative preference shares are less risky than non-cumulative preference shares as they accrue unpaid dividends.

Equity Securities and Company Value

The primary aim of management is to increase the book value and market value of the company. Book value (shareholders' equity on the company's balance sheet) is calculated as total assets less total liabilities. It reflects the historical operating and financing decisions made by the company. Management can directly influence book value (e.g., by retaining net income).

However, management can only indirectly influence a company's market value as it is primarily determined by investors' expectations about the amount, timing and uncertainty of the company's future cash flows. A company may increase its book value by retaining net income, but it will only have a positive effect on the company's market value if investors expect the company to invest its retained earnings in profitable growth opportunities. If investors believe that the company has a significant number of cash flow generating investment opportunities coming through, the market value of the company's equity will exceed its book value.

A useful ratio to evaluate investor's expectations about a company is the price-to-book ratio (also known as the market-to-book) ratio.

- If a company has a price-to-book ratio that is greater than industry average, it suggests that investors believe that the company has more significant future growth opportunities than its industry peers.
- It may not be appropriate to compare price-to-book ratios of companies in different industries because the ratio also reflects investors' growth outlook for the industry itself.

An important measure used by investors to evaluate the effectiveness of management in increasing the company's book value is accounting return on equity.

Accounting Return on Equity

The accounting return on equity (ROE) measures the rate of return earned by a company on its equity capital. It indicates how efficient a firm is in generating profits from every dollar of net assets. The ROE is computed as net income available to ordinary shareholders (after preference dividends have been paid) divided by the average total book value of equity.

$$ROE_t = \frac{NI_t}{\text{Average BVE}_t} = \frac{NI_t}{(BVE_t + BVE_{t-1})/2}$$

An increase in ROE might not always be a positive sign for the company.

- The increase in ROE may be the result of net income decreasing at a slower rate than shareholders' equity. A declining net income is a source of concern for investors.
- The increase in ROE may be the result of debt issuance proceeds being used to repurchase shares. This would increase the company's financial leverage (risk).

Book values and ROE do help analysts evaluate companies, but they cannot be used as the primary means to determine a company's intrinsic value. Intrinsic value refers to the present value of the company's expected future cash flows, and can only be estimated as it is impossible to accurately predict the amount and timing of a company's future cash flows. Astute investors aim to profit from differences between market prices and intrinsic values.

The Cost of Equity and Investors' Required Rates of Return

A company may raise capital by issuing debt or equity, both of which have associated costs.

- A company's cost of debt is easy to estimate as it is reflected in the interest payments that the company is contractually obligated to make to debt holders.
- Estimating cost of equity is difficult because the company is not contractually obligated to make any payments to common shareholders.

Investors' minimum required rates of return refer to the return they require for providing funds to the company.

- For investors who provide debt capital to the company, their minimum required rate of return is the periodic interest rate they charge the company for using their funds. Further, all providers of debt capital receive the same interest rate. Therefore, the company's cost of debt and investors' minimum required rate of return on debt are the same.

- For investors who provide equity capital to the company, the future cash flows that they expect to receive are uncertain (in both timing and amount) so their minimum required rate of return must be estimated. Further, each investor may have different expectations regarding future cash flows. Therefore, the company's cost of equity may be different from investors' minimum required rate of return on equity.

You should think about the cost of equity as the minimum expected rate of return that a company must offer investors to purchase its shares in the primary market and to maintain its share price in the secondary market. If the required rate of return is not maintained, the price of the security in the secondary market will adjust to reflect the minimum rate of return required by investors.

- If investors require a higher return than the company's cost of equity, they will sell the company's shares and invest elsewhere, which would bring down the company's stock price. This decline in the stock price will lead to an increase in the expected return on equity and bring it in line with the (higher) required rate of return.

Note:

- The company's cost of equity can be estimated using the dividend discount model (DDM) and capital asset pricing model (CAPM) which are discussed in other readings.

- The costs of debt and equity are used to estimate a company's weighted average cost of capital (WACC), which represents the minimum required rate of return that the company must earn on its average investment.

INTRODUCTION TO INDUSTRY AND COMPANY ANALYSIS
Cross-Reference to CFA Institute Assigned Reading #48

Industry analysis has the following uses:

- To understand a company's business and business environment.
- To identify active equity investment opportunities.
- To attribute portfolio performance.

APPROACHES TO INDUSTRY CLASSIFICATION

Products and/or Services Supplied

This classification scheme groups companies that make similar products and/or services. Companies are placed in industries based on their principal business activity i.e., the source from which the company derives most of its revenues and/or earnings. Industries that are related to each other are grouped together to form a sector.

Business-Cycle Sensitivities

This approach groups companies based on their relative sensitivity to business cycles.

A cyclical company is one whose performance is positively correlated with the performance of the overall economy. Cyclical companies perform very well when the economy is booming, but perform relatively poorly during recessions. Cyclical companies typically have high operating leverage, which may be accompanied by high financial risk. Examples of cyclical industries include autos, industrials and technology.

A non-cyclical company is one whose performance is relatively independent of the business cycle. Demand for products made by non-cyclical companies remains relatively stable. Examples of non-cyclical industries include healthcare and utilities.

Analysts also often classify industries as defensive or growth industries. Defensive or stable industries are those whose profits are least affected by fluctuations in overall economic activity. Growth industries are industries whose specific demand dynamics override economic factors in determining their performance. These industries generate growth irrespective of overall economic conditions, though their growth rates may decline in recessions.

Limitations of these Classifications:

- The classification of companies as cyclical or non-cyclical is somewhat arbitrary. Economic downturns affect all companies so cyclical and non-cyclical industries are better understood on a relative basis.
- At a given point in time different countries and regions may be undergoing different stages of the business cycle. Comparing companies in the same industry that are currently operating in very different economic conditions may help

identify investment opportunities, but establishing industry benchmark values with the data would be misleading.

Statistical Similarities

Statistical approaches group companies on the basis of correlations of historical returns. This approach has the following limitations:

- The composition of industry groups may vary significantly over time and across geographical regions.
- There is no guarantee that past correlations will continue to hold going forward.
- A relationship may arise by chance.
- A relationship that is actually economically significant may be excluded.

Industry Classification Systems

Commercial Industry Classification Systems

- Global Industry Classification Standard (GICS)
- Russell Global Sectors (RGS)
- Industry Classification Benchmark (ICB)

Governmental Industry Classification Systems

- International Standard Industrial Classification of All Economic Activities (ISIC)
- Statistical Classification of Economic Activities in the European Community (NACE)
- Australian and New Zealand Standard Industrial Classification (ANZSIC)
- North American Industry Classification System (NAICS)

Strengths and Weaknesses of Current Systems

Commercial classification systems generally have an advantage over government systems because of the following reasons:

- Most government systems do not disclose information about specific businesses or companies, so an analyst does not have access to the constituents of a particular category.
- Commercial classification systems are reviewed and updated more frequently than government classification systems.
- Government classification systems do not distinguish between small and large businesses, between for-profit and not-for-profit organizations, or between public and private companies. Commercial classification systems make distinctions between small and large companies automatically by virtue of the companies' association with a particular equity index. Further, commercial classification systems only include for-profit and publicly traded organizations.

Peer Groups

A **peer group** is a group of companies engaged in similar business activities whose economics and valuation are influenced by closely-related factors. Comparing a company to a well-defined peer group is very useful in evaluating company performance and in relative valuation.

Steps in constructing a preliminary list of peer companies:

- Examine commercial classification systems to identify companies operating in the same industry.
- Review the subject company's annual report to identify any mention of competitors.
- Review competitors' annual reports to identify other potential comparable companies.
- Review industry trade publications to identify comparable companies.
- Confirm that comparable companies have primary business activities that are similar to those of the subject company.

Strategic Analysis

Analysis of the industry with a view to examining the implications of the industrial environment on corporate strategy is known as strategic analysis.

Porter's Five Forces Framework

- Threat of substitute product
- Bargaining power of customers
- Bargaining power of suppliers
- Threat of new entrants
- Intensity of rivalry

Barriers to Entry

Generally speaking:

- Low barriers to entry mean that new competitors can easily enter the industry, which makes the industry highly competitive. Companies in relatively competitive industries typically have little pricing power.
- High barriers to entry mean that existing companies are able to enjoy economic profits for a long period of time. These companies have greater pricing power.

However, bear in mind that the above mentioned characteristics of high and low barrier industries are not always observed. Further, it is important to note that:

- Barriers to entry should not be confused with barriers to success.
- Barriers to entry can change over time.

Industry Concentration

Generally speaking:

- If an industry is relatively concentrated i.e., a few large firms dominate the industry, there is relatively less price competition. This is because:
    - It is relatively easy for a few firms to coordinate their activities.
    - Larger firms have more to lose from destructive price behavior.
    - The fortunes of large firms are more tied to those of the industry as a whole so they are more likely to be wary of the long run impact of a price war on industry economics.
- If an industry is relatively fragmented i.e., there is a large number of small firms in the industry, there is relatively high price competition. This is because of the following reasons:
    - Firms are unable to monitor their competitors' actions, which makes coordination difficult.
    - Each firm only has a small share of the market, so a small market share gain (through aggressive pricing) can make a large difference to each firm.
    - Each firm is small relative to the overall market so it tends to think of itself individualistically, rather than as a member of a larger group.

Bear in mind that there are important exceptions to the rules defined above. For example, Boeing and Airbus dominate the aircraft manufacturing industry, but competition between the two remains fierce.

Industry Capacity

Generally speaking:

- Limited capacity gives companies more pricing power as demand exceeds supply.
- Excess capacity results in weak pricing power as excess supply chases demand.

In evaluating the future competitive environment in an industry, analysts should examine current capacity levels as well as how capacity levels are expected to change in the future. Further, it is important to keep in mind that:

- If new capacity is physical (e.g., manufacturing facilities) it will take longer for the new capacity to come online so tight supply conditions may linger on for an extended period. Usually however, once physical capacity is added, supply may overshoot, outstrip demand, and result in weak pricing power for an extended period.
- If new capacity requires financial and human capital, companies can respond to tight supply conditions fairly quickly.

Market Share Stability

Generally speaking:

- Stable market shares indicate less competitive industries.
- Unstable market shares often indicate highly competitive industries with little pricing power.

Market shares are affected by the following factors:

- Barriers to entry
- New products
- Product differentiation

Industry Life-Cycle Analysis

Embryonic: Industries in this stage are just beginning to develop. They are characterized by:

- Slow growth as customers are still unfamiliar with the product.
- High prices as volumes are too low to achieve significant economies of scale.
- Significant initial investment.
- High risk of failure.

Companies focus on raising product awareness and developing distribution channels during this stage.

Growth: Once the new product starts gaining acceptance in the market, the industry experiences rapid growth. The growth stage is characterized by:

- New customers entering the market, which increases demand.
- Improved profitability as sales grow rapidly.
- Lower prices as economies of scale are achieved.
- Relatively low competition among companies in the industry as the overall market size is growing rapidly. Firms do not need to wrestle market share away from competitors to grow.
- High threat of new competitors entering the market due to low barriers to entry.

During this stage, companies focus on building customer loyalty and reinvest heavily in the business.

Shakeout: The period of rapid growth is followed by a period of slower growth. The shakeout stage is characterized by:

- Slower demand growth as fewer new customers are left to enter the industry.
- Intense competition as growth becomes dependent on market share growth.
- Excess industry capacity, which leads to price reductions and declining profitability.

During this stage, companies focus on reducing their costs and building brand loyalty. Some firms may fail or merge with others.

Mature: Eventually demand stops growing and the industry matures. Characteristics of this stage are:

- Little or no growth in demand as the market is completely saturated.
- Companies move towards consolidation. They recognize that they are interdependent so they stay away from price wars. However, price wars may occur during downturns.
- High barriers to entry in the form of brand loyalty and relatively efficient cost structures.

During this stage, companies are likely to be pursuing replacement demand rather than new buyers and should focus on extending successful product lines rather than introducing revolutionary new products. Companies have limited opportunities to reinvest and often have strong cash flows. As a result, they are more likely to pay dividends.

Decline: Technological substitution, social changes or global competition may eventually cause an industry to decline. The decline stage is characterized by:

- Negative growth.
- Excess capacity due to diminishing demand.
- Price competition due to excess capacity.
- Weaker firms leaving the industry.

Limitations of Industry Life-Cycle Analysis

- The following factors may change the shape of the industry life cycle, cause some stages to be longer or shorter than expected, or even result in certain stages being skipped altogether.
  - Technological changes
  - Regulatory changes
  - Social changes
  - Demographics
- Industry life-cycle analysis is most useful in analyzing industries during periods of relative stability. It is not as useful in analyzing industries experiencing rapid change.
- Not all companies in an industry display similar performance.

Price Competition

Generally speaking:

- Industries in which price is the most significant consideration in customers' purchase decisions tend to be highly competitive. A slight increase in price may cause customers to switch to substitute products if they are widely available.

- Price is not as important if companies in an industry are able to effectively differentiate their products in terms of quality and performance. Customers may not focus on price as much if product reliability is more important to them.

Factors Affecting Industry Growth, Profitability, and Risk

- Macroeconomic influences
- Technological influences
- Demographic influences
- Governmental influences
- Social influences

Competitive Strategies

Cost Leadership

Companies pursuing this strategy strive to cut down their costs to become the lowest cost producers in an industry so that they can gain market share by charging lower prices. Pricing may be defensive (to protect market positions when competition is low) or aggressive (to increase market share when competition is intense).

Product/Service Differentiation

Companies pursuing this strategy strive to differentiate their products from those of competitors in terms of quality, type, or means of distribution. These companies are then able to charge a premium price for their products. This strategy is successful only if the price premium is greater than the cost of differentiation and the source of differentiation appeals to customers and is sustainable over time.

Elements that should be Considered in a Company Analysis

A thorough company analysis should:

- Provide an overview of the company.
- Explain relevant industry characteristics.
- Analyze the demand for the company's products and services.
- Analyze the supply of products and services including an analysis of costs.
- Explain the company's pricing environment.
- Present and interpret relevant financial ratios, including comparisons over time and comparisons with competitors.

EQUITY VALUATION: CONCEPTS AND BASIC TOOLS
Cross-Reference to CFA Institute Assigned Reading #49

The aim of equity analysis is to identify mispriced securities. Securities are mispriced or incorrectly priced by the market when their market prices are different from their intrinsic values. Intrinsic or fundamental value refers to a security's true value and is estimated by analysts using a variety of models/techniques.

- If the estimate for a security's intrinsic value is lower than the market price, the security is overvalued by market.
- If the estimate for a security's intrinsic value is greater than the market price, the security is undervalued by the market.
- If the estimate for a security's intrinsic value equals the market price, the security is fairly valued.

EQUITY VALUATION MODELS

Present Value Models

Generally speaking, there are two sources of return from investing in a stock: (1) cash dividends received during the holding period and (2) the change in the stock price over the holding period.

- A cash dividend is a cash distribution made to a company's shareholders. Cash dividends are typically paid out regularly at known intervals, and these are known as regular cash dividends.
- An extra dividend or special dividend refers to a dividend payment by a company that does not usually pay dividends, or a dividend payment on top of the company's regular dividend.
- A stock dividend or a bonus issue occurs when a company issues additional common shares in the company (instead of cash) to shareholders.
  It basically divides the market value of shareholders' equity into smaller pieces without affecting (1) the total value of the pie, or (2) shareholders' proportional ownership in the company. Thus, stock dividends are not relevant for valuation.
- Stock splits and reverse stock splits also have no economic effect on the company or shareholders.
  - A stock split results in an increase in the number of shares outstanding and a consequent decrease in share price.
  - A reverse stock split increases the share price and reduces the number of shares outstanding.
- Share repurchases refer to a company buying back its own shares.
  - Shares that are repurchased by the company are known as treasury shares and, once repurchased, are not considered for dividends, voting, or calculating earnings per share.
  - All other things remaining the same, share repurchases can be viewed as equivalent to cash dividends in terms of their impact on shareholder wealth.

Arguments for Share Repurchases

- Share repurchases send out a signal to the market that management believes that the company's stock is undervalued, or that management will support the stock price.
- They offer the company flexibility in its cash distributions. A share repurchase does not set the expectation of continued distributions in the future as cash dividends might.
- There is a tax advantage to distributing cash through stock repurchases in markets where capital gains are taxed at a lower rate than dividends.
- They can be used to limit the increase in the number of shares outstanding when a significant number of employee stock options have been exercised.

Dividend Payment Chronology

- Declaration date is the date on which a company announces a particular dividend.
- The company also announces the holder-of-record date and the payment date on the declaration date.
- Ex-dividend date or ex-date is the first day that the share trades without the dividend.
- Any investor who holds the stock on the ex-dividend date or who purchased it the day before the ex-dividend date is entitled to receive the dividend.
- On the ex-dividend date, the share price is adjusted for the amount of the dividend.
- Holder-of-record date, also known as the owner-of-record date, shareholder-of-record date, record date, date of record, or date of book closure, is the date at which a shareholder listed in the company's records will be entitled to receive the upcoming dividend.
- Payment date or payable date is the date on which the company actually mails out or transfers the dividend payment to shareholders.

Dividend Discount Model

The dividend discount model (DDM) values a share of common stock as the present value of its expected future cash flows (dividends).

$$\text{Value} = \frac{D_1}{(1+k_e)^1} + \frac{D_2}{(1+k_e)^2} + \ldots + \frac{D_\infty}{(1+k_e)^\infty}$$

$$\text{Value} = \sum_{t=1}^{n} \frac{D_t}{(1+k_e)^t}$$

- When an investor sells a share of common stock, the value that the purchaser will pay equals the present value of the future stream of cash flows (i.e., the remaining dividend stream). Therefore, the value of the stock at any point in time is still determined by its expected future dividends. When this value is discounted to the present, we are back at the original dividend discount model.
- If a company pays no dividends currently, it does not mean that its stock will be worthless. There is an expectation that after a certain period of time the firm will

start making dividend payments. Currently, the company is reinvesting all its earnings in its business with the expectation that its earnings and dividends will be larger and will grow faster in the future. If the company does not make positive earnings going forward, there will still be an expectation of a liquidating dividend. The amount of this dividend will be discounted at the required rate of return to compute the stock's current price.

- The required rate of return on equity (k_e) is usually estimated using the CAPM. Another approach for calculating the required return on equity simply adds a risk premium to the before-tax cost of debt of the company.

One year holding period: If our holding period is just one year, the value that we will place on the stock today is the present value of the dividends that we will receive over the year plus the present value of the price that we expect to sell the stock for at the end of the holding period.

$$\text{Value} = \frac{\text{dividend to be received}}{(1+k_e)^1} + \frac{\text{year-end price}}{(1+k_e)^1}$$

Multiple-Year Holding Period DDM

We apply the same discounting principles for valuing common stock over multiple holding periods. In order to estimate the intrinsic value of the stock, we first estimate the dividends that will be received every year that the stock is held and the price that the stock will sell for at the end of the holding period. Then we simply discount these expected cash flows at the cost of equity (required return).

$$V = \frac{D_1}{(1+k_e)^1} + \frac{D_2}{(1+k_e)^2} + \ldots + \frac{P_n}{(1+k_e)^n}$$

where:
P_n = Price at the end of n years.

Infinite Period DDM (Gordon Growth Model)

The infinite period dividend discount model assumes that a company will continue to pay dividends for an infinite number of periods. It also assumes that the dividend stream will grow at a constant rate (g_c) over the infinite period. In this case, the intrinsic value of the stock is calculated as:

$$PV_0 = \frac{D_0(1+g_c)^1}{(1+k_e)^1} + \frac{D_0(1+g_c)^2}{(1+k_e)^2} + \frac{D_0(1+g_c)^3}{(1+k_e)^3} + \ldots + \frac{D_0(1+g_c)^\infty}{(1+k_e)^\infty}$$

This equation simplifies to:

$$PV = \frac{D_0(1+g_c)^1}{(k_e - g_c)^1} = \frac{D_1}{k_e - g_c}$$

The relation between k_e and g_c is critical:

- As the difference between k_e and g_c *increases*, the intrinsic value of the stock *falls*.
- As the difference *narrows*, the intrinsic value of the stock *rises*.
- Small changes in either k_e or g_c can cause *large* changes in the value of the stock.

For the infinite-period DDM model to work, the following assumptions must hold:

- Dividends grow at a rate, g_c, which is not expected to change.
- k_e must be greater than g_c; otherwise, the model breaks down because of the denominator being negative.

Notice that the DDM formula on the previous page can be rearranged to make the required return, k_e, the subject:

$$k_e = \frac{D_1}{PV_0} + g_c$$

This expression for the cost of equity tells us that the return on an equity investment has two components:

- The dividend yield (D_1/P_0).
- Growth over time (g_c).

Applying Present Value Models

The Gordon growth model is highly appropriate for valuing dividend-paying stocks that are relatively immune to the business cycle and are relatively mature (e.g., utilities). It is also useful for valuing companies that have historically been raising their dividend at a stable rate.

Applying the DDM is relatively difficult if the company is not currently paying out a dividend. A company may not pay out a dividend because:

- It has a lot of lucrative investment opportunities available and it wants to retain profits to reinvest them in the business.
- It does not have sufficient excess cash flow to pay out a dividend.

Even though the Gordon growth model can be used for valuing such companies, the forecasts used are generally quite uncertain. Therefore, analysts use one of the other valuation models to value such companies and may use the DDM model as a supplement. The DDM can be extended to numerous stages. For example:

- A three-stage DDM is used to value fairly young companies that are just entering the growth phase. Their development falls into three stages—growth (with very high growth rates), transition (with decent growth rates) and maturity (with a lower growth into perpetuity).

- A two-stage DDM can be used to value a company currently undergoing moderate growth, but whose growth rate is expected to improve (rise) to its long term growth rate.

Valuation of Common Stock with Temporary Supernormal Growth

The correct valuation model to value such "supernormal growth" companies is the **multi-stage dividend discount model** that combines the multi-period and infinite-period dividend discount models.

$$Value = \frac{D_1}{(1+k_e)^1} + \frac{D_2}{(1+k_e)^2} + \ldots + \frac{D_n}{(1+k_e)^n} + \frac{P_n}{(1+k_e)^n}$$

where:

$$P_n = \frac{D_{n+1}}{k_e - g_c}$$

D_n = Last dividend of the supernormal growth period

D_{n+1} = First dividend of the constant growth period

The Free-Cash-Flow-to-Equity (FCFE) Model

Many analysts assert that a company's dividend-paying capacity should be reflected in its cash flow estimates instead of estimated future dividends. FCFE is a measure of dividend paying capacity and can also be used to value companies that currently do not make any dividend payments. FCFE can be calculated as:

$$FCFE = CFO - FC\ Inv + Net\ borrowing$$

Analysts may calculate the intrinsic value of the company's stock by discounting their projections of future FCFE at the required rate of return on equity.

$$V_0 = \sum_{t=1}^{\infty} \frac{FCFE_t}{(1+k_e)^t}$$

Intrinsic Value of Preferred Stock

When preferred stock is non-callable, non-convertible, has no maturity date and pays dividends at a fixed rate, the value of the preferred stock can be calculated using the perpetuity formula:

$$V_0 = \frac{D_0}{r}$$

For a non-callable, non-convertible preferred stock with maturity at time, n, the value of the stock can be calculated using the following formula:

$$V_0 = \sum_{t=1}^{n} \frac{D_t}{(1+r)^t} + \frac{F}{(1+r)^n}$$

Price Multiples – Relative Valuation

Price multiples are ratios that compare the price of a stock to some sort of value. Price multiples allow an analyst to evaluate the relative worth of a company's stock. Popular multiples used in relative valuation include price-to-earnings, price-to-sales, price-to-book and price-to-cash flow.

Multiples based on Fundamentals

A price multiple may be related to fundamentals through a dividend discount model such as the Gordon growth model. The expressions developed in such an exercise are interpreted as the justified (or based on fundamental) values for a multiple.

The Justified P/E Ratio:

$$\frac{P_0}{E_1} = \frac{D_1/E_1}{r - g}$$

- The P/E ratio is inversely related to the required rate of return.
- The P/E ratio is positively related to the growth rate.
- The P/E ratio appears to be positively related to the dividend payout ratio. However, this relationship may not always hold because a higher dividend payout ratio implies that the company's earnings retention ratio is lower. A lower earnings retention ratio translates into a lower growth rate. This is known as the "dividend displacement" of earnings.

Multiples based on Comparables

This method compares relative values estimated using multiples to determine whether an asset is undervalued, overvalued or fairly valued. The benchmark multiple can be any of:

- A multiple of a closely matched individual stock.
- The average or median multiple of a peer group or the firm's industry.
- The average multiple derived from trend or time-series analysis.

Analysts should be careful to select only those companies that have similar size, product lines, and growth prospects to the company being valued as comparables.

$$\text{Price to cash flow ratio} = \frac{\text{Market price of share}}{\text{Cash flow per share}}$$

$$\text{Price to sales ratio} = \frac{\text{Market price per share}}{\text{Net sales per share}}$$

$$\text{Price to sales ratio} = \frac{\text{Market value of equity}}{\text{Total net sales}}$$

$$\text{P/BV} = \frac{\text{Current market price of share}}{\text{Book value per share}}$$

$$\text{P/BV} = \frac{\text{Market value of common shareholders' equity}}{\text{Book value of common shareholders' equity}}$$

where:
Book value of common shareholders' equity =
(Total assets − Total liabilities) − Preferred stock

Enterprise Value Multiples

Enterprise value (EV) is calculated as the market value of the company's common stock plus the market value of outstanding preferred stock if any, plus the market value of debt, less cash and short term investments (cash equivalents). It can be thought of as the cost of taking over a company.

The most widely used EV multiple is the EV/EBITDA multiple. EBITDA measures a company's income before payments to any providers of capital are made.

- The EV/EBITDA multiple is often used when comparing two companies with different capital structures.
- Loss-making companies usually have a positive EBITDA, which allows analysts to use the EV/EBITDA multiple to value them. The P/E ratio is meaningless (negative) for a loss-making company as its earnings are negative.

Asset-Based Valuation

Asset-based valuation uses market values of a company's assets and liabilities to determine the value of the company as a whole.

Asset based valuation works well for:

- Companies that do not have a significant number of intangible or "off-the-book" assets, and have a higher proportion of current assets and liabilities.
- Private companies, especially if applied together with multiplier models.
- Financial companies, natural resource companies and companies that are being liquidated.

Asset-based valuation may not be appropriate when:

- Market values of assets and liabilities cannot be easily determined.
- The company has a significant amount of intangible assets.
- Asset values are difficult to determine (e.g., in periods of very high inflation).
- Market values of assets and liabilities significantly differ from their carrying values.

STUDY SESSION 16:
FIXED INCOME (1)

FI

FI

FIXED-INCOME SECURITIES: DEFINING ELEMENTS
Cross-Reference to CFA Institute Assigned Reading #50

IMPORTANT RELATIONSHIPS

- The higher (lower) the coupon rate on a bond, the higher (lower) its price.
- An increase (decrease) in interest rates or the required yield on a bond will lead to a decrease (increase) in price, i.e., bond prices and yields are inversely related.
- The more risky the bond, the higher the yield required by investors to purchase the bond, and the lower the bond's price.

OVERVIEW OF A FIXED-INCOME SECURITY

Issuers

- Supranational organizations.
- Sovereign (national) governments.
- Non-sovereign (local) governments.
- Quasi-government entities.

Bond issuers can also be classified based on their credit-worthiness as judged by credit rating agencies. Bonds can broadly be categorized as investment-grade or non-investment grade (or high-yield or speculative) bonds.

Maturity

- Fixed-income securities which, at the time of issuance, are expected to mature in one year or less are known as money market securities.
- Fixed-income securities which, at the time of issuance, are expected to mature in more than one year are referred to as capital market securities.
- Fixed-income securities which have no stated maturity are known as perpetual bonds.

Par Value

The par value (also known as face value, nominal value, redemption value and maturity value) of a bond refers to the principal amount that the issuer promises to repay bondholders on the maturity date. Bond prices are usually quoted as a percentage of the par value.

- When a bond's price is above 100% of par, it is said to be trading at a premium.
- When a bond's price is at 100% of par, it is said to be trading at par.
- When a bond's price is below 100% of par, it is said to be trading at a discount.

FI

Coupon Rate and Frequency

The coupon rate (also known as the nominal rate) of a bond refers to the annual interest rate that the issuer promises to pay bondholders until the bond matures. The amount of interest paid each year by the issuer is known as the coupon, and is calculated by multiplying the coupon rate by the bond's par value.

Zero-coupon (or pure discount) bonds are issued at a discount to par value and redeemed at par (the issuer pays the entire par amount to investors at the maturity date). The difference between the (discounted) purchase price and the par value is effectively the interest on the loan.

Currency Denomination

- Dual-currency bonds make coupon payments in one currency and the principal payment at maturity in another currency.
- Currency option bonds give bondholders a choice regarding which of the two currencies they would like to receive interest and principal payments in.

Yield Measures

- The current yield or running yield equals the bond's annual coupon amount divided by its current price (not par value), expressed as a percentage.
- The yield-to-maturity (YTM) is also known as the yield-to-redemption or the redemption yield. It is calculated as the discount rate that equates the present value of a bond's expected future cash flows until maturity to its current price.
  - Given a set of expected future cash flows, the lower (higher) the YTM or discount rate, the higher (lower) the bond's current price.

THE BOND INDENTURE

A bond is a contractual agreement between the issuer and the bondholder. The trust deed is the legal contract that describes the form of the bond, obligations of the issuer and the rights of bondholders, and it is commonly referred to as the bond indenture. The indenture captures the following information:

- The name of the issuer.
- The principal value of the bond.
- The coupon rate.
- Dates when the interest payments will be made.
- The maturity date.
- Funding sources for the interest payments and principal repayments.
- Collaterals (i.e., assets or financial guarantees underlying the debt obligation above and beyond the issuer's promise to pay).
- Covenants (i.e., actions that the issuer is obligated to perform or prohibited from performing).
- Credit enhancements (i.e., provisions designed to reduce the bond's credit risk).

AREAS THAT INVESTORS SHOULD REVIEW BEFORE PURCHASING A BOND

Legal Identity of the Bond Issuer and its Legal Form

- For sovereign bonds, the legal issuer is typically the institution responsible for managing the national budget.
- Corporate bonds are typically issued by the corporate legal entity.
    - Note that bonds may be issued by the parent company or a subsidiary.
        - If issued by a subsidiary, investors must focus on the creditworthiness of the subsidiary, unless the bond is guaranteed by the parent. Oftentimes, subsidiaries carry a lower credit rating than the parent.
        - If issued by the parent company, it becomes important to analyze the assets actually held by the parent, as investors may not have recourse to assets held by subsidiaries or operating companies.
- In case of securitized bonds, the relationship between the sponsor and the SPE must be evaluated. Investors must ensure that the SPE is structured as a bankruptcy-remote vehicle.

Sources of Repayment Proceeds

- Bonds issued by supranational organizations are usually repaid through (1) proceeds from repayments of previous loans made by the organization or (2) paid-in capital from its members.
- Sovereign bonds are backed by the "full faith and credit" of the national government.
    - Sovereign bonds issued in local currency are usually considered safer than those issued in a foreign currency.
- Non-sovereign government debt can usually be repaid through the following sources:
    - The general taxing authority of the issuer.
    - Cash flows from the project that the bonds were issued to finance.
    - Special taxes or fees specifically set up to make interest and principal payments.
- Corporate bond issuers typically rely on their cash flow-generating ability to repay bonds, which in turn depends on their financial strength and integrity.
- For securitized bonds, repayment depends on the cash flow generated by the underlying pool of financial assets.

Asset or Collateral Backing

- **Seniority ranking:** Secured bonds are backed by assets or financial guarantees to ensure debt repayment in case of default, while unsecured bonds are not protected by a pledge of any specific assets (i.e., they only have a general claim on the issuer's assets and cash flows).

- o In the event of default, unsecured bonds are repaid after secured bonds have been paid off.
  - ■ Senior secured debt is paid off before subordinated or junior secured debt.
- o Investors should review the indenture to identify whether a particular debenture is actually secured or unsecured.
- **Types of collateral backing:**
  - o Collateral trust bonds are secured by securities such as common stock, other bonds, or other financial assets.
  - o Equipment trust certificates are secured by specific types of equipment or physical assets (e.g., aircraft, railroad cars, or oil rigs).
  - o Mortgage-backed securities (MBS) are backed by a pool of mortgage loans. Cash flows generated by the pool are used to make payments on MBS.
  - o Covered bonds are backed by a segregated pool of assets (known as the cover pool).

Credit Enhancements

Credit enhancements are provisions that serve to reduce the credit risk of a bond issue, resulting in a lower yield.

- Internal credit enhancement focuses on the structure of the issue regarding priority of payment or the value of collateral. It includes:
  - o Subordination: This refers to the allocation of cash flows among the various bond classes or tranches based on their seniority.
  - o Overcollateralization: This occurs when the value of the collateral posted to secure an issue exceeds the par value of the securities issued.
  - o Excess spread (or excess interest cash flow): A transaction can be structured in a manner such that the cash flows generated from the collateral pool exceed the amount of interest payable to bondholders so that there is a cushion for making interest payments.
- External credit enhancement refers to guarantees received from a third-party guarantor. Types of external credit enhancement include:
  - o Surety bonds (issued by an insurance company) and bank guarantees: In the event of default, both these forms of enhancement reimburse investors for losses (up to a pre-specified maximum amount known as the penal sum).
  - o Letters of credit: These are lines of credit provided by a financial institution to the issuer to reimburse any shortfalls in the cash flow generated from the collateral pool.

Note that surety bonds, bank guarantees, and letters of credit all expose investors to third party credit risk (i.e., the risk that the guarantor will not be able to fulfill its obligations). This risk can be mitigated by setting up a cash collateral account.

Covenants

Covenants are legally enforceable rules agreed upon by the borrower/issuer and lenders/investors at the time of bond issuance.

- Affirmative covenants are **requirements** placed on the issuer. They are typically administrative in nature so they do not lead to additional costs for the issuer, nor do they significantly restrict the issuer's ability to make business decisions.
- Negative covenants are **restrictions** placed on the issuer. While they entail more costs than affirmative covenants and can constrain the issuer in operating the business, they protect bondholders from dilution of their claims, asset withdrawals or substitutions, and inefficient investments by the issuer.

Legal and Regulatory Considerations

The differences between domestic bonds, foreign bonds, Eurobonds, and global bonds are important to investors as these different types of bonds are subject to different legal, regulatory, and tax requirements. There are also differences in terms of frequency of interest payments and how interest payments are calculated, both of which influence the bond's cash flows and price. Bear in mind however, that the currency denomination has a bigger influence on a bond's price than where it is issued or traded.

National Bond Markets versus Eurobond Market

A national bond market includes all the bonds that are issued and traded in a particular country, and denominated in that country's local currency.

- Bonds issued by entities that are incorporated in that country are known as domestic bonds.
- Bonds issued by entities that are incorporated in another country are known as foreign bonds.

Eurobonds refer to bonds that are denominated in a currency other than the local currency where they are issued. They may be issued in any country and in any currency (including the issuer's domestic currency), and are named based on the currency in which they are denominated.

- Generally speaking, Eurobonds are less regulated than domestic and foreign bonds as they do not fall under the jurisdiction of any single country.

Global bonds are bonds that are issued simultaneously (1) in the Eurobond market and (2) in at least one domestic bond market.

Tax Considerations

- Interest income is generally taxed at the ordinary income tax rate, which is the same rate that an individual pays tax on her wage or salary.
- Municipal bonds in the U.S. are often tax-exempt, in that interest income is often exempt from federal income tax and state income tax in the state of issue.
- In most jurisdictions, capital gains are taxed at a lower rate than interest income.
- In some countries, a prorated portion of any original issue discount must be included in interest income each year for tax purposes.
- In other jurisdictions, investors who have purchased bonds at a premium can either (1) deduct a prorated portion of the premium paid from taxable income each year until the bond matures, or (2) declare a capital loss when the bond is eventually redeemed at maturity.

PRINCIPAL REPAYMENT STRUCTURES

Credit risk is reduced if there are any provisions that call for periodic retirement of some of the principal amount outstanding during the term of the loan.

- A bullet bond is one that only makes periodic interest payments, with the entire principal amount paid back at maturity.
- An amortizing bond is one that makes periodic interest **and** principal payments over the term of the bond.
    - A fully amortized bond is one whose outstanding principal amount at maturity is reduced to zero through a fixed periodic payment schedule.
    - A partially amortized bond also makes fixed periodic principal repayments, but the principal is not fully repaid by the maturity date. Therefore, a balloon payment is required at maturity to repay the outstanding principal amount.

Sinking Fund Arrangements

A sinking fund arrangement requires the issuer to repay a specified portion of the principal amount every year throughout the bond's life or after a specified date.

Sometimes a call provision may also be added to the bond issue. This call provision usually gives the issuer the option to repurchase bonds before maturity at the lowest of (1) market price (2) par, and (3) a specified sinking fund price.

From the bondholders' perspective, the advantage of a sinking fund arrangement is that it reduces credit risk. However, it entails two disadvantages. First, it results in reinvestment risk, and second, if the issue has an embedded call option, the issuer may be able to repurchase bonds at a price lower than the current market price.

COUPON PAYMENT STRUCTURES

Floating-Rate Notes (FRN)

- The coupon rate of a FRN has two components: a reference rate (such as LIBOR) plus a spread (also known as margin).
- FRNs have less interest rate risk (i.e., the risk of bond price volatility resulting from changes in market interest rates) than fixed-rate bonds, but still entail credit risk.
- FRNs may be structured to include a floor and/or a cap on the periodic coupon rate.
- Reverse FRNs or inverse floaters are structured such that the periodic coupon rate is inversely related to the reference rate.

Step-Up Coupon Bonds

A step-up coupon bond (which can be fixed or floating) is one where the periodic coupon rate increases by specified margins at specified dates. Typically, the step-up coupon structure is offered with callable bonds to protect bondholders in a rising interest rate environment. However, note that despite the step-up in coupons (and the consequent increase in interest expense), the issuer may not call the bond if refinancing is less advantageous.

Credit-Linked Coupon Bonds

The coupon rate on credit-linked coupon bonds changes when the bond's credit rating changes. Credit-linked coupon bonds protect investors against a decline in the credit quality, and are therefore attractive to investors who are concerned about the future creditworthiness of the issuer. They also provide some protection against poor economic conditions as credit ratings tend to decline during recessions. A problem with credit-linked coupon bonds is that since a rating downgrade results in higher interest payments for the issuer, it can contribute to further downgrades or even an eventual default.

Payment-in-Kind (PIK) Coupon Bonds

PIK coupon bonds allow the issuer to pay interest in the form of additional bonds instead of cash. They are preferred by issuers that are financially distressed and fear liquidity and solvency problems in the future. Investors usually demand a higher yield on these bonds to compensate them for the higher credit risk and high leverage of the issuer.

Deferred Coupon Bonds (or Split Coupon Bonds)

Deferred Coupon Bonds do not pay any coupon for the first few years after issuance, but then pay a higher coupon than they normally would for the remainder of their terms. Deferred coupon bonds are usually preferred by issuers who want to conserve cash in the short run, or for project financing where cash-generation will commence after an initial development phase.

FI

Investors are attracted to deferred coupon bonds as they are usually priced significantly below par. Further, the deferred coupon structure may help investors manage their tax liability by delaying taxes due on interest income (in certain jurisdictions).

Index-Linked Bonds

These are bonds whose coupon payments and/or principal repayments are linked to a specified index (such as a commodity or equity index). An example of index-linked bonds are inflation-linked bonds (also known as linkers) whose coupon and/or principal payments are linked to an index of consumer prices (e.g., Treasury Inflation Protection Securities or TIPS issued by the U.S. Government are linked to the Consumer Price Index, CPI, in the U.S.). Investors are attracted to inflation-linked bonds because they offer a long-term asset with a fixed **real** return that is protected against inflation risk.

- Zero-coupon-indexed bonds do not pay any coupon so only the principal repayment is linked to a specified index.
- For interest-indexed bonds, only coupon payments are adjusted to changes in the specified index. They repay the fixed nominal principal at maturity.
- Capital-indexed bonds pay a fixed coupon rate, but this rate is applied to a principal amount that is adjusted to reflect changes in the specified index. As a result, both interest payments as well as the principal repayment are adjusted for inflation.
- Indexed-annuity bonds are fully amortized bonds. The annual payment on these bonds is linked to the specified index so effectively that both interest and principal payments reflect changes in the index.

An equity-linked note (ELN) is a fixed-income security whose final payment is linked to the return on an equity index.

- ELNs are generally principal-protected.
- If the underlying index increases in value, investors receive an amount greater than par upon maturity.
- Note that the principal payment is still subject to credit risk of the issuer.

BONDS WITH CONTINGENCY PROVISIONS

Callable Bonds

Callable bonds give the **issuer** the right to redeem (or call) all or part of the bond before maturity. This embedded option offers the issuer the ability to take advantage of (1) a decline in market interest rates and/or (2) an improvement in its creditworthiness.

From the perspective of the bondholder, she would pay less for a callable bond than for an otherwise identical non-callable bond. The difference in the value of a non-callable bond and an otherwise identical callable bond is the value of the embedded call option.

Value of callable bond = Value of non-callable bond − Value of embedded call option
Value of embedded call option = Value of non-callable bond − Value of callable bond

From the perspective of the issuer, it would have to pay more (in the form of a higher coupon or higher yield) to get investors to purchase a callable bond than an otherwise identical non-callable bond. The difference between the yield on a callable bond and the yield on a non-callable bond is the cost of the embedded option to the issuer.

> Yield on callable bond = Yield on non-callable bond +
> Embedded call option cost in terms of yield
>
> Embedded call option cost in terms of yield = Yield on callable bond −
> Yield on non-callable bond

- The more heavily the embedded call option favors the issuer, the lower the value of the callable bond to the investor and the higher the yield that must be offered by the issuer.
- Some callable bonds are issued with an initial call protection period (also known as lockout period, cushion or deferment period), during which the issuer is prohibited from calling the bond. The bond can only be called at or after the specified call date.
- A make-whole provision in a callable bond usually requires the issuer to pay a relatively high lump-sum amount to call the bonds.

Putable Bonds

Putable bonds give **bondholders** the right to sell (or put) the bond back to the issuer at a pre-determined price on specified dates. The embedded put option offers bondholders protection against an increase in interest rates, i.e., if interest rates increase (decreasing the value of the bond), they can sell the bond back to the issuer at a pre-specified price and then reinvest the principal at (higher) newer interest rates.

From the perspective of the bondholder, she would pay more for a putable bond than for an otherwise identical non-putable bond. The difference in the value between a putable bond and an otherwise identical non-putable bond is the value of the embedded put option (which the bond holder has effectively purchased from the issuer):

> Value of putable bond = Value of non-putable bond + Value of embedded put option
>
> Value of embedded put option = Value of putable bond − Value of non-putable bond

From the perspective of the issuer, it would pay out less (in the form of a lower coupon or lower yield) on a putable bond than it would on an otherwise identical non-putable bond. The difference between the yield on a non-putable bond and the yield on a putable bond is the cost of the embedded option borne by the investor.

> Yield on putable bond = Yield on non-putable bond −
> Embedded put option cost in terms of yield
>
> Embedded put option cost in terms of yield = Yield on non-putable bond −
> Yield on putable bond

Note that the more heavily the embedded put option favors the investor, the higher the value of the putable bond to the investor and the lower the yield that must be offered by the issuer.

Convertible Bonds

A **convertible bond** gives the bondholder the right to convert the bond into a pre-specified number of common shares of the issuer.

Convertible bonds are attractive to investors as the conversion (to equity) option allows them to benefit from price appreciation of the issuer's stock. On the other hand, if there is a decline in the issuer's share price (which causes a decline in the value of the embedded equity conversion/call option), the price of the convertible bond cannot fall below the price of an otherwise identical straight bond. Because of these attractive features, convertible bonds offer a lower yield and sell at higher prices than similar bonds without the conversion option. Note however, that the coupon rate offered on convertible bonds is usually higher than the dividend yield on the underlying equity.

- The conversion price is the price per share at which the convertible bond can be converted into shares.
- The conversion ratio refers to the number of common shares that each bond can be converted into. It is calculated as the par value divided by the conversion price.
- The conversion value is calculated as current share price multiplied by the conversion ratio.
- The conversion premium equals the difference between the convertible bond's price and the conversion value.
- Conversion parity occurs if the conversion value equals the convertible bond's price.

Although it is common for convertible bonds to reach conversion parity before they mature, bondholders rarely exercise the conversion option, choosing to retain their bonds and receive (higher) coupon payments instead of (lower) dividend payments. As a result, issuers often embed a call option alongside the conversion option in the convertible bond, making them **callable convertible bonds**.

Warrants

A **warrant** is somewhat similar to a conversion option, but it is not embedded in the bond's structure. It offers the holder the right to purchase the issuer's stock at a fixed exercise price until the expiration date. Warrants are attached to bond issues as sweeteners, allowing investors to participate in the upside from an increase in share prices.

Contingent Convertible Bonds ("CoCos")

CoCos are bonds with contingent write-down provisions. They differ from traditional convertible bonds in two ways:

- Unlike traditional convertible bonds, which are convertible at the **option** of the bondholder, CoCos convert **automatically** upon the occurrence of a pre-specified event.
- Unlike traditional convertible bonds, in which conversion occurs if the issuer's share price **increases** (i.e., on the upside), contingent write-down provisions are convertible on the **downside**.

FIXED-INCOME MARKETS: ISSUANCE, TRADING, AND FUNDING
Cross-Reference to CFA Institute Assigned Reading #51

OVERVIEW OF GLOBAL FIXED-INCOME MARKETS

Classification of Fixed-Income Markets

Type of Issuer

Bond markets can be classified based on the following three types of issuers:

- The government and government-related sector.
- The corporate sector.
- The structured finance (or securitized) sector.

Credit Quality

- Bonds with a credit rating of Baa3 or above by Moody's, or BBB- or above by S&P and Fitch are classified as investment-grade bonds.
- Bonds with ratings below these levels are classified as non-investment grade (or high-yield, speculative or junk) bonds.

Maturity

- Money market securities are fixed-income securities that have a maturity of one year or less at the time of issuance.
- Capital market securities are fixed-income securities that have a maturity of more than one year at the time of issuance.

Currency Denomination

- The currency in which a bond is issued determines which country's interest rates affect its price.

Geography

- Bonds that are issued in a specific country, denominated in the currency of that country and sold in that country are classified as:
  - Domestic bonds, if they are issued by entities incorporated in that country.
  - Foreign bonds, if the issuer is domiciled in another country.
- A Eurobond is issued internationally i.e., outside the jurisdiction of the country whose currency it is denominated in.

Other Classifications of Fixed-Income Markets

- Inflation-linked bonds offer investors protection against inflation by linking the coupon payment and/or the principal repayment to a consumer price index.

- Tax-exempt bonds, such as municipal bonds (or munis) in the U.S. are attractive for investors who are subject to income tax because interest income from these bonds is usually exempt from federal income tax and from state income tax (subject to some restrictions).

Type of Coupon

- The coupon rate for a bond may (1) be fixed throughout its term, or (2) may change periodically based on some reference rate.

Reference Rates

The reference rate used for a particular floating-rate bond issue depends on where the bonds are issued and the currency denomination. For example, a FRN denominated in GBP that pays coupon semi-annually, would typically calculate the coupon as 6-month Libor (or LIBOR-180) plus a spread.

Fixed-Income Indices

Fixed-income indices are generally used by investors (1) to describe a bond market or sector, and (2) to evaluate investment performance.

Investors in Fixed-Income Securities

- Central banks.
- Institutional investors.
- Retail investors.

Primary Markets

In a public offering (or public offer), any member of the public may purchase the bonds.

- In an underwritten offerings (or firm commitment offering), the investment bank guarantees the sale of the issue at that price. The risk associated with selling the bonds is therefore borne by the investment bank (also known as the underwriter).
- In a best efforts offering, the investment bank only acts as a broker and tries its best to sell the bond at the negotiated offering price for a commission.
- In an auction, bonds are sold to investors through a bidding process, which helps in price discovery and allocation of securities.

Shelf Registration allows certain (authorized) issuers to offer additional bonds to the general public without having to prepare a new and separate prospectus for each bond issue. Since shelf issuances are subject to lower levels of scrutiny than standard public offerings, only well-established issuers with proven financial strength can make use of this facility. Further, in some jurisdictions, shelf registrations can only be purchased by qualified investors.

FI

In a private placement, only a selected group of qualified investors (typically large institutional investors) are allowed to invest in the issue.

- The bonds are neither underwritten nor registered, and can be relatively illiquid as there is usually no secondary market to trade them.
- Investors are usually able to influence the terms of the issue, so privately placed bonds typically have more customized and restrictive covenants compared to publicly issued bonds.

Secondary Markets

Secondary markets (or aftermarkets) are those in which existing bonds are traded among investors.

- Organized exchanges are places where buyers and sellers can meet to arrange their trades. Buyers and sellers may come from anywhere, but transactions must be executed at the exchange in accordance with the rules and regulations of the exchange.
- In over-the-counter (OTC) markets, buyers and sellers submit their orders from various locations through electronic trading platforms. Orders are then matched and executed through a communications network.

The vast majority of bond trading occurs in OTC markets.

Sovereign Bonds

Sovereign bonds are bonds that are issued by a country's central government (or their treasuries). They are issued primarily to cover expenditures when tax revenues are insufficient.

- Sovereign bonds are backed by the taxing authority of the national government.
- Sovereign bonds can be issued in the sovereign's local (domestic) currency or in a foreign currency.

Secondary market trading of sovereign bonds is primarily in securities that were most recently issued (known as on-the-run securities or benchmark issues). Generally speaking, as a sovereign issue ages (or becomes more seasoned), it tends to trade less frequently.

Non-Sovereign Government Bonds

Non-sovereign bonds are those issued by levels of government that lie below the national level (e.g., provinces, regions, states, and cities). These bonds can be serviced through the following sources of income:

- The taxing authority of the local government.
- The cash flows from the project that is being financed with bond proceeds.
- Special taxes and fees established specifically for making interest payments and principal repayments.

Generally speaking, non-sovereign bonds are of high credit quality, but they still trade at higher yields (lower prices) than sovereign bonds.

Quasi-Government Bonds

Quasi-government or agency bonds are issued by organizations that perform various functions for the national government, but are not actual governmental entities. These bonds are issued to fund specific financing needs.

- Quasi-government bonds guaranteed by the national government trade at lower yields than similar bonds not carrying the government guarantee.
- Generally speaking, quasi-government entities do not have direct taxing authority, so bonds are serviced with cash flows generated by the entity or from the project that is being financed by the issue.
- In some cases, quasi-government bonds may be backed by collateral.
- Historical default rates on quasi-government bonds have been extremely low.

Supranational Bonds

These bonds are issued by supranational (or multilateral) agencies such as the World Bank (WB) and the International Monetary Fund (IMF). Generally speaking, supranational bonds are issued as plain vanilla bonds. They are typically highly-rated and issued in large sizes (so they tend to be very liquid).

CORPORATE DEBT

Bank Loans and Syndicated Loans

- Most bank loans are floating-rate loans, with Libor, a sovereign rate (e.g., the T-bill rate), or the prime rate serving as the reference rate.
- Bank loans can be customized (with respect to maturity and payment structure) to borrower requirements.
- Access to bank loans depends on (1) the company's financial position and (2) market conditions and capital availability.

Commercial Paper

- Commercial paper is an unsecured debt instrument that is popular among issuers because it is a source of flexible, readily-available, and relatively low-cost financing.
- It can be used to meet seasonal demands for cash and is also commonly used to provide bridge financing.
- Commercial paper is usually "rolled over" by issuers, which is why they tend to retain access to backup bank lines of credit.
- Terms to maturity can range from overnight to one year.
- Historically, defaults on commercial paper have been relatively rare because commercial paper has a short maturity and tends to be rolled over.

- Most investors hold on to commercial paper until maturity, which results in very little secondary market trading in these instruments.
- Yields on commercial paper are higher than yields on short-term sovereign bonds of the same maturity.

Corporate Notes and Bonds

- Corporate bonds can differ based on:
  - Coupon payment structures.
  - Principal payment structures.
    - Bonds with a serial maturity structure have maturity dates that are spread out over the bond's life.
    - Bonds with a term maturity structure are paid off in one lump sum payment at maturity.
  - Terms to maturity.
  - Asset or collateral backing.
  - Contingency provisions.

Medium-Term Notes (MTNs)

- The MTN market can be broken down into three segments:
  - Short-term securities that may be fixed- or floating-rate.
  - Medium- to long-term securities that generally tend to be fixed-rate.
  - Structured notes, which are essentially notes combined with derivative instruments to create special features desired by certain institutional investors.
- MTNs are unique in that they are offered continuously to investors by the agent of the issuer.
- MTNs can be customized/structured to meet investor requirements. While their customized features result in limited liquidity, MTNs offer higher yields than otherwise identical publicly-traded bonds.

STRUCTURED FINANCIAL INSTRUMENTS

Generally speaking, structured financial instruments have customized structures that often combine a bond and at least one derivative. The use of derivatives gives the holder of the instrument exposure to one or more underlying assets, such as equities, bonds, or commodities. The redemption value and often the coupons of structured financial instruments are tied to the performance of the underlying asset(s), as opposed to being tied to the issuer's cash flows (as is the case with traditional bonds).

Capital-Protected Instruments

Capital-protected instruments may offer different levels of capital protection. A guarantee certificate offers full capital protection, but other structured financial instruments may offer only partial capital protection. It is important to note that the capital protection is only as good as the creditworthiness of the issuer of the instrument. Should the issuer of guarantee certificates go bankrupt, investors may lose their entire capital.

Yield Enhancement Instruments

Yield enhancement aims to improve the expected return on an investment by increasing risk exposure. An example of such an instrument is a credit-linked note (CLN), which is basically a bond that pays regular coupons but whose redemption value depends on the occurrence of a well-defined credit event (e.g., a rating downgrade or the default of a reference asset).

- If the specified credit event does not occur, the investor receives the par value of the CLN at maturity.
- However, if the specified credit event occurs, the investor receives the par value of the CLN minus the nominal value of the reference asset to which the CLN is linked.

A CLN allows the issuer to effectively transfer the effect of a particular credit event to investors. The issuer is the protection buyer (as it benefits from having to redeem a lower amount if the credit event occurs), whereas the investor is the protection seller. In return for taking on credit risk, investors are offered higher coupons on CLNs than on otherwise identical bonds. Additionally, CLNs are usually issued at a discount, which further improves the potential return for investors.

Participation Instruments

Participation instruments allow investors to participate in the return of an underlying asset. Floating-rate bonds (whose coupon rates are reset periodically and brought in line with market interest rates) are examples of such instruments, as they offer investors the opportunity to participate in movements of interest rates.

Most participation instruments are designed to give investors indirect exposure to a particular index or asset price that they are precluded from investing in directly. While both may offer equity exposure, it is important to note that participation instruments differ from capital-protected instruments in that they do not offer capital protection.

Leveraged Instruments

Leveraged instruments are structured financial instruments that aim to magnify returns. An inverse floater is an example of a leveraged instrument, where cash flows move in the opposite direction from changes in the reference rate.

An inverse floater's periodic coupon rate is determined as:

$$\text{Inverse floater coupon rate} = C - (L \times R)$$

- Inverse floaters with a coupon leverage greater than zero but lower than 1.0 are called deleveraged inverse floaters.
- Those with a coupon leverage greater than 1.0 are called leveraged inverse floaters.

- Inverse floaters often have a floor that specifies a minimum coupon rate (e.g., a floor may be set at zero to avoid the possibility of a negative coupon).

SHORT-TERM FUNDING ALTERNATIVES AVAILABLE TO BANKS

Retail deposits: These include funds deposited at the bank by individual and commercial depositors into their accounts.

Short-term wholesale funds: These include:

- Central bank funds.
- Interbank funds.
- Certificates of deposit (CDs).

Repurchase and Reverse Repurchase Agreements

A repurchase agreement is an arrangement between two parties, where one party sells a security to the other with a commitment to buy it back at a later date for a predetermined higher price. The difference between the (lower) selling price and the (higher) repurchase price is the interest cost of the loan. Effectively, what is happening is that the seller is borrowing funds from the buyer and putting up the security as collateral.

- The annualized interest cost of the loan is called the repo rate.
- A repurchase agreement for one day is known as an overnight repo, and an agreement for a longer period is known as a term repo.
- Repo rates are usually lower than the rates that a broker or bank would charge on a margin loan.
- The percentage difference between the market value of the security and the amount of the loan is known as the repo margin or haircut.
- Any coupon income received from the bond during the repo term belongs to the seller (borrower).
- Both parties in the repo face counterparty credit risk.
- When looking at things from the perspective of the seller or borrower, the transaction is referred to as a repo.
- When looking at things from the perspective of the buyer or lender, the transaction is referred to as a reverse repo.
  - Reverse repos are used to borrow securities to cover short positions.
- Standard practice is to define the transaction based on the perspective of the dealer.

Factors that Affect the Repo Rate

- Repo rates increase with the level of credit risk in the collateral.
- A longer term typically entails higher repo rates.
- Repo rates are lower when the collateral must be delivered to the lender.
- The more scarce a particular piece of collateral, the lower the repo rate.
- If rates for borrowing from other sources are higher, repo rates will also tend to be higher.

Factors that Affect the Repo Margin

- The longer the term, the higher the repo margin.
- The higher the quality of the collateral, the lower the repo margin.
- The higher the creditworthiness of the counterparty, the lower the repo margin.
- The higher the demand or the lower the supply of the collateral, the lower the repo margin.

FI

INTRODUCTION TO FIXED-INCOME VALUATION
Cross-Reference to CFA Institute Assigned Reading #52

BOND PRICES AND THE TIME VALUE OF MONEY

Bond Pricing with a Market Discount Rate

- If the coupon rate offered on the bond equals the rate of return required by investors to compensate them for the risk inherent in the instrument, the bond will sell for its par value.
- If the coupon rate offered on the bond is higher than the required yield, the bond will sell for a premium.
- If the coupon rate offered on the bond is lower than the required yield, the bond will sell for a discount.
- The higher the discount rate, the lower the present value of each individual cash flow, and the lower the value of the fixed income security.
- The lower the discount rate, the higher the present value of each individual cash flow, and the higher the value of the fixed income security.

Yield-to-Maturity

The yield-to-maturity is the (uniform) interest rate that equates the sum of the present values of the bond's expected future cash flows (when discount at that rate) to its current price. It also represents the internal rate of return on the bond's cash flows given that:

1. The investor holds on to the bond until maturity.
2. The issuer makes all promised payments on time in their full amount.
3. The investor is able to reinvest all coupon payments received during the term of the bond at the stated yield to maturity until the bond's maturity date.

Relationships between the Bond Price and Bond Characteristics

1. A bond's price is inversely related to the market discount rate (the inverse effect). When the discount rate increases (decreases), the price of the bond decreases (increases).
2. Given the same coupon rate and term to maturity, the percentage price change is greater in terms of absolute magnitude when the discount rate decreases than when it increases (the convexity effect).
3. For the same term to maturity, a lower coupon bond is more sensitive to changes in the market discount rate than a higher coupon bond (the coupon effect).
4. Generally speaking, for the same coupon rate, a longer term bond is more sensitive to changes in the market discount rate than a shorter term bond (the maturity effect). Note that while the maturity effect always holds for zero-coupon bonds and for bonds priced at par or premium to par, it does not always hold for long-term low coupon (but not zero-coupon) bonds that are trading at a discount.

Relationship between Price and Maturity

If the yield remains constant:

- A *premium* bond's value *decreases* towards par as it nears maturity.
- A *discount* bond's value *increases* towards par as it nears maturity.
- A *par* bond's value remains *unchanged* as it nears maturity.

Pricing Bonds with Spot Rates

The arbitrage-free valuation approach does not use the same rate to discount each cash flow, but uses the relevant spot rate to discount each cash flow that occurs at a different point in time. A spot rate (or zero rate) is the yield on a zero-coupon bond for a given maturity.

$$PV = \frac{PMT}{(1+Z_1)^1} + \frac{PMT}{(1+Z_2)^2} + \ldots + \frac{PMT+FV}{(1+Z_N)^N}$$

Flat Price, Accrued Interest and the Full Price

When the price of the bond is determined by calculating the present value of future cash flows as of the settlement date, the computed value is known as the full price (also known as the invoice or dirty price). This price includes accrued interest and reflects the amount that the buyer pays the seller. From this full price, the accrued interest is deducted to determine the flat price (also known as the clean price or quoted price) of the bond.

$$PV^{Full} = PV^{Flat} + AI$$

Accrued interest is the seller's proportional share of the next coupon payment. It is calculated as:

$$AI = t\,/\,T \times PMT$$

- For government bonds, the actual/actual day count convention is usually applied. The actual number of days is used including weekends, holidays, and weekdays.
- For corporate bonds, the 30/360 day-count convention is often used.

$$PV^{Full} = PV \times (1+r)^{t/T}$$

PV^{Full} = Full price of the bond (value between coupon payments)
PV = Price of bond at last/previous coupon payment date
r = Discount rate per period
t = Number of last coupon payment date to the settlement date
T = Number of days in coupon period
t/T = Fraction of coupon period that has gone by since last payment

Matrix Pricing

Matrix pricing is used to estimate the market discount rate and price of bonds that are not actively traded. Essentially, prices of comparable (in terms of terms to maturity, coupon rates and credit quality) are used to interpolate the price of the subject bond. Matrix pricing can also be used when underwriting new bonds to estimate the required yield spread over the benchmark rate on the bonds to be issued.

Yield Measures for Fixed-Rate Bonds

The effective annual rate (or effective annual yield) on a fixed-rate bond depends on the assumed number of periods in the year, which is known as the periodicity of the stated annual rate or stated annual yield.

- An **annual-pay bond** would have a stated annual yield for periodicity of one. The stated annual yield would equal the discount rate per year.
- A **semiannual-pay bond** would have a stated annual yield for periodicity of two. The rate per semiannual period would be computed as the stated annual yield divided by two.
- A **quarterly-pay bond** would have a stated annual yield for periodicity of four. The rate per quarter would be computed as the stated annual yield divided by four.

Note that:

- Given the stated annual rate, as the number of compounding periods (periodicity) increases, the effective annual rate increases.
- Given the effective annual rate, as the number of compounding periods (periodicity) increases, the stated annual rate decreases.

The stated annual rate that has a periodicity of two is known as a semiannual bond basis yield or semiannual bond equivalent yield. The semiannual bond basis yield is calculated as the yield per semiannual period multiplied by two.

Converting Stated Annual Rates (SARs)

$$\left(1 + \frac{SAR_M}{M}\right)^M = \left(1 + \frac{SAR_N}{N}\right)^N$$

> **Important:** What we refer to as stated annual rate (SAR) is referred to in the curriculum as APR or annual percentage rate. We stick to SAR to keep your focus on a stated annual rate versus the effective annual rate. Just remember that if you see an annual percentage rate on the exam, it refers to the stated annual rate.

Bond Yield Quoting Conventions

- The street convention yield represents the internal rate of return on the bond's cash flows assuming all payments are made on scheduled dates regardless of whether any scheduled payment dates fall on weekends or holidays.
- The true yield uses these actual payment dates to compute the IRR.

- The government equivalent yield (usually quoted for corporate bonds) restates a yield-to-maturity based on a 30/360 day-count convention to one based on an actual/actual day-count convention.
- The current yield (also called the income yield or interest yield) is calculated as the sum of coupon payments received over the year divided by the flat price. The current yield is a relatively crude measure of the rate of return to an investor.
  - It neglects the frequency of coupon payments in the numerator.
  - It neglects any accrued interest in the denominator.
  - It neglects any gains (losses) from purchasing the bond at a discount (premium) and redeeming it for par.
- The simple yield is calculated as the sum of coupon payments received over the year plus (minus) straight line amortization of the gain (loss) from purchasing the bond at a discount (premium), divided by the flat price.

Yields for Callable Bonds

- The yield-to-call is computed for each call date (based on the call price and the number of periods until the call date), and then determine the yield-to-worst as the worst or lowest yield among the yield to maturity and the various yields to call for the bond.
- The option-adjusted yield is based on the option-adjusted price, which is calculated by adding the value of the embedded call option to the flat price of the callable bond. The option adjusted yield is lower than the yield to maturity on a callable bond because callable bonds offer higher yields than otherwise identical non-callable bonds to compensate investors for effectively selling the embedded call option to the issuer.

Yield Measures for Floating-Rate Notes

The effective coupon rate for a specified period is determined at the beginning of the period but actually paid out at the end of the period (in arrears).

If the quoted margin equals the required margin, the FRN will trade at par at each reset date, but if the quoted margin is lower (greater) than the required margin, the FRN will trade at a discount (premium).

Changes in the required margin can be caused by changes in the issue's (1) credit risk, (2) liquidity and/or (3) tax status.

Risk Exposure of Fixed- versus Floating-Rate Bonds

- Fixed-rate and floating-rate bonds respond very similarly when it comes to credit risk. An increase (decrease) in credit risk leads to a decline (increase) in the value of both types of bonds.
- However, fixed-and floating-rate bonds respond very differently when it comes to changes in benchmark interest rates.

Yield Measures for Money Market Instruments

Money-market instruments are short-term debt securities with maturities ranging from one day (e.g., repos) to one year (e.g., bank certificates of deposit). Money market yields differ from yields in the bond market in the following respects:

1. Bond yields-to-maturity are annualized and compounded. Money market yields are annualized but not compounded (they are stated on simple interest basis).
2. Bond yields-to-maturity can usually be calculated by applying standard time value of money analysis and using a financial calculator. Money market yields are often quoted in terms of nonstandard interest rates so users need to work with various pricing equations.
3. Bond yields-to-maturity are typically stated for a common periodicity for all terms-to-maturity. Money market instruments that have different times-to-maturity have different periodicities for the stated annual rate.

Pricing formula for money market instruments quoted on a discount rate basis

$$PV = FV \times \left(1 - \frac{Days}{Year} \times DR\right)$$

$$DR = \left(\frac{Year}{Days}\right) \times \left(\frac{FV - PV}{FV}\right)$$

A money market discount rate understates the rate of return to the investor and understates the cost of borrowing for the issuer (because PV is generally less than FV).

Pricing formula for money market instruments quoted on an add-on rate basis

$$PV = \frac{FV}{\left(1 + \frac{Days}{Year} \times AOR\right)}$$

$$AOR = \left(\frac{Year}{Days}\right) \times \left(\frac{FV - PV}{PV}\right)$$

The add-on rate a reasonable measure for the yield on a money market investment.

Typically money-market yields are converted to a rate known as the bond-equivalent yield or investment yield for comparisons. The bond equivalent yield is a money-market rate stated on a **365-day year** on an **add-on rate basis**.

Generally speaking, the lower the level of interest rates, the smaller the difference between the stated annual rates for any two periodicities.

The Maturity Structure of Interest Rates

The spot rate curve reflects spot rates for a range of maturities. The distinguishing feature of spot rates is that they are yields that have no element of reinvestment risk. Using spot rates provides a more accurate relationship between yields and terms to maturity relative to using yields to maturity on coupon-bearing Treasuries.

A yield curve for coupon bonds shows the yields-to-maturity for coupon-paying bonds of different maturities. To build the Treasury yield curve, analysts use only the most recently-issued and actively-traded government bonds as they have similar liquidity and tax status. YTMs for maturities where there are gaps can be estimated through a variety of interpolation methods.

A par curve represents a series of yields-to-maturity such that each bond trades at par. The par curve is derived from the spot rate curve.

Forward Curve

A forward rate represents the interest rate on a loan that will be originated at some point in the future. Forward rates are used to construct the forward curve, which represents a series of forward rates, each having the same horizon. Typically the forward curve shows one-year forward rates stated on a semiannual bond basis

Implied forward rates (also known as forward yields) can be computed from spot rates.

If the yields presented are semiannual bond basis:

$$\left(1+\frac{\text{6-mth spot rate}}{2}\right)\left(1+\frac{\text{6-mth forward rate 6 mths from now}}{2}\right) = \left(1+\frac{\text{12-mth spot rate}}{2}\right)^2$$

To calculate the x-period forward rate y periods from today, simply remember the following formula: Note that x and y here respresent the periodic spot rate.

$$(1+{}_y s_0)^y (1+{}_x f_y)^x = (1+{}_{x+y} s_0)^{x+y}$$

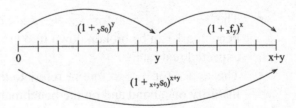

Example: Calculating Forward Rates

Calculate the 1-year forward rate 6 years from today if the 6-year spot rate is 6.25% and the 7-year spot rate is 6%.

Solution:

$$(1 + {}_6s_0)^6(1 + {}_1f_6) = (1 + {}_7s_0)^7$$

$$(1 + {}_1f_6) = \frac{(1.06)^7}{(1.0625)^6} => {}_1f_6 = 4.51\%$$

A forward rate can be looked upon as the marginal or incremental return from expanding the time to maturity by one more year or as a breakeven reinvestment rate. Forward rates are useful to investors in making maturity choice decisions.

Important: Please note that finance authors use different notation when it comes to forward rates. We use ${}_xf_y$, which refers to the x-period forward rate y years from today, or the interest rate on a loan that has a term of x years, where the loan will be originated y years from today. The CFA Program curriculum uses different notation. In the curriculum, the forward rate 2y5y refers to the 5-year rate 2 years into the future and 3y2y refers to the 2-year rate 3 years from now. We have stuck with our (different) notation because we feel it is easier to work with. You can work with either notation, as it won't affect your answers.

YIELD SPREADS

Yield Spreads over Benchmark Rates

- The benchmark yield (or risk-free rate) captures **macroeconomic factors**. The benchmark can be broken down into (1) the expected inflation rate and (2) the expected real rate.
- The spread (or risk premium) refers to the difference between the yield-to-maturity on a bond and on the benchmark. It captures all **microeconomic factors** specific to the issuer.

Types of Yield Spreads

- The yield spread in basis points over an actual or interpolated government bond yield is known as the G-spread.
- The yield spread over the standard swap rate in the same currency and with the same tenor as the subject bond is known as the I-spread or interpolated spread to the swap curve.

- Note that the government bond yield or the swap rate used as the benchmark for a specific bond will change over time as the remaining term to maturity of the bond changes.
- For floating-rate bonds, Libor is often used as a benchmark. Note that Libor is an interbank rate, not a risk-free rate.

Yield Spreads over the Benchmark Yield Curve

Given the term to maturity of a security, the appropriate benchmark yield-to-maturity applies the same discount rate for each cash flow. Theoretically, this method is unappealing because each cash flow received from the bond carries a different amount of risk (typically, cash flows expected to be received further out into the future entail more risk). It makes more sense to use individual spot rate rates to discount each of the bond's expected cash flows as spot rates accurately capture the risk entailed by each corresponding cash flow (i.e., for each time horizon, there is a specific spot rate unless the yield curve is flat). Therefore, practitioners tend to favor use of the z-spread over the G- and I-spreads.

The z-spread (or zero-volatility spread or static spread) of a bond is a constant spread over the government (or interest rate swap) spot rate curve.

The z-spread is also used to calculate the option-adjusted spread (OAS) on a callable bond. The OAS is calculated by subtracting the value of the embedded call option (stated in terms of bps per year) from the z-spread.

OAS = z-spread − Option value (bps per year)

Stated simply, the OAS removes the cost of the option from the z-spread, so the OAS is the spread on top of the spot rate curve that the bond would offer if it were option-free. Since the embedded call option in a callable bond favors the issuer, the OAS (the spread that an otherwise identical option-free bond would offer) is less than the z-spread. An issuer would pay out more (in terms of yield) on a callable bond than on an option-free bond.

FI

INTRODUCTION TO ASSET-BACKED SECURITIES
Cross-Reference to CFA Institute Assigned Reading #53

Benefits of Securitization

- It removes the layer between borrowers and investors.
- It allows investors to have a stronger legal claim on the collateral pool of assets.
- Investors can pick and choose the types of securities they want to invest in (in terms of interest rate and credit risk).
- Financial intermediaries are able to originate more loans (by using financing provided by outside investors to originate loans) than they would be able to if they were only able to issue loans that they could finance themselves.
- The increase in the total supply of loanable funds benefits organizations (governments and companies) that need to borrow.
- Since securitized bonds are sold in the public market, they enjoy much better liquidity (lower liquidity risk) than the original loans on bank balance sheets.
- Financial markets are made more efficient.
- Securitization encourages innovation in investment products, which can offer investors access to (otherwise directly unavailable) assets that match their risk, return, and maturity profiles.
- Even large investors, who may be able to purchase real estate loans, automobile loans, or credit card loans directly, would prefer to invest in asset-backed bonds since they would not be required to originate, monitor, and collect payments from the underlying loans themselves.
- ABS offer companies an alternative means of raising finance that can be considered alongside bond and equity issuance.

Parties to a Securitization

Party	Description	Party in Illustration
Seller	Originates the loans and sells loans to the SPV	ABC Company
Issuer/Trust	The SPV that buys the loans from the seller and issues the asset-backed securities	SPV
Servicer	Services the loans	Servicer

In order for a securitization to serve its purpose, the SPV must be a bankruptcy remote entity, i.e., its obligations remain secure even if the parent company goes bankrupt.

RESIDENTIAL MORTGAGE LOANS

- A mortgage loan is a borrowing that is secured by some form of real estate.
- Upon initiation of the mortgage loan, the borrower's equity equals the down payment, but over time, the borrower's equity changes as a result of (1) changes in the market value of the property and (2) payment of periodic mortgage payments (that include a principal component).

- The lower (higher) the LTV ratio, the higher (lower) the borrower's equity, the less (more) likely the borrower is to default, and the more (less) protection the lender has for recovering the amount loaned in case the borrower defaults.
- Most mortgages around the world are structured as amortizing loans.
- A mortgage loan may allow the borrower to prepay (make a principal repayment that exceeds the scheduled repayment for the month) a portion, or the entire amount, of the outstanding mortgage principal at any point during the term of the mortgage.

RESIDENTIAL MORTGAGE-BACKED SECURITIES

- Agency RMBSs are issued by (1) federal agencies (e.g., Ginnie Mae, which is a federally related institution), and (2) quasi-government entities (e.g., Freddie Mac and Fannie Mae, which are government sponsored enterprises or GSEs).
  - There is no credit risk for agency RMBSs issued by Ginnie Mae as they are backed by the full faith and credit of the U.S. Government.
  - There is minimal credit risk for agency RMBSs issued by GSEs as they are guaranteed by the GSEs themselves.
    - Mortgage loans issued by GSEs must satisfy specific underwriting standards established by various government agencies to qualify for the collateral pool backing agency RMBSs issued by GSEs.
- Non-agency RMBSs are issued by private entities.
  - They typically come with credit enhancements to reduce credit risk.
    - There are no restrictions on the types of non-agency mortgage loans that can be used to back non-agency RMBSs.

MORTGAGE PASS-THROUGH SECURITIES

- A mortgage pass-through security is created when shares or participation certificates in a pool of mortgage loans are sold to investors.
- The cash flow collected from the collateral pool includes scheduled principal and interest payments, and prepayments.
- The amount and timing of cash flows paid to investors in the pass-through securities are different from those of the cash flows collected from the collateral pool of mortgages.
- Payments made by borrowers pass through the government agency (and on to investors) net of servicing and guaranteeing fees. Therefore, the pass-through rate (coupon rate on the pass-through security, which is net interest/net coupon) is lower than the mortgage rate on the underlying pool of mortgages.
- Mortgage loans that are securitized to create pass-through securities do not all carry the same mortgage rate and maturity. Therefore, a weighted average coupon rate (WAC) and weighted average maturity (WAM) are calculated to describe the pool of mortgages that serves as collateral for the pass-through securities.
- Market participants use average life (the weighted average time it will take for all the principal payments, i.e., scheduled repayments and projected prepayments, to be received) as a measure of the interest rate risk of a mortgage-backed security.
  - The average life of an RMBS depends on the assumed prepayment speed—the higher the prepayment speed assumed, the shorter the average life of the mortgage backed security.

- The prepayment rate is measured in terms of the single monthly mortality rate (SMM). It is calculated as the amount of prepayment for a month as a percentage of the mortgage balance that was available to be prepaid that month.

Contraction Risk versus Extension Risk

Prepayment risk encompasses contraction risk and extension risk.

Contraction risk occurs when interest rates fall.

- Option-free bond prices increase when interest rates fall. However, for mortgage loans, the issuer (homeowner) has the right to prepay and can easily do so by refinancing her mortgage. This option to prepay is similar to the call option granted to the issuer of a callable bond. When interest rates fall, it becomes feasible for the mortgage issuer/borrower to prepay (just like it becomes feasible for an issuer to call a callable bond), so the upside potential of the pass-through security is limited. It experiences price compression at low interest rates and exhibits negative convexity.
- To make things worse, when interest rates fall, refinancing activity typically increases and leads to an increase in prepayments, reducing or shortening the average life of the pass-through. The (higher-than-expected) cash flows from the pass-through must then be reinvested at current (lower) rates.

Extension risk occurs when interest rates rise.

- The price of a pass-through (just like the price of any bond) will decline when interest rates increase.
- To make things worse, refinancing activity and prepayment rates slow down when interest rates rise, increasing or lengthening the average expected life of the pass-through. Consequently, a greater-than-anticipated amount remains invested in the pass-through at the coupon rate of the instrument, which is lower than current interest rates.

COLLATERALIZED MORTGAGE OBLIGATIONS

Collateralized mortgage obligations (CMOs) redistribute the cash flows from mortgage pass-through securities into packages/classes/tranches with different risk exposures to prepayment risk.

- For CMOs, the mortgage-related products from which cash flows are obtained are considered the collateral, i.e., a pool of mortgage pass-through security serves as the collateral. For mortgage pass-through securities, a pool of mortgage loans serves as collateral.

Sequential-Pay Tranches

- Each class of bond is retired sequentially.
- Interest payments are periodically made to each tranche based on its coupon rate and principal amount outstanding at the beginning of the period.

- Principal payments are first forwarded to Tranche A, then to Tranche B (after Tranche A has been fully paid off) and so on.
- The principal payment pattern for each of the tranches is not known. However, the shorter-term tranches receive protection from extension risk, while the longer term tranches receive protection from contraction risk.

Planned Amortization Class (PAC) Tranches

- PAC bonds bring increased predictability of cash flows, as they specify a repayment schedule that will be satisfied as long as actual prepayments realized from the collateral fall within a pre-defined band.
- The greater certainty in payments for the PAC tranche comes at the expense of greater uncertainty for the support or companion tranche, which absorbs the prepayment risk.
- The average life of the support tranche fluctuates more wildly than that of the PAC tranche.
- The support tranche provides **two-sided protection** (i.e., protection against extension **and** contraction risk) to the PAC tranche.
- The greater the par value of the support tranche relative to that of the PAC tranche, the greater the prepayment protection for the PAC, the lower the PAC's average life variability, and the greater the support tranche's average life variability.

Floating-Rate Tranches

- Even though the collateral for CMOs carries a fixed rate, it is possible to create a floating-rate tranche (along with an inverse-floater tranche) from any of the fixed-rate tranches in a CMO structure.
- Since the floater varies positively with interest rates, and the inverse floater varies negatively with interest rates, they offset each other.

NON-AGENCY RESIDENTIAL MORTGAGE-BACKED SECURITIES

Non-agency RMBSs are not guaranteed by the government or a GSE, which make the evaluation of credit risk an important consideration when investing in them.

- Cash flows are distributed according to a set of rules that determines the distribution of interest and principal payments to tranches with varying levels of priority/seniority.
- There are also rules for allocating realized losses, with senior tranches having a priority claim over payments and subordinated tranches absorbing losses.
- When it comes to forecasting cash flows on non-agency RMBSs, investors must make assumptions regarding (1) the default rate for the collateral and (2) the recovery rate.

FI

Internal Credit Enhancements

- Reserve funds:
  - Cash reserve funds: The entity seeking to raise the funds deposits some of the proceeds of sale of the loan pool with the SPV. This cash can be used to pay for potential future losses.
  - Excess spread accounts: The excess spread or cash that remains after the payment of net coupon, servicing fees, and all other expenses is kept in reserve to pay for future credit losses on the collateral.
- Overcollateralization: This refers to a situation where the value of the collateral exceeds the par value of the securities issued by the SPV.
  - The amount of overcollateralization for an issue changes over time due to (1) defaults, (2) amortization, and (3) prepayments.
- Senior/subordinate structure: This type of structure has senior bond classes and subordinate bond classes (also known as non-senior/junior bond classes).
  - The structure basically provides credit tranches as the subordinate bond classes provide credit protection to the senior classes.
  - To provide credit protection to investors in the senior bond classes, a shifting interest mechanism is added to the structure. This mechanism locks out subordinated classes from receiving payments for a period of time if the collateral performs poorly.

External Credit Enhancements

External credit enhancements are third-party guarantees for payments to security holders should the issuer not be able to meet payment requirements.

- Monoline insurers are the most common third-party financial guarantors.

Time Tranching versus Credit Tranching

- Time tranching occurs when prepayment risk (or the timing of distribution of cash flows) is redistributed among the various classes of ABS as in a sequential-pay CMO structure.
- Credit tranching occurs when credit risk (or risk of loss from default) is redistributed among the various classes of ABS as in a senior/subordinate structure

COMMERCIAL MORTGAGE BACKED SECURITIES (CMBS)

CMBSs are backed by a pool of commercial mortgage loans on income-generating properties (e.g., apartments, warehouses, shopping centres, etc.). In the U.S. (and many other countries), commercial mortgage loans are non-recourse loans. Therefore, evaluation of credit risk for commercial mortgage loans requires examining the income-generating capacity and value of each property on a stand-alone basis.

Two measures are commonly used to evaluate the potential credit performance of a commercial property:

- The debt-service coverage (DSC) ratio is used to evaluate the adequacy of income generated from the property to service the loan. It is calculated as net operating income (NOI) divided by debt service. NOI is calculated as rental income minus cash operating expenses and a non-cash replacement reserve that reflects depreciation of the property over time.
    - A ratio greater than 1 means that cash flow from the property covers debt servicing costs adequately.
    - The higher the ratio, the lower the credit risk
- The loan-to-value ratio equals the loan amount divided by the appraised value of the property.
    - The lower the ratio, the lower the credit risk.

Basic CMBS Structure

- A credit-rating agency determines the level of credit enhancement required for the issue to attain the credit rating desired by the issuer.
- Different bond classes are created with each class having a different priority on cash flows. The various bond classes are retired sequentially with all principal repayments, prepayments, and proceeds from default (from selling repossessed properties) being used to repay the highest-rated tranche first.
- Losses from loan defaults are charged against the lowest-rated tranche first. If this tranche is not rated by credit-rating agencies, it is known as the first-loss piece, residual tranche, or equity tranche.
- The equity tranche typically has no specific interest rate (as it is the residual tranche). Investors price it based on the expected residual rate of return. Actual returns can be better or worse than expected depending on actual future interest rate movements and actual defaults.
- Interest payments are made to all tranches.
- Typically, CMBS investors have significant call protection, which actually results in these securities trading more like corporate bonds than like RMBSs.
    - Call protection at the loan level can come in form of prepayment lockouts, defeasance, prepayment penalties, and yield maintenance charges.
    - Call protection at the structure level comes from credit tranches.
- Most commercial loans that back CMBSs have balloon maturity provisions, i.e., they require a significant amount of principal to be repaid at maturity (as opposed to during the term of the loan). This exposes investors to balloon risk, which is more like extension risk as there is usually a workout period during which the borrower and lender try to modify the original terms of the loan to ensure eventual repayment.

NON-MORTGAGE ASSET BACKED SECURITIES

The collateral backing asset-backed securities can be classified as either amortizing or non-amortizing assets.

Amortizing loans:

- The periodic cash flows include interest payments, principal repayments (in accordance with an amortization schedule), and (if allowed) prepayments.
- Examples include residential mortgage loans and automobile loans.

Non-amortizing loans:

- These only require a monthly minimum payment with no scheduled principal payment.
- If the payment received is less than the interest amount due, the shortfall is added to the outstanding loan balance.
- If the payment is greater than the interest amount due, the excess serves to reduce the outstanding loan balance.
- Since there is no scheduled principal payment amount, the concept of prepayment does not apply to non-amortizing assets.
- Examples include credit card receivables.

The type of collateral (amortizing versus non-amortizing assets) has a significant effect on the structure of the securitization.

- When amortizing assets are securitized, the total face value (total amount outstanding) declines over time due to scheduled repayments and prepayments, and the number of outstanding loans (composition of the collateral) declines as a result of (1) defaults and (2) full principal repayments or full amortizations.
- On the other hand, securitizations of non-amortizing loans usually take the form of a revolving structure, where the composition of the collateral can change over the term of the securities. This is because principal repayments can either be (1) reinvested by purchasing additional loans, or (2) passed on to security holders.
  - During an initial lockout or revolving period (which immediately follows the origination of the transaction), all principal repayments are reinvested in additional loans with a principal amount equal to the total principal amount received. While this can result in a fewer total number of individual loans comprising the collateral, the total face value outstanding remains the same.
  - During the principal amortization period (which follows the lockout period), principal repayments are not used to purchase additional loans, but are distributed to security holders.

Auto Loan Receivable-Backed Securities

These securities are backed by auto loan and lease receivables. Cash flows for auto loan-backed securities consist of regularly scheduled monthly interest and principal payments and prepayments.

- Generally speaking, auto loan-backed securitizations come with some form of credit enhancement.
- Typically, the securitizations involve a senior/subordinate structure (to provide credit protection to the senior tranches). Further, some securitizations also involve reserve accounts, overcollateralization, and excess interest on the receivables.

Credit Card Receivable-Backed Securities

- The cash flow from a pool of credit card receivables includes (1) finance charges collected (interest charges on the unpaid balance after the grace period), (2) fees (for late payments and membership), and (3) principal repayment.
- Interest payments are made to security holders periodically (monthly, quarterly, or semiannually). The interest rate may be fixed or floating (typically with no cap).
- During the revolving period (also known as the lockout period), any principal repayments from the pool of receivables are used to purchase additional receivables to maintain the size of the pool. During this period, the cash flow passed on to security holders consists only of (1) finance charges and (2) fees collected from the pool of receivables. Principal repayments are only passed on to security holders once the principal-amortizing period sets in.
- Even though receivables in a revolving structure may not be prepaid (since there is no concept of prepayment here), all the bonds may be retired early if an early or rapid amortization provision is triggered.

COLLATERALIZED DEBT OBLIGATIONS

A CDO is a security that is backed by a diversified pool of securities.

- Like an ABS, a CDO also involves the creation of an SPV.
- A CDO manager (also known as collateral manager) is responsible for managing the collateral portfolio of assets (consisting of debt obligations).
- The funds used to purchase the collateral assets are raised from the issuance of bonds to investors. Bond classes may include senior bonds, mezzanine bonds (with credit ratings between senior and subordinated bonds), and subordinated bonds (also known as the residual or equity class).
- Restrictive covenants are placed on the manager to ensure that the credit ratings assigned to the various tranches at issuance are maintained during the term of the CDO.
- Cash flows from the underlying portfolio of assets include (1) coupon interest payments, (2) proceeds from maturing assets, and (3) proceeds from sale of assets. These cash flows are used to make interest and principal payments to the various bond classes.
- From the asset manager/issuer's perspective, the aim is to earn a rate of return on the collateral pool of assets that is higher than the interest costs of bonds issued. This excess return accrues to the equity holders and the CDO manager. Effectively, issuing a CDO is like undertaking a leveraged transaction where the idea is to use borrowed funds (raised from bonds issued) to generate a return that exceeds the funding cost.
- From the investors' perspective, each class of bonds entails a different level of risk. Senior/mezzanine bond investors may be able to earn a potentially higher return than on a comparably-rated corporate bond by gaining exposure to debt products that they may not otherwise be able to purchase. Equity investors can earn an equity-type return by taking the (higher) risk associated with the subordinated class.

- Certain restrictions are placed on the manager (via various tests and limits) to ensure that the senior bond classes are adequately protected and the ratings issued to the bond classes are maintained. Failure to meet these tests may trigger an immediate payoff to the senior bond classes until the tests are satisfied. This payoff would have the effect of deleveraging the CDO (as the asset manager's reliance on its cheapest source of funding, i.e., senior bonds, would be reduced).

The major difference between an ABS and a CDO is that in an ABS the cash flows from the collateral pool are used to pay off bond holders without the active management of collateral. In a CDO, the manager buys and sells debt obligations (assets) to (1) generate the cash flow required to repay bond holders and to (2) earn a competitive return for the equity tranche.

STUDY SESSION 17:
FIXED INCOME (2)

UNDERSTANDING FIXED-INCOME RISK AND RETURN
Cross-Reference to CFA Institute Assigned Reading #54

Sources of Return on a Fixed-Rate Bond

1. Receipt of promised coupon and principal payments.
2. Reinvestment of coupon payments.
3. Potential capital gains/losses if the bond is sold prior to maturity.

If a bond is purchased at a premium/discount, it adds another dimension to the total rate of return.

Horizon Yield, Carrying Value and Capital Gains and Losses

The horizon yield equals the YTM at issuance if the following two conditions hold:

- The bond is sold at its carrying value, i.e., at a price that lies on its constant-yield price trajectory.
- All coupon payments can be reinvested at a rate that equals the bond's YTM at issuance until date of sale.

Carrying value refers to the value of a bond (at any time between the purchase date and maturity date) that entails the same YTM as when the bond was purchased. The carrying value reflects amortization of any premium/discount since the time of purchase. Capital gains/losses arise if a bond is sold at a price different from its carrying value.

Interest Rate Risk

There are two types of interest rate risk, which offset each other:

- **Reinvestment risk.** The future value of any interim cash flows received from a bond (these could be coupon payments as well as principal repayments on amortizing bonds) increases when interest rates rise and decreases when interest rates decline.
- **Market price risk.** The selling price of a bond (at any point during its term or before maturity) decreases when interest rates rise and increases when interest rates decline.

Reinvestment risk matters more to a long-term investors, while market price risk matters more to short-term investors. Therefore, two investors who are holding the same bond can have different exposures to interest rate risk depending on their individual investment horizons.

INTEREST RATE RISK OF FIXED-RATE BONDS

Duration

Duration measures the sensitivity or responsiveness of a bond's **full price** (including accrued interest) to changes in **its yield-to-maturity** (or market discount rate). Broadly speaking, duration can be classified as:

- Yield duration, which measures the responsiveness of a bond's price with respect to **its own yield-to-maturity**. Yield duration statistics include Macaulay duration, modified duration, money duration and the price value of a basis point.
- Curve duration, which measures the responsiveness of a bond's price with respect to **a benchmark yield curve** (e.g., government yield curve, forward curve, or government par curve). Coupon duration statistics include effective duration.

Macaulay Duration

Macaulay duration represents the weighted average of the time it would take to receive all the bond's promised cash flows, where the weights are calculated as the present value of each cash flow divided by the bond's **full price**.

Macaulay duration (in terms of periods) can also be computed using the following closed-form formula:

$$MacDur = \left\{ \frac{1+r}{r} - \frac{1+r+[N\times(c-r)]}{c\times[(1+r)^N - 1]+r} \right\} - (t\,/\,T)$$

Macaulay duration is typically not used as a measure of the interest rate sensitivity of a bond's price. However, it does have has some useful applications, including measurement of the duration gap.

Modified Duration

Modified duration is calculated by dividing Macaulay duration by one plus the yield per period.

$$ModDur = \frac{MacDur}{1+r}$$

Modified duration can be used to estimate the percentage price change for a bond in response to a change in **its yield-to-maturity**.

$$\%\Delta PV^{Full} \approx -AnnModDur \times \Delta Yield$$

- Modified duration only provides a linear estimate of the change in the price of a bond in response to a change in yields.

- It provides good estimates for bond prices in response to relatively small changes in yields, but its estimating accuracy fades with larger changes in yields as the curvature (convexity) of the price-yield profile becomes more pronounced.

If Macaulay duration is not already known, annual modified duration can be estimated using the following formula:

$$\text{ApproxModDur} = \frac{(PV_-) - (PV_+)}{2 \times (\Delta \text{Yield}) \times (PV_0)}$$

- This approximation basically estimates the slope of the line tangent to the price-yield profile for a bond at a particular yield level.
- The value for approximate modified duration obtained by applying this formula gives us the percentage change in the price of a bond in response to a 100 bps (1%) change in yields.
- The percentage price change if yields were to change by 50 basis points would be half the figure obtained from applying the formula.

We can also use the approximate modified duration (ApproxModDur) to estimate Macaulay duration (ApproxMacDur) by applying the following formula:

$$\text{ApproxMacDur} = \text{ApproxModDur} \times (1 + r)$$

Effective Duration

Effective duration (also known as OAS duration) measures the sensitivity of a bond's price to a change in **the benchmark yield curve**.

$$\text{EffDur} = \frac{(PV_-) - (PV_+)}{2 \times (\Delta \text{Curve}) \times (PV_0)}$$

Note that:

- Effective duration is a **curve duration** statistic that measures interest rate risk in terms of a change in the benchmark yield curve (ΔCurve).
- Modified duration is a **yield duration** statistic that measures interest rate risk in terms of a change in the bond's own yield-to-maturity (ΔYield).

Effective duration is the appropriate measure of risk **for bonds with embedded call options**, including callable bonds (and mortgage-backed bonds).

- Modified or Macaulay duration (essentially, just one statistic) can be computed to estimate the percentage price change for a **traditional fixed-rate bond** in response to a change in the benchmark yield and/or credit spread.

- On the other hand, **for bonds with embedded options** (where there is no well-defined internal rate of return), a curve duration statistic must be computed to measure the effects of a change in benchmark yields, and a separate measure (e.g., credit duration) must be computed to measure the effects of a change in the credit spread.

Further, note that unlike modified duration, effective duration does not necessarily provide more accurate estimates for changes in a bond's price if we use a smaller change in benchmark rates.

Finally, although effective duration is the appropriate interest rate risk measure for bonds With embedded options, it is also used for traditional bonds to supplement the information provided by modified and Macaulay duration.

Key Rate Duration

Key rate duration (or partial duration) is a measure of a bond's (or bond portfolio's) sensitivity to a change in the benchmark yield for a given maturity. Key rate durations are used to assess shaping or yield curve risk for a bond, i.e., the bond's sensitivity to changes in the shape of the benchmark yield curve, or non-parallel shifts in the yield curve (e.g., the yield curve becoming steeper or flatter).

For parallel shifts in the benchmark yield curve, key rate durations will suggest the same interest rate sensitivity as effective duration.

Properties of Bond Durations

Fraction of the coupon period that has elapsed (t/T):

All other things remaining the same, Macaulay duration falls as time passes through a coupon period, and then jumps after each coupon payment (creating a saw tooth-like pattern).

Time-to-maturity

- For fixed-rate coupon bonds trading at par or premium to par, longer times-to-maturity correspond to a higher Macaulay duration.
  - However, Macaulay duration for these bonds never rises above a threshold level defined by MacDur = $(1 + r)/r$
- For fixed-rate coupon bonds trading at a discount, longer times-to-maturity **generally** correspond to a higher Macaulay duration.
  - Given a long enough time-to-maturity, Macaulay duration for discount bonds actually rises to a maximum level that lies above MacDur = $(1 + r)/r$.
  - However, after reaching its maximum level, as time-to-maturity further increases, Macaulay duration for discount bonds starts falling back towards $(1 + r)/r$ if the coupon rate is low relative to the yield-to-maturity.
- The Macaulay duration for a zero-coupon bond equals its time-to-maturity.
- For a non-callable perpetuity (or consol) i.e., a bond that pays a fixed coupon forever, Macaulay duration equals the threshold level MacDur = $(1 + r)/r$.

Coupon rate:

All other things remaining the same, a lower-coupon bond has higher duration and more interest rate risk than a higher-coupon bond.

Yield-to-maturity:

All other things remaining the same, a lower yield-to-maturity bond has higher duration and more interest rate risk than a higher yield-to-maturity bond.

Callable Bonds

- The price of a callable bond is always *lower* than the price of an otherwise identical non-callable bond. The difference represents the value of the embedded call option.

When interest rates are **high** relative to the coupon rate:

- It is highly unlikely that the issuer will call the bond, so the value of the embedded call option is relatively low.
- Therefore, the effective durations (slopes of the price-yield profiles) of the callable and non-callable bonds are very similar.

When interest rates are **low** relative to the coupon rate:

- It becomes more likely that the issuer will call the bond (and exercise the option to refinance at a lower cost of funds), so the embedded call option gains value for the issuer.
- As interest rates fall, the callable bond suffers "price compression."
- The effective duration (slope of the price-yield profile) of the callable bond is *lower* than that of an otherwise identical non-callable bond – its expected life shortens as the weighted average time to receipt of cash is reduced.

Putable Bonds

- The price of a putable bond is always greater than the price of an otherwise identical non-putable bond. The difference represents the value of the embedded put option.

When interest rates are **low** relative to the coupon rate:

- It is highly unlikely that the investor will put the bond back to the issuer, so the value of the embedded put option is relatively low.
- Therefore, the effective durations (slopes of the price-yield profiles) of the putable and non-putable bonds are very similar.

When interest rates are **high** relative to the coupon rate:

- It becomes more likely that the investor will put the bond back to the issuer, so the embedded put option gains value for the investor.

- As interest rates rise, the putable bond does not lose as much value as an otherwise identical non-putable bond. The put price effectively serves as a floor on its value.
- The effective duration (slope of the price-yield profile) of the putable bond is lower than that of an otherwise identical non-putable bond—its expected life shortens as the weighted average time to receipt of cash is reduced.

To summarize, the presence of an embedded option (be it a call or a put) *reduces* the duration of the bond and makes it less sensitive to changes in the benchmark yield curve, assuming there is no change in credit risk.

Computing the Duration of a Bond Portfolio

1. Compute the weighted average of time to receipt of the portfolio's aggregate cash flows.

   Under this method, projected cash flows on all (1) traditional bonds and (2) bonds with embedded options held in the portfolio are aggregated to determine the portfolio's cash flow yield (i.e., internal rate of return based on those projected cash flows), which is then used to compute Macaulay and modified duration for the portfolio. While theoretically accurate, this method is difficult to implement in practice.

2. Compute the weighted average of the durations of the individual bonds held in the portfolio.

   Under this method, Macaulay and modified duration statistics for a bond portfolio are computed as the weighted average of the statistics for the individual bonds that comprise the portfolio, where each bond's weight equals the proportion of the total portfolio's market value that it comprises (based on **full prices**).

$$\text{Portfolio duration} = w_1 D_1 + w_2 D_2 + \ldots + w_N D_N$$

Money Duration and Price Value of a Basis Point

Money duration (or dollar duration) is a measure of the *dollar* (or whichever currency the bond is denominated in) *price change* in response to a change in yields.

$$\text{MoneyDur} = \text{AnnModDur} \times PV^{Full}$$

The estimated (dollar) change in the price of the bond is calculated as:

$$\Delta PV^{Full} = -\text{MoneyDur} \times \Delta \text{Yield}$$

The price value of a basis point (PVBP) estimates the change in the full price of a bond in response to a 1 bp change in its yield-to-maturity.

$$PVBP = \frac{(PV_-)-(PV_+)}{2}$$

Bond Convexity

Duration *underestimates* the price increase caused by a reduction in yields, and *overestimates* the decrease in prices when yields rise. Therefore, price estimates of option-free bonds based on duration must be revised upwards to bring them closer to their actual values. This revision is performed via the convexity adjustment. The more the curvature or convexity of the price-yield relationship, the more significant the convexity adjustment becomes.

Annual convexity can be approximated using the following equation:

$$ApproxCon = \frac{(PV_-)+(PV_+)-[2\times(PV_0)]}{(\Delta Yield)^2 \times (PV_0)}$$

The percentage change in a bond's full price can be estimated as:

$$\%\Delta PV^{Full} \approx (-AnnModDur \times \Delta Yield) + \left[\frac{1}{2} \times AnnConvexity \times (\Delta Yield)^2\right]$$

The money convexity of a bond is its annual convexity multiplied by the full price of the bond such that:

$$\Delta PV^{Full} \approx (-MoneyDur \times \Delta Yield) + \left[\frac{1}{2} \times MoneyCon \times (\Delta Yield)^2\right]$$

Factors that Affect Convexity

- The longer the term-to-maturity, the greater the convexity.
- The lower the coupon rate, the greater the convexity.
- The lower the yield-to-maturity, the greater the convexity.
- The greater the dispersion of cash flows, the greater the convexity.

Given the same price, yield-to-maturity and modified duration, a more convex bond will outperform a less convex bond in both bull and bear markets.

Convexity for Bonds with Embedded Options

For callable bonds (and other bonds with embedded options) the first-order effect of a change in the benchmark yield curve is measured by **effective** duration, and the second-order effect of a change in the benchmark yield curve is measured by effective convexity. Effective convexity is a **curve convexity** statistic.

$$EffCon = \frac{[(PV_-)+(PV_+)]-[2\times(PV_0)]}{(\Delta Curve)^2 \times (PV_0)}$$

Negative convexity (also known as concavity) is an important feature of callable bonds. When the benchmark yield is high, callable and non-callable bonds experience similar price changes to changes in benchmark yields. However, as benchmark yields decline, there comes a point where the callable bond moves into negative convexity territory, where the embedded call option holds significant value to the issuer and is highly likely to be exercised.

Putable bonds always have positive convexity.

INTEREST RATE RISK AND THE INVESTMENT HORIZON

Yield Volatility

Changes in bond prices result from two factors:

1. The impact per basis point change in the yield-to-maturity. This factor is captured by duration and convexity; and
2. The number of basis points in the change in yield-to-maturity. This factor is captured by yield volatility.

Investment Horizon, Macaulay Duration and Interest Rate Risk

Given a particular assumption about yield volatility, Macaulay duration indicates the investment horizon for which coupon reinvestment risk and market price risk offset each other. This is one of the applications of duration where "years-based" interpretation is meaningful and where Macaulay duration is used rather than modified duration.

When interest rates rise:

- Money duration measures the immediate decline in the value of the bond.
- Over time, the value of the bond is pulled up to par.
- The gain in future value of reinvested coupon starts out small, but increases at an increasing rate over time.
- At a certain point during the life of the bond, the gain on reinvested coupon and the loss on the sale of the bond offset each other. That point is the Macaulay duration of the bond.

When interest rates fall:

- Money duration measures the immediate increase in the value of the bond.
- Over time, the value of the bond is pulled down to par.
- The loss in future value of reinvested coupon starts out small, but increases at an increasing rate over time.

- At a certain point during the life of the bond, the gain on sale of the bond and the loss on the future value of reinvested coupon offset each other. That point is the Macaulay duration of the bond.

Important Takeaways

1. When the investment horizon is *greater* than the Macaulay duration of the bond, coupon reinvestment risk dominates market price risk. In this case, the investor is concerned about interest rates *falling*.
2. When the investment horizon is *less* than the Macaulay duration of the bond, market price risk dominates coupon reinvestment risk. In this case, the investor is concerned about interest rates *rising*.
3. When the investment horizon equals the Macaulay duration of the bond, coupon reinvestment risk and market price risk offset each other.

The difference between the Macaulay duration of a bond and the investment horizon is known as the duration gap.

$$\text{Duration gap} = \text{Macaulay duration} - \text{Investment horizon}$$

As time passes, (1) the investment horizon falls and (2) the Macaulay duration of the bond also changes, so the duration gap changes as well.

CREDIT AND LIQUIDITY RISK

For fixed-income securities, changes in the components of the overall yield-to-maturity do not occur in isolation i.e., there is interaction between changes in benchmark yields and spreads, between changes in the expected inflation rate and the expected real interest rate, and between changes in credit and liquidity risk. Therefore, for a fixed-rate bond, "inflation duration" or a "credit duration" all refer to the same number and we can use modified duration and convexity to estimate the change in the value of a bond in response to any change in the yield-to-maturity regardless of the source of the yield-to-maturity change.

FI

FUNDAMENTALS OF CREDIT ANALYSIS
Cross-Reference to CFA Institute Assigned Reading #55

Credit risk refers to the risk of loss resulting from a borrower's failure to make full and timely payments of interest and/or principal. It has two components:

- Default risk or default probability refers to the probability of a borrower failing to meet its obligations to make full and timely payments of principal and interest under the terms of the bond indenture.
- Loss severity or loss given default refers to the portion of the bond's value that an investor would lose if a default actually occurred. Loss severity equals 1 minus the recovery rate.

The **expected loss** is calculated as the probability of default multiplied by loss severity.

$$\text{Expected loss} = \text{Default probability} \times \text{Loss severity given default}$$

Spread risk refers to the risk of a widening of the yield spread on the bond. It encompasses:

- Downgrade risk or credit migration risk: This is the risk that the issuer's credit worthiness may deteriorate during the term of the bond, causing rating agencies to downgrade the credit rating of the issue.
- Market liquidity risk: This is the risk that an investor may have to sell her investment at a price lower than its market value due to insufficient volumes (liquidity) in the market. Two issuer-specific factors that affect liquidity risk are the size of the issuer and the credit quality of the issuer.

Seniority Ranking

Companies may issue debt with different rankings in terms of seniority, where the most senior or highest-ranking debt has the first claim on the issuer's cash flows and assets in case of an issuer default or restructuring. Debt may be classified as:

- Secured debt: Holders of secured debt have a direct claim on certain assets and their associated cash flows.
- Unsecured debt or debentures: Holders of unsecured debt only have a general claim on the issuer's assets and cash flow.

In the event of default, secured debt ranks higher than unsecured debt in the priority of claims.

Further, within each category of debt, there are sub-rankings.

Recovery Rates

All creditors at the same level in the capital structure are treated as one class irrespective of (1) the coupon rate offered on their bonds, and (2) when their bonds are maturing. This is referred to as bonds ranking pari passu (i.e., on an equal footing) in right of payment.

Recovery rates are highest for the senior-most class of debt in the priority of claims and fall with each lower rank of seniority. Therefore, the lower the seniority of the bond, the greater the credit risk and this is why investors demand a higher yield to invest in lower ranked debt instruments.

Apart from the relative seniority of a particular bond, recovery rates also vary (1) by industry and (2) depending on when the default occurs in a credit cycle.

Priority of Claims: Not Always "Absolute"

In practice, holders of junior and subordinated debt and even shareholders may recover some value on their interests without more senior creditors being paid in full.

Credit Ratings

Rating agencies issue credit ratings, which reflect an opinion on the potential risk of default of a particular (1) bond issue or (2) bond issuer.

Issuer versus Issue Ratings

Rating agencies usually provide credit ratings for the issuer (referred to as a corporate family rating) and for different issues (referred to as corporate credit rating) as well.

- The corporate family rating (CFR) is based on the overall creditworthiness of the issuer.
- The corporate credit rating (CCR) applies to a specific financial obligation of the issuer and is based on factors such as the issue's relative seniority ranking in the priority of claims and covenants.

The existence of cross-default provisions implies that the **probability of default** for all the different issues of a particular company is the same. However, different issues can be assigned different (higher or lower) credit ratings due to a ratings adjustment known as notching.

Generally speaking:

- For more risky issuers (with lower credit ratings), a larger notching adjustment is applied across seniority rankings. For these issuers, the probability of default is higher, so the potential difference in loss from a lower or higher seniority ranking is a bigger consideration in assessing the issue's credit risk.
- For less risky issuers (with higher credit ratings), the probability of default is lower, so there is less of a need to notch ratings to capture any potential difference in loss severity.

Risks in Relying on Agency Ratings

- Credit ratings can (and generally tend to) change significantly during a bond's term.
- Rating agencies also make mistakes.
- Certain risks (e.g., litigation risk faced by tobacco companies, environmental and business risks faced by chemical companies) cannot be anticipated in advance so rating agencies fail to capture these risks in assigned credit ratings.
- Ratings tend to lag market pricing of credit.

Further, credit ratings primarily focus on the risk of default, whereas (especially for low-quality credits) market price depends more on expected loss (i.e., default probability times loss severity). Therefore, two bonds with similar default risk, but different recovery rates will have similar ratings, but different market values.

The Four Cs of Credit Analysis

Capacity

Capacity refers to a borrower's ability to make its debt payments on time.

Industry Structure

Generally speaking:

- An industry that relies on just a few suppliers has greater credit risk than an industry that has multiple suppliers.
- Industries that rely heavily on just a few customers have greater credit risk than those that sell to a large number of customers.
- The higher the barriers to entry, the lower the level of competition in an industry, and the lower the credit risk of industry participants.
- Industries that offer products and services for which there are no good or cost-effective substitutes have greater pricing power and hence, lower credit risk.
- The greater the intensity of competition among companies in an industry, the lower the industry's profit potential, and the higher the credit risk.
- If an industry is characterized by high fixed costs (e.g., airlines and hotels), companies would find it difficult to cut down costs if they are unable to generate sufficient revenue.

Industry Fundamentals

Evaluation of industry fundamentals is based on:

- Industry cyclicality
- Growth prospects
- Published industry statistics

Company Fundamentals

Analysis of company fundamentals involves an examination of the company's:

- Competitive position
- Track record/operating history
- Management's strategy and execution
- Financial ratios

Collateral

Collateral refers to the quality and value of assets that are pledged against the issuer's debt obligations. Analysts focus more on assessing collateral when the probability of default is significantly high (as is the case with companies with low creditworthiness).

It is sometimes difficult to observe the value and quality of a company's assets directly so analysts should consider the following factors:

- The nature and amount of intangible assets on the balance sheet.
- The amount of depreciation an issuer takes relative to its capital expenditures.

Covenants

Covenants refer to the terms and conditions in a bond's indenture that place restrictions (negative or restrictive covenants) or certain requirements (affirmative covenants) on the issuer.

- While covenants protect bondholders by creating a binding framework for the repayment of debt obligations, they must offer management sufficient flexibility to run the business.
- Covenants provide only limited protection to investment-grade bondholders and slightly stronger protection to high-yield investors.
- Covenants tend to be stronger for bonds that are issued in weak economic times (to induce investors to purchase them).

Character

Character refers to the quality and integrity of management. When evaluating management's character, analysts should:

- Evaluate the suitability and reliability of management's strategy.
- Assess management's track record in executing strategies successfully, while keeping the companies they run clear of bankruptcy, restructuring and other distressed situations.
- Identify the use of aggressive accounting policies and/or tax strategies.
- Look for any history of fraud or malfeasance.
- Look for instances of poor treatment of bond holders in the past.

FI

Ratios and Ratio Analysis

Profitability and Cash Flow Measures

- Earnings before interest, taxes, depreciation, and amortization (EBITDA)
- Funds from operations (FFO)
- Free cash flow before dividends
- Free cash flow after dividends

Leverage Ratios

- Debt / Capital
- Debt / EBITDA
- FFO / Debt

Coverage Ratios

- EBITDA / Interest expense
- EBIT / Interest expense

Issuer Liquidity

All other things remaining same, companies with ready access to liquidity represent lower credit risk. Generally speaking, issuer liquidity is a bigger factor when evaluating credit risk for high-yield companies than for investment grade companies.

Factors Affecting the Yield Spread on Corporate Bonds

This yield spread is composed of the liquidity premium and credit spread.

$$\text{Yield spread} = \text{Liquidity premium} + \text{Credit spread}$$

Yield spreads on corporate bonds are affected by the following:

- Credit cycle: Credit spreads widen (narrow) as the credit cycle deteriorates (improves). They are widest (tightest) at or near the bottom (top) of the credit cycle when financial markets believe that risk is high (low).
- Broader economic conditions: Investors demand a higher (lower) risk premium in relatively weak (strong) economic conditions.
- Financial market performance overall, including equities: Credit spreads widen in weak financial markets, and narrow in strong markets. Credit spreads also narrow in relatively stable, low-volatility market conditions as investors search for yield.
- Broker-dealers' willingness to provide sufficient capital for market making: Credit spreads are narrow when broker-dealers bring sufficient capital to the market, but tend to widen when there is a reduction in broker-provided capital available for market-making purposes.

- General market supply and demand: Credit spreads tend to widen when there is an excess supply of new issues, and tend to narrow when there is excess demand for bonds.

Finally, note that yield spreads on low credit quality bonds tend to be wider that those on high credit quality bonds.

The Return Impact of a Change in the Credit Spread

For small, instantaneous changes in the yield spread, the return impact (i.e., the percentage change in price, including accrued interest) can be estimated using the following formula:

$$\text{Return impact} \approx -\text{Modified duration} \times \Delta\text{Spread}$$

For larger changes in the yield spread, we must also incorporate the (positive) impact of convexity into our estimate of the return impact:

$$\text{Return impact} \approx -(\text{MDur} \times \Delta\text{Spread}) + (1/2 \times \text{Convexity} \times \Delta\text{Spread}^2)$$

- Longer-duration bonds are generally more sensitive to changes in the yield spread.
- Longer-maturity bonds entail more uncertainly than shorter-maturity bonds This is why **spread curves** (also referred to as **credit curves**) are generally upward sloping.

Evaluating the Credit of High-Yield Corporate Debt

High-yield corporate bonds (also referred to as **non-investment-grade corporate bonds** or **junk bonds**) are those that are rated below Baa3/BBB- by the credit rating agencies. High yield bonds entail a greater risk of default than investment grade bonds. As a result, credit analysts pay more attention to recovery analysis (or loss severity in the event of default) when evaluating these bonds.

Special Considerations when Analyzing High Yield Corporate Bonds

- Liquidity: While having cash or the ability to generate cash is important for all debt issuers, it is absolutely critical for high-yield debt issuers. High-yield companies only have access to limited sources of liquidity.
- Financial projections: Analysts should forecast earnings and cash flows several years into the future to assess whether the issuer's credit profile will remain stable, improve, or deteriorate. Analysts should also incorporate required capital expenditures, changes in working capital, and realistic "stress" scenarios in their analysis to identify any vulnerabilities in the business.
- Debt structure: High-yield companies usually have many layers of debt in their capital structures, with each layer having a different seniority ranking and hence, entailing a different potential recovery rate in the event of default. To evaluate the credit risk of a high-yield issuer with many layers of debt in its capital structure, analysts must calculate leverage for each level of the debt structure.

High-yield companies with a relatively high proportion of secured debt (typically bank debt) in their capital structure are said to be "top-heavy." It is generally difficult for such companies to take on more debt in the event of financial stress because of (1) the stringent covenants associated with bank debt and (2) the relatively short maturity of bank debt relative to other forms of debt. Both these factors contribute to a higher risk of default for these companies and lower recovery rates for less secured creditors.

- Corporate structure: High-yield investors need to assess whether debt has been issued by the parent or its subsidiary, and how cash can move between the two. They should compute leverage ratios for each of the debt-issuing entities individually, and on a consolidated basis.
- Covenant analysis: Analysis of covenants takes on even more significance for high-yield bonds than investment-grade bonds. Some of the important covenants for high-yield issuers are:
  - Change of control put
  - Restricted payments:
  - Limitations on liens and additional indebtedness
  - Restricted versus unrestricted subsidiaries

It is also important to analyze covenants in a high-yield issuer's bank credit agreements. Bank covenants can be more restrictive than bond covenants.

Equity-like Approach to High-Yield Analysis

An equity-like approach can be useful for analyzing high-yield bonds. One such approach is to calculate multiples (e.g., EV/EBITDA and debt/EBITDA) and compare them across several issuers. For a given issuer, if there is only a small difference between the EV/EBITDA and debt/EBITDA ratios, it indicates that the issuer has a relatively small "equity cushion," which means higher risk for bond investors.

Evaluating the Credit of Sovereign Debt

Sovereign debt refers to debt issued by national governments. Credit analysis of sovereign bonds entails an evaluation of the government's ability and willingness to service its debt. An assessment of willingness to service debt is particularly important for sovereign debt as bondholders typically have no legal recourse if a national government is unwilling to meet its debt obligations.

Credit rating agencies typically assign a local currency debt rating and a foreign currency debt rating to sovereign issuers. This is because defaults on foreign currency-denominated sovereign bonds have tended to exceed defaults on local currency-denominated sovereign bonds.

FI

Evaluating the Credit of Municipal Debt

Non-sovereign (or sub-sovereign) government entities include local and state governments as well as various agencies and authorities created by them.

General Obligation (GO) Bonds

GO bonds are unsecured bonds issued with the full faith and credit of the issuing entity, and are supported by the taxing authority of the issuer. Credit analysis of GO bonds is quite similar to that of sovereign bonds.

Revenue Bonds

These are issued for financing a specific project (e.g., a toll road, bridge, hospital, etc.) and are serviced with revenues generated from the project. Therefore, analysis of revenue bonds is similar to analysis of corporate bonds. It focuses on the cash-generating ability of the particular project and on the economic base supporting the project (sources of finance).

A key ratio used to analyze revenue-backed municipal bonds is the debt service coverage ratio (DSCR). The higher the ratio, the lower the credit risk of the bond.

FI

STUDY SESSION 18:
DERIVATIVES

DR

© 2019 Wiley

DERIVATIVE MARKETS AND INSTRUMENTS
Cross-Reference to CFA Institute Assigned Reading #56

A derivative is a financial contract or instrument that derives its value from the value of something else (known as the underlying). The underlying on which a derivative is based can be an asset (e.g., stocks and bonds), an index (e.g., S&P 500), or something else (e.g., interest rates).

Exchange-Traded versus Over-the-Counter Derivatives

Exchange-Traded Derivatives Markets

Exchange-traded derivatives (e.g., futures contracts) are traded on specialized derivatives exchanges or other exchanges.

- Standardization facilitates the creation of a more liquid market for derivatives. However, it comes at the cost of flexibility.
  - Liquidity is a function of (1) trading interest and (2) level of uncertainty. Little trading interest and a high level of uncertainty lead to low liquidity.
- Market makers and speculators play an important role in these markets.
  - Market makers stand ready to buy at one (low) price and sell at another (high) price in order to lock in small short-term profits (known as scalping).
  - Speculators are willing to take educated risks to earn profits.
- The exchange is responsible for clearing and settlement through its clearinghouse. The clearinghouse is able to provide a credit guarantee to market participants.
- Exchange markets also have transparency, i.e., information regarding all transactions is disclosed to regulatory bodies. This regulation does bring certain benefits, but also means a loss of privacy.

Over-the-Counter (OTC) Derivatives Markets

OTC derivatives (e.g., forward contracts) do not trade in a centralized market; instead, they trade in an *informal* market. OTC derivatives are customized instruments. Dealers (typically banks) play an important role in OTC markets as they buy and sell these customized derivatives to market participants, and then look to hedge (or lay off) their risks. Due to the customized nature of OTC derivatives, dealers are typically unable to find identical offsetting transactions. Therefore, they turn to similar transactions to lay off some of the risk, and use their specialized knowledge and complex models to manage any remaining exposure.

- Note that there is a tendency to think that the OTC market is less liquid than the exchange market. This is not necessarily true.
- OTC derivative markets are less regulated than exchange-traded derivative markets.
- OTC markets offer more privacy and flexibility than exchange markets.

Forward Commitments versus Contingent Claims

A forward commitment is a legally binding **obligation** to engage in a certain transaction in the spot market at a future date at terms agreed upon today. Forward commitments can be made on exchange-traded derivatives and over-the-counter derivatives.

- **Forwards** are customized and private contracts between two parties, where one party has an obligation to buy an asset, and the counterparty has an obligation to sell the asset, at a price and future date that is agreed upon signing of the contract.
- **Futures** are standardized derivative contracts where one party, the buyer, will purchase an underlying asset from the other party, the seller, at a later date at a price agreed upon contract initiation.
- A **swap** is an over-the-counter derivative contract in which two parties agree to exchange a series of cash flows whereby one party pays a variable series that will be determined by an underlying asset or rate, and the counterparty pays either 1) a variable series determined by a different underlying asset or rate or 2) a fixed series.

A **contingent claim** is a derivative in which the outcome or payoff is determined by the outcome or payoff of an underlying asset, conditional on some event occurring.

- **Options** are contingent claims because their payoffs depend on the underlying's value in the future. Options are derivative instruments that give their holders the choice (not the obligation) to buy or sell the underlying from, or to the seller (writer) of the option. Options can be customized, over-the-counter contracts, or standardized, exchange-traded contracts.
- A **credit derivative** is a contract that transfers credit risk from one party (the credit protection buyer) to another party (the credit protection seller), where the latter protects the former against a specific credit loss. Credit derivatives include credit default swaps (CDS), total return swaps, credit spread options, and credit-linked notes.
- An **asset-backed security (ABS)** is a derivative in which a portfolio of debt instruments is pooled, and claims are issued on the portfolio in the form of tranches, which have different priorities of claims on the payments that come in from the pool of debt securities.

Purposes and Benefits of Derivatives

- Risk allocation, transfer, and management
- Information discovery
- Operational advantages
- Market efficiency

Criticisms and Misuses of Derivatives

- Destabilization and systematic risk
- Speculation and gambling
- Complexity

Arbitrage

Arbitrage opportunities exist whenever similar assets or combinations of assets are selling for different prices. Arbitrageurs exploit these opportunities and trade on mispricings until they are eliminated and asset prices converge to their "correct" levels. Arbitrage plays an important role in the study of derivatives. It is an important feature of efficient markets because it helps:

1. Determine prices
2. Improve market efficiency

BASICS OF DERIVATIVE PRICING AND VALUATION
Cross-Reference to CFA Institute Assigned Reading #57

Pricing the Underlying

The price or value of a financial asset is determined as the present value of expected future price plus (minus) any benefits (costs) of holding the asset, discounted at a rate appropriate for the risk assumed.

$$S_0 = \left[\frac{E(S_T)}{(1+r+\lambda)^T} \right] - \theta + \gamma$$

- The required rate of return includes the risk-free rate and a risk premium.

The Principal of Arbitrage

Arbitrage and Derivatives

When the underlying is combined with the derivative to create a perfectly hedged portfolio, all of the price risk is eliminated and the position should earn the risk-free rate.

> Long asset + Short derivative = Long risk-free asset (lending)
>
> Long asset + Short risk-free asset (borrowing) = Long derivative
>
> Short derivative + Short risk-free asset (borrowing) = Short asset

Risk Aversion, Risk Neutrality, and Arbitrage-Free Pricing

- Derivative pricing models discount the expected payoff of the derivative at the risk-free rate rather than the risk-free rate plus a risk premium.
- Further, the expected payoff is calculated based on what are known as risk-neutral probabilities (not actual or true probabilities of possible outcomes).
- While the risk aversion of investors is relevant to pricing assets, it is not relevant to pricing derivatives. As such, derivatives pricing is sometimes called risk-neutral pricing.

Limits to Arbitrage

- Significant transaction costs
- Large capital requirements
- The possibility of additional capital being required down the line
- Some assets possibly difficult to short
- Modeling risk

DR

Derivatives Pricing versus Valuation

- Price, as it relates to forwards, futures, and swaps (note that options are not a problem in this regard), refers to the fixed price (that is agreed upon at contract initiation) at which the underlying transaction will take place in the future. These securities do not require an outlay of cash at contract initiation, so there is no concept of a price being paid at the beginning.
- The value of these contracts fluctuate in response to changes in the price of the underlying.

FORWARD CONTRACTS

A forward is a contract between two parties, where one (the long position) has the **obligation** to buy, and the other (the short position) has an **obligation** to sell an underlying asset at a fixed forward price (that established at the inception of the contract) at a future date.

- Typically, no cash changes hands at inception.
- The long position benefits when the price of the underlying asset increases, while the short benefits when the price of the underlying asset falls.
- If the party that is adversely affected by price movements defaults on its commitment, the counterparty with the favorable position faces default risk.
- Forwards are a zero-sum game—one party's gain is the other party's loss.

Pricing and Valuation of Forward Contracts

The price of a forward contract is the fixed price or rate at which the underlying transaction will occur at contract expiration. The forward price is agreed upon at initiation of the forward contract. Pricing a forward contract means determining this forward price.

The value of a forward contract is the amount that a counterparty would need to pay, or would expect to receive, to get out of its (already-assumed) forward position.

Valuing a Forward Contract at Expiration (t = T)

$$V_T(0,T) = S_T - F(0,T)$$

Forward Contract Payoffs at Expiration

	$S_T > F(0,T)$	$S_T < F(0,T)$
Long position	$S_T - F(0,T)$ (Positive payoff)	$S_T - F(0,T)$ (Negative payoff)
Short position	$-[S_T - F(0,T)]$ (Negative payoff)	$-[S_T - F(0,T)]$ (Positive payoff)

Valuing a Forward Contract at Initiation (t = 0)

$$V_0(0,T) = S_0 - [F(0,T) / (1+r)^T] = 0$$

No-Arbitrage Forward Price

$$F(0,T) = S_0(1+r)T$$

If the underlying asset entails benefits/costs:

$$F(0,T) = (S_0 - \gamma + \theta)(1+r)^T; \text{ or } F(0,T) = S_0(1+r)^T - (\gamma - \theta)(1+r)^T$$

- The risk premium on the asset does not directly appear in determining the price of a forward.
- Although the forward price is fixed for a particular forward contract, a new contract calling for delivery of the same asset at the same point in time will have a different forward price (depending on the current spot price).

Valuing a Forward Contract During its Life

$$V_t(0,T) = S_t - [F(0,T) / (1+r)^{T-t}]$$

If the underlying asset entails benefits/costs:

$$V_t(0,T) = S_t - (\gamma - \theta)(1+r)^t - [F(0,T) / (1+r)^{T-t}]$$

Value of a Forward Contract

Time	Long Position Value	Short Position Value
At initiation	Zero, as the contract is priced to prevent arbitrage	Zero, as the contract is priced to prevent arbitrage
During life of the contract	$S_t - \left[\dfrac{F(0,T)}{(1+r)^{T-t}} \right]$	$\left[\dfrac{F(0,T)}{(1+r)^{T-t}} \right] - S_t$
At expiration	$S_T - F(0,T)$	$F(0,T) - S_T$

DR

Forward Contracts on Interest Rates (Forward Rate Agreements)

A forward rate agreement (FRA) is a forward contract where the underlying is an interest rate (usually LIBOR). Think about the long position in an FRA as the party that has committed to take a hypothetical loan, and the short as the party that has committed to give out a hypothetical loan, at the FRA rate.

- If LIBOR at FRA expiration is *greater* than the FRA rate, the long benefits.
- If LIBOR at FRA expiration is *lower* than the FRA rate, the short benefits.

A borrower (who would like to lock in a borrowing rate) would take a long position on an FRA, while a lender (who would like to lock in a rate of return) would take a short position on an FRA.

Pricing a Forward Rate Agreement

The price of an FRA (forward price) represents the interest rate at which the long (short) position has the obligation to borrow (lend) funds for a specified period (term of the underlying hypothetical loan) starting at FRA expiration.

- Pricing an FRA is a simple exercise of determining the forward rate consistent with two (given) spot rates.
- Essentially, taking the long position on an FRA is equivalent to holding a longer-term Eurodollar time deposit and at the same time shorting (or owing) a shorter-term Eurodollar time deposit.

FUTURES CONTRACTS

Characteristics of Futures Contracts Vol 6, pgs 17–21

- Futures contracts are standardized.
  - The futures price is the only term set by the two parties involved in the contract; all other terms are established by the exchange including the expiration date of the contract, the underlying, the mode of settlement, and contract size.
- In the futures market, the initial margin is the amount that must be deposited by each party—the long and the short, into her account to be able to trade in the market.
- The maintenance margin is the minimum balance that must be maintained in an investor's account to avoid a margin call (a call for more funds to be deposited in the account).
- Marking-to-market is the process of adjusting the balance in an investor's futures account to reflect the change in value of her futures position since the last mark-to-market adjustment was conducted.
- The clearinghouse is the counterparty to every trade on the exchange. It acts as the short for every long position, and as the long for every short position.
- Taking the position as the counterparty to every trade combined with the ability to enforce periodic mark-to-market adjustments for all market participants makes for a very efficient mechanism for controlling default risk.

- Some futures contracts have price limits. These limits are set by the exchange to restrict the change in the settlement price of a contract from one day to the next.

Forward Prices versus Futures Prices

- If underlying asset prices are positively correlated with interest rates, the futures price will be higher than the forward price.
- If underlying asset prices are negatively correlated with interest rates, the forward price will be higher than the futures price.
- If interest rates are constant, forwards and futures would have the same prices.
- If futures prices are uncorrelated with interest rates, forwards and futures would have the same prices.
- Forward and futures prices would be different if the volatility of the forward price is different from the volatility of the futures price.

SWAPS

A swap is an agreement to exchange a series of cash flows at periodic settlement dates over a certain period of time (known as the tenor of the swap).

Plain-Vanilla Interest Rate Swaps

- A plain-vanilla interest rate swap involves the exchange of fixed interest payments for floating-rate payments.
- The party that wants to receive floating-rate payments and agrees to make fixed-rate payments is known as the pay-fixed side of the swap or the fixed-rate payer/ floating-rate receiver.
- The party that wants to receive fixed payments and make floating-rate payments is the pay-floating side of the swap or the floating-rate payer/fixed-rate receiver.
- There is no exchange of notional principal at initiation or expiration of the swap. The notional principal is simply used to determine the interest payment on each leg of the swap.
- Interest payments are not exchanged in full at each settlement date. Interest payments are netted, and the party that owes more in interest at a particular settlement date makes a payment equal to the difference to the other.
- As with forward contracts, there is an element of counterparty credit risk in swaps as the party that owes the lower amount can default.
- The floating rate is usually quoted in terms of LIBOR plus a spread. The floating rate for any period is known at the beginning of the period, while the settlement payment is actually made at the end of each period.

$$\text{Net fixed-rate payment}_t = [\text{Swap fixed rate} - (\text{LIBOR}_{t-1} + \text{Spread})] \times (\text{No. of days}/360) \times \text{Notional principal}$$

Pricing versus Valuation of Swaps

- At the initiation of the swap, the swap fixed rate is set at a level at which the present value of the floating-rate payments (based on the current term structure of interest rates) equals the present value of fixed-rate payments so that there is zero value to either party. This swap fixed rate therefore represents the price of the swap.

- Over the term of the swap, as there are changes in the term structure of interest rates, the value of the swap will fluctuate.
  - If interest rates increase after swap initiation, the present value of floating-rate payments (based on the new term structure) will exceed the present value of fixed-rate payments (based on the swap fixed rate).
    - The swap will have a positive value for the fixed-rate payer (floating-rate receiver).
    - The swap will be an asset to the fixed-rate payer and a liability for the floating-rate payer.
  - If interest rates decrease after swap initiation, the present value of floating-rate payments will be lower than the present value of fixed-rate payments.
    - The swap will have a positive value for the floating-rate payer (fixed-rate receiver).
    - In this case, the swap will be an asset to the floating-rate payer and a liability for the fixed-rate payer.

Swaps and Forward Contracts

A swap essentially combines a series of forward contracts into a single transaction. For example, a plain vanilla interest rate swap is a combination of FRAs, where one FRA expires on each settlement date over the tenor of the swap, and the FRA rate (forward price) for each FRA equals the swap fixed rate (swap price).

Swaps and Bonds

The payoffs of the pay-fixed side of an interest rate swap are similar to those of a strategy of issuing a fixed-rate bond (on which fixed payments must be made) and using the proceeds to purchase a floating-rate bond (which will return floating-interest payments). On the other hand, the payoffs of the pay-floating side are similar to issuing a floating-rate bond and using the proceeds to purchase a fixed-rate bond.

- If interest rates increase, the fixed-rate payer benefits as there is a positive difference between her (floating-rate) receipts and (fixed-rate) payments.
- If interest rates decrease, the fixed-rate payer loses out as there is a negative difference between (floating-rate) receipts and (fixed-rate) payments.

OPTIONS

European versus American Options

- A European option is one that can only be exercised at the option's expiration date.
- An American option can be exercised at any point in time up to, and including, the option's expiration date.

Moneyness and Exercise Value

Moneyness refers to whether an option is in-the-money or out-of-the-money.

- An option is in-the-money when immediate exercise of the option will generate a positive payoff for the holder.
- An option is out-of-the-money when immediate exercise will generate a negative payoff for the holder.
- An option is at-the-money when immediate exercise will result in neither a positive nor a negative payoff for the holder.

The intrinsic value or exercise value of an option is the amount an option is in-the-money by. It is the amount that would be received by the option holder if he were to exercise the option immediately. An option has zero intrinsic value if it is at- or out-of-the money.

Call Options

- A call option gives the **holder/buyer** the **right** to **buy** (or call) the underlying asset for the given exercise price at the expiration date of the option.
- A call option **writer/seller** has the **obligation** to **sell** the asset to the holder of the call option for the given exercise price, should the option holder choose to exercise the option.

Call Option Payoffs

Option Position	Descriptions	Payoff	
		$S_T > X$	$S_T < X$
		Option holder exercises the option	Option holder does not exercise the option
Call option holder	Choice to buy the underlying asset for X	$S_T - X$	0
Call option writer	Obligation to sell the underlying asset for X if the option holder chooses to exercise the option	$-(S_T - X)$	0

$$\text{Intrinsic value of call} = \max[0, (S_t - X)]$$

Moneyness and Exercise Value of a Call Option

Moneyness	Current Market Price (S_t) versus Exercise Price (X)	Intrinsic Value Max $[0, (S_t - X)]$
In-the-money	S_t is greater than X	$S_t - X$
At-the-money	S_t equals X	0
Out-of-the-money	S_t is less than X	0

Put Options

- A put option gives the **holder/buyer** the **right** to **sell** (or put) the underlying asset for the given exercise price at the option's expiration date.
- A put option **writer/seller** has the **obligation** to **buy** the asset from the put option holder at the option's expiration date for the given exercise price, should the holder choose to exercise the option.

Put Option Payoffs

Option Position	Descriptions	Payoff	
		$S_T < X$	$S_T > X$
		Option holder exercises the option	Option holder does not exercise the option
Put option holder	Choice to sell the underlying asset for X	$X - S_T$	0
Put option writer	Obligation to buy the underlying asset for X if the option holder chooses to exercise the option	$-(X - S_T)$	0

Intrinsic value of a put option = Max $[0, (X - S_t)]$.

Moneyness and Exercise Value of a Put Option

Moneyness	Current Market Price (S_t) versus Exercise Price (X)	Intrinsic Value Max $[0, (X - S_t)]$
In-the-money	S_t is less than X	$X - S_t$
At-the-money	S_t equals X	0
Out-of-the-money	S_t is greater than X	0

Put-Call Parity

$$c_0 + \frac{X}{(1 + R_F)^T} = p_0 + S_0$$

A fiduciary call, which is composed of (1) a call option on a stock and (2) a zero-coupon riskless bond that pays X at maturity (face value equals X) must have the same value as a protective put, which is composed of (1) a European put option on a stock and (2) a share of the same stock as long as:

- The call and put option, and the zero-coupon bond, have the same time to maturity/expiration (T).
- The exercise price of the call and the put, and the face value of the zero-coupon bond, are the same (X).
- The call and the put are options on the same underlying asset as the one held in Portfolio B (S). This asset makes no cash payments and has no carrying costs.
- The call and put can only be exercised at expiration i.e., they are European options.

Combining Portfolios to Make Synthetic Securities

Strategy	Consisting of	Value	Equals	Strategy	Consisting of	Value
Fiduciary call	Long call + Long bond	$c_0 + \dfrac{X}{(1+R_F)^T}$	=	Protective put	Long put + Long underlying asset	$p_0 + S_0$
Long call	Long call	c_0	=	Synthetic call	Long put + Long underlying asset + Short bond	$p_0 + S_0 - \dfrac{X}{(1+R_F)^T}$
Long put	Long put	p_0	=	Synthetic put	Long call + Short underlying asset + Long bond	$c_0 + S_0 - \dfrac{X}{(1+R_F)^T}$
Long underlying asset	Long underlying asset	S_0	=	Synthetic underlying asset	Long call + Long bond + Short put	$c_0 + \dfrac{X}{(1+R_F)^T} - p_0$
Long bond	Long bond	$\dfrac{X}{(1+R_F)^T}$	=	Synthetic bond	Long put + Long underlying asset + Short call	$p_0 + S_0 - c_0$

Factors that Affect the Value of an Option

Value of the Underlying

- The greater (lower) the value of the underlying, the greater (lower) the exercise value of the call option, and the greater its price/value.
- The lower (greater) the value of the underlying, the greater (lower) the exercise value of the put option, and the greater its price/value.
- Note that the value of the underlying serves as an upper boundary on the price of American and European call options.

Exercise Price

- For call options, the higher the exercise price, the *lower* the exercise value of the option.
- For put options, the higher the exercise price, the *higher* the intrinsic value.
- The maximum value of a European put option equals the present value of its exercise price, $X/(1 + RFR)^T$.

Risk-Free Rate

- The value of a call option is *directly* related to the risk-free rate.
- The value of a put option is *inversely* related to the risk-free rate.

Time to Expiration

- The value of a European call option is *directly* related to the time to expiration.
- The value of a European put option can be either *directly* or *inversely* related to the time to expiration. Typically, the direct effect holds, but the inverse effect can prevail if a longer time to expiration comes with a higher risk-free rate, and if the option is deep in-the-money.

Volatility

- Greater volatility in the price of the underlying asset *increases* the value of both calls and puts.
- At any point in time before expiration, an option is worth at least as much as its exercise value. However, on top of its exercise value, there is also an element of speculative value in the option to account for the possibility that the underlying asset's price could move favorably over the remaining time to expiration and result in a payoff greater than the current exercise value. This speculative value is known as the time value of an option, which increases with volatility but decreases as the option nears expiration (known as time value decay). At expiration, no time value remains, and the option is worth its exercise value.

Payments from the Underlying and the Cost of Carry

- For call option holders, benefits from the underlying, which cause a decline in the value of the underlying, are a negative because they lead to a decline in the exercise value. For put option holders, on the other hand, benefits from the underlying are a positive (as the value of the underlying falls).
- Carrying costs have the opposite effect. They are a positive for call options, but a negative for puts.

Lowest Prices of European Calls and Puts

- The lowest value of a European call is the greater of (1) zero and (2) the value of the underlying minus the present value of the exercise price.
- The lowest value of a European put is the greater of (1) zero and (2) the present value of the exercise price minus the value of the underlying.

Put-Call Forward Parity

$$p_0 - c_0 = \frac{[X - F(0,T)]}{(1 + R_F)^T}$$

Assumptions

- The price of the forward contract on the underlying is given by $F(0,T)$.
- The put and the call options expire at the same time as the forward contract.
- X represents the exercise price of the call and put options.
- The options are European options.
- The options and the forward contract are based on the same underlying asset.

Payoffs

	Outcome at T	
	$S_T < X$ Put Expires In-the-Money Call Expires Out-of-the-Money	$S_T > X$ Call Expires In-the-Money Put Expires Out-of-the-Money
Protective put with forward contract		
Risk-free bond	$F(0,T)$	$F(0,T)$
Forward contract	$S_T - F(0,T)$	$S_T - F(0,T)$
Long put	$X - S_T$	0
Total	X	S_T
Protective put with asset		
Asset	S_T	S_T
Long put	$X - S_T$	0
Total	X	S_T
Fiduciary call		
Call	0	$S_T - X$
Risk-free bond	X	X
Total	X	S_T

The One-Period Binomial Model

In the one-period binomial model, the price of the underlying stock starts off at a given level, S, and can either:

- Move up by a factor of u to a new price, S^+, one period later with a probability of q; or

- Move down by a factor of d to a new price, S, one period later with a probability of 1 − q.
- Note that q and 1 − q are actual or real probabilities of the up and down movements respectively.

$$S^+ = Su$$
$$c^+ = Max(0, S^+ - X)$$

$$S$$
$$c = ?$$

$$S^- = Sd$$
$$c^- = Max(0, S^- - X)$$

$$t = 0 \qquad\qquad t = T$$

Value of a Call Option

$$c = \frac{\pi c^+ + (1 - \pi)c^-}{(1 + r)}$$

where

$$\pi = \frac{(1 + r - d)}{(u - d)}$$

The value of an option under this approach is computed by discounting the expected value of the payoff (calculated using risk-neutral probabilities) at the risk-free rate.

American Option Pricing

- Minimum value of an American call option = Max $[0, (S_0 - X/(1 + RFR)^T]$
- Minimum value of an American put option = Max $[0, (X - S_0)]$

American Call Options

- There is no reason to exercise an American call option on an asset that offers no benefits before expiration.
- However, if the asset does offer benefits, early exercise of an American call option may be warranted.
- If there are significant costs of carry on the underlying, there is less of a reason to exercise the American call option early.

American Puts

- It would be beneficial to exercise an American put prior to expiration when a company is in or nearing bankruptcy, and its stock price is close to zero.
- Dividends and coupon interest discourage early exercise for American puts.
- Carrying costs on the underlying encourage exercise for American puts.

DR

STUDY SESSION 19:
ALTERNATIVE INVESTMENTS

AI

INTRODUCTION TO ALTERNATIVE INVESTMENTS
Cross-Reference to CFA Institute Assigned Reading #58

Alternative Investments versus Traditional Investments

Alternative investments differ from traditional investments (long-only positions in stocks, bonds, and cash) with respect to (1) the types of assets and securities invested in and (2) the structure of the investment vehicles in which these assets are held.

Investments in these special vehicles are generally characterized by:

- High fees.
- Large size of investments.
- Low diversification of managers and investments within the alternatives investment portfolio.
- High use of leverage.
- Restrictions on redemptions.

Other Characteristics of Alternative Investments

- Illiquidity of underlying investments.
- Narrow manager specialization.
- Low correlation with traditional investments.
- Low level of regulation and less transparency.
- Limited and potentially problematic historical risk and return data.
- Unique legal and tax considerations.

Portfolio Context: Integration of Alternative Investments with Traditional Investments

Historically, the returns on some categories of alternative investments have been found to have relatively low correlations with returns on traditional investments over long periods. Further, most categories of alternative investments have historically exhibited higher returns than traditional investments.

Considerations When Evaluating the Historical Performance of Alternative Investments

- Reported returns and standard deviations are averages, which may not be representative of returns and standard deviations for sub-periods within the reported period, or for future periods.
- The volatility of returns of alternative investments, as well as the correlation of returns with those of traditional asset classes may be underestimated.
- Hedge fund indices may be inherently biased upwards due to self-selection bias, survivorship bias and backfill bias.
- Differences in weightings and constituents in index construction can have a significant impact on the indices and their results and comparability.

AI

CATEGORIES OF ALTERNATIVE INVESTMENTS

HEDGE FUNDS

General Characteristics

- Hedge funds are aggressively managed portfolios of investments.
- They are not constrained by any significant investment restrictions so they enjoy more flexibility in decision-making.
- They are set up as private investment partnerships, where the fund is the general partner (GP) and the investors are limited partners (LPs).
- Hedge funds are regulated to a much lower extent than traditional investments.
- Hedge funds usually impose restrictions on redemptions.

Funds of funds are funds that invest in a number of hedge funds, hence diversifying across hedge fund strategies, investment regions, and management styles.

Hedge Fund Strategies

Event-driven strategies: These strategies take a bottom-up view, i.e., they begin with company analysis and then aggregate and analyze a larger group. They focus on short-term events that usually involve potential changes in corporate structure (e.g., acquisitions and restructurings) that are expected to affect individual companies. Hedge funds following these strategies may take long and short positions in common stock, preferred stock as well as debt securities and options. Event-driven strategies include:

- Merger arbitrage
- Distressed / restructuring
- Activist
- Special situations

Relative value strategies: These strategies seek to profit from pricing discrepancies (or short-term mispricings) between related securities. Examples of relative value strategies include:

- Fixed income convertible arbitrage
- Fixed income asset backed
- Fixed income general
- Volatility
- Multi-strategy

Macro strategies: These strategies take a top-down view as they focus on the overall macroeconomic environment, taking long and short positions in broad markets (e.g., equity indices, currencies, commodities, etc.) that are expected to benefit based on the manager's view regarding overall market direction.

Equity hedge strategies: These strategies take a bottom-up view and focus on public equity markets, taking long and short positions in equities and equity derivatives. Examples of such strategies include:

- Market neutral
- Fundamental growth
- Fundamental value
- Quantitative directional
- Short bias
- Sector specific

Hedge Funds and Diversification Benefits

It would be inappropriate to make generalized statements regarding hedge fund performance given the wide variety of hedge fund strategies. A specific strategy or fund may generate very high returns in some years, and then perform poorly in subsequent years.

- Studies that have analyzed data over long periods of time suggest that there is a less than perfectly positively correlation between hedge fund returns and equity returns.
- However, there have been (shorter) episodes during which there has been a strong positive correlation between the two.
- The correlation between hedge fund returns and stock market performance tends to increase in times of financial crisis.
- As the hedge fund market has become more crowded, funds have begun to take on more risk to generate competitive returns.

Hedge Fund Fees

Hedge funds usually charge two types of fees:

A management fee (also called base fee) is calculated on **assets under management**.

An incentive fee (or performance fee) is based on realized profits. They may be calculated on profits net of management fees or on profits before management fees. Further, incentive fees may be subject to a **hurdle rate**, or a **high water mark provision**.

Hedge Fund Valuation Issues

- When using market prices for valuing traded securities, it is common practice in the hedge fund industry to use the average of the bid and ask quote.
- For highly illiquid or non-traded investments, reliable market value data is unavailable, so values are estimated using statistical models.

Due Diligence Considerations When Investing in Hedge Funds

- Investment strategy.
- Investment process.
- Competitive advantage.
- Track record.

AI

- Size and longevity.
- Management style.
- Key-person risk.
- Reputation.
- Investor relations.
- Plans for growth.
- Methodology used for return calculations.
- Systems for risk management.

PRIVATE EQUITY

Private Equity Structure and Fees

Private equity funds are also usually structured as partnerships, where outside investors are Limited Partners (LPs) and the private equity firm (which can manage a number of funds) is the General Partner (GP). Most private equity firms charge both a management fee and an incentive fee.

- Management fees are usually calculated as a percentage (usually 1% to 3%) of **committed capital**. Once the committed capital is fully invested, the fee is paid only on the funds remaining in the investment vehicle.
- Incentive fees are usually earned by the GP only after the LPs are paid back their initial investments. The GP typically receives 20% of the total profit of the fund as an incentive fee, while the LPs receive 80% of profits (in addition to the return of their initial investment).

Other private equity strategies include:

- *Development capital* (or *minority equity investing*): This generally involves providing financing to more mature companies to help them expand, restructure operations, enter new markets, or finance major acquisitions.
- *Distressed investing* usually involves buying debt of mature companies that are in financial distress (bankrupt, in default, or likely to default). Distressed debt typically trades at a deep discount to par and the idea is to benefit from an increase in the price of these securities as the company is turned around.

Private Equity Exit Strategies

- Trade sale
- Initial public offerings (IPOs)
- Recapitalization
- Secondary sale
- Write-off/liquidation

Private Equity: Diversification Benefits, Performance, and Risk

Studies have shown that:

- Private equity funds have earned higher returns than equities over the last 20 years.
- Based on the standard deviation of historical annual returns, private equity investments (including venture capital) entail higher risk than equities.
- Private equity returns are less than perfectly positively correlated with returns on traditional investments, so there are diversification benefits of including private equity investments in investment portfolios.

However, it is important to bear in mind private equity return indices are subject to survivorship and backfill biases, both of which lead to overstated returns. Further, in the absence of a liquidity event, private equity firms may not mark-to-market their investment portfolios on a regular basis, which leads to understatement of (1) measures of volatility and (2) correlations with other investments.

Evidence also suggests that identifying skilled private equity fund managers is very important as differences in returns between the top and bottom quartiles of PE funds are significant. Further, top-quartile funds tend to persistently perform better than others.

Portfolio Company Valuation Methods

- Market or comparables approach
- Discounted cash flow approach
- Asset-based approach

Factors That Must Be Considered When Investing in Private Equity

- Current and anticipated economic conditions.
- Interest rates and capital availability expectations.
- The quality of the GP.

REAL ESTATE

Forms of Real Estate Investment

Basic Forms of Real Estate Investments and Example

	Debt	Equity
Private	- Mortgages - Construction lending	- Direct ownership of real estate. Ownership can be through, sole ownership, joint ventures, real estate limited partnerships, or other commingled funds
Public	- Mortgage-backed securities (residential and commercial) - Collateralized mortgage obligations	- Share in real estate corporations - Shares of real estate investment trusts

AI

Real Estate Investment Categories

- Residential property
- Commercial real estate
- REIT investing
- Timberland and farmland

Real Estate Performance and Diversification Benefits

The performance of real estate may be measured using three different types of indices:

- Appraisal indices use estimates of value (based on comparable sales or DCF analysis) as inputs. Appraisal indices tend to understate volatility.
- Repeat sales (transactions-based) indices are constructed using changes in prices of properties that have sold multiple times over the period. These indices suffer from sample selection bias.
- REIT indices are constructed using prices of publicly traded shares of REITs. The reliability of these indices increases with the frequency of trading.

Studies have shown that:

- Real estate as an asset class enjoys less than perfect positive correlation with stocks and bonds, so there may be diversification benefits to adding real estate investments to a portfolio containing traditional investments.
- The correlation between real estate and equities is higher than the correlation between real estate and bonds because real estate and equities are affected similarly by the business cycle.

Note that the low correlation between real estate and other asset classes may be the result of the methods used in index construction so actual diversification benefits may be less than expected.

Real Estate Valuation Approaches

Comparable sales approach: Under this approach, the value of a property is estimated based on recent sales of comparable properties.

Income approach: Two income-based approaches to real estate valuation are the direct capitalization approach and the discounted cash flow approach.

- The *direct capitalization approach* estimates the value of a property by dividing expected net operating income (NOI) generated by the property by a growth implicit capitalization rate (also referred to as the cap rate).
- The *discounted cash flow approach* estimates the value of a property as the present value of its expected future cash flows over a specific investment horizon plus the present value of an estimated resale value (or reversion value) at the end of the holding period.

Cost approach: Under this approach, the value of a property is estimated as its replacement cost, which equals the total cost that would be incurred to buy the land and construct a new, but similar, property on that site. This estimate of current replacement cost is adjusted for the location and condition of the subject property.

REIT Valuation Approaches

Income-based approaches for valuing REITs are similar to the direct capitalization approach for valuing individual properties (described above) in that a measure of income is capitalized into a value using an appropriate cap rate. Two common measures of income used are Funds from operations (FFO) and adjusted funds from operations (AFFO).

Asset-based approaches aim to determine a REIT's net asset value (NAV) by subtracting the value of its total liabilities from the estimated total market value of its assets.

Real Estate Investment Risks

- National and global economic conditions, local real estate conditions, and interest rate levels.
- The ability of fund managers to select, finance and manage the properties.
- Changes in government regulations.
- Regulatory issues, construction delays, and cost overruns.
- Leverage.

COMMODITIES

Investments in physical commodities entail costs for transportation and storage. As a result, most commodity investors prefer to trade commodity derivatives instead of actual physical commodities. Commodity derivatives include futures and forward contracts, options contracts and swaps contracts.

Other commodity investment vehicles include:

- Exchange traded funds (ETFs)
- Common stock of companies exposed to a particular commodity
- Managed futures funds
- Individual managed accounts
- Specialized funds

Commodity Performance and Diversification Benefits

Studies have shown that over a period from 1990 to 2010:

- Commodities earned a lower annual return than stocks and bonds.
- Commodity returns had a higher standard deviation (risk) than stocks and bonds.
- As a result, the Sharpe ratio for commodities as an asset class was much lower than for stocks and bonds.

AI

- Commodities have a relatively low correlation with stocks and bonds, which suggests that there are diversification benefits from adding commodities to a portfolio consisting of traditional asset classes.

Commodity Prices and Investments

Spot prices for commodities are a function of supply and demand, costs of production and storage, value to users, and global economic conditions.

Pricing of Commodity Futures Contracts

The price of a futures contract on a commodity may be calculated as follows:

$$\text{Futures price} = \text{Spot price}\,(1 + r) + \text{Storage costs} - \text{Convenience yield}$$

The futures price may be higher or lower than the spot price of a commodity depending on the convenience yield.

- When futures prices are higher than the spot price (when there is little of no convenience yield), prices are said to be in contango.
- When futures prices are lower than the spot price, prices are said to be in backwardation.

Sources of Return on a Commodity Futures Contract

- Roll yield: The difference between the spot price of a commodity and the futures price, or the difference between the futures prices of contracts expiring at different dates.
- Collateral yield: The interest earned on the collateral (margin) deposited to enter into the futures contract.
- Spot prices: These are influenced by current supply and demand.

INFRASTRUCTURE

- The assets underlying infrastructure investments are real, capital intensive, long-lived assets. They are intended for public use and provide essential services.
- Typically, infrastructure assets are financed, owned, and operated by governments.
- However, increasingly, the private sector is getting involved in infrastructure investments with an intention to (1) lease the assets back to the government, (2) sell newly constructed assets to the government, or (3) hold and operate the assets.
  - Investors are tempted to hold and operate infrastructure assets when (1) there is relatively inelastic demand for the assets and services, and (2) the high costs of the assets create high barriers to entry, both of which result in a strong competitive position for the service provider.
  - Investors expect these assets to generate stable cash flows, which adjust for economic growth and inflation.
  - Investors may also expect capital appreciation depending on the type of investment.

Benefits of Investing in Infrastructure

Investing in infrastructure may enable investors to:

- Add a steady income stream to their portfolios.
- Further diversify their portfolios as infrastructure assets exhibit low correlation with other investments.
- Gain some inflation protection.

Since they typically entail investments in long-lived assets, infrastructure investments may also better match the longer-term liability structure of some institutional investors (e.g. pension funds and life insurance companies).

Categories of Infrastructure Investments

Economic versus Social Infrastructure Assets

- **Economic infrastructure** assets support economic activity. They include assets such as transportation and utility assets.
  - Transportation assets include roads, bridges, tunnels, airports, ports, and railway lines.
  - Utility assets include assets to transmit, store, and distribute gas, water, and electricity; generate power; treat waste; and broadcast and transmit information.
    - Note that assets that broadcast and transmit information may also be categorized separately as communication assets.
- **Social infrastructure assets** are directed toward human activities. They include assets such as education, healthcare, and correctional facilities.

Brownfield versus Greenfield Investments

- **Brownfield investments** refer to investments in **existing** investable infrastructure assets.
  - These assets may be currently owned by a government that wants to (1) privatize the asset, (2) lease the asset out, or (3) sell and lease back the asset.
  - Typically, some financial and operating history regarding the asset is available.
- **Greenfield investments** refer to investments in infrastructure assets that are **to be constructed**.
  - The intent may be to (1) hold and operate the assets or (2) lease or sell the assets to the government after construction

Direct versus Indirect Investments

Direct investments in infrastructure assets result in investors controlling the assets and having the opportunity to capture the entire value on offer. However, they entail a very large capital commitment, which gives rise to concentration and liquidity risk in investor portfolios. Further, investors then bear the responsibility of managing and operating the assets.

AI

Indirect investments include shares of (1) companies, (2) exchange-traded funds, (3) listed funds, (4) private equity funds, and (5) unlisted mutual funds that invest in infrastructure. Investors who are most concerned about liquidity may choose to invest through (1) publicly traded infrastructure securities and/or (2) master limited partnerships.

In addition to liquidity, publicly traded infrastructure securities provide reasonable fees, transparent governance, market prices, and the ability to diversify across underlying assets. Unfortunately however, these securities represent a small segment of the infrastructure investment universe and tend to be relatively concentrated in categories of assets.

Master limited partnerships (MLPs) trade on exchanges and are pass-through entities similar to REITs.

- Regulations regarding MLPs tend to vary across countries.
- Most of the free cash flow is passed on to investors. However, investors are liable for taxes on that income.
- Typically, a general partner manages the partnership, receives a fee, and holds a small partnership interest. Limited partners own the remaining partnership interest.

Risks and Returns Overview

Low risk infrastructure investments have more stable cash flows and higher dividend payout ratios. However, they also typically have less growth and lower expected returns.

- An investment in an MLP with a brownfield investment in an asset that is being leased back to a government, such as a school, is a low risk infrastructure investment.
- An investment in a private equity fund with a greenfield investment is a riskier investment.

Risks of investing in infrastructure include:

- Revenues not meeting expectations.
- Leverage, which may give rise to financing risk.
- Operational risk.
- Construction risk.
- Regulatory risk. Since infrastructure assets often provide services that are very important to society, governments typically regulate certain aspects, including the sale of the underlying assets, operations of the assets including service quality, and prices/profit margins.

Other Alternative Investments

Collectibles include antiques and fine art, fine wine, rare stamps and coins, jewelry and watches, and sports memorabilia.

- They do not provide current income, but have potential for long-term capital appreciation, can diversify a portfolio and can also be a source of enjoyment for owners.

- They can fluctuate dramatically in value and can be relatively illiquid.
- Investors must have some degree of expertise to make wise investing decisions.
- Storage costs can be significant (e.g., for wine and art).

RISK MANAGEMENT

- Investments in certain types of alternative investments require long holding periods. For example, private equity funds and hedge funds have long lockup periods.
- Hedge funds and private equity funds are less transparent than other investments as they may consider their investment strategies to be proprietary information.
- Investments in many alternative investments are relatively illiquid.
- Indices are widely used to track the performance of several types of alternative investments. Historical returns on those indices and the standard deviations of their returns may not really be representative of the risk-return characteristics of alternative investments.
- Reported correlations between alternative investments and traditional investments can be very different from actual correlations.
- There can be significant differences between the performance of an individual portfolio manager or fund and the performance of the overall investment class.
- Large investors can diversify across managers/funds, but small investors cannot.
- Hedge fund managers who have incurred large losses tend to liquidate their funds instead of trying to offset those losses.

Risk-Return Measures

The Sharpe ratio is not an appropriate risk-return measure for alternative investments.

Returns generally tend to be leptokurtic and negatively skewed (positive average returns but with higher than average risk of extreme losses). As a result, measures of downside risk are more useful. These include:

- Value at Risk (VaR)
- Shortfall or safety first measures
- Sortino ratio